MANAGERIAL ACCOUNTING

9th EDITION

Harold M. Sollenberger
D.B.A., C.P.A.
Professor of Accounting
Michigan State University

Arnold Schneider
Ph.D., C.P.A.
Associate Professor of Accounting
Georgia Institute of Technology

SOUTH-WESTERN College Publishing

An International Thomson Publishing Company

Sponsoring Editor: Elizabeth A. Bowers
Developmental Editor: Leslie Kauffman
Production Editor: Peggy A. Williams
Production House: CompuText Productions, Inc.
Cover Designer: D. Betz Design/David Betz
Internal Designer: Lesiak Design
Cover and Internal Illustrator: Peter Sui
Marketing Manager: Steven W. Hazelwood

AQ96IA
Copyright ©1996
by South-Western College Publishing
Cincinnati, Ohio

ISBN: 0-538-84282-2

1 2 3 4 5 6 7 8 9 C5 3 2 1 0 9 8 7 6 5

Printed in the United States of America

I (T) P
International Thomson Publishing
South-Western College Publishing is an ITP Company. The ITP trademark is used under license.

Materials from the Certificate in Management Accounting Examinations, Copyright © 1972, 1974, 1976, 1980, 1983, 1985, 1987, 1988, 1989, 1990, 1991, 1992, 1993 by the National Association of Accountants are reprinted and/or adapted with permission.

Material from Uniform CPA Examination, Questions and Unofficial Answers, Copyright © 1979, 1980, 1982, 1983, 1984 by American Institute of Certified Public Accountants, Inc., is reprinted (or adapted) with permission.

Library of Congress Cataloging–in–Publication Data

Sollenberger, Harold M.
    Managerial accounting / Harold M. Sollenberger, Arnold Schneider.
  -- 9th ed.
      p. cm.
    Rev. ed. of : Managerial accounting / Lande K. Anderson, Harold M. Sollenberger. 8th ed. c1992.
  Includes index.
  ISBN 0-538-84282-2 (hardcover)
  1. Managerial accounting.   2. Cost accounting.   I. Schneider, Arnold, 1953-   . II. Anderson, Lane K. Managerial accounting.
III. Title.
HF5657.4.M66   1995
658. 15' 1--dc20
                                       95-18421
                                         CIP

PREFACE

The managerial task is changing as we move nearer to the 21st century. Managers' information demands are changing. The goal of this text is to merge new ideas from world-class production and service activities, computer-based information systems, quality management, cost management, global business, and ethics, among other subjects, into proven techniques and tools basic to business decision making. The text's perspective is that of the strategic decision maker. The result is a relevant and current text grounded in solid teaching and learning techniques.

THE BASIC PREMISES OF THE TEXT

The text's core question is: How do managers use management accounting information? The answer is: To make decisions. Every page of this text is devoted to helping managers make the best decisions to achieve the goals of their organizations. All decisions concern the future. Today's decisions affect future results. Much more time is given to managing future costs and revenues, and less time is devoted to historical reporting. In today's environment, the emphasis is on customer service, throughput, higher quality, reduced waste, continuous improvement, and global sourcing and marketing.

While managerial accounting is changing dramatically, many fundamentals are still key underpinnings of today's and tomorrow's decision making. The text integrates relevant traditional and leading edge topics into a flow that teaches basic cost analysis, decision definition, relevant information formatting, and decision making itself.

Students must understand that questions cannot be answered "yes" or "no" and that problems cannot be solved merely by calculations. The words "why," "explain," and "justify" appear frequently in exercises, problems, and cases. The student is lead from definition and concept, to mechanical demonstration, to managerial analysis, and to strategy and policy development. Our writing and teaching philosophies are aimed at users of managerial accounting information—future managers. The manager must use all quantitative tools and techniques available but must also apply logic, insight, judgment, and common sense.

Learning should be fun. We attempt to include subtle humor, interesting examples, real-world cases, and student-oriented concerns.

NEW AND IMPROVED FEATURES IN THE NINTH EDITION

The ninth edition of *Managerial Accounting* has moved forward with the fast pace of business. We have incorporated the latest developments in management and management accounting, added and changed materials based on suggestions from users of past editions, and revised numerous areas from our own teaching and research experiences. Among the key changes are:

Activity-Based Costing (ABC), Just-in-Time (JIT), and Activity-Based Management

In addition to Chapter 6 that focuses on ABC and just-in-time costing, we discuss in nearly every chapter the ramifications that these ideas and other new manufacturing and service developments have on decision making and cost management.

Service and Nonprofit Applications and Examples

While most managerial accounting concepts are transferrable across manufacturing, retailing, service, and nonprofit organizations, unique requirements and special adaptations must be recognized and discussed. We make much broader use of service and nonprofit examples and have increased significantly their end-of-chapter coverage.

International Dimensions

Because doing business in Europe, Asia, Africa, South America, and Australia is almost as common as operating on the North American continent, we must be able to think in foreign currencies, understand the impacts of European quality standards for example, and make decisions in increasingly complex global markets. We have added international sections in numerous chapters, increased the number of international-based exercises and problems, and substantially revised the chapter that focuses on specialized international issues, Chapter 16.

Ethics and Ethical Issues

Chapter 1 sets the stage for increased emphasis on ethical issues. Every chapter has a special section to highlight particular ethical concerns. Each chapter also has end-of-chapter exercises and problems that have a strong ethical base and require students to evaluate ethical dilemmas.

Sources of Additional Reference Materials

For each chapter, a set of additional readings is provided to give instructors an opportunity to expand students' exposure to current research and opinions. We have carefully selected these readings for their relevance to text discussions.

Adding Critical Thinking Requirements to End-of-Chapter Materials

As we attempt to challenge the student with qualitative and policy issues, we significantly increased the number of exercises and problems that require the student to think critically. We challenge the student to explain, to justify a viewpoint, to present arguments on both sides of an issue, to provide support for quantitative answers, and to question the basic assumptions and data provided in the exercise or problem. We are convinced that students will understand better and retain more from these challenges.

Leading Edge Topics

We have added Chapter 15 to address recent costing developments. These include the costs of quality, target and kaizen costing, value-added and nonvalue-added activities, nonfinancial performance measures, and strategies to enhance productivity. Elsewhere, we discuss benchmarking, backflushing, and life-cycle costing.

New and Revised End-of-Chapter Materials

Questions, exercises, and problems at the end of chapters are updated, revised, rewritten, deleted, and added. Approximately 30 percent of the problems are new. Requirements on at least another 30 percent are upgraded to add critical thinking approaches. More cases are included. The variety has been broadened to include more service and nonprofit materials. Ethics problems are added to every chapter. Icons indicate service [SI], ethics , international ,and computer applications. Lotus 1-2-3 templates are provided for selected exercises, problems, and cases and are identified with a special icon .

Contemporary Practice Applications and Illustrations

In every chapter, we present live examples from real-world settings or from recent literature. Our intent is to show how concepts we discuss in the text are applied directly in real settings. We also use these Contemporary Practice examples to show the variety of practices that currently do exist.

Other Changes From the Eighth Edition

The organization and presentation is improved in many ways. These include:

- Chapter 1 now links the major decision-making areas to the firm's information systems, its organization structure, the decision-making process itself, and a foundation for managerial accounting ethical standards.
- The cost estimation concepts, formerly in Chapters 4 and 15, are combined in Chapter 3 to give students a better understanding of how cost behavior is determined and used. Regression analysis has

been moved to an Appendix in Chapter 3, and mechanical computations have been replaced by analysis of computer outputs.

■ Chapters 4, 5, and 6 now present a flow of teaching and learning that begins with attaching costs to products, leads to process and job costing, and ends with an extensive integration of activity-based costing into the product and service costing systems. The reciprocal method of service center cost allocation is added to an Appendix in Chapter 4.

■ In Chapter 7, responsibility accounting, flexible budgeting, and performance reports are combined with budgeting to show the linkage between planning and control. Financial modeling is emphasized more in Chapter 8.

■ Chapter 10 introduces a new approach to analyzing changes in profits by combining the substantially revised standard cost variances concepts from Chapter 9 with contribution margin analysis. The discussion of absorption costing versus variable costing has been simplified by focusing the discussion on actual costing systems.

■ Changes to Chapter 14 refocus attention on divisional performance and intracompany business and their impacts on managers.

■ Chapter 15 adds all new contemporary topics. A major section on costs of quality provides powerful support for measuring and assessing the impacts of total quality management programs. Target costing, defining value-added activities, and downsizing are introduced.

■ Chapter 16 complements the increased emphasis on global issues throughout the text. International investment strategies, foreign currency exchange and risks, cross-border budgeting, and ethics issues are discussed.

■ Chapters 17 and 18 have been refined to emphasize the managerial implications of financial statement analysis and cash-flow reporting.

Within each chapter, the sequence of presentation reflects the extensive testing in large enrollment principles courses, stand-alone managerial accounting courses, MBA-level managerial accounting courses, and executive-MBA managerial accounting courses. Examples, illustrations, and end-of-chapter materials have largely come from in-class use by the authors and other managerial professors or from real-world examples provided by working managers or adapted from recent business articles.

THE STRUCTURE OF THE BOOK

The text is divided into six parts. Part One, **Managerial Accounting Framework**, includes Chapters 1, 2, and 3. Chapter 1 sets the stage for managerial uses of accounting data, business environment changes, decision-making steps, organizational structure, and ethical conduct. Chapter 2 presents the basic definitional concepts needed for managerial accounting. This is a critical chapter for students in establishing a firm base for moving into costing and decision-making areas. Chapter 3 expands cost behavior into cost estimation and cost-volume-profit relationships.

Part Two, **Product Cost Framework**, includes Chapters 4, 5, and 6. Chapter 4 sets the cost determination stage by explaining how costs are attached to products and services. Chapter 5 discusses both job and process costing, using the new manufacturing environment as a base. Chapter 6 now presents activity-based costing and management and extends the discussion in JIT and automated manufacturing processes.

Part Three, **Planning and Control Framework**, brings the planning and evaluation tools together in Chapters 7, 8, 9, and 10. Chapters 7 and 8 focus on budgeting and the planning and control system. Chapters 9 and 10 emphasize variance analysis to measure performance by explaining standard costs, contribution margin analysis, and AC and VC costing.

Part Four, **Decision-Making Framework**, includes Chapters 11, 12, 13, and 14. Incremental decision making (Chapter 11) is perhaps the core of decision making in managerial accounting. Capital investments decisions (Chapters 12 and 13) are important to the complete understanding of incremental decisions but are sometimes covered in other courses. Chapter 14 looks at segmental performance evaluation and internal transactions.

Part Five, **Extensions in Managerial Analysis**, includes a new Chapter 15 devoted to leading edge topics. Chapter 16 is expanded to address the growing interest in international business and how it impacts decision making. Topics of Chapters 17 and 18 are financial statement analysis and cash-flow reporting respectively. Use of these two chapters depends on curriculum and course design. Both topics overlap financial and managerial accounting.

CHAPTER FORMAT

Each chapter follows a format or pattern to assist in learning and teaching.

Learning Objectives. Learning objectives identify what the student should be able to do upon completing the chapter. They provide a guide to the study of each chapter and a teaching outline.

Vignette. We start each chapter with a realistic business situation or problem that focuses on topics covered in the chapter. These vignettes provide a framework showing why the chapter topics are important to managers. Many of the vignettes are bases for discussions of chapter or end-of-chapter materials.

Contemporary Practice. These are examples inserted carefully in each chapter to illustrate current practices and presented in either survey or summary form from newspapers, business periodicals, or academic journals.

Chapter Summary. A brief synopsis of each chapter helps the student organize, review, and integrate key concepts. We have structured the summary around the learning objectives so that the student can ascertain if all learning objectives were studied.

Review Problem. Problems with suggested solutions enable the student to test the level of understanding of chapter concepts and to obtain immediate feedback about appropriate answers.

Terminology Review. Important terminology, definitions, and concepts appear in bold type throughout each chapter. These key terms and concepts are listed at the end of the chapter.

Suggested Readings. From six to ten articles are suggested to allow the instructor to add greater detail to certain course topics or to provide students with reference materials to support preparation of papers or specific assignments.

Questions for Review and Discussion. Approximately 20 questions are framed to spark class discussion and to help students confirm their understanding of each chapter's concepts.

Exercises. Exercises usually emphasize one or two simple concepts with basic computations and straightforward "why" or "explain" questions. Each chapter has between 15 and 20 exercises.

Problems. Problems have either more than one issue, challenging situations, complex computations, and/or interpretative issues. Each problem is based on a real-life setting. Each chapter contains between 15 and 20 problems.

Cases. Most chapters have two cases. Cases have greater depth and complexity than problems. They are designed to help students integrate various concepts within the chapter and may cross several chapters. Case complexity and comprehensiveness help students to develop analytical skills.

The lead-in framework, the chapter contents, and the end-of-chapter materials combine to create a powerful learning and teaching package.

WHERE AND HOW TO USE THE TEXT

Managerial Accounting is structured with a great deal of flexibility. This text can easily be used in a number of settings: a second semester principles course, a junior-level course between principles and cost accounting, a junior-level non-accounting major managerial course, and an MBA-level managerial accounting course. The variety of chapters and the mix of materials within chapters allow a course to be structured around a plan for student learning consistent with specific curriculum and course needs.

While we believe that the chapter order as presented is the strongest teaching and learning sequence, many other models can be selected. Most chapters are designed so that they are partially or completely independent of other chapters. Consequently, an opportunity exists to design a unique course for different types or levels of students. Also, we have consciously provided illustrations and end-of-chapter materials for all types of organizations whether manufacturing, service, merchandising, or nonprofit.

The material within each chapter has a mix of conceptual, analytical, interpretative, and management behavioral issues. The text attempts to balance the fine edge of providing a solid reference of what, how, and why, while challenging students to think for themselves. Extensive end-of-chapter materials allow the selection of simple exercises for beginning students and for in-class teaching examples. More difficult problems and cases should challenge students to interrelate concepts, pragmatic issues, and real-world common sense. These materials are easily adapted to both undergraduate and graduate students.

LEARNING AND TEACHING AIDS

For the Instructor

Solutions Manual. The solutions manual contains answers to all review and discussion questions and detailed solutions for every exercise, problem, and case. Additional clarifying notes and suggestions are presented where appropriate.

Solutions Transparencies. A set of transparencies includes solutions to selected exercises, problems, and cases.

Test Bank. (Prepared by Marvin Bouillon, Iowa State University.) A test bank includes a variety of questions and short problems that are compatible and consistent with the text material. The questions provide multiple choice, true-false, and short problem options. Solutions to all questions and problems are included.

MicroSWAT III. This is a microcomputer version of the test bank that permits individualizing each examination to your own circumstances. It is designed to save time in preparing and grading interim and final examinations.

Spreadsheet Applications. (Prepared by John Palipchak, Penn State-Harrisburg.) These template diskettes, using Lotus 1-2-3, format solutions for selected end-of-chapter exercises and problems. These are identified in the textbook with a symbol in the margin ![diskette] 1-2-3 . The templates help students understand problem issues without becoming bogged down with the computations. They also allow instructors to pursue "what if" analysis so that students can see immediately the impacts of changes. These diskettes are provided free of charge from South-Western College Publishing to instructors at educational institutions that adopt this text.

For the Student

Study Guide. (Prepared by Jay Homen, University of Wisconsin-Eau Claire.) A study guide assists you in reviewing each chapter's content, in checking your understanding of concepts, and in preparing for examinations. It provides a means to reexamine the concepts and applications in each chapter from different perspectives. The study guide includes chapter outlines, learning objectives, detailed chapter summaries, self-assessment questions, such as matching, true-false, and multiple choice, and exercises. Solutions for all questions and exercises are included.

Check Figures. Key figures for solutions to the majority of exercises and problems are provided at the end of the text as an aid to students as they prepare their answers.

ACKNOWLEDGMENTS

The ninth edition was completed with the input and assistance of many people. We owe much gratitude to and want to recognize a number of special people, even with the risk that we may omit someone.

We thank the many instructors and students who used the eighth edition and gave us comments for improvements. We particularly thank those who reviewed the manuscript for this edition, including:

James P. Bedingfield, University of Maryland at College Park

Linda Campbell, University of Toledo

Al Chen, North Carolina State University

G. Richard French, Indiana University Southeast

Ginger Parker, Creighton University

Doug Poe, University of Kentucky

Douglas Sharp, Wichita State University

Monte Swain, Brigham Young University

Paul Weber, Aquinas College

Of special note is Lois Sollenberger, who edited many drafts of all chapters and supplemental materials.

Permission has been received from the Institute of Certified Management Accountants to use questions and/or unofficial answers from past Certificate in Management Accounting (CMA) examinations. Also, our appreciation is extended to the American Institute of Certified Public Accountants for permission to use (or to adapt) selected problems from its examinations. These problems bear the notations "ICMA adapted" and "AICPA adapted," respectively.

Harold M. Sollenberger
Arnold Schneider

AUTHORS

Harold M. Sollenberger is Professor of Accounting at Michigan State University. He holds MBA and DBA degrees from Indiana University and a bachelor's degree from Shippensburg University. He is a CPA. He is a member of the Financial Executives Institute, the Institute of Management Accounting, and the American Accounting Association.

At Michigan State University, Professor Sollenberger has served as Chairperson of the accounting and finance faculties and Acting Associate Dean for MBA Programs. He currently serves as Faculty Coordinator of the Advanced Management Program, an executive MBA program. Over the years, he has served as a consultant to CPA firms, governmental units, professional associations, and industrial firms. He was a visiting professor at the University of Southern California and in the People's Republic of China. He has led management study groups to Europe, Japan, Korea, and the PRC.

His teaching experience spans all levels of accounting instruction from introductory courses, to doctoral research seminars, and to working managers. Most recently, he taught managerial accounting to executive MBA students and to undergraduates in large lectures and via live instructional television. Professor Sollenberger has taught for nearly twenty years in a variety of banking and credit union financial management schools. He has taught many continuing education programs. Known for his energetic, humorous, and participatory teaching style, he has received numerous awards for his teaching at both the undergraduate and graduate levels. He has also served as treasurer for several state-wide political campaigns.

Professor Sollenberger has written 10 books and over 20 articles dealing with management information systems, cost analysis, financial institution management, and management reporting systems.

Arnold Schneider is Associate Professor of Accounting at Georgia Institute of Technology, where he teaches and does research in auditing, managerial accounting, and cost accounting. Professor Schneider is a bachelor's graduate of Case Western Reserve University and holds masters and doctoral degrees from Ohio State University. He was an auditor with the U. S. General Accounting Office in Washington, DC. He is a CPA and is a member of the American Accounting Association.

Professor Schneider has also served as a Visiting Fellow in Accounting at Macquarie University in Australia and as a Visiting Associate Professor at Emory University. He has published over 25 articles in various journals, such as *Journal of Accounting Research, Accounting Review, Decision Sciences*, and *Contemporary Accounting Research*. Professor Schneider has served on the editorial boards of the *Accounting Review, Advances in Accounting, Issues in Accounting Education*, and *Southwest Business Review*. In 1986, Georgia Tech's College of Management gave Professor Schneider the Young Investigator Award for his research.

Professor Schneider has taught undergraduate, masters, and doctoral courses. In addition, he has taught financial and managerial accounting courses to working managers. For several years, he has lectured to Chinese executives in the China/U. S. Professional Exchange Program at Georgia Tech. Professor Schneider has served as a consultant with various organizations, including as an expert witness for court cases. He has also held officer and board of director positions for several nonprofit organizations.

To my wife, Lois.
—Harold Sollenberger

To my wife, Marcy.
—Arnold Schneider

BRIEF CONTENTS

C O N T E N T S

3   COST ESTIMATION AND COST-VOLUME-PROFIT RELATIONSHIPS   71

PART *II*   PRODUCT COST FRAMEWORK

4   **PRODUCT COSTING:
ATTACHING COSTS TO PRODUCTS AND SERVICES 137**

5   **PRODUCT COSTING: JOB AND PROCESS COSTING 186**

8 BUDGET DEVELOPMENT AND FINANCIAL MODELING 322

9 COST CONTROL THROUGH STANDARD COSTS 368

10   PROFIT ANALYSIS: VARIANCES AND VARIABLE COSTING   429

PART *IV*   DECISION-MAKING FRAMEWORK

11   MANAGERIAL DECISIONS: ANALYSIS OF RELEVANT INFORMATION   467

12   CAPITAL INVESTMENT DECISIONS   514

13   CAPITAL INVESTMENT DECISIONS: ADDITIONAL ISSUES   554

14   ANALYSIS OF DECENTRALIZED OPERATIONS   587

PART *V* EXTENSIONS IN MANAGERIAL ANALYSIS

**15 COSTS OF QUALITY AND OTHER
COST MANAGEMENT ISSUES   639**

**16 INTERNATIONAL IMPLICATIONS
IN A CHANGING ENVIRONMENT   680**

17 FINANCIAL PERFORMANCE ANALYSIS 722

18 THE STATEMENT OF CASH FLOWS 760

PART I

Managerial Accounting Framework

Managerial Accounting and Management's Need for Information

After studying Chapter 1, you will be able to:

1. Understand the main uses of management accounting information.
2. Explain the changes taking place in the business environment and their impacts on managerial accounting.
3. Identify the major transaction systems and data files in an organization that generate and organize accounting information.
4. Identify the steps in the decision-making process.
5. Distinguish between financial accounting and managerial accounting.
6. Understand the typical organizational structure of a firm and the controller's responsibilities.
7. Recognize the primary ethical responsibilities of the management accountant.

The Controller's Workday: Where Did the Time Go?

It's early October 1998; and Chris Stewart, controller of Olson Software Products, has just arrived at her office at about 7:45 a.m. She scans her e-mail messages, checks her electronic calendar, and looks through her in-basket. She says, "Wow, another busy day!" She wonders if she'll make her tennis date with her husband at 6 p.m. Her calendar shows:

9:00   Meet with division head of Customer Support to discuss 1999 budget numbers. Review preliminary budget numbers before meeting.

10:00   Meet with accounting systems analysts to discuss status of a project to improve the firm's management reporting system.

11:30   Hold a quick session with Louise Haydu, marketing vice-president, to discuss pricing negotiations with new customer.

12:15   Have working lunch with corporate attorney to discuss customer contract wording for a new product to be introduced early next year.

2:00   With budget manager, review September's actual results and budget comparisons and identify problem areas. Also, review third-quarter financial results before her presentation to the president at Friday's staff meeting.

4:00   Review a special cost-volume-profit study of Olson's software products.

She also knows that she needs to:

■ Respond to four e-mail questions about product costs and operating expenses.

■ Talk to Phil Mantua, new product development vice-president, about a serious cost-overrun problem with a new product project.

■ Prepare a presentation on cash flows for the firm's strategic planning meeting next month.

■ Write a memo supporting the spending of $100,000 by the marketing vice-president on media advertising contracts.

Every meeting, discussion, and decision that Chris has today and every day use accounting information. She must generate relevant data in the right form and at the right time. She and her fellow managers must understand cost behavior, cost/benefit analyses, plan versus actual comparisons, and how to use information to achieve Olson Software Products' long-term and short-term goals.

Managers make decisions. Managers select one alternative from a set of choices. Making the best choice depends on the manager's goals, the expected results from each alternative, and the information available when the decision is made. Decision-making information is the focus of this text. Collecting, classifying, reporting, and analyzing relevant information are fundamental to every action that managers take. Management accountants prepare information for decision makers. In this chapter, the stage is set for discussing how managers use information, how the firm is organized, what changes are occurring in business environments, how decisions are framed, and how management accountants are involved in decision making.

Management accountants transform data into information. Data are the raw materials of decision making. Most business data are captured in the transaction systems of the firm. Data that are organized for some purpose or objective becomes information.

HOW MANAGERS USE MANAGEMENT ACCOUNTING INFORMATION

How do managers use management accounting information? The answer is: to make decisions. The major decision areas are:

- Forecasting and planning.
- Performance evaluation.
- Cost determination, pricing, and cost management.
- Operations control and improvement.
- Incremental decision making.
- Financial reporting.
- Motivation of managers.

Every page of this text is devoted to these topics and their interaction. Each decision area uses different information in various formats. This is management accounting.

Forecasting and Planning

Decision making always deals with the future. While historical data are useful in helping to understand past relationships, forecast data are critical. A financial plan common to most organizations is the budget. It sets a plan of action for the coming year. This plan or budget also motivates managers to achieve and creates a basis for evaluating actual results.

Performance Evaluation

After decisions have been made and actions taken, actual results flow in. How did we do? Comparing actual to plan tells a story. Analyzing differences helps evaluate the performance of managers, business segments, or even the entire firm. Comparing actual to plan may also give insights into where changes should be made—perhaps into where and how to improve resource use.

Cost Determination, Pricing, and Cost Management

What is the "true" cost of a product or service? The answer depends on why the question is asked. **Cost determination,** also known as product costing, deals with measuring the resources used to complete an activity or unit of output. **Pricing** can be market based or cost based. For products with market-based prices, pricing must still consider cost in determining profits and returns on investments. For products with cost-based prices, recovering costs is a key management concern for measuring profits. **Cost management** is finding ways to control more efficiently the activities that incur costs. Also, by more careful cost analysis, managers can identify opportunities for cost reduction.

Operations Control and Improvement

By using various accounting tools, we can measure how well operating activities were managed. Tools such as flexible budgets, standard costs, and cost control charts allow managers to monitor operating activities. Yet the real goal is to improve performance in all activities. **Continuous improvement** is a strategy that examines every aspect of a process and of entire processes for increased efficiency, cost reduction, and higher quality. In so-called "new manufacturing" environments, almost revolutionary views of production management are evolving to achieve significant improvements. Cost systems must change with the processes.

Incremental Decision Making

Underlying most decisions is an evaluation of the decision's costs and benefits. Many action-oriented decisions can be grouped by the decision objective: where and when to sell and at what price, whether to make or buy, where to use resources, or whether a segment should be added or deleted. Each decision type has specific information needs, an analysis format, and decision rules. Future incremental revenues and costs are relevant; past costs are irrelevant. Sorting relevant from irrelevant information is a responsibility of every manager.

Financial Reporting

While focusing on assisting managers, the management accountant must remember that financial results are reported to both internal and external users. Financial statements are important internally as indicators of how segments of the business and their managers are performing. In addition, executives report to boards of directors, shareholders, and others on the financial status of the firm. The performance of managers is measured in the light of how investors, shareholders, creditors, tax authorities, and, in the public sector, voters view their results.

Motivation of Managers

The last item listed is far from the least important. As we will see, messages are sent through accounting numbers—some subtle, some blunt and harsh, and others tempered by intent to motivate, encourage, and reward strong performances. Managerial psychology and attitudes are influenced in important ways by information and how it is presented and used.

Contemporary Practice 1.1 reports where managers, responding to a survey, indicate that they use costing systems and cost data in decision making.

T HE OBJECTIVE OF MANAGEMENT

For accounting information to fulfill its roles, management's goals must be clear. The financial goal of a firm is to maximize the long-term wealth of shareholders or, expressed differently, to maximize the present value of shareholders' future cash flows from the firm. Corporate managers have a strong interest in profit. But many organizations do not attempt to produce a profit. The success of a nonprofit enterprise, for instance, is measured by realizing a common goal rather than economic objectives. A governmental agency, for example, is primarily concerned with providing services to its citizens.

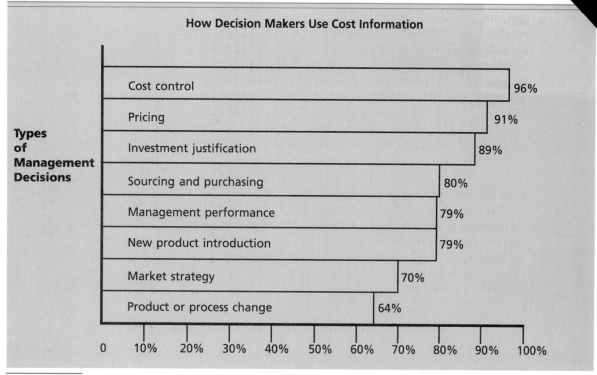

How Decision Makers Use Cost Information

Source: Emore, J. R., and J. A. Ness, "The Slow Pace of Meaningful Change in Cost Systems," *Journal of Cost Management*, Vol. 4, No. 4, pp. 36-45.

In the vast majority of decision-making situations, the same basic decision rules apply to all types of organizations. Economic realities are important in all organizations. At a minimum, management must use its resources in a manner that attains desired goals in an efficient manner.

Contemporary managers recognize that the business enterprise is also responsible to many diverse groups, both inside and outside the organization. Employees depend on the business for a means of livelihood. In addition, the community expects a business to be a positive contributing neighbor. Most businesspersons acknowledge that the goals of each group are best served by the harmonious reconciliation of all interests. Hence, the objective of maximizing profits must be accomplished within socially and legally accepted bounds.

*M*ANAGEMENT ACCOUNTING INFORMATION: USERS AND SYSTEMS

Organizations create or cause events, referred to as economic activity. A manager in a company within any industry will spend large chunks of time organizing personnel and arranging resources to be productive. A manager faces numerous choices, conflicting priorities, organizational politics and culture, and the normal burdens of bureaucracy.

Levels of Management

ddle, and lower-level managers need different information. A rough exists between a manager's level in the organization and the type of ng information needed. Executive or top managers generally face ared or semistructured problems common to strategic planning. Strate-ning deals with market positioning, the economy, competitors, sources of capital, and other outside factors that affect the long-term well-being of the company. Therefore, much information comes from external sources.

Middle management deals with semistructured problems relating primarily to obtaining and using resources effectively and efficiently. Here, managers want information to formulate operating budgets; create capital spending plans; choose product strategies; plan personnel levels; and measure, evaluate, and improve performances of subordinates.

Supervisory or lower management faces more structured tasks. How many control boards are needed on Monday? When should Order 345 be produced? Each manager typically has authority to operate within a particular department or category of work. Decisions, needed information, and decision rules are clearly identified. Supervisors' information needs are detailed, time dependent, and reported routinely.

Sources of Management Accounting Data

In today's world, you can often be data rich but information poor. Internal accounting systems exist as a source of financial and nonmonetary data and convert these data into meaningful information. Accounting systems accumulate, classify, store, and report relevant information in ways that meet each manager's needs. These systems capture transaction data. The common transaction systems in the typical company are:

- **Order entry system**—Sales orders from customers are processed and filled, and customers are billed for their purchases.
- **Cash receipts system**—Cash receipts from customers are recorded, and cash is deposited.
- **Purchases system**—In retail firms, merchandise is ordered, received, and recorded.
- **Production planning and control system**—In manufacturing firms, production schedules are set; purchases made; materials, labor, and equipment are scheduled; and production output is monitored.
- **Cash disbursements system**—All payments for purchases and any other activities are made and recorded.
- **Personnel system**—All personnel events are recorded. The major activities include hiring, benefits, evaluation, and payroll activities.
- **General accounting system**—Data from all other transaction systems are brought together, and most management reports and financial statements are generated. The budgeting process is part of this system.

These seven systems generate the vast majority of data used in most firms for accounting, marketing, production, and general management purposes. The data that managers read in reports and analyses depend on how these systems are designed. In the following chapters, the data we use come from these systems.

Figure 1.1 shows the major databases that exist in many organizations. Depending on the sophistication of data processing systems, databases are accessed by these transaction systems. In nonautomated environments, these databases are file cabinets and manually maintained journals and ledgers. Today, a customer record can be accessed via computers by marketing, shipping, order entry, billing, cash receipts, market research, and any other internal user who needs information on that customer. Today's enormous hardware and software capabilities eliminate most constraints that in the past limited managerial accountants' ability to generate relevant information.

FIGURE 1.1 Major Databases Found in Most Organizations

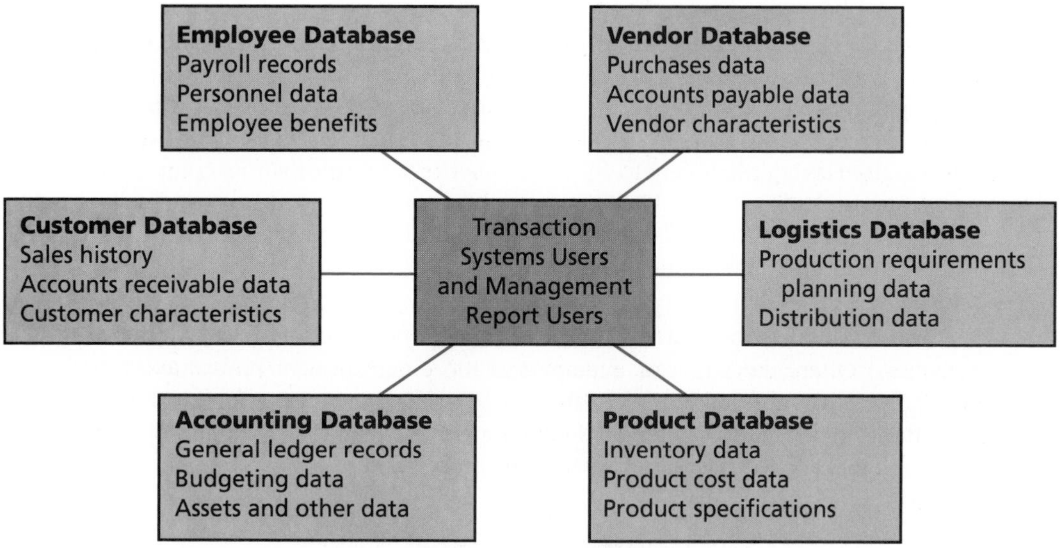

Employee Database
Payroll records
Personnel data
Employee benefits

Vendor Database
Purchases data
Accounts payable data
Vendor characteristics

Customer Database
Sales history
Accounts receivable data
Customer characteristics

Transaction
Systems Users
and Management
Report Users

Logistics Database
Production requirements
planning data
Distribution data

Accounting Database
General ledger records
Budgeting data
Assets and other data

Product Database
Inventory data
Product cost data
Product specifications

A CHANGING BUSINESS ENVIRONMENT

The business environment is changing rapidly, both domestically and globally. These changes influence the way managers conduct business. Consequently, they also affect the information managers use.

Global Competition

The world is now one market. Materials, labor, and technical know-how come from all parts of the world. Markets for our products and services are likewise transnational. It is fair to say that every business has seen competition heighten in the past decade. Shifts in the competitive situation cause managers to identify ways to reduce product and service costs while supplying improved product quality and customer service.

Perhaps the most obvious change is the globalization of business activity. **Globalization** can be defined as being world-wide in scope or application.

Apart from this geographical application, globalization can also be defined as becoming universal. This second meaning implies both a harmonization of rules and a reduction of barriers to allow a free flow of capital, goods, and services and to permit all firms to compete in all markets. GATT (General Agreement on Tariffs and Trade) and NAFTA (North American Free Trade Agreement) are important treaties promoting increased international trade.

A related movement is called **world-class manufacturing**. It emphasizes higher quality, lower inventory investment, faster processing, automation, and organizational flexibility to meet changing needs and advances in information technology. Many business people view companies with world-class manufacturing as pioneers on the "cutting edge" of better ideas.

The Value Chain and Value Added

One way to view a firm's activities is to identify its value chain. A **value chain** looks strategically at each part of the firm's operations and asks what key contribution each part makes to the competitive strength of the firm as a whole. For example, being the low-cost producer in a market gives that firm an advantage. Having the ability to fill a customer order faster than its competitors gives another advantage. Managers are planning and working to develop strength in each link of its business chain. Each link should add value to the firm's operations. Management accountants' challenge is to measure the costs and benefits of adding value.

Value added is the increase in the worth of the firm, its products, and its activities. Often, the target of managers is the elimination of nonvalue-added activities. **Nonvalue-added activities** are essentially wasted effort. Why do something if no value is added? Reduction of waste has helped many firms become more competitive and much more productive.

Quality Assurance

In the past decade, quality has become an obsession in many firms. Customer dissatisfaction with American-made cars, electronic equipment, and many other products paved the way for competitors that delivered high-quality products at low prices—mainly from Japan. Japanese firms, using various quality enhancing techniques including quality circles (QC), statistical quality control, total quality management programs (TQM), continuous improvement programs, and employee empowerment processes, proved that high quality and high productivity are natural allies.

Management accountants focus on the **costs of quality** which come in two forms: voluntary costs and failure costs. Voluntary quality costs include prevention costs, such as training and quality promotion efforts, and appraisal costs, which include quality inspections and testing. Failure costs are either internal, such as scrap and lost work time due to failures, or external, such as warranty costs and lost sales (the most damaging costs). Better training and greater attention to prevention costs should reduce failure costs. Initially, a total quality management program should increase voluntary costs and reduce failure costs.

Over time, failure costs decline; voluntary costs also drop; productivity increases; customer satisfaction grows; sales jump; and profits multiply. This scenario has been proven. The common cry is "Quality is free." The reverse is also true—poor quality, higher costs, lower sales, and financial losses. We measure the quality costs to help managers attack waste and improve quality.

Just-in-Time Management

Just-in-time (JIT) is a method of management that stresses delivering the product or service when it is needed—not before (creating inventory) or after (causing customer dissatisfaction). Often JIT means holding inventories to a minimum. This is a "pull" system, in which sales pull products through the production process. Inventory is expensive. Holding inventory often costs at least 25 percent and as high as 40 percent of its value. Thus, a million dollar inventory costs at least $250,000 just to handle, store, and finance annually.

But JIT is more than just inventory control. It is sometimes called "synchronous manufacturing." The objectives of JIT are to obtain materials just in time for production, to move work in process from one work center to another just in time to meet the needs of the next work center, and to provide finished goods just when the customer wants them.

Technical Evolution

The technical evolution has impacted every business, but manufacturing has, perhaps, experienced the greatest impact. Phrases like focused production, flexible manufacturing, and computer-aided design and manufacturing highlight the changes. **Focused production** attempts to decrease the variety of products made in a plant and to manufacture products and provide services that result in the highest contribution margins. Some companies even organize their plants into cells that focus a group of machines and people toward producing a particular product line.

Flexible manufacturing is a move to increase the variety of products that a given machine or group of machines can produce. The purpose is to reduce space, machinery investment, and setup time and cost, which increases total throughput. By doubling the variety of products that the same machinery can manufacture, a company can substantially cut the equipment required.

Computer-aided design (CAD) is the use of high-quality graphics and software to create new products or to change existing products. CAD leads directly to **computer-aided manufacturing (CAM)**. CAM occurs when machines or entire production lines are run and coordinated by computers. **Computer-integrated manufacturing (CIM)** is a term that ties engineering, production planning, and production processes themselves into a linked process. Reduced lead times for meeting a customer order is one result. The wall between the "people who design" and the "people who make" is torn down and replaced by a team effort.

Management information systems (MIS) handle the major data processing and information handling tasks in organizations. MIS allows information to be literally on the desktop of every manager. In addition, telecommunications technology can communicate vast amounts of data to any place in the world. For example, in an automotive plant as a car is started on the assembly line, an electronic message to begin building the seats for that car is sent to a nearby vendor plant. The seats are completed, trucked to the assembly plant, and delivered to the needed point on the assembly line just as the car arrives. Thus, JIT, CIM, TQM, and MIS all merge into a powerful, high-quality, and very productive manufacturing system.

Management Complexity

Management complexity is such a broad area that only a few points can be mentioned here. Traditional line and staff alignments are becoming blurred. Functional management responsibility (marketing, finance, production, etc.) is being merged with product line responsibility. Matrix organizations are being created, linking functional and product responsibilities.

Downsizing or "rightsizing" is a common approach that many large companies are using to remove entire layers of management and to make the organization "lean and mean." Too many layers of management remove the executive from the day-to-day business. Terms like "reengineering" represent new ways of designing approaches to conducting business in the twenty-first century. **Benchmarking** is a method of comparing operations, costs, and productivity with world-class performers in those areas. Certainly, carefully examining every process, singularly and comprehensively, can add to the long-run success of the organization.

Team approaches are increasingly the norm in tackling business problems. Committees, task forces, project teams, and study groups are terms indicating that work is done through cooperation and integration. Directing and motivating people are at the core of managing.

THE DECISION-MAKING PROCESS

A key to effective decision making is a structured approach. Still, the best process or even the best decision does not guarantee a successful outcome. The future determines its own fate, but the best prepared analysis is most likely to produce the desired result.

The following decision steps outline a structure for decision making.

1. **Define the decision issue.** A careful definition of the problem's scope is fundamental to higher quality analysis in later steps. Defining strategic, competitive, and organizational factors helps to focus on key issues.
2. **Specify the decision objective and decision rule.** Often the **decision objective** is the goal toward which the decision maker is working, such as profit maximization. Other situations may require the greatest efficiency, sales maximization, most persons served, or lowest cost. Knowing the overall goal sets the **decision rule**.
3. **Identify the choices. Choices** are the alternatives available to the decision maker.
4. **Collect relevant data on the choices.** Given time and investigation cost limits, data manipulation is a cost and benefit issue. Theoretically, we should stop collecting data when the marginal cost of collecting more data equals the marginal benefit of making a

better decision. Practically, we are often constrained by time and available data.

5. **Format and analyze information about each choice.** Organizing the decision data often simplifies the decision task. The managerial accountant's responsibility is to organize the relevant data for analysis. A specific format focuses attention on the decision's relevant revenues and costs.

6. **Make the decision.** Given the decision rule, select the choice that gives the greatest benefit. Having said that, we must recognize that basic quantitative analysis is one part of the decision. Strategic issues, long-run impacts, qualitative factors, and even personal biases may influence the decision maker. But relevant data *must* be the foundation of analysis.

7. **Implement the decision.** Now the obvious should take place. A decision has been made; implement it.

8. **Evaluate the results of the decision.** Feedback on actual results enhances the analysis of similar future decisions. Here we close the control cycle.

Each step helps move the decision maker closer to achieving the best outcome for the firm. Performing all eight steps of the decision-making process completes the plan, act, evaluate, and control cycle.

ORGANIZATION OF THE FIRM

Often, to understand an organization, we can look at its structure. Figure 1.2, page 14, presents an abbreviated organization chart for a medium-sized manufacturing firm. The president reports to the board of directors and eventually to shareholders. The board of directors sets general policies for the entity. Responsibility for operating the entity on a day-to-day basis is vested in the president, who in turn delegates authority to vice-presidents of functional areas. Notice that the internal audit function reports to the president. These independent reviewers of internal controls and activities could report to the board of directors.

The marketing organization presents the firm's products and services to customers. It develops marketing strategies, advertises, sends out salespersons, obtains customer orders, and may fill those orders. Production is responsible for all manufacturing activities. The chart in Figure 1.2 shows only basic activities: production planning, purchasing, receiving and moving materials, and production itself. Personnel activities include all hiring, training, and evaluating activities plus dealing with labor unions and developing personnel policies.

The positions of controller and treasurer are shown separately. These might be combined into the position of Chief Financial Officer (CFO). The **treasurer** is responsible for granting credit, collecting and disbursing money, and obtaining credit and long-term funds. **Controller** responsibilities include the duties shown in Figure 1.2. Historically, data processing originated in the controller's area. Now, many companies have a vice-president position responsible for management information systems activities.

FIGURE 1.2   Organization Charts for a Manufacturing Company

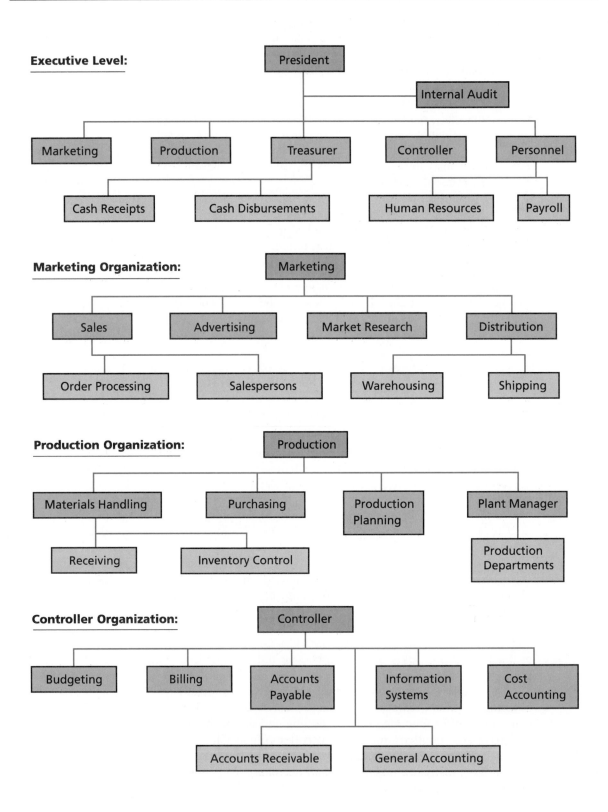

THE DUAL ROLES OF ACCOUNTING INFORMATION

The accounting system generates the information that satisfies two reporting needs that coexist within an organization: financial accounting and managerial accounting. Figure 1.3, page 16, shows the primary interested parties and the typical reports generated to serve these two user groups.

Financial Accounting

Financial accounting is the branch of accounting that organizes accounting information for presentation to interested parties outside the organization. The primary financial accounting reports are the balance sheet (often called a statement of financial position), the income statement, and the statement of cash flows. The balance sheet is a summary of assets, liabilities, and shareholders' equity at a specified point in time. The income statement reports revenues and expenses resulting from the company's operations for a particular time period. The statement of cash flows shows the sources and uses of cash over a time period for operating, investing, and financing activities.

Most businesses are complex, and guidelines (known as generally accepted accounting principles) are provided for financial reporting. The Financial Accounting Standards Board (FASB) and the Securities and Exchange Commission (SEC) oversee the development of these principles. Internationally, while each country has developed its own accounting principles, groups like the International Accounting Standards Committee set guidelines for greater comparability.

Owners, Investors, and Creditors. Shareholder-owned firms rely heavily on owners, investors, and creditors (providers of short-term credit and long-term loans) for sources of capital. Shareholders and investors use accounting reports to decide whether to buy, sell, or hold the firm's stock. Also, creditors assess whether the firm is able to pay its debts on time.

Taxing Authorities. The assessment of many taxes is based on accounting information submitted by the taxpayer. Examples of such taxes include income taxes, sales taxes, use taxes, franchise taxes, excise taxes, property taxes, and gift and estate taxes. In most cases, the dominant taxing authority is the federal government and its tax collection agency, the Internal Revenue Service.

Regulatory Agencies. Local, state, and federal agencies regulate a substantial portion of business activity in the United States. Much regulation is implemented through or involves accounting reports.

Industry Associations. Most industries have an association that gathers important statistics about the national and international industry. A large part of the information they provide comes from accounting reports of member firms.

Managers and Employees. Managers have direct vested interests in their firms' results. Performance bonuses, stock options, and incentive compensation programs are common. Thus, managers are not passive observers as to how certain transactions are recorded. Firm policies, performance evaluation methods, and compensation systems should encourage managers to act in the best interests of themselves and the firm as a whole.

FIGURE 1.3 Scope of Financial and Managerial Accounting

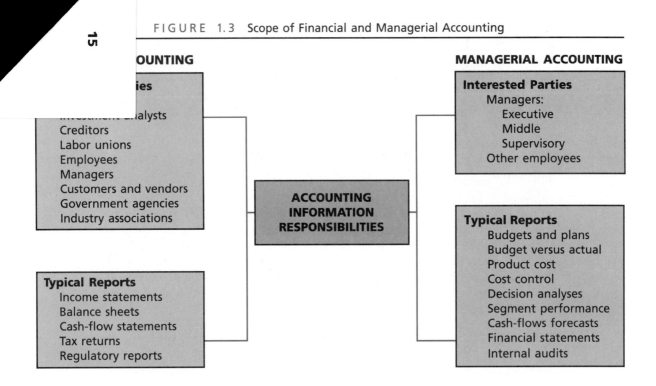

The firm's executives are responsible to the board of directors and shareholders for the firm's financial results. Numerous examples of changes in high-level executive positions reaffirm the importance of achieving strong profits to remain in power and employed. Based in part on financial statement information, employees make decisions about continued employment, union wage demands and contract negotiations, adequacy of pension plans, and employee stock purchase or savings plans. Profit sharing may encourage employees to want the company to be financially successful.

Managerial Accounting

Managerial accounting is the branch of accounting that meets managers' information needs. Because managerial accounting is designed to assist the firm's managers, relatively few restrictions are imposed by regulatory bodies and generally accepted accounting principles. Therefore, a manager must define which data are relevant for a particular purpose and which are not.

Differences Between Managerial and Financial Accounting

Several important differences distinguish managerial accounting from financial accounting. First, managerial accounting is not subject to the same rules and principles as is financial accounting. In many cases, "common sense" is the most important guide for decision makers.

A second difference is that financial accounting relies on accounting principles structured around the accounting equation. Management reports, on the other hand, are designed to meet managers' needs. These reports often use estimates and forecasts, use different values for the same events, do not balance in a debit/credit sense, and are designed for particular decisions or analyses. The expression *different costs for different purposes* has long been used to describe relevance. Relevant information has an impact on the decision analysis. Irrelevant data have no impact.

Another difference is that managerial accounting focuses on segments of the organization as well as on the whole organization. The primary interest of financial accounting is the company as a whole. In managerial accounting, however, the segment is of major importance. Segments may be products, projects, divisions, plants, branches, regions, or any other subset of the business. Tracing or allocating costs, revenues, and assets to segments creates difficult issues for managerial accountants.

Two important similarities do exist. The transaction and accounting information systems discussed earlier are used to generate the data inputs for both financial statements and management reports. Therefore, when the system accumulates and classifies information, it should do so in formats that accommodate both types of accounting. The other similarity is the manner in which accountants measure costs, define assets, and specify accounting periods. Many concepts underlie accounting information, whether the data are later used for financial or managerial reporting. Recording the results of events is often based on rationales that are common to both financial and managerial accounting. We must be careful to know what is a common thread and what must be independently collected.

*R*OLE OF THE MANAGEMENT ACCOUNTANT

Although the top accounting-oriented people in an organization are the chief financial officer and the controller, the accounting and financial management functions contain a range of jobs. A variety of careers is available as shown in Figure 1.4 (page 18); these careers can frequently be paths to executive management.

Management Accountant

A **management accountant** maintains accounting records, prepares financial statements, generates managerial reports and analyses, and coordinates budgeting efforts. The management accountant is an advisor, an internal consultant, and an integral part of management. The controller, as shown in Figure 1.2, is responsible for managing the entire accounting function. The controller influences management when answering questions like: What information should be reported? What format best displays the information? How can data be collected and processed? By the nature of the job, the management accountant applies management principles and often is a major player in decision making itself.

Certified Management Accountant

The Certified Management Accountant program recognizes a person's achievement of a specific level of knowledge and professional skill. Becoming

FIGURE 1.4   Management Accounting Job Titles

Accounting systems analyst	Internal auditor
Bid cost estimator	International controller
Budget performance analyst	Labor negotiations cost analyst
Capital investment analyst	Master budget coordinator
Cash disbursements manager	Payroll accountant
Cash flow analyst	Physical asset accountant
Cash receipts manager	Plant controller
Computer controls auditor	Product cost/profit analyst
Corporate financial accountant	Project controller
Corporate tax planner	Quality cost analyst
Cost accountant	Risk management analyst
Cost forecasting analyst	Statistical cost analyst
Customer or sales analyst	Strategic planner
Efficiency cost analyst	Transfer pricing analyst

a **Certified Management Accountant (CMA)** is considered an important professional step for anyone desiring to become a management accountant or financial executive. The CMA program was founded on the principle that a management accountant is a contributor to and a participant in management.

To qualify for the CMA designation, candidates must pass a comprehensive examination and meet specific educational and professional standards. To remain a CMA, a person must meet continuing educational requirements and adhere to the program's "Standards of Ethical Conduct for Management Accountants." The Institute of Management Accountants (IMA) is the professional organization of management accountants and sponsors the CMA designation.

The four-part examination covers the areas important for the work of a management accountant. Part 1 examines economics, finance, and management. Part 2 covers financial accounting and reporting. Part 3 deals with management reporting, analysis, and behavioral issues. Part 4 tests decision analysis and information systems.

Ethical Conduct of Management Accountants

In the preceding pages, we discussed managers' needs for accounting information. We assumed that whatever information the accounting system generates is presented and used in an ethical manner. Ethical conduct is a necessary asset of a managerial accountant. The credibility of the information provided, analyses done, and opinions offered depends heavily on the reputation of the responsible accountant. Independence, competence, lack of bias or favoritism, trust, and objectivity are key elements in establishing credibility.

While true for all managers, management accountants in particular must maintain integrity and ethical behavior and must make top management aware of unethical behavior on the part of others within the organization. This does not mean that the management accountant is a police officer. Rather, the management accountant promotes and encourages ethical behavior in all aspects of business life.

Ethical standards of businesspersons have been given much more visibility and scrutiny in recent years. Issues that appear again and again in management careers test the ethical standards of everyone. Among common ethical issues are:

- **Business practices and policies.** Practices that seem harmless on the surface may encourage or require employees or managers to be deceitful or dishonest.

- **Objective reporting.** Because situations exist where prejudiced reporting of certain numbers may influence decisions, accountants are guided by goals of unbiased reporting and professional judgment.

- **Colleague behavior.** Even if we have high ethical standards, people around us may not be so blessed. Many policies and internal controls are in place in organizations to prevent wrongdoing and to encourage proper behavior. But, your personal integrity should not condone unethical behavior in others.

- **Competitors.** Winning is part of the business "game." But to do so in a fair environment is critical. Using true product and competitor data, following corporate policies, and abhorring bribes, kickbacks, and other similar payments are easy examples. Many firms provide behavior guidelines and policies to purchasing and sales personnel who are at special risk in giving and receiving favors and improper inducements.

- **Tax avoidance and evasion.** Tax burdens can be significant. Proper planning and careful use of tax laws to minimize the organization's tax liability are acceptable. Tax avoidance is legitimate. Inappropriate use of the same laws or use of deceit to hide income or overstate deductions is tax evasion, which is unethical as well as illegal.

- **Confidentiality.** Keeping secrets is still "in." Internal data are developed for managers' use. Disclosures outside the firm often require review and approvals. Privacy of competitive, personnel, and negotiating data is critical. Negative examples of overheard conversations in elevators, on golf courses, and at lunches that lead to lost business, embarrassment, and lawsuits are unfortunately common. Confidentiality also asserts that "insider" information should not be used for anyone's personal advantage.

- **Appearance of independence.** The accountant should be independent in situations where the resulting information is used for analysis and decision making. Independence applies to both real independence and the appearance of independence. If it appears that the management accountant is biased because of that person's conduct, associations, or vested interests (possible promotion, salary increases or bonuses, or investments), the information provided is tainted and open to doubt by other decision makers.

- **Corporate loyalty and personal advancement.** Many situations exist where, because of an unethical act, the reputation of the firm itself is in danger. Or an unethical act may ensure your personal enhancement in some manner. Also, to report an unethical act may endanger the future of the person reporting the act. These are all difficult dilemmas pitting right against wrong, but not always in an obvious way.

While space and time do not allow us to develop approaches for resolving these problems here, it is clear that ethical issues underlie management accountants' professional and day-to-day activities. Each chapter will raise and discuss ethical issues related to those special topics.

Each person must develop a method of handling ethical problems. Of primary importance is the ability to see an ethical dilemma when it faces us. Once identified, the situation may well cause us to request advice. Numerous sources are available for guidance including:

- **Our own personal values.** We would like to think that our own value system is "ethical" and provides enough guidance. Clearly, this is our main line of defense against "wrong."

- **Corporate policies and ethics statements.** Many firms have statements on expected employee behavior or written policies and procedures on how a range of situations should be handled. These statements do set limits or barriers and may describe expected levels of behavior.

- **Laws.** "If it's legal, it must be okay" is often used a basis for defining ethical behavior. This is absolutely not true. Laws are man-made in a political process, often without much serious consideration for the ethical conduct of any parties involved. But at least if it's illegal, the behavior is likely unethical.

- **Professional standards.** Most professions have developed a statement of ethical standards for their members. Figure 1.5 presents a statement developed for management accountants. These statements are basic standards of behavior and give professional guidance in many areas.

- **Supervisors, internal auditors, and other company officials.** These are often persons with more experience and broader understanding of conflicting issues and of corporate attitudes. An ethical situation, however, may involve a supervisor or other corporate official, which may make the dilemma much more sensitive and severe. A few companies have created an ombudsperson position to assist employees in handling delicate situations.

- **Counselors from outside of the organization.** This is a last resort and generally violates another ethical consideration—confidentiality. While close friends, a spouse, or a personal counselor may seem like logical sources of advice and support, the nature of the dilemma may well require confidentiality until all other avenues of resolution are exhausted. Merely consulting outsiders presents serious risks of unauthorized disclosure which may only further complicate an issue.

Even though all of these options may exist, we each need to develop a rational approach to identifying, analyzing, and deciding on ethical issues that confront us. Management accountants must be aware of ethical dilemmas, perhaps more than the typical manager, because of their responsibility for decision-making information and their involvement in many decision-making processes.

The Institute of Management Accountants believes ethics is a cornerstone of its organization and recognizes the importance of providing ethical guidance. The IMA has developed *Standards of Ethical Conduct for Management Accountants.* That statement is presented in Figure 1.5. The Standards are grouped into four sections: competence, confidentiality, integrity, and objectivity.

FIGURE 1.5   Standards of Ethical Conduct for Management Accountants

E THICAL CONDUCT

Competence

Management accountants have a responsibility to:

■ Maintain an appropriate level of professional competence by ongoing development of their knowledge and skills.

■ Perform their professional duties in accordance with laws, regulations, and technical standards.

■ Prepare complete and clear reports and recommendations after appropriate analyses of relevant and reliable information.

Confidentiality

Management accountants have the responsibility to:

■ Refrain from disclosing confidential information acquired in the course of their work, except when authorized, unless legally obligated to do so.

■ Inform subordinates as appropriate regarding the confidentiality of information acquired in the course of their work and monitor their activities to assure the maintenance of that confidentiality.

■ Refrain from using or appearing to use confidential information acquired in the course of their work for unethical or illegal advantage either personally or through third parties.

Integrity

Management accountants have the responsibility to:

■ Avoid actual or apparent conflicts of interest and advise all appropriate parties of any potential conflict.

■ Refrain from engaging in any activity that would prejudice their ability to carry out their duties ethically.

■ Refuse any gift, favor, or hospitality that would influence or would appear to influence their actions.

■ Refrain from either actively or passively subverting the attainment of the organization's legitimate and ethical objectives.

■ Recognize and communicate professional limitations or other constraints that would preclude responsible judgment or successful performance of an activity.

■ Communicate unfavorable as well as favorable information and professional judgments or opinions.

■ Refrain from engaging in or supporting any activity that would discredit the profession.

Objectivity

Management accountants have the responsibility to:

■ Communicate information fairly and objectively.

■ Disclose fully all relevant information that could reasonably be expected to influence an intended user's understanding of the reports, comments, and recommendations presented.

Source: *Standards of Ethical Conduct for Management Accountants*, Montvale, NJ: Institute of Management Accountants (formerly the National Association of Accountants), 1983.

CONTEMPORARY   PRACTICE   1 . 2

"Let's Eavesdrop on Managers"

Secret electronic monitoring of employee computer, telephone, and face-to-face communications is rapidly increasing. Employees feel invaded, demeaned, and untrusted. Advocates of surveillance believe monitoring increases productivity, provides job improvement through feedback, protects innocent employees from unfair accusations, and ensures better customer service. One employee suggested that "the more central a position and the higher the cost of poor performance, the greater should be the degree of monitoring," implying that maybe the president needs the most monitoring.

Source: Marx, G. T., "Let's Eavesdrop on Managers," *Computerworld*, April 20, 1992, p. 29.

Competence refers to the skills that the accountant brings to the job. Confidentiality defines protecting the access and use of information. Integrity focuses primarily on the personal behavior and interactions of the management accountant. Objectivity, as defined here, is primarily directed toward disclosure of unbiased information.

SUMMARY

Managers in all types of organizations need accounting information to aid them in making decisions as efficiently and effectively as possible. Managerial uses of accounting information include forecasting and planning, performance evaluation, cost determination and management, pricing, operations control, incremental decision making, financial reporting, and motivation of managers. All managerial decision making should be made with the mission and the strategic goals of the firm in mind. Frequently, the main goal is profit making. In all cases, a defined and structured decision-making process should be followed.

An organization's structure often can be presented on a chart. The structure of an organization determines responsibility and reporting relationships. The controller is the executive responsible for accounting information, budgets, information systems, cost accounting, accounts payable and receivable, and general accounting.

Accounting information is provided from a system that handles the requirements of two branches of accounting: financial accounting and managerial accounting. Financial accounting presents accounting information to parties outside the organization. Managerial accounting organizes accounting information for internal management. Internal reporting is generally directed to the decision areas mentioned earlier.

The ethical conduct and integrity of the management accountant are critical to the success of the accountant's mission. Ethical situations are common and often complex. Management accountants have a special responsibility to their management colleagues and to themselves to uphold high ethical standards.

TERMINOLOGY REVIEW

SUGGESTED READINGS

Brown, V. H., "The Tension Between Management Accounting and Financial Reporting," *Management Accounting*, Vol. 68, No. 11, pp. 39-41.

Collins, D., and T. O'Rourke, *Ethical Dilemmas in Accounting*, South-Western Publishing Co., Cincinnati, OH, 1994.

Coppage, R. E., "Supervision: A Significant Dimension of Ethics for Management Accountants," *Advances in Management Accounting*, 1992, pp. 231-242.

Johnson, H. T., and R. S. Kaplan, *Relevance Lost: The Evolution of Management Accounting*, Harvard Business School Press, Boston, MA, 1987.

Krause, P., and D. E. Keller, "Bringing World-Class Manufacturing to a Small Company," *Management Accounting*, Vol. 70, No. 5, pp. 28-33.

McKinnon, S. M., and W. J. Bruns, "Management Information and Accounting Information: What Do Managers Want?" *Advances in Management Accounting*, 1992, pp. 55-80.

Mihalek, P. H., A. J. Rich, and C. S. Smith, "Ethics and Management Accountants," *Management Accounting*, Vol. 69, No. 6, pp. 34-36.

QUESTIONS FOR REVIEW AND DISCUSSION

1. Explain how forecasting and planning are related to performance evaluation.

2. Identify the major managerial decision areas. What is the main purpose of each?

3. Review the vignette at the beginning of the chapter. Review Chris Stewart's schedule and additional action items. Into which managerial decision area does each item fall?

4. Distinguish between cost determination and cost management.

5. Which of the following areas of decision making is most important? (If management did not do this, the company would be out of business.) Explain.

   (a) Forecasting and planning

   (b) Performance evaluation

   (c) Cost management, pricing, and cost determination

   (d) Operations control and improvement

   (e) Financial reporting

   (f) Motivation of managers

6. Compare and contrast the characteristics of accounting information needed by top management with accounting information used by lower management.

7. Identify the major transactions systems that generate most of the data used in organizations. What is the main purpose of each of these systems?

8. What are the major data files that exist in most organizations? What data elements would you expect to find in these files?

9. For each transaction system discussed, which of the data files discussed would be used?

10. What is the difference between "value chain" and "value added?" What is a "nonvalue-added activity?"

11. What are TQM, CIM, and JIT? How are they related?

12. What is meant by "world-class manufacturing?"

13. What are the differences among focused production, flexible manufacturing, and computer-integrated manufacturing?

14. What objectives, other than profit, might be important to managers in an organization?

15. Identify the eight steps in the decision-making process. Which steps are primarily information handling activities? Describe the activities.

16. Making the decision may actually be the easiest part of the process. Which part of the decision-making process is the most expensive? Most time-consuming? Most difficult analytical process?

17. What groups (both inside and outside an organization) have an interest in financial statements issued by the organization? Give reasons for each group's interest.

18. Briefly describe three ways in which financial accounting and managerial accounting are different. Name two ways in which they are the same or similar.

19. What major activity areas report to the controller? To the treasurer?

20. Referring to the major transaction systems and the organization chart presented in the chapter, who is probably responsible for each transaction system?

21. A management accountant is both an information provider and a part of management. Explain.

22. Carlos Garcia, president of Garcia Food Processors, stated: "The controller in our organization frequently has more influence over the lower-level managers than our upper-level people have. This seems to also be the case with most of our clients." Why would he say this? Do you agree or disagree with the assessment of the president? Explain.

23. Briefly describe the management accountant's responsibility for ethical behavior with respect to competence, confidentiality, integrity, and objectivity.

24. What is the payoff for an organization to have a code of ethics that employees will follow?

25. What are sources of counsel and guidance on ethical dilemmas available to a manager?

26. Give examples of ethical dilemmas that would arise from objective reporting, colleague behavior, confidentiality, tax evasion, and personal advancement.

E XERCISES

1-1. You have purchased using company funds the latest version of SuperSpreadSheet for your work station in your office. Comment on the following situations.

   (a) Stan, a friend in another department, is thinking of buying the same product and wants to try yours for several days.

   (b) You would like to use the same spreadsheet on your home computer to handle your household budget records.

   (c) Mary, your boss, asks for a copy of the diskettes for use on her computer.

1-2. You are on your way to lunch, and the elevator is packed. Two persons from a competing firm happen to be talking about a business deal which involves one of your customers. Your computer-like mind lists your alternatives: plug your ears; tell them that you are with a competitor; listen and then delete the information from your brain; immediately go back to the office and act on the new information; or call their supervisor and report the conversation you just overheard. What should you do?

1-3. You have been involved in high-level discussions about downsizing. Certain departments will be eliminated. Your best friend is in one of these departments. Should you try to change the downsizing plan to save your friend's job? Should you mention to your friend that a transfer to another department would be wise? Should you tell your friend not to buy a house that he and his wife are considering? Discuss each consideration.

1-4. Comment on the following frequently heard statements about ethical conduct:

   (a) "You can't teach ethics. If people don't know right from wrong by now, they'll never learn."

   (b) "It's legal. My attorney says so. Therefore, it's okay."

   (c) "Are you trying to impose your values on me?"

   (d) "I believe in situational ethics. What's right or wrong depends on the situation."

   (e) "I can't be ethical all the time. My competitors would eat me alive!"

   (f) "Everyone does it."

Cost Concepts

After studying Chapter 2, you will be able to:

1. Define, distinguish, and illustrate key cost concepts.

2. Understand the differences in cost flows among service, merchandising, and manufacturing enterprises.

3. Explain product cost elements.

4. Describe and formulate a cost function.

5. Distinguish between the behavior of variable and fixed costs.

6. Differentiate among planning, decision, and control cost terms.

What's It Cost?

Professor Jacobs enters the classroom a few minutes before the start of the first class of Accounting 202, Principles of Management Accounting. He looks around the room, sees about 40 students, and wonders how this class will evolve. He moves to the front of the room, takes his notes and text from his briefcase, faces the class, and says, "Hi! What does it *cost* you to take this course?" He pauses and looks for reactions on the faces of the students. He points to the first hand to go up.

The volunteer is Karen who says, "Let's see. Tuition is $248 a credit. This is a 3 credit course; so that's $744."

Another person, Sidney, says, "Hey, you forgot this textbook and the course packet. That's another 50 bucks, even for a used book. Also, I had to buy a calculator; I lost my other one."

Mike, getting a few winks and not hearing the question, awoke because of the noise; he asks the woman next to him, "Who is this guy, and what'd he say?" Professor Jacobs notices Mike's lost look and compliments him on his arrival on the scene. He asks Mike for a cost estimate. Mike replies without much thought, "A lot, probably $5,000."

By now, several more hands are up. Randy says, "Being here means I have to eat and sleep. That runs $2,500 a semester in the dorm."

Randy's friend reminds him, "You forgot the financial aid package you got. That reduces your out-of-pocket cost by a bunch."

Another student, Barb, says, "I quit a good job to come back to school. I was making about 300 a week. Now, I'm only getting 50 a week from my part-time job." But Mike, now aroused, tells Barb, "Yea, but you can't blame all that on Professor Jacobs' class. You're taking four or five courses, aren't you?"

Professor Jacobs asks for any other thoughts. Kim responds, "I've got to have a social life! That costs money—maybe $20 a week. Oh, then there's clothes. Wow, I mean that really costs money— hundreds of dollars every couple of months. I forgot the ordinary stuff like my hair, toothpaste, dues for clubs, and things like that— probably another $100 a month on average."

Professor Jacobs smiles and says, "Well, we're off to a great start. These costs are relevant for specific decisions we all make. But which ones for which decision? Looks like it'll take us the rest of the semester to sort this out."

Mike groans, "Looks like sleep is out for a while in this class."

To understand cost behavior and to know which costs to consider and which to ignore are critical factors not only for business decisions but also in everyday life situations. This chapter explains the terminology needed to analyze these decisions. Most analyses require only basic common sense. Assemble the relevant facts and make a rational decision. Even when we know the relevant quantitative facts, qualitative and strategic factors may cause us to select an alternative that is economically less attractive on the surface but might help us to achieve other goals.

Managers use cost information in many different ways. Cost data are especially important in these areas:

- **Planning**.   Estimating future costs in preparing budgets and in projecting operating activities.
- **Decision making**.   Selecting and formatting costs relevant to a wide variety of decision-making processes.
- **Cost control**.   Measuring costs incurred; comparing these costs with budgets, goals, targets, or standards; and evaluating differences or variances.
- **Income measurement**.   Determining the costs of products and services sold to determine this time period's profitability for the entire business or some segment of the business, such as a contract, a product, or a customer.

THE NATURE OF COST

Cost, broadly defined, is the amount of resources given up to gain a specific objective or object. Generally, cost refers to the monetary measurement (exchange price) attached to acquiring goods and services consumed by some activity. Cash outlays are monetary measurements; but occasionally, goods and services are also obtained by exchanging other assets, such as receivables or property, or by taking on debt.

The **cost objective** is defined as any purpose for accumulating costs. A cost objective may be making decisions, costing products, planning spending levels, or evaluating actual performances. It is the "why" of cost analysis.

Businesspersons undertake activities to achieve some output or result. Often these activities incur costs—purchasing materials, hiring people, and renting space—and are known as **cost drivers**. To achieve a cost objective, activities occur and resources are used. And resources cost money. Determining a product's cost means finding the cause-and-effect connection between inputs and outputs. A cost driver links activities that create outputs and resources that are used.

Cost, in many respects, is an elusive term. It is a noun that needs an adjective, such as incremental, average, or avoidable. Cost has meaning only for a particular purpose and situation. Consequently, meaningful use of the term "cost" requires an adjective to define its use. Each adjective indicates certain attributes, and those attributes dictate the relevance of each cost.

Costs, Expenses, and Profit Measurement

Since costs are resources given up to obtain a specific good or service, that good or service may be consumed; or, it may still be an asset at the end of a period. In many managerial analyses, the distinction among cost, expense, and asset is clouded. The words "cost" and "expense" are used interchangeably, as is done throughout this text. Yet for profit measurement, cost dollars imply assets; and expenses are subtracted from revenues.

Cash Versus Accrual Accounting

Clearly, cash flows strongly influence managerial decisions. Yet, profit measurement must include proper revenue recognition and expense matching rules. Accrual-based accounting methods, such as those measuring receivables and payables, depreciation and amortization expenses, taxation expenses and payments, and historical costs of assets, are used to determine a company's financial profit. Often, however, this accrual-based accounting information is at odds with management's need for cash-based accounting information. Occasionally, differences between cash and accrual numbers have major impacts on specific decisions.

COMPARING SERVICE, MERCHANDISING, AND MANUFACTURING ORGANIZATIONS

Many similarities exist. Providing a service to a client in a law firm or repairing a washing machine in a fix-it shop has strong similarities to manufacturing pencils in spite of different physical settings. In service industries, resources are brought together to provide the service, just as they are brought together to create a product in a factory environment.

Differences in measuring profits for various types of organizations are largely a function of inventoried costs. Service firms have only supplies inventories. Merchandising firms buy and sell products and hold merchandise inventories. Manufacturing firms buy materials and convert these inputs into saleable products. Inventories here include yet-to-be-used materials, work in process inventory (partially complete products), and finished goods inventory (completed and ready-to-sell products). Figure 2.1, page 30, compares income statements and selected balance sheet accounts for the three business types.

Service Organizations

A service business performs an activity for a fee. Costs of performing the service may include salaries of professionals and support personnel, supplies, purchased services, and routine costs such as rent and utilities. In Figure 2.1, the expenses of Hopp Consultants, a public relations firm, are reported as either direct client expenses or operating expenses. Some service organizations report all expenses as operating expenses.

Essentially, all operating costs incurred by the firm are **period costs**; they become expenses of the time period in which the costs are incurred. Only receivables, payables, supplies, depreciation, and perhaps costs not yet billed to clients would cause accrual net income to differ from operating cash flow.

In a service organization, the problems of measuring performance, such as the profitability of specific contracts, and matching direct costs with specific revenues are surprisingly similar to manufacturing costing problems.

Internally, financial reports for service firms often separate revenues and expenses by type of service or customer. For example, hospitals track revenues by procedure type and attempt to measure costs and expenses of those procedures. Professional firms, such as accountants, lawyers, and architects, measure the direct costs of performing services by client. Lawyers record time spent on each case, both for billing purposes and for tracing salary costs. In Figure 2.1, Hopp Consultants apparently serves multiple clients and can identify professional time, service costs, and other traceable costs with specific client contracts.

Merchandising Organizations

A merchandising business purchases products for resale. Generally, a merchandising firm is a link in the physical distribution chain, acting as a wholesaler or retailer. Figure 2.1 introduces cost of goods sold to the income statement of Gonzales Supermarket, a retail grocery store. Again, supporting the reported totals would be detailed revenues and costs of sales for various segments such as produce, hardware, meat, and grocery departments.

Merchandise costs are inventoriable costs and **product costs**. All other expenses in the supermarket operation are treated as period costs.

FIGURE 2.1 Measuring Income in Service, Merchandising, and Manufacturing Firms

Income Statements for the Year Ended December 31, 1998

	Service Firms	Merchandising Firms	Manufacturing Firms
	Hopp Consultants	Gonzales Supermarket	Felspausch Products
Sales	$8,000,000	$ 8,000,000	$ 8,000,000
Cost of goods sold:			
Cost of goods manufactured:			
Purchases of direct materials			$ 2,300,000
+ Beginning direct materials inventory			360,000
- Ending direct materials inventory.................			(310,000)
Materials used			$ 2,350,000
+ Direct labor			920,000
+ Manufacturing overhead			2,100,000
Total manufacturing costs.........................			$ 5,370,000
+ Beginning work in process			320,000
- Ending work in process			(340,000)
Cost of goods manufactured			$ 5,350,000
Purchases..		$ 6,800,000	
+ Beginning finished goods inventory..............		510,000	650,000
- Ending finished goods inventory		(480,000)	(620,000)
Cost of goods sold		$ 6,830,000	$ 5,380,000
Direct client expenses.............................	5,800,000		
Gross margin	$2,200,000	$ 1,170,000	$ 2,620,000
Operating expenses:			
Selling expenses	$ 510,000	$ 550,000	$ 980,000
Administrative expenses	1,270,000	260,000	1,030,000
Total operating expenses	$1,780,000	$ 810,000	$ 2,010,000
Net operating income	$ 420,000	$ 360,000	$ 610,000

Selected Balance Sheet Information for December 31, 1998

Accounts receivable	$1,350,000	$ 80,000	$ 1,020,000
Materials inventory			310,000
Work in process inventory			340,000
Finished goods inventory...........................		480,000	620,000
Accounts payable	220,000	110,000	460,000

Manufacturing Organizations

Manufacturing generally occurs in a factory. What is a factory? It is a place where resources are brought together to produce a product. Examples include:

- Soft-drink bottling company—mixing batches and filling bottles of red pop.
- Pharmacy—filling prescriptions.
- University dorm cafeteria—preparing and serving "delicious" food.

- Print shop—printing a variety of requests from customers.
- Breakfast cereal manufacturer—processing grains into "grrrrreat" cereal.
- Automotive assembly plant—joining parts and subassemblies for a minivan.
- Telephone company—processing local, long-distance, and information calls.
- Tax return preparation firm—preparing tax returns.
- Hospital surgery department—performing heart bypass operations.

Only a few of these are what we normally consider to be a "factory," but all "produce" a product or service. Most costing concepts are readily adaptable to a broad range of service, merchandising, and manufacturing organizations.

As Figure 2.1 illustrates, manufacturing firms have more complexity in determining cost of goods sold. A new income statement section, **cost of goods manufactured**, is introduced. It includes:

- The costs of inputs to the manufacturing process: direct materials, direct labor, and manufacturing overhead.
- Direct materials inventory and work in process inventory, which represents production in the factory.

The sum of the product inputs is **total manufacturing costs**, the total cost of resources used in production during a time period.

Figure 2.2 compares a factory to a large bucket. When the whistle blows to start the production period, the bucket already has resources in it—beginning work in process inventory. During the period, more resources are poured into the bucket—total manufacturing costs. Flowing from the bucket are all products that are finished during the period and either sold or added to finished goods inventory. This is cost of goods manufactured. When the whistle blows to end the period, ending work in process inventory remains in the bucket.

F I G U R E   2 . 2   The Factory as a "Bucket" of Costs

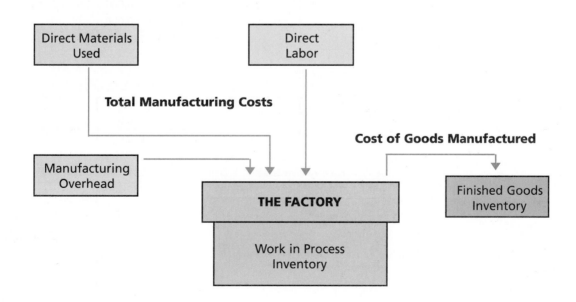

Figure 2.3 illustrates a flow of costs through the T-accounts of Felspausch Products. To calculate the cost of goods manufactured, it is important to understand how costs are accumulated. Flows of physical resources and their costs are parallel and end in finished goods inventory with their costs attached.

Transaction Events

(a) Purchase $2,300,000 of production materials.
(b) Issue $2,350,000 of materials to production—work in process.
(c) Pay $920,000 to production workers, including most employee benefits.
(d) Add cost of production workers to work in process.
(e) Pay $2,100,000 for all other production costs, such as utilities, supervision salaries, and supplies.
(f) Add all other production costs to work in process.
(g) Complete and transfer products costing $5,350,000 to finished goods inventory.
(h) Sell products costing $5,380,000 to customers for $8,000,000.

Account balances from Figure 2.1 are included for certain assets and liabilities.

We use T-accounts in many situations throughout the text to illustrate the flows of costs through a firm's accounts. It is a convenient learning approach to visualize the flows of physical resources through various processes and the flows of costs and revenues through the accounting system.

FIGURE 2.3 Manufacturing Cost Flows Through T-Accounts for Felspausch Products

Accounts Payable	
	—
—	(a) 2,300,000
	12/31 460,000

Direct Materials Inventory	
1/1 360,000	
(a) 2,300,000	(b) 2,350,000
12/31 310,000	

Work in Process Inventory	
1/1 320,000	
(b) 2,350,000	
(d) 920,000	(g) 5,350,000
(f) 2,100,000	
12/31 340,000	

Cash, Accrued Payables, & All Other Accounts	
—	—
—	(c) 920,000
	(e) 2,100,000

Payroll	
(c) 920,000	(d) 920,000

Finished Goods Inventory	
1/1 650,000	
(g) 5,350,000	(h) 5,380,000
12/31 620,000	

Factory Overhead	
(e) 2,100,000	(f) 2,100,000

Cost of Goods Sold	
(h) 5,380,000	

Accounts Receivable	
—	
(h) 8,000,000	—
12/31 1,020,000	

Sales	
	(h) 8,000,000

Figure 2.4, page 34, illustrates a simplified version of the Felspausch Products factory. Here, resources are brought together for producing automotive components. An assembly line in the factory is the focus of "manufacturing" activities.

Materials (primarily parts and components) are purchased for production, and factory employees work to convert parts into finished products. Many support services are used; and expenses are incurred for materials handlers, equipment maintenance people, heat, power, employee benefits, factory accountants, supervisors, and depreciation on equipment and the building.

In Figure 2.4, the firm is divided into office and factory areas. Obviously, this example is simplified and avoids many business complexities. But, it shows:

- **Product and period costs.** In general, any expense incurred in the office area is an operating expense and a period cost. Any cost incurred in the factory is a manufacturing cost, an inventoriable cost, and a product cost.
- **Location of inventories.** Manufacturing requires three production inventories—materials, work in process, and finished products. Materials purchases are received and stored in the materials warehouse, and their costs recorded in **Materials Inventory**. When materials are requisitioned for use on the factory floor, direct materials costs are transferred to **Work in Process Inventory**. This is production that is started but not completed. Completed products are physically sent to the finished goods warehouse; and their work in process costs are moved to **Finished Goods Inventory**. These products are ready for sale to customers. And when a sale occurs and is shipped, finished goods product costs are moved to **Cost of Goods Sold**, an expense account.
- **Flow of costs and products.** Figure 2.4 assumes an assembly process, but many different production systems exist. Materials are added, workers process, and other activities support; a physical flow and a cost flow coexist.

Traditional Groupings of Product Costs

Figure 2.1 illustrates the income measurement for Felspausch Products. Product cost accounting combines three groups of manufacturing costs—direct materials, direct labor, and factory overhead. While automated manufacturing and costing systems can create many more or fewer cost groups, these three have historically been used in nearly all manufacturing costing.

Direct materials costs are costs of physical components of the product. The range of materials includes natural resources, such as oil, flour, or lumber, to partially processed components (another company's finished product). Often, a complete list of all materials used in a product is prepared and is called a **bill of materials**. Materials issued to production are **direct materials used**. To find materials used, take materials purchases, add beginning materials inventory, and subtract ending materials inventory. Supplies like nails, glue, lubricants, and paints could be included in direct materials or, more commonly, called indirect materials, which are factory overhead costs.

Direct labor costs are wages paid to workers who directly process the product. In Figure 2.4, assembly line workers would be direct labor. Direct labor costs could include fringe benefit costs, such as health insurance, pension

FIGURE 2.4   The Felspausch Products Factory

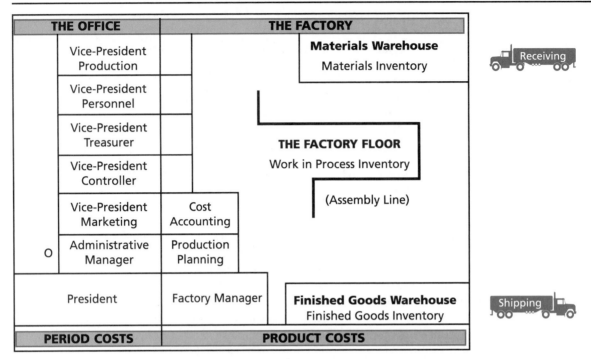

costs, and various employer payroll taxes. For example, a $15 per hour wage rate might increase to nearly $30 per hour when all employer-paid benefit costs are added.

Factory overhead costs include all manufacturing costs that are not materials or direct labor. Manufacturing overhead, factory burden, and indirect manufacturing costs are other names for these costs. Obviously, a wide variety of costs exists, such as maintenance employees' wages, factory managers' salaries, factory utilities costs, and factory equipment depreciation and repair costs. Hundreds of different cost accounts could be grouped under manufacturing overhead. Definitions are not universal. Certain workers' tasks could be overhead in one company and direct labor in another. For example, materials handlers and quality-control personnel costs could be accounted for as either direct or indirect labor. Generally, if the worker has direct contact with the product, the cost is direct labor. Costs of support tasks are indirect labor—part of overhead.

Historically, the three cost groups were assumed to be about equal portions of total product cost. Today, automation reduces direct labor and causes factory overhead to increase. As more production is generated from the same capacity, materials as a percentage of total cost may also increase. In a recent internal cost study at a major automaker, these percentages were found:

	Type of Plant		
	Stamping	*Assembly*	*Machining*
Materials	59%	41%	42%
Direct labor	6	10	11
Manufacturing overhead	35	49	47
Total product costs	100%	100%	100%

Thus, managers' attention to purchasing and to nonvalue-added overhead cost results directly from the growth in importance of these costs.

Types of Product Costs.   Materials and direct labor costs are often viewed as **direct product costs**, since they are easily identified with specific products and units of product. Factory overhead is usually thought of as **indirect product costs**. Factory overhead is not easily traced to specific products or units. For example, the plant manager's salary cannot be tied to specific product units in a multiproduct factory, since the manager is responsible for all activities in the factory. As an exception, a few overhead costs may be traceable to specific products or activities and be considered direct costs. Figure 2.5 illustrates these concepts and shows a dotted line between manufacturing overhead and direct costs to indicate this possibility. In more sophisticated costing systems, these direct overhead costs are separately identified and accounted for similar to direct labor, as we will discuss in Chapter 6.

FIGURE 2.5   **Product Costs and Product Cost Groups**

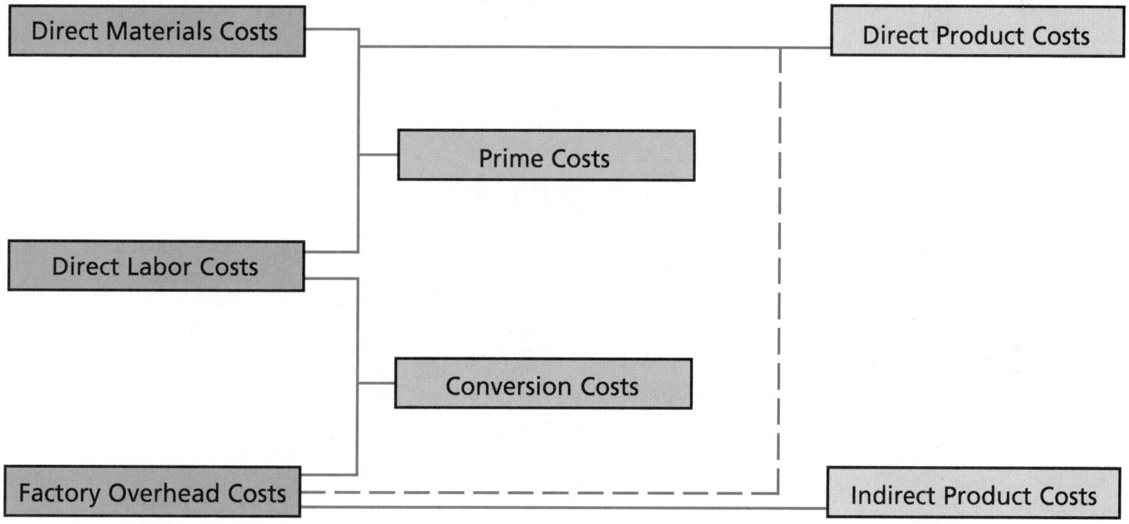

Direct materials and direct labor are also known as the **prime costs** of a product. These costs are easily traceable to a specific product. Direct labor and factory overhead are called **conversion costs**. In the factory, materials are "converted" into finished product using labor and all of the factory's supporting resources.

Calculating Unit Costs.   Product costing attaches costs to units of product. The simplest approach is to divide the number of units produced into total manufacturing costs.   For example, a highly automated factory produces a variety of handheld calculators. The same production processes are used for all models with minimal changeover costs. Three million calculators roll off the line every month. Different circuit boards distinguish the models.   March production data by product line are as follows:

	Business	Scientific	General Purpose	Total
Direct materials costs	$ 3,600,000	$ 4,200,000	$ 1,500,000	$ 9,300,000
Indirect other costs				6,000,000
Total costs				$15,300,000
Units produced	1,200,000	1,200,000	600,000	3,000,000
Direct materials costs per unit	$ 3.00	$ 3.50	$ 2.50	$ 3.10
Indirect other costs per unit	2.00	2.00	2.00	2.00
Product cost per unit	$ 5.00	$ 5.50	$ 4.50	$ 5.10

Many approaches to product costing could be used. The easiest is to divide the total costs of $15,300,000 by 3,000,000 calculators. However, the $5.10 average cost hides the different direct costs of specific circuit boards for each model. A second approach identifies materials costs as direct to each model and averages all other costs over all units. This produces a high cost of $5.50 for scientific models and a low cost of $4.50 for general purpose models. More complex costing is needed if the production processes for each model use different amounts of resources. The goal is to find the most detailed unit cost, given our decision-making needs.

COST BEHAVIOR

To say that a cost "behaves" in a certain way is somewhat misleading. Costs result from taking actions or from the mere passage of time. Something drives a cost—some activity, decision, or event. Selling one more hamburger involves a burger, a bun, a container, a napkin, and any condiments used. But selling one more hamburger has no impact on supervision, equipment rental, or advertising costs. Building lease expense will not change unless the lease includes a rental payment based on a percentage of sales. **Cost behavior**, then, is the impact that a cost driver has on a cost.

Which costs can be expected to remain constant when the amount of work activity increases or decreases? Also, which costs increase as more work is performed? If costs are to be estimated and controlled, we need to know whether or not costs will change if conditions change and, if so, by what amount.

Cost behavior is often viewed as a dichotomous pattern—either variable or fixed. In the real world, many behavior patterns exist since most costs are not strictly variable or fixed. Thus, the concepts of semivariable and semifixed costs add complexity to cost behavior studies. It may oversimplify the analysis, but a split between variable and fixed is common and is used frequently.

Variable Costs

A **variable cost** changes in total in direct proportion to changes in activity or output. A decrease in activity brings a proportional decrease in total variable cost, and vice versa. For example, direct materials costs are usually variable costs since each unit produced requires the same amount of materials. Thus, materials costs change in direct proportion to the number of units manufactured.

A proportional relationship between activity and cost has these important characteristics:

> Variable cost by its observed nature is a rate per unit of activity or output. A variable cost per unit remains constant across a reasonable range of activity. And, the slope of the total variable cost curve is the variable cost per unit—the added cost divided by the added units.

For example, if a product costs $4.00 per unit, the expression $4X yields the total variable cost at X level. Figure 2.6 shows the behavior of variable costs on a per unit basis and in total and also includes a slope of the total variable costs line.

FIGURE 2.6 Behavior of Variable Costs

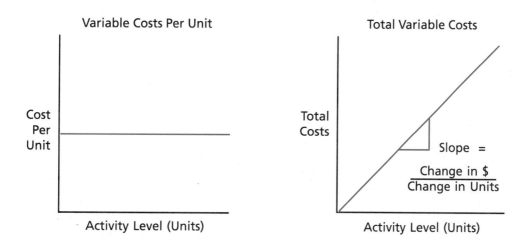

Fixed Costs

A **fixed cost** is constant in total amount regardless of changes in activity level. Costs such as the plant manager's salary, depreciation, insurance, and rent usually remain the same regardless of whether the plant is above or below its expected level of operations. Important characteristics of a fixed cost are:

> Fixed cost by its observed nature is a lump of costs that is not normally divisible. A fixed cost remains constant across a reasonable range of activity. The fixed cost per unit decreases as activity or volume increases and increases as activity or volume decreases.

For example, April's rent is quoted as a dollar amount for that month, not as an amount per unit of output or even per hour of use.

By definition, total fixed costs are constant, causing the fixed cost per unit to vary at different levels of activity. Figure 2.7, page 38, shows the behavior of fixed costs on a per unit basis and in total. When a company produces a greater number of units, the fixed cost per unit decreases. Conversely, when fewer units are produced, the fixed cost per unit increases. This variability of fixed costs per unit creates problems in product costing. The cost per unit depends on the number of units produced or on the level of activity.

FIGURE 2.7   Behavior of Fixed Costs

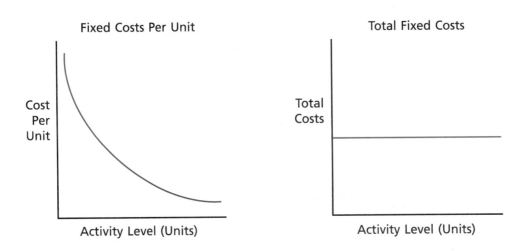

Certain fixed costs can be changed by management action. These are **discretionary fixed costs**. Discretionary fixed costs are expenditures that managers can elect to spend or not to spend. For example, a company might budget the cost of consultants at $20,000 per month for the coming year. But the contract states that the company can cancel the contract at any time. Management maintains discretionary control over the spending. On the other hand, if the contract guarantees the consultant a 12-month relationship and the contract has been signed, a **committed fixed cost** has been created. A committed fixed cost is one over which a manager has no control and must incur.

An interesting observation is necessary here. Managers can, with time and intent, change the cost behavior of certain activities. For example, variable direct labor costs can be converted into a fixed cost by guaranteeing full-time employment for some period, such as a three-year union contract. Or equipment could be leased on a short-term basis (day-to-day or even hourly) instead of purchased—converting a fixed cost into a variable cost. Also, automated equipment with a fixed rent or depreciation could replace variable cost manual labor. Thus, we recognize that managers can act to change certain cost behavior, particularly over time.

Expressing Variable and Fixed Costs—A Cost Function

Since a variable cost is a rate, it is a function of an independent variable—an activity or output level. Variable costs can be converted into total variable costs only by knowing the activity or output level. Fixed costs are first expressed as an amount, a constant. Fixed costs can be converted into a rate per unit only if the activity or output level is known. In the example shown at the top of the next page, the cost per unit of $7 and total costs of $700,000 can be found only if the output of 100,000 units is known.

If the production level increases to 120,000 units, both the cost per unit and total costs change. A decrease in the cost per unit from $7 to $6.50 results from spreading fixed costs of $300,000 over more units—120,000 instead of 100,000.

	Costs of 100,000 Units		Costs of 120,000 Units	
	Cost Per Unit	Total Costs	Cost Per Unit	Total Costs
Variable costs	**$ 4.00** →	$ 400,000	**$ 4.00** →	$ 480,000
Fixed costs	3.00 ←	**300,000**	2.50 ←	**300,000**
Total	$ 7.00	$ 700,000	$ 6.50	$ 780,000

The increase in total costs equals the variable costs for the additional 20,000 units.   A decrease in volume has similar reverse impacts—the cost per unit increases, but total costs decline.

Three factors must generally be known to perform analyses:

1. The variable cost rate.
2. The fixed cost amount.
3. The level of activity or output.

Notice that if we know the bold numbers in the previous example and the activity level, we can calculate all other numbers.

These factors can be brought together in a **cost function**—an expression that mathematically links costs, their behavior, and their cost driver.   In the example, the expression is:

Total costs = $300,000 + $4X, where X is the number of units produced.

This expression can be symbolically shown as:

Total costs = a + bX, where a is fixed costs and b is variable cost per unit.

This is an important formula in managerial accounting. Understanding these relationships can give insight into cost behavior for planning, control, and decision making.   By knowing the activity level and cost function, we can find either total costs or costs per unit.   The reverse is also true.

Finding the Cost Function From Total Costs and Activity Levels.   In this example, let's assume we know the total costs ($700,000 and $780,000) at both activity levels (100,000 and 120,000 units).   How do we find the cost function? First, we calculate the variable cost per unit as follows:

$$\frac{\text{Change in total costs}}{\text{Change in activity level}} = \frac{(\$780{,}000 - \$700{,}000)}{(120{,}000 - 100{,}000)} = \frac{\$80{,}000}{20{,}000} = \$4 \text{ per unit}$$

This is the b in our cost function.   The change in cost from a change in activity yields the **slope** of the total variable cost line.

To find the fixed costs, we take the total costs at either activity level and subtract the variable costs at that level as follows:

$780,000 - ($4 x 120,000 units) = $300,000 **or**

$700,000 - ($4 x 100,000 units) = $300,000

We now have both a and b.   The cost function is $300,000 + $4X.

Finding the Cost Function From Per Unit Costs and Activity Levels. Using the same example, per unit costs were $7 at the 100,000 units activity level and $6.50 at 120,000 units. First, we find total costs at each level by multiplying the total cost per unit by the activity level as follows:

$7 per unit x 100,000 = $700,000   **and** $6.50 per unit x 120,000 = $780,000

Second, we follow the same procedure used previously in converting total costs into the cost function. The same calculations could be applied separately to total variable costs for *b* and to total fixed costs for *a*. Calculations at both levels produce the same cost function.

One danger in converting fixed cost lumps into costs per unit is that the unit cost can be misinterpreted. It might be assumed that $7 is the variable cost—forgetting that the $300,000 is a fixed cost. At different activity levels, the per unit cost will be different. Even in solving homework problems, students are in danger of missing the impact of volume changes on total costs and unit costs if only costs per unit or total costs are used in their analyses.

Relevant Range

In Figures 2.6 and 2.7, activity is assumed to start at zero and go to very high levels. Realistically, the cost function holds only for a much narrower range of activity—a relevant range. A **relevant range** is the normal range of expected activity. Management does not expect activity to exceed a certain upper bound nor to fall below a lower bound. Production activity is expected to be within this range, and costs are budgeted for these levels. In cost analysis, costs are expected to behave as defined within the relevant range. The cost function is assumed to be valid for this range of activity. Usually, past experience establishes the relevant range.

Fixed costs are fixed and variable costs are variable within the relevant range. In the previous example, the volume range was between 100,000 and 120,000 units. The cost function of $300,000 plus $4 per unit is valid between 100,000 and 120,000 units as shown in Figure 2.8. If planned production was 130,000 units, our cost function may not be valid or useful.

FIGURE 2.8 Cost Patterns Using a Relevant Range

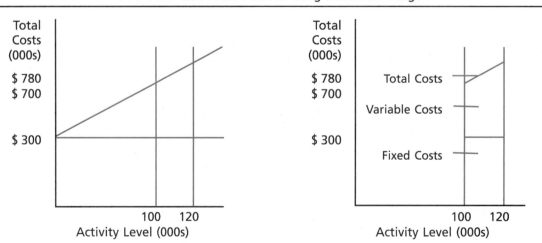

Semivariable and Semifixed Costs

Figure 2.9 illustrates cost functions that are neither strictly variable nor fixed. In the real world, very few costs are truly variable or fixed. **Semivariable costs** change but not in direct proportion to the changes in output. Some semivariable costs, called **mixed costs**, may be broken down into fixed and variable components, thus making it easier to budget and control costs. Using the cost function techniques shown previously, fixed and variable parts can be identified. In Example A of Figure 2.9, telephone expenses may include a monthly basic connection fee (fixed) plus a charge for each local call (variable).

Semifixed costs or **step-fixed costs** are typified by step increases in costs with changes in activity as shown in Example B. Activity can be increased somewhat without a cost increase. However, at some activity level, additional fixed cost must be incurred to expand capacity. If many narrow steps exist, a step-cost pattern may approximate a variable cost. Or with wide steps, one step may encompass the entire relevant range; and the step cost appears as a fixed cost.

FIGURE 2.9   Examples of Semivariable and Semifixed Cost Patterns

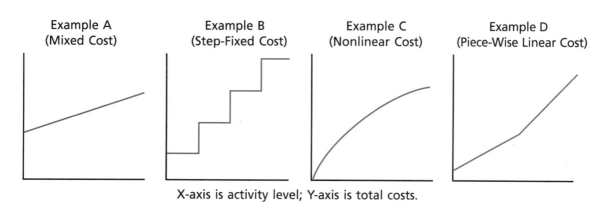

| Example A
(Mixed Cost) | Example B
(Step-Fixed Cost) | Example C
(Nonlinear Cost) | Example D
(Piece-Wise Linear Cost) |

X-axis is activity level; Y-axis is total costs.

CONTEMPORARY   PRACTICE   2.1

Step-Fixed Costs in a Telecommunications Company

"Traffic sensitive costs are the costs of providing telecommunications services that have a direct relationship to the number of messages or volume of traffic handled by the network. TS (traffic sensitive) costs tend to exhibit a 'stair step' cost behavior pattern. For example, toll circuit equipment is classified as a traffic sensitive investment. However, these costs are not variable until toll volumes exceed the existing capacity of toll circuits so that more toll circuits must be added."

Source: Cardullo, J. P., and R. A. Moellenberndt, "The Cost Allocation Problem in a Telecommunications Company," *Management Accounting*, September 1987, p. 40.

Example C shows a cost that increases but at a lower cost per unit as activity increases. An example is increased worker efficiency as activity increases, resulting in a lower per unit cost. This is a **nonlinear cost**. Example D shows a **piece-wise linear cost**. It is a constant variable rate until a certain activity level is reached, then the variable cost per unit increases. Perhaps an electric utility offers a low per kilowatt rate for the first 500 kilowatts and a higher rate beyond that level.

Many expenses have both fixed and variable components. Chapter 3 examines techniques that can help separate the fixed and variable portions and that can quantify the cost function.

COST CONCEPTS FOR PLANNING AND CONTROLLING

Often, cost terms can be explained using contrasts. In other situations, great care must be exercised to distinguish different cost meanings, even subtle differences. For others, similar terms can be substituted for each other.

Direct Costs Versus Indirect Costs

Costs are often defined as being direct or indirect with respect to a cost objective—an activity, a department, or a product. If a cost can be specifically traced to the cost objective, it is a **direct cost** of that objective. A direct cost is also called a **traceable cost**. The cost of installing a sun roof on a Chevy Camaro is a direct cost of the Camaro because it is traceable to that model. If no clear link between a cost and the cost objective is apparent, the cost is an **indirect cost**. For example, the heating cost at an assembly plant is an indirect cost of all models assembled there.

The same cost can be direct for one purpose and indirect for another. For example, the salary of the St. Louis office manager is a direct cost of that branch. But within the branch office where different products are sold, the manager's salary is an indirect cost of specific products.

Common and Joint Costs. An indirect cost is often called a common cost or a joint cost. A **common cost** is incurred to benefit more than one activity. In a university setting, the College of Business dean's salary is a direct cost to the College of Business; however, the dean's salary is a common cost to all departments within the College of Business.

The term **joint cost** is applied to situations where multiple outputs are derived from one resource. For example, a barrel of crude oil can be processed into literally thousands of products. The crude oil and the initial refining process costs are joint costs of the products produced. It is impossible to trace specific portions of crude oil costs to specific products; therefore, allocations of the joint costs must be made to those products.

Cost Allocations. Indirect costs not traceable to particular products or departments may need to be allocated to those objectives. A cost objective may use a resource, but the amount used may not be easily measured. For example, a shoe department occupies 2,000 square feet of a 50,000 square foot store and

C O N T E M P O R A R Y   P R A C T I C E   2 . 2

Drop the Football Team, No . . . .

In 1987, the football program at Utah State University came under attack after a report showed that the Athletic Department had a large operating deficit. This triggered a resolution calling for the elimination of the football program. While the excess of expenditures over revenues for the football program amounted to $56,450 during the 1987-1988 fiscal year, an analysis of relevant costs and revenues revealed that Utah State would be worse off by at least $307,000 if football was dropped but NCAA Division A-1 status was retained in other sports. "Needless to say, USU is still playing football."

Source: Skousen, C. R., and F. A. Condie, "Evaluating a Sports Program: Goalposts vs. Test Tubes," *Management Accounting*, November 1988, pp. 43-49.

accounts for 10 percent of sales and 6 percent of profits. If the rent for the entire store is $300,000 per year, how much should be allocated to the shoe department—$12,000 (space), $18,000 (profits), $30,000 (sales), or some other amount? No cost allocation is absolutely correct, and different viewpoints will argue for different allocations. The allocation process should attempt to link the cost, the use of the resource, and the activity or output.

Incremental Costs Versus Average Costs

A basic distinction in cost analysis is made between the cost of adding one more unit and the average cost of all units produced. **Incremental costs** are the costs incurred by adding more activity—more sales, another project, or a new department. **Marginal cost**, a similar term, is the increase in costs from adding one more unit of output or doing one more task. Incremental or marginal costs are often variable costs but can include any additional fixed costs resulting from increased activity.

The concept also applies to deleting a segment. An **avoidable cost** will be deleted if a specific segment or activity is eliminated. An **unavoidable cost** cannot be eliminated. For example, in a retail bakery chain, the Wealthy Street store has revenues and direct expenses. If that store is closed, most operating expenses can be eliminated or avoided. However, if two years remain on the lease, the lease payments are unavoidable.

The per unit **average product cost**, or **full cost**, generally includes production costs for all units, including materials, direct labor, and manufacturing overhead costs. The average cost will generally decline as production volume increases since the same fixed costs are spread over more units.

The incremental cost concept extends the cost behavior discussion. Which costs will change if a change in activity occurs? For example, if a supermarket manager considers adding a pharmacy to the store, what costs will change? Incremental costs will include:

- One-time costs of preparing facilities (equipment and remodeling).
- Annual fixed costs of salaries of pharmacists and trained assistants, advertising, and security.
- Variable costs, including costs of sales, utilities, and supplies.

If no space is added to the store, another department will lose space and presumably sales. To make the decision, all expected changes in revenues and costs must be included. This is **incremental cost analysis**.

Relevant Costs Versus Irrelevant Costs

The key to incremental costing is knowing which costs are relevant and which are irrelevant to a particular decision. To be a **relevant cost**, a cost:

- Must differ when decision choices are compared. If a cost increases, decreases, appears, or disappears as different actions are evaluated, it is relevant.
- Must be a current or future value.

The definition of irrelevant should be obvious. An **irrelevant cost** is one that does not change across alternatives. Being irrelevant does not mean that this cost can be forgotten. Merely, it will not quantitatively affect this particular decision.

A **sunk cost** is an irrelevant cost, a past or committed cost, and an irreversible cost. We cannot go back and change a sunk cost. Also, any future payments that we must make are committed and sunk costs. All historical costs are sunk costs.

To illustrate relevance, assume that Summers Township owns a water purification filter that originally cost $7,000. The township trustees are considering using the filter to reduce other water treatment expenses of $15,000. Or, if not used, it could be resold for $5,000. Note that the filter's $7,000 cost has already been incurred, does not affect the decision of whether to use or dispose of the filter, and can be ignored as a sunk cost. The analysis is:

	Include Past Filter Cost		Exclude Past Filter Cost	
	Use	*Dispose*	*Use*	*Dispose*
Reduced treatment expenses	$ 15,000		$ 15,000	
Proceeds from filter		$ 5,000		$ 5,000
Original cost of filter	(7,000)	(7,000)		
Net benefit	$ 8,000	$ (2,000)	$ 15,000	$ 5,000

The economic advantage of using instead of selling the filter is $10,000, whether the filter's historical cost is included or excluded.

Historical costs, common to most balance sheets, have little or no significance in managerial analysis. Only current and future values have meaning. Even tax effects based on historical costs impact only current and future taxes. The temptation to continue to use historical costs in decision making is great. But using past costs will quickly distort the decision-making process.

Indifference Points and Opportunity Cost

The **indifference point** is the activity level where a decision maker would accept either alternative. For example, if Alternative A's cost function is $1,000 plus $5 per unit and Alternative B's cost function is $500 plus $10 per unit, the indifference point would be 100 units, found as follows:

	Alternative A		*Alternative B*
	$1,000 + $5X	=	$500 + $10X
	X	=	100 units

When X equals 100, we are indifferent between the two alternatives. To choose the lower cost alternative, select Alternative B if volume is under 100; or select Alternative A if volume is over 100.

An opportunity cost is another version of differential cost. An **opportunity cost** is the benefit foregone by selecting another alternative. It is generally the value of the best alternative not taken. For example, we might have three job offers with salaries of $40,000, $35,000, and $28,000 per year. By selecting the best offer of $40,000, our opportunity cost is $35,000, the next best alternative. We give up $35,000 to gain $40,000. The general decision rule is that the opportunity cost should not exceed the value of the option selected.

Controllable Costs Versus Noncontrollable Costs

Another important aspect of cost is the distinction between costs that can and cannot be controlled by a given manager. This cost classification, like the direct and indirect cost classification, depends on a point of reference. If a manager is responsible for a cost, that cost is a **controllable cost** with respect to that manager. If that manager is not responsible for incurring a cost, it is a **noncontrollable cost** with respect to that manager. The entire cost control system rests on who can control each cost.

All costs are controllable at some level of management. Every cost in an organization is controllable by some manager in that organization. Costs should be planned or budgeted by the manager who has responsibility for those costs.

Planned Costs Versus Actual Costs

The plan sets the course of action. A plan, also known as a **budget**, shows what and how resources are to be used to achieve certain goals. Actual results are compared to the plan. The very essence of control rests on the knowledge that actual results will be compared to the plan, used to revise the ongoing plan, and used to evaluate managers.

Periodic control reports monitor the plan-versus-actual status. Generally, this month's actual results are compared to this month's budget as are year-to-date results. Expense variances are shown as over (unfavorable) or under (favorable) budget. What caused the variance? Will the variance recur in the future? What actions will reduce future variances? The budget itself may need revision. Control reports are like flashing warning lights to get management's attention.

As an example, DaQing Qi is plant manager of the Hong Kong Plant of Altman Fabrics, Inc. He has three department supervisors reporting to him.

Each month he receives a report similar to Figure 2.10 showing summary costs incurred by him and his departmental supervisors. The June report is converted into U.S. dollars. If Qi believes that costs incurred in Department 2 are excessive, he can review that department's detailed cost report. After an analysis, the Department 2 supervisor and Qi may find that materials costs were excessive. At this point, he would ask the supervisor to explain why the variances occurred and to find ways to control future materials costs.

Each manager receives a similar report, showing costs controlled by that manager. A network of reports showing a comparison of controllable costs with budget extends from the lowest level of management to the president's office.

*C*ONTRIBUTION MARGIN AND ITS MANY VERSIONS

Thus far, we have defined cost terms. But managerial responsibility for profit measurement is even more important. Revenue is added to the analysis. While net profit evaluates the entire firm, measuring profitability of parts of a firm requires more finely tuned profit yardsticks. The term we use is **contribution margin**, which is the revenue minus certain costs, a margin. This margin contributes to covering all remaining costs and to earning a net profit. Figure 2.11 shows five versions used in different situations.

FIGURE 2.10 Management Control Report Comparing Actual to Plan

ALTMAN FABRICS, INC.
Monthly Cost Report

Plant: Hong Kong
Manager: DaQing Qi
Period: June 1998

	June			Year-to-Date		
	Budget	Actual	(Unfav.) Fav. Variance	Budget	Actual	(Unfav.) Fav. Variance
Plant supervision:						
Salaries & wages........	$ 8,830	$ 9,460	$ (630)	$ 53,550	$ 55,320	$ (1,770)
Employee benefits	760	710	50	4,870	4,880	(10)
Insurance..............	250	250	0	1,500	1,500	0
Utilities	430	320	110	2,680	3,290	(610)
Miscellaneous	1,680	1,880	(200)	10,160	10,800	(640)
Total costs...........	$ 11,950	$ 12,620	$ (670)	$ 72,760	$ 75,790	$ (3,030)
Department 1	68,210	68,970	(760)	386,420	385,280	1,140
Department 2	46,300	49,500	(3,200)	263,140	278,230	(15,090)
Department 3	23,970	23,920	50	143,810	143,670	140
Total plant costs	$150,430	$155,010	$ (4,580)	$ 866,130	$ 882,970	$ (16,840)

FIGURE 2.11 Versions of Contribution Margin

Variable Contribution Margin:

| Total sales |
| - Total variable costs |
| Variable contribution margin |
| or Contribution margin |

| Sales price per unit |
| - Variable cost per unit |
| Contribution margin per unit |

| Sales percentage |
| - Variable cost percentage |
| Contribution margin percentage |
| or Contribution margin ratio |

Controllable Contribution Margin:

| Total sales |
| - Controllable costs |
| Controllable contribution margin |

Direct (or Segment) Contribution Margin:

| Total sales |
| - Direct (or Segment) costs |
| Direct (or Segment) contribution margin |

Variable Contribution Margin—Per Unit, Ratio, and Total Dollars

The basic and most common definition of contribution margin is sales minus variable costs. **Variable contribution margin** is a more explicit term because only variable items (revenue and costs) are included in the calculation. This contribution margin pays for fixed costs and includes any net profit. We use this definition of contribution margin in Chapter 3.

As an example, a salesperson is selling a product for $20 per unit. The firm buys the item for $12 per unit and pays the salesperson a 10 percent commission. The firm expects to sell 10,000 units. Variable contribution margin can be shown as follows:

| | Variable Contribution Margin | | |
	Per Unit	Ratio	Total Dollars
Sales (10,000 units)	$20	100%	$200,000
Variable costs:			
Cost of sales and commissions			
($12 plus 10 percent of $20)	14	70	140,000
Variable contribution margin	$ 6	30%	$ 60,000

Thus, the contribution margin can be expressed as $6 per unit, 30 percent of sales, or $60,000. Depending on the analysis needed, we may use one, two, or all three versions. From total variable contribution margin, we subtract fixed expenses—the remaining expenses—to arrive at net profit.

Controllable and Direct Contribution Margins

The next contribution margin concept looks at managerial control and is used when a manager has revenue and cost responsibility. Costs controllable by the manager are typically variable costs and controllable fixed costs. These costs are subtracted from sales to yield **controllable contribution margin** or controllable margin. This represents the money available to pay any noncontrollable expenses and includes any company net profit. Note that the definitions of controllable and noncontrollable developed previously are used for both

C O N T E M P O R A R Y   P R A C T I C E   2 . 3

Sell a Lube, Generate Contribution Margin

In 1990, 28 franchisers operated 4,000 fast lube outlets in the U.S. A survey shows that a typical service package offers an oil change, checks of other fluids, and maybe a car wash for about $24. Direct contribution margin is estimated at $15 to $16 per vehicle. A recent study shows that to be profitable, a lube center has to service over 50 vehicles a day and have a population of 80,000 with an average household income of $26,000 within a 3-mile radius.

Source: Strischek, D., "Lending to Quick Lube Shops," *Journal of Commercial Lending*, September 1990, pp. 40-47.

revenue and costs. Controllable contribution margin is used to evaluate managerial performance. However, this is not the net profit that the manager generates for the company, since noncontrollable costs must be paid before any net profit is earned.

Direct or **segment contribution margin** or segment margin is a segment's revenue minus all of its direct costs. A segment might be a product, a region, or a division. Definitions of direct and indirect were discussed earlier and focus on traceability. As an example, the direct contribution margin of a product line is sales less product-line cost of sales, product-line advertising costs, and any other costs traceable to that product line. The product line's direct contribution margin is the revenue remaining to pay for company common costs and to earn company profits.

Illustration of All Contribution Margin Concepts

Celeste Rudd owns three Burgers Plus locations. Figure 2.12 presents a summary income statement, expanded for the Grand Avenue location. Variable

FIGURE 2.12   Contribution Margin Analysis By Store

Contribution Analysis by Store for the Month of September					
	River Road	**Pine Street**	**Grand Avenue**		**Totals**
Sales......................................	$ 120,000	$ 96,000	$ 185,000	100 %	$ 401,000
Variable food expenses	$ 55,500	$ 46,000	$ 85,100	46 %	$ 186,600
Other variable expenses.....................	6,000	4,500	11,100	6	21,600
Total variable expenses	$ 61,500	$ 50,500	$ 96,200	52 %	$ 208,200
Variable contribution margin	$ 58,500	$ 45,500	$ 88,800	48 %	$ 192,800
Direct controllable fixed expenses	12,600	13,900	20,400		46,900
Controllable contribution margin	$ 45,900	$ 31,600	$ 68,400		$ 145,900
Direct noncontrollable fixed expenses	24,400	21,300	38,900		84,600
Direct contribution margin	$ 21,500	$ 10,300	$ 29,500		$ 61,300
Common corporate expenses					36,900
Net profit					$ 24,400

contribution margin is shown in total dollars for each store and also as a ratio for the Grand Avenue store.   **Direct controllable fixed expenses** include assistant managers' salaries, maintenance services, and other fixed costs that the store manager controls.   The controllable contribution margin is the profit on which the Grand Avenue manager will be evaluated and rewarded (a bonus for strong profit or profit improvement).   **Direct noncontrollable fixed expenses** include rent on the building and the outlet manager's salary, which are probably controlled by Rudd.

The direct or store contribution margin is used to measure the profit performance of each store.   Measuring store profitability stops at the direct contribution margin.   Direct contribution margin is the finest tuned profit measure that is free of allocations.   Common corporate expenses, which include Rudd's salary and other corporate expenses, cannot be traced to the three locations.

Contribution margin per unit requires more detail.   Rudd has set target contribution margins for her three main burger products as follows:

	Cheap Burger	Double Burger	Triple Burger	Average for All Burgers
Selling price per unit	$ 1.00	$ 2.00	$ 3.00	$ 1.95
Variable food costs per unit	.65	1.20	1.50	1.15
Variable contribution margin per unit	$ .35	$ .80	$ 1.50	$ .80
Variable contribution margin ratio	35 %	40 %	50 %	41 %

Note that the "other variable expenses" (probably supplies and condiments) in Figure 2.12 cannot be traced accurately to each product.   Also, actual burger margins can be compared across all stores and to the targets.

Ms. Rudd now has numerous versions of profitability for each location.   She will use each to answer specific questions about her products, managers, and stores.

Common use of the term contribution margin frequently means variable contribution margin.   But play it safe—define which contribution margin you are using.

$\mathcal{S}$ UMMARY

Cost analysis and income measurement are equally important to service, merchandising, or manufacturing firms.   Tracing cost flows is important to understanding the conversion of materials, direct labor, and overhead into a product or service.   The cost driver is the link between resources used and outputs.

Different decisions need different costs.   A "cost" must have an adjective attached to give it meaning.   In general, costs have many attributes, but the three most important ones for using cost concepts are cost behavior, traceability, and controllability.

Variable and fixed costs behave differently when activity levels change.   Variable costs are naturally expressed as a rate; fixed costs are naturally a lump of costs.   Fixed and variable costs can be expressed as a cost function, such as $a + bX$, where a is the fixed cost, b is the variable rate, and X is the level of activity.

Direct costs are traceable; indirect costs are nontraceable. Controllability refers to a specific manager's authority to incur the cost and responsibility to use the resource generating the cost.

Contribution margin is revenue minus a subset of costs. Variable contribution margin can be expressed as an amount per unit, a ratio, or total dollars. Controllable contribution margin is used to evaluate the manager, and direct or segment contribution margin is used to evaluate the segment.

P ROBLEMS FOR REVIEW

Review Problem A

Ballou Corporation operates sales, administrative, and printing activities from a facility in Dayton. It prints and sells a variety of products. The following selected costs relate to the firm's activities and particularly to the factory's Printing Department.

(a) Production paper used in Printing Department.

(b) Hourly wages of production personnel in Printing Department.

(c) Factory property taxes and insurance.

(d) Supplies used which changes with printing volume in Printing Department.

(e) Contract signed by Printing Department manager for an annual maintenance fee on special machinery.

(f) Equipment depreciation in Printing Department.

(g) Building depreciation.

(h) Sales commissions.

(i) Advertising agency contract costs for a special program.

(j) Annual computer staff; uses the same staff level all year—half for factory operations, including the Printing Department, and half for administrative work.

Required:

Based on reasonable assumptions about Ballou Corporation, classify each cost as:

1. Variable or fixed cost.

2. Controllable or noncontrollable by the supervisor of the Printing Department.

3. Direct or indirect product costs or period costs.

Solution:

Cost Item	Cost Behavior		Under Control Of Department Manager		Product Cost		Period Cost
	Variable Cost	Fixed Cost	Yes	No	Direct Cost	Indirect Cost	
(a)	X		X		X		
(b)	X		X		X		
(c)		X		X		X	
(d)	X		X			X	
(e)		X	X			X	
(f)		X		X		X	
(g)		X		X		X	
(h)	X			X			X
(i)		X		X			X
(j)		X		X		X*	X*

* An allocation between the factory and the office is required.

Review Problem B

Wild Eddie's Appliances operates in 15 states and has 45 outlets. February data from Store 13 have just arrived at headquarters as follows:

Sales	$ 300,000
Cost of goods sold	166,000
Other variable expenses	17,000
Direct controllable fixed expenses	25,000
Direct noncontrollable fixed expenses .	30,000
Allocated headquarters expenses	22,000

The store manager reported selling 1,000 appliances in February.

Required:
Identify as many versions of contribution margin as possible.

Solution:

	Total Dollars	Ratio	Per Unit
Sales..	$ 300,000	100 %	$ 300
Variable costs:			
Cost of goods sold	$ 166,000		
Other variable expenses	17,000		
Total variable expenses.........................	$ 183,000	61	183
Variable contribution margin	**$ 117,000**	**39 %**	**$ 117**
Direct controllable fixed expenses....................	25,000		
Controllable contribution margin	**$ 92,000**		
Direct noncontrollable fixed expenses.................	30,000		
Direct (or Segment) contribution margin	**$ 62,000**		

Three different definitions of contribution margin are variable, controllable, and direct (or segment) contribution margin. Variable contribution margin can be expressed three ways: total dollars, ratio or percentage, and per unit. Notice that allocated headquarters expenses are not used.

TERMINOLOGY REVIEW

Average product cost, *43*
Avoidable cost, *43*
Bill of materials, *33*
Budget, *45*
Committed fixed cost, *38*
Common cost, *42*
Contribution margin, *46*
Contribution margin ratio, *47*
Controllable contribution margin, *47*
Controllable cost, *45*
Conversion costs, *35*
Cost, *28*
Cost behavior, *36*
Cost drivers, *28*

Cost function, *39*
Cost objective, *28*
Cost of goods manufactured, *31*
Cost of goods sold, *43*
Direct contribution margin, *48*
Direct controllable fixed expenses, *49*
Direct cost, *42*
Direct labor costs, *33*
Direct materials cost, *33*
Direct materials used, *33*
Direct noncontrollable fixed expenses, *49*
Direct product costs, *35*
Discretionary fixed costs, *38*

SUGGESTED READINGS

Baiman, S., and J. Noel, "Noncontrollable Costs and Responsibility Accounting," *Journal of Accounting Research*, Autumn 1985, pp. 486-501.

Hunt, R., L. Garrett, and C. M. Merz, "Direct Labor Cost Not Always Relevant at H-P," *Management Accounting*, February 1985, pp. 58-62.

Nanni, A. J., J. G. Miller, and T. E. Vollmann, "What Shall We Account For? A Matrix Approach to Corporate Goals and Strategies," *Management Accounting*, January 1988, pp. 42-48.

Sandretto, M. J., "What Kind of Cost System Do You Need?" *Harvard Business Review*, January-February 1985, pp. 110-118.

Schneider, A., "Indirect Cost Allocations and Cost-Plus Pricing Formulas," *Journal of Cost Analysis*, Fall 1986, pp. 47-57.

Young, D. W., "Cost Accounting and Cost Comparisons: Methodological Issues and Their Policy and Management Implications," *Accounting Horizons*, March 1988, pp. 67-76.

QUESTIONS FOR REVIEW AND DISCUSSION

1. Why must "cost" have an adjective attached for it to have meaning to a manager?

2. Define the terms "cost objective" and "cost driver." How do they relate to resources and resource costs?

3. What characteristics distinguish accounting for revenues and expenses for service, merchandising, and manufacturing organizations?

4. Distinguish among the following terms: cost of goods manufactured, cost of goods sold, and total manufacturing costs.

5. Use the letters for the following product costs to create a formula for each term listed.

A.	Fixed factory overhead	**F.**	Direct materials purchases
B.	Variable factory overhead	**G.**	Direct materials used
C.	Total manufacturing overhead	**H.**	Direct labor
D.	Beginning work in process	**I.**	Ending work in process
E.	Beginning finished goods inventory	**J.**	Ending finished goods inventory

Terms: Prime costs, conversion costs, direct costs, indirect costs, total manufacturing costs, costs transferred to finished goods inventory, and cost of goods sold.

6. Period costs differ from product costs. How do they differ? Why is the distinction important?

7. Name the three traditional cost elements in a manufactured product. How can these elements be attached to the product?

8. Describe the basic cost behaviors of variable, fixed, and semivariable costs, both in total amount and on a per unit basis.

9. Identify at least two ways in which fixed costs pose difficulties for cost accountants and managers.

10. A fixed product cost is a lump of dollars. A variable product cost is a rate per unit. What other data do we need to know or calculate to find total product costs or the cost per unit?

11. What does the mathematical expression $100,000 + $12X$ mean in terms of measuring product cost?

12. **(a)** Controller, Maria Burroughs, in a recent speech said, "I rarely see a real variable cost or a truly fixed cost." What did she mean?

(b) She also commented, "Some of my friends define semivariable costs, semifixed costs, step costs, and mixed costs differently. Other friends often use these terms interchangeably. And I like all of my friends." Was she just trying to be funny, or is there truth in her quip? Explain.

13. Comment on the validity of the following statements:

(a) All sunk costs are irrelevant.

(b) All irrelevant costs are past costs.

(c) All relevant costs are present or future amounts.

(d) All future costs are relevant costs.

(e) A cost can be relevant for one decision and irrelevant for another decision.

14. How can an individual cost be both a direct and an indirect cost? A controllable and a noncontrollable cost? Give examples.

15. Assume that you are a student in a managerial accounting course. You are analyzing your costs of taking this course. Give an example of a direct cost, common cost, indirect cost, controllable cost, variable cost, fixed cost, opportunity cost, and avoidable cost.

16. Assume that you are the Accounting Department chairperson at a college. You are considering hiring an instructor and offering an advanced managerial accounting course. Give an example of a direct cost, common cost, indirect cost, controllable cost, variable cost, fixed cost, opportunity cost, avoidable cost, and out-of-pocket cost of offering the course.

17. Will an indirect cost be reduced by eliminating a product? Explain. Give an example of where an indirect cost might be reduced and of where it might not be reduced.

18. Mary Minard supervises the Admissions Department at Tender Care Hospital. The hospital accountant includes Mary's salary among the direct expenses in her departmental expense report. Mary claims she cannot control her own salary; and, therefore, it should not be in the Admissions Department's expense report. Is Mary correct? Explain.

19. What is contribution margin? How is variable contribution margin used? How is controllable contribution margin used? How is direct contribution margin used?

20. We have 15 subsidiaries. All corporate costs are allocated to the subsidiaries. In evaluating the profitability of our French subsidiary, we find it generates a net loss. Why might this number not be a good indicator of the profit contribution that this subsidiary makes to the corporation as a whole?

E XERCISES

2-1. Classifying Cost Behavior.   Don Rameriz operates a pizza shop near a major university. During critical periods, like registration and final exams, he is open 24 hours a day. Half of his business is takeout. He has these expenses:

(a) Cost of dough used in pizzas.

(b) Salary of the supervisor of the overnight shift when needed.

(c) Wages of the delivery persons.

(d) Straight-line depreciation on equipment.

(e) Power costs to operate the ovens.

(f) Monthly lease partially based on sales.

(g) Cost of drinks served.

(h) Insurance premiums covering his equipment.

(i) Equipment maintenance costs.

(j) Cost of supplies (i.e., napkins, toothpicks, and pizza boxes).

Required:
Classify each cost as variable, fixed, semivariable, or semifixed costs. Add any assumptions or comments you need to clarify your answers.

2-2. Cost Flows in Manufacturing.   The following data are from the Best Company for July production activities:

Inventories:	July 1	July 31
Direct materials	$ 15,000	$ 20,000
Work in process	12,000	16,000
Finished goods	45,000	38,000

	Month of July
Factory overhead.	$ 100,000
Cost of goods manufactured	?
Direct materials purchased	80,000
Direct labor	30,000

Required:

1. What was the cost of direct materials used during July? What was the cost of goods manufactured?

2. Use T-accounts to show the flows of costs through the appropriate accounts for July.

2-3. Cost Classification.   Selected costs associated with a variety of business situations are shown below:

(a) Salary of the plant manager.

(b) Lubricating oils for machines.

(c) Brass rods used in making plumbing products.

(d) Property taxes on a building that includes both the factory and home office.

(e) Labor in the repairs and maintenance section.

(f) Salary of the supervisor in the Grinding Department.

(g) Crude oil used in a refining process which results in numerous products.

(h) Wages of artists preparing ads for a grocery chain.

(i) Depreciation on administrative office furniture.

(j) Salaries of quality assurance personnel who test products during production.

(k) Salaries of software engineers in a production plant using robots.

(l) Sales commissions of the marketing staff.

Required:
Create columns to classify each cost by cost behavior (variable, semivariable, or fixed) with respect to activity; as a product or period cost; and, if it is a product cost, as a direct or indirect product cost.

2-4. Cost of Goods Manufactured.   The following data are available about the Biroscak Company:

	1997 Balances	1998 Balances	1999 Balances
Beginning materials inventory	$ 10,000	$?	$ 12,000
Ending materials inventory	15,000	?	11,000
Beginning work in process inventory	30,000	?	18,000
Ending work in process inventory	24,000	?	21,000
Direct labor		20,000	
Manufacturing overhead		40,000	
Materials purchases		30,000	

Required:
Find cost of goods manufactured.

2-5. Relevant Inventory Costs.   Wild Side Clothes manufactures designer jeans. At the end of the current year, one line of jeans was out of style. These jeans were carried in inventory at $50,000. Geri Wilder, a product line manager, estimates that, with a little rework costing $8,000, she could sell the entire lot to a discount clothing outlet for $15,000. Or, Geri figures, the jeans could be sold "as is" to a company in northern Mexico for $6,000, although Wild Side would have to pay $750 in freight charges. She could also sell the jeans as waste material to a recycling firm for $2,200.

Required:
1. What is the sunk cost in this situation?
2. Which is the best choice? Why?
3. Geri could store the jeans for a cost of $150 per month. She says, "I think this style will return in, oh, maybe 8 or 10 years." She guesses that the jeans might be sold for "up to $30,000" then, assuming no storage damage and no inflation. Does this information affect your analysis? Explain.

2-6. Finding Production Costs.   Jean Smith knows the following about the production process in her plant:

Department 1: Prime costs are 40 percent of total manufacturing costs.
Direct labor is 25 percent of factory overhead costs.
Factory overhead is $600,000.

Required:
Find total manufacturing costs.

Department 2: Direct product costs are materials and direct labor.
Conversion costs are 300 percent of materials.
Indirect product costs are 50 percent of conversion costs.
Total manufacturing costs are $600,000.

Required:
Find materials costs.

Department 3: Conversion costs are $100,000.
Prime costs are $100,000.
Materials purchases are $70,000.
Increase in materials inventory is $10,000.
Decrease in work in process inventory is $20,000.

Required:
Find factory overhead costs.

2-7. Cost Term Definitions.   For each definition, indicate what cost term is being defined.

(a) Cost per unit that decreases as more units are made during a time period.

(b) Activity levels within which the firm is expected to operate.

(c) Costs that are not inventoried.

(d) Costs that management has obligated itself to incur in the future.

(e) Costs that will go away if an activity is eliminated.

(f) Profit that is given up by accepting a different alternative.

(g) Costs that are the responsibility of a specific manager.

(h) Costs incurred while producing more than one product but cannot be easily traced to each product.

(i) Total product costs divided by total units produced.

(j) Costs of adding one more unit of output.

(k) Costs that are traceable to a particular cost objective but cannot be controlled by the manager responsible for that cost objective.

(l) Product cost that is not materials or direct labor.

2-8. Cost Measurement in Manufacturing.   Zhang Manufacturing Company of Hong Kong used materials costing HK$180,000 in the production of 10,000 units of product. Labor costs of HK$50,000 were incurred. Other costs of manufacturing, such as factory supervision, utilities, taxes, and insurance, are all fixed costs and amounted to HK$100,000 for the year. Administrative and marketing costs were HK$60,000. No finished goods inventory existed at the beginning of the year, and 8,000 units of product were sold during the year.

Required:

1. Find the cost per unit to manufacture the product. Break down the cost by traditional product cost elements.
2. Show where total manufacturing costs were at the end of the year.

2-9. Cost Functions.   Consider each of the following cases.

a. On Laskey's Turkey Farm, Laskey produced one batch of 5,000 turkeys at a cost of $20,000. Another batch of 6,000 turkeys cost $22,000. Estimate the cost function.

b. Bradburn Laboratories handled 50,000 tests in 1997. Total costs are $500,000; and fixed costs are $200,000. If volume is expected to be 60,000 tests in 1998, what is Bradburn's forecast of 1998 costs using the 1997 cost function?

c. For Benman Services, Inc., the cost function is $4,000 per service contract plus $30,000 per month. What is the average cost of handling a service contract this month if the activity level is 50 contracts? 30 contracts?

2-10. Indifference Point.   Joyce and Chris each operate local french fry shops. Joyce's place is called AutoFries and is highly automated. She pours potatoes into one end of an expensive machine, and fries come out at the other end. Her costs are $10,000 per month plus $0.10 per box of fine fries.

Chris's place is called Human Touch Fries. She uses manual peelers and frypersons. Her costs are $2,000 per month plus $0.30 per box of fine fries.

Required:

At what volume of boxes would the cost per box be the same for both? What if sales were higher than this volume? Lower? Comment on their relative profits.

 2-11. Finding a Cost Function.   Grey Corporation, located in London, UK, has collected the following data on the costs of electricity and machine hours for the last three months of 1997:

	Cost of Electricity	Machine Hours
October	£17,000	3,000
November	22,000	4,000
December	12,000	2,000

Required:

The production manager thinks that a pattern exists for electricity costs. Using the approach discussed in the chapter, does a cost function exist for electricity? If so, does one cost function work for all three months? Explain.

2-12. Opportunity Cost and Relevant Costs.   Cynthia Good already has credits toward a MBA degree from Edgewater University and thinks that she can finish the degree requirements in one year. To do this, however, she must give up her job that pays a salary of $25,000 per year. Living costs, whether or not she returns to complete the degree requirements, are estimated at $16,000 for the year. In addition, the costs of tuition and books at the university will amount to $9,000.

Required:

Write a memo to Good highlighting her opportunity cost if she decides to return to school. What are the relevant and irrelevant costs of the decision? Include comments on any information that is missing that is critical to her decision.

 2-13. Direct and Controllable Costs.   Marie Heltzel is manager of Department 7 in the Frankfurt, Germany, plant and has the authority to buy supplies, hire labor, and maintain equipment for the department. Costs in German marks for April 1998 are:

Plant superintendent's salary	DM 8,000
Plant heat and light	3,200
Plant maintenance and repairs	1,700
Equipment maintenance charges—Department 7	2,600
Supplies used—Department 7	1,400
Salary—Marie Heltzel	2,500
Labor cost—Department 7	14,600
Plant depreciation	3,000
Equipment depreciation—Department 7	2,300
Total	DM39,300

Required:
1. Identify costs that can be controlled by Marie Heltzel.
2. Identify costs that can be traced directly to Department 7.
3. Identify costs that might be allocated to Department 7 based on a cost driver. Suggest a cost driver.

2-14. Cost Flows in Manufacturing.   Analyze the following cases:

a. Work in process inventory of Page Corporation increased $11,500 from the beginning to the end of November. Costs incurred during November were $12,000 for materials used, $63,000 for direct labor, and $21,000 for overhead. Find cost of goods manufactured for November.

b. In the Essells Company, costs incurred during November were $15,000 for materials purchased, $40,000 for direct labor, and $50,000 for overhead. Materials inventory decreased by $4,000. If cost of goods manufactured in November was $99,000 and beginning work in process inventory was $28,000, find ending work in process inventory.

c. In the Emeric Company, the cost of goods sold for November was $156,000, finished goods inventory decreased by $13,000, and work in process inventory increased by $9,000.   Find the total manufacturing costs for November.

2-15. Searching for Unknowns in Manufacturing Costs Flows.   Three Japanese firms—Kumamoto, Kawasaki, and Kanazawa—produce musical products. Operating results for 1997 follow (all numbers are in millions of yen):

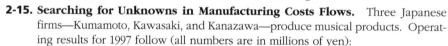

	Kumamoto Co.	Kawasaki Co.	Kanazawa Co.
Sales	¥ ?	¥ 90,000	¥ ?
Materials used	15,000	?	22,000
Direct labor	30,000	20,000	15,000
Factory overhead	60,000	25,000	?
Total manufacturing costs	?	?	?
Beginning work in process	4,000	9,000	9,000
Ending work in process	12,000	4,000	6,000
Cost of goods manufactured	?	69,000	61,000
Beginning finished goods	6,000	?	8,000
Ending finished goods	21,000	22,000	?
Cost of goods sold	?	?	65,000
Gross margin	?	24,000	24,000
Operating expenses	25,000	?	13,000
Net income	6,000	(1,000)	?

Required:
Find the missing values. Helpful hint: Format a manufacturing cost of sales section, and insert the known amounts.

2-16. Product Line Profits.   The Meyers Parts Company has divided its business into three product lines. Product Line A is expected to generate sales revenue of $900,000 a year, with costs of sales amounting to $490,000. Product Line B should yield sales of $600,000 a year, with costs of sales of $390,000. Product Line C should have sales of $1,500,000, with costs of sales of $1,040,000. Traceable fixed costs of each line are $250,000, $200,000, and $350,000, respectively. Costs common to all product lines are $300,000.

Required:
1. Measure the profit performance of each product line.
2. Which of the three product lines earns the best profit level? How did you measure "best?"
3. Would your answer change if the common costs were allocated on the basis of sales dollars? In equal shares (1/3 each)? Explain.

2-17. Income Statement Formatting. A partial list of account balances for the Jahn Corporation as of December 31, 1997, follows:

Revenue and Expenses:		January 1 Inventories:	
Purchases of raw materials . . .	$ 160,000	Raw materials	$ 45,000
Direct labor.	225,000	Work in process	30,000
Indirect labor	40,000	Finished goods	125,000
Rent—factory	84,000		
Depreciation—machinery	35,000	December 31 Inventories:	
Insurance—factory	18,000	Raw materials.	$ 40,000
Salespersons' salaries	72,000	Work in process	35,000
Maintenance—machinery. . . .	12,000	Finished goods	110,000
Administrative salaries	50,000		
Miscellaneous—factory.	26,000		
Miscellaneous—office.	40,000		
Sales.	850,000		

Required:
Prepare an income statement with a cost of goods manufactured section.

2-18. Contribution Margin. As a recent marketing graduate of Big Time University, you landed a job with General Food Mills as product manager for Red Pop. Recent operating results are:

Sales of Red Pop	$2,000,000
Costs of Red Pop.	500,000
Direct noncontrollable fixed marketing expenses	600,000
Variable selling expenses	300,000
Direct controllable fixed marketing expenses	100,000
Allocated product marketing expenses (percentage of sales)	400,000
Allocated corporate office costs (per employee)	200,000

Required:
1. Evaluate the profitability of Red Pop.
2. What data should be used to evaluate you as manager of Red Pop?

 **2-19. Variable Contribution Margin.** Maser Testing performs soil tests for toxic chemicals in its laboratory. Data from the third quarter of 1998 include:

Selling price	$15	per test
Variable lab costs	$8	per test
Variable administrative and shipping expenses	$3	per test
Total fixed lab costs	$25,000	per quarter
Total fixed administrative expenses	$15,000	per quarter
Tests performed	12,000	tests

Required:
Prepare an income statement showing several forms of variable contribution margin plus net income.

 2-20. Ethics in Cost Control. Carla Freed, regional manager of Gold Medal Sports Shops, is reviewing the results of 15 stores in her region. Store managers are moved annually. Each store manager's income is very dependent on the direct contribution margin of that store. For the past year, Store 9 has been managed by a person who has operated several other profitable stores in recent years and is about to be promoted to a larger store. Carla notices several items that bother her.

1. Store 9 has almost no personnel training expenses relative to other stores.
2. Store 9 has stopped participating in numerous community events that gave the store significant visibility but did incur substantial expenses.
3. Store 6, where this store manager worked the prior year, has had a severe drop in profits due to higher operating expenses.
4. The advertising budget was spent almost entirely in the first four months of the year, with almost nothing spent in the last several months.

Required:

Comment on a possible negative managerial scenario that the regional manager may be sensing. Might the manager of Store 9 be an exceptional manager? Explain.

P ROBLEMS

2-21. Identifying Cost Patterns.   Match the following graphs with the numbered descriptions. Indicate any assumptions you are making. The X-axis is activity; the Y-axis is total dollars of cost.

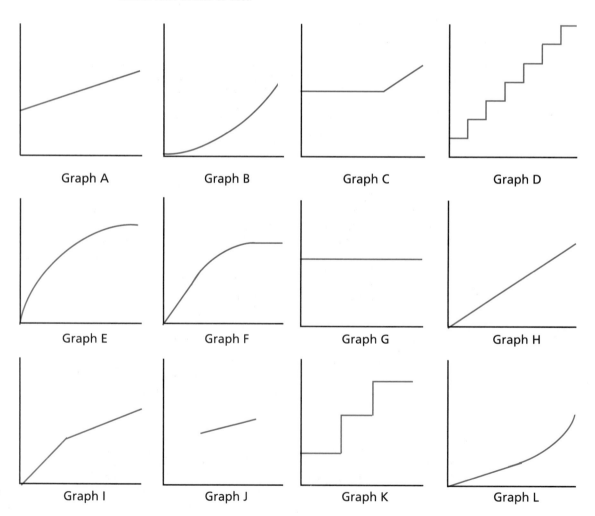

Graph A   Graph B   Graph C   Graph D

Graph E   Graph F   Graph G   Graph H

Graph I   Graph J   Graph K   Graph L

_____ **1.** Straight-line depreciation expense (a classic fixed cost).

_____ **2.** Shift supervision salaries (shifts added as demand increases).

_____ **3.** Delivery costs as a pizza shop serves a wider and wider area from one location.

_____ **4.** Sales commissions paid to salespersons.

_____ **5.** Workers' wages plus overtime premium. Overtime is needed after a certain activity level is reached. Workers are less efficient when they work a lot of overtime.

_____ **6.** a + bX, where "a" and "b" are not equal to zero.

_____ **7.** Water and waste water costs with a fixed-cost base charge plus a per gallon rate beyond a certain level.

_____ **8.** Payroll taxes that are based on the first $30,000 of each employee's wages. All employees earn more than this at high activity levels.

_____ **9.** Mixed costs within a relevant range.

_____ **10.** Cost of hourly messenger service for a regional bank with a reduced rate after 2,000 hours of chargeable time.

_____ **11.** Wage costs as more hourly telephone callers are added in a telemarketing campaign.

_____ **12.** Materials costs where cost per pound decreases as quantity purchased increases.

2-22. Determining Unknowns.   Find the missing values in the following manufacturing income statement:

	1997	*1998*	*1999*
Sales	$?	$ 113,700	$?
Cost of goods sold:			
Direct materials inventory, 1/1	$ 8,000	$?	$?
+ Direct materials purchases	?	20,000	30,000
Direct materials available.	$?	$ 26,000	$?
- Direct materials inventory, 12/31	?	(9,000)	(12,300)
Direct materials used	$?	$?	$?
Direct labor	20,000	23,500	?
Manufacturing overhead	16,000	?	24,000
Total manufacturing costs	$ 53,000	$?	$ 90,900
+ Work in process inventory, 1/1	12,000	18,000	?
- Work in process inventory, 12/31. . . .	?	(16,300)	(22,300)
Cost of goods manufactured	$?	$ 63,500	$ 84,900
+ Finished goods inventory, 1/1	?	?	?
Goods available for sale	$ 62,000	$ 84,500	$ 103,200
- Finished goods inventory, 12/31	(21,000)	?	?
Cost of goods sold	$?	$?	$ 83,200
Gross profit	$ 49,000	$?	$ 46,800

2-23. Unit Cost and Volume.   Benedek Service Company refurbishes utility meters in older neighborhoods. Estimated costs for the next three months of activity are:

	Meters Serviced	
	500	*1,000*
Labor costs	$15,000	$ 30,000
Replacement parts	10,000	20,000
Other variable refurbishing expenses	6,000	12,000
Fixed refurbishing expenses	18,000	18,000
General and administrative expenses	12,500	15,000

Required:

1. Using only refurbishing costs, what does it cost to refurbish a meter at each activity level? Prepare a cost function.
2. How do the general and administrative expenses appear to behave? Analyze this cost.
3. What is the firm's average total cost per meter at each level?

2-24. Cost Flows Through T-Accounts. Use T-accounts to show the flow of costs and revenues through the accounts of Blotkamp Corporation during July 1998 for the transactions listed. Accounts, with beginning balances, include:

Cash	$ 36,000	Accumulated depreciation	$ 56,000
Accounts receivable	122,000	Accounts payable	49,000
Direct materials inventory . .	128,000	Sales	0
Supplies inventory	65,000	Cost of goods sold	0
Work in process inventory . .	82,000	Direct labor cost	0
Finished goods inventory . . .	172,000	Factory overhead expenses	0

Transactions:

1. Materials and supplies purchased on account: $346,000 and $98,000, respectively.
2. Direct materials requisitioned for production: $385,000.
3. Supplies used in production: $93,000.
4. Direct labor wages paid: $98,000.
5. Depreciation expense on factory building and equipment: $22,000.
6. Indirect labor wages and supervisory salaries paid: $186,000.
7. Utilities expenses paid: $26,000.
8. Other factory expenses paid: $83,000.
9. Completed production: $845,000.
10. Sales on account recorded: $1,262,000.
11. Accounts receivable collected: $1,195,000.
12. Cost of goods sold: $870,000.
13. Cash payments made to vendors: $468,000.

2-25. Cost Identification of Product Costs. A regional bakery, Aunt Bird's Goodies, normally produces 200,000 pies per year in the Pie Department. The cost report for the Pie Department for the year is:

Direct materials	$ 93,000
Direct labor	91,000
Supervision	135,000
Supplies used	36,000
Depreciation on pie department equipment	32,000
Telephone expenses	8,000
Other pie department expenses	25,000
Utilities, insurance, and taxes	52,000
Rent	48,000
Total costs	$ 520,000

Direct materials, supplies used, and direct labor are the only costs that vary with production. Plant-wide costs (utilities, insurance, taxes, and rent) have been allocated to the Pie Department based on the space occupied by pie making.

Required:
1. Determine variable costs, direct fixed costs, and allocated costs per unit.
2. If a pie sells for $2.90:
   (a) What is the variable contribution margin per pie? ratio? in total?
   (b) What is the direct contribution margin?
   (c) What is the gross margin from selling pies?
3. Assume that next year only 150,000 pies will be manufactured. Find the price needed just to cover total product costs.

2-26. Actual Versus Budget.   Consider the following two situations:

Situation A: Barrett Resume Service provides the following data for January:

	Budget	**Actual**	**Difference**
Number of resumes prepared	5,000	4,500	(500)
Variable costs	$ 7,500	$ 7,000	$ 500
Fixed costs	2,000	2,100	(100)
Total costs	$ 9,500	$ 9,100	$ 400

Required:
Using Barrett's cost function, comment on each of the following statements.
(a) Barrett spent $400 less than it should have in January.
(b) Barrett spent $100 more than it should have for fixed costs.
(c) Barrett spent $250 more than it should have for variable costs.

Situation B: Dan Reynolds prepares hand-drawn maps for history buffs. He budgets costs as follows:

Prime costs	$20 per map produced
Production overhead	$10 per map produced plus $30,000
Selling expenses	$ 5 per map sold plus $20,000

He made 1,000 maps and sold 900 maps at $100 per map. He spent $19,000 on prime costs, $38,500 on production overhead costs, and $25,000 on selling expenses.

Required:
Using Reynolds' cost function, comment on his budget performance.

2-27. Product Costs and Control.   Metal barrels, used as containers for roofing asphalt and various industrial materials, are manufactured by MVM Containers Company. Materials cost for each container is $7.25, and labor cost per container is $2.00. Various supplies used in production cost $1.50 per container. Other direct operating costs of the barrel department, where these containers are made, are fixed and estimated for the year as follows:

Supervision	$ 85,000
Equipment and operating costs	6,000
Repairs and maintenance of equipment	3,500
Equipment depreciation	1,500
Total	$ 96,000

The supervisor of this department controls all of these costs with the exceptions of equipment depreciation and the supervisor's own salary of $48,000, which is included in supervision costs. Plant-wide overhead is allocated to departments based on a factor that combines space occupied with the number of employees. The barrel department expects to be allocated 30 percent of plant-wide overhead costs of $240,000.

Required:

1. What are prime costs per container? What are variable costs per container?
2. What are conversion costs per container if 50,000 containers are produced?
3. Identify the costs controlled by the department supervisor.
4. What are the total costs per container, if MVM produces 40,000 containers per year? If MVM produces 50,000 containers per year?

2-28. Product Cost in a Service Business. Robyn Pike developed a budget for 1998 for her Sun City Pharmacy. Her accounting firm has provided the following report for the first quarter of 1998:

	Budget	Actual	(Over) Under
Number of prescriptions filled	20,000	22,000	(2,000)
Pharmacists salaries.	$ 60,000	$ 66,000	$ (6,000)
Variable overhead costs.	20,000	21,500	(1,500)
Fixed overhead costs	60,000	59,000	1,000

Pharmacists salaries are considered fixed because they receive no overtime pay for extra hours worked.

Required:

1. What was the cost function that allowed her to create the 1998 budget?
2. What was the budgeted and actual average cost of filling a prescription for the first quarter of 1998?
3. Using her cost function and the actual first quarter 1998 activity level, what amounts should have been budgeted for filling 22,000 prescriptions?
4. Prepare a revised budget and compare it to her actual costs to find a new difference between budgeted and actual expenses. Comment.

2-29. Changing Unit Costs. Metalstar Company manufactures rivets from special alloys in a plant in Guadalajara. Its manufacturing costs in Mexican pesos for the first two months of 1998 were as follows:

	Monthly Budget	Actual Costs	
		January	February
Direct materials and direct labor	M$100,000	M$ 91,000	M$108,000
Utilities for the factory	20,000	22,000	23,000
Depreciation of machinery and building . .	30,000	30,000	30,000
Supervision and other factory costs.	60,000	60,500	62,000
Rivet output (units)	200,000	180,000	210,000

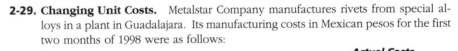

1-2-3

Direct materials, direct labor, and utilities are considered to be variable costs; and the other costs are fixed costs.

Required:

1. What was the budgeted average cost per rivet? Find the cost function.
2. What was the actual average cost per rivet for each month?
3. What is the budget variance for each expense for each month based on the actual rivets produced? Comment on the variances.

2-30. Ethics of Contract Costs and "Fairness." The Bureau of Business and Economics Research (BBER) at Western State University has contracted with the Fiscal Planning Office (FPO) of the state legislature to do economic analyses and forecasting. Most of the work involves computer operations using a large planning model and databases that the state Department of Commerce has assembled.

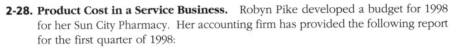
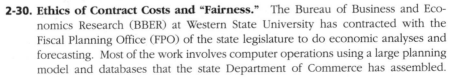

The contract calls for payment of all direct costs of personnel with limits on the amount of chargeable time per quarter. An overhead rate is applied to personnel charges at 60 percent of direct personnel costs. This rate is developed by the university to cover common costs of operating the university plus personnel benefits of the persons working on the project.

Data processing costs are reimbursed on a cost basis and include additional equipment needed to perform the analyses, purchase of modeling software, computer time, and data storage.

An auditor from the state's Auditor General's Office has just finished a routine audit of this contract and has written a report critical of the BBER. Among the items noted are:

(1) A large copy machine was leased by the BBER to prepare reports for the FPO and charged to the contract. The BBER uses the machine for preparing many other reports for the university, including course materials.

(2) Computer time is billed at the "average cost of computing time at priority level." This rate is approximately eight times the rate faculty and students are charged for work done on the university's mainframe. The same rate is used for other outside customers of the computer center.

(3) Personnel time was billed to the contract using a rate based on the contracting faculty person's annual salary divided by 250 work days. But the auditor found that the work was actually done by a graduate student earning about 20 percent of the faculty person's salary.

(4) The software model purchased for FPO contract use has been adapted at low cost to perform analyses for several other BBER corporate clients. It is also used by two faculty members who are doing outside consulting on their own. Corporate clients are charged for the use of the model. The faculty use the model at night and on weekends when the model is not otherwise used.

Required:

1. Identify the parties that have an economic interest in these issues.

2. Does the BBER appear to be costing the contract with the FPO fairly? Evaluate each issue given the information available.

2-31. Cost Behavior. Cristache Food Corporation makes frozen appetizers from spinach. The president finds that sales and variable costs are consistently proportional. Data for 1998 follow:

Sales		$100,000
Cost of appetizers made and sold:		
Spinach and direct labor	$ 33,000	
Processing overhead: Variable	4,000	
Fixed	18,000	55,000
Gross margin		$ 45,000
Less operating expenses:		
Selling expenses:	Variable	$ 5,000	
	Fixed	12,000	
General expenses:	Variable	2,000	
	Fixed	16,000	35,000
Net operating income		$ 10,000

Required:

Express the above data in a cost function format. What is the variable contribution margin ratio (percentage)?

2-32. Estimating Costs.   Dillon Wordprocessors prepares grant requests for scientific research funding.   The firm's relevant range is 200 to 300 requests per quarter. Costs at these levels are:

	For 200 Requests	*For 300 Requests*
Typists wages	$ 1,000	$ 1,500
Rent, supplies, and utilities	1,000	1,200
Total costs	$ 2,000	$ 2,700

Required:

The firm expects to prepare 220 requests in the fourth quarter.   Budget operating expenses.

2-33. Cost Behavior and Planning.   McConnell Inc. manufactures and sells a single product with a price of $50 per unit.   The following annual cost data have been estimated for the firm's upper and lower levels of its relevant range of activity:

	Lower Level	*Upper Level*
Production (units)	5,000	7,500
Manufacturing costs:		
Direct materials	$ 50,000	$ 75,000
Direct labor	40,000	60,000
Overhead:		
Indirect labor.	21,000	28,500
Supplies.	20,000	30,000
Depreciation	12,000	12,000
Distribution expenses:		
Salespersons	45,000	62,500
Travel and advertising.	13,000	13,000
Other.	29,000	41,500
General and administrative expenses	30,000	37,500
Total	$ 260,000	$ 360,000

Required:

1. Classify each cost according to its apparent behavior pattern (fixed, variable, or semivariable).
2. Prepare diagrams showing (1) revenue, (2) total variable costs, (3) total semivariable costs, and (4) total fixed costs.
3. Express revenues and costs in an equation format.

2-34. Finding Unknown Amounts.   For each firm, find the unknown amounts designated by letters.   Each case is independent.

	Firm 1	*Firm 2*	*Firm 3*	*Firm 4*
Direct materials inventory, 1/1	$ 6,400	$ F	$ 6,900	$ 1,500
Direct materials inventory, 12/31	5,400	4,600	5,500	P
Direct labor.	13,000	8,000	K	6,000
Factory overhead	29,000	7,600	13,000	Q
Purchases of direct materials.	9,000	7,000	L	8,000
Direct materials used	A	G	9,400	5,600
Sales.	B	33,800	55,000	40,000
Cost of goods sold.	C	22,000	M	17,000
Cost of goods manufactured	50,000	H	N	18,100
Total manufacturing costs	D	21,500	O	18,100
Finished goods inventory, 1/1	8,000	4,000	7,800	6,000
Finished goods inventory, 12/31	5,300	5,300	6,200	R
Gross profit	11,300	I	12,000	S
Work in process, 1/1	E	4,800	1,300	T
Work in process, 12/31	2,000	J	300	2,500

2-35. Finding Cost of Goods Sold.   The McCurry Outfitters makes Artic Warmsuits.
The general manager has a special board on his office wall where he writes key
statistics. On the board for March, he has written the following:

1-2-3

Production output	25,000 suits
Materials costs	$50,000
Direct labor costs	2,000 hours at $10 per hour
Factory overhead.	$2 per outfit produced plus $40,000 per month
Selling expenses	$1 per outfit sold plus $50,000 per month

He heard the sales manager brag about selling 20,000 suits this month.

Required:

1. From the data, what was the cost of producing an Artic Warmsuit in March?
2. What was cost of goods sold in March?
3. What are the total product and period costs that will appear on McCurry Outfitters' income statement for March?

2-36. Relevant Costs.   Alpine Sheet Metal uses one area of its plant for file storage.
The plant superintendent complains that this wasted space should be used produc-
tively or at least be rented to some other company. The files could be microfilmed
at a one-time cost of $20,000. Annual maintenance and updating would cost
$4,000. The space could be leased to Deneau Truck Lines at an annual rental of
$25,000.

A second option is to manufacture a new product line in this space. Marketing
and cost estimates show that the new product can be expected to produce the
following results each year:

Net sales		$ 268,000
Direct materials costs	$ 50,000	
Direct labor costs	32,000	
Supervision and other costs	50,000	
Allocated plant costs (based on space occupied):		
Plant utilities, taxes, and insurance . . . . $ 34,000		
Plant supervision 52,000		
Plant maintenance and depreciation 42,000	128,000	
Total costs of new product line		260,000
Income before income tax.		$ 8,000

The superintendent is disappointed to learn that the new product will contribute relatively little profit and is inclined to rent the space to Deneau Truck Lines.

Required:

1. Identify the relevant costs for each alternative.
2. What would each alternative contribute to Alpine's profits?
3. What questions should the superintendent ask about the cost analysis?

2-37. Cost Analysis Without Profit as a Bottom Line.   Three Oaks Public Library has
three areas, classified by type of books and services provided. The three areas are
Technical, General, and Children. The library board of trustees is reviewing budget
data and actual spending. Budget and actual direct costs of operating each area for
the first quarter of 1997 are as follows:

	Technical	*General*	*Children*	*Total*
Budgeted direct costs	$ 120,000	$ 70,000	$ 50,000	$ 240,000
Actual direct costs:				
Salaries	$ 78,000	$ 50,000	$ 43,000	$ 171,000
Books and periodicals	47,700	16,300	11,500	75,500
Supplies	2,900	2,800	4,600	10,300
Total actual expenses	$ 128,600	$ 69,100	$ 59,100	$ 256,800

Quarterly administrative overhead costs of operating the library were:

Building occupancy and utilities.	$ 30,000
Library administrative personnel.	45,000

Other data with respect to library areas are:

	Recent Monthly Activity			
	Percentage of Useful Space Occupied	Number of Employees	Number of Customers Serviced	Number of Books Checked Out
Technical	30 %	6	500	1,200
General	30	5	2,800	3,000
Children	30	4	1,700	1,800
Administration . . .	10	5		
Total	100 %	20	5,000	6,000

Required:

1. Compare the actual results relative to budgeted direct costs.
2. Why would a cost analysis be important to the library board of trustees?
3. Discuss alternative ways of analyzing operating costs and services provided.
4. Would allocating the administrative overhead costs to the three areas be helpful to your analysis? Comment.

2-38. Income Statement Preparation. The Giffin Corporation produces heavy-duty riding garden tractors and has the following balances in its operating accounts (in millions of dollars) for 1998:

Sales	$700
Selling and administrative expenses	100
Factory supplies used	10
Factory utilities	30
Indirect labor	60
Purchases of direct materials	125
Direct labor	100
Factory building and equipment depreciation expense	80
Factory supervisory salaries	40
Miscellaneous factory overhead	35

Direct materials, 12/31/97 . . .	$ 15	Direct materials, 12/31/98	20
Work in process, 12/31/97 . .	10	Work in process, 12/31/98	5
Finished goods, 12/31/97 . . .	70	Finished goods, 12/31/98	?

Records show that 120,000 units were transferred to finished goods inventory in 1998. Sales were 110,000 units. Giffin uses first-in, first-out for all inventories.

Required:

Prepare an income statement including the cost of goods manufactured and sold for 1998.

*C*ASE 2A—THE GINGERBREAD LADY

The Gingerbread Lady has a part-time business of producing and selling gingerbread houses at Christmas craft shows. Production starts in late October and runs four consecutive weeks. To meet health codes, she rents a kitchen at a nearby preschool and bakes and decorates the houses there. She can only use the kitchen on Friday evenings and all day on Saturdays and can produce 300 houses in one weekend. The rent per weekend is $60. Consequently, the Gingerbread Lady can produce, at most, 1,200 houses for the season. Materials and labor costs amount to $2.50 per house.

The houses are sold at various bazaars throughout the community. The Gingerbread Lady charges whatever the market will bear at each bazaar. Four bazaars have been announced this year. For some reason, all of this year's bazaars are being held at the same time, thus forcing the Gingerbread Lady to choose which bazaar she will attend. A description of each bazaar with the anticipated selling price and specific costs is as follows:

Alternative A: A private athletic club with an elite membership sponsors this two-day bazaar. It charges a flat fee of $25 per day for each seller. The Gingerbread Lady feels a selling price of $6.75 per house is appropriate. From past experience, she knows she can sell 200 houses with followup orders for 150 houses.

Alternative B: A two-day neighborhood bazaar is held in the lower-middle income section of the city. She will charge $5.95 per house and must pay a flat fee of $15 per day. She can sell, at most, 400 houses.

Alternative C: This two-day bazaar is held in a community center in another lower-middle income section of the city. Here the price of each house would be a bit lower at $5.45. The center charges $12 per day for each seller. Based on last year's records, the Gingerbread Lady can sell 500 houses in the two days.

Alternative D: The local university sponsors a three-day bazaar and charges each seller 10 percent of the gross revenue from sales as a fee. Because of the student population, the Gingerbread Lady will charge $5.00 per house. But she thinks she can sell 600 houses during the three days.

She has already determined that it is not worthwhile to be in business if she cannot make a minimum of $1.25 per house, since other income options would give her at least that income.

Required:

1. Prepare an analysis showing which bazaar, if any, the Gingerbread Lady should pick to attend this year.
2. If the Gingerbread Lady could hire someone to handle the next most attractive (profitable) bazaar for her, what is the maximum amount she could pay and at least break even (after her minimum profit per house)?
3. If the Gingerbread Lady could hire other people to handle additional bazaars and pay them 50 percent of any profits over $1.25 per house as their wage, to which bazaars should she commit?

C ASE 2B—WALTER'S BUS ROUTES

Illinois Transportation runs passenger and freight services between Chicago airports and downstate cities. The owner, Walter Gruber, is an operations-wise manager. He recently heard about a "segment contribution margin" approach at a university continuing education program. His actual results for the first half of 1998 have just arrived.

Total revenue was $5.0 million, of which $3.5 million was freight traffic and $1.5 million was passenger traffic. Of the passenger revenue, 60 percent was generated by Route 1, 30 percent by Route 2, and 10 percent by Route 3.

Total direct controllable fixed costs were $600,000, of which $500,000 was spent on freight traffic. Of the remainder, $40,000 could not be traced to specific routes, although it was clearly applicable to passenger traffic in general. Routes 1, 2, and 3 incurred costs of $30,000, $18,000, and $12,000, respectively.

Total direct costs not controllable by segment managers were $500,000, of which 80 percent was traceable to freight traffic. Of the 20 percent traceable to passenger traffic, Routes 1, 2, and 3 should be charged $40,000, $20,000, and $15,000, respectively. The balance was not traceable to a specific route.

Total variable costs were $3.2 million, of which $2.0 million was freight traffic. Of the $1.2 million traceable to passenger traffic, $670,000, $400,000, and $130,000 were incurred by Routes 1, 2, and 3, respectively.

The common fixed costs not clearly traceable to any part of the company amounted to $500,000. Walter has always allocated these on a percentage of sales basis.

Required:

1. Walter asks you to prepare an earnings statement that shows the performance of each segment of the firm by various types of contribution margin.
2. Comment on what the results tell Walter.

C H A P T E R *3*

Cost Estimation and Cost-Volume-Profit Relationships

*L*EARNING OBJECTIVES

After studying Chapter 3, you will be able to:

1. Understand the significance of cost behavior to decision making and control.
2. Obtain cost functions by account analysis, the engineering approach, the scattergraph approach, and the high-low method.
3. Identify the interacting elements of cost-volume-profit analysis.
4. Explain the break-even formula and its underlying assumptions.
5. Calculate the effect on profits of changes in selling prices, changes in variable costs, or changes in fixed costs.
6. Calculate operating leverage; determine its effects on changes in profit; and understand how margin of safety relates to operating leverage.
7. Find break-even points and volumes that attain desired profit levels when multiple products are sold in combination.
8. Estimate and examine cost functions using regression and correlation analyses. (Appendix)

"Can You Lose a Little on Each One, But Make It Up on Volume?"

Skip Johnson, owner of C&J Electronics, began manufacturing hand-held calculators fifteen years ago. During that time, he enjoyed a number of upswings and weathered several downturns in the economy. Generally, the business has had profitable years and has provided a high standard of living for Skip and his family.

But times are changing. Personnel costs continue to rise, particularly fringe benefits like medical insurance premiums. Other costs continue to rise as well. At the same time, because of increased competition from calculator manufacturers and from computer products, prices of calculators have fallen dramatically over the years. Skip has begun to slash operating costs, but he still faces shrinking profit margins.

Because of high profitability in the past, Skip never analyzed how his costs change in relation to changes in activity levels; nor did he analyze the relationships among revenues, costs, and volume to see how they relate to profit levels. Now, Skip is wondering how far sales can drop before he sees the red ink in losses. With that information, he hopes to identify what changes will keep operations profitable. Skip sees many other businesses closing their doors and is fearful he will have to follow suit someday. He just doesn't know what factors will influence his future costs and revenues.

Managers like Skip Johnson of C&J Electronics need to understand cost behavior and cost estimation to be in a better position to plan, make decisions, and control costs. As we discussed in Chapter 2, cost behavior describes the relationship between costs and an activity as the level of activity increases or decreases. Determining cost behavior is important to management's understanding of overhead costs, marketing costs, and general and administrative expenses and for proper implementation of budgets and budgetary controls. With a knowledge of cost behavior, managers can also estimate how costs are affected as future activity levels change, which can lead to better decisions. In addition, knowledge of cost behavior can assist managers in analyzing the interactions among revenues, costs, and volume for profit-planning purposes. These interactions will be covered later in this chapter.

SIGNIFICANCE OF COST BEHAVIOR TO DECISION MAKING AND CONTROL

To understand more fully the significance of a manager's analysis of cost behavior, we look at three areas: decision making, planning and control, and trends in fixed costs.

Decision Making

Cost behavior affects the decisions management makes. Variable costs are the incremental or differential costs in most decisions. Fixed costs change only if the specific decision includes a change in the capacity-providing activities that result in increasing or decreasing the level of fixed costs.

Cost-based pricing requires a good understanding of cost behavior because fixed costs pose conceptual problems when converted to per unit amounts.

Fixed costs per unit assume a given capacity level. If the volume of production and sales is different from the capacity contemplated in determining the cost-based price, the fixed cost component of total costs yields a misleading price. Managers must know which costs are fixed, as well as anticipated capacity levels, to make good pricing decisions.

Planning and Control

A company plans and controls variable costs differently than it plans and controls fixed costs. Variable costs are planned in terms of input/output relationships. For example, for each unit produced, the materials cost consists of a price per unit of materials times the number of units of materials; and the labor cost consists of the labor rate times the number of labor hours. Once operations are underway, levels of activities may change. The input/output relationships identify changes in resources necessary to respond to the change in activity. If activity levels increase, this signals that more resources (materials, labor, or variable overhead) are needed. If activity levels decrease, the resources are not needed; and procedures can be triggered to stop purchases and reassign or lay-off workers. In cases where more materials or labor time is used than is necessary in the input/output relationship, inefficiencies and waste are in excess of the levels anticipated; and managers must investigate causes and eliminate or reduce the financial impact of the unfavorable variances.

Fixed costs, on the other hand, are planned for on an annual basis, if not longer. Control of fixed costs is exercised at two points in time. The first time is when the decision is made to incur a fixed cost. Management evaluates the necessity of the cost and makes the decision to move forward or reject the proposal. Once fixed costs are incurred, another point of control enters, that being the daily decision of how best to use the capacity provided by the cost. For example, a university makes a decision to build a new classroom and faculty office building. That decision is the first point of control. After construction, control is implemented in using the building to its maximum capacity. That will occur if classes are scheduled throughout the day and evening.

Another difference in the planning and control of variable and fixed costs is the level at which costs are controllable. Variable costs can be controlled at the lowest supervisory level. Fixed costs are often controllable only at higher managerial levels.

Trends in Fixed Costs

With the many changes taking place in the manufacturing environment, organizations are finding that an increasing portion of their total costs are fixed costs. The following are a few of the more critical changes taking place.

Implementation of more automated equipment is replacing variable labor costs and a major share of the variable overhead costs. Thus, fixed costs are becoming a more significant part of total costs. Costs such as depreciation, taxes, insurance, and fixed maintenance charges are substantially higher. Some industries, for example the steel and automobile industries, are becoming essentially fixed cost industries, with variable costs playing a less important role than was once the case.

Another factor that has helped to increase fixed costs significantly is the movement in some industries toward a guaranteed annual wage for production workers. Employees who were once hourly wage earners are now becoming salaried. With the use of more automated equipment, the workers of a company may not represent "touch labor," that is they do not work directly on the product. Instead, the production worker may merely observe that the equipment is operating as it should and is properly supplied with materials or may monitor production by means of a television screen. The production line employee is handling more of the functions normally associated with indirect labor, and the cost is a fixed cost.

Although a significant shift to automation has occurred in many larger industries and even in some medium-sized industries, many companies and service organizations still operate in a more conventional way, without automated equipment and with direct labor on an hourly basis. Society seldom changes completely. For example, you can travel from one place to another by jet plane, but the automobile is also still used. Likewise, different cost behavior patterns will likely coexist.

C OST ESTIMATION

Cost estimation is the process of determining a cost relationship with the activity for an individual cost item or a grouping of costs. We typically express this relationship as an equation that reflects the cost behavior within the relevant range. In Chapter 2, we referred to this equation as a cost function. The **dependent variable** (Y) of the equation is what we want to predict (i.e., costs, in our case). The **independent variable** (X) (i.e., the activity base for cost behavior) is used to predict the dependent variable. The cost function can be written as follows:

$$Y = a + bX$$

This equation states that Y, the total cost, is equal to a value a plus a factor of variability applied to the activity level X. The value a represents the fixed cost. The factor b represents the change in Y in relation to the change in X, i.e., the variable cost per unit of activity.

Although a number of techniques exist for estimating a cost-to-activity relationship, we will discuss four techniques: (1) account analysis, (2) engineering approach, (3) scattergraph and visual fit, and (4) high-low method. A fifth method, regression analysis, is discussed in the Appendix to this chapter since it requires some knowledge of statistics. Contemporary Practice 3.1 displays the results of a survey on the usage of overhead cost estimation techniques. The survey reveals that account analysis is the predominant approach used.

Account Analysis

In **account analysis**, accountants estimate variable and fixed cost behaviors of a particular cost by evaluating information from two sources. First, the accountant reviews and interprets managerial policies with respect to the cost. Second, the accountant inspects the historical activity of the cost. All cost accounts are classified as either fixed or variable. If a cost shows semivariable or semifixed

C O N T E M P O R A R Y   P R A C T I C E   3 . 1

Survey on Cost Estimation Techniques

A survey of 155 controllers from Fortune 500 firms revealed the following frequency of usage for methods of identifying fixed and variable overhead expenses:

Account analysis	71%
High-low method	8%
Regression analysis	8%
Scattergraph and visual fit	5%
Other methods	8%
	100%

Source: Cornick, M., W. D. Cooper, and S. B. Wilson, "How Do Companies Analyze Overhead?" *Management Accounting*, June 1988, pp. 41-43.

cost behavior, the analyst either (1) makes a subjective estimate of the variable and fixed portions of the cost or (2) classifies the account according to the preponderant cost behavior. Unit variable costs are estimated by dividing the total variable costs by the quantity of the cost driver.

As an example, suppose for cost control purposes, the sales manager of C&J Electronics wishes to estimate the sales staff's automobile expenses as a function of miles driven. Costs for the past year during which 58,000 miles were driven are classified as follows:

Item	Cost	Classification
Fuel	$ 3,200	Variable
Depreciation	11,200	Fixed
Insurance	3,900	Fixed
Maintenance	1,800	Variable
Parking	2,100	Fixed

The fixed costs total $17,200, while the variable cost per mile is 8.62 cents [($3,200+$1,800) ÷ 58,000]. Hence, the cost function would be expressed as:

$$Y = \$17,200 + \$.0862\ X$$

The sales manager believes that costs should be stable for the coming year for which the staff's auto travel budget would be 65,000 miles. Accordingly, the auto expenses should total $22,803 [$17,200 + ($.0862 x 65,000)]. The sales manager intends to investigate any significant deviation from this budgeted cost.

Account analysis is fairly accurate for determining cost behavior in many cases. Vendor invoices, for instance, show that direct materials have a variable cost behavior; leasing costs are fixed. A telephone bill is a semivariable cost. One portion is fixed for the minimum monthly charge, and the remainder may be variable with usage.

Account analysis has limited data requirements and is simple to implement. The judgment necessary to make the method work comes from experienced managers and accountants who are familiar with the operations and management policies. Because operating results are required for only one period, this method is particularly useful for new products or situations involving rapid changes in products or technologies.

The two primary disadvantages of this method are its lack of a range of observations and its subjectivity. Using judgment generates two potential issues: (1) different analysts may develop different cost estimates from the same data; and (2) the results of analysis may have significant financial consequences for the analyst, therefore the analyst will likely show self-serving estimates. Another potential weakness in the method is that data used in the analysis may reflect unusual circumstances or inefficient operations, as is likely to occur with new products. These factors then become incorporated in the subsequent cost estimates. This method is also dependent on the quality of the detailed chart of accounts and transaction coding.

Engineering Approach

The **engineering approach** uses analysis and direct observation of processes to identify the relationship between inputs and outputs and then quantifies an expected cost behavior. A basic issue in manufacturing a product is determining the amount of direct materials, direct labor, and overhead required to run a given process. For a service, the question relates primarily to the labor and overhead costs.

One method of applying this approach to a product, such as C&J Electronics' calculators, is to make a list of all materials, labor tasks, and overhead activities necessary for the manufacturing process. Engineering specifications and vendor information can be used to quantify the units of the various materials and subassemblies. Time and motion studies can help estimate the amount of time required for the tasks to be performed. Other analyses are used to assess the overhead relationships to the process. Once quantities and time are determined, the costs related to those amounts are established using appropriate materials prices, labor rates, and overhead rates.

A major advantage of the engineering approach is that it details each step required to perform a task. This permits transfer of information to similar tasks in different situations. It also allows an organization to review productivity and identify strengths and weaknesses in the process. Another advantage is that it does not require historical accounting data. It is, therefore, a useful approach in estimating costs of new products and services. The major disadvantage is the expensive nature of the approach. For example, time and motion studies require in-depth examinations of each task and close observations of individuals performing those tasks. An additional disadvantage is that estimates made by the engineering approach are often based on near-optimal working conditions. Since actual working conditions are generally less than optimal, cost estimates using the engineering approach will generally understate the actual costs.

Scattergraph and Visual Fit

An approach that yields rough approximations to fixed and variable costs is called **scattergraph and visual fit**. With the advent of personal computers, the mechanical nature of this approach loses its appeal. When the analyst has data, the computer can graph the observations and estimate cost behavior quickly. However, we present the details because, in many cases, it can be used in a preliminary analysis and can easily be applied.

The first step in applying the approach is to graph each observation, with cost on the vertical axis and activity or cost driver on the horizontal axis. The second step is to fit visually and judgmentally a line to the data. Care should be taken so that the distances of the observations above the line are approximately equal to the distances of the observations below the line. Figure 3.1 shows a graph of maintenance cost and hours of operation for ten weeks of activity in one of C&J Electronics' operating departments. The data for this graph are as follows:

Hours (X)	Maintenance Cost (Y)
50	$120
30	110
10	60
50	150
40	100
30	80
20	70
60	150
40	110
20	50

FIGURE 3.1   A Visually Fitted Cost Function

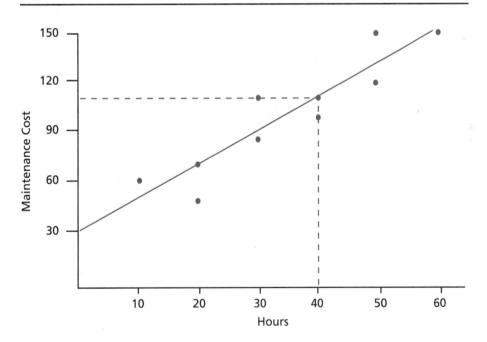

The third step is to estimate the cost behavior from the plotted line. The variable cost per hour is indicated by the slope of the line, and the fixed cost is measured where the line begins at zero hours of activity. In the maintenance cost example, the fixed cost is at the line's Y-axis intercept and is $30. The variable costs can be calculated by subtracting the fixed costs from the total costs at some point along the line. For example, the total costs indicated by the line at 40 hours are approximately $110. Compute variable costs as follows:

Total costs at 40 hours of operation	$110
Less fixed costs	30
Variable costs	$ 80

$80 variable costs ÷ 40 hours = $2 per hour of operation

This analysis yields the following cost function:

$$Y = \$30 + \$2X$$

When used by itself, the scattergraph and visual fit approach is limited by the judgment of the person drawing the line through the data. Even reasonable people will disagree on the slope and intercept for a given graph. However, lines that are drawn visually will tend to be fairly consistent near the center of the data. Therefore, a visual fit may be a useful way to obtain rough approximations near the center of the data. Care should be taken with estimates away from the center. The further from the central area, the larger are the errors that may occur in estimates of fixed and variable costs.

High-Low Method

Another method for obtaining rough approximations to fixed and variable costs is the **high-low method**. The first step is to list the observed costs for various levels of activity from the highest level in the range to the lowest. This method chooses observations associated with the highest and the lowest activity levels, not the highest and lowest costs. The second step is to divide the difference in activity between the highest and the lowest levels into the difference in cost for the corresponding activity levels to arrive at the variable cost rate. As an example, suppose a manager for a pest control service wishes to estimate supplies costs as input for bidding on jobs. Its costs of supplies for several recent jobs, along with the hours of activity, are as follows:

	Hours of Activity	*Supplies Costs*
High	95	$ 397
	90	377
	87	365
	82	345
	78	329
	75	317
	66	281
	58	239
Low	50	217

The difference in hours is 45 (95 - 50), and the difference in cost is $180 ($397 - $217). The variable supplies cost per hour is computed below:

$$\frac{\text{Cost at highest activity - Cost at lowest activity}}{\text{Highest activity - Lowest activity}} = \frac{\$180}{45} = \$4 \text{ Variable cost per hour}$$

The fixed cost is estimated by using the total cost at either the highest or lowest level and subtracting the estimated total variable cost for that level:

Total fixed cost = Total cost at highest activity - (Variable cost per unit x Highest activity)

or

Total fixed cost = Total cost at lowest activity - (Variable cost per unit x Lowest activity)

If the variable cost is calculated correctly, the fixed cost will be the same at both the high and low points. For the preceding illustration, the calculation of total fixed cost is as follows:

$$\text{Total fixed cost} = \$397 - (\$4 \text{ variable cost per hour} \times 95 \text{ hours})$$
$$= \$397 - \$380$$
$$= \$17$$

or

$$\text{Total fixed cost} = \$217 - (\$4 \text{ variable cost per hour} \times 50 \text{ hours})$$
$$= \$217 - \$200$$
$$= \$17$$

The cost function that results from the high-low method is:

$$Y = \$17 + \$4X$$

If the pest control service manager forecasts that a particular job would require 75 hours, the bid would include an estimate of $317 for supplies costs.

Occasionally, either the highest or lowest activity or the cost associated with one of those points represents an unusual situation that is obviously unrelated to the remaining data. When this happens, use the next highest or lowest observation that appears to align better with the data.

The high-low method is simple and can be used in many situations. Its primary disadvantage is that two points from all of the observations will only produce reliable estimates of fixed and variable cost behavior if the extreme points are representative of the points in between. Otherwise, distorted results may occur. Sometimes only two data points are available; and, in effect, these are used as the high and low points.

If enough quality data are available, statistical techniques can provide more objective cost estimates than we have discussed thus far. These techniques are covered in the Appendix to this chapter, pages 100-110.

Ethical Considerations in Estimating Costs

All cost estimation methods involve some degree of subjectivity. With account analysis, managers judgmentally classify costs. In the engineering method, the manager must often subjectively adjust data obtained from near-optimal working conditions to reflect normal working conditions. The scattergraph approach involves a subjective fitting of a line to data points. With the high-low method, one must decide whether the high and low points are representative data points.

The subjectivity inherent in cost estimation can lead to biased cost estimates. Indeed in certain instances, incentives exist for managers to bias cost estimates. In developing budgets or cost-based prices, managers may want to overestimate costs. In developing proposals for projects or programs, incentives may exist to underestimate costs. Managers must take care not to use subjectivity as an opportunity to act unethically.

COST-VOLUME-PROFIT (CVP) ANALYSIS

The separation of fixed costs from variable costs contributes to an understanding of how revenues, costs, and volume interact to provide profits. With this understanding, managers can perform any number of analyses that fit into a broad category called **cost-volume-profit (CVP) analysis**. Examples of such analyses include:

1. The number of unit sales required to break even.
2. The dollar amount of revenues needed to achieve a specified profit level.
3. The effect on profits if selling prices and variable costs increase by 10 percent.
4. The increase in selling price needed to cover a projected fixed cost increase.

CVP analysis, as its name implies, examines the interaction of factors that influence the level of profits. Although the name gives the impression that only cost and volume determine profits, several important factors exist that determine whether we have profits or losses and whether profits increase or decrease over time. The key factors appear in the *basic CVP equation:*

(Selling price) (Sales volume) - (Unit variable cost) (Sales volume) - Total fixed cost = Pretax profit

The basic CVP equation is merely a condensed income statement, in equation form, where variable costs are separated from fixed costs. This equation, as well as other variations which will be discussed later, appears as formula (1) in Figure 3.2.

The excess of total sales over total variable cost is called the **contribution margin**. From the basic CVP equation, we see that the contribution margin contributes towards covering fixed costs as well as providing net profits. The contribution margin, as well as the **contribution margin ratio**, often plays an important role in CVP analysis. The latter measure is the ratio of the contribution margin to total sales (or, equivalently, the ratio of the contribution margin per unit to the selling price).

Fundamental assumptions about CVP analysis are as follows:

1. Relevant range: CVP analysis is limited to the company's relevant range of activity.
2. Cost behavior identification: Fixed and variable costs can be identified.
3. Linearity: The selling price and the unit variable cost are constant over all sales volumes within the company's relevant range of activity.
4. Equality of production and sales: The volumes of sales and production are equivalent.
5. Activity measure: The primary cost driver is volume of units.
6. Constant sales mix: The sales mix of a multiproduct firm is constant.

FIGURE 3.2 Formulas for CVP Analysis

CVP Formulas

(1)	Basic CVP equation:	$(p - v)x - FC = PP$
(2)	CVP equation with taxes:	$[(p - v)x - FC](1 - t) = AP$
(3)	Break-even point, in units:	$\dfrac{FC}{c}$
(4)	Break-even point, in revenues:	$\dfrac{FC}{CM\%}$
(5)	Target pretax profit, in units:	$\dfrac{(FC + PP)}{c}$
(6)	Target pretax profit, in revenues:	$\dfrac{(FC + PP)}{CM\%}$
(7)	Target aftertax profit, in units:	$\dfrac{[FC + AP \div (1 - t)]}{c}$
(8)	Target aftertax profit, in revenues:	$\dfrac{[FC + AP \div (1 - t)]}{CM\%}$

Notation:

p = Selling price per unit

v = Variable cost per unit

x = Volume of units

FC = Total fixed cost

PP = Pretax profit

t = Tax rate

AP = Aftertax profit

c = Contribution margin per unit ($= p - v$)

$CM\%$ = Contribution margin ratio ($= \dfrac{p - v}{p}$)

Assumptions (1) through (3) are straightforward. Assumption (4) is required because, if sales and production are not equal, some amount of variable and fixed costs is treated as assets (inventories) rather than expenses. As long as inventories remain fairly stable between adjacent time periods, this assumption does not seriously limit the applicability of CVP analysis. Regarding assumption (5), factors other than volume may drive costs as we have discussed earlier in this chapter and will discuss further in later chapters. Costs that vary with cost drivers other than volume can be added to the fixed cost component. Assumption (6) will be discussed in detail later in this chapter.

While our discussion may appear to presume that CVP analysis is applicable only to companies that sell physical products, these techniques are just as applicable to service organizations. Contemporary Practice 3.2, page 82, provides an illustration of CVP analysis at a trucking firm.

C O N T E M P O R A R Y   P R A C T I C E   3 . 2

Break-Even Analysis for a Trucking Firm

An article published in the *Journal of Accountancy* discusses how The Motor Convoy, Inc., a Georgia-based trucking firm, determines break-even points for various volumes of freight. The cost driver used is length of trip (in miles). The article reports that break-even points computed for volumes of 2,000, 2,500, 3,000, and 3,500 pounds were trip lengths of 190, 260, 320, and 410 miles, respectively.

Source: Camp, R. A., "Multidimensional Break-Even Analysis," *Journal of Accountancy,* January 1987, pp. 132-133.

Basics of CVP Analysis

CVP analysis is often called **break-even analysis** because of the significance of the **break-even point**, which is the volume where total revenue equals total costs. It indicates how many units of product must be sold or how much revenue is needed to at least cover all costs.

Each unit of product sold is expected to yield revenue in excess of its variable cost and thus contribute to the recovery of fixed costs and provide a profit. The point at which profit is zero indicates that the contribution margin is equal to the fixed costs. Sales volume must increase beyond the break-even point for a company to realize a profit.

Let's look at CVP relationships in the context of C&J Electronics. Assume that price and costs for its calculators are as follows:

	Dollars Per Unit	Percentage of Selling Price
Selling price	$25	100%
Variable cost	15	60%
Contribution margin	$10	40%
Total fixed cost	$100,000	

Each calculator sold contributes $10 towards the recovery of fixed costs and the creation of a profit. Hence, the company must sell 10,000 calculators to break even. The 10,000 calculators sold will result in a total contribution margin of $100,000, equaling the total fixed cost.

In general, the break-even point can be calculated by the following rearrangement of the basic CVP equation, which appears as formula (3) in Figure 3.2:

Total fixed cost ÷ Unit contribution margin = Break-even point (in units)

For C&J Electronics, the break-even point is determined as follows:

$100,000 ÷ $10 = 10,000 calculators

A break-even point measured in dollars of revenue can be computed by multiplying the 10,000 calculators by the $25 selling price, or it can be computed directly using formula (4) of Figure 3.2 as follows:

Total fixed cost ÷ Contribution margin ratio = Break-even point (in revenues)

$100,000 ÷ 40% = $250,000

A Desired Pretax Profit

In business, a break-even operation is not satisfactory but serves as a base for profit planning. If we have a target profit level, we can insert that number into the basic CVP equation. This yields the following general formulas, which appear as formulas (5) and (6) in Figure 3.2:

(Fixed cost + Pretax profit) ÷ Unit contribution margin = Units required to attain pretax profit

(Fixed cost + Pretax profit) ÷ Contribution margin ratio = Revenues required to attain pretax profit

Continuing with the C&J Electronics illustration, suppose that Skip Johnson had set a profit objective of $200,000 before income taxes. The units and revenues required to attain this objective are determined as follows:

($100,000 + $200,000) ÷ $10 = 30,000 calculators

($100,000 + $200,000) ÷ 40% = $750,000

A Desired Aftertax Profit

The profit objective may be stated as a profit after income taxes. Rather than changing with volume of units, income taxes vary with profits after the break-even point. When income taxes are to be considered, the basic CVP equation is altered as follows:

[(Selling price - Unit variable cost)(Sales volume) - Total fixed cost](1 - Tax rate) = Aftertax profit

This CVP equation with taxes appears as formula (2) in Figure 3.2. Rearrangement of this equation results in the following general formulas, which appear as formulas (7) and (8) in Figure 3.2:

[Total fixed cost + Aftertax profit ÷ (1 - Tax rate)] ÷ Unit contribution margin = Units required to attain aftertax profit

[Total fixed cost + Aftertax profit ÷ (1 - Tax rate)] ÷ Contribution margin ratio = Revenues required to attain aftertax profit

Suppose that Skip Johnson had budgeted a $105,000 aftertax profit and that the income tax rate was 30 percent. We use the above general formulas to obtain the following volume and revenue:

[($100,000 + $105,000 ÷ (1 - .30)] ÷ $10 = 25,000 calculators

[($100,000 + $105,000 ÷ (1 - .30)] ÷ .40 = $625,000

Desired Profit as an Amount per Unit or a Percentage of Sales

Managers sometimes state the profit objective as either an average profit per unit or as a percentage of sales revenue (also called profit margin). Suppose

Skip Johnson had stated the profit objective as $2 pretax profit per unit. We can use the basic CVP equation to determine the number of calculators to be sold to meet this target:

$$(\$25 - \$15)(\text{Sales volume}) - \$100,000 = (\$2)(\text{Sales volume})$$

$$\text{Sales volume} = 12,500 \text{ calculators}$$

Suppose instead that Skip Johnson had stated the profit objective as a 20 percent profit margin before taxes. Again, we use the basic CVP equation, as follows:

$$(\$25 - \$15)(\text{Sales volume}) - \$100,000 = (.2)[(\$25)(\text{Sales volume})]$$

$$\text{Sales volume} = 20,000 \text{ calculators}$$

GRAPHICAL ANALYSIS

Total revenue and total cost at different sales volumes can be estimated and plotted on a graph. The information shown on the graph can also be given in conventional reports, but it is often easier to grasp the fundamental facts when they are presented in graphic or pictorial form. Let's look at two common forms of graphical analysis—the **break-even chart** and the profit-volume graph.

The Break-Even Chart

Dollars are shown on the vertical scale of the break-even chart, and the units of product to be sold are shown on the horizontal scale. The total costs are plotted for the various quantities to be sold and are connected by a line. This line is merely a combination of the fixed and variable cost diagrams from Chapter 2. Total revenues are similarly entered on the chart.

The break-even point lies at the intersection of the total revenue and the total cost lines. Losses are measured to the left of the break-even point; the amount of the loss at any point is equal to the dollar difference between the total cost line and the total revenue line. Profit is measured to the right of the break-even point and, at any point, is equal to the dollar difference between the total revenue line and the total cost line. This dollar difference is the contribution margin per unit multiplied by the volume in excess of the break-even point.

In Figure 3.3, a break-even chart has been prepared for C&J Electronics using the following data associated with sales levels between 5,000 and 30,000 calculators.

	Number of Calculators Produced and Sold					
	5,000	*10,000*	*15,000*	*20,000*	*25,000*	*30,000*
Total revenue	$125,000	$250,000	$375,000	$500,000	$625,000	$750,000
Total cost:						
Variable	$ 75,000	$150,000	$225,000	$300,000	$375,000	$450,000
Fixed	100,000	100,000	100,000	100,000	100,000	100,000
Total cost	$175,000	$250,000	$325,000	$400,000	$475,000	$550,000
Profit (loss)	$ (50,000)	$ 0	$ 50,000	$100,000	$150,000	$200,000

FIGURE 3.3   Break-Even Chart

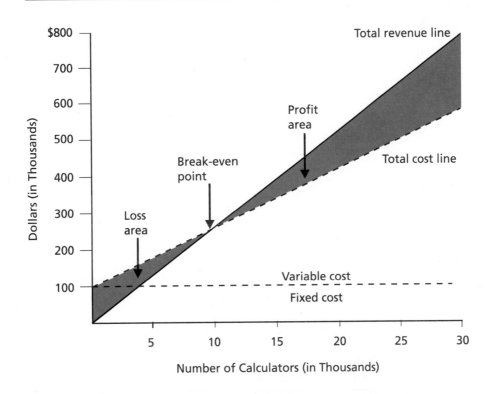

Curvature of Revenue and Cost Lines

In some cases, revenues and costs cannot be represented by straight lines. If more units are to be sold, management may have to reduce selling prices. Under these conditions, the revenue function is a curve instead of a straight line. Costs may also be nonlinear depending on what changes take place as volume increases. The cost curve may rise slowly at the start, then rise more steeply as volume is expanded. This occurs if the variable cost per unit becomes higher as more units are manufactured. Also, fixed costs might change as volume increases. For example, volume increases might cause a jump in supervision, equipment, and space costs. Therefore, it may be possible to have two break-even points as shown in Figure 3.4, page 86.

The Profit-Volume Graph

A **profit-volume graph**, or **P/V graph**, is sometimes used in place of or along with a break-even chart. Data used in the earlier illustration of a break-even chart in Figure 3.3 have also been used in preparing the P/V graph shown in Figure 3.5, page 86. In general, profits and losses appear on the vertical scale; and units of product, sales revenue, and/or percentages of capacity appear on the horizontal scale. A horizontal line is drawn on the graph to separate profits from losses. The profit or loss at each of various sales levels is plotted. These

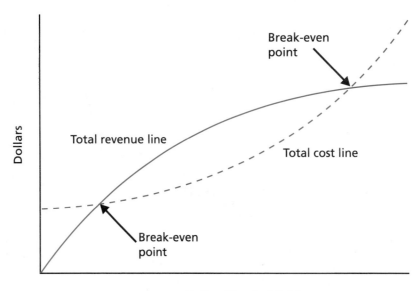

Units of Product Sold

points are then connected to form a profit line. The slope of the profit line is the contribution margin per unit if the horizontal line is stated as units of product or the contribution margin ratio if the horizontal line is stated as sales revenue.

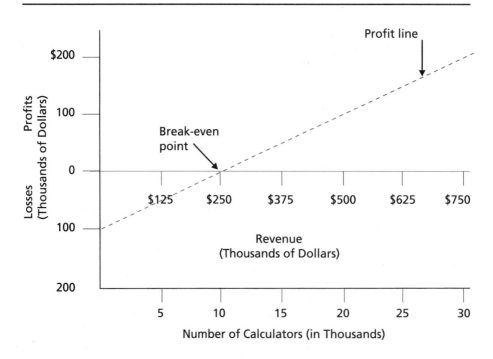

The break-even point is the point where the profit line intersects the horizontal line. Dollars of profit are measured on the vertical scale above the horizontal line, and dollars of loss are measured below the line. The P/V graph may be preferred to the break-even chart because profit or loss at any point is shown specifically on the vertical scale; but the P/V graph does not clearly show how cost varies with activity. Break-even charts and P/V graphs are often used together, thus obtaining the advantages of both.

ANALYSIS OF CHANGES IN CVP VARIABLES

Break-even charts and P/V graphs are convenient devices to show how profit is affected by changes in the factors that impact profit. For example, if unit selling price, unit variable cost, and total fixed cost remain constant, how many more units must be sold to realize a greater profit? Or, if the unit variable cost can be reduced, what additional profit can be expected at any given volume of sales? The effects of changes in sales volume, unit variable cost, unit selling price, total fixed cost, and sales mix are discussed in the following paragraphs.

Sales Volume

For some companies, substantial profits depend on high sales volume. For example, if each unit of product is sold at a relatively low contribution margin, high profits are a function of selling in large quantities. This is more significant when the fixed cost is high.

For an illustration, consider a company that handles a product with a selling price of $1 per unit. Assume a variable cost of $0.70 per unit and a fixed cost of $180,000 per year. The contribution margin, therefore, is $0.30 per unit ($1 - $0.70). Before any profit is realized, the company must sell enough units for the total contribution margin to recover the fixed cost. Therefore, 600,000 units must be sold just to break even:

$$\$180,000 \div \$.30 = 600,000 \text{ units}$$

For every unit sold in excess of 600,000, a $0.30 profit before tax is earned. In such a situation, the company must be certain that it can sell substantially more than 600,000 units to earn a reasonable profit on its investment.

When products sell for relatively high contribution margins per unit, the fixed cost is recaptured with the sale of fewer units; and a profit can be made on a relatively low sales volume. Suppose that each unit of product sells for $1,000 and that the variable cost per unit is $900. The fixed cost for the year is $180,000. The contribution margin ratio is only 10 percent, but this is equal to $100 from each unit sold. The break-even point will be reached when 1,800 units are sold. The physical quantity handled is much lower than it was in the preceding example, but the same principle applies. More than 1,800 units must be sold if the company is to produce a profit.

A key relationship between changes in volume and pretax profit is the following:

Contribution margin per unit x Change in sales volume = Change in pretax profit

This relationship presumes that the contribution margin per unit remains unchanged when the sales volume changes. It also presumes that fixed costs have not been changed. Suppose that Skip Johnson of C&J Electronics wishes to know how the sale of an additional 500 calculators would impact profits. The above relationship reveals that pretax profits would increase by $5,000 ($10 contribution margin per unit x 500 units).

Variable Costs

The relationship between the selling price of a product and its variable cost is important in any line of business. Even small savings in the variable cost can add significantly to profits. A reduction of a fraction of a dollar in the unit cost becomes a contribution to fixed cost and profit. If 50,000 units are sold in a year, a $0.10 decrease in the unit cost becomes a $5,000 increase in profit. Conversely, a $0.10 increase in unit cost decreases profit by $5,000.

Management is continually searching for opportunities to make even small cost savings. What appears trivial may turn out to be the difference between profit or loss for the year. In manufacturing, it may be possible to save on materials cost by using cheaper materials that are just as satisfactory.   Using materials more effectively can also result in savings. Improving methods of production may decrease labor and overhead costs per unit.

A small savings in unit cost can give a company a competitive advantage. If prices must be reduced, the low-cost producer will usually suffer less. At any given price and fixed cost structure, the low-cost producer will become profitable faster as sales volume increases.

The following operating results of three companies show how profit is influenced by changes in the variable cost pattern. Each of the three companies sells 100,000 units of one product line at a price of $5 per unit. Each has an annual fixed cost of $150,000. Company A can manufacture each unit at a variable cost of $2.50. Company B has found ways to save costs and can produce each unit for a variable cost of $2, while Company C has allowed its unit variable cost to rise to $3.

	Company A	*Company B*	*Company C*
Number of units sold	100,000	100,000	100,000
Unit selling price	$ 5.00	$ 5.00	$ 5.00
Unit variable cost	2.50	2.00	3.00
Unit contribution margin	2.50	3.00	2.00
Contribution margin ratio	50%	60%	40%
Total revenue	$500,000	$500,000	$500,000
Total variable cost	250,000	200,000	300,000
Total contribution margin	$250,000	$300,000	$200,000
Fixed cost	150,000	150,000	150,000
Income before income tax	$100,000	$150,000	$ 50,000

A difference of $0.50 in unit variable cost between Company A and Company B or between Company A and Company C adds up to a $50,000 difference in profit when 100,000 units are sold. The low-cost producer has a $1 per unit profit advantage over the high-cost producer. If sales volume should fall to 60,000 units per company, Company B would have a profit of $30,000,

Company A would break even, and Company C would suffer a loss of $30,000. The same results are shown in the break-even graph in Figure 3.6.

The fixed cost line for each company is drawn at $150,000, the amount of the fixed cost. When 40,000 units are sold, a difference of $20,000 occurs between each total cost line. The lines diverge as greater quantities are sold. At the 100,000-unit level, the difference is $50,000 between each total cost line. Company B can make a profit by selling any quantity in excess of 50,000 units, but Company C must sell 75,000 units to break even. With its present cost structure, Company C will have to sell in greater volume if it is to earn a profit equal to profits earned by Company A or Company B. Company C is the inefficient producer in the group and, as such, operates at a disadvantage. When there is enough business for everyone, Company C will earn a profit but will most likely earn less than the others. When business conditions are poor, Company C will be more vulnerable to losses.

Price Policy

One of the ways to improve profit is to get more sales volume; and, to stimulate sales volume, management may decide to reduce prices. Bear in mind, however, that if demand for the product is inelastic or if competitors also reduce prices, volume may not increase at all. Moreover, even if the price reduction results in an increase in sales volume, the increase may not be enough to overcome the handicap of selling at a lower price. This point is often overlooked by optimistic managers who believe that a small increase in volume can compensate for a slight decrease in price.

Price cuts, like increases in unit variable costs, decrease the contribution margin. On a unit basis, price decreases may appear to be insignificant; but when the unit differential is multiplied by thousands of units, the total effect may be tremendous. Many more units may need to be sold to make up for the

FIGURE 3.6 **Effects of Variable Cost Changes**

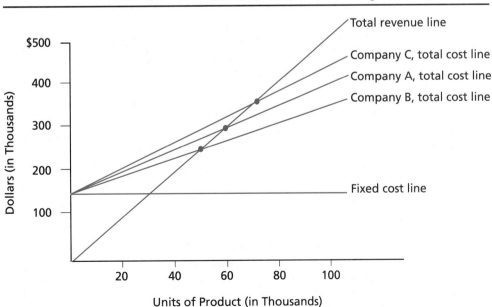

difference. Company A, for example, hopes to increase profit by stimulating sales volume; and, to do so, it plans to reduce the unit price by 10 percent. The following tabulation portrays its present and contemplated situations:

	Present Situation	Contemplated Situation
Selling price	$5.00	$4.50
Variable cost	2.50	2.50
Contribution margin	$2.50	$2.00
Contribution margin ratio	50%	44.4%

At present, one-half of each revenue dollar can be applied to fixed cost and profit. When revenues are twice the fixed cost, Company A will break even. Therefore, 60,000 units yielding revenues of $300,000 must be sold if the fixed cost is $150,000. But when the price is reduced, less than half of each dollar can be applied to fixed cost and profit. To recover $150,000 in fixed cost, unit sales must be 75,000 ($150,000 ÷ $2 per unit contribution margin). Thus, to overcome the effect of a 10 percent price cut, unit sales must increase by 25 percent:

$$(75,000 - 60,000) \div 60,000 = 25\% \text{ increase}$$

Similarly, revenue must increase to $337,500 (75,000 units x $4.50 per unit). This represents a 12.5 percent increase, as follows:

$$(\$337,500 - \$300,000) \div \$300,000 = 12.5\% \text{ increase}$$

Not only must total revenue be higher; but, with a lower price, more units must be sold to obtain that revenue. A break-even chart showing these changes appears in Figure 3.7.

The present pretax income of $100,000 can still be earned if 125,000 units are sold. This is obtained using formula (5) of Figure 3.2:

$$(\$150,000 + \$100,000) \div \$2 = 125,000 \text{ units}$$

Fixed Costs

A change in fixed cost has no effect on the contribution margin. Increases in fixed cost are recovered when the contribution margin from additional units sold is equal to the increase in fixed cost. Presuming that the contribution margin per unit remains unchanged, the following general relationship holds:

(Contribution margin per unit x Change in sales volume) - Change in fixed cost = Change in pretax profit

Suppose Skip Johnson estimates that if he spends an additional $30,000 on advertising he should be able to sell an additional 2,500 calculators. The above equation reveals that pretax profit would decrease by $5,000 [($10 x 2,500) - $30,000].

FIGURE 3.7 **Effect of a Price Reduction**

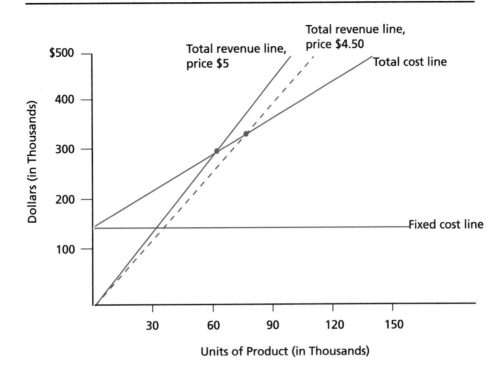

Because fixed cost is not part of the contribution margin computation, the slope of the total cost line on a break-even chart is unaffected by changes in fixed cost. The new total cost line is drawn parallel to the original line; and the vertical distance between the two lines, at any point, is equal to the increase or the decrease in fixed cost.

The break-even chart in Figure 3.8, page 92, shows the results of an increase in fixed cost from $100,000 to $130,000 at C&J Electronics. Under the new fixed cost structure, the total cost line shifts upward; and, at any point, the new line is $30,000 higher than it was originally. To break even or maintain the same profit as before, C&J Electronics must sell 3,000 more calculators.

Decreases in fixed cost would cause the total cost line to shift downward. The total contribution margin can decline by the amount of the decrease in fixed cost without affecting profit. The lower sales volume now needed to maintain the same profit can be calculated by dividing the unit contribution margin into the decrease in fixed cost.

Ethical Considerations When Changing CVP Variables

Managers are often under pressure to reduce costs—both variable and fixed costs. Many companies have downsized in recent years by eliminating jobs and even closing plants. Managers must be careful not to cut costs in an unethical manner. Changing a price can also involve ethical issues. For instance, immediately after a hurricane hit southern Florida several years ago, some sellers of building supplies were accused of "price gouging."

FIGURE 3.8 Effect of an Increase in Fixed Cost

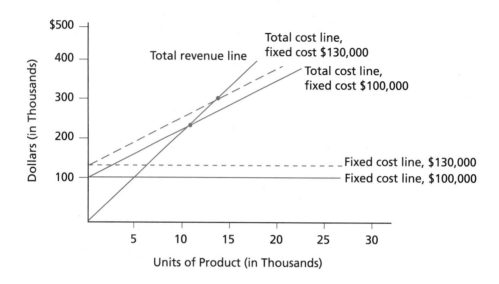

*M*EASURES OF RELATIONSHIP BETWEEN OPERATING LEVELS AND BREAK-EVEN POINTS

Companies want to know where they are with respect to the break-even point. If they are operating around the break-even point, management may be more conservative in its approach to implementing changes and mapping out new strategies. On the other hand, if they are operating well away from the break-even point, management will be more aggressive because the downside risk is not as great. Two measures that relate to this distance between a break-even point and the current or planned operating volume are operating leverage and margin of safety. These measures are the subject of the following sections.

Operating Leverage

Operating leverage measures the effect that a percentage change in sales revenue has on pretax profit. It is a principle by which management in a high fixed cost industry with a relatively high contribution margin ratio (low variable costs relative to sales revenue) can increase profits substantially with a small increase in sales volume. We typically call this measure the operating leverage factor or the degree of operating leverage, and it is computed as follows:

$$\frac{\text{Contribution margin}}{\text{Pretax profit}} = \text{Operating leverage factor}$$

As pretax profit moves closer to zero, the closer the company is to the break-even point. This will yield a high operating leverage factor. As sales volume increases, the contribution margin and pretax profit both increase; and, consequently, the operating leverage factor becomes progressively smaller. Hence, the operating leverage factor is related to the distance between the break-even point and a current or expected sales volume. With an increase in sales volume, profits will increase by the percentage increase in sales volume multiplied by the operating leverage factor.

Suppose C&J Electronics is currently selling 15,000 calculators. With its unit contribution margin of $10 and fixed costs of $100,000, the operating leverage factor is 3, computed as follows:

$$\frac{(15,000)(\$10)}{(15,000)(\$10) - \$100,000} = \frac{\$150,000}{\$50,000} = 3$$

At a sales volume of 15,000, if sales volume can be increased by an additional 10 percent, profit can be increased by 30 percent:

Percentage increase in sales volume		Operating leverage factor		Percentage increase in pretax profit
10%	x	3	=	30%

A 10 percent increase in sales volume will increase sales from 15,000 units to 16,500 units. Operating leverage suggests that the pretax profit should be $65,000 ($50,000 x 1.3). Indeed, when we deduct the $100,000 fixed cost from the new contribution margin of $165,000 (16,500 x $10), we obtain a pretax profit of $65,000.

A company with high fixed costs will have to sell in large volume to recover the fixed costs. However, if the company also has a high contribution margin ratio, it will move into higher profits very quickly after the break-even volume is attained. Hence, a fairly small percentage increase in sales volume (computed on a base that is already fairly large) will increase profits rapidly.

Margin of Safety

The **margin of safety** is the excess of actual (or expected) sales over sales at the break-even point. The excess may also be computed as a percentage of actual (or expected) sales. The margin of safety, expressed either in dollars or as a percentage, shows how much sales volume can be reduced without sustaining losses. The formulas for calculating margin of safety are:

Margin of safety in dollars = Actual (or expected) sales - Break-even sales

Margin of safety in percentage form $= \dfrac{\text{Margin of safety in dollars}}{\text{Actual (or expected) sales}}$

For our purposes, margin of safety is the percentage form. Therefore, unless otherwise specified, a reference to margin of safety will mean a percentage.

Recall that the break-even sales level for C&J Electronics was $250,000. At an actual sales level of 15,000 calculators, its safety margin is one-third, calculated as follows:

$$\frac{[(15,000)(\$25) - \$250,000]}{(15,000)(\$25)} = \frac{\$125,000}{\$375,000} = .333 \text{ or } 1/3$$

Note that one-third is the reciprocal of the operating leverage factor computed earlier for C&J Electronics. The margin of safety will always be the reciprocal of the operating leverage factor.

T HE SALES MIX

When selling more than one product line, the relative proportion of each product line to the total sales is called the **sales mix**. With each product line having a different contribution margin, management will try to maximize the sales of the product lines with higher contribution margins. However, a sales mix results because limits on either sales or production of any given product line may exist.

When products have their own individual production facilities and fixed costs are specifically identified with the product line, cost-volume-profit analysis is performed for each product line. However, in many cases, product lines share facilities; and the fixed costs relate to many products. For such a situation, cost-volume-profit analysis requires averaging of data by using the sales mix percentages as weights. Consequently, a break-even point can be computed for any assumed mix of sales; and a break-even chart or P/V graph can be constructed for any sales mix. But any one graph will reflect a constant sales mix for the entire range of volumes covered by the cost and revenue lines. If the sales mix changes, a new set of cost and revenue lines is needed.

Let's consider cost-volume-profit analysis with a sales mix. Suppose that Skip Johnson of C&J Electronics has decided to upgrade the type of calculators produced by replacing the current ones with programmable models. He has also decided to diversify product lines by introducing the production of telephones and telephone answering machines. Assume that the following budget is prepared for the sale of these three product lines. Fixed costs are budgeted at $500,000 for the period.

Product Lines	Sales Volume (Units)	Unit Selling Price	Unit Variable Cost	Contribution Margin Dollars	Contribution Margin Ratio
Programmable calculators	20,000	$50	$20	$30	60%
Telephones	10,000	50	30	20	40
Answering machines	10,000	50	40	10	20
Total	40,000				

The break-even point in units is computed using a weighted average contribution margin as follows:

Product Lines	Sales Mix Proportions		Unit Contribution Margin	Weighted Contribution Margin
Programmable calculators	50%	x	$30	$15.00
Telephones	25%	x	20	5.00
Answering machines	25%	x	10	2.50
Weighted contribution margin				$22.50

$$\frac{\text{Fixed cost}}{\text{Weighted contribution margin}} = \frac{\$500,000}{\$22.50} = 22,222 \text{ total units}$$

The detailed composition of sales and contribution margins at this level is as follows:

Product Lines	Sales Mix Proportions		Total Units		Units of Product		Unit Contribution Margin		Contribution Margin
Programmable calculators	50%	x	22,222	=	11,111	x	$30	=	$333,330
Telephones	25%	x	22,222	=	5,555	x	20	=	111,100
Answering machines	25%	x	22,222	=	5,555	x	10	=	55,550
Break-even contribution margin*									$499,980

* Approximately equal to fixed cost of $500,000. Difference is due to rounding.

To obtain the sales revenue at the break-even point directly, we calculate it as we did earlier in the chapter. Simply divide the weighted contribution margin ratio into the fixed costs. Individual product line revenues will be the total revenues multiplied by individual sales mix proportions. Continuing with our illustration, we have:

	Product Lines			
	Programmable Calculators	Telephones	Answering Machines	Total
Units to be sold	20,000	10,000	10,000	40,000
Sales	$1,000,000	$500,000	$500,000	$2,000,000
Variable cost	400,000	300,000	400,000	1,100,000
Contribution margin . . .	$ 600,000	$200,000	$100,000	$ 900,000
Less fixed cost				500,000
Budgeted pretax profit . .				$ 400,000

As shown in the following calculations, the weighted contribution margin ratio is 45 percent; and revenue at the break-even point is $1,111,111.

$$\frac{\text{Total contribution margin}}{\text{Total sales revenue}} = \frac{\$900,000}{\$2,000,000} = 45\%$$

$$\frac{\text{Fixed cost}}{\text{Weighted contribution margin ratio}} = \frac{\$500,000}{45\%} = \$1,111,111$$

If the actual sales mix changes from the budgeted sales mix, the break-even point and other factors of cost-volume-profit analysis may change. Suppose that C&J Electronics actually operated at the budgeted capacity with fixed costs of $500,000. The unit selling prices and variable costs were also in agreement with the budget. Yet, with the same revenue of $2,000,000, the pretax profit was considerably lower than anticipated. The difference was due to a changed sales mix. Assume the following actual results:

Product Lines	Sales Volume (Units)	Unit Contribution Margin	Total Contribution Margin	Sales Revenue
Programmable calculators . . .	5,000	$30	$150,000	$ 250,000
Telephones	20,000	20	400,000	1,000,000
Answering machines	15,000	10	150,000	750,000
Totals			$700,000	$2,000,000
Less fixed cost			500,000	
Actual pretax profit			$200,000	

Instead of earning $400,000 before income taxes, the company earned only $200,000. Sales of the telephones and answering machines, the less profitable products, were much better than expected. At the same time, sales of the best product line, the programmable calculators, were less than expected. As a result, the total contribution margin was less than budgeted, so pretax income was also less than budgeted.

One way to encourage the sales force to sell more of the high contribution margin lines is to compute sales commissions on the contribution margin rather than on sales revenue. If sales commissions are based on sales revenue, a sales force may sell a high volume of less profitable product lines and still earn a satisfactory commission. But if sales commissions are related to contribution margin, the sales force is encouraged to strive for greater sales of more profitable products and, in doing so, will help to improve total company profits.

SUMMARY

Four methods for identifying variable and fixed cost behavior are account analysis, the engineering approach, the scattergraph and visual fit, and the high-low method. In account analysis, the analyst determines the cost behavior of a specific cost by reviewing and interpreting managerial policies with respect to the cost and by inspecting the historical activity of the cost. The engineering approach uses analysis and direct observation of processes to identify the relationship between inputs and outputs and then quantifies an expected cost behavior. In the scattergraph and visual fit method, the analyst graphs each observation, with cost on the vertical axis and activity or cost driver on the horizontal axis. Then, the analyst visually and judgmentally fits a line to the data. The Y-axis intercept of the line is the estimate of fixed cost, and the slope of the line is the estimate of variable cost per unit. The high-low method is a simple method in which the rate of cost variability is determined from data taken only at the high and low points of a range of data.

In planning profit, management considers sales volume, selling prices, variable costs, fixed costs, and the sales mix. When the contribution margin is equal to fixed costs, the company breaks even. A desired profit level can be attained when the contribution margin is equal to the fixed costs plus the desired profit before income taxes. Break-even charts or profit-volume graphs are visual representations of profits or losses that can be expected at different volume levels.

In making plans, management can review various alternatives to see how they will affect profit. For example, what will likely happen if the selling price is increased or if the variable cost is decreased? Often a relatively small change in variable cost per unit will have a relatively large effect on profit. Prices may be cut to increase sales volume, but this will not necessarily increase profit.

Recent developments such as increased automation tend to increase the importance of fixed costs in the total cost structure. With a relatively high contribution margin ratio and relatively high fixed costs, a small percentage increase in sales volume can be translated into a substantial increase in profits. This principle is known as operating leverage. When a company is operating at volume levels higher than the break-even point, the margin of safety becomes an important part of a cost-volume-profit analysis.

When more than one product line is sold, the relative proportion of total sales for each product line is known as the sales mix. To maximize profit, management will try to maximize the sales of product lines with higher contribution margin rates. A break-even point and break-even units for each product line can be computed for any given sales mix.

P ROBLEMS FOR REVIEW

Review Problem A

Cox Company's costs for equipment maintenance during the last eight weeks are given as follows:

Week	Hours	Actual Costs
1	45	$400
2	60	540
3	64	560
4	65	600
5	55	520
6	50	470
7	40	450
8	35	360

Required:

1. Using the scattergraph and visual fit approach, estimate a cost function from the above data.

2. Using the high-low approach, estimate a cost function from the above data.

3. For each of the methods in Parts (1) and (2), predict the cost of equipment maintenance for a week during the following month when 58 hours are expected to be worked.

Solution:

1. First, we plot the data and draw a line by visual inspection, as follows:

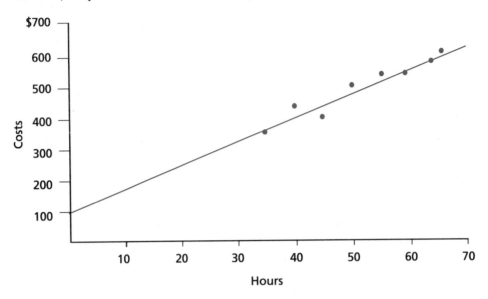

Looking at the graph, it appears that the Y-intercept of the line drawn is approximately $100. This is our estimate of the fixed cost. To obtain the variable cost, we arbitrarily choose 30 hours and its associated cost of approximately $300 from the graph. We compute as follows:

Total cost at 30 hours	$300
Less fixed cost	100
Variable cost	$200

$200 ÷ 30 = $6.67 per hour

Our cost function is: $Y = \$100 + \$6.67X$

2. We see from the data that the high activity was during Week 4, while the low activity was during Week 8. Thus, we compute our variable cost per hour as follows:

($600 - $360) ÷ (65 - 35) = $8 per hour

Next, we choose the high point or low point to obtain the fixed cost:

Fixed cost = $600 - 65($8) = $600 - $520 = $80

or

Fixed cost = $360 - 35($8) = $360 - $280 = $80

Our cost function is: $Y = \$80 + \$8X$

3. From Part (1), the cost prediction would be:

$100 + $6.67(58) = $100 + $386.86 = $486.86

From Part (2), the cost prediction would be:

$80 + $8(58) = $80 + $464 = $544

Review Problem B

Foxx Company manufactures a water sealant at the Orange County Plant. This sealant is used to stop leaks in basements or in concrete retainer walls. In 1996, the company sold 1,600,000 gallons of the sealant at a price of $3.00 per gallon with a variable production cost per gallon of $1.50. The fixed manufacturing costs were $1,550,000.

In 1997, new automated equipment will be used in production. This will increase the fixed manufacturing costs for the year to $1,785,000. The variable production cost per gallon has been estimated at $1.30 per gallon. The sales division estimates that sales volume can be increased by 12.5 percent in 1997.

Required:

1. For 1996, compute the break-even point in gallons and revenues.

2. For 1997, compute the break-even point in gallons and revenues.

3. Using the cost and revenue data for 1996, consider each of the following situations independently:

   (a) What is the effect in gallons on the break-even point for the decrease in variable cost from $1.50 per gallon to $1.30 per gallon?

   (b) What is the effect in gallons on the break-even point for the increase in fixed cost of $235,000?

4. For 1997, calculate the operating leverage factor and the margin of safety, after making all estimated changes.

Solution:

1. For 1996, break-even point in gallons and revenues:

$$\frac{\$1,550,000 \text{ (Fixed cost)}}{\$1.50 \text{ (Unit contribution margin)}} = 1,033,333 \text{ gallons}$$

$$\frac{\$1,550,000 \text{ (Fixed cost)}}{50\% \text{ (Contribution margin ratio)}} = \$3,100,000$$

2. For 1997, estimated break-even point in gallons and revenues:

$$\frac{\$1,785,000 \text{ (Fixed cost)}}{\$1.70 \text{ (Unit contribution margin)}} = 1,050,000 \text{ gallons}$$

$$\frac{\$1,785,000 \text{ (Fixed cost)}}{56.67\% \text{ (Contribution margin ratio)}} = \$3,150,000$$

3. **(a)** New break-even point given a change in variable cost:

$$\frac{\$1,550,000 \text{ (Fixed cost)}}{\$1.70 \text{ (Unit contribution margin)}} = 911,765 \text{ gallons}$$

Old break-even point.	1,033,333 gallons
Decrease in break-even point	121,568 gallons

   (b) New break-even point given a change in fixed cost:

$$\frac{\$1,785,000 \text{ (Fixed cost)}}{\$1.50 \text{ (Unit contribution margin)}} = 1,190,000 \text{ gallons}$$

Old break-even point.	1,033,333 gallons
Increase in break-even point	156,667 gallons

4. Operating leverage and margin of safety for 1997:
Estimated sales for 1997:

$$(1,600,000)(1.125)(\$3.00) = \$5,400,000$$

Estimated contribution margin for 1997:

$$\$5,400,000 - (1,600,000)(1.125)(\$1.30) = \$3,060,000$$

Estimated profit before tax for 1997:

$$\$3,060,000 - \$1,785,000 = \$1,275,000$$

Operating leverage:

$$\frac{\$3,060,000\,(\text{Contribution margin})}{\$1,275,000\,(\text{Profit before tax})} = 2.40$$

Margin of safety:

$$\frac{\$5,400,000\,(\text{Current revenues}) - \$3,150,000\,(\text{Break-even revenues})}{\$5,400,000\,(\text{Current revenues})} = 41.7\%$$

❖ *APPENDIX*

*R*EGRESSION AND CORRELATION ANALYSES

Regression and correlation analyses are statistical techniques that can be used to estimate and examine cost functions. **Regression analysis** fits a line to the cost and activity data using the least squares method. **Correlation analysis** deals with the "goodness of fit" in the relationship between costs and activity as identified by the **regression line**. Both analyses are important in finding relationships and establishing the significance of those relationships.

Linear Regression

Linear regression is a statistical tool for describing the movement of one variable based on the movement of another variable. In determining cost behavior, it is important to know if the movement in costs is related to the movement in activity. The cost behavior is expressed as a line of regression. A line of regression can be fitted precisely to a large quantity of data by the **least squares method**. The high-low method is a rough approximation computed from data taken only at the high and low points of the range, but the least squares method includes all data within the range. The line of regression is determined so that the algebraic sum of the squared deviations from that line is at a minimum when the best fitting straight line is drawn through the observations.

We will explain the application of linear regression through an illustration. Suppose that the buildings manager of the Atlanta Juvenile Community Center is asked to assist in budgeting for the buildings-related costs. During the past year, electricity costs for various hours of monthly activity in a particular building have been recorded as follows:

Hours (X)	Electricity Cost (Y)
30	$500
50	650
20	300
10	300
60	900
50	750
40	650
60	700
30	450
10	350
40	600
20	450

The advent of the personal computer and spreadsheet software has greatly simplified the application of linear regression. By entering the data and using a few function commands, the results appear on the screen. Using spreadsheet software analysis, the data for our example of electricity cost and hours of activity yield the following results:

Regression Output	
Constant	200
Std Err of Y Est	67.08
r^2	0.886
No. of observations	12
Degrees of freedom	10
X coefficient(s)	10

The information necessary to obtain a cost function can be read from the output. The constant is the fixed cost of $200. The X coefficient is our variable cost per hour, $10. Hence, our cost function is:

$$Y = \$200 + \$10X$$

The number of observations is given as a check. The degrees of freedom amount is 10 which equals 12 - 2, where 2 is the number of parameters we are estimating (a and b). The remaining terms in the regression output will be discussed later.

The buildings manager can now use the derived cost function to budget the electricity cost. Suppose that 35 hours of activity is expected in the building during the next month. In this case, $550 will be budgeted for electricity cost [$200 + ($10 x 35)].

Quality of the Regression

In measuring the relationship between the cost and activity, we are interested in more than just an equation for estimating cost. We also want to know the "goodness of fit" for the correlation of the regression line to the cost and activity data and the "reliability" of the cost estimates. This section discusses some of the measures available for assessing goodness of fit and reliability.

Goodness of Fit.   The relationship between cost and activity is called correlation. At times, costs may be randomly distributed and are not at all related to the cost driver used in defining the relationship. This is illustrated in Figure 3.9, page 102.

FIGURE   3.9   No Correlation

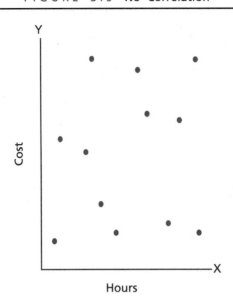

At the other extreme, the relationship may be so close that the data can almost be plotted on a line, as shown in Figure 3.10.

Between these extremes, the degree of correlation may not be so evident. A high degree of correlation exists when the regression line explains most of the variation in the data. The preceding example of electricity costs has all data lying relatively close to the regression line, as shown on the graph in Figure 3.11.

FIGURE   3.10   Positive Correlation

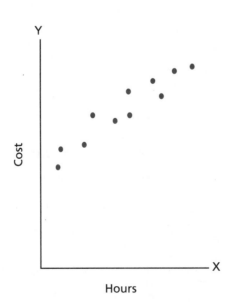

FIGURE 3.11 Explanation of Correlation

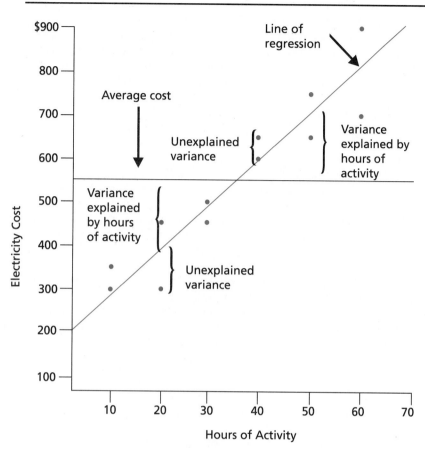

The average cost is computed in the conventional way by adding the costs and dividing by the number of data points. In this case, the average is $550. Any variance between the line of regression and the average can be explained by hours of activity. The unexplained variances are the variances between the actual costs and the line of regression. In this illustration, a large part of the variance from the average can be explained by hours of activity; only a small amount is unexplained. Hence, a good correlation exists between cost and hours.

The degree of correlation is measured by the correlation coefficient, most frequently designated as r. A related measure, r^2, is often used to assess the "goodness of fit" between the data and the regression line. The r^2 figure can vary from 0 to 1. An r^2 close to 0 would indicate that the regression line does not describe the data. That is, the regression line is nearly horizontal, and little of the variation in Y is explained by the variation in X. If the regression line is very descriptive of the data, the r^2 will be close to 1. Such is the case for the above example of electricity cost estimation. Recall that the regression output showed an r^2 (r^2 in the regression output on page 101) of 0.886. This means that 88.6 percent of the variation in electricity costs could be explained by hours of activity.

Reliability.   Because a regression equation will not result in a perfect fit on the data observations, a measure of variability in the data is necessary with respect to the regression equation.   The **standard error of the estimate** (S_e) is a measure of the deviation between the actual observations of Y and the values predicted by the regression equation. In other words, S_e gives an estimate of the amount by which the actual observation might differ from the estimate. For our example of electricity costs, the regression output showed an S_e of 67.08, labeled as "Std Err of Y Est."

Statistical data often form a pattern of distribution designated as a normal distribution. In a **normal distribution**, data can be plotted as a smooth, continuous, symmetrically bell-shaped curve with a single peak in the center of distribution. We will assume that the cost data in this Appendix are normally distributed. A table of probabilities for a normal distribution shows that approximately two-thirds of the data (more precisely, 68.27 percent) lie within plus and minus one standard deviation of the mean. In our example, then, approximately two-thirds of the cost observations should lie within plus and minus one standard error of the estimate of the line of regression or lie between $67.08 above the line of regression and $67.08 below it. To understand how this works with our data, examine the plot in Figure 3.12 of differences between the actual cost and predicted cost.

An interrelationship exists between r^2 and S_e. For example, as the deviations between actual cost and the predicted cost decrease, our measure for "goodness of fit" (r^2) increases in amount and S_e decreases in amount. That is, the higher the r^2, the lesser the deviation, the higher the correlation, and the closer actual observations fit the line of regression. The significance of this interrelationship is that the higher the r^2 and the lower the standard error of the estimate, the more reliable is our estimate of b (the variable cost per hour).

FIGURE 3.12 **Graph of Differences**

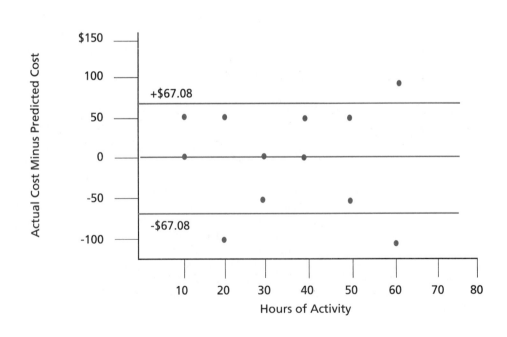

Sources of Errors. The cost equation derived from a set of data has a certain degree of error due to imperfections in the data, data collection, and other processing issues. These imperfections will appear in the difference between an actual cost and a cost predicted by the regression equation. Understanding the sources of errors is a step toward eliminating the impact of those errors on the results. The most common sources of errors fall into one of the following three categories: (1) major errors in the original data, (2) errors in keying data, and (3) inappropriate measures of activity.

Major errors in the original data are minimized through (1) reviewing the cutoff procedures that separate costs into periods, especially for unusual data, and (2) examining the data for procedural errors, such as classification of transactions into the wrong account. For errors in keying data and calculation, look for unusual cost data (i.e., observations with large differences between the actual cost and the cost predicted by the regression line). If multiple cost drivers are available in the data, try other cost drivers to locate one with a higher r^2 value.

C HECKING SOME INFERENCES

Before making use of a sample of cost data for cost estimation and control, we must have assurance that inferences with respect to cost behavior are correct. Otherwise, the cost data may be misleading. An overriding concern with regression analysis or any other cost estimation technique is that of extrapolating beyond the relevant range of activity. Cost behavior may change drastically once the activity falls below or rises above the relevant range. For instance, assume the relevant range of activity for our electricity cost estimation example is 10 to 60 hours. We wish to predict the electricity cost for the coming month during which 80 hours of activity are expected. Since this level is above the relevant range, the cost function we derived earlier may not be appropriate to use.

Additionally, our electricity cost data are suitably represented by a straight line (linear) and not by a curve. In some situations, the linear relationship may not be appropriate. Costs, for example, may not increase at a constant rate but instead may change at an increasing or a decreasing rate as the measure of activity increases. Hence, the cost data would be represented by a curve rather than a straight line. The shape of the line or curve can be revealed by plotting a sufficient amount of data for various hours of activity.

Also, the data may not be uniformly dispersed along the line of regression. At the extremes, for example, the data may be more widely dispersed than at the middle portion of the range. As a result, lines drawn for plus and minus one standard error of the estimate may not be parallel. This is illustrated on the graph in Figure 3.13, page 106. In situations where the degree of dispersion varies over the range, it is necessary to determine the standard error of the estimate for each position in the range.

C ONTROL LIMITS

From the data given in our example, the fixed electricity cost is estimated at $200; and the variable electricity cost is estimated at the rate of $10 per hour. For 30 hours of activity, the total cost is estimated at $500. This is a predicted cost, however; and it is

FIGURE 3.13 Wide Dispersion at Extremes

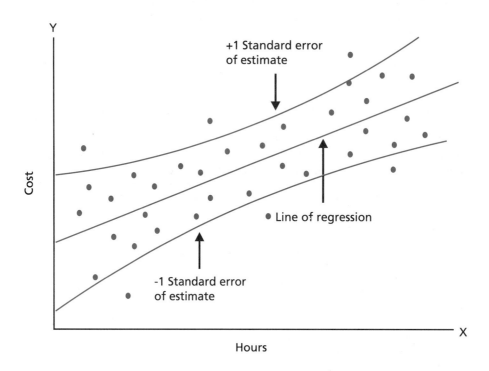

unlikely that the actual cost will be precisely $500. Because some variation in cost can be expected, management should establish an acceptable range of tolerance. Costs that lie within the limits of variation can be accepted. Costs beyond the limits, however, should be identified and investigated.

In deciding on an acceptable range of cost variability, management may employ the standard error of the estimate discussed earlier. Recall that a table of probabilities for a normal distribution shows that approximately two-thirds of the data lies within plus and minus one standard error of the estimate of the regression line. For the electricity cost illustration, the standard error of the estimate amounts to $67.08. At 40 hours of activity, for example, the cost is expected to lie between $532.92 and $667.08 about two-thirds of the time:

	Upper Limit *(+1 Standard Error)*	*Lower Limit* *(-1 Standard Error)*
Regression prediction [$200 + ($10 x 40)]	$ 600.00	$ 600.00
Standard error of the estimate	+ 67.08	- 67.08
	$ 667.08	$ 532.92

If more tolerance is permitted for control purposes, the limits may be extended. For instance, a 95 percent probability (also known as a confidence interval) occurs for a range of costs of plus and minus 1.96 standard deviations. From the data given, the 95 percent probability is for a cost range between $468.52 and $731.48 at 40 hours of activity [$600 plus and minus $131.48 (1.96 x $67.08)]. Management must make a decision by balancing two alternatives:

1. A relatively narrow range of cost variation with a relatively low probability of a cost being within the range.

2. A relatively wide range of cost variation with a relatively high probability of a cost being within the range.

In other words, the wider the range, the fewer the costs that will be considered for investigation and the higher the likelihood that waste and inefficiencies will go uncorrected.

M ULTIPLE REGRESSION

In many situations, more than one factor will be related to cost behavior. Electricity costs in the preceding example may vary not only with changes in the hours of activity but also with the number of people using the building, temperature changes, or other cost drivers. Or, telephone service costs may be a function of the basic monthly charge, in-state long distance calls, out-of-state long distance calls, and features such as call waiting or call forwarding. Insofar as possible, all factors that are related to cost behavior should be brought into the analysis. This will provide a more effective approach to predicting and controlling costs. In simple regression, only one factor is considered; but, in **multiple regression,** several factors are considered in combination. The basic form of the multiple regression model is:

$$Y = a + b_1X_1 + b_2X_2 + \ldots + b_mX_m$$

The X's represent different independent variables, and the a's and b's are the coefficients. Any b is the average change in Y resulting from a one unit change in the X_i.

Concerns in Using Multiple Regression

Sometimes a factor affecting the amount of cost is not (or only partially) quantitative in nature. For example, bank charges for various services may be different for senior citizens than they are for people under 65 years of age. A multiple regression model will have one independent variable that will have a value of 1 for a senior citizen and 0 for other customers. These variables are called "dummy variables."

Another concern in using a multiple regression model is the potential existence of a very high correlation between two or more independent variables. The variables move so closely together that the technique cannot tell them apart. We call this situation **multicollinearity**. For example, direct labor hours and direct labor costs would be highly correlated. Multicollinearity is not an issue if we are interested only in predicting the total costs. However, when we need accurate coefficients, a definite problem exists. The coefficients on the b's in the model are variable costs for that independent variable, and accurate coefficients can be used in pricing decisions and cost-volume-profit analyses.

Multicollinearity, when severe, will be indicated by one or more of the following symptoms:

1. A coefficient is negative when a positive one is expected.
2. A coefficient is insignificant which, in theory, should be highly significant.
3. An unreasonably high coefficient exists that does not make economic sense.

If one or more of the symptoms appear, we need to think through our theory supporting the equation. Remove one of the independent variables that is less critical to the setting. Adding two problem variables together may be a solution in some cases.

T IME SERIES APPROACHES

Regression and correlation analyses are concerned with the linear relationship between two or more variables. Knowledge of the independent variable(s) X is used to predict the dependent variable Y. In **time series analysis**, the independent variable is time. The dependent variable Y assumes different values over time. Thus, any variable classified chronologically is a time series. The time periods may be years, quarters, months, weeks, days, hours, or any other interval. Time series analysis is commonly used in budgeting and financial planning. Time series are analyzed to discover past patterns of growth and change that can be used to predict future patterns and needs of an organization's operations.

A number of time series analysis techniques exist. These techniques use historical information about the cost (its trends and movements over time) to predict future values for that cost. The advantage of time series techniques is that they are economical to use, although computers are required. The only data needed are the variable's historical information (total cost for some cost category or some performance statistic). Most of these methods require application of complex statistical computations that are beyond the scope of managerial accounting. The following sections describe an approach to analyzing trends.

Trend Analysis

The trend is the component that underlies the growth or decline in a time series. These movements can be described by a straight line or a curve. In a production operation, forces affecting the trend might be price changes, technological changes, or productivity changes. In a service operation, a population change might also be a factor.

Before the analyst develops a measurement for the trend, the data are plotted on a graph. Remember that the independent variable is time. The plot gives the analyst the general shape of the data. If a plot of the series indicates a straight-line movement, a straight trend line will be fitted to the data. The method most widely used to describe straight-line trends is the least squares method in simple linear regression. If a nonlinear trend is apparent, the least squares method in multiple regression is used.

As a short example of the trend line concept, consider the monthly overhead cost data for a management consulting firm:

Month	Overhead Cost	Month X, Coded From X = 0
January	$7,170	0
February	5,955	1
March	5,982	2
April	4,655	3
May	6,041	4
June	6,577	5
July	5,855	6
August	6,939	7
September	7,571	8
October	8,065	9
November	9,314	10
December	9,009	11

The regression results for this situation are as follows:

Constant	5,358.65
Standard error of the estimate	960.16
r^2	0.558
Number of observations	12
Degrees of freedom	10
X coefficient	285.29

Figure 3.14 shows the foregoing data points plotted on a graph with the regression trend line superimposed over the data points.

The regression trend line explains only 55.8 percent of the variability in the data. That is not as good a fit as a manager would like to have for predicting costs in the future and in setting control limits. Since the data are time series data, other factors may

FIGURE 3.14   Graph of Data and Regression Trend Line

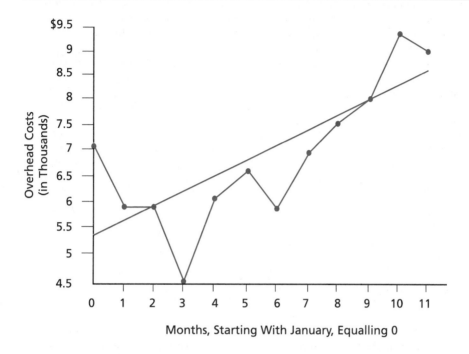

be included in the data, such as seasonal variations. The next section looks at decomposition as a technique for further analysis.

Decomposition

Because many fluctuations and variations occur that obscure the trend in data, it is necessary to identify the component factors that influence each of the periodic values in a series. This identification procedure is called decomposition. In addition to trend, three other components are found in time series analysis: (1) cyclical variations, (2) seasonal variations, and (3) irregular fluctuations.

The cyclical component is a series of irregular wavelike fluctuations or cycles of more than one year's duration due to changing economic conditions. It is the difference between the expected values of a trend and the actual values—the residual variation fluctuating around the trend. In our previous example of 12 months, a cyclical variation would not occur because the time period was not long enough.

Seasonal fluctuations are typically found in data classified quarterly, monthly, or weekly. Seasonal variation refers to a pattern of change that recurs regularly over time. The movement is completed within the duration of a year and repeats itself year after year. In our example of overhead costs, we see relatively lower costs from February through August and relatively higher costs the rest of the year. This situation could be the result of seasonal fluctuations.

The irregular fluctuations component can be caused by unpredictable or nonperiodic events. Economic behavior, for example, is influenced by weather changes, strikes, wars, rumors of wars, elections, and the passage of certain federal or state legislation. An index for the irregular fluctuations of the past can be estimated and included in the analysis.

To study these components of a time series, we usually treat the original data of a time series as a product of the components. That is, a monthly series is a product of trend, seasonal variations, and irregular fluctuations, expressed as T x S x I. T is measured in units of actual data, and S and I are index values. The index values may be related to a price index or some other index. If the time series data were in terms of years, a C for cyclical fluctuations would replace the S for the seasonal fluctuations.

For our example, let's include a seasonal index adjustment, as follows:

Month	Index	Adjusted Data*
January	111.45	6,433
February	90.62	6,572
March	89.15	6,710
April	67.97	6,849
May	86.46	6,987
June	92.30	7,125
July	80.61	7,264
August	93.74	7,402
September	100.40	7,541
October	105.03	7,679
November	119.15	7,817
December	113.25	7,956

* Original data x (100 ÷ index) = Adjusted data

The regression run on this adjusted data is as follows:

Constant	6,433.33
Standard error of the estimate	0.259
r^2	0.999
Number of observations	12
Degrees of freedom	10
X coefficient	138.40

The r^2 value is so near perfect that we do not need to graph the adjusted data and the regression trend line to know that the points and the line are almost identical. The seasonal adjustment accounted for the original difference. We now have a trend line for predicting the direction of costs in the future if other factors do not change.

T ERMINOLOGY REVIEW

Account analysis, *74*
Break-even analysis, *82*
Break-even chart, *84*
Break-even point, *82*
Contribution margin, *80*
Contribution margin ratio, *80*
Correlation analysis, *100*
Cost estimation, *74*
Cost-volume-profit (CVP) analysis, *80*
Dependent variable, *74*
Engineering approach, *76*
High-low method, *78*
Independent variable, *74*
Least squares method, *100*

Linear regression, *100*
Margin of safety, *93*
Multicollinearity, *107*
Multiple regression, *107*
Normal distribution, *104*
Operating leverage, *92*
Profit-volume (P/V) graph, *85*
Regression analysis, *100*
Regression line, *100*
Sales mix, *94*
Scattergraph and visual fit, *76*
Standard error of the estimate, *104*
Time series analysis, *108*

S UGGESTED READINGS

Cheung, J. K., and J. Heaney, "A Contingent-Claim Integration of Cost-Volume-Profit Analysis With Capital Budgeting," *Contemporary Accounting Research*, Spring 1990, pp. 738-760.

Greenberg, R. R., "Estimating Cost Functions With Autocorrelated Errors: A Time Series Approach," *Journal of Cost Analysis*, Spring 1988, pp. 19-33.

Koch, B. S., "Evaluating Offshore Energy Leases Using Cost-Volume-Profit Analysis," *Journal of Petroleum Accounting*, Summer 1986, pp. 35-42.

Lau, A. H., and H. Lau, "Maximizing the Probability of Achieving a Target Profit in a Two-Product Newsboy Problem," *Decision Sciences*, Spring 1988, pp. 392-408.

Rankin, L. J., and R. J. Campbell, "Regression Analysis in Planning and Testing," *CPA Journal*, May 1986, pp. 50-58.

Robinson, L. E., and L. A. Robinson, "Increasing Small Business Profit by Use of Management Accounting Techniques," *Journal of Cost Analysis*, Spring 1986, pp. 63-67.

Schneider, A., "Cost-Volume-Profit Models Containing Earnings-Based Bonus Expenses," *Accounting Enquiries*, August 1992, pp. 168-190.

Thakkar, R. B., D. R. Finley, and W. M. Liao, "A Stochastic Demand CVP Model With Return on Investment Criterion," *Contemporary Accounting Research*, Fall 1984, pp. 77-86.

Q UESTIONS FOR REVIEW AND DISCUSSION

1. Why is cost estimation so important?
2. Distinguish between the dependent variable and the independent variable in a cost-estimating equation.
3. Describe the two major steps involved in the account analysis method of cost estimation.
4. Explain the engineering approach in cost estimation.
5. Describe the steps for preparing an estimate of fixed and variable costs using the scattergraph and visual fit method.
6. When using the high-low method, what criteria should be used in selecting the two points?
7. Describe the high-low method of cost estimation.
8. Identify the interrelated factors that are important to profit planning.
9. When the total contribution margin is equal to the total fixed cost, is the company operating at a profit or at a loss? Explain.
10. If the total fixed cost and the contribution margin per unit of product are given, explain how to compute the number of units that must be sold to break even.
11. Describe the components of a break-even chart.
12. If the total fixed cost and the percentage of the contribution margin to revenue are given, explain how to compute the revenue at the break-even point.
13. If the total fixed cost and the percentage of the variable cost to revenue are given, is it possible to compute the revenue at the break-even point? Explain.

14. Can two break-even points exist? If so, describe how the revenue and cost lines would be drawn on the break-even chart.

15. In conventional practice, only one break-even point exists. Why?

16. Is it possible to compute the number of units that must be sold to earn a certain amount of profit after income tax? Explain.

17. How does a P/V graph differ from a break-even chart? Which form of presentation is superior? Why?

18. What does the slope of the profit line on the P/V graph represent?

19. What is operating leverage?

20. Define margin of safety. How is a margin of safety related to operating leverage?

21. What is the meaning of a break-even point where multiple products are present? Explain the meaning in terms of the individual products.

22. How is regression analysis different from the other methods of cost estimation? **(Appendix)**

23. What is r^2? What range of values can it take? **(Appendix)**

24. What does a standard error of the estimate measure? **(Appendix)**

25. In a normal distribution of data, what proportion of the data should lie within plus and minus one standard deviation from the mean? **(Appendix)**

26. Is it possible to predict costs beyond the range of X values used in determining a line of regression? Explain. **(Appendix)**

27. What is multiple regression? When would it be used in cost estimation? **(Appendix)**

28. What is multicollinearity? How does it pose problems in multiple regression analysis? **(Appendix)**

29. What is a time series? **(Appendix)**

E XERCISES

3-1. Cost Segregation by High-Low Method. The costs of equipment lubrication in the machining operation of Tellit Products Company have been recorded as follows:

Hours	Costs
18,500	$61,700
16,000	54,200
17,200	57,800
18,000	60,200
21,000	69,200
16,400	55,400
16,700	56,300
15,000	51,200
17,600	59,000
18,100	60,500

Required:

Determine the average rate of cost variability per hour and the fixed cost by the high-low method.

3-2. High-Low Method. Joyce Mason sells various ceramics and crafts at flea markets in the area. She uses a motor home for transportation and lodging. She recognizes that travel costs with the home are relatively high and would like to estimate costs so that she can decide how far she can travel and still operate at a profit.

Records from one round trip of 150 miles show that the total cost was $320. On another round trip of 340 miles, the total cost was $472. A local round trip of 50 miles cost $240. She is convinced that the time and cost for trips of more than 300 miles are too high unless the sales potential is very high.

Required:

Calculate the variable cost per mile and the fixed cost per trip by the high-low method.

3-3. Other Cost Behavior.   Luke Reeves has power saws that he uses to produce wooden components used by other companies in interior building construction and in furniture making. He would like to estimate the costs of operation as a guide in billing customers. Reeves has not been in business long enough to develop much cost information, but he senses that the variable cost per hour is somewhat higher on jobs that require less time.

On a job that took 20 hours, the cost was $230. Another job that took 50 hours cost $275. The cost of a project that required 200 hours was only $400, and another project at 300 hours cost $500.

Required:

1. Using the information given, what is the estimated variable cost per hour in the range extending from 20 to 50 hours? What is the fixed cost for this range?
2. What is the estimated variable cost per hour in the range extending from 200 to 300 hours? What is the fixed cost for this range?
3. What factors might exist that would cause the variable cost per hour to change?

3-4. Account Analysis.   Your spouse volunteered you as the social chairperson of the local United Way campaign. One of the major activities under your direction is the Christmas dinner and dance for about 220 people. Renting the hall at the local Festive Inn will cost $250. The hall will seat up to 300 people. Decorations for the head table, which will seat 16 people, will cost $50. Decorations for each table will cost $10, and each table will seat up to 8 people. For $25, you can hire the choir director from one of the local high schools to play the piano and sing softly during dinner. The dance band (a prominent college student group) will cost $250. Typesetting and printing 300 copies of the program cost $75. The caterer has offered a full-course meal for $10 per person, but you must guarantee one week in advance. To help serve the meals, you have arranged for the voluntary services of a local Campfire Girls group. You expect 25 people to help serve, and their meal costs will be added to the total costs.

At the time the guarantee was required, you had 205 confirmed reservations for the dinner, including all speakers and dignitaries, but not including servers. You guarantee 224 people plus the servers. Assume that the servers will eat in an adjoining room, which is furnished free of charge and that their tables will not be decorated.

Required:

1. Estimate the total cost of the Christmas dinner and dance for the number of people guaranteed.
2. Estimate the total costs if you had to guarantee 272 people plus servers.
3. Which costs vary with the number of people? Which costs vary with the number of tables (or which costs are fixed per table)? Which costs are fixed for the dinner and dance?

3-5. Visual Fit, High-Low Method, and Ethics.   The cost of maintenance for animated exhibits at Auckland Amusement Park in New Zealand is partly variable and partly fixed. Supplies and other materials tend to vary with hours of operation, while the salaries of the maintenance workers are fixed. Cost data (in New Zealand dollars) for various hours of operation are as follows:

Hours	Total Cost
500	NZ$ 9,000
700	11,200
450	8,600
800	12,000
600	9,800
900	13,000

Required:

1. Using the scattergraph and visual fit approach, determine the variable cost per hour and the fixed cost.
2. Compute the variable cost per hour and the fixed cost using the high-low method.
3. Explain why the variable cost per hour and the fixed cost are different under the two methods of computation.
4. Suppose that for some reason the cost analyst at Auckland Amusement Park wanted to provide intentionally biased estimates of the variable cost per hour and the fixed cost. Discuss how this could have been done with the visual fit approach versus the high-low method.

3-6. Visual Fit and the Extremes.   The cost of utilities at Harrison Supply varies according to hours of operation, but a portion of the cost is fixed. Hour and cost data for several months are given as follows:

Hours	Total Cost
100	$ 800
200	700
300	800
400	900
500	1,000
600	1,100
700	1,200
800	1,300
900	1,600

Required:

1. Fit a line to the data by visual fit. (Place the line so that it is representative of most of the data.)
2. Using your line, compute the variable cost per hour and the fixed cost per month.
3. Determine the variable cost per hour and the fixed cost by the high-low method.
4. Explain in which of the foregoing two variable cost per hour numbers and two fixed cost numbers you have more confidence for making business decisions.

3-7. Cost Estimation and Break-Even Point.   Water is supplied to Lake Arthur Township by pumping water from a lake to a storage tank at the highest elevation in town, from which it then flows to the customers by gravity. The town council notes that the costs to pump water vary to some extent by the number of gallons pumped, but fixed costs are also included in the pumping costs. A record of gallons consumed per month and total pumping cost per month is as follows:

Gallons Consumed (000)	Pumping Cost	Gallons Consumed (000)	Pumping Cost
1,750	$29,100	1,800	$29,700
1,900	30,800	2,300	35,900
2,150	34,000	2,000	31,800
2,050	32,600	1,500	25,500

In addition to pumping costs, 1.1 cents per gallon in variable costs and $75,000 in fixed costs are incurred to supply water to the residents. Lake Arthur Township charges its residents 4.6 cents per gallon consumed.

Required:
1. Use the high-low method to obtain a cost function for Lake Arthur Township's pumping costs.
2. At what level of water consumption would Lake Arthur Township break even?

3-8. Break-Even Point.   Vin de Guillet of southern France conducts tours through its wine processing facility. The tours are free and are included as part of the sales promotion program. Estimates show that the cost per tourist is 25 francs plus an additional fixed cost for the year of 350,000 francs. An average of 30,000 tourists can be expected each year. The average contribution margin per case of wine sold is 90 francs.

Required:
Calculate how many cases of wine must be sold to cover the total average cost of the tours.

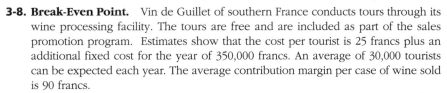

3-9. Break-Even Point and Fixed Cost Increase.   Abba Spero operates a health club in Cleveland. Annual memberships are sold, and nonmembers may pay for individual sessions. Spero states that the average revenue amounts to $18 per patron visit. He has estimated variable cost at $2.20 per patron visit and fixed cost per year at $42,000. Next year, fixed cost is expected to increase to $49,500.

Required:
1. How many patron visits are required this year for Spero to break even?
2. Under the new fixed cost structure for next year, how many patron visits are needed to break even?
3. How many patron visits above the break-even point are required next year to earn a profit of $13,900?

3-10. Break-Even Point and Variable Cost Increase.   The owner of Fuerbringer's, a hardware retailer in Germany, is concerned about increased costs to purchase a hardware item that is sold by the company through one of its retail outlets. This year the variable cost per unit of product (in deutsche marks) is DM28. Next year the variable cost is expected to increase to DM32 per unit. The selling price per unit, however, cannot be increased and will remain at DM39 per unit. The fixed costs amount to DM90,000.

Required:
1. What is the break-even point in units of product this year?
2. What is the break-even point in revenues for this year?
3. How many units of product must be sold next year to break even?
4. How much revenue will generate break-even volume for next year?

3-11. Planned Profit Before Income Taxes.   Huseman Appliances, Inc. is planning operations for the next year. The total contribution margin has been estimated at 40 percent of sales revenue. The 40 percent contribution margin ratio is considered to be more probable, but there is a possibility that the contribution margin ratio will only be 35 percent. The owner has budgeted fixed costs at $840,000 for the year and has set a pretax profit goal of $560,000.

Required:
1. How much revenue will be needed to reach the profit goal if the contribution margin ratio is 40 percent?
2. How much revenue will be needed to reach the profit goal if the contribution margin ratio is 35 percent?
3. What possible explanations could account for a change in the contribution margin ratio estimate from 40 percent to 35 percent?

3-12. Planned Profit After Income Taxes.   Jessica VanBakel notes that if her company is to keep up with the competition, she must obtain the latest type of equipment. If new equipment is obtained, fixed costs are expected to increase from $640,000 a year to $1,000,000. On the other hand, the contribution margin ratio is expected to increase from 30 percent to 40 percent. VanBakel has set a profit objective of $300,000 after income taxes at a tax rate of 40 percent.

Required:
1. Compute the sales revenue needed to meet the profit objective with a 30 percent contribution margin ratio and lower fixed costs.
2. Compute the sales revenue needed to meet the profit objective with a 40 percent contribution margin ratio and higher fixed costs.
3. What possible explanations could account for a change in the contribution margin ratio from 30 percent to 40 percent?

3-13. Planned Profit After Income Taxes.   WestOak Catering Service has budgeted a 12 percent of sales aftertax profit. Management has agreed that this level of profit is needed to yield a reasonable return on the owners' investment. Fixed costs have been budgeted at $456,000 for the year, and the contribution margin ratio has been estimated at 30 percent. The income tax rate is 40 percent.

Required:
1. How much revenue will be needed to realize the profit objective?
2. By how much does this revenue exceed the break-even revenue?

3-14. Break-Even Point and Profits.   Kerri Mayo has noticed a demand for small tables for personal computers and printers. Retail office furniture outlets are charging from $400 to $600 for a table. Kerri believes that she can manufacture and sell an attractive small table that will serve the purpose for $210. The costs of materials, labor, and variable overhead per table are estimated at $110. The fixed costs consisting of rent, insurance, taxes, and depreciation are estimated at $25,000 for the year. She already has orders for 180 tables and has established contacts that should result in the sale of 150 additional tables.

Required:
1. How many tables must Kerri make and sell to break even?
2. How much profit can be made from the expected production and sale of 330 tables?
3. How many tables need to be produced and sold to meet a profit objective of $11,000?

3-15. Effect of a Price Reduction.   Vacation Motel is presently charging $45 per night for a room. The variable cost per room per night has been estimated at $20. Fixed costs for the year have been estimated at $236,250. The motel has the capacity to operate at 15,000 room days a year. Room days are equal to the number of rooms multiplied by number of days. With the present price structure, the motel has been operating at only 9,500 room days a year.

The manager believes that the motel cannot compete on a service basis with chain motels and that occupancy can be increased by reducing the room rate to $30 per night. The owner states that, with a rate of $30 per night, the motel cannot earn a profit even with 100 percent occupancy.

Required:
1. How much profit is earned per year now operating at 9,500 room days?
2. Calculate the degree of operating leverage at 9,500 room days.
3. With the new price structure, how many room days will be needed to earn the same profit that is being earned now?
4. Is the owner correct in stating that a profit cannot be earned with a rate of $30 per night? Explain.

3-16. Effect of a Variable Cost Increase. Jason Fabricators produces a component that is sold for $80 per unit. This year the variable cost to produce and sell each unit is $60. Next year, materials and labor costs are expected to increase, so the variable cost per unit will increase to $65. The selling price cannot be increased. The fixed costs this year are $285,000 and are expected to be the same next year. The president of the company is concerned about the amount of additional sales volume required next year to earn the same pretax profit, which averaged $12 per unit this year.

Required:
1. How many units are sold this year?
2. How many more units must be sold next year to earn the same average profit per unit as this year?
3. Compare the margin of safety for each of the two points.
4. Comment on the likelihood of sustaining this year's profit level.

3-17. Effect of a Fixed Cost Increase. The owner of a Mexican manufacturing company is concerned about increased fixed manufacturing costs. Last year, the fixed manufacturing costs (in pesos) were M$600,000. This year, the fixed manufacturing costs increased to M$750,000. The fixed selling and administrative costs of M$540,000 were the same for both years. The company operated in both years with an average contribution margin ratio of 30 percent. It earned a profit before income taxes of M$910,000 last year.

Required:
1. What was the sales revenue last year?
2. How much would sales revenue have to increase this year for the company to earn the same profit as it did last year?
3. Calculate the margin of safety for each year. Which year was better?

3-18. Multiple Product Analysis. Thomas Company sells Products X, Y, and Z. Thomas sells three units of X for each unit of Z and two units of Y for each unit of X. The contribution margins are $1.00 per unit of X, $1.50 per unit of Y, and $3.00 per unit of Z. Fixed costs are $600,000.

Required:
How many units of each product would Thomas sell at the break-even point?

(AICPA adapted)

3-19. Multiple Product Analysis. A division of Roswell Products, Inc. manufactures and sells two grades of canvas. The contribution margin per roll of Lite-Weight canvas is $25, and the contribution margin per roll of Heavy-Duty canvas is $75. Last year, this division manufactured and sold the same amount of each grade of canvas. The fixed costs were $675,000, and the profit before income taxes was $540,000.

During the current year, 14,000 rolls of Lite-Weight canvas were sold, and 6,000 rolls of Heavy-Duty canvas were sold. The contribution margin per roll for each line remained the same; also, the fixed cost remained the same.

Required:
1. How many rolls of each grade of canvas were sold last year?
2. How much profit was earned during the current year?
3. Assuming the same sales mix experienced in the current year, compute the number of units of each grade of canvas that should have been sold during the current year in order to earn the $540,000 profit that was earned last year.

3-20. Describing Regression Results (Appendix). As controller of Well-Kept Lawn and Garden Service, you are concerned about the cost behavior of overhead costs. You gathered the appropriate data and asked a statistician friend to perform a regression analysis. You are given the following results:

$$Y = 1{,}750 + 7.25\ X$$

$$r^2 = .91$$

$$S_e = 24.50$$

where: Y = Overhead cost

X = Labor hours

Required:

1. Explain the meaning of the equation: $Y = 1{,}750 + 7.25\ X.$

2. What is the percentage of the variance of overhead cost that is associated with changes in labor hours?

3. The president wants to know what S_e means and how it might be used in evaluating actions. Give a brief answer.

3-21. Explaining Regression Results (Appendix).   J. D. Carter & Associates is a tax preparation service. Each month, J. D. watches the Cost of Services Rendered account which contains the direct costs and certain support costs for the various tax services performed. He believes a relationship exists between the costs of services rendered and revenues. He has asked you to analyze the cost behavior of the account. You pull together data covering two years and do a regression analysis which yields the following output:

Constant	870.6
Std. Err. of Y Est.	137.54
r^2	.8473
No. of observations	24
Degrees of freedom	22
X coefficient(s)	0.639

Required:

Explain what information this regression output gives about cost behavior and how management might use it.

3-22. Explaining Multiple Regression Results (Appendix).   The Computer Services Department of Worldwide Market Research, Inc. provides services to all other departments. Demand by other departments has grown to a point where the manager wants to bill for services rendered. A decision has been made to analyze computer services operating costs compared to input device time, to CPU time, and to output device time. Operating cost data and the various times were given to a statistician for analysis. The statistician returned the following summary:

Constant	2,250
Std. Err. of Y Est.	221
r^2	0.95142
Number of observations	12
Degrees of freedom	8

	Input	CPU	Output
X coefficient(s)	0.335	0.458	0.189

Required:

Explain what information this regression output gives about cost behavior and how management might use it.

*P*ROBLEMS

3-23. Account Analysis.   The following is a partial list of account titles appearing in the chart of accounts for Edlestein Industrial Supply Company:

1. Direct Materials
2. Supervisory Salaries—Factory
3. Heat, Light, and Power—Factory
4. Depreciation on the Building
5. Depreciation on Equipment and Machinery (units-of-production method)
6. Janitorial Labor
7. Repair and Maintenance Supplies
8. Pension Costs (as a percentage of employee wages and salaries)
9. FICA Tax Expense (employer's share)
10. Insurance on Property
11. Sales Commissions
12. Travel Expenses—Sales
13. Telephone Expenses—General and Administrative
14. Magazine Advertising
15. Bad Debt Expense
16. Photocopying Expense
17. Audit Fees
18. Dues and Subscriptions
19. Depreciation on Furniture and Fixtures (double-declining-balance method)
20. Group Medical and Dental Insurance Expenses

Required:
1. Discuss each account title in terms of whether the account represents a variable, fixed, or semivariable cost.
2. For accounts designated as variable or semivariable, indicate the most likely cost driver with which the cost varies.
3. Explain the problems associated with using the account analysis approach to establish cost behavior patterns.

3-24. Rough Approaches.   Evelyn Dement, an insurance claims adjuster for Chapparal Casualty Company, notes that the cost to process a claim has both fixed and variable components. She believes that she can estimate costs more accurately if she can separate the costs into their variable and fixed components. The monthly record of the number of claims and the costs for the past year is given as follows:

Month	Number of Claims	Cost
January	120	$20,600
February	134	20,670
March	142	20,710
April	156	20,780
May	160	20,800
June	220	21,100
July	250	21,250
August	330	21,650
September	114	20,570
October	280	21,400
November	274	21,370
December	230	21,150

Required:
1. Estimate the variable cost per claim and the fixed cost per month by the high-low method.

2. Estimate the variable cost per claim and the fixed cost per month by the scattergraph and visual fit method.

3. Explain the differences between the two methods in the amounts determined for variable cost per claim and fixed cost per month.

3-25. High-Low Method. The manager of the Shipping Department at Gorman Fixtures Company in Windsor, Canada, recognizes that the cost of supplies is partly variable and partly fixed. A record of the number of shipments and costs (in Canadian dollars) per month is as follows:

Month	Number of Shipments	Total Cost
January	50	C$2,650
February	45	2,635
March	20	2,600
April	60	2,780
May	85	2,855
June	90	2,950
July	75	2,825
August	40	2,720
September	35	2,705
October	80	2,840

Required:

1. Calculate the variable cost per shipment and the fixed cost per month by the high-low method.

2. Calculate the expected cost of supplies for November if 55 shipments are made.

3-26. High-Low Method. For years, Case Metals Company paid equipment maintenance personnel on an hourly rate basis. The fixed cost of maintenance labor was relatively low. With the installation of automated equipment, the nature of their work has changed. Now, maintenance personnel monitor the operations and are paid salaries. Therefore, fixed cost has increased, but variable cost per hour has been reduced. Past records show the following monthly information with respect to hours and cost for maintenance labor:

Hours	Cost		Hours	Cost
1,500	$15,000		700	$ 8,000
800	9,400		500	7,600
1,200	12,600		1,100	11,800
1,600	15,800		1,000	11,000
1,400	14,200		600	7,800

Since the installation of automated equipment, costs for monthly maintenance labor are as follows:

Hours	Cost		Hours	Cost
1,200	$17,600		1,500	$17,800
1,000	16,800		900	17,000
1,700	18,400		1,200	17,500
800	16,500		1,000	17,000
2,000	19,000		1,400	17,700

Required:

1. Using the high-low method, compute the variable costs per hour and the fixed costs per month under the conditions that existed in the past.

2. Using the high-low method, compute the variable costs per hour and the fixed costs per month under present conditions with automated equipment.

3. How will management now plan and control maintenance labor costs differently with the automated equipment as opposed to past practices?

3-27. Account Analysis and CVP.   Hoepen Company, a Dutch publisher of academic journals, has the following information available pertaining to the 1997 costs of publishing *The Journal of Cost Accounting*:

Account	Cost (in Florin)
Paper	20,000
Binding materials	1,000
Covers	4,000
Equipment depreciation	35,000
Rent	24,000
Production wages	66,000
Staff and managers' salaries	220,000
Utilities	48,000
Printing ink	13,000
Insurance	7,000

The journal's subscription price is F93, and 8,000 subscriptions were sold in 1997. Hoepen's target pretax profit from *The Journal of Cost Accounting* for 1998 is F250,000. Assume that the number of journals produced is the same as the number of subscriptions sold and that the cost structure will remain unchanged for 1998.

Required:
1. Using the account analysis approach, derive a cost function from the preceding information.
2. How many subscriptions to *The Journal of Cost Accounting* must Hoepen sell to break even with this journal in 1998?
3. How many subscriptions will be needed in 1998 to achieve the target pretax profit?

3-28. Cost, Volume, and Profit Relationships.   Data with respect to a basic product line sold by Carroll Stores are as follows:

Selling price per unit	$ 50
Variable cost per unit	30
Contribution margin per unit	$ 20

The fixed costs for the year are $360,000. The income tax rate is 40 percent.

Required:
1. Determine the number of units that must be sold to break even.
2. If a profit before income taxes of $270,000 is to be earned, how many units of product must be sold?
3. If a profit after income taxes of $180,000 is to be earned, how many units of product must be sold?
4. If the selling price per unit is reduced by 10 percent, how many units must be sold to earn a profit of $8 per unit before income taxes?
5. Assume that the selling price remains at $50. How many units must be sold to earn a profit of $8 per unit before income taxes if the variable cost per unit increases by 10 percent?
6. Why does a 10 percent decrease in the selling price have more effect on the contribution margin than a 10 percent increase in the variable unit cost?

3-29. Margin of Safety and Operating Leverage.   The Waterford Division of Maxus Products manufactures a component used in the production of garden tractors. Marty Story, the president of the division, states that the division has the capacity to produce 5,000 units of this component each month. The fixed costs of production are $10,000 each month.

Story admits that it will take some time before the plant has enough orders to operate at capacity but that sales should range between 3,000 and 4,000 units per month. She is interested in examining what happens to the margin of safety and the operating leverage over a range of activity. To help with this analysis, the accountant tells you that each unit is sold for $20, and the variable unit cost is $15.

Required:
1. Calculate the margin of safety for 3,000 and 4,000 units.
2. Calculate the degree of operating leverage for 3,000 and 4,000 units.
3. Determine the expected manufacturing profit or loss at 3,000 and 4,000 units.
4. What do the margin of safety and degree of operating leverage tell you about what will happen to profit as sales move from 3,000 to 4,000 units?

3-30. CVP and Ratios.   The vice-president of sales, Neal Mermelstein, estimates that the variable cost per product unit will increase from $80 to $95. The selling price is expected to remain at $120. The fixed costs for the year amount to $340,000. Last year the company sold 30,000 units of product and expects to sell the same quantity this year. Mermelstein is concerned about the loss in profitability because of increased costs. He asks you to prepare an evaluation of what changes are taking place.

Required:
1. What is the contribution margin percentage (ratio) for this year and last year?
2. What is the break-even point in sales dollars for this year and last year?
3. Calculate the margin of safety for last year and this year.
4. Calculate the degree of operating leverage for last year and this year.
5. Explain what would happen to profits this year if the sales volume could be increased by 15 percent.

3-31. Effects of Fixed Cost Changes.   R. A. Ro and Company, maker of quality hand-made pipes, has experienced a steady growth in sales for the past five years. However, increased competition has led Mr. Ro, the president, to believe that an aggressive advertising campaign will be necessary next year to maintain the company's present growth. To prepare for next year's advertising campaign, the company's accountant has provided Mr. Ro with the following data for the current year, 1997:

Variable Costs	*Per Pipe*
Direct labor	$ 8.00
Direct materials	3.25
Variable overhead	2.50
Total variable costs	$13.75

Fixed Costs	
Manufacturing	$ 25,000
Selling	40,000
Administrative	70,000
Total fixed costs	$135,000
Selling price, per pipe	$ 25.00
Expected sales, 1997 (20,000 units)	$500,000
Tax rate: 40%	

Mr. Ro has set the sales target for 1998 at a level of $550,000 (or 22,000 pipes).

Required:
1. What is the projected aftertax net income for 1997?

2. What is the break-even point in units for 1997?

3. Mr. Ro believes an additional selling expense of $11,250 for advertising in 1998, with all other costs remaining constant, will be necessary to attain the sales target. What will be the aftertax net income for 1998 if the additional $11,250 is spent?

4. What will be the break-even point in dollar sales for 1998 if the additional $11,250 is spent for advertising?

5. If the additional $11,250 is spent for advertising in 1998, what sales level in dollars is required to equal 1997's aftertax net income?

6. At a sales level of 22,000 units, what is the maximum amount that can be spent on advertising if an aftertax net income of $60,000 is desired?

(ICMA adapted)

3-32. Effects of Variable Cost Changes.   All-Day Candy Company is a wholesale distributor of candy. The company services grocery, convenience, and drug stores in a large metropolitan area. Small but steady growth in sales has been achieved by the All-Day Candy Company over the past few years while candy prices have been increasing. The company is formulating its plans for the coming fiscal year. The data used to project the current year's aftertax net income of $110,400 are as follows:

Average selling price per box....................................	$4.00
Average variable costs per box:	
Cost of candy	$2.00
Selling expenses	.40
Total	$2.40
Annual fixed costs:	
Selling......................................	$160,000
Administrative..	280,000
Total	$440,000

Tax rate: 40%

Expected annual sales volume is 390,000 boxes. Manufacturers of candy have announced that they will increase prices of their products an average of 15 percent in the coming year due to increases in raw materials (sugar, cocoa, peanuts, etc.) and labor costs. All-Day Candy Company expects that all other costs will remain at the same rates or levels as the current year.

Required:

1. What is All-Day Candy Company's break-even point in boxes of candy for the current year?

2. What selling price per box must All-Day Candy Company charge to cover the 15 percent increase in the cost of candy and still maintain the current contribution margin ratio?

3. What volume of sales in dollars must the All-Day Candy Company achieve in the coming year to maintain the same net income after taxes as projected for the current year if the selling price of candy remains at $4.00 per box and the cost of candy increases 15 percent?

(ICMA adapted)

3-33. Sales Promotion and Ethical Considerations.   Kleen Kar Wash charges $5.95 for a car wash. The variable costs of supplies, labor, etc., are estimated at $3.25 per car. The fixed overhead is $2,000 per month. During an average month, the company will wash 1,400 cars.

Jerry Cummings, the manager, has made arrangements with a fast food outlet nearby to distribute coupons valued at $1 toward food purchases. Kleen Kar Wash will pay 50 cents for each coupon and will distribute one coupon with each car wash. The cost to promote this premium will be $150 each month. With the coupons, Cummings believes that volume will increase to 1,800 cars per month.

Required:
1. What is the average profit each month without the premium?
2. What will be the profit with the premium if Cummings' estimates are correct?
3. Cummings so strongly believes in this promotion that the owner of Kleen Kar Wash wonders whether Cummings might have been biased. Which items should the owner carefully scrutinize?
4. Suppose that Cummings is incorrect and that only 1,200 cars are washed each month, even with the promotion. Compute the profit.

3-34. Costs and Profit Planning.   Meng Tan recently retired from the Coast Guard and plans to use his boat for fishing excursions. He has estimated costs as follows:

Per person:	
Pole rental	$ .75
Bait bucket	.75
Per season:	
Fuel cost	$ 800.00
Dock rental	400.00
Boat maintenance	1,200.00
Depreciation of boat	3,000.00
Taxes and permits	400.00
His own salary	3,000.00

A part-time worker is to be hired to dress the fish for the customers. This worker will receive a salary of $1,000 for the season plus a per person fee for each customer. Tan would like to earn a profit of $5,000 each season after his own salary and estimates that the revenue from 4,000 customers will be $46,000.

Required:
To meet his profit objective, what is the maximum per person fee that Tan can pay to a part-time worker?

3-35. Estimating a Selling Price.   Kaylene Bays and her brother, Francis, would like to make extra money when they have time away from their studies at Wisconsin State University. They are skilled in carpentry and plan to build and sell rustic lawn chairs. Estimates of the cost to make and sell each chair are as follows:

Lumber and other materials	$30
Labor (wages to student helpers)	15
Commission to stores selling the chairs	8% of selling price

The costs of radio and direct mail advertising are estimated at $5,000. A pickup truck to transport the chairs can be rented for $1,000. Kaylene and Francis each plan to earn a profit of $4,500 for their efforts. This amount was calculated by considering what they could earn if they used their time in another way.

Kaylene believes that 800 units can be made and sold. Francis is more optimistic and believes that 900 units can be made and sold. Both agree that the price must be less than the commercial price of $98 per chair.

Required:
1. Compute a selling price to obtain the desired profit if 800 chairs are sold.
2. Compute a selling price to obtain the desired profit if 900 chairs are sold.
3. Assume that the selling price is based on the sale of 800 chairs but that 900 chairs are actually sold. How much additional profit will Kaylene and Francis each make?
4. Assume that the selling price is based on the sale of 800 chairs but that only 700 chairs are actually sold. Will Kaylene and Francis achieve their profit objectives? Explain.

3-36. Operating Leverage and Margin of Safety.   The vice-president of sales, Walter Speed, observed that the company has operated with a 40 percent contribution margin ratio but that the fixed costs are relatively large at $2,000,000 per year. The income before taxes this year was only $400,000 on sales of $6,000,000. He sees an opportunity to increase sales to $6,300,000 next year but is concerned that such a small increase in sales will have relatively little impact on profits inasmuch as the fixed costs are so high.

Required:

1. Compute the degree of operating leverage for both this year and next year. Assume sales revenue for next year can be increased to $6,300,000.

2. Explain why the profits can be increased by a relatively large amount with only a modest increase in revenue.

3. Calculate the margin of safety for both this year and next year, assuming sales revenue can be increased to $6,300,000 for next year.

4. Does the margin of safety give any additional information not available through the operating leverage? Explain.

1-2-3

3-37. Change in Sales Mix.   Lindfield Gift Shop in Sydney, Australia, sells three types of stuffed animals: koalas, kangaroos, and crocodiles. Budgeted sales and profits (in Australian dollars) for this year are estimated as follows:

	Koalas	Kangaroos	Crocodiles	Total
Sales.............	A$400,000	A$900,000	A$700,000	A$2,000,000
Variable costs	300,000	450,000	510,000	1,260,000
Contribution margin ..	A$100,000	A$450,000	A$190,000	A$ 740,000
Fixed costs				350,000
Income before taxes ..				A$ 390,000

In reviewing actual results for the year, the manager wonders why the actual profit for the year was less than the budgeted profit, considering that selling prices and costs conformed to the budget and that total sales revenue agreed with the budget. Actual sales by product line were:

Koalas	A$ 700,000
Kangaroos	400,000
Crocodiles	900,000
Total revenue	A$2,000,000

Required:

1. Compute the sales revenue of each product at the break-even point under the budgeted data.

2. Compute the sales revenue of each product that would be sold at the break-even point under the actual sales mix.

3. Calculate the profit before income taxes for the actual sales mix, assuming variable costs maintained the budgeted relationship and actual fixed costs equaled budgeted fixed costs.

4. Explain why the actual profit is lower than the budgeted profit.

3-38. Break-Even Analysis.   The owners of Evening Star Motel want to know the potential maximum profits and the break-even occupancy for the operation. Evening Star Motel is a low-cost operation that attracts business people and families traveling on low budgets. A study of costs shows a difference between summer and winter operations. Swimming pool maintenance adds to summer costs, while utilities (heat and light) add to winter costs. Variable costs have been determined on the basis of cost per room occupied per day and are as follows:

	Cost Per Room
Laundry.	$1.90
Heat and light (summer)	1.10
Heat and light (winter)	2.20
Repairs	.75
Supplies	1.60
Taxes and insurance	3.60
Maintenance.	1.50
Pool maintenance (summer only)	.60

Fixed costs per month have been estimated as follows:

Housekeeping	$ 14,000
Management	17,000
Desk service	2,700
Repairs and maintenance	1,600
Taxes.	1,430
Insurance	1,120
Heat and light	1,000
Depreciation—motel	26,000
Depreciation—furnishings	12,500
Pool maintenance and personnel (summer only)	1,800

Evening Star has 300 rooms and charges $40 per room per night. Summer is relatively short and is defined as June, July, and August. All other months are designated as winter months. A month consists of 30 days for making calculations. Maximum capacity for a month would be 9,000 room days (300 rooms x 30 days).

Required:

1. Compare the maximum operating net incomes that can be expected for a summer month versus a winter month.
2. How do the break-even points (in terms of room days) compare for summer versus winter? Also, state each break-even point as a percentage of maximum capacity.
3. Based on advance reservations and normal expectations, Evening Star Motel plans for 5,000 room days in August. Determine the estimated operating income for August. Also, determine the percentage of capacity expected for August.

3-39. Effect of Changes on Profits.   The management of Allison Plastics, Inc. is in the process of preparing a budget for the next year. The company manufactures car mats, dishware, and figures that can be used as decorations or as toys for children. Some changes in prices and costs are expected along with changes in sales volume. Data from operations for the past year are as follows:

	Figures	Mats	Dishware
Units sold	550,000	1,200,000	350,000
Unit selling price	$12.00	$8.00	$40.00
Variable costs per unit:			
Materials.	$ 3.00	$ 3.00	$12.00
Indirect materials and supplies	.40	.40	1.00
Labor	1.50	1.50	6.00
Packing and shipping	.60	.60	1.50
Utilities	.50	.50	.50

Fixed Costs

Supervision	$ 230,000
Employee benefits	765,000
Postage and telephone	73,000
Property taxes and insurance	126,000
Heat and light	192,000
Repairs and maintenance	94,000
Depreciation	86,000
Advertising	549,000
Travel and entertainment	162,000
Sales office and other sales expenses	236,000
Office and administration	372,000
Total fixed costs	$2,885,000

The sales volume of figures for next year is expected to be 80 percent of the volume for the past year. The sales volume of mats is expected to remain constant. The volume of dishware sales should increase by 10 percent if the advertising budget is increased by $170,000. The selling price of figures is to be reduced to $10 per unit, and the selling price of mats is to be increased to $9 per unit.

Materials prices per unit of product for next year have been estimated as follows:

Figures	$ 3.50
Mats	3.50
Dishware	14.00

Labor cost for next year is estimated at $2 per unit for both figures and mats. For dishware, labor cost is estimated at $7 per unit. The utility costs are estimated at $1 for each unit of each product line. Fixed costs, with the exception of the advertising referred to previously, will probably increase by 10 percent. Income taxes are at 40 percent of pretax income.

Required:

1. Compute the contribution margin per unit and contribution margin ratio for each product during the past year.
2. Compute the contribution margin per unit and contribution margin ratio for each product according to the estimates for the next year.
3. Determine the net income for the past year. (Show contribution margin by product line.)
4. Determine the expected net income for next year. (Show contribution margin by product line.)
5. Will the expected volume increase in dishware sales more than compensate for the expected dishware cost increases? Show computations.
6. Compute the break-even point for the given sales mix of each year. Explain the break-even point change between years.

3-40. Control Limits (Appendix).   The supervisor of the Heat Treatment Department at Rockville Technics, Inc. has estimated that power cost varies at the rate of $0.80 per hour and that the fixed cost for the month is $500. The standard error of the estimate from the line of regression is $60. The supervisor investigates the cost of any month that is more than plus or minus one standard deviation from the line of regression. Actual monthly hours and costs for last year are given at the top of page 128.

Month	Hours	Cost
January	600	$ 980
February	550	970
March	600	960
April	650	1,050
May	550	940
June	500	980
July	700	1,180
August	800	1,150
September	750	1,050
October	900	1,330
November	850	1,180
December	450	900

Required:

1. Using the formula $Y = a + bX$, what should be the cost for each month?
2. Calculate the difference between the actual cost and the predicted cost for each month.
3. Plot the differences in Part (2) on a graph, and draw lines that represent plus or minus one standard error of the estimate.
4. For which month or months should the cost be investigated? Why?

3-41. Selection of a Control Limit (Appendix).   For the last five years, the management of Ramsay Fasteners of Singapore has followed the practice of investigating variations if a cost differs by more than one standard error of the estimate from the line of regression. One standard error of the estimate is S$205 (Singapore dollars).

A new supervisor, hired to manage the machining operation, asks, "Did you ever consider that you may be overdoing it by investigating every cost that is over one standard error from the line of regression? After all, you still have a probability of about 1 in 3 that the variation will be random. Then you have gone to a lot of bother for nothing. For example, last March in this operation you investigated the cost of lubrication and found nothing wrong."

The supervisor of the fabrication operation replies, "I'll grant that we may whip a few dead horses, but your idea of investigating anything over 1.96 standard error would have missed a very important variance for one month that was brought under control."

The cost of lubrication is estimated to vary at S$6 per hour in the machining operation with a fixed cost of S$3,500 each month. The actual costs for last year that the supervisors were discussing are given as follows:

Month	Hours	Cost	Month	Hours	Cost
January	1,200	S$10,850	July	500	S$ 6,350
February	1,400	12,000	August	700	7,700
March	1,000	9,800	September	900	9,100
April	1,100	10,000	October	1,000	9,850
May	1,000	9,650	November	1,200	10,600
June	600	7,600	December	1,300	11,450

Required:

1. Calculate the difference between the actual cost and the predicted cost for each month.
2. Identify the months which were investigated with the control limit set at one standard error of the estimate from the line of regression.
3. Identify the months which would have been investigated if the control limit had been set at 1.96 standard error of the estimate from the line of regression.
4. The supervisor of the fabrication operation has stated that one very important month would have been missed using the rule suggested by the supervisor of

the machining operation. Which month would have been missed? What was the variance for that month?

3-42. Cost to Investigate Variances and Control (Appendix).   "You are spending too much money to investigate cost variances!" Kelli Tunnell exclaims. "Last year we sent someone to the plant four times, and only once did we find a cost difference that should be controlled."

Tunnell's partner, Jeffrey Crowfoot, replies, "It costs nothing to send someone to the plant, and you admit that once we found a cost variance worth looking at."

"But it does cost something to send someone to the plant," Tunnell persists. "It may not be additional cost, but we lose work that the employee could have done in that time and that has a value or a cost."

The company has been following the practice of investigating the cost of steam treatment whenever the cost is more than one standard error from the line of regression. One standard error is equal to $600. Kelli Tunnell wants to investigate costs only when they are more than 1.96 standard error from the line of regression.

A record of line of regression costs and actual costs for last year is given below:

Month	Hours	Line of Regression Cost	Actual Cost
January	600	$19,000	$19,350
February	850	22,750	22,980
March	580	18,700	19,350
April	740	21,100	21,600
May	800	22,000	21,700
June	850	22,750	23,550
July	900	23,500	24,700
August	930	23,950	23,700
September	920	23,800	24,200
October	870	23,050	23,750
November	760	21,400	21,500
December	720	20,800	20,600

Required:

1. What were the four months in which the costs were investigated with the upper control limit set at a plus one standard error?

2. Assume that the cost that did require control, the cost Jeffrey Crowfoot mentioned, was incurred in June. Would this variance have been investigated if the upper limit had been set at plus 1.96 standard error?

3. If the upper control limit had been set at plus 1.96 standard error, for which months would the costs have been investigated?

4. Is Kelli Tunnell correct in stating that a cost of lost work occurs even if no added cost is incurred? Explain.

3-43. Linear Regression (Appendix).   Motomation Corporation plans to acquire several retail automotive parts stores as part of its expansion program. Motomation carries out extensive review of possible acquisitions prior to making any decision to approach a specific company. Projections of future financial performance are one of the aspects of such a review. One form of projection relies heavily on using past performance (normally ten prior years) to estimate future performance.

Currently, Motomation is conducting a preacquisition review of Atlas Auto Parts, a regional chain of retail automotive parts stores. Among the financial data to be projected for Atlas is the future rental cost for its stores. The following schedule presents the rent and revenues (in millions of dollars) for the past ten years.

Year	Revenues	Annual Rent Expense
1988	$ 22	$1.00
1989	24	1.15
1990	36	1.40
1991	27	1.10
1992	43	1.55
1993	33	1.25
1994	45	1.65
1995	48	1.60
1996	61	1.80
1997	60	1.95

The following three alternative methods have been developed for estimating future rental expense.

Alternative A: A linear regression using time as the independent variable was performed. The resultant formula is as follows:

$$\text{Rental expense} = .93 + .0936X$$

$$r = .895$$

$$\text{Standard error of the estimate} = .150$$

where: X is equal to (actual year - 1988), e.g., 1997 = 9

Alternative B: The annual rental expense was related to annual revenues through linear regression. The formula for predicting rental expense in this case is as follows:

$$\text{Rental expense} = .5597 + .02219X$$

$$r = .978$$

$$\text{Standard error of the estimate} = .070$$

where: X is equal to (revenues ÷ 1,000,000), e.g., X for 1997 is 60

Alternative C: The third alternative is to calculate rental expense as a percentage of revenues using the arithmetical average for the ten-year period of 1988-1997 inclusive.

Required:

1. Calculate for each of the three alternatives the rental expense estimate for Atlas Auto Parts for 1998 assuming the 1998 projected revenue will be the same as the 1997 revenue, i.e., $60 million.

2. Using the data presented for Alternative B, approximate the range of values that would provide a 95 percent confidence interval for the 1998 rental expense estimate.

3. **(a)** Discuss the advantages and disadvantages of each of the three alternative methods for estimating the rental expense for Atlas Auto Parts.

   (b) Identify one method from Alternatives A, B, or C that you would recommend Motomation Corporation use to estimate rental expense. Explain why you selected that alternative.

4. Explain whether a statistical technique is an appropriate method in this situation for estimating rental expense.

(ICMA adapted)

C ASE 3A—BEDFORD HOSPITAL

Bedford Hospital operates a general hospital but rents space and beds to separately owned entities providing specialized services such as pediatrics and psychiatrics. Bedford charges each entity for common services, such as patients' meals and laundry, and for administrative services, such as billings and collections. Space and bed rentals are fixed amounts per year, based on the number of beds.

Bedford charged the pediatrics service with the following costs for the year ended June 30, 1998:

	Patient Days (Variable)	Bed Capacity (Fixed)
Dietary.	$ 600,000	—
Janitorial	—	$ 70,000
Laundry	300,000	—
Laboratory	450,000	—
Pharmacy.	350,000	—
Repairs and maintenance	—	30,000
General and maintenance	—	1,300,000
Rent.	—	1,500,000
Billings and collections	300,000	—
Total	$ 2,000,000	$ 2,900,000

During the year ended June 30, 1998, pediatrics charged patients an average of $300 per day, had a capacity of 60 beds, and had total revenue of $6,000,000. Pediatrics also employed the following personnel:

	Annual Salaries (Each)
Supervising nurses	$25,000
Nurses	20,000
Aides	9,000

Bedford requires that separately owned departments employ the following minimum numbers of personnel, based on patient days:

Annual Patient Days	Aides	Nurses	Supervising Nurses
Up to 21,900	20	10	4
21,901 - 26,000	26	13	4
26,001 - 29,200	30	15	4

Pediatrics always employs the minimum requirements in each category. These salaries are, therefore, fixed within ranges of annual patient days.

Pediatrics operated at 100 percent of capacity on 90 days in 1998. It is estimated that during those 90 days, the demand for beds exceeded the capacity by about 20. Bedford could make an additional 20 beds available for pediatrics during the year ending June 30, 1999. The additional beds would increase pediatrics' fixed charges.

Required:

1. Determine the break-even point for pediatrics, expressed as the number of patient days, for the year ending June 30, 1999, if it does not rent the additional 20 beds. Assume that the revenue, cost per patient day, cost per bed, and salary rates will remain the same as they were in the previous year.

2. Assume that all of the data related to 1998 will hold for 1999, except that pediatrics will rent the additional 20 beds and, therefore, increase its per bed charges. Demand for beds will be the same in 1999 as it was in 1998. Determine the increase or decrease in profit for pediatrics that would accompany renting the additional beds.

(AICPA adapted)

1-2-3

CASE 3B—RADEN PAPER COMPANY

Raden Paper Company produces four basic paper product lines at one of its plants: computer paper, paper napkins, place mats, and poster board. Materials and operations vary according to the line of product. The market has been relatively good. The demand for napkins and place mats has increased with more people eating out, and the demand for the other lines has been growing steadily.

The plant superintendent, Marcella Owens, while pleased with the prospects for increased sales, is concerned about costs:

"We hear talk about a paperless office, but I haven't seen it yet. The computers, if anything, have increased the market for paper. Our big problem now is the high fixed cost of production. As we have automated our operation, we have experienced increases in fixed overhead and even variable overhead. And, we will have to add more equipment since it appears that we need even more plant capacity. We are operating over our normal capacity as it is.

"The place mat market concerns me. We may have to discontinue printing the mats. Our specialty printing is driving up the variable overhead to the point where we may not find it profitable to continue with that line at all."

Cost and price data for the next fiscal quarter are as follows:

	Computer Paper	Napkins	Place Mats	Poster Board
Estimated sales volume in units	30,000	120,000	45,000	80,000
Selling prices	$14.00	$7.00	$12.00	$8.50
Materials costs.	6.00	4.50	3.60	2.50

Variable overhead includes the cost of hourly labor and the variable cost of equipment operation. The fixed plant overhead is estimated at $420,000 for the quarter. Direct labor, to a large extent, is salaried; and the cost is included as a part of fixed plant overhead. The superintendent's concern about the eventual need for more capacity is based on increases in production that may reach and exceed the practical capacity of 60,000 machine hours.

In addition to the fixed plant overhead, the plant incurs fixed selling and administrative expenses per quarter of $118,000.

"I share your concern about increasing fixed costs," the supervisor of plant operations replies. "We are still operating with about the same number of people we had when we didn't have this sophisticated equipment. In reviewing our needs and costs, it appears to me that we could cut fixed plant overhead to $378,000 a quarter without doing any violence to our operation. This would be a big help."

"You may be right," Owens responds. "We forget that we have more productive power than we once had, and we may as well take advantage of it. Suppose we get some hard figures that show where the cost reductions will be made."

Data with respect to production per machine hour and the variable cost per hour of producing each of the products are as follows:

	Computer Paper	Napkins	Place Mats	Poster Board
Units per hour	6	10	5	4
Variable overhead per hour	$9.00	$6.00	$12.00	$8.00

"I hate to spoil things," the vice-president of purchasing announces. "But the cost of our materials for computer stock is now up to $7.00. Just got a call about that this morning. Also, place mat materials will be up to $4.00 a unit."

"On the bright side," the vice-president of sales reports, "we have firm orders for 35,000 cartons of computer paper, not 30,000 as we originally figured."

Required:

1. From all original estimates given, prepare estimated contribution margins by product line for the next fiscal quarter. Also, show the contribution margins per unit.
2. Prepare contribution margins as in Part (1) above with all revisions included.
3. For the original estimates, compute each of the following:
   (a) Break-even point for the given sales mix.
   (b) Operating leverage factor for the estimated sales volume.
   (c) Margin of safety for the estimated sales volume.
4. For the revised estimates, compute each of the following:
   (a) Break-even point for the given sales mix.
   (b) Operating leverage factor for the estimated sales volume.
   (c) Margin of safety for the estimated sales volume.
5. Comment on Owens' concern about the variable cost of the place mats.

PART *II*

Product Cost Framework

Product Costing: Attaching Costs to Products and Services

*L*EARNING OBJECTIVES

After studying Chapter 4, you will be able to:

1. Understand why and how costs are attached to products and services.
2. Identify the circumstances in which a job cost system and a process cost system are appropriate.
3. Describe how direct materials, direct labor, and factory overhead are costed to products.
4. Explain why predetermined overhead rates are usually used for product costing.
5. Calculate plant-wide and departmental factory overhead rates.
6. Identify the main differences among alternative measures for the denominator in the overhead rate.
7. Explain why services or products should be costed for pricing purposes by using an overhead rate computed at normal volume levels.
8. Describe how to allocate service center costs so that they can be included in overhead rates of operating departments.

What Is the Cost of a Backpack?

As a government employee working out of Denver, Julie Freeman satisfied her love for the outdoors by working as a part-time wilderness guide and cross-country ski instructor. She also found herself either redesigning or making the equipment she needed, such as pull-along sleds and backpacks. When people started buying her sleds, she used her savings as seed money for a new business, Colorado Recreational Products. Now her most notable product is a unique collapsible teepee-shaped tent.

Freeman started her enterprise with a firm hope of making a profit, and she has realized profits. However, times are changing. Revenues for this year have reached over $2 million and are expected to increase in the future. Costs, on the other hand, are increasing faster than revenues. Freeman does not know what her profit margins

are for sleds, backpacks, and tents because she has no idea what it costs her to make a product. Most of her accounting has been a "shoebox approach" where receipts, deposit slips, and invoices go into a box. Periodically, a local CPA firm sends a staff accountant to sort the box's contents and prepare financial statements.

Freeman needs cost information about production, and her accounting system does not provide it. For example, she needs to know: What does it cost to produce one unit of each of her products? Are production costs higher this month than last month? With profits going down, which products are losing profit margin? And, behind all of these questions is: Which costs are production costs? Freeman needs an accounting system that will provide cost information for her current needs and for the future.

Product costs are used by entrepreneurs like Julie Freeman of Colorado Recreational Products to accomplish an assortment of needs: to evaluate the profitability of their goods and services; to aid in pricing and bidding decisions; to plan and budget operations; to evaluate performance; to control costs; and to establish inventory values for the balance sheet and cost of goods and services sold for the income statement.

This chapter discusses accounting for production costs and presents ways to identify costs with products. Accounting for direct materials and direct labor comes first. Then, accounting for factory overhead covers simple to more complex situations. Finally, we discuss how service center costs are included in product cost. The chapter describes the types of manufacturing environments that are appropriate for job cost and process cost systems. However, detailed product costing differences between these two systems will be covered in Chapter 5.

P RODUCT COST SYSTEMS

The production of goods and services involves resources. As mentioned in Chapter 2, the costs of these resources are typically classified as materials, labor, and factory overhead. The costs are accumulated by jobs or by departments. Then they are assigned to each unit of output (product or service) based on each unit's use of the resources. These relationships for assigning costs to products or services are depicted in Figure 4.1.

The principles underlying product costing are applicable to manufacturing companies, wholesalers, retailers, and service organizations. For example, a hospital may be interested in determining the cost of a specific medical treatment or the cost of outpatient care. A furniture store may wish to know the

FIGURE 4.1   A View of Cost Linkage

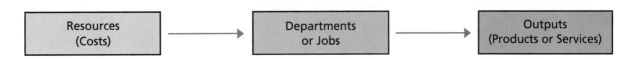

costs associated with carrying and selling a particular line of sofas. A building contractor, on the other hand, will accumulate costs by project. If a contractor is constructing a new bridge for the state for instance, the contractor will identify and trace the costs to the bridge project. A university may be interested in the estimation, measurement, and control of program costs to train mathematics teachers. A museum may want to determine the cost of a particular exhibit for a season.

Regardless of the type of organization, costs are identified as direct costs when they can be readily connected to a cost objective. Indirect costs, which cannot as easily be connected to an objective, must be allocated using some reasonable basis for allocation. Because the principles used in tracing costs are more clearly identified in a manufacturing setting, the same manufacturing cost methods can often be adapted to a wide variety of applications. Manufacturing costs are accumulated and assigned to products by using one of two basic cost accounting systems:

1. The job cost system.
2. The process cost system.

The production environment, which translates into the nature of the product or service and the type and number of operations, is the primary consideration in selecting a cost accounting system. Therefore, we consider the different production environments and whether job cost or process cost is appropriate.

Production Environment for a Job Cost System

The environment appropriate for a **job cost system** is typified by one-of-a-kind, customized, or special-order products and services. These products and services have two dominant characteristics:

1. They are unique and are produced or provided individually, in lots, in batches, or in some other grouping.
2. Various particular products or services use different amounts of inputs such as materials, labor, and overhead.

Examples of products that fit these characteristics are office buildings, residential housing, NASA spacecraft, custom equipment, and office furniture. Examples of services include healthcare procedures, accounting tasks, legal cases, family counseling sessions, real estate appraisals, auto repair jobs, plays and concerts, and fund-raising campaigns.

The uniqueness of a product or service determines what work will be performed and the type and sequence of operations. This, in turn, determines the amount of materials, labor, and overhead related to the work. Since the amount of input will differ, unit costs can easily vary among similar products. In many cases, as a result, prices for these products or services are cost based; i.e., costs are accumulated by customer order or job. For example, a company that builds military equipment to support soldiers in a desert setting will generally have cost-based prices; and the company will use a job cost system.

Production Environment for a Process Cost System

Process costing is appropriate when operations represent mass production or continuous processing. In this situation, each unit of product or service within the same category is identical or nearly so. Examples include food processing, candy making, oil refining, rubber production, and automobile assembly. Products or services in this environment have two dominant characteristics:

1. Products or services are identical or similar and are produced or provided on a continuous basis.
2. Products or services receive substantially identical amounts of materials, labor, and overhead.

The main difference between mass-produced services and mass-produced products is that labor and overhead are the significant cost elements for services. Although materials may be present, their costs are generally insignificant in service situations. Examples include most banking services, baggage handling at bus depots or airports, insurance claims processing, credit checking, and dry cleaning.

The production environment is typically categorized as yielding commingled products, fabricated products, or assembled products. **Commingled products** exist when one unit cannot be distinguished from any other unit. One pound of sugar is indistinguishable from another pound unless contained in some way. Products in this category include flour, oil, electricity, soft drinks, textiles, processed foods, and paper. **Fabricated products** involve reshaping materials through a cutting, stamping, or molding operation. Examples include tires, nuts and bolts, sugar-coated breakfast cereals, and silverware. **Assembled products** bring parts and subassemblies together for an assembly operation. Each product passes through the same assembly operations. Examples include kitchen appliances, calculators, computers, telephones, and pick-up trucks. The sleds, backpacks, and tents produced by Colorado Recreational Products are also examples of assembled products.

Many situations exist where a production process has characteristics of both costing systems. For example, an automated assembly line sends all cars through the same assembly steps; but every car is unique in some way. Often, high volumes of production make process costing easier and more common. In other cases, the uniqueness of each unit causes job costing to provide more relevant unit costs.

COSTING OF DIRECT COSTS

We now discuss how to determine the manufacturing costs that are directly traceable to products or jobs. These costs consist of direct materials and direct labor.

Costing of Direct Materials

Materials include raw materials, purchased parts, and purchased or subcontracted assemblies and subassemblies. **Direct materials** are those that are identified with the production of a specific product and are easily and economically traced to the product; their costs represent a significant part of the total product cost. All other materials and supplies that become part of a product or are consumed in production are called **indirect materials**, which is part of factory overhead.

The costs associated with acquiring materials and having them ready for production typically fall into five categories:

1. The acquisition cost (purchase price or production cost) of the materials.
2. In-transit charges, such as freight, insurance, storage, and customs and duty charges.
3. Credits for trade discounts, cash discounts, and other discounts and allowances.
4. The costs of purchasing, receiving, inspecting, and storing activities.
5. Miscellaneous items, including income from the sale of scrap and spoiled units, obsolescence, and other inventory losses.

Categories 1 through 3 are typically included in the cost of materials, whether direct or indirect materials. Categories 4 and 5 are treated as factory overhead. We allocate those costs to products with one of the several approaches that will be discussed later in the chapter.

The document that lists all materials needed to produce one unit of each product is the **bill of materials**, which is generated by product design engineers. It lists the sequence in which the materials will enter production. Once a decision is made about the quantity of products to produce, the bill of materials is used to determine the amount of materials to be acquired.

Suppose that Colorado Recreational Products purchased materials on account for $75,000. Upon receipt of the materials, we increase Materials and Accounts Payable by $75,000 as follows:

Materials		Accounts Payable	
75,000			**75,000**

Production managers requisition the materials required for a specific job or product from the storeroom. Thus, each requisition becomes the basis for charging the cost of materials to a specific job or product. Assume that a month's requisitions at Colorado Recreational Products show that direct materials costing $60,000 have been transferred from the materials inventory to production. The total of $60,000 is moved from Materials to Work in Process. The latter account is a focal account for the entry of production costs. The costs of the three cost elements—direct materials, direct labor, and factory overhead—are funneled through this account, as will be shown later. It is, therefore, the control account for all in-process activity. The movement of materials used in production for the month is shown as:

Materials		Work in Process	
75,000	**60,000**	**60,000**	

The costs included in the $60,000 are also charged to the processing departments that used the materials. In a job cost system, the costs would be charged to each job. These itemizations form the subsidiary ledger that supports the work in process control account.

Costing of Direct Labor

Factory labor cost is the total labor cost expended for the benefit of production. **Direct labor** can be specifically identified with a product in an economically feasible manner. **Indirect labor** is not readily traced to a product. Because of the changes in the production environment in many companies and the emphasis on a just-in-time philosophy, a new term, value-added direct labor, is being used. **Value-added direct labor** changes materials into a finished product. For example, value-added direct labor fabricates parts, assembles products, and finishes products. Nonvalue-added direct labor moves, inspects, stores, examines, or otherwise handles the product without adding value to the product. For our purposes, we will generally define direct labor as value-added and indirect labor as nonvalue-added, even though the differences are not always clear.

Labor-related costs include the wages and salaries of the employees plus any additional expenditures made by an employer on behalf of an employee. These typically include bonuses, overtime premiums (i.e., the *additional* wages for overtime), shift differentials, idle time, employer's payroll taxes, and fringe benefits. These additional expenditures are usually treated as part of the factory overhead costs. Some of these expenditures cannot easily be traced to individual production orders. Others, such as overtime premiums and shift differentials, are treated as factory overhead so that those products worked on during overtime hours or late shifts are not unfairly penalized.

Labor time tickets or labor time reports will show how much of the labor time and cost is charged to each job or production order. Periodically, factory payroll is recorded by a debit to Payroll with offsetting credits to Wages Payable, Employees' Income Tax Payable, and other liability accounts for payroll deductions. Suppose that during one month, the labor costs for Colorado Recreational Products were $10,000; and the workers' take-home pay totaled $7,400. The resulting transaction is shown:

Payroll		Wages Payable	
10,000			**7,400**

Other Labor-Related Payables	
	2,600

For the sake of simplicity, we will assume that all of Colorado Recreational Products' labor is direct labor. We transfer the Payroll balance to Work in Process as follows:

Payroll		Work in Process	
10,000	**10,000**	60,000	
		10,000	

COSTING FACTORY OVERHEAD

Factory overhead, unlike direct materials and direct labor, cannot be requisitioned or measured directly as a cost of any particular job, production order, or service. Factory overhead consists of a variety of costs such as indirect materials, indirect labor, insurance, depreciation, utilities, repair and maintenance, and taxes—all of which are indirectly related to the products. The indirect nature of overhead costs with respect to the products or services creates a difficulty in identifying production costs with each unit. For our purposes at this point, we take an overall, simplified approach to costing of factory overhead to products. This is to convey the concepts involved. Later in the chapter, we explain overhead costs by employing departmental rates. In Chapter 6, we extend the discussion to include activity-based costing.

For the discussion that follows, factory overhead is attached to products or services by means of a cost driver that links costs to the products or services. The cost driver chosen as a basis for overhead allocation should be related logically to both the overhead and the product or service. If machinery plays an important role in the manufacturing operation, the overhead costs likely consist of power, lubrication, maintenance, repairs, depreciation, and other costs closely related to machine operation. The benefits received by the products can probably be best measured against the cost of the machine hours used in their production. Therefore, these overhead costs should be allocated to the products on the basis of machine hours used to produce the products. For other plants whose operations are more labor intensive than capital intensive, direct labor cost or direct labor hours may be more appropriate for overhead allocation.

The most common cost drivers chosen for overhead allocation are direct labor hours, machine hours, and direct labor cost. A recent survey of manufacturing firms found that over 41 percent of the respondent companies used direct labor (hours or cost) to allocate overhead cost.[1] Another survey found this figure to be 62 percent.[2]

The total cost driver activity for the plant is divided into the total overhead cost to obtain an **overhead rate**. Products then are assigned overhead cost by multiplying the actual quantities of the activity by the rate calculated. Suppose that Colorado Recreational Products uses direct labor cost to allocate overhead. During the month in the earlier example for which direct labor cost was $10,000, the total overhead for the plant was $15,000. Consequently, the overhead rate would be 150 percent of direct labor cost. During that month, the direct labor cost incurred to produce backpacks amounted to $2,700. Hence, $4,050 ($2,700 x 1.5) of overhead cost would be allocated to the backpacks.

Predetermined Overhead Rate

Thus far, we have discussed an **actual costing** system, where the product costs consist of actual direct materials used, actual direct labor cost, and overhead allocation based on total actual overhead costs and total actual activity. Most companies, however, use a normal costing system or a standard costing system.

---

[1] Szendi, J.Z. and R.C. Elmore, "Management Accounting: Are New Techniques Making In-Roads with Practitioners?" *Journal of Accounting Education*, Spring 1993, p. 66.

[2] Cohen, J.R. and L. Paquette, "Management Accounting Practices: Perceptions of Controllers," *Journal of Cost Management*, Fall 1991, p. 75.

The latter will be covered in Chapter 9. **Normal costing** differs from actual costing in that overhead is allocated using a **predetermined overhead rate**, defined as:

Predetermined overhead rate = Budgeted factory overhead ÷ Budgeted cost driver activity

With normal costing, the **applied factory overhead** would be determined by multiplying the predetermined overhead rate by the actual cost driver activity for the job or product. Typically, companies use a one-year time horizon to calculate predetermined overhead rates.

Two major reasons exist for the use of normal costing rather than actual costing. The first is the timing of factory overhead cost incurrence. For example, air-conditioning costs in the summer for many companies in the Sunbelt tend to be higher than heating costs are in the winter. Should we allocate the higher air-conditioning costs to products that were manufactured during the summer? The facilities and workers must be maintained regardless of the weather. In addition, discretionary costs may fluctuate widely from month to month. For instance, managers may decide to incur substantial maintenance costs during some months and very little during other months. Because of the seasonal and discretionary aspects of overhead, a more stable overhead rate requires a longer time horizon, such as one year.

The second reason for the use of normal costing is the potential fluctuation in the activity represented by the cost driver. Most companies do not have a constant level of activity every month. For example, employees take vacations during the summer months; operations are scaled back to accommodate major repairs and maintenance; production ceases while a changeover in tooling occurs; or the company is closed for the week between Christmas and New Year's Day. Normal costing, by using a one-year time horizon for the overhead rate, averages costs over the units of work regardless of when work is performed. Therefore, a product is not penalized because it is produced during a period of low volume.

Calculating an actual overhead rate using a one-year time horizon means that prices and other cost-based decisions cannot be made until the end of the year. Clearly, companies cannot operate this way. The use of a predetermined overhead rate allows costs of products and jobs to be calculated throughout the year as necessary. Moreover, a predetermined overhead rate helps managers to prepare bids on major orders or to price business from prospective customers.

To illustrate the application of overhead in a normal costing system, suppose that, for 1997, Northeast Publishing Company has budgeted $50,000 for fixed overhead costs and $3 per direct labor hour for variable overhead costs. This is its overhead cost function. These budgeted costs correspond to a budgeted activity level of 10,000 direct labor hours. The predetermined overhead rate would be computed as:

$$[\$50,000 + \$3(10,000)] \div 10,000 = \$8 \text{ per direct labor hour}$$

Assume there were 10,000 direct labor hours during 1997. During production, various entries were made to cost the individual jobs. We could quite literally add $8 to Work in Process every time one more hour of direct labor is worked. In normal accounting activity, however, these transfers to Work in Process are done periodically, perhaps weekly or monthly. If done in aggregate, a summary transfer to Work in Process of all overhead applied to all jobs would show the following:

Factory Overhead		Work in Process	
	80,000	60,000	
		10,000	
		80,000	

As each job goes through production, an overhead charge at the predetermined rate of $8 for each direct labor hour is made to the job. Suppose Northeast Publishing Company published an economics textbook (Job 1018) that required $20,000 of direct materials and 2,000 hours of direct labor at $10 per hour. The completed cost for Job 1018 can be summarized as:

Direct materials	$ 20,000
Direct labor (2,000 hours at $10 per direct labor hour)	20,000
Factory overhead (2,000 hours at $8 per direct labor hour)	16,000
Total cost	$ 56,000

At its completion, the cost of a job is transferred from Work in Process to Finished Goods. For Job 1018, the transfer would be:

Finished Goods		Work in Process	
56,000		60,000	**56,000**
		10,000	
		80,000	

Disposition of the Overhead Variance

While the products are costed by using a predetermined overhead rate and crediting the Factory Overhead account, actual overhead costs are incurred and recorded as debits to Factory Overhead. Suppose Northeast Publishing Company incurred actual overhead costs amounting to $81,500 during 1997. These costs included depreciation of $11,500, expired insurance of $10,000, salaries of $40,000, and utilities of $20,000. The entries to record these actual costs are:

Factory Overhead		Accumulated Depreciation	
81,500	80,000		**11,500**

Prepaid Insurance		Wages Payable	
	10,000		7,400
			40,000

Utilities Payable	
	20,000

Notice that expense accounts were not debited because the preceding items represent product costs rather than period costs, as discussed in Chapter 2. Nonmanufacturing, or selling and administration, costs would be debited to expense accounts. Suppose Northeast Publishing Company had selling expenses of $29,000, office rent of $45,000, executive salaries of $320,000, and office utilities of $33,000. The following entries would be recorded:

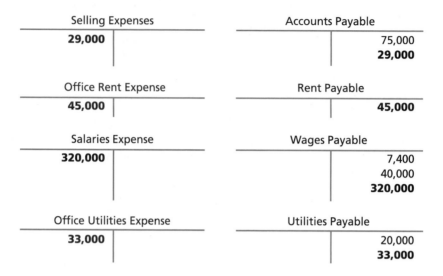

Selling Expenses			Accounts Payable	
29,000				75,000
				29,000

Office Rent Expense			Rent Payable	
45,000				**45,000**

Salaries Expense			Wages Payable	
320,000				7,400
				40,000
				320,000

Office Utilities Expense			Utilities Payable	
33,000				20,000
				33,000

Since only $80,000 of factory overhead was applied during 1997, not all of the actual factory overhead spent was charged to jobs. The difference, or variance, of $1,500 can be closed to Cost of Goods Sold at the end of the year or, if desired, can be allocated to Cost of Goods Sold, Finished Goods, and Work in Process on the basis of their account balances. Since these variances tend to be relatively small, most companies simply close them out to Cost of Goods Sold. Using this approach, Northeast Publishing's entry to close out the variance is:

Factory Overhead			Cost of Goods Sold	
81,500	80,000		**1,500**	
	1,500			

Notice that since Northeast Publishing did not attach all $81,500 of spending to production, cost of goods sold is increased by $1,500.

If too little overhead is costed to the products, as in the preceding example, the variance is called **underapplied** or **underabsorbed overhead.** When this occurs, expenditures for overhead expenses exceed the amount attached to the products during the accounting period. On the other hand, if too much overhead is costed to the products, the variance is called **overapplied** or **overabsorbed overhead**. In this situation, the amount of overhead costs attached to the period's output is more than the amount actually spent for overhead.

Underapplied factory overhead means nothing more than the actual costs were not absorbed by the products manufactured. Underapplied overhead occurs in either of these situations:

1. We produced less than expected.
2. We spent more than expected.

When overhead is overapplied, the variance is credited to (i.e., subtracted from) Cost of Goods Sold. Overapplied overhead occurs in either of these situations:

1. We produced more than expected.
2. We spent less than expected.

In the Northeast Publishing Company example, 10,000 direct labor hours were worked. This was exactly the amount of activity that was budgeted. Therefore, the reason for the underapplied overhead variance was overspending. According to the company's cost function ($50,000 + $3 per direct labor hour), spending should have been $80,000 but was actually $81,500.

More detailed reasons for overhead variances are discussed in Chapter 9.

Multiple Overhead Rates

Some reasonable, causal, or beneficial relationship should exist among the costs accumulated in factory overhead accounts, the cost driver selected, and the products or services to which the costs will be allocated. Simply stated: The activity (as represented by the cost driver) is the link between the output of products or services and factory overhead spending. The implication is that more output requires more activity and, therefore, more spending. For example, if a company uses direct labor hours as a cost driver for the labor activity, factory overhead costs should consist primarily or exclusively of costs that support direct workers. Such costs may include supervision and facilities for work places, as well as travel, training, and fringe benefits of workers.

In the examples to this point in the chapter, we have assumed that only one cost driver is appropriate for the total factory overhead. However, diversity of products and services will often result in distorted cost allocations when only one cost driver is used. The greater the differences in products, the greater the diversity that exists in the operations. The more diverse the operations, the more likely it is that one cost driver cannot assign costs to all products fairly. In these situations, departmental overhead rates will assign costs more accurately to products than will one plant-wide overhead rate. A plant-wide factory overhead rate can only be justified for a company making few and similar products. Contemporary Practice 4.1 displays results from a recent survey on the types of overhead rates most commonly used by manufacturing companies in Korea, Japan, and the United States.

C O N T E M P O R A R Y   P R A C T I C E   4 . 1

Survey on Types of Overhead Rates	
Country	*Most Common Type of Overhead Rate*
Korea	Single plant-wide rate (43% of respondent companies).
United States	Departmental rates (38% of respondent companies).
Japan	Rates for groups of departments (68% of respondent companies).

Source: Kim, I. and J. Song, "U.S., Korea, and Japan: Accounting Practices in the Three Countries," *Management Accounting*, August 1990, p. 28.

For an example, consider The Paint Farm. It finishes furniture for local manufacturers. The furniture passes through two major activity centers that form the two departments in the process: Sanding and Painting. A summary of direct labor and factory overhead costs for each department during the last month follows:

	Sanding	*Painting*	*Total*
Direct labor..........................	$ 37,000	$ 26,500	$ 63,500
Factory overhead......................	74,000	79,500	153,500

Factory overhead is allocated to products on the basis of direct labor dollars. Dividing the factory overhead costs by direct labor dollars gives the following departmental and plant-wide overhead rates:

Sanding ($74,000 ÷ $37,000)   = 200%
Painting ($79,500 ÷ $26,500)   = 300%
Plant-wide ($153,500 ÷ $63,500) = 241.7%

Using the different rates in allocating factory overhead costs to a job that has $86 of Sanding direct labor and $32 of Painting direct labor (i.e., total labor costs of $118) gives the following amounts:

Plant-wide overhead rate ($118 x 241.7%)		$ 285.21
Departmental overhead rates:		
Sanding ($86 x 200%).............................	$172.00	
Painting ($32 x 300%).............................	96.00	$ 268.00

The departmental rates allocate costs considering the characteristics of the product or job involved. The plant-wide rate averages all products and jobs.

For The Paint Farm, the same cost driver was selected for each department. A more common situation is where departments have different cost drivers. For example, a Fabrication Department may use direct labor hours; a Machining Department, machine time; a Production Engineering Department, direct labor cost. As a company considers ways to trace costs to products more accurately, it will look at the production and support activities more closely and choose an appropriate cost driver to allocate the overhead costs.

Alternative Concepts of Volume

When selecting the denominator for the overhead rate, volume can be measured in one of four ways:

1. Ideal capacity.
2. Practical capacity.
3. Expected volume.
4. Normal volume.

Ideal capacity is the maximum amount of product that can be manufactured or the maximum service that can be rendered with available facilities. This is often a too perfect goal to be realized and is generally recognized to be the absolute limit and beyond realistic expectations. Certain interruptions and inefficiencies in production are to be expected.

Practical capacity is full utilization of facilities with allowance made for normal interruptions and inefficiencies. For example, production will be slowed or stopped at times because of breakdowns, shortages of labor and materials, or retooling. These possibilities are considered in arriving at practical plant capacity.

Expected volume is the level of operation budgeted or estimated for the current period. This may be at or below practical plant capacity. It is the level at which management expects to operate during the next month or year.

Normal volume is generally a balance between practical plant capacity and sales demand in the long run. Over a period of years, the peaks and valleys of customer demand are leveled by averaging; and the average level of plant utilization is considered to be normal volume.

It may seem, at first, that factory overhead per unit should be calculated at the expected level of operation for the next year. Indeed, this is the practice of most companies. However, for product pricing purposes, a better approach is to use the normal volume. Why should normal volume be used when you already know that the company may be operating below that level? After all, a rate computed at the expected level of operation will come closer to costing all of the overhead to the products, and product cost will be more in line with actual cost.

The problem with using an overhead rate based on expected, rather than normal, volume is illustrated by the following example. Assume that the normal level of operation is 200,000 machine hours and that 100,000 units of the product can be manufactured in that time. The fixed overhead for the year is budgeted at $500,000. The normal fixed overhead per unit of product is then $5, computed as:

$$\frac{\text{Budgeted fixed overhead}}{\text{Units produced at normal volume}} = \frac{\$500,000}{100,000} = \$5 \text{ Fixed overhead per unit}$$

But management expects to operate at only 100,000 machine hours next year and to produce 50,000 units of product. An overhead rate at expected volume would be $10 per unit of product:

$$\frac{\text{Budgeted fixed overhead}}{\text{Units produced at expected volume}} = \frac{\$500,000}{50,000} = \$10 \text{ Fixed overhead per unit}$$

If the company plans to operate below normal volume, an overhead rate computed at the expected level of operations will result in more fixed overhead being assigned to each unit of product. If selling prices are set by adding a markup to total cost, the price will be higher when fewer units are produced. With a higher price under competitive conditions, customers may be lost, thereby aggravating a condition where volume is already below normal.

For this reason, the objective is not necessarily to assign all overhead costs to products. The products should bear the normal overhead costs, and any unabsorbed fixed overhead should be recognized as a period expense. (Overabsorbed fixed overhead would likewise result in a reduction of period expenses.) Rather than allocating unabsorbed fixed overhead to products produced, this approach treats the costs of idle capacity as the costs of products that the company did *not* produce.

C OST OF PROVIDING SERVICES

An entity that provides services instead of tangible products may not operate with a formal cost accounting system but will nevertheless measure performance by type of service and by customer groups. A hotel, for example, may provide an exercise room for its guests. The cost of supplies used exclusively for the exercise room, such as rubbing lotions and bandages, along with the salaries and wages of the room's employees, such as the manager and exercise class instructors, are identified with the exercise activities. Also, costs of special equipment used, such as depreciation and maintenance expenses, and other overhead costs increased by operating this service will be included. These costs can be used as a basis for deciding how much must be added to a guest's bill to cover all costs and allow for profit. Also, does the amount of customer patronage justify continuance of the service? Can other features be provided at a certain cost to attract more customer attention? Properly assigning costs to the exercise room will give the manager the accounting information needed to answer these questions.

Accounting and legal services are examples where the organization may want costs accumulated by client number or case. In this situation, each client number or case becomes a job, with costs traced to the individual jobs. No formal inventory account for work in process exists; but an account is used that serves as the equivalent, such as Costs of Unbilled Work.

A PRODUCT COSTING ILLUSTRATION

Summarized cost data are presented in this section for Clark Machine Company to illustrate product costing procedures using a normal costing system. Note that the entries given are in composite form. In practice, many repetitious entries are made to record individual transactions that take place during the year. The sequential order of the cost transactions should also be considered. For example, the preparation of the budget for factory overhead and the overhead rate calculations are completed before the beginning of the year. The predetermined overhead rate must be calculated from a budget of factory overhead so that products will be assigned the proper overhead cost. Only at the end of the year will the company know that 220,000 direct labor hours were used and that the actual factory overhead cost was $1,336,200. Throughout the year, the company purchases materials and incurs labor and factory overhead costs as products are continually processed, completed, and sold. At the same time, costs are traced to the products and released as expenses when the products are sold.

Clark Machine Company transactions data for the fiscal year ended April 30, 1997, are as follows:

1. Materials purchased during the fiscal year totaled $840,000.
2. Direct materials requisitioned for production cost $631,400. Indirect materials costing $47,200 were also requisitioned.
3. Factory payrolls amounted to $1,874,000. The income taxes withheld from the employees' wages totaled $393,400, and the deduction for FICA taxes withheld amounted to $106,600.
4. A distribution of the factory labor cost of $1,874,000 shows that $1,760,000 was direct labor, while the remaining $114,000 was indirect labor.

5. Factory overhead at the normal operating level of 250,000 direct labor hours results in an overhead rate of $6 per direct labor hour. During the year, direct labor workers recorded 220,000 labor hours.
6. The factory overhead, in addition to indirect materials and indirect labor, amounted to $1,175,000. Included in this amount is depreciation of $120,000 and the employer's share of FICA taxes of $106,600. The balance of the overhead was acquired through accounts payable.
7. Jobs completed and transferred to stock during the year had costs of $2,945,200.
8. The cost of goods sold during the year was $2,320,000.
9. The Factory Overhead account is closed to Cost of Goods Sold at the end of the fiscal year.

The transactions are entered in the accounts as follows:

1. **Purchase of materials.** (The cost of each type of material is also entered on the individual materials inventory cards.)

Materials		Accounts Payable	
840,000			840,000

2. **Materials issued to production.** (Requisitions are the basis for entries reducing materials inventory, for posting direct materials costs to each job, and for posting indirect materials costs to Factory Overhead.)

Materials		Work in Process	
840,000	678,600	631,400	

Factory Overhead	
47,200	

3. **Aggregate factory payrolls.**

Payroll		Wages Payable	
1,874,000			1,374,000

Employees' Income Taxes Payable		FICA Taxes Payable	
	393,400		106,600

4. **Payroll distribution for the year.** (A classification of labor time by jobs is shown on labor time tickets. These tickets are the basis for distributing direct labor cost to individual jobs and for posting indirect labor cost to the factory overhead subsidiary ledger.)

Work in Process		Payroll	
631,400		1,874,000	1,874,000
1,760,000			

Factory Overhead	
47,200	
114,000	

5. **Factory overhead applied.** (Factory overhead applied to products on direct labor hour basis is: 220,000 hours x $6 rate = $1,320,000.)

Work in Process		Factory Overhead	
631,400		47,200	**1,320,000**
1,760,000		114,000	
1,320,000			

6. **Actual factory overhead.** (This is in addition to indirect materials and indirect labor.)

Factory Overhead		Accumulated Depreciation	
47,200	1,320,000		**120,000**
114,000			
1,175,000			

FICA Taxes Payable		Accounts Payable	
	106,600		840,000
			948,400

7. **Work completed during the year and transferred to stock.** (Completed jobs are removed from the file of jobs in process and moved to the subsidiary ledger supporting finished goods inventory. Ending Work in Process is $766,200.)

Work in Process		Finished Goods	
631,400	**2,945,200**	2,945,200	
1,760,000			
1,320,000			
766,200			

8. **The cost of goods sold.** (Deductions are recorded in the finished goods inventory ledger. Entries are also made in records supporting billings to customers for the sales. Ending Finished Goods is $625,200.)

Finished Goods		Cost of Goods Sold	
2,945,200	**2,320,000**	2,320,000	
625,200			

9. **Closing of Factory Overhead.** (Total actual overhead costs from entries in Items (2), (4), and (6) is $1,336,200. Actual overhead amounting to $16,200 is not absorbed as a part of the product cost. The underapplied overhead is closed to Cost of Goods Sold.)

Factory Overhead		Cost of Goods Sold	
47,200	1,320,000	2,320,000	
114,000	**16,200**	**16,200**	
1,175,000			

SERVICE CENTER COSTS

Most companies have several departments or functions involved directly or indirectly in producing goods or providing services. The development of departmental overhead rates depends on the interrelationships among these different departments.

Operating departments are organizational units most closely tied to the productive effort that results in products or services to customers. In manufacturing organizations, these units are typically called **producing departments**. On the other hand, **service centers** (or **support functions**) provide supporting services that facilitate the activities of the operating departments. Often, service centers provide support services to one another. Service centers include, for example, maintenance, quality control, cafeterias, internal auditing, personnel, accounting, production planning and control, and medical facilities. Although they do not have a direct relationship to output, service center costs support operating departments and, therefore, become part of the cost of a finished product or service. In some limited cases, a service center provides support services for operating departments as well as services for outside customers. Examples include engineering consulting, research and development, computer systems design, copying services, and laboratory work.

Service center costs are allocated to operating departments by means of a cost driver. Depending on the nature of the support activity, any one of a number of cost drivers may be appropriate for calculating a rate. Examples of cost drivers that could be used are given in Figure 4.2. The allocated service center costs become part of the total overhead costs of the operating departments.

FIGURE 4.2   Cost Drivers Used for Service Centers

Possible Cost Drivers for Selected Service Centers	
Service Center	*Cost Drivers*
Purchasing	Number of orders, cost of materials, line items ordered.
Receiving and inspection	Cost of materials, number of units, number of orders, labor hours.
Storerooms	Cost of materials, number of requisitions, number of units handled, square or cubic footage occupied.
Personnel	Number of employees, labor hours, turnover of labor.
Laundry	Pounds of laundry, number of items processed.
Cafeteria	Number of employees.
Custodial services	Square footage occupied.
Repair and maintenance	Machine hours, labor hours.
Medical facilities	Number of employees, hours worked.
Factory administration	Total labor hours, number of employees, labor cost.
Power	Kilowatt hours, capacity of machines.

Occasionally, companies may not allocate service center costs to operating departments to ensure that the services are fully utilized by the operating managers. Some examples of this phenomenon include internal audit departments, credit-check services, libraries, and computer services. An illustration of the latter appears in Contemporary Practice 4.2.

Three common approaches are available for allocating the costs of service centers: direct method, step (sequential) method, and reciprocal method. The latter approach, which requires the solution of simultaneous equations, is discussed in the Appendix to this chapter.

To illustrate the allocation of service center costs, we will use data from the School of Business at Hardknox University. The School of Business wishes to determine overhead costs per credit hour for its Undergraduate and Graduate Programs. We will treat these programs as the two operating departments. The School of Business has three service centers: Building Services, Staff Services (e.g., secretarial support, computer support, and photocopying), and Administration. Budgeted data for the coming year appear as follows:

	Square Feet Occupied	Employees	Overhead Costs
Service centers:			
Building Services.....................	1,000	30	$165,000
Staff Services	2,000	20	90,000
Administration	8,000	20	330,000
Operating departments:			
Graduate Program	10,000	30	265,000
Undergraduate Program..............	20,000	90	420,000

Building Services costs are allocated based on square footage of classroom and office space. Staff Services and Administration costs are allocated based on number of employees (i.e., faculty and staff). Budgeted credit hours for the year are 20,000 for the Graduate Program and 60,000 for the Undergraduate Program.

Direct Method

Direct method allocations are made from each service center to the operating departments in proportion to activity performed for each operating department. Thus, the direct method does not assign the costs of a service center to other service centers for work performed for them. Allocation of service center costs uses only those cost drivers pertaining to operating departments. Once the

C O N T E M P O R A R Y   P R A C T I C E   4 . 2

Cost Allocation in a Data Processing Service Department

"For many years, managers of the Corporate Data Processing Services (CDPS) department of the Boise Cascade Corporation did not allocate any of the costs of supporting personal computers (PC), such as purchasing, set-up, and application assistance, to the PC users because they wanted to stimulate PC use. These costs were charged/allocated to all of the other CDPS users, primarily consumers of mainframe computer resources."

Source: Merchant, K.A. and M.D. Shields, "When and Why to Measure Costs Less Accurately to Improve Decision Making," *Accounting Horizons*, June 1993, p. 78.

service centers have their costs allocated, operating department overhead rates per unit of activity are calculated.

Space associated with the Graduate Program is 10,000 square feet; and, for the Undergraduate Program, the space used is 20,000 square feet. The allocation base, therefore, totals 30,000 square feet. Building Services costs are then pro-rated over the two programs as follows:

Graduate Program.......	10,000 sq. ft.	1/3 x $165,000 =	$ 55,000
Undergraduate Program..	20,000	2/3 x $165,000 =	110,000
Total	30,000 sq. ft.	Total cost........	$165,000

The same approach follows for Staff Services and Administration. These are summarized as follows:

Graduate Program	30 employees	1/4 x $ 90,000 =	$ 22,500
Undergraduate Program..	90	3/4 x $ 90,000 =	67,500
Total	120 employees	Total cost	$ 90,000
Graduate Program	30 employees	1/4 x $330,000 =	$ 82,500
Undergraduate Program..	90	3/4 x $330,000 =	247,500
Total	120 employees	Total cost........	$ 330,000

Another way to perform these allocations is to divide the service center costs by the cost driver and apply the resulting rate to the operating department usage amount. For example, Building Services would have a rate of $5.50 per square foot ($165,000 ÷ 30,000).

The results of service center allocations and the subsequent calculation of overhead rates for the operating departments are summarized below:

	Building Services	Staff Services	Administration	Graduate Program	Undergraduate Program
Costs	$ 165,000	$ 90,000	$ 330,000	$ 265,000	$ 420,000
Building Services	(165,000)			55,000	110,000
Staff Services		(90,000)		22,500	67,500
Administration			(330,000)	82,500	247,500
	$ 0	$ 0	$ 0	$ 425,000	$ 845,000
Credit hours.............				÷ 20,000	÷ 60,000
Overhead rate per credit hour				$ 21.25	$ 14.08

Step (Sequential) Method

The **step (sequential) method** is an attempt to consider services performed for other service centers. However, recognition of those services is a one-way process. The service centers are arranged in a sequence, and their costs are allocated one after the other. Once a service center's costs are allocated, no other costs are allocated back to that service center even though it may use resources of other service centers. The first service center's costs are allocated to all subsequent service centers and operating departments. The second service center's costs are then allocated to all subsequent service centers and operating departments but not to the first service center. This process continues until the costs of all service centers have been allocated to operating departments. The number of allocation steps will equal the number of service centers.

Since there are three service centers in the Hardknox University School of Business, there are three steps in the allocation process. We begin by allocating the costs of Building Services. The square footage for Staff Services is 2,000; Administration is 8,000; Graduate Program is 10,000; and Undergraduate Program is 20,000. The allocation base, therefore, totals 40,000 square feet. Building Services costs are then prorated over the remaining service centers and operating departments as follows:

Staff Services.	2,000 sq. ft.	5% x $165,000 =	$ 8,250
Administration	8,000	20% x $165,000 =	33,000
Graduate Program	10,000	25% x $165,000 =	41,250
Undergraduate Program . . .	20,000	50% x $165,000 =	82,500
Total	40,000 sq. ft.	Total cost.	$165,000

Staff Services receives an allocation of Building Services costs. This allocation must be added to the costs already charged to the Staff Services Department to determine the allocation of Staff Services costs. The new total Staff Services costs are $98,250 ($90,000 + $8,250). The next step in the allocation process follows:

Administration	20 employees	2/14 x $ 98,250 =	$ 14,035*
Graduate Program	30	3/14 x $ 98,250 =	21,054
Undergraduate Program . .	90	9/14 x $ 98,250 =	63,161
Total	140 employees	Total cost.	$ 98,250

* This figure has been rounded down.

After allocating Building Services and Staff Services costs, the Administration costs for the next step of the allocation are $377,035 ($330,000 + $33,000 + $14,035). These costs are allocated as follows:

Graduate Program	30 employees	25% x $ 377,035 =	$ 94,259
Undergraduate Program . .	90	75% x $ 377,035 =	282,776
Total	120 employees	Total cost.	$ 377,035

The results of service center allocations and the subsequent calculation of overhead rates for the operating departments are summarized as follows:

	Building Services	Staff Services	Administration	Graduate Program	Undergraduate Program
Costs	$ 165,000	$ 90,000	$330,000	$ 265,000	$ 420,000
Building Services	(165,000)	8,250	33,000	41,250	82,500
	$ 0	$ 98,250			
Staff Services		(98,250)	14,035	21,054	63,161
		$ 0	$377,035		
Administration			(377,035)	94,259	282,776
			$ 0	$ 421,563	$ 848,437
Credit hours				÷ 20,000	÷ 60,000
Overhead rate per credit hour				$ 21.08	$ 14.14

How do you arrange the order of service centers? The general rule is to sequence service centers according to the amount of services provided to other service centers—going from greatest to least. What constitutes "greatest amount of service?" One interpretation is the number of other service centers being served. Another is the amount of costs in the service center; the service center with the highest costs has its costs allocated first. It is not clear which interpretation should be applied. The real issue is to set up a sequence that will provide reasonable and logical allocations.

Two other issues influence the way we allocate service center costs: treatment of revenues and allocation of costs by behavior. These issues are presented next.

Treatment of Revenues

Most service centers simply incur costs and generate no revenues. A few, such as a cafeteria, may charge employees or other outside parties for the services they perform. Any revenues generated should be offset against the service center costs. For both the direct method and the step method, we allocate the costs less the offset. In this manner, other service centers and operating departments will not be required to bear costs for which the service center has already been reimbursed.

Allocation of Costs by Behavior

Whenever possible, service center costs should be separated into variable and fixed classifications and allocated separately. This approach helps give a better link between the cost driver and the costs to avoid possible inequities in allocation, as well as to provide data for planning and decision making, performance evaluation and control, and cost management.

As a general rule, variable costs should be charged to other service centers and operating departments on the basis of the actual activity that controls the incurrence of the costs involved. The service centers and departments directly responsible for the incurrence of servicing costs are, therefore, required to bear the cost in proportion to their actual usage of the service involved.

The fixed costs of service centers represent the cost of providing capacity. As such, these costs are most equitably allocated to consuming service centers and operating departments on the basis of predetermined amounts. In this way, the amount of costs allocated is determined in advance of the period in which service is provided. Once determined, the amount does not change from period to period. Typically, the amount allocated is based either on peak-period or long-run average servicing needs. This approach of allocating variable costs on the basis of actual activity and fixed costs using predetermined percentages is sometimes referred to as the **dual-rate method** of allocation.

E THICAL ISSUES FOR COST ALLOCATION

Often, a department's or division's performance is evaluated on the basis of profits after overhead costs have been allocated. Consequently, the choice of cost drivers can affect performance evaluation. One wishing to reward some managers and penalize others could attempt to do so by unethically selecting cost drivers that would shift overhead costs to the desired entities.

When the prices of certain jobs or products are cost based, while others are market driven, managers are often tempted to shift much of the overhead costs to those cost-based jobs or products. This can be accomplished by:

1.   Including items in the overhead cost pool that are not business expenses (e.g., entertainment expenses unrelated to the business).
2.   Arbitrary selection of cost drivers.

When using the step method of allocating support costs, another way to shift overhead costs is:

3.   Arbitrary ordering of support centers.

Clearly, the inclusion of nonbusiness expenses is unethical. The arbitrary selection of cost drivers or ordering of support centers is not as clear. On one hand, management has an obligation to the company's owners to maximize profits using any allowable methods. On the other hand, there is a question of fairness to the parties purchasing the products. Moreover, when the government happens to be the other party, the issue extends to one of fairness to taxpayers.

SUMMARY

One of the objectives in cost accounting is to determine the cost to provide a given service, to manufacture a given quantity of product, or to complete some project. The two most common cost accounting systems for achieving this objective are job cost and process cost systems. A job cost system is appropriate when the product or service is one-of-a-kind, customized, or a special order by a customer. A process cost system is appropriate when the operations represent mass production or continuous processing. This production environment is typically characterized by commingled products, fabricated products, or assembled products.

We accumulate the costs of materials, labor, and overhead separately. Materials are identified as direct or indirect. If direct, the materials are charged directly to the specific product. Indirect materials costs are included in factory overhead costs. Labor costs follow the same type of distinctions.

Factory overhead is budgeted and then divided by a cost driver that relates overhead cost to the products. This yields an overhead rate that is used to allocate overhead to services or products. If overhead consists largely of labor-related costs and labor support costs, such as supervision and fringe benefit costs, the cost driver selected may be direct labor hours. The cost driver "direct labor hours" serves as a bridge between the product and the overhead costs. On the other hand, machine hours may be more appropriate if a large part of the overhead is lubrication, maintenance, and other costs generally related to machine operation. Other cost drivers may, however, be better links between costs and outputs. Both the overhead cost and the cost driver should be budgeted at a normal level of operations rather than just the expected volume for the coming period. Factory overhead rates can be plant wide or departmental, depending on the diversity of the products.

Actual costs are accumulated, and comparisons of actual and estimated costs for each product help management to control costs. Actual overhead incurred can be compared with the overhead applied to the services or products. If actual factory overhead is less than the overhead applied to products (or if overhead is overapplied), the variance is usually closed out to Cost of Goods Sold.

The overhead costs of operating departments include allocations of service center costs. The direct method allocates service center costs directly to operating departments without any intervening allocations to other service centers. The step method involves a sequence of allocations where service center costs are allocated to other service centers as well as to operating departments. Any revenues earned by service centers should be deducted from the costs to be allocated. Ideally, variable costs should allocated separately from fixed costs.

P ROBLEMS FOR REVIEW

Review Problem A

Johnson Schuman owns and operates a plumbing and heating company. Two overhead rates are used in applying overhead costs to the jobs. One rate is based on direct labor hours, and the other is based on machine hours. The machine is a backhoe used in digging service lines. Overhead costs of operating the backhoe are kept separately so that only the jobs requiring the use of the backhoe are charged an overhead rate per machine hour. For the year, $126,000 of general overhead costs were budgeted for 6,000 direct labor hours; and $21,600 of backhoe-related overhead costs were budgeted for 1,800 machine hours (hours of backhoe operation).

On February 1, the cost in Work in Process is $440 and consists of only one job, the job for W. Hartenstine. Costs and other data pertaining to jobs worked on during February are:

	Direct Materials	Direct Labor	Labor Hours	Machine Hours
W. Hartenstine	$ 135	$ 320	16	-
C. Lasher	246	560	28	-
P. Romero	230	365	12	5
M. Tellerico	84	60	3	-
All other jobs	842	14,000	500	160
Totals........................	$1,537	$15,305	559	165

All orders were finished during February with the exception of the Tellerico order which is still in process.

Required:

1. Compute an overhead rate per direct labor hour and an overhead rate per machine hour.

2. Prepare a summary of costs incurred for work performed in February.

3. Determine the cost of work completed during February.

Solution:

1.

$$\frac{\text{Budget of overhead for direct labor hours}}{\text{Budget of direct labor hours}} = \frac{\$126,000}{6,000} = \$21 \text{ per direct labor hour}$$

$$\frac{\text{Budget of overhead for machine hours}}{\text{Budget of machine hours}} = \frac{\$21,600}{1,800} = \$12 \text{ per machine hour}$$

2. Costs of work performed during February:

Materials	$ 1,537
Direct labor	15,305
Applied overhead—labor (559 hours x $21)	11,739
Applied overhead—machine (165 hours x $12)	1,980
Cost of work performed during February	$ 30,561

3. Cost of work completed during February:

Work in process at February 1	$ 440
Add February costs.	30,561
	$ 31,001
Less cost of incomplete Tellerico job	207*
Cost of work completed in February.	$ 30,794

* Work in process at February 28 for Tellerico job:

Direct materials	$ 84
Direct labor	60
Overhead labor (3 hours x $21)	63
Total cost	$ 207

Review Problem B

The Lemler Company manufactures 3-1/2 inch computer disks with two service centers and three producing departments. The budgeted data for June 1998 are:

	Overhead Cost	Labor Hours	Machine Hours	Employees
Service centers:				
Plant Administration	$ 50,000	10,000		20
Personnel	35,000	20,000		25
Producing departments:				
Cutting	225,000	25,000	200,000	150
Assembly	375,000	35,000	150,000	225
Finishing	400,000	30,000	20,000	175

Plant Administration costs are allocated on the basis of labor hours, and the Personnel allocation is based on the number of employees. The overhead rates in Cutting and Assembly are based on machine hours. The overhead rate in Finishing is based on labor hours.

Required:

1. Using the direct method, allocate the service center costs to the producing departments, and calculate overhead rates for each producing department.

2. Using the step method, allocate the service center costs to the producing departments, and calculate overhead rates for each producing department. If necessary, round all allocations to producing departments to the nearest dollar. (Allocate service centers' Plant Administration first and Personnel second.)

Solution:

1.   Direct Method:

	Plant Admin.	Personnel	Cutting	Assembly	Finishing
Total departmental costs	$ 50,000	$ 35,000	$ 225,000	$ 375,000	$ 400,000
Allocation of support costs:					
(25 ÷ 90) x $50,000	(13,889)		13,889		
(35 ÷ 90) x $50,000	(19,444)			19,444	
(30 ÷ 90) x $50,000	(16,667)				16,667
	$ 0				
(150 ÷ 550) x $35,000		(9,546)	9,546		
(225 ÷ 550) x $35,000		(14,318)		14,318	
(175 ÷ 550) x $35,000		(11,136)			11,136
		$ 0	$ 248,435	$ 408,762	$ 427,803
Machine hours			200,000	150,000	
Labor hours					30,000
Departmental overhead rate			$ 1.242	$ 2.725	$ 14.260

2.   Step Method:

	Plant Admin.	Personnel	Cutting	Assembly	Finishing
Total departmental costs	$ 50,000	$ 35,000	$ 225,000	$ 375,000	$ 400,000
Allocation of support costs:					
(20 ÷ 110) x $50,000	(9,091)	9,091			
(25 ÷ 110) x $50,000	(11,364)		11,364		
(35 ÷ 110) x $50,000	(15,909)			15,909	
(30 ÷ 110) x $50,000	(13,636)				13,636
	$ 0	$ 44,091			
(150 ÷ 550) x $44,091		(12,025)	12,025		
(225 ÷ 550) x $44,091		(18,037)		18,037	
(175 ÷ 550) x $44,091		(14,029)			14,029
		$ 0	$ 248,389	$ 408,946	$ 427,665
Machine hours			200,000	150,000	
Labor hours					30,000
Departmental overhead rate			$ 1.242	$ 2.726	$ 14.256

❖ APPENDIX

RECIPROCAL METHOD FOR SERVICE CENTER COSTS

Neither the direct method nor the step method of service center cost allocation recognizes mutual rendering of services among service centers. A third method, the **reciprocal method**, does consider that service centers can perform services in a mutual fashion for each other. The method, however, is more complex than the direct and step methods because it involves solving simultaneous equations. Specifically, the number of simultaneous equations will equal the number of service centers. When this number is large, a computer becomes necessary to solve the equations. For simplicity, we will restrict our analyses to cases with two service centers.

The reciprocal method involves a two-stage procedure:

Stage 1: Set up and solve the following two equations for S_1 and S_2:

$$S_1 = DC_1 + k_1 S_2$$
$$S_2 = DC_2 + k_2 S_1$$

where: S_i = Cost of service center i *after* the reciprocal allocation (i = 1, 2)

DC_i = The direct costs traceable to service center i (i = 1, 2)

k_1 = The percentage of S_2 cost allocated to S_1

k_2 = The percentage of S_1 cost allocated to S_2

Stage 2: Allocate the costs of each service center derived in Stage 1 (i.e., S_1 and S_2) to *all* other service centers and operating departments.

To illustrate, suppose Bleier Brothers, Inc. manufactures portable metal home and office safes. It has two producing departments: the Press Department with directly traceable overhead costs of $200,000 and the Finishing Department with directly traceable overhead costs of $320,000. The departmental overhead rates are based on direct labor hours. There are also two service centers: Storerooms having directly traceable costs of $48,000 and Custodial Services having directly traceable costs of $250,000. Storerooms costs are allocated on the basis of number of storeroom requisitions, while Custodial Services costs are allocated on the basis of square footage of space occupied. These facts are summarized in the following table:

Department	Costs	Requisitions	Square Footage	Labor Hours
Press	$200,000	1,000	8,400	40,000
Finishing	320,000	8,000	1,200	160,000
Storerooms	48,000	–	2,400	–
Custodial Services	250,000	1,000	–	–

First, we set up the two equations for Stage 1:

$$S = \$48,000 + .2C$$
$$C = \$250,000 + .1S$$

where: S = Cost of Storerooms after the reciprocal allocation

C = Cost of Custodial Services after the reciprocal allocation

The allocation percentages were determined as follows:

$$k_1 = 2,400 \div (2,400 + 1,200 + 8,400) = 2,400 \div 12,000 = .2$$

$$k_2 = 1,000 \div (1,000 + 8,000 + 1,000) = 1,000 \div 10,000 = .1$$

Notice that the denominators for calculating the allocation percentages consist of all centers and departments other than the one from which the costs are being allocated. In Stage 2, the costs will be allocated to all other service centers and producing departments.

We now solve the two equations by first substituting the second equation into the first:

$$S = \$48,000 + .2(\$250,000 + .1S)$$

$$.98S = \$98,000$$

$$S = \$100,000$$

Now we obtain C by inserting $100,000 into our second equation:

$$C = \$250,000 + .1(\$100,000)$$

$$C = \$260,000$$

Having solved for S and C, we proceed to Stage 2, where we allocate these costs as follows:

(a) Of the $100,000 from S, 10 percent ($1,000 \div 10,000$) is allocated to Custodial Services, 10 percent ($1,000 \div 10,000$) is also allocated to the Press Department, and 80 percent ($8,000 \div 10,000$) is allocated to the Finishing Department.

(b) Of the $260,000 from C, 20 percent ($2,400 \div 12,000$) is allocated to Storerooms, 70 percent ($8,400 \div 12,000$) is allocated to the Press Department, and 10 percent ($1,200 \div 12,000$) is allocated to the Finishing Department.

The resulting allocations, total producing department overhead costs, and departmental overhead rates are summarized in the following table:

	Storerooms	Custodial Services	Press Department	Finishing Department
Costs	$ 48,000	$250,000	$200,000	$320,000
Storerooms	(100,000)	10,000	10,000	80,000
Custodial Services	52,000	(260,000)	182,000	26,000
Totals (after allocation)	$ 0	$ 0	$ 392,000	$426,000
Direct labor hours			40,000	160,000
Overhead rate per direct labor hour			$ 9.80	$ 2.67

All $298,000 of service center costs ($48,000 + $250,000) have been fully allocated to the producing departments. To confirm: $10,000 + $80,000 + $182,000 + $26,000 = $298,000.

T ERMINOLOGY REVIEW

S UGGESTED READINGS

Bailey, C. D., G. B. Harwood, and W. Hopwood, "Removing the Computational Burden from Reciprocal Cost Allocation," *Journal of Accounting Education*, Fall 1984, pp. 169-174.

Chen, J. T., "Cost Allocation and External Acquisition of Services When Self-Services Exist," *Accounting Review*, July 1983, pp. 600-605.

Dierks, P. A., "Applying Cost Accounting to Transit System Financing," *Management Accounting*, December 1978, pp. 20-23.

Hoshower, L. B., and R. P. Crum, "Controlling Service Center Costs," *Management Accounting*, November 1987, pp. 44-48.

Schwarzbach, H. R., "The Impact of Automation on Accounting for Indirect Costs," *Management Accounting*, December 1985, pp. 45-50.

Sunder, S., "Simpson's Reversal Paradox and Cost Allocation," *Journal of Accounting Research*, Spring 1983, pp. 222-233.

Zimmerman, J. L., "The Costs and Benefits of Cost Allocations," *Accounting Review*, July 1979, pp. 504-521.

Q UESTIONS FOR REVIEW AND DISCUSSION

1. Under what conditions would a job cost system be appropriate? A process cost system?

2. What is the distinguishing characteristic of a commingled product?

3. What is the difference between a fabricated product and an assembled product?

4. Describe briefly how costs flow through the accounts for a manufacturer. How would this change for a service organization?

5. What is a bill of materials? Why is it important to the acquisition of materials?

6. What are the cost elements associated with the materials acquisition process? Which ones are likely to be included in the cost of materials charged as direct or indirect materials?

7. What are the three criteria for determining whether materials are direct or indirect?

8. What are the cost elements associated with labor? Which ones are likely to be included in the cost of direct or indirect labor?

9. Explain why a budget is used in costing factory overhead rather than assigning actual overhead cost after the end of the year.

10. What is the basis for selecting a cost driver to be used in costing factory overhead?

11. What account is credited when factory overhead is added to work in process?

12. How is the difference between the actual factory overhead and the overhead applied to the products handled at the end of the year?

13. Explain under what circumstances departmental rates are preferred to a plant-wide factory overhead rate.

14. What is the difference between theoretical and practical capacity?

15. Explain the difference between practical capacity and normal volume.

16. If the company does not expect to operate at normal volume during the next year, why should the products be costed by using an overhead rate determined at normal volume?

17. What is the difference between a service center and an operating department?

18. How do service center costs enter into the final cost of products and services?

19. How are service center costs allocated to other service centers and operating departments under the direct method? Under the step method?

20. If a service center generates revenues, how do these revenues enter into the allocation of service costs to other service centers and operating departments?

21. Why is the reciprocal method for service center allocation more justifiable than the step method or direct method? **(Appendix)**

22. Describe the two stages of cost allocation under the reciprocal method. **(Appendix)**

E XERCISES

4-1. Cost of Orders.   Costello Repair Services specializes in the routine maintenance and repair of power lawn mowers and other small machines. Three orders (#721, #722, and #723) were started and completed in March. Materials costing $41 were used on order #721; materials costing $17 were used on order #722; and materials costing $8 were used on order #723. Labor is paid at a uniform rate of $8.50 per hour, and overhead is applied at 80 percent of labor cost. During the month, 3 labor hours were used for order #721, 2 hours for order #722, and 4 hours for order #723.

Required:
Compute the cost of each order, showing separately the cost of materials, labor, and overhead.

4-2. Entries for Cost Flow.   Svensson Tool & Die Company of Malmo, Sweden, spent Skr6,400,600 for direct materials used in April for the production of various orders. Direct labor cost for the month was Skr2,453,800. Factory overhead is costed to production at 150 percent of direct labor cost. No orders were in process at the beginning and the end of the month. All work was delivered to customers.

Required:

Using T-accounts, show how the costs entered production and were transferred to Finished Goods and to Cost of Goods Sold.

4-3. Overtime and Late-Shift Labor Costs.   Evan's Enterprises operates its factory on a two-shift basis and pays a late-shift differential of 15 percent above the regular wage rate of $18 per hour. The company also pays a premium of 50 percent for overtime work. During 1998, work occurred in the following categories:

Number of hours worked during the regular shift	10,000
Number of overtime hours for regular shift workers	300
Number of hours worked during the late shift	6,000

Required:

1. Compute the total cost to assign to direct labor.
2. Compute the amount of labor-related cost to assign to factory overhead.

4-4. Factory Overhead Rates.   Jensen Supply Company normally operates at 450,000 direct labor hours a year. At this level of operation, variable overhead has been budgeted at $337,500, and fixed overhead has been budgeted at $1,012,500.

Required:

1. Compute the total factory overhead rate per direct labor hour at normal volume.
2. Determine the variable portion of the overhead rate at normal volume. What would be the variable overhead rate if normal volume were 400,000 direct labor hours instead of 450,000 hours? Assume that variable cost changes in direct proportion with hours of operation.
3. Determine the fixed portion of the overhead rate at normal volume. What would be the fixed overhead rate if 400,000 direct labor hours were considered normal volume? Explain why the rate differs depending on the level set as normal volume.

4-5. Overhead Rates for a Service Enterprise.   Mountain Horn Hostel was purchased by a naturalist who hopes to show people the value of wildlife and also to provide them with a pleasant vacation retreat. Costs are budgeted for the year and will be allocated over the 120 days of the tourist season. The hostel has a normal volume of 100 persons per day. Using the cost information, the owner hopes to develop a billing rate per person per day that will yield an acceptable profit.

Costs for the year were estimated as follows:

Kitchen and dining room costs	$ 172,000
Housekeeping costs	68,000
Taxes and insurance	18,000
Repairs and maintenance	21,000
Utilities	37,000
Grounds and pool maintenance	11,000
Salaries of drivers and guides	54,000
Operating costs—buses and vans	9,000
Depreciation—buses and vans	18,000
Depreciation—buildings	12,000
Total estimated cost	$ 420,000

A friend of the naturalist offers advice: "Your idea of normal volume is full capacity. What about rainy days and cancellations? You'll be lucky to have 80 people a day. And if snow comes early, count on a 100-day season. That's my idea of normal."

Required:

1. Compute a cost per person per day using the naturalist's concept of normal.

2. Compute a cost per person per day using the friend's figures.

3. Explain the difference in the results of the two computations.

4-6. Applied Factory Overhead.   Avery Co. uses a predetermined factory overhead rate based on direct labor hours. For the month of October, Avery's budgeted overhead was $300,000 based on a volume of 100,000 direct labor hours. Actual overhead amounted to $325,000 with actual direct labor hours totaling 110,000.

Required:

How much was the overapplied or underapplied overhead?

(AICPA adapted)

4-7. Applied Factory Overhead.   Jabotinsky Company, an Israeli manufacturer of olive wood products, uses a predetermined factory overhead application rate based on direct labor cost. For 1997, Jabotinsky's budgeted factory overhead was 900,000 shekels, based on a volume of 50,000 direct labor hours and a budgeted wage rate of 9 shekels per hour. Actual factory overhead amounted to 963,000 shekels. For 1997, the overapplied factory overhead was 33,000 shekels.

Required:

Compute the amount of actual direct labor cost for 1997.

4-8. Overhead Rate Computation.   Davis Company applies overhead using direct labor cost. The following T-accounts pertain to 1998 operations:

Work in Process			Factory Overhead	
(a)	10,000		70,000	60,000
(b)	50,000	120,000		
(c)	20,000			
(d)	?			
(e)	?			

(a) Beginning balance; **(b)** Direct materials; **(c)** Direct labor; **(d)** Factory overhead; **(e)** Ending balance

Required:

Compute the overhead rate that was used for 1998.

4-9. Flow of Cost.   During 1998, Danzi Company purchased materials costing $152,600. Materials requisitioned for jobs cost $98,000, and indirect materials costing $42,000 were charged to Factory Overhead. Factory payrolls were $212,000 with income taxes withheld of $43,000 and FICA taxes withheld of $17,000. Indirect labor of $71,000 included in the payrolls was charged to Factory Overhead. All other labor was direct labor charged to the jobs. Factory overhead was applied to the jobs at the rate of $8 per machine hour. During the year, the company operated at 45,000 machine hours and incurred factory overhead costs of $259,000 (in addition to the indirect materials and indirect labor previously stated). Depreciation of $47,000 was included in the $259,000 of factory overhead costs.

Products costing $465,000 were completed during the year, and the cost of goods sold was $480,000. At the beginning of the year, Danzi had the following balances:

Materials	$ 27,000
Work in Process	48,000
Finished Goods	34,000

Required:

Use T-accounts to show the flow of costs for the 1998 transactions of Danzi Company. Close out Factory Overhead to Cost of Goods Sold.

4-10. Analysis of Work in Process. The following debits (credits) appeared in Worrell Corporation's Work in Process account for March 1996:

March 1, balance	$ 12,000
March 31, direct materials.	40,000
March 31, direct labor	30,000
March 31, factory overhead	27,000
March 31, to finished goods	(100,000)

Worrell applies overhead to production at a predetermined rate of 90 percent of direct labor cost. Job #232, the only job still in process at the end of March 1996, has been charged with factory overhead of $2,250.

Required:
What was the amount of direct materials charged to Job #232?

(AICPA adapted)

4-11. Overhead Variance Computation. Zaleski Corporation applies overhead on the basis of machine hours. Budget and actual data for direct labor hours, machine hours, and overhead for 1997 are as follows:

	Budget	*Actual*
Direct labor hours	20,000	19,600
Machine hours	50,000	48,000
Factory overhead costs	$400,000	$389,000

Required:
Compute the overapplied or underapplied overhead for 1997.

4-12. Incomplete Data. Kyoto Corporation, a Japanese manufacturer of television sets, provides the following data for 1999:

Budgeted overhead cost	¥20,000,000
Budgeted activity	20,000 machine hours
Actual overhead cost	¥21,500,000
Overapplied overhead	¥500,000

Required:
Determine the amount of machine hours worked at Kyoto Corporation during 1999.

4-13. Departmental and Plant-Wide Overhead Rates. Yellowhouse Toy Company manufactures small battery-powered cars that children under eight years of age can drive in a house or yard. Currently, the company has two models: Speed Demon and Luxury Classic. Both cars sell well. The company processes the cars in three departments: Fabrication, Assembly, and Painting. The departmental budgets for the current year are as follows:

	Overhead Costs	*Machine Hours*
Fabrication	$ 730,000	25,000
Assembly	260,000	13,000
Painting	10,000	12,000
Totals	$1,000,000	50,000

The estimated machine hours for 50 units of each model are:

	Speed Demon	*Luxury Classic*
Fabrication	50	90
Assembly	75	40
Painting	35	20
Totals	160	150

Required:
1. Compute overhead rates for each department and for the plant.

2. Compute the estimated overhead cost of 50 units of each model using:
   (a) A plant-wide rate.
   (b) Departmental rates.
3. Explain why a different cost exists for the cars depending on the use of a plant-wide rate or departmental rates.

4-14. Divisional and Facility-Wide Overhead Rates.   Goshen Research Laboratories performs contract research for government and commercial applications. It is located in the Salt Lake Valley where it has access to a labor market with advanced scientific and engineering degrees. Utah has several major universities graduating people who want to pursue careers while remaining in Utah. The company consists of six divisions with appropriate support and ancillary facilities. Each division is housed in its own building within the industrial complex.

The company bills its customers based on costs of research work. Costs included are for direct equipment, direct labor hours, and overhead. The current overhead rate used for billing purposes is the facility-wide rate of $31.25 per hour for this year. The overhead costs and labor hours by division are as follows:

	Overhead (in Thousands)	Labor Hours (in Thousands)
Thermal	$ 3,760	160
Solar................................	13,120	800
Aquatic.............................	2,975	170
Laser................................	113,400	2,250
Gases	16,471	910
Mechanical	37,290	1,695
Totals	$ 187,016	5,985

Several customers, particularly government agencies, question the overhead rate because it is too high for their projects.

Required:
1. Calculate overhead rates for the overall facility and for each of the six divisions.
2. Show how much overhead would be charged to each of the following projects with a facility-wide overhead rate and then with divisional rates:

   (a) Project #96106: *Soil Conservation of Semi-Arid Lands.* (Funded by the U.S. Department of the Interior.) During 1996, this project had 31,400 hours of work recorded. Sixty percent of those hours were from the Thermal Division, and 40 percent were from the Solar Division.

   (b) Project #96111: *Coal Gasification Project.* (Funded 30 percent by the State of Utah, 50 percent by the U.S. Department of Energy, and 20 percent by a private utilities company.) This project absorbed 47,500 hours, of which 23,200 were in the Laser Division and the remaining hours in the Mechanical Division.

3. Which of these two project sponsor groups would have a more legitimate complaint about the overhead rate? Explain.

4-15. Departmental Factory Overhead Rates.   Chin Chow Products, Inc. operates with two manufacturing departments. The Shaping and Forming Department uses more machinery and equipment, and the overhead rate is based on machine hours. Assembly is more labor intensive, and the overhead rate is based on direct labor hours. Budgeted hours and budgeted overhead at normal volume are given below for each department:

	Departments	
	Shaping and Forming	Assembly
Budgeted machine hours	150,000	
Budgeted direct labor hours		50,000
Budgeted overhead.........................	$ 450,000	$ 250,000

Order #878 required 50 hours of machine time in Shaping and Forming and 30 direct labor hours in Assembly.

Required:
1. Compute the overhead rates for each of the two departments.
2. Determine the factory overhead applied to Order #878 in each of the two departments.

4-16. Direct Method, Step Method, and Ethical Analysis.   Jacksboro Manufacturing, Inc. shows the following estimated operating statistics for this year:

	Personnel Transactions Processed	Number of Employees	Space Occupied (Square Feet)
Service centers:			
Utilities	10	80	1,000
Cafeteria	20	25	8,000
Personnel	15	50	2,000
Producing departments:			
A	80	900	70,000
B	20	600	30,000

Budgeted overhead costs for the year and the cost driver for each department are as follows:

	Overhead	Cost Driver
Utilities	$ 30,000	Square footage
Cafeteria	20,000	Number of employees
Personnel	10,000	Number of personnel transactions
Producing Dept. A	80,000	Machine hours
Producing Dept. B	60,000	Direct labor hours

Producing Dept. A budgeted 20,000 machine hours for the year, while Producing Dept. B budgeted 15,000 direct labor hours.

Required:
1. Using the direct method, allocate the service center costs to the producing departments, and calculate overhead rates for each producing department.
2. Using the step method, allocate the service center costs to the producing departments, and calculate overhead rates for each producing department. Allocate service center costs in the order of utilities, cafeteria, and personnel. If necessary, round all allocations to producing departments to the nearest dollar.
3. Suppose Producing Dept. A sells its products to the government on a cost-plus basis, while Producing Dept. B sells its products on the open market where the price is determined by supply and demand. Assume the step method of allocation is used and that any ordering of the three service centers is permitted. How might management decide on the ordering of the service centers? Discuss the ethical issues.

1-2-3

4-17. Direct and Step Methods for Developing Overhead Rates.   Dabling Creations is in the process of developing overhead rates for the coming year. The budgeted information for its three support functions (Repair, Factory Office, and Personnel) and two operating departments (Fabrication and Finishing) is as follows:

	Repair	Factory Office	Personnel	Fabrication	Finishing	Total
Overhead	$ 22,500	$ 29,000	$ 21,000	$ 44,250	$ 46,750	$163,500
Service hours	200	800	1,200	9,000	7,000	18,200
Square footage	2,000	1,000	500	6,500	8,000	18,000
Number of employees . .	30	20	80	240	620	990

The Repair Department is responsible for providing maintenance to all departments. Its costs are allocated using service hours as the cost driver. Factory Office includes factory scheduling, storage, and all accounting functions. Its costs are allocated using square footage. Personnel handles the hiring, training, and terminating of all employees for the company. Its costs are allocated using number of employees as the cost driver. Fabrication is machine intensive, so the cost driver is machine hours. Fabrication has budgeted 10,000 machine hours. Finishing is labor intensive and uses direct labor hours as the cost driver. The budget calls for 20,000 direct labor hours during the period.

Dabling Creations has used the direct method of allocating support function costs in the past. For the coming year, management is considering using the more sophisticated step method.

Required:
1. Calculate the overhead rates for Fabrication and Finishing assuming the support functions are allocated using the direct method.
2. Calculate the overhead rates for Fabrication and Finishing assuming the support functions are allocated using the step method. Use the sequence of Repair, Factory Office, and Personnel to allocate the costs of the support functions.
3. Discuss whether Dabling Creations should incur costs to switch over to the step method.

4-18. Reciprocal Method of Allocating Service Center Costs (Appendix). Zurich Cheese Company, a Swiss manufacturer of cheese products, has two service centers and two producing departments. Data for October are as follows:

	Service Centers	
	Maintenance	Utilities
Costs (Swiss francs)	46,000	30,000
Services provided to:		
Maintenance.	—	10%
Utilities	20%	—
Producing Department 1	40%	30%
Producing Department 2	40%	60%
Totals	100%	100%

Required:
Using the reciprocal method, allocate the costs of the service centers to the producing departments.

4-19. Reciprocal Method of Allocating Service Center Costs (Appendix). Wilner Airlines has two operating departments (Freight and Passenger) and two service centers (Maintenance and Administration). The following table shows June 1998 data:

	Service Centers		Operating Departments	
	Maintenance	Administration	Freight	Passenger
Costs	$ 630,000	$ 950,000	$ 1,800,500	$ 5,260,470
Labor hours	8,000	9,000	30,000	51,000
Number of employees	40	50	80	200

Maintenance costs are allocated using labor hours, while Administration costs are allocated using number of employees.

Required:
Using the reciprocal method, allocate the costs of the service centers to the operating departments.

P ROBLEMS

4-20. Factory Overhead Rates.　Guadalajara Glass Company, a Mexican manufacturer, produces a glass product that has a direct materials cost (in pesos) of M$21 per unit and a direct labor cost of M$14 per unit. Factory overhead is applied to production on the basis of machine hours with five units of product produced each machine hour. Under normal conditions, the company operates at 150,000 machine hours each year and produces 750,000 units of product. At this level, the company budgeted M$900,000 for variable overhead and M$600,000 for fixed overhead.

Required:

1. Compute the overhead rate per machine hour at normal operating volume.
2. Determine the total unit cost of the product at the normal operating volume.
3. If normal operating volume were 200,000 machine hours, what would be the overhead rate per machine hour?
4. Suppose the company operated at 200,000 machine hours and incurred overhead costs totaling M$1,960,000 during the year. Would the overhead be overapplied or underapplied? Compute the amount. (Use 150,000 machine hours as normal operating volume.)

4-21. Fixed Overhead and Hours of Operation.　Jack Bickham has prepared a budget of overhead costs for Sutherland Industries, Inc. at the normal level of operations and at the expected level of operations for the next year, shown as follows:

	Normal Level	*Expected Level*
Direct labor hours	150,000	120,000
Variable overhead	$ 750,000	$ 600,000
Fixed overhead	1,200,000	1,200,000
Total overhead	$ 1,950,000	$ 1,800,000

Bickham states, "We cost our products by using an overhead rate computed at normal volume; but it seems to me that if we used a rate computed at expected volume, we wouldn't have such a large overhead variance at the end of the year. What makes the variance worse is that we have so much fixed overhead."

During the next year, the company operated at 120,000 direct labor hours and incurred overhead costs as follows:

Variable overhead	$ 605,000
Fixed overhead	1,200,000
Total overhead	$ 1,805,000

Required:

1. Compute an overhead rate per direct labor hour at normal operating volume.
2. Compute an overhead rate per direct labor hour at the expected level of operations.
3. Determine the underapplied or overapplied overhead amount when the rate is figured at normal volume and when the rate is figured at expected volume.
4. Point out the fallacy in Bickham's argument.
5. Is Bickham correct in stating that the variance is worse because of the relatively large fixed overhead? Explain.

4-22. Cost of Service.　Calico Library, located in a small western city, depends on donations and membership dues for support. The membership dues are applied to the annual cost of operation, and donations are used to make additions to the library.

In 1998, the library plans to add bookmobile service for subscribers living in outlying areas. Each person would pay an annual subscription fee, based on miles driven and number of persons served in each district. Miles driven and number of persons to be served by the bookmobile have been estimated for 1998 as follows:

District	Miles Per Year	Number of Subscribers
Dry Canyon	6,000	600
Sand Valley	1,000	200
Castle District	2,000	400
Little Stream	5,000	800
Totals	14,000	2,000

Costs of van operation each year, including depreciation, have been estimated at $10,500 plus the salary of a driver at $31,500. These costs are to be apportioned first on the basis of mileage driven per district and then by the number of subscribers per district.

The library board believes that the subscribers in outlying areas should also bear their share of general library overhead estimated at $210,000 for 1998. A total of 50,000 subscribers (including those in outlying areas) are to share this cost.

Required:

1. Based on the information given, determine the fee for a subscriber in each district served by the bookmobile.

2. If the membership dues are also based on full operating costs, should the dues rate change as a result of the bookmobile service? Explain.

4-23. Costs of Individual Orders.   During August, Altamont Machine Company started production orders 116, 117, and 118. Order 115 was in process at the beginning of the month with direct materials costs of $35,000, direct labor costs of $21,000, and applied factory overhead of $25,200. During the month, direct materials were requisitioned, and direct labor was identified with the orders as follows:

Order No.	Direct Materials	Direct Labor
115	—	$ 26,000
116	$ 39,000	45,000
117	53,000	47,000
118	47,000	16,000

Factory overhead is applied to the orders at 120 percent of direct labor cost. Orders 115, 116, and 117 were completed and sold in August. Order 118 was incomplete on August 31.

Required:

1. Determine the cost of each order by cost element.

2. What was the total cost of direct materials requisitioned in August and charged to Work in Process?

3. Determine the cost of goods sold in August.

4. What was the Work in Process balance on August 31?

4-24. Cost of Contracts.   Pfeffer Contracting Company repaves highways and does excavation work. On January 1, 1999, the Eastern Highway Project was in process with costs as follows:

Materials	$ 810,000
Labor	420,000
Contract overhead	210,000

During 1999, the company incurred costs for various projects as follows:

	Eastern Highway	State University	Clover Estates	Route 691	Market Street	Totals
Materials .	$ 215,000	$ 1,780,000	$ 170,000	$ 3,720,000	$ 350,000	$ 6,235,000
Labor	170,000	1,420,000	590,000	1,480,000	260,000	3,920,000
Overhead .	85,000	710,000	295,000	740,000	130,000	1,960,000
Totals . .	$ 470,000	$ 3,910,000	$ 1,055,000	$ 5,940,000	$ 740,000	$ 12,115,000

Contract overhead is costed to the projects at 50 percent of labor cost. Actual overhead cost for 1999 was $2,090,000. Pfeffer Contracting Company uses a Contracts in Process instead of a Work in Process account. Projects completed are charged directly to Cost of Contracts Completed.

All projects, with the exceptions of the State University Project and the Market Street Project, were completed during the year.

Required:

1. Determine the costs transferred to Cost of Contracts Completed. Use T-accounts to show this transfer.
2. Using T-accounts, close the underapplied or overapplied contract overhead directly to Cost of Contracts Completed.
3. Determine the total cost of the Eastern Highway Project and the cost of each contract in process at the end of the year. (Show detail by project and cost element.)

4-25. Cost Flows.   A summary of manufacturing cost transactions for Modern Motors, Inc. for 1997 is as follows:

(a)   Materials costing $995,650 were purchased from suppliers on account.

(b)   Materials were requisitioned during the year as follows:

Direct materials	$ 791,000
Indirect materials (factory overhead)	147,000

Included were direct materials requisitions of $21,000 for Order 115.

(c)   The factory payroll for the year amounted to $488,000. FICA taxes withheld was $33,000; income taxes withheld was $87,000; and the amount paid to the employees was $368,000.

(d)   The factory labor was utilized as follows:

Direct labor	$ 338,000
Indirect labor (factory overhead)	150,000

Included in the direct labor cost was $22,500 identified by labor time tickets with Order 115.

(e)   Factory overhead was applied to production at 150 percent of the direct labor cost.

(f)   Factory overhead cost during the year, in addition to the cost of indirect materials and indirect labor previously mentioned, amounted to $173,000. Included in this amount was depreciation of $52,000. Credit the balance of this cost to Accounts Payable.

(g)   Orders costing $1,117,000 were completed during the year. Order 115 is included among the completed orders.

(h)   Goods costing $944,000 were sold to customers on credit terms for $1,552,000.

Required:

1. Record transactions (a) through (h) using T-accounts, and close the factory overhead variance to Cost of Goods Sold.

2. Compute the total cost and cost per unit of Order 115 assuming that 15,000 units were produced for that order.

4-26. Cost Flows. The Paddle Shop, Inc. keeps accounting and cost records on a personal computer. During the month of January, data were lost as a result of errors made by a new operator. Fortunately, some data were retrieved and are set forth as follows:

(a) The debit balance in the Payroll account was $130,000. This balance included $20,000 in indirect labor that was charged to the Factory Overhead account.

(b) The debit balance in the Factory Overhead account totaled $166,000. This balance included the indirect labor amount in (a).

(c) Factory overhead is applied to the products at 150 percent of direct labor cost.

(d) The Work in Process account showed a January 1 balance of $91,000. Materials requisitioned and charged to Work in Process during the period amounted to $98,000. The balance in Work in Process on January 31 was $82,000.

(e) The Finished Goods balance at January 1 was $48,000.

(f) Cost of Goods Sold had a debit balance of $389,000. This amount did not include underapplied or overapplied factory overhead.

Required:
1. From the information given, determine the direct labor and the factory overhead applied to production in January.
2. What was the cost of work completed and transferred to the finished goods inventory for the month?
3. Determine the finished goods inventory cost on January 31.
4. Determine the underapplied or overapplied factory overhead in January.

4-27. Incomplete Data. You find that the cost records at Sabath Tool & Die Company have been poorly maintained. Some information has been entered, but other information is missing. Fortunately, the information given is correct.

The costs for Jobs 686, 687, and 688 are to be determined. The direct materials cost is $528 for Job 686 and $715 for Job 687. The cost of direct materials requisitioned during the month for all other jobs, except Job 688, is $4,820. No jobs were in process at the beginning of the month. The total cost of direct materials requisitioned during the month was $6,913.

Labor is paid at a uniform rate of $10 an hour. Job 686 required 82 direct labor hours, and Job 688 required 43 direct labor hours. A total of 760 direct labor hours were worked during the month. The direct labor cost of all other jobs, with the exception of the three jobs being considered, was $5,850.

Two machine hours are used for each direct labor hour. Overhead is applied at a rate of $4 per machine hour. The actual overhead cost for the month was $6,320. Jobs 686, 687, and 688 were completed during the month.

Required:
1. Compute the costs for Jobs 686, 687, and 688. Show costs by cost element.
2. Determine the amount of factory overhead applied to all orders during the month.
3. What was the amount of the underapplied or overapplied factory overhead?
4. You have received a telephone call from the plant manager requesting the total cost per unit on Job 686. There were 50 units of product on this order. What is the total cost per unit?

4-28. Factory Overhead Cost Control. Kathryn Kjaersgaard is the supervisor of Department 5 in the Arhus plant of Copenhagen Instrument Company. She is responsible for the cost of direct materials, direct labor, and variable overhead costs incurred in this department. The fixed overhead cost is not under her jurisdiction.

During a recent week, actual factory overhead costs (in Danish krone) for Department 5 were as follows:

Actual Variable Overhead:

Indirect materials	DKr19,400	
Supplies	14,200	
Telephone	700	
Heat and light	1,600	
Power	7,000	
Repairs and maintenance	3,200	
Total variable overhead		DKr 46,100

Actual Fixed Overhead:

Indirect labor	DKr61,000	
Supervision	42,000	
Heat and light	7,000	
Repairs and maintenance	9,000	
Depreciation	21,000	
Total fixed overhead		140,000
Total actual overhead		DKr186,100

The department operated at 45,000 direct labor hours during the week. A budget of factory overhead for 45,000 direct labor hours is as follows:

Budgeted Variable Overhead:

Indirect materials	DKr16,500	
Supplies	12,400	
Telephone	700	
Heat and light	1,550	
Power	7,000	
Repairs and maintenance	2,350	
Total variable overhead		DKr 40,500

Budgeted Fixed Overhead:

Indirect labor	DKr61,000	
Supervision	42,000	
Heat and light	7,000	
Repairs and maintenance	9,000	
Depreciation	21,000	
Total fixed overhead		140,000
Total budgeted overhead		DKr180,500

Variable overhead is costed to the products at the rate of DKr0.9 per direct labor hour, and fixed overhead is costed to the products at the rate of DKr2.8 per direct labor hour.

Required:

1. How much overhead was costed to the products during the week?
2. Compute the underapplied or overapplied factory overhead for the week.
3. Prepare a report for Kjaersgaard showing all actual variable overhead costs, all budgeted variable overhead costs, and variances for each cost listed.
4. Identify any items of overhead that are over the budgeted amount by more than 10 percent.

4-29. Automation and Cost. In 1998, Pioneer Motors, Inc. automated its production lines. As a result, virtually all of the labor that directly related to creating the products was eliminated. A smaller labor force is required, and the remaining workers are primarily monitoring machine operation and product quality. What was once classified as direct labor is now reclassified as indirect labor.

Total budgeted manufacturing costs for 1998 as a labor-intensive operation are compared with the budgeted costs for 1999 with a machine-intensive operation, as shown in the following table:

	Budgets	
	Labor-Intensive Operation	Machine-Intensive Operation
Direct materials	$ 4,870,000	$ 4,630,000
Direct labor.	3,260,000	0
Supervision	730,000	550,000
Indirect labor	880,000	2,720,000
Payroll taxes and fringe benefits	421,000	344,000
Supplies and indirect materials	310,000	325,000
Lubrication	76,000	217,000
Power.	142,000	319,000
Maintenance—equipment	115,000	436,000
Repairs—equipment	132,000	117,000
Depreciation—equipment.	48,000	382,000
Taxes and insurance	126,000	133,000
Heat and light	38,000	46,000
Other utilities	17,000	19,000
Depreciation—plant	80,000	80,000

When the company operated with more labor, overhead was assigned to the products on the basis of 400,000 direct labor hours. Under the automated operation, the rate is based on 500,000 machine hours.

One of the production managers states that the total overhead costs of manufacturing are higher than they were before and that the company did not save anything by automating the production lines. The vice-president of production disagrees: "While total overhead costs may be higher, the increased productivity makes it possible for us to serve a growing market with lower costs per unit of product."

The following table shows the cost data for a large order assuming it was produced under each production process:

	Labor-Intensive Operation	Machine-Intensive Operation
Direct materials	$ 640,000	$ 615,000
Direct labor.	$ 680,000	$ 0
Direct labor hours	60,000	0
Machine hours	0	30,000
Number of product units	100,000	100,000

Required:
1. Compute an overhead rate for both the labor-intensive operation and the machine-intensive operation.
2. Determine the total and unit cost of the large order under both types of operation.
3. Comment on the positions taken by the production manager and the vice-president of production.

1-2-3

4-30. Departmental and Plant-Wide Rates.   Purinton Printing Products has one division that makes rollers for printing presses. The rollers vary in size from 1/4 inch to 8 inches in diameter. Fabrication and Finishing are the two departments within this division. The company uses machine hours as the base for allocating factory overhead costs to products. The budgeted data for the two departments for the coming year are:

	Fabrication	Finishing	Totals
Machine hours	90,000	30,000	120,000
Overhead costs	$ 2,232,000	$ 252,600	$ 2,484,600

The machine hours for a batch of 100 units for two different products are given as:

	Fabrication	Finishing	Totals
1/2" roller	4	8	12
6-1/2" roller	9	6	15

The prime costs per batch for these two products are:

	1/2" roller	6-1/2" roller
Direct materials:		
Fabrication	$ 18.90	$ 33.40
Finishing	9.70	11.50
Direct labor:		
Fabrication	48.10	187.30
Finishing	37.80	32.20
Total prime costs	$114.50	$264.40

Required:

1. Compute the departmental overhead rates for Fabrication and Finishing using machine hours as the cost driver.

2. Compute a plant-wide overhead rate using machine hours as the cost driver.

3. Compute the overhead cost per batch of product assuming:
  (a) The plant-wide rate.
  (b) The departmental rates.

4. Is the total cost *per unit of each product* distorted by using a plant-wide rate instead of departmental rates? Explain with supporting computations.

1-2-3

4-31. Departmental Rates Versus Company-Wide Rates.   Kool-Air Galore, Inc. manufactures air conditioners for automobiles. The company designs its products with flexibility to accommodate many makes and models of automobiles. The main products are MaxiFlow and Alaska. MaxiFlow uses a few complex fabricated parts, but these have been found easy to assemble and test. On the other hand, Alaska uses many standard parts but has complex assembly and test processes. The following planning information is available for 1996 for each department:

	Overhead Cost	Machine Hours
Radiator parts fabrication	$ 80,000	10,000
Radiator assembly, weld, and test	100,000	20,000
Compressor parts fabrication	120,000	5,000
Compressor assembly and test	180,000	45,000
Total	$ 480,000	80,000

A production batch of 20 units requires the following number of hours in each department:

	MaxiFlow	Alaska
Radiator parts fabrication	28	16
Radiator assembly, weld, and test	30	74
Compressor parts fabrication	32	8
Compressor assembly and test	26	66
Total	116	164

Required:

1. Compute the departmental overhead rates using machine hours as the cost driver.

2. Compute a company-wide overhead rate using machine hours as the cost driver.

3. Compute the overhead cost per batch of MaxiFlow and Alaska assuming:

(a) The company-wide rate.

(b) The departmental rates.

4. Compute the total cost per unit of MaxiFlow and Alaska assuming:

(a) The company-wide rate.

(b) The departmental rates.

5. Is one product affected more than the other by use of departmental rates rather than a company-wide rate? Why or why not?

1-2-3

4-32. Service Center Allocation and Dual-Rate Method. MumsDay Corporation manufactures a complete line of fiberglass attaché cases and suitcases. MumsDay has three manufacturing departments—Molding, Component, and Assembly—and two service centers—Power and Maintenance.

The sides of the cases are manufactured in the Molding Department. The frames, hinges, locks, etc., are manufactured in the Component Department. The cases are completed in the Assembly Department. Varying amounts of materials, time, and effort are required for each of the various cases. The Power Department and the Maintenance Department provide services to the three manufacturing departments.

MumsDay has always used a plant-wide overhead rate. Direct labor hours are used to assign the overhead to its product. The predetermined rate is calculated by dividing the company's total estimated overhead by the total estimated direct labor hours to be worked in the three manufacturing departments.

Whit Portlock, manager of Cost Accounting, has recommended that MumsDay use departmental overhead rates. The planned operating costs and expected levels of activity for the coming year have been developed by Portlock and are presented by department in the following schedules (000s omitted):

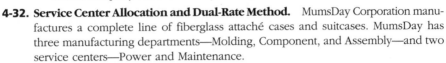

	Manufacturing Departments		
	Molding	*Component*	*Assembly*
Departmental activity measures:			
Direct labor hours	500	2,000	1,500
Machine hours	875	125	0
Departmental costs:			
Raw materials	$ 12,400	$ 30,000	$ 1,250
Direct labor	3,500	20,000	12,000
Variable overhead	3,500	10,000	16,500
Fixed overhead	17,500	6,200	6,100
Total departmental costs	$ 36,900	$ 66,200	$ 35,850
Use of service centers:			
Maintenance—estimated usage in labor hours for coming year	90	25	10
Power (in kilowatt hours):			
Estimated usage for coming year	360	320	120
Practical capacity	500	350	150

	Service Centers	
	Power	*Maintenance*
Departmental activity measures:		
Practical capacity	1,000 KWH	Adjustable
Estimated usage in coming year	800 KWH	125 hours
Departmental costs:		
Materials and supplies	$ 5,000	$1,500
Variable labor	1,400	2,225
Fixed overhead	12,000	275
Total service center costs	$18,400	$4,000

Required:

1. Calculate the plant-wide overhead rate for MumsDay Corporation for the coming year using the same method as used in the past.
2. Whit Portlock has been asked to develop departmental overhead rates for comparison with the plant-wide rate. The following steps are to be used in developing the departmental rates:
    (a) The Maintenance Department costs should be allocated to the three manufacturing departments using the direct method.
    (b) The Power Department costs should be allocated to the three manufacturing departments using the dual-rate method, i.e., the fixed costs allocated according to practical capacity and the variable costs according to planned usage.
    (c) Calculate departmental overhead rates for the three manufacturing departments using a machine hour base for the Molding Department and a direct labor hour base for the Component and Assembly Departments.
3. Should MumsDay Corporation use a plant-wide rate or departmental rates to assign overhead to its products? Explain your answer.

(ICMA adapted)

1-2-3

4-33. Support Function Allocation—Direct and Step Methods.   Thatcher Women's Clothing of Manchester, England, specializes in designer skirts which it manufactures to customer order. The budgeted data (in British pounds) for its main plant for 1996 are:

	Support Functions		Producing Departments	
	Adminis-tration	Mainten-ance	Cutting	Sewing
Overhead cost	£ 80,000	£ 30,000	£ 500,000	£ 600,000
Labor hours		10,000	50,000	80,000
Machine hours			100,000	150,000
Square meters of space occupied	4,500	7,000	50,000	25,000

During the year, Skibells Co. placed an order that was started and completed by year's end. Data for this job include the following information:

	Cutting	Sewing
Direct materials cost	£ 95,000	£ 21,000
Direct labor hours	7,000	15,000
Direct labor cost	£ 56,000	£120,000
Machine hours	16,000	30,000

Required:

Treat each of the following requirements independently:

1. The company follows a policy of applying overhead for the entire plant on the basis of machine hours.
    (a) Calculate a plant-wide overhead rate based on machine hours.
    (b) Apply overhead to the Skibells job.
2. The company follows a policy of allocating support function costs to the producing departments using the direct method. Administration costs are allocated on direct labor hours; Maintenance on square meters of space occupied; Cutting on machine hours; and Sewing on direct labor hours.
    (a) Allocate support function costs to producing departments.
    (b) Calculate overhead rates for producing departments.
    (c) Apply overhead to the Skibells job.
3. The company follows a policy of allocating support function costs to the producing departments using the step method. Administration costs are allocated first using direct labor hours; Maintenance using square meters of space occupied; Cutting using machine hours; and Sewing using direct labor hours.
    (a) Allocate support function costs to producing departments.

(b) Calculate overhead rates for producing departments.

(c) Apply overhead to the Skibells job.

4. Prepare a summary of the results of allocating overhead to the Skibells job in each of the three alternatives. Explain why the differences in overhead costs occur.

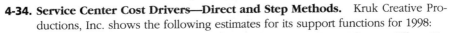

4-34. Service Center Cost Drivers—Direct and Step Methods. Kruk Creative Productions, Inc. shows the following estimates for its support functions for 1998:

	Number of Employees	Square Meters of Floor Space	Hours of Repairs and Maintenance Used	Kilowatt Hours of Power Used
Support functions:				
Administration	45	12,000	20	6,000
Personnel	5	1,000	5	500
Cafeteria	20	5,000	10	4,000
Building and Grounds	10	1,000	40	2,000
Repairs and Maintenance . . .	10	1,000	80	500
Power	25	5,000	100	1,000
Producing departments:				
Cutting	45	20,000	380	80,000
Grinding	100	30,000	460	66,000
Assembly	90	40,000	240	30,000
Finishing	50	10,000	170	50,000

Administration, Personnel, and Cafeteria costs are allocated using the number of employees. Building and Grounds cost allocation uses square meters of floor space. Repairs and Maintenance uses repair hours. Power is based on kilowatt hours used.

Required:

1. Prepare a summary that shows the percentage of each support function allocated to the producing departments, assuming the direct method of allocating support functions is used. (Round calculations to four decimal places.)

2. Prepare a summary that shows the percentage of each support function allocated to the remaining functions and producing departments, assuming the step method of allocating support functions is used. (Round calculations to four decimal places.) For purposes of this allocation, assume a sequence in the same order listed in the table above.

3. Prepare a summary that shows the percentage of each support function allocated to the remaining functions and producing departments, assuming the step method of allocating support functions is used. (Round calculations to four decimal places.) For purposes of this allocation, assume the following sequence: Administration, Power, Personnel, Cafeteria, Repairs and Maintenance, and Building and Grounds.

4. Explain why the sequencing of support functions is important for step method allocations.

4-35. Service Center Allocation—Reciprocal Method (Appendix). Hwang's Health Club is organized into two operating departments—Programming & Classes and Individual Fitness. There are also two service centers—Janitorial and Cafeteria. Janitorial costs are allocated based on square footage, while Cafeteria costs are allocated based on number of employees. The costs traceable to the operating and service centers during 1999 were as follows:

	Service Centers		Operating Departments	
	Janitorial	Cafeteria	Programming & Classes	Individual Fitness
Materials	$ 10,000	$ 200,000	$ 8,000	$ 5,000
Labor	100,000	300,000	265,000	150,000
Overhead	20,000	40,000	75,000	90,000
Totals	$ 130,000	$ 540,000	$ 348,000	$ 245,000

In addition to these costs, the Cafeteria generated revenues of $480,000. Other data are as follows:

	Service Centers		Operating Departments	
	Janitorial	Cafeteria	Programming & Classes	Individual Fitness
Square footage	1,600	8,000	24,000	32,000
Number of employees	5	14	19	6

Required:

Compute the total overhead cost for each operating department after allocation of service center costs. Use the reciprocal method to allocate the service center costs.

4-36. Ethics.   Tom Savin has recently been hired as a cost accountant by the Offset Press Company, a privately held company that produces a line of offset printing presses and lithograph machines. During his first few months on the job, Savin discovered that Offset has been underapplying factory overhead to the Work in Process account, while overstating expenses through the general and administrative account. This practice has been going on since the start of the company, which is in its sixth year of operation. The effect in each year has been favorable, having a material impact on the company's tax position. No internal audit function exists at Offset, and the external auditors have not yet discovered the underapplied factory overhead.

Prior to the sixth year audit, Savin had pointed out the practice and its effect to Mary Brown, the corporate controller, and had asked her to let him make the necessary adjustments. Brown directed him not to make the adjustments but to wait until the external auditors had completed their work and see what they uncovered.

The sixth year audit has now been completed, and the external auditors have once more failed to discover the underapplication of factory overhead. Savin again asked Brown if he could make the required adjustments and was again told not to make them. Savin, however, believes that the adjustments should be made and that the external auditors should be informed of the situation.

Since there are no established policies at Offset Press Company for resolving ethical conflicts, Savin is considering following one of three alternative courses of action:

(a) Follow Brown's directive and do nothing further.

(b) Attempt to convince Brown to make the proper adjustments and to advise the external auditors of her actions.

(c) Tell the Audit Committee of the Board of Directors about the problem and give it the appropriate accounting data.

Required:

1. For each of the three alternative courses of action that Tom Savin is considering, explain whether or not the action is appropriate. Refer to "Standards of Ethical Conduct for Management Accountants" in Chapter 1, page 21, to support your answer.

2. Without prejudice to your answer in Part 1, assume that Tom Savin again approaches Mary Brown to make the necessary adjustments and is unsuccessful. Describe the steps that Tom Savin should take in proceeding to resolve this situation.

(ICMA adapted)

C ASE 4A—UPTON, INC.

Upton, Inc. manufactures a line of home furniture. The company's single manufacturing plant consists of the Cutting, Assembly, and Finishing Departments. Upton uses departmental rates for applying manufacturing overhead to production and maintains separate manufacturing overhead accounts for each of the three production departments.

The following predetermined departmental manufacturing overhead rates were calculated for Upton's fiscal year ending May 31, 1999:

Department	*Rates*
Cutting.	$2.40 per machine hour
Assembly	$5.00 per direct labor hour
Finishing	$1.60 per direct labor dollar

Information regarding actual operations for Upton's plant for the six months ended November 30, 1998, is presented below:

	Department		
	Cutting	*Assembly*	*Finishing*
Manufacturing overhead costs	$ 22,600	$ 56,800	$ 98,500
Machine hours	10,800	2,100	4,400
Direct labor hours	6,800	12,400	16,500
Direct labor dollars	$ 40,800	$ 62,000	$ 66,000

Based upon this experience and updated projections for the last six months of the fiscal year, Upton revised its operating budget. Projected data regarding manufacturing overhead and operating activity for each department for the six months ending May 31, 1999, are presented as follows:

	Department		
	Cutting	*Assembly*	*Finishing*
Manufacturing overhead costs	$ 23,400	$ 57,500	$ 96,500
Machine hours.	9,200	2,000	4,200
Direct labor hours	6,000	13,000	16,000
Direct labor dollars	$ 36,000	$ 65,000	$ 64,000

Diane Potter, Upton's controller, plans to develop revised departmental manufacturing overhead rates that will be more representative of efficient operations for the current fiscal year ending May 31, 1999. She has decided to combine the actual results for the first six months of the fiscal year with the projections for the next six months to develop revised departmental overhead rates. She then plans to adjust the manufacturing overhead accounts for each department through November 1998, to recognize the revised overhead rates. The following analysis was prepared by Potter from general ledger account balances as of November 30, 1998.

Account	*Direct Materials*	*Direct Labor*	*Manufacturing Overhead*	*Account Balance*
Work in Process Inventory	$ 53,000	$ 95,000	$ 12,000	$ 160,000
Finished Goods.	96,000	176,000	48,000	320,000
Cost of Goods Sold	336,000	604,000	180,000	1,120,000
	$485,000	$875,000	$240,000	$1,600,000

Required:

1. Determine the amount of manufacturing overhead applied as of November 30, 1998, before any revision for the:

   (a) Cutting Department.

   (b) Assembly Department.

   (c) Finishing Department.

2. How should Upton, Inc. revise the departmental manufacturing overhead rates for the remainder of the fiscal year ending May 31, 1999? Show supporting calculations.
3. Prepare an analysis that shows how the manufacturing overhead applied should be adjusted as of November 30, 1998.

(ICMA adapted)

C ASE 4B—WADSWORTH & CAPELL LEGAL SERVICES

Wadsworth & Capell Legal Services is a large law office in St. Louis. It is organized into three operating departments: Criminal, Civil, and Personal & Family Services. Support functions include a secretarial pool and a research center. An administrative function is responsible for managing the entire company. Wadsworth & Capell follows the practice of allocating support functions to the three operating departments in order to establish a cost-based charge for pricing the various legal services to clients. Administrative costs are not allocated (they are treated as period costs in the income statement), but they are recovered through the profit margin developed as a percentage of all other costs.

Budgeting for the upcoming fiscal year has resulted in the following costs charged directly to all functions and departments:

	Secre-tarial	Research	Criminal	Civil	Personal & Family
Salaries and wages...	$ 80,000	$ 120,000	$ 300,000	$ 400,000	$ 100,000
Fringe benefits	5,600	11,200	30,000	40,000	10,000
Depreciation........	8,000	16,000	24,000	32,000	8,000
Supplies	16,000	3,200	4,500	6,000	1,500

The indirect costs that are prorated to administration, support functions, and operating departments are of four varieties: insurance, leasing, utilities, and janitorial services. The following means are used to prorate indirect costs:

(a) Insurance costs ($160,000) are for malpractice coverage and for equipment, fixtures, and furniture. The premium ($36,000) representing coverage on equipment, fixtures, and furniture is prorated on the basis of book value. The remainder of the $160,000 is for malpractice. Since malpractice relates to people, the proration is based on the number of people in each department.

(b) Leasing costs ($96,000) are incurred for the office space occupied by the firm. Therefore, these costs are prorated based on square footage occupied.

(c) Utilities costs ($60,000) are for heat, light, and water. They are prorated on the basis of square footage occupied.

(d) Janitorial services ($36,000) to keep the offices clean are contracted out. These costs are prorated on square footage.

In allocating the support functions to the operating departments, the secretarial pool cost is allocated on the basis of secretarial time. The research center cost is allocated based on salaries and wages. Overhead rates for the operating departments are determined by using salaries and wages in the Criminal and Civil Departments and staff time in Personal & Family Services. The following budgeted data are available for the allocation bases:

	Adminis-tration	Secre-tarial	Research	Criminal	Civil	Personal & Family
Number of people	2	4	6	4	6	2
Book values	$ 10,000	$70,000	$ 80,000	$120,000	$160,000	$ 40,000
Square footage	1,000	2,000	2,000	1,500	2,500	1,000
Staff time (hours)	4,000	8,500	12,500	9,000	12,500	5,000
Secretarial time (hours)....	500	200	2,000	2,000	3,000	1,000

Required:

1. Complete the proration of indirect costs to all support functions and operating departments. Show the sum of direct and indirect costs in each function and department.

2. Explain why the proration of indirect costs is necessary.

3. Using the direct method, allocate the service functions to the operating departments and develop the overhead rates for each of the operating departments. (Round allocations to the nearest dollar and overhead rates to four decimal places.)

4. Using the step method, allocate the service functions to the operating departments and develop the overhead rates for each of the operating departments. The secretarial pool is allocated first. (Round allocations to the nearest dollar and overhead rates to four decimal places.)

5. Compare the answers in Part (3) and Part (4) and explain why the differences occurred. Is the direct method used in Part (3) or the step method used in Part (4) preferred? Why?

Product Costing: Job and Process Costing

*L*EARNING OBJECTIVES

After studying Chapter 5, you will be able to:

1. Differentiate among job, process, modified, and hybrid costing systems.
2. Analyze costs in a job cost system for the purpose of cost control.
3. Describe the cost elements and cost flows in a process cost system.
4. Compute the equivalent units of production and unit costs using FIFO.
5. Prepare a cost of production report.
6. List several ways in which management can use departmental unit costs as a tool in evaluating departmental performance.
7. Explain the impact that JIT inventory systems have on process cost accounting.
8. Compute the equivalent units of production and unit costs using the weighted average method. (Appendix)

> ### Finding Unit Costs in Different Cost Environments
>
> When Evan Deming founded Shirts Unlimited, he envisioned a manufacturing enterprise involving the mass production of t-shirts and sweatshirts in standard colors and fabrics. Because he kept his costs low, while his quality and service were excellent, his first few years were very successful. Deming was supplying department stores throughout the country with his shirts.
>
> Periodically, Deming was approached by customers who wished to have specialized t-shirts and sweatshirts manufactured for certain events such as rock concerts or sporting events. Deming was reluctant to accept these orders because he was operating near full capacity. Moreover, because these specialized items required different types of cutting, sewing, and dyeing operations (according to customer specifications), Deming did not feel his current operating process was amenable to the production of customized orders. Therefore, he would routinely turn down these requests.
>
> One day, Deming decided to invest his growing profits into a new plant that would be oriented to producing specialized t-shirts and sweatshirts. One of Deming's many concerns was how he would determine the costs of these customized jobs. He knew that the process costing system used for his current plant would not be suitable for his new job shop.

This chapter discusses how to determine the costs of products produced in a process costing environment as well as products produced in a job costing environment. Although we focus on manufactured products, the concepts presented are appropriate in service and merchandising organizations.

OVERVIEW OF JOB AND PROCESS COSTING

A **job costing system** identifies manufacturing costs with individual jobs or products. A separate tracking of costs is associated with each job or product. The costs accumulated for a job in process can be determined at any point in time.

A **process costing system** identifies manufacturing costs with individual departments for an interval of time such as one month. Costs are not charged to specific units or orders as work is performed, but unit costs are based on costs incurred during a time period and on the volume of output during the same period. The unit cost of a final product will be the sum of all manufacturing costs allocated to the product by each department through which the product passed during manufacturing.

Several other characteristics distinguish job costing from process costing.

Manufacturing Environment

Job costing is most appropriate when jobs or products manufactured are different from one another. These products use different types or amounts of materials, labor, and overhead. Examples include building construction, defense contracting, consulting engagements, and printing shops. Also, products manufactured in just-in-time (JIT) inventory environments tend to use job costing since these organizations produce only what is needed and when it is needed.

Process costing is most appropriate in a manufacturing environment where products are mass produced or result from continuous processing. Each unit going through the same manufacturing process is identical to other units. Examples include candy, soft drinks, clothing, chemicals, and most processed foods. In addition, individual operations can be suitable for process costing if every product passing through the operation has the same work performed on it. For instance, various models of televisions or video cassette recorders on an assembly line may have the same operations performed during the assembly process.

In a job cost environment, sales orders usually precede production. Production is for a specific order. In a process cost environment, however, production usually precedes sales. Goods are produced for anticipated sales.

Materials, Labor, and Overhead Costs

A process cost environment will generally use materials that are standard. In a job cost setting, materials requirements are often unique to each job and perhaps even the types of materials needed are unknown. Hence, process cost manufacturers usually have larger inventories of materials.

Tasks in a process cost environment are generally routine. Less skilled labor is usually needed than in a job cost environment, where workers need to perform a greater variety of tasks because of the different types of jobs. Automation is found more often in process cost settings. Therefore, the proportion of factory overhead cost in the total product cost will generally be higher than for job cost settings.

Focal Point for Cost Accumulation

In process cost systems, we identify materials, labor, and factory overhead costs with specific departments or operating centers. This differs from job cost systems which identify costs with specific batches or customer orders. In this chapter, the term department will be used as a generic term and will cover the traditional concepts of department, operating or work center, operation, task, activity center, and responsibility center. As a result of charging costs to departments, few detailed records are needed with process costing.

M ODIFIED AND HYBRID SYSTEMS

Classifying an accounting system as a job cost or process cost system is often not easy. This is especially true when companies have a wide variety of products and processes. Modifications and adaptations are made to the accounting system to meet the needs of specific situations. These result in systems we categorize as modified cost systems and hybrid cost systems.

A **modified cost system** has one or more elements of cost using job costing, while the other cost elements use process costing. For example, a manufacturer of shoes will make different sizes and styles and use different grades of leather. However, the operations of cutting and sewing the leather and attaching the heels and souls are essentially the same for each shoe. Consequently, the manufacturer can group the shoes by sizes, styles, and grades of leather and treat the costing of materials using job costing. Then, the labor and factory overhead costs for the operations can use a process cost system.

A **hybrid cost system** exists when one type of costing system (job costing or process costing) is used for one phase of the production process and another system is used for a subsequent phase. For example in manufacturing cars, the various parts, subassemblies, engines, transmissions, and so forth may be produced where a job costing system is used. In a JIT environment, most parts are produced in small batches only when needed. In assembly, every car, regardless of model, has the same assembly operations performed. Therefore, the labor and factory overhead costs of the assembly operations may be accounted for using a process cost system. Hybrid cost systems can involve various sequences of job and process costing depending on the particular production process.

Operation costing is a term often used to refer to modified or hybrid cost systems. Contemporary Practice 5.1 conveys the results of a survey on the frequency of job, process, and operation costing systems used by manufacturing firms.

Except in the simplest of cases, pure job costing or process costing does not exist. There is usually some modification. Managers need to understand their own organization's costing system to evaluate the cost information generated by that system. The remainder of this chapter provides detailed discussions of job cost and process cost systems.

THE JOB COST SYSTEM

The job cost system accumulates separately the costs of materials, labor, and overhead for each job, whether a job of one unit or a job of many units. Every job is assigned a number which is used for accumulating the costs of that job. Daily, weekly, or monthly cost summaries for each job are generated. These summaries are referred to as **job, work,** *or* **production orders**. The file of production orders in process constitutes a subsidiary ledger in support of the work in process account in the general ledger. An example of a completed production order (Order No. 216) for the new plant at Shirts Unlimited is shown in Figure 5.1, page 190.

Chapter 4 discussed the accounting for the cost elements—direct materials, direct labor, and applied factory overhead—that make up a job. Now, let's look at issues related to job cost control.

C O N T E M P O R A R Y   P R A C T I C E   5 . 1

Frequency of Costing Systems

A survey of 112 manufacturing companies revealed the following frequencies of use of different costing systems:

Costing Systems	Percentage
Job costing	28%
Process costing	36
Operation costing	18
More than one of the above	18
	100%

Source: Schwarzbach, H. R., "The Impact of Automation on Accounting for Indirect Costs," *Management Accounting*, December 1985, p. 46.

FIGURE 5.1   A Completed Production Order

```
Shirts Unlimited Production Order No: 216

Customer No: 3122          Customer Name: Nigrini Enterprises

Order Date: 1/10/97        Order Due: 1/30/97

Order Started: 1/19/97     Order Completed: 1/27/97

Quantity: 1,000            Style: Arizona Sun. w/pocket and embossing

Date Description      Code    Quantity Price  Materials     Labor       Overhead      Total
                      No.

1/19  Cloth           0052     2,504  $1.25  $ 3,130.00
1/19  Trim            0068     7,000    .05       350.00

1/23  Payroll         1004       140  $8.00                $ 1,120.00
1/30  Payroll         1005        60   8.00                    480.00

1/23  Factory O/H     2004       140  $6.00                             $   840.00
1/30  Factory O/H     2005        60   6.00                                 360.00

Totals                                 $ 3,480.00  $ 1,600.00  $1,200.00  $6,280.00

Unit cost                              $   3.4800  $   1.6000  $  1.2000  $  6.2800
```

Cost Control in a Job Cost System

Production supervisors, in planning their operations, may estimate the direct materials and direct labor costs for each job for which they are responsible. They subsequently measure actual costs and compare them with the estimated costs of each job, taking into account the stage of completion. For example, a report on production materials may be prepared as follows:

Direct Materials

Job Number	Estimate	Actual	Dollar Variance Under (Over)	Percentage of Completion
1017	$ 22,000	$ 21,000	$ 1,000	100%
1018	19,500	20,000	(500)	100
1019	10,000 *	14,000	(4,000)	50
1020	5,000 *	5,000	-0-	25
Total	$ 56,500	$ 60,000	$(3,500)	

* Estimates adjusted to percentage of completion basis.

The variance column shows the differences between estimated and actual amounts. The total estimates for each job have been adjusted by the percentage completed so that a valid comparison can be made with the actual amounts. The total direct materials cost of Job 1019 was estimated to be $20,000. Since the job is 50 percent complete as to direct materials, the estimated cost is $10,000 (50 percent of $20,000).

A report that compares actual direct labor hours with the estimated hours will reveal whether more hours are being used on a job than expected. Again, the estimates are made comparable with actual results by determining the percentage of work completed and applying that percentage to the total estimate. For example, Job 1020 is only 10 percent complete for direct labor. The total estimate on that job for direct labor hours must be 4,500 hours if 450 hours is 10 percent of the total estimate, as shown:

Direct Labor Hours

Job Number	Estimate	Actual	Direct Labor Hour Variance Under (Over)	Percentage of Completion
1017	4,450*	4,000	450	80%
1018	1,800*	2,000	(200)	50
1019	3,300*	3,500	(200)	50
1020	450*	500	(50)	10
Total	10,000	10,000	-0-	

* Estimates adjusted to percentage of completion basis.

The report on direct labor hours can be converted to a direct labor cost report by multiplying the direct labor hours by the direct labor hour rate (in this case, $10), as shown in the following report:

Direct Labor Cost

Job Number	Estimate	Actual	Direct Labor Dollar Variance Under (Over)	Percentage of Completion
1017	$ 44,500 *	$ 40,000	$ 4,500	80%
1018	18,000 *	20,000	(2,000)	50
1019	33,000 *	35,000	(2,000)	50
1020	4,500 *	5,000	(500)	10
Total	$100,000	$100,000	-0-	

* Estimates adjusted to percentage of completion basis.

Supervisors are able to use such cost information to follow each job from its inception to its completion. As a **cost overrun** (unfavorable variance from estimate) develops, they can take corrective measures. The preceding example shows that Job 1019 is 50 percent complete with respect to both direct materials and direct labor. More materials and more hours were used than anticipated. Knowing what caused the overrun may enable the supervisor to find ways to reduce costs. Or, perhaps the estimate was unrealistically low; in this case, budgets could be revised.

Whereas a job cost system accumulates costs by jobs, a process cost system accumulates costs by departments. This difference, as well as other differences, changes the approach in determining unit costs in a process cost environment. However, as outlined in the remaining sections of this chapter, many of the product costing concepts of Chapter 4 apply as well to process costing.

THE COST ELEMENTS IN A PROCESS COST SYSTEM

The cost elements in a process cost system depend on whether the organization is a manufacturing, merchandising, or service organization. A manufacturer typically has more detailed costs; therefore, we focus on manufacturing firms in the following sections. We will discuss the two major elements of manufacturing costs in a process cost system—materials and conversion costs.

Materials

Materials are requisitioned for use in a specific department, and the materials costs are accumulated by the department for a specific time period. Although materials can be added in any department, they are often issued from the storeroom to the first operating department in the process. The concept of accounting for materials costs does not depend on whether materials are added in the first department or in subsequent departments. Distinguishing between direct materials and indirect materials is not considered critical in obtaining accurate unit costs.

Two major differences between the job cost system and the process cost system in accumulating materials costs should be noted. Materials costs are identified first with departments and then assigned to individual units in a process cost system. Materials costs bypass departments and are charged directly to specific jobs in a job cost system. In process costing, materials costs are accumulated for a period of time and averaged over all units receiving materials during the period. This averaging of costs is broader in a process cost system than in a job cost system, where costs would be averaged only over the batch of units comprising a particular job.

Conversion Costs

Labor and overhead costs are incurred to convert materials into a finished product; hence, labor and overhead costs are called **conversion costs**. Because labor and overhead costs often enter the process at the same time, we combine them for illustrations throughout the chapter. This assumes that overhead is applied to production using direct labor hours or dollars. Where another cost driver is used, we separate the two cost elements.

Labor cost is measured monthly, by department, and without identifying specific orders. Labor time tickets may be used for payroll accounting but are not needed to measure the time to complete a single order because each unit of product in a process cost setting is presumed to take the same amount of time. Like materials, little emphasis is placed on distinguishing precisely between direct labor and indirect labor.

Factory overhead costs are accumulated by department. Typically, they are recorded in a departmental overhead control ledger by type of cost (e.g., depreciation, utilities). Overhead costs are charged to production through predetermined overhead rates for each department. In most of our illustrations, manufacturing overhead appears to be actual overhead. However, the costs represent charges based on predetermined overhead rates under a normal costing system. Since normal costing was discussed in Chapter 4, we will not repeat the coverage here. We assume that factory overhead is accumulated and applied using departmental rates.

Cost Flows

In a process system, a product may flow through several operations before completion. For example, production of cellular phones may start in a fabricating operation, as shown in Figure 5.2. Both the physical units and costs will be identified for the fabricating operation over a period of time, such as a month. When the inner components of the phones are completed in the fabricating operation, the units with their costs are transferred by automatically guided vehicles to the next operation—in this case, the molding operation where the casings are formed. Additional costs will be incurred and accounted for in the molding operation. At the completion of the molding operation, the units and accumulated costs of preceding operations will be transferred to the last operation in this example, the finishing operation.

Because costs need to be identified with departments, a process cost system normally involves accounting transfers between departmental work in process inventory accounts. Each department has its own work in process account; and when goods are completed in one department, their costs are transferred to the work in process account of the next department.

FIGURE 5.2 **Flow of Units and Costs in a Process Manufacturing System**

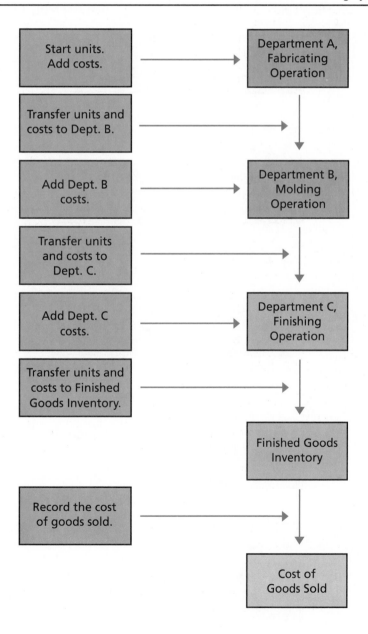

In some types of operations, a subassembly may be produced on a separate production line for addition to the product at a later stage. For example, assume that the main production line for computer disk drives extends from Department A (Fabricating) to Department C (Assembly). A subassembly line, consisting of Departments W (Forming) and X (Soldering), uses numerically controlled machines to produce a component that converts physical measures like velocity and pressure into digital form. These components are brought into the main line in Department C. A diagram showing the flow of units and costs for this example appears in Figure 5.3.

FIGURE 5.3 Flow of Units and Costs for Subassembly Components

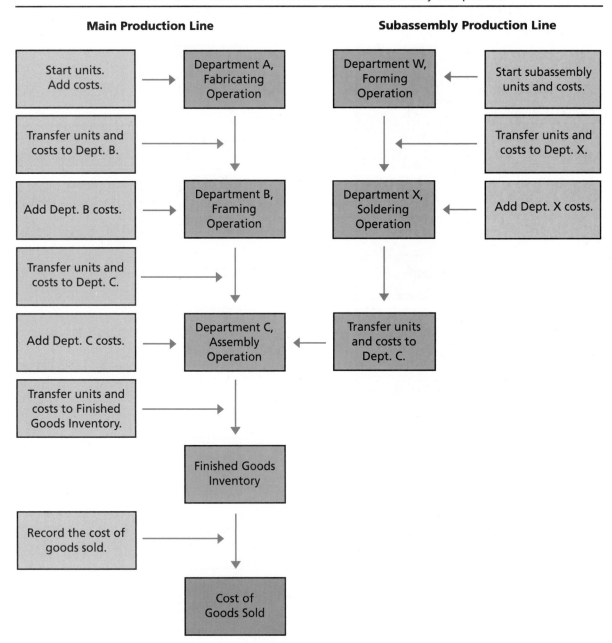

THE EQUIVALENT UNIT CONCEPT

A primary goal of any cost accounting system is to identify product costs for determining ending inventories of work in process and finished goods and for establishing the cost of goods sold amount. Costs are attached to units in inventories whether the units are wholly or partially completed. The mechanism for tracing costs to units is a unit cost.

Unit Costs

When calculating unit costs, we typically think of a formula similar to the following:

$$\text{Unit cost} = \frac{\text{Total costs}}{\text{Units produced or work done}}$$

Applying this formula to the typical process cost situation is complicated by two major factors: (1) the stage of completion of units in work in process inventories; and (2) the different points in time that materials and conversion costs enter a departmental process. We will discuss point (2) in more detail later in the chapter.

The number of units completed is not a good measure for determining an appropriate unit cost when partially completed units are in beginning or ending inventories. Consequently, an equivalent unit must be identified. An **equivalent unit** amount represents the theoretical number of units that could have been produced had the resources been applied to units that were started and completed during the period. We can also think of equivalent units as representing the actual work done on the physical units. For instance, two physical units 50 percent complete represent the equivalent of one unit 100 percent complete.

Flow of Physical Units

For each department, the flow of *physical* units can be viewed as follows:

Units in beginning work in process inventory + Units of product started during the period
  = Units completed and transferred out + Units in ending work in process inventory

This relationship among physical units is also shown in Figure 5.4, page 196. As diagramed, the number of units started and completed during the period can be computed two ways:

Units completed and transferred out – Units in beginning work in process inventory
  =   Units started and completed

or

Units of product started during the period – Units in ending work in process inventory
  =   Units started and completed

FIGURE 5.4   Relationship Among Physical Units Within a Department

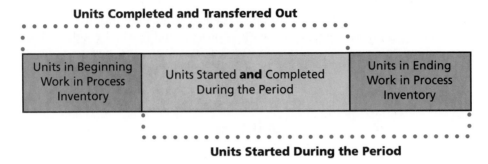

Knowing where all units are in a production process is an important starting point for calculating unit costs. Figure 5.4 represents the location and flow of physical units through a production process for a given time period.

Stage of Completion

In a process cost system, the units in the beginning and ending inventories are usually at different stages of completion. The **stage of completion** is the average percentage of work completed on a unit of product at any point in time. For a department, it is useful to identify three distinct groupings of products when computing equivalent units:

1. Partially completed units in the beginning inventory which are completed during the current period. The work to complete these units is represented by 100 percent minus the stage of completion when the period started. We generally assume a first-in, first-out flow.
2. Units started and completed during the period. The work completed is represented by 100 percent.
3. Partially completed units at the end of the period. The work completed is represented by the percentage of completion at the end of the period.

When all three of these groups are summed, the result is equivalent units of output for this time period—the work done by the workers in this department. This is the number of units that could have been produced if all production were started and completed during the period, assuming no beginning or ending work in process inventories.

For example, Seminole Metal Works has a machining department. On March 1, 15,000 units were in process and were 60 percent completed. During March, the department started work on 200,000 units. On March 31, 20,000 units were in process and were 30 percent completed.   From our flow of physical units formula, we calculate the number of units completed as follows:

Units in beginning inventory	15,000
+ Units started during period	200,000
− Units in ending inventory	(20,000)
Units completed and transferred	195,000

Next, we compute the units started and completed using both methods described previously:

Units completed and transferred	195,000
– Units in beginning inventory	(15,000)
Units started and completed	180,000

or

Units started during the period	200,000
- Units in ending inventory	(20,000)
Units started and completed	180,000

We now have the three groups of units and their stages of completion which are necessary to find the number of equivalent units. One way to calculate the equivalent units of output for the period, referred to as the "units started and completed method," is as follows:

Units Started and Completed Method:

Current period work to complete beginning inventory [15,000 x (100% - 60%)] .	6,000
Units started and completed (180,000 units x 100%)	180,000
Current period work in ending inventory (20,000 units x 30%)	6,000
Equivalent units of output (work done during the period)	192,000

Two other methods are available for calculating these equivalent units. One is called the "units completed method," and the other method is the "units started method." They give the same equivalent units results, as follows:

Units Completed Method:

Units completed (195,000 units x 100%)	195,000
+ Current period work in ending inventory (20,000 units x 30%)	6,000
– Prior period work in beginning inventory (15,000 units x 60%)	(9,000)
Equivalent units of output (work done during the period)	192,000

Units Started Method:

Units started (200,000 units x 100%)	200,000
+ Current period work to complete beginning inventory [15,000 x (100% - 60%)] .	6,000
– Next period work to complete ending inventory [20,000 x (100% - 30%)]	(14,000)
Equivalent units of output (work done during the period)	192,000

Any one of these three methods may be used if a manager is working only with equivalent units and unit costs. However, in preparing the cost of production report which we will discuss later, the units started and completed method is most suitable. Hence, this is the approach we will use.

Timing of Inputs

Materials, labor, and factory overhead are the inputs to the production process. These inputs may enter at different points during the process. The most common situation is for materials to enter at the beginning of a departmental process and for labor and factory overhead to be added continuously throughout the process. Consequently, it is possible for some units in process to have all of their materials content but only part of the labor and factory overhead. In other processes, the materials may be added continuously or at the end of the process. For our purposes, unless otherwise stated, presume that materials are added at the beginning of the process, and labor and factory overhead enter the process together and are added continuously or evenly throughout the process.

To calculate unit costs when inputs have different timing for entering a process, we need to calculate the equivalent units for each cost input. Therefore, one equivalent unit computation is for materials; and another computation is for conversion costs. The computational steps developed in the next section will show how separate equivalent units quantities are used to establish unit costs.

Computational Steps

Tracing physical units to a department and accounting for those units are generally clerical functions. Likewise, the identification of the costs charged to a department is a relatively simple function. However, distributing the costs to work completed and ending inventories requires an understanding of several steps. These steps are:

1. Determine flow of physical units.
2. Calculate equivalent units.
3. Compute unit costs.
4. Distribute total costs to units.
5. Reconcile the costs.

The last step checks whether the four previous steps were completed accurately. This step verifies that the total costs distributed to the units equal the total costs charged to the department. Each of these steps is presented in detail as part of developing a cost of production report.

We assume a **first-in, first-out (FIFO) cost method** in progressing through the five computational steps. The beginning inventory is completed before new units are completed. Costs incurred flow in the same manner. A recent survey of manufacturing companies using process costing found that most (58%) were using the FIFO cost method.[1] Another frequently used method, the weighted average cost method, is discussed in the Appendix to this chapter.

Under FIFO, the older units and costs are transferred out first, and the more current units and costs are transferred out next. Only the most recent costs are held as ending inventory. With the FIFO cost method, the equivalent units of output are literally the units that could have been completed if all efforts during the period were devoted to starting and completing units, allowing no partially completed units. Usually, however, some units will be in a stage of partial completion at both the beginning and at the end of the period. The beginning work in process units are completed during the period, and a start has been made on the units in ending work in process.

To illustrate the computational steps, consider the current plant of Shirts Unlimited which we encountered in the opening vignette of this chapter. Sweatshirts are produced in three departments: Cutting, Sewing, and Finishing. Our illustra-

---

[1] Hauser, R. C., F. R. Urbancic, and D. E. Edwards, "Process Costing: Is It Relevant?" *Management Accounting*, December 1989, p. 53.

tion will focus on the Cutting Department. All cloth materials enter production at the beginning of the Cutting Department operations. The cloth is cut there. Both materials and conversion costs are incurred in the Cutting Department. Its activity for May 1998 is summarized as follows:

Work in process, May 1, 1998:	
Units	4,000
Stage of completion:	
Materials	100%
Conversion costs	40%
Costs:	
Materials	$ 400,000
Conversion costs	80,000
Beginning inventory total cost	$ 480,000
Units started	12,000
Units completed and transferred	14,000
Current period costs:	
Materials	$1,200,000
Conversion costs	650,000
Total costs added	$1,850,000
Work in process, May 31, 1998:	
Units	2,000
Stage of completion:	
Materials	100%
Conversion costs	30%

Step 1: Determine Flow of Physical Units. Determining the flow of physical units for a department involves identifying the units in the beginning inventory, the units started and completed during the period, and the units in the ending inventory. These are whole units; stage of completion is not an issue here. For the Cutting Department of Shirts Unlimited, we have:

Units in beginning work in process	4,000
Units started and completed (12,000 - 2,000 *or* 14,000 - 4,000)	10,000
Units in ending work in process	2,000
Total units	16,000

Step 2: Calculate Equivalent Units. Equivalent units are computed by multiplying physical units by the percentage of work completed on them. For our example, using the units started and completed method, we have the following calculations:

	Materials	*Conversion*
Current period work to complete beginning inventory:		
4,000 x (100% - 100%)	0	
4,000 x (100% - 40%)		2,400
Units started and completed in May:		
10,000 x 100%	10,000	10,000
May's work in ending inventory:		
2,000 x 100%	2,000	
2,000 x 30%		600
Equivalent units (work done during May)	12,000	13,000

Step 3: Compute Unit Costs. We begin this step by itemizing the costs for which the Cutting Department will be held accountable.

Costs Charged to Department:	Materials	Conversion	Total
Beginning inventory	$ 400,000	$ 80,000	$ 480,000
May's costs.	1,200,000	650,000	1,850,000
Total costs	$1,600,000	$ 730,000	$2,330,000

The unit costs for materials and conversion costs are calculated from the *current* month's costs and equivalent units. Last month's costs and equivalent units of work will be treated separately. The costs for May are divided by the equivalent units for May to obtain unit costs:

Unit Costs for May:

Unit cost for materials   = $1,200,000 ÷ 12,000 = $100

Unit cost for conversion = $650,000 ÷ 13,000   = $50

The beginning work in process cost provides useful information for managers. These dollars represent costs from the prior period, in this case, the previous month. Thus, unit cost information about the beginning inventory is obtained by dividing the beginning inventory costs by the prior period work (i.e., equivalent units) in beginning inventory:

April's Unit Costs in May's Beginning Inventory:

Unit cost for material   = $400,000 ÷ 4,000 = $100

Unit cost for conversion = $80,000 ÷ 1,600   = $50

These unit costs are identical to those for the current period, although such a case will not occur very often.

Step 4: Distribute Total Costs to Units.   The distribution of costs to units using the unit costs and equivalent units derived earlier is shown at the top of page 201.

Note the sequence of computations. First, the old costs in the beginning work in process are listed. Then, we compute the cost to complete the beginning work in process in the current period. Next, we calculate the costs associated with units started and completed. The sum of these costs is the cost of goods completed and transferred out. This is also called the cost of goods manufactured. Finally, we determine the costs of the work done on the units still in process on May 31.

Often the unit cost calculations result in the need to round to some decimal place. The more decimal places used, the less the rounding error in total dollars assigned to units completed and units in ending inventory. If rounding errors occur, it is customary to adjust the costs assigned to units completed to compensate for the rounding error.

Costs Accounted for:	Materials	Conversion	Total
Completed and transferred to Sewing:			
Work in process, May 1:			
Prior period costs	$ 400,000	$ 80,000	$ 480,000
May: Equivalent units	0	2,400	
Times cost per unit	$ 100	$ 50	
Costs	$ 0	$ 120,000	120,000
Completed cost of beginning inventory . . .	$ 400,000	$ 200,000	$ 600,000
Started and completed:			
Units	10,000	10,000	
Times cost per unit	$ 100	$ 50	
Costs	$ 1,000,000	$ 500,000	1,500,000
Total cost of completed and transferred units .	$ 1,400,000	$ 700,000	$ 2,100,000
Work in process, May 31:			
Equivalent units	2,000	600	
Times cost per unit	$ 100	$ 50	
Costs	$ 200,000	$ 30,000	$ 230,000
Total costs accounted for	$ 1,600,000	$ 730,000	$ 2,330,000

Step 5: Reconcile the Costs. This final step in the computational process is really a check to ensure that all department costs are charged to units completed and units in the ending inventory. As shown in Step 3, the total costs charged to the Cutting Department are $2,330,000. After distributing the costs to the units completed and units in the ending inventory, the sum of the costs distributed should also equal $2,330,000. This is confirmed by the total costs accounted for in Step 4. This check shows that materials and conversion costs charged to the department have indeed been distributed to all units.

Cost of Production Report

The five computational steps provide all of the calculations needed to prepare a **cost of production report** for May. This report, which presents information about units, costs charged to the department, and how the costs are accounted for, is shown in Figure 5.5 on page 202.

In T-account form, the transactions reflected in the cost of production report would be summarized as shown in Figure 5.6 on page 203.

We use the same procedures to determine costs for subsequent departments in the processing operation. In departments after the first, however, unit costs must be combined with the accumulated costs of work done in earlier departments. For example, if operations cover ten departments, Department 10 would obtain a unit cost for the total work done in all preceding nine departments and calculate a unit cost for its own work.

FIGURE 5.5 Cost of Production Report for Cutting Department

SHIRTS UNLIMITED **Cutting Department** **Cost of Production Report for the Month of May 1998**			

Units:	**Physical Units**	**Materials Equivalent Units**	**Conversion Equivalent Units**
Beginning work in process	4,000		
Prior month:			
4,000 x 100%		4,000	
4,000 x 40%			1,600
May's work:			
4,000 x (100% – 100%)		0	
4,000 x (100% – 40%)			2,400
Units started and completed	10,000		
10,000 x 100%		10,000	10,000
Ending work in process	2,000		
2,000 x 100%		2,000	
2,000 x 30%			600
Total units	16,000		
Equivalent units of output		12,000	13,000

Costs Charged to Department:	**Materials**	**Conversion**	**Total**
Beginning work in process:			
Costs	$ 400,000	$ 80,000	$ 480,000
Divided by equivalent units	4,000	1,600	
Cost per unit	$ 100	$ 50	
May's production:			
Costs	$1,200,000	$ 650,000	$1,850,000
Divided by equivalent units	12,000	13,000	
Cost per unit	$ 100	$ 50	
Total costs charged	$1,600,000	$ 730,000	$2,330,000

Costs Accounted for:	**Materials**	**Conversion**	**Total**
Completed and transferred to Sewing:			
Work in process, May 1:			
Prior period costs	$ 400,000	$ 80,000	$ 480,000
May: Equivalent units	0	2,400	
Times cost per unit	$ 100	$ 50	
Costs	$ 0	$ 120,000	120,000
Completed cost of beginning inventory	$ 400,000	$ 200,000	$ 600,000
Started and completed:			
Units	10,000	10,000	
Times cost per unit	$ 100	$ 50	
Costs	$1,000,000	$ 500,000	1,500,000
Total cost of completed and transferred units	$1,400,000	$ 700,000	$2,100,000
Work in process, May 31:			
Equivalent units	2,000	600	
Times cost per unit	$ 100	$ 50	
Costs	$ 200,000	$ 30,000	$ 230,000
Total costs accounted for	$1,600,000	$ 730,000	$2,330,000

FIGURE 5.6   Flow of Cost From Cutting Department to Sewing Department

Work in Process—Cutting				Work in Process—Sewing	
Beg. Inventory	480,000	Completed	2,100,000 →	Transferred in 2,100,000	
Materials	1,200,000				
Conversion	650,000				
End. Inventory	230,000				

M ANAGEMENT'S USE OF COST OF PRODUCTION REPORTS

Internal accounting reports often serve only to attach dollars to the events about which managers already know. For example, managers know about volumes, inefficiencies, and scrap; but they do not know the costs related to them. However, the information provided by a cost of production report can be used by managers in several different ways.

When unit costs for materials and conversion costs change from one period to the next, a manager should ask why. Why is a materials price higher or lower? What causes conversion costs to change? The manager has to find the answers to ensure that the numbers reported represent reality and are accurate. Sometimes managers intuitively know the numbers are either correct or incorrect because of their experiences.

Cost of production reports for several periods in succession can show trends. Here certain questions arise. Are figures related to inventories bouncing around, or are they stable? Why? Why are unit costs steadily moving up, or why are they erratic? Are we changing the mix of workers as reflected in labor cost changes? The answers to these and many other questions help managers understand their working environment and the company's focus much better.

If unit costs are identified as variable and fixed costs, a manager can perform various cost-volume-profit analyses. Naturally, a sequence of departments that depend on one another must cooperate in some of these analyses for the company to have the greatest benefit.

Many other uses are available. In Chapters 7 and 8, we compare these costs to budgeted costs. In Chapters 9 and 10, we analyze variances from expected costs in more detail. These uses are cited only to show that the cost of production reports are more than mere printing on paper.

Ethical Considerations

As with all financial reports, production reports can easily be manipulated. Estimating the stage of completion of the work in process is an area particularly susceptible to manipulation by production managers. These estimates are very subjective. Two reasons explain why managers might be motivated to overestimate the stage of completion. First is pressure to meet production quotas of units or equivalent units produced. A second reason relates to minimizing unit costs. A higher estimate for the degree of completion of the work in process inventory results in a greater number of equivalent units of output for the period. This, in turn, generates a lower cost per equivalent unit. Notice, however, that any overestimate in one period results in an opposite impact in the following period. Management accountants, nevertheless, need to be aware that temptations to overestimate the stage of completion may exist.

SIMPLIFICATIONS OF JIT AND AUTOMATED PRODUCTION PROCESSES

For companies adopting a **just-in-time (JIT) philosophy**, the expectation is to reduce or eliminate inventories. If a company implements JIT throughout its operations, the final departments in the process finish the products just in time to be shipped; parts, components, and subassemblies are manufactured just in time to meet the final department's needs and so on back through the process. Even in the beginning, materials are received just in time to enter the appropriate department.

JIT can significantly simplify accounting for a process cost system. One such example is highlighted in Contemporary Practice 5.2. Partially completed units within each department will be kept as low as possible. Thus, little difference exists between units completed and work done during the period. Consequently, the costs incurred during the period are largely tied to goods completed. As a result, unit costs are more accurate in a JIT environment because they are less influenced by stage of completion estimates. This is true of automated factories as a whole, since they tend to have fairly uniform amounts of beginning and ending work in process inventories. Thus, work done during the period will be approximately equal to the number of units completed during the period.

In addition, little need exists to transfer costs from one department to the next. The costs of the period can be recorded directly to the cost of goods sold account. Process costs per unit can still be computed but on a daily or weekly basis. The unit costs will be calculated using units produced rather than equivalent units. Further aspects of JIT product costing are discussed in Chapter 6.

Also, in JIT factories, certain departments remain idle until their outputs are needed by the next department. This may cause a particular department to appear inefficient in one period and very efficient in another. Therefore, evaluations of managers and costs in JIT plants need to consider the flow of production and who controls decisions of what and when to produce.

Many managers believe that a system truly operating under JIT will have no inventories and, therefore, no need for a process cost system. Because the process flow time is not zero, some items are always in production in a partially completed stage. Process costing becomes greatly simplified in such a setting, but it is not eliminated.

CONTEMPORARY   PRACTICE   5.2

Simplification of Accounting With JIT

A JIT inventory system is used at the printed circuit fabrication facility of Hewlett-Packard's Disc Memory Division. "By simplifying the accounting for work in process inventories, an estimated 100,000 journal entries per month were eliminated!"

Source: Hunt, R., L. Garrett, and C. M. Merz, "Direct Labor Cost Not Always Relevant at H-P," *Management Accounting*, February 1985, p. 58.

SUMMARY

In a job cost environment, costs are identified with specific batches or customer orders. In a process cost environment, products are continuously manufactured through a series of departments. Physical units and costs are identified with the departments. Unit costs are used in tracing the costs through the various departments and to the finished goods inventory account.

Because manufacturing situations will vary from one company to another, modifications and adaptations to the cost accounting system must be made. Modified and hybrid cost systems are common. A modified cost system will have some elements of cost using job costs and other elements of cost using process costs. A hybrid cost system will have one department on a job cost basis and another department on a process cost basis.

For control purposes, actual costs of jobs are compared to estimates, taking into account the stage of completion for each job. If a cost overrun develops before the completion of a job, corrective measures can be taken.

Unit costs in a process cost system are computed by dividing the appropriate current costs by the related equivalent units. The inventory costing method used is the first-in, first-out method. This assumes the beginning inventory is completed before new units are completed. Costs incurred are assumed to flow in the same manner. The cost of production report summarizes the costs charged to departments and how the costs are distributed between completed units and ending work in process.

Changes taking place in the manufacturing environment have an impact on a process cost system. Some changes, such as JIT, can simplify the calculation of unit costs.

PROBLEMS FOR REVIEW

Review Problem A

Wyncote Repair Shop has three jobs in process at the end of 1999. The following cost information for parts and labor is provided:

Job Number	Parts			Labor		
	Original Estimate	Percentage Complete	Cost to Date	Original Estimate	Percentage Complete	Cost to Date
9936	$ 960	60%	$ 600	$ 800	30%	$ 200
9937	380	50	210	950	10	150
9938	500	90	440	250	60	180

Required:
For both parts and labor, determine which of the jobs in process are underbudget and which are overbudget.

Solution:

Job Number	Parts				
	Original Estimate	Percentage Complete	Adjusted Estimate	Cost to Date	Variance Under (Over)
9936	$ 960	60%	$ 576	$ 600	$ (24)
9937	380	50	190	210	(20)
9938	500	90	450	440	10

| Job | *Labor* | | | | |
Number	Original Estimate	Percentage Complete	Adjusted Estimate	Cost to Date	Variance Under (Over)
9936	$ 800	30%	$ 240	$ 200	$ 40
9937	950	10	95	150	(55)
9938	250	60	150	180	(30)

Review Problem B

The following data pertain to the Forming Department of Decatur Corporation:

Work in process, May 1, 1998:	
Units.	3,000
Stage of completion:	
Materials	0%
Conversion costs	10%
Conversion costs	$ 6,000
Units started	13,000
Units completed.	15,000
May's costs:	
Materials	$ 225,000
Conversion costs	$ 260,100
Work in process, May 31, 1998:	
Units.	1,000
Stage of completion:	
Materials	0%
Conversion costs	60%

Required:

1. Perform the computational steps on the Forming Department.
2. Prepare a cost of production report for May 1998.

Solution:

1. **Computational Steps:**

   Step 1: Determine physical flow:

Units in beginning work in process.	3,000
Units started and completed (13,000 - 1,000 or 15,000 - 3,000)	12,000
Units in ending work in process	1,000
Total units	16,000

   Step 2: Calculate equivalent units:

	Materials	**Conversion**
Current period work to complete beginning inventory:		
3,000 x (100% - 0%)	3,000	
3,000 x (100% - 10%)		2,700
Units started and completed:		
12,000 x 100%	12,000	12,000
Current period work in ending inventory:		
1,000 x 0%	0	
1,000 x 60%		600
Equivalent units (work done during the period)	15,000	15,300

   Step 3: Compute unit costs:

   $$\text{Unit cost for materials} = \$225{,}000 \div 15{,}000 = \$15$$

   $$\text{Unit cost for conversion} = \$260{,}100 \div 15{,}300 = \$17$$

Step 4: Distribute total costs to units:

Costs Accounted for:	Materials	Conversion	Total
Completed and transferred:			
Work in process, May 1:			
Prior period costs......................	$ 0	$ 6,000	$ 6,000
May: Equivalent units	3,000	2,700	
Times cost per unit	$ 15	$ 17	
Costs	$ 45,000	$ 45,900	90,900
Completed cost of beginning inventory.....	$ 45,000	$ 51,900	$ 96,900
Started and completed:			
Units	12,000	12,000	
Times cost per unit	$ 15	$ 17	
Costs	$180,000	$204,000	384,000
Total cost of completed and transferred units	$225,000	$255,900	$480,900
Work in process, May 31:			
Equivalent units	0	600	
Times cost per unit	$ 15	$ 17	
Costs	$ 0	$ 10,200	$ 10,200
Total costs accounted for...................	$225,000	$266,100	$491,100

Step 5: Reconcile costs:

Costs Charged to Department:	Materials	Conversion	Total
Beginning inventory........................	$ 0	$ 6,000	$ 6,000
Current month	225,000	260,100	485,100
Total costs	$225,000	$266,100	$491,100

2. **Cost of Production Report:**

Steps 1 through 4 provide all of the calculations needed to prepare a cost of production report for May, as follows:

DECATUR CORPORATION Forming Department Cost of Production Report for the Month of May 1998			
Units:	Physical Units	Materials Equivalent Units	Conversion Equivalent Units
Beginning work in process:	3,000		
Prior month:			
3,000 x 0%.....................		0	
3,000 x 10%.....................			300
May's work:			
3,000 x (100% - 0%)		3,000	
3,000 x (100% - 10%)			2,700
Units started and completed:	12,000		
12,000 x 100%....................		12,000	12,000
Ending work in process:	1,000		
1,000 x 0%......................		0	
1,000 x 60%			600
Total units	16,000		
Equivalent units of output..............		15,000	15,300

(continued on page 208)

Costs Charged to Department:	Materials	Conversion	Total
Beginning work in process:			
Costs	$ 0	$ 6,000	$ 6,000
Divided by equivalent units	0	300	
Cost per unit	—	$ 20	
May's production:			
Costs	$225,000	$260,100	$485,100
Divided by equivalent units	15,000	15,300	
Cost per unit	$ 15	$ 17	
Total costs charged	$225,000	$266,100	$491,100

Costs Accounted for:	Materials	Conversion	Total
Completed and transferred:			
Work in process, May 1:			
Prior period costs	$ 0	$ 6,000	$ 6,000
May: Equivalent units	3,000	2,700	
Times cost per unit	$ 15	$ 17	
Costs	$ 45,000	$ 45,900	90,900
Completed cost of beginning inventory	$ 45,000	$ 51,900	$ 96,900
Started and completed:			
Units	12,000	12,000	
Times cost per unit	$ 15	$ 17	
Costs	$180,000	$204,000	384,000
Total cost of completed and transferred units	$225,000	$255,900	$480,900
Work in process, May 31:			
Equivalent units	0	600	
Times cost per unit	$ 15	$ 17	
Costs	$ 0	$ 10,200	$ 10,200
Total costs accounted for	$225,000	$266,100	$491,100

❖ APPENDIX

W EIGHTED AVERAGE COST METHOD

An alternative to the first-in, first-out cost method for calculating equivalent units is the **weighted average cost method**. This method averages the beginning work in process inventory (last period's costs) and the current production (this period's costs). The method assumes that the started and completed units for the period are the units completed and transferred out (regardless of when the units were started). In computing unit costs, equivalent units are calculated as the sum of (1) the units completed during the period and (2) the ending work in process inventory multiplied by its stage of completion. Whereas the equivalent units for the FIFO unit cost represent only work done during the current period, equivalent units for the weighted average method represent all units completed during this period (including work already done in the beginning work in process) plus any work done on ending work in process units.

The weighted average cost method is easier and simpler than FIFO because it does not require tracking the costs in the beginning inventory separately from those costs added during the current period. It is justified on the basis of convenience and simplicity. One can argue that a process which produces identical or similar units should generate the same unit costs from one month to the next. In addition, if beginning and ending inventories do not differ significantly from period to period, the costs per unit are relatively stable. However, the weighted average method commingles costs and production efforts of two time periods. The resulting product costs do not match production management's measures of inputs and outputs. Thus, many managers view the extra effort for FIFO as worthwhile.

WEIGHTED AVERAGE COMPUTATIONAL STEPS

We apply the same computational steps to the weighted average cost method as we had for the FIFO cost method. A slight difference occurs in the "Costs Accounted for" section of the cost of production report. In this section, costs are distributed to units completed and units in the ending inventory. The weighted average cost method will usually have different unit costs than FIFO.

We continue the example of the Shirts Unlimited illustration in the chapter. For the Cutting Department, we prepared the cost of production report using the FIFO cost method. Now, we apply the weighted average cost method to the data.

Step 1: Determine Flow of Physical Units

Determining the flow of physical units for a department is the same as for the FIFO method:

Units in beginning work in process	4,000
Units started and completed (12,000 - 2,000 **or** 14,000 - 4,000)	10,000
Units in ending work in process	2,000
Total units	16,000

Step 2: Calculate Equivalent Units

The weighted average method computes unit costs by aggregating costs to date (for the completed units and ending work in process) and dividing these by work done to date. Thus, to obtain the equivalent units of work done to date on the completed units and ending work in process, we need only consider the 14,000 units completed (4,000 + 10,000) and the 2,000 units in ending work in process. For our example, we would have the following calculation:

	Materials	*Conversion*
Units completed: 14,000 x 100%	14,000	14,000
Ending inventory:		
2,000 x 100%	2,000	
2,000 x 30%		600
Equivalent units of work done to date	16,000	14,600

Step 3: Compute Unit Costs

The unit costs for materials and conversion costs are calculated from the total costs and the equivalent units. The costs for which the Cutting Department will be held accountable are:

	Materials	Conversion	Total
Beginning inventory	$ 400,000	$ 80,000	$ 480,000
Current month	1,200,000	650,000	1,850,000
Total costs	$1,600,000	$730,000	$2,330,000

We calculate unit costs by using the equivalent units determined earlier and dividing them into the total costs:

$$\text{Unit cost for materials} \quad = \quad \$1{,}600{,}000 \div 16{,}000 \quad = \quad \$100$$

$$\text{Unit cost for conversion} \quad = \quad \$730{,}000 \div 14{,}600 \quad = \quad \$50$$

These unit costs are identical to those calculated using the FIFO cost method because April unit costs were the same as those for May. Usually, some difference will occur in the numbers but generally not a significant one.

Step 4: Distribute Total Costs to Units

The distribution of costs using the unit costs from Step 3 is as follows:

Costs Accounted for:	Materials	Conversion	Total
Completed and transferred to Sewing:			
Units	14,000	14,000	
Divided by cost per unit	$ 100	$ 50	
Costs	$1,400,000	$ 700,000	$2,100,000
Work in process, May 31:			
Equivalent units	2,000	600	
Divided by cost per unit	$ 100	$ 50	
Costs	$ 200,000	$ 30,000	230,000
Total costs accounted for	$1,600,000	$ 730,000	$2,330,000

Step 5: Reconcile the Costs

As shown in Step 3, the total costs charged to the Cutting Department are $2,330,000. After distributing the costs to the units completed and units in the ending inventory, the sum of that distribution should equal $2,330,000. This is confirmed by the total costs accounted for in Step 4.

Cost of Production Report

The five computational steps provide all of the calculations needed to prepare a cost of production report for May. The report prepared under the weighted average cost method appears in Figure 5.7.

FIGURE 5.7   Cost of Production Report for Cutting Department (Weighted Average Method)

SHIRTS UNLIMITED
Cutting Department
Cost of Production Report for the Month of May 1998

Units:	Physical Units	Materials Equivalent Units	Conversion Equivalent Units
Units completed:	14,000		
14,000 x 100%		14,000	14,000
Ending work in process:	2,000		
2,000 x 100%		2,000	
2,000 x 30%			600
Total units	16,000		
Equivalent units of work to date		16,000	14,600

Costs Charged to Department:	Materials	Conversion	Total
Prior period costs	$ 400,000	$ 80,000	$ 480,000
Current month costs	1,200,000	650,000	1,850,000
Total costs	1,600,000	730,000	2,330,000
Divided by equivalent units	16,000	14,600	
Cost per unit	$ 100	$ 50	

Costs Accounted for:	Materials	Conversion	Total
Completed and transferred to Sewing:			
Units	14,000	14,000	
Times cost per unit	$ 100	$ 50	
Costs	$1,400,000	$700,000	$2,100,000
Work in process, May 31:			
Equivalent units	2,000	600	
Times cost per unit	$ 100	$ 50	
Costs	$ 200,000	$ 30,000	230,000
Total costs accounted for	$1,600,000	$730,000	$2,330,000

TERMINOLOGY REVIEW

SUGGESTED READINGS

Doney, L. D., "Using Expert Systems for Job Cost Estimates," *Management Accounting*, December 1987, pp. 63-64.

Schiff, J. B., and A. I. Schiff, "High-Tech Cost Accounting for the F-16," *Management Accounting*, Vol. 70, No. 3, pp. 43-48.

Schwan, E. S., "Process Costing via Reaction Accounting," *Management Accounting*, Vol. 56, No. 3, pp. 45-50.

Siegel, J. G., and M. Stevens, "Reporting and Appraisal of Process Cost Data," *Accountants Record*, March-April 1984, pp. 10-13, 19.

Stallman, J. C., "Framework for Evaluating Cost Control Procedures for a Process," *Accounting Review*, October 1972, pp. 774-790.

Wolk, H. I., and M. G. Tearney, "Job Order Costing and Normal Spoilage: An Equational Approach," *Government Accounting Journal*, Fall 1977, p. 53.

QUESTIONS FOR REVIEW AND DISCUSSION

1. Distinguish between a job cost system and a process cost system as to the timing of sales versus production.

2. What is the focal point for cost accumulation in a process cost system?

3. Distinguish between a modified cost system and a hybrid cost system.

4. What is the purpose of a job, work, or production order?

5. For job cost control purposes, what amounts are compared with actual costs?

6. List the five computational steps necessary to account for costs in a process cost system.

7. Explain how equivalent units are computed under the FIFO method of inventory accounting.

8. How are the unit costs computed under the FIFO method of inventory accounting?

9. Why are equivalent units for materials usually different from equivalent units for conversion costs?

10. What accounting report is the major document for a process cost system?

11. How can one check to ensure that cost distribution to completed units and ending inventory has been done properly?

12. How can management use a cost of production report?

13. Which aspect of determining unit costs in a process cost system is particularly susceptible to manipulation by production managers?

14. Explain how a just-in-time environment can simplify a process cost system.

15. What is the distinction between equivalent units under the FIFO method and equivalent units under the weighted average method? **(Appendix)**

16. Under what circumstances will both FIFO and weighted average yield the same equivalent units? **(Appendix)**

17. On a cost of production report, the costs of units completed and transferred out are treated one way under the FIFO method and a different way under the weighted average method. Explain this difference. **(Appendix)**

E XERCISES

5-1. Analysis of Job Orders.   Data from three production orders completed by Araceli Products Company are as follows:

	Production Orders		
	163	*164*	*165*
Direct materials	$ 5,600	$ 3,800	$ 2,600
Direct labor	4,500	2,700	3,000
Applied factory overhead	2,400	900	1,200
Total costs	$12,500	$ 7,400	$ 6,800
Direct labor hours	600	300	400
Number of units produced	1,000	500	200

Required:
1. What was the direct labor rate per hour on each of the orders?
2. What was the overhead rate per hour on each of the orders, assuming this rate was based on direct labor hours?
3. Compute the total cost per unit of product on each order.

5-2. Job Cost Control.   Greenberg & Campbell, an engineering consulting firm, has three jobs in process at the end of 1996. The following labor cost information is provided:

Job Number	Original Estimate	Percentage Complete	Labor Costs to Date
9611	$12,000	20%	$ 2,525
9612	17,500	40	6,080
9613	10,800	75	8,020

Required:
Determine which of the jobs in process are underbudget and which are overbudget.

5-3. Job Cost Flows.   Amy Devorah prints brochures for clients and uses job costing. She applies her overhead costs to jobs each month by adding 20 percent to prime costs. In February, she had the following job activity:

Job	Beginning Inventory	Materials Added	Direct Labor Added
115	$25,000		$ 10,000
116		$ 20,000	20,000
117		20,000	10,000

Job 117 was incomplete at the end of February.

Required:
Determine the cost of jobs completed in February.

5-4. Analysis of Work in Process in a Job Cost System.   The Atkinson Corp. uses a job cost system and a predetermined overhead rate based on labor cost. The following T-account summarizes January 1998 activity relating to work in process:

Work in Process Inventory

1/1/98	Balance	30,000	1/31/98 Jobs completed	120,000
	Materials used	50,000		
	Labor cost	60,000		
	Overhead applied	40,000		
1/31/98	Balance	60,000		

Required:
If jobs in the work in process inventory on 1/31/98 contain $10,000 of materials, how much labor cost is in the work in process inventory on 1/31/98?

5-5. Physical Flow.   The work in process inventory in Operation 1 on July 1 was 2,500 units. During July, 60,000 units were completed in Operation 1 and transferred to Operation 2. The ending work in process inventory in Operation 1 was 3,500 units.

Required:
1. Compute the number of units started into production.
2. Compute the number of units started and completed.
3. Why is the stage of completion for the work in process inventories irrelevant for these computations?

5-6. Physical Flow.   Newman Co. had 8,800 units in work in process at January 1. These units were 85 percent complete as to conversion cost. During January, 22,000 units were completed. At January 31, 7,100 units remained in work in process. These were 25 percent complete as to conversion cost. Direct materials are added at the beginning of the process.

Required:
How many units were started during January?

5-7. Equivalent Units in a Nonmanufacturing Setting.   Carroll Fisheries raises cutthroat trout for local restaurants. The process involves three ponds: raising, growing, and fattening. Fingerlings are grown after hatching in the raising pond. At a specified point, the fingerlings are moved to the growing pond, where they mature. After maturing, the fish are transferred to the fattening pond. The growing pond had 5,000 fingerlings on April 1 that were 10 percent complete for the growing pond. The fish represent materials. During the month, an additional 30,000 fingerlings were put into the pond. By the end of April, 28,000 fish had been moved to the fattening pond. The fingerlings remaining in the growing pond were 30 percent complete.

Required:
1. Determine the equivalent units for fingerlings.
2. Determine the equivalent units for conversion costs.

5-8. Unit Cost Computation.   Kloss Equipment, of Oslo, Norway, manufactures ski poles. On November 1, 15,000 poles were in process in Department 1 that were 100 percent complete for materials and 60 percent complete for conversion costs. Materials are added at the beginning of the process. The cost of the beginning work in process inventory (in Norwegian krone) was NKr150,000 for materials and NKr45,000 for conversion costs. In November, 200,000 units were started in process. Materials costs for the month were NKr2,050,000. Conversion costs amounted to NKr3,700,000. On November 30, 30,000 units were in process that were 30 percent complete for conversion costs.

Required:
1. Compute the equivalent units and unit cost for materials.
2. Compute the equivalent units and unit cost for conversion costs.
3. How would the computational process in Part (2) change if labor and factory overhead were not incurred at the same rate?

5-9. Total Cost Distribution and Ethics.   There were 5,000 units in process in the Cutting Department of Rosella Company at the beginning of February. These units had materials and conversion costs of $48,000 and were 60 percent complete for conversion costs. Materials are added at the beginning of the process. During February, 60,000 units were started. The ending inventory for the month totaled 8,000 units, 25 percent complete for conversion costs. The unit cost calculation shows $4 for materials and $8 for conversion costs.

Required:

1. Compute the cost of units completed and transferred to the next department.

2. Compute the cost of units in the ending inventory for the month.

3. Why might the production manager wish to inflate the estimate of the degree of completion of the ending inventory from 25 percent to 50 percent? Support your answer with computations.

5-10. Cost of Production Report.   Schulteis Chicken Farms raises chicks to the egg-laying stage and then moves the hens to the laying sheds. Information about the Chick Raising Operation for March is:

(a) Beginning inventory of chicks is 12,000, 100 percent complete for chicks and 20 percent for raising costs.

(b) Beginning inventory costs are $12,960 for chicks and $1,153 for raising costs.

(c) Chicks added during March totalled 20,000.

(d) Costs incurred during the month are $20,000 for chicks and $12,180 for raising costs.

(e) Ending inventory at March 31 consisted of 2,000 chicks, 100 percent complete for chicks and 70 percent for raising costs.

Required:

Prepare a cost of production report for the Chick Raising Operation for March.

5-11. Unit Costs in a Bank.   BancTwo of Columbus, Ohio, processes nonroutine checks in its Check Clearing Department. No materials costs are incurred in this department. On June 1, 4,000 checks in process were 25 percent complete with an associated processing cost of $200. During June, 100,000 checks were started in process. By the end of June, 70,000 checks had been started and completed. The direct processing costs in June amounted to $22,000. On June 30, the checks in process were one-third complete.

Required:

Calculate equivalent units and the unit cost of work done during June.

5-12. Units Costs.   Cochrane Candy Company manufactures candy bars in unit lots consisting of 24 bars to a unit. The January 1 inventory consisted of 6,000 units in process that were two-thirds complete. The work in process on January 1 included costs of $30,000 for materials and $4,000 for processing. During the month of January, the company started 50,000 units.

Processing costs in the month of January amounted to $55,400. All materials are added at the beginning of the process. During January, $272,400 of materials costs were incurred. By the end of January, the company completed and transferred 53,000 units to the finished goods inventory. On January 31, 3,000 units in process were one-third complete.

Required:

Compute the equivalent units and unit cost of work done during January for both materials and processing.

5-13. Units Costs (Appendix).   Work Exercise 5-12 using the weighted average cost method.

5-14. Cost Distribution.   Axiom Products, Inc. manufactures a vitamin product. On July 1, it had 8,000 units in process that were 25 percent complete for conversion costs. Materials (a coating) are added at the end of the process. The cost of the beginning work in process was $1,800. July conversion costs were $36,000, and the materials costs were $17,000. Axiom started and completed 60,000 units in July. The work in process inventory on July 31 of 10,000 units was 60 percent complete.

Required:

1. What was the total cost of work transferred to the finished goods inventory in July?
2. Determine the cost of work in process inventory on July 31.

5-15. Cost Distribution (Appendix).

Required:

1. Work Exercise 5-14 using the weighted average cost method.
2. Under what circumstances would the conversion cost per unit be identical to that computed by the FIFO method? Explain.

5-16. Unit Cost—Weighted Average Cost Method (Appendix).   On December 1, S&M Vineyards ("we whip 'em till they wine") had 10,000 bottles of wine in process that were 40 percent complete for conversion costs. The conversion cost in the beginning work in process inventory was $20,000. In December, 150,000 bottles were started in process. Conversion costs in December amounted to $790,000. On December 31, 20,000 bottles in process were 40 percent complete for conversion costs.

Required:

1. Compute the equivalent units (bottles).
2. Determine the conversion cost per bottle.

5-17. Cost Accounting—Weighted Average Cost Method (Appendix).   Maple Leaf Enterprises of Saskatoon, Saskatchewan, manufactures hockey sticks for distribution throughout Canada. The beginning work in process in Department A1 on September 1 consisted of 40,000 units (hockey sticks). During the month of September, 150,000 units were completed and transferred to Department A2. The September 30 work in process inventory in Department A1 consisted of 60,000 units that were 20 percent complete in that department. The unit cost, as computed by the weighted average cost method, was C$6.

Required:

1. Compute the total cost of work transferred to Department A2.
2. Compute the total cost of work in process at September 30.
3. Why might you expect more accurate unit costs if the hockey sticks were produced in an automated factory?

5-18. Equivalent Units With Incomplete Data.   Calculate the equivalent units for the period with respect to *conversion costs* for each of the following independent situations.

(a) Department MK had 5,000 units in process on April 1 which were 60 percent complete for conversion costs. Materials are added at the beginning of the departmental process, and conversion costs are added uniformly throughout the process. On April 30, the in-process inventory consisted of 8,000 units that had 25 percent of the work completed. There were 83,000 equivalent units of output for the period with respect to *materials.*

(b) At the beginning of July, 12,000 units were in process in Department XY, 90 percent complete for materials and 70 percent complete for conversion costs. On July 31, the in-process inventory was 10,000 units, which were 50 percent complete for materials and 40 percent complete for conversion costs. There were 176,200 equivalent units of output for the period with respect to *materials.*

5-19. Costing Completed Goods.   Hubert Products Company of Wellington, New Zealand, produces a kiwi fruit drink. The units and equivalent units (in liters), as well as unit costs, for the Initial Mix Department are as follows:

	Materials	Conversion
Equivalent units in beginning work in process	6,000	1,200
Units started and completed	40,000	40,000
Equivalent units in ending work in process	3,000	1,800
Unit costs	NZ$0.10	NZ$0.20

Required:
1. Compute the current period costs for:
   (a) Materials.
   (b) Conversion costs.
2. If the beginning work in process inventory was valued at NZ$12,600, what would be the cost of goods completed?

5-20. T-Account Flow With Process Costs. Southwest Paper Company manufactures paper from pine logs in a continuous process. Its operations are divided into three activity centers: Stripping, Mixing, and Pressing. The Stripping Center strips the bark from the logs, and chips the logs into small pieces. The Mixing Center mixes the chips with chemicals in a vat. The Pressing Center presses the chemically dissolved pulp into paper.

The process does not change, and the company's operations move at a constant speed so that beginning and ending inventories are always in the same amount and at the same stage of completion. For this reason, costs are transferred out of work in process inventories by the end of each period.

The company completed the following transactions during one week in August:

(a) Purchased on credit three car loads of logs for $2,700 and one tank car of chemicals for $1,000.

(b) Placed two car loads of logs and half of the chemicals into process.

(c) Labor for the week was as follows:

Stripping Center.	$1,500
Mixing Center.	700
Pressing Center.	900
Factory indirect labor.	800

(d) Manufacturing overhead (other than indirect labor) was as follows:

Depreciation	$ 400
Machinery repairs	100
Power.	100
Supplies	50
Taxes	100

(e) The company applies manufacturing overhead to departments on the basis of 50 percent of direct labor costs.

Required:
Show the flow of costs for each of the transactions using T-accounts. Separate work in process accounts exist for each activity center.

P ROBLEMS

5-21. Job Cost Control. Pollack Photography Studio has four jobs in process at the end of 1996. The following cost information for materials and conversion costs is provided:

Job Number	Materials			Conversion		
	Original Estimate	Percentage Complete	Cost to Date	Original Estimate	Percentage Complete	Cost to Date
K98	$120	10%	$ 20	$ 550	20%	$ 125
L76	100	75	65	850	80	655
T45	180	50	95	950	70	620
P90	145	20	30	600	25	185

Required:

1. For both materials and conversion costs, determine which of the jobs in process are underbudget and which are overbudget.

2. Does any job have a total cost overrun? Identify.

5-22. Flow of Process Cost. LeMay Cookie Company manufactures a line of chocolate cookies in three processing operations. The product is perishable; therefore, there are no work in process inventories in any of the operations at the end of the month. During the month of June, 500,000 units were processed completely in all three operations, transferred to finished goods inventory, and sold. Processing costs for the month were as follows:

```
Department A:
    Materials . . . . . . . . . . . . . . . . .    $165,000
    Labor  . . . . . . . . . . . . . . . . . .       25,000
    Overhead applied  . . . . . . . . . .           20,000    $210,000

Department B:
    Labor. . . . . . . . . . . . . . . . . .      $ 80,000
    Overhead applied  . . . . . . . . . .           40,000     120,000

Department C:
    Labor  . . . . . . . . . . . . . . . . .      $ 60,000
    Overhead applied  . . . . . . . . . .           45,000     105,000
```

Required:

1. Using T-accounts for the work in process inventories of each operation, trace the flow of costs through the three operations and into cost of goods sold.

2. Determine the total unit manufacturing cost.

3. Determine the addition to unit cost by each of the three operations.

5-23. Flow of Process Cost. A vitamin product is manufactured in three operations by Bocian Health Products, Inc. No work in process existed on August 1 in any of the three operations, but 10,000 units were in process in each operation at the end of August. All costs within each department, including materials, are added uniformly throughout the department's production process. The percentage of the work in process that was completed in each operation at August 31 is as follows:

```
Department 1 . . . . . . . . . . . . . . . . . . . . . . . . . . . . .    40%
Department 2 . . . . . . . . . . . . . . . . . . . . . . . . . . . . .    60
Department 3 . . . . . . . . . . . . . . . . . . . . . . . . . . . . .    20
```

Costs in the three departments for August were as follows:

	Departments		
	1	2	3
Materials	$ 94,000	$ 0	$ 0
Labor	47,000	30,000	14,400
Overhead applied	47,000	21,600	7,200
Totals	$188,000	$ 51,600	$ 21,600

During August, 100,000 units were started in process in Department 1.

Required:

1. For each department, compute the unit cost of work completed in that department and the cumulative unit cost of work done (i.e., including preceding departments' costs).
2. Using T-accounts for each department, trace the flow of costs through the three departments and into finished goods inventory.
3. Assume that 50,000 units were sold during the month. What amount will appear in the Cost of Goods Sold account?

5-24. Cost of Production Report and Ethics.   Pfeffer Specialty Foods, Inc. prepares and cans tasty Italian foods in three processing operations. All materials are added at the beginning of the first operation. Data for the month of May in Operation A are given as follows:

	Units
Work in process, May 1	5,000
Units started in process	120,000

	Costs
Work in process, May 1:	
Materials	$ 15,000
Labor and overhead	2,500
May's costs:	
Materials	$360,000
Labor and overhead	232,000

The beginning work in process was 20 percent complete for labor and overhead. During the month, 115,000 units were completed and transferred to Operation B; and 10,000 units that were 20 percent complete as to labor and overhead were in process in Operation A at May 31.

Required:

1. Prepare a cost of production report for Operation A for the month of May.
2. Explain how management might use this cost of production report.
3. What might motivate the production manager to inflate the estimate of the degree of completion of the ending inventory from 20 percent to 40 percent? Support your answer with computations.

5-25. Cost of Production Report.   McDuffy Robotics, a subsidiary of U.S.-based International Robotics, located in Dublin, Ireland, manufactures a small robot which looks like a leprechaun and can be moved by remote control. It can be used as a novelty to serve food and drinks to guests; and, with a special attachment, it can vacuum the carpet.

The materials are all added at the beginning of the Assembly Operation (the first operation). Labor and overhead are added during the month. Data for the month of July in the Assembly Operation are as follows:

	Units
Work in process, July 1	20,000
Units started in process	250,000

	Costs (in U.S. Dollars)
Work in process, July 1:	
Materials	$ 240,000
Labor and overhead	80,000
July's costs:	
Materials	$3,500,000
Labor and overhead	1,457,280

The inventory of work in process on July 1 was complete as to materials but only one-fourth complete as to labor and overhead. On July 31, the inventory consisted of 20,000 units that were 40 percent complete with respect to labor and overhead.

Required:

1. Prepare a cost of production report for the Assembly Operation for the month of July.

2. Explain how management could use this report.

5-26. Explanation of Approach to a Cost of Production Report.   A partial cost of production report for the month of May is as follows for Department 1 of Enid Chemical Company:

Physical units:

Work in process, May 1 (40% complete)	500
Started and completed	1,700
Work in process, May 31 (50% complete)	300
Total units	2,500

Costs charged to department:

Work in process, May 1	$ 800.00
Processing cost, May.	9,020.00
Total costs charged	$ 9,820.00

Costs accounted for:

Transferred to Department 2:	
Work in process, May 1	$ 800.00
Cost to complete work in process, May 1	1,258.60
Started and completed	7,132.09
	$ 9,190.69
Work in process, May 31	629.30
Total costs accounted for	$ 9,819.99*

  * Difference caused by rounding.

Required:

1. Explain what the partial cost of production report shows about the quantity flow and the cost flow.

2. Explain why equivalent units are preferred to total units produced in determining costs of units completed and units in ending inventory.

3. What additional information can this report give a manager?

4. Calculate how many units were completed during the month of May.

5-27. Cost Accountability—Two Months.   Conrad George, Inc. manufactures a single product that goes through a mixing operation followed by a drying operation. The data for the Mixing Department for October and November are:

	October	November
Units in beginning inventory	0	600
Units started during month	12,400	13,100
Units completed and transferred	11,800	13,300
Costs put into production:		
Materials	$258,640	$271,760
Labor and factory overhead	$526,860	$569,770
Units in ending inventory	600	400
Stage of completion for ending inventory:		
Materials	90%	50%
Labor and factory overhead	60%	30%

Required:

1. Prepare a cost of production report for October. Round unit costs to five decimal places and total dollars to the nearest dollar.

2. Prepare a cost of production report for November. Round unit costs to five decimal places and total dollars to the nearest dollar.

5-28. Cost Accountability—Two Months (Appendix).   Work Problem 5-27 using the weighted average cost method.

5-29. A Comparison of Actual and Estimated Unit Costs. Owen Tu ("The Count") has estimated unit costs at various production stages in manufacturing baseballs. The unit cost of work done in Operation 1, according to budget estimates, should be $2.50, consisting of a unit cost of $1.60 for materials and a unit cost of $0.90 for labor and overhead. All materials are added at the beginning of the operation, and labor and overhead are added as the work progresses. Cost and production data for Operation 1 are as follows for the month of October:

Quantities:

Units in work in process, October 1 (40% complete)	10,000
Units started in production	150,000
Units in work in process, October 31 (20% complete)	5,000

Costs charged to operation:

Work in process, October 1:		
Materials	$ 16,000	
Labor and overhead	5,400	$ 21,400
October's costs:		
Materials	$240,000	
Labor and overhead	182,400	422,400
Total costs charged		$443,800

Required:

1. Determine unit costs for materials and for conversion costs.

2. Compare the actual unit costs with the estimated unit costs. Identify separately any variance of materials cost and any variance of conversion cost.

5-30. A Comparison of Actual and Estimated Unit Cost (Appendix). Work Problem 5-29 using the weighted average cost method.

5-31. Cost of Production Report and Cost Flows. Bao Brothers is a manufacturer of men's neckties in Singapore. Materials are added to production at the beginning of the manufacturing process, and factory overhead is applied to each unit at the rate of 60 percent of direct labor costs. Its operations for June show the following ending inventories of work in process and finished goods as reflected in the general ledger:

	Units	Costs
Work in process (50% complete for labor and overhead)	300,000	S$ 870,000
Finished goods	200,000	900,000

No finished goods inventory existed on June 1. The operating data for the month are:

			Costs	
	Units	**Materials**	**Labor**	
Work in process, June 1				
(80% complete for labor and overhead)	200,000	S$ 200,000	S$ 315,000	
Units started during June	1,000,000			
June's materials costs		1,300,000		
June's labor costs.			1,780,000	
Units completed	900,000			

Required:

1. Calculate the unit costs for June for:

  (a) Materials.

  (b) Labor.

  (c) Overhead.

2. Determine the cost of completed units and ending work in process.

3. Using T-accounts, prepare a summary of cost flows from Work in Process Inventory through Finished Goods Inventory to Cost of Goods Sold.

1-2-3

5-32. Analysis for Several Months.   Hansen Industries started operations three years ago and is gaining a reputation for the manufacturing of quality paint. The accounting system is evolving and has not been fully formalized. A chief accountant, Deborah Turner, has been hired to bring order to the paper shuffling. In the process, Turner has gathered data to prepare cost of production reports for Activity Center A for the first three months of the current fiscal year (April, May, and June). This information is as follows:

	April	**May**	**June**
Gallons:			
Beginning inventory	10,000	?	?
Started in production	80,000	65,000	70,000
Completed	70,000	60,000	?
Ending inventory	?	?	20,000
Stage of completion:			
Beginning inventory	60%	30%	70%
Ending inventory.	30%	70%	40%
Cost data:			
Beginning inventory:			
Materials	$ 10,000	?	?
Conversion costs	20,000	?	?
Current period:			
Materials	$ 80,000	$ 66,000	$ 70,000
Conversion costs	170,000	142,000	156,000

Materials are added at the beginning of Activity Center A. Conversion costs flow uniformly throughout the process.

Required:

1. Compute the physical flows of product for each of the three months.
2. Prepare a cost of production report for each of the three months. Round unit costs to four decimal places and total dollars to the nearest dollar.
3. Analyze the cost of production reports for each month, and comment on production stability and unit costs for materials and conversion costs.

5-33. Cost Flows Through T-Accounts.   Lupe Manufacturing Company produces a single product. Its operations are a continuous process through two activity centers: Machining and Finishing. Materials are added at the start of production in each department. For November, the following transactions took place:

(a) Purchased materials on credit costing $435,400.
(b) Started 80,000 units in production in the Machining Center. The direct materials cost $240,000, and indirect materials cost $8,100. The Machining Center had no beginning work in process inventory.
(c) Paid the following salaries and wages for the month:

	Machining	**Finishing**
Direct labor	$ 140,000	$ 141,500
Factory indirect labor	30,000	6,700

(d) Applied factory overhead at 100 percent of direct labor cost in Machining and at 20 percent of direct labor cost in Finishing.
(e) Incurred actual factory overhead costs for Machining, other than indirect materials and indirect labor, of $100,000.
(f) Completed 60,000 units in Machining and transferred them to Finishing. The units remaining in Machining were 100 percent complete for materials and 50 percent complete for conversion costs.
(g) Added $88,500 of direct materials costs in Finishing. Indirect materials were $2,400. No beginning inventory was in Finishing on November 1.
(h) Incurred actual factory overhead costs for Finishing, other than indirect materials and indirect labor, totaling $16,600.

Required:

Using T-accounts, trace the costs reflected in the transactions through the appropriate accounts.

5-34. Analysis of a Work in Process Account.   Broadway Pharmaceutical Company manufactures a tablet for allergy sufferers. All ingredients are added at the beginning of the Blending Operation. Conversion costs flow uniformly throughout the process. Tabulating and Coating are operations downstream from Blending. Information on the Blending Operation for October is as follows:

Work in Process—Blending Operation

October 1, balance (100,000 units, 40% complete for conversion costs)	151,760	Completed and transferred to Tabulating:	
		Units - ?	
		Costs - ?	
Direct materials added (1,000,000 units)	1,310,000		
Direct labor cost	?		
Factory overhead (applied at 180% of direct labor cost)	396,000		
October 31, balance (200,000 units, 70% complete for conversion costs)	?		

The October 1 balance consists of the following cost elements:

Direct materials	$ 128,000
Direct labor	8,800
Factory overhead	14,960
Total costs	$ 151,760

Required:

1. Compute the amount of direct labor cost for the period.
2. Calculate the unit costs for direct materials, direct labor, and factory overhead for the current month (October). Direct labor and factory overhead should be separate; do not combine them into one figure.
3. Calculate the unit costs for direct materials, direct labor, and factory overhead in the inventory at the beginning of October.
4. Compare the unit costs computed in Parts (2) and (3). Explain what information this comparison gives to a manager.

5-35. Analysis of a Work in Process Account (Appendix).   Work Problem 5-34 using the weighted average cost method.

1-2-3

5-36. Unit Cost Computations (Appendix).   Kristina Company, which manufactures quality paint sold at premium prices, uses a single production department. Production begins with the blending of various chemicals, which are added at the beginning of the process, and ends with the canning of the paint. Canning occurs when the mixture reaches the 90 percent stage of completion. The gallon cans are then transferred to the Shipping Department for crating and shipment. Labor and overhead are added continuously throughout the process. Factory overhead is applied on the basis of direct labor hours at the rate of $3.00 per hour.

Prior to May, when a change in the process was implemented, work in process inventories were insignificant. The change in the process enables greater production but has resulted in significant amounts of work in process for the first time. The company has always used the weighted average method to determine equivalent production and unit costs. Now, production management is considering changing from the weighted average method to the first-in, first-out method.

The following data relate to actual production during the month of May:

Costs for May	
Work in process inventory, May 1:	
(4,000 gallons, 25% complete)	
Direct materials—chemicals	$ 45,600
Direct labor ($10 per hour)	6,250
Factory overhead	1,875
May's costs added:	
Direct materials—chemicals	228,400
Direct materials—cans	7,000
Direct labor ($10 per hour)	35,000
Factory overhead	10,500

Units for May	Gallons
Work in process inventory,	
May 1 (25% complete)	4,000
Sent to Shipping Department	20,000
Started in May	21,000
Work in process inventory,	
May 31 (80% complete)	5,000

Required:

1. Prepare a schedule of equivalent units for each cost element using the:

    (a) Weighted average method.

    (b) First-in, first-out method.

2. Calculate the cost (to the nearest cent) per equivalent unit for each cost element using the:

    (a) Weighted average method.

    (b) First-in, first-out method.

3. Discuss the advantages and disadvantages of using the weighted average method versus the first-in, first-out method, and explain under what circumstances each method should be used.

(ICMA adapted)

5-37. Adjusting Inventory Records (Appendix). You have been sent to Panama City, Panama, to audit the December 31, 1998, financial statements of Canal Fashions, a manufacturer of sandals. You are attempting to verify the costing of the ending inventories of work in process and of finished goods, which were recorded on Canal Fashions' books (in Panamanian balboas) as follows:

	Units	Cost
Work in process (50% complete as to conversion cost)	300,000	B 660,960
Finished goods	200,000	1,009,800

Materials are added to production at the beginning of the manufacturing process, and overhead is applied to each product at the rate of 60 percent of direct labor costs. There was no finished goods inventory on January 1, 1998. A review of Canal Fashions' inventory cost records disclosed the following information:

		Costs	
	Units	Materials	Labor
Work in process, January 1, 1998			
(80% complete as to conversion cost) . . .	200,000	B 200,000	B 315,000
Units started:	1,000,000		
Materials cost		1,300,000	
Labor cost			1,995,000
Units completed	900,000		

Required:

1. Determine the unit costs for materials, labor, and overhead using the weighted average cost method.

2. Determine the cost of finished goods and work in process inventories.

3. Using T-accounts, make entries to correctly state the inventories of finished goods and work in process. Assume the books have not been closed.

(AICPA adapted)

CASE 5A—BOZEMAN HI-TECH PRODUCTS

Bozeman Hi-Tech Products manufactures a product that is accounted for under a process cost system in the Assembly and Finishing departments. Recently, the production superintendent was reviewing the April cost of production reports for the two departments. His intuition suggested something was wrong with the reports. He asked the departmental managers if they had reviewed the reports. Both indicated that they had. However, both managers acknowledged that the reports must be in error because they did not agree with the operating facts. One manager suggested the Accounting Department had screwed up again.

You have been asked to review the departmental cost of production report for the Assembly Department and determine what adjustments should be made. You have the following information available to you for the Assembly Department:

Units:	
Beginning inventory	10,000
Units started	20,000
Units completed and transferred	26,000
Ending inventory	4,000

Costs:	
Materials	$ 22,000
Labor	8,000

In the Assembly Department, materials are added at the beginning of the process, and conversion costs enter evenly throughout the operation. Beginning work in process was 50 percent complete for conversion costs. Beginning inventories include $6,000 for materials and $2,000 for conversion costs. Overhead is applied at the rate of 50 percent of labor dollars. Ending inventory was 40 percent completed. The FIFO method is used.

Excerpts from the Assembly Department's cost of production report are as follows:

Cost of goods completed (26,000 x $1.2667)		$ 32,934
Ending inventory:		
Materials (4,000 x $.9333)	$ 3,733	
Conversion costs (4,000 x $.3333)	1,333	5,066
Total costs accounted for		$ 38,000

Additional Computations	*Materials*	*Conversion Cost*
Costs in process, beginning	$ 6,000	$ 2,000
Current period costs	22,000	12,000
	$ 28,000	$ 14,000
Computation of equivalent units:		
Units completed	26,000	26,000
Ending inventory	4,000	4,000
Equivalent units	30,000	30,000
Equivalent unit cost	$ 0.9333	$ 0.3333

Required:

Prepare a corrected cost of production report for the Assembly Department. Identify the errors, if any, in the original cost of production report.

C ASE 5B—GULF COAST PIPELINES

Gulf Coast Pipelines, Inc. is a liquid petroleum pipeline transportation company. The line running from Corpus Christi to Kansas City is a 30-inch, high pressure line which moves product at an average of 8 miles per hour. A filled line contains 28 million barrels of product which travel an average 192 miles per day. The line speed can be increased safely to about 280 miles per day or slowed to almost a stop. The line can be filled to capacity or be partially empty. Over certain segments, the line moves faster than elsewhere as more product is added and taken out. The line carries various products including crude oil of varying weights, home heating oil, and numerous other petroleum products.

As a transportation company, Gulf Coast Pipelines does not own the products transported. Instead, it is paid a fee for its services based on moving 10,000 barrels (420,000 gallons) of product one mile. The variable cost of running the line is for the 30 pumping stations along the line: the higher the traffic, the higher the fuel cost for pumping. The other cost of running the line is overhead cost, which relates to line maintenance. One unit is considered to be moving 10,000 barrels of product one mile.

On April 1, the Corpus Christi to Kansas City line had 1.44 million units in process (18 million barrels that were to be transported an average of 800 miles), which were 60 percent complete. During the month, the line completed 12 million units of delivered product and had ending units in process of two million units (20 million barrels to be transported 1,000 miles) that were 40 percent complete. The beginning units in transit had accumulated costs of $8,800,000 of which $2,400,000 were variable costs. During the month, the Corpus Christi to Kansas City line had $33,420,800 in variable costs and $81,168,800 in fixed costs. The completed deliveries were billed at $134,400,000 for services.

Required:

1. What is the nature of the costs incurred as to direct materials, direct labor, and variable or fixed overhead?
2. Why should this application be considered for a modified process cost system?
3. Compute the equivalent units of production for the Corpus Christi to Kansas City line. (Round to four decimal places, if needed.)
4. Compute a cost per unit of output for variable and fixed costs.
5. What were the profits before administrative expenses and taxes during April?
6. What were the costs of the units in transit on April 30?

CHAPTER 6

Activity-Based Costing and Just-in-Time Costing

LEARNING OBJECTIVES

After studying Chapter 6, you will be able to:

1. Explain the interrelationships among cost drivers, activities, and products in an activity-based costing system.

2. Describe the key components and cost flows in an activity-based costing system.

3. Distinguish between the two stages of cost allocation in an activity-based costing system.

4. Apply activity-based costing in a manufacturing setting.

5. Understand how activity-based costing is extended to nonmanufacturing settings.

6. Relate activity-based management to activity-based costing.

7. Describe the key elements of a just-in-time costing system.

Why Profitable Products Aren't Necessarily as Profitable as They Look

Alexus Plumbing Fixtures is a $100 million manufacturer of plumbing fixtures. It has a vertically integrated 720,000-square-foot factory encompassing die casting, screw machines, pipe threading, chrome plating, stamping, polishing, and assembly. It also sells product variations extending into the hundreds of thousands, including different functions, styles, finishes, and substitutions. These factors contribute to a large overhead structure that amounts to almost 60 percent of cost of goods sold. The cost accounting system identifies materials, labor, and overhead costs with each department; and the departmental costs are allocated to products on the basis of direct labor identified with that department. Alexus is losing money. Management wants to reduce costs and improve profitability.

Members of the management team recently attended a management seminar and heard a speaker mention the benefits of activity-based costing. The speaker said that companies similar to Alexus, that permit many options in their products, are losing money because the companies push products that look profitable based on a faulty cost accounting system. Alexus executives believe they should study their business to see if activity-based costing would alleviate some of their cost problems and help them control costs better.

Stan Stanslovsky, a plant controller and something of a computer jock, came back from the meeting and began to think about alternative costing approaches. He figured that a major change in the product costing system would take months, maybe years, and would cost hundreds of thousands of dollars. He remembered his younger days as a budget analyst in the sales division of a food products company. It always had test markets to try new ideas. Why couldn't he "test" a different product costing approach, he wondered.

Stan selected a small product line of water filters. Two departments were almost exclusively devoted to the filter products. Most products were simple assembly tasks; a few were complex; and some required either manual or automated steps. He studied past costs and activity levels. He talked to the plant's production planners and engineers and to workers and managers in both departments.

After about a month of work, Stan recreated the unit costs of the filters for the first quarter of the year. He emphasized links between costs incurred and activities. He found that frequent setups to change from producing one filter to another took time and stopped production. Some filters had low demand; others were high-volume sellers. He linked some costs to machine usage and others to direct labor hours expended. Instead of merely materials, direct labor, and overhead cost pools, Stan had grouped costs by materials, materials handling, all labor wages and benefits, machine usage costs, setup costs, supervision, and general factory overhead.

He found that some products were undercosted, some overcosted, while about half didn't change much. The new costs of certain key products were off by over 50 percent. Were the old costs or his new costs right? Well, he knew his new numbers were only estimates, but they were so different that Alexus' pricing formulas, cost analyses, and decision-making data could all be substantially off base.

He began to show his results to others who had gone to the seminar—production, sales, and financial people. A few scoffed, but Stan got many responses like: "I thought that might be the case" and "I always wondered about those cost numbers."

But Stan knew the big test would be to get budget money to make changes in the cost accounting system itself. Would people be willing to pay for better information?

Two major forces have combined to put great pressure on managerial accountants like Stan Stanslovsky to provide improved cost information about their firms' products and services. These are global competition and automation in the workplace.

1. **Global competitiveness.**   Most companies in nearly every industry face increased competition from direct competitors, whether from across the street or halfway around the world. Whether the technology is old

(making iron and steel) or new (making high-definition televisions), the needs for accurate and relevant product cost data have grown dramatically. Competitiveness also means knowing the costs of product quality, reliable delivery, and waste (unproductive effort). Cost control takes on new meaning if a competitor can sell an item at a price that is 10 percent lower than another company's production cost and still make money on the sale. Increasingly, companies are realizing that traditional volume-based cost systems are not using the "right" variables or collecting cost data in enough detail.

2. **Automation of the workplace.**   Dramatic changes in production have also taken place. Another "industrial revolution" is what some people have called it. Computer power has introduced concepts like computer-aided design (CAD), computer-aided manufacturing (CAM), flexible manufacturing systems (FMS), and robotics. Computer power has allowed precise tasks to be programmed and machines to be designed to do those tasks. Likewise, computer power has enabled production managers to coordinate thousands of events, transactions, and possible courses of action. One outcome is a shift from heavy dependence on labor to technology. Direct labor costs were often a major product cost, and labor activity often reflected general activity in the plant. Now, in many factories, direct labor is a minor portion of a product's total cost. Other production costs have grown tremendously because of equipment costs and support personnel needed to coordinate production. New activity measures are needed to link resources used with production activities. The traditional approach of allocating overhead costs using direct labor hours or direct labor cost is no longer relevant in companies that are highly automated.

The very computer power that has changed production must also be applied to cost accounting. First, due to costliness, the days of separate cost accounting systems for financial reporting and for production management are past. Second, what had been cost prohibitive in terms of cost systems is now reasonable. Memory capacities, computation speed, communication networks, and equipment availability are building blocks that make data collecting, analyses, and reporting relatively inexpensive when compared to the value created.

Competition and automation have focused attention on getting more accurate, timely, and relevant product costs. The same concern can be expressed for all uses of cost information, applicable to all cost objectives. The concepts are very simple and have always been at the heart of cost accounting: Link the cost of resources used to the activity using the resources, and link the activity to the product being produced. Traditionally, the activity measure used most often has been a volume measure—direct labor hours (or dollars). In recent years, there has been a recognition that the complexity of production, rather than the volume, is the most important determinant of overhead costs. Costing systems known as activity-based costing reflect this new orientation.

This chapter presents the conceptual foundation for activity-based costing as a means of improving the accuracy of assigning costs to cost objectives—primarily to products and services. Many companies that have adopted activity-based costing systems have also instituted just-in-time inventory systems. Later in the chapter, we discuss how adoption of just-in-time inventory systems has affected product costing.

ACTIVITY-BASED COSTING

Activity-based costing focuses on finding the cost of producing a product or service. In Chapter 2, we introduced cost of goods manufactured and the three traditional groups of costs—direct materials, direct labor, and factory overhead. At one time, direct materials and direct labor were linked with products because of their obvious direct relationships; all other manufacturing costs were traditionally lumped together as overhead. One activity measure, often direct labor, was used to attach all overhead costs to products. Many different overhead costs were combined and included, such as:

1. Plant supervision salaries.
2. Materials handling costs.
3. Plant engineering costs.
4. Setup or changeover costs.
5. Supplies and indirect materials.
6. Depreciation, taxes, and insurance on equipment.
7. Energy and other utility costs.
8. Repair and maintenance costs.

Ideally, every overhead cost item could be traced directly to specific products. However, this is just not possible. If we produce a million units of different types and sizes of batteries in a factory, can the manager's $100,000 salary be traced to the different batteries? No. Can we link the manager's salary to certain factory activities, then link the activity costs to the different batteries? Yes, but only with careful analysis and application.

Issues Influencing Cost Management Systems Design

Product costs are so critical to managerial decisions that greater precision and accuracy are needed today than were demanded in the past. Thus, a major effort is underway in many companies to upgrade their product costing systems.

The level of detail that a product costing system needs is based on the following considerations:

1. The competitive environment, which will impact the degree of accuracy needed and the toleration of product costing errors.
2. The homogeneity or heterogeneity of the products produced.
3. The complexity of the production process.
4. The volumes of each product produced.
5. The costs of measuring and collecting activity and cost data.
6. The impacts that more accurate and relevant data will have on managerial behavior.

Detailed product costing systems are expensive to design and to operate. Yet the value of better product cost information can also be extremely high. This detail is illustrated in Contemporary Practice 6.1.

Definition of Activity-Based Costing

Activity-based costing (ABC) is a system of accounting that focuses on activities performed to produce products or services. Activities become the

C O N T E M P O R A R Y   P R A C T I C E   6 . 1

Product Costing Change at Chrysler

The Warren Stamping Plant of Chrysler Corporation changed its product costing approach to activity-based costing. The diagram below compares costs of one vehicle's side panel produced in this plant for both of the costing methods. Notice the more elaborate detail with the ABC method.

Current Cost Method

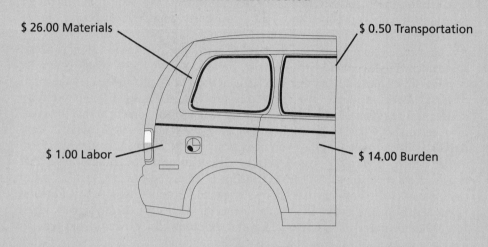

$ 26.00 Materials

$ 0.50 Transportation

$ 1.00 Labor

$ 14.00 Burden

ABC Method

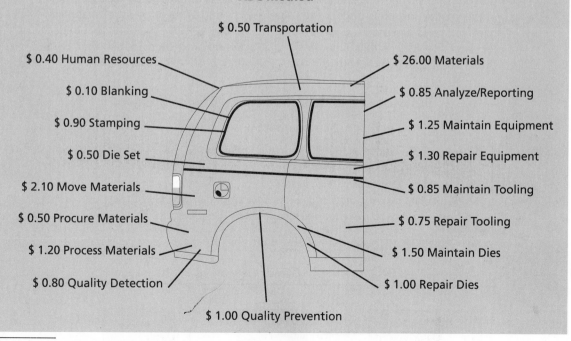

$ 0.50 Transportation

$ 0.40 Human Resources

$ 0.10 Blanking

$ 0.90 Stamping

$ 0.50 Die Set

$ 2.10 Move Materials

$ 0.50 Procure Materials

$ 1.20 Process Materials

$ 0.80 Quality Detection

$ 1.00 Quality Prevention

$ 26.00 Materials

$ 0.85 Analyze/Reporting

$ 1.25 Maintain Equipment

$ 1.30 Repair Equipment

$ 0.85 Maintain Tooling

$ 0.75 Repair Tooling

$ 1.50 Maintain Dies

$ 1.00 Repair Dies

Source: Chrysler Corporation personnel, October 1991.

fundamental cost accumulation points. Costs are traced to activities, and activities are traced to products based on each product's use of the activities. We show these relationships for allocating costs to products in Figure 6.1.

Under activity-based costing, an effort is made to identify and account for as many costs as possible as direct costs of production. Any cost that can reasonably be traced to a particular product or product line is treated as a direct cost. For example, under the traditional costing system, the cost of setup time (the factory downtime incurred in converting from producing one product to producing another) is included in manufacturing overhead and applied to products on the basis of direct labor hours. Under ABC, setup time might be measured for each product line; and setup costs would be directly assigned to each part or product manufactured.

An ABC system identifies the major activities in a production process, aggregates those activities into activity centers, accumulates costs in activity centers, selects cost drivers that link activities to products, and traces the costs of activities to products. We show this process in Figure 6.2. An **activity center** is a segment of the organization for which management wants the costs of a set of activities to be reported separately. A mechanism called a **cost driver** is used for linking a given activity's pool of costs. A cost driver is an event, action, or activity that results in cost incurrence. It is any factor that causes costs to change. The basic concept is that cost drivers, such as setup time, measure the amount of resources a specific product uses. A cost function is created from the activity's costs and the planned cost driver activity level.

Although not always obvious, several different cost drivers could link an activity's costs and the cost objective. In the materials handling case in Figure 6.2, four possible cost drivers are listed. Assume that *pounds of materials moved* are considered to be the most appropriate cost driver. We therefore divide the planned materials handling costs by the planned pounds to be moved. Cost per pound is the cost function. Then, the actual pounds handled in the production of a product × the cost per pound is the amount of materials handling costs assigned to that product. Again, the overall process is to identify the best cost driver that links costs and activities and then to use that cost driver to link activities with products (or other cost objectives).

Flow of Costs Under Activity-Based Costing

In applying ABC to a specific organization, we follow five basic steps:

1. Assemble similar actions into activity centers.
2. Classify costs by activity center and by type of expense.
3. Select cost drivers.
4. Calculate a cost function to link costs and cost drivers with resource use.
5. Assign costs to the cost objective—often the product cost.

These steps are consistent with Figure 6.2.

FIGURE 6.1   **An Overall View of ABC Cost Linkage**

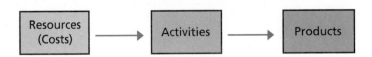

FIGURE 6.2   An Overall View of the ABC Process

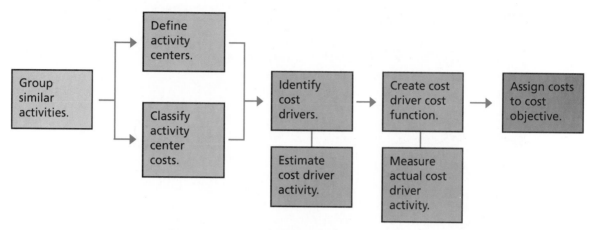

Example: Moving and handling materials in the factory:

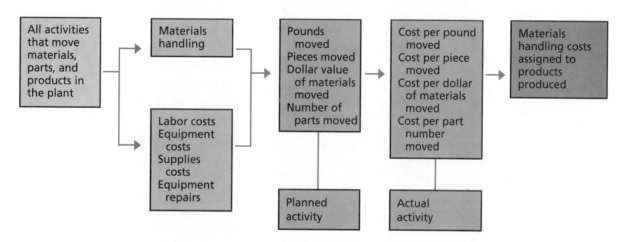

Step 1:   Assemble Similar Actions into Activity Centers.   The number of actions performed in any organization can be quite large. Although the ideal is to relate the cost of every action to a cost driver and then to the product, the expenses of doing this can far exceed the benefits. Therefore, we combine actions into activity centers. Treating collections of actions as activity centers eliminates the need to measure and track the performance of individual actions and costs.

One meaningful way of grouping actions is to classify them with different levels of activities. A common outline is unit-level activities, batch-level activities, product-level activities, and facilities-level activities. Figure 6.3, page 234, illustrates the four types. **Unit-level activities** are performed each time a unit is produced. These are repetitive activities. Direct labor or machining activities are examples. Costs of these activities vary with the number of units produced. **Batch-level activities** are performed each time a batch of goods is produced. Machine setups, order processing, and materials handling are related to batches rather than individual units. The costs of these activities vary according to the

164

FIGURE 6.3　Levels of ABC Activity Groups

Unit-Level Activities

Activities:
　Assembly
　Stamping
　Machining

Resources used:
　Direct labor
　Direct materials
　Supplies
　Electricity

Cost drivers:
　Direct labor hours
　Machine hours
　Number of units produced

Batch-Level Activities

Activities:
　Batch changeovers (setups)
　Materials handling
　Order processing
　Inspections

Resources used:
　Labor costs of setups
　Labor costs of materials handling
　Labor costs to process orders
　Labor costs to inspect

Cost drivers:
　Number of batches
　Number of setups
　Number of orders processed

Product-Level Activities

Activities:
　Production scheduling
　Product designing
　Parts and product testing
　Special handling and storing

Resources used:
　Specialized equipment
　Labor costs of design
　Testing facility costs

Cost drivers:
　Number of products
　Number of parts

Facility-Level Activities

Activities:
　Plant supervision
　Building occupancy
　Personnel administration

Resources used:
　Plant depreciation
　Insurance and property taxes
　Salaries of plant management

Cost drivers:
　Number of employees
　Number of units produced
　Labor hours

number of batches but are common or fixed for all units in the batch. **Product-level activities** are those performed as needed to support the production of each different type of product. Maintaining bills of materials and routing information, processing engineering changes, testing routines, and handling materials are examples of activities in this category. **Facility-level activities** are those which simply sustain a facility's general manufacturing process. Examples would include plant supervision and building occupancy. These costs are common to a variety of products and are the most difficult to link to product-specific activities. For this reason, many people question whether facility-level costs should be linked to products.

　Traditionally, we classify factory overhead costs as variable or fixed. Relative to volume of outputs, costs of unit-level activities are predominately variable, while costs of the other three levels are predominately fixed. However, identifying batch-, product-, and facility-level activity centers helps in selecting cost drivers. Often, the cost perspective changes; many costs that are fixed relative to units of output are now variable relative to the cost driver. This is particularly true for batch- and product-level activities. Costs of facility-level activities remain primarily in the fixed category and are often apportioned or allocated to products in some arbitrary manner.

Step 2:   Classify Costs by Activity Center and by Type of Expense.
Once the actions are grouped into activities, the next step is to identify the costs with the activities. The coding and classifying of cost data at this early point determine the level of detail and the breakdowns of cost data available to management for all cost analysis purposes later. A chart of accounts or a database classification scheme will identify the type of cost by natural classification: salary, postage, telephone, repair, supplies, etc. A second code will identify the activity center. Often, this is called a cost center. An activity center and a cost center are both commonly defined as the smallest part of an organization for which costs are accumulated. In fact, in most carefully defined cost systems, the terms activity center and cost center can be used interchangeably.

Step 3:   Select Cost Drivers.   Direct costs can be traced immediately to a product without the need for a cost driver. All other manufacturing costs need links between cost, activity, and product. Cost drivers are the links. A cost driver can link a pool of costs in an activity center to the product. Or a cost driver can link costs in one activity center to activities in another activity center. Multiple layers of activities can exist. One activity relates to another activity, which may relate to still another activity before relationships to products are identified. Figure 6.4, page 236, gives an example of the variety of these relationships. The first box at the top is the total costs of manufacturing during a production period. The costs are classified by activity center code and by natural expense type. A manager is responsible for each activity center and the costs incurred in that center.

A **preliminary stage cost driver** links costs of resources consumed (inputs) in one activity center to other activity centers. A **primary stage cost driver** links costs in an activity center directly with products. Some costs, such as batch-level activity center costs in Figure 6.4, are initially assigned to a primary stage activity center and only need a single-stage assignment process. These primary stage centers may collect reassigned costs from numerous preliminary stage activity centers—based on cost drivers that reflect activities and resources used.

The activity centers are typically one of four types as described above. Direct costs of unit-level activity centers are assumed in Figure 6.4 to be always traceable to specific products. Batch-level activity center costs should also be traceable to specific products but often use a cost driver. Product-level activity center costs may be related to a specific product or may be grouped by activities before being assigned to products at the primary stage. Facility-level activity center costs may go through multiple preliminary stages before being assigned to products.

ABC systems differ from traditional volume-based cost accounting systems in the number and variety of cost drivers used to trace costs. Traditional cost accounting systems use very few drivers—often only direct labor hours or dollars. ABC systems, on the other hand, may use a multitude of cost drivers that relate costs more closely to the resources being consumed and the activities occurring.

FIGURE 6.4   Relationships of Activity (Cost) Centers, Cost Drivers, Cost Functions, and Product Costs

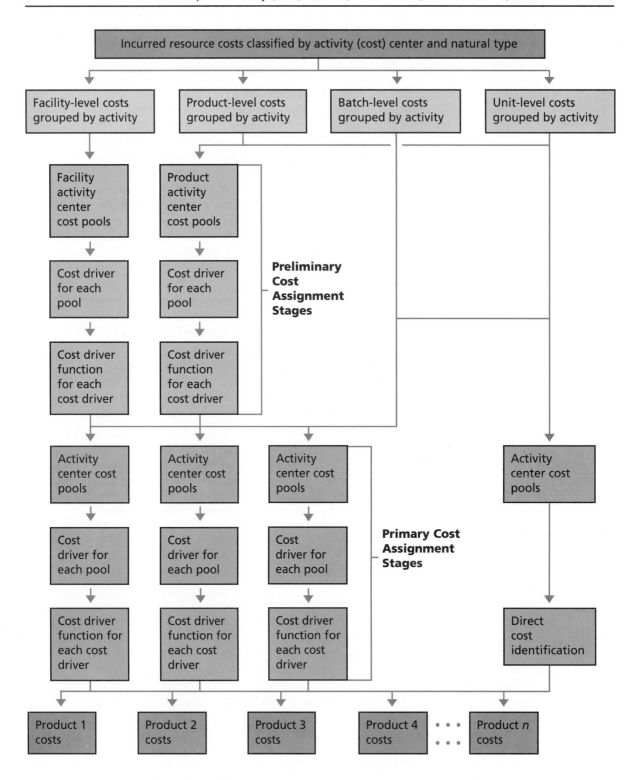

Although not comprehensive, Figure 6.5 gives examples of cost drivers that might be found in an ABC system.

Accountants must work with management to discover and identify activities and cost drivers. This is done through interviewing, process observation, simulation, diagramming, and analyses of current information systems.

Step 4: Calculate a Cost Function. In Figure 6.4, a cost function is used to convert the pool of costs and cost driver data into a rate per cost driver unit, a percentage of other cost amounts, or an allocation percentage. This cost function could be based on either planned or actual activity levels. In Chapter 4, we discussed the creation of predetermined overhead rates using planned activity levels. Using planned activity levels and costs for example, if costs of the setup activity center cost pool totaled $25,000, if setup hours were the cost driver, and if 500 hours were expected, the cost function would be $50 per setup hour. Costs are then distributed to products as setup hours are incurred. This approach is the same as that discussed in Chapter 4, except for the use of a different type of cost driver.

Step 5: Assign Costs to the Cost Objective. The final step is distributing costs to the users of the resources. The cost pool, the cost driver, and the cost function now combine to determine how much cost is charged to each resource user. If this is at a preliminary stage, the users are predominately other activity centers. Thus, a group of costs are now reassigned to other cost pools based on use. If the activity center is at the primary stage, the users are the products themselves. In the setup example, if 60 hours of setup time were used for Product A's production, $3,000 would be charged to Product A. All costs entering the manufacturing process during a given time period are eventually assigned to products.

Influence of Product Mix Complexity

The primary goal of ABC for product costing is to generate accurate product costs. In general, this means that the cost accounting system must handle the

FIGURE 6.5   Cost Drivers Used in Actual ABC Systems

Number of products or units.	Number of machine hours used.
Number of labor minutes per piece.	Number of vendors.
Amount of labor cost incurred.	Number of purchasing and ordering hours.
Value of materials in a product.	Number of customer options per product.
Number of materials moves.	Number of accessories.
Number of materials handling hours.	Number of times ordered.
Number of times handled.	Number of units scrapped.
Number of parts received per month.	Number of engineering change orders.
Number of part numbers maintained.	Number of die impressions.
Number of part numbers in a product.	Number of units reworked.
Amount of hazardous materials.	Volume of scrap—by weight or units.
Number of new parts introduced.	Number of customer orders processed.
Number of setup hours.	Square feet used by an activity.
Number of setups.	Number of employees.

complexity of production while minimizing possible distortions caused by cost assignment processes. The complexity of product mix plays a significant role in determining whether the costs of two or more activities can be combined and traced to a product by means of a single cost driver and still be assigned accurately. If a company wants more accurate product costs, it must increase the number of activity centers, cost pools, and cost drivers. Since the introduction of a new cost driver in the system has a cost/benefit value, most companies face a trade-off between more cost drivers, greater detail, and more expensive data processing versus more data aggregation and less expensive data processing. Several important issues relate to selecting cost drivers, and they include:

1. Product diversity (homogeneity or heterogeneity).
2. Batch-size diversity.
3. Relative costs of activities aggregated.

Product diversity refers to the degree to which products differ in the number of activities (that is, resources or inputs) required by each product. The greater the difference in how two products use resources or inputs, the greater the distortion a single cost driver will make in tracing costs to these products. For example, producing an ornate bathroom faucet fixture may consume labor-intensive production resources while producing a kitchen sink faucet may consume machine-intensive resources.

Some products are simply larger than other products. A console model versus a portable model is an example. The size influences how the product is produced and which resources are required. The complexity of a product is determined by the differences in how a product is manufactured and by the number of options a manufacturer has for its products. For example, deluxe models and products with many customer options increase the manufacturing difficulty. Each option adds an extension to the production process. However, supervision and other departmental costs are not necessarily influenced by these options. Materials inputs may differ by product. Some materials may require more handling from the receiving dock through the storeroom to the production floor. In other cases, certain materials may require longer machining time or more time in trimming processes. Some products may have a high degree of vertical integration—from raw materials to finished products. Others are merely assembled from purchased parts.

Batch-size diversity occurs when products are manufactured in different-sized batches. Batches refer not only to production orders but also to order quantities of raw materials and to shipping batch sizes. In an automotive stamping plant, a weekly run of hood stampings for a popular model may be 3,000 units, while a very similar but higher priced model hood may have a biweekly run of 500.

Although we normally think of differing batch sizes when we produce different products, batch-size diversity can also occur with the same product over time. For instance, this week the production order consists of 500 units. Due to an increase in demand, the production schedule for next week calls for 800 units. Just-in-time production encourages producing only what is needed immediately—often smaller batches and more frequently. Frequent batch runs may also require that more attention be given to minimizing setup time and cost. In traditional cost systems, setup costs are added to other overhead costs, losing the separate identity and cost detail of setup activities. In ABC systems, a separate cost pool for setup costs would typically be formed, and these costs would be assigned to products using cost drivers such as setup hours or number of setups. Both of these cost drivers reflect batch-size diversity, with the former measure being more detailed and, thus, often more appropriate.

Relative differences in activity costs, depending on the level of aggregation, influence whether more cost drivers are necessary to assign costs of activities to products. The rule of thumb is that activities can be grouped until the costs assigned to a product using a grouped cost driver differ materially from the assignment that would take place if the individual activities used their own unique cost driver.

If computer resources were free and if managers had unlimited amounts of analysis time, more and more detail could be captured and evaluated. Since this is not the case, very practical decisions must be made. In large ABC applications, the number of cost drivers (both preliminary and primary) used across an entire plant may be as low as 20 or as high as several hundred. Often, a high percentage of costs is assigned using a small number of drivers. The cost system's design should allow judgments to be made about the number of cost pools and cost drivers and should allow for cost pools and cost drivers to be changed easily when the need arises.

A COMPREHENSIVE ACTIVITY-BASED COST EXAMPLE

The controller and the production manager of Freeman Metal Products have just completed the installation of an activity-based costing system in their factory. The firm's products are primarily replacement parts sold to construction and farm equipment industries. The actual plant is a complex of nearly 20 producing and 15 support departments; and several hundred basic products, plus many custom variations, are routinely produced. Many orders are for small quantities, while others are standing orders for thousands of units per month. To simplify the example, only four support activity centers and two producing activity centers are illustrated. Also, only three products are shown. Production volume for October is as follows:

	Product A	Product B	Product C
Units produced	22,000	15,000	12,000

The activity centers' traceable costs for October and cost drivers are as follows:

Activity Center Information

Activity Center Code	Activity Center	Materials	Labor	Other Costs	Cost Driver
	Support centers:				
120	Occupancy			$ 60,000	Square feet used
130	Data Processing			30,000	Transactions processed
140	Personnel Benefits			9,000	Payroll cost
220	Materials Handling			16,000	Materials cost
	Producing centers:				
410	Heat Treating	$ 18,000	$ 10,000	20,000	Treatment hours
420	Machining	14,000	20,000	15,000	Machine hours
	Totals	$ 32,000	$ 30,000	$ 150,000	

Activities are grouped and activity centers determined as a result of special studies. Each activity center has one cost driver. For example, the cost driver selected for Occupancy is square feet of plant used by each activity.

The materials and labor costs are directly traceable to the three products as follows:

	Materials	Labor
Product A:		
Heat Treating	$ 1,000	$ 2,000
Machining.	4,000	2,000
Product B:		
Heat Treating	6,000	2,000
Machining.	2,000	8,000
Product C:		
Heat Treating	11,000	6,000
Machining.	8,000	10,000
Totals	$32,000	$30,000

As for the other costs, cost drivers are selected after analysis of past cost behavior and activity levels within each activity center. First, the other costs of the support centers are assigned to the producing centers. This is the preliminary stage allocation.

Preliminary Stage Allocation

The cost driver data for the preliminary stage cost assignments are as follows:

Cost Driver Data—Preliminary Stage Allocation

Activity Center Code	Activity Center	Cost Driver	Activity Centers Using Resources	
			410	420
120	Occupancy	Square feet used	80,000	40,000
130	Data Processing	Transactions processed	120,000	180,000
140	Personnel Benefits	Payroll cost	$10,000	$20,000
220	Materials Handling	Materials cost	$18,000	$14,000

Cost functions for each of the support centers are developed as follows:

Activity Center	Calculation	Cost Function
Occupancy	$60,000 ÷ (80,000 + 40,000)	$0.50 per square foot
Data Processing	$30,000 ÷ (120,000 + 180,000)	$0.10 per transaction
Personnel Benefits	$9,000 ÷ ($10,000 + $20,000)	30% of payroll cost
Materials Handling	$16,000 ÷ ($18,000 + $14,000)	50% of materials cost

Using these cost functions, the following costs are assigned to the two producing centers:

Heat Treating: $0.50(80,000) + $0.10(120,000) + .30($10,000) + .50($18,000) = $64,000

Machining: $0.50(40,000) + $0.10(180,000) + .30($20,000) + .50($14,000) = $51,000

Having made these preliminary cost assignments, the producing centers contain both direct product costs and costs to be assigned to products using primary cost drivers.

Primary Stage Allocation

The activities and cost drivers are as follows for each product:

Cost Driver Data—Primary Stage Allocation

Activity Center Code	Activity Center	Cost Driver	Cost Driver Activity Linked to Each Product		
			Product A	Product B	Product C
410	Heat Treating	Treatment hours	2,000	3,000	5,000
420	Machining	Machine hours	2,500	1,500	1,000

As can be seen, different products use different amounts of the resources in each activity center. Overhead cost functions for each of the producing centers are developed as follows:

Activity Center	Calculation	Overhead Cost Function
Heat Treating ..	($20,000 + $64,000) ÷ (2,000 + 3,000 + 5,000)	$ 8.40 per treatment hour
Machining	($15,000 + $51,000) ÷ (2,500 + 1,500 + 1,000)	$13.20 per machine hour

Using these cost functions, the following overhead costs are assigned to the three products:

Product A: $8.40(2,000) + $13.20(2,500) = $49,800

Product B: $8.40(3,000) + $13.20(1,500) = $45,000

Product C: $8.40(5,000) + $13.20(1,000) = $55,200

Materials and labor costs which are directly traceable are added to determine the total product costs:

Cost Item	Product A	Product B	Product C
Materials	$ 5,000	$ 8,000	$19,000
Labor	4,000	10,000	16,000
Overhead	49,800	45,000	55,200
Total cost	$58,800	$63,000	$90,200

Note that the total costs assigned to these products equal the sum of the costs reported by the six activity centers (i.e., $58,800 + $63,000 + $90,200 = $32,000 + $30,000 + $150,000 **or** $212,000). Per unit costs for each product are:

Product A: $58,800 ÷ 22,000 = $2.67

Product B: $63,000 ÷ 15,000 = $4.20

Product C: $90,200 ÷ 12,000 = $7.52

Comparing ABC to Traditional Volume-Based Costing

As discussed, traditional volume-based costing systems unfortunately have paid less attention to the cause-and-effect relationships between resources used and production activities. Assume that the prior costing system in use by Freeman Metal Products assigned overhead costs to products using labor dollars. This is a common approach to assigning overhead. Let us also assume that the preliminary cost assignment steps are the same under either approach. Since $150,000 of total overhead costs are incurred and total labor cost is $30,000, an overhead rate of $5 for each $1 of labor is added to each product. The product costs would be as follows:

	Total	Product A	Product B	Product C
Direct materials	$ 32,000	$ 5,000	$ 8,000	$ 19,000
Direct labor	30,000	4,000	10,000	16,000
Overhead cost (500% of labor) .	150,000	20,000	50,000	80,000
Total product cost	$212,000	$29,000	$68,000	$115,000
Units produced		22,000	15,000	12,000
Traditional cost per unit		$ 1.32	$ 4.53	$ 9.58
ABC cost per unit from above ..		$ 2.67	$ 4.20	$ 7.52
Difference:				
Traditional minus ABC cost ..		$ (1.35)	$ 0.33	$ 2.06
Percentage of ABC cost		(50.6%)	7.9%	27.4%

A dramatic picture appears. Using a costing system very common in many companies today, two of the three products have large cost differences— Products A and C. Freeman had been using a cost overstated by 27.4 percent for Product C. This is a far more profitable product than Freeman management had thought. Freeman may be losing Product C business because of its higher than necessary price. Conversely, Product A is less profitable than previously thought. With traditional costing, it received a disproportionately low amount of overhead allocation because its labor cost of $4,000 was much lower than labor costs of Products B and C ($10,000 and $16,000, respectively). However, Product A consumed more overhead resources, namely machine hours per unit, comparable to the other two products. Product A prices might need to be raised to cover its actual use of production resources.

ABC is also considered superior to volume-based costing when a company's product mix includes the following two types of products:

- High volume, low complexity.
- Low volume, high complexity.

To illustrate, suppose Bedingfield Corporation produces 50,000 boxes of "Bland," a breakfast cereal where each piece has the same shape, color, and flavor (high volume, low complexity). The company also produces 10,000 boxes of "Wow!," a cereal having a variety of shapes, colors, and flavors (low volume, high complexity). Setup costs of $2,000 and materials handling costs of $9,000 are to be assigned to the two cereals. The following activity information is obtained:

	"Bland"	*"Wow!"*
Direct labor hours	25,000	2,500
Production runs	10	20
Materials moves	50	40

Volume-based costing, using direct labor hours, would assign the costs as follows:

"Bland":   ($2,000 + $9,000) x (25,000 ÷ 27,500) = $10,000

"Wow!":   ($2,000 + $9,000) x (2,500 ÷ 27,500) = $1,000

An ABC system would use the number of production runs to assign setup costs and the number of materials moves to assign materials handling costs, as follows:

"Bland":   [$2,000 x (10 ÷ 30)] + [$9,000 x (50 ÷ 90)] = $5,667

"Wow!":   [$2,000 x (20 ÷ 30)] + [$9,000 x (40 ÷ 90)] = $5,333

After dividing these assigned costs by 50,000 boxes for "Bland" and 10,000 boxes for "Wow!," we obtain the following costs per box:

	"Bland"	*"Wow!"*
Volume-based costing	$ 0.20	$ 0.10
Activity-based costing	$ 0.11	$ 0.53

Compared to ABC, volume-based costing has overcosted the high volume, low complexity product ("Bland"), while undercosting the low volume, high complexity product ("Wow!"). This distortion is known as **product cross-subsidization** and has caused companies that use volume-based costing to set high prices for high volume, low complexity products and low prices for low volume, high complexity products. Signals that companies may be experiencing product cross-subsidization include the inability to break into new markets or to maintain current market share as a result of competitors' seeming ability to price below cost.

Whether ABC costs are "correct" or not, they would appear to be more accurate than the traditional costs. ABC makes a greater effort to match resource use, costs, activities, and products.

C O N T E M P O R A R Y   P R A C T I C E   6 . 2

Survey of ABC Usage

A recent survey found that about one-fifth of the respondent firms have turned to ABC for pricing, performance measurement, and budgeting. Moreover, about one-half expected to use ABC within 18 months for pricing, while approximately 60 percent planned to use ABC within 18 months for performance measurement and budgeting.

Source: Szendi, J. Z., and R. C. Elmore, "Management Accounting: Are New Techniques Making Inroads with Practitioners?" *Journal of Accounting Education*, Spring 1993, p. 67.

ABC AND NONMANUFACTURING ACTIVITIES

Our emphasis in ABC thus far has focused on those costs associated with manufacturing activities. Historically, manufacturing-related costs comprised the bulk of a manufacturing organization's total costs. Furthermore, only manufacturing-related costs are considered product costs for external reporting purposes. In recent times, emphasis on accounting for nonmanufacturing costs such as selling, distribution, general administration, and research and development has grown. One reason is that nonmanufacturing costs are a growing portion of companies' total costs. Another reason is that, due to computerization, it has become less costly to develop alternate accounting systems within a company. Therefore, in addition to the cost system needed for external reporting, companies now find it worthwhile to maintain alternate systems more useful for internal purposes such as pricing, control, decision making, and performance evaluation. With the growing emphasis on accounting for nonmanufacturing costs, manufacturing firms who have adopted ABC for manufacturing-related activities are increasingly expanding their implementation of ABC to include nonmanufacturing activities. Contemporary Practice 6.3 illustrates this.

In addition to manufacturing firms, the usage of ABC is growing in the service sector. Competitive pressures in industries such as health care, financial services, telecommunications, and transportation have led to increased cost consciousness. (See Contemporary Practice 6.4.) Not only is ABC being used to assess costs associated with various services but, increasingly, it is being used to determine costs associated with particular customers. Customer profitability analysis is becoming an increasingly important issue with management.

ACTIVITY-BASED MANAGEMENT

Aside from product costing purposes, ABC systems are also used to improve the operations of an organization. This extension of ABC is often referred to

CONTEMPORARY   PRACTICE   6 . 3

ABC for General Administrative Costs

The Financial Services Department at Weyerhaeuser Company is a unit in the corporate controller's department responsible for central accounting activities. Management has designated the following activity centers: General Accounting, Salaried Payroll, Accounts Payable, Accounts Receivable, Consolidation and Data Base Administration, and Invoicing. Within each of these activity centers, major activities have been identified, and separate cost drivers have been chosen for each of these major activities. For instance, the Accounts Receivable activity center contains two major activities—cash application and customer file. Cash application costs are assigned to Weyerhaeuser's divisions based on number of invoices, while customer file costs are assigned based on number of customers on the file.

Source: Johnson, H. T., and D. A. Loewe, "How Weyerhaeuser Manages Corporate Overhead Costs," *Management Accounting*, August 1987, pp. 20-26.

CONTEMPORARY PRACTICE 6.4

ABC in a Bank

American Bank and Trust Co. of Reading, Pennsylvania, offered two types of savings accounts—regular passbook account and statement savings account. Management believed it was much cheaper to handle statement savings accounts. An ABC analysis, however, revealed that the yearly cost of the statement savings account was $36.81 per customer, while the cost for the regular passbook account amounted to only $34.58.

Source: Harvard Business School, "American Bank," Case No. 187-194, 1987.

as **activity-based management (ABM)**. The ABM philosophy is that the activities identified for ABC can also be used for cost management and performance evaluation purposes.

One aspect of ABM which evolves from activity analysis is the identification and elimination of **nonvalue-added costs**. Activities and their costs that can be eliminated without deterioration of product quality and value can reduce total production time and increase profitability. For instance, many companies have adopted just-in-time production systems in an effort to eliminate activities related to storing and handling inventories.

Another aspect of ABM is the determination of efficiency and effectiveness measures for all cost generating activities. Traditionally, accountants have been concerned only with financial performance measures. With ABM, performance evaluation of activities has been expanded to include many nonfinancial measures. Measures dealing with quality and productivity have become particularly prominent. Indeed, the phenomenon of total quality management is considered part of ABM. Examples of nonfinancial quality measures include product defect rates, number of customer complaints, number of engineering change orders, and amount of rework. Examples of nonfinancial productivity measures include the ratio of value-added time to total production time, amount of production per day per employee, and square footage required per day per unit of output.

ABM also encompasses innovations such as target costing, continuous (KAIZEN). improvement, employee empowerment, and benchmarking. These cost (190) management and performance evaluation issues are discussed in detail in Chapter 15. The remainder of this chapter covers an ABM topic which deals with product costing—JIT costing.

*J*IT COSTING

To reduce nonvalue-added costs, many companies in recent years have adopted **just-in-time (JIT) systems**. These systems generally have the following characteristics:

1. Raw materials, work in process, and finished goods inventories are reduced as much as possible, if not eliminated. Costs associated with inventories, such as storage and moving, are considered to add no value

to the product. As such, the production system operates on a **demand-pull** basis. Raw materials are purchased only as demanded by production needs; production is scheduled only as demanded by sales orders.

2. Since little or no inventory buffers exist at various work stations, problems such as defective materials or machine breakdowns not only stop work at that station but also cause shutdowns at subsequent stations. Thus, total quality programs are emphasized in JIT environments.

3. Long-term agreements are negotiated with a small number of suppliers. The criteria for selecting suppliers focus on dependable delivery and quality.

4. Layouts of production facilities are structured in the form of **focused factories**, i.e., "factories within a factory." To simplify activities, especially materials handling, machines are grouped in arrangements that allow a worker or a team of workers to perform a variety of sequential operations. These arrangements are often referred to as **manufacturing cells**.

5. JIT is facilitated by automation in various forms—flexible manufacturing systems, automated materials handling systems, numerically controlled machines, computer-integrated manufacturing systems, etc. Thus, in JIT environments, direct labor cost is usually not significant and sometimes even nonexistent.

Due to these characteristics, firms with JIT systems sometimes record costs differently than was discussed in Chapter 4. **Just-in-time (JIT) costing** differs from traditional costing with regard to the accounts used and the timing of cost recording. Specifically, three major differences exist. First, instead of using separate accounts for Raw Materials and Work in Process, JIT costing combines these into a Raw and In-Process Inventory (RIP) account. The rationale is that the amount of work in process at any particular time will be low.

A second difference is that since direct labor is usually a minor cost item in a JIT setting, no separate account for direct labor in JIT costing is created. Rather, direct labor is combined with factory overhead into a Conversion Cost account. In some companies, direct labor is actually included in the Factory Overhead account.

The third difference relates to the application of factory overhead. In traditional manufacturing environments, overhead is applied to products as they are being produced. As such, overhead is applied to and recorded into the Work in Process account. In JIT costing, overhead is not applied to products until they are completed. No Work in Process account exists to accumulate conversion costs. When products are completed under JIT costing, conversion cost is applied to the Finished Goods account. In "purer" JIT systems, the conversion cost is applied or added to Cost of Goods Sold, since the goods are sold soon after production is completed. JIT costing is sometimes termed **backflush costing** because the product costs are "flushed" out of the accounting system and are attached to the products only *after* they are completed. This is the reverse of the traditional approach which attaches costs to products, via the Work in Process account, as products are being produced.

To illustrate JIT costing, suppose that Ho Corporation manufactures cellular telephones in a plant located in Shenzhen, China, which uses a JIT production system. The following transactions occurred during January (monetary amounts are in yuan):

(a) Ho purchased Y17,000 of raw materials.
(b) All materials purchased were requisitioned for production.
(c) Ho incurred direct labor costs of Y8,000.
(d) Actual factory overhead costs amounted to Y125,000.
(e) Ho applied conversion costs totaling Y130,000. This includes Y8,000 of direct labor.
(f) All telephones were completed.

These transactions would be recorded in a traditional costing system as follows:

Raw Materials				Accounts Payable		Work in Process			
(a)	17,000	(b)	17,000	(a) 17,000		(b)	17,000	(f)	147,000
				(d) 125,000		(c)	8,000		
						(e)	122,000		

Wages Payable		Factory Overhead		Finished Goods	
	(c) 8,000	(d) 125,000	(e) 122,000	(f) 147,000	

Under JIT costing, no entries are made for transactions (b), (c), and (e). Entry (b) is not necessary because the placement of materials into production is implied in transaction (a) when the materials are first received. No separate entry for (c) is made because direct labor is combined with factory overhead and recorded as a debit to Conversion Cost as part of entry (d). Finally, entry (e) is omitted because conversion cost is not applied until the goods are completed. The entry for conversion cost application, therefore, becomes part of entry (f).

The JIT costing system would record the January transactions in the following manner:

Raw and In-Process Inventory				Accounts Payable		Conversion Cost			
(a)	17,000	(f)	17,000	(a) 17,000		(d) 133,000		(f) 130,000	
				(d) 125,000					

Wages Payable		Finished Goods	
	(d) 8,000	(f) 147,000	

As noted earlier, in a "purer" JIT costing system, the debit in entry (f) would be to Cost of Goods Sold rather than to Finished Goods. Also note that the JIT costing system is much simpler and less expensive than the traditional system because fewer entries are needed.

SUMMARY

Activity-based costing is a system of accounting that focuses on activities performed to produce items or services. The activities are the primary building blocks in cost accumulation. Cost drivers are used to identify costs with activities and to identify activities with products. Preliminary stage cost drivers assign support activity costs to other activity centers. Primary stage cost drivers relate costs of activities to products or services.

In designing an activity-based costing system, five basic steps are followed. First, assemble similar actions into activity groups. This process involves categorizing activities as unit level, batch level, product level, and facility level. Second, classify costs by activity group and by expense. Third, select the appropriate preliminary stage and primary stage cost drivers. This process eliminates distortions in cost allocations to products that result from product mix complexity. Fourth, calculate a cost function to link costs and the cost driver activity. Finally, fifth, assign costs to the cost objective (often the product cost).

ABC can also be applied to nonmanufacturing activities and to nonmanufacturing organizations. Activity-based management involves the analysis of activities for cost management and performance evaluation issues.

JIT costing differs from traditional costing systems in three respects. First, JIT costing does not use a Work in Process account. Second, JIT costing combines direct labor and factory overhead into one account. Third, in JIT costing, overhead is not applied to products until the products are completed.

*P*ROBLEM FOR REVIEW

Silber Piping Products uses activity-based costing. It has assigned all of the factory overhead costs into seven overhead cost pools. The budgeted amounts for these cost pools and their associated cost drivers are as follows:

Overhead Cost Pool	Budgeted Costs	Cost Driver	Budgeted Level for Cost Driver
Purchasing and materials-related . . .	$ 250,000	Materials costs	$2,000,000
Product engineering	110,000	Engineering hours	5,500 hours
Factory occupancy	300,000	Machine hours	100,000 hours
Fringe benefits	80,000	Direct labor cost	$1,000,000
Machine depreciation	450,000	Machine hours	100,000 hours
Machine setup costs	75,000	Number of setups	1,000 setups
General manufacturing costs	200,000	Machine hours	100,000 hours
Total	$1,465,000		

The company has just completed a customer order with the following cost driver information related to the order:

Materials cost	$40,000
Direct labor cost	$10,000
Engineering hours	45
Number of setups	3
Machine hours	28

Required:

1. Determine the total overhead cost that would be assigned to the customer order.

2. Compare the total overhead cost computed in Part (1) with one obtained by using a plant-wide overhead rate based on machine hours.

Solution:

1. The total factory overhead cost charged to this order is calculated as follows:

Purchasing and materials-related costs [($250,000 ÷ $2,000,000) x $40,000] . . .	$ 5,000
Product engineering [($110,000 ÷ 5,500) x 45]	900
Factory occupancy [($300,000 ÷ 100,000) x 28].	84
Fringe benefits [($80,000 ÷ $1,000,000) x $10,000]	800
Machine depreciation [($450,000 ÷ 100,000) x 28]	126
Machine setup costs [($75,000 ÷ 1,000) x 3]	225
General manufacturing costs [($200,000 ÷ 100,000) x 28].	56
Total overhead costs charged to order	$ 7,191

2. Using a plant-wide rate based on machine hours, the overhead rate would be:

$$\$1,465,000 \div 100,000 \ = \ \$14.65 \text{ per machine hour}$$

The cost charged to the customer order would only be $410.20 ($14.65 x 28 machine hours). This plant-wide rate leads to a major distortion in cost allocation. Other orders would have to subsidize this order if a plant-wide rate is used. Activity-based costing is better because it more accurately traces costs to the order that uses the resources and causes the activities incurring the costs.

TERMINOLOGY REVIEW

Activity-based costing (ABC), *230*
Activity-based management (ABM), *245*
Activity center, *232*
Backflush costing, *246*
Batch-level activities, *233*
Batch-size diversity, *238*
Cost driver, *232*
Demand-pull, *246*
Facility-level activities, *234*
Focused factories, *246*

Just-in-time (JIT) costing, *246*
Just-in-time (JIT) systems, *245*
Manufacturing cells, *246*
Nonvalue-added costs, *245*
Preliminary stage cost driver, *235*
Primary stage cost driver, *235*
Product cross-subsidization, *243*
Product diversity, *238*
Product-level activities, *234*
Unit-level activities, *233*

SUGGESTED READINGS

Babad, Y. M., and B.V. Balachandran, "Cost Driver Optimization in Activity-Based Costing," *Accounting Review,* July 1993, pp. 563-575.

Betts, M., "As Easy as ABC?" *Computerworld,* May 23, 1994, pp. 107-108.

Cooper, R., and R. S. Kaplan, "Measure Costs Right: Make the Right Decisions," *Harvard Business Review,* Vol. 66, No. 5, pp. 96-103.

Griffin, L., and A. Harrell, "An Empirical Examination of Managers' Motivation to Implement Just-in-Time Procedures," *Journal of Management Accounting Research,* Fall 1991, pp. 98-112.

Hwang, Y., J. H. Evans, and V.G. Hegde, "Product Cost Bias and Selection of an Allocation Base," *Journal of Management Accounting Research,* Fall 1993, pp. 213-242.

Jones, S. K., and K. M. Poston, "An Alternative Formulation for Activity-Based Cost Functions," *Advances in Management Accounting,* 1992, pp. 141-150.

MacArthur, J. B., "Activity-Based Costing: How Many Cost Drivers Do You Want?" *Journal of Cost Management,* Vol. 6, No. 3, pp. 37-41.

Mackey, J.T., "JIT Jitters About Responsibility Accounting," *CMA Magazine,* July-August 1989, pp. 22-25.

QUESTIONS FOR REVIEW AND DISCUSSION

1. Describe the relationships among resources, activities, and products.

2. What is a cost driver? What is its role in tracing costs to products?

3. Identify the five basic steps in applying activity-based costing to a costing problem.

4. Why are actions grouped into activities instead of treated individually?

5. Define an activity center. How many activity centers can exist in one production department? Explain.

6. What is the purpose for grouping actions into specific categories of unit-level activities, batch-level activities, product-level activities, and facility-level activities?

7. Describe the differences among unit-level activities, batch-level activities, and product-level activities.

8. How might the definitions of variable and fixed costs be changed in an activity-based costing system?

9. Explain the difference between a preliminary stage cost driver and a primary stage cost driver.

10. Explain the purpose of a cost function that will use cost driver data.

11. What is meant by product diversity? Why is it important in product costing?

12. How can batch-size diversity influence the costs assigned to products?

13. What factors have led to an increased emphasis on accounting for nonmanufacturing costs such as selling, distribution, general administration, and research and development?

14. How does activity-based management relate to activity-based costing?

15. Identify the key characteristics associated with JIT systems (other than cost recording issues).

16. How does JIT costing differ from traditional costing?

17. Why is JIT costing sometimes referred to as backflush costing?

E XERCISES

6-1. Grouping of Similar Activities.   Seguin Electronics, Inc. makes avionics equipment for private aircraft manufacturers. The production process takes place in three departments. The following costs were budgeted for February:

Computer programming—production	$ 18,000
Custodial wages—plant	4,500
Depreciation—machinery	120,000
Depreciation—plant	60,000
Electricity—machinery	11,600
Electricity—plant	7,400
Engineering design	45,000
Equipment maintenance—parts and supplies	2,900
Equipment maintenance—wages	14,100
Heating—plant	3,200
Inspection—production	3,800
Insurance—plant	10,000
Property taxes	9,300
Raw materials, components, subassemblies	330,000
Setup wages	14,000

Required:
1. Identify each of the costs as one of the following:
   (a) A unit-level activity.
   (b) A batch-level activity.
   (c) A product-level activity.
   (d) A facility-level activity.
2. Specify an appropriate cost driver for tracing to the products the costs that are associated with the various activity levels previously identified.

6-2. Activity Groupings and Cost Drivers.   Wind-Driven Products, Inc. uses JIT manufacturing and has the production process organized into manufacturing cells where each cell produces either a few products or major subassemblies. Cell workers are responsible for completing a quality product, setting up machinery, and maintaining all machinery in the cell. The following are the costs incurred either within each cell or for the benefit of each cell:

(a) Raw materials
(b) Direct labor
(c) Salary of a cell supervisor
(d) Salary of the plant manager
(e) Salaries of janitors
(f) Salary of an industrial engineer
(g) Overtime wages for cell workers
(h) Plant depreciation
(i) Depreciation on machinery
(j) Oil for lubricating machinery
(k) Cell equipment maintenance
(l) Parts for machinery
(m) Power
(n) Costs to set up machinery
(o) Taxes on plant and equipment
(p) Insurance on plant and equipment
(q) Pencils and paper for cell supervisor

Required:
1. Indicate the costs that can be identified directly with products without the use of cost drivers.
2. Group the remaining costs by similar activities.
3. Suggest an appropriate cost driver for assigning the costs of grouped activities to the product. (It is possible for some groupings to have a cost driver to trace the costs to another grouping of activities before assigning costs to products.)

6-3. Appropriateness of ABC.   Wacker Company has identified the following activity centers and cost drivers:

Activity Center	Cost Driver
Purchasing	Number of purchase orders
Materials Handling	Number of parts
Setups	Number of setups
Cutting	Number of parts
Assembly	Direct labor hours
Painting	Number of units painted

Two customer orders came in for the month. The cost drivers appearing on each order are as follows:

	Order 1	Order 2
Number of purchase orders	1	2
Number of parts	10	5
Number of setups	3	1
Direct labor hours	25	15
Number of units painted	12	24

Required:
Assuming the company traditionally allocated these costs using direct labor hours, how would activity-based costing, with the indicated cost drivers, improve the allocation of costs to products on the two customer orders?

6-4. Preliminary Stage Cost Drivers. Potter Manufacturing has the following groupings of activities and primary stage cost drivers:

Activity (Cost Center) Grouping	Primary Stage Cost Driver
Purchasing	Number of parts
Production—Labor-Paced Assembly	Direct labor hours
Production—Machine-Paced Assembly	Machine hours
Production—Quality Testing	Testing hours
Marketing and Distribution	Number of finished units sold

The costs that have been identified either directly or indirectly with "Production—Labor-Paced Assembly" are as follows:

(a) Production manager's salary and office expenses. (An analysis of production manager's time shows that he/she spends 70 percent on labor-paced assembly, 20 percent on machine-paced assembly, and 10 percent on quality testing.)

(b) Supervisor's salary.

(c) Supplies and other indirect materials costs.

(d) Repair and maintenance costs. (This work is performed by a separate support function called "Maintenance.")

(e) Fringe benefit costs of all workers in the labor-paced assembly activity.

(f) Heat, light, and power costs.

(g) Depreciation on equipment.

(h) Janitorial costs. (This work is performed by a separate janitorial support function.)

(i) Plant security.

(j) Plant insurance.

Required:
Explain how preliminary cost drivers are used to trace each of the costs to Production—Labor-Paced Assembly activity grouping. Include in your discussion a suggested cost driver for each cost.

6-5. Choosing an Activity Base. Costs and activity levels over the past three months are as follows for the Mixing Department of the Ballou Company:

	December	January	February
Activity center total costs	$20,000	$30,000	$40,000
Labor hours	1,000	1,000	1,000
Machine hours	3,000	4,500	6,000
Pounds of materials used	10,000	12,000	14,000
Units produced	120,000	130,000	140,000

Required:
Which activity measure would appear to be the best cost driver for this cost center? Comment.

6-6. Primary Stage Allocation. In the Materials Handling activity center, the following costs were incurred:

Direct costs	$ 50,000
Assigned from Plant Administration	4,000
Assigned from Occupancy	8,000
Assigned from Data Processing	16,000
Assigned from Personnel Benefits	7,000
Activity center total costs	$ 85,000

Materials Handling distributed $1,700,000 of materials to five producing departments. The cost driver selected was costs of materials distributed. The Fabricating Department received $900,000 of materials.

Required:

What costs were assigned to Fabricating from Materials Handling?

6-7. Cost Control With ABC.   The Flying Llama Travel Agency of Lima, Peru, budgets its agents' expenses based on the following activities, cost drivers, and cost functions:

Operations	Kilometers traveled	0.60 New Sol per kilometer
Entertainment	Admission expenses	15.00 New Sol per passenger
Trips	Trip agent costs	300.00 New Sol per trip

Juanita Garcia spent 8,200 New Sol in September. She ran 10 trips, had 20 persons per trip, and went a total of 4,000 kilometers. Other agents' spending averaged 8,600 New Sol.

Required:

Using activity-based costing, comment on Garcia's spending for September. Also, comment on the spending of the other agents.

6-8. Finding the Unknown Overhead Rate.   Product 43 uses 200 hours of direct labor and has 2,000 machine steps. Sue Greenberg, the cost accountant, has been considering using either direct labor hours or machine steps as the cost driver. The ratio of overhead cost to direct labor hours is $60. The assignment of overhead cost to Product 43 using direct labor hours would result in a higher charge by $4,000 than if machine steps were used as the cost driver.

Required:

Determine the ratio of overhead cost to machine steps.

6-9. Assigning Overhead Costs to a Job.   Ovadia Enterprises is an Israeli exporter of souvenir items manufactured in the capital city of Jerusalem. The following overhead cost data have been accumulated:

Activity Center	*Cost Driver*	*Amount of Activity*	*Center Costs (in Shekels)*
Materials Handling	Grams handled	100,000 grams	50,000
Painting	Units painted	50,000 units	200,000
Assembly	Labor hours	4,000 hours	120,000

Job 1234 contains 3,000 units. It weighs 10,000 grams and uses 300 hours of labor.

Required:

Compute the total overhead cost that should be assigned to Job 1234.

6-10. Activity-Based Costing and Cost Drivers.   Jilliard Company manufactures two types of medical syringes: low-unit and med-unit. The overhead activities, costs, and related data are as follows:

	Low-Unit	*Med-Unit*	*Activity Center Costs*
Receiving orders	100	150	$ 7,500
Machine hours	12,000	13,000	125,000
Setups.	45	20	9,750
Shipping orders	200	400	30,000

Required:

1. Identify the appropriate cost driver for each activity center and compute a rate for each center.

2. Allocate the overhead costs to the two products using the rates from Part (1).

3. Assume the total costs of all activity centers are allocated on the basis of machine hours. Calculate the overall rate and allocate overhead costs to the two products using that rate.

4. Explain why the costs allocated to the two products differ between Parts (2) and (3).

6-11. Product Cost Buildup. Delerico Manufacturing Company makes a variety of backpacks. The activity centers and budgeted information for the year are:

Activity Center	Overhead Costs	Cost Driver	Activity Center Rate
Materials Handling	$ 300,000	Weight of materials	$ 0.30 per pound
Cutting.........	1,800,000	Number of shapes	3.00 per shape
Assembly	4,600,000	Direct labor hours	12.00 per labor hour
Sewing	1,200,000	Machine hours	8.00 per machine hour

Two styles of backpacks were produced in December, the EasyRider and the Overnighter. The quantities and other operating data for the month are:

	EasyRider	Overnighter
Direct materials weight in pounds.................	50,000	15,000
Number of shapes	35,000	15,000
Assembly direct labor hours	7,500	1,200
Sewing machine hours	12,500	1,800
Units produced	5,000	1,000

Required:

1. Using the activity center rates, find the total overhead costs charged to each product during the month.
2. Calculate a per unit cost for each backpack.
3. With the information given, compute the budgeted level for each cost driver upon which the activity center rates were based.

6-12. Product Costing. Rick Young, the controller of Buckeye Electronics, wishes to use activity-based costing for a new circuit board produced for personal computers. Young has identified the following activities associated with circuit board production and the related conversion costs forecast for the period:

Activity	Conversion Cost
Purchasing of parts.....................................	$ 72,000
Starting the product	60,000
Inserting the components................................	150,000
Soldering the boards....................................	180,000
Testing the quality	140,000

The cost drivers that Young intends to use, as well as the amounts of activity forecast for the period, are:

Activity	Cost Driver	Cost Driver Amounts
Purchasing of parts.........	Number of parts purchased	12 per board
Starting the product	Number of boards started	60,000
Inserting the components	Number of insertions	10 per board
Soldering the boards........	Number of boards soldered	60,000
Testing the quality	Number of testing hours	2,000

Each circuit board has anticipated direct materials costs of $46. In addition, each circuit board takes on average 15 minutes to test.

Required:
Determine the cost of a circuit board produced by Buckeye Electronics.

6-13. Comparison of Product Costs. Sekar Company of Bangalore, India, manufactures two types of field hockey sticks—Regular and SuperPro. The following data have been obtained:

	Regular	SuperPro
Direct materials cost per unit (in rupees)	Rs33.00	Rs38.00
Direct labor cost per unit (in rupees)	Rs32.00	Rs44.00
Direct labor hours	12,000	3,000
Machine hours	2,000	4,000
Engineering hours	450	450
Number of setups	5	20
Number of units	8,000	2,200

Overhead costs are assigned to products on the basis of direct labor hours. The overhead costs consist of the following items:

Overhead Cost Item	Amount (in Rupees)
Setup costs	Rs 250,000
Engineering costs	180,000
Machine costs	900,000
Total	Rs 1,330,000

Required:

1. Using direct labor hours to allocate overhead costs, determine the cost per unit for each product.
2. Using activity-based costing, determine the cost per unit for each product.
3. Comment on the reasons for the differences between costs in Parts (1) and (2).

6-14. Finding Missing Costs. Jim Tackett, the production manager for Tackett Tire Division, is unable to locate the 1999 budget. You have managed to recover the following information for him:

Activity Center	Budgeted Overhead Cost	Cost Driver	Budgeted Cost Driver Level
Quality Control	$ 14,000	Inspection hours	350 hours
Engineering	42,000	Engineering hours	600 hours
Waste Disposal	15,000	Pounds of waste	5,000 pounds
Miscellaneous Overhead .	?	Direct labor hours	10,000 hours

You have also obtained the following information pertaining to the most recent customer order, which you learned was assigned an overhead cost of $9,500:

Direct labor hours	2,000
Inspection hours	50
Engineering hours	55
Amount of waste disposed in pounds	430

Required:

Determine the amount of miscellaneous overhead that was budgeted for 1999.

6-15. Preliminary and Primary Stage Allocations. Barcelona Supply Company, a Spanish manufacturer of clothing for matadors, has provided the following information about overhead costs traceable to its activity centers:

Activity Center	Overhead Cost (in Pesetas)	Cost Driver
Maintenance	P 950,000	Maintenance hours
Receiving	830,000	Receiving orders
Production (manual)	2,880,000	Labor hours
Production (automated)	3,980,000	Machine hours

The following activities were reported:

Activity Center	Maintenance Hours	Receiving Orders	Labor Hours	Machine Hours
Production (manual)	100	25	1,500	300
Production (automated) . . .	900	75	500	1,200

The overhead allocations involving Maintenance and Receiving are performed in the preliminary stage, while overhead costs for the two production centers are assigned to products in the primary stage.

Required:
Compute the overhead rates used for product costing in the two production activity centers.

6-16. Preliminary and Primary Stage Allocations. Crimson Tide Industries manufactured 1,000 lawnmower engines (LE) and 1,400 motorcycle engines (ME) during the year. The following traceable costs are reported by Bill Cready, the controller, for its activity centers:

Activity Center	Materials	Labor	Other Costs
#1100			$75,000
#1200			60,000
#2300			25,000
#3100	$36,000	$45,000	80,000
#3200	52,000	88,000	92,000

Data for the preliminary stage cost assignment are as follows (in the order shown):

Activity Center	Activity Centers Using Resources and Receiving Costs		
	#2300	#3100	#3200
#1100	10%	40%	50%
#1200	25%	60%	15%
#2300		80%	20%

Data for the primary stage cost assignment are as follows:

Activity Center	Products Using Resources and Receiving Costs	
	LE	ME
#3100	70%	30%
#3200	20%	80%

One-fourth of the materials and labor costs is traceable to lawnmower engines and the remainder to motorcycle engines.

Required:
Determine the per unit costs for lawnmower engines and for motorcycle engines.

6-17. Preliminary and Primary Stage Allocations. Gamecock Forklift Manufacturing produced 100 electric forklifts and 150 propane forklifts during 1996. Jesse Dillard, the controller, reported the following traceable costs, other than direct materials and direct labor, for its activity centers:

Activity Center	Costs
Plant Administration	$ 66,000
Setup Operations	24,000
Materials Handling	47,000
Machining	180,000
Assembly	150,000

Data for the preliminary stage cost assignment are as follows:

Activity Center	Activity Centers Using Resources and Receiving Costs		
	Setup Operations	Machining	Assembly
Plant Administration	5%	40%	55%
Materials Handling		55%	45%

Data for the primary stage cost assignment are as follows:

Activity Center	Cost Driver Activity Linked to Each Product		
	Cost Driver	Electric	Propane
Setup Operations	Number of setups	30 setups	20 setups
Machining............	Machine hours	250 hours	150 hours
Assembly	Labor hours	6,000 hours	9,000 hours

Required:
Determine the overhead cost per unit assigned to each type of forklift.

6-18. Account Balances Under JIT Costing.   Tom Selling, general manager of Cornell Corporation's Midwest Division, has provided the following information for transactions that occurred during March. This division uses a JIT costing system.

(a) Raw materials were purchased at the cost of $97,000.

(b) All materials purchased were requisitioned for production.

(c) Direct labor costs of $77,000 were incurred.

(d) Actual factory overhead costs amounted to $225,000.

(e) Applied conversion costs totaled $300,000. This included $77,000 of direct labor.

(f) All units were completed.

Required:
1. Determine the March 31 balance in the Conversion Cost account.
2. Determine the March 31 balance in the Finished Goods account.

6-19. Recording Transactions Under JIT Costing.   Manyong Park, owner of Taegu Supply Company in South Korea, which manufactures chopsticks for restaurants, has recently decided to implement a JIT costing system. Transactions (in South Korean won) for August are as follows:

(a) Raw materials were purchased at the cost of W950,000.

(b) All materials purchased were requisitioned for production.

(c) Direct labor costs of W2,500,000 were incurred.

(d) Actual factory overhead costs amounted to W6,000,000.

(e) Applied conversion costs totaled W8,100,000. This included W2,500,000 of direct labor.

(f) All units were completed.

Required:
Enter the August transactions into T-accounts. Label these entries by the identifying letters.

6-20. Comparing JIT Costing to Traditional Costing.   Hagerty, Inc., a manufacturer of computer diskettes, currently uses a conventional process costing system. During February, Hagerty plans to purchase $40,000 of raw materials. Of this amount, 80 percent will be used for current production, while the remainder will serve as a buffer in inventory. Direct labor cost is expected to be $10,000 during February, and the actual factory overhead is anticipated to total $65,000.

Jim Kinard, the owner, has been considering the use of a JIT inventory system. If implemented at the beginning of February, only the materials needed for current production would be purchased.

Required:
1. Using T-accounts, enter the February transactions for the purchase and usage of materials under:

(a) Conventional costing.

(b) JIT costing.

2. Using T-accounts, enter the February transactions for the labor and overhead costs under:

(a) Conventional costing.

(b) JIT costing.

Do not record the entry for applied overhead.

*P*ROBLEMS

6-21. Activity Identification and Cost Driver Selection.   Stemmons Company has the following chart of accounts:

(a)   Salaries of Purchasing Agents

(b)   Secretarial and Clerical Costs in the Purchasing Department

(c)   Personnel and Supplies in the Receiving Department

(d)   Personnel and Supplies in Production Scheduling and Control

(e)   Personnel and Supplies in Inventory Storerooms

(f)   Direct Materials

(g)   Direct Labor

(h)   Indirect Materials

(i)   Indirect Labor

(j)   Factory Supervision

(k)   Factory and Equipment Maintenance

(l)   Personnel Training Programs

(m)   Hiring Costs

(n)   Personnel and Supplies in Industrial Engineering

(o)   Personnel and Supplies in Packing and Shipping

(p)   Personnel and Supplies in the Accounting Department

(q)   Personnel and Supplies in the Advertising Department

(r)   Personnel and Supplies in Market Research

(s)   Personnel and Supplies in Product Design Engineering

(t)   Cost of Product Advertising

(u)   Cost of Institutional Advertising

(v)   Research and Development

(w)   Charitable Donations

(x)   Dues to the Trade Association

The controller has identified the following cost drivers:

1. Number of purchase orders placed.

2. Pounds, gallons, and so forth, of items purchased.

3. Number of production shop orders active.

4. Number of machine hours.

5. Number of direct labor hours.

6. Number of units manufactured.

7. Number of persons employed.

8. Number of customer orders shipped.

9. Dollar volume of sales.

Required:

1. Identify each of the accounts with one of the following:
   (a) Unit-level activities.   **(c)** Product-level activities.
   (b) Batch-level activities.   **(d)** Facility-level activities.

2. Specify an appropriate cost driver from the list given that can be used for tracing costs associated with the various levels of activities to the next cost objective or products, whichever is appropriate. If an appropriate cost driver is not on the list, suggest one.

6-22. Grouping Similar Activities—Manufacturing and Nonmanufacturing.
HealthCare Products is organized functionally into three divisions: Operations, Sales, and Administrative. Purchasing, receiving, materials and production control, manufacturing, factory personnel, inventory stores, and shipping activities are under the control of the vice-president for operations. Advertising, market research, and sales are the responsibility of the vice-president for sales. Accounting, budgeting, the firm's computer center, and general office management are delegated to the controller (Administrative). The following cost categories are found in the company as a whole:

(a) Depreciation on factory equipment.

(b) Depreciation on office equipment.

(c) Depreciation on factory building.

(d) Advertising manager's salary.

(e) Assembly foreman's salary.

(f) Salespersons' salaries.

(g) Salespersons' travel expenses.

(h) Supplies for the Machining Department.

(i) Advertising supplies.

(j) Electricity for the Assembly Department.

(k) Lost materials (scrap) in the Machining Department.

(l) Direct labor in the Assembly Department.

(m) Supplies for the Sales Office.

(n) Sales commissions.

(o) Packing supplies.

(p) Cost of hiring new employees.

(q) Payroll fringe benefits for workers in the Shipping Department.

(r) Supplies for Production Scheduling.

(s) Cost of repairing parts improperly manufactured in the Machining Department.

(t) Paint for the Assembly Department.

(u) Heat, light, and power for the factory.

(v) Leasing of computer equipment for the Accounting Department.

Required:

1. Identify each of the costs with the appropriate division: Operations, Sales, Administrative.

2. Identify each of the costs with one of the following:
   (a) Unit-level activities.   **(c)** Product-level activities.
   (b) Batch-level activities.   **(d)** Facility-level activities.
   Organize these classifications by division: Operations, Sales, Administrative.

3. Specify an appropriate cost driver for tracing costs associated with the various levels of activities to the next cost objective or products, whichever is appropriate.

6-23. Preliminary Stage and Primary Stage Cost Drivers.   Refer to the data in Problem 6-22. HealthCare Products is interested in using activity-based costing to identify as many costs as possible with the products. These costs will be used for planning and control decisions rather than for inventory valuation. The controller decided that all operation costs will be related to products, but only those sales and administrative costs that are classified as unit-level, batch-level, or product-level costs should be related to products.

Required:

1. Using preliminary stage cost drivers, explain how individual items of costs will be traced to activity groupings.
2. Using primary stage cost drivers, show how the costs should be related to products.
3. Explain why it is necessary to use preliminary stage and primary stage cost drivers.

1-2-3

6-24. Application of Activity-Based Costing.   Heidkamp Manufacturing has grouped activities into five categories: Building, Repair, Computer, Machine, and Finishing. Building charges its costs to all of the other groupings based on square footage of floor space used. Repair charges its costs only to Machine and Finishing. Computer has both outside and inside business. It uses computer hours as the cost driver for charging costs of work performed. Currently, 30 percent of the computer service is provided to outside customers, while 70 percent goes to inside users. Machine uses setup hours as the cost driver for 40 percent of its costs. Machine hours is the cost driver for the other 60 percent. All costs of Machine are charged to products. Finishing uses transactions as the cost driver for 70 percent of its costs, and the other 30 percent has product flow time as the cost driver. All costs of Finishing are assigned to products.

The current month's costs for each grouping, prior to charging costs from one grouping to another, are as follows:

Building	$864,800
Repair	500,000
Computer	300,000
Machine	400,000
Finishing	200,000

The operating statistics for the month for each category follow:

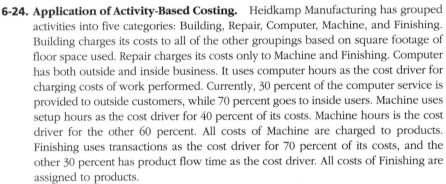

	Building	*Repair*	*Computer*	*Machine*	*Finishing*
Floor space (in sq. ft.) . . .		9,000	19,000	14,400	57,600
Repair hours	8,000			22,400	9,600
Computer hours*				16,800	4,200
Setup hours				5,000	
Machine hours.				100,000	
Transactions					400,000
Product flow time (hours)					20,000

* The total computer hours are 30,000, but 30 percent of those relates to outside work. Therefore, 30 percent of the computer costs should be designated for outside work.

During the month, a number of jobs were active. Two jobs were started and completed during the month. Following are the operating statistics for these two jobs:

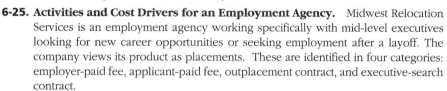

	#TK451	**#RG566**
Setup hours	200	50
Machine hours	100	300
Transactions	200	100
Product flow time	80	900

Required:

1. Using the indicated preliminary stage cost drivers, determine the total costs that will be charged to Machine and Finishing.

2. Using the indicated primary stage cost drivers, determine the total amount of costs charged to each of the two jobs.

6-25. Activities and Cost Drivers for an Employment Agency.   Midwest Relocation Services is an employment agency working specifically with mid-level executives looking for new career opportunities or seeking employment after a layoff. The company views its product as placements. These are identified in four categories: employer-paid fee, applicant-paid fee, outplacement contract, and executive-search contract.

The agency incurs a number of costs in performing its services. Those costs are classified as operating expenses as follows:

Acct. #	Account Title
402	Salaries and Wages
403	Payroll Taxes
404	Employee Benefits
408	Office Supplies (postage, stationery, etc.)
409	Dues and Publications
410	Utilities
412	Rent
413	Repairs and Maintenance (contracted from outside)
420	Business Promotion
421	Auto Expenses
422	Travel Expenses
430	Professional Fees
432	Collection Expenses
435	License
441	Property Taxes
444	Insurance Costs
445	State Franchise Tax
447	Bad Debt Expense
448	Depreciation and Amortization
449	Miscellaneous

Required:

1. Classify each cost as related to unit-level, batch-level, product-level, or facility-level activities. Indicate an appropriate cost driver for each cost.

2. With the information from Part (1), group costs into logical activity groups and specify a cost driver for each activity group.

3. Explain what differences exist between applying activity-based costing to a manufacturing firm and to an employment agency.

6-26. Comparing ABC With Traditional Costing.   In manufacturing roller blades, Radzelli Company's plant used 400 direct labor hours, 500 machine hours, and 20 setups. The following overhead costs were taken from the factory accounts:

Overhead Expenses		Volume of Activities
Machining center	$120,000	20,000 machine hours
Setup center	40,000	100 setups
Total expenses	$160,000	4,000 direct labor hours

The plant was using a factory-wide overhead rate based on direct labor hours. A new ABC system will use machine hours in the Machining Department and number of setups in the Setup Department as cost drivers.

Required:

By what amount would the overhead costs assigned to roller blades differ between the prior system and the ABC system?

6-27. Impact of Grouping Activities.   Perrington Water Treatment Services has one division that manufactures two models of residential water treatment systems. The controller is considering implementing an activity-based costing system for overhead costs. In looking at the operations for the past year, the following overhead costs were reported:

Materials handling	$120,000
Receiving	40,000
Engineering	90,000
Depreciation on machinery	60,000
Power	30,000
Setups	84,000
Maintenance	80,000
Packing for shipment	35,000
Total	$539,000

The controller is looking at two alternative approaches. The first is to find a cost driver for each cost. The second is to group some of the costs and to select a cost driver for the grouping. Tentative groupings and their cost drivers are:

(a) Materials-related costs (Cost driver = Materials dollars):
   Materials handling.
   Receiving.

(b) Engineering (Cost driver = Engineering labor hours).

(c) Manufacturing overhead (Cost driver = Machine hours):
   Depreciation on machinery.
   Power.
   Setups.
   Maintenance.

(d) Packing for shipment (Cost driver = Number of orders shipped).

The following activity information is available for the past year for the two models:

	Standard	Deluxe
Units produced	10,000	20,000
Direct labor hours	10,000	20,000
Machine hours	20,000	40,000
Number of moves for materials handling	2,000	4,000
Engineering labor hours	5,000	3,000
Number of orders received	600	400
Number of setups	70	30
Maintenance hours used	1,500	2,500
Kilowatt hours of electricity used	15,000	30,000
Number of orders shipped	2,000	3,000
Materials	$80,000	$240,000

Required:

1. Using the costs and activity information, determine how much of the overhead costs would be charged to each model if costs were traced to products under the controller's first alternative.

2. Using the costs and activity information, determine how much of the overhead costs would be charged to each model if costs were traced to products under the controller's second alternative.

3. Explain how grouping of costs influences the costs traced to the products.

6-28. Distortion of Product Profitability.   The Chromosome Manufacturing Company produces two products, X and Y. The company president, Gene Mutation, is concerned about the fierce competition in the market for product X. He notes that competitors are selling X for a price well below Chromosome's price of $12.70. At the same time, he notes that competitors are pricing product Y almost twice as high as Chromosome's price of $12.50.

Mr. Mutation has obtained the following data for a recent time period:

	Product X	Product Y
Number of units	11,000	3,000
Direct materials cost per unit	$3.23	$3.09
Direct labor cost per unit	$2.22	$2.10
Direct labor hours	10,000	2,500
Machine hours	2,100	2,800
Inspection hours	80	100
Purchase orders	10	30

Mr. Mutation has learned that overhead costs are assigned to products on the basis of direct labor hours. The overhead costs for this time period consisted of the following items:

Overhead Cost Item	Amount
Inspection costs	$16,200
Purchasing costs	8,000
Machine costs	49,000
Total	$73,200

Required:

1. Using direct labor hours to allocate overhead costs, determine the gross margin per unit for each product.
2. Using activity-based costing, determine the gross margin per unit for each product.
3. How do your answers to Parts (1) and (2) help explain the observations made by Gene Mutation about competitors?

6-29. Comparison of Plant-Wide Rate to ABC.   The controller of G'Day Chemical Supply of South Australia has established the following activity centers with overhead costs (in Australian dollars) and related cost drivers:

Activity Centers	Budgeted Overhead Costs	Cost Driver	Budgeted Level for Cost Driver
Materials Handling	A$120,000	Weight of raw materials	60,000 pounds
Machine Setups	240,000	Number of setups	120 setups
Hazardous Waste	60,000	Weight of hazardous materials	12,000 pounds
Quality Control	85,000	Number of inspections	1,000 inspections
Other	205,000	Machine hours	102,500 hours

An order for 1,000 boxes of a powdered chemical has the following production requirements:

Raw materials (in pounds)	10,500
Machine setups	5
Hazardous materials (in pounds)	1,850
Inspections	13
Machine hours	490

Required:

1. Compute the overhead rates for each activity center.
2. Using the rates determined in Part (1), charge overhead costs to the order for 1,000 boxes of powdered chemical.

3. Calculate the cost per box of powdered chemical.
4. Assume the company allocates overhead costs on a plant-wide basis using machine hours.
   (a) Compute the plant-wide overhead rate.
   (b) Charge overhead costs to the order for 1,000 boxes of powdered chemical.
   (c) Calculate the cost per box of powdered chemical.
5. Explain why the cost per box differs under the two methods.

6-30. Overhead Rates and Cost Comparisons. Hertzlott Machine Shop makes replacement parts for automotive transmissions. It produces three basic products: gears, shafts, and casings. The company is budgeting activity for 1998. The activity centers, costs, and cost drivers are as follows:

Activity Center	Budgeted Costs	Cost Driver
Materials Handling	$ 312,400	Direct materials cost
Production Scheduling	116,000	Number of production orders
Setups.	144,600	Number of setups
Manual Machinery	986,000	Direct labor hours
Automated Machinery	3,212,000	Machine hours
Finishing	1,798,000	Direct labor hours
Packaging and Shipping . . .	234,000	Number of orders shipped

The following data are predicted for 1998:

	Gears	Shafts	Casings
Units produced	10,000	2,000	700
Direct materials cost per unit	$60	$80	$100
Number of production orders	40	20	10
Number of setups	20	10	14
Direct labor hours	20,000	10,000	8,400
Machine hours	30,000	15,000	2,800
Number of orders shipped	1,000	1,500	70

Required:

1. Compute an overhead rate for each activity center. Round calculations to four decimal places.
2. Compute an overall rate for the combined activities based on direct labor hours. Round calculations to four decimal places.
3. Show how much overhead is budgeted for gears, shafts, and casings using the activity-center rates and the overall rate.
4. Calculate an overall rate for the combined activities based on the total number of units.
5. Show how much overhead is budgeted for gears, shafts, and casings using the rate in Part (4).
6. Explain why the overhead costs differ in Parts (3) and (5).

6-31. ABC and Selling Costs. Redwood Company sells craft kits and supplies to retail outlets and through its catalog. Some of the items are manufactured by Redwood, while others are purchased for resale. For the products it manufactures, the company currently bases its selling prices on a costing system that accounts for direct materials, direct labor, and the associated overhead costs. In addition to these product costs, Redwood incurs substantial selling costs; and Roger Jackson, controller, has suggested that these selling costs be included in the product pricing structure.

After studying the costs incurred over the past two years for one of its products, skeins of knitting yarn, Jackson has selected four categories of selling costs and developed cost drivers for each of these costs. The selling costs actually incurred during the past year and the cost drivers are as follows:

Cost Category	Amount	Cost Driver
Sales commissions	$ 675,000	Boxes of yarn sold to retail stores
Catalogs	295,400	Catalogs distributed
Cost of catalog sales	105,000	Skeins sold through catalog
Credit and collection	60,000	Number of retail orders
Total selling costs	$1,135,400	

The knitting yarn is sold to retail outlets in boxes, each containing twelve skeins of yarn; the sale of partial boxes is not permitted. Commissions are paid on sales to retail outlets but not on catalog sales. The cost of catalog sales includes the wages of personnel who process the catalog orders and the telephone costs. Jackson believes that the selling costs vary significantly with the size of the order. Order sizes are divided into three categories as follows:

Order Size	Catalog Sales	Retail Sales
Small	1-10 skeins	1-10 boxes
Medium	11-20 skeins	11-20 boxes
Large	Over 20 skeins	Over 20 boxes

An analysis of the previous year's records produced the following statistics:

	Order Size			
	Small	Medium	Large	Total
Retail sales in boxes				
(12 skeins per box)	2,000	45,000	178,000	225,000
Catalog sales in skeins	79,000	52,000	44,000	175,000
Number of retail orders	485	2,415	3,100	6,000
Catalogs distributed	254,300	211,300	125,200	590,800

Required:

1. Prepare a detailed schedule showing Redwood Company's total selling cost for each order size and the per skein selling cost within each order size.

2. Explain how the analysis of the selling costs for skeins of knitting yarn is likely to impact future pricing and product decisions at Redwood Company.

(ICMA adapted)

6-32. Traditional Costing vs. ABC Costing.   Coffee Bean, Inc. (CBI) is a distributor and processor of a variety of different blends of coffee. The company buys coffee beans from around the world and roasts, blends, and packages them for resale. CBI currently has 15 different coffees that it offers to gourmet shops in one-pound bags. The major cost is raw materials; however, there is a substantial amount of manufacturing overhead in the predominantly automated roasting and packing process. The company uses relatively little direct labor.

CBI competes primarily on the quality of its products. Some of the coffees are very popular and sell in large volumes, while a few of the newer blends have very low sales volumes. CBI prices its coffee at cost plus a markup of 30 percent. If prices for certain coffees are significantly higher than market, adjustments are made, since customers are price conscious as well.

Data for the 1997 budget include manufacturing overhead of $3,000,000, which has been allocated on the basis of each product's direct labor cost. The budgeted direct labor cost for 1997 totals $600,000. Purchases and use of raw materials (mostly coffee beans) are expected to total $6,000,000.

The expected prime costs for each one-pound bag of two of the company's products are:

	Mona Loa	Malaysian
Raw materials	$4.20	$3.20
Direct labor	.30	.30

CBI's controller believes the traditional costing system may be providing misleading cost information and has developed an analysis of the 1997 budgeted manufacturing overhead costs, as follows:

Activity	Cost Driver	Budgeted Activity	Budgeted Cost
Purchasing	Purchase orders	1,158	$ 579,000
Materials handling ...	Number of setups	1,800	720,000
Quality control	Number of batches	600	144,000
Roasting	Roasting hours	96,100	961,000
Blending	Blending hours	33,600	336,000
Packaging..........	Packaging hours	26,000	260,000
Total manufacturing overhead cost...........................			$3,000,000

Data regarding the 1997 production of the Mona Loa and Malaysian coffees are presented as follows. No raw materials inventory exists for either of these coffees at the beginning of the year.

	Mona Loa	Malaysian
Expected sales	100,000 lbs.	2,000 lbs.
Batch size	10,000 lbs.	500 lbs.
Setups	3 per batch	3 per batch
Purchase order size	25,000 lbs.	500 lbs.
Roasting time	1 hr. per 100 lbs.	1 hr. per 100 lbs.
Blending time	0.5 hr. per 100 lbs.	0.5 hr. per 100 lbs.
Packaging time	0.1 hr. per 100 lbs.	0.1 hr. per 100 lbs.

Required:

1. Using Coffee Bean, Inc.'s current costing approach:
   (a) Determine the company's predetermined overhead rate using direct labor cost as the single allocation base.
   (b) Determine the expected costs and selling prices of one pound of Mona Loa coffee and one pound of Malaysian coffee.
2. Using the controller's analysis of budgeted manufacturing overhead, develop a new cost, using an activity-based costing approach, for one pound of:
   (a) Mona Loa coffee.
   (b) Malaysian coffee.
3. What are the implications of the activity-based cost of the two products with respect to the use of direct labor as a basis for allocating overhead to products and to the use of the existing cost system as a basis for pricing?

(ICMA adapted)

6-33. ABC and Charging for Support Services. Marfrank Corporation is a manufacturing company with six functional departments—Finance, Marketing, Personnel, Production, Research and Development (R&D), and Information Systems—each administered by a vice-president. The Information Systems Department (ISD) was established in 1996 when Marfrank decided to acquire a new mainframe computer and develop a new information system.

While systems development and implementation is an ongoing process at Marfrank, many of the basic systems needed by each of the functional departments were operational at the end of 1997. Thus, calendar year 1998 is considered the first year for which the ISD costs can be estimated with accuracy. Marfrank's president wants the other five functional departments to be aware of the magnitude of the ISD costs by reflecting the allocation of ISD costs in the reports and statements prepared at the end of the first quarter of 1998. The allocation of ISD costs to each of the departments was based on their actual use of ISD services.

Jon Werner, vice-president of ISD, suggested that the actual costs of ISD be allocated on the basis of the number of pages of actual computer output. This basis was suggested because the departments use reports in evaluating their operations and in making decisions. The use of this basis resulted in the following allocations:

Department	Percentage	Allocated Cost
Finance	50	$ 112,500
Marketing	30	67,500
Personnel	9	20,250
Production	6	13,500
R & D	5	11,250
Total	100	$ 225,000

After the quarterly reports were distributed, the Finance and Marketing Departments objected to this allocation method. Both departments recognized that they were responsible for most of the output in terms of reports, but they believed that these output costs might be the smallest of ISD costs and requested that a more equitable allocation basis be developed.

After meeting with Werner, Elaine Jergens, Marfrank's controller, concluded that ISD provided three distinct services—systems development, computer processing represented by central processing unit (CPU) time, and report generation. She recommended that a predetermined rate be developed for each of these services from budgeted annual activity and costs. The ISD costs would then be assigned to the other functional departments using the predetermined rate times the actual activity used. Any difference between actual costs incurred and costs allocated to the other departments would be absorbed by ISD.

Jergens and Werner concluded that systems development costs could be charged on the basis of hours devoted to systems development and programming, that computer processing charges be based on CPU time used for operations (exclusive of database development and maintenance), and that report generation charges be based on pages of output. The only cost that should not be included in any of the predetermined rates would be purchased software; these packages were usually acquired for a specific department's use. Thus, Jergens concluded that purchased software would be charged at cost to the department for which it was purchased. In order to revise the first quarter allocation, Jergens gathered the following information on ISD costs and services:

Information Systems Department Costs

	Estimated Annual Costs	Actual First Quarter Costs	Percentage Devoted to		
			Systems Develop.	Computer Processing	Report Generation
Wages and benefits:					
Administration	$ 100,000	$ 25,000	60 %	20 %	20 %
Computer operators . .	55,000	13,000		20	80
Analysts/programmers	165,000	43,500	100		
Maintenance:					
Hardware	24,000	6,000		75	25
Software	20,000	5,000		100	
Output supplies	50,000	11,500			100
Purchased software	45,000	*16,000	-	-	-
Utilities	28,000	6,250		100	
Depreciation:					
Mainframe computer .	325,000	81,250		100	
Printing equipment . .	60,000	15,000			100
Building improvements	10,000	2,500		100	
Total department costs . .	$ 882,000	$ 225,000			

* Note: All software purchased during the first quarter of 1998 was for the benefit of the Production Department.

Information Systems Department Services

	Systems Development	Computer Operations (CPU)	Report Generation
Annual capacity	4,500 hours	360 CPU hours	5,000,000 pages
Actual usage during first quarter–1998:			
Finance	100 hours	8 CPU hours	600,000 pages
Marketing	250	12	360,000
Personnel	200	12	108,000
Production	400	32	72,000
R & D	50	16	60,000
Total usage	1,000 hours	80 CPU hours	1,200,000 pages

Required:

1. Develop predetermined rates for each of the service categories of ISD—systems development, computer processing, and report generation.
2. Using the predetermined rates developed in Part (1), determine the amount each of the other five functional departments would be charged for services provided by ISD during the first quarter of 1998.
3. With the method proposed by Elaine Jergens for charging the ISD costs to the other five functional departments, there may be a difference between ISD's actual costs incurred and the costs assigned to the five user departments.
   (a) Explain the nature of this difference.
   (b) Discuss whether this proposal by Jergens will improve cost control in ISD.
   (c) Explain whether Jergens' proposed method of charging user departments for ISD costs will improve planning and control in the user departments.

(ICMA adapted)

6-34. Analysis of Accounts With JIT Costing.   L.D. Ferreira, general manager of a highly automated coffee production plant in Sao Paulo, Brazil, has provided the following information for transactions that occurred during October. All amounts are in Brazilian cruzeiro. The production plant uses a JIT costing system.

(a) Raw materials costing Cr$300,000 were purchased.
(b) All materials purchased were requisitioned for production.
(c) Direct labor costs of Cr$200,000 were incurred.
(d) Actual factory overhead costs amounted to Cr$995,000.
(e) Applied conversion costs totaled Cr$1,300,000. This includes the direct labor cost.
(f) All units were completed and immediately sold.

Required:

1. Determine the October 31 balance in the Cost of Goods Sold account. No adjustment has been made for overapplied or underapplied conversion cost.
2. What was the amount of overapplied or underapplied conversion cost for the month?

6-35. Recording Transactions Under JIT Costing.   Jensen's Jewelry Factory manufactures a variety of costume jewelry. The owner, Dan Jensen, has recently decided to implement a JIT costing system. Transactions during September were as follows:

(a) Raw materials totaling $45,000 were purchased.
(b) All materials purchased were requisitioned for production.
(c) Direct labor costs of $11,000 were incurred.
(d) Indirect labor costs amounted to $120,000.
(e) Utilities costs totaled $15,000.
(f) Other actual factory overhead costs amounted to $85,000.

(g)   Applied conversion costs totaled $221,000. This includes the direct labor cost.

(h)   All units were completed.

Required:

1.   Enter the September transactions into T-accounts. Label these entries by the identifying letters.

2.   Determine the amount of overapplied or underapplied conversion cost for the month.

6-36.   Comparing JIT Costing to Traditional Costing.   Murdock and Associates manufactures automated materials-handling systems. The company currently uses a conventional job costing system. During November, the company plans to purchase $96,000 of raw materials. Of this amount, 75 percent will be used for current production, while the remainder will serve as a buffer in inventory. Direct labor cost is expected to be $18,000 during November, and the actual factory overhead is anticipated to total $85,000. The applied factory overhead is expected to be $90,000. By the end of the month, two materials-handling systems should be completed; no systems were in process at the beginning of the month.

Rick Murdock, the owner, has been considering the use of a JIT inventory system. If implemented at the beginning of November, only the materials needed for current production would be purchased.

Required:

1.   Using T-accounts, enter the November transactions for the purchase and usage of materials under:

   (a)   Conventional costing.

   (b)   JIT costing.

2.   Using T-accounts, enter the November transactions for the labor and actual overhead costs under:

   (a)   Conventional costing.

   (b)   JIT costing.

3.   Using T-accounts, enter the November transactions for the application of overhead costs and the completion of the materials-handling systems under:

   (a)   Conventional costing.

   (b)   JIT costing.

1-2-3

C ASE 6A—ALAIRE CORPORATION

Alaire Corporation manufactures several different types of printed circuit boards; however, two of the boards account for the majority of the company's sales. The first of these boards, a television (TV) circuit board, has been a standard in the industry for several years. The market for this board is competitive and, therefore, price-sensitive. Alaire plans to sell 65,000 of the TV boards in 1999 at a price of $150 per unit. The second high-volume product, a personal computer (PC) circuit board, is a recent addition to Alaire's product line. Because the PC board incorporates the latest technology, it can be sold at a premium price; the 1999 plans include the sale of 40,000 PC boards at $300 per unit.

Alaire's management group is meeting to discuss strategies for 1999, and the current topic of conversation is how to spend the sales and promotion dollars for next year. The sales manager believes that the market share for the TV board could be expanded by concentrating Alaire's promotional efforts in this area. In response to this suggestion, the production manager said, "Why don't you go after a bigger market for the PC board? The cost sheets show that the contribution from the PC board is more than double the contribution from the TV board. I know we get a premium price for the PC board; selling it should help overall profitability."

Alaire uses a conventional cost system, and the following data apply to the TV and PC boards:

	TV Board	PC Board
Direct materials	$ 80	$ 140
Direct labor	1.5 hours	4.0 hours
Machine time	0.5 hours	1.5 hours

Variable factory overhead is applied on the basis of direct labor hours. For 1999, variable factory overhead is budgeted at $1,120,000, and direct labor hours are estimated at 280,000. The hourly rates for machine time and direct labor are $10 and $14, respectively. Alaire applies a materials handling charge at 10 percent of materials cost; this materials handling charge is not included in variable factory overhead. Total 1999 expenditures for materials are budgeted at $1,060,000.

Ed Welch, Alaire's controller, believes that before the management group proceeds with the discussion about allocating sales and promotional dollars to individual products, it might be worthwhile to look at these products on the basis of the activities involved in their production. As Welch explained to the group, "Activity-based costing integrates, by using cost drivers, the cost of all activities into individual product costs rather than including these costs in overhead pools." Welch has prepared the following schedule to help the management group understand this concept.

"Using this information," Welch explained, "we can calculate an activity-based cost for each TV board and each PC board and then compare it to the costs we have been using. The only cost that remains the same for both cost methods is the cost of direct materials. The cost drivers will assign the direct labor, machine time, and overhead costs in the current costing approach."

Budgeted Costs		Cost Driver	Annual Activity for Cost Driver
Materials overhead:			
Procurement	$ 400,000	Number of parts	4,000,000 parts
Production scheduling	220,000	Number of boards	110,000 boards
Packaging and shipping	440,000	Number of boards	110,000 boards
	$1,060,000		
Variable overhead:			
Machine setup	$ 446,000	Number of setups	278,750 setups
Hazardous waste disposal	48,000	Pounds of waste	16,000 pounds
Quality control	560,000	Number of inspections	160,000 inspections
General supplies	66,000	Number of boards	110,000 boards
	$1,120,000		
Manufacturing:			
Machine insertion	$1,200,000	Number of parts	3,000,000 parts
Manual insertion	4,000,000	Number of parts	1,000,000 parts
Wave soldering	132,000	Number of boards	110,000 boards
	$5,332,000		

Required Per Unit	TV Board	PC Board
Parts:		
Machine insertions	24	35
Manual insertions	1	20
Total	25	55
Machine setups	2	3
Hazardous waste in pounds	.02	.35
Inspections	1	2

Required:

1. On the basis of the current (conventional) cost approach being used, calculate the total contribution expected in 1999 for Alaire Corporation's:
   (a) TV board.
   (b) PC board.
2. On the basis of activity-based costs, calculate the total contribution expected in 1999 for Alaire Corporation's:
   (a) TV board.
   (b) PC board.
3. Explain how the comparison of the results of the two costing methods may impact the decisions made by Alaire Corporation's management group.

(ICMA adapted)

C ASE 6B—FRANZEL COMPANY

Franzel Company manufactures several different models of luggage in its four manufacturing departments. These four departments and one service department (Equipment Maintenance) are housed in one facility. Due to the distinctive characteristics of the costs and operations of the different manufacturing departments, departmental manufacturing overhead rates are employed for each manufacturing department.

Franzel has been reviewing its operations and plans to implement some changes in the budgeting and reporting for the manufacturing departments during the next fiscal year. The Molding Department is being reviewed first, and its cost and operating data for six months of the current fiscal year are presented in the following chart:

Molding Department
Manufacturing Overhead Activity Measures and Actual Costs

	Jan.	Feb.	March	April	May	June
Activity measures:						
Pounds of materials	25,000	27,000	30,000	24,000	20,000	22,000
Machine hours	11,500	13,500	12,500	8,500	9,500	10,000
Units produced	50,000	45,000	52,000	42,000	48,000	40,000
Machine setups	15	20	16	18	19	21
Materials handling costs ($1.40/lb.)	$ 35,000	$ 37,800	$ 42,000	$ 33,600	$ 28,000	$ 30,800
Setup costs	11,500	15,250	12,000	14,000	14,500	22,750
Machine hour costs:						
Indirect labor ($5/machine hr.) . .	57,500	67,500	62,500	42,500	47,500	50,000
Power ($0.20/kwhr.)	21,250	24,250	22,750	16,750	18,250	19,000
Equipment maintenance	15,000	18,000	12,000	19,000	16,000	35,000
Fixed costs	335,000	335,000	335,000	335,000	335,000	335,000
Total overhead	$475,250	$497,800	$486,250	$460,850	$459,250	$492,550

This information has been accumulated to assist in developing the manufacturing overhead budget for the coming year. These costs are traceable (direct) to the Molding Department except for a portion of the fixed costs and the equipment maintenance costs. The fixed costs include the common building and operating costs which are allocated to each of the manufacturing departments on the basis of square feet of space occupied. The Equipment Maintenance Department costs are charged to the operating departments for services rendered. These costs represent the actual costs of parts and supplies

($150,000 for the current fiscal year), plus a charge of $50 per hour. The manager of the Equipment Maintenance Department determines the preventive maintenance schedule for each of the production departments; all other repairs are made on a "first come, first served" basis.

Management is comfortable with using the six-month data as the basis for the preliminary budget estimates because most of the activity measures and costs appear to be representative. However, the following adjustments will have to be made for the coming year:

Cost Item	Cost Adjustment
Indirect labor	Cost increase of 8 percent
Equipment maintenance . . .	Cost increase of 10 percent for parts, supplies, and the hourly charge
Fixed costs	$360,000 per month

In the past, the overhead application base in the Molding Department has been machine hours for all costs. However, management has used scattergraphs to analyze the behavior of some costs and has concluded that more than one cost driver exist in this department. As shown in the scattergraph below, which captures data for the 12-month period through June of this year, the number of setups clearly represents the behavior of the setup costs and is now the application base for these costs. Similarly, the cost driver that is most appropriate as an application base for materials handling costs is pounds of materials processed. Machine hours will continue to be used as an application base for the remaining costs of the Molding Department.

Jon Stein, vice-president of manufacturing, has indicated that he wants to employ a responsibility accounting system where each manufacturing department will be held accountable for all costs included in its manufacturing overhead budget. Actual monthly costs will be compared to the annual budget, and each department is expected to operate at or below budgeted monthly costs.

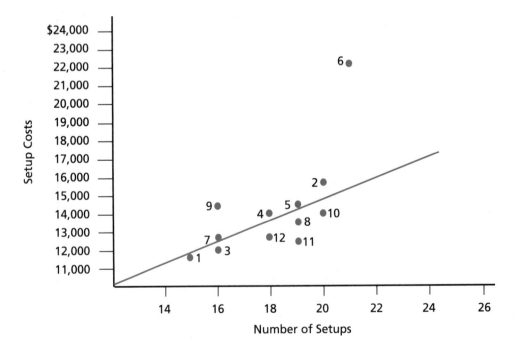

The numbers next to the points on the graph refer to the month of occurrence, i.e., January = 1, etc.

Based on the production budgets, the activity measures for the Molding Department will be at the following levels for the coming fiscal year:

Activity Measure	Estimated Annual Amount
Pounds of materials	280,000
Machine hours	135,000
Units produced	520,000
Machine setups...........................	200
Power usage in kilowatt hours per unit produced ..	2.5
Equipment maintenance in hours	1,600

Required:

1. Using the cost data presented for the 6-month period of the current year, adjusted for the estimated changes expected to occur and the estimated activity measures for the coming year, develop a manufacturing overhead budget for the Molding Department for the coming year. Use the high-low method to determine the fixed and variable components of the setup costs.

2. Develop the overhead rate that should be employed in the Molding Department for the coming year for the costs to be applied on the basis of machine hours.

3. Describe the likely behavior of the manufacturing departmental managers with respect to their accountability for equipment maintenance costs.

(ICMA adapted)

PART III

Planning and Control Framework

C H A P T E R *7*

Budgeting for Operations

*L*EARNING OBJECTIVES

After studying Chapter 7, you will be able to:

1. Identify the major elements of a financial planning and control system.
2. Explain the major purposes of budgeting.
3. Define responsibility accounting including cost, profit, and investment centers.
4. Describe how control can be accomplished through responsibility accounting.
5. Diagram and explain the major steps in preparing a master budget.
6. Discuss preparing and formatting budget schedules.
7. Understand the role of flexible budgeting in planning and control.
8. Use probabilistic budgeting.
9. Identify the major human behavior factors that affect budgets and the budgeting process.

To Budget or Not to Budget . . . The Answer Is Clear!

If you mention the words "plans" or "budgets" to Pat Shockley, president of National Alliance Industries, you get a reaction ranging from disdain to outright hostility. She has been heard to say:

- "How can I plan? Things always change so fast!"
- "My business isn't suited to anything so formal. My managers and I need to be flexible, fast on our feet, and ready to change direction overnight, if we have to do so."
- "The budget always says we can't do it. I just say, 'Do it!'"
- "The budget reports tell me where I've been, never where I'm going."
- "That's the accountant's budget; it doesn't tell me what my problems are and what to do about them!"
- "We can't wait for approvals and reports. Budgets hold us back!"

Shockley even has a coffee cup with "Budgets Are for Wimps!" printed on it. She believes that intuition and drive, not reports, got the company to where it is today. "The easiest way to lose our edge is to start acting like paper shufflers!" she exclaims. Each of her comments has some truth in it; but, more likely, the comments together reflect serious deficiencies in the firm's management process—little or no planning and little ability to measure performance.

A close friend says plans and budgets strike terror in Shockley because her "style" is threatened. She likes to operate quickly, often keeping others in the dark. The friend says that Pat's afraid to admit that she has no idea where the company is going.

Recently, a situation arose where Shockley thought employees were making too many "bad calls" on key decisions. She was surprised by the responses she got when she asked several department managers what was wrong. Each complained about lack of direction at the top, how management kept changing its mind, and how employees found it hard to get things done.

A simple concept is a key to budgeting: Planning is not deciding what to do in the future; it is deciding what to do now to assure a future. This chapter discusses concepts, tools, and processes used in a planning and control system.

*B*UDGETING: A PLANNING AND CONTROL SYSTEM

Planning and control consist of an overall management system. **Planning** can be viewed as a framework within which managers anticipate future events, develop a plan of action, and estimate future revenues and costs. **Control** is the process of using feedback on actual operating results to compare to the plan, to evaluate performance in achieving the plans and goals, and to make changes. A **budget** is a plan showing what and how resources are to be used over a specified time period.

The plan, act, control, and evaluate cycle is shown in Figure 7.1. The master plan is prepared; decisions are made and actions taken; reports are prepared and analyzed; and the plan is reviewed and updated.

A **mission statement** sets the purposes of the organization. **Goals and objectives** are statements about its future position and its long-term direction. They describe specific performance targets and often give specific timeframes for achieving certain targets. A profit goal might be, for example, to earn an annual 15 percent aftertax return on shareholders' equity or to generate sales of $1 billion by 1999. Once goals (direction and motivations) and objectives

FIGURE 7.1 The Planning and Control Cycle

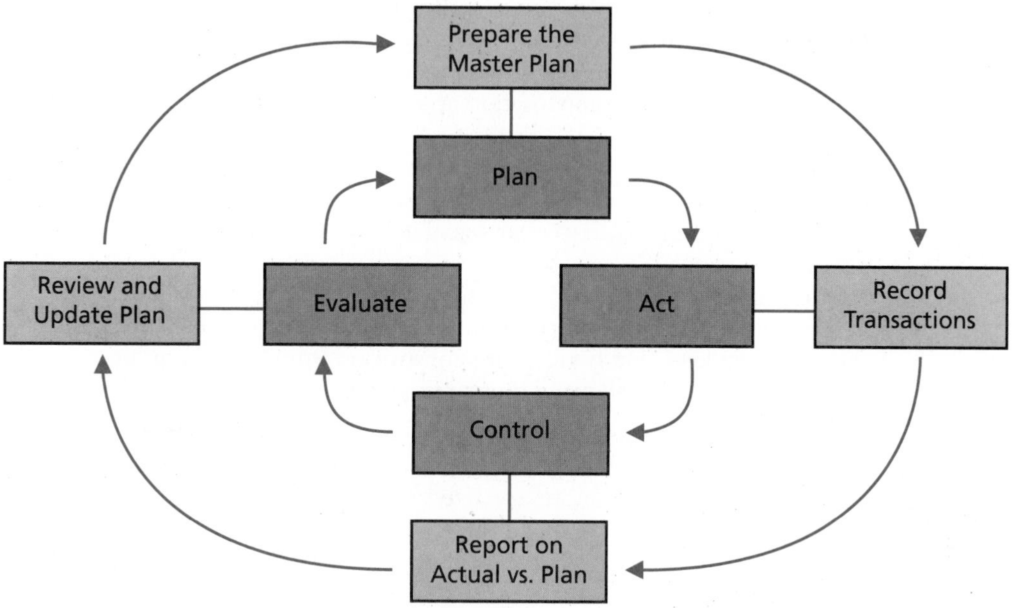

(quantified performance targets) are set, desired outputs can be defined. The budgeting process determines the inputs needed to achieve the forecast outputs.

A planning and control system includes tools, methods, and attitudes. The following set of common elements appears:

1. **Strategic planning process.** This long-range planning effort must define the firm's mission (why the firm exists), the **long-range goals** (what level of achievement it expects), and a **strategic plan** (what markets, price policies, resource needs, and production capabilities the firm will have).

2. **Set of goals, objectives, and planning assumptions for annual planning.** Specific annual goals and objectives that move the firm toward the longer run strategic goals form the planning targets for the annual budgeting process.

3. **Business plan and management-by-objectives (MBO) goals.** Creating the annual business plan is the task of evaluating the firm's strengths, weaknesses, opportunities, and tactics to build firm-wide priorities for the coming year. Also, each manager develops a personal set of goals and a plan of achievements which are consistent with firm's business plan.

4. **Planning process and timetable.** A budgeting time schedule includes dates to start the process, submit budgets, and review and approve budgets at various management levels—formalizing who does what and when. Also, the planning process includes an updating process, often called **continuous budgeting**. As one month's actual results arrive (say March of 1997), a new month's forecast is added (March of 1998). A twelve-month planning horizon is maintained.

5. **Responsibility accounting system.**   This is a planning and control system that combines responsibility centers, charts of accounts, control reports, and activity centers and cost drivers from activity-based costing.

6. **Reward or incentive system.**   Rewards can provide incentives for managers who achieve their unit's budget goals and/or MBO targets. Tying performance to compensation appears to be an increasingly common practice.

7. **Financial modeling.**   Ability to evaluate alternative or "what if" scenarios is now an expected part of any financial planning system. Simulation can test a plan to assess goal achievement and evaluate alternative actions.

8. **Participatory budgeting.**   It is assumed that every manager in the firm is involved in planning and control. Often, budget objectives are set at the executive level; but budgets are constructed from the bottom up. This is sometimes called "grassroots" budgeting.

A budget period may be a week, month, quarter, year, or longer.   But normally, a master budget is for a year's activities and is divided into months or quarters. Long-term budgets may be for five or more years.

R ESPONSIBILITY ACCOUNTING

Responsibility accounting has no universal definition but does link authority and control. Managers prepare plans for their areas of responsibility and exert control over those activities by making decisions and evaluating results.   A responsibility accounting system brings discipline to planning and control tasks. The same basic elements remain visible in accounting systems of small firms to sophisticated planning systems in large, complex organizations.   The basic elements of responsibility accounting are:

1. **Responsibility center definitions**—to segment the organization into small sets of similar activities.

2. **Chart-of-accounts classifications**—to classify accounting data by their natural characteristics.

3. **Control reports**—to report actual versus plan for expenses, revenues, and other financial and activity measures such as cost drivers.

4. **Roll-up reporting capability**—to summarize lower level activities at higher levels along responsibility channels.

Strictly speaking, cost control is less cost control and more management of people who incur costs. In Chapter 2, controllable and noncontrollable costs were defined.   Here, controllable costs are tied to organizational structure, activities management, and performance assessment.

Responsibility Centers

From a firm's perspective, planning and control focus on responsibility centers. A **responsibility center** is an organizational unit that has a specific manager with authority and control over spending, earning, or investing. Responsibility centers can be classified into three groups—cost centers, profit centers, and investment centers. Figure 7.2 illustrates these responsibility centers.

FIGURE 7.2   Responsibility Centers: Investment, Profit, and Cost Centers

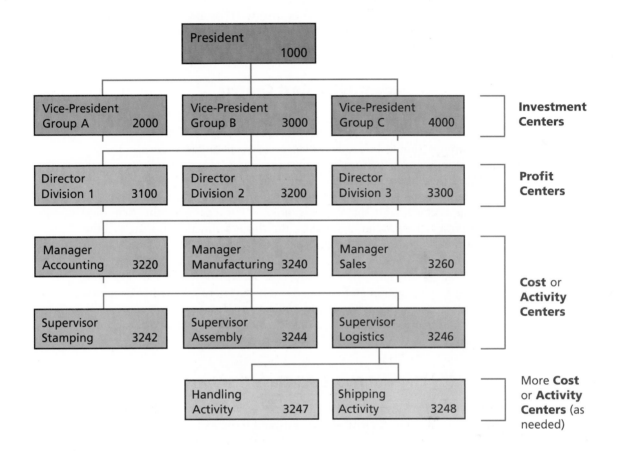

A **cost center** is a responsibility center where control exists over incurring costs. Often, cost centers are defined by an organization chart and may be further subdivided into more cost centers if costs and activities can be better linked for cost determination and management purposes. It is here that quality costs, setups, and other ABC relationships are integrated into the cost system. A cost center is the smallest unit of an organization within which costs and activities are measured. **Activity centers**, discussed in Chapter 6, are much like cost centers. At the detail level, the terms are used interchangeably. If a cost center has several cost drivers, it should be subdivided into more cost or activity centers so that homogeneous activities and their costs can be linked.

A **profit center** is a responsibility center where control exists over generating revenue and incurring its related costs. A profit center manager has both cost and revenue responsibilities. Often, sales organizations are profit centers—with product revenues, cost of sales, and marketing expenses. Managers with product-line responsibility might include both manufacturing and marketing departments. Branch or regional managers often have sales and expense control. The term **revenue center** can be used where a manager has revenue responsibility but controls few expenses, such as in an airline reservation department.

An **investment center** is a responsibility center where control exists over costs, revenues, and investments in assets used or managed. Managers must have the authority to acquire or dispose of assets. Typically, divisions of large firms are considered to be investment centers and are viewed by top management essentially as separate business entities.

Identifying Cost Centers

In many cases, cost centers parallel the boxes on the organization chart. Figure 7.2 illustrates the link between a firm's organization and its cost center coding. Activity groupings should be studied before cost centers are defined. In fact, ABC, TQM, nonmonetary performance measures, and other management needs may well determine the responsibility center structure. A logic is often created by a numbering system—defining different parts of the organization, levels of management, and superior/subordinates links. For example, the first digit indicates a group; the second, a division; the third, a functional area; and the last digit provides even greater detail if needed.

Design of the cost system is critical. If activities are grouped too finely, too many cost centers are created; and key cost information is subdivided too finely. Yet, data aggregation and summarization start here. A greater danger is losing important cost relationships if cost and activity detail are too summarized. Cost centers defined too broadly lose detail needed in later analyses, and this detail can be recreated only at great cost.

Chart of Accounts Classifications

Designing a **chart of accounts** or a database is hardly one of life's exciting tasks. However, a detailed chart of accounts and the cost center structure form responsibility accounting's classification system. Expenses are classified by their basic nature: wages, supplies, telephone, repairs, depreciation, etc. Costs are now classified in two ways—by who and where in the cost center and by what in the chart of accounts. Having too few accounts loses the fineness needed for later reporting, and reporting too much detail can smother analysis. But today, the cost of data storage has fallen; and the ability to access huge amounts of detailed information in an organized manner expands a manager's sphere of inquiry.

Figure 7.3 presents a sample structure of a chart of accounts for the firm organized as shown in Figure 7.2. For example, 3248-6320 would be the code for equipment repairs in the shipping department. Each cost center should have its uniquely defined set of expense accounts for its own special needs but should also use the same account numbers for expenses common to all cost centers.

Control Reports and Roll-Up Reporting

Control reports are prepared routinely for each cost center for a specific time period. Figure 7.4, page 284, is a cost center report from a metal-forming factory. This is from Cost Center 3242 in Figure 7.2 and uses the basic chart of accounts outlined in Figure 7.3. This factory has nearly forty cost centers and uses approximately 400 different expense accounts. Thirty to forty of these accounts are used in a typical cost center.

FIGURE 7.3 Partial Chart of Accounts Structure

Partial Chart of Accounts

1000	Assets		5000	Selling & Administrative Expenses
1100	Cash		5100	Salary Expenses
1110	Checking Accounts		5110	Manager Salary Expense
•	•		5120	Staff Salary Expense
1200	Accounts Receivable		•	•
•	•		5400	Advertising Expenses
•	•		•	•
1300	Inventories		6000	Manufacturing Expenses
•	•		6100	Direct Manufacturing Expenses
2000	Liabilities		6110	Direct Labor Wages
•	•		6160	Direct Materials
•	•		6200	Manufacturing Overhead
3000	Equities		6210	Machine Expenses
•	•		6211	Machine Setup
•	•		•	•
4000	Revenues		6320	Repairs—Equipment
4100	Product Line A		•	•
4110	Product A-1		6520	Depreciation Expense—Equipment
•	•		•	•
4900	Miscellaneous Revenue		7000	Gain and Loss Items

Several observations should be made about the control report in Figure 7.4. The breakdown among controllable, semicontrollable, and allocated expenses is an excellent approach to signal which costs and variances are the responsibility of that cost center's manager. Monthly and year-to-date comparisons of actual costs to budget amounts report the current situation, annual trends, and magnitude and direction of variances from budget. Activity measures, including cost drivers that relate overhead costs to outputs, are reported at the bottom of the report.

The overall performance of supervisor Kannisoni in controllable and semicontrollable categories was close to budget for September. But because of an extra large administrative allocation in account 6780, the cost center's total overhead expenses appear to be about $6,000 over budget. While including allocated expenses may be useful for other purposes, it has little beneficial budget impact and violates a basic responsibility accounting rule—account for what you control.

Roll-up reporting aggregates results for each higher management level. Middle and upper levels of management receive reports containing summarized results for all cost centers under their control. The report in Figure 7.4 is reviewed by supervisor Kannisoni and his superior. Results from this cost center are summarized at the next higher level—in the control report for the manufacturing manager in Cost Center 3240 from Figure 7.2. All cost centers in Division 2, Profit Center 3200, are summarized in the Division 2 director's control report. Division 2 is then summarized in the Group B vice-president's Investment Center 3000 control report along with all divisions reporting to the Group B vice-president. All responsibility center reports are eventually summarized into one firm-wide control report for the president. In all reports, actual amounts are compared to budget amounts on monthly and year-to-date bases.

FIGURE 7.4 Example of a Cost Center Control Report

| Cost Center: Stamping | | | | Period: September 98 | | |
| Cost Center No.: 3242 | | | | Supervisor: Tatso Kannisoni | | |

	Monthly		Fav./	Year-to-Date		Fav./
	Actual	Budget	(Unfav.)	Actual	Budget	(Unfav.)
6110 Total direct labor	23465	24192	727	206211	209520	3309
6160 Total direct materials	79560	80000	440	712344	715000	2656
6211 Machine setup	3703	3424	(279)	29920	30608	688
6212 Downtime	1076	1680	604	13357	13286	(71)
6215 Maintenance labor	430	639	209	4205	3016	(1189)
6245 Hourly overtime premium	761	0	(761)	3094	0	(3094)
6271 Hourly fringe benefits	11222	12000	778	106112	103506	(2606)
6330 Repairs—dies & fixtures	10671	7319	(3352)	78971	77446	(1525)
6441 Rework	68	22	(46)	479	206	(273)
6443 Scrap	1247	1242	(5)	8730	13827	5097
6490 Miscellaneous expenses	118	160	42	1901	1434	(467)
Total controllable o/h expenses	29296	26486	(2810)	246769	243329	(3440)
6220 Other indirect labor	2498	2389	(109)	21111	20732	(379)
6260 Salaries	2107	2045	(62)	16914	18105	1191
6272 Salaried benefits	424	518	94	4138	4812	674
6320 Repairs—equipment	7066	10069	3003	82987	80253	(2734)
6420 Factory utilities	337	139	(198)	2564	3888	1324
Total semicontrollable o/h exp	12432	15160	2728	127714	127790	76
6510 Depreciation—building	271	267	(4)	1588	962	(626)
6520 Depreciation—equipment	4070	4070	0	36630	36630	0
6540 Property taxes	1342	1342	0	12078	12078	0
6780 Administrative allocations	33945	27503	(6442)	260230	244201	(16029)
Total allocated o/h expenses	39628	33182	(6446)	310526	293871	(16655)
Total cost center overhead	81356	74828	(6528)	685009	664990	(20019)
Total cost center expenditures	184381	179020	(5361)	1603564	1589510	(14054)
Activity measures:			Diff			Diff
Workers	12.0	12.0	0.0	11.7	11.8	0.1
Direct labor hours	1920.0	2016.0	96.0	16450.0	17460.0	1010.0
Number of stampings (000)	179.7	175.0	4.7	1563.0	1575.0	12.0
Operating machine hours	1145.0	1209.6	64.6	10419.0	10476.0	57.0

WHY BUDGET?

Advantages of budgeting nearly always outweigh the costs and efforts required by the process. Although many reasons exist for budgeting, key purposes include:

1. Formalize the planning process.
2. Create a plan of action.
3. Create a basis for performance evaluation.
4. Promote continuous improvement.
5. Coordinate and integrate management's efforts.
6. Aid in resource allocation.
7. Create an "aura of control."
8. Motivate managers and employees positively.

Formalize the Planning Process.   Perhaps the foremost purpose of budgeting is to compel managers to think about the future, which forces them to set goals, consider potential future problems, and formulate strategies. Budgeting moves managers from merely reacting to opportunities, problems, and actions to anticipating these situations.

Create a Plan of Action.   The planning process brings together ideas, forecasts, resource availabilities, and financial realities to create a course of action to achieve the firm's goals and objectives. Now what? Use it! Make decisions to implement the plan. Follow the budgeted marketing plan. Schedule production according to the sales forecast. Buy materials according to the production budget. The budget should be the operating bible for all managers in the firm. Yes, conditions do change and budgets do need regular updating.

Create a Basis for Performance Evaluation.   Actual results lack meaning unless they are compared to a target, a plan, or a budgeted number. A budget is a **benchmark** against which actual results are measured and managers' performances are evaluated. Significant variances between actual and planned amounts require explanations and, often, corrective actions. Likewise, target costing and continuous improvement imply that unfavorable variances may be decreasing toward a goal of zero or may become increasingly favorable as improvements are made. One major benefit of a benchmark is that managers know what is expected of them and can work toward that outcome. For judging performance, a budget is regarded as a more relevant comparative base than is past actual performance.

Promote Continuous Improvement.   Budgeting efforts should strive to improve operations continuously. Redesigning processes, increasing productivity expectations, eliminating nonvalue-adding activities, and erasing quality problems are integral parts of planning for future performance. The budgeting system is where these improvement processes are quantified and locked into operating plans.

Coordinate and Integrate Management's Efforts.   The budget is a plan of action for the entire organization and reflects the coordinated efforts of all managers. Budgeting processes open lines of communication within the organization: (1) up and down organizational lines from subordinates to supervisors and (2) across organizational lines to integrate functional tasks.

Aid in Resource Allocation.   "We'll do it, if we get budget approval to hire another person." "If I can convince my boss to budget more funds for market-ing, we can expand our market penetration." These are typical comments about resources and budgets. Budget time is when resources are allocated or reas-signed. Once dollars are in or not in a budget, they are difficult to move or to change.

Create an "Aura of Control."   The expression "in control" can mean many things; but, in a management sense, effective controls ensure that managers understand their authority, responsibilities, and limits. A budget system can serve as a disciplinarian or "cop" for fiscal issues. An "aura of control" gives employees a sense that management has control over business activities and that policies are being followed.

Motivate Managers and Employees Positively.   Budget systems often have negative images. But the good news is:

1. People who help to prepare budgets for their domain will have a commitment to the budget and take pride in achieving "their" plans.
2. Through the budget, managers can see how their parts of the puzzle fit together to form a whole—the firm-wide plan.
3. Promotions, raises, and incentives are based on job performance, which includes achieving budget targets.

Budgeting systems promote improved teamwork, more involvement in pro-cess improvement, and greater goal congruency throughout the organization. If the president treats budgets as important, each manager and employee will also do so.

*M*ASTER BUDGET—AN OVERVIEW

The annual budgeting effort is commonly called the **master budget** or, in some firms, the **profit plan** or **comprehensive budget**. Although a master budget usually covers a one-year period in detail, it may be prepared on a month-by-month basis for the year and may be extended in summary form for several years into the future. Regardless of the period of time, the master budget begins with a sales budget and concludes with pro forma financial statements. The components of a master budget differ for manufacturing and nonmanufacturing companies.

Master Budget for a Manufacturer

Master budget terminology and classifications may differ among manufacturing organizations, but a common set is shown in Figure 7.5 to describe the master budget and its supporting schedules. In Chapter 8, a comprehensive example is developed to illustrate each schedule and its format. Figure 7.5 references the appropriate Chapter 8 schedules.

The interrelationships among master budget components can be flowcharted as in Figure 7.6, page 288. While much budget work can be done simulta-neously, a stepping-stone procedure generates a sequential flow of planning information.

FIGURE 7.5 The Master Budget Structure

The Structure of a Master Budget for a Manufacturer

I.   Annual Goals and Planning Assumptions
   A. Operating and financial goals
   B. Planning assumptions
       1. Product cost and price data (Chapter 8, Schedule 1)
       2. Operating and financial activity assumptions (Schedule 2)
       3. Beginning balance sheet

II. Operating Budget
   A. Sales forecast (Schedule 3)
   B. Production plan (Schedule 4)
   C. Manufacturing cost budgets
       1. Materials requirements (Schedule 5)
       2. Direct labor (Schedule 6)
       3. Manufacturing overhead budgets
           (a) Flexible budget (Schedule 7)
           (b) Manufacturing overhead expense (Schedule 8)
   D. Supporting schedules
       1. Accounts receivable—credit and collections (Schedule 9)
       2. Inventories—levels and valuation (Schedule 10)
       3. Accounts payable—purchases and payments (Schedule 11)
   E. Cost of goods manufactured and sold (Schedule 12)
   F. Operating expenses budgets
       1. Selling expenses (Schedule 13)
       2. Administrative expenses (Schedule 14)
   G. Cash-flow forecast (Schedule 16)

III. Project Budgets (Schedule 15)
   A. Capital expenditures
   B. Research and development and other special projects

IV. Forecast Financial Statements
   A. Forecast statement of income and expense
   B. Forecast balance sheet

Operating Budgets. The **operating budget** is a formal document that takes a sales forecast and converts it into a plan of action. Planned operating results are summarized in a cash-flow forecast and forecast financial statements.

The day-to-day activities of any business are the interdependent parts of an operating cycle. The **operating cycle** is illustrated in Figure 7.7, page 289, as a circular sequence of events from purchasing on account to paying those bills with cash collected from sales. The cycle can be viewed as a "cash-to-cash" process. Inventories are financed by payables. Sales reduce inventories and create receivables. Customers are billed; and cash is collected. Since cash is now available, the cycle repeats itself.

Broad budget numbers are then broken down into specific activities. For example, a cash-flow budget for March can be broken down into weekly cash-flow schedules to anticipate payroll, loan payment, and other critical short-term cash-flow dates. Detailed weekly or even daily production plans by specific machine or person are developed from the monthly production plan.

FIGURE 7.6 Components of the Master Budget

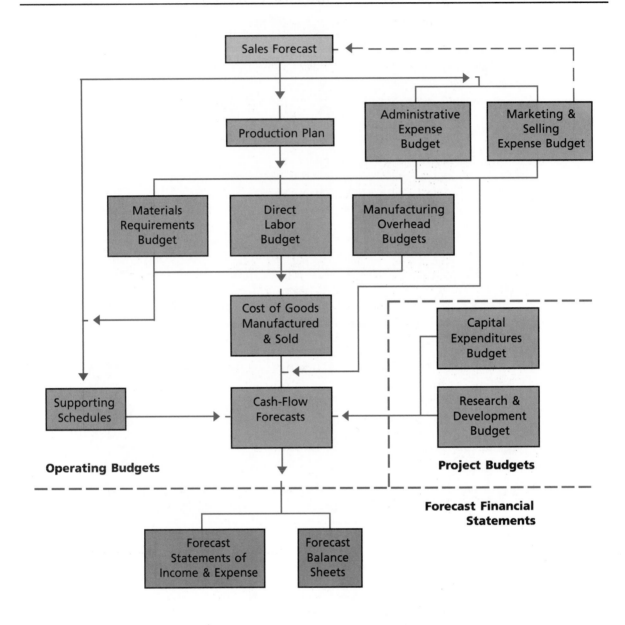

Cash-Flow Forecast.   Cash-flow forecasting is a key to cash management. **Cash management** is planning and controlling cash balances over time. Often, three timeframes can be identified: long term, annual, and short term which may be daily or weekly. Each fits into the firm's planning process.

An organization must have adequate cash flow to survive. For example, a public relations firm provides services to its clients but must pay salaries, travel, rent, and other costs. Clients are billed but wait perhaps 30 days or longer to pay. Thus, it is possible that a firm collects cash 30, 60, or 90 days after paying many expenses. The financing of these timing differences must be arranged.

FIGURE 7.7 The Operating Cycle

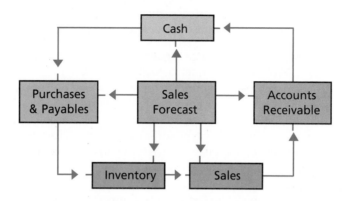

Project Budgets. While much budgeting uses a 12-month timeframe to plan repetitive activities, a number of activities do not have traits that are compatible with this timeframe. They may overlap years, have shorter lives, and be unique. These activities use a **project budget**. Examples include capital expenditures for new construction and equipment, research and development programs, and information systems development projects. Project costs are planned around resources and the project's timeline. Project budgets, however, are integrated into annual plans as well.

Forecast Financial Statements. **Forecast financial statements** summarize the financial results from operating, cash-flow, and project budgets. Forecast income statements and balance sheets provide managers with information needed to judge how adequately the master plan achieves the firm's financial goals and objectives. Most financial goals are expressed as ratios of balance sheet and income statement numbers. Financial ratios are discussed in Chapter 17. The forecast financial data then become the basis for evaluating actual results.

Master Budget for Nonmanufacturing Organizations

How does a master budget differ for a merchandising or service organization? The basic budgeting concepts are essentially the same; however, variations do exist.

Merchandising Organizations. A merchandiser replaces production in Figures 7.5 and 7.6 with purchases. The budget cycle for merchandisers will have the following different traits:

- Often, multiple locations exist and have individual budgets. Budgets for all segments are consolidated into one sales and operating expense budget.
- Revenue and expense budgets for store operations are created.
- If distribution systems and warehousing are involved, these budgets must be linked to sales forecasts and store budgets.
- A greater proportion of managers are profit center managers (product lines, branches, or departments) with both revenue and expense responsibilities.

Most merchandising companies will concentrate on a gross margin or contribution margin plan, which combines sales and cost of sales budgets. Operating expenses may differ in nature in merchandising firms, but the functional classifications of selling and administrative expenses remain.

Service Organizations.   A service organization often depends heavily on human resources. Planning personnel capacity and staffing levels is critical. In many service organizations, personnel expenses, which include salaries and benefits, account for well over 75 percent of all expenses. This is the case, for example, in school systems and accounting, legal, and consulting firms. Here personnel may be organized by type of service, skill, customer, or project. Staffing plans using headcounts may be more valuable for planning and control than dollar plans.

In complex organizations, such as hospitals and banks, budgets develop around services provided. Forecasts of customer or patient work volumes, equipment used, support services required, and revenue generated are developed in responsibility centers and are combined vertically and linked horizontally. Interdependencies force budgeters to analyze both direct and indirect impacts of changes in planned activities. In financial institutions, for example, interest income from loans and investments is forecast along with interest expense on deposits. Yet, operating expenses for the people who make loans and get deposits require traditional expense budgeting.

Many service firms, such as engineering and design firms, advertising agencies, and an array of repair companies, will budget revenues by project, client, or job. Project budgets are based on the resources needed to accomplish the task. Traceable costs are planned like prime costs. Overhead expenses for project support are similar to manufacturing overhead, based on cost drivers and activities. Providing a service is still much like making a product.

Nonprofit Organizations.   Many nonprofit organizations operate similar to merchandising and service firms. Yet, two characteristics of nonprofit organizations require special attention: (1) lack of clearly defined outputs and (2) fixed or legislated inputs or revenues. These commonly arise with governmental and philanthropic services. Budgets are determined by a legislative process with legal constraints placed on how much can be spent and what type of spending can be incurred. The outputs might be better fire protection, natural resource conservation, or national defense. In certain areas, workloads can be defined, such as in issuing drivers licenses or processing tax returns. Given the legislated revenue side, the budgeter's tasks are to work with managers to define desirable goals and outcomes, to allocate resources (people and dollars) to the programs that generate the greatest benefit, and to evaluate performance based on comparisons of predefined goals and results across units and for given benchmarks.

THE STARTING POINT AND BEYOND

Successful budgeting rests on strong and visible support of planning by top management. If executives emphasize planning, updating budgets, and evaluating performances using budget comparisons, all managers can see that financial planning and control are major parts of the "corporate culture."

The controller sets the wheels in motion by providing time schedules, forecast support data, and forms. The executive team meets to set goals, targets, and assumptions. But given these basics, where is the starting point of the planning cycle? What is planned first?

Finding the Controlling Constraint

The starting point of the budget effort should always be the most constraining variable. Generally, this is sales. Most managers work to generate more sales. But other variables might be limiting in specific cases, such as:

- Machine capacity in a specialized production area (plastic extruding equipment in a plastic bottle plant).
- Floor space in a retail outlet (the first floor in a major downtown department store).
- Salespersons' time to make calls on customers (traveling sales reps who must decide on which customers to call).
- Tables in a restaurant (where demand for reservations cannot be met).

Most constraints are temporary. Seasonal peaks may exceed normal capacity. Also, personnel limits can be eliminated by hiring or training more people. Maximizing the profitability of floor space in a retail store means eliminating items that generate low contribution margins given the space they use. When a variable other than sales limits growth, it becomes the starting point for planning. However, the sales volume continues to be the primary limiting factor over years and across most firms.

Sales Forecasting

A realistic sales budget is the foundation of a master budget, as can be seen from the master budget flowchart in Figure 7.6, page 288, and the operating cycle diagram in Figure 7.7, page 289. The **sales forecast** is based on a variety of interlocking factors, such as pricing policy, economic outlook, industry conditions, advertising, historical patterns, and the firm's strategic market position. In large companies, economic forecasting is done in a separate planning department or by the controller's staff, with forecasts prepared for many timeframes.

C O N T E M P O R A R Y   P R A C T I C E   7 . 1

Multiple Sales Forecasts at Lowe's Companies

"The sales budget is key to the entire budgeting process, and an accurate sales budget is based on an accurate sales forecast," says a Lowe's executive. Three sales forecasts are prepared and then merged. The controller's forecast is based on historical sales, general economic conditions, industry competition, and market research studies. Individual store managers prepare a local sales forecast. Regional managers make a forecast for their areas of responsibility. The three forecasts are brought together at the corporate offices, and a single approved sales budget results.

Source: Howell, K. A., "Lowe's Companies' Statistical Approach to Sales Forecasting," *Corporate Controller*, May-June 1991, pp. 24-28.

A sales forecast is built using data from many sources, including:

1. **Analysis of historical trends to create a momentum forecast.** Product life cycles, seasonal patterns, customer demand growth, and sales trends allow market research managers to predict sales.

2. **Grassroots forecasts by products and by customers prepared by salespersons.** Salespersons ask customers for input—what each expects to purchase over the coming year. Specific sales budgets are set by product and by customer. These estimates are combined locally, regionally, and finally nationally or internationally.

3. **Statistical analysis of sales and economic data.** Time series and correlation analysis, discussed in Chapter 3, are used to compare variables over time. Forecasts are generated by correlating sales to published statistics, such as employment, consumer price indices, spending patterns, and population trends.

4. **Market research analysis of promotion, sales efforts, and market share.** Promotional and advertising resources are budgeted to maximize sales or to maximize contribution margin. The objective is to spend until the last marginal dollar of spending equals the marginal dollar of revenue generated.

These approaches are not independent. More likely, all are involved in solving the forecasting problem. Each method tests the assumptions and the data of the others. The marketing plan and the sales forecast are interdependent. Figure 7.6 shows the reciprocal relationship with solid and dotted lines.

Using Activity-Based Costing Relationships

Activity-based costing implies that formal links have been identified among resource inputs and their costs, operating activities, and outputs. The budgeting process must include these relationships in converting expected sales volumes into production and operating expense budgets. A carefully developed ABC system will greatly simplify the budgeting process by using the cost functions developed for product costing to plan expenses. From the ABC studies comes a much greater understanding of cost-causing relationships. While sales is still the starting point for firm-wide budgeting, budgeting in each activity or cost center starts with determining the activity levels of each cost driver.

Quality assessment, JIT performance, and employee involvement and empowerment measures are part of the planning and evaluation process. These are predominately nonmonetary indicators but still part of budgeting. Financial modeling can include these linkages in a computer-based simulation of operations and operating budgets. Budgeting, benchmarking, and continuous improvement are integrated and on-going activity-based management processes.

Independent and Dependent Variables

Planning assumptions, management inputs, product cost and price data, and sales forecasts are called **independent variables**; they can be changed by the planner or budget analyst. These can also be called exogenous values, since they are often external inputs. Most remaining values in budgets are formula driven, using the independent variables or other already determined values.

These calculated values are called **dependent variables**. Independent variables are used to calculate dependent variables. For example, sales units, prices, and the percentage of sales collected in the month of sale are independent variables and combined to find cash collected, a dependent variable. In spreadsheet software logic, independent variables are constants or external inputs. The dependent variables are found by creating a cell formula.

Through modeling, a "what if" change in an independent variable will allow alternative scenarios to be tested. The impacts of the changes can be seen on the dependent variables.

Preparing and Formatting Budget Schedules

Budget preparation uses forecasts, planning assumptions, basic logical and mechanical relationships, and management experience and judgment. Yet, making a coordinated whole from budget inputs from many sources is a major responsibility of the controller.

A few calculation guidelines help, such as:

- While budgeting does not follow debit and credit rules, a final test of the master budget is whether the balance sheet balances.
- Budget relationships are defined quantitatively to allow the same formulas to be repeated in later time periods, such as in spreadsheet cell formulas.
- Ideally, initial planning assumptions, management inputs, and beginning values should be sufficiently complete to calculate all other variables.

To these budgeting guidelines, we can add a few mechanical rules:

- Prepare schedules in order of the sequential chain of events, such as the sales forecast, production plan, and then the purchases schedule.
- Align time periods by columns—month by month or quarter by quarter. This pattern allows repetitive calculations to be duplicated easily.
- Put independent variables in an initial schedule for easy access when making "what if" changes for later analyses.
- Avoid circular reasoning. For example, sales may be a function of advertising. Yet, the advertising budget may be a percentage of sales.

Structure and format simplify budget preparation. Frequently, data from one period are needed in the prior or next period. Or data in one schedule are used in a following schedule. A structure keeps data and calculations organized.

An Example.   Assume that:

1. Sales for the first four months of 1998 are forecast to be $50,000, $60,000, $80,000, and $70,000, respectively. Sales price is $5 per unit.
2. Cost of sales will be 60 percent of sales or $3 per unit.
3. Beginning inventory is $18,000. Ending inventory is expected to be 40 percent of next month's cost of sales.
4. Cash from sales will be collected as follows: 60 percent in the month of sale, 20 percent in the month after the sale, and 20 percent in the second month after the sale. Uncollectibles are ignored here.

5. Beginning accounts receivable is $40,000, composed of 25 percent from November sales and 75 percent from December sales.
6. Beginning accounts payable is $20,000, all from December purchases.
7. Cash payments are made for 30 percent of purchases in the month of purchase and for the remaining 70 percent in the month after purchase.

The format and data for cash receipts forecasting for 1998's first quarter are:

	January	February	March
Sales	$50,000	$60,000	$80,000
Cash collections of receivables from:			
November sales ($40,000 x .25)	$10,000		
December sales ($40,000 x .75 x .5; .5)	15,000	$15,000	
January sales ($50,000 x .6; .2; .2)	30,000	10,000	$10,000
February sales ($60,000 x .6; .2)		36,000	12,000
March sales ($80,000 x .6)			48,000
Total cash collected from sales	$55,000	$61,000	$70,000

The January *column* contains all data needed to find cash collections for January. The sales *row* provides the data to find cash collections for January, February, and March. This columnar format can be used in all master budget schedules.

The format and data for forecasting purchases for the first quarter are:

	January	February	March	April
Sales	$ 50,000	$ 60,000	$ 80,000	$ 70,000
Cost of sales (60%)	30,000	36,000	48,000	42,000
Product needs:				
Cost of sales	$ 30,000	$ 36,000	$ 48,000	
Ending inventory (40% of next month's cost of sales)	14,400	19,200	16,800	
Total needs	$ 44,400	$ 55,200	$ 64,800	
Product available:				
Less beginning inventory	18,000	14,400	19,200	
Required purchases	$ 26,400	$ 40,800	$ 45,600	

As can be seen from the arrows, organizing data by columns and rows sets a repeating pattern for calculations. Also, an important pattern is established—sales plus ending inventory set the total amount needed, while beginning inventory and purchases meet the need.

A partial cash-flow schedule showing payments for purchases appears as follows:

	January	February	March
Cash payments:			
Current month's purchases (30%)	$ 7,920	$ 12,240	$ 13,680
Prior month's purchases (70%)	20,000	18,480	28,560
Total payments for purchases	$ 27,920	$ 30,720	$ 42,240

To complete the cash-flow schedule, all other cash generating and using activities would be added. Also, with the beginning cash balance, the ending cash balance can be found. The formatting guides and calculation sequences presented in Chapter 8 can be used as examples of particular schedules.

Budgets in Physical Units.   Often, budgets are expressed in physical units, not dollars. Using the preceding example, sales are forecast at 10,000, 12,000, 16,000, and 14,000 units for the first four months of 1998. Assume that instead of purchasing the units, the firm manufactures them. For the first quarter, the production plan format would be:

	January	*February*	*March*	*April*
Units of production needed:				
Sales (sales dollars ÷ $5 per unit) . . .	10,000	12,000	16,000	14,000
Ending inventory (40% of next				
month's sales)	4,800	6,400	5,600	
Total units needed	14,800	18,400	21,600	
Less beginning inventory	6,000	4,800	6,400	
Required production	8,800	13,600	15,200	

OTHER BUDGETING TECHNIQUES

So far, we have discussed budgeting in terms of a master budget and its components. The concept of budgeting can incorporate other tools where needed.

Flexible Budgeting

In Chapter 2, we introduced cost functions. We suggested that expense budgets can be based on a variable rate and a fixed amount of costs. By knowing the cost function, we can plan costs for any activity level within our relevant range. This is a **flexible budget**. Initially, when the master budget is prepared, an expected activity level is the basis for the expense budget.

For example, Bill Cron provides local area delivery services. He is developing a home delivery service for local restaurants to be called Your Favorite Foods. This would utilize unused capacity in his delivery services. Activity is the number of deliveries. Following are expense items, which include variable, fixed, and semivariable behaviors.

Expense Item	*Fixed Expenses*	*Variable Expenses*
Driver payments		$1.50 per delivery
Supplies expense		.15
Added management expenses	$3,000	
Depreciation expense	1,000	
Added communications expenses	600	.10
Miscellaneous expenses	400	.05
Totals	$5,000	$1.80 per delivery

The cost function is: $5,000 + ($1.80 x deliveries). Bill thought he would handle about 10,000 deliveries this year but made only 9,000. Figure 7.8 presents his original budget, a flexible budget for the actual 9,000 deliveries, and a comparison of his actual expenses to the adjusted budget. The original budget is based on 10,000 deliveries and therefore cannot be used to evaluate actual results. The flexible budget is based on the actual activity level, 9,000 deliveries. **Remember:** Fixed expenses are fixed, and variable expenses adjust to the actual activity level. For example, miscellaneous expenses are $400 plus 10,000 times $0.05 or $900 in the original budget and are $400 plus 9,000 times $0.05 or $850 in the flexible budget. The manager is expected to spend no more than $850 for miscellaneous expenses since only 9,000 deliveries were made.

Actual expenses come from the responsibility accounting system. Total spending was $22,100, $900 above the flexible budget. Notice that overspending and underspending can occur in both variable and fixed areas. Here, problem expenses are driver payments and added communications expenses. Bill will investigate these variances. If we compare actual results with the original expense budget, his spending would have been under budget. But 1,000 fewer deliveries were made than planned. Thus, variable expense amounts of those 1,000 nondeliveries should not be spent. This is the difference between the original and flexible budgets—$1,800 (1,000 x $1.80).

Flexible budgeting can also be tied to applying overhead in product costing. In Chapter 4, we developed overhead rates to apply factory overhead to products. Applied overhead was found by using the cost function and actual activity. Actual overhead minus applied overhead produced either an overapplied or underapplied overhead variance. This variance includes any spending variance and any mismatch in applying fixed overhead. These variances are discussed in detail in Chapter 9.

Project Budgeting

Project budgets are oriented to specific events or tasks and use time schedules, financial budgets, and responsibility assignments for planning and control. Project budget examples include:

FIGURE 7.8 Flexible Budgeting Performance Report for *Your Favorite Foods*

	Original Expense Budget	Flexible Budget Based on Actual Deliveries	Actual Expenses	Budget Variances Fav. (Unfav.)
Variable expenses:				
Driver payments	$15,000	$13,500	$14,050	$ (550)
Supplies expense	1,500	1,350	1,300	50
Fixed expenses:				
Added management expenses	3,000	3,000	3,100	(100)
Depreciation	1,000	1,000	1,000	0
Semivariable expenses:				
Added communication expenses	1,600	1,500	1,900	(400)
Miscellaneous expenses	900	850	750	100
Total expenses	$23,000	$21,200	$22,100	$ (900)

C O N T E M P O R A R Y   P R A C T I C E   7 . 2

When Volume Varies

Raritan Bay Medical Center uses a flexible budget to manage costs based on a patient census, which is a ratio of patients to beds. The patient census has peaks and valleys. Also, the nursing staff uses "benefit time" during March, July, August, and December, often peak census months. The budget was out of balance. Nursing managers decided to view the budget variance as a credit card balance that had to be paid off by year end. Steps they took were to (1) give the variance visibility at monthly unit meetings, (2) encourage staff to take benefit time during low census periods, (3) discourage end-of-shift overtime, (4) trade work and staff with other units to balance workloads, and (5) cross-train nurses to increase staff flexibility.

Source: Wilburn, D., "Budget Response to Volume Variability," *Nursing Management*, February 1992, pp. 42-44.

1. Construction projects.
2. Information systems projects.
3. Engineering and design projects.
4. Entertainment events.
5. Government defense contracts.

Project management has been a source of many problems, such as exceeding deadlines and spending overruns. Many projects are one-time efforts. Research often presents another management dilemma—working in technologically unknown areas with no predictable output or timetable. Project budgets are developed around stages and segments of work. Timetables, deadlines, decision points, and spending authorizations are linked. Actual costs can be compared with budget time and dollar amounts to monitor the project periodically and at specific review points.

Two management concerns exist. How did we do? And, what should we do now? The first is control oriented, and the second is planning oriented. One looks back at resources used, and the other looks forward to completing the project. As an example, assume that a systems development project is budgeted at $90,000 and should take six months to complete. It is now three months into the project, and $40,000 has been spent. The manager in charge estimates that it is one-third done and will take another six months and $80,000 to complete. How should the current status be evaluated? If the project is now one-third complete, the manager is over budget in both time and money as follows:

		Performance to Date			Total Project	
	Original Budget	*Resources Used to Date*	*Original Budget for Portion Completed*	*Budget Overrun to Date*	*Revised Projected Budget*	*Projected Budget Overrun*
Costs	$ 90,000	$ 40,000	$ 30,000	$(10,000)	$120,000	$ 30,000
Time	6 months	3 months	2 months	(1 month)	9 months	3 months

Using the original budget, at this point the project is a month behind schedule and overspent by $10,000. If the total project budget is revised for time and dollars, the project will be $30,000 and three months over budget.

The following observations are useful:

1. The original budget is valuable as a base for the initial "go, no go" decision and for evaluating actual performance for the entire project. We approved a $90,000, 6-month project.
2. The revised budget serves as a base for resource planning. We expect to spend $80,000 more and to need six more months.
3. At each stage, a decision point exists. Should the project be cancelled, revised, or continued?

Careful monitoring of project status (costs and accomplishment) is critical to avoid out-of-control situations and wasted resources.

Probabilistic Budgeting

Probabilities reflect the likelihood that certain business conditions will occur. When risk exists that a particular variable may move within a range of values, probabilistic expressions of those outcomes help the budget to be more realistic. The sensitivity of profits to changes in factors, such as sales volume and prices, can be tested; then management can focus on the sensitive variables.

An illustration shows how **expected values** of sales, costs, and any other budgeted variable are calculated from probabilities. Assume, for example, that a company plans to sell a product next year for $20 a unit with a variable cost of $14. Probability estimates have been made for three sales volume levels.

	Sales Volume (Units)		Probabilities		Expected Value (Units)
Conservative	150,000	x	.20	=	30,000
Most likely	200,000	x	.70	=	140,000
Optimistic	250,000	x	.10	=	25,000
			1.00		
Expected sales volume (units)					195,000

In this case, sales volume probabilities are the basis for finding the expected contribution margin, as follows:

Expected sales (195,000 units x $20)	$3,900,000
Expected variable costs (195,000 units x $14)	2,730,000
Expected contribution margin	$1,170,000

The detail calculation of expected contribution margin is as follows:

Possible Outcomes:	Sales Revenue		Variable Cost		Contribution Margin		Sales Probabilities		Expected Value
Sales of 150,000 units: (20% likelihood)	$3,000,000	-	$2,100,000	=	$900,000	x	.20	=	$180,000
Sales of 200,000 units: (70% likelihood)	$4,000,000	-	$2,800,000	=	$1,200,000	x	.70	=	840,000
Sales of 250,000 units: (10% likelihood)	$5,000,000	-	$3,500,000	=	$1,500,000	x	.10	=	150,000
Total expected value of contribution margin									$1,170,000

Price, volume, variable cost, fixed costs, and many other variables can be assigned probabilities in many combinations reflecting the levels of uncertainty. Past experience coupled with a careful analysis of the future can serve as a basis for establishing probability estimates. For each particular circumstance, expected profits will vary according to combinations of expected conditions. Admittedly, probability estimates will not be precise, but they should represent the best inputs managers can generate and be more accurate than rough approximations or intuitive estimates.

*B*EHAVIORAL SIDE OF BUDGETING

People perform a multitude of activities in pursuit of the organization's goals and objectives. Managers should know what effects planning and control tools and techniques have on people. Budgets have the potential of motivating workers to reach higher levels of efficiency and productivity. Therefore, this section explores common behavioral implications of the budgeting process.

Top-Management Support

Heavy top-management involvement in the planning and control process is correlated with budgeting success at middle- and lower-management levels. Nothing will destroy the effectiveness of the budgeting process quicker than managers' perceptions that their superiors do not support the process. Top-management actions must cement the impression that a commitment exists for planning and budget-related performance evaluations.

Demonstration of support involves at least five important steps. First, establish clearly delineated lines of authority and responsibility. Second, involve managers in the planning process. Third, set appropriate goals and objectives that can be easily translated into plans and actions at lower-management levels. Fourth, review, critique, and approve budgets thoroughly. And fifth, follow-up and review budget reports with the intent of encouraging budget updates and goal-oriented actions.

Managers who participate in preparing budgets and who sense that budgets represent "fair" standards receive personal satisfaction from accomplishing the objectives set forth in the budget. Personnel "buy into" the budget goals and plan of action.

Budgetary Slack

Budgetary slack, also called "padding the budget," occurs when managers intentionally request more funds than needed. A common instance of padding occurs when lower-level managers know from past experience that their budget requests will be cut by upper-level managers without careful review. Their response is to inflate or "pad" certain expenses or to "low-ball" revenue estimates. In turn, upper-level managers, knowing that lower-level managers pad their budgets, automatically raise the level of anticipated revenues and cut budgeted expenses. Now the organization has a vicious circle of lack of trust and counterproductivity.

Another problem arises during budget downsizing when upper management requires all segments to cut expenses by some percentage, say 10 percent. Managers may make noneconomic decisions or resort to gamesmanship for self-preservation, perhaps creating protective slack for the next cuts. While upper-level management may think its cost-cutting approach is "fair," this approach suffers from three weaknesses: (1) organizational differences are ignored; (2) specific resource reallocations needed to support the firm's long-run goals are obliterated; and (3) executive management is viewed as capricious and uncaring.

The most effective weapon against "slack" is a careful and rigorous review of budgets by line managers. To be effective, reviewers must know the inner workings of the activities reporting to them. Nonaccounting managers must be able to read and interpret budget data and control reports.

Human Factors and Budget Stress

Budgets are bases for directing and controlling activities and establishing a discipline within an organization. The tightness of budgets necessarily depends on a number of factors, including the ability to predict future results for a given function, the manager's experience, and the closeness of supervision. Some people need close guidance and a "fear of God" approach, while others operate best with broad degrees of freedom. Supervisors and upper-level managers must make careful judgments about how tight budget standards should be for each manager. Remember, the goals are to generate the greatest benefit from each manager's area of responsibility and to maximize goal achievement for the whole organization.

Ethics of Budgeting

"Gamesmanship" often rears its head in budgeting. Budgets are future estimates. Management judgment is heavily involved. We expect ethical behavior, objective allocations of resources based on need and returns, and a managerial attitude of fairness and equity to permeate the organization. We have already mentioned the problem of budget slack—budgeting expenses too high or revenues too low to cover later budget cuts. Other problems involve overestimating revenues or understating expenses to justify approval of projects,

C O N T E M P O R A R Y   P R A C T I C E   7 . 3

When Budgets Shrink, What Do You Do?

Marketing budgets are favorite whipping posts when expenses must be cut. Several marketers offer a few remedies: One suggests that the best defense is a strong offense. Write a solid business plan, highlighting customer information, strategies, and links to corporate goals and including supporting data. Another says his highest priority is salespersons' compensation and the lowest is advertising. Another priority setter says that sales training should come first. All agree that a limited budget forces sales managers to spend more wisely.

Source: "You Said It: How Do You Balance Your Sales Budget?" *Sales and Marketing Management,* September 1992, pp. 24-26.

charging expenses for one purpose which is overspent to another account or project which has excess funds, blaming controllable budget variances on non-controllable events, and creating budget pressures on subordinates that encouraged them to act unethically "to meet the budget." In the public sector where budgets are legislated, spending unused appropriations near the end of a fiscal year on nonessential or wasteful activities to help justify budget requests for the next fiscal year is common and borders on unethical use of public funds.

Executive management must be alert to messages that the budget system sends to all employees. The discussions of "aura of control," top-management support, budget slack, and human factors all combine to highlight the importance of a structured control system with clear responsibilities and feedback. Planning and control systems can move a firm to a higher ethical plane and also create more dilemmas. The managers involved in the budget-setting process and in the control reporting process are the most effective weapons in upholding the integrity of the planning and control system.

Budgets—Only One Aspect of Planning and Control

While responsibility accounting and budgeting systems are key parts of an organization's planning and control activities, other planning and control tools act as a support or as a substitute for budgeting. Training, policies and procedures, supervision, staff support, standards, and the degree of centralization or decentralization all influence the level of importance attached to budgeting processes. And this level of dependence changes over time as organizations become more mature, change managerial philosophies, or encounter operating or financial problems.

*I*MPACTS OF NEW MANUFACTURING APPROACHES

The evolution of manufacturing approaches has in some cases had major impacts on budgeting. The following observations can be made:

- Just-in-time systems reduce inventory needs and may even eliminate their role in production budgeting. Certainly, lower inventory levels are needed. Some firms have reduced major component inventories to under two hours of production requirements. Shorter lead times place greater pressure on production planning. Small mistakes or delays cause entire plants to stop—losing product output and incurring nonproductive costs.
- Activity-based costing will increase the number of cost drivers and cost centers. Budgeting may actually be easier since costs and activities are more closely related. Greater budgeting emphasis is on cause and activity.
- Flexible manufacturing and team production activities shift the collection of cost data. Obviously in cost forecasting, shifts will occur in how costs are grouped for planning and control. Also, greater emphasis is placed on certain costs and operating data, such as costs of quality, manufacturing cycle times, value-added labor, and manufacturing throughput.

- Team approaches reemphasize the importance of collective inputs from various sources to build the strongest plan given the goals and the constraints.

The reduction of lead times and buffers throughout the production process places greater importance on planning. Without planning, the new manufacturing efficiencies cannot be achieved.

SUMMARY

One major management function is to plan and control the activities of an organization. A planning and control system includes a strategic plan, a responsibility accounting system, and financial modeling. Responsibility accounting provides the infrastructure for collecting and reporting plan and actual data. Cost or activity, profit, and investment centers define a manager's sphere of responsibility. The "glue" that holds planning activities together is the budget. The purposes of budgeting are outlined. Budgeting is a versatile tool and a framework for carrying out management's expectations and responsibilities.

The master budget is an integrated set of schedules and ties operating, project, and financial budgets together. The operating budget begins with the constraining variable, most commonly the sales forecast. Budget sequences of sales/production/purchases/payables/cash payments *and* sales/receivables/cash collections are common to many types of organizations. All operating budgets are integrated into the cash-flow budget and forecast financial statements. Understanding how to organize budget data and how to format budget schedules can ease the assimilation of the huge amount of budget data brought together to create an operating plan.

Other budgeting approaches were presented. Flexible budgeting allows managers to be evaluated according to the actual activity they experience. Project budgeting prepares plans that span normal annual timeframes or are nonroutine in nature. Probabilistic budgeting gives managers an opportunity to bring a range of estimates for key variables into the budgeting process.

Concluding considerations are given to managers' budget-related behavior and the impacts that budgets have on people. Areas of particular importance are top-management's support of the budget, managerial expectations, budgetary slack, and budget stress.

PROBLEM FOR REVIEW

The production manager of the Morris Company maintains an inventory of materials equal to production needs for the next month because of potential delays in shipments from his Korean supplier. Each unit takes 4 pounds of materials, which cost $3 per pound. Finished goods inventory is usually maintained at 20 percent of the following month's budgeted sales. Budgeted sales in units for the first five months of 1998 are:

Month	Budgeted Sales		Month	Budgeted Sales
January	12,000		April	16,000
February	16,000		May	20,000
March	15,000			

As of December 31, 1997, 60,000 pounds of materials and 3,000 units of finished goods were on hand.

Required:

Prepare a budget for production in units and a budget for purchases in pounds and dollars for the first three months of 1998.

Solution:

Production plan in units budget:

	January	February	March	April	May
Sales	12,000	16,000	15,000	16,000	20,000
Ending inventory (20% of next month's sale)	3,200	3,000	3,200	4,000	
Total units needed	15,200	19,000	18,200	20,000	
Beginning inventory available	3,000	3,200	3,000	3,200	
Production required	12,200	15,800	15,200	16,800	

Purchases budget:

	January	February	March	April
Production required	12,200	15,800	15,200	16,800
Pounds per unit	x 4	x 4	x 4	x 4
Pounds required	48,800	63,200	60,800	67,200
Ending inventory (next month's production requirements)	63,200	60,800	67,200	
Total pounds needed	112,000	124,000	128,000	
Beginning inventory available	60,000	63,200	60,800	
Materials purchases in pounds	52,000	60,800	67,200	
Cost per pound	x $3	x $3	x $3	
Materials purchases in dollars	$156,000	$182,400	$201,600	

*T*ERMINOLOGY REVIEW

SUGGESTED READINGS

Anthony, R. A., *Planning and Control Systems: A Framework for Analysis*, 1965, Division of Research, Harvard Graduate School of Business, Boston, MA.

Caplan, E. H., "Behavioral Assumptions of Managerial Accounting," *Accounting Review*, Vol. 41, No. 3, pp. 496-509.

Churchill, N. C., "Budget Choice: Planning vs. Control," *Harvard Business Review*, July-August 1984, pp. 150-157.

Emmanuel, C., D. Otley, and K. Merchant, *Accounting for Management Control*, Second Edition, 1990, Chapman and Hall, London, United Kingdom. Chapters 7, 8, and 9.

Merchant, K. A., "Budgeting and the Propensity to Create Budget Slack," *Accounting, Organizations and Society*, Vol. 10, No. 2, 1985, pp. 201-210.

Schiff, M., and A. Y. Lewin, "The Impact of People on Budgets," *Accounting Review*, Vol. 45, No. 2, pp. 259-268.

Sollenberger, H. M., "The Five Phases of Budgeting" and "Responsibility Accounting: Creating a Framework for Budgeting," *Credit Union Executive*, Winter 1990, pp. 30-35 and Spring 1990, pp. 24-36.

QUESTIONS FOR REVIEW AND DISCUSSION

1. What is a budget? How is budgeting related to performance evaluation?

2. List the major components of a planning and control system.

3. Identify and explain at least five purposes of budgeting.

4. Reread the vignette about Pat Shockley at the beginning of the chapter. Respond to each of her comments about budgeting. Give reasons why she thinks that way. What retort could you give to each comment?

5. Which is a better basis for judging actual results: budgeted performance or past actual performance? Explain.

6. How do the individual elements of a responsibility accounting system help link planning and control?

7. What are the similarities and differences among an activity center, a cost center, a profit center, and an investment center?

8. Why are well-designed organization charts and charts of accounts important elements in responsibility accounting?

9. Since the limiting factor is the starting point for budgeting, identify the most common limiting variable. Explain. Now, pick four specific businesses and identify another variable that might be the limiting factor.

10. Name the major budget schedules that create data needed for the cost of goods manufactured budget. What data are provided by each? See Figures 7.5 and 7.6.

11. Why is formatting important in preparing budget schedules? What are three key formatting guidelines?

12. What is the difference between an independent variable and a dependent variable in the budgeting process? Give three examples of each.

13. How is a cash budget used in planning short-term borrowings and investing?

14. How does a cost function help in budgeting? In evaluating budget performance?

15. Explain why variable and fixed costs behave differently when a budget is "flexed" from the expected to the actual level of activity.

16. For what kinds of business activities are project budgets useful?

17. When probabilities are estimated for various possible selling prices, sales volumes, or unit costs, what is meant by "expected value of contribution margin?"

18. Why are the human behavioral concerns important in budgeting? Identify and explain the concerns.

19. What is "budgetary slack?" Is it good or bad? Why "yes" *and* "no?"

E XERCISES

7-1. Responsibility Accounting.   Using Figures 7.2 and 7.3, the following codes were taken from documents within the company:

(a) 3260-4110

(b) 3242-6211

(c) 1000-5110

(d) 3100-5000

(e) 3244-6160

Required:
Explain what each digit in each code means. Give an example of what each code probably represents.

7-2. Needed Purchases.   Stew Crumbaugh, controller of Ink Supply, Inc. estimated sales for the third and fourth quarters at $750,000 and $800,000, respectively. The estimated cost of sales rate is 40 percent. The June 30 inventory at cost is $120,000. The targeted inventory at the end of the third quarter is to be 20 percent of estimated fourth quarter sales volume.

Required:
What quantity of inventory should be purchased in the third quarter?

7-3. Purchases Requirements.   Marv Chiddick uses Material A1 in manufacturing two products, T-1 and T-2. Material A1 is forecast to cost $10 per pound.

Production Plan	T-1 Units	T-2 Units		Products	Pounds of Material A1 Needed Per Unit
January	300	100			
February	400	120		T-1	2
March	600	150		T-2	3
April	500	200			

Inventory of A1 should be 200 pounds at all times.

Required:
Prepare a schedule showing forecast purchases quantities and dollars of Material A1 needed for the four months.

7-4. Materials Requirements.   Stewart Co. produces plastic buckets. The following budget data are available:

(a) Ending finished goods inventory: 20 percent of next quarter's sales.

(b) Ending materials inventory: 30 percent of next quarter's production.

(c) Forecast sales for each quarter of 1998 are 1,000, 1,100, 1,200, and 1,300 buckets, respectively.

(d) Two pounds of plastic are needed for each bucket. January 1, 1998, inventories are at the correct planned levels.

Required:

How many pounds of plastic must be purchased for the first two quarters of 1998 to meet the bucket sales forecast?

7-5. Sales to Materials Needs.   Milano Treasures produces statues. Inventory policy states that ending finished inventory should be 30 percent of next month's forecast sales units. Also, the policy requires that next month's estimated clay usage should be in ending inventory. Each statue uses 5 pounds of clay. The sales forecast for the fourth quarter is:

	October	November	December
Forecast unit sales	1,000	1,200	1,400

Inventories at October 1 are at the correct planned levels.

Required:

How much clay does Milano's buyer need to purchase in October?

7-6. Cash Payments.   We know the following about Best's Goodies budget for 1998:

May 1, 1998, inventory	1,000 units
Cost of 1 unit	$10.00
Desired ending inventory	10 percent of next month's unit sales
Purchases paid for in:	
Month of purchase	60 %
Month following purchase	40 %

	May	June	July
Sales forecast in units	10,000	12,000	16,000

Required:

Calculate the forecast cash payments to vendors during June.

7-7. Cash Receipts.   Hudson Company, located in Manchester, U. K., prepared the following sales budget for 1998's first six months:

	January	February	March	April	May	June
Sales units	8,000	7,000	7,500	8,500	7,800	8,300

Units sell for £20 each. Twenty percent of sales is for cash, and the remainder is on account. The firm forecasts collection of sales on account to be 60 percent in the month of sale with the remainder collected in the next month. Beginning receivables at January 1 are £40,000.

Required:

1. Find the forecast cash receipts for each month.
2. If more customers use bank cards causing cash sales to increase to 40 percent of total sales, by how much is cash increased in the second quarter?

7-8. Sales and Purchases.   Dawe Company sells course note packets for classes with high enrollments at Prestige University. Each packet sells for $10, and the purchase cost is $6 per packet. Dawe keeps an inventory of 40 percent of next month's forecast sales. Each month Dawe pays suppliers 70 percent of the current month's purchases, and the remainder is paid in the following month. The Spring semester's sales budget is:

	January	February	March	April	May
Sales	$6,000	$4,000	$3,000	$6,000	$1,000

Required:

1. Calculate Dawe's budgeted purchases per month through April.
2. Show Dawe's cash payments to suppliers per month from February through April.

7-9. Forecast Cash Receipts. The Hackstock Co., located in Sweden, sells saw blades for industrial use. Company sales are 80 percent on account and 20 percent for cash. Sales on account are collected at 30 percent in the month of sale, 50 percent in the next month, and the remainder in the second month after the sale.

The accounts receivable balance in Swedish krona on January 1 was SKr40,000 (SKr5,000 from November sales and SKr35,000 from December sales). The sales forecast for the first half of next year is:

January	SKr100,000	April	SKr140,000
February	90,000	May	150,000
March	120,000	June	160,000

Required:
Prepare a forecast of cash receipts for each month of the first quarter.

7-10. Forecast Cash Payments. Hal's Soft Shoe Shop is preparing its cash budget for the month of November. The following information is available about its operation:

November beginning inventory.	$ 18,000
Estimated November cost of goods sold	90,000
Estimated November ending inventory	16,000
Estimated November payments for purchases made prior to November . . .	21,000
Estimated November payments for purchases made in November.	80%

Required:
What are the estimated cash payments in November for Hal?

7-11. Flexible Budgeting. The Cuney Company operates a mobile pizza business. Budgeted estimates of monthly expenses at two levels of sales are as follows:

	20,000 Pizzas	*30,000 Pizzas*
Pizza ingredients	$ 20,000	$ 30,000
Truck rental and salaries	25,000	25,000
Gas, part-time help, etc.	20,000	26,000

Cuney sales for the month were 28,000 pizzas. The expenses were $27,500, $25,100, and $25,000, respectively, for each expense.

Required:
1. Comment on the behavior of each expense group.
2. Prepare a budget report for the month that shows how well expenses were controlled.

7-12. Flexible Budgeting. The Gilbert Bicycle Co. operates a repair shop on Louis Street. Jim, the owner, has calculated his overhead costs per year to be $10,000 plus $10 per bike repaired. In late 1997, he prepared a budget for repairing 500 bikes in 1998. He actually repaired 550 bikes in 1998 and spent $15,200 for overhead expenses.

Required:
Comment on each of the following statements about 1998 activities?

(a) His cost function is ($10,000/500) + $10, or $30 per bike.

(b) His spending was $300 under his adjusted budget; therefore, he did control costs well.

(c) His original budget for 1998 (prepared in late 1997) was $15,500.

(d) His spending was $200 over his original budget; therefore, he did not control costs well.

7-13. Forecasting Profits. Mrs. Davis is budgeting 1999 operations and assembled the following data for January and February for her mail order Jelly Bean Factory:

	January	February
Sales	$200,000	$250,000
Cost of sales	$ 80,000	$100,000
Advertising expenses............................	30,000	30,000
Operating expenses	80,000	90,000
Total expenses...............................	$190,000	$220,000
Net profit	$ 10,000	$ 30,000

Required:

Costs "behave" the same during each month. If Davis thinks sales for March will be $240,000, what net profit should she expect for March?

7-14. Linking Applied Overhead and Flexible Budgeting. At budgeted volume of 400 units for the Anaya Corporation, variable overhead costs were $400,000 and fixed overhead costs were $200,000. The cost driver for budgeting and applying overhead is units. Actual production was 450 units. Actual variable costs were $444,000, and actual fixed costs were $209,000.

Required:

1. Did Anaya control costs well? Explain.

2. Was overhead overapplied or underapplied? Explain.

7-15. Linking Applied Overhead and Flexible Budgeting. Rudolph Steins, a Bavarian ceramic stein maker, has an overhead cost function in German marks of DM400,000 plus DM4 per stein. The original budget for 1998 used 200,000 steins as its normal capacity. This cost function and the normal capacity are used to cost each stein. Sales were unusually good in 1998. Rudolph produced and sold 245,000 steins. Variable costs totaled DM992,000, and fixed costs were DM445,000. Because of the higher volume, extra overtime of DM40,000 was incurred and added to variable costs. Also, extra supervision salaries added DM40,000 to fixed costs.

Required:

1. Looking only at total variable and fixed costs, were Rudolph's costs well controlled in 1998? Explain.

2. If the extra production costs are excluded for the analysis, were Rudolph's other costs well controlled? Explain.

3. Show how much overhead cost was added to products. Comment on overapplied or underapplied overhead.

7-16. Evaluation of a Responsibility Report. Acosta Bank Security Services prepared the following responsibility report for its Armored Car cost center:

Responsibility Report for the Week Ended April 9, 1998

Supervisors responsible: Kelli Tunnell Cheryl Broadway	Budget	Actual	Fav. (Unfav.) Variance
Cost driver—personnel hours	800	850	(50) U
Variable costs:			
Delivery personnel	$16,000	$16,500	$ (500) U
Departmental fixed costs:			
Equipment maintenance.................	30,000	29,250	750 F
Supervision and depreciation	10,000	10,610	(610) U
Administrative overhead—allocated by payroll ..	8,000	9,000	(1,000) U
Total costs	$64,000	$65,360	$(1,360) U

Required:

Given the concepts of responsibility accounting, evaluate the appropriateness of this report. If necessary, revise the report.

7-17. Types of Responsibility Centers. The following list describes a variety of business situations:

(a) A convenience store that is owned by a chain organization. The goods to be sold and the selling prices are all determined by the corporate office.

(b) The wing assembly department of a private airplane manufacturer.

(c) The janitorial department of an office furniture manufacturer.

(d) The women's shoe department in a large retail store. The buyer, an assistant department manager, decides which styles, sizes, etc., are purchased. The department supervisor sets selling prices.

(e) The marketing department of a local TV station.

(f) The purchasing department for a large electronics company.

(g) The parts department of an automobile dealership.

(h) The PC product line of a major computer manufacturer that is organized by product lines.

(i) The technical support department for a large computer software company. Customers call an 800 number and ask questions about problems they are experiencing with software purchased from the company.

(j) The car pool operation for a city government. City officials needing cars check them out for the days of travel.

Required:

For each business segment, indicate how it is most likely to be organized, as a cost center, a profit center, or an investment center. State any additional assumptions you feel are necessary to clarify a situation.

7-18. Performance Report With a Budget Formula. Desert Rat Rentals, operating in Quartzite, Arizona, has one department totally dedicated to dune buggies. The company rents them at a daily rate plus mileage. The company's accountant, Dusty Aire, developed the following annual budget formula for each cost related to the dune buggies and provided the actual costs for this season, which just ended:

Cost Item	Formula		This Season's Actual Costs
Fuel and oil.	$ 0.35 per mile		$ 8,735
Chassis and other lubricants	0.05 per mile plus	$1,000	2,190
Repairs	0.06 per mile plus	1,200	2,705
Depreciation		2,500	2,500
Licenses, taxes, and fees		2,600	2,930
Insurance expenses		1,600	1,735
Total budget formula	$ 0.46 per mile plus	$8,900	$ 20,795

During the season, records of Desert Rat Rentals show that the dune buggies were driven 24,000 miles.

Required:

Prepare a responsibility performance report for Dusty that will show the budget, actual results, and variances for the Dune Buggy Department for this season.

7-19. Cash Budgeting. Caveney Corporation, a Melbourne, Australia, firm, is preparing a cash budget for 1999 using the following data:

(a) Each month, 60 percent of sales is on credit. Of credit sales, 70 percent is collected in the month of sales and 30 percent in the next month.

(b) Cost of goods sold is 70 percent of sales. Of purchases, 60 percent is paid when purchased; and the remainder is paid in the next month.

(c) Planned inventory is 40 percent of the next month's sales. Budgeted purchases in February were A$60,000.

(d) Operating expenses are A$30,000 per month, including A$2,000 of depreciation expense. These are paid when incurred.

(e) Forecast cash balance as of March 1 is A$20,000, which is the target level.

Budgeted sales, in Australian dollars, for a portion of 1999 are: February, A$90,000; March, A$120,000; April, A$110,000; and May, A$100,000.

Required:

1. Create a cash forecast for March.

2. If Caveney plans to buy a computer system for A$20,000, can the firm pay for it and keep a "safe" cash level? What are the main risks?

7-20. Project Budgeting.   We have approved a 6-month, $200,000 systems project to improve office communications. We are now 4 months into the project. People and equipment expenses have been $160,000, and we think it will take another 3 months and $80,000 to finish the project.

Required:

1. From a control perspective, how is the project coming along?

2. From a planning perspective, how does the project look as we view the future?

7-21. Budget Comments.   Comment briefly on the following quotes about budgeting from a financial planning textbook:

(a) "One major criticism of budgeting is that it is used as a 'cost reduction' tool rather than a 'cost control' tool. The objective of the budget is to control costs at an efficient level of operation."

(b) "There are generally three benefits from allowing employees to participate in developing the budget: (1) Employees tend to accept the budget as their own plan of action. (2) Participation tends to increase morale among employees and toward management. (3) Employee cohesiveness is increased, and productivity will also increase if dictated by the group norm."

(c) "Even though budgets are quantitative tools, considerable emotion is connected to budgeting. The individual in control often sees the budget as a means of getting things done. People being controlled often have feelings of anxiety because their success and promotion are tied directly to the budget."

7-22. Expected Value of Profit.   The sales manager of the Zweng Corporation's Economic Forecasting Department has estimated that a 40 percent probability exists that sales volume for next year will be 600,000 units with a selling price of $7 per unit. A 60 percent probability exists that sales will be 500,000 units with a selling price of $8 per unit. Variable cost per unit is estimated at $6 (with a probability of 20 percent) or $5 (with a probability of 80 percent). Fixed costs for the next year have been estimated at $800,000.

Required:

1. Compute the forecast net income for next year.

2. Comment on the resulting net income.

7-23. Responsibility Problems.   Refer to Figure 7.4 and discuss the following responsibility situations:

Case A: Notice the September and the year-to-date budget variances in account 6780 Administrative Allocations. Why might these variances occur? Where does control over this expense probably exist? Comment on the budget planning and control implications.

Case B: Assume that the unexpected overtime costs in account 6245 arise from rework that had to be done on several major jobs this month. The cause of the rework is disputed. Mr. Kannisoni claims the materials either were defective when purchased or were prepared improperly in the preceding department. He feels this expense should be charged to Materials Preparation or to Purchasing. Comment on his problem.

Case C: The Assembly Department, the next production department after Stamping, has experienced a production problem; and the manager must stop the assembly line. The manager asks Mr. Kannisoni to stop the transfer of stampings to Assembly until the problem is solved. If it stops, the Stamping Department will lose output and incur extra costs to catch up again. If Stamping does not stop, Assembly will have to handle the stampings several times, incurring more costs. Who should do what? Who should bear the additional costs?

7-24. Ethical Budget Issues. Don Bjorn, a salesperson with Great Lakes Steel, is working on his 1999 sales budget. Don is paid on a half-salary and half-commission basis for a target salary of $90,000. Based on his approved sales budget, Don would receive commissions equivalent to one-third of his target salary if he achieves the sales budget. By exceeding his sales budget he could, and has, earned 50 percent above his target salary. Last year he sold 8,000 tons of all grades of steel. This was a little over the prior year's total and well above his 1998 sales budget of 6,000 tons. He did well.

So far Don has filled in the preliminary sales forecast forms. This is a first estimate of 1999 sales on a product-by-product estimate. Don's total adds up to 5,200 tons. His sales manager has sent the forms back for a redo, since he obviously missed some sales someplace. His second version showed 5,400 tons. The third round requested a customer-by-customer breakdown in addition to the product estimates. A memo from the vice-president of marketing asks that each salesperson be as accurate as possible in estimating sales. Don has just mailed his estimates. They call for 5,600 tons.

The process from this point, as Don describes it, is that he will receive a call from his manager telling him to redo the latest estimate and make sure it is 10 percent above last year's budgeted number. Don will "hem and haw" on the phone, redo the form, and send it in showing 6,600 tons, exactly a 10 percent increase. Don says everyone will be happy, particularly him. Don says he has one last hurdle to jump—a visit to corporate and a conference with the vice-president and sales manager. Under great protest, Don will agree to a 6,750-ton 1999 target. The 1999 budget will then be approved.

Don, an effective salesperson in all respects, has done it again. He checks his early order book for 1999 and his penciled notes, adds up the first-quarter early bookings, sees orders adding up to nearly 3,200 tons, and smiles. "Ah, yes! 1999 should be a great year. Maybe this is the year for that 38-foot sailboat!"

Required:
Evaluate Great Lakes Steel's sales budgeting and incentive systems. Comment on Don's approach to the process. How could it be strengthened?

*P*ROBLEMS

7-25. Purchases Budget. In producing a glass-based product, Young-Ho Nam Industries, located near Seoul, Republic of Korea, uses 10 pounds of Material R and 2 pounds of Material S. All materials are purchased one month before the units are scheduled for completion. The production cycle takes less than one day, and all units of product are sold in the following month.

1-2-3

Materials costs (in won) per unit are estimated to be W4 for Material R and W7 for Material S. A production plan for June 1998 through January 1999 inclusive is:

Units to Be Completed:		Units to Be Completed:	
June 1998	42,000	October 1998	51,000
July 1998	46,000	November 1998	54,000
August 1998	48,000	December 1998	60,000
September 1998	47,000	January 1999	65,000

Required:

1. Prepare a monthly schedule for the last six months of 1998 showing how many pounds of each materials should be purchased.
2. Convert the materials purchases budget in pounds into Korean won (W).
3. Compute the cost of materials in cost of goods sold for October, November, and December.

7-26. Budget Constraints.   Rollin Parts, Inc. has the capacity to manufacture 400,000 units of a certain product line each year. Each unit of product requires 2 pounds of a metal that is difficult to obtain. The Sales Department estimates that 300,000 units of product can be sold next year. The Purchasing Department states that 30,000 pounds of the metal are on hand at the beginning of the year and that only 290,000 pounds can be purchased on the market next year. The Purchasing Department has found a company that is willing to produce 100,000 units of product on a contract basis. That company has enough of the required metal on hand to make the 100,000 units.

Required:

1. What is the limiting factor in budgeting next year? Why?
2. How many units of the product can be produced internally *and* sold next year?
3. What is the maximum forecast sales possible for next year?

7-27. Responsibility Reporting.   The chart of accounts for Giacomazza Company shows expense classifications as follows:

5000	Selling Expenses
6000	Manufacturing Expenses
6100	Direct Materials
6200	Direct Labor
6300	Manufacturing Overhead
7000	Administrative Expenses

The following accounts and amounts (with 000s omitted) were taken from the accounting and budgeting records for June:

Acct. No.	Account Name	June Actual	June Budget	Year-to-Date Actual	Year-to-Date Budget
5110	Advertising	$ 125	$ 135	$ 833	$ 810
5120	Bad Debt Expense	37	36	218	216
5130	Sales Commissions	109	111	754	670
6100	Direct Materials	1,319	1,388	8,178	8,328
6200	Direct Labor	749	751	4,599	4,506
6310	Depreciation—Factory Machinery	45	45	275	280
6320	Factory Rent	244	244	1,464	1,464
6330	Factory Utilities	34	33	237	218
6340	Indirect Labor	176	174	1,056	1,044
6350	Property Taxes—Factory Machinery . .	19	21	114	126
6360	Repairs and Maintenance— Factory . .	47	50	351	320
7120	Property Taxes—Office Equipment . . .	7	8	42	48
7130	Salaries of Administrative Personnel . .	1,687	1,601	9,122	9,606

Required:

Prepare a responsibility performance report for manufacturing operations. Use a format you think will best show budget performance.

7-28. Responsibility Accounting and Roll-up Reporting. Pampa Packaging Corporation has two plants, one in Illinois and one in Singapore. Each plant has a forming and a packing department. Production for the Forming Department of the Illinois Plant is estimated at 1,600 tons for June. The budgeted costs per ton are as follows:

Direct materials	$ 8
Direct labor	15
Factory overhead (half fixed and half variable)	10
Total per ton	$33

Total budgeted production costs for the Packing Department are $33,000 for June. Budgeted costs for the plant manager's office are $57,000.

Budgeted costs for the Singapore plant total $67,000. The vice-president of production is responsible for both plants and has $54,000 of budgeted expenses. Budgeted expenses for the company's vice-president of marketing's office are $112,600. The president's office budget is $60,000.

In June, 1,500 tons were produced; and actual expenses were as follows:

President's office	$ 62,300	Illinois plant:	
Vice-president of marketing . . .	109,800	Plant manager's office .	$ 58,300
Vice-president of production . . .	55,500	Packing Department . .	34,900
Singapore plant—total costs . . .	70,100	Forming Department:	
		Direct materials	10,600
		Direct labor	23,400
		Overhead	13,200

Required:

Prepare responsibility reports showing the appropriate budget, actual expenses, and variances from budget for each of the following:

(a) Forming Department in Illinois plant.

(b) Plant manager for the Illinois plant.

(c) Vice-president of production.

(d) President of the company.

7-29. Performance Report for a Grocery Store. McInnes Groceries of Heber Valley maintains tight control on its operating expenses through the use of budgets. The monthly and year-to-date budgets are based on formulas that the chief accountant developed. The accounts, monthly budget formulas, and May and year-to-date activities are:

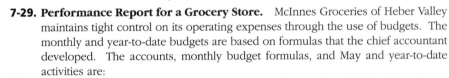

	Budget Information	Actual Results May	Year-to-Date
Payroll	$50,000 + 6.0% of revenues	$ 69,000	$ 362,000
Store Supplies	1.0% of revenues	3,600	15,000
Advertising	$ 4,000 + 1.0% of revenues	6,010	38,150
Equipment Rental	$ 8,000	8,100	37,220
Payroll Taxes	15.0% of payroll	9,940	51,860
Accounting, Legal, Fees . . .	$ 4,000 + 0.5% of revenues	5,760	29,800
Training Expenses	$ 2,000 + 1.5% of revenues	8,000	41,740
Charitable Contributions . .	$ 1,000 + 0.5% of revenues	1,600	8,000
Utilities and Telephone	$ 2,700 + 0.5% of revenues	6,100	21,900
Leasing	$ 9,000	9,000	45,000
Insurance	$ 2,600	2,800	14,200
Depreciation on Equipment	$ 4,700	5,000	25,000
Transportation Expenses . . .	$ 2,900 + 2.0% of revenues	8,480	41,950
Revenues		300,000	1,700,000

Required:

Prepare a responsibility performance report for the operating expenses. Show the May and year-to-date information for actual, budget, and favorable and unfavorable budget variances. Separate the report into three sections: variable costs, semivariable costs, and fixed costs.

7-30. Budgeting Cash.   The following data for the month of May are part of the information being used to prepare the master budget for Hillman Sports Wholesalers:

Planned cash balance, May 1	$ 60,000
Sales	800,000
Merchandise purchases	500,000
Inventory increase	20,000
Payroll earned	95,000
Payroll paid	88,000
Other expenses (payable in May)	41,000
Depreciation	2,000
Accrued taxes (payable in December)	6,000
3-month bank note: Principal due May 31	250,000
Interest payable due May 31	9,000
Accounts payable, May 1 (for merchandise purchases)	240,000
Customer receivables, May 1 ($70,000 from March	
sales and $450,000 from April sales)	520,000

Assumptions:

Accounts receivable: 50 percent is collected in the month of sale, 40 percent in the next month, and 10 percent in the second month after the sale.

Accounts payable: 40 percent is paid in the month of purchase and 60 percent in the next month.

Required:

Using the preceding information, prepare a cash budget showing expected cash receipts and disbursements and a pro forma income statement for the month of May.

7-31. Cash Forecasting.   John Iannotti is preparing his budgets for 1999. He has written the following on a pad of legal paper:

Forecast Sales		Actual 12/31/98 Balance Sheet Data	
January	$ 70,000	Cash	$ 8,000
February	90,000	Accounts Receivable	20,000
March	80,000	Inventory	40,000
April	60,000	Accounts Payable	45,000

Other data are as follows:

(a) Sales are on credit with 40 percent collected in the month of sale and 60 percent in the next month.

(b) Cost of sales is 60 percent of sales.

(c) Other variable costs are 10 percent of sales, paid in the month incurred.

(d) Inventories are to be 80 percent of next month's budgeted sales requirements.

(e) Purchases are paid in the month after purchase.

(f) Fixed expenses are $3,000 per month; all are paid in the month incurred.

Required:

1. Prepare a cash budget for February.

2. Comment on which assumptions may be the most tenuous and which may be the most certain.

7-32. Budgeted Income Statement for a Service Organization.   The Ole Route 66 Motel is a low-priced motel in Winslow, Arizona, along Interstate 40. It has 50 rooms, each with two double beds. The rates are $18 for one person, $10 for the second person, and $3 each for the third and fourth persons. Rollaway beds are available for $2 per night.

During April, the motel manager expects an 80 percent occupancy rate. Past experience suggests that 20 percent of the rooms rented will be to only 1 person, 20 percent to 2 persons, 30 percent to 3 persons, and 20 percent to 4 persons. Ten percent will have 5 persons and use rollaway beds.

Laundry costs average $1.00 per person per night. Cleaning workers earn $6.00 per hour, and it takes 30 minutes to clean each room. Other variable operating costs (utilities, for example) are $4 per occupied room per night. Maintenance and grounds personnel costs are about $1,500 per month. Two clerks each have a salary of $1,200 per month. Depreciation is $2,000 per month. Other cash fixed expenses are $3,500 per month.

Required:

1. Prepare a budgeted income statement for April.

2. Suggest an average occupancy percentage needed to break even if the average number of people staying in a room is three.

7-33. Labor Cost Budget. Budget plans of Baxter Medical Services are being revised for the last two quarters of 1999. Two main procedures are provided to patients referred by area physicians. Under the revised plan, the forecast volume of procedures is estimated as follows:

	Procedure 1	*Procedure 2*
Third quarter	1,200	1,500
Fourth quarter	1,600	1,800

Personnel schedules indicate that 15 minutes are required for Procedure 1 and 20 minutes for Procedure 2. Technicians labor rate per hour is $15 during the third quarter. On October 1, a $1.00 per hour raise contained in the Baxter labor contract with its union will go into effect.

In preparation of the budget, provision is to be made for fringe benefit costs such as pensions and medical health insurance. The total fringe benefit cost is estimated to be 55 percent of the hourly labor cost for the third quarter. Increased health insurance cost will increase the fringe benefit cost to 60 percent of the hourly labor cost for the fourth quarter.

Required:

1. Prepare a budget showing the direct labor cost per procedure and in total dollars for each quarter.

2. Add a section to the direct labor cost schedule showing the estimated fringe benefit cost and total labor cost for each quarter. Comment on the increase in costs and its possible implications.

7-34. Flexible Budgeting and Profits. The Ota Company provides package delivery services in Osaka, Japan. All monetary figures are in millions of Japanese yen (¥). Flexible budgets for possible 1998 activity levels of 125,000, 150,000, and 175,000 deliveries are as follows:

Units of deliveries	125,000	150,000	175,000
Sales	¥ 125.0	¥ 150.0	¥ 175.0
Variable expenses	¥ 37.5	¥ 45.0	¥ 52.5
Semivariable expenses	35.0	40.0	45.0
Fixed expenses	30.0	30.0	30.0
Total expenses	¥ 102.5	¥ 115.0	¥ 127.5
Net income	¥ 22.5	¥ 35.0	¥ 47.5

Deliveries in 1998 were 135,000. Sales revenues were ¥130 million. Actual variable expenses were ¥42 million; semivariable expenses were ¥37.5 million; and fixed expenses were ¥29.6 million.

Required:

1. Using flexible budgeting based on units, what should Ota have earned? What was earned?
2. If the flexible budget is based on sales in yen, what should Ota have earned?
3. Comment on the comparison of the two flexible budgets you prepared.

7-35. Production and Inventories.   Handorf Company has irregular sales volume during the year, and management is planning to produce at a uniform rate with inventories increasing or decreasing throughout the year. A sales budget in product units is forecast for the first six months of 1998 as follows:

Months	Units	Months	Units
January	40,000	April	25,000
February	25,000	May	40,000
March	20,000	June	50,000

The production cycle is short, and work in process inventories are insignificant. An inventory of 10,000 units was on hand at January 1, and 20,000 units of inventory are planned for June 30.

Required:

Prepare a production schedule that will have level production each month while showing the expected inventories at the end of each month. Comment on the problems this approach creates. Why is it attractive?

7-36. Supplies and Labor Costs.   The Greenberg Health Clinic serves as an outpatient clinic for citizens in Brant City. Medicines, drugs, and various medical supplies must be purchased; and cost estimates must be made for each month. In addition to physicians who are available on a contract basis at a cost of $50,000 a month, nurses salary costs are $40,000 a month. Other employees are engaged on a part-time basis at a cost of $12.00 per hour. Past experience shows that one part-time person is required for every 50 patients served in a month. The typical part-time employee works 100 hours in a month.

The costs of medicines and various supplies average $5 per patient served plus a fixed cost of $15,000 each month. A forecast of patients to be served in the last quarter is:

	Number of Patients
October	900
November	1,100
December	1,200

Required:

1. Prepare a schedule showing the costs of the medicines and other supplies for each month.
2. According to the estimates, how many part-time people will be needed each month, and at what cost?
3. Prepare a budget schedule showing the costs of contract services, salaries, medicines and other supplies, and part-time labor for each month.

7-37. Direct Labor Cost Budget.   Gonzalez, Inc., in Monterrey, Mexico, manufactures three electric gardening tools: a grass trimmer, a hedge trimmer, and a brush cutter. There are 15 skilled employees at the present time, and new employees will be engaged as production increases. Each employee works approximately 160 hours a month and is paid in Mexican pesos at the rate of M$11 per hour. They assemble and test each unit. The production plan in units is:

	Product Lines		
	Grass Trimmer	Hedge Trimmer	Brush Cutter
March	6,000	3,000	1,000
April	9,000	3,000	1,000
May	12,000	6,000	2,000
June	15,000	7,500	2,000
July	12,000	6,000	3,000
August	9,000	3,000	1,000
Labor to assemble and test:	10 minutes	15 minutes	30 minutes

Required:

1. Prepare a budget of direct labor hours for each month and convert it into a budget of direct labor costs in Mexican pesos.

2. How many employees will be needed for production each month?

3. If by spending M$2,500 per month to lease a semiautomatic machine, assembly and test labor could be reduced by 20 percent. Should the change be made? Explain.

7-38. Sales Budget From Incomplete Data.   You have been working on the budget for 1999 for WWWW Company, located in Windsor, Canada. The president, Will Nelson, is holding a key meeting in a Seoul, Republic of Korea, parts supplier plant at 9:00 a.m. on Thursday. Mr. Nelson wants the sales and production budgets in units and the quantities of materials purchases for the Windsor plant for next year faxed to him. It's now 2:00 p.m. on Wednesday in Windsor, twelve hours behind Seoul.

   You have certain data on your desk but nothing about units to be sold. Available information reveals that 4 pounds of materials are required for each unit of product manufactured. Materials are used in the quarter acquired except for changes in materials inventory. An inventory of 20 percent of next month's usage should be planned for materials at all times. You remember seeing the December 31, 1999, forecast balance sheet which showed 400,000 pounds in materials inventory. Planned usage for the year is:

	Pounds of Materials
First quarter	1,200,000
Second quarter	1,500,000
Third quarter	2,000,000
Fourth quarter	2,500,000

Each pound of materials purchased costs C$2.40. The inventory of finished goods is 12,000 units at the beginning of the year. Plans call for this inventory to increase by 2,000 units each quarter until year end, when it will be 20,000 units.

Required:

1. Prepare schedules to support the forecast of production and sales units by quarters.

2. Prepare a budget of sales in Canadian dollars assuming a selling price per unit of product of C$60.

3. You have finished the sales schedule by 4:00 p.m. Now convert the materials used in a purchases budget in pounds and dollars and determine the costs of materials in cost of goods sold and in inventory by quarter.

7-39. Project Management.   In the Osann Corporation, an advertising project is forecast to cost $100,000, generate $200,000 in additional variable contribution margin, and take 6 months to complete.

   It is now 4 months into the project, and $60,000 has been spent. Osann estimates that it is one-third done and that it will take another 8 months and $100,000 to complete the project. Current estimates now show that the forecast additional variable contribution margin will be $160,000. Osann is at a "go" or "no go" point on this project.

Required:

1. How does Osann report the project relative to the budget?

2. How does Osann report this project in its "plan of action," if approved for continuation?

3. Should the project be "canned" or continued at this "go" or "no go" point? Explain.

7-40. Probabilistic Budgeting.   Anderson Manufacturing Company is in the process of preparing its operating budget for next year. Bill McCarthy, controller, wants to include in the budget documents a budgeted income statement based on probabilities. In visiting with selling, production, and administrative personnel, McCarthy has obtained estimates and probabilities for each area.

Unit sales estimates, with associated selling prices and probabilities, are:

Units	Selling Price	Probability
800,000	$ 25	.20
700,000	28	.30
600,000	32	.40
500,000	36	.10

Variable manufacturing costs will either be $8 per unit, with a probability of 80 percent, or $10 per unit, with a probability of 20 percent. Fixed manufacturing costs have a 90 percent chance of being $4,000,000 and a 10 percent chance of being $5,000,000. Variable selling and administrative expenses are estimated at $2, $3, or $4, with probabilities of 20 percent, 70 percent, and 10 percent, respectively. Fixed selling and administrative expenses have a 60 percent chance of amounting to $5,000,000 and a 40 percent chance of being $6,000,000.

Required:

Prepare a budgeted income statement based on expected values.

7-41. Behavioral Effects of Budgeting.   Ecourse Steel Corporation is a medium-size company in the steel industry with six divisions located in different geographical sectors of the United States. Considerable autonomy in operational management is permitted in the divisions, partly due to the products produced and the markets served. Corporate management establishes divisional budgets using prior year data. Budgets are prepared by year and then divided by four to establish a quarterly plan, with top management attempting to recognize problems unique to each division. Once the year's divisional budgets are set by corporate management, they cannot be modified by division management.

The budget for calendar year 1999 projects total corporate net income before taxes of $6,600,000, including $1,650,000 for the first quarter. Results of first quarter operations presented to corporate management in early April showed corporate net income of $1,475,000. The Gary Division operated at 4.5 percent above its projected divisional net income, while the other five divisions showed net incomes with variances ranging from 1.5 to 22 percent below budgeted net income.

Corporate management is concerned with the first quarter results because it believed strongly that differences among divisions had been recognized. An entire day in late November of last year was spent presenting and explaining the corporate and division budgets to the division managers and their division controllers. A mid-April meeting of corporate and division management has generated unusual candor. All five division managers with net income below plan cited reasons why first quarter results in their respective divisions represented effective management and were the best that could be expected. Corporate management has remained unconvinced and informs division managers, "Results will be brought into line with the budget by the end of the second quarter!"

Required:

1. Identify and explain the major disadvantages in the procedures apparently employed by Ecourse Steel's corporate management in preparing and implementing divisional budgets.
2. Discuss the behavioral problems that may arise by requiring Ecourse Steel's division managers to meet the quarterly budgeted net income figures, as well as the annual budgeted net income.

(ICMA Adapted)

7-42. Expected Cash Flow. Knevil Equipment Company is planning to expand beyond the industrial market of its materials handling equipment to produce trailers for the sports and recreation markets. The president, Spike Knevil, estimates that the company must invest $1,800,000 in new equipment up front. He wants to know how much cash flow can be provided by operations next year to apply toward acquiring the equipment and how much of the cost will have to be financed.

His sales staff estimates revenue next year at $8,500,000. However, if economic conditions deteriorate, sales revenue may be only $6,500,000.

Cost of goods sold has historically been 70 percent of revenue. A possibility exists that the company will have to absorb cost increases that cannot be passed along to customers. In this case, the cost of goods sold will be 80 percent of revenue. With sales down to $6,500,000, the cost of goods sold will definitely be 80 percent of revenue. Probabilities of occurrence have been estimated for each of three alternatives as follows:

Revenues and Cost of Goods Sold	Operating Expenses	Probabilities
Sales at $8,500,000, cost of goods sold at 70 percent . . .	$ 1,050,000	30%
Sales at $8,500,000, cost of goods sold at 80 percent . . .	1,200,000	50
Sales at $6,500,000, cost of goods sold at 80 percent . . .	1,100,000	20

Depreciation of $280,000 is included in operating expenses under each alternative, and depreciation of $350,000 is included in cost of goods sold for each alternative. Income taxes are estimated at 40 percent of income before income taxes.

In making the transition, equipment will be sold for $600,000, net of income taxes. A payment of $350,000 must be made on long-term notes payable. Spike wants dividends of $300,000 to be paid under each alternative.

Required:

1. What is the "worst case" cash-flow scenario that Spike could face?
2. Prepare a statement to show the forecast cash flow provided by operations under each assumption and the expected value of cash flows.
3. Continue the forecast statement to show how much additional cash will be needed to finance the new project after considering the information given. Show the impact of all three assumptions on expected cash flows.

C ASE 7A—ALPENA COUNTY HOSPITAL

The Alpena County Hospital is located in a well-known summer resort area. The county population doubles during vacation months. The hospital is organized into several departments. Although it is a relatively small hospital, its pleasant surroundings have attracted a competent and well-trained medical staff.

An administrator, Jim Rainey, was hired a year ago to slow cost increases and to improve the business activities of the hospital. Among the new ideas he has introduced is responsibility accounting. This program was announced along with quarterly cost reports supplied to department heads. Previously, cost data were presented to department heads infrequently. Excerpts from the announcement and the report received by the laundry supervisor are as follows:

> "The hospital has adopted a '**responsibility accounting system**.' From now on, you will receive quarterly reports comparing the costs of operating your department with budgeted costs. The reports will highlight the differences (variations) so you can zero in on departures from budgeted costs. (This is called 'management by exception.') Responsibility accounting means you are accountable for keeping the costs in your department within the budget. Variations from budget will help you to identify which costs are out of line. Your first such report accompanies this announcement."

Performance Report: Laundry Department
July, August, and September

	Budget	Actual	Fav. (Unfav.) Budget	Percentage Fav. (Unfav.) Budget
Patient days	9,500	11,900	(2,400)	(25)
Pounds processed—laundry . .	125,000	156,000	(31,000)	(25)
Costs:				
Laundry labor	$ 9,000	$ 12,500	$ (3,500)	(39)
Supplies	1,100	1,875	(775)	(70)
Water: heating and				
softening	1,700	2,500	(800)	(47)
Maintenance	1,400	2,200	(800)	(57)
Supervisor's salary	3,150	3,750	(600)	(19)
Allocated administration costs	4,000	5,000	(1,000)	(25)
Equipment depreciation	1,200	1,250	(50)	(4)
	$21,550	$ 29,075	$ (7,525)	(35)

Administrator's comments: Costs are significantly above budget for the quarter. Particular attention needs to be paid to labor, supplies, and maintenance.

The annual budget for the year was constructed by the new administrator. Quarterly budgets were computed as one-fourth of the annual budget.

The administration compiled the budget from an analysis of the prior three years' actual costs. For that 3-year period, costs were increasing from one year to the next, with more rapid increases occurring between the second and third years. The administrator considered establishing the budget at an average of the prior three years' costs, hoping that the installation of the system would reduce costs to this level. However, in view of increasing costs, he finally chose last year's costs less 3 percent for the current budget. The activity level, measured by patient days and pounds, was set at last year's volume, which was approximately equal to the volume of each of the past three years.

Required:

1. Comment on the method used to construct the budget.

2. What information should be communicated by variations from budgets? (**Hint:** Consider those factors over which the manager of the Laundry Department has control.)

3. Explain the strengths and weaknesses of this report.

(ICMA adapted)

CASE 7B—LETA LEARNING SYSTEMS

LETA Learning Systems specializes in education and training. One responsibility center in the Professional Seminar Division is Government Contract Seminars. It is treated as a profit center for performance evaluation purposes.

Because the Department of Defense is downsizing, many companies are cutting back and sending people to fewer training seminars. Actual results and variances for the last fiscal year for Government Contract Seminars are as follows:

	Actual	Fav. (Unfav.) Budget
Seminar participants	7,020	1,380
Number of seminars given	175	25
Revenues	$1,404,000	$(396,000)
Costs which vary with number of participants:		
Food	$ 70,200	$ 10,800
Workbooks and handouts	274,890	85,110
Costs which vary with number of seminars:		
Instructors' fees	280,000	40,000
Rental of sites	21,600	(2,630)
Equipment rental (overhead projectors, etc.)	8,110	(510)
Fixed costs of Government Contract Seminars:		
Salaries of managers and assistants	124,000	(4,000)
Office expenses	13,000	(640)
Promotion of seminars	89,000	7,500
Divisional overhead allocated to this profit center	389,000	9,000
Total expenses	$1,269,800	$ 144,630
Profits	$ 134,200	$(251,370)

Seminars are for one, two, and three days. The budget expected the average class days per seminar to be 2.5 days; the actual average was 2 days. The manager's salary, included above, is $60,000 and was budgeted at that level.

Required:

1. Since Government Contract Seminars is a profit center, the presumption is that the manager controls revenues. The factors influencing revenues are the number of seminar participants and the number and length of seminars. Does the manager really control these factors? Explain.

2. In general, are the variances in this report controllable by the manager of the profit center? Which costs and related variances are not controllable by the manager?

3. Suggest improvements in the report. Prepare a performance report which you believe better describes the manager's performance than the preceding report.

CHAPTER 8

Budget Development and Financial Modeling

After studying Chapter 8, you will be able to:

1. Prepare schedules for all elements of the master budget.
2. Identify independent and dependent budget variables.
3. Understand the basic format and calculation sequences necessary for preparation of budgets and supporting schedules.
4. Show the purpose of flexible budgeting in a master budget.
5. Identify the primary components of financial planning models.
6. Understand the need for simulation capabilities in budget preparation and for "what if" analyses.

Ben's Budget Inquisition and Renee's Response

Ben Hall, president of Hall Associates, Inc., has just reviewed a first draft of the 1998 budget for his labor relations consulting firm. The firm has 25 employees, operates in a three-state area in the northeastern United States, provides services to small businesses, and participates in mediation and arbitration activities in the public sector. Increases in his costs, uncertainty about future revenue sources, and questions about how his staff reacts to budgets and budget pressures have him concerned about what he calls "the ethics and realities" of financial planning. He shares much of the budget information with his managers since the firm has a profit-sharing system. Ben knows that people costs and their benefit program costs have risen at an annual rate of 12 percent for three years. Business revenues have grown only 8 percent per year over that same time period.

Recently, Renee Foresman, controller of Hall Associates, purchased a budgeting software package from a firm specializing in financial planning for consulting firms. After some work with the software firm, Renee has installed the master budgeting module on her PC. She first entered

monthly 1996 and 1997 actual and budget numbers from each department into the software's database. She then entered her best estimates about 1998. A first budget draft for Ben was printed and given to him. This morning she met with Ben about her budget. He had a long list of questions about the budget assumptions, the numbers, and meeting the firm's financial goals. Most of the questions will take hours, if not days, to get solid answers. Another module of the software package is a planning model that will allow Renee to change many variables in the master budget database and quickly recalculate a "new" budget.

Ben tells Renee to "play with her new toy" and to come back tomorrow with answers to his questions. Renee finds that the financial model answers many of the questions, but the answers give Ben a chance to ask more informed questions. A number of the questions Ben raises really need inputs from his operating managers. How he, Renee, and the other managers act and react to the simulation results will impact the budget and the future directions of Hall Associates.

Chapter 8 illustrates a comprehensive master budget. Based on the budgeting discussion in Chapter 7, a master budget is developed for a hypothetical firm. Financial modeling is presented as a powerful tool to test budget numbers, planning assumptions, and goal achievement. Modeling leads to "what if" analysis where independent variables can be altered to measure the impacts of the changes. Financial modeling is explained and discussed, and several "what ifs" will be presented as illustrations of financial simulation.

A MASTER OPERATING BUDGETING EXAMPLE

To illustrate the master budget sequence of planning activity and budget schedule formats, a comprehensive example is presented.[1] The firm is Hoffman Products Company, a small manufacturer of wood-based products. In recent years, its primary products are ceremonial speaker podiums, which are sold to chapters of the Effective Speakers Society of America (ESSA). Graduates of the Society's speaker training programs are awarded a wooden podium as a symbol of public speaking prowess. Hoffman Products produces a high-quality product at a very competitive price. The firm has an exclusive arrangement with the ESSA that requires the local chapters to purchase Hoffman podiums at previously agreed upon prices. Two styles are produced—the JR EXEC and

---

[1] The Hoffman Products Company case is accompanied by a software spreadsheet template on an instructor's diskette for in-class display and course assignments.

the EXEC. Chapters of the ESSA give the EXEC model to honors graduates and the JR EXEC to all others.

In the Hoffman Products factory, wood is cut, finished, and assembled; a polyurethane finish is applied; and packing and shipping are done. A small sales office and administrative staff complete the organization.

Each year, Hoffman Products prepares a master budget on a quarterly basis and generally follows the structure shown in Chapter 7, Figure 7.4 on page 284. As in most budgeting situations, Hoffman Products' dollar amounts are rounded to the nearest dollar. The model used to prepare the budget will track decimal places. When amounts are rounded throughout the budget example, certain columns or rows may appear to add incorrectly; however, overall accuracy is maintained.

Annual Goals and Planning Assumptions

Hoffman Products begins its planning process with a meeting organized by the controller at a local resort each August. All managers discuss their areas of responsibility and present strengths, opportunities, problems, and last year's results.

Operating and Financial Goals. At the planning session, a set of goals and targets for the coming calendar year is established. For 1998, the following goals were selected:

Operating and Financial Goals		*1998 Forecast Value*
Growth:	Sales dollar growth of 15 percent ($680,000 in 1997)	17.47%
Profitability:	Return on equity of at least 10 percent	9.02%
Capital:	Total debt to equity ratio below 25 percent	21.73%
Liquidity:	Current ratio above 3:1	5.54:1
Other goals:	Inventory reduction of 10 percent from beginning levels	14.35%
	Cost of podiums below 65 percent of sales—JR EXEC	63.42%
	Cost of podiums below 65 percent of sales—EXEC	63.26%

Beginning and ending balance sheet and annual income statement numbers are used. Based on the forecast developed by Hoffman for 1998 (shown in later schedules), all goals except for the return on equity are met. Other operating goals and targets related to efficiency and operating management are also prepared but are not listed here, since they are not directly related to the budget process.

Planning Assumptions. Certain data and relationships are needed to begin the planning process. These include beginning balances, product costs and prices, operating activity assumptions, and financing assumptions.

Product Cost and Pricing Data. The first planning data are costs of both JR EXEC and EXEC models. For both podiums, materials, labor, and overhead are listed in Schedule 1 by price and quantity of each resource used. A list of materials is often called a **bill of materials**. Direct labor shows costs and hours. A more detailed set of labor processes is used to plan labor schedules in each department.

Manufacturing overhead is identified as fixed or variable. After extensive analysis of activities, cost drivers, and cost behaviors, direct labor hours were

Schedule 1: Product Quantities, Costs, and Price Sheet

Product Costs	Cost	JR EXEC		EXEC	
		Quantity	Per Unit	Quantity	Per Unit
Materials:					
Plywood (square feet)	$ 0.275	12.00	$ 3.300	15.00	$ 4.125
Trim (feet)	0.085	15.00	1.275	18.00	1.530
Total materials			$ 4.575		$ 5.655
Direct labor:					
Preparation and finishing hours.	$ 12.00	0.75	$ 9.000	1.00	$12.000
Manufacturing overhead:					
Variable—Based on direct labor hours	$ 7.10	0.75	$ 5.325	1.00	$ 7.100
Fixed—Based on machine hours	10.40	0.50	5.200	0.60	6.240
Total manufacturing overhead			$10.525		$13.340
Total product cost			$24.100		$30.995
Sales price			$ 38.00		$ 49.00

selected as the cost driver for variable overhead. Much activity in the plant is linked to the labor-intensive processes that generate the majority of variable overhead costs. The cost driver for fixed overhead is machine hours, since most fixed overhead is generated by equipment costs. Shipping costs per unit are considered to be selling expenses and are not product costs. Podium prices are negotiated between the ESSA and Hoffman Products each fall as an early part of the planning process.

Operating and Financing Assumptions. A variety of planning details is needed to prepare budget schedules. Most of these come from past experience, estimates of beginning balances, and 1998 forecasts. Schedule 2, page 326, presents the initial assumptions.

Operating assumptions include percentages, specific budgeted amounts for certain accounts to prepare overhead rates, and any other constant that will be needed in calculations. In real life, predicted inflation rates, salary increase percentages, growth rates in certain activities, and staffing levels are also included.

Borrowing details, cash policies, taxes, dividends, and the beginning balance sheet figures are the independent variables for financing assumptions. These starting points are needed to complete the cash-flow forecast and **pro forma (or forecast) financial statements**. Also, the beginning balance sheet is shown in the December 31, 1997, column of the forecast balance sheet statements on page 339.

Sales Forecast

The sales forecast, the only remaining independent variable needed, is based on past sales, the ESSA's enrollment forecast, and contacts with major chapters. It is prepared using a rolling five-quarter timeframe. A fifth quarter of sales data is needed to complete a number of fourth-quarter schedules.

Physical quantities are independent variables. Dollar amounts are found by using the physical units and prices from Schedule 1. A small sales returns

Schedule 2: Operating and Financing Assumptions

			Products	
Inventory Data:	**Plywood (Sq. Feet)**	**Trim (Feet)**	**JR EXEC**	**EXEC**
December 31, 1997, inventory	10,000	9,000	1,300	200
Ending inventory (percentage of next quarter's usage) . .	20%	10%	25%	25%

Accounts receivable:

Sales percentage collected this quarter	75%
Uncollectible accounts percentage	2
Sales return percentage expected	1
Cash discount percentage for receipt of this quarter's sales.	2

Accounts payable:

Purchases percentage paid this quarter	60%
Cash discount percentage for payment of this quarter's purchases	2

Manufacturing activity base:

Normal labor hour activity rounded to the nearest 500 hours	16,000
Normal machine hour activity rounded to the nearest 500 hours	10,000
(See Schedule 7 for budgeted variable rates and annual fixed amounts.)	

Selling and administrative expense data:

Sales commissions. . . . . 4% Shipping expenses	$1.30
(See Schedule 13 for annual budgeted selling expense amounts.)	
(See Schedule 14 for annual budgeted administrative expense amounts.)	

Financial assumptions and balances:

Cash balance: Minimum balance . . . $ 5,000; Maximum balance	$ 10,000
Borrowing and investment incremental amount	5,000
Quarterly principal payment on notes payable	3,000
Capital stock—outstanding shares (24,000 shares).	240,000
Dividend rate—per share per quarter	0.05
Income tax rate (federal, state, and local)	40%
Interest rate on bank borrowings and investments (annual)	9%
(See December 31, 1997, balance sheet for beginning balances.)	

Project Expenditures:	**First Quarter**	**Second Quarter**	**Third Quarter**	**Fourth Quarter**
Equipment purchases	$ 8,000	$ 0	$ 10,000	$12,000
Research and development.	0	0	0	4,000

allowance of 1 percent of sales is forecast. Also, the format of the four quarters, an annual total, and a fifth quarter (or the first quarter of 1999) is provided by marketing and sales managers.

From the sales dollars in Schedule 3 through the end of the master budget, all numbers are calculated using data and instructions in Schedules 1 through 3. All values from this point are dependent variables using the independent variables.

Production Plan

A production plan (see Schedule 4) is prepared for each product using the beginning finished podium inventory, the sales forecast, and the desired ending inventory levels for each product. In this example, work in process inventory is assumed to be so small and unchanging that it is immaterial to both planning and product costing tasks. If work in process were substantial,

Schedule 3: Sales Forecast by Product and by Quarter

	First Quarter	Second Quarter	Third Quarter	Fourth Quarter	Total	Fifth Quarter
Unit sales:						
JR EXEC	3,200	3,200	3,600	3,800	13,800	3,500
EXEC	1,200	1,400	1,500	1,500	5,600	1,300
Sales dollars:						
JR EXEC	$121,600	$121,600	$136,800	$144,400	$524,400	$133,000
EXEC	58,800	68,600	73,500	73,500	274,400	63,700
Total gross sales	$180,400	$190,200	$210,300	$217,900	$798,800	$196,700
Less returns.	(1,804)	(1,902)	(2,103)	(2,179)	(7,988)	(1,967)
Net sales dollars.	$178,596	$188,298	$208,197	$215,721	$790,812	$194,733

the beginning level would be known; a desired ending level would be set; and production would be determined.   Hoffman is implementing a just-in-time system of production and customer shipments.   A goal is to reduce all inventories by 10 percent this year.   The plan shows a 14 percent reduction.

Key relationships in this production plan are the percentages of sales that should be on hand at the end of each quarter.   Note the format of Schedule 4. Each product's production schedules would be built by day, week, or month and by specific operation within each producing department.   A company may choose to operate at a fairly uniform level throughout the year; or, conversely, it may prefer to manufacture products as needed.   When production moves with sales, the inventories will vary slightly.   Just-in-time processes argue that the benefits of producing only when needed more than compensate for the costs of fluctuating production.

If production is level, manufacturing costs tend to be more uniformly distributed throughout the year.   However, other problems arise when production is stabilized.   Inventories of finished goods will grow when sales volume

Schedule 4: Production Plan by Product and by Quarter

	First Quarter	Second Quarter	Third Quarter	Fourth Quarter	Total	Fifth Quarter
JR EXEC:						
Unit sales.	3,200	3,200	3,600	3,800	13,800	3,500
Ending finished goods	800	900	950	875	875	800
Total units needed.	4,000	4,100	4,550	4,675	14,675	4,300
Beginning finished goods	(1,300)	(800)	(900)	(950)	(1,300)	(875)
Production.	2,700	3,300	3,650	3,725	13,375	3,425
EXEC:						
Unit sales.	1,200	1,400	1,500	1,500	5,600	1,300
Ending finished goods	350	375	375	325	325	350
Total units needed.	1,550	1,775	1,875	1,825	5,925	1,650
Beginning finished goods	(200)	(350)	(375)	(375)	(200)	(325)
Production.	1,350	1,425	1,500	1,450	5,725	1,325

is low and will fall during high-demand periods. Variations in inventory create carrying costs. Handling and storing are nonvalue-adding activities. Funds invested in inventories could be used elsewhere. Carrying costs often run at least 25 percent of inventory value.

Materials Requirements and Purchases Schedule. Quantities of materials used in each unit (the bill of materials) are specified in Schedule 1. Estimated quantities are based on experience or engineering studies and help set standard costs, which are discussed in Chapter 9. Quantities of materials needed to meet production requirements are determined by multiplying the units to be made by the amount of materials required for each unit.

Ending plywood inventory for the first quarter of 12,195 square feet is 20 percent (Schedule 2) of the second quarter's production needs of 60,975 square feet. The 32,400 square feet of plywood needed for JR EXEC production in the first quarter is found by multiplying 12 square feet per unit (Schedule 1) times the 2,700 units to be produced (Schedule 4). Thus, the rules from Schedules 1 and 2 and the quantities from Schedule 4 determine all amounts needed to calculate the purchases requirements in Schedule 5.

In more complex production situations, the accumulation of parts and materials needs is called a **bill of materials explosion**. All uses of the same part in different products are summed to find the total usage across the entire product line for a time period. Computer software for production planning, such as Materials Requirements Planning (MRP), is used to calculate needs and to issue purchase orders when inventory levels reach certain points.

The purchasing department furnishes data with respect to estimated prices. It maintains contact with suppliers and tracks prices offered by competing firms. Freight on incoming materials and costs of purchasing, handling, and storing materials are a part of materials cost. Usually, these transit costs are difficult to trace to specific materials items; for expediency, they are often budgeted in factory overhead.

Direct Labor Budget. The direct labor budget is estimated first by the direct labor time required per unit (Schedule 1) times the units to be made (Schedule 4). Hours per podium are set by past experience or industrial engineering studies. New production processes may create labor savings and change past patterns. Also, allowances are made for idle and setup time and training. Using 1,800 hours per year (50 weeks times 40 hours minus 10 percent for training and other nonproductive work) as a per employee estimate, nearly 9 hourly direct laborers are needed.

Labor cost per hour can be the "straight" wage rate, with all payroll taxes and fringe benefits included in manufacturing overhead. Or the rate could be a "loaded" wage rate, which includes most fringes and expected overtime premiums. The differences can be dramatic. For example, the 1994 United Auto Workers contract with the major U.S. auto companies provided an average straight wage of over $15 per hour, while the loaded rate was over $30 per hour.

In Schedule 6, the 2,025 total hours for JR EXEC in the first quarter are found by multiplying 0.75 hours per unit (Schedule 1) times 2,700 units to be produced (Schedule 4). Hours are summed and multiplied by the wage rate from Schedule 1.

Direct and indirect labor definitions vary considerably from firm to firm. Even within the same company, a union contract in one plant may separate

Schedule 5: Materials Requirements and Purchases

	First Quarter	*Second Quarter*	*Third Quarter*	*Fourth Quarter*	*Total*	*Fifth Quarter*
Plywood requirements (square feet):						
Ending inventory	12,195	13,260	13,290	12,195	12,195	
Production:						
JR EXEC production requirements . . .	32,400	39,600	43,800	44,700	160,500	41,100
EXEC production requirements	20,250	21,375	22,500	21,750	85,875	19,875
Production requirements	52,650	60,975	66,300	66,450	246,375	60,975
Total needs	64,845	74,235	79,590	78,645	258,570	
Beginning inventory	(10,000)	(12,195)	(13,260)	(13,290)	(10,000)	
Purchases in square feet	54,845	62,040	66,330	65,355	248,570	
Dollar cost of plywood purchases	$15,082[2]	$17,061	$18,241	$17,973	$68,357	
Trim requirements (linear feet):						
Ending inventory	7,515	8,175	8,198	7,523	7,523	
Production:						
JR EXEC production requirements . . .	40,500	49,500	54,750	55,875	200,625	51,375
EXEC production requirements	24,300	25,650	27,000	26,100	103,050	23,850
Production requirements	64,800	75,150	81,750	81,975	303,675	75,225
Total needs	72,315	83,325	89,948	89,498	311,198	
Beginning inventory	(9,000)	(7,515)	(8,175)	(8,198)	(9,000)	
Purchases in feet	63,315	75,810	81,773	81,300	302,198	
Dollar cost of trim purchases	$ 5,382	$ 6,444	$ 6,951	$ 6,911	$ 25,687	
Total materials purchases	$ 20,464	$ 23,505	$ 25,191	$ 24,883	$ 94,044	

Schedule 6: Direct Labor Requirements

	First Quarter	*Second Quarter*	*Third Quarter*	*Fourth Quarter*	*Total*
Direct labor hours needed:					
JR EXEC production	2,025.00	2,475.00	2,737.50	2,793.75	10,031.25
EXEC production	1,350.00	1,425.00	1,500.00	1,450.00	5,725.00
Total direct labor hours	3,375.00	3,900.00	4,237.50	4,243.75	15,756.25
Total direct labor payroll	$ 40,500	$ 46,800	$ 50,850	$ 50,925	$ 189,075

[2] The purchase cost is actually $15,082.375. This number is rounded to the nearest dollar, $15,082. This is the first of many rounded amounts in the comprehensive example. Spreadsheet software tracks all significant digits in calculations and rounds to the specified level. Therefore, certain columns and rows which include rounded numbers may appear to add incorrectly. For example, the third-quarter purchase costs of plywood and trim add to $25,192 (the sum of rounded costs of $18,241 plus $6,951), while third-quarter total purchases show $25,191 (the rounded sum of the two full costs). Budgeting rarely needs detail beyond whole dollars. Financial modeling software maintains high levels of accuracy that computers can automatically provide. Having a column of rounded numbers not add up exactly every time is a minor inconvenience in the overall model's accuracy level.

direct and indirect job classifications, which are combined in a second plant. Average rates are used to calculate the labor cost budget to account for employees with varying seniority and skill levels earning different wage rates.

With an increasing trend toward automation, many employees who once were hourly workers are now salaried. They work as monitors as opposed to direct converters of materials into finished products. These workers' earnings could be accounted for as fixed and added to manufacturing overhead. Or production time wages could be direct labor and variable, with the remaining portion of salary from nonproduction time added to manufacturing overhead. Or, even though it is fixed, the entire salary could be classified as direct labor, with supervisors being responsible for coordinating employees and work to met productivity expectations.

Manufacturing Overhead Budgets.   Planning manufacturing overhead takes two forms—creating the expected overhead spending patterns using a flexible budget and budgeting spending and applied overhead levels.

Cost Estimation Using ABC and Statistical Techniques.   Detailed cost estimates come from several sources already discussed in prior chapters. Cost estimation techniques presented in Chapter 3 (regression analysis, high-low method, etc.) are used by managers and accountants to budget expenses that track well against one or more activity variables. More commonly, the same cost drivers used in Chapters 4 and 6 to build cost functions and assign costs to cost objectives are now applied to another cost objective—budgeting. Companies with well-designed activity-based costing systems can now use these defined relationships to budget future costs given expected levels of activity. Also, activity-based management can identify nonvalue-adding activities, activities that use more resources than similar well-managed activities in other companies or departments, and areas for improvement.

Manufacturing Overhead Flexible Budget.   Selecting activity bases for applying overhead, setting normal activity levels, planning variable and fixed overhead items, and setting the overhead rates are all part of the annual budgeting process. Schedule 7 is the result. Independent variables are the variable overhead rates and the fixed overhead annual amounts. Separate cost drivers were selected for variable and fixed overhead. The variable overhead cost driver is direct labor hours. Fixed overhead is applied using machine hours. Annual normal direct labor and machine hours are rounded (16,000 labor hours and 10,000 machine hours). Budgets are prepared for various ranges of activity, in both cases in increments of 500 hours around normal levels. Using budgeted expenses and normal activity levels given in Schedule 2, variable and fixed overhead rates are set. These are calculated on Schedule 7 and added to product costs in Schedule 1.

For many companies, the best opportunity for cost savings lies in manufacturing overhead, since it has grown rapidly in recent years. Direct materials costs and direct labor costs have been scrutinized by management. Overhead costs are not easily traceable to outputs. Measures of efficiency and productivity, discussed in Chapter 15, are recent attempts to manage these costs more carefully.

Manufacturing Overhead Expense Budget.   With overhead rates and budgeted activity levels, quarterly budgets for manufacturing overhead and applied

Schedule 7: Manufacturing Overhead Flexible Budget

				Cost Driver Activity Levels		
					Normal	
Variable cost driver: Direct labor hours			15,000	15,500	16,000	16,500
Fixed cost driver: Machine hours			9,000	9,500	10,000	10,500
Variable expenses:	**Rate/Hour**					
Supplies and maintenance expenses.	$ 1.00		$ 15,000	$ 15,500	$ 16,000	$ 16,500
Indirect labor expenses.	1.50		22,500	23,250	24,000	24,750
Fringe benefits expenses	4.20		63,000	65,100	67,200	69,300
Variable power expenses	0.40		6,000	6,200	6,400	6,600
Total variable overhead expenses	$ 7.10		$106,500	$110,050	$113,600	$117,150
Fixed expenses:	**Amount**					
Depreciation expense	$ 20,000		$ 20,000	$ 20,000	$ 20,000	$ 20,000
Utilities and taxes expenses	15,000		15,000	15,000	15,000	15,000
Supervision salaries	41,000		41,000	41,000	41,000	41,000
Other fixed overhead expenses	28,000		28,000	28,000	28,000	28,000
Total fixed overhead expenses	$104,000		$104,000	$104,000	$104,000	$104,000
Total manufacturing overhead expenses.			$210,500	$214,050	$217,600	$221,150
Overhead rates:					**Normal**	
Variable rate per direct labor hour			$ 7.10	$ 7.10	$ 7.10	$ 7.10
Fixed rate per machine hour			$ 11.56	$ 10.95	$ 10.40	$ 9.90

overhead are prepared. Again, direct labor and machine hour activity levels come from the hours per unit in Schedule 1 and the production plan. Variable expense budgets for each quarter are the expected spending levels given that activity level. The first quarter's supplies and maintenance expenses of $3,375 in Schedule 8, page 332, result from multiplying $1.00 per direct labor hour (Schedule 7) times 3,375 hours (Schedule 6). Budgeted fixed costs are divided equally among quarters.

Near the bottom of Schedule 8 is the planned applied overhead. This will differ from the budgeted spending level because of the difference between budgeted fixed cost and applied fixed overhead. The quarter's planned activity level for machine hours (2,160 hours) does not equal one quarter of the annual normal activity level (10,000 hours ÷ 4 quarters). Fixed overhead is budgeted at $26,000 for the quarter, one-fourth of $104,000. Using the fixed overhead rate of $10.40 per machine hour developed in Schedule 7, the applied fixed overhead is $22,464. Fixed overhead is underapplied by $3,536, which is $26,000 minus $22,464 (or $10.40 per hour x 340 hours).

Variable overhead is *budgeted* and *applied* at $7.10 per direct labor hour. Therefore, no budgeted overapplied or underapplied variable overhead exists.

It may seem strange to budget overapplied or underapplied overhead; but, unless the normal activity is exactly equal to the budgeted production activity, a budgeted overhead variance exists.

Schedule 8: Manufacturing Overhead Budget by Budgeted Activity Levels

	First Quarter	Second Quarter	Third Quarter	Fourth Quarter	Total
Budgeted direct labor hour activity level	3,375.0	3,900.0	4,237.5	4,243.8	15,756.3
Budgeted machine hour activity level	2,160.0	2,505.0	2,725.0	2,732.5	10,122.5
Variable expenses:					
Supplies and maintenance expenses	$ 3,375	$ 3,900	$ 4,238	$ 4,244	$ 15,756
Indirect labor expenses	5,063	5,850	6,356	6,366	23,634
Fringe benefits expenses	14,175	16,380	17,798	17,824	66,176
Variable power expenses	1,350	1,560	1,695	1,698	6,303
Total variable expenses	$23,963	$27,690	$30,086	$30,131	$111,869
Fixed expenses:					
Depreciation expense.	$ 5,000	$ 5,000	$ 5,000	$ 5,000	$ 20,000
Utilities and taxes expenses	3,750	3,750	3,750	3,750	15,000
Supervision salaries	10,250	10,250	10,250	10,250	41,000
Other fixed overhead expenses	7,000	7,000	7,000	7,000	28,000
Total fixed expenses.	$26,000	$26,000	$26,000	$26,000	$104,000
Total manufacturing overhead	$49,963	$53,690	$56,086	$56,131	$215,869
Manufacturing overhead cash outflow	$44,963	$48,690	$51,086	$51,131	$195,869
Applied manufacturing overhead:					
Variable overhead applied	$23,963	$27,690	$30,086	$30,131	$111,869
Fixed overhead applied	22,464	26,052	28,340	28,418	105,274
Total applied overhead.	$46,427	$53,742	$58,426	$58,549	$217,143
Overapplied/(underapplied) overhead	$ (3,536)	$ 52	$ 2,340	$ 2,418	$ 1,274
Overapplied/(underapplied) overhead YTD	$ (3,536)	$ (3,484)	$ (1,144)	$ 1,274	$ 1,274

Supporting Schedules

Several supporting schedules are prepared by the accounting staff and are important to cash-flow forecasting and in the calculation of costs of podiums manufactured and sold. Assumptions about collections, payments, and ending balances were given in Schedule 2. We can now develop forecasts for accounts receivable (Schedule 9), inventories (Schedule 10), and accounts payable (Schedule 11).

For accounts receivable, the percentage of net sales collected in the current quarter is 75 percent; uncollectible accounts are 2 percent of net sales and are written off in the next quarter; and cash discounts are 2 percent of collections of the current quarter's net sales. Inventory values use quantities from Schedules 4 and 5 and costs from Schedule 1. For accounts payable, Schedule 2 indicates that 60 percent of purchases are paid in the current quarter less a 2 percent discount. The remainder is paid in the next quarter.

Cost of Goods Manufactured and Sold Schedule

Now all the elements are in place to prepare a schedule of the cost of goods manufactured and sold. These costs are forwarded in summary form to the income statement.

Schedule 9: Accounts Receivable

	First Quarter	Second Quarter	Third Quarter	Fourth Quarter
Beginning balance	$ 58,000	$ 44,649	$ 47,074	$ 52,049
Net sales	178,596	188,298	208,197	215,721
Total receivables	$236,596	$232,947	$255,272	$267,770
Decreases in receivables:				
Collections from prior quarter's sales	$ 53,360	$ 41,077	$ 43,309	$ 47,885
Collections from this quarter's sales	131,268	138,400	153,025	158,555
Total cash collections	$184,628	$179,477	$196,333	$206,440
Cash discounts	2,679	2,824	3,123	3,236
Uncollectibles from prior quarter's sales	4,640	3,572	3,766	4,164
Total credits	$191,947	$185,873	$203,222	$213,840
Ending balance	$ 44,649	$ 47,074	$ 52,049	$ 53,930

Schedule 10: Ending Inventories—Cost Basis

	December 31, 1997	First Quarter	Second Quarter	Third Quarter	Fourth Quarter
Materials inventory:					
Plywood (square feet)	$ 2,750	$ 3,354	$ 3,647	$ 3,655	$ 3,354
Trim (linear feet)	765	639	695	697	639
Total materials inventory	$ 3,515	$ 3,992	$ 4,341	$ 4,352	$ 3,993
Finished goods inventory:					
JR EXEC units	$31,330	$19,280	$21,690	$22,895	$21,088
EXEC units	6,199	10,848	11,623	11,623	10,073
Total finished goods inventory	$37,529	$30,128	$33,313	$34,518	$31,161
Total inventories	$41,044	$34,121	$37,655	$38,870	$35,154

Schedule 11: Accounts Payable

	First Quarter	Second Quarter	Third Quarter	Fourth Quarter
Beginning balance	$10,300	$ 8,186	$ 9,402	$10,077
Purchases on account	20,464	23,505	25,191	24,883
Total payables	$30,764	$31,691	$34,593	$34,960
Decrease in payables:				
Payments of prior quarter's purchases	$10,300	$ 8,186	$ 9,402	$10,077
Payments of this quarter's purchases	12,033	13,821	14,813	14,631
Total cash payments	$22,333	$22,007	$24,214	$24,708
Cash discounts	246	282	302	299
Total debits to payables	$22,579	$22,289	$24,516	$25,007
Ending balance	$ 8,186	$ 9,402	$10,077	$ 9,953

Using Schedule 12, page 334, a useful proof can be made. With product costs from Schedule 1 and sales from Schedule 3, total costs of JR EXEC and EXEC sold can be calculated quickly. These numbers can be checked against the sums of materials, labor, and applied overhead and the changes in inventories. For each product in each quarter, these numbers should match. Notice that the overapplied or underapplied overhead adjusts the total cost of podiums sold.

Schedule 12: Cost of Podiums Manufactured and Sold

	First Quarter	Second Quarter	Third Quarter	Fourth Quarter	Total
JR EXEC manufacturing costs:					
Materials costs:					
Plywood used....................	$ 8,910	$ 10,890	$ 12,045	$ 12,293	$ 44,138
Trim used	3,443	4,208	4,654	4,749	17,053
Total materials used	$ 12,353	$ 15,098	$ 16,699	$ 17,042	$ 61,191
Direct labor	24,300	29,700	32,850	33,525	120,375
Manufacturing overhead applied	28,418	34,733	38,416	39,206	140,772
Cost of JR EXECs manufactured	$ 65,070	$ 79,530	$ 87,965	$ 89,773	$ 322,338
Plus: Beginning JR EXEC inventory	31,330	19,280	21,690	22,895	31,330
Less: Ending JR EXEC inventory	(19,280)	(21,690)	(22,895)	(21,088)	(21,088)
Cost of JR EXECs sold	$ 77,120	$ 77,120	$ 86,760	$ 91,580	$ 332,580
EXEC manufacturing costs:					
Materials costs:					
Plywood used....................	$ 5,569	$ 5,878	$ 6,188	$ 5,981	$ 23,616
Trim used	2,066	2,180	2,295	2,219	8,759
Total materials used	$ 7,634	$ 8,058	$ 8,483	$ 8,200	$ 32,375
Direct labor	16,200	17,100	18,000	17,400	68,700
Manufacturing overhead applied	18,009	19,010	20,010	19,343	76,372
Cost of EXECs manufactured	$ 41,843	$ 44,168	$ 46,493	$ 44,943	$ 177,446
Plus: Beginning EXEC inventory	6,199	10,848	11,623	11,623	6,199
Less: Ending EXEC inventory..........	(10,848)	(11,623)	(11,623)	(10,073)	(10,073)
Cost of EXECs sold	$ 37,194	$ 43,393	$ 46,493	$ 46,493	$ 173,572
Total cost of podiums sold................	$114,314	$120,513	$133,253	$138,073	$ 506,152
Overapplied/(underapplied) overhead......	(3,536)	52	2,340	2,418	1,274
Adjusted cost of podiums sold.............	$117,850	$120,461	$130,913	$135,655	$ 504,878

Selling and Administrative Expense Budgets

Expenses of promoting, selling, and distributing the products are budgeted by combining the costs into a selling or marketing expenses budget (Schedule 13). Although the selling expenses are not product costs, they are frequently broken down by product lines, sales regions, customers, and salespersons.   Cost

Schedule 13: Selling Expenses Budget

	First Quarter	Second Quarter	Third Quarter	Fourth Quarter	Total
Sales commission expenses	$ 7,216	$ 7,608	$ 8,412	$ 8,716	$ 31,952
Advertising expenses	1,500	1,500	1,500	1,500	6,000
Sales salaries expenses	7,500	7,500	7,500	7,500	30,000
Other sales expenses...........................	2,500	2,500	2,500	2,500	10,000
Shipping expenses	5,720	5,980	6,630	6,890	25,220
Bad debt expense	3,572	3,766	4,164	4,314	15,816
Total selling expenses.........................	$28,008	$28,854	$30,706	$31,420	$118,988
Cash selling expenses	$24,436	$25,088	$26,542	$27,106	$103,172

analysis can be applied to sales activities, revealing the costs of selling each product and to service specific customers. The goal is to match sales spending with sales revenue and profit potential. Thus, selling expenses are budgeted by area of responsibility and can be used as a basis for control.

Promotional expenses depend upon sales; but they also influence sales. Shipping expenses vary according to the destination of the products and the agreements with customers.

The cost of administration and the cost of maintaining the business entity are frequently combined into an administrative expenses budget (Schedule 14). Administrative expenses are also broken down for control purposes. In this illustration, annual fixed amounts are divided equally among the four quarters. In reality, each quarter would be budgeted separately.

Few administrative expenses are volume related. With major swings in volume or growth over time, these expenses will shift and increase. All organizations must guard against growth in these nonproducing areas. Governments, universities, and major corporations alike have an ability to grow layers of "white collar" staff, which represents overhead that must be supported by the revenue generating activities of the organization. This has been the focus of downsizing efforts by many organizations in recent years. The expression "lean and mean" implies reducing administrative and other overhead costs to minimal levels.

Project Budgets

Few project budgets exist in this example. Hoffman Products has a small capital investment and research and development budget, which is listed in Schedule 2. Equipment purchases are capitalized, and research and development costs are expensed. These expenditures are brought together in Schedule 15.

Schedule 14: Administrative Expenses Budget

	First Quarter	Second Quarter	Third Quarter	Fourth Quarter	Total
Clerical salaries expense	$ 10,000	$ 10,000	$ 10,000	$10,000	$ 40,000
Executive salaries expense	12,500	12,500	12,500	12,500	50,000
Other administrative expenses	3,500	3,500	3,500	3,500	14,000
Total administrative expenses	$ 26,000	$ 26,000	$ 26,000	$26,000	$104,000

Schedule 15: Capital Investment Project Budget

	First Quarter	Second Quarter	Third Quarter	Fourth Quarter	Total
Projects:					
Equipment purchases	$8,000	$ 0	$10,000	$12,000	$ 30,000
Research and development	0	0	0	4,000	4,000
Total project expenditures	$8,000	$ 0	$10,000	$16,000	$ 34,000

Cash-Flow Forecasts

Now that all operating and project budgets are in place, the time for summarizing has arrived. The first summary is the preparation of the cash-flow forecast. Nearly every schedule impacts cash. The basic structure is to list receipts and disbursements, sum to a cash balance, and show any planned investing or borrowing activities.

This cash-flow forecast is different in structure from the statement of cash flow discussed in Chapter 18. Generally, all inflows are listed, and then all outflows are listed. In Schedule 16, a source document for each cash-flow item is cited. Cash flows for whatever purpose are included here.

A key part of cash-flow forecasting is to anticipate cash deficits or surpluses. If the cash balance falls below the minimum desired level (given in Schedule 2), bank borrowings or investment sales are needed. If the cash balance exceeds the maximum level, excess cash should be invested to ensure

Schedule 16: Cash-Flow Forecast

	Source	First Quarter	Second Quarter	Third Quarter	Fourth Quarter	Total
Cash inflows:						
Collections from sales	Schedule 9	$175,428	$179,476	$196,333	$206,440	$757,678
Interest received	Balance sheet	0	0	113	113	225
Total cash inflows		$175,428	$179,476	$196,446	$206,553	$757,903
Cash outflows:						
Purchases payments	Schedule 11	$ 22,333	$ 22,007	$ 24,214	$ 24,708	$ 93,262
Direct labor payroll	Schedule 6	40,500	46,800	50,850	50,925	189,075
Manufacturing overhead . . .	Schedule 8	44,963	48,690	51,086	51,131	195,869
Selling expenses	Schedule 13	24,436	25,088	26,542	27,106	103,172
Administrative expenses	Schedule 14	26,000	26,000	26,000	26,000	104,000
Interest payments	Balance sheet	1,350	1,350	1,283	1,215	5,198
Income taxes payments	Balance sheet	2,000	1,182	3,708	6,662	13,552
Dividend payments	Schedule 2	1,200	1,200	1,200	1,200	4,800
Project budget payments . . .	Schedule 15	8,000	0	10,000	16,000	34,000
Note payable repayment . . .	Schedule 2	3,000	3,000	3,000	3,000	12,000
Total cash outflows		$173,781	$175,316	$197,883	$207,947	$754,928
Cash inflows minus outflows		$ 1,647	$ 4,160	$ (1,438)	$ (1,394)	$ 2,975
Plus: Beginning cash		6,000	7,647	6,806	5,369	6,000
Cash available		$ 7,647	$ 11,806	$ 5,369	$ 3,975	$ 8,975
Less: Excess cash on hand		0	(5,000)	0	0	(5,000)
Plus: Cash needed		0	0	0	5,000	5,000
Ending cash balance		$ 7,647	$ 6,806	$ 5,369	$ 8,975	$ 8,975
Cumulative borrowings		$ 0	$ 0	$ 0	$ 0	$ 0
Cumulative investments		$ 0	$ 5,000	$ 5,000	$ 0	$ 0

Making Managers Aware of Cash

When a firm's cash management is centralized to increase cash efficiency, cash generation may be negatively affected. Managers of business units may no longer worry about cash. To instill a cash discipline in a multidivisional firm, a cash generating incentive system should be in place. It includes a monthly cash-flow budget for each business unit, cash-flow achievement as part of the incentive compensation package, and interest income credit for excess cash inflows or expense charge for excess cash outflows. This gets managers' attention.

Source: Seidensticker, H. B., "Maximize Cash Generation by Internal Cash Flow Reporting," *Journal of Cash Management*, March-April 1990, pp. 36-40.

maximum earnings. Calculations at the bottom of Schedule 16 show that Hoffman Products is forecast to generate extra cash in one quarter and to need extra cash in another quarter. Using $5,000 increments for borrowing or investing cash as indicated in Schedule 2, no net change is forecast in the investments or borrowings balances between the beginning and the end of 1998.

THE EXAMPLE COMPLETED: FORECAST FINANCIAL STATEMENTS

Operating budgets build the base for the coming year's activities. But the operating data also determine the financial results for the year. Consolidation of operating numbers into forecast financial statements is frequently the controller's responsibility. These statements are reviewed carefully by the firm's executives. The results are compared to the annual financial goals set earlier. In this example, the source schedule for each account balance is listed to help explain income statement and balance sheet numbers.

Forecast Income Statements

The forecast or pro forma income statement is a summary of the expected revenue and expense budgets and shows whether the annual profit goals can be realized. Management can compare its actual income statements with the estimated statements as the year progresses. If budgeted profits are to be realized, adjustments may have to be made. Perhaps the budget itself requires revision.

As can be seen, most amounts are summarized from earlier schedules. Only the interest income and expense and income tax expense are computed here from data in Schedule 2 and from amounts already calculated.

Forecast income statements are often subdivided into months or weeks. Also, analyses are made by product lines, sales regions, and customer groupings.

HOFFMAN PRODUCTS COMPANY
Forecast Income and Expense Statements

	First Quarter	Second Quarter	Third Quarter	Fourth Quarter	Total	Source
Sales:						
Sales of JR EXEC	$121,600	$121,600	$136,800	$144,400	$524,400	Schedule 3
Sales of EXEC	58,800	68,600	73,500	73,500	274,400	Schedule 3
Total gross sales	$180,400	$190,200	$210,300	$217,900	$798,800	
Less: Sales returns	(1,804)	(1,902)	(2,103)	(2,179)	(7,988)	Schedule 3
Net sales	$178,596	$188,298	$208,197	$215,721	$790,812	
Cost of podiums sold:						
Cost of JR EXECs sold	$ 77,120	$ 77,120	$ 86,760	$ 91,580	$332,580	Schedule 12
Cost of EXECs sold	37,194	43,393	46,493	46,493	173,572	Schedule 12
Total cost of podiums sold	$114,314	$120,513	$133,253	$138,073	$506,152	
Manufacturing variances.	(3,536)	52	2,340	2,418	1,274	Schedule 8
Net cost of podiums sold ...	$117,850	$120,461	$130,913	$135,655	$504,878	
Gross margin on sales	$ 60,746	$ 67,837	$ 77,285	$ 80,067	$285,934	
Selling expenses	$ 28,008	$ 28,854	$ 30,706	$ 31,420	$118,988	Schedule 13
Research and development expenses	0	0	0	4,000	4,000	Schedule 15
Administrative expenses	26,000	26,000	26,000	26,000	104,000	Schedule 14
Total operating expenses ...	$ 54,008	$ 54,854	$ 56,706	$ 61,420	$226,988	
Operating income	$ 6,738	$ 12,983	$ 20,579	$ 18,646	$ 58,946	
Other: Interest income	$ 0	$ 113	$ 113	$ 0	$ 225	Calculated
Purchase cash discounts	246	282	302	299	1,129	Schedule 11
Interest expense	(1,350)	(1,283)	(1,215)	(1,148)	(4,995)	Calculated
Sales cash discounts	(2,679)	(2,824)	(3,123)	(3,236)	(11,862)	Schedule 9
Total other items	$ (3,783)	$ (3,712)	$ (3,923)	$ (4,085)	$ (15,504)	
Net income before taxes	$ 2,955	$ 9,271	$ 16,655	$ 14,561	$ 43,442	
Income tax expense	(1,182)	(3,708)	(6,662)	5,825	17,377	Calculated
Net income	$ 1,773	$ 5,562	$ 9,993	$ 8,737	$ 26,065	

Forecast Balance Sheets

The forecast or pro forma balance sheet indicates the firm's financial position at a future date. Like the income statement, it is a summary statement that depends on individual budgets which have been prepared. Rarely will an account be budgeted directly on the balance sheet. Again, source schedules are cited for each account. Analyses of budgeted and actual balances show how accounts are affected by operations during the budget year. The same type of financial performance analysis discussed in Chapter 17 should be applied to forecast financial statements.

The forecast balance sheet also serves as a point of reference during the year. Interim statements prepared at various dates can be compared with corresponding budget statements.

HOFFMAN PRODUCTS COMPANY					
Forecast Balance Sheets					
	December 31, 1997	*March 31, 1998*	*June 30, 1998*	*September 30, 1998*	*December 31, 1998*	*Source*
Assets:						
Cash	$ 6,000	$ 7,647	$ 6,806	$ 5,369	$ 8,975	Schedule 16
Short-term investments . .	0	0	5,000	5,000	0	Schedule 16
Accounts receivable	48,000	44,649	47,074	52,049	53,930	Schedule 9
Allowance for bad debts	(3,840)	(3,572)	(3,766)	(4,164)	(4,314)	Schedule 9
Inventories	41,044	34,121	37,655	38,870	35,154	Schedule 10
Interest receivable	0	0	113	113	0	Income Stmt
Total current assets	$ 91,204	$ 82,844	$ 92,882	$ 97,236	$ 93,745	
Building and equipment . .	360,000	368,000	368,000	378,000	390,000	Schedule 15
Accumulated depreciation	(100,000)	(105,000)	(110,000)	(115,000)	(120,000)	Schedule 8
Total assets	$351,204	$345,844	$350,882	$360,236	$363,745	
Liabilities and equity:						
Accounts payable	$ 10,300	$ 8,186	$ 9,402	$ 10,077	$ 9,953	Schedule 11
Taxes payable	2,000	1,182	3,708	6,662	5,825	Income Stmt
Bank borrowings	0	0	0	0	0	Schedule 16
Interest payable	1,350	1,350	1,283	1,215	1,148	Income Stmt
Total current liabilities .	$ 13,650	$ 10,718	$ 14,393	$ 17,954	$ 16,925	
Long-term notes payable .	60,000	57,000	54,000	51,000	48,000	Schedule 16
Total liabilities	$ 73,650	$ 67,718	$ 68,393	$ 68,954	$ 64,925	
Capital stock	$240,000	$240,000	$240,000	$240,000	$240,000	Schedule 3
Retained earnings	37,554	38,127	42,489	51,282	58,819	Schedule 16 and Income
Total equity	$277,554	$278,127	$282,489	$291,282	$298,819	Statement
Total liabilities and equity . .	$351,204	$345,844	$350,882	$360,236	$363,745	

Master Budget Summary

Several observations should be made about the master budget example. The budget should be tested for reasonableness in all areas. Tests include:

1. Review of the reasonableness of critical independent variables (most often the sales forecast) as a key evaluation step.
2. Sensitivity analysis to determine whether small changes in key variables will cause major changes in profitability or cash flows.
3. "What if" analyses to determine whether a better combination of budgeted efforts could produce a stronger plan.
4. Budget review and approval by each manager involved in the planning effort.
5. Analysis to determine whether management's goals and objectives are realized.

Many iterations may be needed to arrive at a budget that managers can "buy into," that meets management's goals, and that pushes the firm toward its long-range goals. This budgeting process assumes active participation of all managers at all levels.

*F*INANCIAL PLANNING MODELS

We are living in a rapidly changing environment. The problem is how to cope with change. One tool now widely available for managing change is financial modeling. **Modeling** is a meaningful abstraction of reality where key variables and relationships are mathematically represented. In the past ten years, computer capabilities have brought financial modeling and simulation to even the smallest firms. **Simulation** uses a model to test policies, decisions, and alternative forecast scenarios. This section defines a financial planning model and examines the uses of financial simulation. The major application, testing plans using "what if" analysis, is illustrated.

Defining the Financial Planning Model

A **financial planning model** converts an organization's accounting and other processes into a series of equations. These equations represent interrelationships that exist within an organization. The aims are to simulate, using computer power, all significant processes that may affect the decision problem and, thereby, to arrive at realistic approximations of actual results. Successful modeling depends on defining relationships, identifying key variables, and inputing accurate data. The master budget is an excellent example of defining the interrelationships that describe an organization's operating and financial functions, its inputs, and its outputs.

Financial planning models:

1. Evaluate and test planning goals and operating and financial policies.
2. Perform "what if" analyses to:
   (a) Weigh the results of complex decisions.
   (b) Measure impacts of policy changes.
   (c) Measure impacts of price and cost changes.
   (d) Measure the potential for achieving financial goals and targets.
3. Assess long-range impacts of specific strategies.
4. Without incurring costs of decision making in the real world:
   (a) Identify warning signals that may require managerial attention.
   (b) Fine tune decisions to find optimal points.
   (c) Allow advocates of competing strategies to "strut their stuff."
5. Speed the budget consolidation task to give fast feedback and more time for decision analysis.

Output from a financial planning model is typically in financial statement form plus analysis schedules of specific decisions. Financial models come in all sizes, modes, and complexities. Usually, a model is used repeatedly. The range of model types includes:

1. **Manual calculations** that involve few steps, require limited data and interrelationships, and rarely need many iterations.
2. **Spreadsheet software** (generally personal computer based) that is developed or purchased for specific user applications.
3. **Stand alone programmed software** developed for personal computers, networks, and mainframes. These models are more powerful versions of spreadsheet software and operate separately from a firm's accounting transaction and reporting systems. Needed data can be downloaded and uploaded between the model and the accounting systems.

4. **Modeling capabilities integrated into the firm's accounting systems** designed as an integral part of the accounting systems. All accounting and finance functions are modeled as a normal activity and not as a separate process.

While modeling costs are decreasing, the variety of products is large and growing as are modeling applications.

Elements of the Model

A financial planning model consists of three significant elements: inputs, the model, and outputs. These are combined to create a mathematical representation of the organization or task it models. In Figure 8.1, page 342, the basic modeling elements are illustrated and linked.

Inputs. Inputs are historical databases, economic indicators, operating and financial parameters, management policies, planning assumptions, and model queries as shown in Figure 8.1. Historical databases include detailed financial statement account balances, transaction summaries, statistical relationships, economic data, nonfinancial data, and other databases needed in specific industries, such as banking. The forecast information may be generated internally, developed from external sources, or even purchased from data vendors.

Operating factors represent constraints, physical relationships and processes, customer and product data files, purchasing and distribution linkages, and staffing. Financial factors include cash patterns, borrowing and investing policies, capitalization issues, taxes, and accounting policies and practices.

Management policies involve goal setting, pricing, marketing practices, borrowings, dividends, salary and benefits practices, and other decision rules that affect the financial affairs of the firm directly and indirectly. Often guidelines or constraints are needed to serve as **parameters** or boundaries for model variable values and to keep the model "in control." Planning assumptions include the items already illustrated in the master budget example plus anticipated inflation rates, salary and benefits changes, and market growth.

Model queries are questions that managers ask the model. The questions often represent changes in independent variables. These are "what ifs." The query defines the modeling problem and includes any new assumptions or data required. Also, **management overrides** may be allowed to provide managers with a mechanism to supersede statistical projections or other modeled values that are unrealistic.

C O N T E M P O R A R Y   P R A C T I C E   8 . 2

What Makes a Model Work?

In building a spreadsheet-based financial model for a hospital, two major flaws occur frequently—an inappropriate level of detail and a fundamental structural flaw. The following practical steps are critical to building a model: (1) define the problem, (2) specify the desired output, (3) demarcate the planning horizon, (4) determine the level of detail required, (5) structure the model, (6) define major variables and their interrelationships, (7) review the assumptions, (8) build the model, and (9) test the model.

Source: Porter, M., and T. R. Miller, "Uses and Abuses of Financial Modeling," *Topics in Health Care Financing*, Fall 1992, pp. 34-45.

FIGURE 8.1 Elements of the Financial Planning Model

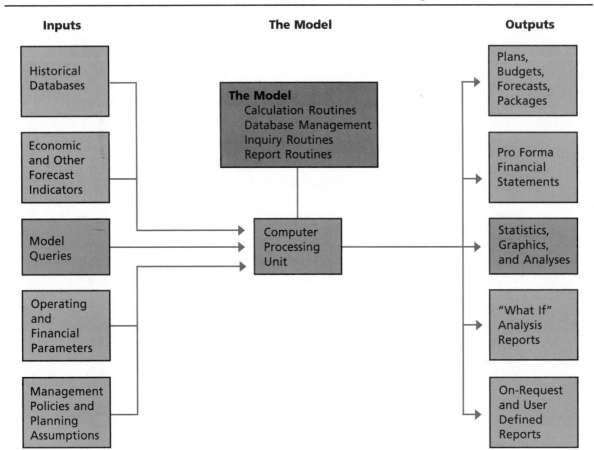

The Model. The second element is the **model** itself—a core of programs, software routines, and computer power that makes the model work. Calculation routines, file management systems, reporting routines, and user query routines are prime components. While the essential resource is often computer power, models also contain:

1. Statistical routines for projections, curve fitting, confidence interval setting, and probability measurement.
2. Formulas for expressing constraints, cost and production functions, input/output relationships, and other fixed or known interrelationships.
3. Optimization routines to find maximums or minimums for particular goals.
4. Interactive capability to allow users to perform on-line "what ifs."
5. Ability to upload and download data from other information systems.
6. Accrual accounting and balancing rules and report preparation routines.

Most of these tools are not visible to the user. For example, a bank financial planning model needs to know that February 1996 has 29 days and not 28. But few users will consciously think about this minute detail. Many models use mathematical formulas to express relationships among independent and dependent variables. An example is provided in the "Problem for Review" section. Such a set of formulas is used to create budget numbers for successive time periods.

Outputs. The third element is the model's output: revised plans, pro forma financial statements, statistical summaries, "what if" analyses, and other reports requested by managers. Outputs can be hard copy, screen displays, or computer files. The model's output often moves through a report-generating package that allows managers to create relevant report formats and comparisons.

Structuring the Interrelationships

In structuring the model, a primary purpose is to transfer the computational burden from the user to the computer. Which relationships should be modeled, and which should be ignored? Criteria should include:

1. Materiality: Is it large enough to be significant?
2. Controllability: Can management do something about it?
3. Sensitivity: If it changes, will the change have an impact on key variables?
4. Explainability: Can the relationship be logically defined?
5. Historical support: Do past data support the linkage?

Care must be taken when building the model to keep it simple enough to manage and use and yet sophisticated enough to capture the essence of the decision.

"What If" Analysis

To demonstrate "what if" analysis in financial modeling, several changes in independent variables are tested using the Hoffman Products example. Let us assume that the controller of Hoffman Products prepared the budget as shown earlier. But specific questions are bothering the president. Three "what ifs" are run with the results compared to the original forecast data. These "what ifs" involve:

1. Product cost changes.
2. Sales forecast changes.
3. Collections and payables assumptions changes.

Example 1—Product Cost Changes. Wood prices may increase substantially over the next year. The increases may be as much as 10 percent on plywood and 8 percent on trim and affect net income and the earnings goals of Hoffman Products. Materials costs from Schedule 1 and the new prices show:

| | **Original Forecast** | | | | | **"What If" Changes** | | |
| | | *JR EXEC* | | *EXEC* | | *New* | *JR EXEC* | *EXEC* |
	Price	*Quantity*	*Costs*	*Quantity*	*Costs*	*Price*	*Costs*	*Costs*
Materials:								
Plywood (sq. feet)	$0.275	12.00	$3.300	15.00	$4.125	$0.3025	$3.630	$4.538
Trim (feet)	0.085	15.00	1.275	18.00	1.530	0.0918	1.377	1.652
Materials total			$4.575		$5.655		$5.007	$6.190

The impacts of the changes on net income and on certain goals are:

	Original Forecast	"What If" Change	Percentage Change
Net income	$26,065	$20,553	(21.15%)
Goals:			
Profitability goal: Return on equity of 10%	9.04%	7.18%	(20.58%)
Product cost below 65% of sales price—JR EXEC	63.42%	64.56%	1.80%
Product cost below 65% of sales price—EXEC	63.26%	64.35%	1.72%

The 10 and 8 percent changes in wood materials costs translate into a more than 20 percent decrease in net income. The drop in net income causes the return on equity percentage to fall further below the 10 percent goal. Wood cost increases can be absorbed and still meet the goals. Cost to sales percentages are dangerously near the 65 percent management maximum. This "what if" approach can also be applied to labor wage negotiations, overhead cost increases, and marketing and administrative cost changes.

Example 2—Sales Forecast Changes.   For Hoffman Products to sell 13,800 units of JR EXEC and 5,600 units of EXEC, the Effective Speakers Society of America will need to increase orders by about 10 percent.   If economic conditions cause growth to be only 5 or 6 percent, sales could be 100 units less each quarter for each product. The president asks what will be the impacts of the smaller growth on net income and on the sales and earnings goals of Hoffman Products.   "What if" analysis provides the following information:

	Original Forecast	"What If" Change	Percentage Change
Units of sales (17,650 units sold in 1997)	19,400	18,600	(4.12%)
Net income	$26,065	$17,777	(31.80%)
Goals:			
Growth goal: Sales dollar growth of 15%	17.47%	12.35%	(29.31%)
Profitability goal: Return on equity of 10%	9.04%	6.25%	(30.86%)
Product cost below 65% of sales price—JR EXEC	63.42%	64.14%	1.14%
Product cost below 65% of sales price—EXEC	63.26%	63.93%	1.06%

The slower growth (5 percent instead of 10 percent) has a dramatic impact on profits.   Sales dollar growth drops to 12.35 percent, which is below the desired 15 percent growth goal. Net income drops by over 30 percent. Return on equity falls far below the 10 percent target to 6.25 percent. These numbers should concern management if a recession develops or ESSA has lower enrollment growth than planned. An interesting aspect is the increase in unit costs. With lower volumes, the activity bases for overhead application in the factory drop, causing increased manufacturing overhead rates or a large underapplied overhead. Again, as in Example 1, the unit costs are close to the 65 percent maximum.

Example 3—Collections and Payables Assumptions Changes.   Recent national economic conditions may make credit tighter. The president thinks ESSA chapters will pay Hoffman Products more slowly, thus changing the receivables collected in the month of sale assumption from 75 to 50 percent. To offset this, Hoffman Products could reduce the payment of its purchases in the month incurred—dropping the percentage from 60 to 50 percent without hurting its credit rating. The president wonders what this would do to Hoffman Product's cash-flow pattern. The results of the "what if" analysis are as follows:

	Original Forecast	"What If" Change	Total or Percentage Change
Annual total cash receipts minus disbursements	$ 2,975	$(45,699)	$(48,674)
Yearend investments and borrowings positions:			
Short-term investments	$ 0	$ 0	$ 0
Bank borrowings	0	45,000	45,000
Total change in cash position			$(45,000)
Goals:			
Capital: Total debt to equity below 25%	21.73%	37.74%	73.68%
Liquidity goal: Current ratio above 3:1	5.54:1	2.20:1	(60.29%)

The drain on cash is large, approaching $50,000 for the year. By yearend, no short-term investments will exist; and new bank borrowings will be $45,000. Receivables and payables will grow, but the biggest impact is moving from an excess cash position to a serious cash deficit. The current ratio falls by more than 60 percent and is below the acceptable goal level. If a credit crunch occurs, interest rates probably will also increase, causing interest expenses to grow. The president will want to study this forecast with great care.

"What if" analysis can be applied to any independent variable. Often obvious impacts show up; but surprising results also appear, particularly when multiple variable changes are examined.

SUMMARY

A master budget example was developed to show the integrative nature of the various budget schedules. These schedules were brought together as a complete set, as new forecast financial statements were built and balanced.

A major development over the past ten years is the computer power available for simulation and application of financial modeling. In developing a financial planning model, the master budget is an excellent example for understanding the interrelationships that describe the operating and financial functions and the organization's objectives, inputs, and outputs. The abilities to model the master budget and to test every controllable variable and assumption have tremendously increased the analyses opportunities during planning phases. Even testing goals and objectives for realism has increased budgeting believability for management. This chapter defined modeling, described its benefits, explained its elements, and illustrated the "what if" analytical power.

PROBLEM FOR REVIEW

Dupere Wholesalers is implementing a financial planning model to aid in its monthly and annual budgeting process. Tom Denomme, controller, has identified the following relationships among key planning variables.

1. Sales volume (in units) is increasing at the rate of 4 percent per month. The selling price is $25 per unit.

2. All sales are on credit. Cash collections are received 40 percent in the month of sale and 60 percent in the month after the sale.

3. Inventory is maintained at 30 percent of next month's sales forecast.

4. Purchases are paid 50 percent in the month of purchase and 50 percent in the month after purchase. Each unit costs $13.

5. The operating expenses are both variable and fixed. The variable expenses average 20 percent of each month's revenue. Fixed expenses, including depreciation of $30,000, total $65,000 per month. All expenses are paid in the month incurred.

The following notations have been defined by Tom:

S_t	= Volume for current month (units)		P	= Price per unit
$S\$_t$	= Revenue for current month (dollars)		G	= Growth rate
Pur_t	= Current period's purchases in units		C	= Cost per unit
$Pur\$_t$	= Current period's purchases in dollars		D	= Depreciation expense
CGS_t	= Cost of goods sold for current month		t	= Current month
NI_t	= Net income for current month		$t-1$	= Last month
CR_t	= Cash receipts for current month		$t-2$	= Two months ago
CD_t	= Cash disbursements for current month		$t+1$	= Next month
Co_1	= Percentage of sales collected in current month			
Co_2	= Percentage of sales collected in next month			
Py_1	= Percentage of purchases paid in current month			
Py_2	= Percentage of purchases paid in next month			
I_t	= Inventory at the end of current month			
EI%	= Inventory as a percentage of next month's sales			
VO%	= Variable operating expenses as a percentage of sales			
FO$	= Fixed operating expenses			

Required and Solution:

Using the defined notations, prepare a series of equations that may be used to calculate the budget variables listed.

1. Sales volume for the current month: $S_t = (1 + G) * S_{t-1}$

2. Revenue for current month: $S\$_t = P * S_t$

3. Purchases for current month (units):

    $P_t = S_t + I_t - I_{t-1}$; **where** $I_t = EI\% * S_{t+1}$ **and** $I_{t-1} = EI\% * S_t$

4. Purchases for current month (dollars): $Pur\$_t = C * Pur_t$

5. Cost of goods sold for current month: $CGS_t = C * S_t$

6. Net income for current month: $NI_t = S\$_t - CGS_t - (VO\% * S\$_t) - FO\$$

7. Cash receipts for current month: $CR_t = (Co_1 * S\$_t) + (Co_2 * S\$_{t-1})$

8. Cash disbursements for current month:

    $CD_t = (Py_1 * Pur\$_t) + (Py_2 * Pur\$_{t-1}) + (VO\% * S\$_t) + (FO\$ - D)$

TERMINOLOGY REVIEW

SUGGESTED READINGS

Benson, F. D., "Effective Operational Budgeting Techniques," *Corporate Accounting*, Summer 1985, pp. 3-12.

Block, L. J., S. Umapathy, and R. L. May, "Accounting and Behavior in Budgeting: A Literature Review," *Massachusetts CPA Review*, Summer 1984, pp. 22-28.

Collins, F., P. Munter, and D. W. Finn, "The Budgeting Games People Play," *Accounting Review*, January 1987, pp. 29-49.

Covaleski, M. A., and M. W. Dirsmith, "The Use of Budgetary Symbols in the Political Arena: An Historically Informed Field Study," *Accounting, Organizations, and Society*, Vol. 13, No. 1, 1988, pp. 1-24.

Gordon, L. A., and F. E. Sellers, "Accounting and Budgeting Systems: The Issue of Congruency," *Journal of Accounting and Public Policy*, Winter 1984, pp. 259-292.

Harwood, G. B., J. L. Pate, and A. Schneider, "Budgeting Decisions as a Function of Framing: An Application of Prospect Theory's Reflection Effect," *Management Accounting Research*, September 1991, pp. 161-170.

Kanodia, C., "Participative Budgets as Coordination and Motivational Devices," *Journal of Accounting Research*, Autumn 1993, pp. 172-189.

Walker, K. B., and C. E. Bain, "Sales Volume Forecasting: A Comparison of Management, Statistical, and Combined Approaches," *Journal of Management Accounting Research*, Fall 1989, pp. 119-135.

QUESTIONS FOR REVIEW AND DISCUSSION

1. Why do the formats suggested in Chapter 7 make the preparation of the schedules in the example in Chapter 8 easier to complete?

2. What independent and dependent variables are needed to create a production budget?

3. If Hoffman Products Company were a wholesaler and not a manufacturer, how would the master budget sequence as presented change?

4. If Hoffman Products Company provided interior design services and were not a manufacturer, how would the master budget sequence as presented change?

5. From the master budget example, identify the independent variables. Which schedules contain only dependent variables?

6. Why is it important that the balance sheet balance in preparing budgets?

7. Explain why preparing the cash-flow forecast requires that all operating and project budget schedules be completed first.

8. Explain the difference between budgeted manufacturing overhead spending and budgeted applied overhead.

9. Considering the master budgeting example, what steps could be taken to even out the effect of differences in the flow of cash over the year?

10. What does "what if" analysis mean?

11. In the Hoffman Products Company example, what are the approximate impacts of the following changes?

    (a) On accounts receivable, "what if" the price of EXEC decreased by $4 per unit?

    (b) On cash payments, "what if" the direct labor time per unit increased by 10 percent?

(c) On net income, "what if" sales commissions were eliminated and sales salaries were increased by $25,000?

(d) On short-term investments, "what if" the percentages of ending inventory to next month's needs are increased?

What other major related changes would you expect in each case?

12. In the Hoffman Products Company example, trace the following numbers back to independent variables:

(a) On Schedule 5, first-quarter ending inventory—12,195 square feet.

(b) On Schedule 6, third-quarter direct labor hours for JR EXEC—2,737.5 hours.

(c) On Schedule 8, second-quarter fringe benefits expenses—$16,380.

(d) On Schedule 11, third-quarter payment of prior quarter's purchases—$9,402.

13. Describe the primary components of the three basic elements of a financial planning model.

14. What factors cause a computer to be essential for financial modeling in today's business environment?

15. How can a simulation model be used to create a better budget?

16. A model in its most basic sense is a meaningful abstraction of reality. Explain how this concept applies to financial planning models.

17. A financial planning model should help management perform its functions better. Give an example of how a financial planning model could be helpful to a bank. To a travel agency. To an automobile manufacturer.

18. From a "what if" perspective, could the pattern of collecting accounts receivable affect planned cash disbursements? Explain.

19. Considering the "what if" examples presented in the chapter, what other "what ifs" could you suggest, and why would they be important?

20. John Gaetz, controller of a local hospital, said the following about financial modeling at a recent meeting of the Tri-City Accountants Society: "The first financial model was A = L + E." Comment.

E XERCISES

8-1. Purchases and Cash Payments. A production plan by quarter for Storr Company is:

First quarter..........	24,000 units	Third quarter......	32,000 units
Second quarter	30,000	Fourth quarter.....	42,000

Four units of materials are used in producing each unit of product. Each unit of materials costs $0.60. Ending materials inventory is to be equal to 25 percent of production requirements for the next quarter. This requirement was met at the beginning of the year. Production for the first quarter following the budget year is estimated at 28,000 units. Accounts payable for materials purchased is estimated at $38,400 at the beginning of the current budget year. Forecast accounts payable at the end of the quarter should equal 40 percent of the purchases during the quarter.

Required:

1. Determine the units of materials to be purchased each quarter.

2. Determine the cost of materials purchases by quarter.

3. Estimate the payments to be made each quarter for materials.

8-2. Purchases and Collections.   Murphy Neat Shirts Co. sells shirts and is budgeting for 1998. The beginning accounts receivable, inventory (at cost), and accounts payable balances and partial 1998 sales data are:

Beginning balances (1/1/98):

Accounts receivable	$ 200,000
Inventory (at cost).	150,000
Accounts payable	100,000

1998 Data:	**First Quarter**	**Second Quarter**
Sales	$600,000	$800,000
Cost of sales	360,000	480,000

Required:

1. Quarterly ending inventory should be 60 percent of the next quarter's expected sales volume. Find the budgeted purchases of shirts during the first quarter.

2. Sales are all on credit, and 80 percent is collected in the quarter of sale. The remainder is collected in the next quarter. Find the budgeted cash collections for the second quarter.

8-3. Revised Production Budget.   By mid-September, the sales manager of Pillai Supplies, Inc. realized that the original forecast for the fourth quarter would have to be revised. The original and revised forecasts appear as follows:

	Original Forecast	**Revised Forecast**
October	160,000 units	150,000 units
November	220,000	200,000
December	270,000	230,000
January	300,000	240,000

Normally, 200 units can be produced in one hour of machine time. An inventory equal to 20 percent of next month's estimated sales should be on hand at the end of each month, and the company plans to have 32,000 units in inventory on September 30.

Required (Use of spreadsheet software is recommended.):

1. Prepare production and machine-hour budgets for the three months of the fourth quarter using the original sales forecast.

2. Revise the production and machine-hour budgets for Part (1) using the revised forecast.

3. How many hours of production machine time can be released each month for other work because of the expected reduction in sales?

8-4. Forecast Cash Payments.   January 1 actual inventory for Stock & Stem Company was $5,000, and payables were $3,000. Cost of goods sold figures for January, February, and March were $30,000, $35,000, and $40,000, respectively. The purchases policy says that ending inventory should be 20 percent of next month's cost of sales. Of purchases, 40 percent is paid in the current month and the remainder in the next month.

Required:

Find the forecast cash payments for February.

8-5. Direct Materials Purchases and Cash Payments.   The Campbell Company prepared a production budget for the first months of 1999 as follows:

January	18,000 units
February	16,000
March	20,000
April	24,000

Two units of Material 03 are required for each pound of product at a cost per unit of $1.50. One unit of Material 08 is required for each pound of product at a cost per unit of $5.

Forty percent of both materials needed in a month must be purchased in the preceding month. Thirty percent of the materials cost is paid during the month of purchase, and the other 70 percent is paid in the following month. Accounts payable at the beginning of January for materials purchases is estimated to be $44,000.

Required:

1. Determine the number of units to be purchased each month.
2. Determine the cost of purchases by month.
3. Prepare a budget of cash payments for materials by month.

8-6. Labor Cost Budget.   Coats Cartons, Inc. manufactures two basic product lines—Sturdee and Rain-Proof. Past experience has shown that 10 units of Sturdee can be produced per labor hour and 8 units of Rain-Proof per labor hour. Direct labor is paid at the rate of $12 per hour, and each employee works approximately 400 hours of productive time each quarter. Production has been estimated for 1999 as follows:

	Sturdee Units	*Rain-Proof Units*
First quarter	12,600	12,000
Second quarter	16,200	9,000
Third quarter	14,400	15,000
Fourth quarter	14,400	18,000

Required:

1. Prepare a schedule showing the total direct labor hours needed each quarter to meet the production requirements. Convert hours to dollars.
2. How many employees will be needed each quarter?

8-7. Purchases and Cash Receipts.   Olympia Candies is preparing a budget for the second quarter of the current calendar year. The March ending inventory of merchandise was $106,000, which was higher than expected. The company prefers to carry ending inventory amounting to the expected sales volume of the next two months. Purchases of merchandise are paid half in the month of purchase and half in the month following purchase, and the balance due on accounts payable at the end of March was $24,000. Budgeted sales are as follows:

April	$ 40,000	July	$ 72,000
May	48,000	August	56,000
June	60,000	September	60,000

Required:

1. Assume that a 25 percent gross profit margin is budgeted. Prepare a budget schedule that shows the following for April, May, and June:
   (a) Cost of goods sold.
   (b) Purchases required.
   (c) Cash payments for merchandise.
2. Assume that the accounts receivable balance on April 1 was $35,000 and that three-fourths of all customers pay in the month of sale and one-fourth in the month following the sale. Prepare a budget showing the cash receipts from accounts receivable for April, May, and June.

8-8. Cash Collections and Receivables.   Past experience has demonstrated that 70 percent of the net sales billed in a month by Henry Company is collected during the month, 20 percent is collected in the following month, and 10 percent is collected in the second following month.

A record of estimated net sales by month is given as follows:

1998 November	$450,000	1999 March	$500,000
December	460,000	April	550,000
1999 January	480,000	May	600,000
February	420,000	June	700,000

On January 1, 1999, the forecast net accounts receivable balance is $183,000.

Required:

Prepare a schedule of expected collections on accounts receivable for each of the first six months of 1999, and show the estimated balance of net accounts receivable at the end of each month.

8-9. Cash Receipts From Sales.   Ponytail Productions has forecast revenues as follows:

July	$67,000	October	$75,000
August	69,000	November	80,000
September	72,000	December	90,000

The controller has maintained a record of collections and has estimated the following pattern:

Month of sale	60%
First month after sale	30
Second month after sale	8
Uncollected	2

Required (Use of spreadsheet software is recommended.):

1. Calculate the amount of cash receipts the company is budgeting by month in the fourth quarter.

2. If the collection pattern changed to 40, 40, 15, and 5 percent, respectively, what is the impact on fourth quarter cash receipts?

8-10. Budget Schedules and Changes.   Gardner Hardware provided these budget data:

Forecast Sales for 1998		Balance Sheet Data, December 31, 1997	
January	$60,000	Cash	$ 8,000
February	50,000	Accounts receivable:	
March	80,000	From November sales	16,000
April	90,000	From December sales	50,000
		Inventory	54,000
		Accounts payable	37,000

Other data are as follows:

(a) Sales are on credit, with 60 percent of sales collected in the month after sale and 40 percent in the second month after sale.

(b) Cost of sales is 60 percent of sales.

(c) Other variable costs are 10 percent of sales, paid in the month incurred.

(d) Inventories are to be 150 percent of next month's sales forecast.

(e) Purchases are paid in the month after purchase.

(f) Fixed expenses of $3,000 are paid each month.

Required:

1. Create the budget schedules needed to support a cash-flow forecast for the first three months of 1998.

2. Prepare a budgeted income statement for the first quarter of 1998.

8-11. Production Cost Budget.   A manufacturing budget for 1999 was prepared for Sequeira Metals, of Barcelona, Spain, and is as follows:

First quarter.	48,000 units	Third quarter	64,000 units
Second quarter	56,000	Fourth quarter	60,000

Budgeted cost estimates in Spanish pesetas are based on the previous year's actual costs. Direct materials cost per unit is estimated at P600. Direct labor cost is budgeted at P400 per unit, and factory overhead is to be applied at 200 percent of direct labor cost. Factory overhead spending is based on a cost function of P200 per unit plus P36,000,000 per quarter. Of the quarter's production, 75 percent is sold in the current quarter, and 25 percent is sold in the next quarter. December 31, 1998, inventory is 12,000 units.

Required:
1. Prepare a schedule showing production costs for each quarter and for 1999.
2. Compute estimated cost of goods sold for each quarter and for 1999.
3. Analyze factory overhead.

8-12. Cash Payments for Operations. Drescher Paper Products, Inc. averages a gross profit of 30 percent. Sales for August were $500,000. The beginning inventory balance for August was $15,000 higher than the ending inventory balance. The accounts payable balance was $45,000 at the beginning of August and $52,000 at month end. The selling and administrative expenses are paid in the month incurred. Such expenses follow the formula of 5 percent of sales plus $25,000 per month, including depreciation expense of $10,000.

Required:
Compute the cash payments for operations during August.

8-13. Estimated Income Statement. Ridgway Appliances, Inc. prepared a budget for 1998 by quarters. Budget data appear as follows:

	Budgeted Sales	Materials Purchases	Beginning Materials Inventory
First quarter	$ 860,000	$ 280,000	$ 75,000
Second quarter . . .	940,000	360,000	65,000
Third quarter	990,000	400,000	50,000
Fourth quarter . . .	960,000	300,000	45,000
First quarter, 1999 .	—	—	40,000

Ridgway is trying to reduce inventories. Direct labor is budgeted at $140,000 each quarter with factory overhead estimated at 200 percent of direct labor costs. Selling and general expenses are budgeted at $115,000 each quarter. The amount of finished goods is estimated to be $140,000 at the beginning of the year. Finished goods inventory is to be decreased by $10,000 per quarter.

Required:
1. Prepare an estimated income statement for each quarter and for the year. Income tax is estimated at 40 percent of income before income tax.
2. If the inventory reductions did not occur and other given amounts remain the same, what changes might you see in 1998 operating results?

8-14. Adequacy of Cash Flow With "What Ifs." Jennifer Victor is preparing a budget of cash receipts and disbursements for Gourmet Food Services, Inc. Some sales are for cash, and the remainder is billed on a contract basis. Sales for April to August are:

	Cash Sales	Billed Sales	Total Sales
April	$ 65,000	$40,000	$105,000
May	72,000	46,000	118,000
June	84,000	68,000	152,000
July	88,000	72,000	160,000
August	86,000	70,000	156,000

Of the billed sales, 65 percent is collected during the month of sale; and the other 35 percent is collected in the next month. Food costs amounting to 75 percent of sales must be paid during the month of sales. Monthly operating costs are $24,000. The cash balance at May 1 amounted to $7,000. If the cash balance is over $20,000 on August 31, Victor and the other shareholders will receive the excess as dividends.

Required (Use of spreadsheet software is recommended.):

1. Prepare a budget of cash receipts and disbursements for each month, May to August, inclusive.

2. Compute the amount, if any, that can be paid in dividends at the end of August.

3. What is the impact on possible dividend payments in the following situations?

(a) "What if" competitive pressures cause food costs to increase to 80 percent of sales.

(b) "What if" collections of billed sales slow to 50 percent in the month of sale and 50 percent in the next month.

8-15. Budgeted Balance Sheet. The balance sheet for Griffith Stores, Inc. at December 31, 1998, is:

Assets:		Liabilities and Equity:	
Cash	$ 82,000	Accounts payable.	$ 62,000
Accounts receivable	112,000		
Inventory	136,000	Capital stock	300,000
Building and fixtures, net	358,000	Retained earnings	326,000
Total assets	$688,000	Total liabilities & equity	$688,000

Cash receipts for the year are collections on accounts receivable amounting to $846,000. Cash payments are budgeted at $838,000. Included in those payments is $126,000 for various expenses that do not flow through accounts payable. Credits to accounts payable for the year are estimated at $715,000, all merchandise purchases. All cash payments are for expenses or purchases. Depreciation expense is $75,000. Net sales are estimated at $930,000. The inventory of merchandise is expected to increase to $147,000 by the end of the year.

Required:

From the information given, prepare a budgeted balance sheet at December 31, 1999. Prove the retained earnings balance by computing the net income. Income tax is estimated at 40 percent and will be paid after December 31, 1999.

8-16. Expense Budgeting. An expense budget for next year is being prepared by Ballard Testing Services. Past studies show the expense behavior pattern as:

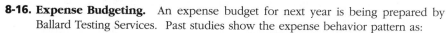

Expense:	Per Testing Hour	Per Test	Per Year
Payroll taxes	$3.25		
Support labor	2.00		$42,000
Disposable test materials		$ 2.00	
Supplies		1.25	
Heat, light, and power		1.50	22,000
Supervision			86,000
Employee benefits			60,000
Taxes and insurance			20,000
Depreciation			10,000

A wide variety of tests is performed. Some take as much as an hour to perform. Most take 10 minutes. An average of 4 tests per hour appears to be a good measure of productivity and for planning.

Required:

1. Budget expenses for the first quarter of the year based on the following activity levels:

	January	February	March
Number of testing hours	2,000	1,800	2,100
Number of tests planned	8,000	7,400	8,200

2. Calculate the planned cost of a test for each month.
3. What alternatives exist for attaching the annual costs to tests?

8-17. Managerial Behavior and Budget Ethics. Stoller Corporation has seen a new revision of the budget system each year for the past five years. Bonuses followed strong budget performances. The following are changes made during the past few years:

Change 1: One year top management felt that, since wages were 60 percent of total expenses, the budget should simply focus on keeping next year's headcounts equal or below the current year's level. Most managers did this by shifting work to outside contractors.

Change 2: Concern over customer service caused top management to budget the number of back orders issued because an item was not available from existing inventory. A trip to Tahiti was given to managers with zero actual back orders.

Change 3: Because corporate expenses were viewed as being too high, the president decided to allocate all home office expenses to the nine divisions. Each division head budgeted down to "net income" and was evaluated on the comparison of actual to planned "net income."

Change 4: Also, at the final budget approval stage for the last several years, the president forced each division to reduce its total expenses by an even five percent across the board. This year, the president increased the across-the-board cuts to 10 percent.

Required:

Comment on Stoller Corporation's approach to budgeting and the possible impacts each change might have on the budget process and managers' behavior.

P ROBLEMS

8-18. Payments for Materials. Emory Mills, Inc. is hard pressed for cash to meet scheduled payments for materials and other costs. Materials are purchased as needed for production. A month is required for production because of an aging process. Thus, production starts in Month 1 and ends in Month 2; sales occur in Month 3. In the production operation, a natural loss of materials occurs. The final output is equal to only 80 percent of the input. Sales by month have been budgeted as follows:

June	200,000 units	September	280,000 units
July	240,000	October	300,000
August	320,000	November	320,000

Each unit is sold for $6.50. Half of the amount billed is collected during the month sold, with the other half being collected during the next month. Production materials cost $0.65 per gallon, and 4 gallons are needed to produce each unit of finished product. Costs of operation, other than materials costs, amount to $500,000 each month and must be paid during the month incurred. Purchases are paid in the following month.

Required:

1. Determine the cost of materials purchases for July, August, and September.

2. Compute the expected cash inflow from customers and subtract estimated disbursements for July, August, and September.

3. Can the company meet the demands for cash each month? Comment.

8-19. Expenses and Cash Disbursements.   Danell Andersen, the treasurer of Danish Ancient Studies Association, is planning an expense budget for 1999 in Danish krone. Rent for the office is expected to amount to DKr6,000 for the year and will be paid in a lump sum during January 1999. Insurance costing DKr840 for the year is to be prepaid in January for the entire year. Salaries for the employees have been budgeted at DKr72,000 for the year and are evenly distributed throughout the year.

An outside service has been engaged to obtain speakers and to schedule visits to archaeological digs during the year. The entire cost for the year, estimated at DKr36,000, must be paid during September. It is estimated that the services will be distributed throughout the year as follows:

First quarter	DKr 3,000
Second quarter	12,000
Third quarter	15,000
Fourth quarter	6,000

Telephone and postage have been budgeted at DKr600 each quarter with payment being made during the quarter. Travel expenses for the year of DKr6,000 will be paid during the second quarter with the cost being equally divided between the second and third quarters of the year.

Depreciation on office furniture and various implements has been estimated at DKr600 for the year. Supplies costing DKr300 are to be used each quarter with payment for the entire year being budgeted for February.

Required:

1. Prepare an accrual expense budget for Danell Andersen for 1999 by quarters.

2. Convert the expense budget into a cash payments budget for 1999 by quarters.

8-20. Budgeted Cost of Goods Manufactured.   Saleem Plastic Products had an inventory of 25,000 units of finished product on January 1. Sales forecasts for the first six months are as follows:

January	40,000 units	April	70,000 units
February	55,000	May	60,000
March	50,000	June	70,000

Saleem maintains a finished goods inventory equal to 40 percent of the forecast sales of the next month. Each unit of product requires 3 pounds of raw materials at $5 per pound. The budgeted direct labor cost is $8 per hour, and each finished unit requires 30 minutes. Variable factory overhead is 40 percent of raw materials costs. Fixed factory overhead, including depreciation of $10,000, totals $90,000 per month and is applied using units. Normal volume is 60,000 units per month.

Required (Use of spreadsheet software is recommended.):

1. Determine the total cost of producing a unit.

2. Prepare budgeted gross profits for January, February, March, and April. Assume that a unit sells for $32.

3. Comment on the following:

(a) "What if" finished goods inventory level is only 20 percent of next month's sales?

(b) "What if" normal capacity is 50,000 units per month?

8-21. Cash Forecasting.   Mr. Otley started a used computer store in London and is looking at cash flows very carefully. He collected the following budget figures for 1998 in pounds:

	12/31/97	*12/31/98*		*12/31/97*	*12/31/98*
Cash	£ 4,000	£ 7,000	Accounts payable	£19,000	£26,000
Accounts receivable .	12,000	20,000	Wages payable	4,000	6,000
Inventory	40,000	30,000	Income taxes payable .	10,000	6,000
Prepaid expenses . . .	5,000	7,000	Interest payable	2,000	1,000

1998 Income Statement

Sales	£100,000
Cost of goods sold	75,000
Gross profit	£ 25,000
Operating expenses	11,000
Operating income	£ 14,000
Interest expense	3,000
Income before taxes	£ 11,000
Taxes expense	5,000
Net income	£ 6,000

(Including depreciation expense of £3,000)

Required:

Prepare a cash forecast for 1998 for Otley's budgeted operations.

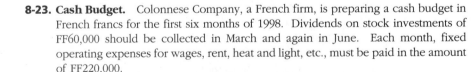

8-22. Cash Flows and "What If."   M. W. Cope, a member of the board of directors of Bryja Markets, Inc., is concerned about the ability of the company to repay a loan in the amount of $250,000 that matures on June 30, 1999. In addition to the principal of the loan, the company must pay interest of $50,000.

The cash balance at January 1, 1999, is $82,000. Sales for December 1998 through June 1999 are budgeted as follows:

	Net Sales		*Net Sales*
December 1998	$ 236,000	April	$170,000
January 1999	137,000	May	156,000
February	142,000	June	148,000
March	182,000		

Cash sales each month are equal to approximately 30 percent of net sales. Collections on accounts receivable are expected as follows:

> 60 percent collected during the month of sale
> 40 percent collected in the following month

Total cash disbursements are estimated at $115,000 each month.

Required (Use of spreadsheet software is recommended.):

1. Prepare a cash budget for each month and in total for the six months of 1999.

2. Will the company be able to pay the loan with interest and still maintain a cash balance of no less than $60,000 on June 30? Explain.

3. If actual sales are 10 percent lower than the forecast each month while cash expenses drop by only $5,000 per month, what will happen to Bryja's ability to pay off the loan and keep the cash balance at the desired level?

4. If the sales and expenses fall as in Part (3) and collections patterns change to 40 percent collected in the current month and 60 percent in the following month, what will happen to the Bryja's cash situation?

8-23. Cash Budget.   Colonnese Company, a French firm, is preparing a cash budget in French francs for the first six months of 1998. Dividends on stock investments of FF60,000 should be collected in March and again in June. Each month, fixed operating expenses for wages, rent, heat and light, etc., must be paid in the amount of FF220,000.

Collections on accounts receivable are estimated as follows:

> 60 percent collected in month of sale
> 25 percent collected in month following the sale
> 15 percent collected in second month following the sale

Payments for merchandise purchased are scheduled so that 70 percent of the payments are made in the month of purchase with the balance paid in the following month. The cash balance is estimated at FF175,000 for January 1, 1998.

Estimated net sales and purchases by month are as follows:

	Net Sales	Purchases		Net Sales	Purchases
November 1997 ..	FF560,000	FF320,000	March	FF 650,000	FF 350,000
December	550,000	380,000	April	580,000	280,000
January 1998	640,000	420,000	May	460,000	260,000
February........	700,000	400,000	June	520,000	260,000

Income tax payments of FF100,000 and FF150,000 are to be made in February and June, respectively. A bond payable principal payment of FF80,000 will be made in February with interest of FF12,000 added. Assume that interest expense is 12 percent annually or 1 percent per month on the loans outstanding and that monthly interest is paid when accrued.

Required:

Prepare a budget of cash receipts and cash payments for each month. Since a minimum cash balance of FF150,000 must be available at the end of each month, identify the months, if any, when short-term loans will be required and the amounts of the loans. Also, indicate months, if any, when short-term loans can be repaid.

8-24. Interpreting Overhead Budget Data. The following data come from a manufacturing overhead section of a master budget for Reed Products:

Manufacturing Overhead Flexible Budget:

	Activity Levels in Units		
	6,500	7,000	7,500
Variable overhead expenses ($1.50 per unit)	$ 9,750	$ 10,500	$ 11,250
Fixed overhead expenses ($10,500 per quarter)	10,500	10,500	10,500
Total flexible overhead budget	$ 20,250	$ 21,000	$ 21,750
Variable overhead rate per unit		$ 1.50	
Fixed overhead rate per unit		1.50	
Manufacturing overhead rate per unit		$ 3.00	

Manufacturing Overhead Spending Budget by Quarter:

	Q - 1	Q - 2	Q - 3	Q - 4	Total
Budgeted volume (units)	6,800	6,500	6,900	7,400	27,600
Budgeted spending:					
Variable overhead expenses ...	$ 10,200	$ 9,750	$10,350	$11,100	$41,400
Fixed overhead expenses	10,500	10,500	10,500	10,500	42,000
Total overhead expenses ...	$ 20,700	$20,250	$20,850	$21,600	$83,400
Budgeted applied:					
Variable overhead applied	$ 10,200	$ 9,750	$10,350	$11,100	$41,400
Fixed overhead applied	10,200	9,750	10,350	11,100	41,400
Total overhead applied	$ 20,400	$19,500	$20,700	$22,200	$82,800
Overapplied or (underapplied) .	$ (300)	$ (750)	$ (150)	$ 600	$ (600)

Required:

1. What was the apparent normal volume? Explain how you know this.
2. Explain the overapplied or underapplied overhead variance for each quarter and for the year. Why is it underapplied for the year?
3. Based on the data and your knowledge of flexible budgeting, what is Reed Products expected to spend on manufacturing overhead for the year?

8-25. Working Capital Needs and Short-Term Loans.   Every year Blue Knob, Inc. has operated at about the same level, but sales vary substantially by season. As a result, the company needs short-term borrowings which are repaid when the cash position improves. Key month-end balances are given below:

	Cash	Accounts Receivable	Inventories	Accounts Payable
December 1998 actual	$100,000	$ 80,000	$200,000	$190,000
January 1999	90,000	100,000	240,000	220,000
February	70,000	110,000	280,000	170,000
March	40,000	150,000	250,000	140,000
April	30,000	250,000	190,000	100,000
May	70,000	275,000	110,000	80,000
June	120,000	160,000	80,000	70,000

A target cash balance of $100,000 each month is desired for transaction purposes. Cash in excess of that amount is to be invested in U.S. treasury bills, and loans are to be made as necessary. A short-term borrowing line of credit has been arranged with Blue Knob's lead commercial bank.

Required:

Assume that at December 31, 1998, the balance sheet shows no short-term investments or short-term borrowings. No major balance changes are expected in other accounts during the next six months. Plan borrowings and investments by month for the first half of 1999.

8-26. Product Cost Budget.   The management of Ingham Glass Products is aware of increased competition in the industry and has taken steps to improve cost control. Product costs on a per unit basis for last year are as follows:

	Product Lines		
	Red	White	Blue
Direct materials	$ 6	$ 3	$ 5
Direct labor	3	2	3
Applied factory overhead	3	2	3
Total unit cost	$12	$ 7	$11
Units produced last year	300,000	240,000	340,000

The direct materials are manufactured by another division of the company, which agreed to lower its price by 10 percent for this year. Direct labor cost will increase from $12 to $15 an hour, but increased productivity is planned. The revision of the production process will make it possible to manufacture 6 units of Red per hour, 8 units of White, or 10 units of Blue. Fixed overhead cost will, however, increase by $100,000 a year.

This year's planned volumes are the same as last year's actual output. Last year the company operated at a normal activity level set at 200,000 direct labor hours with budgeted and actual factory overhead costs of $2,400,000. This year, normal activity is to be reset at 150,000 direct labor hours with factory overhead amounting to $2,100,000 (including the fixed overhead increase).

Required:

1. Determine the cost of production this year in total and on a per unit basis.
2. Compute the expected cost savings in total. Comment on the impact of the changes.

8-27. Estimated Financial Statements.   Ranval Fasteners, Inc. has budgeted operations for each quarter of 1998 as follows:

	Net Sales	Production Costs	Operating Expenses
First quarter	$750,000	$480,000	$145,000
Second quarter	800,000	500,000	160,000
Third quarter	850,000	520,000	170,000
Fourth quarter	900,000	500,000	175,000
First quarter, 1999	800,000	520,000	170,000

Forecast finished goods inventory is planned as follows:

March 31	$135,000	September 30	$140,000
June 30	130,000	December 31	125,000

All production costs and operating expenses with the exception of depreciation are to be paid during the quarter incurred. Each quarter, depreciation expenses included in production costs and in operating expenses are $40,000 and $20,000, respectively.

Collections on sales are planned at 60 percent during the quarter of the sale and 40 percent during the quarter following the sale. Materials are purchased as needed in production and are not held in inventory. Income tax is estimated at 40 percent of income before income tax and is paid during the subsequent quarter. Dividends of $100,000 are to be paid in June and again in December if covered by sufficient profits. No dividends will be paid if the profits for the year are expected to be less than $300,000.

A summary balance sheet at December 31, 1997, shows:

Cash	$ 115,000	Income taxes payable	$ 55,000
Accounts receivable	280,000		
Inventory	120,000	Capital stock	1,500,000
Net plant and equipment . .	1,450,000	Retained earnings	410,000
Total assets	$1,965,000	Total liabilities & equity	$1,965,000

Required:

1. Prepare an estimated income statement for each quarter and for the year.

2. Prepare a balance sheet at the end of each quarter of 1998.

3. Comment on changes in assumptions that might endanger the dividend payments.

8-28. Financial Planning Model. Hool Contract Engineering would like to develop a financial planning model to aid in its monthly and annual financial planning. Bob Johannes, accountant, has identified the following relationships among the key planning variables for 1998:

1. Revenues are constrained by the number of skilled computer-aided design (CAD) engineers employed by Hool. Each engineer works 2,000 hours per year and has a billing time ratio of 75 percent. All available billable time is utilized. Salaries, billing rates, and headcounts by skill levels are:

	Salary	Billing Rate	Number Employed
Professional grade 1	$90,000	$120 per hour	20
Professional grade 2	60,000	90 per hour	30
General design engineer	45,000	80 per hour	15
Administration	70,000		10

2. Customers are billed during the first week of the next month for engineering time. About 75 percent of the customers pay by the end of the billing month. The remainder pays during the following month.

3. Equipment and software lease costs are forecast to be $1,890,000 annually but are paid monthly.

4. Other annual administrative expenses include cash expenses of $500,000 plus $10,000 per employee and 10 percent of total salaries. Per employee costs are paid one month in advance (i.e., health insurance). The percentage of salaries expenses (i.e., payroll taxes) is paid in the month following the payroll expense.

5. Income taxes are 40 percent.

Required:

Using symbols similar to those shown in the Problem for Review in this chapter, prepare a series of equations that can represent the following relationships:

1. Engineering revenue for the current month.

2. Costs of engineers for the current month.

3. Total payroll for the current month.

4. Cash inflow from customers for the current month (dollars).

5. Cash outflow for all nonpayroll administrative expenses for the current month.

6. Net income before taxes for the current month.

7. Income taxes for the current month.

8. Ending cash account balance for the current month.

Use subscripts of t for the current month, $t-1$ for last month, $t+1$ for next month, and $t+2$ for two months after the current month.

8-29. Budgeted Savings—Materials and Labor.   Paul Horton is concerned about losses of materials in production, especially since the prices of materials may increase. Data with respect to materials for one product line are:

	Quantity Per Unit in Final Product	Materials Price Per Pound
Material A	24 pounds	$ 0.12
Material B	12 pounds	0.08
Material C	12 pounds	0.08

The product weight yield is 75 percent of the input for all three materials.

The labor rate is $14.40 an hour, and 12 finished units are made each hour. Variable overhead is $2 per unit of product. Fixed overhead is budgeted at $2,700,000 for the next quarter. The company includes only variable costs as product costs.

Horton believes that the yield from materials should be increased to 80 percent of materials inputs. Also, with some changes in production methods, 15 finished units could be made each hour. During the next quarter, the company plans to produce and sell 1,800,000 finished units at a price of $14 per unit.

Required (Use of spreadsheet software is recommended.):

1. Prepare a budgeted income statement for the manufacturing operation under present conditions without savings in materials or labor time.

2. Comment on the following:

   (a) "What if" Horton achieves the planned savings in materials yield?

   (b) "What if" Horton implements the planned labor saving changes?

   (c) "What if" Horton achieves the planned savings in materials yield and the planned labor saving changes?

8-30. Comprehensive Operating Budget.   Shell Environmental Systems, Inc. distributes portable air purification and drinking water treatment systems. Casey Heydari, controller, is in the process of budgeting operations by quarter for the upcoming year of 1998.

The air purifier unit sells for $500, and sales volume is expected to grow by 5 percent quarterly over the next two years. A water treatment unit sells for $200, and sales volume will grow by 3 percent quarterly for the next 18 months. Selling expenses are budgeted at 20 percent of total sales dollars plus advertising expenses of $40,000 per quarter. General and administrative expenses are approximately 3 percent of sales plus $50,000 per quarter. The income tax rate is 40 percent.

Purchase costs are $275 per unit for an air purifier and $130 per unit for a water treatment system. The company sold, during the fourth quarter of 1997, 1,000 air purifiers and 2,000 water treatment units. The ending inventory for 1997 was 50 percent of forecast sales for the first quarter of 1998 and should remain at that same percentage. The forecast unit costs for 1998 are the same as those experienced in 1997.

Required (Use of spreadsheet software is recommended.):

1. Assist Casey in the budget review process by preparing spreadsheet schedules to show forecast 1998 net income by quarter and in total. (Round sales units to nearest whole unit.)
2. Comment on each of the following changes to the 1998 forecast:
   (a) Sales growth rates of only 2 percent per quarter for both products.
   (b) Per unit product costs of $295 for air purifiers and $110 for water treatment systems.
   (c) Selling expenses cost function of 10 percent of sales plus $100,000 per quarter.

8-31. Forecasting Income and Cash.   Newton Company recently (late December 1997) negotiated a $100,000 bank loan from the 3rd National Bank of Cincinnati. As part of the loan agreement, the bank requires a cash-flow forecast for the current year to help determine whether Newton can repay the loan. The following December 31, 1997, data are available:

Assets:		*Liabilities & Equities:*	
Cash	$ 15,000	Accounts payable	$ 56,000
Accounts receivable	110,000	Wages payable	15,000
Inventory	100,000	Bank loan	100,000
Equipment	600,000	Capital stock	250,000
Accumulated depreciation	(250,000)	Retained earnings	154,000
Total assets	$ 575,000	Total liabilities & equities . . .	$ 575,000

Other data relating to 1998 include:

(a) Sales are expected to be $1,000,000. Accounts receivable at yearend is expected to be $140,000.

(b) Cost of goods sold is expected to be $400,000, and yearend inventory is expected to be $150,000.

(c) Accounts payable is expected to increase by $15,000.

(d) Wages payable is expected to be $22,000 at yearend, and the wages expense is expected to be $230,000.

(e) Depreciation expense will be $50,000.

(f) Other expenses, all paid in cash, are expected to be $95,000, including interest on the loan.

(g) Cash expenditures for plant and equipment are expected to be $160,000.

(h) Newton expects to pay a dividend of $40,000.

Required:

1. Calculate the forecast net income for 1998.
2. What is the anticipated cash provided by operations in 1998? Is this cash flow adequate to meet the bank's expectation of loan repayment? Comment.

8-32. Ethical Use of Modeling.   Stu Williams, a personal financial planning consultant, uses a "personal wealth builder" financial model to help evaluate his clients' current financial positions and desired retirement and estate goals. Most clients are relatively naive about financial matters. He represents a national life insurance company, a set of mutual fund companies, and other investment programs such as real estate and energy partnerships, precious metals, and annuities. He is properly licensed to provide counsel and to sell these products. He derives the majority of his income from insurance and mutual fund sales. He also does personal advising on a fee-only basis, a minor part of his business.

Stu's model has numerous assumptions built in to allow quick evaluation of a person's wealth potential given that person's current investment program and income levels. Stu knows about these assumptions, many of which he can change given the client situation and need. Much data must be provided by the client, mostly current and historical data and some forecast or desired future needs and goals. From the model comes a set of suggestions for financial planning. These suggestions identify (1) serious gaps in current financial protection, such as disability insurance and accidental death coverage; (2) changes in current investments to increase rates of return or safety; (3) actions needed to achieve near-term financial goals, such as paying for college tuition; (4) retirement planning to ensure adequate income and financial safety to enjoy the "golden years;" and (5) estate planning to ensure that the client's heirs receive their maximum entitlements.

Required:

Stu has found that the "personal wealth builder" financial model has great credibility with clients. They see it as a "black box" that provides financial answers to difficult questions. Identify possible ethical problems with using this model in Stu's normal client contracts. Give suggestions to Stu about how he can assure his clients of a fair evaluation.

8-33. Financial Planning Model. For a number of years, Brugge Company of Brussels, Belgium, has had difficulty in budgeting its monthly income statement and cash flows. As an outside consultant, you have been hired by the controller to develop a rudimentary financial planning model that will lead to a budgeted monthly income statement and cash receipts and cash disbursements schedules. Upon investigation, you find the following relationships:

(a) Sales revenue is growing at 0.5 percent per month.

(b) Sixty percent of each month's sales are for cash; the remaining 40 percent are credit sales.

(c) Credit sales are collected at 50 percent in the month of sale, 45 percent in the month after the sale, and 5 percent in the second month after the sale.

(d) Cost of goods sold averages 75 percent of sales.

(e) Purchases in units each month equal the forecast sales units for the next month.

(f) Seventy percent of purchases are paid in the month of purchase, with half of these qualifying for a 2 percent cash discount. The remaining 30 percent is paid in the following month.

(g) The monthly operating expenses are 1 percent of monthly sales revenue plus fixed costs in Belgian francs of BF20,000, of which BF2,000 is depreciation. These expenses are paid in the month incurred.

(h) Income taxes are ignored on a monthly basis.

Required:

Prepare a series of equations, based on the foregoing relationships, that will allow the company to budget net income and cash flow. Define independent and dependent variables by symbols or abbreviations. Use subscripts to indicate time periods, such as $_t$ for the current month, $_{t-1}$ for the prior month, and $_{t+1}$ for the next month.

8-34. Estimated Cash Flow.   The controller of Vardallas Services, Inc. observes that accounts receivable are expected to decrease by $47,000 from March 31, 1998, to June 30, 1998.   In preparation for increased activity in the summer months, however, inventory of materials and supplies will increase by $62,000.   Also, accounts payable will likely increase by $38,000.

Early in July, short-term loans of $150,000 must be paid along with the regular quarterly dividend of $0.40 per share on 60,000 outstanding shares of stock.   Plans have been made to acquire new office equipment at a cost of $38,000, with payment to be made by mid-July.   The cash balance on March 31, 1998, was $142,000.   An estimated income statement for the next quarter is:

Estimated Income Statement for the Quarter Ended June 30, 1998	
Service revenue	$528,000
Cost of materials and supplies used	$136,000
Operating expenses (including depreciation of $81,000)	177,000
Interest expense	23,000
Total deductions from revenue	$336,000
Income before income taxes	$192,000
Income taxes	78,000
Net income	$114,000

Required:

Without considering the results of operations in early July, does it appear that operations in the quarter ended June 30, 1998, can supply sufficient cash to meet payment obligations in early July, while maintaining a cash balance of at least $120,000?   Prepare a forecast cash-flow schedule to support your position.

8-35. Forecast Balance Sheet.   Adelberg Electronics, Inc. designs and assembles electronic systems used by a variety of organizations.   Its principal products are medical measurement systems and instrumentation systems for chemical analyses.

As a member of the budgeting team, your assignment is to prepare the budgeted balance sheet, based on information provided by other team members.   The latest actual balance sheet shows:

Balance Sheet, December 31, 1998 (in Millions)					
Current assets:			Current liabilities:		
Cash	$ 479		Accounts payable	$ 249	
Accounts receivable	590		Accrued income taxes	132	
Inventories	511		Other liabilities	280	$ 661
Prepaid expenses	30		Long-term debt		143
Total current assets		$1,610	Total liabilities		$ 804
Plant and equipment	$1,397		Shareholders' equity:		
Less: Depreciation	462		Common stock	$ 356	
Net plant and equipment		935	Retained earnings	1,385	1,741
Total assets		$2,545	Total liabilities & equity		$2,545

Joe Silk, another member of the team, has given you the following budgeted income statement for the coming year:

Forecast Income Statement for 1999 (in Millions)		
Sales		$3,253
Cost of goods sold		1,583
Gross profit		$1,670
Operating expenses:		
Marketing	$ 590	
General and administrative	358	
Research and development	343	1,291
Net income before taxes		$ 379
Provision for income taxes		134
Net income after taxes		$ 245

The controller has also furnished you with a number of assumptions, policies, and other information as follows:

1. The company has made arrangements to acquire plant and equipment during the year for $339 million. Long-term debt will finance $18 million, and cash will be used for the remainder.

2. All sales are on credit. Collections on credit sales for the year are scheduled to be $3,218 million.

3. Changes in several account balances are planned.
   (a) Inventories will decrease by $15 million.
   (b) Other accrued liabilities will increase by $70 million.
   (c) Prepaid expenses will increase by $10 million.

4. Depreciation expense in the forecast income statement totals $105 million.

5. Payments of accounts payable will total $2,682 million and on accrued income taxes will be $179 million.

6. Common stock will be sold to employees in a special stock purchase plan for $34 million.

7. Dividends of $29 million will be declared and paid during the year.

Required:
1. Prepare a forecast balance sheet.
2. Does the proposed financing of new plant and equipment strain the cash position? Explain.
3. Identify several danger areas in the forecast that might cause the asset acquisition to be difficult to finance. What other sources of cash might exist?

C ASE 8A—BRIDGES & BRIDGES

Bridges & Bridges is a regional food distribution company. Ms. Bridges, CEO, has asked your assistance in preparing cash-flow information for the last three months of 1999. Selected accounts from an interim balance sheet dated September 30, 1999, have the following balances:

Cash	$ 142,100	Accounts payable	$ 354,155
Marketable securities	200,000	Other payables	53,200
Accounts receivable	1,012,500		
Inventories	150,388		

Mr. Bridges, CFO, provides you with the following information based on experience and management policy. All sales are credit sales and are billed the last day of the month of sale. Customers paying within 10 days of the billing date may take a 2 percent cash discount. Forty percent of the sales are paid within the discount period in the month following billing. An additional 25 percent pay in the same month but do not receive the cash discount. Thirty percent is collected in the second month after billing; the remainder is uncollectible. Additional cash of $24,000 is expected in October from renting unused warehouse space.

Sixty percent of all purchases, selling and administrative expenses, and research and development expenses are paid in the month incurred. The remainder is paid in the following month. Ending inventory is set at 25 percent of the next month's budgeted cost of goods sold. The company's gross profit averages 30 percent of sales for the month. Selling and administrative expenses follow the formula of 5 percent of the current month's sales plus $75,000, which includes depreciation of $5,000. Research and development expenses are budgeted at 3 percent of sales.

Actual and budgeted sales information is as follows:

Actual:		*Budgeted:*	
August	$ 750,000	October	$ 826,800
September	787,500	November	868,200
		December	911,600
		January	930,000

The company will acquire equipment costing $250,000 cash in November. Dividends of $45,000 will be paid in December.

The company would like to maintain a minimum cash balance at the end of each month of $120,000. Any excess amounts go first to repayment of short-term borrowings and then to investment in marketable securities. When cash is needed to reach the minimum balance, the company policy is to sell marketable securities before borrowing.

Required (Use of spreadsheet software is recommended.):

1. Prepare a cash budget for each month of the fourth quarter of 1999 and for the quarter in total. Prepare supporting schedules as needed. (Round all budget schedule amounts to the nearest dollar.)

2. You meet with the two Bridges to present your findings and happen to bring along your PC with the budget model software. They are worried about your findings in Part (1). They have obviously been arguing over certain assumptions you were given.

(a) Mr. Bridges thinks that the gross margin may shrink to 27.5 percent because of higher purchase prices. He is concerned about what impact this will have on borrowings. Comment.

(b) Ms. Bridges thinks that "stock outs" occur too frequently and wants to see the impact of increasing inventory levels to 30 and 40 percent of next quarter's sales on their total investment. Comment on these changes.

(c) Mr. Bridges wants to discontinue the cash discount for prompt payment. He thinks that maybe collections of an additional 20 percent of sales will be delayed from the month of billing to the next month. Ms. Bridges says "That's ridiculous! We should increase the discount to 3 percent. Twenty percent more would be collected in the current month to get the higher discount." Comment on the cash-flow impacts.

1-2-3

CASE 8B—DEWEY'S INVISIBLE DOG PRODUCTS

Dewey's Invisible Dog Products (DIDP) markets items it purchases from select suppliers. The current products are novelty items—two forms of dog leashes for "invisible dogs."

The items are called Lil Feefee and Big Bowser. Dewey has obtained agreements with several beach resort shops and a few tourist traps to provide leashes to their various locations. These stores are good customers, and the present demand for both leashes is expected to hold for several years. Business is somewhat seasonal as tourist locations have particularly strong sales only during summer months. Each year, Dewey negotiates volumes and prices with the representatives of these stores and estimates his operating costs. Based on these negotiations and other factors, Dewey begins to plan for 1998. DIDP prepares a profit plan for each year on a quarterly basis. The profit plan uses basic inputs given in Schedules 1 and 2.

DIDP uses spreadsheet software to assist the profit plan preparation. Using this system DIDP is able to construct a comprehensive profit plan and is able to test or change key factors quickly by asking "what if" questions.

Schedule 1—Profit Planning Assumptions

	Lil Feefee	Big Bowser
Product information:		
Unit sales price	$11.00	$14.00
Unit purchase cost	5.50	6.00
Percentage of sales collected in next quarter		40%
Percentage of purchases paid in next quarter		30%
Ending inventory level:		
Percentage of next quarter's sales		30%
12/31/97 Lil Feefee inventory—units		5,000 units
12/31/97 Big Bowser inventory—units		3,000 units
Selling and administrative expenses: (annual)		
Shipping costs	$	0.50 per unit
Sales commissions		10 %
Wages and salaries	$86,000	
Depreciation expense	12,000	
Other cash expenses	98,000	
Lil Feefee fixed expenses	12,000	
Big Bowser fixed expenses	15,000	

Beginning balance sheet (12/31/97):

Cash	$ 15,000	Accounts payable	$ 20,000
Accounts receivable	42,000	Taxes payable	2,000
Equipment (net)	100,000	Capital stock	40,000

Semiannual dividends paid in 1st and 3rd quarters	$4,000
Income tax rate (Taxes are accrued on positive net income only and paid in the next quarter.)	40%

Schedule 2—Sales Forecast

	Total 1998	Q - 1	Q - 2	Q - 3	Q - 4	Q - 5
Units:						
Lil Feefee units	48,000	10,000	15,000	12,000	11,000	11,000
Big Bowser units	12,000	2,500	3,600	3,200	2,700	3,000
Total units	60,000	12,500	18,600	15,200	13,700	14,000

Required (Use of spreadsheet software is recommended.):

1. Prepare the following 1998 budgeted statements, plus any needed supporting schedules:

(a) Cash-flows forecast.

(b) Forecast statement of income.

(c) Forecast balance sheet.

To facilitate "what ifs," avoid the use of actual independent variable values in cell formulas of schedules.

2. Using the spreadsheet developed in Part (1), identify the major changes in Dewey's financial condition that the following "what if" scenarios will cause. Give particular emphasis to cash flows and net income changes.

(a) Changes in the sales forecast for Lil Feefee:

Revised Schedule 2—Sales Forecast

	Total 1998	Q - 1	Q - 2	Q - 3	Q - 4	Q - 5
Units:						
Lil Feefee	42,000	10,000	12,000	10,000	10,000	10,000

(b) Changes in costs and prices of Lil Feefee and Big Bowser:

	Lil Feefee	*Big Bowser*
Product information:		
Unit sales price	$12.00	$16.00
Unit purchase cost	6.00	7.00

(c) Changes in the following percentages:

First:	Percentage of sales collected in next quarter	60%
Second:	Percentage of purchases paid in next quarter	20%
Third:	Ending inventory level percentage of next quarter's sales	50%
Fourth:	All three changes occur together.	

3. Suggest additional elements, variables, and schedules that might be helpful to Dewey in budgeting using this model. Comment on the difficulty of incorporating these items in the model you created.

CHAPTER 9

Cost Control Through Standard Costs

LEARNING OBJECTIVES

After studying Chapter 9, you will be able to:

1. Explain the significance of profit analysis for an organization.
2. Describe the major characteristics and conditions of a standard cost system.
3. Compute materials price and usage variances, and identify probable causes of such variances.
4. Compute labor rate and efficiency variances, and identify probable causes of such variances.
5. Describe the interrelationships that exist among materials and labor variances.
6. Explain the major considerations that are the basis of standard costs for overhead.
7. Distinguish between a budget variance and a capacity variance for overhead.
8. Explain why the capacity variance is related only to fixed overhead costs.
9. Explain how standard costs can be used in a process cost system.

Where Do I Start With Standard Costs?

Claude Cormier, president of Rue de Pierre, a chain of fast food restaurants in central France, just returned from a reunion of his INSEAD graduating class. During the day of activities in the Riviera, he talked with several of his classmates who have become extremely successful in various businesses. One of those classmates suggested to Claude that adoption of a standard cost system eliminated most of her firm's unacceptable scrap and spoilage, caused an examination of nonvalue-added activities, and substantially reduced several inefficient operations.

Claude did not know whether his restaurant chain would really benefit from a standard cost system. If he did make the change, which costs should be put on standards? How does he set up standards? When do variances mean something? Isn't a standard cost system expensive to use? Isn't it a pain in the derriere? Wouldn't a tight budget do the same thing?

These questions were more than Claude could deal with. He decided to bounce the idea of standard costs off his controller.

In measuring success in any undertaking, a comparison is usually made between actual performance and expected performance. Any difference is a variance. A manager is then left with the responsibility to explain the what, why, and how of the variance. In doing so, the manager must understand the influence of key variables on the actual results, focus on areas that deserve more detailed investigation, and determine changes that must be made in future planning and control.   This chapter introduces the concept of profit analysis and then concentrates on variances associated with a standard cost system for direct materials, direct labor, and factory overhead. Chapter 10 extends these concepts to analyzing revenues and operating expenses.

*P*ROFIT ANALYSIS

Profit is an overall measure of how well an organization is doing. A profit variance then is the difference between the actual net income and the planned net income for the same period. The causes of such a variance are related to the various elements that make up net income: revenues, cost of goods sold, and operating expenses. The following table shows a disaggregation of the profit variance into more detailed elements.

	Actual	*Budget*	*Variance*
Revenues	$385,000	$365,000	$20,000 Favorable
Cost of goods sold	282,500	227,250	55,250 Unfavorable
Gross margin	$102,500	$137,750	$35,250 Unfavorable
Operating expenses	81,250	90,000	8,750 Favorable
Net income	$ 21,250	$ 47,750	$26,500 Unfavorable

To have a variance, a baseline with which to compare actual results is necessary. Common baselines are results of a prior month or year, a budget, a flexible budget, or a standard. The analysis of a profit variance necessarily looks at each significant area in the income statement, and each area has a baseline that management feels is appropriate for the circumstances. The analysis then looks at causes of variation from the baseline.

The cost of goods sold, comprised of the costs of materials, labor, and factory overhead, is generally the most significant cost in the income statement. Consequently, companies expend great effort to manage and control these costs. Managers can easily cite examples of how small savings on a unit basis or on a single operation or task performed add many dollars to profit. Analysis of cost variances helps managers to find cost savings.

Besides cost control, cost variances are also used to evaluate the performance of managers who are responsible for particular costs. For example, a plant manager might examine materials, labor, and overhead cost variances in the grinding department to evaluate the performance of the grinding department manager.

Cost variances are often based on comparisons between actual and standard costs.

THE USE OF STANDARDS

Although a standard may be used as a basis for management and control by service industries, retailers, manufacturers, or governmental and not-for-profit entities, the procedures discussed here are focused on a manufacturing setting. However, the concepts discussed have wide application to other organizations and to other types of costs. For example, the driver of a delivery truck is expected to handle a certain number of deliveries in a normal day. The number of expected or normal deliveries serves as a standard for the measurement of performance.

Standard costs are appropriate when an organization has standard products, services, or repetitive operations and when management controls the factors comprising a standard cost. Some examples of where these conditions can exist are:

1. Filling prescriptions in a pharmacy.
2. Picking orders in a warehouse.
3. Preparing food in a restaurant.
4. Answering telephones in travel agencies, airline offices, customer service departments, and computer technical hotlines.
5. Processing orders in a mail-order house.
6. Calling on customers (by phone or door-to-door).
7. Processing computer center transactions from a modem.

Definition of Standard Costs

A **standard cost** for a product consists of a **price standard** (a generic term indicating price for materials, rate for labor, and rate for factory overhead) and a **quantity standard** (a generic term indicating amount for materials, time for labor, and activity or volume for factory overhead). Setting standards for price and quantity involves management judgments, industrial engineering studies, work measurement studies, vendor analyses, union bargaining, as well as a number of other techniques.

Standards are generally stated on a per unit basis: per unit of quantity, per unit of time, per unit of activity, or per unit of product. Once set, these standards remain unchanged as long as no changes occur in operating methods, in factors that influence quantities, or in unit prices of materials, labor, and factory overhead.

Advantages of Standards

A standard cost system presents many advantages to an organization. Although the primary purpose has always been cost control, properly set standards have many other advantages. This section covers five major advantages of standard costs.

Cost Control.   **Cost control** is comparing actual performance with the standard performance, analyzing variances to identify controllable causes, and taking action to correct or adjust future planning and control. As discussed later in this chapter and the next chapter, costs can change for at least four reasons: (1) changes in levels of prices or rates, (2) changes in efficiency, (3) changes in activity or volume, and (4) changes in the mix or yield. Variance analysis must identify these changes as well as the managers responsible for them so that adjustments can be made to the standards or that good performance can be rewarded.

Standard cost accounting follows the principle of **management by exception.** Actual results that correspond with the standards require little attention. The exceptions, however, are emphasized. Management by exception can be desirable because it highlights only those weak areas that require management's attention. However, a behavioral effect can occur when management by exception is applied to people. If a worker is ignored when operating according to the standard and is noticed only when something is wrong, the worker may become resentful and perform less satisfactorily. While it may be argued that the worker is being paid to operate at standard, the human factor cannot be ignored. Without recognition, the worker becomes discontented; and this discontentment may spread throughout the organization with a loss of both morale and productivity.

Cost Management.   Cost management is related to cost control, but here the emphasis is on establishing the level of costs that becomes the benchmark for measuring performance. It can be as simple as decreasing the costs of operations through improved methods and procedures, using better selection of resources (human, materials, and facilities), or eliminating unnecessary (nonvalue-added) activities. As standards are set and periodically reviewed, operations can be analyzed to identify waste and inefficiency and to eliminate their sources. These reviews can also highlight better than expected performance; appreciation will motivate employees to continue looking for better ways to operate. A standard cost system creates an environment in which people become cost conscious, always looking for continuous improvements in the process.

Decision Making. If standards are set at currently attainable levels (a concept discussed later in the "Quality of Standards" section), the standard costs are useful in making many types of decisions. For example, some common decisions involve regular, special order, or transfer pricing; sell or process further; make or buy; and cash planning. When an analysis is used as the basis for setting the standard costs, managers need not perform a new analysis for each decision.

Recordkeeping Costs. A standard cost system saves recordkeeping costs, not during the initial startup but in the long-run operation of the system. When using actual costs, each item of materials issued from a storeroom has its cost that came from a specific purchase order. The cost transferred to work in process inventory is calculated using an inventory flow method: specific identification, FIFO, LIFO, moving average, or weighted average. For companies with thousands of different materials categories in stock, identifying costs to move to work in process inventory can be an enormous task. When standard costs are in place, each item in the same materials classification has the same standard cost. Therefore, costs transferred to work in process inventory are the standard cost per unit times the number of units issued. This same process applies to work in process inventory transfers to finished goods. All inventories have their standard costs, and balances are always stated at standard.

Inventory Valuation. A standard cost system records the same costs for physically identical units of materials and products; an actual cost system can record different costs for physically identical units. Differences between the two costs tend to be waste, inefficiency, and nonvalue-added activities. Such items, if incurred at all, are period costs and excluded from inventory amounts. They should not be capitalized and deferred in inventory values. Therefore, standards provide a more rational cost in valuing inventories.

Occasionally, differences between actual and standard costs show positive efficiencies. Performance has been better than expected. If this situation will continue, the standards are revised. Otherwise, the current standards still provide a rational basis for costing products.

The Quality of Standards

The term "standard" has no meaning unless we know on what the standard is based. A standard may be very strict at one extreme or very loose at the other extreme. We broadly classify standards as strict or tight standards, attainable standards, and loose or lax standards.

No easy solution exists as to how standards should be set. The objective, of course, is to obtain the best possible results at the lowest possible cost. Often human behavior becomes the dominant concern in setting standards. A very rigorous standard may motivate some employees to produce exceptional results. On the other hand, a standard that is too strict and cannot be reached may discourage employees and produce only modest results. In setting a level of standards, management must consider the employees, their abilities, their aspirations, and their degree of control over the results of operations.

Strict Standards. **Strict standards** are set at a maximum level of efficiency, representing conditions that can seldom, if ever, be attained. They ignore normal materials spoilage and idle labor time due to such factors as machine breakdowns. These standards appear to represent perfection, something few employees will achieve. Although a standard should challenge people, a standard that is virtually unattainable will not motivate most employees to do their best. An employee is more likely to put forth increased effort when feeling successful. In other words, a person's aspirations increase with success and decrease with failure.

In addition, variances from strict standards have little significance for control purposes. There will never be a favorable variance, only zero or unfavorable variances. In fact, most variances will be large and unfavorable. The question is: "What does such a variance measure?"

Loose Standards. **Loose standards** tend to be based on past performance and represent an average of prior costs. They include all inefficiency and waste in past operations. Such standards are not likely to motivate employees to high performance. The very nature of loose standards means less than efficient performance. As a result, variances from loose standards are almost always favorable and provide little useful information for cost control. Again, the question is: "What does such a variance measure?"

Attainable Standards. **Attainable standards** can be achieved with reasonable effort. Perhaps the standards should be somewhat lower than what can be achieved by earnest effort. With success, the employees gain confidence and tend to be more productive. For a more experienced group of workers, an exacting standard may serve as a challenge that motivates an employee to higher levels of performance. With less experienced workers, standards may have to be set at a lower level at first. As learning takes place, the standards may be raised. Increases in standards should be made with caution and should be accepted by the employees as being fair.

Managers should expect to see favorable and unfavorable variances with an attainable standard. Some employees will meet and exceed the standard with reasonable effort, while others will not meet the standard because of poor performance.

Revising the Standards

Standard costs should be reviewed periodically to see if revisions are necessary to keep them at the selected level of quality. Although many factors may combine that determine the best time to review standard costs, they should be reviewed at least once a year. Otherwise, they may not be current. This does not mean waiting until the end of the year. Companies with thousands of items on standards will have a department dedicated to reviewing standards throughout the year.

A key for reviewing standards is to identify changes taking place that outdate existing standards. Changes that typically call for a revision to one or more standard costs include:

1. Increases or decreases in the price levels of specific materials and supplies.

2. Changes in personnel payment plans or wage schedules.
3. Modifications of materials type or specifications.
4. Acquisitions of new equipment or disposition of old equipment.
5. Modifications of operations or procedures.
6. Additions or deletions of product lines.
7. Expansions or contractions of facilities.
8. Changes in management policies that affect the amount of costs and the way costs are accumulated and identified with activities, operations, and products.
9. Increased experience of employees.

Management policies can have a significant impact on standard costs. Examples of the most common policy areas are the definition of capacity, the classification of fringe benefits, depreciation methods, and capitalization and expense policies. Capacity definitions influence the level of waste and inefficiency that management will tolerate and the amount of fixed costs applied to individual units of an operation, task, or product. A redefinition of capacity can be due to changes in the number of shifts, in hours of operation with given shift schedules, or in demand for the product or service. Fringe benefits can appear in several ways, any of which can influence a product cost significantly. Management can classify any element of fringe benefit cost as a direct cost of the product, an indirect cost through a labor-related cost pool, an indirect cost through a factory overhead cost pool, or a period cost through a general and administrative cost pool. Management determines which depreciation methods are in use. One common policy is to change from a declining-balance method for existing equipment to a straight-line method at about the mid-life point of the asset life. Occasionally, management will change the method applied to new equipment purchased. The criteria for capitalization and expense decisions determine which costs are capitalized as assets and charged to operations through depreciation and amortization and which costs are charged immediately upon incurrence. Any change in the criteria alters the treatment of those costs affected.

Throughout the chapter, we assume that standards are entered into the formal accounting system. As such, product costing is determined through a standard cost system. Many companies do not follow this practice. Instead, they use standards as a part of statistical supplements in arriving at information for control purposes. Revision of standards is much more critical if the standards are the basis for product costing.

S TANDARD COST SHEET

Once standards have been set for each cost component, the costs are summarized in a **standard cost sheet**. Here the cost of each category of direct materials used, the cost of each direct labor operation employed, and the cost of all overhead tasks, operations, processes, and support functions applied to a unit of final product are itemized. Standard cost sheets can be extremely lengthy or very simple depending on the product and manufacturing process.

Suppose that Colexus, Inc. uses a standard cost system in accounting for its only product, Colex. The standards are:

Component	Total Cost of Component	Unit Cost
Materials	3 lbs. at $4.00 per pound	$12.00
Direct labor	.5 hour at $7.00 per hour	3.50
Variable overhead	.5 hour at $6.00 per hour	3.00
Fixed overhead	.5 hour at $9.00 per hour	4.50
Total cost per unit		$23.00

This standard cost sheet gives the total unit cost of each product produced. For each completed unit, three pounds of direct materials at a total cost of $12 are taken from materials inventory and charged to work in process inventory. Also, $3.50 is charged for direct labor; and a total of $7.50 in overhead costs is applied. Nothing is noted here about the actual costs incurred because all production is carried only at standard cost. Thus, when a completed unit of product is transferred from work in process inventory to finished goods inventory and later to cost of goods sold, the cost is $23. The standard cost sheet becomes the basis for all accounting entries related to the product.

To explain standards for materials, direct labor, and factory overhead, we need to know the volume of output and the materials quantities allowed for that volume in order to calculate certain variances. The standard cost sheet lists the allowed amounts. The volume of output will be expressed as units of product or equivalent units, depending on the circumstances in production.

STANDARDS FOR MATERIALS

Standards are established for the cost of obtaining materials and for the quantities to be used in production. Managers then compare actual costs against these standards to ascertain variances. Basically, two types of variances exist: price and usage. Different variances may be developed for specialized purposes, but they can always be classified as variations in the price of materials or in the quantities used, or as a combination of price and usage. If the actual cost is greater than the standard cost, the variance is an **unfavorable variance**; if actual cost is less than standard cost, the variance is a **favorable variance.**

Materials Price Variance

A **materials price variance** measures the difference between the prices at which materials are acquired and the prices established in the standards. What is in the standard, how a variance is calculated, and what are potential causes of variances are now explained.

Setting the Price Standard.   A standard price is set for each item of materials the company expects to use. The cost elements that make up the standard are a matter of management policy. Although the purchase price is the dominant element, other costs may also be included, such as the cost of insurance for materials in transit, the cost of transporting materials, various cash and trade discounts, and costs of receiving and inspecting materials at the receiving dock. Once management decides on the elements, the next step is assessing prices. The estimation techniques are not discussed here, but common approaches to determining amounts include:

1. Statistical forecasting.
2. Knowledge and experience in the particular type of business.
3. Weighted average of prices in most recent purchases.
4. Prices agreed upon in long-term contracts or purchase commitments.

Accounting for a Price Variance.   A materials price variance is isolated at the time of purchase. The actual quantity of materials purchased is entered in the materials inventory at standard prices. The liability to the supplier is recorded at actual quantities and actual prices. Any difference between the two amounts is recorded as a price variance.

To illustrate, assume that the Purchasing Department of Colexus, Inc. bought 40,000 pounds of materials for $159,200, which is $3.98 per pound. To make the example easier to follow, we will use the following symbols:

$$AQP = \text{Actual quantity purchased}$$

$$AP = \text{Actual price}$$

$$SP = \text{Standard price}$$

$$MPV = \text{Materials price variance}$$

The cost flow of actual and standard costs would appear in T-account form as follows:

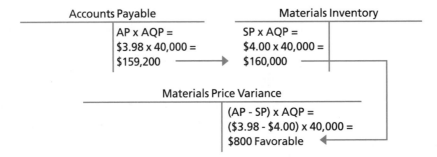

To calculate the variance without thinking in terms of accounts, the information from the T-accounts can be summarized into convenient formulas.

$$AP \times AQP = \$3.98 \times 40,000 = \$159,200$$

$$SP \times AQP = \$4.00 \times 40,000 = \$160,000$$

$$MPV = (AP - SP) \times AQP = -\$0.02 \times 40,000 = \$800 \text{ Favorable}$$

Note that the actual quantity is used in all calculations. Only the prices differ. A materials price variance can be either favorable or unfavorable when actual costs are compared with standard costs. In this illustration, the materials price variance is favorable because the materials were purchased at a cost below the standard.

Causes of the Price Variance.   A variance occurs for any number of reasons. If the variance is significant, we must identify causes. If performance is deemed good, the responsible people should be praised and, where appropriate, rewarded. If the investigation finds out-of-control situations, corrections can be made so variations are eliminated in the future. In some cases, outdated standards are being used and need to be adjusted.

Although many causes for variances pertain to any given situation, a list of the common sources is as follows:

1. Random fluctuations in market prices.
2. Materials substitutions.
3. Market shortages or excesses.
4. Purchases from vendors other than those offering the terms used in the standard.
5. Purchases of higher or lower quality materials.
6. Purchases in nonstandard or uneconomical quantities.
7. Changes in the mode of transportation.
8. Changes in the production schedule that result in rush orders or additional materials.
9. Unexpected price increases or decreases.
10. Fortunate buys.
11. Failure to take cash discounts.

Responsibility for the Price Variance.   The purchasing department is usually charged with the responsibility for price variances. If the purchasing function is carried out properly, the standard price should be attainable. When lower prices are paid, a favorable materials price variance is recorded, indicating that the purchasing department was under the standard. Higher prices are reflected in an unfavorable materials price variance. In some circumstances price variances really should be charged to a production department instead of to the purchasing department. As examples, a rush order is caused by last minute production changes; or production people request a specific brand name for materials rather than allowing the purchasing department to buy by specifications.

Periodic reports show how actual prices compare with standard prices for the various types of materials purchased. Reports on price variances may be made as frequently as daily but will generally be weekly and monthly. They reveal which materials, if any, are responsible for a large part of any total price variation and can help the purchasing department in its search for more economical vendors.

Materials Usage Variance

Materials are put into production, but the actual quantity used may be more or less than specified by the standards. The variation in the use of materials is called a **materials usage variance**. Other names for the variance are materials quantity variance, materials use variance, and materials efficiency variance.

Setting the Quantity Factor.   The quantity factor in a materials standard is based on engineering specifications, blueprints and designs, bills of materials, and routings. Taken together, these items specify the quality, size, thickness, weight, and any other factors necessary for a good unit of final product. Also included in the quantity factor are any desired allowances for normal acceptable waste, scrap, shrinkage, and spoilage that may occur during the manufacturing process.

Accounting for a Usage Variance. As materials are used, the work in process account is increased by the standard quantity used multiplied by the standard price. The materials inventory account is decreased by the actual quantity used multiplied by the standard price. Returning to Colexus, Inc., assume that 31,000 pounds of materials are withdrawn from Materials Inventory for use in the production of 10,000 units of final product. Because the standard cost sheet indicates only three pounds should be used for each final product, the standard quantity of materials that should have been used is 30,000 pounds (3 pounds x 10,000 units of final product).

For our example, we will use the following symbols:

SP   =   Standard price

AQU =   Actual quantity used

SQ   =   Standard quantity allowed

MUV =   Materials usage variance

The cost flow of actual and standard costs would appear in T-account form as follows:

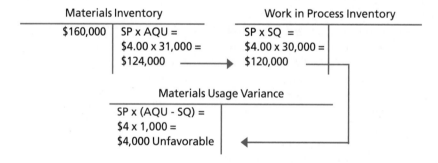

To calculate the variance without thinking in terms of accounts, the preceding information can be summarized into convenient formulas.

$$SP \times AQU \quad = \quad \$4.00 \times 31{,}000 \quad = \quad \$124{,}000$$

$$SP \times SQ \quad \; = \quad \$4.00 \times 30{,}000 \quad = \quad \$120{,}000$$

$$MUV = SP \times (AQU - SQ) = \$4.00 \times 1{,}000 = \$4{,}000 \text{ Unfavorable}$$

In the first two equations, the standard unit price is used; but the quantities differ. In one case, the actual quantities issued from the storeroom are used. In the other, the standard materials quantity allowed for each good unit of final product is used. Because only quantities can differ in the equations, any variation is a usage variance. The variance for Colexus, Inc. is unfavorable because the amount of materials used is greater than the amount called for by the standard.

Causes of the Usage Variance.   What causes a materials usage variance? To answer this question, we look at the elements that make up the quantity standard and the specific situation.   Examples of common causes include:

1. Changes in product specifications.
2. Materials substitutions.
3. Breakage during the handling of materials in movement and processing.
4. Improper use of materials by workers.
5. Machine settings operating at nonstandard levels.
6. Waste.
7. Pilferage.

Responsibility for the Usage Variance.   Ordinarily, materials usage variances are chargeable to production departments. They often arise as a result of wasteful practices in working with materials, or they arise because of products that must be scrapped through faulty production.

Reports on the quantities of materials used are made to the responsible production department supervisor. A production supervisor, for example, may receive daily or weekly summaries showing how the quantities used in the department compare with the standards. At the operating level, managers can directly control the use of materials. Often, reports on variations from standard are for physical quantities only. Managers may not need immediate feedback from a cost report. Daily or weekly cost reports simply tell managers the financial magnitude of variations and serve as a reminder that corrections should be made before losses become too great.

Summary reports of actual and standard materials consumption given in dollars, with variances and variance percentages, also go to the plant superintendent at least monthly. If the variances in any department are too large, the superintendent can take steps to reduce them. During the month, of course, the operating managers will watch materials usage; and, if they have been doing their jobs properly, the accumulated variances for the month should be relatively small.

Interrelationships of Price and Usage Variances

We have treated the materials price and usage variances as though they are independent and unrelated. In many cases, the event that causes one variance also causes the other. For example, assume the purchasing department buys lower-grade materials at a substantially reduced price. This generates a favorable price variance for purchasing. When those materials reach production, they result in a higher than normal waste. This gives the operating supervisors unfavorable usage variances. Keeping the two variances in isolation makes the purchasing agent look good, while the operating supervisors turn in poor performances. In reality, both variances are the responsibility of the purchasing department. If the variances net out favorable, the purchasing decision has benefited the company. On the other hand, a net unfavorable variance is a loss to the company.

The operating people can also influence the price variance. If improperly adjusted machines, for instance, generate a higher than usual waste, more materials may be needed from the storeroom. When a production supervisor requisitions the materials and the storeroom manager realizes sufficient quantities are not available, a request is made to the purchasing department to order more. To keep the production schedule current, a rush order is issued. The higher prices paid for a rush order will result in an unfavorable price variance.

The warning of these situations is simple: Investigation of variances must not be done in isolation.

STANDARDS FOR LABOR

We set standards for direct labor and measure variances from the standards in much the same way as we did for materials. The price factor is called rate; the quantity factor is time. When referring to variations in time, we use the term efficiency. The **labor rate variance** measures the portion of the total labor cost variance caused by the difference between the actual wage rate paid and the standard wage rate. The **labor efficiency variance** measures the portion of the total labor cost variance caused by the difference between the actual hours worked and the standard hours required for production.

When discussing standards for labor, we assume direct labor only. Indirect labor consists of the costs for people working in the production departments but not directly on products and for the time of direct laborers classified as training time, break time, overtime premium, and idle time. These costs are often distributed from payroll to factory overhead and become part of overhead standards. Therefore, indirect labor is discussed later as part of overhead.

Setting Rate Standards

Standard cost systems rely on individual labor rates by skill-level classification for better control and accuracy. However, in some cases, standard rates can be set for entire cost centers or departments. Regardless of how it is structured, the underlying wage or salary rate used as the standard rate will be either established through contract negotiations or by the prevailing rates in the location where the work is performed. The details for selecting wage-level classifications cover training, education, experience, special physical abilities, and set of task skills.

When setting the standard rates, management must decide whether to use a basic labor rate or a "loaded" labor rate as the standard. A "loaded" labor rate includes labor-related costs such as overtime premiums, shift premiums, bonuses and incentives, payroll taxes, and fringe benefits. Those factors not included in the labor rate standard will be included in overhead. Therefore, management will look at the advantages of treating these cost factors as direct costs or as indirect costs. For example, if the company is performing contracted work for the federal government, the company would typically recover more of its costs through the "loaded" standard labor rate.

Setting Time Standards

Time standards are more difficult to establish than materials quantity standards. People's productivity is the basis for setting time standards; and people tend to differ in behavior from one time to the next. Setting time standards involves answering two questions: (1) What operations are performed? and (2) How much time should be spent on each operation for the product or service? The answer to the first question is determined by reviewing operations and procedures, process charts, and routing lists. The answer to the second question will be determined in one or more of the following ways:

1. Operation and body movement analysis. (This involves dividing each operation into the elementary body movements such as reaching, pushing, turning over, etc. Published tables of standard times are available for each movement. These standard times are applied to the individual movements and added together for the total standard time per operation.)
2. Time and motion studies conducted by industrial engineers.
3. Averages of past performance, adjusted for anticipated changes.
4. Test runs through the production process for which standards are to be set.

Accounting for the Rate and Efficiency Variances

Unlike materials, labor cannot be purchased and stored until needed. We purchase and use labor at the same time. Therefore, accounting for both variances is combined.

Colexus, Inc. shows a payroll for its direct workers of $38,584 and 5,200 hours worked. That gives an actual rate of $7.42 per hour. The standard cost sheet shows that each completed unit requires one-half hour of direct labor time. Since the company produced 10,000 good units, 5,000 hours should have been worked (.5 hour x 10,000 units).

For our example, we will use the following symbols:

$$AR \ = \ \text{Actual rate}$$

$$SR \ = \ \text{Standard rate}$$

$$AH \ = \ \text{Actual hours}$$

$$SH \ = \ \text{Standard hours allowed}$$

$$LRV \ = \ \text{Labor rate variance}$$

$$LEV \ = \ \text{Labor efficiency variance}$$

The cost flow of actual and standard costs would appear in T-account form as follows:

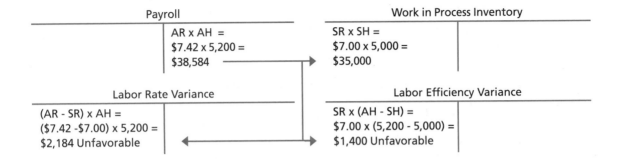

The labor rate variance is commonly calculated first. It results whenever the actual rate paid to a worker differs from the standard rate. Calculating a labor rate variance requires holding the actual hours constant while comparing the difference in rates, as follows:

$$AR \times AH = \$7.42 \times 5,200 = \$38,584$$

$$SR \times AH = \$7.00 \times 5,200 = \$36,400$$

$$LRV = (AR - SR) \times AH = \$0.42 \times 5,200 = \$2,184 \text{ Unfavorable}$$

The variance is unfavorable because the actual rate exceeds the standard rate.

The labor efficiency variance (also called quantity, time, or usage variance) results when employees' total actual hours worked differ from the standard. We calculate the variance by holding the rate constant while comparing the difference in hours. The following summarizes this procedure:

$$SR \times AH = \$7.00 \times 5,200 = \$36,400$$

$$SR \times SH = \$7.00 \times 5,000 = \$35,000$$

$$LEV = SR \times (AH - SH) = \$7.00 \times 200 = \$1,400 \text{ Unfavorable}$$

The variance is unfavorable because the actual hours worked are more than the standard hours allowed for the 10,000 units of final product produced.

Because the hours are purchased and used at the same time, an alternate approach to calculating the variances can be used:

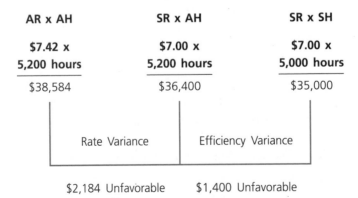

Causes of Labor Variances

Labor rates are usually set by contract, negotiations, management, or federal laws or regulations. So, why would a labor rate variance occur? Two basic reasons exist. First, labor rates often represent an average for a task, operation, or work center. If a departmental manager shifts workers' assignments because of sudden changes in personnel requirements or a shortage of personnel, the average rate can easily change depending on how the shift relates to higher-paid or lower-paid workers. A second reason is that standard labor rates may include cost elements beyond the basic labor rate. Any changes in overtime worked, shift differentials, payroll taxes, or fringe benefits will show up in a labor variance if these elements are part of the standard rate.

Labor efficiency relates to how many units are completed per actual hour for each task, operation, or process. Many reasons exist for why productivity varies from the level assumed in the standard time. Some of the common causes of a labor efficiency variance include:

1. Use of lower-skilled or higher-skilled workers.
2. Effects of a learning curve.
3. Use of lower-quality or higher-quality materials.
4. Changes in production methods.
5. Changes in production scheduling.
6. Installation of new equipment.
7. Poorly maintained equipment or machine malfunction.
8. Delays in routing work, materials, tools, or instructions.
9. Insufficient training, incorrect instructions, or worker dissatisfaction.

Responsibility for Labor Variances

Labor rate and efficiency variances are charged to the department managers who have control over the use of workers. Labor rate variances are often the responsibility of personnel managers who manage hiring, union contracts, and perhaps labor scheduling. Although a labor rate variance is important to understand and control, managers tend to concentrate more on the labor efficiency variance because it has a greater impact on capacity utilization and the department's ability to meet production schedules. Labor efficiency is compared by department and by job with established standards. Daily or weekly reports to department managers and the plant superintendent help to locate and solve difficulties on a particular job or in a department. Differences between standard costs and actual costs incurred by a job or department may show that a job cannot be handled at the standard labor cost or that a department is not managed properly.

Interrelationships of Variances

As we saw with materials, variances should not be analyzed in isolation from one another. The event that causes one variance can easily be the cause for one or more other variances. Future cost planning and control can be improved when interrelationships among labor variances and between materials and labor variances are identified and understood.

Labor Rate and Efficiency Variances. People perform the productive effort; thus, the rate of pay and the time required are related. Because so many relationships can exist between the two factors, only a few examples are cited to aid in identifying what to look for in a specific operation.

Assume a number of employees are in various military reserve units that have been called to active duty. As a short-term solution, a manager has two options: (1) employ temporary workers or (2) shift other workers internally and add overtime. Using temporary workers may be cheaper or more expensive depending on the situation. They are not as experienced with the equipment, procedures, and processes. They may take more time than the standard allows. Therefore, hiring temporary workers can result in both rate and efficiency variances. The second option is to shift existing workers and use overtime. The move will put differently skilled workers on new jobs. The move can create either a favorable or an unfavorable rate variance depending on the mix of workers. Their experience levels may be higher or lower than the specific job requires and can result in an efficiency variance. Adding overtime could affect a rate variance, depending on how the company treats the overtime premium. Efficiency should not be an issue of overtime unless the workers become less productive through fatigue.

In another case, suppose an employee is having difficulties working on a particular machine. The worker is taking more time than standard to complete good units. The manager, trying to keep production on schedule and not lose capacity to inefficiency, shifts a more skilled, higher-paid worker to the job. The higher-paid worker will yield an unfavorable rate variance but can reduce the unfavorable efficiency variance or create a favorable one.

Materials and Labor Variances.   Materials and labor variances can also be related to the same source. Assume, for instance, that a purchasing agent made a fortunate buy on a lower-quality grade of material. The "good buy" yields a favorable materials price variance for purchasing. However, when the materials are used in production, they crumble and create more waste than anticipated. More materials are needed, and an unfavorable materials usage variance arises. A department manager, desiring to minimize the lost time, moves higher-skilled people to the operation where the higher waste occurs. This action leads to a labor rate variance and may influence the magnitude or the direction of a labor efficiency variance.

In another case, a worker starts the shift fatigued and stressed. Lack of concentration results in higher waste which takes more time. This results in unfavorable materials usage and labor efficiency variances. Because more materials are needed, the manager requisitions additional materials from the storeroom. The storekeeper finds fewer materials available than are now required. Purchasing is asked to place a rush order so that production can proceed with minimum delay. The rush order increases the purchasing costs, causing an unfavorable materials price variance.

The Influence of Automation

We are seeing a trend where many companies are automating various aspects or even all aspects of their production. The purpose of this movement is to increase productivity and quality while keeping unit costs low. With automatic equipment, the need for high skill levels of direct labor is substantially reduced. Direct labor in such an environment becomes such an insignificant element of cost that variances have little meaning.

In some industries, automation may not go beyond a certain point; in which case, direct labor will remain a smaller but significant cost element. However, with a great deal of automation, direct labor time becomes more dependent upon the speed of a machine operation than upon the speed of individual workers. Hence, labor efficiency is more related to machine efficiency than to employee efficiency. Therefore, a labor efficiency variance will carry little meaningful information.

*J*OINT VARIANCE

Figure 9.1 graphically presents the labor variances discussed. We arbitrarily assigned to the labor rate variance the added cost resulting from the higher rate paid for the extra hours worked. This is traditionally done.

Figure 9.2, page 386, shows an alternative approach. Here, the added cost resulting from the higher rate paid for the extra hours of work is included. The formulas that correspond to this approach are:

$$LRV = (AR - SR) \times SH$$

$$LEV = SR \times (AH - SH)$$

$$\text{Joint rate/efficiency variance} = (AR - SR) \times (AH - SH)$$

FIGURE 9.1 **Labor Rate and Efficiency Variances**

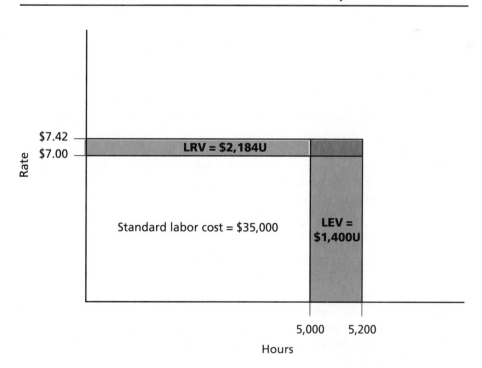

FIGURE 9.2   Joint Rate/Efficiency Variance

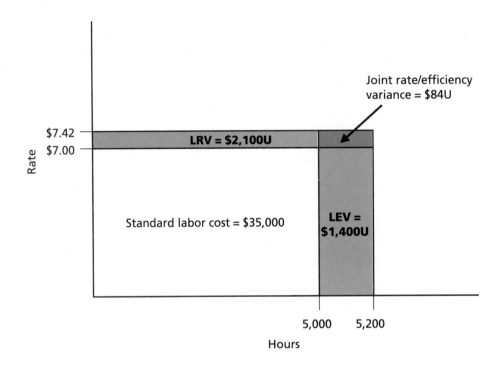

For the preceding example:

$$LRV = (\$7.42 - \$7.00) \times 5,000 = \$2,100 \text{ Unfavorable}$$

$$LEV = \$7.00 \times (5,200 - 5,000) = \$1,400 \text{ Unfavorable}$$

$$\text{Joint rate/efficiency variance} = (\$7.42 - \$7.00) \times (5,200 - 5,000) = \$84 \text{ Unfavorable}$$

Of the $2,184 labor rate variance in our earlier approach, only $2,100 was a pure rate variance. The alternative approach has shifted $84 into a joint rate/efficiency variance.

Similarly, this alternative approach can be used for materials to obtain a joint price/usage variance. However, when the quantity of materials used in production differs from the quantity purchased, as in the earlier illustration, the alternative approach for materials variances becomes more complex.

STANDARDS FOR OVERHEAD

The factory overhead costs consist of all manufacturing costs that are not classified as direct materials and direct labor. Examples of factory overhead costs include indirect materials and supplies, indirect labor, maintenance and repairs, lubrication, power, factory property taxes and insurance, and depreciation. Service organizations will have similar overhead costs related to providing services.

In a standard cost system, a standard overhead rate is used to apply these costs to products and services. The actual overhead costs are accumulated and compared to the applied amounts to determine whether the standards were met. Variances from the standard help to direct management's attention to situations where costs should be controlled more closely, where managers should be praised and rewarded for good performance, or where the standards should be revised.

Development of Overhead Rates

Standard costs for manufacturing overhead have price and quantity factors, just like direct materials and direct labor. Price is reflected in one or more overhead rates; quantity is the measure of activity. Price and quantity in this case are closely linked. In developing standard overhead rates, five major considerations must be evaluated.

First, which cost elements are included in manufacturing overhead? We need to identify the costs such as indirect materials, indirect labor, fringe benefits, payroll taxes, utilities, property taxes, insurance, depreciation, and security. When certain variances occur, these items will be examined for specific changes.

The second consideration is the measure of activity for relating overhead costs to products. A **measure of activity** for this purpose represents the factor that best expresses how costs change as volume increases or decreases. As noted in earlier chapters, we refer to the measure of activity as an allocation base or cost driver. Although many factors can influence costs, we select the dominant cost driver. Common ones are direct labor hours or costs, machine hours, and units of products. In Chapter 6, we examined activity-based costing and identified other cost drivers that cause costs to be incurred. Our use of the measure of activity is the same as a primary-stage cost driver in those discussions. For standard costs, the appropriate measure must be selected if variances are to provide any meaningful information.

Third, and closely related to the measure of activity, is the concept of capacity and the anticipated volume level for the current period. We discussed several capacity concepts in Chapter 4. The capacity or volume concept selected and the determination of the current period level significantly influence overhead rates because of the presence of fixed costs.

A fourth consideration is cost behavior. The behavior of each cost within factory overhead is important because management plans and controls variable costs differently than it plans and controls fixed costs. Consequently, distinguishing variable from fixed overhead costs aids in analyzing variances for cause and responsibility. Standard cost systems often use dual overhead rates for variable overhead costs and for fixed overhead costs. In separating the variable and fixed cost rates, different cost drivers may be used for each cost behavior.

The fifth consideration is the level at which overhead rates should be set: by task, by machine or labor operation, by activity center, by department, or by plant. For a single product operation, plant-wide rates for variable and fixed costs are sufficient. The greater the product and operation diversity, the more likely it is that rates are set for smaller groupings of costs. For our illustration with Colexus, Inc., we assume a plant-wide level merely to illustrate the concepts. The same considerations will apply should a company compute rates by task, activity center, and so forth.

Flexible Overhead Budgets

As we have noted in previous chapters, a **flexible overhead budget** is based on a formula that expresses the budgeted overhead at any point within the relevant range. The formula recognizes that some costs are variable and some are fixed. The following schedule shows the flexible overhead budget formula for Colexus, Inc. We assume here that the measure of activity is direct labor hours.

Cost Item	Fixed Cost	Variable Cost Per Direct Labor Hour
Indirect materials	—	$1.90
Hourly indirect labor	—	1.27
Supervision.	$21,000	—
Repair and maintenance	3,600	1.11
Utilities and occupancy	10,580	1.00
Depreciation.	13,800	—
Miscellaneous costs	520	0.72
Total	$49,500	$6.00

The flexible budget cost function is: $49,500 + ($6.00 x number of hours). Since we know that the hours are related to units of product in terms of two units per hour, we can restate the formula as: $49,500 + ($3.00 x units of product). Typically, we would have multiple products using different amounts of direct labor which would require the use of the basic formula.

As a sidelight, the overhead rates are also available from these numbers, if we assume a volume of 5,500 direct labor hours or 11,000 units of product. For variable costs, the rate is $6.00 per hour or $3.00 per unit (.5 hour x $6.00). The fixed costs are $9.00 per hour ($49,500 ÷ 5,500 hours) or $4.50 per unit (.5 hour x $9.00).

The significance of the flexible overhead budget becomes apparent in the next section where we identify variances for overhead costs.

Framework for Two-Way Overhead Variance Analysis

Because different factors give rise to underapplied or overapplied overhead, we need a framework to identify the areas of potential causes of variations. In our framework, we compare actual overhead costs with a flexible budget and with the applied overhead to arrive at two possible variances: budget variance and capacity variance.

To begin, we need to know the actual overhead costs and the applied overhead costs. We have already seen for Colexus, Inc. that the company produced 10,000 units during the month. Actual overhead costs for the month are $31,500 variable and $50,000 fixed. The factory overhead accounts would then show the following information:

Actual costs:		
Variable	$31,500	
Fixed	50,000	$81,500
Applied costs:		
Variable ($3.00 x 10,000 units)	$30,000	
Fixed ($4.50 x 10,000 units)	45,000	75,000
Underapplied		$ 6,500

Remember, the cost per unit for variable and fixed overhead is calculated in advance and appears on the standard cost sheet for individual products. Therefore, the rates used in the example are applied directly to actual units or equivalent units of product.

The next step is to compare the actual costs and applied costs with the flexible budget for 10,000 units produced. Figure 9.3 summarizes this information. Note that the two-way overhead variance analysis actually produces three variances: variable and fixed overhead budget variances plus the fixed overhead capacity variance.

Budget Variance. A **budget variance** is the difference between actual overhead costs and the flexible budget for actual units produced. It is also called a **controllable variance**. This variance is deemed controllable by the appropriate operating departments. In the foregoing example, the variance is unfavorable; more dollars were spent than were budgeted for 10,000 units. A more detailed examination of the variance is necessary to identify areas where managers need to take action. One approach for providing greater detail is to show the budget variance by individual cost item with the use of the flexible overhead cost function, as shown in the following table:

Cost Item	Actual Overhead	Flexible Budget for 10,000 Units	Budget Variance	
Indirect materials	$10,250	$ 9,500	$ 750	U
Hourly indirect labor	6,250	6,350	100	F
Supervision.	21,400	21,000	400	U
Repair and maintenance	9,050	9,150	100	F
Utilities and occupancy	15,930	15,580	350	U
Depreciation.	13,800	13,800	0	
Miscellaneous costs	4,820	4,120	700	U
Total	$81,500	$79,500	$2,000	U

FIGURE 9.3   Overhead Variances for Colexus, Inc.

Overhead	Actual Overhead Costs	Flexible Budget for 10,000 Units	Standard Costs of Units Produced (Applied Costs)
Variable	$31,500	$ 30,000*	$ 30,000
Fixed	50,000	49,500	45,000
Total.	$81,500	$ 79,500	$ 75,000

	Budget Variance	Capacity Variance	
Variable	$1,500 Unfavorable	$ 0	
Fixed	500 Unfavorable	4,500 Unfavorable	
Total.	$2,000 Unfavorable	$4,500 Unfavorable	

$6,500 Unfavorable and Underapplied

*$6 x .5 hour x 10,000 units

A number of causes may exist for either a favorable or an unfavorable budget variance. The common causes will fall into one of four categories:

1. Price changes in the individual cost components comprising overhead costs.
2. Quantity changes in individual items within overhead cost components, probably in the variable overhead area.
3. Estimation errors in segregating variable and fixed costs.
4. Any overhead costs that are incurred or saved because of inefficient or efficient use of the underlying activity measure (machine hours or labor hours, for example).

The estimation errors come in two varieties: (1) the inaccuracies in predicting what will occur in the future, and (2) the reliability of approximations made in separating overhead costs into variable and fixed categories. The inefficient or efficient use of activity relates to the fact that in an activity (labor worked, for example) overhead costs are incurred to support that activity. If the activity is inefficient, overhead costs support inefficiency. On the other hand, if less activity occurs, lower total overhead costs are incurred to support it. Therefore, efficient resource use also saves overhead costs.

Capacity Variance.   The **capacity variance** (also called a volume variance) is the difference between the flexible budget for the actual units produced and the amounts applied to work in process inventory. In Figure 9.3, because the variable overhead costs are the same in each column, the capacity variance is the difference between the budgeted fixed overhead and the applied fixed overhead. Therefore, the capacity variance is the amount of budgeted fixed overhead not applied (unfavorable) or the amount applied in excess of the budgeted fixed costs (favorable). A capacity variance, then, occurs when actual production differs from the capacity level used to calculate the standard fixed overhead rate.

Continuing with the example, we know that fixed overhead for the month was budgeted at $49,500; and we presume that 5,500 direct labor hours or 11,000 units of product constitute a normal level of operation. We see that the standard overhead rate for costing products is computed at the normal volume, so in this case it is $4.50 per unit of product. We determine this rate by first computing the hourly overhead rate:

$$\frac{\$49,500 \text{ (Budgeted fixed overhead)}}{5,500 \text{ (Hours of direct labor)}} = \$9.00 \text{ per hour}$$

We then convert the hourly rate to a rate per unit of product with the following computation:

$$1/2 \text{ hour per unit x } \$9.00 \ = \ \$4.50 \text{ per unit}$$

During the month, Colexus, Inc. manufactured 10,000 units of product. Fixed overhead is costed to the products by multiplying the standard rate of $4.50 per unit by the 10,000 units of output.

$$\$4.50 \text{ x } 10,000 \text{ units of product} = \$45,000 \text{ applied}$$

Fixed overhead budget	$ 49,500
Fixed overhead applied	45,000
Capacity variance (unfavorable)	$ 4,500

Figure 9.4 illustrates a graphical approach to the capacity variance concept. The diagonal line on the graph represents the amount of fixed overhead applied for various units of product manufactured. It rises at the rate of $4.50 per unit of product and reaches the $49,500 budgeted fixed overhead level at the normal volume of 11,000 units. However, the company only produced 10,000 units of product. With the rate of $4.50 per unit, only $45,000 of the budgeted fixed overhead was applied. The difference between the budgeted fixed overhead and the fixed overhead applied is the capacity variance, as designated on the vertical scale.

Earlier we presented the budget variance for individual categories of overhead costs. We could extend the idea to the capacity variance, but we do not gain additional information from further detail. The capacity variance is an overall issue and has little to do with individual costs.

P LANT CAPACITY AND CONTROL

In general, we consider the capacity variance as an item that production departments do not control. The plant produces what marketing identifies as the sales requirements. Therefore, the production departments cannot be held responsible if the sales demand exceeds or falls below production at a normal level of plant operation. Other factors, however, may contribute to producing

FIGURE 9.4   Analysis of Capacity Variance

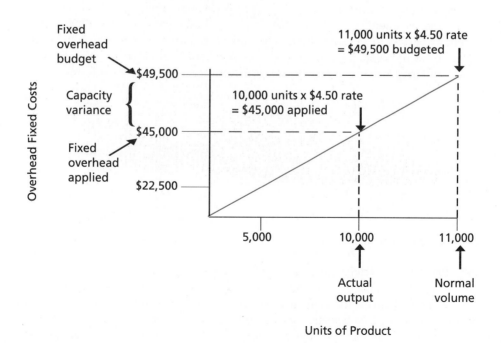

below capacity. Some of these factors are controllable (or somewhat controllable) by production departments. Excessive machine downtime (due to poor maintenance, for example) or inefficient production scheduling could be problems traceable to production managers. Lack of rapidity in completing tasks due to unskilled workers is a factor that is expected to some degree, but an excess of this condition may also be traceable to one or more production managers.

For Colexus, Inc., normal volume was defined at 5,500 direct labor hours or 11,000 units of product. Normal volume, as defined in Chapter 4, represents the average level of actual plant operation over several years. Practical plant capacity, on the other hand, is the level at which the plant can operate if all facilities are used to full extent. Some allowance is made under this definition for expected delays because of changes in machine setups, necessary maintenance time, and other interruptions. Hence, practical capacity is less than theoretical maximum capacity which could be obtained only under ideal conditions.

A comparison of the actual output with the output for practical plant capacity broadly measures the failure of the plant to operate at the level for which the plant was designed. Assume that Colexus, Inc. has a plant that can reasonably be expected to produce 15,000 units a month. Yet only 10,000 units were produced. The **idle capacity** is defined as the difference between the practical capacity and the actual production for a given month. The idle capacity for Colexus, Inc. is determined as follows:

Practical capacity	15,000 units
Actual production	10,000
Total idle capacity	5,000 units

The idle capacity can be analyzed further to determine why plant capacity was not used as intended. Assume that the sales budget shows that 12,000 units were expected to be sold during the month but that orders for only 11,500 units were received. The differences between practical capacity, sales budget, sales orders received, and actual production are illustrated as follows:

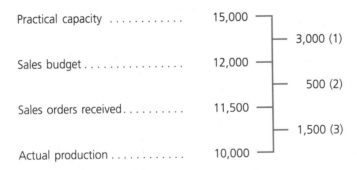

(1) Practical capacity minus sales budget. The difference between the practical plant capacity and the sales budget for the month requires further investigation. Perhaps the company was overly optimistic and provided too much plant capacity or is anticipating growth in future years. Or the Sales Department may not be obtaining potential available sales. Additional analysis may reveal the nature of the problem and provide a foundation for improvements.

(2) Sales budget minus sales orders received. The difference between the sales budget for the month and the sales orders received is a measurement of the inability of the Sales Department to meet the budget quota. Perhaps the sales quota was too high, or the Sales Department was not sufficiently aggressive.

(3) Sales orders received minus actual production. The difference between the sales orders received and actual production reflects a mixture of idle time and inefficiency. Suppose that Colexus, Inc. used 5,200 hours to produce 10,000 products and 5,000 hours were allowed. The 200 hours of inefficiency, in this case, used time that could have been used for production of an additional 400 units (200 hours ÷ .5 hour per unit). The difference between the sales orders received and the expected production for the time used (11,500 - 10,400 = 1,100 units) is a measurement of idle time. The idle time may be traced to poor production scheduling or to some other lapse in production management that caused production to fall below scheduled customer deliveries.

To simplify our example, we gave no allowance for inventories at either the beginning or the end of the period. In practice, adjustments must be made for units carried over as inventory or for units remaining on hand at the end of the month.

The significance of the variances may be emphasized by considering the dollar effect. If the sales department fails to meet the sales quota, the company loses profit on lost sales. Arguments can be made that the additional units could only be sold by reducing prices or that the cost estimates are not entirely accurate. Nevertheless, this approach to the problem can be helpful in that it points out how dollars of profit may be sacrificed by not using the facilities as intended.

V ARIANCE INVESTIGATION

When cost variances occur, managers need to know what caused them. Knowing the amount of variance does not disclose the cause(s); rather, investigation is required. However, managers must decide whether the benefits of investigation and corrective action exceed the related costs. Obviously, a $10 unfavorable materials usage variance from a standard cost of $50,000 would not be worth investigating. But where should the line be drawn?

Ideally, if the costs and benefits of investigating and correcting can be estimated, these costs and benefits should be compared in deciding whether to investigate. In practice, however, this is extremely difficult. Instead, many companies use simple decision rules based on prescribed dollar limits, such as "investigate any variance over $500." The main problem with this method is that $500 may be significant when the standard cost is $2,000 but may be insignificant when the standard cost is $20,000. Therefore, other companies use a percentage rule, such as "investigate any variance of 10% or more." Some companies use more sophisticated statistical approaches that set limits based on standard deviations from the standard cost. As Contemporary Practice 9.1 on page 394 illustrates, however, most companies do not seem to have formal decision rules; rather, managers are instructed to use "judgment."

C O N T E M P O R A R Y   P R A C T I C E   9 . 1

Survey On Variance Investigation

A survey of controllers from 115 U.S. manufacturing firms reported the following distribution of policies used regarding the investigation of direct labor cost variances:

Policy	Percentage
Investigate all variances....................................	5.3%
Investigate variances over prescribed dollar limits	31.0
Investigate variances over prescribed percentage limits.........	14.1
Statistical procedures....................................	0.9
Variances never investigated..............................	0.9
Judgment (no formal rule)	47.8
	100.0%

Source: Gaumnitz, B. R., and F. P. Kollaritsch, "Manufacturing Variances: Current Practices and Trends," *Journal of Cost Management*, Volume 5, No. 1, pp. 58-64.

S UMMARY OF STANDARD COST VARIANCES

We have completed a number of variance computations for the cost elements of production. Figure 9.5 contains a summary of all variances and the methods of calculating them. It also emphasizes that the costs charged to units produced are the standard costs. Therefore, work in process inventory and all subsequent accounts containing product costs will be stated at standard. Notice that costs on the far left side are all actual costs, while costs on the far right side are standard costs. If dollar amounts become smaller as we move from left to right, we experience unfavorable variances. If amounts become larger, we experience favorable variances.

D ISPOSITION OF VARIANCES

In our discussion of materials and labor variances, we set up separate variance accounts. Factory overhead variances, although identified separately in worksheet analysis, are combined in the underapplied or overapplied amounts. At the end of each period, variances accounts must be closed. Where do these variances go? As a practical matter, all standard cost variances eventually go to cost of goods sold. The most common practice is to close the variance accounts directly to cost of goods sold, thus, to treat them as period costs. Occasionally, if the variances are significant in amount, they will be prorated to cost of goods sold and to the appropriate materials, work in process, and finished goods inventories. We assume here that variances are closed to the cost of goods sold account.

FIGURE 9.5   Summary of Standard Cost Variances

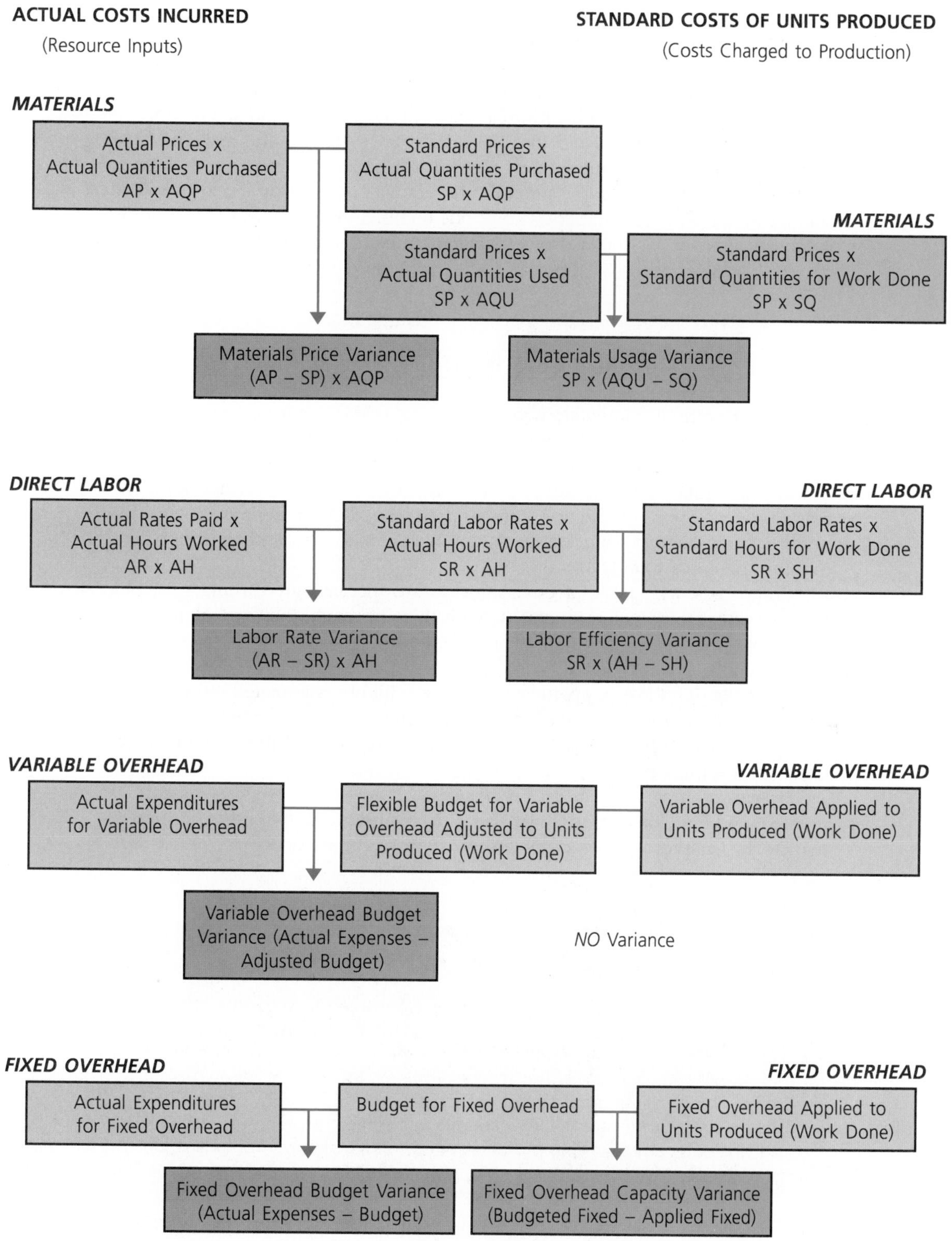

ACTUAL COSTS INCURRED
(Resource Inputs)

STANDARD COSTS OF UNITS PRODUCED
(Costs Charged to Production)

MATERIALS

Actual Prices x Actual Quantities Purchased AP x AQP	Standard Prices x Actual Quantities Purchased SP x AQP

MATERIALS

Standard Prices x Actual Quantities Used SP x AQU	Standard Prices x Standard Quantities for Work Done SP x SQ

Materials Price Variance (AP – SP) x AQP	Materials Usage Variance SP x (AQU – SQ)

DIRECT LABOR

DIRECT LABOR

Actual Rates Paid x Actual Hours Worked AR x AH	Standard Labor Rates x Actual Hours Worked SR x AH	Standard Labor Rates x Standard Hours for Work Done SR x SH

Labor Rate Variance (AR – SR) x AH	Labor Efficiency Variance SR x (AH – SH)

VARIABLE OVERHEAD

VARIABLE OVERHEAD

Actual Expenditures for Variable Overhead	Flexible Budget for Variable Overhead Adjusted to Units Produced (Work Done)	Variable Overhead Applied to Units Produced (Work Done)

Variable Overhead Budget Variance (Actual Expenses – Adjusted Budget)	*NO* Variance

FIXED OVERHEAD

FIXED OVERHEAD

Actual Expenditures for Fixed Overhead	Budget for Fixed Overhead	Fixed Overhead Applied to Units Produced (Work Done)

Fixed Overhead Budget Variance (Actual Expenses – Budget)	Fixed Overhead Capacity Variance (Budgeted Fixed – Applied Fixed)

STANDARD COSTS IN A PROCESS COST SYSTEM

Throughout this chapter, we have alluded to units as actual units of production or equivalent units. Standard costs are appropriate for job cost systems or process cost systems. Where we have a process cost system, the equivalent units are calculated using the FIFO method discussed in Chapter 5. Remember that equivalent units can be different for materials, labor, and overhead.

One convenience realized in a standard cost system is the availability of unit costs without the computations we did in Chapter 5. Since standard costs are predetermined, we simply multiply the equivalent units by the appropriate standard costs to determine costs of goods completed and costs of the ending inventory. Except for the use of equivalent units, variance analysis in a process cost system does not differ from the analysis used in a job cost system.

STANDARD COSTS IN JIT/CIM ENVIRONMENTS

In JIT and computer-integrated manufacturing (CIM) environments, standard cost systems face greater challenges. These environments are often characterized by rapid technological changes in production processes and products produced, which make it very difficult to set standards. Furthermore, the prevalence of short production runs and the need for real-time information require variance reporting on a much more timely basis than the typical monthly or even weekly basis.

Companies with JIT/CIM environments are increasingly turning to a philosophy of continuous improvement. With this approach, the focus is more on trends of variances rather than their magnitudes.

Generally, fewer types of cost variances are computed in JIT/CIM environments. Since JIT/CIM companies tend to be highly automated, direct labor variances are of little or no relevance. Also, materials price variances have little relevance because JIT companies usually have long-term contracts with a small number of suppliers.

In many companies with JIT/CIM processes, cost variances are being supplemented and, in some cases, replaced by nonfinancial measures of performance. In Chapter 15, we discuss these types of measures.

C O N T E M P O R A R Y   P R A C T I C E   9 . 2

Cost Standards at NEC

NEC, the large Japanese electronics company, installed its standard cost system in the 1950s when it was producing a stable range of products. Currently, NEC has a large range of fast-changing products due to rapid obsolescence. This has presented severe problems for the standard cost system. "The cost standards cannot be revised quickly enough for many products, so variance reports are increasingly open to question . . . As a result, the company is relying more heavily on departmental budgets than product-by-product variances from standard costs."

Source: Hiromoto, T., "Another Hidden Edge—Japanese Management Accounting," *Harvard Business Review*, July-August 1988, pp. 22-26.

STANDARD COSTS IN SERVICE ORGANIZATIONS

Standard costs are also applicable to service organizations. As with manufacturing companies, the more routine the service organization's activities, the easier it is to set standards. Generally, though, a service organization's activities are less routine than those of a manufacturing company.

Standard costing in a service setting will tend to emphasize labor and overhead, since materials are usually not a significant item. Notable exceptions, however, would be restaurants and auto repair shops, where food ingredients and car parts, respectively, are sizable cost elements. Calculating standard costs and variances for service organizations is similar to what we have seen for manufacturing companies. The main difference is that in determining standard quantities, the output of a service organization is often not as clear as for a manufacturing company. The following list contains examples of output measures that might be chosen in various service settings:

1. Number of claims processed in an insurance company.
2. Number of loan applications processed at a bank.
3. Number of deliveries made by a delivery service.
4. Number of patients treated in a particular department of a hospital.
5. Number of passengers transported by an airline.

TARGET COSTING AND KAIZEN COST TARGETS

Recognizing that most costs of production are determined when products are developed and designed, many companies are turning to a technique developed by Japanese companies known as **target costing**. After a target selling price and a target profit are established, an allowable cost consistent with these targets is obtained for the product. The company then designs the product and sets cost standards based on the allowable (target) cost. To promote continuous improvement, these cost targets, known as **kaizen cost targets**, are reduced in each successive period. Target costing and kaizen cost targets are discussed more fully in Chapter 15.

ETHICAL CONSIDERATIONS

Because cost variances are used to evaluate performance of cost center managers, there may be temptation to compromise ethics. This might happen in the standard setting process or in reporting actual costs. A manager who has input in setting standards might deliberately provide inaccurate information in an attempt to produce loose standards. Likewise, a manager who plays a role in gathering or reporting actual costs might intentionally distort actual data. Top management should be aware that performance evaluation based on cost variances can produce these behaviors. Cost center managers must guard against compromising their integrity for a possible short-term gain.

A more subtle form of unethical behavior results when managers avoid doing their best for fear of causing the standards to be tightened. A manager might believe that cost decreases in the current period are unlikely to be replicated due to some unique conditions. In that case, the manager should prepare a convincing argument to upper management not to revise standards significantly. Upper management can alleviate these types of problems by not automatically adjusting the cost standard by the full amount of cost reduction. For instance, if the production manager knows that any cost reduction will cause next period's cost standards to decrease by only 50 percent of the cost reduction, the manager would tend to put more effort into cutting costs than if the standards were to be adjusted by the full cost reduction.

S UMMARY

When actual performance varies from expectations, explanations for the differences are sought. Once causes of variations are identified, changes can be made through the planning process or control mechanisms. One aid to the analysis is the use of a standard cost system for costs that ultimately flow into cost of goods sold. Standard cost systems operate effectively in situations where standardized products or standardized operations exist. Although the primary advantage of such a system is cost control, several other advantages can also be achieved: cost management, improved decision making, savings in recordkeeping costs, and more rational inventory valuation.

A standard cost consists of a price factor and a quantity factor. The quality of a standard is expressed as strict, attainable, or loose. The preferred standard for all purposes is one that is current and attainable. A standard cost sheet is a basic element of the standard cost system. Here the standard quantities and prices are stated for direct materials, direct labor, and all factory overhead. The standard cost sheet gives the total unit cost that is attached to a completed unit of a given product.

Materials variances are set after considering the purchase price and other dollar amounts to be included and after determining the quantities needed for the intended operations. A materials price variance occurs anytime the actual price differs from the standard price. The variance is calculated as the actual quantity purchased times the difference between the actual price and the standard price. A materials usage variance is caused by using more or less materials than set by the standard. This variance is calculated as the standard price times the difference between the actual quantity used and the standard quantity allowed. Price variances are generally the responsibility of the purchasing department, while usage variances are generally the responsibility of production department managers.

In establishing labor standards, management looks at what operations are performed, how much time should be spent in each operation, what labor skills are needed to perform the operations, and what rate should be paid. The standard labor rate is the base rate of pay plus any other costs associated with labor that management chooses to include. A labor rate variance occurs any time the actual rate differs from the standard rate. The variance is the actual hours worked times the difference between the actual rate and the standard rate. A labor efficiency variance is caused by using more or less time than the standard specifies. This variance is calculated as the standard rate times the difference between actual hours worked and the standard hours allowed. Both variances generally are the responsibility of production department managers.

Standards for factory overhead are set after considering five important factors: the cost elements to include in the standards, the measure of activity that best relates the costs to the work done, the capacity concept for the selected measure of activity, the cost behavior of each element of overhead cost, and the rate structure, whether by task, operation, process, department, or overall. During any period, the actual overhead cost can differ from the overhead applied to products. To understand the significance of the underapplied or overapplied amounts, we calculate a budget variance and a capacity variance. A budget variance is the difference between actual overhead costs incurred and the flexible budget for the actual number of units produced. It represents those overhead cost elements over which department managers have control. The capacity variance is the difference between the flexible budget for the actual units produced and the amounts applied to products. This variance consists only of fixed overhead costs and represents the amount by which actual production differs from planned capacity.

*P*ROBLEM FOR REVIEW

The Houston plant of Enrico Instruments, Inc. manufactures an electrical surge protector. The standard cost per unit of this product is as follows:

Direct materials:	5 units of materials x $2 standard price	$ 10
Direct labor:	.5 hour x $6 standard labor rate	3
Overhead:	3 machine hours x $8 standard overhead rate	24
	Standard production cost per unit	$ 37

The total factory overhead at normal operating volume has been budgeted at $480,000; and 60,000 machine hours or 20,000 units of product have been budgeted as normal volume. The overhead rate per machine hour is $8.

Summary transactions and cost data pertaining to the year are as follows:

1. Materials purchases were 100,000 units at a unit cost of $2.04.

2. Direct materials issued to production were 93,000 units. Actual units of product manufactured during the year totaled 18,000 units.

3. Factory payroll totaled $159,500, of which indirect labor was $110,000.

4. Actual direct labor hours and rates were 7,500 hours at $6 and 500 hours at $9.

5. Factory overhead other than indirect labor was:

Indirect materials	$129,000
Reduction of prepaid insurance	2,000
Accrued expenses	109,500
Depreciation	86,000

Variable factory overhead costs totaled $146,500. Fixed costs were $290,000. These amounts include indirect labor and the previously listed costs.

6. Actual machine hours totaled 54,500 hours.

7. No units were in process at either the beginning or the end of the year. During the year, 18,000 units of product were manufactured, and 17,000 units were sold.

8. A portion of the flexible overhead budget in summary form is as follows:

	Percentage of Normal Operating Volume			
	70%	80%	90%	100%
Standard production (units of product)..	14,000	16,000	18,000	20,000
Budgeted machine hours	42,000	48,000	54,000	60,000
Variable overhead.	$126,000	$144,000	$162,000	$ 180,000
Fixed overhead	300,000	300,000	300,000	300,000
Total overhead	$426,000	$444,000	$462,000	$ 480,000

Required:

Compute the following standard cost variances:

1. Materials price variance and materials usage variance.

2. Labor rate variance and labor efficiency variance.

3. Overhead variances: budget variance and capacity variance. Show what portions of the variances are variable and fixed.

Solution:

1. Materials price variance and materials usage variance:

    (a) Materials price variance:

$$AP \times AQP = \$2.04 \times 100{,}000 = \$204{,}000$$

$$SP \times AQP = \$2.00 \times 100{,}000 = \$200{,}000$$

$$MPV = (AP - SP) \times AQP = \$0.04 \times 100{,}000 = \$4{,}000 \text{ Unfavorable}$$

    (b) Materials usage variance:

$$SP \times AQU = \$2.00 \times 93{,}000 = \$186{,}000$$

$$SP \times SQ = \$2.00 \times 90{,}000 = \$180{,}000$$

$$MUV = SP \times (AQU - SQ) = \$2.00 \times 3{,}000 = \$6{,}000 \text{ Unfavorable}$$

2. Labor rate variance and labor efficiency variance:

    (a) Labor rate variance:

$$AR \times AH = \$49{,}500^*$$

$$SR \times AH = \$6.00 \times 8{,}000 = \$48{,}000$$

$$LRV = (AR - SR) \times AH = \$1{,}500 \text{ Unfavorable}$$

    * 7,500 hours at $6.00 + 500 hours at $9.00

(The actual labor rate is not necessary to calculate the labor rate variance. However, the actual rate is required if the formula LRV = (AR - SR) x AH is used. The actual rate is found by dividing actual cost of $49,500 by 8,000 actual hours. The rate is $6.1875.)

    (b) Labor efficiency variance:

$$SR \times AH = \$6.00 \times 8{,}000 = \$48{,}000$$

$$SR \times SH = \$6.00 \times 9{,}000 = \$54{,}000$$

$$LEV = SR \times (AH - SH) = \$6.00 \times (1{,}000) = \$6{,}000 \text{ Favorable}$$

3. Overhead variances:

    (a) Underapplied or overapplied overhead:

        Actual costs:

Indirect labor	$110,000	
Indirect materials	129,000	
Reduction of prepaid insurance	2,000	
Accrued expenses	109,500	
Depreciation	86,000	$436,500
Applied costs:		
$24.00 x 18,000 units		432,000
Underapplied		$ 4,500

    (b) Budget variance:

Actual overhead costs		$436,500
Budgeted overhead costs at 18,000 units:		
Variable	$162,000	
Fixed	300,000	462,000
Budget variance—favorable		$ 25,500

    (c) Capacity variance:

Budgeted overhead costs at 18,000 units:		
Variable	$162,000	
Fixed	300,000	$462,000
Applied overhead		432,000
Capacity variance—unfavorable		$ 30,000

    (d) Summary of overhead variances:

Overhead	Actual Overhead Costs	Flexible Budget for 18,000 Units	Standard Costs of Units Produced (Applied Costs)
Variable	$146,500	$ 162,000	$162,000
Fixed	290,000	300,000	270,000
Total	$436,500	$ 462,000	$432,000

	Budget Variance	Capacity Variance
Variable	$15,500 Favorable	$ 0
Fixed	10,000 Favorable	30,000 Unfavorable
Total	$25,500 Favorable	$ 30,000 Unfavorable

$4,500 Unfavorable
Underapplied

❖ *APPENDIX 1*

THE LEARNING CURVE

In many industries, labor is a substantial part of the cost of production. Management applies quantitative methods in attempting to calculate how much labor time should be used in carrying out certain functions. Time and motion studies, that take into account human limitations, can help to determine how much labor time is required for an operation.

Management can obtain additional profit from increased productivity. With more units manufactured in a given time period, a greater manufacturing margin occurs even after sharing the benefits of increased productivity with the employees. Management is constantly trying to upgrade the skills of employees and to increase their efficiency through education and motivation.

We call the rate of learning a new task a **learning curve**. The curve shows that the average time to manufacture a unit will decrease as workers gain experience with a task. The initial or start-up phase is called the **learning phase.** Assume, for example, that the first batch of 100 units to be manufactured is produced in 500 labor hours. After this experience, the workers can produce the next 100-unit batch in less time. Perhaps the second 100-unit batch can be produced in 300 hours. An additional batch of 200 units may be produced with an additional 480 hours. When an optimum point is reached, no further increases in productivity can be expected; and productivity is said to be at the **static phase.** Many, however, would argue that further improvement is always possible.

The foregoing example illustrates an 80 percent learning curve. This rate of learning means that when production doubles, the cumulative average time per unit decreases to 80 percent of the previous cumulative average time. The following table shows this relationship.

Units Per Batch	Cumulative Number Of Units	Hours Per Batch	Cumulative Hours	Cumulative Average Hours Per Unit*
100	100	500	500	5.0
100	200	300	800	4.0*
200	400	480	1,280	3.2*

* Cumulative average is 80 percent of previous cumulative average.

The learning rate may be such that when the production is doubled, the cumulative average time per unit is 70 percent, 60 percent, or any other percentage of the previous cumulative average time per unit. At some point, the learning stage is completed; and further increases in productivity may not be expected. Experience with the learning rates for certain types of functions may be used in predicting expected results. Figure 9.6 shows the data for the 80 percent learning curve plotted on a graph.

FIGURE 9.6   An 80 Percent Learning Curve

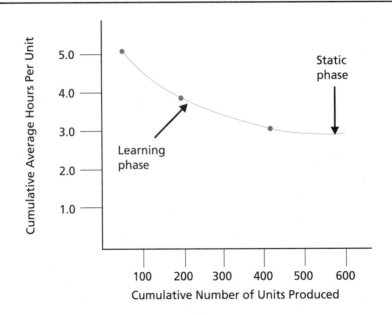

❖ *APPENDIX 2*

*T*HREE-VARIANCE METHOD FOR OVERHEAD

In many business situations, management needs more information about factory overhead costs to investigate variances and make appropriate adjustments. For example, measuring efficiency through comparing input activity bases with output activity bases provides a particularly helpful expansion to the variance analysis in certain situations where overhead cost behavior parallels resource input activity more closely than production output volumes. Consequently, we move from the two-variance approach discussed in the chapter to a three-variance method. The information is available also to expand to four variances.

*F*RAMEWORK FOR THREE-WAY OVERHEAD VARIANCE ANALYSIS

The difference between the two-way and the three-way variance analysis is the treatment of the budget or controllable variance. The budget variance is divided into a spending variance and an efficiency variance. The capacity variance is the same in both approaches.

To show how the variances fit together, remember that overhead costs for Colexus, Inc. are related to direct labor hours. The actual direct labor hours worked were 5,200. Since Colexus produced 10,000 units of product, it was allowed 5,000 (.5 hour x 10,000 units) direct labor hours. Based on the variable and fixed costs we have shown in the chapter, and remembering that the underapplied overhead was $6,500, we adapt Figure 9.3 to obtain Figure 9.7.

FIGURE 9.7   Three-Way and Four-Way Overhead Variance Analyses

Overhead	Actual Overhead Costs	Flexible Budget for 5,200 Hours	Flexible Budget for 10,000 Units (5,000 Hours)	Standard Costs of Units Produced (Applied Costs)
Variable	$31,500	$31,200*	$30,000	$30,000
Fixed	50,000	49,500	49,500	45,000
Total	$81,500	$80,700	$79,500	$75,000

Variable	$300 Unfavorable	$1,200 Unfavorable	$ 0
Fixed	500 Unfavorable	0	4,500 Unfavorable
Total	$800 Unfavorable	$1,200 Unfavorable	$4,500 Unfavorable

Spending Variance   **Efficiency Variance**   **Capacity Variance**

Variable	$1,500 Unfavorable
Fixed	500 Unfavorable
Total	$2,000 Unfavorable

Budget Variance

$6,500 Unfavorable
Underapplied

*($6 x 5,200 hours)

Spending Variance

A **spending variance** is the difference between the actual overhead cost and the flexible overhead budget for the actual activity base (hours of operation in our example). The variance assumes that the best measure of the amount spent on overhead is based on the actual activity base. Therefore, the actual overhead for the preceding data is the cost of 5,200 direct labor hours; and this amount is compared with the budget for those hours.

A spending variance is similar to the combination of the price (or rate) variances and the usage (or efficiency) variances in direct materials and direct labor. It shows that either the prices paid for overhead goods or services and/or the quantity used were not in agreement with the budget. A separate price or usage variance could be calculated.

The causes of variations include three of those categories presented for the budget variance:

1. Price changes in the individual cost components compressing overhead costs.

2. Quantity changes in individual items within overhead cost components.

3. Estimation errors in segregating variable and fixed costs.

Efficiency Variance

The **efficiency variance** is the difference between the flexible budget for the actual activity base and the flexible budget for the standard activity base allowed for actual units of product produced. Because fixed overhead costs are identical in both budgets, the efficiency variance consists only of differences in variable overhead costs. Therefore, we have an alternate means of calculating the variance. The formula is similar to that used for materials usage and labor efficiency variances: standard variable overhead rate per hour times the difference between the actual activity base and the standard activity base allowed. For Colexus, Inc., the efficiency variance is unfavorable because the workers used more than the standard hours allowed to complete the 10,000 units of product.

The term "efficiency" is in some sense a misnomer because it does not measure the efficient or inefficient use of individual overhead items. These are included in the spending variance. The efficiency variance measures the additional overhead costs incurred or saved as a result of inefficient or efficient use of the overhead activity base. That is, overhead must be incurred to support the cost driver. If the cost driver is inefficient, overhead costs are incurred to support inefficiency.

When direct labor hours are the measure of activity, a relationship exists between the labor efficiency variance and the overhead efficiency variance—they move in the same direction. If labor hours are inefficiently used, the labor efficiency variance measures the labor costs incurred for that inefficiency; and the overhead efficiency variance is the additional overhead cost incurred to support the inefficient labor. A favorable labor efficiency variance indicates the overhead efficiency variance must be favorable also. Consequently, to find the causes of an overhead efficiency variance for a direct labor activity base, look for the causes of inefficient or efficient labor.

Four-Way Analysis

Some managers prefer an additional level of detail. We already know that an efficiency variance involves variable cost only and a capacity variance involves fixed cost only. Since the spending variance can be split into variable and fixed components, we have four variances: variable overhead spending, variable overhead efficiency, fixed over-head spending, and fixed overhead capacity. These variances are also shown in Figure 9.7.

TERMINOLOGY REVIEW

Attainable standards, *373*
Budget variance, *389*
Capacity variance, *390*
Controllable variance, *389*
Cost control, *371*
Efficiency variance, *404*
Favorable variance, *375*
Flexible overhead budget, *388*
Idle capacity, *392*
Kaizen cost targets, *397*
Labor efficiency variance, *380*
Labor rate variance, *380*
Learning curve, *402*
Learning phase, *402*

Loose standards, *373*
Management by exception, *371*
Materials price variance, *375*
Materials usage variance, *377*
Measure of activity, *387*
Price standard, *370*
Quantity standard, *370*
Spending variance, *404*
Standard cost, *370*
Standard cost sheet, *374*
Static phase, *402*
Strict standards, *373*
Target costing, *397*
Unfavorable variance, *375*

SUGGESTED READINGS

Campbell, R. J., M. Janson, and J. Bush, "Developing Strategic Cost Standards in a Machine-Paced Environment," *Journal of Cost Management*, Vol. 4, No. 4, pp. 18-28.

Chen, K. H., and S. J. Lambert, "Impurity of Variable Factory Overhead Variances," *Journal of Accounting Education*, Spring 1985, pp. 189-196.

Chow, C. W., M. D. Shields, and A. Wong-Boren, "A Compilation of Recent Surveys and Company-Specific Descriptions of Management Accounting Practices," *Journal of Accounting Education*, Vol. 6, No. 2, pp. 183-207.

Cohen, J. R., and L. Paquette, "Management Accounting Practices: Perceptions of Controllers," *Journal of Cost Management*, Vol. 5, No. 3, pp. 73-83.

Jaouen, P. R., and B. R. Neumann, "Variance Analysis, Kanban, and JIT: A Further Study," *Journal of Accountancy*, June 1987, pp. 164-166.

Laudeman, M., and F. W. Schaeberle, "The Cost Accounting Practices of Firms Using Standard Costs," *Cost and Management*, July-August 1983, pp. 21-25.

Lipe, M. G., "Analyzing the Variance Investigation Decision: The Effects of Outcomes, Mental Accounting, and Framing," *Accounting Review*, October 1993, pp. 748-764.

Robbins, W. A., and F. A. Jacobs, "Cost Variances in Health Care: When Should Managers Investigate?" *Healthcare Financial Management*, September 1985, pp. 36-42.

Thomas, M. F., and J. T. Mackey, "Activity-Based Cost Variances for Just-in-Times," *Management Accounting*, April 1994, pp. 49-54.

QUESTIONS FOR REVIEW AND DISCUSSION

1. Explain the significance of profit analysis for an organization.

2. Under what conditions will a standard cost system work best?

3. Define a standard cost. Explain what constitutes the components of a standard cost.

4. What are the five major categories of advantages for a standard cost system? Why are they important?

5. Point out advantages and disadvantages of following the principle of management by exception.

6. What are some of the aspects of human behavior that must be considered in setting standards? Relate these to the quality of standards.

7. Which level of standard (tight, attainable, or loose) will give the lowest standard cost per unit? Explain.

8. Standards should be reviewed from time to time and examined for possible revision. What events would call for a review of standards?

9. A standard cost sheet is a key component of a standard cost system. Describe a standard cost sheet and explain why it is significant.

10. Define a materials price variance. What determines whether it is favorable or unfavorable?

11. In purchasing materials, what amounts are recorded in Accounts Payable and what amounts in Materials Inventory? What happens to the difference?

12. Describe five potential causes of a materials price variance.

13. Define a materials usage variance.

14. As materials are issued from the storeroom, what amounts are credited to Materials Inventory and what amounts are charged to Work in Process? What happens to the differences?

15. List and explain five potential causes of materials usage variances.

16. Who is responsible for a materials price variance? For a materials usage variance?

17. Explain how the purchase of materials at less than the standard price may have an adverse effect on other production variances.

18. How are labor rate variances and labor efficiency variances computed?

19. The departmental supervisor assigned three people with a labor rate per person of $10 an hour to a project with a standard labor rate of $9 an hour. Each person spent 70 hours on this project. What effect will this have on the labor rate variance?

20. List five causes of a labor rate variance.

21. List five causes of a labor efficiency variance.

22. Give an example of how a labor rate variance and a labor efficiency variance are related.

23. Give an example of how labor variances and materials variances are related.

24. Discuss the major considerations in the development of factory overhead rates.

25. Explain briefly how underapplied or overapplied factory overhead can be analyzed into a budget variance and a capacity variance.

26. Define a budget variance and list the major causes of a budget variance.

27. Define a capacity variance and explain why it consists solely of fixed factory overhead costs.

28. Can a capacity variance be controlled? Explain.

29. What is the primary difference between using standard costs in a job cost system and a process cost system?

EXERCISES

9-1. Standard Cost Sheet.   Murry Company manufactures special electronic equipment and parts. It has adopted a standard cost system with separate standards for each part. A special electronic "black box" has standards set with the following components. Materials include both iron and copper. Each "black box" requires 5 sheets of iron which cost $3 per sheet and 4 spools of copper at $3.50 per spool. Four hours of direct labor are needed for producing each box, and the standard rate per hour is $6. Overhead costs are charged to products on the basis of direct labor time. The overhead rates are $3 per hour for variable costs and $2 per hour for fixed costs.

Required:
Prepare a standard cost sheet that shows the standard cost per unit for each "black box."

9-2. Standard Cost Sheet.   Hermes Enterprises, of Patras, Greece, installed a standard cost system to achieve better cost control and to facilitate the task of charging costs to its product. The company produces specialized square bricks, known as Chi Squares. Each brick requires six kilograms of direct materials that cost (in drachmas) Dr300 per kilogram. The standard calls for two hours of direct labor time with a rate of Dr1,500 per hour. Manufacturing overhead is applied on the basis of machine hours at the rate of Dr800 per machine hour. The product uses 1.5 machine hours. Three-fourths of the manufacturing overhead rate is for fixed costs.

Required:
Prepare a standard cost sheet that shows the standard cost per brick.

9-3. Materials Variances.   A printed circuit used in the production of fuel-injected engines has a standard cost of $3 per unit. The standard calls for one printed circuit per engine. Last month, Capetini Automotive purchased 150,000 printed circuits at a cost of $2.91 per unit and 30,000 circuits at a cost of $3.15 per unit. The Production Department required 180,000 printed circuits to produce 178,500 engines.

Required:
1. Determine the materials price variance.
2. Determine the materials usage variance.
3. Using T-accounts, show the accounts and amounts involved in the purchasing of the printed circuits and in the issuing of the printed circuits to work in process.

9-4. Materials Price Variance.   Three types of materials, designated as Basic, Filler, and Lining, are used by VanErik Construction Suppliers in the production of insulating blocks. Data with respect to April purchases are as follows:

Materials	Number of Units Purchased	Standard Unit Cost	Actual Unit Cost
Basic	15,000	$ .60	$ .65
Filler	7,000	1.00	1.15
Lining	9,000	2.00	1.80

Required:
1. Determine the total materials price variance for the month of April.
2. Determine the individual materials price variances for the month of April.

3. Which calculation gives more information about price variances: the total price variance or the individual price variances? Explain.

9-5. Materials Variances—Missing Information.   In May, Liu Equipment Company, of Shanghai, China, purchased 50,000 parts at the total cost (in yuan) of Y600,000. During the month, 46,000 parts having a standard unit cost of Y11 were used in production. The materials usage variance for the month was unfavorable by Y33,000. According to the standards, 5 parts should be used for each unit of product.

Required:
1. Calculate the materials price variance.
2. How many units of product were made?
3. How many units of parts should have been used in production?
4. How many dollars should be charged to Work in Process for materials requisitioned?

9-6. Materials Variances.   Standard quantities and costs of parts for a tricycle manufactured by Cycle Specialties, Inc. are as follows:

Description	Parts Per Tricycle	Cost Per Unit of Part
Wheels	3	$ 3.00
Frame	1	2.50
Handle bars	2	0.80
Fenders	3	0.60
Steering assembly	1	1.00

This year, the company assembled 60,000 tricycles. No materials were on hand either at the beginning or at the end of the year. The quantities purchased and used in production at actual costs are as follows:

Description	Number of Parts Used	Actual Cost
Wheels	182,000	$582,400
Frames	60,800	145,920
Handle bars	121,000	84,700
Fenders	183,000	109,800
Steering assemblies	60,000	72,000

Required:
1. Compute the materials price variance and the materials usage variance for each component.
2. Determine the total materials price variance and the total materials usage variance.
3. Identify components with relatively large price variances and components with relatively large usage variances.

9-7. Materials Variances and T-accounts.   The Kala Company has the following data for the month of November:

Materials purchased, 2,600 kilograms	$ 8,580
Materials used in production	1,320 kilograms
Units of product manufactured	17,000
Materials usage variance	$ 384 Unfavorable
Standard price per kilogram	$ 3.20

Required:
1. Find the standard quantity of materials allowed for the units of product manufactured.
2. Determine the materials price variance.
3. Trace the materials costs and variances through T-accounts with Work in Process Inventory as the final account.

9-8. Selection of Labor Standards. Four employees each work 38 hours a week in an assembly operation. Standard production for the week was established at 2,280 assemblies or at a rate of production of 15 assemblies per labor hour. A time study person has observed that it is possible to make 20 assemblies an hour, and this rate has been set as the new standard.

Production data for one week under the new standard are as follows:

Employee	Hours Worked	Units Assembled
1	38	660
2	38	590
3	38	630
4	38	620

The standard labor rate per hour is $12. During this week, an unfavorable materials usage variance due solely to above normal scrap and waste was $2,500. Also, 500 units that had been fully assembled were rejected by an inspector.

Required:

1. What was the standard labor cost per assembly under the old standard of 15 assemblies per hour?
2. What was the anticipated labor cost per assembly under the new standard of 20 assemblies per hour?
3. What was the actual labor cost per assembly during the week (after deducting the rejected units)?
4. Comment on the new labor standard and possible reasons for the losses.

9-9. Labor Variances. Karlsruhe Mueslix Werke manufactures a popular German breakfast cereal. The company adopted a standard cost system that has the following labor standards for 10,000 cartons of Mueslix:

Department	Rate	Hours	Standard Cost
Crushing	DM20	100	DM2,000
Baking	12	40	480
Mixing	16	20	320
Packaging	12	40	480
Total		200	DM3,280
Labor cost per carton			DM0.328

During September, the company produced 830,000 cartons and had the following actual costs and hours:

Department	Cost	Hours Worked
Crushing	DM159,358	8,400
Baking	52,752	3,820
Mixing	29,172	1,410
Packaging	29,368	2,653
Total	DM270,650	16,283

Required:

1. Calculate the labor rate variance for each of the four departments.
2. Calculate the labor efficiency variance for each of the four departments.
3. Using T-accounts, show the amounts recorded in the Payroll account, the variance accounts, and the Work in Process account.

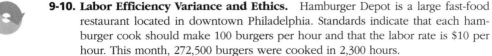

9-10. Labor Efficiency Variance and Ethics. Hamburger Depot is a large fast-food restaurant located in downtown Philadelphia. Standards indicate that each hamburger cook should make 100 burgers per hour and that the labor rate is $10 per hour. This month, 272,500 burgers were cooked in 2,300 hours.

Required:
1. What was the labor efficiency variance this month?
2. Why might the restaurant manager be tempted to report to top management a smaller variance than actually occurred?

9-11. Labor Variances.   The payroll for Medical Claims Processors for the year was $516,000. Income taxes of $105,000 and FICA taxes of $42,000 were withheld, and employee voluntary withholdings totaled $4,000. The net amount paid to employees was $365,000. Included in the total payroll was indirect labor of $141,000 (not on an hourly basis).

The standard labor rate of $5.00 per hour was paid for 60,000 hours, and $7.50 per hour was paid for 10,000 hours. The company processed 550,000 claims during the year. Standards show that eight claims should be processed each hour.

Required:
1. Calculate the labor rate variance.
2. Calculate the labor efficiency variance.
3. Using T-accounts, show what direct labor cost was charged to Work in Process Inventory, to the various payroll-related accounts, and to the appropriate variance accounts.

9-12. Materials and Labor Variances With Incomplete Data.   Paul Shenk, the cost accountant for Billings Plastics, Inc. has provided you with actual and standard cost data for one of the basic product lines for the month of February:

	Direct Materials	Direct Labor
Purchased and used at actual cost, 38,000 units.....	$104,500	
Actual direct labor payroll......................		$63,000
Standard materials units per product unit..........	2	
Standard labor time per product unit		20 minutes
Standard price per unit of materials	$2.50	
Standard direct labor rate per hour...............		$10
Labor rate variance (unfavorable)		$6,000

During February, 18,000 units of product were manufactured.

Required:
1. Determine the materials price variance.
2. What was the standard cost of the standard units of direct materials used in production?
3. Compute the materials usage variance.
4. How many direct labor hours were used in February?
5. Compute the labor efficiency variance.
6. What was the standard cost of direct labor charged to work in process?

9-13. Overhead Variances.   Carrollton Delivery Service hires drivers to deliver packages in Dallas. An average standard time to make a delivery has been established as one hour. The office is centrally located, and it takes about as much time to deliver to one location as it does to another. Fixed costs have been budgeted at $240,000 for the year. Under normal conditions, the company expects to make 60,000 deliveries a year. Variable cost has been budgeted at $12 per hour. Last year, the company made 63,000 deliveries in 59,000 hours and incurred total costs of $988,000, including fixed costs.

Required:
1. Compute the standard cost of making a delivery.
2. How much overhead costs were charged to deliveries in total during the year?
3. Determine the budget variance.
4. Determine the capacity variance.

9-14. Overhead Variance Analysis. A flexible budget for Jimbo Casting Company is in summary form as follows:

Machine hours	60,000	70,000	80,000	90,000
Variable overhead	$240,000	$280,000	$320,000	$360,000
Fixed overhead	480,000	480,000	480,000	480,000
Total overhead	$720,000	$760,000	$800,000	$840,000

The standard rate of production is 6 units per machine hour, and normal volume has been defined at 80,000 machine hours. The company manufactured 420,000 units of product in 70,000 machine hours. Actual variable overhead was $287,000, and the fixed overhead was $475,000.

Required:

1. Compute the amount of underapplied or overapplied overhead.
2. Compute the budget variance.
3. Explain the major causes of a budget variance.
4. Compute the capacity variance.
5. Cite three possible reasons for the existence of this capacity variance.

9-15. Budget Variance for Individual Costs. Suzi Greenberg, manager of the Machining Department at Mayfield Industries, Inc. has estimated overhead costs for August at an expected operating level of 6,000 machine hours. Past experience indicates a rate of cost variability per hour as follows:

Lubrication	$.75
Supplies	.30
Power	.25
Repairs	.50
Maintenance	.80

Costs that are fixed for the month are budgeted as follows:

Supervision	$ 4,500
Indirect labor	11,500
Heat and light	3,200
Taxes and insurance	1,600
Depreciation	1,800

During the month of August, the department worked 5,500 hours and produced the quantity of product that should have been produced in 5,000 hours. The department incurred the following overhead costs:

Lubrication	$ 3,900
Supplies	1,700
Power	1,500
Repairs	2,800
Maintenance	4,300
Supervision	4,000
Indirect labor	12,000
Heat and light	3,200
Taxes and insurance	1,400
Depreciation	1,600
Total	$ 36,400

Required:

1. Prepare a budget of overhead costs for 5,000 machine hours.
2. Compare the actual overhead costs with the budget for 5,000 machine hours. Show budget variances for each item.
3. Explain what factors could cause the budget variance to occur.

9-16. Fixed Overhead Relationships.   University Medical Center has a radiology department that operated at 50,000 standard hours last year. The standard calls for five patients per hour, and the department actually handled 9,000 patients. Fixed overhead data are as follows:

Fixed overhead charged to patients	$630,000
Unfavorable capacity variance	350,000

Required:
1. What was the fixed overhead budget last year?
2. What was the fixed overhead rate per patient?
3. How many patients were considered to be normal volume?
4. Would the capacity variance have been smaller or larger if the Radiology Department had processed 12,000 patients? Explain.

9-17. Learning Curve (Appendix 1).   Skyway Technic, Inc. is planning to submit a bid on equipment to be used in space exploration. Experience on similar contracts indicates that a 70 percent learning curve may be appropriate in estimating labor hours and costs. The first 500 units of this equipment will require an estimated 10,000 labor hours. The next 500 units should be completed in 4,000 hours. Another 1,000 units should follow the 70 percent learning curve, after which the learning process will be completed. The labor rate per hour is $20.

Required:
1. What will be the cumulative average hours per unit after production of the third batch (1,000-unit batch)? (Assume a 70 percent learning curve.)
2. Estimate the labor cost per unit after the completion of the learning process.

9-18. Learning Curve (Appendix 1).   A potential customer approaches Elliot, Inc. with a proposal to buy seven complex agricultural pumps for a total of $2,000. The pump is a new product, and only one unit has been produced at the request of another customer. The following cost data are available on the first pump:

Direct materials (15 pounds at $2 per pound)	$ 30
Direct labor (50 hours at $10 per hour)	500
Variable overhead ($2 per direct labor hour)	100
Fixed overhead ($1 per direct labor hour)	50
Total cost	$ 680

The Engineering Department believes an 80 percent learning curve exists for this situation. Also, if the bid is accepted, the company will be eligible for a 3 percent quantity discount on direct materials.

Required:
Estimate the incremental profit or loss Elliot, Inc. would realize if it accepted the proposal for the seven pumps.

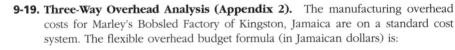

9-19. Three-Way Overhead Analysis (Appendix 2).   The manufacturing overhead costs for Marley's Bobsled Factory of Kingston, Jamaica are on a standard cost system. The flexible overhead budget formula (in Jamaican dollars) is:

Fixed costs	J$100,000 per period
Variable costs	J$ 10 per bobsled

Each bobsled requires 2 hours of machine time. Normal production is 25,000 bobsleds per month. During the most recent period, 42,000 hours of work produced 20,000 bobsleds. The actual manufacturing overhead costs totaled J$350,000, of which J$120,000 was fixed cost.

Required:
1. Calculate the underapplied or overapplied manufacturing overhead.

2. How much of the total overhead variance is fixed cost and how much is variable cost?

3. Compute the spending and efficiency variances.

4. Compute the capacity variance.

5. Prove that the spending, efficiency, and capacity variances account for the total overhead variance.

9-20. Labor and Three-Way Overhead Analysis (Appendix 2). Direct labor and overhead standards per finished unit for Hereford Metals Company are as follows:

Direct labor	10 hours at $5.00 per hour
Variable overhead	10 hours at $2.00 per hour
Fixed overhead	10 hours at $3.00 per hour

Budgeted fixed overhead costs per month are $150,000. During March, 5,000 finished units were produced. Direct labor costs were $234,000 (52,000 hours). Actual variable overhead costs were $103,000, and actual fixed overhead costs were $147,000.

Required:

1. Determine the rate and efficiency variances for direct labor for March.

2. Compute the underapplied or overapplied manufacturing overhead for the month.

3. Calculate the spending, efficiency, and capacity variances for the month.

4. Explain how the labor efficiency and overhead efficiency variances are related.

5. Split the spending variance into its variable and fixed components.

P ROBLEMS

9-21. Standard Cost Sheet—Materials and Labor. An industrial solvent with the brand name Velocidad is produced by Proveedor Chemical Company in Caracas, Venezuela, and sold in 25-liter drums. Data with respect to materials and labor are as follows:

1. A batch of 1,500 liters of Velocidad is made from an input of 1,500 liters each of Destino and Promesa. In the boiling operation, 50 percent of the volume of both Destino and Promesa is lost through evaporation.

2. At the end of the boiling operation, 2 kilograms of Bono are added to each 1,500-liter batch. (This has no measurable effect on volume.)

3. A worker can process one 25-liter drum in 20 minutes.

4. At the final inspection, two 25-liter drums are rejected out of every ten drums received from the production line.

5. Standard materials prices and the labor rate (in bolivars) are as follows:

Destino	B 200 per liter
Promesa	B 150 per liter
Bono	B 600 per kilogram
Labor rate	B1,200 per hour

Required:

Prepare a standard cost sheet that shows the standard materials and labor cost for each 25-liter drum of completed product.

9-22. Standard Cost Sheet—All Cost Elements. Wellington Office Furniture is a well-known supplier of quality office furniture. It is currently setting up a standard cost system to cover all of its products. One product is the Home Office Workstation for those who operate a business in their homes. The production process for this workstation involves four departments: Cutting, Assembly, Staining, and Finishing. Materials, labor, and overhead costs are accumulated by department.

Raw materials include lumber, stain, drawer handles and fixtures, screws, dowels, and glue. Each workstation requires 64 feet of lumber at $1.60 per foot. Drawer handles and other drawer fixtures are $16.80 per workstation. Stain required is 0.8 gallons at $16.70 per gallon. Screws, dowels, and glue are included in the overhead costs of the Assembly Department. Lumber enters the process in the Cutting Department; drawer handles and other drawer fixtures in the Assembly Department; and stain in the Staining Department.

Direct labor occurs in Cutting, Assembly, and Finishing. Cutting requires 30 minutes per workstation with labor costs of $9.50 per hour. Assembly requires two hours per workstation with labor costs of $11.60 per hour. Finishing requires 20 minutes with labor costs of $7.80 per hour. Staining is an automated department and has no direct labor.

Factory overhead is applied to workstations by department on the basis of direct labor hours in the three departments with direct labor. Cutting is $10 per hour; Assembly is $9.50 per hour; and Finishing is $9 per hour. The Staining Department overhead is applied on the basis of machine time, and the rate is $18 per machine hour. Each workstation requires one-fourth of an hour of machine time.

Required:

Prepare a standard cost sheet that shows all of the elements of cost for a completed workstation. For convenience, identify the cost elements by department.

9-23. Comparison of Materials Cost, Two Plants. Redwood Coatings Company manufactures a roof coating and sealant product in 5-gallon pails in both the Holton plant and the McHugh plant. Materials cost is a large part of the total cost and varies from month to month. Standard quantities of materials used to manufacture each 5-gallon pail and the standard prices are as follows:

	Standard Quantities	*Standard Prices*
Oil	5 gallons	$3.00 per gallon
Metal	2 pounds	2.50 per pound
Sealer	10 ounces	0.10 per ounce

Production and cost data for the two plants for both June and July are as follows:

	Holton Plant	*McHugh Plant*
Product units manufactured:		
June	80,000	50,000
July	85,000	60,000
Quantity of materials used:		
June:		
Oil.	416,000 gals.	252,000 gals.
Metal	163,000 lbs.	102,000 lbs.
Sealer	800,000 oz.	502,000 oz.
July:		
Oil.	427,000 gals.	320,000 gals.
Metal	170,000 lbs.	126,000 lbs.
Sealer	855,000 oz.	604,000 oz.

All materials purchased were used in production. The actual prices for the materials purchased and used were the same for both plants. Actual prices are as follows:

	Actual Unit Prices	
	June	July
Oil	$3.40	$3.45
Metal	2.30	2.40
Sealer	0.12	0.13

Required:

1. Compute the total materials price variance by ingredient for both June and July.
2. Compute the materials usage variance by ingredient for each plant for each month.
3. Which plant had the larger usage variance in June? Which had the larger usage variance in July?

9-24. Substituting Factors of Production.   Denise Warren, vice-president of production at Vanity Fabrics, Inc., believes that a net savings in production cost can be realized by using stronger and more expensive yarn in production. In her opinion, far too much labor time is wasted in working with poor grade yarn that breaks or gets jammed in the knitting machines.

At the present time, 20,000 product units are made with 200,000 yards of yarn costing $0.12 a yard. With a better grade of yarn costing $0.25 a yard, the same number of units could be made with 160,000 yards of yarn.

The standard labor rate is $8.50 per hour, and the standard time to make 20,000 units with the cheaper yarn is 20,000 hours. Warren estimates that with the better yarn, only 16,000 hours will be needed for 20,000 product units.

Required:

1. Calculate the standard costs of yarn and labor when using the cheaper yarn.
2. Calculate the standard costs of yarn and labor when using the more expensive yarn.
3. Does a net cost savings exist with the better yarn?
4. Besides the factors previously mentioned relating to current cost savings, give other reasons why better yarn might be favored.

9-25. Reconstructing Actual Inputs.   Azcue Company manufactures a number of different products. Its most profitable product comes from a division in northern Mexico, which has the following standard cost sheet (all monetary amounts are in pesos):

Materials (2 kilograms at M$8.5 per kilogram)	M$17
Labor (.5 hour at M$12 per hour)	6
Overhead (M$18 per labor hour)	9
Total product cost	M$32

Income statements are prepared for each product line on a monthly basis. At the end of a recent month, the following income statement information was available for the product:

Sales (M$45 x 92,000 units)		M$4,140,000
Cost goods sold at standard (M$32 x 92,000 units)		2,944,000
Gross profit at standard		M$1,196,000
Manufacturing cost variances:		
Materials price	M$ 7,500 F	
Materials usage	8,500 U	
Labor rate	5,900 U	
Labor efficiency	12,000 F	5,100
Adjusted gross profit		M$1,201,100

Materials purchases for the month were 300,000 kilograms. The division produced 120,000 units, with no work in process inventories at the beginning or end of the month. All variances are closed to the Cost of Goods Sold account at the end of each month.

Required:

1. Calculate the actual materials price per kilogram.
2. Calculate the number of kilograms of materials actually used in production.
3. Calculate the actual number of labor hours worked.

9-26. Interrelationship of Materials and Labor Variances.   Vicki Jaedicke, purchasing agent for Rainelle Products, Inc., was pleased to report that she bought 50,000 units of a plastic part for $15,000, which was lower than the $22,500 cost at its standard price. The part also was a lower grade than called for by the standard. According to standards, five of these parts should be used in the production of each unit of product.

When these parts were used in production, breakage was higher than normal. To keep the abnormal breakage to a minimum, the operating manager shifted more skilled workers into the operations where breakage occurred. The standard labor rate for this operation was $7 per hour. One-half hour is the standard time for the production of each final product.

Last month, the company used 42,000 plastic parts and 3,300 hours in the production of 6,000 units of product. The labor cost was $31,750.

Required:

1. Compute materials price and materials usage variances.
2. Compute labor rate and labor efficiency variances.
3. Combine the four variances to obtain the net effect. Did the purchasing agent save the company money in buying the nonstandard plastic parts?
4. Which variance amounts would be assigned to the purchasing agent and which would be assigned to the operating manager?

1-2-3

9-27. Evaluation of Four Plants.   Bethel Motors, Inc. produces an automotive product at four plants: Hill, Valley, Ridge, and River. Standard materials and labor costs per unit of product are the same at all plants and are as follows:

Direct materials per product unit:
Metal sheets (5 units at $2). . . . . $ 10
Purchased part (3 units at $1)   3
Standard materials costs . . . . $ 13

Direct labor per product unit:
.5 hour at $10.   5
Standard materials and labor cost . . . . $ 18

Actual production data for each of the four plants for June, July, and August are as follows:

| | **Plants** | | | |
	Hill	Valley	Ridge	River
June:				
Units produced	80,000	50,000	60,000	100,000
Units of materials used:				
Metal sheets	402,000	252,000	335,000	510,000
Purchased part	241,000	151,000	215,000	305,000
Labor hours.	42,000	27,000	40,000	49,000
July:				
Units produced	95,000	40,000	70,000	110,000
Units of materials used:				
Metal sheets	480,000	212,000	375,000	550,000
Purchased part	275,000	122,000	225,000	335,000
Labor hours.	48,000	21,000	42,000	53,000

		Plants		
	Hill	Valley	Ridge	River
August:				
Units produced	100,000	45,000	65,000	120,000
Units of materials used:				
Metal sheets	505,000	230,000	330,000	608,000
Purchased part	310,000	140,000	200,000	362,000
Labor hours.	50,000	23,000	38,000	58,000

Required:

1. Compute the materials usage variance for each month for each plant.

2. Compute the labor efficiency variance for each month for each plant.

3. If the market weakens, which plant is most likely to be closed down? Explain.

9-28. Materials and Labor—Missing Information. You have been asked to provide your supervisor with cost information about operations in the South Euclid plant. Unfortunately, you are furnished with only partial information; you must calculate much of what is needed. The information you have to work with is as follows:

1. The company purchased 350,000 units of direct materials for the South Euclid plant during the month. The standard price is $3.10.

2. Raw materials at the beginning of the month at the standard price cost $52,700. The standard price has not changed during the past two months.

3. Raw materials at the end of the month at the standard price cost $108,500.

4. The materials price variance was unfavorable by $175,000.

5. The materials usage variance was unfavorable by $21,700.

6. Actual direct labor cost was $320,000, but the labor rate variance was unfavorable by $10,000.

7. Actual direct labor hours were 32,000.

8. The plant manufactured 65,000 units of product.

9. The labor efficiency variance was favorable by $15,000.

Required:

Using the data provided, furnish the following information:

(a) Actual quantity of raw materials withdrawn from inventory for use in production at the standard price.

(b) Actual cost of materials purchased.

(c) Number of units of raw materials needed for each unit of product according to the standard.

(d) Standard direct materials cost of production.

(e) Standard direct labor cost of production.

(f) The standard labor rate per hour.

(g) Standard labor hours per product unit.

9-29. Overhead in an Automated Operation. Sachi Kato observes, "The nature of costs has changed since Kato Windings Company installed more automated equipment. At one time, direct labor was an important factor. With automation, direct labor is essentially a fixed cost with workers monitoring the operation on television screens. Variable overhead cost is lower, and is related to hours of machine operation. On the other hand, fixed cost is much higher than it was in a labor-oriented operation. However, the production line can only move so fast. If it is stepped up, too many pieces are broken."

Yoko Kato, the production manager, says, "We may not obtain much more savings from increases in productivity. Additional savings will have to come by holding down fixed costs and receiving a large volume of orders."

Data from last year are as follows:

Variable cost per machine hour	$4
Number of standard units of product per machine hour	100
Fixed overhead budget	$6,000,000
Normal number of product units produced in a year	60,000,000
Actual hours of operation	500,000
Actual product units produced	58,000,000
Actual overhead cost:	
Variable overhead	$1,935,000
Fixed overhead	$6,030,000

Required:

1. What was the standard variable overhead cost per product unit and the standard fixed overhead cost per product unit?
2. How much overhead was applied to production for the year?
3. Determine the following variances:
   (a) Overhead budget variance.
   (b) Overhead capacity variance.
4. Prepare a graph that shows how a capacity variance occurs in this case.

9-30. Complete Variance Analysis and Cost Flow. Sudan Machine Company operates with a standard cost accounting system and uses cost variances as a means of detecting costs that may require more control. A standard cost sheet for a component that is manufactured exclusively in one plant is as follows:

Direct materials (6 units at $4)	$ 24.00
Direct labor (.5 hour at $8)	4.00
Variable overhead (.75 machine hour at $4)	3.00
Fixed overhead (.75 machine hour at $16)	12.00
Standard unit cost	$ 43.00

Data from the past year are as follows:

1. Purchased 2,000,000 units of materials at a cost of $7,540,000.
2. Manufactured 300,000 units of product.
3. Budgeted $6,400,000 for fixed overhead for the year.
4. Used 1,812,000 units of material in production.
5. Used 200,000 direct labor hours.
6. Spent $1,610,000 for direct labor.
7. Worked 190,000 actual machine hours.
8. Spent $880,000 for variable overhead.
9. Spent $6,321,000 for fixed overhead.
10. Completed 300,000 units and sold 250,000 units.

Required:

1. Determine the following variances:
   (a) Materials price variance.
   (b) Materials usage variance.
   (c) Labor rate variance.
   (d) Labor efficiency variance.
   (e) Overhead budget variance.
   (f) Overhead capacity variance.
2. Which is the largest unfavorable variance that may be controllable by production management? Explain.
3. If the capacity variance is unfavorable by a large amount, what steps may be taken to correct it?

4. Using T-accounts, trace all costs through the accounts and close all variances to Cost of Goods Sold. Show the ending balances in the following accounts:
(a) Materials Inventory.
(b) Work in Process Inventory.
(c) Finished Goods Inventory.
(d) Cost of Goods Sold.

9-31. Budget and Capacity Variances.   Revchek Manufacturing bases its factory overhead on the flexible budget cost function of:

$$\$33,000 + (\$2.40 \times direct\ labor\ hours)$$

Normal production is based on 12,000 direct labor hours. Standards call for two direct labor hours per unit of completed product. For the current period, the operating results were as follows:

Actual direct labor hours worked	11,400
Units produced	5,800
Actual variable overhead costs	$28,460
Actual fixed overhead costs	$31,950

Required:
1. Calculate the rates for variable and fixed overhead that would be used to apply overhead to products.
2. Calculate the underapplied or overapplied overhead for the period.
3. Determine the following variances:
(a) Overhead budget variance.
(b) Overhead capacity variance.
4. How much of the budget variance is due to variable costs and how much to fixed costs?

9-32. Overhead Variances for a Department.   The following flexible budget information has been prepared for the Fabrication Department of Abbott Industries:

Machine hours at normal capacity	5,000
Variable overhead:	
Indirect labor	$ 3,500
Supplies	2,500
Repairs and maintenance	1,000
Electricity, other than lighting	5,000
Total variable overhead	$12,000
Fixed overhead:	
Supervision	$ 3,000
Supplies	1,700
Repairs and maintenance	3,000
Depreciation on machinery	6,500
Insurance	1,800
Property taxes	1,000
Heating	600
Lighting	400
Total fixed overhead	$18,000

Factory overhead is allocated on the basis of machine hours. The standard calls for ten units of product per machine hour.

During May, 4,650 machine hours were actually worked; and 48,530 units of product were produced. The following actual overhead costs were incurred:

Variable overhead:

Indirect labor.	$ 3,400
Supplies	2,200
Repairs and maintenance	960
Electricity, other than lighting	4,740
Total variable overhead	$11,300

Fixed overhead:

Supervision	$ 3,100
Supplies	1,650
Repairs and maintenance	3,200
Depreciation on machinery	6,500
Insurance	1,900
Property taxes	1,100
Heating	845
Lighting	405
Total fixed overhead	$18,700

Required:

1. Prepare a report that shows each category of overhead cost with individual budget variances.

2. What are the major potential causes of the budget variances?

3. Calculate an overall capacity variance for the department.

9-33. Comprehensive Variance Analysis. Alexander Company uses a standard cost system and isolates the following six variances for the appropriate departments:

Materials price variance	Labor efficiency variance
Materials usage variance	Overhead budget variance
Labor rate variance	Overhead capacity variance

The company uses direct labor as the measure of activity for each of the producing departments.

Required:

For each of the following *independent* events, indicate which variances would be affected. Briefly explain why they would be affected, and indicate whether the effect is favorable or unfavorable. If more than one variance is influenced in a given situation, limit your discussion to the two or three most important variances for that situation.

(a) Demand exceeded expectation, and the number of units produced during the year was much greater than the number planned.

(b) Because of an improperly adjusted machine, more materials were wasted than anticipated. When the department supervisor requisitioned more materials from the storeroom, no materials were there. A rush order for more materials was placed, and the materials arrived by special delivery before the end of the day.

(c) A purchasing agent bought substandard materials at a large savings. Because of the lower quality of the materials, more scrap was produced; and an additional employee was hired to assist in the cutting operation.

(d) Several customer rush orders were accepted and placed into production. The orders were completed within the standard time allotted; however, overtime was required to meet the customers' delivery schedules.

(e) A new union contract at the beginning of the year required an increase in labor rates. Adjustments to the standard wage rates were made as required at the beginning of the year. During the year, the rate of inflation in the economy was lower than what was predicted for the contract wage rates.

(f) Due to food poisoning in the plant cafeteria, several highly skilled employees from one department were sick for two days. The department supervisor hired temporary, unskilled production-line workers to substitute for the skilled workers. The wages for the temporary help were less than standard; and the output was also less than standard.

(g) Because of more than usual machine breakdowns, repair and maintenance personnel used more supplies than called for in the overhead budgets.

(h) A brownout caused by the overload of extra power usage in the city resulted in the inability to run machines at full power for four hours during a second shift.

(i) A forklift driver inadvertently ran into a large machine, dumping his load and stopping the machine. Several direct labor workers and the machine operator helped clean up the mess and got the machine going again.

(j) A new quality control inspector was less strict than policy standards required; and units that should have been reworked were passed over, released to the finished goods warehouse, and sold to customers.

9-34. Standard Costs and Ethics.   Quincy Farms is a processor of items made from local farm products that are distributed to supermarkets. For many years, Quincy's products have had strong regional sales on the basis of brand recognition. However, other companies have begun marketing similar products in the area, and price competition has become increasingly important. Doug Gilbert, the company's controller, is planning to implement a standard cost system for Quincy and has gathered considerable information from his co-workers on production and materials requirements for Quincy's products. Gilbert believes that the use of standard costing will allow Quincy to improve cost control and make better pricing decisions.

Quincy's most popular product is strawberry jam. The jam is produced in ten-gallon batches, and each batch requires six quarts of good strawberries. The fresh strawberries are sorted by hand before entering the production process. Because of imperfections in the strawberries and normal spoilage, one quart of berries is discarded for every four quarts of *acceptable* berries. Three minutes of sorting is the standard direct labor time required to obtain one quart of acceptable strawberries. These strawberries are then processed with the other ingredients; processing requires 12 minutes of direct labor time per batch. After processing, the jam is packaged into quart containers. Gilbert has gathered the following information from Joe Adams, Quincy's cost accountant, relative to processing the strawberry jam.

■ Quincy purchases strawberries at a cost of $0.80 per quart. All other ingredients cost a total of $0.45 per gallon.

■ Direct labor is paid at the rate of $9.00 per hour.

■ The total cost of materials and labor required to package the jam is $0.38 per quart.

Adams has a friend who owns a strawberry farm that has been losing money in recent years. Because of good crops, there has been an oversupply of strawberries; and prices have dropped to $0.50 per quart. Adams has arranged for Quincy to purchase strawberries from his friend and hopes that $0.80 per quart will put his friend's farm in the black.

Required:

1. Develop the standard cost for the direct cost components of a ten-gallon batch of strawberry jam. For each direct cost component, the standard cost should identify the:
   (a) Standard quantity.
   (b) Standard rate.
   (c) Standard cost per batch.

2. Citing the specific standards of competence, confidentiality, integrity, and/or objectivity from "Standards of Ethical Conduct for Management Accountants" found in Chapter 1, explain why Joe Adams' behavior regarding the cost information provided to Doug Gilbert is unethical.

(ICMA adapted)

9-35. Learning Curves (Appendix 1).   Western Space Systems, Inc. is developing a new but complex part for a sophisticated Star Wars missile. In making the first unit, the company used 500 direct labor hours at a cost of $8,000. The Engineering Department is estimating a learning curve but hasn't decided whether it is 80 percent or 90 percent.

Required:

1. Determine the cumulative average work hours per unit under an 80 percent and a 90 percent learning curve for a total of:

   (a) 2 units.
   (b) 4 units.
   (c) 8 units.
   (d) 16 units.

2. After completing the first unit, a prime contractor has ordered 15 additional units. What is the estimated direct labor cost for this order:

   (a) for an 80 percent learning curve?
   (b) for a 90 percent learning curve?

3. Suppose the actual learning curve realized in producing the additional 15 units was 85 percent, what is the additional cost or savings on the order as compared to an 80 percent and a 90 percent learning curve?

9-36. Learning Curves and CVP Analysis (Appendix 1).   CalMain Industries, Inc. is considering introducing a new product which will sell at $1,700 per unit. The Engineering Department has studied the product design and the production process and arrived at the following estimates:

1. Labor will follow an 80 percent learning curve.

2. The first unit of product will require 100 direct labor hours.

3. The labor rate is $10 per hour.

4. Variable factory overhead is $4 per direct labor hour.

5. Fixed factory overhead will increase $5,000 per year as a result of this product.

6. Materials will cost $100 per completed unit of product.

Required:

1. Assuming there is no constraint on the available labor time during the year, how many units of the new product would have to be produced and sold to break even?

2. Assuming that maximum labor time available is 300 hours during the year, how many units of the new product can be produced? Will the company break even within that constraint? Explain.

3. Returning to Part (1), if the company could improve its learning rate to 75 percent, how many more units could it produce at the break-even point for an 80 percent learning curve?

9-37. Learning Curves (Appendix 1).   The Henderson Equipment Company has produced a pilot run of 50 units of a recently developed cylinder used in its finished products. The cylinder has a one-year life, and the company expects to produce and sell 1,650 units annually. The pilot run required 14.25 direct labor hours for the 50 cylinders, averaging 0.285 direct labor hours per cylinder. The last cylinder in the pilot run required 0.194 direct labor hours. Henderson has experienced an 80 percent learning curve on the direct labor hours needed to produce new cylinders. Past experience indicates that the learning phase tends to cease by the time 800 parts are produced.

Henderson's manufacturing costs for cylinders are:

Direct labor	$12.00 per hour
Variable overhead	10.00 per direct labor hour
Fixed overhead	16.60 per direct labor hour
Materials	4.05 per unit

Required:

1. If the cylinders are manufactured by Henderson Equipment Company, determine:

   (a) the average direct labor hours per unit for the first 800 cylinders (including the pilot run) produced. Round calculations to three decimal places.

   (b) the total direct labor hours for the first 800 cylinders (including the pilot run) produced.

   (c) the marginal direct labor hours for the 800th cylinder produced. Round calculations to three decimal places.

2. After completing the pilot run, Henderson Equipment Company must manufacture an additional 1,600 units to fulfill the annual requirement of 1,650 units. Without prejudice to your answer in Part (1), assume that the first 800 cylinders produced (including the pilot run) required 100 direct labor hours and the 800th unit produced (including the pilot run) required 0.079 hours. Calculate the total manufacturing costs for Henderson to produce the additional 1,600 cylinders required.

(ICMA adapted)

9-38. Efficiency or Capacity Variance (Appendix 2).   Argentina Metals Company produces a magnetic instrument at its Buenos Aires plant. A standard cost accounting system is used. When operating at a normal volume of 300,000 machine hours, the plant should produce 1,200,000 units of this instrument. In the past few years, the company has been able to sell only 800,000 units of this product line each year. Management is aware of the relatively high fixed overhead costs budgeted at 4,800,000 pesos for the year and of the need to operate as closely to normal volume as possible.

The company has two categories of variable overhead: one varies at the rate of 3 pesos per unit of product; the other, which is based on machine hours, varies at 2 pesos per unit of product. Therefore a total of 5 pesos is charged to each product for variable overhead.

Last year the plant operated at 250,000 machine hours and produced 800,000 units of the magnetic instrument. The standard variable overhead cost is 8 pesos per machine hour, and the company incurred 2,050,000 pesos of actual variable overhead. It incurred 4,800,000 pesos in fixed overhead.

One of the production supervisors, Ernesto Valdez, has stated that some improvement has been made in operating more closely to normal volume. "By operating at 250,000 machine hours, the plant is up to 5/6 of normal volume. If the plant had operated at only 200,000 hours, as it did the year before last, we would have absorbed only 2/3 of the fixed overhead. This year the unfavorable capacity variance is only 800,000 pesos. The year before that, the unfavorable capacity variance was 1,600,000 pesos."

The supervisor of another department, Julio Diaz, disagreed and replied, "You can't eliminate a capacity variance by using more hours. Ernesto, you are confusing the concept of a capacity variance with an efficiency variance."

Valdez answered by saying, "An efficiency variance involves only the variable overhead and has nothing to do with what we are discussing, the absorption of fixed overhead."

Required:

1. Calculate both the overhead efficiency variance and the capacity variance for both years.
2. Explain what the efficiency variance measures as compared to what the capacity variance measures.
3. Which of the two supervisors is correct? Explain.

9-39. Multiple Products and Overhead Analysis (Appendix 2). Ohio Electrical Instruments manufactures three product lines used by the military: electronic support devices (SD), electronic counter measure devices (CMD), and electronic counter counter measure devices (CCD). The company has one large production facility in Columbus. Most of the components are manufactured by various divisions, although a few components are purchased from outside vendors. The Assembly Department is responsible for the final assembly of all three products.

Assembly operations are labor intensive and operate under a standard cost system. Because overhead costs are driven by direct labor hours, overhead is applied to each product on that basis. The standard overhead costs for Assembly on each of the three products are as follows:

	Hours	Variable	Fixed	Total	Per Unit
SD..............	3.0	$10.00	$7.50	$17.50	$52.50
CMD............	4.0	10.00	7.50	17.50	70.00
CCD	5.0	10.00	7.50	17.50	87.50

Normal volume for Assembly is 36,000 direct labor hours per month. During January, the Assembly Department had the following production performance:

	Units	Hours Worked
SD	3,800	10,900
CMD	2,700	10,400
CCD	2,200	11,500

Actual variable overhead amounted to $326,540 for the month. Actual fixed overhead totaled $271,000. No in-process inventories existed at the beginning or the end of the month.

Required:

1. How many standard direct labor hours were allowed for actual production in Assembly during the month?
2. Calculate the underapplied or overapplied overhead for the month.
3. Calculate the following overhead variances:
   (a) Variable spending variance.
   (b) Variable efficiency variance.
   (c) Fixed spending variance.
   (d) Fixed capacity variance.
4. Explain how the variable efficiency variance is related to direct labor.
5. Explain how the variable efficiency variance and the fixed capacity variance are related.

1-2-3

9-40. Standard Cost and Variances (Appendix 2). Edinburgh Garment Company has four operating divisions in Scotland. Each division manufactures a different type of kilt. The controller wants monthly reports on the operations for each division and for the total company. Data for each of the divisions are as follows: (All figures are in thousands.)

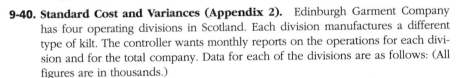

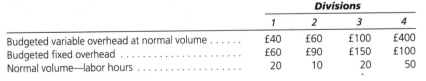

	Divisions			
	1	2	3	4
Budgeted variable overhead at normal volume	£40	£60	£100	£400
Budgeted fixed overhead	£60	£90	£150	£100
Normal volume—labor hours	20	10	20	50

Operating data for the months of August, September, and October are as follows: (All figures are in thousands.)

	Divisions			
	1	2	3	4
August:				
Actual manufacturing overhead	£92	£155	£240	£487
Actual labor hours	14	10	19	48
Standard labor hours for work done	15	8	20	45
September:				
Actual manufacturing overhead	£83	£188	£226	£498
Actual labor hours	12	15	16	50
Standard labor hours for work done	14	12	12	50
October:				
Actual manufacturing overhead	£76	£197	£233	£475
Actual labor hours	9	16	18	47
Standard labor hours for work done	10	15	16	50

Required:

1. Prepare monthly reports for each division and for the company as a whole for August, September, and October. Show the following variances:
   (a) Manufacturing overhead spending variance.
   (b) Manufacturing overhead efficiency variance.
   (c) Manufacturing overhead capacity variance.
2. Identify the division(s) with the worst spending variance, the worst efficiency variance, and the worst capacity variance for each of the three months.
3. If the economy were to turn downward, which division would be most likely to run into problems first? Explain.

C ASE 9A—WINN'S BICYCLES, INC.

Winn's Bicycles, Inc. is a large manufacturer located in Denver. Its usual production of bicycles is 10,000 units per year. The company has been a leader in the 21-speed bike industry for several years. However, with increasing competition and a higher public emphasis on quality, Winn has been searching for ways to maintain quality and cut costs. John Jackson, production planner, suggested that starting at the beginning of 1999 the company invest in higher quality materials and hire more experienced workers at a slightly higher pay rate.

The company has used a standard cost system for the past five years. The current standard costs for one bicycle, based on production of 10,000 units, are as follows:

Materials.	$ 60
Direct labor (4 hours at $10)	40
Variable overhead (based on labor)	20
Fixed overhead (based on labor)	8
Standard cost per bicycle	$128

Jeffrey Winn, president, is skeptical about decreasing costs by increasing materials and labor costs. However, after much debate, he agrees to try the changes for one year beginning with January 1999. Because the exact costs of changes were not known at the beginning of 1999, the existing standard costs were retained. Therefore, the changes will be in the variances from standard costs.

During 1999, the company produced only 9,500 bicycles because the marketplace showed a decreasing demand. The following data show the actual results for 1999:

1. Materials costing $617,500 were purchased and used. No usage variance existed, so any differences were due solely to price changes.
2. Direct labor was $249,375 for 23,750 direct labor hours.
3. Actual variable overhead totaled $163,000.
4. Actual fixed overhead totaled $80,000.

Mr. Winn was pleased with the results. Even though production was down by 500 bicycles, the difference in costs was significant. He would like to know why.

Required:

1. Compute all appropriate variances for the following categories:
   (a) Materials.
   (b) Labor.
   (c) Overhead.
2. Explain how any of the variances interrelate (have the same basic cause).
3. Explain which of the variances are controllable.
4. Assuming that the actual cost results for 1999 represent the new standard performance, calculate the new standard cost per bicycle, showing separately the materials, labor, and overhead components. (Normal production is still based on 10,000 bicycles.)

CASE 9B—AUTOMOBILE SUPPORT COMPANY[1]

The following transcript was prepared from a recording of a recent meeting of executives of the Automobile Support Company.

Location:	Seventh Floor Conference Room
Time:	10:00, Monday morning
Meeting:	Special Executive Meeting
Present:	Bob Sharp—President
	Gloria Finan—Controller
	Charlie Smith—Assistant Controller
	Bill Plankton—Plant Manager
	Henry Wills—Sales Manager
	Julie Sheehan—Purchasing Manager

Bob Sharp: Good morning. As you recall, Thursday's operations review meeting was chaotic. Many of the variances from standard costs that showed up in the interim financial statements did not seem to be controllable, and some of you questioned the entire accounting system. I asked Gloria to look into our standard costing methods and report back to us today. Gloria, have you come up with anything?

Gloria Finan: I think so, Bob. As you know, for many years we have used a standard costing system in which standards are only adjusted annually. At year end, we determine the actual cost to produce the products then in inventory. These costs become the standards for the next year. This has worked well for the interim financial reports that we must provide to shareholders and others. We are able to create these reports without the need of expensive and disruptive interim costing of inventories. But the system has been less than satisfactory for internal purposes such as controlling costs through variance calculation and analysis. I asked my new assistant, Charlie Smith, to work out a system that would satisfy both shareholders and management. Charlie recently received an MBA from State University and has strong opinions about proper feedback and control. I brought Charlie with me today so that he could give us his recommendations in person. Charlie?

Charlie Smith: Thanks, Gloria. I think I have a solution that will satisfy everybody. The basic complaint about the present system is that the standards are out-of-date every time costs change. My proposal is simple—let's use two sets of standards. One set will be changed only once a year as is our current practice and will be used for our interim financial statements. This will satisfy that need. The other set will be changed continually to keep materials, labor, and overhead costs (and standard quantities) current. This will result in variances that reflect true efficiencies and inefficiencies and should satisfy our internal needs. I've worked out current standards and could implement them this week if you wish.

Bill Plankton: This looks very interesting, Charlie; but I wonder if I might ask a couple of questions?

Charlie Smith: Of course.

Gloria Finan: (aside to Charlie) Look out!

Bill Plankton: Under your proposed system two sets of books for inventories are needed. There will be two sets of variances, which may differ in amount considerably, and two sets of inventory values for Raw Materials, Work in Process and Finished Goods. Would this not be both confusing internally and a concern externally to tax officials, regulatory agencies, and even shareholders if word leaked out in the press about our having dual sets of books? I say we go with one system; and, since we all understand the old one, I see nothing wrong with sticking with it, imperfect though it may be.

While I'm at it, I may as well get something else off my chest. Our internal reports always show production inefficiencies as variances which are blamed on the plant, while the sales department gets none of the blame and all of the glory. Can't we have a system that shows variances from budget for (1) sales prices, (2) sales volume, and (3) changes in sales mix? Aren't these more important to the company's long-term success than cost variances, regardless of whether you look at them from a current or an old standard?

Charlie Smith: Well. . .

Henry Wills: Now Bill, let's not get worked up over things we can't control. Don't blame Sales when the market is soft. Let's concentrate on controlling costs.

Bill Plankton: How can we control costs when we keep getting rush orders that we have to fill? Our guys have to interrupt production runs and work overtime two to three times a week just to help your salesmen keep their customers happy. And guess who gets blamed for those cost overruns?

Julie Sheehan: Well, I like Charlie's idea of using current standards; but I think in the future we should take his plan one step further. Why not develop "prospective" standards? By this I mean, when we set our standards at the beginning of the year, we should anticipate the cost increases which will occur during the year and build these into the standards. In the purchasing department this would reward timely purchasing decisions with favorable price variances. Right now the only time we get favorable price variances is when we get quantity discounts for purchasing in bulk.

Henry Wills: That might help with price variances, but it would not help with efficiency variances. It would also mean we would still need two sets of standards—the current standards for use in providing sales with current product costs and the prospective standards for the cost system.

Charlie Smith: We could set price standards prospectively and efficiency standards currently. The latter would require that we devise a procedure to keep our book inventory from going out of whack. I agree that we would need two sets of standards.

Gloria Finan: Since you brought it up, Julie, I must tell you that a number of purchasing's bulk orders have cost us more in inventory carrying costs than we have saved in price discounts. So even the favorable variances you mention were erroneous indicators of good performance. I don't think Charlie's plan addresses that issue, and it probably should.

Bob Sharp: Sorry Charlie, but I think that there are a number of additional ideas mentioned today that deserve attention: the use of two sets of standards; the use of prospective standards; the changing of standards as costs change; and the repricing of inventories, so inventory variances are not created. Gloria, could you and Charlie report back to us on Friday after considering the strengths and weaknesses of the issues brought up today? Thank you. This meeting stands adjourned.

Charlie Smith: (to Gloria as they head back to their offices) I thought you were on my side, Gloria.

Required:
1. What are the objectives for a standard cost system? How are these objectives being met and not being met with the current system?
2. Prepare a set of recommendations for changes in the system. What implementation issues will be raised by your recommendations?

Profit Analysis: Variances and Variable Costing

*L*EARNING OBJECTIVES

After studying Chapter 10, you will be able to:

1. Identify the differences between planned and actual net income.
2. Calculate these sales variances: sales price, sales quantity, and sales mix.
3. Calculate these cost variances: cost performance, cost quantity, and cost mix.
4. Explain why actual contribution margin or gross margin differs from budget.
5. Recast absorption income statements into variable costing statements.
6. Reconcile the differences between absorption costing net income and variable costing net income.
7. Understand arguments supporting both variable costing and absorption costing.

A Credit Union's Interest Margin: Where're the Earnings?

Joyce Clouse, president of Roaring Spring Community Credit Union, has just received the first quarter financial statements from her vice-president and controller, Hal Hoover. She immediately sees that net income is up, return on assets is now 1.2 percent, and total assets have grown to $125 million. From the income statement, she notes that interest margin (interest income minus interest and dividends expense) is up by $150,000 over the same quarter of last year. It's also $50,000 ahead of this quarter's financial plan. Pondering, she asks, "What'd we do? Yes, we're bigger, and interest rates jumped more than we expected." She calls Hal and asks, "Have we run the interest margin variance report for last quarter?" Hal responds, "No, but I'll have it in half an hour."

Like clockwork, Hal knocks on the president's door, enters, and hands Joyce the one-page report. "Ah yes, of that $50,000 interest margin variance, we earned $60,000 on the asset side and only lost $10,000 to budget in higher dividends on member deposits," Joyce says with a smile. She also notes that the $50,000 was split almost equally among higher rates, more deposits than expected, and a higher earning mix of loans. "You know," Joyce tells Hal, "we can't take much credit for higher interest rates and getting more deposits, but all that work we put into shifting our loan mix really did pay off. Our variable-rate loan yield shifted right with the rates."

While in financial institutions this analysis is called interest margin variance analysis, it is the same tool used by other firms to analyze changes in gross margin and contribution margin. It is a powerful tool for both planning and control if used and interpreted carefully by managers.

In many situations, managerial performance focuses on how actual net income compares to budgeted net income. When differences occur, management is interested in where and why. To answer these questions, the income statement is divided into sections and then dissected into individual variances that can highlight the major causes.

In Chapter 8, flexible budgeting helped analyze variable cost budget variances. Chapter 9 discussed standard costs and how actual product costs are compared to a performance standard. Product cost variances are important, but they explain only a portion of why net income varies from budget. Figure 10.1 provides a framework for analyzing the total income statement. **Contribution margin variance analysis** focuses on measuring revenue and product variable cost variances. Figure 10.2 shows the same structure using **gross margin variance analysis**. The difference between the two methods rests with how fixed costs are handled. Later in the chapter, we discuss fixed costs within variable and absorption costing.

To explain the net income variance in Figure 10.1, revenues, variable production costs, variable operating expenses, and fixed production and operating expenses are analyzed separately. Revenues and variable production costs are part of contribution margin variance analysis. Then variances for variable operating expenses and finally fixed manufacturing and operating expenses are discussed.

These analyses can be used to make a number of comparisons such as:

- Actual results for this period to budget.
- Actual results for this period to actual results for a prior period.
- A "what if" plan to a base plan.

The period may be a day, week, month, or year, depending on the needed timeframe.

C ONTRIBUTION MARGIN ANALYSIS

Using Figure 10.1 as a discussion base, product contribution margin is revenue minus variable product costs. Then, after subtracting variable operating expenses, we have variable contribution margin. A product contribution margin analysis framework views sales and variable product cost variances as a symmetric picture—price, quantity, and mix on both sides.

FIGURE   10 . 1   Net Income Variance Analysis—Contribution Margin Approach

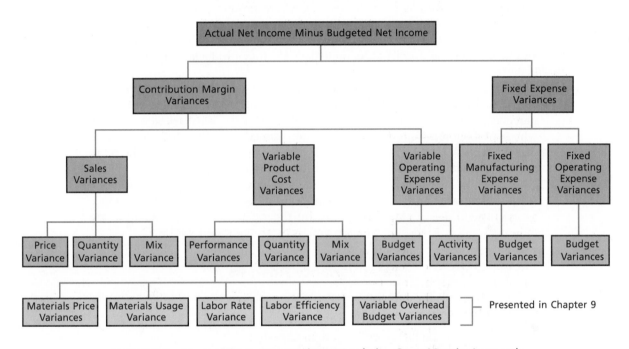

FIGURE   10 . 2   Net Income Variance Analysis—Gross Margin Approach

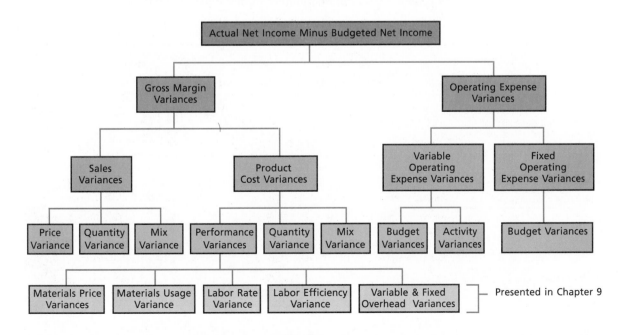

Product Contribution Margin Analysis

Product contribution margin analysis can be used in a wide variety of situations. But certain conditions should be met. These include:

- Product lines where individual products are similar in price and type.
- Products that are complementary or substitutes.
- Product mixes that can vary as total quantity increases or decreases.

While products are emphasized, services also fit the analysis well. Margin analysis also applies to financial institutions where certain types of assets and liabilities are viewed as products. Cases where products are diverse, such as paper clips and washing machines, are not easily adaptable to this tool.

As an illustration, Anderson Wholesalers in Figure 10.3 includes budget and actual units and dollars per unit data for four products from its product line.

Important variables are total quantity of units, sales mix, and price and variable cost per unit. Quantity is total units of all products. Sales mix is the percentage that each product represents of total sales. The task is to explain why contribution margin dropped from the planned $54,000 to $52,350. Notice that Products A and B have high contribution margins per unit, while the more popular products, C and D, have rather low margins.

Figure 10.4 presents the sales, cost, and contribution margin variances. Actual results are at the left with variances from budget presented in sequence as calculated. Budgeted amounts are on the right. Favorable variances are indicated with a *F*, and unfavorable variances are indicated with a *U*.

Sales Variance Analysis

In any sales analysis, only three changes can cause actual and budgeted sales to differ. These are:

1. Prices can be higher or lower than expected.
2. The quantity of total units sold can be higher or lower than expected.
3. The mix of products sold can be different from the planned mix of sales.

FIGURE 10.3 **Product Line Quantity, Price, and Variable Cost Data**

Products	Budgeted Units	Mix	Price	Cost	Actual Units	Mix	Price	Cost
A	1,000	10.0%	$30	$18	1,200	11.76%	$28	$17.50
B	2,000	20.0	20	10	1,500	14.71	25	11.00
C	3,000	30.0	10	8	3,000	29.41	11	8.50
D	4,000	40.0	15	11	4,500	44.12	14	11.50
Total quantity	10,000	100.0%			10,200	100.00%		

Products	Budgeted Contribution Margin	Actual Contribution Margin
A	1,000 x ($30 - $18) = $12,000	1,200 x ($28 - $17.50) = $12,600
B	2,000 x ($20 - $10) = 20,000	1,500 x ($25 - $11.00) = 21,000
C	3,000 x ($10 - $8) = 6,000	3,000 x ($11 - $8.50) = 7,500
D	4,000 x ($15 - $11) = 16,000	4,500 x ($14 - $11.50) = 11,250
Total margin	$54,000	$52,350

F I G U R E 10 . 4 Contribution Margin Variance Analysis—An Example

Sales Variances:

Product	Actual Sales	Price Variances	Adjusted Sales $M_a x Q_a x P_b$	Quantity Variances	Adjusted Sales $M_a x Q_b x P_b$	Mix Variances	Budgeted Revenue
A............	$ 33,600	$2,400 U	$ 36,000	$ 706 F	$ 35,294	$ 5,294 F	$ 30,000
B............	37,500	7,500 F	30,000	588 F	29,412	10,588 U	40,000
C............	33,000	3,000 F	30,000	588 F	29,412	588 U	30,000
D............	63,000	4,500 U	67,500	1,324 F	66,176	6,176 F	60,000
Totals	$167,100	$3,600 F	$163,500	$ 3,206 F	$160,294	$ 294 F	$160,000

Cost Variances:

Product	Actual Costs	Purchase Price Variances	Adjusted Costs $M_a x Q_a x C_b$	Quantity Variances	Adjusted Costs $M_a x Q_b x C_b$	Mix Variances	Budgeted Costs
A............	$ 21,000	$ 600 F	$ 21,600	$ 424 U	$ 21,176	$ 3,176 U	$ 18,000
B............	16,500	1,500 U	15,000	294 U	14,706	5,294 F	20,000
C............	25,500	1,500 U	24,000	471 U	23,529	471 F	24,000
D............	51,750	2,250 U	49,500	971 U	48,529	4,529 U	44,000
Totals	$114,750	$4,650 U	$110,100	$2,160 U	$107,940	$ 1,940 U	$106,000

Contribution Margin Variances:

Product	Actual Contribution Margin	Price Variances	Adjusted Margin $M_a x Q_a x (P_b - C_b)$	Quantity Variances	Adjusted Margin $M_a x Q_b x (P_b - C_b)$	Mix Variances	Budgeted Contribution Margin
A............	$ 12,600	$1,800 U	$ 14,400	$ 282 F	$14,118	$ 2,118 F	$12,000
B............	21,000	6,000 F	15,000	294 F	14,706	5,294 U	20,000
C............	7,500	1,500 F	6,000	117 F	5,883	117 U	6,000
D............	11,250	6,750 U	18,000	353 F	17,647	1,647 F	16,000
Totals	$ 52,350	$1,050 U	$ 53,400	$1,046 F	$52,354	$ 1,646 U	$54,000

The analytical task separates the single difference in sales into three variances—price, quantity, and mix. Figure 10.5, page 434, presents the framework for calculating these variances. Actual sales is an array of product prices (P) times the total quantity of units (Q) times an array of mix percentages (M).

As shown in Figure 10.5, each variance is the difference found by changing one variable at a time from actual to budget. The subscripts indicate actual ($_a$) or budget ($_b$). Typically, the analysis runs from actual back to budget. One variance is found at each step. Any sequence of variance calculations could be used, but the most common is price, quantity, and finally mix. Remember that price is the first variance calculated in standard costing in Chapter 9.

Let us follow Product A through the calculation sequence. Actual sales are $33,600 from selling 1,200 units (11.76 percent of total unit quantity of 10,200 units) at $28 per unit. A price cut apparently generated more volume.

Sales Price Variances. The **sales price variance** is the difference between actual and budgeted sales caused by price changes. From Step 1 in Figure 10.5, the sales price variance is computed as: $(P_a - P_b) \times Q_a \times M_a$. For all

FIGURE 10.5 Matrix for Calculating Sales Price, Quantity, and Mix Variances

Actual:	Actual sales	$P_a \times Q_a \times M_a$	
			→ Sales price variances
Step 1:	Use budgeted prices	$P_b \times Q_a \times M_a$	
			→ Sales quantity variances
Step 2:	Use budgeted quantity	$P_b \times Q_b \times M_a$	
			→ Sales mix variances
Step 3:	Use budgeted sales	$P_b \times Q_b \times M_b$	

products, an additional $3,600 in sales was earned from price differences. For Product A, sales dollars decreased by $2,400 [($28 - $30) x 10,200 x (1,200 ÷ 10,200) = $2,400]. The variance is the difference between the actual and the budgeted price per unit, using actual total quantity and mix percentages.

Sales Quantity Variance. The **sales quantity variance** is important for the total product line but not very meaningful for individual products. The impact of total quantity increases or decreases is analyzed by the quantity variance. The variance is the difference between actual and budgeted total units, using budgeted prices and actual mix percentages. From Step 2 of Figure 10.5, the formula is: $P_b \times (Q_a - Q_b) \times M_a$. Broken down for Product A, it is: $30 x (10,200 - 10,000) x (1,200 ÷ 10,200) = $706. The total sales quantity variance for all four products is $3,206, which is the weighted-average revenue per unit (apparently $16.03) multiplied by the sale of an additional 200 units (10,200 - 10,000).

Sales Mix Variances. The **sales mix variance** measures the change in each product's portion of total sales. The mix variance measures the impacts of fast and slow selling products. The variance is the difference between the actual and budgeted mix percentages, using budgeted prices and total quantity. Using Step 3 of Figure 10.5, the formula is: $P_b \times Q_b \times (M_a - M_b)$. From Figure 10.3, the sales mix variance for Product A is calculated as follows: $30 x 10,000 x [(1,200 ÷ 10,200) - (1,000 ÷ 10,000)] = $5,294. This is Product A's increased portion of total unit sales. Notice that some products increased and others decreased, a normal situation. Did high-priced products increase or decrease relative to lower-priced products? The small positive sales mix variance of $294 implies that a slight shift to higher-priced products occurred.

The three sales variances must be viewed together. A drawback is the fact that one product's changes can impact the others' variances. A large sales jump for Product A will cause quantity and mix variances for the other products. Thus, quantity and mix variances must be interpreted carefully.

Single Product Variances. In single product situations, the mix variance disappears; and only sales price and quantity variances are calculated. The same formulation in Figure 10.5 is used but without the mix component.

Product Cost Variance Analysis

In any product cost analysis, only three changes can cause actual product variable cost of sales to differ from budgeted costs. These are:

1. Variable product costs can be higher or lower than expected.
2. The quantity of total units sold can be higher or lower than expected.
3. The mix of products sold can be different from the planned mix of sales.

The causes of product cost and sales variances are similar. In fact, sales and cost quantity and mix variances will have the same direction and magnitude. The sales price and cost performance or purchase price variances are independent. Figure 10.6 shows that the sequence of calculation is cost performance variances, to total quantity variance, and finally to product mix variance. The data are from Figure 10.3, and the variances are shown in Figure 10.4. Let us follow Product A through the calculation sequence.

Cost Performance or Purchase Price Variances. The **cost performance variances** here are the same variable standard cost variances discussed in Chapter 9. This variance could also be a **purchase price variance** if the firm purchases it products, as does Anderson Wholesalers in this example. The difference between the budgeted, or standard, unit cost of $18 for Product A and the actual unit cost of $17.50 is $0.50 per unit. In manufacturing, the $0.50 per unit variance is the sum of the materials, direct labor, and variable overhead variances. From Step 1 in Figure 10.6, the purchase price variance is computed as: $(C_a - C_b) \times Q_a \times M_a$. For all products, additional costs of $4,650 were incurred from unit cost differences. For Product A, costs decreased by $600 [($18 - $17.50) \times 10,200 \times (1,200 \div 10,200) = $600].

If the firm is a manufacturer and has a standard costing system, cost performance variances are identified and recorded in the factory. Products are inventoried at standard costs, and no cost performance variances will appear here.

Also, remember cost variances are based on units produced, while contribution margin variances are based on units sold. Changes in inventory levels will require adjustments to equate the two sets of variances.

Cost Quantity Variances. The **cost quantity variance** is a mirror image of the sales quantity variance. While the total quantity variance is important, variances for specific products are of little significance. The variance is the difference between actual and budgeted total quantity, using budgeted unit costs and actual mix percentages. From Step 2 of Figure 10.6, the formula is: $C_b \times (Q_a - Q_b) \times M_a$. Broken down for Product A, it is: $18 \times (10,200 - 10,000) \times (1,200 \div 10,200) = 424. The total cost quantity variance for all four products is $2,160.

FIGURE 10.6   **Matrix for Calculating Cost Performance, Quantity, and Mix Variances**

Actual:	Actual product costs	C_a	x	Q_a	x	M_a	Cost purchase price variances or
Step 1:	Use budgeted unit costs	C_b	x	Q_a	x	M_a	Cost performance variances
Step 2:	Use budgeted quantity	C_b	x	Q_b	x	M_a	Cost quantity variances
Step 3:	Use budgeted product costs	C_b	x	Q_b	x	M_b	Cost mix variances

Cost Mix Variances. The **cost mix variances** are also mirror images of the sales mix variances. The cost mix variance measures the impacts of faster and slower selling products on total variable costs. The variance is the difference between the actual and budgeted mix percentages, using budgeted unit costs and total quantity. Using Step 3 of Figure 10.6, the formula is: $C_b \times Q_b \times (M_a - M_b)$. From Figure 10.3, the cost mix variance for Product A is calculated as $18 \times 10,000 \times [(1,200 \div 10,200) - (1,000 \div 10,000)] = \$3,176$.

The three product cost variances sum to the difference between total actual and total budgeted costs. As with the sales variances, product cost variances must be analyzed individually and together and with the sales variances.

Contribution Margin Variances—Bringing Together Sales and Product Costs

By combining the sales and cost variances, changes in contribution margin can be seen. Figure 10.4 concludes with the summed sales and cost variances.

Many interrelationships can be examined. For Product A, Anderson Wholesalers apparently reduced the price to increase volume. Combined with a cost per unit reduction, contribution margin increased by $600. Similar impacts arose from the opposite actions with Product B—higher price, lower volume, and higher cost per unit. Product B's actions earned a $1,000 higher contribution margin. Product C's higher price had a no impact on volume. But Product D experienced a serious drop in contribution margin per unit, from $4 to $2.50 per unit, because of price and cost changes. The positive changes in Products A, B, and C were overwhelmed by the contribution margin loss from Product D.

Calculation Issues

In any multiple-variance situation, the calculation order issue arises. We have used the price, quantity, and mix sequence. Other sequences produce different variances, but the magnitude (large or small) and the direction (positive or negative) rarely change. It is worthwhile to note that these analyses focus on magnitude and direction and not on precision.

Moving from actual to budget, or vice versa, and having the three variances add to 100 percent of the total variance are intuitively appealing. Other approaches are occasionally used in the real world. For example, the Security and Exchange Commission requires financial institutions to file an interest margin variance report that uses the base period (last year) as the starting point for calculating each variance. The sum of the individual variances does not equal the total variance. Any residual is allocated to the other variances, but that's government regulation.

Variable Operating Expense Variances

From Figure 10.1, the next step is to evaluate performance of variable operating expenses. Since these expenses vary with sales activities, their budgets are based on expected activity levels. A flexible budget is the best approach to build the budget and to evaluate performance. The discussion of flexible budgeting in Chapter 7 focused on determining the relationships among activities, resource use, and costs—the cost function.

Any variable operating expenses that can be traced to specific products should be analyzed as part of the product cost variance analyses discussed previously. ABC techniques can identify these direct relationships. Differences between actual and budgeted expense levels would appear in the cost performance variance section as spending variances. An example of these expenses might be commissions paid as a percentage of revenue or of contribution margin.

In comparing actual performance to budget, variable expenses are adjusted to the actual activity level. As an example, a cost function for a package transfer service is $4 per delivery. If expected activity were 4,000 transfers, the variable expense budget would be $16,000. But if 4,200 transfers were performed and $17,000 were spent, variances could be identified as follows:

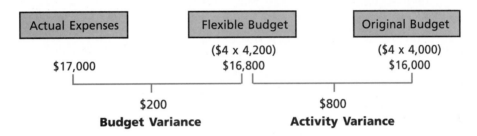

The budget variance is unfavorable. The activity variance reflects the difference between planned and actual activity, in this case an actual higher spending level—viewed as unfavorable. The responsible manager is allowed to spend $800 more than the original budget because of the higher activity, but that amount plus an additional $200 was spent.

In certain situations, the budget variance can be separated into price and usage variances. A brief example at the top of page 438 illustrates this concept. Hudson-Field Department Store operates a gift wrapping department. The departmental variable operating expense budget is developed around an estimate of parcels wrapped, which is forecast based on total sales quantity of the store. Two variable expense items are wrapping materials and wages of associates (employees).

C O N T E M P O R A R Y   P R A C T I C E   1 0 . 1

Menu Engineering: Restaurant Contribution Margins

A restaurant's revenues can be viewed as a sales mix of individual menu items, categories of offerings (e.g., appetizers, entrees), and meal periods or categories (e.g., breakfast, banquets). Variable costs of foods and other direct expenses can be subtracted to find contribution margin per item. A contribution margin per seat per hour could be determined. High and low performers can be identified to help decide which items should be dropped, added, repriced, or reconfigured. A 1992 survey of over 100 restaurants showed that 72 percent broke down their costs into variable and fixed. And, 55 percent used a direct cost approach for menu items, which is the basis for contribution margin analysis.

Source: Bayou, M. E., and L. E. Bennett, "Profitability Analysis for Table-Service Restaurants," *Cornell Hotel and Restaurant Administration Quarterly*, April 1992, pp. 49-55.

	Actual Results	Flexible Budget	Original Budget	Price Variance	Usage Variance	Budget Variance	Activity Variance
Parcels wrapped	1,020	1,020	1,000				
Hours worked	110	102	100				
Budget: 10 parcels per hour							
Yards of wrapping paper	980	1,020	1,000				
Budget: 1 yard per parcel							
Associates wages	$ 850	$ 816	$ 800	$ 30 F	$64 U	$34 U	$16 U
Budget: $8 per hour worked							
Cost of wrapping paper used	$1,010	$1,020	$1,000	$ 30 U	$40 F	$10 F	$20 U
Budget: $1 per parcel							

Associates wage price variance was calculated as: ($8 x 110) - $850 = $30 favorable. The usage variance was: $880 - $816 = $64 unfavorable. The associates worked slower than expected (used more labor), but the average wage was lower than budgeted. The wrapping paper variances are found similarly. The paper price variance was: ($1 x 980) - $1,010 = $30 unfavorable. The paper usage variance was: (1,020 - 980) x $1 = $40 favorable. Wrapping paper costs were higher than budgeted, but they used less paper than expected.

*G*ROSS MARGIN VARIANCES

In Figure 10.2, gross margin variances appear in place of contribution margin variances. The main difference is where product fixed overhead costs are analyzed. If Anderson Wholesalers manufactured its products and used the gross margin approach, fixed manufacturing product costs would be included in the product cost variances. Thus, performance cost variances include the fixed overhead budget and volume variances in addition to materials, labor, and variable overhead variances. Calculations based on Figure 10.3 data and outlined in Figures 10.5 and 10.6 are the same under both versions.

In many sales organizations, the terms contribution margin and gross margin are used interchangeably. In manufacturing, the two approaches differ because of fixed overhead. In sales organizations, other variable operating expenses may be included in contribution margin analysis.

*U*SES AND LIMITS OF CONTRIBUTION MARGIN AND GROSS MARGIN VARIANCE ANALYSIS

Margin variance analyses identify reasons for change in performance. They are predominately sales tools. Sales managers are typically responsible for increases or decreases in sales quantities and shifts in sales mix. Uses of variance analysis include:

- Planning pricing strategies to set optimal prices and volume forecasts.
- Planning interrelationships among products to find complementary (Higher sales of one product generates higher sales of another product.) and substitution effects (Higher sales of one product causes lower sales of another product.).
- After-the-fact analysis of actual results for comparison to budgets.
- Analysis of changes from period to period.

Linking contribution margin variances and standard costing variances developed in Chapter 9 gives managers powerful tools for analyzing market and manufacturing environments.

Unfortunately, these analyses identify variances, but answers must be assembled from the parts presented. In the real world, a skilled manager can review a profit margin variance report in a few minutes and be prepared to ask penetrating questions about results and operations.

One problem with quantity and mix variances is the impacts a change in one product's volume has on other products' variances. For example, if one product's sales units double, the other unchanged products will show unfavorable mix and favorable quantity variances, as did Product C in the Anderson Wholesalers example.

*F*IXED COST VARIANCE ANALYSES—MANUFACTURING AND OPERATING EXPENSES

Because of the nature of fixed costs, variance analysis is often an actual versus budget comparison. Under flexible budgeting, fixed costs remain constant. Fixed is fixed. Therefore, the analysis merely identifies a variance from budget. Many fixed costs are planned using a **static budget**, which is oblivious to volume or activity changes. The budgeted amount is the expected spending level. Any variation from that amount is a budget variance.

In prior chapters, we discussed creating cost functions, applying fixed costs to products, budgeting fixed product costs, and analyzing fixed overhead variances. We linked a cost's behavior, activities, and resource use. Fixed operating expenses include fixed costs of engineering, administration, distribution, marketing, and many staff functions.

Managing fixed cost budget variances can be challenging. If a cost is fixed, why did we spend more than budgeted? Many fixed costs are fixed only over a narrow relevant range, are largely fixed but contain a small variable element, or are a variety of expenses that together appear fixed but have numerous cost behavior patterns. Fixed cost budget variances may require careful follow-up analyses.

Activity-Based Cost Analysis

Planning and controlling fixed expenses are related to management activities in each responsibility center. Variances are primarily spending, but activity factors come into play because of the diversity involved. In ABC applications, all variances are activity based or spending based. Thus, fixed costs in a product output sense may really be variable if linked to other activity bases.

If activity-based costing is applied to nonproduction areas, certain fixed costs may also become variable, linked to their respective activity bases. For example, many data processing operations collect activity data, particularly for certain on-line applications such as inventory systems and customer databases. In fact, data processing costs are often "billed" to users to reassign costs to departments using the data processing resources. These "transfer prices" are based on planned volumes and costs. A comparison of costs transferred to actual costs is one measure of operating performance. Such systems are also used for maintenance, training, and multimedia departments.

By relating costs to activities in staff and support service areas, cost management is exercised. Detailed costs can highlight expensive activities and processes that add little or no value. Improvement goals can be linked to cost functions from ABC. Process reengineering can change the way work is done and improve cost efficiency and productivity measures.

Use of Benchmarking

Many nonproducing areas need a basis for evaluation. World-class manufacturing comparisons can be paralleled in nonmanufacturing units. This is called **benchmarking**. In accounting areas, the cost of processing a payment to a vendor can be measured by activity-based costing. That cost can be compared to other units within the company or, more likely, to world-class operators. Networks of companies willing to share benchmarking data are growing rapidly.

Benchmarking in many areas has been going on for years through trade and industry association work. Sharing operating data along with financial statement information can help firms create a "peer group" for comparing operating methods, expenses, and improvement factors. Peers should be selected carefully to represent high-quality performances and challenges for improvement.

As an example, Stein Company is attempting to get better control over customer order inquiries. The firm uses an ABC system to find the cost of servicing customer calls. Through an information sharing arrangement, monthly cost data from three other firms are compared to Stein data over several years as follows:

	1996 Costs	1997 Costs	1998 Actual Costs	1998 Budgeted Costs	Peer Firm A	Peer Firm B	Peer Firm C
Inquiries per month	1,120	1,322	1,954	1,800	5,000	1,200	7,500
Customer inquiry costs	$ 6,455	$ 6,835	$10,004	$ 9,000	$16,400	$ 5,300	$29,500
Cost per inquiry	$ 5.76	$ 5.17	$ 5.12	$ 5.00	$ 3.28	$ 4.42	$ 3.93

"World-class performers" are ahead of Stein. Care must be taken to have comparable work requirements, cost pools, and activities. Growth in activity levels may be causing Stein's inability to meet the budgeted cost per inquiry goal in 1998. Yet, the peer data indicate that potential for significant cost reductions exists.

VARIABLE COSTING

Variable costing (also known as **direct costing**) is an approach to product costing that assigns only variable manufacturing costs (direct materials, direct labor, and variable factory overhead) to items produced. Thus, inventoriable costs are limited to the variable manufacturing costs; and period costs include all fixed costs and variable nonmanufacturing costs. **Absorption costing**, the method typically used for external income statement reporting, allocate manufacturing costs (variable and fixed) to products. This section compare these two costing methods.

Variable costing, like absorption costing, can be used in conjunction with actual, normal, or standard costing systems. For simplicity, we will restrict our discussion in this chapter to situations in which actual costing is used.

Characteristics of Variable Costing

The two costing methods vary as to the cost elements for product costs, the difference in inventory values, and the difference in profits. These differences all result from one basic item—the treatment of fixed manufacturing costs. Absorption costing includes these costs in product costs while variable costing considers them as period costs to be included with the operating expenses. The following summary contrasts the two costing approaches:

Cost Category	Variable Costing	Absorption Costing
Direct materials	Product	Product
Direct labor	Product	Product
Variable factory overhead	Product	Product
Fixed factory overhead	Period ⟷	Product
Marketing expenses	Period	Period
Administrative expenses	Period	Period

Variable costing typically uses a contribution margin approach as a reporting format. Variable marketing and administrative costs are included in the computation of the contribution margin. However, variable marketing and administrative costs are not product costs.

Selecting variable costing or absorption costing has an impact on inventory values and profits because of the variation in the treatment of fixed factory overhead. Although the profit can differ between the two costing methods, profit under variable costing is not always higher or lower than absorption costing. The difference between profits under the two methods is determined

CONTEMPORARY PRACTICE 10.2

Usage of Variable Costing

In a survey of 219 U. S. manufacturing firms, managers were asked whether variable costing was used in reports to top management. Their responses were:

	Frequency
Variable costing used as the primary format	23.2%
Variable costing used as a supplemental format	28.9
Variable costing not used	47.9
	100.0%

Source: Cress, W. P., and Pettijohn, J. B., "A Survey of Budget-Related Planning and Control Policies and Procedures," *Journal of Accounting Education*, Vol. 3, No. 2, p. 77.

of production to sales. Assuming that the fixed manufactur-
main the same from one period to the next, we have three
ws:

	Net Income
ual sales units	AC = VC
eater than sales units (building inventory)	AC > VC
ss than sales units (liquidating inventory)	AC < VC

AC = Absorption costing

VC = Variable costing

The magnitude of any difference in profits is a function of the fixed manufacturing costs per unit and the changes in inventory levels, as we shall discuss
later.

Comparing Variable Costing and Absorption Costing

Let's assume that West Africa Furniture Company of Monrovia, Liberia, produces
a single product, a vibrating sofa chair. In its first year, 1997, the company
produced 100,000 chairs and sold 75,000 chairs at $135 wholesale. The costs for
the year are:

Manufacturing costs (per unit):
Materials	$19.00
Labor	18.00
Variable overhead	15.00
Fixed overhead ($1,200,000 ÷ 100,000 units)	12.00

Marketing and administrative costs:
Variable	$13.00 per unit sold
Fixed	$800,000

The absorption costing income statement that reflects these results is as
follows:

Absorption Costing Income Statement For the Year Ended December 31, 1997		
Sales revenue ($135 x 75,000)		$10,125,000
Cost of sales:		
Variable ($52 x 75,000)	$3,900,000	
Fixed ($12 x 75,000)	900,000	4,800,000
Gross profit		$ 5,325,000
Marketing and administrative expenses:		
Variable ($13 x 75,000)	$ 975,000	
Fixed	800,000	1,775,000
Net profit		$ 3,550,000

A variable costing income statement would be as follows:

Variable Costing Income Statement For the Year Ended December 31, 1997		
Sales revenue ($135 x 75,000)		$10,125,000
Variable costs:		
Manufacturing ($52 x 75,000)	$3,900,000	
Marketing and administrative ($13 x 75,000) . . .	975,000	4,875,000
Contribution margin		$ 5,250,000
Fixed costs:		
Manufacturing	$1,200,000	
Marketing and administrative	800,000	2,000,000
Net profit.		$ 3,250,000

Notice that the variable costing profit is lower than the profit from absorption costing. Why does this happen? The next section answers this question.

Reconciliation of Variable and Absorption Costing

The difference in net profit figures is due solely to the treatment of fixed manufacturing costs. Absorption costing includes those costs in the inventory costs; variable costing treats them as expenses to be charged to the period incurred. During any given time period, the amount of fixed costs in inventory will increase or decrease as production differs from sales. If production is greater than sales (as is the case with West Africa Furniture Company in 1997), fixed costs in the ending inventory are deferred to future periods under absorption costing. Alternatively, all fixed costs are expensed under variable costing. Therefore, absorption costing will show a higher net profit. Conversely, if sales are greater than production, fixed costs in the beginning inventory are expensed in the current period and added to the fixed costs incurred during the current period. Therefore, fixed costs in the income statement under absorption costing are higher than under variable costing; and the result is a lower net profit for absorption costing.

In the simplified case in which fixed overhead costs per unit are the same in beginning and ending inventories, the difference in net profits is exactly equal to the change in inventory units times the fixed overhead rate per unit. For West Africa Furniture Company, the change in inventory is:

Units produced	100,000
Units sold	75,000
Increase in inventory	25,000

Using a fixed overhead rate of $12 per unit, the difference in net profit figures is: $12 x 25,000 units = $300,000. Let's check this result:

Absorption costing net profit	$ 3,550,000
Variable costing net profit	3,250,000
Difference	$ 300,000

When the fixed overhead rates are different in beginning and ending inventories, the reconciliation of net profit figures is performed as follows:

	Absorption costing net profit
+	Fixed overhead in beginning inventory
-	Fixed overhead in ending inventory
=	Variable costing net profit

To illustrate, suppose that in 1998, West Africa Furniture Company produces 80,000 chairs and sells 100,000. We will presume the same total fixed costs, unit variable costs, and selling price as in 1997. West Africa Furniture Company uses a FIFO cost flow. As a result, the fixed overhead per unit produced during 1998 is $15 ($1,200,000 ÷ 80,000).

The 1998 absorption costing income statement would be as follows:

Absorption Costing Income Statement **For the Year Ended December 31, 1998**		
Sales revenue ($135 x 100,000)		$13,500,000
Cost of sales:		
Variable ($52 x 100,000)	$5,200,000	
Fixed [($12 x 25,000) + ($15 x 75,000)]	1,425,000	6,625,000
Gross profit		$ 6,875,000
Marketing and administrative expenses:		
Variable ($13 x 100,000)	$1,300,000	
Fixed	800,000	2,100,000
Net profit		$ 4,775,000

Note that the fixed portion of cost of sales is consistent with the FIFO cost flow assumption. The first 25,000 units come from 1997 production, which had a unit cost of $12 for fixed overhead; the remaining 75,000 units come from 1998 production, which had a unit cost of $15 for fixed overhead.

The 1998 variable costing income statement would be as follows:

Variable Costing Income Statement **For the Year Ended December 31, 1998**		
Sales revenue ($135 x 100,000)		$13,500,000
Variable costs:		
Manufacturing ($52 x 100,000)	$5,200,000	
Marketing and administrative ($13 x 100,000) . .	1,300,000	6,500,000
Contribution margin		$ 7,000,000
Fixed costs:		
Manufacturing	$1,200,000	
Marketing and administrative	800,000	2,000,000
Net profit		$ 5,000,000

We reconcile the 1998 net profits as follows:

	Absorption costing net profit.	$ 4,775,000
+	Fixed overhead in beginning inventory ($12 x 25,000)	300,000
-	Fixed overhead in ending inventory ($15 x 5,000).	(75,000)
=	Variable costing net profit	$ 5,000,000

The reconciliation of net profits between the two costing methods is independent of inventory cost-flow assumptions. A company can use FIFO, LIFO, or some average cost method, and the reconciliation of net profits follows the same procedures.

Another observation about the difference between the two methods relates to the profit patterns over time with respect to production and sales strategies. Let's consider the case of a constant production schedule over time while sales fluctuate each period. The absorption costing net income will fluctuate up and down with sales, but the constant production will have a leveling effect on the swings. The peaks will not be as high nor as low as the corresponding sales changes. Variable costing net income, on the other hand, will have swings that match those of sales, in both direction and relative magnitude. For the situation where production fluctuates while sales remain rather constant, a different picture appears. Absorption costing net income will fluctuate with production, in both direction and relative magnitude. Variable costing net income will remain constant, corresponding with sales levels.

While the absorption and variable costing methods yield different profit figures during periods when units sold do not equal units produced, these are merely timing differences. If over the course of several time periods, aggregate production equals aggregate sales, then the aggregate profits will be the same for both costing methods despite differences in profits during specific periods.

Arguments for Either Costing Method

Neither variable costing nor absorption costing is correct or incorrect. Their usefulness correlates with management's attitudes and with philosophies of organizational behavior. Some companies will find variable costing extremely useful, while other companies will find it less meaningful. Any manager can make a valid case for either variable or absorption costing. The primary arguments, for and against, are discussed next.

Short Term Versus Long Term. Those who favor variable costing (We call them the variable costers.) believe that it focuses on the short-term consequences of accounting and is more realistic of the way managers make decisions. Those who favor absorption costing (We call them the absorption costers.) assume that long-run performance is more important and that absorption costing more appropriately reflects long-term consequences.

Unethical Behavior by Managers. Variable costers assume that managers can easily adapt to a new accounting method with little additional cost. They further argue that managers will be rewarded for playing games with absorption costing reports. They specifically refer to a manager's ability to manipulate net profit by increasing or decreasing inventory levels that are valued under absorption costing. The absorption costers admit that occasional short-term decisions (e.g., amount of ending inventory to hold) will be made incorrectly. However, over the long term, the mistakes will be more obvious; and the "games" will be discovered by competent superiors. Absorption costers might assert that unethical managers cannot be suddenly rehabilitated by a change in accounting methods.

Variable Versus Fixed Costs. Variable costers believe that costs can be easily and meaningfully divided into variable and fixed categories and that using a contribution margin is much more useful for planning and decision making and for control and performance evaluation. Since absorption costing is primarily for external reporting purposes, absorption costers do not see this distinction as meaningful for reports. They will also argue that managers can still make the cost behavior distinctions for internal purposes. They point out that the variable/fixed split is not easily made in practice.

External Versus Internal Reports.   Financial statement reporting using generally accepted accounting principles, as well as tax reporting for the Internal Revenue Service, requires absorption costing. Variable costers argue that allowing external reporting requirements to dominate how useful and meaningful information should be reported is not a valid philosophy for competent management. Since information should be geared to the needs of management, external requirements should not drive the internal accounting system. Absorption costers argue that to have one set of requirements for external reporting and another set for internal reporting gives managers conflicting and inconsistent information. It also forges an image that the company is hiding something in the two approaches.

Effects of New Manufacturing Environments

Since the major variation between the two costing methods is the treatment of fixed costs as product or period costs, the difference in net profits disappears when little or no inventory of work in process or finished goods exists. For companies implementing JIT production procedures, inventories will be eliminated or substantially reduced. Hence, the particular costing method chosen loses significance in this environment. Also, this controversy is irrelevant to service organizations which do not carry inventories.

In automated production environments, whether JIT or not, the bulk of labor and factory overhead costs is fixed. Variable costs represent a low percentage of total manufacturing costs. In these environments, therefore, variable costing loses much of its appeal because the product cost will be a small fraction of the total manufacturing cost.

S UMMARY

The analysis of income statement variances can identify the source of the difference between planned net income and actual net income. This difference can be broken into sales, product cost, and variable and fixed operating variances.   Each of these variances can be subdivided into more detailed variances to point to causes.   The sales variance is the sum of the sales price, quantity, and mix variances.   In a parallel analysis, the product cost variance is the sum of cost performance or purchase price, quantity, and mix variances. Together the sales and product cost variances explain the variation in contribution margin or gross margin.   Similar analyses compare plan and actual for operating expenses.

Variable costing includes only variable manufacturing costs as an element of product cost. The traditional method of income statement preparation is called absorption costing. It includes fixed manufacturing costs as an element of product cost. As a result of this difference, net profit under the two methods will not necessarily be the same. Anytime production exceeds sales, absorption costing yields a higher net profit; when sales exceeds production, variable costing yields a higher net profit.   The arguments for and against using either costing method apply to individual situations and management philosophy. Neither method is inherently correct or incorrect.

PROBLEMS FOR REVIEW

Review Problem A

The Safe Bank provided the following information about its 1998 and 1999 earning assets and interest-paying liabilities:

($ in Millions)	1998 Results Average Balance	Mix Percentage	Interest Amount	Rate	1999 Results Average Balance	Mix Percentage	Interest Amount	Rate
Assets:								
Short-term investments	$ 1,000	10.0%	$ 40	4.0%	$ 1,500	12.5%	$ 51	3.4%
Long-term investments	2,000	20.0	100	5.0	1,800	15.0	81	4.5
Commercial loans	4,000	40.0	400	10.0	4,500	37.5	414	9.2
Consumer loans	3,000	30.0	240	8.0	4,200	35.0	315	7.5
Total	$10,000	100.0%	$780	7.8%	$12,000	100.0%	$861	7.2%
Liabilities:								
Demand deposits.	$ 4,000	40.0%	$ 120	3.0%	$ 6,000	50.0%	$ 210	3.5%
Certificates	6,000	60.0	300	5.0	6,000	50.0	288	4.8
Total	$10,000	100.0%	$420	4.2%	$12,000	100.0%	$498	4.2%
Interest margin			$360	3.6%			$363	3.0%

Required:
Kurt Schneck, president, is depressed about the lack of growth in interest margin in spite of a 20 percent growth in assets. He asks you for an analysis of 1999's interest margin relative to 1998's.

Solution:
Among the first steps in the analysis will be to perform an interest margin variance analysis. The format and variances are as follows:

($ in Millions)	1999 Interest Margin	Rate Variance	Quantity Variance	Mix Variance	1998 Interest Margin
Interest income:					
Short-term investments . . .	$ 51	$ 9 U	$ 10 F	$10 F	$ 40
Long-term investments. . . .	81	9 U	15 F	25 U	100
Commercial loans	414	36 U	75 F	25 U	400
Consumer loans	315	21 U	56 F	40 F	240
Total	$861	$ 75 U	$156 F	$ 0 -	$ 780
Interest expense:					
Demand deposits	$ 210	$ 30 U	$ 30 U	$30 U	$ 120
Certificates	288	12 F	50 U	50 F	300
Total	$ 498	$ 18 U	$ 80 U	$20 F	$ 420
Interest margin	$ 363	$ 93 U	$ 76 F	$20 F	$ 360

As an example of the calculations, short-term investment variances are found as follows (all dollars in millions):

Rate variance: $(0.04 - 0.034) \times (\$12{,}000 \times 0.125) = \$ 9$ unfavorable

Quantity variance: $0.04 \times (\$10{,}000 - \$12{,}000) \times 0.125 = \$10$ favorable

Mix variance: $0.04 \times \$10{,}000 \times (0.10 - 0.125) = \$10$ favorable

The analysis shows that interest rates declined in general. The interest margin line shows that $93 million was lost due to rate changes. Most of this came from lower earnings on assets. But a big problem was the higher rate paid on demand deposits, a management decision. This drew an additional $2 billion in deposits, but the bank paid 0.5 percent more in 1999 than in 1998. The bank grew in total in interest margin and earned a net $76 million more from that growth. It did shift its mix of liabilities to a lower cost source of funds (demand deposits) and saved $20 million.

Also, if interest rates are falling in general, the bank may want to be less dependent on certificates of deposit that appear to be longer term. Also, certificates showed a very small decline in interest rates from 5 to 4.8 percent while loans appear to be either variable rate or short term because their rates dropped much more. These are policy and decision questions that Kurt must review.

Review Problem B

Hedy Silber, the sales manager of Meadowbrook Machine Company, Inc., objects to the accounting procedure in costing the manufactured products. She states that sales were lost from a failure to grant price concessions to customers. By including fixed overhead as a part of product cost, the costs are, of course, higher than they would be under variable costing. As a result, the president is reluctant to authorize sales below the full cost. But at any price above the unit variable cost, Ms. Silber states that the company can earn additional profits. Furthermore, she believes that the income statements give a false picture by shifting fixed costs from one year to another as a part of inventory cost.

Joey Pollack, the chief financial officer, defends the accounting policy. The objective, he says, is to maintain prices and gain a reputation for quality products at an established price. Too many companies, he continues, have been shortsighted and have spoiled their markets at an established price by granting price concessions merely to increase volume. Profits are not earned until all costs are covered, and each unit of product should bear a share of the fixed overhead.

The following cost and sales data are given for the past three years:

Year	Units Produced	Units Sold
1996.....................	20,000	16,000
1997.....................	25,000	22,000
1998.....................	25,000	30,000

No inventories were on hand at the beginning of 1996. The company increased inventories over the three years in anticipation of growth in sales volume. Variable manufacturing cost per unit was constant throughout the three years and appears as:

Materials.....................................	$ 140
Labor	80
Variable overhead	40
Variable manufacturing cost per unit	$ 260

The fixed factory overhead was $8,750,000 each year. The administrative expenses have averaged $40 per unit sold for variable costs and a total of $750,000 per year for fixed costs. The selling price remained the same throughout the three years at $720 per unit. The company uses a FIFO cost flow.

Required:

1. Prepare income statements using absorption costing for each of the three years.
2. Prepare income statements using variable costing for each of the three years.
3. Reconcile the differences in profits between the two statements for each of the three years.

Solution:

1. Income statements with absorption costing:

Absorption Costing Income Statement For the Years 1996, 1997, and 1998			
	1996	**1997**	**1998**
Units sold...................	16,000	22,000	30,000
Units produced	20,000	25,000	25,000
Sales	$11,520,000	$15,840,000	$21,600,000
Cost of goods sold:			
Inventory, beginning	$ 0	$ 2,790,000	$ 4,270,000
Current production	13,950,000	15,250,000	15,250,000
	$13,950,000	$18,040,000	$19,520,000
Inventory, ending.............	2,790,000	4,270,000	1,220,000
Cost of goods sold	$11,160,000	$13,770,000	$18,300,000
Gross profit	$ 360,000	$ 2,070,000	$ 3,300,000
Administrative expenses:			
Variable	$ 640,000	$ 880,000	$ 1,200,000
Fixed	750,000	750,000	750,000
	$ 1,390,000	$ 1,630,000	$ 1,950,000
Net profit (loss)...............	$ (1,030,000)	$ 440,000	$ 1,350,000

2. Income statements with variable costing:

Variable Costing Income Statement For the Years 1996, 1997, and 1998			
	1996	**1997**	**1998**
Units sold....................	16,000	22,000	30,000
Units produced	20,000	25,000	25,000
Sales	$11,520,000	$15,840,000	$21,600,000
Variable cost of goods sold:			
Inventory, beginning	$ 0	$ 1,040,000	$ 1,820,000
Current production...........	5,200,000	6,500,000	6,500,000
	$ 5,200,000	$ 7,540,000	$ 8,320,000
Inventory, ending	1,040,000	1,820,000	520,000
Variable cost of goods sold	$ 4,160,000	$ 5,720,000	$ 7,800,000
Administrative expenses:			
Variable	640,000	880,000	1,200,000
Total variable costs	$ 4,800,000	$ 6,600,000	$ 9,000,000
Contribution margin	$ 6,720,000	$ 9,240,000	$12,600,000
Fixed costs:			
Manufacturing	$ 8,750,000	$ 8,750,000	$ 8,750,000
Administrative...............	750,000	750,000	750,000
Total fixed costs	$ 9,500,000	$ 9,500,000	$ 9,500,000
Net profit (loss)...............	$ (2,780,000)	$ (260,000)	$ 3,100,000

3. Reconciliation of net profits between the two costing methods:

	1996	**1997**	**1998**
Net profit—absorption costing	$(1,030,000)	$ 440,000	$ 1,350,000
Add: Fixed costs in beginning inventory........	0	1,750,000	2,450,000
	$(1,030,000)	$ 2,190,000	$ 3,800,000
Less: Fixed costs in ending inventory	1,750,000	2,450,000	700,000
Net profit—variable costing	$(2,780,000)	$ (260,000)	$ 3,100,000

TERMINOLOGY REVIEW

Absorption costing, *440*

Benchmarking, *440*

Contribution margin variance analysis, *430*

Cost mix variance, *436*

Cost performance variance, *435*

Cost quantity variance, *435*

Direct costing, *440*

Gross margin variance analysis, *430*

Purchase price variance, *435*

Sales mix variance, *434*

Sales price variance, *433*

Sales quantity variance, *434*

Static budget, *439*

Variable costing, *440*

SUGGESTED READINGS

Bastable, C. W., and D. H. Bao, "The Fiction of Sales-Mix and Sales-Quantity Variances," *Accounting Horizons*, June 1988, pp. 10-17.

Boer, G., "What Gross Margins Do Not Tell You," *Management Accounting*, October 1984, pp. 50-53, 91.

Chen, J. T., "Full and Direct Costing in Profit Variance Analysis," *Issues in Accounting Education*, June 1986, pp. 282-292.

Govindarajan, V., and J. K. Shank, "Profit Variance Analysis: A Strategic Focus," *Issues in Accounting Education*, Fall 1989, pp. 396-410.

Hilton, R. W., R. J. Swieringa, and M. J. Turner, "Product Pricing, Accounting Costs and Use of Product Costing Systems," *Accounting Review*, April 1988, pp. 195-218.

Lere, J. C., "Product Pricing Based on Accounting Costs," *Accounting Review*, April 1986, pp. 318-324.

Olson, R. L., and H. Sollenberger, "Interest Margin Variance Analysis: A Tool for Current Times," *The Magazine of Bank Administration*, May 1978, pp. 45-51.

Schiff, M., "Variable Costing: A Closer Look," *Management Accounting*, February 1987, pp. 36-39.

QUESTIONS FOR REVIEW AND DISCUSSION

1. What are the major causes of actual net income differing from budgeted net income?

2. Using contribution margin analysis in an appliance store:

    (a) What changes could cause February's revenue to be greater than January's revenue?

    (b) What changes could cause February's cost of sales to be greater than January's cost of sales?

3. If a firm has only one product, what changes would contribution margin analysis identify?

4. What are the differences between gross margin and contribution margin analyses?

5. Explain the difference between purchase price variances and cost performance variances.

6. Why would a manager be interested in the variances generated by a contribution margin or gross margin analysis?

7. Explain how a change in mix:

    (a) Can result from price changes.

    (b) Can cause profits to drop even if the same total quantity is sold.

    (c) Will have similar impacts on both the revenues and product costs.

8. Under what conditions can a spending variance be divided into price and quantity variances?

9. Does it matter in what sequence the mix, quantity, and price variances are calculated? Is there a traditional sequence? Will the sequence change the importance of specific variances? Explain.

10. In nonproductive areas, how can benchmarking be used to measure expense control performance?

11.　Differentiate between variable costing and absorption costing.

12.　Explain whether variable costing or absorption costing will have the higher net income under each of the following conditions:

(a)　Production equals sales.

(b)　Production exceeds sales.

(c)　Production is less than sales.

13.　How is it possible to increase net profit using absorption costing when sales are not increasing?

14.　Identify the four major areas of argument for and against variable costing or absorption costing.

15.　A company had a highly labor-intensive manufacturing process. Recently it implemented robotics and a number of other technological changes that made the process capital intensive. What impact would this change make on the inventory valuations for variable costing and for absorption costing?

16.　How is it possible to show zero profit at a break-even point using variable costing but show a profit using absorption costing?

E XERCISES

10-1. Variance Analysis With a Single Product.　Information for May from the Colby Corporation is as follows:

	Budget	*Actual*
Sales units.	2,500	3,000
Sales	$20,000	$22,500
Cost of sales	15,000	19,500
Gross margin	$ 5,000	$ 3,000

Required:
Explain why gross margin declined by $2,000 from the budgeted level.

10-2. Contribution Margin and Expenses With a Single Product.　Yuma Lamps has a subsidiary in Mexicali, Mexico. The subsidiary is operating under the following approved profit plan for June (in pesos):

Sales revenue (24,000 lamps)		M$528,000
Variable costs:		
Cost of goods	M$312,000	
Variable operating expenses	24,000	336,000
Contribution margin		M$192,000
Direct fixed costs		46,000
Product net profit		M$146,000

Actual operations produced and sold 25,000 units at an average selling price of M$20 per unit. Actual cost of goods equaled M$12.50 per unit, and variable operating expenses were M$28,000. Actual fixed costs were M$50,000.

Required:
1.　Prepare an income statement that compares budget and actual results.
2.　Prepare an analysis that explains the variance in contribution margin. Include the variable operating expenses as part of the variance analysis.
3.　Explain why the actual product net profit is not M$146,000.

10-3. Sales Variances.   Hinsky Publishing sells four reference books through local book-stores. Salespersons have authority to match competitors' prices and are encouraged to maximize revenues. Following are sales figures for the third quarter of this year and last year.

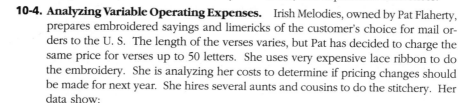

Reference Books	3rd Quarter Sales—Last Year		3rd Quarter Sales—This Year	
	Units	Price	Units	Price
Medical dictionary	12,000	$41	10,000	$43
Bible concordance	20,000	20	18,000	19
Thesaurus..............	8,000	26	9,000	25
Global dictionary	35,000	44	43,000	41
Total quantity	75,000		80,000	

Required:

Compare last year's revenue to this year's results, and explain the differences.

10-4. Analyzing Variable Operating Expenses.   Irish Melodies, owned by Pat Flaherty, prepares embroidered sayings and limericks of the customer's choice for mail orders to the U. S. The length of the verses varies, but Pat has decided to charge the same price for verses up to 50 letters. She uses very expensive lace ribbon to do the embroidery. She is analyzing her costs to determine if pricing changes should be made for next year. She hires several aunts and cousins to do the stitchery. Her data show:

	Actual Results	Original Budget
Embroidered verses	250	200
Letters embroidered	8,250	6,000
Inches of lace used	67,650	48,000
(budgeted at 8 inches per letter)		
Cost of lace used (in Irish pounds)	£16,024	£12,000

Required:

Given the data available, prepare an analysis, in as much detail as possible, to explain the £4,024 difference in lace costs. Use variance names that would be appropriate, such as "letter variance."

10-5. Analysis of Operating Expenses.   Sonora Company has marketing and administrative expenses that follow a cost function of $15,000 plus 6 percent of sales. Sales were budgeted at $150,000 for the month. Actual sales were $160,000, and marketing and administrative expenses were $24,000.

Required:

Identify all variances possible from the data provided. Which variances are the marketing manager's responsibility? Why?

10-6. Contribution Margin Analysis.   Marathon Auto Cleaners has two services that it provides to its customers. Data from 1998 and 1999 show the following:

	1998 Results		1999 Results	
	Partial	Complete	Partial	Complete
Services provided	200,000	300,000	120,000	380,000
Sales price per service...........	$5.00	$6.00	$5.50	$5.90
Variable cost per service	3.00	3.20	3.10	3.18

Required:

1. Determine the change in contribution margin between the two years.
2. Analyze the revenue, variable cost, and contribution margin changes.
3. Comment on the changes from 1998 to 1999.

10-7. Contribution Margin Analysis.   Ross Distributing sells two items, Cheap and Expensive. Joe Ross is pleased that the June contribution margin is above budget, but he believes something strange happened as he sold less and made more money. The data are as follows:

	Budgeted Results			Actual Results		
	Cheap	Expensive	Total	Cheap	Expensive	Total
Sales units	240,000	120,000	360,000	250,000	100,000	350,000
Revenues	$2,400,000	$2,160,000	$4,560,000	$2,750,000	$1,800,000	$4,550,000
Variable costs	1,200,000	930,000	2,130,000	1,350,000	750,000	2,100,000
Contribution margin . . .	$1,200,000	$1,230,000	$2,430,000	$1,400,000	$1,050,000	$2,450,000

Required:
1. Prepare an analysis of revenues, variable costs, and contribution margin.
2. Explain to Joe how he could sell less and make more.

10-8. Analysis of Performance. Assume a dry cleaning firm has an operating expense function of $200,000 plus $1 per garment processed and expects to handle 100,000 garments. Units is the cost driver. Actual fixed costs were $203,000, actual variable costs were $101,000, and 102,000 garments were handled.

Required:
How did the firm perform? Show all variances from budget.

10-9. Comparing Net Incomes. Soneral Company started business in 1994 and had the following sales and production experiences:

	1994	1995	1996	1997	1998
Sales (units)	1,000	1,000	1,100	1,100	1,300
Production (units)	1,000	1,500	900	1,100	1,000

The selling price was $2 per unit. Product costs were $1 per unit for all variable costs plus $1,000 for fixed costs. Fixed overhead was applied using 1,000 units as the expected production level each year ($1 per unit). Operating expenses were the same in each year.

Required:
Comment on each of the following:
A. Net income under variable costing is the same for 1996 and 1997.
B. Net income in 1994 is the same for both absorption costing and variable costing.
C. The total 5-year net income for absorption costing will be greater than the 5-year net income for variable costing.
D. Under absorption costing, which year will show the highest profit? Why?
E. Under variable costing, which year will show the highest profit? Why?
F. Why is net income for the two methods different in 1996? Explain in dollars.

10-10. Unit Costs. Cheng Industries operates a plant in Kaohsiung, Taiwan, which manufactures table tennis paddles for export throughout the world. During December, Cheng produced 24,000 paddles. Costs incurred by Cheng during December were (in New Taiwanese dollars):

Direct materials	NT$ 44,000
Direct labor	17,000
Variable manufacturing overhead	8,000
Variable selling and general	1,000
Fixed manufacturing overhead	15,000
Fixed selling and general	19,000
Total	NT$104,000

Required:
1. Compute the cost of each paddle under absorption costing.
2. Compute the cost of each paddle under variable costing.

10-11. Variable and Absorption Costing Income Statements.   Casselton Agricultural Products, Inc. started producing and selling a new product. Selected operating results for this new product line for its first year of operations are as follows:

Units:	
Produced	16,000
Sold	14,500
Sales price per unit	$ 12
Variable costs:	
Direct materials	$44,000
Direct labor	36,000
Factory overhead	16,000
Marketing and administration	12,000
Fixed costs:	
Factory overhead	$40,000
Marketing and administration	20,000

Required:

1. Prepare an income statement for the year using the variable costing method.

2. Prepare an income statement for the year using the absorption costing method.

3. Prepare a reconciliation of net profits resulting from the two methods. Comment on the difference in profits.

10-12. Variable Costing.   Last year, Rhao & Sons Co. operated at 250,000 units. The income statement for the year, prepared on an absorption costing basis, is as follows:

Units made and sold	250,000
Sales revenue	$2,000,000
Cost of goods sold	1,500,000
Gross profit	$ 500,000
Operating expenses (includes variable costs of $125,000)	225,000
Profit before income taxes	$ 275,000
Income taxes	110,000
Profit after income taxes	$ 165,000

The fixed manufacturing cost per unit of product is $3.00.

Required:

Revise the income statement on a variable costing basis.

10-13. Variable Costing and Inventory Increase.   In 1998, Criswell Manufacturing Company plans to operate at normal capacity and manufacture 400,000 units of product, as in 1997. Sales for 1998 have been estimated at 350,000 units, with total revenue at $17,500,000. The cost of the 20,000 units in the finished goods inventory on January 1, 1998, was $600,000. Included in this amount was $400,000 in fixed manufacturing overhead. No changes in fixed manufacturing costs are expected in 1998, and the variable cost per unit of product will also remain unchanged.

Required:

1. Prepare an estimated income statement for 1998 under absorption costing.

2. Prepare an estimated income statement for 1998 under variable costing.

3. Explain why the income from manufacturing is higher under absorption costing than under variable costing. Your explanation should identify the fixed costs in beginning inventory and in ending inventory.

10-14. Unequal Sales and Production and Variable Costing.   Treadwell Memory Chips reduced its finished goods inventory in 1998 from 80,000 units at the beginning of the year to 50,000 units. Fixed manufacturing overhead of $1,360,000 was incurred, and 170,000 units were produced during the year. The fixed overhead cost per unit was the same as in 1997. Variable manufacturing cost per unit was $9. Each unit of product was sold for $20.

Required:

1. Prepare an income statement for the manufacturing operation in 1998 using absorption costing.

2. Prepare an income statement for the manufacturing operation in 1998 using variable costing.

3. Provide a reconciliation for the difference in profit between the two methods. Comment.

P ROBLEMS

10-15. Salespersons Behavior.   Don McMillan, controller of Poland Sales, has an ear-to-ear smile. He tosses an analysis of last year's gross margin on president Ron Poland's desk and says a soft "I told you so." Ron looks up and says, "I hope this is good news; volume is way down from the first half."

Salespersons had been paid 5 percent of sales. At midyear, Don convinced Ron to change the commission payment to 10 percent of gross margin. The analysis Don gave Ron showed an average budget month, an average month from the first half of last year, and an average month from the second half of last year. All costs are purchase prices. He used the following data:

Products	Budget Month			Average Month-1st Half			Average Month-2nd Half		
	Price	Cost	Quantity	Price	Cost	Quantity	Price	Cost	Quantity
Able	$20	$10	10,000	$18	$10	12,000	$22	$10	9,000
Baker	30	15	10,000	25	15	14,000	29	15	11,000
Charlie	40	20	10,000	38	20	11,000	43	20	10,000

Required:

1. Prepare an analysis similar to the one that Don probably just gave Ron, comparing an average actual month from both halves to an average budget month using gross margin variance analysis.

2. Compare the salespersons' commission results for the two time periods relative to the budget.

3. Should Ron and Don both be smiling? Comment on the salespersons' behavior.

10-16. Analyzing Results.   Chavez Walkie-Talkie markets two models of its main product line. Budgeted and actual results for 1998 are as follows:

	Budget	Actual
Sales revenue	$1,080,000	$1,120,850
Cost of sales	756,000	829,445
Gross margin.	$ 324,000	$ 291,405
Operating expenses	174,000	198,000
Net profit	$ 150,000	$ 93,405

	Budget		Actual	
	NearBy	FarAway	NearBy	FarAway
Units sold	3,000	6,000	3,200	6,300
Selling price per unit	$166.00	$ 97.00	$162.25	$ 95.50
Cost of sales per unit	116.20	67.90	120.07	70.67

Operating expenses follow a budget formula of $10 per unit sold plus $84,000.

Required:
1. Analyze the change in gross margin.
2. Analyze the change in operating expenses.
3. Identify and comment on the three main reasons for the decline in net profit.

10-17. Interest Margin Analysis. The "Say Yes" Bank, the friendliest in the East, had a profit plan that showed a $34.8 million interest margin for 1998. Results are in. The president, Ann Friendly, called the CFO, Jim Friendly, and asked how the bank could have earned so much more interest margin than expected. She recalls that some rates went up but others went down. She knows growth was higher than expected. Operating expenses were right on target. She plans to share the good news with all the other Friendlys working at the bank (43 at last count); but she needs some answers. Jim hands you the following data and a calculator.

($ in Millions)	1998 Budget				1998 Results			
	Average Balance	Mix Percentage	Interest Amount	Interest Rate	Average Balance	Mix Percentage	Interest Amount	Interest Rate
Assets:								
Investments	$ 300	33.3%	$ 12.0	4.0%	$ 250	26.9%	$ 10.5	4.2%
Short-term loans	300	33.3	27.0	9.0	400	43.0	35.6	8.9
Long-term loans	300	33.3	30.0	10.0	280	30.1	26.6	9.5
Total	$ 900	100.0%	$ 69.0	7.7%	$ 930	100.0%	$ 72.7	7.8%
Liabilities:								
Deposits	$ 900	100.0%	34.2	3.8%	$ 930	100.0%	37.2	4.0%
Interest margin			$ 34.8	3.9%			$ 35.5	3.8%

Required:
Explain how the bank earned $0.7 million more in interest margin in 1998 than planned. How much of this comes from having more assets than expected?

10-18. The CPA Firm. Tom Brodbeck, administrative partner in a CPA firm, has developed a concept of the perfect mix of personnel to handle the type of client work load this firm has enjoyed for several years. He thinks the ratio should be one partner, three managers, and eight staff accountants. The firm's budget for the work year called for 36 persons and an ideal mix. Because of promotions, new hires, and resignations, the average mix for the year was four partners, seven managers, and 29 staff accountants. The budgeted and actual salary expenses (with headcounts in parentheses) were:

	Budgeted Salaries		Actual Salaries	
Partners	$ 360,000	(3)	$ 440,000	(4)
Managers	720,000	(9)	630,000	(7)
Staff accountants	936,000	(24)	1,102,000	(29)
Total salaries	$2,016,000	(36)	$2,172,000	(40)

Tom is reviewing this year's results. He sees that salaries are $156,000 above budget.

Required:
1. Prepare an analysis that will show the mix and yield variances for the firm's staff this year. Remember to identify the salary variance first.
2. Comment on the $156,000 salary difference between budget and actual.
3. The ideal staffing ratio should generate 1,500 hours of billable time per person. Billable time is the time charged to clients. Tom knows that 64,000 billable hours were worked this year. Comment on the impact of this fact on the firm's profitability, and explain how you might analyze the chargeable hours data.

10-19. Travel Packages Contribution Margin. Duncan Tours arranges and conducts travel tours for retirees in eastern Pennsylvania. Three basic tours are the most popular: New York City, Cape Cod, and Williamsburg. Prices and variable costs per person for each tour are:

	Prices	Variable Cost
New York City..........................	$400	$250
Cape Cod.............................	350	175
Williamsburg..........................	540	360

The fixed costs, such as managers' and tour guides' salaries and office rent, have been estimated at $800,000 per year and are allocated to each tour based on the estimated number of customers served. A forecast income statement shows:

	New York City	Cape Cod	Williamsburg	Total
Number of customers	6,000	1,500	2,500	10,000
Revenues...............	$2,400,000	$525,000	$1,350,000	$4,275,000
Total costs	1,980,000	382,500	1,100,000	3,462,500
Estimated income	$420,000	$142,500	$250,000	$812,500

Actual results for the year include $810,000 for fixed costs and are as follows:

	New York City	Cape Cod	Williamsburg
Number of customers	7,000	1,000	4,000
Price realized...........	$390	$330	$500
Variable cost incurred	255	175	350

Required:
1. Develop comparative income statements on a contribution margin basis for forecast and actual.
2. Explain the variation in contribution margin through variance analysis.
3. Comment on the major reasons for the change in net income for the year.

10-20. Comprehensive Operating Expense Variance Analysis. Miko Computer Programmers provides contract programming services to major corporations. It budgets around programming hours sold (worked). For the third quarter, Miko budgeted 180,000 hours of sales. An hour is billed at $45 and has a "loaded" cost of $35.50. Miko's flexible operating expense budget formulas are:

Administrative salaries..................	$90,000	+	$0.04 per hour sold
Sales salaries......................	60,000	+	0.06 per hour sold
Utilities and supplies	11,500	+	0.25 per hour sold
Training costs			2.05 per hour sold
Depreciation expense	61,000		
Property taxes......................	2,000		

Actual results for the third quarter showed that 195,000 hours generated revenue of $8,190,000 and programmer costs of $6,630,000. Actual operating costs were:

Administrative salaries...................................	$96,800
Sales salaries..	73,600
Utilities and supplies	58,060
Training costs	415,250
Depreciation expense	61,000
Property taxes...	1,850

Required:
1. Prepare income statements that show the original budget, a flexible budget based on actual hours sold, and actual results.
2. Prepare an analysis of gross margin differences.
3. What type of cost behavior appears in the operating expense spending variances?

10-21. Contribution Margin Analysis.   Kang Temps provides temporary employees for general office services. The services are classified as clerical and secretarial. Assignments can be for one day or for several months. Employees are paid based on classification and experience. Jim Kang, the owner, bills clients an average of $15 per hour for clerical time and $20 per hour for secretarial time. Kang pays clerical workers an average of $9 per hour and secretaries $13 per hour.   The workers are paid only for hours worked. Wages are the only variable expenses. Kang forecasts monthly overhead costs of $35,000.

During November, Kang's clerical workers generated 4,400 hours and $63,500 in revenue.   Secretarial workers generated 3,600 hours and $73,200 in revenue. Wages and related expenses were $43,122 for clerical workers and $44,565 for secretarial workers. Kang's actual November overhead was $36,400.

Jim Kang's budget for November showed 4,500 hours and 3,500 hours, respectively, for clerical and secretarial work.

Required:

Evaluate November's contribution margin. Using variance analysis, highlight the major causes of November's difference in profits.

10-22. Variable Costing and Two Product Lines.   Presupuesto Co. manufactures lawn rakes and shovels at its San Juan, Puerto Rico, plant. Data with respect to sales and production have been estimated by Javier Clemente, the controller, for next year as follows:

	Rakes	Shovels
Estimated units to be sold	240,000	160,000
Unit selling price	$3.50	$6.00
Unit variable cost of manufacturing	$1.75	$2.75
Production time per unit of product	10 min.	30 min.

The fixed factory overhead of the San Juan plant is apportioned to the products at the rate of $3.00 per production hour. Total corporate fixed overhead of $300,000 has been apportioned to the San Juan plant, but this is not apportioned to the products.

Required:

1. Assuming a variable costing approach, prepare an income statement that will show for each product line and in total:
   (a) The contribution margin.
   (b) The apportioned fixed factory overhead.
   (c) The profit for each product.
   (d) The final profit after recognizing apportionment of the corporate fixed overhead.
2. What is the expected total unit cost of each product line without apportioning the corporate fixed overhead?
3. Apportion corporate fixed overhead to each product on the basis of production time. Now, what is the expected total unit cost of each product line?
4. Which unit cost number would be best to use in establishing a cost-based selling price? Why?

10-23. Variable and Absorption Costing and Profit at the Break-Even Point.   The president of Schaucer Supply Company, Lola Schaucer, is surprised to learn that the company earned a profit in 1999 even though sales were at the break-even point.

"When we were going over the budget for 1999," she said, "I was told that we would have a poor year and could expect to break even with sales of only 206,000 units. Now, I find that we earned a modest pretax profit with sales of 206,000 units, although selling prices and costs were as budgeted. I am not complaining about a profit, mind you, but I can't understand how a profit can be made when operating at the break-even point."

Data pertaining to 1999 are as follows:

Unit selling price	$35
Unit variable cost	20
Unit contribution margin	$15

$$\frac{\$3{,}090{,}000 \text{ (fixed production cost)}}{\$15 \text{ (unit contribution margin)}} = 206{,}000 \text{ units break even}$$

Fixed production costs are applied to products at $10 per unit. The inventory of finished goods was 30,000 units on January 1, 1999, and 133,000 units on December 31, 1999. The marketing and administrative expenses were fixed at the amount of $90,000.

Required:

1. Prepare an income statement for 1999 using absorption costing.

2. Prepare an income statement for 1999 using variable costing.

3. Explain to the president how a profit was made when using absorption costing even though sales were at the break-even point.

4. Explain whether the absorption costing income statement or the variable costing income statement gives the more realistic results.

1-2-3

10-24. Conversion of Absorption Costing to Variable Costing. Vanguard Electrical Supply Company manufactures electric switches and timing devices in three operating divisions: Utility, Household, and Commercial. An income statement, showing the results for each division, is given for 1997. The company had total fixed manufacturing overhead of $8,900,000. Inventories were increased during the year in anticipation of more sales volume in 1998.

VANGUARD ELECTRICAL SUPPLY COMPANY Income Statement for the Year 1997 (in Thousands)				
	Utility	*Household*	*Commercial*	*Total*
Net sales	$6,200	$5,150	$6,300	$17,650
Cost of goods sold:				
Inventory, beginning	$ 540	$ 240	$ 150	$ 930
Production cost	5,400	4,000	4,200	13,600
Cost of goods available for sale	$5,940	$4,240	$4,350	$14,530
Less inventory, ending	900	640	900	2,440
Cost of goods sold	$5,040	$3,600	$3,450	$12,090
Manufacturing profit	$1,160	$1,550	$2,850	$ 5,560

The plant controller, Margaret Hubert, believes that profits may be higher than they would be otherwise because of fixed costs being carried over to the next year as a part of inventory. She would like to have the statement revised to a variable costing basis and would like to know the manufacturing contribution margin for each division.

Additional analyses show the units and unit variable costs as follows. There are no partially completed units.

	Utility	Household	Commercial
Units in beginning inventory	30,000	15,000	10,000
Units produced	300,000	250,000	280,000
Units in ending inventory	50,000	40,000	60,000
Unit variable manufacturing cost	$6	$6	$5

Required:

1. Prepare an income statement on a variable costing basis that shows the contribution margin and direct profits by division and in total.
2. Prepare a reconciliation between the variable costing and absorption costing income statements. This reconciliation should show results by division and in total.
3. How much of the fixed cost was carried over to 1998 as a part of ending inventory cost for each division?

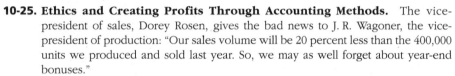

10-25. Ethics and Creating Profits Through Accounting Methods. The vice-president of sales, Dorey Rosen, gives the bad news to J. R. Wagoner, the vice-president of production: "Our sales volume will be 20 percent less than the 400,000 units we produced and sold last year. So, we may as well forget about year-end bonuses."

Wagoner smiles and replies, "We'll just pump the inventories up by producing 500,000 units. There is plenty of storage area in the warehouse."

"We'll never get away with it. The president will see what we are doing," Rosen answers.

"No, he knows nothing about accounting. Let me handle it, and we'll still get our bonuses."

A summary manufacturing income statement for last year is given as follows:

Net sales	$18,000,000
Cost of goods sold:	
Inventory, January 1	$ 175,000
Production cost	14,000,000
Cost of merchandise available for sale	$14,175,000
Less inventory, December 31	175,000
Cost of goods sold	$14,000,000
Income from manufacturing	$ 4,000,000

Product cost for last year included fixed manufacturing overhead of $20 per unit. Unit variable costs and total fixed costs are expected to remain the same next year. The company uses a FIFO cost flow.

Required:

1. How is Wagoner planning to build up the profits?
2. Prepare an estimated income statement for this year assuming that Rosen's estimate of sales is correct and that 500,000 units of product are manufactured. Use absorption costing.
3. Recast the last year's manufacturing income statement and the estimated statement for this year on a variable costing basis.
4. Discuss whether J. R. Wagoner is behaving in an ethical manner.

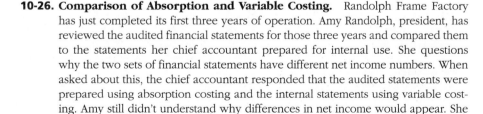

10-26. Comparison of Absorption and Variable Costing. Randolph Frame Factory has just completed its first three years of operation. Amy Randolph, president, has reviewed the audited financial statements for those three years and compared them to the statements her chief accountant prepared for internal use. She questions why the two sets of financial statements have different net income numbers. When asked about this, the chief accountant responded that the audited statements were prepared using absorption costing and the internal statements using variable costing. Amy still didn't understand why differences in net income would appear. She wants an analysis of the two results.

The selling price and cost data are identical for each of the three years and appear as follows:

Selling price per unit	$15.00
Manufacturing costs:	
Direct materials cost per unit	$2.80
Direct labor cost per unit	4.70
Variable factory overhead per unit	.50
Fixed factory overhead in total	$120,000.00
Marketing and administrative expenses:	
Variable	25% of sales
Fixed	$ 35,000

	Units	
Year	Production	Sales
1997	60,000	50,000
1998	60,000	55,000
1999	50,000	60,000

The company uses a FIFO cost flow.

Required:

1. Prepare a three-year comparative income statement using absorption costing.
2. Prepare a three-year comparative income statement using variable costing.
3. Reconcile the net income figures of absorption costing and variable costing for each of the three years.
4. Using a graph with sales units on the horizontal axis and net income (dollars) on the vertical axis, plot and connect the following points:
   (a) Net income and sales units assuming absorption costing.
   (b) Net income and sales units assuming variable costing.
   (c) The difference in net income between the two costing methods and their related sales units.
5. What conclusions can you derive from the graph in Part (4) about the advantages of the variable costing approach?

C ASE 10A—KEROBO DIVISION

The Kerobo Division of BASE Industries manufactures and sells two versions of patio chairs—plastic and fiberglass. The division markets chairs to retail and catalog outlets. Generally, a sale includes both types of chairs.

The two chairs are produced on different assembly lines located in adjoining buildings. Division management and sales staff occupy a third building on the property. Control reports separate sales and production activities for planning and control purposes. The operating results for the first quarter as compared to budget are as follows:

	Actual Results		Budget Results	
	Plastic	Fiberglass	Plastic	Fiberglass
Sales in units.	60,000	20,000	50,000	25,000
Sales revenue	$630,000	$300,000	$500,000	$375,000
Less variable costs:				
Manufacturing (standard).........	480,000	200,000	400,000	250,000
Selling expenses	37,800	18,000	30,000	22,500
Contribution margin..............	$112,200	$ 82,000	$ 70,000	$102,500
Other expenses:				
Variable production variances............	$ 48,600		$ 0	
Fixed manufacturing expenses	49,200		48,000	
Fixed selling and general expenses	38,500		36,000	
Corporate office allocation..............	18,500		17,500	

The budget for the current year was based on the assumption that Kerobo would maintain its present market share of the estimated total patio chair market. It appears that industry volume is about 10 percent higher than forecast. A status report was sent to BASE headquarters at the end of the second month indicating that the division operating income would be about 45 percent below budget.

Manufacturing activity for the first quarter resulted in 55,000 plastic and 22,500 fiberglass chairs being produced. The costs incurred were:

	Plastic	Fiberglass
Materials purchased	$339,000 for 60,000 units	$180,000 for 30,000 units
Materials used	280,000 for 56,000 units	138,000 for 23,000 units
Direct labor	55,800 for 9,300 hours	44,800 for 5,600 hours
Factory overhead:		
Variable: Supplies	43,000	18,000
Power.............	49,000	15,000
Benefits	19,000	12,000
Fixed: Supervision	14,000	11,000
Depreciation........	12,000	9,000
Other fixed costs	1,900	1,300

Variable standard costs per unit and budgeted monthly fixed costs are:

	Plastic		Fiberglass	
Direct materials (1 unit per chair)	$ 5.00		$ 6.00	
Direct labor	1.00	(1/6 hour x $6)	2.00	(1/4 hour x $8)
Variable factory overhead	2.00	(40% of materials)	2.00	(1/4 hour x $8)
Standard variable cost	$ 8.00		$ 10.00	
Budgeted monthly fixed costs:				
Supervision	$4,500		$ 3,500	
Depreciation	4,000		3,000	
Other fixed costs	600		400	
Total monthly fixed costs	$9,100		$ 6,900	

Required:

1. Explain Kerobo's higher than expected contribution margin by using variance analysis.
2. Can part of the contribution margin variance be attributed to Kerobo's change in market share? Explain.
3. Analyze the manufacturing cost variances in as much detail as possible.
4. Based on your analysis in Parts (1), (2), and (3):
   (a) Identify the major causes of Kerobo's unfavorable profit performance.
   (b) Discuss steps Kerobo's management could have undertaken to prevent the profit decline.

(ICMA adapted)

CASE 10B—KRQ INDUSTRIES, INC.

The management of the Brownville Plastics Division of KRQ Industries, Inc. is considering ways to improve profitability by expanding the sales volume of the more profitable lines. The Brownville Division makes five plastic product lines as follows:

1. Clear plastic handles for small tools, such as screwdrivers.
2. Plastic cases for flashlights, cameras, projectors, etc.
3. Kitchenware (plates, cups, and saucers).
4. Ornamental light globes.
5. Novelties and toys.

In trying to rank the five product lines by profitability, there is a question of how the fixed manufacturing costs should be allocated. The materials vary according to the product line. In some cases, a clear plastic is processed; and, in other cases, colors are added. Also, the processing operation depends on the type of product made.

Sales and production cost data for the year are as follows:

	Handles	Cases	Kitchenware	Light Globes	Novelties
Units sold*	150,000	80,000	120,000	90,000	60,000
Selling price	$9.00	$15.00	$16.00	$14.00	$5.00
Materials cost	1.80	3.50	4.80	4.20	1.60
Labor time per unit ...	20 min.	30 min.	40 min.	20 min.	10 min.

*Units are batches or lots as defined for each product line.

The sales volume as given is considered to be typical. The labor rate per hour is $9.00, and variable overhead is $6.00 per labor hour. The fixed manufacturing overhead for the year has been budgeted at $550,000. Selling and administrative costs follow a budget formula of four percent of total revenue plus fixed costs of $325,000.

The president of the company, Holly Mercer, asks, "How should we allocate the fixed costs of production in calculating the profitability of each product line? I have heard suggestions that the costs should be allocated on the basis of the relative market values. Joe Henderson, our production superintendent, has suggested that the fixed costs should be allocated on the basis of the revenues minus the direct costs of production. Any other thoughts?"

"Does it really matter how the fixed costs are allocated if we are trying to find out which lines are more profitable?" inquires Dave Lopez, the sales manager. "As I understand it, we are operating at normal volume now. We can handle more business, but we should be concentrating on the promotion of the more profitable lines."

Henderson breaks in, "But, Dave, there can be no profit until all costs are recovered. If a product line can't cover its share of fixed costs, we shouldn't be making it."

"Can you determine exactly how much fixed cost should be identified with any one product line?" Lopez asks.

"Why don't we work it out both ways?" the president answers. "Let's get an income statement showing fixed production costs allocated on the basis of revenue, another income statement with the fixed costs allocated on the basis of revenue minus the variable costs, and still another income statement showing the contribution of each line over its variable costs. On that last statement, we should have the contribution margin per unit of product. While we are at it, let's determine contribution margin per product line per hour. Then, we can see how our time can be used to the best advantage. That will give Dave a better idea about which lines are more important to us."

Required:

1. Prepare income statements as requested by the president.
2. Comment on the positions taken by Joe Henderson and Dave Lopez.
3. Which income statement approach gives the most meaningful information for the managers involved? Explain.

PART IV

Decision-Making Framework

CHAPTER 11

Managerial Decisions: Analysis of Relevant Information

LEARNING OBJECTIVES

After studying Chapter 11, you will be able to:

1. Understand the use of differential analysis in making basic decisions.

2. Identify and use relevant costs and revenues in decision making.

3. Recognize the decision type; know the basic decision rule and guidelines; identify major constraints, assumptions, and underlying concerns; format the problem data for analysis; and apply the decision logic to similar real-life problems.

4. Evaluate make or buy, special sales pricing, scarce resource, process further, and add or delete a segment decisions.

5. Explain the role of market and cost information in pricing decisions.

Decisions, Decisions, Decisions

Kristin Rich operates a chain of take-out ribs and sandwich shops, called Rich Ribs, in the city's suburbs. Before leaving on vacation, Kristin asked her controller, Jack Lintol, to prepare cost analyses of several decisions she has been considering. She met with Jack to outline each decision.

Decision 1: A major employer in the area called Kristin and asked whether a deal could be arranged to serve Rich Ribs at a company picnic and later perhaps regularly in its cafeteria, depending on the employees' reaction. Kristin's company name may or may not be identified. The company's offering price is roughly 60 percent of Rich's a la carte menu price.

Decision 2: The Riverwood shop has been showing a monthly net operating loss for the last six months. The shop's lease expires at yearend. Also, a new mini shopping mall is opening in a growing part of the city not presently served by Kristin's shops. Kristin could close the Riverwood shop and shift the manager to the new mall shop.

Decision 3: A local bakery with an excellent reputation in the area has offered to sell bread sticks to Kristin. Rich Ribs includes a serving of bread sticks with every take-out dinner order. Now Kristin bakes her own bread sticks in her kitchen every day and is proud of their quality, but the bakery price offer seems very low.

Decision 4: Kristin is thinking of adding pizza to her menu, but the kitchen's oven capacity would be stretched severely if she keeps all other menu items. She wants to use her kitchen capacity in the most profitable way.

Kristin has a "common sense feel" about the answers to these decisions, but she needs economic proof. She looks to Jack to assemble, analyze, and present the relevant information for each issue. She must then weigh all the quantitative and qualitative factors and decide.

Yes, "decisions, decisions, decisions" is a common lament. But decision making creates action. It is the exciting part of management. Managers' experiences and skills are applied to specific problems. The decision may be significant, such as when and where to build a new $1 billion manufacturing facility. Or it may be mundane, such as sending a customer contract by first-class mail or overnight by Federal Express. In either case, consciously or subconsciously, managers follow a process: define the problem, consider choices, collect and analyze relevant data, make a decision, and act.

This chapter examines groups of decisions that require particular decision rules, relevant data, and formats. These decisions commonly occur in all business activities and even in our personal lives. These groups are:

1. **Make or buy**—where to get resource inputs.
2. **Special sales pricing**—where and at what price to sell.
3. **Use scarce resources**—how to get the most out of limited resources.
4. **Sell or process further**—when to sell.
5. **Add or delete a segment**—which to do.

Other decision groups, such as replace equipment and expand capacity, are explored in Chapters 12 and 13.

Decisions discussed here are necessarily simplified. The real world offers much more complexity. Decisions are about the future, where much uncertainty exists. The printed page implies a certainty about the future that actual decision makers strangely do not enjoy. In textbook problems, we consider only a few variables that impact decision results. In reality, literally hundreds of variables are moving in different directions at the same time. Therefore, an ized approach helps managers use a process, select relevant variables, and at to their analysis.

THE DECISION-MAKING PROCESS

Every managerial decision is made with the mission and the strategic goals of the organization in mind. A critical key to effective decision making is an organized approach. Organization implies structure and methodology, but not arbitrariness or rigidity. In Chapter 1, an eight-step process was outlined:

1. Define the decision issue.
2. Specify the decision objective and decision rule.
3. Identify the choices or alternatives.
4. Collect relevant data on the choices.
5. Format and analyze information about each choice.
6. Make the decision.
7. Implement the decision.
8. Evaluate the results of the decision.

Chapter 11 focuses on certain steps. For Step 2, we outline a decision rule and guidelines. For Step 4, we define relevant data. For Step 5, we present formats for analyses. In addition to quantitative analysis, major qualitative issues that influence the decision are raised. And for Step 6, we apply differential analysis to select the preferred choice, given the facts.

An important element underlying the processes explained here is the empowerment of managers throughout the firm to make decisions. Decisions are based on a clear understanding of organizational goals, training in decision analysis, sharing decision-making information, the authority to act, and an evaluation process.

DIFFERENTIAL ANALYSIS

Differential analysis uses relevant revenues and costs to make decisions. It is the result of defining a decision rule and quantifying and formatting relevant information.

The Basic Decision Rule

The basic differential analysis decision rule is:

Select the choice that yields the greatest incremental profit.

Incremental profit is the difference between the relevant revenues and the relevant costs of each choice. **Relevant revenues and costs** are defined as the current and future values that differ among the choices considered. In most cases, the term "incremental" is used as a substitute for "relevant." In choosing among choices, all past and committed costs (often referred to as **sunk costs**) and all costs that remain the same across all choices are ignored.

A decision is frequently a choice of:

Do it or **don't do it**.   *or*   **Do A**, or **do B**, or **do C**, or **etc**.

In the first case, "don't do it" is the status quo; and "do it" has incremental revenues and costs attached. In the second case, incremental revenues and costs for each choice are measured. In either case, the decision is based on which choice generates the highest incremental profit—incremental revenues minus incremental costs.

Relevant revenues are often assumed to be cash inflows, and relevant costs are cash outflows. **Out-of-pocket costs** refer to costs that are cash outflows. If cash flow and accrual numbers differ, the managerial emphasis is often on cash.

In many cases, capacity impacts decisions. Capacity costs are frequently fixed and are irrelevant to most short-term decisions. A relevant factor is the **opportunity cost** of using capacity. If excess capacity exists and no alternative uses are apparent, the opportunity cost is zero—the unused capacity has no next-best use. If capacity is fully used, earnings from its alternative uses and costs of acquiring additional capacity are weighed.

Incremental Analysis Versus Total Analysis

Differential analysis contrasts choices by comparing incremental contribution margins. Two commonly used approaches are applicable to all decision types —the incremental analysis approach and the total analysis approach. The **incremental analysis approach** includes only incremental revenues and costs of each choice. The **total analysis approach** shows the results for the total entity, including the alternative and then excluding the alternative. To evaluate adding a new product, the format is:

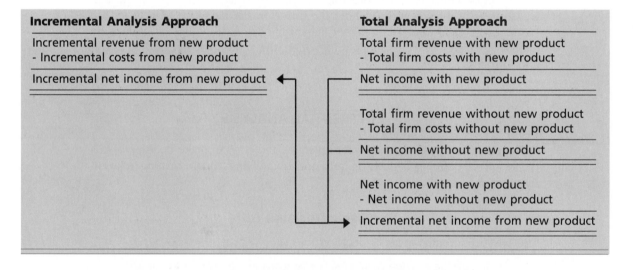

Incremental Analysis Approach	**Total Analysis Approach**
Incremental revenue from new product - Incremental costs from new product	Total firm revenue with new product - Total firm costs with new product
Incremental net income from new product	Net income with new product
	Total firm revenue without new product - Total firm costs without new product
	Net income without new product
	Net income with new product - Net income without new product
	Incremental net income from new product

Clearly, the two approaches yield the same incremental net income. The incremental analysis approach has the advantage of showing only relevant amounts. All sunk and nonchanging amounts are ignored. The total analysis approach reports the firm's gross results, with and without the decision's impacts.

An Example of Differential Analysis

BeanTown Caps is located in Boston, with a factory in South Carolina. Bill O'Connell, CEO, recently purchased this small manufacturer of baseball-type caps. It produces several styles in a variety of materials, but all caps are essentially the same. The caps are marketed under the name BT Caps. Bill has just finished an initial budget for 1998, including this income statement:

Sales (100,000 units at $10 per unit).............		$1,000,000
Production costs:		
Variable production costs ($3 per unit)..........	$300,000	
Fixed factory costs	300,000	600,000
Gross profit		$ 400,000
Operating expenses:		
Selling expenses (15 percent of sales)	$150,000	
Administrative expenses	150,000	300,000
Net income		$ 100,000

Bill's factory operates at 80 percent of capacity. He is currently weighing several alternatives to increase capacity utilization and profits. His analysis shows the choices as:

1. Maintain the status quo.
2. Expand sales of BT Caps to 125,000 by lowering the selling price from $10 to $9 per unit.
3. Use the remaining capacity to make an insulated cap for cold weather runners, called HotHat. He estimates a sales price of $8 per unit, selling expenses of 15 percent, variable costs of $4 per unit, and no change in fixed costs.

The three choices are compared in Figure 11.1 using a total analysis approach. Choice 2 increases net income to $131,250, a differential increase of $31,250. With Choice 3, the HotHat, net income increases by $70,000.

FIGURE 11.1 Total Analysis Approach to Differential Analysis

			Choice 3		
	Choice 1	*Choice 2*	*BT Caps*	*HotHats*	*Total*
Units of sales..................	100,000	125,000	100,000	25,000	
Sales price	$10.00	$9.00	$10.00	$8.00	
Variable costs:					
Production costs	$ 3.00	$3.00	$ 3.00	$4.00	
Selling costs..................	1.50	1.35	1.50	1.20	
Total variable costs...........	$ 4.50	$4.35	$ 4.50	$5.20	
Contribution margin per unit	$ 5.50	$4.65	$ 5.50	$2.80	
Sales	$1,000,000	$1,125,000	$1,000,000	$ 200,000	$1,200,000
Variable costs:					
Production costs	$ 300,000	$ 375,000	$ 300,000	$ 100,000	$ 400,000
Selling costs..................	150,000	168,750	150,000	30,000	180,000
Total variable costs...........	$ 450,000	$ 543,750	$ 450,000	$ 130,000	$ 580,000
Variable contribution margin	$ 550,000	$ 581,250	$ 550,000	$ 70,000	$ 620,000
Fixed costs:					
Fixed factory costs..............	$ 300,000	$ 300,000			$ 300,000
Administrative costs.............	150,000	150,000			150,000
Total fixed costs	$ 450,000	$ 450,000			$ 450,000
Net income	$ 100,000	$ 131,250			$ 170,000

The incremental analysis approach is shown in Figure 11.2. No mention is made of the original sales of 100,000 units or fixed costs which do not change. All comparisons are incremental to Choice 1, the status quo. Therefore, while Choice 1 is not shown in Figure 11.2, the other choices show the contribution margin differential to Choice 1's $100,000 of net income.

Based on quantitative facts, O'Connell will select Choice 3. But before the decision is made, long-term considerations should be evaluated. Is the HotHat consistent with the firm's product plans? Will it take resources from Bill's primary market—BT Caps? Because Bill is an avid runner, are his personal biases confusing his thinking? Are additional equipment or worker skills needed? Although supposedly a short-term decision, these policy issues concern Bill.

Policy Issues Affecting Relevant Costing Decisions

As with all real-world issues, the decision-making path is more complex than the basic rules imply. The differential analysis model is so simple and appealing that we can easily be lulled into a false sense of objectivity.

ABC and Relevant Costs. Companies with well-developed activity-based costing systems are in a more powerful position to make relevant costing decisions. With carefully selected cost drivers and cost functions, changes in costs from a change in activity can be more clearly seen. In our discussions here, activity bases are frequently assumed to be units of product or sales dollars, but often the costing system itself is used to estimate incremental costs.

The Timeframe. Certain assumptions are made in differential analysis. A short-term horizon is assumed, variable costs are relevant, and most fixed costs are irrelevant. However, managers must recognize that all important decisions have both short-term and long-term impacts. In many cases, investments must be made that last longer than the immediate timeframe. Decisions made today often are not easily reversed tomorrow. Also, decisions made on a one-time basis or made for an immediate gain may change the options available in the long run. By selecting Choice 3 in our preceding example, Bill has committed all unused capacity. If BT Caps sales grow, he must somehow expand capacity or lose sales.

Strategic Planning Issues. A firm's strategic plan looks at product offerings, pricing strategies, competitive positions, and financial performance goals. Also,

FIGURE 11.2 Incremental Analysis Approach to Differential Analysis

	Choice 2	Choice 3
Incremental sales of BT Caps ($9 x 25,000)	$225,000	
Incremental production costs of BT Caps ($3 x 25,000)	(75,000)	
Lost revenue from price reduction [($9 - $10) x 100,000]	(100,000)	
Sales of HotHats ($8 x 25,000)		$200,000
Incremental production costs of HotHats ($4 x 25,000)		(100,000)
Incremental sales commissions (15% x increased revenue)	(18,750)	(30,000)
Incremental contribution margin	$ 31,250	$ 70,000

growing globalism means sources of resources and sales markets are now international in nature and must be considered by nearly every firm. "Long haul" policies are implemented in the short run by tactics and decision guidelines. By overaggressive use of marginal costing principles, managers may be letting the "tail wag the dog." Incremental decisions are often just that, additions at the margin. The major pricing, production, and marketing decisions must follow long-term strategies that have been carefully thought through.

Often decisions are masked as incremental decisions, when they are really policy-making, long-term decisions. For example:

1. A one-time sale at a low price becomes repeat business.
2. Regular customers seek price breaks to compete with off-brand look-a-likes.
3. Purchasing cheaper, lower-quality parts eventually hurts a firm's image as a high-quality producer. This same outsourcing may undermine harmony that the company and its labor union have worked hard to develop.
4. Stopping and starting production of a temporarily unprofitable product may cause losses of market share for an entire product line and of skilled employees who make the product.

These examples of "profitable" short-term decisions could have long-term negative impacts. While relevant costing is a powerful analytical tool, no decision can be made in isolation.

*M*AKE OR BUY DECISIONS

The decision question is:

> ***Should we make an item or perform the service ourselves,
> or should we purchase the item or service from a vendor?***

Nearly all products and services offered on the market today result from basic make or buy decisions. A sample of these decisions includes:

The "Make" Alternative	The "Buy" Alternative
Make the component part in our factory in Indiana.	Buy it from a nearby supplier, a nonunion vendor in another state, a Taiwanese producer, or another division of our own company.
Operate our fleet of delivery trucks.	Hire various freight companies.
Run our printing shop.	Contract with local printers.
Employ our own cleaning staff.	Hire a cleaning service.
Manage our data processing operation.	Hire a facilities management company.
Cook for ourselves.	Eat in the dorm cafeteria.

Managers consider make or buy decisions for various reasons, including to:

1. Reduce costs.
2. Use or free up capacity.
3. Improve quality or delivery performance.
4. Encourage greater productivity from internal operations by forcing competition with outsiders.
5. Get new technology.
6. Free scarce investment funds for other uses.

Key Decision Rule and Guidelines

The key decision rule is:

> ***Buy it if the out-of-pocket costs of buying the product or service are less than the out-of-pocket costs of making the product or service; otherwise make it.***

Out-of-pocket costs are the relevant costs in this decision. The decision rule is still to earn the highest profit. But since make or buy decisions generally deal only with costs, the decision rule minimizes cost. If we buy from a vendor, we **outsource**. We are **in-house sourcing** if we make the item ourselves.

Relevant make costs are the direct costs of producing an item plus any opportunity costs. Direct costs include direct materials and direct labor and variable manufacturing overhead. Included also are any incremental fixed costs caused by the make decision plus any traceable costs, such as unique tooling costs. These are called avoidable costs if the decision is to buy.

Relevant buy costs are the item's purchase price, shipping and handling costs, and any costs incurred to get the purchased item into usable form. Inspection and testing costs are examples. Another relevant cost issue is alternative uses of space vacated, if a formerly produced part is now purchased. The space could be rented at some market rate, used by another department, or used to make other parts.

Data Analysis Format

The make or buy analysis lists the relevant costs to make and the relevant costs to buy in a two-column format, shown as follows:

Make Costs		*Buy Costs*	
Materials and direct labor	$	Purchase cost plus handling costs . .	$
Variable overhead costs	$		
Avoidable fixed overhead costs	$		
Other avoidable or incremental costs. .	$		
Opportunity costs of additional resources needed	$	Incremental revenue or earnings from use of released resources . .	($)
Total make costs	$	Total buy costs.	$

Any costs that do not change are ignored, since they are irrelevant. Direct product costs and purchase costs are easily listed. Items can be either an additional cost on one side or a negative cost on the other. For example, if by outsourcing, office space is no longer needed and can be leased for $5,000, the revenue reduces the buy costs. Or, it can be viewed as an additional make cost, since by performing the service ourselves we incur a $5,000 opportunity cost. Either way works. The bottom line is the comparison of the total make cost and the total buy cost. Select the alternative with the lower cost.

An Example

Tomlin Company has bids from several suppliers for a control device, a unit used in several models of its Hibeam Line of lighting fixtures. Tomlin made these devices for the past several years and needs 30,000 units for 1998 production requirements. Walker Wiring returned the most attractive bid at $3 per unit delivered. Quality control checks of purchased units would cost Tomlin $3,000. Tomlin's costs for 25,000 units made in 1997 were:

	Per Unit	Total Costs
Materials.	$1.25	$31,250
Direct labor.	.60	15,000
Variable overhead	.50	12,500
Fixed overhead applied	1.00	25,000
Total	$3.35	$83,750

All costs are direct costs, except fixed manufacturing overhead. The only direct and avoidable fixed manufacturing overhead is $6,000, the cost of leasing specialized equipment required to make the control device. If the device is purchased, Tomlin could return the specialized equipment, void the lease, and use the space for storage. Renting storage space would cost $4,000 next year.

The decision rule of least cost is set; and the choices are:

1. Make the control device.
2. Buy the control device, eliminate the specialized equipment, and use the space for storage.

The relevant make and buy costs are:

Make Costs		Buy Costs	
Materials ($1.25 x 30,000).	$37,500	Purchase cost ($3 x 30,000). .	$90,000
Direct labor ($0.60 x 30,000)	18,000	Quality control costs.	3,000
Variable overhead ($0.50 x 30,000). .	15,000	Rent savings	(4,000)
Equipment lease cost	6,000		
Total make costs	$76,500	Total buy costs	$89,000
Net make advantage	$12,500		

We can make several observations:

1. The variable costs on both sides are relevant.
2. The $6,000 cost of leasing the equipment is relevant because the equipment lease payment is avoided under the buy choice. The remaining fixed factory overhead is unavoidable and irrelevant to the decision.
3. The $4,000 rent savings is relevant because it occurs only in the buy choice.

4. The relevant volume is 30,000 units (the 1998 expected volume).
5. Comparing the 1997 make full cost of $3.35 per unit to the buy cost of $3 hides important cost behavior patterns.

The recommendation is to continue to make and save $12,500.

Strategic and Qualitative Factors

The make or buy decision is a least cost choice. But many subtleties surround the decision. In the preceding example, only quantitative monetary facts were considered. Quality, delivery, labor force, and investment implications are frequently key issues.

Often, product and service quality is the highest ranking factor and could support either the make or buy side. By making the product, we can control quality in all aspects of production. On the other hand, a particular task may require specialized knowledge. We may not have this expertise. Whereas, an outside specialist may be faster and produce higher quality output. Quality can be so important that cost differentials are ignored.

Delivery capability in just-in-time systems is critical. Again, perhaps in-house sourcing has an advantage since our production planners can schedule production on an "as needed" basis. Or, the outside supplier may use delivery capability as a key competitive issue and be better able to meet complex requirements. Vendor certification programs have allowed buying firms to set benchmarks for performance and to narrow possible suppliers to a group known for high achievement.

Labor stability is another major make or buy consideration. For the United Auto Workers Union (UAW) and American auto producers, outsourcing is a major area of contention in labor negotiations. The auto companies have historically been vertically integrated. These companies, to be competitive with foreign producers and to increase internal productivity, are searching for the most efficient suppliers. Many suppliers are "lean and mean," more so than the auto makers' own captive divisions. The UAW, concerned about member job losses, is demanding labor contract provisions that guarantee in-house production. Also, a sense of community responsibility affects how managers decide where work and, therefore, jobs are located.

C O N T E M P O R A R Y   P R A C T I C E   1 1 . 1

The Ethics of Getting the Best Price

Pressures from purchasing agents to force price reductions from vendors create ethical and legal dilemmas. A purchasing agent tells a vendor that a competitor has offered a lower price. If the vendor wants to keep the business, it must meet or beat the lower price. What if the "lower price" offer doesn't exist? Merely saying that something can be bought elsewhere for a lower price is typically insufficient. The supplier may think that the price is just "too low" to be legitimate. But suppliers must deal with the Robinson-Patman Act that forbids price discrimination without justification. Also, the Sherman Antitrust Act prevents suppliers from discussing prices with each other.

Source: Murry, John E., "To Control Costs—Walk the Ethical Tightrope," *Purchasing*, December 16, 1993, pp. 21-24.

Global business transactions expand the decision beyond whether to make or buy. Now, if we make, where do we make it? If we buy, where do we buy it? Brazil, Mexico, China, Korea, and eastern or western Europe are possible sources. Also, many multinational firms have facilities in several countries and can shift production depending on costs, quality, materials proximity, and product demand.

S PECIAL SALES PRICING DECISIONS

The decision question is:

> ***Will we benefit from special sales generally made at prices lower than those charged to our regular customers?***

This decision evaluates added sales opportunities using contribution margin analysis. Often, one company's make or buy problem is another company's special sales pricing problem. Examples of special pricing decisions include:

1. Generating discount-priced sales to use excess production capacity.
2. Accepting sales that only cover out-of-pocket costs to keep a workforce employed during a recession.
3. Making a one-time sale to move stale merchandise.
4. Responding to a request for a special feature from a regular customer.
5. Pricing to enter a new competitive marketplace.

Clearly, knowledge of cost behavior, volumes, and capacities is a major influence on pricing and marketing.

Key Decision Rule and Guidelines

The key decision rule is:

> ***Subject to the following specific guidelines, make the special sale if we earn a positive contribution margin from the special sale.***

The guidelines or assumptions necessary to allow the basic rule to work are:

1. Excess capacity exists, with no alternative use of the capacity. The opportunity cost of using the capacity is zero or at least very low.
2. Special sales should not interfere with regular sales. The special sale should be in a different market segment than our regular business.
3. The special sale is a one-time order and will not become repeat business.

If all of these guidelines are not met, the analysis will have additional relevant revenues and costs to consider.

The minimum price must cover out-of-pocket costs plus any opportunity cost of making the sale (lost profits from regular sales or lost production). The economic rule is to produce and sell until the marginal revenue equals the marginal cost—until a zero incremental profit is reached.

CONTEMPORARY PRACTICE 11.2

Fill the Seat, Get the Marginal Dollar

In December 1993, Delta Airlines tried to fill its excess capacity anticipated on Christmas day by offering round-trip fares of $79 for flights of 500 miles or less. Passengers would have to depart and return on Christmas day. This was expected to fill otherwise empty seats without significantly affecting flights before and after Christmas.

Source: Thurston, S., "Delta Reduces Prices on Some Holiday Flights," *Atlanta Constitution*, December 23, 1993, p. F1.

Data Analysis Format

The format of relevant data for special sales decisions appears as follows:

Incremental revenue	$
Incremental costs:	
Additional variable costs	($)
Additional direct fixed costs	($)
Incremental profits	$

Only relevant revenues and costs are shown. Variable costs are often taken from the variable costs of regular business adjusted for any changes in features, such as different formulas for baby foods, heavy-duty shock absorbers for police cars, and overtime police wages for a special concert on campus. Any additional supervision, preparation time, shipping, and packaging are relevant. Generally, variable costs are relevant; and fixed costs remain unchanged and are irrelevant unless otherwise indicated.

An Example

Assume that North Comm's capacity is 90,000 units of a cellular phone receiver, including 15,000 units made on overtime. North Comm is currently producing and selling 80,000 units per year at $8 per unit. Variable production costs are $3 per unit, and annual fixed factory overhead costs are $200,000. Variable shipping costs are $0.50 per unit; all administrative expenses are $120,000 and fixed.

The profit calculation is as follows:

Sales (80,000 units x $8)		$ 640,000
Factory and shipping costs:		
Variable (80,000 units x $3.50)	$ 280,000	
Fixed overhead	200,000	480,000
Gross profit		$ 160,000
Administrative expenses		120,000
Net income		$ 40,000

An Argentine communications company approaches North Comm with an offer to buy 10,000 receivers at $6 each. Sales in Argentina should not affect

North Comm's regular sales. The special units would require minor modifications and force more overtime, adding $0.80 per unit to variable costs. Additional supervision would cost $3,000. The entire lot would be packed and shipped to Argentina for $2,000. The analysis shows:

Incremental sales..................................	$ 60,000
Incremental costs:	
Incremental variable factory costs (10,000 x $3).........	(30,000)
Additional variable factory costs (10,000 x $0.80).......	(8,000)
Additional fixed supervision costs	(3,000)
Additional shipping costs..........................	(2,000)
Incremental profits	$ 17,000

Incremental profits of $17,000 are added to the net income from regular sales to create a forecast of $57,000 for net income. The special sale adds to North Comm's total profit even though the $6 price is $1.50 below the average cost of $7.50 (total product and administrative expenses of $600,000 divided by 80,000 units). The decision rule and the criteria are met. Do it.

Nonsegmented Markets. Accepting special prices is a sound policy only if the special market can be kept separate from the regular market. For example, in the preceding illustration, assume that the international market begins to affect the domestic market to the extent that the domestic price drops from $8 per unit to $7.60 per unit (a 5 percent drop). In this case, the firm's profit calculation for the next period would appear as follows:

Incremental profits from the Argentine sale	$ 17,000
Less lost revenue from price reduction (80,000 units x $0.40) ..	(32,000)
Incremental profits	$(15,000)

If the special market price influences the domestic market, profits decrease from $40,000 to $25,000—a loss of $15,000. Don't do it.

No Excess Capacity. Assume that North Comm's capacity was only 85,000 units instead of 90,000 units and that the Argentine sale is all or nothing. By accepting the order, 5,000 units of regular business must be given up. The profit calculation is as follows:

Incremental profits from Argentine sale	$ 17,000
Less contribution margin on lost regular sales (5,000 x $4.50)..	(22,500)
Incremental profits	$ (5,500)

Losing 5,000 units of regular sales to accommodate the 10,000-unit Argentine sale will cost North Comm profits. Don't do it.

Not a One-Time Sale. This may be a sample order, with an unknown probability of larger future contracts. If repeat sales are expected, North Comm must be very careful not to commit itself to a low-margin business.

Strategic and Qualitative Factors

Product pricing is a key market positioning tool. Capacity use is a resource management decision. Low-priced special sales can preempt strategic plans. The first question: How does the sale fit our long-term marketing goals? Tied to this is a second question: Is using capacity for this sale consistent with the strategic use of production capabilities? The decision guidelines previously presented (excess capacity, segmented markets, and one-time sale) are tactical rules to help prevent subtle economic errors. If we want a premium product and price image, discount deals may tarnish it. Our dealers probably depend on our pricing and product image stability. Will customers not really see differences between our regular-priced products and our special-priced products?

Accepting one more one-time sale is an easy path to follow. More of our capacity becomes allocated to low-profit business on a routine basis. If the market segmentation guideline does not hold, regular business begins to shrink; and special sales expand. Fewer and fewer customers are paying prices that cover all costs, while more sales at special prices pay only a portion of the firm's operating costs.

USE OF SCARCE RESOURCES DECISIONS

The decision question is:

> ***When a productive resource is limited, how do we allocate the use of the scarce resource?***

The scarce or limited resource decision is an extension of the special sales pricing decision except that no excess capacity exists. Some constraint exists. Several examples are shown in Figure 11.3.

FIGURE 11.3   Scarce Resource Examples

Scarce Resource	Issue
Specialized machine time	What are the most profitable products per machine hour to produce?
Shelf space in a grocery store	What mix of footage use earns the most profits?
Salesperson time during sales calls	Which products should they attempt to sell during the limited time allowed them?
A seat in a popular restaurant	Which menu items generate the most profit per seat per dinner hour?
A fixed advertising budget	Which media expense generates more profit?
Your study time	How should you allocate available study hours to earn the highest average grade?

All of these examples use **contribution margin per unit of scarce resource**, which is contribution margin per unit divided by the amount of scarce resource used by each unit. For example, assume that Product 28 has a $10 per unit contribution margin and needs 30 minutes on a polishing machine that is a major factory bottleneck. Then, $20 per hour ($10 ÷ 0.5 hours) is the contribution margin per hour of polishing machine time when producing Product 28. Expressed differently, what price should be charged for a product or service that uses a given amount of the scarce resource?

Key Decision Rule and Guidelines

The scarce resource decision rule is:

> *Optimize profits from a scarce resource by selecting the products or services with the highest contribution margin per unit of the scarce resource.*

This rule yields the product mix that maximizes total profits. Products are ranked by their ability to generate the highest contribution margin per unit of scarce resource used. The scarce resource constraint is often a temporary situation. Over time, we can train more skilled workers, buy more equipment, or rent more space to eliminate the constraint.

Guidelines for selecting the most profitable set of products or services are:

1. We must know the amount of scarce resource needed (input) to produce a unit of output.
2. The product with the highest contribution margin per unit of scarce resource is selected, then the second highest, and so on until the scarce resource is used.
3. Commonly, the analysis uses variable contribution margin.
4. Allocated, common, or indirect fixed costs are irrelevant to the decision.

When substantial incremental direct fixed costs exist, we must also incorporate these costs into the analysis.

Data Analysis Format and an Example

The format uses the contribution margin per unit of output and the scarce resource input needed to produce that unit. The result is a profit ranking of all products based on a contribution margin per unit of scarce resource.

As an example, the Museum Repro Company (MRC) markets reproductions of well-known sculptures. Finish work is done by four highly skilled artists. MRC cannot find additional artists to meet the sales demand. Data on four of MRC's pieces are:

	Roman	*Greek*	*Aztec*	*Egyptian*
Sales price per unit	$250	$ 350	$ 600	$1,000
Variable costs per unit	150	150	240	550
Indirect fixed costs per unit . . .	50	110	120	200
Sales demand.	1,000 units	200 units	500 units	500 units
Hours of work per unit	2 hours	5 hours	6 hours	10 hours

The data format uses contribution margin analysis as follows:

	Roman	Greek	Aztec	Egyptian
Sales price per unit	$250	$350	$600	$1,000
Variable costs per unit	150	150	240	550
Contribution margin per unit	$100	$200	$360	$ 450
Hours of detail work per unit	÷ 2	÷ 5	÷ 6	÷ 10
Contribution margin per hour of work ..	$ 50	$ 40	$ 60	$ 45
Priority ranking....................	2nd	4th	1st	3rd

Assume that the four artists each work about 2,000 hours per year. MRC will use the 8,000 hours available as follows:

Priority	Piece	Hours Per Unit	Units			Hours Required	Remaining Available Hours	Contribution Margin Per Hour	Contribution Margin
							8,000		
1st.......	Aztec	6	x	500	=	3,000	5,000	$60	$180,000
2nd	Roman	2	x	1,000	=	2,000	3,000	$50	100,000
3rd	Egyptian	10	x	300	=	3,000	0	$45	135,000
Total contribution margin generated									$415,000

Sales Demand Not Met:

Egyptian	200 units
Greek	200 units

If MRC produces all needed Aztec and Roman units and only 300 Egyptian units, the detail artists' 8,000 hours are entirely used. This product mix generates the highest contribution margin given the artists' available time. Note that indirect fixed costs are ignored in the analysis because these costs will not change regardless of the production mix.

Qualitative Factors

The qualitative issues in the scarce resource analysis are questions of price and product offerings. Why is MRC's capacity limited? Is the marketplace demand driven? Prices should be set based on competition and customer demand. Scarce resource analysis can highlight possible poor pricing. In the MRC example, Egyptian and Greek prices might be raised to improve the contribution margin per hour of artist time to match or exceed Aztec's contribution margin. Also, the basic analysis ignores the complementary aspect of various items in a product line. To compete in a market may require a complete offering, a full menu, or a complete set of selling departments.

Also of concern is the use of the scarce resource itself. Can steps be taken to conserve capacity, to substitute less critical resources, or to buy additional capacity? MRC can get an estimate of the value of additional capacity. In the MRC example, another employee working 2,000 hours per year would produce the following additional contribution margin:

	Hours Per Unit		Units		Hours Required		Contribution Margin Per Hour		Additional Contribution Margin
Egyptian.............	10	x	200	=	2,000	x	$45	=	$90,000

The added contribution margin is $90,000, which results after the variable labor costs have been deducted. At that price, should MRC train another detail artist? Yes.

SELL OR PROCESS FURTHER DECISIONS

The decision question is:

> **Should the product be sold as is, or should it be processed further?**

A common sell or process further decision deals with a product that can be sold now or processed further and sold later as another product. Other times, processing further can spawn multiple products from a common input. These are called **joint products**, and the further processing becomes a **split-off point**. Until this point, the common input is a single product. An example of a split-off point is the refining process where crude oil is processed into joint products of gasoline, heating oil, and motor oil. The decision is to sell the crude oil or process it into the joint products and sell those.

Key Decision Rule and Guidelines

The key decision rule is:

> **Process further if the incremental revenue from processing further is greater than the incremental costs of processing further.**

The basic guidelines are:

1. All additional processing costs are assumed to be incremental.
2. Costs incurred prior to the split-off point are common to both sell and process further choices and are irrelevant to the process further decision.
3. The decision is independent of product costing. Product costing attaches all product costs to units, including common and past costs. In

C O N T E M P O R A R Y   P R A C T I C E   1 1 . 3

Best Use of Andre's People and Space

Andre was disappointed with profits from his hairstyling business. He worked at controlling costs and advertised to increase his client base. Revenues increased, but profits lagged. A consultant analyzing his operations suggested increasing the contribution margin per hour of stylists time. This meant converting fixed stylist salaries to a commission basis to get stylists to work more efficiently, changing prices to reflect higher costs of certain services, and advertising discounts during slack periods. Bingo! More profits.

Source: Sprohge, H., and J. Talbott, "How Contribution Margin Analysis Helped Andre's Salon," *Journal of Accountancy*, August 1990, pp. 110-117.

process further decisions, only present and future revenues and costs are relevant.

4. The decision assumes that products are *either* sold as is *or* processed further. If capacity allows, we could do *both* if both generate a positive contribution margin.

The decision task is to always look forward and never look backward. We are standing here today with something of value and looking into the future. We can sell it now. Or, we can do additional work, spend more money, and sell in the future. Past costs cannot be changed and are common to both choices.

Data Analysis Format and Examples

Assume, for example, that unfinished hardwood desks for home offices sell for $180, with a manufacturing cost of $100. The company can stain the desks at an additional cost of $30 each, yielding a desk that sells for $225. Due to market demand, the company could only sell 500 stained desks. The data format shows:

Revenue from sale of stained desks (500 units x $225)...............	$112,500
Less revenue from sale of unstained desks (500 units x $180)	90,000
Incremental revenue..	$ 22,500
Less cost of staining (500 units x $30)	15,000
Incremental contribution margin from processing further	$ 7,500

The decision is obvious: Stain and sell 500 desks.

Three important assumptions were made. First, the desk's manufacturing cost is assumed to be irrelevant because it is the same for unstained or stained desks. Second, the company is assumed to have capacity to process desks further without losing sales of other products. And third, the process further costs are assumed to be avoidable costs.

Joint Products—Process All or None. A common situation is the joint product decision. Assume that we produce an industrial wax with a sales value of $4 per gallon. The manufactured cost is $3.25 per gallon. We can convert 60,000 gallons of industrial wax through a process that yields equal amounts of three high-quality auto waxes: Super Gloss, Shiner, and Deep Glow. Costs of converting industrial wax into the three products are $40,000. The market values of the three waxes are $6, $5, and $4.80 per gallon, respectively. Should we process further? The data format is as follows:

	Quantity		Price		Revenue
Super Gloss	20,000 gallons	x	$6.00	=	$120,000
Shiner	20,000	x	5.00	=	100,000
Deep Glow......................	20,000	x	4.80	=	96,000
Total revenue after processing					$316,000
Less revenue lost from industrial wax ($4 x 60,000 gallons)					240,000
Incremental revenue from processing further..........................					$ 76,000
Less cost of processing further.....................................					40,000
Incremental contribution margin					$ 36,000

The decision is to process further. Notice that the industrial wax production cost is not included since it is a sunk cost.

Joint Products—Which Products Should Be Processed Further?   If processing costs are variable and if each auto wax can be produced independently, what should be done? Assume that variable costs per gallon were $1, $1.25, and $0.40, respectively. The analysis on a per gallon basis is:

	Process Further Price		Industrial Wax Price		Additional Revenue		Additional Processing Costs		Additional Contribution Margin	Process Further Decision
Super Gloss	$ 6.00	-	$ 4	=	$ 2.00	-	$1.00	=	$ 1.00	Yes
Shiner	5.00	-	4	=	1.00	-	1.25	=	(0.25)	No
Deep Glow.	4.80	-	4	=	0.80	-	0.40	=	0.40	Yes

Super Gloss and Deep Glow should be produced, but Shiner has a negative incremental contribution margin and should not be made. If we have a limited supply of industrial wax, we would make Super Gloss first and then Deep Glow.

Joint Products—Setting Priorities.   If we could produce as much as we can sell of all products, our priorities would be Super Gloss, Deep Glow, industrial wax, and finally Shiner. Shiner is the least attractive product, but it still generates a profit [$5.00 - ($3.25 + $1.25)]. The $3.25 is relevant in this process further decision if we cannot sell all of the industrial wax that we can produce.

Qualitative Factors

The short-term version of this decision assumes further processing stages can be shut down or started up with few impacts. Rarely is this the case. Fixed costs will continue, skilled labor may be difficult to keep available, and product market shares may be difficult to maintain. Thus, the best short-run quantitative choice may not achieve the planned results, or the long-run damages may overwhelm the short-run benefits.

In many processing operations, significant capacity costs exist. In real life, metals commodity prices often determine whether copper, zinc, and gold mines operate or temporarily suspend production. In beef cattle, pork, and poultry operations, prices of retail, wholesale, and "on the hoof" products and processing costs are constantly monitored and forecast at each stage to make optimal sell versus process further decisions.

A DD OR DELETE A SEGMENT DECISION

The decision question is:

Is the firm more profitable with or without the segment?

Examples of this decision include:

1. Opening or closing a branch of a retail store.
2. Adding or eliminating a product or an entire product line.
3. Adding or eliminating a specialized service in a hospital.
4. Combining purchasing departments in two plants into one unit.

In each of these examples, the question is whether the firm is better off with or without the particular segment and hinges on the direct or segment contribution margin, which excludes allocated common costs. The analysis must resist the temptation to focus on net income of the segment. Also, the decision must consider the strategic value of the segment to the firm's long-term success.

Key Decision Rules and Guidelines

The key decision rules are:

> *Add the segment if the firm's profits are higher after adding it. Delete the segment if the firm's profits are higher after eliminating it.*

These rules assume that the following guidelines are in place:

1. Segment evaluations use direct contribution margin.
2. Segment eliminations focus on lost revenue and avoidable costs.
3. Segment additions focus on incremental revenues and costs.

Figure 11.4 shows two income statements for Narasimhan Clothiers and its three departments. One format shows net income for each department, after allocating common indirect expenses equally to the three departments. The other shows direct contribution margin for the three departments. Amounts are in thousands.

Department C appears to be losing $30,000 under the net income format. It is tempting to evaluate a segment's performance based on its net income. But is Department C a loser? By reorganizing the data into a contribution margin format, Department C shows a $20,000 contribution to common expenses and profits. And, no indirect costs are eliminated if Department C is deleted.

The net income format often hides the expense behavior (variable and fixed) and traceability (direct and indirect). The contribution margin format generally presents a clearer story.

FIGURE 11.4 **Department Performance for Narasimhan Clothiers—A Merchandiser**

	Net Income Approach				Contribution Margin Approach			
	Dept. A	Dept. B	Dept. C	Totals	Dept. A	Dept. B	Dept. C	Totals
Sales	$400	$500	$100	$1,000	$400	$500	$100	$1,000
Cost of sales	200	320	60	580	$200	$320	$60	$580
Variable sales commissions . .					40	50	10	100
Total variable costs					$240	$370	$70	$680
Gross margin	$200	$180	$40	$420				
Variable contribution margin . . .					$160	$130	$30	$320
Expenses:								
Direct expenses	$80	$90	$20	$190				
Direct fixed expenses					40	40	10	90
Direct contribution margin					$120	$90	$20	$230
Expenses:								
Common indirect expenses . .	50	50	50	150				150
Total operating expenses . .	$130	$140	$70	$340				
Net income	$70	$40	$(30)	$80				$80

Data Analysis Format and an Example

Narasimhan's president sees the net loss for Department C and considers eliminating the department. Assume that deleting Department C has no impact on Departments A and B or on indirect expenses. An incremental analysis in thousands shows:

Department C revenue lost.	$(100)
Department C cost of sales avoided	60
Department C variable selling expenses avoided	10
Department C direct fixed expenses avoided	10
Lost direct contribution margin from Department C.	$ (20)

Narasimhan would lose $20,000 in profits if Department C is dropped. Department C should be kept unless a higher earning alternative exists.

Strategic and Qualitative Factors

This decision is tied to the scarce resource decision. To drop or add a segment is rarely an isolated decision. What will replace the dropped segment? What does the new segment replace? The opportunity cost is generally not zero, must be quantified, and is compared to the incremental change in contribution margin. In the preceding example, a Department D and its incremental revenues and expenses would replace Department C's column.

While complementary and substitution effects have been shown already, the subtle impacts on other products and departments are often difficult to measure. While direct contribution margin is used, certain direct costs may be neither entirely avoidable nor controllable by the decision maker. History shows that contraction is much more difficult to manage than expansion.

Many companies are "downsizing," which includes a variety of strategies. Simple cost reduction should mean eliminating expenses which are contributing least to organizational goals. Seeking out waste, nonvalue-adding activities, should be part of normal budgeting and cost control systems. Major organizational restructuring may include the elimination of product lines, entire factories, or a layer of management or the consolidation of support staffs. Each of these is a version of the delete a segment decision. The same analytical process applies.

E QUIPMENT REPLACEMENT DECISIONS

The basic question asks:

> *Is greater benefit received from acquiring new equipment or continuing to use the old equipment?*

To answer this question, expenses incurred or revenues earned from using the old and the new equipment must be known. New equipment has two relevant measures: the incremental investment in new equipment and the increased contribution margin earned from the new equipment. Decision rules that include multiyear investment analyses are discussed in Chapter 12. For illustration purposes here, we assume new equipment is rented and not purchased.

For example, a computer center has reached an activity level that requires two Model 310 mainframe units. These machines have a total annual rental cost of $500,000. Operating costs add another $100,000 per machine. A larger and faster Model 420 would have more capacity than both Model 310s combined. A Model 420 rents for $480,000 per year and has an operating cost of $150,000 per year. With this simplified data, the analysis is:

Rent of two Model 310s avoided	$ 500,000
Operating costs of two Model 310s avoided	200,000
Rent of Model 420 incurred	(480,000)
Operating costs of Model 420 incurred	(150,000)
Savings from renting Model 420	$ 70,000

The quantitative analysis says rent Model 420. Qualitatively, we also get more capacity, which actually is a quantifiable benefit.

While renting or leasing equipment is a common financing alternative, purchasing is the basic method of acquiring new assets. An investment is made today, and benefits are earned over the asset's life. Evaluating all aspects of these decisions is a Chapter 12 task.

E THICAL CONSIDERATIONS

The fundamental ethical issue in incremental decision making is validity of estimates of future revenues and costs. "Show me a proposal, and I can make it look good or bad" epitomizes the ethical problem facing many managerial accountants. The objective approach, reflected in another quote of "just give me the facts," is often easier stated than done. Facts are often estimates of the future. Biases, known or unrealized, can easily influence these estimates. What does the boss want the analysis to show? How can I make this project look good enough to get approved? These are pressures and influences that can destroy the basic decision-making process. Steps can be taken to reduce the likelihood that decision analyses are subverted by biases, intentional or unintentional, and include:

- In-depth management reviews of assumptions and supporting data before a decision is made to ensure management's conspicuous attention to objectivity.
- Development of managerial attitudes that support critical evaluations and avoid "kill the messenger bearing bad news" attitudes.
- Creation of known criteria that emphasize the importance of validating relevant revenue and cost data estimates.
- Post-decision audits to validate past estimates of future results.

In many cases, managerial attitudes toward objective assessments begin at the top of the organization and "trickle down" to the lowest management levels.

*C*OSTS AND PRICING DECISIONS

One of the most difficult and critical decisions facing a manager is pricing. A firm's pricing policy is a major part of its overall strategic positioning. A great pricing debate centers on whether prices are based on market conditions (supply and demand) or on production costs (recovery of cost). Certain environments tend to emphasize one or the other as shown in Figure 11.5.

In spite of the characteristics shown in Figure 11.5, market prices are still strongly influenced by cost functions. For example, competitive copy center pricing near college campuses pushes the per copy price close to actual cost, given volume and cost behavior. Cost-based pricers nearly always have competitors with different cost functions or markups. And, conditions do change. The long-distance telephone industry has moved from a regulated industry to a highly price-competitive situation, while becoming even more capital intensive.

Global competitiveness has introduced market price as a starting point in product design and costing—a target market price minus a desired markup equals an allowable product cost. This is discussed in Chapter 15.

In cost-based pricing, **markup pricing methods** are widely used. To arrive at the price, a cost is computed; and a **markup** stated as a percentage of cost is added. The purpose of the markup is to cover nonproduct costs and generate a profit. The term "cost" as used in this method is ambiguous until carefully defined.

Full Cost Pricing

The most widely used markup pricing approach is full cost. **Full cost pricing** is a price commonly based on total manufacturing costs, including fixed and variable product costs. Proper treatment of fixed cost presents a problem in full cost pricing. As volume increases, the fixed cost and full cost per unit decrease. If price follows cost, the price goes down, which further spurs demand. Unfortunately, volume decreases create serious distress. Per unit full costs increase, forcing up prices. Demand falls more, costs go up again, and so on. Full cost pricing does have the following potential problems:

1. A full cost per unit is accurate at only one level of volume.
2. Rarely does a full cost reflect incremental costs when volume changes.
3. To calculate a full cost, often arbitrary cost allocations are made.

FIGURE 11.5 **Characteristics That Encourage Certain Pricing Behaviors**

Market-Driven Prices— Common Conditions and Products:	Cost-Based Prices— Common Conditions and Products:
Consumer products	Industrial and durable goods
Service activities	Capital intensive industries
Highly competitive markets	Regulated industries
Few distribution layers	Many distribution layers
Primarily direct costs	Many indirect costs
Adaptable capacity	Government contracting (low bidder)
New products	Intermediate products
Commodities	Entrenched industries

4. Given a market framework in which price is set where marginal cost equals marginal revenue, full cost-based pricing almost guarantees a "wrong" price.

However, full costing does offer some countering benefits:

1. Using full costs causes all products to bear a "fair share" of all common costs that must be covered.
2. Full cost will include long-term cost patterns in pricing strategies.
3. For certain ranges of activity (perhaps the relevant range), the per unit full cost may change very little as volume increases or decreases.
4. Being the long-term low cost provider is a very effective competitive strategy, particularly when cost includes product and nonproduct costs.

Variable Cost Pricing

Another pricing approach uses variable cost as the cost base. One advantage is that difficulties with allocating indirect and fixed costs are avoided. Also, if reasonably accurate estimates of demand given various prices exist, it may be possible to find a price that produces maximum profits. In long-term planning, more costs are subject to management action and can be changed. Pricing to maximize long-term profits is often a key financial goal.

If variable cost is used, any added markup must be large enough to cover all fixed costs and to provide a profit. A danger always exists that variable costs may be thought of as full costs. Prices that cover only a portion of total costs will, in the long run, lead to serious financial problems. If the markup is too high, the firm may price itself out of the market. If the markup is too low, the firm experiences low profits or losses.

The Market-Based Side

If prices are market driven, the debate over full or variable costs does not disappear. Market price minus cost yields a profit measure: (1) using full cost, a gross margin or a net profit and (2) using variable cost, a version of contribution margin. These margins can be linked to return on investment in evaluating the performance of existing investments (more in Chapter 14) and in making new investments (more in Chapters 12 and 13). Prices are nearly always part of return-on-investment analyses. Thus, even when prices are not cost based, cost influences how managers view product profitability, attack market segments, and decide whether to enter or exit markets.

SUMMARY

Managers in any organization make decisions; some are short-run decisions, while others have long-run implications. This chapter creates a structured approach to make and implement decisions involving costs and revenues.

Differential analysis can be applied to a wide variety of decisions. The basic rule is to select the choice that gives the greatest incremental profit.

Incremental profit is the difference between the relevant revenues and the relevant costs of each choice. Relevant revenues and costs are defined as the current and future values that differ among the choices considered.

The decision groups examined were make or buy, special sales pricing, scarce resource, sell or process further, and delete or add a segment. For each decision group, a key decision rule and guidelines were stated; and a format for analyzing relevant data was developed. While the basic decision assumes a short-term timeframe, the real-world applications often include long-term elements. Qualitative issues affect every decision, with strategic and policy concerns looming in the background.

Cost information is relevant to pricing analyses regardless of whether prices are market driven or cost based. Finally, full cost and variable cost pricing approaches give a different base for determining a markup for cost-based prices.

PROBLEMS FOR REVIEW

Review Problem A—Special Sale

DeStefano Company, of Milano, Italy, sells a consumer electronics product called Teris at a price of 35,000 Italian lira per unit. Teris costs per unit are:

Prime costs	L 15,000
Overhead	15,000 (60 percent of which is fixed)
Total costs	L 30,000

A special order for 20,000 units was received from Chou Distributors, an import/export firm in Beijing, PRC. Additional shipping costs on this sale are L4,000 per unit.

Required:

1. If DeStefano is operating at full capacity, what is the minimum price per unit that should be set for the Beijing order? Comment.

2. If DeStefano has excess capacity, what is the minimum price per unit? Comment.

Solution:

This is a special pricing problem. DeStefano must determine whether:

1. Excess capacity exists—"no" for Part (1) and "yes" for Part (2).

2. The order will not interfere with regular business—probably not since the order is from an importer in Beijing.

3. A positive contribution margin exists—will depend on the price selected.

For Part (1), DeStefano must take sales from regular customers and, thus, must earn at least the same contribution margin from the Beijing sale as from regular sales. Since the Beijing sale will cost L4,000 per unit more in shipping costs, the selling price should be L39,000 per unit.

For Part (2), the price per unit should cover only incremental costs of the additional units: L15,000 for prime costs, L6,000 for variable overhead (.4 x L15,000), and L4,000 for shipping costs. The minimum price must, therefore, be greater than L25,000 to earn a positive contribution margin.

Review Problem B—Sell or Process Further

The Eckel Corporation creates Products A, B, and C from a joint process costing $60,000. This cost is divided equally among A, B, and C. Each product can be sold at the split-off point or processed further. Additional processing costs are $1 per gallon. Available data are:

Product	Gallons From Joint Process	Sales Price Per Gallon at Split-Off	Sales Price Per Gallon if Processed Further
A	10,000	$3	$6
B	5,000	4	8
C	20,000	7	9

Required:

If Eckel has only $12,000 available for further processing, which product should be processed further to earn the highest incremental contribution margin? Why?

Solution:

First, find the incremental profit per gallon of processing further:

Product	Sales Price if Processed Further		Sales Price at Split-Off		Incremental Revenue		Incremental Cost		Incremental Profit	Priority Rank
A	$6	-	$3	=	$3	-	$1	=	$2	2nd
B	8	-	4	=	4	-	1	=	3	1st
C	9	-	7	=	2	-	1	=	1	3rd

Eckel can process 12,000 gallons ($12,000 ÷ $1). Using the priorities, processing Product B costs $5,000, leaving $7,000 to process Product A. Even though a positive contribution margin could be earned from processing more A and then C, no funds remain to do so. Eckel's incremental contribution margin is $29,000 as follows:

Product B: ($4 x 5,000 gallons) - ($1 x 5,000 gallons)	$ 15,000
Product A: ($3 x 7,000 gallons) - ($1 x 7,000 gallons)	14,000
Incremental contribution margin	$ 29,000

Note that the joint costs of $60,000 already spent do not impact the decision.

Review Problem C—Delete a Segment

Vanderbeek, Inc. has three product lines. Last year's data in thousands are:

	Alpha	Beta	Gamma	Total
Sales	$ 230	$ 270	$ 360	$ 860
Variable costs	(120)	(150)	(170)	(440)
Unavoidable fixed costs	(60)	(60)	(60)	(180)
Avoidable fixed costs	(80)	(50)	(80)	(210)
Net income	$ (30)	$ 10	$ 50	$ 30

Rebecca, the company president, is not impressed with the performance of product line Alpha and is considering its elimination.

Required:

Is eliminating Alpha a good decision? Comment on the impact of eliminating Alpha.

Solution:

Using the incremental analysis approach, lost revenues and avoidable costs of Alpha are:

Sales lost	$(230,000)
Variable costs avoided	120,000
Fixed costs avoided	80,000
Contribution margin lost	$ (30,000)

If Alpha is dropped, Vanderbeek's profits will decline by $30,000. Unavoidable fixed costs are ignored since they will not change regardless of the decision. The total approach shows the same impact as follows:

	With Alpha	Without Alpha
Sales	$ 860,000	$ 630,000
Variable costs	(440,000)	(320,000)
Unavoidable fixed costs	(180,000)	(180,000)
Avoidable fixed costs	(210,000)	(130,000)
Net income	$ 30,000	$ 0

After Alpha is dropped, Vanderbeek just breaks even instead of earning $30,000. Rebecca should keep Alpha, unless a more profitable alternative is found.

*T*ERMINOLOGY REVIEW

Contribution margin per unit of scarce resource, *481*
Differential analysis, *469*
Full cost pricing, *489*
Incremental analysis approach, *470*
Incremental profit, *469*
In-house sourcing, *474*
Joint products, *483*
Markup, *489*
Markup pricing methods, *489*

Opportunity cost, *470*
Out-of-pocket costs, *470*
Outsource, *474*
Relevant buy costs, *474*
Relevant make costs, *474*
Relevant revenues and costs, *469*
Split-off point, *483*
Sunk costs, *469*
Total analysis approach, *470*

*S*UGGESTED READINGS

Institute for Management Accounting, *Criteria for Make-or-Buy Decisions*, New York, NY, 1973.

Lere, J., "Product Pricing Based on Accounting Costs," *Accounting Review*, Vol. 61, No. 2, pp. 318-324.

Schneider, A., "Simultaneous Determination of Cost Allocation and Cost-Plus Prices for Joint Products," *Journal of Business Finance and Accounting*, Summer 1986, pp. 187-195.

Shank, J., and V. Govindarajan, "Strategic Cost Management: The Value Chain Perspective, *Journal of Management Accounting Research*, Fall 1992, pp. 179-197.

"The Price Is Right at Hewlett-Packard," *Financial Executive*, Vol. 10, No. 1, pp. 22-25.

*Q*UESTIONS FOR REVIEW AND DISCUSSION

1. What is the basic decision rule in differential analysis? Explain each noun in the rule.

2. Refer to the decision steps defined in Chapter 1. In which steps does the managerial accountant play major roles?

3. Why is identifying a decision's choices one of the most important steps in the decision-making process?

4. Ann Hayhow, owner of several small local businesses, said recently, "The general rule I follow in making short-run decisions is that variable costs are almost always relevant and fixed cost are almost always irrelevant." Do you agree? Why or why not?

5. Distinguish between:

(a) Incremental analysis approach and total analysis approach.

(b) Relevant cost and irrelevant cost.

(c) Out-of-pocket cost and opportunity cost.

6. Joe French of Quick Supplies says he prefers the incremental analysis method because it eliminates all unnecessary data. Jan Dutch of Office Managers, Inc. prefers the total analysis approach because she can see the "big picture." Comment.

7. Why is the timeframe—short term or long term—important in decision making?

8. "Accounting is common sense! Any rational person should be able to look at the relevant dollars and cents and make a decision." Do you agree or disagree? Why?

9. The president of Bethany Company said, "Accounting data are useful for predicting the results of various choices; but, in my company, the final decision often depends on other factors." Explain this statement.

10. For each of the five major decision types discussed, give an example that has not been mentioned in the text.

11. Identify the guidelines that should be met for a special sales pricing decision. Explain why they are important. What happens when each is violated?

12. What is the decision rule in a make or buy decision? Define relevant costs on both sides.

13. If capacity is scarce, how can opportunity costs be used to decide whether a product should be sold now (an intermediate product) or finished and sold as a completed product?

14. Nehlsen Company prepares tax returns and charges $40 for simple returns and $100 for more complicated returns. Nehlsen's receptionist is making customer appointments for the second weekend of April. Write the receptionist a memo as a guide to which customers should be scheduled and which should be told to go elsewhere. Before you write the memo, list the assumptions you are making.

15. Explain how a special sales decision in one firm might be a make or buy decision in another firm.

16. Why might a company produce a subassembly at a higher cost rather than buy the same subassembly from an outside supplier?

17. If a restaurant owner considers adding a new main course and deleting another for profitability purposes, what decision rule should be applied? What type of decision is this?

18. Although a firm has unused capacity and a special order would contribute $75,000 to profits, a manager rejected the order. Why might the manager do this?

19. In markup pricing, what elements must be covered by the markup when full costs are used? When variable costs are used?

20. The marketing vice-president of Janelle Fabrics says that product prices should always be set by supply and demand in the marketplace to ensure high sales levels. The controller says that product prices should always be based on costs to ensure profitability. Who's right? Explain.

E XERCISES

11-1. Special Sales. A. A. Anthony Company sells Product A for $30 per unit. Anthony's per unit cost on the full capacity of 200,000 units is:

Direct materials	$10
Direct labor	5
Overhead	12
Manufacturing costs	$27

The manufacturing overhead is one-third variable and two-thirds fixed.

A Japanese firm has offered to buy 20,000 units. Additional shipping costs of this order would be $2 per unit. Anthony has sufficient existing capacity to manufacture the additional units. The Anthony sales manager wants to earn an incremental profit of $40,000 from this sale.

Required:
What is the minimum price per unit Anthony should charge?

11-2. Additional Processing. Kiser Company produces a vitamin supplement from a common mixture at a cost of $50 per pound. Kiser sells this mixture as HiEnergy for $80 per pound. Or, any one or all of three new products (called GoGetEm, ReallyGo, and SuperGo) can be made from the mixture. Kiser can sell all HiEnergy produced.

	Additional Production Costs Per Pound	Sales Value Per Pound
HiEnergy		$ 80
GoGetEm	$15	100
ReallyGo	35	110
SuperGo	40	130

Required:
Define and apply Kiser's production decision rule.

11-3. Sales Priorities. Martinez Company employees highly skilled native American artists to produce sand paintings for sale in craft stores. The artists make large, medium, and small paintings. The sales and production data are:

	Large	Medium	Small
Sales price	$80	$50	$25
Materials and artists' time costs	38	25	16
Hours per piece	1 hour	0.5 hour	0.2 hour

Required:
If artists' time is scarce, what size priorities should be set?

11-4. Incremental vs. Total Analysis Approaches. Taylor Company currently produces 6,000 units of its major product per month. Financial data for last month are:

Sales	$240,000
Variable costs	144,000
Fixed costs	60,000

The company would like to expand its operations to 7,000 units per month. Fixed costs would increase $10,000 because of the expansion.

Required:
Prepare both a total analysis approach and an incremental analysis approach to evaluate the decision. Compare the results.

11-5. Production Choice. Li Lieu, owner of Emperor of Xi'an Restaurant in Xi'an, PRC, uses 5,000 fancy dumplings per month. Current costs in Chinese yuan are:

Ingredients costs	Y3
Labor and other variable expenses	Y2

Wang Cao offers to sell Li Lieu dumplings at Y5 each. If Li Lieu buys dumplings, he can eliminate Y4,000 per month in fixed making costs. He thinks he can also earn an additional Y3,000 per month in contribution margin by adding three tables where the dumplings had been made.

Required:
Should Li Lieu make or buy? Comment on concerns you might have.

11-6. Incremental Sales. Clouse Dairy produces and sells 10,000 gallons per month of Joyce's Sweet Cream, a premium ice cream. Capacity is 12,000 gallons. A supermarket in another city has offered to buy 3,000 gallons of ice cream for $1 per gallon. Clouse would give up some regular sales to fill the new order. Costs and revenues per unit are:

Ingredients and labor	$ .60
Variable overhead	.20
Fixed overhead	.30
Cost per gallon	$1.10
Sales price	$1.30

Required:

1. Using only quantitative facts, should Clouse sell to the supermarket? Explain your reasoning.

2. Comment on strategic and qualitative issues that might concern Clouse.

11-7. Department Profits. Biroscak Sales runs several small department stores. In 1999, his Toledo store showed the following results:

	Dept. 1	Dept. 2	Dept. 3	Dept. 4	Totals
Sales.	$ 700	$1,000	$ 800	$1,500	$ 4,000
Cost of goods sold	(350)	(500)	(450)	(800)	(2,100)
Gross margin	$ 350	$ 500	$ 350	$ 700	$ 1,900
Direct expenses	(100)	(400)	(400)	(300)	(1,200)
Common expenses	(100)	(300)	(100)	(300)	(800)
Net income.	$ 150	$ (200)	$(150)	$ 100	$ (100)

Required:
Comment on the impact of each of the following actions.

(a) Delete Department 2.

(b) Delete Department 3.

(c) Delete Departments 2 and 3.

(d) Replace Departments 2 and 3 with a new Department 5 which would earn a positive direct contribution margin of $25.

(e) Reallocate the common expenses.

11-8. Special Hat Sales. A. J., Inc. can make 10,000 caps per year. A. J. can sell 9,000 caps per year to NASCAR racing fans for $10 per hat. The company's cost per hat based on making 10,000 caps is:

Prime costs	$ 5.00	
Overhead costs	3.00	(Overhead is two-thirds fixed at that volume.)

Sugar Ray Hinsky offers to buy 1,000 hats with special boxing insignias for $7 per hat. Attaching special insignias will cost A. J. $200.

Required:
What should A. J. do? Explain.

11-9. Eating—A Student Dilemma.   For the next academic year, Clare is deciding whether to buy a meal coupon at a nearby dining hall or to cook in her own apartment. She has estimated the following costs and benefits:

Meal coupon cost	$1,000
Cost of additional snack items if she buys the coupon	200
Cost of food if she cooks	600
Value of pleasure of eating in her own apartment	300
Value of her time spent preparing meals	400

Required:
Comment on her costs and benefits estimates. What should she do?

11-10. Incremental Pricing.   Hinds Copies prepares course packets used in many courses. Prof. Sollenberger has asked for a price for his managerial accounting course packet. Jo Ann, the owner, really wants this business. She calculates incremental costs to be $6 each for 400 packets and $5 each for 600 packets. Also, she generally adds $1 to each packet to help cover her common fixed overhead. All costs are either fixed or variable. Sollenberger also needs 30 complimentary copies for his teaching assistants. Enrollment estimates are for 600 students, of which 80 percent of students buy the packets.

Required:
What is the lowest price she can offer and cover incremental costs?

11-11. Studying—Another Student Dilemma.   Evan is concerned about grades in four courses he is taking this semester. Between now and his final exams, he has a maximum of 40 hours of study time. He can also sleep, watch TV, and goof off. The grade system uses 4.0, 3.5, 3.0, 2.5, 2.0, 1.5, 1.0, and 0.0, where 4.0 is an *A*. If he does not study for a course, he thinks he can keep his current grades. His grades now and after studying and the time needed to earn the higher grades are:

	Grade Now	*Forecast Final Grade*	*Study Hours Required*
Course 1	2.0	3.5	25 hours
Course 2	3.0	4.0	20 hours
Course 3	1.0	3.0	20 hours
Course 4	1.0	2.0	15 hours

Required:
Prioritize his study time to earn the highest grade average.

11-12. Equipment Replacement.   Merle Murphy, owner of Murphy Farms, is considering plans to rent a new sprinkler system for his navy bean business. He currently uses a system that rents for $20,000 per year and has annual operating costs of $10,000 plus $100 per acre. The new system will rent for $10,000 per year and have annual operating costs of $30,000 plus $40 per acre. Both systems will perform the same function. He will plant 200 acres of beans. The 1998 contribution margin from beans is estimated to be $100,000.

Required:
Should Murphy change to the new system? Explain your conclusion.

11-13. Sell or Process.   Zaleski produces three products: X, Y, and Z. They can each be sold as is or processed further. They are produced from a common batch of materials costing $30,000. Quantities, market values, and additional costs are:

Products	*Gallons*	*Market Value Now*	*Additional Costs*	*Market Value After*
X	10,000	$1.00 per gallon	$10,000	$3.20 per gallon
Y	10,000	2.00 per gallon	20,000	3.75 per gallon
Z	10,000	3.00 per gallon	15,000	5.00 per gallon

Required:

What should Zaleski do? Identify several assumptions you made.

11-14. Scarce Resource Decision. The Soma Company can produce three different products: Able, Baker, and Charlie. Because of unusual demand, all orders cannot be filled. Fixed costs allocations are based on production time. Soma has 2,000 hours of production time.

	Able	*Baker*	*Charlie*
Sales price	$ 50	$ 40	$ 30
Variable costs	30	25	20
Fixed costs	10	10	10
Production time per unit	0.8 hour	0.5 hour	0.2 hour

Required:

1. Assume that Soma must produce at least 500 units of each product. What should be produced?
2. Assume that Soma can sell only 3,000 units of each product. What priorities should be set for Soma to maximize profits?

11-15. Make or Buy. Gramlich Corporation operates its own cafeteria for employees. The cafeteria prices are only 75 percent of the full costs of preparation. Management feels this is an important employee benefit. ASF, Inc. offers to operate the cafeteria and promises to increase the quality of menu items, reduce prices, and reduce the needed subsidy. ASF would use Gramlich's existing facilities and even transfer current cafeteria employees to its staff. ASF submitted a formal bid based on comparable services. As Gramlich's controller, you have summarized the 1998 budget for cafeteria operations and ASF's numbers from its proposal as follows:

	Internally Managed	*ASF Managed*
Food costs	$ 500,000	$ 450,000
Preparation costs	200,000	180,000
Administrative overhead	300,000	
Management fee		200,000
Total cafeteria costs	$1,000,000	$ 830,000
Cafeteria revenue	800,000	750,000
Operating subsidy	$ 200,000	$ 80,000

Required:

Comment on the numbers. Outline key issues that are of concern to you. What data will you need to collect and analyze to resolve the issues?

11-16. Process Further Decision. Silver Bullet Refining produces naphtha, kerosene, and other distillates from a joint process costing $120,000 for a certain volume of crude oil. From this process, 1,000 barrels of naphtha can be produced and are allocated $35,000 of joint costs. This can be sold at the split-off point for $60 per barrel or further processed into other products and sold for $85 per barrel. The processing cost for further refining 1,000 barrels of naphtha is $20,000.

The other distillates can be sold now for $80,000 or processed further for $40,000 and sold for $110,000. Kerosene can be sold for $60,000 at the split-off point. Kerosene is also allocated $35,000 of the joint costs.

Required:

1. Which products should be sold at the split-off point or processed further?
2. What is the most Silver Bullet can pay for crude oil and not lose money on the refining process?

11-17. Eliminating a Department. ABCDE Department Store has five departments—A, B, C, D, and E. Department E's future is being evaluated using the following data:

	All Others	Department E	Total
Sales..............................	$ 4,500,000	$ 500,000	$ 5,000,000
Cost of sales......................	2,200,000	300,000	2,500,000
Gross margin	$ 2,300,000	$ 200,000	$ 2,500,000
Rent and services	$ 800,000	$ 200,000	$ 1,000,000
Direct salaries.....................	450,000	50,000	500,000
Advertising expenses	450,000	50,000	500,000
Total expenses	$ 1,700,000	$ 300,000	$ 2,000,000
Net profit (loss)....................	$ 600,000	$(100,000)	$ 500,000

Rent and services are corporate committed fixed expenses and are allocated evenly to the five departments. Half of the advertising expenses varies with sales; the other half will not change regardless of the decision and is allocated using sales dollars.

Required:

Comment on the following statements:

(a) Department E is earning $150,000 in variable contribution margin for ABCDE.

(b) Department E is earning $100,000 in direct contribution margin for ABCDE.

(c) The company's overall profitability without Department E would be $600,000.

11-18. Make or Buy Indifference Point. Dave Simmet contacted a Malaysian manufacturer that will charge $40 per unit plus $200,000 for special equipment and dies for a lens assembly for an overhead projector. But he thinks he can make it himself for the following costs:

Prime costs	$ 21
Other variable costs	3
Total variable costs	$ 24

Simmet knows that incremental salaries, equipment rentals, and other fixed costs to make the assembly will run $360,000 per year. Common costs of manufacturing are applied to products at 60 percent of prime costs. Simmet plans to sell these projectors for $150 per unit.

Required:

Find the sales volume in units where Simmet would be indifferent between making the lens assembly or buying it.

11-19. Product Combination Decision. Data concerning four product lines are as follows:

	Product Line			
	A	B	C	D
Selling price per unit	$ 300	$ 250	$ 130	$ 70
Variable cost per unit	250	80	50	40
Hours required for each unit	5	10	4	2
Maximum market potential (units) ...	No limit	6,000	8,000	4,000
Total fixed costs.....................................		$100,000		
Total hours available		96,000 hours		

Required:

1. Based on these data, choose the best product combination.

2. How would the answer change if the company were required to deliver 2,000 units of each product line to a major distributor? The maximum market potential includes the distributor's units.

11-20. Process or Sell Decision. The Smokey Meat Company produces a meat product which can be sold after the slaughtering process, or it can be smoked and then sold. For next month the company has scheduled production of 30,000 pounds which, if sold unsmoked, would bring a selling price of $2.30 per pound. Costs associated with producing the unsmoked product are $1.20 per pound plus fixed facilities costs of $30,000 for the month. If 30,000 pounds are produced, the entire slaughtering capacity will be used.

If the 30,000 pounds are smoked, smoking capacity, which would otherwise be idle, will be used entirely also. The additional variable costs, mainly for heat and smoking ingredients, are estimated to be $0.40 per pound; and the selling price of the smoked product is $3.30 per pound. The monthly committed fixed costs on the portion of the facility used for smoking the meat amount to $8,000, and avoidable fixed costs are $5,000.

Required:

Prepare an analysis to help the manager decide whether the 30,000 pounds should be smoked or not be smoked.

11-21. Buying Legal Services. Jon Jenkins, a local attorney, was contacted by a doctors' professional corporation to represent it in a series of legal matters. After a negotiating conference, Jon offers to provide up to 400 hours of legal services during the next year if the corporation will pay a retainer of $3,000 per month plus direct expenses. After 400 hours, his rate is $100 per hour. Or he could charge the corporation $130 for each billable hour plus direct expenses.

Dr. Beall, chief administrator for the doctors' group, thinks that a competent attorney could be hired full time for $90,000 per year including direct support costs. He knows that the firm has used about 15 hours of legal services per month for the past two years. He sees a 50 percent probability that this trend will continue for the coming year, a 20 percent chance that 20 hours per month will be needed, and a 20 percent chance that 40 hours per month will be needed. A 10 percent likelihood exists that one particular case may force the firm to need 100 hours per month.

Required:

Recommend an approach to analyzing Dr. Beall's purchase of legal services. What decision does your approach suggest?

11-22. Equipment Replacement. Last week Janovits Enterprises purchased a new irrigation system called Spray costing $60,000. Its annual cash operating costs are estimated to be $35,000. It has a four-year useful life and no residual value. Today, a salesman has offered Janovits a new system called Sprinkle that will cost $60,000 and will also have a four-year useful life with no residual value. The Spray equipment can be used as a trade-in for a $10,000 allowance. The annual cash operating costs of Sprinkle are estimated to be $20,000. Sales of $400,000 and other operating expenses of $180,000 per year will be the same under either alternative.

Required:

Ignoring the time value of money to be discussed in Chapter 12, should Janovits purchase the Sprinkle system? Explain.

11-23. Sell or Process Further. Maslowski Company produces Green Awfully Sticky Stuff (GASS) at a cost of $10,000 per batch. A GASS batch can be sold as is for $50,000 or processed through Department A where Products A and AA are made. Or the GASS batch can be processed through Department B where Products B and BB are made. Costs and revenues of processing further in Departments A and B are:

	Incremental Costs	Products	Market Value
Department A	$ 20,000	A	$ 13,000
		AA	$ 72,000
Department B	$150,000	B	$100,000
		BB	$ 95,000

Required:

What should be done with a batch of GASS that Maslowski has on hand? Show calculations to support your decision.

11-24. Changing Product Lines.   Kelley Peck, president of Peck Department Store, thinks that the Paint Department should be dropped. She wants to add a Peanut Butter Boutique in the same space. Data for 1998 in thousands are:

	Paint	All Other Departments	Store Total	Proposed Peanut Butter Boutique
Sales.	$10,000	$ 90,000	$100,000	$ 20,000
Cost of sales	(6,000)	(54,000)	(60,000)	(15,000)
Gross margin	$ 4,000	$ 36,000	$ 40,000	$ 5,000
Direct expenses	(1,000)	(14,000)	(15,000)	(3,000)
Allocated expenses . .	(4,000)	(16,000)	(20,000)	(1,000)
Net income	$ (1,000)	$ 6,000	$ 5,000	$ 1,000

Allocated expenses are common costs and are assigned by a mathematical formula.

Required:

Ignoring your attitude toward peanut butter, what should she do to maximize profits? Explain.

11-25. Special Sales Pricing.   Chung Company, in Hong Kong, is selling 80,000 units of a product at HK$10 per unit. The variable cost is HK$6 per unit, and the annual fixed cost is HK$120,000. A discount house has offered to buy 10,000 additional units of the product which would be slightly modified, but the modifications would not affect production cost. The discount house will pay HK$7 per unit.

Required:

1. If the two markets can be distinguished, should the order be accepted (assuming capacity exists and has no other use)? Explain.
2. The manager feels that the two markets might not be distinguished and that the lower price would cause regular sales to fall by 5,000 units. Should Chung accept the discount house offer? Explain.
3. If the discount house offer is raised to HK$9 per unit and competition resulting from the special sale causes the regular price to drop to HK$9.50 to maintain the same regular sales volume, should Chung accept the discount house offer? Explain.

11-26. Make or Buy.   Roto, Inc. makes steel blades for lawn mowers that it heat treats, assembles, and sells. The cost accounting system gives the following data:

Prime costs	$ 80,000
Variable manufacturing overhead	60,000
Fixed manufacturing overhead	90,000
Units produced	100,000 units

Roto has an opportunity to purchase its 100,000 blades from an outside supplier at a cost of $2.20 per blade. Inspection of the purchased blades will cost an additional $5,000 in the Quality Assurance Department. Certain leased equipment, which costs $30,000 and is included in fixed overhead, can be avoided if the blades are purchased. The released space could be used to make a part that is now purchased, which would save Roto $46,000.

Required:

1. In quantitative terms, should Roto buy the blades from the outside supplier? Explain your decision.
2. What major factors might change the decision?

11-27. Segment Profit Performance Analysis.   Blaufuss Sausages has a central processing plant and three stores. Recently, profits have been declining. The projected 1999 income statement for the three stores appears below:

	Main Street	*King Street*	*Queen Street*	*Total*
Sales	$ 200	$175	$190	$ 565
Product cost of sausages	(120)	(100)	(110)	(330)
Gross margin	$ 80	$ 75	$ 80	$ 235
Direct store expenses	(60)	(85)	(35)	(180)
Allocated administrative expenses . .	(25)	(15)	(20)	(60)
Net income	$ (5)	$ (25)	$ 25	$ (5)

Required:

What will each of the following actions do to Blaufuss' profits?

(a) Eliminate the Main Street store.

(b) Eliminate the King Street store.

(c) Eliminate the Main and King Street stores.

(d) Close all stores.

(e) Open a fourth store and divide allocated administrative expenses among four stores. (Assume that the new store will have a zero net income.)

11-28 Ethics of Product Pricing.   Vine Resources (VR) provides office equipment systems development and maintenance services. Its customers are in a wide array of businesses. Maintenance services are provided on an annual contract with a fixed annual fee or with a fixed per hour rate, on a one-time as needed basis, or as defined in a contract with the customer. VR won a competitive bid with the City of Dermit to maintain a large number of office work stations. The contract is for three years and calls for routine maintenance checks to be done quarterly as part of the annual fee, emergency calls to be billed at the "full" cost per hour of service representatives, and parts to be replaced for free except for major hardware components. This rate will be updated annually.

It is now a year and a half into the contract. The city controller is concerned with the growing cost of machine maintenance. After examining the situation, the controller has found:

1. Emergency calls have doubled in the past six months and are growing.

2. The "full" cost service rate has gone from $15 per hour last year to $20 per hour this year.

3. Office workers are complaining about too much downtime.

A meeting with the VR representative found that all routine maintenance has been performed on schedule. Also, while some personnel costs have increased, the main reason for the jump in service rate was a change made in how certain fringe benefit costs were assigned to service personnel. The VR representative also mentioned the aging nature of the equipment and the need to upgrade the entire system.

Required:

Comment on possible implications of the controller's findings and the VR representative's explanations.

11-29. Markup Pricing.   Assume that the following cost analysis has been performed for a specific customer order for Lila Products, Inc. The president, Lila Ganong, is experimenting with different pricing strategies. She thinks 100,000 units can be sold. Fixed costs have been allocated using various activity bases.

	Per Unit	Total
Manufacturing costs—variable	$4.25	$425,000
Manufacturing costs—direct fixed	1.50	150,000
Manufacturing costs—indirect fixed	3.75	375,000
Manufacturing costs—total	$9.50	$950,000
Selling expenses—variable	$1.80	$180,000
Selling expenses—indirect fixed	1.45	145,000
Selling expenses—total	$3.25	$325,000

Required:

What markup percentage is required to earn $120,000 if the price is set:

1. Assuming that the order is a one-time sale?

2. Assuming that the order will become part of Lila's regular product line?

11-30. Cost Analysis and Pricing.   Sales in the Jackson office of Fast Print Company for 1998 were $475,000. Costs were:

Materials and variable supplies expenses	$200,000
Direct labor expenses	100,000
Occupancy and other fixed operating expenses	100,000
Total expenses	$400,000

For most printing jobs, a cost-plus pricing policy is used. To find a job's cost, estimated labor costs are doubled to cover labor and overhead and then added to estimated materials costs. The total job costs are then multiplied by 120 percent to calculate customer price.

The advertising manager for a regional supermarket has proposed a deal. She has a weekly advertising piece which will be mailed to local residents. The printing job would require $200 of materials and supplies and $100 of direct labor time. She is willing to pay $420 per week and would like a one-year contract. The Jackson office manager rejects the offer since it violates his pricing strategy.

Required:

1. Would the supermarket business be profitable for Fast Print:

   (a) On a one-time basis?

   (b) On a regular (annual) basis?

2. What qualitative issues might impact your answer?

P ROBLEMS

11-31. Elimination of a Product Line.   The Halverson's Old General Store is currently divided into three departments. Over the past several months, sales and profit have declined, although the situation is now considered stable. Department 2 has begun to show a loss; and the owner, Joan Halverson, is thinking of discontinuing it. The space could be rented to a chain shoe store which would pay a flat fee of $12,000 a month.

Below is last month's income statement, considered to be typical. Sales salaries are fixed but traceable to each department and could be avoided if the department were eliminated. Total fixed administrative costs (allocated equally to all departments) are common costs.

	Department 1	Department 2	Department 3	Total
Sales	$185,000	$80,000	$135,000	$400,000
Costs:				
Cost of goods sold	$ 96,000	$ 44,000	$ 70,000	$210,000
Sales salaries	28,000	8,000	24,000	60,000
Administrative expenses	30,000	30,000	30,000	90,000
Total costs	$154,000	$ 82,000	$124,000	$360,000
Income before income tax	$ 31,000	$ (2,000)	$ 11,000	$ 40,000

Required:

Prepare an analysis to show Halverson whether Department 2 should be discontinued and the space rented.

11-32. Make or Buy Decision.   Ling Automotive Systems developed a new windshield cleaning system for the original-equipment auto market. The system requires an electronic motor that the firm does not currently produce but is available from suppliers. The best bid is from Fiero Electronics, an Italian firm, at $23 per unit for any volume within the firm's relevant range.

Ling's production manager believes that the motor can be made in-house, although additional space and machinery would be required. The firm now leases, for $80,000 per year, space that could be used to make the new motors. However, another subsystem is now assembled in this space. Ling would have to lease additional space which rents for $175,000 per year in an adjacent building for the assembly process. It is suitable for assembly work but not for motors production. Additional equipment needed would rent for $200,000 per year.

The controller has developed the following unit costs based on the expected demand of 100,000 units per year:

Prime costs	$14.00
Rent for space	.80
Machinery rental	2.00
Variable overhead	4.00
Allocated fixed overhead	6.00
Total costs	$26.80

Required:

Should Ling make or buy the motors? What assumptions are you making?

11-33. Special Sales Pricing.   Aoi Company manufactures study lamps in Osaka, Japan. Next year's budget estimates sales to be 500,000 lamps at ¥1,700 each. Variable costs are ¥900 per lamp, and fixed costs are budgeted at ¥300 million or ¥600 per lamp. Recently, a purchasing agent from Nationwide Superstores in the U. S. offered to buy 100,000 lamps at a price of ¥1,350 each. By working overtime and adding extra shifts, Aoi would have sufficient capacity. Additional overtime premiums would be ¥7.5 million. Additional supervision costs are ¥2 million. Total selling and administrative expenses will not change if the order is accepted.

Aoi's finance manager argues, "With the extra volume, the full cost of regular sales would be reduced from ¥1,500 per unit to ¥1,400. At this level Aoi would make an extra ¥100 per unit on all regular sales but still lose money on the special sales because of overtime costs and the lower price." He thinks that the "economics of the deal" are too risky and that it violates the firm's strategic pricing policies that have helped Aoi create a reputation for quality.

Required:

1. Is the finance manager's quantitative analysis sound? Explain your decision.
2. What does the finance manager mean by "too risky?"
3. Why might this be a violation of the firm's pricing policies?

11-34. Evaluating a Segment.   The Yablanka family has developed an extensive bakery business in Chicago and now has 90 shops. Annually, several new outlets are opened, and old ones are closed. Fred, the controller, reviews the performance of each location and of all store managers. He is currently evaluating Store 54, operated by a relatively experienced manager. Business statistics for the company and Store 54 data are:

	Average Store Percentages	Store 54
Sales	100%	$400,000
Expenses:		
Cost of baked goodies	35%	$150,000
Store salaries and wages	20	110,000
Store occupancy costs	30	120,000
Home office expenses	10	50,000
Total expenses	95%	$430,000
Net income	5%	$ (30,000)

The store's lease is a three-year commitment for $30,000 per year. If Store 54 is closed, a nearby Yablanka store would attract $50,000 of Store 54's lost gross margin. Store 54's manager has a five-year personal services contract for $30,000 per year and could be transferred to a new store. All other salaries and occupancy costs can be eliminated. Home office expenses are allocated evenly among the 90 stores.

Required:

1. Should Store 54 be closed now? Why or why not?

2. If Store 54 gets a 6-month reprieve, in which areas should the manager attempt to improve?

11-35. Evaluating a New Sales Segment.   Huang Automotive in Taiwan is presently operating at 75 percent of practical capacity and producing about 200,000 units annually of a power steering system component. Huang recently received an offer from a Korean truck manufacturer to purchase 40,000 components at NT$225 (new Taiwanese dollars) per unit. Flexible budgets for production of 200,000 and 250,000 units are:

	200,000 Units	250,000 Units
Direct materials	NT$18,000,000	NT$22,500,000
Direct labor	6,000,000	7,500,000
Factory overhead	24,000,000	27,000,000
Total costs	NT$48,000,000	NT$57,000,000
Cost per unit	NT$240	NT$228

Peter Wu, vice-president of sales, thinks accepting the order will get the company's "foot in the door" of an expanding international market, even if the company loses a little on this order.

T. J. Chan, vice-president of engineering, feels that any new market should first show its profitability and that this offer is below last year's cost per unit of NT$240. "This guarantees a loss on the order," he says.

Lili Zhang, treasurer, has made a quick computation which indicates that accepting the order will actually increase dollars of gross margin.

Required:

1. Estimate Huang's variable cost per unit.

2. Show how Mr. Chan and Ms. Zhang are analyzing the situation. Using the given facts, what does the incremental analysis of the Korean sale show?

3. What major nonquantitative factors might affect the decision to accept or reject the special order?

11-36. Scarce Resources With Other Constraints. Data for four products are as follows:

	Product A	Product B	Product C	Product D
Selling price per unit	$13	$20	$5	$25
Variable cost per unit	6	5	2	16
Allocated costs per unit	4	8	1	3
Units produced per hour	4 units	2 units	8 units	3 units
Maximum sales limit.	5,000 units	5,000 units	10,000 units	No limit
Minimum requirements	1,000 units	None	2,000 units	1,200 units

Total capacity is 6,000 hours. Minimum requirements meet existing sales commitments. Marketing has provided a "best estimate" of maximum sales expected for each product.

Required:

Based on the preceding data, choose the best product combination.

11-37. Alternative Uses of Capacity. Harris Equipment built a new facility five years ago but is using only 60 percent of its capacity to produce several machining equipment product lines. Management would like to use the excess capacity and has three possibilities. Only one of the three can be selected.

(a) Harris could produce an additional 600 units per year of its most popular machine and focus marketing efforts on European metal parts producers. Management estimates that additional freight costs would amount to $550 per machine and fixed factory overhead would increase by $150,000. To cover the additional cost, the selling price per machine on European sales would be increased by $800 per machine. Incremental international selling costs would be about $200,000 per year. Harris has earned a contribution margin of $1,800 on each unit in the past.

(b) Harris could produce and market a smaller model of an existing laser lathe. The capacity could be used to produce 200 units per year that would sell for $15,500 each. Management has estimated the following unit variable costs.

Prime costs	$ 4,500
Variable overhead	2,000
Variable selling.	500
Total costs	$ 7,000

The new lathe would add fixed costs of $700,000 to fixed overhead expenses and $250,000 to fixed selling expenses.

(c) Olson Testing Company has offered to lease the facilities at $30,000 per month plus 2 percent of the net revenues generated from the facilities by Olson. Net revenues are estimated at $15,000,000 per year.

Required:

1. Which of the three alternatives should management select? Comment on the relative riskiness.

2. What is the opportunity cost of this decision?

11-38. Dropping a Product. Bob Leverenz, an old prospector, runs a side business. He buys rattlesnakes from "snake hunters" in west Texas, paying an average of $10 per snake. Each snake comes complete. He produces canned snake meat, cures hides, and makes souvenir rattles. At the end of a recent season, Bob is evaluating his financial results:

	Meat	*Hides*	*Rattles*	*Total*
Sales	$ 30,000	$ 8,000	$ 2,000	$ 40,000
Cost of snakes	(18,000)	(4,800)	(1,200)	(24,000)
Gross profit	$ 12,000	$ 3,200	$ 800	$ 16,000
Processing expenses ..	$ (6,000)	$ (900)	$ (600)	$ (7,500)
Common expenses.......	(4,000)	(600)	(400)	(5,000)
Operating expenses ...	$(10,000)	$(1,500)	$(1,000)	$(12,500)
Income (loss)	$ 2,000	$ 1,700	$ (200)	$ 3,500

Cost of snakes assigned to each product is based on a ratio of cost to revenue. Processing expenses are direct costs. Common expenses are allocated on the basis of direct processing expenses and are Bob's basic living expenses. Bob has a philosophy of "every tub on its own bottom" and is determined to cut his losses on rattles.

Required:

1. Is he really "losing" money on rattles? Explain.

2. An old miner has offered to buy every rattle "as is," without processing, for $0.50 per rattle. Will this eliminate the "loss" problem and improve Bob's profitability? Explain your reasoning.

11-39. Purchasing Ethical Dilemmas. Over the years, Don Dremmen has been "on the road" selling a variety of industrial goods for several different distributors. He keeps a small diary of "problems" that he has encountered over the years that concern him. Among these are:

(a) A competing salesperson, selling a high-quality product at a high price, would routinely give tickets to Bulls' basketball games to the purchasing agents of certain large customers.

(b) A close friend, also a salesperson, died recently of serious health problems that Don thinks was brought on by excessive entertaining of potential clients for years.

(c) When he was selling certain heavy equipment, he had the most difficulty competing with a rival salesperson that actually moved a service representative into his territory to be close to several large construction firms headquartered there. The service rep visited with their service personnel almost every week and even taught maintenance courses for free.

(d) One particular customer worked out a schedule to have him and several other sales representatives bring in donuts for the office staff on Fridays. His turn was always the third Friday of the month.

(e) Another current customer called him last week and said, "You know that fastener we buy from you? I just got a quote from a Singapore supplier at $23.50 a thousand. You gotta meet it, or I drop ya. Well?"

Required:

Comment on whether these are a typical salesperson's laments or ethical issues?

11-40. Costing a Service. Up-and-Away Airlines, a regional commuter airline, flies routes among mid-sized cities in the Midwest. The firm owns six airplanes, which can hold 150 passengers each. All routes are about the same distance, and all fares are $55 one way. The line operates 200 flights per month. Each flight costs $2,000 for gasoline, crew salaries, and so forth. Variable costs per passenger are $5, to cover meals and head taxes levied for each passenger departure at each airport. Other fixed costs are $60,000 per month.

Required:

1. How many passengers must the airline carry on 200 flights to earn a $30,000 per month profit? What percentage of capacity does this number represent?

2. What impact does a $1 increase in airfare have on the capacity percentage needed to break even?

3. Comment on the cost behavior of each cost element.

11-41. Use of Capacity. Bucien Specialty Compounds manufactures chemical compounds for industrial use. Department 23 produces related products—Pre and Post. Pre can be sold for $3 per pound or processed further and sold as Post. Pre can also be bought at a market price of $3 per pound plus $0.25 per pound for hauling. One pound of Pre is used to produce one pound of Post. Post has been selling for $7.20 for several years but has recently fallen to $6.80 per pound. Production could be Pre only, Pre and Post, or Post only.

Department 23's available capacity is 1,500 ton hours. (Processing one ton for one hour is a ton hour.) It takes three hours to process 10 pounds of Pre and Post —one hour for Pre and two for Post.

Marcia Bailey, marketing vice-president, has analyzed the markets and costs. She thinks that Post production should be halted when its price falls below $6.55 per pound. At that point, the profit from a pound of Post would be less than two times the profit from a pound of Pre. She says this is important since Post uses twice as much production time as Pre. She cites the following data:

Department 23 Analysis of Pre:

Selling price, net of any selling costs		$ 3.00
Direct materials and labor	$ 1.95	
Manufacturing overhead	.60	2.55
Operating profit per pound		$ .45

Department 23 Analysis of Post:

Selling price, net of any selling costs		$ 6.80
Cost of 1 pound of Pre (from above)	$ 2.55	
Additional direct materials and labor	1.90	
Manufacturing overhead	1.20	5.65
Operating profit per pound		$ 1.15

Direct materials and labor costs are variable. Manufacturing overhead is fixed and is allocated to products by budgeting the total overhead for the coming year and dividing it by the total ton hours of capacity available.

Required:

1. Is Ms. Bailey correct? Why or why not?

2. Recommend a production plan given current prices.

3. Suggest a market price decision rule to guide production.

11-42. Direct Contribution Margins. Zehnder Company, a Swiss firm, sells three products. Financial data for a typical month are (in thousands of Swiss francs):

	Products			
	J	K	L	Total
Sales	SFr 300	SFr 500	SFr 800	SFr 1,600
Variable costs	90	200	400	690
Contribution margin	SFr 210	SFr 300	SFr 400	SFr 910
Fixed costs:				
Separable and avoidable	SFr 90	SFr 100	SFr 120	SFr 310
Joint, allocated on sales dollar basis . .	60	100	160	320
Total fixed costs	SFr 150	SFr 200	SFr 280	SFr 630
Profit	SFr 60	SFr 100	SFr 120	SFr 280

Required:

1. The firm is considering the introduction of a new Product M to replace Product J. Product M sells for SFr12 per unit, has variable costs of SFr5 per unit, and has separable fixed costs of SFr104,000. How many units of Product M must be sold to maintain the existing income of SFr280,000?

2. Revenues of Product K could increase by 20 percent by reducing variable contribution margin to 45 percent and increasing separable and avoidable fixed costs by SFr40,000. Should Zehnder do this? Show your logic.

3. Rank each product by total sales, variable contribution margin percentage, direct contribution margin percentage, and net profit percentage. Comment on how Zehnder might use each ranking.

11-43. **"Lose a little on each one, and make it up on volume."** Adams Company currently sells three products whose quantities, selling prices, and variable costs are:

Product	Quantity	Selling Price	Variable Cost
110	10,000	$ 22	$ 14
111	15,000	12	7
112	25,000	27	16

The plant is currently operating at capacity. Each unit requires the same production time. Fixed operating costs are $350,000 and are applied using units as the cost driver. An analysis shows that Product 111 is not profitable:

Selling price per unit		$12
Variable cost per unit	$ 7	
Fixed cost per unit	7	14
Profit (loss) per unit		$ (2)

Part A: The sales manager argues that Product 111 should be dropped, stating that it is difficult to make profits on volume when every unit loses money.

Required:

1. Under what conditions should Product 111 be dropped? Should not be dropped?
2. If Product 111 is dropped, comment on profits per unit of Product 110.
3. If Product 111 is dropped, how many more units of Product 112 need to be sold to maintain current profit levels?

Part B: The sales manager finds another product, 113, to replace Product 111. No additional sales of Product 110 or Product 112 will occur. Product 113 can be sold for $8 and has a variable cost of $6. But, it uses only half of the production time per unit that Product 111 uses. Sufficient sales can be generated to use all of Product 111's current capacity.

The sales manager argues that Product 113 should be added and Product 111 should be dropped by saying, "It is true that the contribution margin of Product 113 is only $2.00 per unit; but since more units of Product 113 can be produced, the fixed cost per unit will go down. Look, the fixed cost per unit on all units will drop by $1.62—from $7 to $5.38 ($350,000 ÷ 65,000)—if we switch to Product 113. It'll increase profits on Products 110 and 112, too."

Required:

1. Is the sales manager right? Explain.
2. What price must Adams charge for Product 113 for profits to equal current profits with Product 111?

11-44. **Department Profitability.** White's Grocery Store is a small-town operation being threatened by a national discount store outlet being built nearby. Mickey White, the owner, is studying the addition of a department to sell either garden supplies or beer and wine. He has talked to several other owners of similar stores and has reached the following conclusions:

1. A garden supplies department would generate sales of $40,000 per year with a gross profit of 60 percent. No other variable costs would be added. Additional fixed costs would be $12,000. Grocery sales would increase by 5 percent because of increased traffic through the store.

2. A beer and wine department would generate sales of $60,000 per year with a gross profit of 40 percent. No other variable costs would be added, but fixed costs would increase by $18,000. Grocery sales would increase by 8 percent.

The income statement for a typical year for grocery sales alone is as follows:

Sales	$600,000
Cost of goods sold (variable)	240,000
Gross profit	$360,000
Other variable costs	120,000
Contribution margin	$240,000
Fixed costs	140,000
Income	$100,000

Required:

1. Recompute the effects on income of adding each department.

2. Which department should be added? What qualitative issues appear important?

11-45. Make or Buy Decision. Hillman Company produces a line of iron and steel building products. The product lines include numerous subassemblies and parts. Many of these parts can be either produced in Department 8 or outsourced. Four parts are listed below with their related cost and production data, including normal batch sizes and estimated setup costs:

	Iron Frames # 10	Steel Frames # 11	Steel Housing # 12	Assembly Unit # 13
Materials cost	$5.00	$6.00	$18.00	$8.00
Variable labor cost	1.50	1.00	5.00	3.00
Overhead cost (excluding setup costs)	4.50	3.00	15.00	9.00
Time required per unit	1 hour	4 hours	5 hours	2 hours
Units required	80,000	40,000	15,000	100,000
Batch size (in units)	10,000	10,000	3,000	5,000
Estimated setup costs per batch	$4,000	$3,000	$3,000	$2,000
Outsourcing prices	$10.00	$11.00	$32.00	$18.00

Department 8's facilities are flexible in that these parts can be produced in any combination. Department 8's capacity is 300,000 machine hours. Materials and labor costs are considered variable. Batch sizes and setup costs are estimated based on past experience. Overhead costs, except for setup costs, are fixed. Total overhead is assigned to products at the rate of 300 percent of direct labor cost, established after preparing the factory overhead budget.

Required:

Write a memo presenting your recommendation and describing your decision logic for producing and outsourcing.

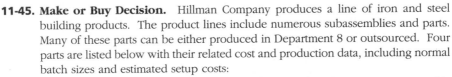

C ASE 11A—TEDDY BEAR HOUSE

Teddy Bear House is a day-care center/preschool which operates as a partnership of Linda Rivera and Marilou Clarke. The center is in a city which has a large base of two-income families who have a need for quality day care. The two women started the center this year. Clarke contributed $40,000 to get the business started—to purchase equipment and to operate through the early months. Rivera, who previously managed another center, is the director of the center and draws $2,000 per month for her services. Partnership profits and losses, after Rivera's salary, are split 75 percent for Clarke and 25 percent for Rivera.

Teddy Bear House operates from 6 a.m. to 6 p.m., Monday through Friday, is in a single building which has a capacity limit of 120 children, and meets city and state regulations. At present, the center has six classes, all at maximum sizes, structured as follows:

Age	Number of Classes	Children Per Class	Total Children	Monthly Tuition Per Child
2-to-3	2	10	20	$320
3-to-4	1	15	15	280
4-to-5	1	15	15	280
5-to-6	2	15	30	260

Class sizes are determined by state law which sets a limit on the number of children per instructor. The center uses one instructor per classroom.

Tuition is charged monthly. Minor adjustments are made on an individual basis. In October, the most recent month with data available, revenues were $21,500 ($22,600 less $1,100 adjustments). Monthly revenues should be rather stable since classes are full most of the time. Expenses for October were:

Salaries for instructors	$ 9,600
Salary of director	2,000
Salary of part-time cook.................................	900
Food expenses	2,200
Staff benefits expenses	2,450
Supplies expenses	600
Occupancy and other administrative expenses	3,250
Total expenses	$ 21,000

Fixed expenses are the salary of the part-time cook and occupancy and other administrative expenses. The salary of the director is fixed; but, as a partnership, this is in reality a distribution of profits but is included in expenses for comparative purposes.

Food is $1.25 per student per day. Staff benefits are 10 percent of salaries plus $200 per person for benefit programs for instructors and the part-time cook. Supplies are $1 per student per month. Step costs are salaries for instructors, averaging $1,600 per instructor per class.

Rivera wants to increase the quality of service by decreasing class sizes and also expanding student enrollments. These alternatives are interrelated. Rivera thinks that the class sizes are too large and that children are not getting the individual attention they require. Rivera surveyed parents of all 80 students to measure their support for a tuition increase tied to a reduction in class size. For children ages 2 to 5, most parents would support a 25 percent tuition increase, and nearly 50 percent would support a 50 percent increase. Of the 5-to-6 age group parents, nearly three-fourths did not want any increase. The remainder said they would support a 25 percent increase but no more.

Proper class size is very subjective. However, Rivera feels that she could achieve a child/instructor ratio of 6 to 1 for the 2-to-3 age group; an 8 to 1 ratio for the 3-to-4 and 4-to-5 age groups; and a 10 to 1 ratio for the 5-to-6 age group.

The center has easily maintained the 80 student level, with each class full. Rivera keeps in touch with waiting-list parents to make certain each is still interested. This list provides children when someone leaves the center. The current waiting list is as follows:

Age Group	Number of Children	Age Group	Number of Children
2-to-3	5	4-to-5	4
3-to-4	7	5-to-6	11

Rivera does not start a new class unless more students are on the waiting list than are required per class. Obviously, enough students are on the 5-to-6 age group waiting list to start a new class. Lately, however, she has wondered if the center could make a profit by starting classes with fewer than the requisite number, taking the chance that new students would appear and could be added immediately.

Information from her various inquiries implies that a potential market for quality infant care (0 to 24 months) exists. Rivera doesn't think this expansion would be profitable. However, she has never done an analysis of the situation and has not thought about an appropriate tuition. She believes that the infant/instructor ratio in her center should be no higher than 5 infants to one instructor. The center would have no food costs for the infants.

Clarke will only agree to Rivera's suggested changes if the center will continue to operate at or above the current profit level.

Required:

1. Look at each decision separately, as incremental to the current situation, and evaluate the marginal profit:

   (a) If class size is decreased (keeping the same 80 students), what increase in tuition is necessary to keep the current monthly profit level?

   (b) Without regard to (a) above, is it profitable to create the new class from the waiting list? Explain.

   (c) Use the new fee structure as found in Part (1) (a). Is it profitable to move to smaller class sizes if new full classes are created and filled to their new maximums using the waiting list? Show calculations.

   (d) Is a class for infant care profitable if tuition is the same as the small class tuition for the 2-to-3 age group? Using the current tuition rate?

2. Write a brief memo to Rivera and Clarke highlighting any concerns that underlie the analyses you have performed in Part (1).

C ASE 11B—KAHN PRODUCTS

Bernie Steer, the production vice-president at Kahn Products, located in Amsterdam, complains that the quality of a part used in manufacturing is poor. He states that this part costs F23 per unit (in Dutch florin) but that 10 percent of the parts breaks in the assembly process. This part is now purchased from a supplier that uses a lighter gauge of steel. As a result of bending operations in assembly, it can snap at a stress point. The supplier has been willing to split the cost of replacement parts with Kahn. The best alternative supplier using the higher gauge of steel was a quoted price of F28. Any price increase to cover the higher costs would cause serious competitive problems for Kahn's salespersons.

Breakage of this part during assembly has caused rework and scrap costing Kahn about F150,000 in addition to the cost of broken parts. Also, the engineering and customer service staffs estimate that about 25 percent of the firm's warranty claims of F660,000 last year was related to in-service failures of this part.

Sue Svatik, the controller, states that idle plant capacity exists and suggests that Kahn make its own higher quality parts. Svatik believes that the suppliers are unwilling to reduce their profits and are cheapening their products instead of absorbing higher metals costs.

The company needs 50,000 of these parts each year. A study reveals that if Kahn produced the parts, the following additional costs would be incurred:

Direct materials (including higher gauge of steel)	F1,050,000
Direct labor (15,000 labor hours)	225,000
Variable overhead (30,000 machine hours)	180,000

Engineering believes that failure rates will become negligible.

Steer is not convinced that the components can be made at a lower cost than the purchase cost. The plant's substantial fixed overhead must be absorbed at a F10 per machine hour rate. In Steer's opinion, use of any idle capacity should cover at least this fixed overhead.

Required:

1. Based on the quantitative data given, how should the part be sourced? Show computations.
2. Evaluate Steer's argument. Does he make a valid point?
3. Discuss the possible long-term ramifications of this decision on the factory, on sales, on customers, and on profits.

Capital Investment Decisions

*L*EARNING OBJECTIVES

After studying Chapter 12, you will be able to:

1. Explain the nature and importance of capital investment decisions.

2. Identify the relevant cash inflows and outflows in an investment proposal.

3. Know how to format the relevant cash flows in an investment proposal.

4. Understand how to apply present value evaluation methods to capital investment decisions.

5. Understand how to apply payback period and accounting rate of return methods to capital investment decisions.

6. Compare strengths and weaknesses of capital investment evaluation methods.

7. Comprehend how income taxes impact the cash flows of capital investments.

Capital Investment Alternatives

John Victory, president of Fine Tone Instruments, grabbed his briefcase and headed for the airport. After running through the airport and just making his flight, John settled into his coach seat, right in front of two screaming kids and behind two salespersons who apparently just made the deal of the century. He opened his briefcase and found the capital spending proposals file. The deadline for submitting proposals to him was yesterday. He plans to review these on his cross-country flight. The variety surprises him and includes:

- Engineering is pushing to integrate a newly announced semiconductor into an aging product. The new technology will push Fine Tone into new markets with great sales potential but against stiff competition.
- Adding space to the corporate headquarters will bring three administrative departments together, increase efficiency, and reduce operating expenses.
- His production planning manager proposes rearranging several work centers to improve production efficiency for a family of current products.
- Another project adds capacity to a specialized assembly operation.

- The plant manager requests funding for an air purification system which must be installed by yearend to meet new state air quality requirements.
- An information systems proposal would automate several manual operations, save personnel, and slice inventory by an estimated 10 percent.
- His finance manager is negotiating for controlling interest in a firm with technical expertise that Fine Tone needs for new product development.
- Marketing has proposed a major jump in advertising spending for a product line that has not been meeting sales targets.

John clearly wants to get the "biggest bang for the bucks" in Fine Tone's limited capital investment budget. But, a quick calculation shows him that this year's investment dollars will fund about half of the these proposals. Some proposals are risky, while others have predictable outcomes. Some are straightforward, but many include many extraneous issues. Also, data are overstated for some proposals and understated for others. Some generate immediate returns; others promise big cash flows years from now.

This chapter extends the study of incremental analysis begun in Chapter 11 into multiperiod decisions, which are called **capital investment decisions**. Chapters 12 and 13 discuss:

1. Identification of relevant cash flows in capital investments.
2. Techniques and methods for analyzing project data.

Chapters 12 and 13 depend on an understanding of the time value of money. For those who are unfamiliar with the time value of money or have not applied present values in financial accounting or other courses, the Appendix to this chapter, pages 532-538, explains the concept. Present value tables necessary for **discounting** future cash flows are also in the Appendix on pages 535 and 536.

Relevant operating revenues and costs for multiperiod decisions are defined as cash inflows and cash outflows. Since these decisions extend over a period of years, opportunity costs and the timing of these cash flows are major factors. For short timeframes, opportunity costs are small and may be ignored. But when days become years, the time value of money becomes an important decision factor.

Capital investment analysis is a planning task and is directly linked to budgeting as discussed in Chapters 7 and 8. **Capital budgeting** is the process of evaluating specific proposals, budgeting the spending level, and selecting which projects to fund.

THE IMPORTANCE OF CAPITAL INVESTMENT DECISIONS

Capital investment is the acquisition of assets with an expected life greater than one year. These decisions attract managers' interest with good reasons:

1. **Long-term commitments.** Capital decisions often lock the firm into assets for many years.
2. **Large amounts of dollars.** Capital projects often have big price tags. From Ford Motor Company with an annual investment budget of $7 billion to a small firm buying a $30,000 truck, large relative dollar amounts get attention.
3. **Key areas of the firm.** New products, new production technology, and research efforts are crucial to a firm's ongoing competitiveness.
4. **Source of future earnings.** Investing with foresight is the key to the firm's future profits and financial performance.
5. **Scarce capital dollars.** In most firms, more demands exist for capital funds than the firm can generate. Only the best opportunities should be funded.

Excellent analysis and decisions increase the firm's capacity, technology, efficiency, and cash generating power. Poor decisions waste resources, lose opportunities, and impact firm profits for many years.

THE CAPITAL INVESTMENT DECISION

Capital investments generally include cash outflows, which are the investments, and cash inflows, which are the returns on the investments. The decision maker expects cash inflows to exceed cash outflows. The typical investment project has cash outflows at the beginning and cash inflows over the life of the project.

Cash Flows

Cash flows are the key data inputs in capital investment analyses. Cash has an opportunity cost, since it could be used to buy a productive or financial asset with earning power. Cash is a basic asset. Prices, costs, and values can all be expressed in cash amounts. If the decision impacts several time periods, cash-flow timing becomes a relevant factor.

Cash outflows commonly include:

- The cash cost of the initial investment plus any startup costs.
- Incremental cash operating costs incurred over the project's life.
- Incremental working capital such as inventories and accounts receivable.
- Additional outlays needed to overhaul, expand, or update the asset during the project's life.
- Additional taxes owed on incremental taxable income.

Cash inflows include:

- Incremental cash revenues received over the project's life.

- Reduced operating expenses received over the project's life.
- Cash received from selling old assets being replaced in the new project, net of any tax impacts.
- Released working capital, perhaps at the project's end.
- Salvage value realized from asset disposition at the project's end.

These relevant cash flows occur after the "go" decision is made to proceed with the project. Therefore, we estimate future cash flows. Certain cash flows are estimated based on current prices and known technology; whereas others are estimates based on vague facts and unproven methods. Often, cost savings and project benefits are not easily quantified. Much time and expense is spent to develop supporting forecast data. Of major importance, the *same cash-flow estimates* are used regardless of the project evaluation method used.

Decision Criteria

Winning projects generally have the highest rates of return on investment. Decisions are either:

Accept or reject   *or*   Select A or B or C or etc.

In the first type, we decide whether the return is acceptable or unacceptable. This is a screening decision. Is the return "good enough?" The second type is a preference or ranking decision—select the best choice from a set of mutually exclusive projects. By picking A, we reject B, C, and any other choices. A possible choice is to do nothing—the status quo.

Generally, projects are ranked on a scale of high to low returns. The highest ranking projects are selected until the capital investment budget is spent. Often, funds are limited; and many acceptable projects will go unfunded. The firm's goal is to select projects with the highest returns. As in Chapter 11, pertinent nonquantitative factors may sway a decision and cause lower ranked projects to be selected.

Time Perspectives

In the real world, every conceivable combination of cash-flow timing can exist. But, we assume a simplified timeline. The present point in time is today, Year 0. This is when we assume investments are made—new assets acquired, old assets sold, and any tax consequences of these changes felt. In real life, several years of cash outflows may precede the start of a project's operation.

Generally, annual time periods are used. Using shorter time periods is possible, such as one-month periods for monthly lease payments. Annual flows of cash are assumed to occur at yearend. In the Appendix, Tables 1 and 2 show "end of period" present value factors. Other tables exist that can reflect smooth cash flows within a time period. But this fine tuning is probably necessary only in specialized situations.

An Example—Equipment Replacement and Capacity Expansion

As an illustration, Quartz Timepieces, a Seattle firm, is considering a device costing $100,000 to replace an obsolete production device:

1. The new device has an expected life of five years and can probably be sold at the end of Year 5 for $10,000.
2. The vendor recommends an updating in Year 3 at a cost of $20,000.
3. Capacity will increase by 1,000 units per year. Each unit sells for $55 and has $30 of variable costs.
4. Additional inventory of $3,000 is needed and will be released at the project's end.
5. Operating costs will be reduced by $15,000 per year.
6. The old device can be sold for $8,000 now, which is its book value. But, it could be used for five more years with no salvage or book value.

Remember that any cash revenue or cost that does not change is irrelevant and can be ignored. Any cash flow that differs among decision choices is relevant. Added taxes or tax savings on incremental income or expenses are also relevant cash flows. But, until income tax issues are discussed, taxation implications are ignored.

Formatting the Relevant Data

As in Chapter 11, adopting a uniform format for analysis of capital investments helps to organize data and to present it in a logical pattern. Using data from the previous example, the timeframe format shown in Figure 12.1 is used throughout our capital investment discussions.

Cash outflows are negative numbers, and inflows are positive numbers. Project years begin now, Year 0 or today, and are shown as columns. Specific cash-flow items are shown as rows. The investment of $100,000 in equipment and $3,000 in inventory costs is reduced by the sale of old equipment for $8,000. The **net initial investment** is $95,000. The additional 1,000 units of sales generate incremental contribution margin of $25,000, using a $55 sales price less a $30 variable cost per unit.

Remember that volumes of analytical support may be developed to backup each number in Figure 12.1. The $100,000 device cost would result from evaluation of many devices and negotiations with vendors. Estimates of additional revenues and variable costs come from marketing studies and capacity use. Cost savings come from production, industrial engineering, and cost accounting analyses. Each dollar amount is the best estimate that Quartz personnel can provide.

FIGURE 12.1   Format for Relevant Capital Investment Data—Quartz Timepieces

| | | Life of the Project | | | | |
Cash Flows:	Today	Year 1	Year 2	Year 3	Year 4	Year 5
New device	$(100,000)					
Salvage value						$10,000
Sale of old device	8,000					
Added inventory	(3,000)					3,000
Added contribution margin		$25,000	$25,000	$25,000	$25,000	25,000
Operating cost savings		15,000	15,000	15,000	15,000	15,000
Updating costs				(20,000)		
Net cash investment	$ (95,000)					
Net cash inflows		$40,000	$40,000	$20,000	$40,000	$53,000

THE EVALUATION METHODS

The evaluation methods discussed here are:

1. Present value methods (also called discounted cash-flow methods).
   (a) Net present value method.
   (b) Internal rate of return method.
2. Payback period method.
3. Accounting rate of return method.

Nearly all managerial accountants agree that methods using **present values** (Methods 1a and 1b) give the best assessment of long-term investments. The methods that do not involve the time value of money (Methods 2 and 3) have serious flaws. But since they are commonly used for investment evaluation, their strengths and weaknesses are discussed.

Net Present Value Method

The **net present value (NPV) method** includes the time value of money by using an interest rate that represents the desired rate of return or, at least, sets a minimum acceptable rate of return. The decision rule is:

> *If the present value of incremental net cash inflows is greater than the incremental investment net cash outflow, approve the project.*

Using Tables 1 and 2 in the Appendix, the net cash flows for each year are brought back to Year 0 and summed for all years. An interest rate must be specified. This rate is often viewed as the cost of funds needed to finance the project and is the minimum acceptable rate of return. Note that the present value of cash flows in the Today column is the amount itself—no discounting is needed. In Figure 12.2, page 520, the net cash investment ($95,000) is subtracted from the sum of cash-inflow present values ($137,331). When the residual is positive, the project's rate of return (ROR) is greater than the minimum acceptable ROR. *If:*

Present value of incremental net cash inflows $\geq$ Incremental investment cash outflows

   then: Project's ROR $\geq$ Minimum acceptable ROR

If net present value is zero or positive, the project is acceptable. When the sum is negative, the project's ROR is less than the discount rate. *If:*

Present value of incremental net cash inflows $<$ Incremental investment cash outflows

   then: Project's ROR $<$ Minimum acceptable ROR

If net present value is negative, the project should be rejected.

The Interest Rate. What is the source of the interest rate for discounting? This rate has many names that help explain its source and use. Among them are:

1. **Cost of capital**—a weighted-average cost of long-term funds. Only projects that can earn at least what the firm pays for funds should be accepted. Later, we illustrate a calculation of cost of capital.

FIGURE 12.2 Net Present Value of Capital Investment Cash Flows

Cash Flows:	Today	Life of the Project				
		Year 1	Year 2	Year 3	Year 4	Year 5
Net cash flows (Figure 12.1)	$ (95,000)	$40,000	$40,000	$20,000	$40,000	$53,000
Present value factors at 12%	x 1.000	x .893	x .797	x .712	x .636	x .567
Present values at 12%	$ (95,000)	$35,720	$31,880	$14,240	$25,440	$30,051
Sum of PVs for Years 1 to 5	137,331					
Net present value	$ 42,331					

2. **Minimum acceptable rate of return**—a particular rate that is considered to be the lowest ROR that management will accept.
3. **Desired rate of return**, **target rate of return**, or **required rate of return**—a rate that reflects management's ROR expectations.
4. **Hurdle rate**—a level that a project's ROR must "jump over" or exceed.
5. **Cutoff rate**—the rate at which projects with a higher ROR are accepted and those with a lower ROR are rejected, often the rate where all available capital investment funds are committed.

A firm will use one or more of these terms as its **discount rate**. We use these terms interchangeably. Generally, if a project's ROR is below this percentage, it is rejected; above this rate, the project is acceptable. Still, whether it is funded depends on the availability of capital funds.

The Example. In the Quartz Timepieces example, we assume that management has decided that 12 percent is the minimum acceptable rate of return. Calculations needed to obtain a net present value are shown in Figure 12.2. The net present value is a positive $42,331; therefore, the project earns more than a 12 percent ROR. The net present value method does not give the project's exact ROR.

If we had selected other discount rates, the net present values we find are:

Percentage	Present Value of Net Cash Inflows	−	Investment	=	Net Present Value
16%	$124,328		$95,000		$29,328
20	113,246		95,000		18,246
24	103,713		95,000		8,713
28	95,523		95,000		523
30	91,797		95,000		(3,203)

Notice that as the interest rate increases, the present values of the future cash flows decrease. At 30 percent per year, the project's net present value is negative, and the project is unacceptable. The project's rate of return must be between 28 and 30 percent.

Project Ranking. Even though a project has a positive net present value, too many attractive projects may exist, given the investment dollars available.

A ranking system is needed. We can rank projects by the amount of net present value each generates, but this ignores the relative size of the initial investments. An extension of the net present value method is the **profitability index**. It is found by dividing the present value of a project's *net cash* *inflows* by its *net initial investment*. The resulting ratio is cash in to cash out. The higher the ratio is, the more attractive the investment becomes. Notice that an acceptable project should have a profitability index of at least 1. The following projects are ranked by the profitability index.

Project	Present Value of Net Cash Inflows	Initial Investment	Net Present Value	Profitability Index	Ranking
A	$235,000	$200,000	$35,000	1.18	5
B	170,000	140,000	30,000	1.21	4
C	80,000	60,000	20,000	1.33	1
D	98,000	80,000	18,000	1.23	3
E	52,000	40,000	12,000	1.30	2

We would typically accept projects with the highest profitability index until we exhaust the capital budget or the list of acceptable projects.

Internal Rate of Return Method

The **internal rate of return (IRR)** is the project's ROR and is the rate where the:

Net initial investment cash outflow = Present value of the incremental net cash inflows

Without calculator or computer assistance, the specific ROR is found by trial and error. We search for the rate that yields a zero net present value.

In the Quartz Timepieces example, the internal rate of return was found to be between 28 and 30 percent. The net present value at 28 percent is positive and at 30 percent is negative. By interpolation, we can approximate a finer-tuned rate as follows:

Rate of Return	Net Present Value	Calculations	
28%	$ 523	Base rate	= 28.00%
30	(3,202)	($523 ÷ $3,725) x 2%	= 0.28
2% difference	$ 3,725 absolute difference	Internal rate of return	28.28%

In most cases, however, knowing that the rate is between 28 and 30 percent is adequate. Also, calculators and software do this automatically.

Estimating the Internal Rate of Return. By using Table 2 and knowing certain project variables, we can estimate other unknown variables including a project's internal rate of return. This estimate requires that the annual net cash inflows be an annuity. The variables and a sample set of data are:

Variable	**Example Data**
A = Initial investment cash outflow	$ 37,910
B = Life of project	5 years
C = Annual net cash inflow	$ 10,000 per year
D = Internal rate of return	10 percent
E = Present value factor at 10 percent (Table 2)	3.791

If we know any three of *A, B, C, or D*, we can find *E* and the missing variable. A variety of questions can be answered:

1. What is the internal rate of return of the project? If *A, B,* and *C* are known, we can calculate *E* and find *D* as follows:

$$E = A \div C \qquad \$37,910 \div \$10,000 = 3.791$$

On Table 2, we go to the 5-period (year) row and move across until we find 3.791 in the 10 percent column (D). At 10 percent, the cash outflow ($37,910) equals the present value of the net cash inflows (3.791 x $10,000). The internal rate of return is 10 percent.

2. What annual cash inflow will yield a 10 percent IRR from the project? If *A, B,* and *D* are known, we can find *E* and calculate *C.* *E* is found in Table 2 by using five years and 10 percent ROR. The annual cash inflow is found as follows:

$$C = A \div E \qquad \$37,910 \div 3.791 = \$10,000 \text{ per year}$$

We need $10,000 per year in cash inflow to earn a 10 percent IRR.

3. What can we afford to invest if the project earns $10,000 each year for five years, and we want a 10 percent IRR? If we know *B, C,* and *D*, we can find *E* in Table 2 and then calculate *A.* The investment is found by using the annual net cash inflow and 3.791 (E) as follows:

$$A = C \times E \qquad \$10,000 \times 3.791 = \$37,910$$

We can pay no more than $37,910 and still earn at least a 10 percent return.

4. How long must the project last to earn at least a 10 percent IRR? If we know *A, C,* and *D*, we calculate *E* and find *B* as follows:

$$E = A \div C \qquad \$37,910 \div \$10,000 = 3.791$$

For a 10 percent IRR, 3.791 is on the 5-period row (B) of Table 2. The project's life must be at least five years.

Most business calculators and spreadsheet software have built-in functions to find the internal rate of return. This simplifies the calculation burden that has limited its use in the past.

Ranking Projects. Since each project has a specific rate of return, ranking projects under the IRR method is relatively simple. All projects are listed according to their rates of return from high to low. The cost of capital or a cutoff rate can establish a minimum acceptable rate of return. Then, projects are selected by moving down the list until the budget is exhausted or the cutoff rate is reached.

Reinvestment Assumption. The internal rate of return method assumes that cash flows are reinvested at the project's internal rate of return. While this assumption may be realistic for cost of capital rates, it may be wishful thinking for projects with high internal rates of return. This issue, however, is best left to finance texts and courses.

High Discount Rates. Applicable to present value methods is a general business concern about high discount rates. Any project with significant long-term payoffs will not appear strong because the long-term payoffs will be discounted so severely. Even huge cash inflows due ten years or more into the future appear to be less valuable than minor cost savings earned in the first year of another project. Concern exists that high discount rates encourage managers to think only short term, to ignore research, market innovation, and creative product development projects, and to ignore long-term environmental effects. These are strategic impacts of using accounting tools and policies in wise or unwise ways.

The Payback Period Method

The **payback period method** is a "quick and dirty" evaluation of capital investment projects. It is likely that no major firm makes investment decisions based solely on the payback period, but many ask for the measure as part of their analyses. The payback period method asks:

How fast do we get our initial cash investment back?

No ROR is given, only a time period. If annual cash flows are equal, the **payback period** is found as follows:

Net initial investment ÷ Annual net cash inflow = Payback period

If the investment is $120,000 and annual net cash inflow is $48,000, the payback period is 2.5 years. We do not know how long the project will last nor what cash flows exist after the 2.5 years. It might last 20 years or 20 days beyond the payback point.

If annual cash flows are uneven, the payback period is found by recovering the investment cost year by year. In the Quartz Timepieces example:

Year	Cash Flows	Unrecovered Investment
0	$(95,000)	$95,000
1	40,000	55,000
2	40,000	15,000
3	20,000	0

In Year 3, the cost is totally recovered, using only $15,000 of Year 3's $20,000 (75 percent). The payback period is 2.75 years.

The payback method is viewed as a "bail-out" risk measure. How long do we need to stick with the project just to get our initial investment money back? It is used frequently in short-term projects where the impact of present values is not great. Such projects as efficiency improvements, cost reductions, and personnel savings are examples. Several major companies set an arbitrary payback period, such as six months, for certain types of cost-saving projects.

Using the Payback Reciprocal to Estimate the IRR.   The payback period can be used to estimate a project's IRR, assuming a fairly high ROR (over 20 percent) and project life that is more than twice the payback period. For example, if a $40,000 investment earns $10,000 per year and could last 12 years, the payback period is four years. The reciprocal of the payback period is 1 ÷ 4 and gives an IRR estimate of 25 percent. From Table 2 for 12 years, the present value factor (payback period) of 4 indicates a rate of return of between 22 and 24 percent. The payback reciprocal will always overstate the IRR somewhat. If the project's life is very long, say 50 years, the **payback reciprocal** is an almost perfect estimator. (See the present value factor of 4.000 for 25 percent and 50 periods on Table 2.)

Ranking Projects.   When the payback period is used to rank projects, the shortest payback period is best. Thus, all projects are listed from low to high. A firm's policy may say that no project with a payback period of over four years will be considered. This acts like a cutoff point. Then, projects would be selected until capital funds are exhausted. The major complaints about the payback period method are that it ignores:

1. The time value of money.
2. The cash flows beyond the payback point.

These are serious deficiencies, but the method is easily applied and is a rough gauge of potential success.

Accounting Rate of Return Method

This method:

1. Ignores the time value of money.
2. Presumes uniform flows of income over the project's life.
3. Includes depreciation expense and other accounting accruals in the calculation of project income, losing the purity of cash flows.

In fact, we only discuss this approach because many internal corporate performance reporting systems use accrual accounting data. Many companies use discounted cash flows for investment decisions but report actual results using accrual income and expense measures.

The **accounting rate of return (ARR) method** attempts to measure *accrual net income* from the project. The ARR subtracts depreciation expense on the incremental investment from the annual net cash inflows. Other accrual adjustments may also be made. The general formula is:

$$\frac{\text{Annual net operating cash inflow} - \text{Annual depreciation expense on incremental investment}}{\text{Average investment}} = \text{Accounting rate of return}$$

The average investment, the denominator, is the average of the net initial investment and the ending investment base ($0 if no salvage value exists). This is the average book value of the investment over its life. Some analysts prefer to use the original cost of the investment or replacement cost as the denominator. The numerator is the incremental accrual net income from the project. To illustrate, assume the following:

Initial investment	$110,000	Salvage value	$10,000
Annual cash inflow . . .	35,000	Project life	5 years
Depreciation expense . .	20,000		

ARR calculations are:

$$\frac{\$35,000 - \$20,000}{(\$110,000 + \$10,000) \div 2} = \frac{\$15,000}{\$60,000} = 25 \text{ percent}$$

The 25 percent must be viewed relative to other projects' ARR and cannot be compared to present value rates of return. For ranking purposes, projects are ranked from high to low. An arbitrary percentage may be set as a minimum rate, similar to an accrual return on equity.

Another problem with the ARR is the impression it gives of an increasing ROR on an annual basis as an asset grows older. A manager would see this project's performance on annual investment center responsibility reports as follows:

	Average Investment (Book Value)	Project Net Income	Annual ARR
Year 1	$100,000	$15,000	15.0%
Year 2	80,000	15,000	18.8
Year 3	60,000	15,000	25.0
Year 4	40,000	15,000	37.5
Year 5	20,000	15,000	75.0

The average annual book value declines each year; and net income is assumed to remain constant. As the asset gets older, the ARR increases. It is tempting for managers to reject any proposal that will make their performance reports look less favorable. This is particularly true when their bonuses are tied to accrual accounting performance numbers. Managers will be biased toward sticking with older assets with higher accounting rates of return. They forego new investments that offer new technology, lower operating costs, and greater productivity.

*E*THICAL ISSUES AND PRESSURES ON MANAGEMENT

In many corporate situations, managers are under pressure to earn high rates of return in the short run. All capital investment analysis depends on the credibility of future cash-flow estimates. Unlike past facts which are measured very objectively, future values are based on predictions, opinions, judgments,

C O N T E M P O R A R Y   P R A C T I C E   1 2 . 1

Capital Budgeting in Major Lodging Chains

In a 1990 study, major lodging chains were surveyed about their capital budgeting methods. The reported frequencies of use of each method for making four types of investment decisions were:

	ARR	Payback	NPV	IRR
Asset replacement ...	13%	46%	19%	35%
Facility renovation ...	17	35	28	44
Facility expansion	20	39	37	57
Property acquisition ..	15	37	46	57

When compared to a similar 1980 study, IRR tripled in its popularity, NPV nearly doubled, and payback declined slightly. Notice that more than one method was used since the sum of the four methods exceeds 100 percent. Payback was often used as supporting information but not as the major decision variable.

Source: Schmidgall, R. S., and J. Damitio, "Current Capital Budgeting Practices of Major Lodging Chains," *Real Estate Review*, Fall 1990, pp. 40-45.

and perhaps wishful thinking. The quality of decision making rests on a premise that future estimates are made objectively and in good faith. A manager trying to get a needed project approved may unintentionally develop estimates that are too optimistic because of the manager's enthusiastic support of the idea. On the other hand, a manager can easily bias a project's estimates on purpose.

Company policies compound the problem by setting very high hurdle or cutoff rates that encourage proposal developers to overestimate future revenues and underestimate investment costs. Managers have been heard to say, "Show me the hurdles, and I'll make the project jump over them." In fact, a vicious cycle may develop—higher hurdles, more bias in estimates, higher hurdles, and so on.

To control these problems, many firms have special analysts that evaluate proposals independent of the sponsoring managers. Others perform post-audits (discussed in Chapter 13) to compare actual results to the estimates. Tying responsibility for the project's promises to the manager's future evaluations may help solve some of these problems.

The second issue is the severe pressure on managers to show growth in immediate earnings. Key investment analysts and shareholders watch quarterly earnings announcements and other short-term information about the company to make almost daily buy and sell decisions. Capital investment proposals include a mix of short-term and long-term projects. Short-term projects often emphasize cost savings, which may be worthwhile but not strategically important. Long-term projects include research and development and new technology. Unfortunately, these projects often have long payback periods but with very significant future potential. If hurdle rates are high, long-term projects will rarely rank as high as short-term projects. The long-run competitiveness and success of a firm may be damaged severely if its managers are biased toward short-term rewards.

C O N T E M P O R A R Y   P R A C T I C E   1 2 . 2

Political Risk in International Capital Investments

In a recent interview survey, managers indicate that political events and changes in political relationships between countries are important risks in evaluating capital investments in other countries. But they also report that the evaluation is subjective rather than formal. Little use is made of external consultants. And these decisions are often made without determining if the expected ROR is high enough to compensate for the higher international risk.

Source: Goddard, S., "Political Risk in International Capital Budgeting," *Managerial Finance*, Vol. 16, Issue 2, 1990, pp. 7-12.

Japanese firms, for a number of reasons, are said to have a much longer term investment horizon. They are less concerned about the immediate profitability of new products and markets. Market penetration and market share are more important. This allows managers to develop a strategic plan that emphasizes the long-run success of the firm.

T AXES AND DEPRECIATION

The illustrations have thus far ignored income taxes. Also, depreciation, being a noncash expense, was used only in the accounting rate of return method. These factors impact capital budgeting significantly.

Income Taxes and Capital Investments

Except for nonprofit organizations, the real world is a tax-paying world, and capital investment analysis must consider taxes. Taxation rules are complex and impact many cash flows. Taxable income and gains include:

- Incremental revenues minus incremental expenses.
- Incremental operating expense savings.
- Gains on sales of the old assets now and of the new assets at the project's end.

Incremental expenses and losses reduce taxes and include:

- Incremental operating expenses.
- Losses on sales of assets now and at the end of a project's life.

The tax rate should be the expected **marginal tax rate** for the future year being analyzed. The marginal tax rate is the tax rate applied to any incremental taxable income. While the corporate federal income tax maximum rate is currently 35 percent, many companies also pay state and local income taxes. For simplicity, we assume that the marginal income tax rate is 40 percent for all income tax-related issues. Clearly, income taxes reduce the ROR on capital projects by reducing net cash inflows.

Depreciation Expense

The only role that depreciation expense plays in cash-flow-based capital investment analysis is as a deduction for calculating income taxes. If taxes are ignored or are not applicable, as in nonprofit organizations, depreciation expense is also ignored.

The Internal Revenue Code uses the terms **Accelerated Cost Recovery System (ACRS)** and the **Modified Accelerated Cost Recovery System (MACRS)** to depreciate tangible assets for tax purposes. ACRS, MACRS, and their impacts are discussed in Chapter 13. To simplify our depreciation expense and taxation discussions, we assume: *(1) straight-line depreciation is used; (2) depreciation expense calculations ignore salvage values; and (3) salvage values are net of tax consequences.*

To understand the tax and depreciation expense impacts, let us look again at the Quartz Timepieces example in Figure 12.2 and now apply a tax rate of 40 percent to the incremental operating cash flows. For now, we ignore the effects of depreciation. This is shown in Figure 12.3.

As Figure 12.3 shows, suddenly a very profitable project (just under 30 percent ROR on a no-tax basis) now has a negative net present value using a 12 percent discount rate. We assume that the overhaul in Year 3 is a deductible expense, salvage value is net of taxes, and inventory recovery has no tax effects.

The Tax Shield. Depreciation expense is a noncash expense, is a legitimate deduction for tax purposes, and creates a **tax shield**. By reducing taxable income, cash paid for taxes is reduced. Depreciation saves cash by reducing tax payments. Thus, if depreciation expense increases, tax payments decrease. Cash outflow is reduced. A reduced outflow has the same effect as an increased inflow. Remember, cash was paid out when the asset was originally purchased.

The depreciation impact is seen in the Quartz example. The increase in depreciable assets is $92,000 ($100,000 - $8,000) and is spread over five

FIGURE 12.3 Net Present Value Analysis With Taxes but Without Depreciation

Cash Flows:	Today	Year 1	Year 2	Year 3	Year 4	Year 5
		*Life of the Project*				
Net investment cash flows	$(95,000)					$13,000
Annual cash inflows (taxable)		$40,000	$40,000	$20,000	$40,000	$40,000
Taxes on taxable income (40%).		(16,000)	(16,000)	(8,000)	(16,000)	(16,000)
Aftertax cash inflows...............		$24,000	$24,000	$12,000	$24,000	$24,000
Net annual cash flows..............	$(95,000)	$24,000	$24,000	$12,000	$24,000	$37,000
Present value factors at 12%	x 1.000	x .893	x .797	x .712	x .636	x .567
Present values at 12%	$(95,000)	$21,432	$19,128	$ 8,544	$15,264	$20,979
Sum of PVs for Years 1 to 5	85,347					
Net present value	$ (9,653)					

years.   Currently, salvage value is ignored in most IRS depreciation calculations.   Assuming straight-line depreciation, the *incremental* depreciation expense is $18,400 per year.   Aftertax cash flows are:

	Year 1
Incremental revenues	$ 55,000 *
- Incremental cost of sales	(30,000) *
+ Operating cost savings	15,000 *
Incremental cash inflow	$ 40,000
- Depreciation expense	(18,400)
Taxable income	$ 21,600
- Incremental taxes (40 percent)	(8,640) *
Aftertax project net income	$ 12,960
+ Add back depreciation expense	18,400
Aftertax cash inflow	$ 31,360

* Cash flows

The project's Year 1 aftertax profit, $12,960, and the incremental depreciation expense, $18,400, are summed to find the Year 1 aftertax cash flow.   This is similar to the indirect method of finding cash flow from operations on the statement of cash flows discussed in Chapter 18.   Tax cash outflows for the entire project are added to the Figure 12.4 analysis.   The increased tax deduction for depreciation moves the net present value of the project from a negative $9,653 to a positive $16,879, a $26,532 change.   This is the present value of the depreciation expense tax savings and can be determined as follows:

Depreciation Expense	x	Tax Rate	x	Present Value Factor (for 5 years at 12 percent)	=	Present Value of Tax Shield
$18,400	x	.40	x	3.605	=	$26,533

FIGURE 12.4   **Net Present Value Analysis With Depreciation and Taxes**

Cash Flows:	Today	Year 1	Year 2	Year 3	Year 4	Year 5
		Life of the Project				
Net investment cash flows	$ (95,000)					$13,000
Annual cash flows (taxable).		$40,000	$40,000	$20,000	$40,000	$40,000
Incremental income taxes		(8,640)	(8,640)	(640)	(8,640)	(8,640)
Aftertax cash inflows.		$31,360	$31,360	$19,360	$31,360	$31,360
Net annual cash flows.	$ (95,000)	$31,360	$31,360	$19,360	$31,360	$44,360
Present value factors at 12%	x 1.000	x .893	x .797	x .712	x .636	x .567
Present values at 12%	$ (95,000)	$28,004	$24,994	$13,784	$19,945	$25,152
Sum of PVs for Years 1 to 5	111,879					
Net present value	$ 16,879					

Accelerated Depreciation Benefits. The cash saving power of depreciation can be increased by using **accelerated depreciation** to deduct more depreciation earlier in a project's life. Deferring taxes has a time value of money. Merely by changing depreciation methods, the net present value increases. This is strictly from speeding up the depreciation expense deductions and the time value of the tax deferrals. Chapter 13 will further discuss the advantages of accelerated depreciation and shorter tax lives for assets. The MACRS methods now in use provide both of these benefits.

COST OF CAPITAL

Throughout our discussions, cost of capital is mentioned frequently. Long-term money has a cost, either real, as in interest paid on bonds payable, or an opportunity cost, as in the use of retained earnings. A basic approach is explained here to show the source of this rate.

A **weighted-average cost of capital** pools a firm's long-term funds and is used because the relative amount of each funds source affects the average cost. Debt generally is less costly than equity since the creditor assumes less risk and interest is deductible for tax purposes. If a firm has a pretax debt cost of 10 percent and a 40 percent tax rate, the aftertax cost is 6 percent. Dividends, on the other hand, are not deductible for tax purposes and are profit distributions to owners, not a business expense.

Assume that a firm has the following long-term funds structure and cost of funds:

	Book Value	Mix Percentage	Pretax Cost	Aftertax Cost	Weighted Average
Bonds payable	$10,000,000	25%	10%	6%	1.5%
Preferred stock	4,000,000	10	12	12	1.2
Common stock	14,000,000	35	18	18	6.3
Retained earnings	12,000,000	30	18	18	5.4
Total long-term funds . .	$40,000,000	100%			14.4%

The pretax cost percentages come from financial markets calculations. The weighted-average cost of capital is 14.4 percent. Often, financially strong companies have low cost of funds. High risk, financially unstable, or new firms have high costs.

SUMMARY

Capital investment decisions are critical to the firm's long-term success. The relevant data for making investment decisions are incremental cash flows, using criteria established in Chapter 11. Capital investments generally have multiperiod cash flows, requiring the use of the time value of money. The opportunity cost of cash to be received in the future can be a significant variable in measuring returns.

Four methods are discussed to evaluate the cash flows. Two methods use present values for all cash flows:

- Net present value, where a rate of return is set and decisions are made based on whether the net present value is positive or negative.

- Internal rate of return, where the rate of return is found by setting the initial investment equal to the present value of future net cash inflows.

Two other methods discussed that do not use the time value of money are the payback period and the accounting rate of return methods.

Rarely are funds available to finance all attractive projects. Projects are selected based on rankings of their relative attractiveness. The cost of capital is often used to develop a minimum acceptable rate of return.

*P*ROBLEM FOR REVIEW

Baxter Insurance is evaluating a new processor to prepare personalized reports for insurance clients. Baxter will serve 200,000 clients per year for the foreseeable future. The report is currently prepared on a 3-year old machine that could be used for another five years. The machine cost $160,000 new and was to last eight years. It is now worth $85,000 net of taxes, or it will have a $15,000 salvage value net of taxes in five years.

The new machine will have a useful life of five years, cost $275,000, and have a $25,000 salvage value net of taxes. Comparative cash operating expenses are:

	Old Machine	New Machine
Variable cost	$2.00 per client	$1.70 per client
Fixed cost	$100,000	$80,000

Assume straight-line depreciation, a 40 percent tax rate, and a 14 percent cost of capital.

Required:

1. Find the relevant cash flows for the machine replacement decision.
2. Using the NPV method, should the new machine be acquired?
3. Find the IRR, the payback period, and the ARR.

Solution:

1. The differential cash flows are:

		Life of the Project				
Cash Flows:	**Today**	**Year 1**	**Year 2**	**Year 3**	**Year 4**	**Year 5**
New machine	$(275,000)					
Sale of old machine	85,000					
Incremental salvage value						$ 10,000[1]
Variable cost savings		$ 60,000[2]	$ 60,000	$ 60,000	$ 60,000	60,000
Fixed cost savings		20,000[3]	20,000	20,000	20,000	20,000
Incremental income taxes.		(18,000)[4]	(18,000)	(18,000)	(18,000)	(18,000)
Net cash flows	$(190,000)	$ 62,000	$ 62,000	$ 62,000	$ 62,000	$ 72,000

---

[1] Salvage value of the new machine minus the salvage value of the old machine.

[2] Variable cost savings are $0.30 per unit on 200,000 units, $60,000 per year.

[3] Fixed cost savings are $20,000 per year ($100,000 - $80,000).

[4] Incremental tax payment is based on:

Variable cost savings	$ 60,000	Annual depreciation expense:	
Fixed cost savings	20,000	Old machine ($160,000 ÷ 8) . .	$ 20,000
Incremental depreciation	(35,000)	New machine ($275,000 ÷ 5) .	55,000
Incremental taxable income	$ 45,000	Incremental depreciation	$ 35,000
Incremental cash taxes (40%) . .	$ 18,000		

2. Using the Part (1) cash flows, the net present value method shows:

		Life of the Project				
Cash Flows:	**Today**	Year 1	Year 2	Year 3	Year 4	Year 5
Net cash flows.	$(190,000)	$62,000	$62,000	$62,000	$62,000	$72,000
Present value factors at 14%.	x 1.000	x .877	x .769	x .675	x .592	x .519
Present value of cash flows	$(190,000)	$54,374	$47,678	$41,850	$36,704	$37,368
Sum of PVs for Years 1 to 5	217,974					
Net present value	$ 27,974					

The investment earns a positive net present value. If a 14 percent rate of return or better is the goal, we should approve the investment.

3. To find the **internal rate of return**, we use the trial and error method. Using various discount rates, a negative net present value is found at 20 percent:

	18%	20%
Net present value.	$8,244	$(538)

The rate of return is between 18 and 20 percent, actually nearer to 20 percent. Using a business calculator, the rate is determined to be 19.88 percent.

The **payback period** is:

$$\$190,000 \div \$62,000 = 3.06 \text{ years}$$

The **accounting rate of return** is:

$$\frac{(\$60,000 + \$20,000 - \$35,000 - \$18,000)}{[(\$190,000 + \$10,000) \div 2]} = 27.0 \text{ percent}$$

❖ APPENDIX

T HE TIME VALUE OF MONEY

Dollars promised in the future are not equal to dollars received now. When given a choice, we all prefer getting $100 today versus $100 two years from now. Dollars due in different time periods should be valued on a uniform scale that recognizes the **time value of money**. **Present value** converts future dollars into current dollar equivalents. **Future value** converts all dollars into equivalent dollars as of some future date. To find these values, we need an interest rate and the number of time periods between today and the future cash flows.

Money has earning power. Dollars today grow to a larger sum through investment. The investment principal plus **compound interest** is the future value (FV). The future value of $100 in two years, with interest compounded at the rate of 10 percent annually, is $121. The formula for the future value of $1 is:

$$FV = (1 + i)^n$$

where   i = interest rate

n = number of years

In the example, the future value is computed as follows:

$$FV \text{ of } \$1 = (1.10)^2 = \$1.21$$

$$FV \text{ of } \$100 = \$100 \times \$1.21 \textbf{ or } \$121$$

An investor who is happy with a 10 percent rate of return (ROR) looks at the receipt of $121 in two years as equivalent to $100 today, assuming certainty. This investor is indifferent between $100 today or $121 in two years.

The interest rate influences the values.[1] If a decision maker has a choice of investments, the preferred choice is the investment with the highest ROR. The reason, of course, is that the investment with the highest ROR will yield the largest future amount or require the smallest current investment. For example, an alternative investment will earn a 15 percent ROR. Assuming certainty, the future value in two years of the $100 at 15 percent is:

$$\$100 \times (1.15)^2 = \$100 \times 1.3225 = \$132.25$$

Since $132.25 (future value of $100 in two years at 15 percent) is larger than $121, the project earning 15 percent is preferred to the 10 percent project.

Present Value of Money

Because decisions are made today and because future cash flows come in many different patterns and time periods, present values of future dollars are more useful and easier to analyze. It is conventional to use present value analysis.

How much money must we invest today to earn a given dollar amount in the future? Or, given an investment, how much will be earned in the future? Or, given an investment and a set of future cash inflows, what is the ROR? Answers to these questions can be found by computing the present value of the future cash flows and comparing it with the amount invested.

The **present value** (PV) of a future value can be computed by multiplying the future value by the present value of $1. The present value of $1 is:

$$PV \text{ of } \$1 = 1 \div (1 + i)^n$$

Assume, for example, that $121 is needed in two years; and the rate of interest is 10 percent. How much must be invested today to have $121 after two years? We first determine the present value of $1 due in two years with interest compounded annually at 10 percent:

$$PV \text{ of } \$1 \text{ for 2 years at 10 percent} = 1 \div (1.10)^2 = 0.8264$$

---

[1] Calculations to equate future dollars should not be confused with price-level adjustments. The two calculations are made for different purposes. Differences in timing must be recognized even if the price level does not change.

Next, we multiply by the future value:

$$\text{PV of \$121 for 2 years at 10 percent} = \$121 \times 0.8264 = \$100$$

The computation can be viewed as:

$$\$121 \div 1.10 = \$110 \text{ is the value at the end of Year 1}$$

$$\$110 \div 1.10 = \$100 \text{ is the investment at the start of Year 1, or today.}$$

This is summarized as follows:

$$\$121 \div (1.10)^2 \quad \textbf{\textit{or}} \quad [1 \div (1.10)^2] \times \$121 = \$100$$

The process of reducing a future amount to a present value is called **discounting**. The present value is sometimes called the **discounted value**. The rate of interest is the **discount rate**. The 0.8264 is called the **present value factor** or **discount factor**.

It is seldom necessary to calculate either future values or present values as done here. Calculators and spreadsheet software easily perform these functions. Tables 1 and 2 give present value factors for various discount (interest) rates for various time periods expressed in years. Table 1 gives the present value of \$1 to be received at the end of the various time periods at interest or discount rates shown across the top row of the table. Thus, it is a tabulation of the factor $1 \div (1 + i)^n$, where n is the number of years and i is the discount rate. The factor for two years at 10 percent is 0.826, and the present value (PV) of \$121 to be received in two years is calculated as follows:

$$\text{PV} = \$121 \times 0.826 = \$100 \text{ (rounded)}$$

The discount factors appearing in Tables 1 and 2 are rounded to the third digit, which is sufficient precision for most capital investment problems.

The Present Value of a Series of Future Cash Flows

Often, a series of future cash inflows are earned from an investment instead of one cash inflow. As an example, a machine costing \$3,500 today is forecast to generate cash inflows of \$1,000 each year for five years. The time interval for most decisions is annual, but any time interval (a day, week, month, quarter, etc.) can be used as long as the interest rate (i) is adjusted to correspond to the time period.

Calculating present values depends on whether the series of cash flows involves equal or unequal amounts. An **annuity** refers to a series of equal cash flows. In either case, however, the underlying concepts are the same. The present value of a series is the sum of the present values of the individual amounts. The present value of the five annual receipts of \$1,000 using a 10 percent discount rate is computed as follows:

Year	Computation		Explanation
1	$\$1,000 \times (1 \div 1.10)$	=	\$ 909 PV of \$1,000 received at the end of Year 1
2	$1,000 \times [1 \div (1.10)^2]$	=	826 PV of \$1,000 received at the end of Year 2
3	$1,000 \times [1 \div (1.10)^3]$	=	751 PV of \$1,000 received at the end of Year 3
4	$1,000 \times [1 \div (1.10)^4]$	=	683 PV of \$1,000 received at the end of Year 4
5	$1,000 \times [1 \div (1.10)^5]$	=	621 PV of \$1,000 received at the end of Year 5
			\$3,790 PV of an annuity of \$1,000 for 5 years

Present Value Tables

Table 1
Present Value of $1

Where: P = Present value factor
i = Interest rate
n = Number of periods

$$P = \frac{1}{(1+i)^n}$$

Periods (n)	1%	2%	4%	5%	6%	8%	10%	12%	14%	15%	16%	18%	20%	22%	24%	25%	30%	40%
0	1.000	1.000	1.000	1.000	1.000	1.000	1.000	1.000	1.000	1.000	1.000	1.000	1.000	1.000	1.000	1.000	1.000	1.000
1	0.990	0.980	0.962	0.952	0.943	0.926	0.909	0.893	0.877	0.870	0.862	0.847	0.833	0.820	0.806	0.800	0.769	0.714
2	0.980	0.961	0.925	0.907	0.890	0.857	0.826	0.797	0.769	0.756	0.743	0.718	0.694	0.672	0.650	0.640	0.592	0.510
3	0.971	0.942	0.889	0.864	0.840	0.794	0.751	0.712	0.675	0.658	0.641	0.609	0.579	0.551	0.524	0.512	0.455	0.364
4	0.961	0.924	0.855	0.823	0.792	0.735	0.683	0.636	0.592	0.572	0.552	0.516	0.482	0.451	0.423	0.410	0.350	0.260
5	0.951	0.906	0.822	0.784	0.747	0.681	0.621	0.567	0.519	0.497	0.476	0.437	0.402	0.370	0.341	0.328	0.269	0.186
6	0.942	0.888	0.790	0.746	0.705	0.630	0.564	0.507	0.456	0.432	0.410	0.370	0.335	0.303	0.275	0.262	0.207	0.133
7	0.933	0.871	0.760	0.711	0.665	0.583	0.513	0.452	0.400	0.376	0.354	0.314	0.279	0.249	0.222	0.210	0.159	0.095
8	0.923	0.853	0.731	0.677	0.627	0.540	0.467	0.404	0.351	0.327	0.305	0.266	0.233	0.204	0.179	0.168	0.123	0.068
9	0.914	0.837	0.703	0.645	0.592	0.500	0.424	0.361	0.308	0.284	0.263	0.225	0.194	0.167	0.144	0.134	0.094	0.048
10	0.905	0.820	0.676	0.614	0.558	0.463	0.386	0.322	0.270	0.247	0.227	0.191	0.162	0.137	0.116	0.107	0.073	0.035
11	0.896	0.804	0.650	0.585	0.527	0.429	0.350	0.287	0.237	0.215	0.195	0.162	0.135	0.112	0.094	0.086	0.056	0.025
12	0.887	0.788	0.625	0.557	0.497	0.397	0.319	0.257	0.208	0.187	0.168	0.137	0.112	0.092	0.076	0.069	0.043	0.018
13	0.879	0.773	0.601	0.530	0.469	0.368	0.290	0.229	0.182	0.163	0.145	0.116	0.093	0.075	0.061	0.055	0.033	0.013
14	0.870	0.758	0.577	0.505	0.442	0.340	0.263	0.205	0.160	0.141	0.125	0.099	0.078	0.062	0.049	0.044	0.025	0.009
15	0.861	0.743	0.555	0.481	0.417	0.315	0.239	0.183	0.140	0.123	0.108	0.084	0.065	0.051	0.040	0.035	0.020	0.006
16	0.853	0.728	0.534	0.458	0.394	0.292	0.218	0.163	0.123	0.107	0.093	0.071	0.054	0.042	0.032	0.028	0.015	0.005
17	0.844	0.714	0.513	0.436	0.371	0.270	0.198	0.146	0.108	0.093	0.080	0.060	0.045	0.034	0.026	0.023	0.012	0.003
18	0.836	0.700	0.494	0.416	0.350	0.250	0.180	0.130	0.095	0.081	0.069	0.051	0.038	0.028	0.021	0.018	0.009	0.002
19	0.828	0.686	0.475	0.396	0.331	0.232	0.164	0.116	0.083	0.070	0.060	0.043	0.031	0.023	0.017	0.014	0.007	0.002
20	0.820	0.673	0.456	0.377	0.312	0.215	0.149	0.104	0.073	0.061	0.051	0.037	0.026	0.019	0.014	0.012	0.005	0.001
21	0.811	0.660	0.439	0.359	0.294	0.199	0.135	0.093	0.064	0.053	0.044	0.031	0.022	0.015	0.011	0.009	0.004	0.001
22	0.803	0.647	0.422	0.342	0.278	0.184	0.123	0.083	0.056	0.046	0.038	0.026	0.018	0.013	0.009	0.007	0.003	0.001
23	0.795	0.634	0.406	0.326	0.262	0.170	0.112	0.074	0.049	0.040	0.033	0.022	0.015	0.010	0.007	0.006	0.002	0.000
24	0.788	0.622	0.390	0.310	0.247	0.158	0.102	0.066	0.043	0.035	0.028	0.019	0.013	0.008	0.006	0.005	0.002	0.000
25	0.780	0.610	0.375	0.295	0.233	0.146	0.092	0.059	0.038	0.030	0.024	0.016	0.010	0.007	0.005	0.004	0.001	0.000
30	0.742	0.552	0.308	0.231	0.174	0.099	0.057	0.033	0.020	0.015	0.012	0.007	0.004	0.003	0.002	0.001	0.000	0.000
35	0.706	0.500	0.253	0.181	0.130	0.068	0.036	0.019	0.010	0.008	0.006	0.003	0.002	0.001	0.001	0.000	0.000	0.000
40	0.672	0.453	0.208	0.142	0.097	0.046	0.022	0.011	0.005	0.004	0.003	0.001	0.001	0.000	0.000	0.000	0.000	0.000
45	0.639	0.410	0.171	0.111	0.073	0.031	0.014	0.006	0.003	0.002	0.001	0.001	0.000	0.000	0.000	0.000	0.000	0.000
50	0.608	0.372	0.141	0.087	0.054	0.021	0.009	0.003	0.001	0.001	0.001	0.000	0.000	0.000	0.000	0.000	0.000	0.000
∞	0.000	0.000	0.000	0.000	0.000	0.000	0.000	0.000	0.000	0.000	0.000	0.000	0.000	0.000	0.000	0.000	0.000	0.000

Present Value Tables

Table 2
Present Value of $1 Received Periodically for n Periods

$$P = \dfrac{1 - \dfrac{1}{(1 + i)^n}}{i}$$

Where:
P = Present value factor
i = Interest rate
n = Number of periods

Periods (n)	1%	2%	4%	5%	6%	8%	10%	12%	14%	15%	16%	18%	20%	22%	24%	25%	30%	40%
0	1.000	1.000	1.000	1.000	1.000	1.000	1.000	1.000	1.000	1.000	1.000	1.000	1.000	1.000	1.000	1.000	1.000	1.000
1	0.990	0.980	0.962	0.952	0.943	0.926	0.909	0.893	0.877	0.870	0.862	0.847	0.833	0.820	0.806	0.800	0.769	0.714
2	1.970	1.942	1.886	1.859	1.833	1.783	1.736	1.690	1.647	1.626	1.605	1.566	1.528	1.492	1.457	1.440	1.361	1.224
3	2.941	2.884	2.775	2.723	2.673	2.577	2.487	2.402	2.322	2.283	2.246	2.174	2.106	2.042	1.981	1.952	1.816	1.589
4	3.902	3.808	3.630	3.546	3.465	3.312	3.170	3.037	2.914	2.855	2.798	2.690	2.589	2.494	2.404	2.362	2.166	1.849
5	4.853	4.713	4.452	4.329	4.212	3.993	3.791	3.605	3.433	3.352	3.274	3.127	2.991	2.864	2.745	2.689	2.436	2.035
6	5.795	5.601	5.242	5.076	4.917	4.623	4.355	4.111	3.889	3.784	3.685	3.498	3.326	3.167	3.020	2.951	2.643	2.168
7	6.728	6.472	6.002	5.786	5.582	5.206	4.868	4.564	4.288	4.160	4.039	3.812	3.605	3.416	3.242	3.161	2.802	2.263
8	7.652	7.325	6.733	6.463	6.210	5.747	5.335	4.968	4.639	4.487	4.344	4.078	3.837	3.619	3.421	3.329	2.925	2.331
9	8.566	8.162	7.435	7.108	6.802	6.247	5.759	5.328	4.946	4.772	4.607	4.303	4.031	3.786	3.566	3.463	3.019	2.379
10	9.471	8.983	8.111	7.722	7.360	6.710	6.145	5.650	5.216	5.019	4.833	4.494	4.192	3.923	3.682	3.571	3.092	2.414
11	10.368	9.787	8.760	8.306	7.887	7.139	6.495	5.938	5.453	5.234	5.029	4.656	4.327	4.035	3.776	3.656	3.147	2.438
12	11.255	10.575	9.385	8.863	8.384	7.536	6.814	6.194	5.660	5.421	5.197	4.793	4.439	4.127	3.851	3.725	3.190	2.456
13	12.134	11.348	9.986	9.394	8.853	7.904	7.103	6.424	5.842	5.583	5.342	4.910	4.533	4.203	3.912	3.780	3.223	2.469
14	13.004	12.106	10.563	9.899	9.295	8.244	7.367	6.628	6.002	5.724	5.468	5.008	4.611	4.265	3.962	3.824	3.249	2.478
15	13.865	12.849	11.118	10.380	9.712	8.559	7.606	6.811	6.142	5.847	5.575	5.092	4.675	4.315	4.001	3.859	3.268	2.484
16	14.718	13.578	11.652	10.838	10.106	8.851	7.824	6.974	6.265	5.954	5.668	5.162	4.730	4.357	4.033	3.887	3.283	2.489
17	15.562	14.292	12.166	11.274	10.477	9.122	8.022	7.120	6.373	6.047	5.749	5.222	4.775	4.391	4.059	3.910	3.295	2.492
18	16.398	14.992	12.659	11.690	10.828	9.372	8.201	7.250	6.467	6.128	5.818	5.273	4.812	4.419	4.080	3.928	3.304	2.494
19	17.226	15.678	13.134	12.085	11.158	9.604	8.365	7.366	6.550	6.198	5.877	5.316	4.843	4.442	4.097	3.942	3.311	2.496
20	18.046	16.351	13.590	12.462	11.470	9.818	8.514	7.469	6.623	6.259	5.929	5.353	4.870	4.460	4.110	3.954	3.316	2.497
21	18.857	17.011	14.029	12.821	11.764	10.017	8.649	7.562	6.687	6.312	5.973	5.384	4.891	4.476	4.121	3.963	3.320	2.498
22	19.660	17.658	14.451	13.163	12.042	10.201	8.772	7.645	6.743	6.359	6.011	5.410	4.909	4.488	4.130	3.970	3.323	2.498
23	20.456	18.292	14.857	13.489	12.303	10.371	8.883	7.718	6.792	6.399	6.044	5.432	4.925	4.499	4.137	3.976	3.325	2.499
24	21.243	18.914	15.247	13.799	12.550	10.529	8.985	7.784	6.835	6.434	6.073	5.451	4.937	4.507	4.143	3.981	3.327	2.499
25	22.023	19.523	15.622	14.094	12.783	10.675	9.077	7.843	6.873	6.464	6.097	5.467	4.948	4.514	4.147	3.985	3.329	2.499
30	25.808	22.396	17.292	15.372	13.765	11.258	9.427	8.055	7.003	6.566	6.177	5.517	4.979	4.534	4.160	3.995	3.332	2.500
35	29.409	24.999	18.665	16.374	14.498	11.655	9.644	8.176	7.070	6.617	6.215	5.539	4.992	4.541	4.164	3.998	3.333	2.500
40	32.835	27.355	19.793	17.159	15.046	11.925	9.779	8.244	7.105	6.642	6.233	5.548	4.997	4.544	4.166	3.999	3.333	2.500
45	36.095	29.490	20.720	17.774	15.456	12.108	9.863	8.283	7.123	6.654	6.242	5.552	4.999	4.545	4.166	4.000	3.333	2.500
50	39.196	31.424	21.482	18.256	15.762	12.233	9.915	8.304	7.133	6.661	6.246	5.554	4.999	4.545	4.167	4.000	3.333	2.500
∞	100.00	50.000	25.000	20.000	16.667	12.500	10.000	8.333	7.143	6.667	6.250	5.556	5.000	4.545	4.167	4.000	3.333	2.500

The present value can also be computed as follows:

$$\$1,000 \times \left[\frac{1}{1.10} + \frac{1}{(1.10)^2} + \frac{1}{(1.10)^3} + \frac{1}{(1.10)^4} + \frac{1}{(1.10)^5} \right] = \$3,790$$

The decimal equivalents of the fractions can be found in Table 1 and applied to the annual cash inflow:

$$(.909 + .826 + .751 + .683 + .621) = 3.790$$

$$\$1,000 \times 3.790 = \$3,790$$

Note that the factor, 3.791, can be read from Table 2 using the 10 percent column and the 5-period row. The factors in Table 2 are the sums of the present value factors in Table 1. The difference between 3.790 and 3.791 is due to rounding. The following calculations using interest rates of 8 percent, 10 percent, and 12 percent for five years illustrate this point.

Years	8% Table 1	8% Table 2	10% Table 1	10% Table 2	12% Table 1	12% Table 2
1	0.926		0.909		0.893	
2	0.857		0.826		0.797	
3	0.794		0.751		0.712	
4	0.735		0.683		0.636	
5	0.681		0.621		0.567	
Total	3.993	3.993	3.790*	3.791*	3.605	3.605

* Difference due to rounding.

When calculating, it is easier to add the annual factors and make one computation. Thus, Table 2 is more convenient for evaluating equal cash flows. If the annual cash-flow amounts are not equal, it is necessary to use Table 1.

Present Value Analysis Applied

Assume that we sell machinery and offer financing to our customers using long-term notes payable. When a contract is signed the customer makes two promises:

1. To pay the principal amount (the **face value** of the note) at maturity.
2. To pay interest periodically at the rate stated in the contract.

We can either hold the note (earning interest and collecting the principal at the end of the contract) or sell the contract to an investor to get the cash for the sale now. The contract's market value depends on several factors including the **market rate of interest** for similar contracts. The sum of the present values of the two promises is the contract's market price. As the market rate of interest rises, the contract's value declines, and vice versa.

To illustrate, assume that we sell a $100,000 machine. The buyer signs a 10-year $100,000 contract with an interest rate of 10 percent, paid annually. This contract calls for the following cash payments:

Year	Interest at 10 Percent	Payment of Principal	Total Cash Outflow
1	$10,000		$ 10,000
2	10,000		10,000
. . . .	.	.	.
. . . .	.	.	.
9	10,000		10,000
10	10,000	$100,000	110,000

Suppose that the current market rate of interest is 12 percent. In this case, investors are not willing to buy the contract at face value, because they could earn 12 percent elsewhere. To sell the contract, we must price the contract below face value. Selling at a price below face value allows the investor to increase the rate of return by paying less for the two promises. The selling price and discount are determined as follows:

Promise 1:	$100,000 x .322 (10 periods at 12 percent from Table 1)	$ 32,200
Promise 2:	$ 10,000 x 5.650 (10 payments at 12 percent from Table 2)	56,500
	Proceeds from sale of the contract	$ 88,700
	Discount	$ 11,300

The investor who purchases the contract from us at $88,700 (with a **discount** of $11,300) will earn 12 percent interest on the $88,700 invested. The 12 percent earned is usually called the **yield** or the effective rate of interest. An **effective interest rate** or **yield to maturity** is the rate of interest earned regardless of the compounding period or the stated interest rate.

Likewise, if the current market rate of interest is 8 percent, an investor will pay a **premium** for a contract with a 10 percent interest rate. The selling price and premium are determined as follows:

Promise 1:	$100,000 x .463 (10 periods at 8 percent from Table 1)	$ 46,300
Promise 2:	$ 10,000 x 6.710 (10 payments at 8 percent from Table 2)	67,100
	Proceeds from sale of the contract	$113,400
	Premium	$ 13,400

*T*ERMINOLOGY REVIEW

Accelerated Cost Recovery System (ACRS), *528*
Accelerated depreciation, *530*
Accounting rate of return method (ARR), *524*
Annuity, *534*
Capital budgeting, *515*
Capital investment, *516*
Capital investment decisions, *515*
Compound interest, *533*
Cost of capital, *519*
Cutoff rate, *520*
Desired rate of return, *520*
Discount, *538*
Discount factor, *534*
Discount rate, *520, 534*
Discounted value, *534*
Discounting, *515, 534*
Effective interest rate, *538*
Face value, *537*
Future value, *532*
Hurdle rate, *520*
Internal rate of return method (IRR), *521*

Marginal tax rate, *527*
Market rate of interest, *537*
Minimum acceptable rate of return, *520*
Modified Accelerated Cost Recovery System (MACRS), *528*
Net initial investment, *518*
Net present value method (NPV), *519*
Payback period, *523*
Payback period method, *523*
Payback reciprocal, *524*
Premium, *538*
Present value, *519, 533*
Present value factor, *534*
Profitability index, *521*
Project ranking, *520*
Required rate of return, *520*
Target rate of return, *520*
Tax shield, *528*
Time value of money, *532*
Weighted-average cost of capital, *530*
Yield, *538*
Yield to maturity, *538*

SUGGESTED READINGS

Bennet, R. E., and J. A. Hendricks, "Justifying the Acquisition of Automated Equipment," *Management Accounting*, July 1987, pp. 39-46.

Bierman, Jr., H., and S. C. Schmidt, *The Capital Budgeting Decision*, 7th Edition, MacMillan, New York, NY, 1988.

Haka, S., L. A. Gordon, and G. E. Pinches, "Sophisticated Capital Budgeting Techniques and Firm Performance," *Accounting Review*, Vol. 60, No. 4, 1985, pp. 651-669.

Howell, R. A., S. R. Soucy, and A. H. Seed, *Management Accounting in the New Manufacturing Environment*, Institute of Management Accountants and CAM-I, Montvale, NJ, and Arlington, TX, 1987.

Kaplan, R. S., "Must CIM Be Justified by Faith Alone?" *Harvard Business Review*, March-April 1986, pp. 87-93.

Mensaw, Y. M., and P. J. Miranti, "Capital Expenditure Analysis and Automated Manufacturing Systems: A Review and Synthesis," *Journal of Accounting Literature*, 1989, pp. 181-207.

QUESTIONS FOR REVIEW AND DISCUSSION

1. Why is timing important in a capital investment decision? What is meant by the time value of money?

2. Why do capital investment decisions receive so much management time and attention?

3. What is meant by "net initial investment" in a capital investment decision?

4. Could the net present value method and the internal rate of return use the same interest rate? Explain.

5. Are the returns from an investment the same as the accounting profit? Explain.

6. What are the advantages and disadvantages of the payback method?

7. What are the advantages and disadvantages of the accounting rate of return method?

8. John Bassey, a sales representative for a machine tool company, used the following phrase over and over with his customers: "Buy this thing; depreciate it; and watch the cash come rolling in from Uncle Sam!" What does he mean?

9. Explain the difference between the internal rate of return method and the net present value method.

10. The net present value of a certain investment is zero. Does this mean the investment earns no profit? Explain the significance of a zero net present value.

11. How can project rankings using the internal rate of return and the profitability index differ?

12. Why can the terms cutoff rate, hurdle rate, minimum acceptable rate of return, target rate of return, and desired rate of return be used interchangeably?

13. Explain the tax shield. Tie this explanation to the comment: "Depreciation is a source of cash."

14. How would you estimate the internal rate of return if you know the life of the project? How would you estimate the project's life if you know its internal rate of return?

15. Are the definitions of relevant costs and revenues different for capital investment analysis than the definitions used in Chapter 11? Explain.

16. Doris Myers is buying a car for $12,000. After a downpayment of $3,000, she finances the remainder at 12 percent annual interest with monthly payments. If she signs a 50-month financing contract, what will be her monthly payment?

17. What is the advantage of accelerated depreciation over straight-line depreciation in a capital investment decision?

18. Cash, accounts receivable, and inventory are classified as current assets. How can they be considered part of a long-term capital investment?

19. Knowing the cost of capital is a necessary part of present value analysis. What does it represent? Explain one way to measure it.

20. The formula used to derive the numbers in Table 1 is:

$$P = \frac{1}{(1 + i)^n}$$

Where: P = Present value factor

i = Interest rate

n = Number of periods

Explain the math in words.

E XERCISES

12-1. Time Value of Money.   Walt Zarnoch has won second prize in THE BIG Lottery. Friends who he never knew have offered him several "opportunities of a lifetime." He would like a 14 percent annual return. The lottery prize was a check for $300,000. Among the "opportunities" were:

(1) $50,000 per year for ten years.

(2) $400,000 on the same date in the next U. S. presidential election year.

(3) $20,000 per year for the rest of his life (about 50 years).

(4) A penniless friend told Zarnoch that he wrote him a check for $1,000,000 and has put it "in the mail."

(5) $500,000 to be paid on this same date five years from now.

Required:
After judging uncertainty, which should he select? Explain.

 12-2. Determining the Life of an Investment.   Edward's Electronics is considering expanding its business by adding one more store in Amsterdam. The building and its operating contents will cost F1 million (Dutch florin) and generate about F150,000 in cash inflows each year after taxes. The manager feels the investment should not be made unless the store realizes a 10 percent rate of return on the cash invested.

Required:
For how many years must the store operate to earn a 10 percent return?

12-3. Four Methods.   Crandall Company purchased a farm tractor for $100,000. The cash inflow from using the tractor is expected to be $25,000 per year for eight years. Crandall uses a 15 percent cutoff rate.

Required:
Use straight-line depreciation where needed, and ignore taxes. What is the payback period, the estimated IRR, the NPV, and the ARR?

12-4. Payback Method.   Hanley Company purchased a machine for $125,000 and will depreciate it on a straight-line basis over a 5-year period with an aftertax salvage value of $15,000.   The related cash operating savings, before income taxes, are expected to be $50,000 a year.

Required:
1. Find the payback period ignoring taxes.
2. Assume that Hanley's effective income tax rate is 40 percent and that salvage value is ignored when calculating depreciation.   What is the payback period?

12-5. Different Capital Investment Methods.   Miko Center Company plans to acquire equipment costing $600,000.   Depreciation on the new equipment would be $120,000 each year for five years.   The annual cash inflow before income tax from this equipment has been estimated at $220,000.   The tax rate is 40 percent.

Required:
1. Find the payback period.
2. Find the ARR using the average investment.
3. Find the NPV if Miko's minimum acceptable rate of return is 16 percent.
4. Estimate the IRR from Table 2 (e.g., between 10 and 12 percent).

12-6. Determining the Required Investment.   The Wheeler Company would like to initiate an advertising campaign to increase its annual sales volume.   Data show that the proposed advertising will add $80,000 to the annual cash flow for each of the next two years and $30,000 in the third year.

Required:
What is the maximum amount that Wheeler would invest in this campaign if the company sets a minimum rate-of-return objective of 18 percent?

12-7. Investments With Uneven Cash Flows.   Icon Consolidated has data on two $100,000 investment opportunities.   With only $100,000 in cash available, the owners must decide which is the better opportunity.   The controller has gathered the following data:

Investment 1: $30,000 of cash inflow for each of the first three years and $90,000 for each of the last three years.

Investment 2: $80,000 of cash inflow in the first year, $60,000 in the next four years, and $40,000 in the sixth year.

Required:
If 14 percent ROR is needed, which investment will be preferred?   Why?

12-8. Comparing Alternatives.   The Mohr Company is considering a new popper for one of its portable caramel popcorn stands.   The analysis is narrowed to the "Bang" or the "Pow."   Information on the two devices is:

	Bang	*Pow*
Purchase price	$ 90,000	$ 60,000
Annual cash inflows	34,000	24,000
Salvage value in 5 years	8,000	5,000
Useful life	5 years	5 years

Either device will do the job equally as well.   Mohr uses a 16 percent cost of capital.   Ignore taxes.

Required:
1. Which machine has the higher NPV?
2. Using the profitability index, which machine is more attractive?
3. If Mohr has $180,000 to invest in popping machines, what should it do?   Why?

 12-9. Equipment Replacement.   By replacing an old refrigeration unit, Ann Bacon of Bacon's Produce in Liverpool, U. K., thinks that sales from the greater capacity will increase by £100,000 per year and that cash operating costs will decline by £60,000 per year. The new refrigerator will cost £350,000. Her variable contribution margin is 40 percent. The old equipment is fully depreciated but can be sold for £8,000. The new refrigerator will use straight-line depreciation, has a 5-year life, and is expected to have a salvage value of £40,000. Ignore taxes.

Required:
Format the cash flows for the refrigeration unit proposal.

12-10. Selecting Between Two Investments.   Meridian Township has $60,000 of surplus cash in a fund that will not be used for one year. The township treasurer has two investment possibilities available:

(a)   Invest in 10 percent corporate commercial paper for six months and then reinvest the proceeds in an 8 percent corporate bond for the remaining six months.

(b)   Invest now in an 8 percent corporate bond maturing in three months, reinvest the proceeds in 10 percent treasury bills for six months, and hold the proceeds in the township's 4 percent interest-bearing checking account for the remaining three months.

Required:
Which choice gives the township the higher amount at yearend? Show calculations.

12-11. Net Returns and Discounted Rate of Return.   The Echols Company is considering new word processing equipment that can reduce personnel costs by an estimated $60,000 a year. The new equipment is also expected to generate annual intangible customer service benefits of $70,000. The new equipment will cost $400,000 and will be depreciated on a straight-line basis for tax purposes. The asset will have no residual value at the end of ten years, the estimated life of the equipment. Income tax is estimated at 40 percent.

Required:
1. Determine the annual net cash inflow from the proposed investment.
2. Will the investment earn an 18 percent aftertax rate of return?
3. Comment on the NPV.

12-12. Selecting the Better Machine.   A Topeka party store owner is considering the purchase of a new ice machine. Two firms offer machines that promise the same sales. Both will last five years. The Hawkeye uses hamsters for power, and the Jayhawk uses solar power. The owner wants a 10 percent return. Ignore taxes.

	The Hawkeye	*The Jayhawk*
Cost of machine	$ 25,000	$ 50,000
Annual cash operating costs	9,000	1,000
Salvage value	2,000	10,000

Required:
1. Using NPV, which machine is preferred; and what is the advantage?
2. For the same money, should the owner buy two Hawkeye machines instead of one Jayhawk?

12-13. Sales Offer as Investment.   The owner of a self-storage business has just received an offer that is worth $600,000 after taxes for the storage buildings. The owner is interested in another investment opportunity that can probably yield an annual discounted return of 15 percent after taxes. The storage business is expected to continue to yield an annual cash inflow, before taxes, of $170,000 for a period of 15 years. The book value of the storage buildings is $660,000, and straight-line depreciation is used for tax purposes. Zero salvage value is predicted. A 40 percent tax rate applies.

Required:
Should the offer for the storage business be accepted? Explain.

12-14. Different Investment Goals.   Three projects are being evaluated. All have the same initial investment and expected life. Data from the projects are:

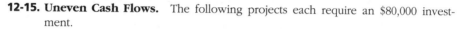

	Net Present Value (Using 16%)	Payback	Accounting Rate of Return
Project A	$22,000	2.8 years	18%
Project B	23,000	2.7	16
Project C	21,000	2.6	17

Required:
1. If present value and profitability are important, rank the projects.
2. If we want the project that will make us look best in accrual accounting reports, rank the projects.
3. If avoiding risk and getting our cash investment back quickly are key factors, rank the projects.

12-15. Uneven Cash Flows.   The following projects each require an $80,000 investment.

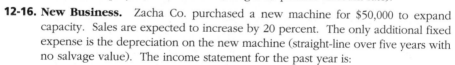

Cash Inflows:	Project				
	98-A4	98-G3	98-K1	98-P6	98-S4
Year 1	$20,000	$10,000	$40,000		$60,000
Year 2	20,000	10,000			30,000
Year 3	20,000	15,000	40,000		10,000
Year 4	20,000	15,000		$160,000	(60,000)
Year 5	20,000	25,000	40,000		
Year 6	20,000	25,000			40,000
Year 7	20,000	30,000	40,000		
Year 8	20,000	30,000			80,000

Required:
1. For each project, find the payback period.
2. For each project, find the ARR.
3. For each project, find the NPV (using a 15 percent discount rate).

12-16. New Business.   Zacha Co. purchased a new machine for $50,000 to expand capacity. Sales are expected to increase by 20 percent. The only additional fixed expense is the depreciation on the new machine (straight-line over five years with no salvage value). The income statement for the past year is:

Sales	$ 300,000
Variable expenses	(180,000)
Fixed expenses	(100,000)
Net income before taxes	$ 20,000
Taxes (40%)	(8,000)
Net income after taxes	$ 12,000

Required:
1. What is the expected annual aftertax cash inflow from the new machine?
2. Find the NPV using a hurdle rate of 15 percent and the payback period.

12-17. Equipment Replacement.   By replacing present equipment with more efficient equipment, Willie Company estimates that cash operating costs can be reduced by $65,000 a year. In addition, increased sales volume can result in a larger contribution margin of $25,000 a year without considering the efficiency savings. Depreciation of $50,000 per year will be taken on new equipment. Depreciation on present equipment is $10,000 per year. The income tax rate is 40 percent.

Required:
What is the estimated incremental annual aftertax cash inflow on this investment?

12-18. Investment in Another Company. The management of Musser Enterprises, in Cologne, Germany, is considering a DM10,000,000 investment to acquire the assets of Ener-Tec Company, a small company that has developed a more economical means of using electrical energy. Last year, Ener-Tec reported net sales of DM20,000,000 and operating expenses of DM18,000,000. Included in the operating expenses is depreciation of assets in the amount of DM800,000. This level of earnings is expected to continue for five years, after which the technology will be outdated and the assets will have no value.

Required:

Ignoring income taxes and using present value, what is the approximate rate of return earned by the investment?

12-19. Capital Budgeting Ethics. Tadd and Todd manage similar stores of Tough Tires. They met at a recent managers' conference and discussed their need for new car lifts at their stores. At the meeting, the company's controller made a presentation on next year's capital investment budget. Funds are scarce, proposals will be studied carefully, the cutoff rate will be raised, and fewer proposals approved. Tadd and Todd return to their stores and prepare competing proposals for the lifts. Tough Tires assumes a 40 percent tax rate. Their data show the following:

	Tadd's Proposal	Todd's Proposal
Cost of equipment	$100,000 in Year 0	$100,000 in Year 0
Installation costs	15,000 in Year 0	5,000 in Year 0
Sale of old equipment net of taxes	5,000 in Year 0	10,000 in Year 0
Incremental depreciation expense each year . .	11,500 per year	7,000 per year
Reduced operating expenses per year	20,000 per year	25,000 per year
Increased contribution margin per year	15,000 per year	25,000 per year
Salvage value of new machine net of taxes . .	10,000 in Year 10	30,000 in Year 15
Life of equipment	10 years	15 years

Required:

1. Develop a rough estimate of the IRR for the two proposals.

2. Why would the two sets of estimates differ so much?

3. How might the Tough Tires controller test the managers' estimates?

12-20. Find the Missing Values. For these projects, provide the missing value, if:

A = Initial investment   **D** = Internal rate of return

B = Life of project   **E** = Present value factor from Table 2 for "B"

C = Annual net cash inflow   periods at "D" internal rate of return

	A	B	C	D	E
Project 1	$118,932	6 years	$34,000	?%	?
Project 2	?	5 years	12,000	?%	3.605
Project 3	68,000	15 years	?	16%	?
Project 4	84,750	? years	15,000	12%	?
Project 5	?	? years	20,000	20%	2.991
Project 6	111,925	20 years	?	8%	?

12-21. Ranking Projects. The following projects have been evaluated using four capital budgeting techniques.

	Project A	Project B	Project C	Project D
Net present value (using 14%) . .	$3,440	$8,550	$300	$(2,000)
Internal rate of return	18%	16%	20%	12%
Payback period	3 years	2 years	4 years	5 years
Accounting rate of return	25%	18%	22%	20%

Required:

1. Based only on the information provided, rank the projects for each of the capital investment methods shown.

2. What additional information is needed to make better rankings? Discuss what might cause the differences in the rankings.

12-22. Tax Shield.   Your boss is considering a new parking lot for employees that will cost $200,000. The company is in the 40 percent tax bracket. Your boss says, "It will only cost us $120,000 after taxes to put in the lot." The firm has a 14 percent cost of capital and would depreciate the lot over eight years using the straight-line method.

Required:

Tell your boss what the net cost, in present value terms, will be to build the new parking lot. Comment on the absence of "benefits."

P ROBLEMS

12-23. Payback and Discounted Returns.   Ignore tax impacts. Carol Towel, manager of Timber Ridge Investments, uses the payback method in selecting investment alternatives. She states that, "If I can recover the investment in three years, I'm virtually in the same position as another investor who earns an 18 percent internal rate of return on a 5-year investment." In her business, investments produce uniform returns over a 5-year period and have no salvage value. Three investment choices are outlined as follows:

	Choice 1	*Choice 2*	*Choice 3*
Investment	$90,000	$24,000	$44,000
Annual return for each of 5 years	30,000	9,000	12,500

Required:

1. Which, if any, of the investment choices meet the 3-year payback criterion?
2. Evaluate the three choices by the NPV method with a minimum rate of return of 18 percent, and compare the results with those found in Part (1).
3. Comment on her statement.

12-24. Relevant Costs.   Aussie Auto Wash Company has just installed a special machine for washing cars in its Perth outlet. The machine cost A$20,000. Its operating costs, based on a yearly volume of 100,000 cars, total A$15,000, exclusive of depreciation. After the machine has been used one day, a salesperson offers a different machine that promises to do the same job at a yearly operating cost of A$9,000, exclusive of depreciation. The new machine will cost A$24,000, installed. The "old" machine is unique and can be sold outright for only A$8,000, less A$2,000 removal cost. The old and new machines will have a 4-year useful life and no residual value. Sales, all in cash, will be A$150,000 per year; and other cash expenses will be A$110,000 annually, regardless of this decision.

Required:

1. Ignore taxes. Calculate net income for each of the four years assuming that the new machine is not purchased and then assuming that it is purchased. Sum the net incomes for the four years for each alternative. What should be done?
2. Ignore taxes, and consider the time value of money. If a 15 percent return on investment is desired, what should be done?

12-25. Incremental Costs and Revenues.   The Sopariwala Company has the opportunity to market a new product. The sales manager believes that the firm could sell 5,000 units per year at $14 per unit for five years. The production manager has determined that machinery costing $60,000 and having a 5-year life and no salvage value would be required. The machinery will have annual fixed cash operating costs of $4,000. Variable costs per unit will be $8. Straight-line depreciation is to be used for both book and tax purposes. The tax rate is 40 percent, and the firm's cost of capital is 14 percent.

Required:
1. Determine the NPV of the investment if taxes are ignored.
2. Determine the NPV of the investment if taxes are paid but no depreciation is taken.
3. Determine the NPV of the investment if taxes and depreciation are included.
4. Comment on the differences in net present values.

12-26. Improving Investment Returns.   For many years Emilio Perez has been successful in the retail garment industry in Nogales, Mexico. Recently he has learned of an opportunity to purchase a two-story modern building for M$750,000. He believes that he can operate successfully by using only one of the two floors. At the present time, his business is operating in an older building where he uses three floors. This has sales and production constraints, he admits.

With uncertainties about inflation and interest rates, he would hesitate to invest unless he could obtain a discounted rate of return of at least 15 percent. Yet, he estimates that the annual returns from his business after income tax would probably increase by M$150,000 for each of the next ten years if he moved. This investment opportunity does not appear that good to him, and he is inclined to continue the current arrangements.

His daughter, who has recently graduated from medical school, disagrees with his position: "You forget that this area is growing. We have no professional building; and I know of several doctors, dentists, and attorneys who would be happy to have offices on the second floor if you did some remodeling. I already have estimates and find that you can have the second floor remodeled for M$100,000. The offices should yield annual aftertax rental income of M$40,000."

Required:
1. From the data given, what is the approximate IRR on the building itself?
2. What is the approximate IRR on the building and the remodeling investment together?
3. Comment on the worthiness of the incremental investment.

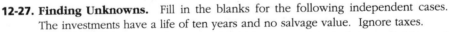

12-27. Finding Unknowns.   Fill in the blanks for the following independent cases. The investments have a life of ten years and no salvage value. Ignore taxes.

	Annual Cash Inflow	Investment	Cost of Capital	Internal Rate of Return	Net Present Value
Case 1 . . .	$ 45,000	$188,640	14%	?	$?
Case 2 . . .	80,000	?	12%	18%	?
Case 3 . . .	?	300,000	?	16%	81,440
Case 4 . . .	?	450,000	12%	?	115,000
Case 5 . . .	100,000	?	?	14%	(38,300)

12-28. Investment Returns and Sales Volume.   D. D. Ward, whose uncle whispered "plastics" into his ear soon after he graduated from college years ago, founded Plastic Opportunities, Inc. Ward is considering an investment of $2,000,000 in a new product line. Depreciation of $200,000 is to be deducted in each of the next ten years. Salvage value is estimated at zero. A selling price of $50 per unit is decided upon; unit variable cost is $30. The sales division believes that a sales estimate of 50,000 units per year is realistic. His controller states that a solid market exists for only 20,000 units a year. Projects must meet a minimum rate-of-return requirement of 15 percent. Income tax is estimated at 40 percent of income before tax.

Required:
1. Evaluate the project using each of the sales volume estimates. Use the NPV method.

2. At what volume will the project earn exactly a 15 percent return?

12-29. Change in the Value of Money. Ann Aust, manager of Town Company, states that she used to accept investments that yielded discounted returns (after income taxes) of 18 percent. With a decreasing cost of capital, she now expects to earn a 12 percent discounted rate of return. Two competing investment proposals are now awaiting her evaluation. The estimated data are as follows:

	Proposal 1	*Proposal 2*
Investment life.	6 years	6 years
Net investment	$180,000	$192,000
Annual cash inflows before depreciation and taxes:		
Year 1	$ 50,000	$ 80,000
Year 2	50,000	70,000
Year 3	50,000	60,000
Year 4	90,000	50,000
Year 5	60,000	50,000
Year 6	60,000	50,000

Depreciation is based on the straight-line method, and estimated salvage values will equal disposal costs at the end of the projects' lives. Taxes are estimated to be 40 percent of income before taxes.

Required:

1. Do either or both of the proposals provide an 18 percent return?

2. Do either or both of the proposals provide a 12 percent return?

3. Comment on the implications of the results in Parts (1) and (2).

12-30. Management Ethics and Cost Savings. Keefer Company operates several factories, one of which was built some 70 years ago and is in poor condition. The factory has a fire insurance policy covering machinery, inventory, and the building itself. Premiums on the policy are $40,000 per year. The president has refused to approve several proposals for modernizing the fire safety system.

Recently, a fire inspector from the insurance company has recommended that the premium be increased to $80,000 per year because the older factory's fire protection has been diminished. The existing sprinkler system has stopped functioning and cannot be repaired at a reasonable cost. The plant manager was told by the inspector that a new system, costing $200,000 with a 10-year life and no salvage value, is needed to continue the policy at the current premium level.

The system would be depreciated on a straight-line basis. The tax rate is 40 percent, and Keefer's cost of capital is 12 percent. The manager resubmitted the fire safety system proposal with the new insurance data.

Required:

1. In a quantitative sense, should the sprinkler system be installed? Explain.

2. Discuss other issues that should be considered in making this decision.

3. How can sound capital budgeting decisions be made while still considering human issues?

12-31. Alternative Uses. The Edo Building Company owns an office building in the business center of Tokyo. The building has a large unused lobby area. The facilities manager for the firm, Yuri Misatuni, is planning to get a greater financial return from the unused space and believes that a convenience shop should be placed in the lobby. She talked to managers of several other office buildings and projected the following annual operating results if the company establishes the shop:

Sales	¥8,500,000
Cost of sales	4,000,000
Salaries and benefits of clerks	2,400,000
Licenses and permits	100,000
Share of utilities on the building	200,000
Share of building depreciation	100,000
Advertising for the shop	100,000
Allocation of Edo administrative expense	150,000

The investment required would be ¥5,000,000, all for equipment that would be worthless in ten years. Before presenting the plan to the executive manager, Yuri learned that the space could be leased to an outside firm that would operate a convenience shop. The lease firm would pay a commission of ¥500,000 per year for ten years. Because the lobby is heated and lighted anyway, Edo would supply utilities at a minimal added cost. Edo's cost of capital is 12 percent. Ignore taxes.

Required:

1. Determine the best course of action for Edo Building Company.

2. Determine how much annual rent Edo would have to receive to equalize the attractiveness of her options.

12-32. Basic Replacement Decision. You are given the following data:

Existing machine:		Replacement machine:	
Cost	$70,000	Cost	$180,000
Current value (net of taxes) . .	32,000	Salvage value (net of taxes) . . .	20,000
Salvage value (end of life)	0	Annual cash operating costs . .	8,000
Annual depreciation	5,000	Useful life	6 years
Annual cash operating costs . .	50,000		
Remaining life	6 years		

The income tax rate is 40 percent. The target rate of return is 14 percent. Straight-line depreciation is used. Assume that salvage value is ignored in calculating depreciation expense.

Required:

1. Determine the NPV of the replacement decision.

2. What is the profitability index of the replacement decision?

12-33. Value of a Business. Jawbreaker, Ltd., a Hong Kong firm, makes and sells candy in large lots for other firms that package and sell the candy under various brand names. The firm could acquire a small candy exporting firm that has sold about 800,000 kilograms of candy annually to Korea and Japan. To operate the firm, Jawbreaker would have to hire a specialized salesperson for HK$1,200,000 annually, including travel and entertainment expenses. Additional packaging machinery costing HK$1,600,000 must be acquired. The machinery would last five years, have no salvage value, and be depreciated on a straight-line basis.

Other data are as follows:

(a) Variable costs are HK$0.80 per kilogram.

(b) Selling price on the export business is HK$4 per kilogram.

(c) Annual cash costs of operating the new machinery are HK$320,000.

(d) Tax rate is 40 percent. (Assume that Hong Kong and U. S. tax rules are the same.)

(e) Cost of capital is 16 percent.

Required:

On the basis of this information and a 5-year time horizon, what is the most Jawbreaker should pay for this investment opportunity?

12-34. Expanding a Product Line.   Ghafari Brothers Company makes office equipment, such as tables, desks, computer equipment consoles, and work tables. The sales manager is trying to decide whether to expand the relatively new computer equipment console product line. The average desk will sell for $300 and has a variable cost of $140 per unit. Volume is expected to be 4,000 units per year for five years. To make the desks, the firm will have to buy additional machinery that will cost $900,000, has a 5-year life, and has a $100,000 salvage value net of taxes. Straight-line depreciation is used, and salvage value is ignored in depreciation calculations. Additional fixed cash operating costs will be $200,000 per year. Ghafari has a 40 percent tax rate, and its cost of capital is 16 percent.

Required:

1. Using NPV, determine whether the computer console line should be expanded.
2. Compute the payback period.
3. Determine the approximate IRR that the firm expects to earn on the investment. Ignore salvage value.

12-35. Changes in the Economic Environment.   Four years ago, Belanger Properties, Inc. invested $10,000,000 in a venture in an economic development zone in another country. The investment was estimated to have a 10-year life and was expected to produce a cash inflow of $2,500,000 each year before income taxes.

It did exactly this for four years. Conditions are less favorable now, and the revised estimate indicates that the annual cash inflow will be only $1,300,000 but will last for eight more years. Because of its foreign investment classification, it has a special tax status and is not subject to normal income taxes. The investment can now be sold for $5,400,000. At present, an investment can be justified only if the IRR is expected to be at least 18 percent.

Required:

Should the investment be sold for $5,400,000 or be continued? Show computations using the NPV method. Comment on the changed estimates.

1-2-3

12-36. Equipment Replacement Concerns.   The Molding Department of Hornus, Inc. has been investigating the acquisition of new equipment costing $100,000. Cash savings before income taxes from the use of this equipment are estimated to be $40,000 per year for ten years. At the end of five years, the new equipment must be overhauled at a cost of $35,000. The new equipment will have no salvage value after ten years. The new machine would replace an old machine that would need a $30,000 overhaul now and again in five years, if it is not replaced. The old machine is fully depreciated but can still function. To remove the old machine, environmental precautions (mainly an asbestos problem) will cost the firm $40,000. The rate used in evaluating investments is 10 percent. The income tax rate is 40 percent. Hornus uses straight-line depreciation.

Required:

1. Calculate the NPV. Make a recommendation.
2. If the asbestos will need to be removed within two years anyway, how does this impact your answer to Part (1)? Comment.

12-37. Break-Even Volume and Investment.   For several years, Grabski Company has used a combination of its own equipment and rental equipment to handle materials. The company has its own equipment to handle routine work but must rent equipment to handle particularly bulky materials. The cost to rent equipment has been estimated to average $4,000 a year.

An evaluation of cash operating expenses indicates that the company can save $0.15 per cubic yard of materials by buying its own equipment instead of renting equipment. An equipment manufacturer offers the necessary additional equipment at a cost of $80,000. The equipment will probably have a useful life of six years with no salvage value.

Uncertainty exists with respect to how much work will be required from the new equipment if it is purchased. Estimates of the number of cubic yards that might possibly be handled in each of the six years are 80,000 cubic yards, 100,000 cubic yards, or 120,000 cubic yards. On this type of investment, a 15 percent discounted return is considered to be appropriate. Ignore taxes.

Required:

1. Can the investment meet the minimum rate-of-return requirement if 80,000 cubic yards are handled? 100,000 cubic yards? 120,000 cubic yards?
2. Determine the break-even volume, that is, the number of cubic yards at which the investment can just meet the 15 percent return requirement. Round all amounts to the nearest dollar.

12-38. Ranking Investment Alternatives. Mazzeo Industries has designated $1.2 million for capital investment expenditures during the upcoming year. Its cost of capital is 14 percent. Any unused funds will earn the cost of capital rate. The following investment opportunities along with their required investment and estimated net present values have been identified:

Project	Net Investment	NPV	Project	Net Investment	NPV
A	$200,000	$ 22,000	F	$250,000	$30,000
B	275,000	21,000	G	100,000	7,000
C	150,000	6,000	H	200,000	18,000
D	190,000	(19,000)	I	210,000	4,000
E	500,000	40,000	J	250,000	35,000

Required:

1. Rank the projects using the profitability index. Considering the limit on funds available, which projects should be accepted?
2. Using the NPV, which projects should be accepted considering the limit on funds available?
3. If the available investment funds are reduced to only $1,000,000:
   (a) Does the list of accepted projects change from Part (2)?
   (b) What is the opportunity cost of the eliminated $200,000?

12-39. Proposal Preparation. Yoder Instruments Company manufactures a variety of products. The sales manager of Yoder, Dave Shockley, has stated repeatedly that he could sell more units of one of the firm's products if they were available. To prove his claim, the sales manager conducted a market research study last year at a cost of $60,000 to determine potential demand for this product. The study indicated that Yoder could sell 25,000 units annually for the next five years. A unit sells for $20 per unit.

The machinery currently used has capacity to produce 15,000 units annually. This machinery has a book value of $80,000 and a remaining useful life of five years. The salvage value of the machinery is negligible now and will be zero in five years. The variable production costs using this equipment are $12 per unit.

New machinery could produce 30,000 units annually. The new machinery costs $250,000 and has an estimated useful life of five years with no salvage value at the end of the five years. Yoder's production manager, Jean Smith, has estimated that the new equipment would provide increased production efficiencies, reducing the variable production costs to $10 per unit. She also explains that the machine's higher capacity would cause factory administrative overheads to be reallocated. She thought a charge of $4 per unit for the additional 10,000 units produced would be the amount calculated by the Cost Accounting Department.

Dave Shockley felt so strongly about the additional capacity that he prepared an economic justification for the equipment. His analysis, which follows, excited him because it covered all expenses including the bank's 9 percent prime interest rate and "still returned a small sum to the bottom line." He was last seen on his way to the president's office to schedule a meeting with the executive finance committee. A quick peek at his analysis shows:

Initial investment:

Purchase price of new machinery		$250,000
Disposal of present equipment:		
Loss on disposal	$80,000	
Less benefit of tax loss (40%)	32,000	48,000
Market research study costs		60,000
Total new investment needed		$358,000

Additional annual profit:

Contribution margin from product:		
New machinery output:		
30,000 x [$20 - ($10 + 4)]		$180,000
Existing machinery output:		
15,000 x [$20 - ($12 + 4)]		60,000
Added contribution margin		$120,000
Less depreciation on new machinery		50,000
Increase in taxable income		$ 70,000
Income tax (40%)		28,000
Increase in income.		$ 42,000
Cost of borrowed funds (0.09 x $358,000)		32,220
Net annual return on the new machinery		$ 9,780

Required:

Dave Shockley's executive secretary, who has kept him out of "hot water" in the past, is worried about his numbers. She asks you to evaluate his project numbers and see if he has his "gear together." You recall that the firm's cost of capital has been 16 percent, and tax rate is 40 percent. Straight-line depreciation is used. Revise the numbers as you feel necessary.

CASE 12A—NEW TECHNOLOGY ARRIVES

1-2-3

The Wildhaber Machine Shop purchased a new grinding machine one year ago at a cost of $68,000. The machine has been working very satisfactorily, but the shop manager, Fred, has just received information on an electronically controlled grinder that is vastly superior to the machine which he now uses. While both machines can meet all required existing quality standards and tolerances, the new machine's quality potential can far exceed the old machine's capabilities. Comparative data on the two machines follow:

	Present Machine	Proposed New Machine
Purchase cost new (including installation costs).	$70,000	$90,000
Salvage value today	35,000	
Salvage value at end of life	5,000	10,000
Annual costs to operate	95,000	75,000
Estimated useful life when new	7 years	6 years

Fred makes a few quick computations and exclaims, "Wow! We need that machine and its capabilities. But, no way can I sell it upstairs. When the boss sees the loss on the old machine, he'll have kittens." He's looking at this:

Remaining book value of the old machine	$60,000
Salvage value now of the old machine	35,000
Net loss from disposal (before tax deduction of the loss)	$25,000

Wildhaber uses straight-line depreciation and ignores salvage value in its depreciation calculations. Sales from the grinding operation are expected to remain unchanged at $300,000 per year indefinitely. Other cash costs of the grinding operation total $80,000 annually. The corporate tax rate is 40 percent.

Required:

1. Prepare summary income statements covering the next six years for the grinding operation, assuming that:
   (a) the new machine is not purchased.
   (b) the new machine is purchased.
2. What do you recommend? Show any needed additional analysis.
3. Comment on the reality of the $25,000 loss Fred has calculated. Can or should this be ignored?
4. Comment on why introducing new technology is difficult to justify to management.
5. Develop a policy that would encourage investment in new technology and yet would avoid wasting scarce capital investment money.

CASE 12B—KRANTZ HOSES

The production manager of Krantz Hoses is considering a project to modernize its equipment. The company produces assorted rubber and metal hoses and pipes needed by a variety of automotive and appliance manufacturers. One of Krantz's major customers is Phillips Appliances which purchases specialized hoses. Krantz has negotiated an annual contract with Phillips in each of the past eight years. In the past, requirements have averaged about 800,000 hoses per year.

The present arrangement of the factory includes four hose forming machines currently devoted to the Phillips business. Each machine is operated by a skilled worker. The management is considering replacing these manual machines with an automatic forming, pressing, and testing machine, capable of performing all operations necessary for making hoses. This machine would produce hoses at a rate equal to five existing machines.

The four existing manual machines are four years old. Each can produce 200,000 hoses on a 2-shift, 5-day per week basis. Their total cost new was $570,000. The remaining useful life of these machines is estimated to be eight years. The salvage value at the end of their useful life is estimated to be $5,000 each net of taxes and was ignored in depreciation calculations. Depreciation totalling $190,000 has been accumulated on the four machines. Cash for the purchase of these machines was partially supplied by a 10-year, 14 percent, unsecured bank loan, of which $250,000 is still outstanding. The best estimate of the current selling price of the four machines in their present condition is $200,000, after removal costs. A writeoff of the loss on disposal will net an immediate tax savings of $72,000.

The automatic machine needs only one highly skilled operator to feed raw rubber and metal sleeves, observe its functioning, and make necessary adjustments. It would have an output from two shifts of 1,000,000 hoses annually. No present use exists for the extra capacity. The machine's cost is estimated to be $900,000, delivered and installed. The useful life is estimated to be ten years. No reliable estimate of its salvage value can be made. An educated guess is that the residual value would equal its book at any time in its life. No salvage value is used in depreciation calculations.

From a study prepared by the cost accountant, the following information has been compiled. The direct labor rate for machine operators is $15 per hour. The new machine would use less floor space, which would save $16,000 annually on the allocated charges for square footage of space used, although the layout of the plant is such that the freed space would not be used for other purposes. Miscellaneous cash expenses for supplies and power would be $20,000 less per year if the automatic machine is used. Assume that all depreciation calculations will use straight-line depreciation.

If purchased, the new machine would be financed by a 12 percent secured bank loan, that would include paying off the loan on the old machines. Outstanding notes payable are at 9 percent. The company treasurer assumes that the weighted-average cost of equity and debt is about 16 percent.

Required:

1. Summarize the net investment and net cash flows for the proposed project.
2. Evaluate the project using the capital investment methods you have studied.
3. Comment on the important qualitative factors in evaluating this project.
4. What decision would you recommend? Why?

Capital Investment Decisions: Additional Issues

Based on your understanding of Chapter 12, studying the Chapter 13 material will enable you to:

1. Analyze several issues which complicate calculations in capital investment decisions.

2. Evaluate the financing decision independent of the acquisition decision.

3. Understand the significance of accelerated depreciation and MACRS.

4. Understand the use of life-cycle costing in capital budgeting.

5. Use sensitivity analysis and expected values to help assess risk in capital investment decisions.

6. See the importance of a post-audit of capital investment decisions in improving control and in evaluating future capital investments.

7. Integrate the evaluation of social costs of capital investments into the quantitative analysis.

More Complexities in Capital Investments

At the beginning of Chapter 12, John Victory, president of Fine Tone Instruments, is reviewing investment proposals. He is amazed by the complexity of the decisions. Few projects are straightforward cash out and cash in propositions. Inflation is a worry. Alternatives may have different lives, initial investments, and promised RORs. Also, why purchase equipment when it could be leased? Then, there are taxes. Depreciation appears to make certain capital investments more attractive. But should Victory make investment choices based on tax advantages? Comparisons often appear to be between apples and oranges.

In making capital investment decisions, he thinks it's important to include all relevant money over the entire life of a project, including any environmental impacts. In a few years, he would like to look at the proposals again, then with the wisdom of hindsight. Can differences in key variables be reduced to a manageable level? He knows that the success of certain projects depends heavily on one or two key variables. If estimates for these key variables are off by a small amount, the feasibility of the entire project may be in doubt. Victory shakes his head and digs into the stack of proposals.

Based on Chapter 12 discussions about capital investment decisions, Chapter 13 contains a set of more complex issues and extensions of basic analyses. While certain topics in Chapter 13 are relevant to undergraduate managerial accounting courses, the majority of topics are more appropriate for extending capital investment discussions in graduate courses.

Since capital investment projects vary widely and depend heavily on estimates of the future, additional issues and levels of complexity often need to be considered. Among these are calculation issues, financing alternatives, taxation and depreciation concerns, and risk analysis. Finally, the planning and control cycle is closed with a post-audit of the investments' results.

*C*ALCULATION ISSUES

Sufficient calculation issues arise in capital investment analyses that textbooks have been written to address them. Several have been examined in Chapter 12, and others are discussed now.

Inflation and Future Cash Flows

Inflation is a common economic problem. Over the past 20 years in the United States, annual inflation rates have ranged from a high of over 13 percent to a low of under 2 percent. These levels are moderate compared to rates in many other countries. Yet, capital investment decisions must consider inflationary impacts on future cash flows.

While several approaches could be used to incorporate inflation into the analysis, the approach we suggest is to build the impacts of inflation into the expected future cash flows. This allows the use of specific inflation rates for each cash-flow component. Also, rates could be changed for each future period. The discount rate will be the noninflation desired rate of return times one plus the expected general inflation rate.

To illustrate inflation impacts on estimates of future cash flows, assume that Beall Motors plans to enter the engine diagnostic business. The equipment will cost about $120,000 and should last about three years. At that time, automotive technology advances will require more powerful computer capabilities. Annual revenues are expected to be $150,000; personnel costs are $60,000; and other support costs would be about $30,000. Beall uses a 10 percent desired rate of return.

Economic forecasts indicate that inflation will be 6 percent per year for the next few years. But Beall feels that, at best, prices could be raised no more than 4 percent per year. Personnel costs will probably increase at a 10 percent rate, primarily because of benefits costs. Other costs will increase at an average of 6 percent annually. The equipment, which has no salvage value, will be depreciated on a straight-line basis. Assume a 40 percent tax rate. The cash flows related to the equipment are as follows:

	Investment	Life of the Project		
Cash Flows:	Year 0	Year 1	Year 2	Year 3
Initial investment	$(120,000)			
Revenues		$150,000	$156,000	$162,240
Personnel costs		(60,000)	(66,000)	(72,600)
Other costs		(30,000)	(31,800)	(33,708)
Incremental taxes*		(8,000)	(7,280)	(6,373)
Net cash flows	$(120,000)	$ 52,000	$ 50,920	$ 49,559

* Taxes in Year 1: ($150,000 - $60,000 - $30,000 - $40,000) x 0.4 = $8,000

  Taxes in Year 2: ($156,000 - $66,000 - $31,800 - $40,000) x 0.4 = $7,280

  Taxes in Year 3: ($162,240 - $72,600 - $33,708 - $40,000) x 0.4 = $6,373

Notice that depreciation, being based on the historical cost of the investment, is $40,000 in each year. While all other revenues and costs have inflation built into them, the tax law requires that the depreciation expense is always expressed in historical-cost dollars from the year of acquisition. Using historical cost-based depreciation in tax calculations often leads to higher tax payments since profits grow from inflated revenues. The discount rate would be [(1 + 0.10) x (1 + 0.06)] - 1 or 16.6 percent. This includes the compounding impacts of inflation.

It is dangerous to ignore inflation. To do so, assumes that all inflation effects sum to zero, which is rarely the case. Certain cost areas, such as health care, have had unusually high increases in recent years. Forecasting these costs should include estimated inflationary impacts to make cash-flow estimates credible.

Working Capital

When expansion occurs, inventories and receivables often grow. Financing **working capital** growth is an integral part of a project's total investment. Unlike depreciable equipment and fixed assets, working capital is committed and can probably be recovered at the end of the project. Often, working capital requirements grow slowly over time as sales increase. Increases in these inventories and accounts receivable can easily be overlooked and omitted from a project's analysis. In contrast, JIT projects often release working capital by reducing inventories, which can help finance the project itself.

Assume that Athletic Champs operates a chain of sporting goods stores in shopping malls. Opening a new store requires layout, equipment, and fixtures costing about $450,000. In addition, about $200,000 of inventory is needed to stock a new store. Experience shows that inventory and other working capital needs will grow at about $20,000 per year for the first five years. If Athletic Champs uses an 8-year timeframe for evaluating a store location, assumptions will be needed about the equipment salvage value and the recovery of the working capital investment. The fixed assets' salvage values are estimated to be $50,000 net of taxes, and the entire working capital investment (now $300,000) is thought to be recoverable. The cash flows would look like:

Cash Flows:	Today	Life of the Project			
		Year 1	Year 2	Year 5	Year 8
Initial construction	$(450,000)				$ 50,000
Working capital needs . .	(200,000)	$(20,000)	$(20,000)	$(20,000)	300,000

Working capital recovery is not automatic. Inventory may be obsolete, and receivables might not be collectible. A going-concern assumption can generally be made if the business is expected to continue past the timeframe cutoff.

Uneven Project Lives

When comparing projects, lives of each project may not match. How can a 3-year solution to a problem be compared to a 5-year or a 8-year solution? The decision must be viewed from the timeframe of the job to be done. Do we want a solution for 3, 5, or 8 years? How long can the physical asset last? Often, technological changes make an asset's economic life shorter than its physical life. A 3-year solution may be sought, while an asset's physical life might well be twice that long.

If the time period is based on the needs of the problem, the task is to find salvage or market values for assets at the end of the defined time period. If the time period is based on the physical lives of the proposed assets, different useful lives of the proposed solutions must be somehow matched. One approach is to use a shorter lived project as the comparison time period. This requires finding salvage or market values for assets at midpoints in their lives. While no specific rule exists, the investment's timeframe as defined by management seems to be the better choice. Management's intent and common sense, rather than the physical lives of assets, should govern the time period choice.

Evaluation of Projects With Different Initial Investments

Up to this point, most of the illustrations have assumed that a single investment alternative existed. The firm had to decide whether to invest in that project. Actually, a firm may have several alternatives but still have to select only one. In such a case, care must be exercised in using the internal rate of return method, because the project with the highest internal rate of return may not be the most desirable. This can happen in those cases where the dollar investment is not the same among alternatives. The dollar amount of the return from a larger investment, in many cases, will exceed the dollar return from a smaller investment having a better internal rate of return.

Assume that Vista Transit Company must choose between two dump trucks. Each has an estimated life of five years with annual returns as follows:

	Truck I	Truck II
Net investment	$75,000	$100,000
Net cash inflow for each of 5 years	26,000	33,000

Investments are expected to earn a desired rate of return of at least 12 percent. Truck II requires an investment of an additional $25,000 versus Truck I. The approximate internal rate of return is computed for each alternative and for the incremental investment as follows:

	Truck I	Truck II	Incremental (II - I)
Net investment	$(75,000)	$(100,000)	$(25,000)
Annual return	26,000	33,000	7,000
Payback period	2.885	3.030	3.571
Nearest PV factor on Table 2 for 5 periods	2.864	2.991	3.605
Nearest internal rate of return given on Table 2	22%	20%	12%

It appears that Truck I should be selected because the internal rate of return is higher. The additional $25,000 investment needed by Truck II yields a much lower rate of return—12 percent. But, if the rate of return on the incremental investment is greater than the hurdle rate of return, the larger investment should still be made. In this example, an additional $7,000 per year is returned on an additional investment of $25,000. The rate of return on the incremental investment barely meets the 12 percent desired rate of return.

In other situations, Truck I could be a Phase I of a pair of sequential jobs, and Truck II could be Phases I and II combined. Phase I may be executed without Phase II but not vice versa. Advocates of Phase II would clearly argue that both phases be approved at one time. However, as we have seen, Phase II has an IRR of about 12 percent. If the cutoff rate is 15 percent, Phase I and the combined phases are acceptable. But Phase II by itself is unacceptable. Breaking down projects into their subcomponents can give useful insight into the yields on incremental investments.

Gains and Losses on Asset Disposals

If assets are sold at more or less than their book values, gains or losses appear with tax implications. The book value is an asset's original cost minus its accumulated depreciation. In the real world, accounting book values and tax cost bases often differ. Unless specifically mentioned, these two amounts are assumed to be the same in our discussions. If the sale is for more than the book value, a gain occurs; and if for less, a loss occurs.

Gains and losses on disposals and their impacts on cash flows arise at two points in the capital investment decision:

1. Old assets may be sold as part of investing in a new asset.
2. New assets may be sold at the end of the project's expected life.

Sales and trade-ins are handled differently for tax purposes. In trade-ins, the market value of the old asset reduces the cash paid to acquire the new asset. For tax purposes, the old book value is added to the cash cost of the new asset to create the new asset's book value. For example, assume that a new asset is purchased for $20,000 cash plus the trade-in of an old asset having a book value of $5,000. Also, assume that the new asset will have a 5-year life and no salvage value. Straight-line depreciation over five years will be $5,000 per year [($20,000 + $5,000) ÷ 5]. No gain or loss is recognized.

When old assets are sold and new assets are purchased in separate transactions, a gain or loss on the old asset is recognized; and the new asset's cost is depreciated. Tax-related issues surrounding gains and losses on sales depend on current legislation applicable to capital gains and losses. At present, capital gains tax rates and ordinary income rates are the same.

Most issues related to taxation of gains and deductibility of losses are beyond the scope of this text. The concern here is to recognize cash inflows from asset sales and to identify the basic tax impacts of the gains and losses. It is assumed here that gains are taxed at 40 percent and that losses are deducted from other income and the firm's tax liability is reduced by the 40 percent rate.

F INANCING VERSUS INVESTMENT DECISIONS

Many capital investments are directly tied to how the investment outlay will be financed. Often debt is issued; stock is sold; bank borrowing is arranged; or **leases** are signed. The general capital investment decision rules about financing are:

1. Make the capital investment decision without regard to the method of financing by assuming a cash purchase.
2. Then, make the financing decision.

The general rule says that the "go" or "no go" decision should be dependent on the project's basic cash flows. Financing choices may increase or decrease the firm's financing costs but should not change the inherent quality of the project.

A common situation is the choice of using the firm's own cash reserves, borrowing from a bank, or leasing the asset. The timing of cash flows and the interest cost of these alternatives can differ dramatically.

Leases have an interest rate embedded in the lease payment. Aside from tax issues, the financing decision can depend on whether the embedded lease interest rate is higher or lower than either the firm's borrowing or investment rate. Using either a short-term borrowing rate or the cost of capital rate may be a function of the length of the lease. A 24-month auto lease might be compared to the firm's bank borrowing rate, while a building lease for ten years would use the cost of capital rate.

Assume a copying machine can be leased for $10,000 per year for five years with payments due at the beginning of the year. The alternative is to buy the machine for $43,120 cash. The **embedded interest rate** is found as follows:

Cash price - Initial cash payment = Present value of future cash flows

Present value of future cash flows ÷ Annual cash payment = Present value factor

$43,120 - $10,000 = $33,120 present value

$33,120 ÷ $10,000 = 3.312 present value factor

We use Table 2 and the 4-period row because the first payment is made immediately. We are paying the copying equipment firm 8 percent interest for financing. The cash flows are shown in Figure 13.1.

If the lease's embedded rate is lower than the cost of funds rate, the advantage is often to lease. This commonly occurs in two situations. First, some businesses use an artificially low interest rate for leases either to give them a competitive advantage or to encourage customers to lease instead of buy. It is through promotional efforts such as this that the "tail (the financing decision) might wag the dog (the acquisition decision)." In these cases, the cash purchase cost would be the present value (using the cost of capital) of the annual lease payments. The vendor's lease present value would be below its cash purchase price. See the Contemporary Practice 13.1 example.

Second, the financial condition of some firms is so poor that they may have exhausted both debt and equity sources of additional funds. Leasing may be their only way to acquire needed new assets, regardless of the embedded interest rate. Yet, lessors generally perform credit checks on lessees for credit worthiness.

*A*CCELERATED DEPRECIATION, MACRS, AND THE TAX SHIELD

Accelerated depreciation has been in tax law since the 1950s. Cumbersome and complex rules developed around methods, asset lives, and capitalization. In the early 1980s, as part of a series of "tax reform" laws, a new depreciation

FIGURE 13.1   Financing Cash Flows for a Lease and a Purchase

Cash Flows:	Today	Year 1	Year 2	Year 3	Year 4	Year 5
		Life of the Lease				
Lease cash outflows	$(10,000)	$(10,000)	$(10,000)	$(10,000)	$(10,000)	$0
Present value factors (8%)	x 1.000	x .926	x .857	x .794	x .735	x .681
Sum of lease present values	$(43,120)					
Purchase cash outflow.	$(43,120)					

C O N T E M P O R A R Y   P R A C T I C E   1 3 . 1

Yes, I _Can_ Drive a Cadillac!

In early 1994, television and newspaper ads announced a special Cadillac leasing opportunity called 24-Month SmartLease Plus. Pay $12,405 at the signing date, and drive off in a Seville SLS. Or you can pay $2,200 plus $499 per month for 24 months under a regular 24-Month SmartLease. Ads say you save $1,771, the difference between the sums of the two cash payment streams. Are present values involved? Yes, that's how the monthly payments are set, considering residual values and special fees. But GMAC, the lessor, also changed the embedded lease interest rate from 4.0 percent to 2.5 percent for this promotion. The car's MSRP is $43,143, and leases include numerous conditions. Present values impact this deal in many ways, but you have to analyze your options yourself.

Source: General Motors Acceptance Corporation personnel.

system was introduced—the **Accelerated Cost Recovery System (ACRS)**. Currently, the **Modified Accelerated Cost Recovery System** or **MACRS** is applicable to assets acquired since 1987. Figure 13.2 lists the eight classes of assets.

MACRS Classes and Deduction Percentages

For each class, specific percentages of cost are deducted annually. The percentages for 3-, 5-, 7-, and 10-year classes are shown in Figure 13.3, page 562. MACRS uses the declining-balance depreciation method as the base for determining the annual percentages. The deduction percentage declines each year and eventually falls below the annual straight-line percentage deduction for the asset's remaining life. In that year, the MACRS method assumes a switch to straight-line depreciation for the rest of the asset's life. A series of accounting conventions, such as the half-year deduction, are used. The half-year convention says that only one half of the first year's depreciation can be taken in the first tax year. The remaining half of the first year's depreciation is taken in the second tax year, along with half of the second year's depreciation. This explains the transition from normal declining-balance percentages to MACRS percentages.

The advantage of MACRS, the current form of tax-law accelerated depreciation, is the present value of greater depreciation deductions earlier in

F I G U R E   1 3 . 2   MACRS Classes by Life and Type

Class	Type of Assets
3 Year	Certain tools and assets of specialized industries
5 Year	Autos and trucks, research equipment, and computers
7 Year	Office equipment and most production equipment
10 Year	Machinery and equipment in selected industries
15 Year	Certain utility facilities and land improvements
20 Year	Certain agricultural buildings and utility equipment
27½ Year	Residential rental property
31½ Year	Nonresidential real property

FIGURE 13.3   MACRS Accelerated Depreciation Percentages

Recovery Year	Property Class			
	3-Year	5-Year	7-Year	10-Year
1	33.33	20.00	14.29	10.00
2	44.45	32.00	24.49	18.00
3	14.81	19.20	17.49	14.40
4	7.41	11.52*	12.49	11.52
5		11.52	8.93*	9.22
6		5.76	8.92	7.37
7			8.93	6.55*
8			4.46	6.55
9				6.56
10				6.55
11				3.28

* Year of switch to straight-line to maximize depreciation.

a project's life. In total dollars, no more depreciation is taken; and no fewer tax dollars are paid. The key is when the tax dollars are paid.

An Example of MACRS

Assume that a company is considering the purchase of computer equipment costing $100,000, with an estimated useful life of six years. The income tax rate is 40 percent, and the firm's minimum acceptable rate of return on investments is 16 percent. The tax savings and present values of the savings are shown in Figure 13.4. The equipment falls into the 5-year class with no salvage value. The half-year convention is also used for both straight-line and MACRS depreciation. The comparative advantage of the MACRS method can be seen.

The advantage of using MACRS depreciation over straight-line depreciation is $2,625 using a 16 percent discount rate. Incrementally, this is a significant addition to the net present value. Thus, the early deductions of depreciation can be an important macroeconomic policy tool. Unfortunately, the legislative process often prevents quick implementation of changes to promote investment when economic stimuli are needed.

Immediate Expensing of Assets for Small Businesses

Another feature of current tax law is to allow an immediate tax deduction for up to $10,000 of new assets. Firms purchasing new depreciable assets over $210,000 lose this option. Companies immediately expensing any amount must deduct that amount from the basis of the asset to determine the asset's depreciable base. This provision is to assist small firms.

*L*IFE-CYCLE COSTING AND INVESTMENT ANALYSIS

A concept that has increased in managerial importance in recent years is **life-cycle costing**, which tracks and accumulates costs and revenues over the

FIGURE 13.4   Comparing Tax Impacts of MACRS and Straight-Line Depreciation Methods

	Today	Life of the Project					
		Year 1	Year 2	Year 3	Year 4	Year 5	Year 6
MACRS depreciation:							
Tax depreciation expense		$20,000	$32,000	$19,200	$11,500	$11,500	$ 5,800
Tax savings (40%)		$ 8,000	$12,800	$ 7,680	$ 4,600	$ 4,600	$ 2,320
Straight-line depreciation:							
Tax depreciation expense		$10,000	$20,000	$20,000	$20,000	$20,000	$10,000
Tax savings (40%)		$ 4,000	$ 8,000	$ 8,000	$ 8,000	$ 8,000	$ 4,000
Advantage of MACRS over Straight-Line (S-L):							
MACRS over S-L depreciation . .		$10,000	$12,000	$ (800)	$(8,500)	$(8,500)	$(4,200)
MACRS over S-L tax savings . . .		$ 4,000	$ 4,800	$ (320)	$(3,400)	$(3,400)	$(1,680)
Present value factors at 16%		x .862	x .743	x .641	x .552	x .476	x .410
Present values at 16%		$ 3,448	$ 3,566	$ (205)	$(1,877)	$(1,618)	$ (689)
MACRS advantage over S-L	$2,625						

entire life span of a product. As innovative products appear, flourish, and disappear with increasing frequency, the need to measure the total results becomes more important than year-to-year accrual accounting profit measurements. **Product life cycles** have been plotted for many years and typically include four phases: development, introduction and growth, maturation, and decline. Life-cycle analysis affects managerial accounting in several areas:

1. Budgeting revenues and costs for the entire project or product life.
2. Accounting for performance on a cumulative basis rather than on annual slices.
3. Developing a pricing strategy for each phase of the product's life cycle to maximize market penetration and total product profits.
4. Reporting on projects that have significant timing mismatches of cash inflows and outflows.
5. Recognizing and including hidden or ignored costs such as environmental impacts.

While this is not exclusively a capital investment issue, life-cycle analysis must begin at the stage where estimates of all future cash flows are prepared.

While many patterns exist, Figure 13.5, on page 565, illustrates the cash flows over the phases of a product's life cycle. Without details, observe the unit sales patterns, the pricing strategy, and the drop in unit costs over the product's life. These estimates require involvement of research, marketing, and production personnel very early in the project's life. An integrative team approach to planning and development is becoming more critical to successful project planning.

C O N T E M P O R A R Y   P R A C T I C E   1 3 . 2

Contemporary? Not Quite! But Still Apropos.

Shakespeare's *Merchant of Venice* is a classic application of this "new idea" in management literature, life-cycle investment analysis. How did the merchant operate? This man, with considerable wealth, commissioned a sailing captain, contracted to build a ship, hired a crew, filled the ship with merchandise, sent the ship off to the Orient, and waited for its return. Upon its arrival, he sold the commodities and treasures, compensated the captain and crew, sold the ship, and accounted for the venture. With the profits, he made more investments. If he experienced losses, Shylock was always nearby.

Source: William Shakespeare, *The Merchant of Venice.*

Year-by-year product income statements could be very misleading. In Figure 13.5, of the 6-year life, only three years show a profit; and only in the fifth year does the cumulative cash flow turn positive. In fact, these last three years are the product's most visible period with production and sales activities. By this time the initial research and introduction costs were recorded and perhaps forgotten. Product responsibility may have shifted several times, from research to market research to sales and production. The ability to measure life-cycle revenues and costs may be dissipated throughout the accounting system. Coding of revenues and costs is needed to continue monitoring the actual cash flows similar to the estimated patterns shown in Figure 13.5.

In the trucking industry, it is common to track vehicle costs during the life of a vehicle to assist in replacement decisions. Many use computer models to track mileage, repairs, overhauls, and operating costs. Thus, life-cycle costs are estimated in the acquisition decision, monitored during operation for operations management, and evaluated for disposal purposes. By being included in the initial analysis, lifetime financial consequences of asset ownership can be assessed under a variety of assumptions.

Combining the NPV and Payback Methods—Break-even Time

Pressure to reduce the time needed to introduce new products has brought an interesting twist to the financial analysis of product life cycles. Product developers want to know if a project's life will have a positive return. Figure 13.5 shows a positive cumulative cash flow. We could estimate the payback period for this project in terms of years. But since the payback method ignores the time value of money, this measure is less useful than a discounted approach. By building in a discount rate (12 percent in Figure 13.5), we can find a discounted payback period. This is called the **break-even time**. In the example, the changeover from a negative cumulative net present value to a positive position occurs near the end of Year 5. Thus the break-even time using a 12 percent ROR is 4.87 years, found by interpolation.

Environmental Costs

Of particular importance to life-cycle costing advocates is the inclusion of environmental costs in the initial project evaluation. If reforestation, land

F I G U R E   13.5   Product Life-Cycle Cash-Flow Patterns

	Year 1	Year 2	Year 3	Year 4	Year 5	Year 6
	Develop & Design		**Introduce & Grow**		**Mature**	**Decline**
Life-Cycle Phases:						
Product data:						
Units produced and sold			5,000	15,000	20,000	10,000
Price per unit			$ 80	$ 60	$ 45	$ 30
Production cost per unit			30	20	18	16
Cash revenues			$ 400,000	$ 900,000	$900,000	$300,000
Cash expenses:						
Research & design expenses . .	$ 100,000	$ 300,000	$ 100,000	$ 10,000		
Production preparation		80,000	100,000	50,000		
Marketing expenses			150,000	150,000	$100,000	$ 20,000
Production costs			150,000	300,000	360,000	160,000
Total expenses	$ 100,000	$ 380,000	$ 500,000	$ 510,000	$460,000	$180,000
Net cash flow	$(100,000)	$(380,000)	$(100,000)	$ 390,000	$440,000	$120,000
Cumulative cash flows	$(100,000)	$(480,000)	$(580,000)	$(190,000)	$250,000	$370,000
Present value (12%)	$ (89,300)	$(302,860)	$ (71,200)	$ 248,040	$249,480	$ 60,840
Cumulative present value	$ (89,300)	$(392,160)	$(463,360)	$(215,320)	$ 34,160	$ 95,000

Life of the Project

Graph of Cash Flows

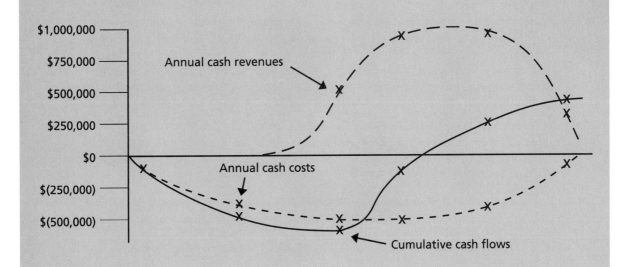

reclamation, pollution prevention safeguards, environmental impact studies, and asset disposals are involved, costs of these activities are relevant to the projects' ROR analyses. The advantage is that these costs are recognized and considered when the decision to incur them is made.

MONITORING AND POST-COMPLETION AUDITING OF CAPITAL INVESTMENTS

Many capital investments are one-time undertakings. In many firms, project management is more difficult than managing repetitive tasks. Having strong project managerial tools and controls is necessary to avoid cost overruns, missed timetables, lost benefits, and disruption of normal business activities.

Once an investment proposal is approved, controls over expenditures and a reporting system to keep managers apprised of the project's status are needed. An essential key is a project control system. All expenditures should be traced to the project. Oversight should be applied to ensure that expenditures are consistent with the approved investment proposal. Systematic status reporting of each project allows those persons who manage projects and those who approved the investment to track project progress and compare it to the original plan.

After equipment is acquired or after a project is completed, performance should be monitored. Results, both from technical and economic points of view, need to be audited or evaluated at the end of a "shakedown period." During this period, it may be found that certain corrections or changes have to be made if the project is to realize its promised potential. Also as noted in Chapter 12, managers may make exaggerated promises to get initial project approval. Knowledge that these claims must be verified is in itself a control. A post-completion audit or evaluation shows whether the forecast benefits are being achieved and may indicate ways in which operations can be improved.

The audit referred to is not an audit in the strict financial accounting sense. In reality, it is a management review and, like the original evaluation, may have estimation problems. Quantification of intangible benefits after-the-fact may be just as difficult as when the original investment proposal was evaluated. The review may also be limited by the available accounting

CONTEMPORARY   PRACTICE   13.3

Post-Audits in the United Kingdom

A United Kingdom study showed that 36 percent of U. K. firms used a formal post-audit process. The audits were used as an "educational device to improve future forecasts. This enlightened view is necessitated by the changes in inflation, market conditions, etc., that are normally outside the divisional manager's control, but that nevertheless occur between the time of making the forecasts and operating the project for at least one year." One participant stated that the benefits of post-audits are "60 percent psychological and 40 percent technical."

Source: Emmanuel, C., D. Otley, and K. Merchant, *Accounting for Management Control*, Second Edition, Chapman and Hall, London, UK, 1990, p. 328.

information. For a special project where a new segment is added, the operating results may be shown separately in the accounting records. But on an individual piece of equipment, which is part of a larger project, separate accounting data may not exist. How much additional effort should be exerted to separate relevant revenues and costs depends on the importance of the investment and the costs of data collection.

The **post-audit** is a mechanism that:

1. Compares actual operating results with forecast cash flows to improve the estimation process in future capital investment proposals.
2. Makes managers aware of a control that will evaluate their forecasts and recommendations and reflect on their ability to produce promised results.
3. Can review project management and evaluate cost and technical performance.
4. Can detect early operating problems.

The post-audit closes the planning and control cycle. Both better control and improved planning should be the long-term expectations.

*P*ROBLEMS OF UNCERTAINTY

The future is never certain. Capital investment analysis depends heavily on estimates of future cash flows. All estimates are risky. How can the risk be measured and incorporated into the analysis? Several steps can be taken:

1. Test the forecast data for source credibility and reasonableness.
2. Test the assumptions underlying the forecasts and the project itself.
3. Create managerial responsibility for the estimates.

The goal is to create the strongest estimates possible. Responsibility for developing the proposal and for executing the project is linked to performance. An audit trail is developed.

Basically, risk can be added to capital investment analysis in three ways:

1. Adding a risk percentage factor to the cost of capital to compensate for risk and differences in risk.
2. Performing a sensitivity analysis of key project variables.
3. Incorporating expected values into cash-flow forecasting.

Risk Percentage Factor

Adding a **risk percentage factor** to the cost of funds is an approach used to recognize the risk of error in estimates. By adding a percentage to the cost of capital, a safety shield is created. The minimum acceptable rate of return is now higher than the cost of capital by the risk factor. This represents a cushion against the prospect that a project's costs were understated, revenues were overstated, or other key estimates were too optimistic.

A number of firms extend this idea still further to recognize differences among divisions or types of projects within a firm. Divisions with histories of strong earnings and successful capital investments might be assigned a lower desired ROR, with a smaller risk factor. New divisions or ones in high-risk areas, such as research and development, might be assigned a desired ROR with a higher risk factor. The following is an example:

	Cost of Capital	Risk Factor	Desired Rate of Return
High-risk division	12%	8%	20%
Normal risk	12	4	16
Low-risk division	12	2	14

However, difficulties exist. Not all projects in a given division deserve the same risk "penalty." Also, past results may not be good indicators of future risks and returns. Yet, adding a risk factor does attempt to recognize **uncertainty** in future cash-flow forecasts.

Sensitivity Analysis

All examples presented thus far assume that estimates of future revenues and costs are valid. However, the possibility always exists that forecast variables could change. **Sensitivity analysis** measures how much key variables can change and still not affect the capital investment decision. Among variables commonly tested are:

1. Sales prices and volumes.
2. Operating and product costs.
3. Life of the project.
4. Development costs.

Many firms have simulation capabilities available to test "what if" scenarios. If sales volume were to drop by 10 percent from the forecast level, what is the impact on ROR or NPV? If because of technological advances a particular machine's life is cut from six years to four years, how badly will losing Years 5 and 6 cash flows hurt the proposal?

For example, assume that the net present value of Project 52 is $80,000. Project 52 will add 10,000 units of productive capacity to our factory per year. We earn a $10 contribution margin per unit. The expanded capacity should last five years. Our desired rate of return is 15 percent. Thus, ignoring taxes, the value of 1 unit of sales per year for five years is $33.52 (from Table 2, 3.352 x $10). We can answer several questions:

1. What if sales only reach 80 percent of new capacity?

    PV of the lost contribution margin: 2,000 units x $33.52 = $67,040

    NPV of project if sales equal 8,000 units: $80,000 - $67,040 = $12,960

    The project still earns better than a 15 percent return.

2. What unit sales are needed to earn at least 15 percent?

    Units of allowed lost sales: $80,000 ÷ $33.52 = 2,386 units

    Units of sales to have a 15 percent ROR: 10,000 - 2,386 = 7,614 units

This means that a 23.86 percent drop in expected new sales will cause the project to have a zero net present value—a return of 15 percent. A drop of 3,000 units would cause the project to have a negative net present value and to be rejected.

3. What if the project lasted only four years, not five years?

PV of Year 5 sales: 10,000 x $10 x 0.497 = $49,700

NPV of Project 52 if Year 5 is eliminated: $80,000 - $49,700 = $30,300

The project is still acceptable.

Cutting years off the end of a project's life is a common method of reducing uncertainty. We have less confidence in estimates that are further into the future.

Using Expected Values

Incorporating multiple estimates for key variables into the analysis has long been attempted. We suggested this approach in budgeting in Chapter 7. One method of incorporating multiple estimates uses optimistic, most likely, and pessimistic estimates of sales, costs, and lives. Another similar method assigns probabilities to various values of key variables. Weighted averages are then used to generate the cash-flow estimates called **expected values**. Using the Project 52 example from the last section, a sales forecast with probabilities could be created:

Sales Level		Probability of Occurrence		
10,000 units	X	0.4	=	4,000 units
9,000 units	X	0.3	=	2,700 units
8,000 units	X	0.2	=	1,600 units
7,000 units	X	0.1	=	700 units
Expected value of sales volume				9,000 units

Obviously, "what ifs" of many variable changes can be analyzed. Spreadsheet capabilities now make these simulations routine and a normal part of project evaluation.

*C*APITAL INVESTMENTS IN NONPROFIT ORGANIZATIONS

In most cases, capital investment decisions in nonprofit organizations are no different than in profit-making concerns. A notable exception is that nonprofit organizations need not consider income tax effects on each flow. The goal is to obtain the highest benefit from the money spent. For example, in choosing between two firefighting trucks with equal operating ratings, the choice is the lowest NPV of operating costs. Often, the legislative and appropriation processes in governmental units may obscure the basic purposes of public spending. Solving social problems, providing public services, and operating quasi-business activities must include cost and benefit analyses to help select efficient and effective solutions.

In special cases, a project's profits and cash flows may not be the primary goal of the expenditure. In the case of a city government, an investment may be made for the general welfare of the citizens. A city will attempt to obtain the highest level of benefits for its citizens at a given cost. For example, neighborhood playgrounds may be built in various sections of the city. The benefits for the children and young people of the city are evident, but how can they be measured? Can the quality of life be quantified? What is the value of a life saved? Intangible benefits are sometimes difficult or impossible to quantify or even to estimate. But estimation of benefits and costs can often help in selecting from among alternatives. Decisions can be and are made that include public good tradeoffs. In many cases, publicly elected officials make those judgments based on their assessments of citizens' preferences. Yet, the managerial accountant must collect, format, and report the quantitative facts as clearly in nonprofit situations as in all others.

*S*OCIAL COSTS OF CAPITAL INVESTMENT DECISIONS

Social costs are growing in importance in the capital investment decisions of both public and private organizations. **Social costs** and **social benefits** are costs and benefits that the community shares. The community can be defined locally, nationally, or globally. Social cost concerns arise from a wide variety of sources and include the costs of:

1. Protecting the health of employees, consumers, and persons in the community.
2. Providing employment and training for workers in the community.
3. Handling substances that endanger the environment.
4. Evaluating environmental impacts prior to capital development.
5. Choosing among various benefits for employees, taxpayers, and other groups given limited resources.
6. Considering public policy, political pressures, and public opinion in allocating capital resources.

Many of these considerations have intangible costs and benefits, legal requirements, and no direct positive cash-flow possibilities for the firm. Pollution controls are often legally required. Good citizenship would expect a firm to want to prevent air and water pollution. But few "win/win" situations exist. New regulations may impose additional costs on a firm that has been experiencing marginal profitability. Capital spending on pollution equipment may mean that equipment purchases to improve the firm's technology and competitiveness must be delayed or eliminated, threatening the firm's survival.

An additional difficulty is that diverse viewpoints value social costs and benefits very differently. Nuclear power plants are classic examples of strong opinions on all sides, which have largely brought a halt to nuclear power development in the United States. Increased and changing regulations, public protests, strong "not-in-my-back-yard" reactions, and major project management problems have caused public utilities to shelve new nuclear power plant construction.

The analysis task is to incorporate the relevant impacts of social costs on the firm into the capital proposal. This means recognizing tangible costs of compliance, of solving environmental problems, and even of public relations. Converting intangibles to dollar estimates can be done easily in some cases and only with great difficulty in others. Equipment costs to achieve air particulate content compliance can be estimated. Valuing clean air, a human life, and wetlands is nearly impossible (but has been attempted), even though we know great value exists. Thus, quantitative analysis should be as complete an assessment of the impacts of social costs on the firm as possible.

The real difficulty arises in the analysis of the qualitative issues. Reducing social costs and maintaining the firm's short-term profitability are often in natural conflict. Enlightened managers have seen that a firm's single goal of profit maximization has evolved into a multipronged set of goals that includes employees', consumers', and the community's concerns.

S UMMARY

This chapter examines additional complexities of capital investment decisions. Even after this chapter's discussion, a student of capital investment decisions can see the difficult task managers have in forecasting the future, considering relevant costs and revenues, and assessing qualitative competitive and social issues. Computational issues such as uneven lives, working capital needs, incremental investment analysis, and inflationary impacts on forecasts were examined. The discussion of tax and accelerated depreciation actually only scratched the surface of tax impacts on capital decisions.

A distinction was drawn between the acquisition and financing decisions. A project proposal must stand on its own merits. Selecting a financing alternative is another decision where relevant cash flows must be evaluated to find the low-cost alternative.

Life-cycle costing is almost assumed in capital investment analysis. But the concept is also useful in measuring the project's performance. Risk analysis, sensitivity analysis, and expected values are tools used to incorporate risk into the cash-flow analysis.

Having a post-audit of capital investment projects closes the planning and control cycle. This post-completion management review is a control tool to evaluate original proposal data, implementation, and actual performance. It is a control tool to improve the planning process for future capital spending.

Social costs and benefits are both difficult to measure and often highly controversial. Many types of social costs bring legal, political, and community pressures to managers who make capital investment decisions. The same reasons that make capital investing critical to a firm make these decisions important to employees and to local and global communities.

P ROBLEM FOR REVIEW

Amarillo Metal Works is considering the replacement of a precision cutting machine. The new machine would cost $40,000 and generate annual cost savings of about $20,000. The

$20,000 estimate is the most likely to be correct (a 50 percent likelihood), but the cost savings could be lower by 20 percent (20 percent likelihood) or higher by 20 percent (30 percent likelihood). Inflation will increase the savings by 5 percent per year. The machine has a useful life of six years, and it qualifies as a 5-year class asset under MACRS. The current cutting machine has a book value of $18,000 and could be made to last six more years. Depreciation on this machine is straight-line. If the machine were sold now, proceeds would be $10,000. Amarillo has a cost of capital of 12 percent and has added a 4 percent risk factor. The company's current tax rate is 40 percent.

Required:

1. Calculate the net initial investment assuming the old machine is sold.

2. Calculate the aftertax annual cash flows assuming the new machine will be used for six years with tax depreciation for five years. Consider the cost savings, expected probabilities, and the estimated inflation rate.

3. Evaluate this investment using the net present value method.

Solution:

1. Net investment:

Investment in new machine	$(40,000)
Less proceeds from the sale of old machine	10,000
Less income tax reduction [.40 x ($18,000 - $10,000)]	3,200
Net investment.	$(26,800)

2. Annual net cash flows for six years:

Inflation Adjustment:	Year 1	Year 2	Year 3	Year 4	Year 5	Year 6
Cash cost savings	$20,000	$20,000	$20,000	$20,000	$20,000	$20,000
Inflation factor	x1.0000	x1.0500	x1.1025	x1.1576	x1.2155	x1.2763
Inflation-adjusted cash savings	$20,000	$21,000	$22,050	$23,152	$24,310	$25,526

Expected Cost Savings:	Probability	Year 1	Year 2	Year 3	Year 4	Year 5	Year 6
Optimistic (+20%)	30% x	$24,000	$25,200	$26,460	$27,782	$29,172	$30,631
Most likely	50 x	20,000	21,000	22,050	23,152	24,310	25,526
Pessimistic (-20%)	20 x	16,000	16,800	17,640	18,522	19,448	20,421
Expected value	100%	$20,400	$21,420	$22,491	$23,615	$24,796	$26,037

Incremental Depreciation:	Year 1	Year 2	Year 3	Year 4	Year 5	Year 6
New depreciation (MACRS):						
Year 1—20.00%	$ 8,000					
Year 2—32.00%		$12,800				
Year 3—19.20%			$ 7,680			
Year 4—11.52%				$ 4,608		
Year 5—11.52%					$ 4,608	
Year 6— 5.76%						$ 2,304
Old depreciation (S-L)	(3,000)	(3,000)	(3,000)	(3,000)	(3,000)	(3,000)
Incremental depreciation	$ 5,000	$ 9,800	$ 4,680	$ 1,608	$ 1,608	$ (696)

Calculation of Annual Cash Inflows:	Year 1	Year 2	Year 3	Year 4	Year 5	Year 6
Cash cost savings	$20,400	$21,420	$22,491	$23,616	$24,795	$26,037
Incremental depreciation	(5,000)	(9,800)	(4,680)	(1,608)	(1,608)	696
Taxable income	$15,400	$11,620	$17,811	$22,008	$23,187	$26,733
Incremental tax (40%)	(6,160)	(4,648)	(7,124)	(8,803)	(9,275)	(10,693)
Aftertax cash flow	$14,240	$16,772	$15,367	$14,813	$15,520	$15,344

3. Net present value method:

Calculations:	Year 0	Year 1	Year 2	Year 3	Year 4	Year 5	Year 6
Net investment	$(26,800)						
Net cash inflow		$14,240	$16,772	$15,367	$14,810	$15,517	$15,351
PV factors (16%) . . .	x 1.000	x .862	x .743	x .641	x .552	x .476	x .410
Present values	$(26,800)	$12,275	$12,462	$ 9,850	$ 8,175	$ 7,386	$ 6,294
Total PV of inflows	56,442						
Net present value	$ 29,642						

T ERMINOLOGY REVIEW

Accelerated Cost Recovery System (ACRS), *561*
Break-even time, *564*
Embedded interest rate, *560*
Expected value, *569*
Inflation, *555*
Lease, *559*
Life-cycle costing, *562*
Modified Accelerated Cost Recovery System (MACRS), *561*

Post-audit, *567*
Product life cycles, *563*
Risk percentage factor, *567*
Sensitivity analysis, *568*
Social benefits, *570*
Social costs, *570*
Uncertainty, *568*
Working capital, *556*

S UGGESTED READINGS

Atkinson, A. A., "Life-Cycle Costing," *CMA Magazine*, July-August 1990, pp. 7-10.

Fellingham, J. C., and R. A. Young, "The Value of Self-Reported Costs in Repeated Investment Decisions," *Accounting Review*, October 1990, pp. 837-856.

Gordon, L. A., M. P. Loeb, and A. W. Stark, "Capital Budgeting and the Value of Information," *Management Accounting Research*, March 1990, pp. 21-35.

Hertz, D. B., "Risk Analysis in Capital Investment," *Harvard Business Review*, January-February 1964, pp. 175-186.

Klammer, T., B. Koch, and N. Wilner, "Capital Budgeting Practices—A Survey of Corporate Use," *Journal of Management Accounting Research*, Fall 1991, pp. 113-130.

Mukherjee, T. K., "A Survey of Corporate Leasing Analysis," *Financial Management*, Autumn 1991, pp. 96-107.

Q UESTIONS FOR REVIEW AND DISCUSSION

1. How can projects be ranked when initial capital investments are different?

2. Why is an initial investment in additional inventory different than an investment in machinery? Explain the difference in cash flows.

3. How can inflation be incorporated into capital investment analysis?

4. What problem arises if alternative investments have different useful lives? Identify at least one solution.

5. By incorporating inflation into the discount rate, what assumptions are made?

6. A project can be divided into Phase I and Phase II. Phase II is a continuation of Phase I, cannot be developed by itself, and may or may not be developed. Phase I looks like a sure "winner," but Phase II is questionable. Capital investment analysis is done on Phase I and on Phases I and II together. What might be learned from each of the analyses? What extension might you suggest?

7. What is meant by financing decisions and investing decisions? Why should they be analyzed separately?

8. Why would the annual cost of leasing differ from the annual cost of buying? Identify factors on both sides.

9. How are the ideas of social costs, environmental costs, and intangible benefits linked to life-cycle costing in capital investment analysis?

10. What depreciation methods are built into most of the annual MACRS depreciation percentages?

11. If capital investment analysis depends so heavily on estimates of future cash flows, what controls exist to prevent overoptimistic estimates from inflating a given project's rate of return?

12. **(a)** ABC Company uses a 14 percent hurdle rate. XYZ Company uses a 20 percent hurdle rate. What could cause this difference in rates?

    (b) In DEF Corporation, Division G uses a 12 percent hurdle rate; Division H uses a 14 percent hurdle rate; and Division I uses a 16 percent hurdle rate. What could cause these differences in rates?

13. What information does sensitivity analysis provide that net present value analysis does not?

14. What does the term "expected value" mean? Is it real? How can it replace a specific estimate of a key variable?

15. How can intangible benefits and costs be incorporated into capital investment analysis?

16. A business analyst recently said, "Social costs of many decisions often far outweigh the business dollars and cents amounts." Why might this be true?

17. A local not-for-profit organization's director was heard to say, "Capital investment analysis works for profit-making organizations but not for us. We're trying to maximize benefits to the people whom our organization serves and not trying to maximize profits." Comment on the pros and cons of the quote.

18. Suggest several advantages of using life-cycle costing for capital project analysis.

E XERCISES

13-1. Gains and Losses on Disposal. A company is considering the purchase of a new machine for $200,000 which would have a 5-year life. The company would sell for $50,000 its old machine which cost $180,000 and has a book value of $20,000. Gains, losses, and profits have a tax rate of 40 percent. The new machine will require about $30,000 less in raw materials inventory to operate.

Required:
What is the net cash outflow for the investment?

13-2. Net Investment.   The management of Westport Metal Fabricators plans to re-place a forming machine that was acquired several years ago at a cost of $45,000. The machine has been depreciated to its salvage value of $5,000. A new machine can be purchased for $80,000. The dealer will grant a trade-in allowance of $6,000 on the old machine. If a new machine is not purchased, the company will spend $20,000 to repair the old machine. Gains and losses on trade-in transactions are not subject to income tax. The cost to repair the old machine can be deducted in the first year for computing income tax. Income tax is estimated at 40 percent of the income subject to tax.

Required:
Show the net investment in the new machine for decision-making purposes.

13-3. Working Capital.   Kim Andrews sells a very successful line of skin protection creams to Scottish golfers. She can spend £100,000 now on additional inventory. The added inventory will increase earnings after taxes by £40,000 per year. She is looking at a 6-year time horizon. She expects to recover the £100,000 inventory investment at the end of the six years. She must earn a 16 percent ROR.

Required:
What is the NPV of this decision? Is this a wise use of funds? Why?

13-4. Incremental Investment and Discounted Rate of Return.   A manufacturer of equipment quotes a price of ¥1,300,000 for a unit of equipment that is being considered by Tatso Products, Inc. This equipment should be able to produce net returns of ¥400,000 each year for five years. Another equipment manufacturer offers a similar unit at a price of ¥1,800,000. This unit of equipment is expected to yield ¥550,000 in net returns each year for five years. These are mutually exclusive investment alternatives. An investment of this type is expected to yield a dis-counted ROR of no less than 16 percent. Ignore taxes.

Required:
1. Which investment alternative is more attractive if a minimum acceptable ROR of 16 percent is expected? Show computations.
2. What is the approximate IRR for each project?
3. What is the approximate IRR for the incremental investment?
4. Comment on the differences between solutions to Part (1) and Parts (2) and (3).

13-5. MACRS Depreciation.   The Buccalo Company will buy tooling equipment for research purposes for $800,000. No salvage value is expected at the end of the 5-year life. The equipment qualifies as a 3-year class asset for MACRS depreciation. Annual net cash inflow before taxes is $300,000.   The tax rate is 40 percent. Buccalo wants at least a 16 percent ROR.

Required:
Find the NPV, the ARR, the payback period, and the approximate IRR.

1-2-3

13-6. Basic MACRS Application.   Sizemore Company is considering an investment opportunity involving a cash outlay of $120,000 for new office building machinery that would last about ten years and have no estimated residual value. The machin-ery would reduce annual cash operating costs by $25,000. The firm's tax rate is 40 percent, and its cost of capital is 14 percent. The company considers this asset to be a 7-year asset for MACRS purposes.

Required:
Find the NPV, the payback period, and the approximate IRR.

13-7. Environmental Costs and Ethical Issues.   Mark Johnson, controller of St. Johns Hospital, is reviewing capital proposals for next year's capital budget. The pro-posals have been put together by the managers responsible for their respective areas. He is concerned that the figures in several proposals do not seem to reflect some sensitive factors. The proposals include:

Building expansion: A new wing will use a site that included a vacant gasoline station. Mark is aware of problems at other similar sites with underground contamination from leaking storage tanks. Cleanup costs have ranged from several thousand to nearly half a million dollars at other sites. The only cost shown in the proposal is demolition costs to remove the building.

Equipment acquisition: A new diagnostic machine is being requested by the Endocrinology Department. The machine uses radioactive isotopes. The proposal includes costs of handling these radioactive wastes as part of the hazardous materials management policies. Mark, however, knows that this machine will significantly increase the hospital's involvement with these materials and will change its status for handling and storage. He does not know what these additional requirements are. These costs are not mentioned.

Parking lot improvement: Expansion of the parking area will include removal of several older homes, owned by the hospital and rented to low-income families. Several community organizations have voiced concerns about losing more quality housing in the area. One group threatens to protest the loss of housing. No mention of this is given in the proposal.

Required:

1. Mark has asked you for suggestions as to how the issues he has raised regarding these proposals might be incorporated into the decision-making process.
2. He is also interested in preventing these omissions in the future. Prepare an addition to the capital investment policy manual that would ensure specific consideration of such issues.

13-8. Net Investment and Discounted Rate of Return. A unit of equipment used in research and development can be acquired from a manufacturer at a $200,000 cost. If this equipment is acquired, an old unit of equipment that is fully depreciated will be sold for $20,000. Annual savings from using the new equipment, before deducting depreciation or taxes, have been estimated at $80,000. The new equipment is a 3-year class asset for MACRS depreciation purposes, should have a 5-year life, and will have no salvage value. Income tax rate is 40 percent for all taxation items.

Required:

1. Determine the net investment in the new equipment.
2. Will this investment be acceptable if the minimum ROR has been established at 16 percent? Explain.

13-9. Ethics of Financing. Jane Outslay, a community activist, has just opened the first community development credit union in the Overton section of Metro City. Its goal is to provide credit to low-income persons living in Overton, the poorest area of Metro City. For several years, no financial institution has operated in this square-mile area. Jane has made many presentations to community groups and needs illustrations of how the credit union can help low-income people establish credit to buy furnishings, remodel homes, and buy autos. She has these facts:

Buying living room furniture: Sam's Rent-to-Own offers a low-quality living room set, table, lamps, and entertainment center for $2,000 cash or a monthly payment of $75 per month, with nothing down and 48 months to pay. The monthly payment includes simple interest of 18 percent for 48 months plus a small monthly service charge of $3.33, common terms in the area.

Somewhat better quality furniture at a reputable store some distance away would cost $1,500. Jane's credit union could provide credit to a working person for 48 months at a 9 percent interest rate. A 10 percent downpayment is required.

Buying a car: Joe's Deal and Drive will sell and finance a $10,000 new car. The monthly payment includes 15 percent simple interest on the $10,000 for four years, a required $1,800 per year insurance policy, a credit checking fee of $500, and a required $5 per month credit life policy.

Mike's Autos will lease the same car on a 24-month lease with a 12 percent imbedded interest rate. The lease on the $9,000 car includes a residual value for the car of $3,000 at the end of the lease period. Insurance from an independent agent will cost $100 per month. A $500 up-front lease contract fee is required.

Jane's credit union will lend 90 percent of the car's cost of $9,000. A 48-month loan can be made at 9 percent. Insurance is again $100 per month.

Required:

Prepare a comparative analysis for each situation for Jane to use in community talks. Highlight qualitative advantages and disadvantages of each financing choice in each situation.

13-10. MACRS and the Replacement Decision.   You are given the following data:

Existing machine:		Replacement machine:	
Cost	$70,000	Cost	$180,000
Book value	30,000	Estimated salvage value	10,000
Salvage value	0	Annual cash operating costs	8,000
Annual depreciation	5,000	MACRS depreciation method . . .	5 years
Annual cash operating costs . .	50,000	Useful life	6 years
Present sales value	50,000		
Remaining life	6 years		

Required:

Determine the NPV of the replacement decision assuming a desired ROR of 16 percent and a 40 percent income tax rate.

13-11. Lease Versus Purchase.   Zalka and Daughters, a Finnish publisher, is considering the purchase of a photocopy machine. The dealer has offered a sale or a lease contract. Maintenance and supplies costs are the same under either arrangement. The cash purchase price in Finnmarks is Fmk45,000. The lease arrangement is monthly payments of Fmk2,000 for 24 months. Zalka's annual cost of funds is approximately 12 percent (or 1 percent per month). Assume that the machine will have a technological life of two years. Ignore taxes.

Required:

Which is the more appealing financial arrangement? Explain.

13-12. Inflation and Investment Analysis.   Sittin'-in-the-Sun Health Spas is evaluating an expansion of its existing facilities this fall. The proposal calls for a 6-year building rental contract at $10,000 a year. Equipment purchases and facility improvements are expected to cost $60,000. Straight-line depreciation ignoring the half-year convention is used. Other cash operating expenses are estimated at $25,000 annually. Based on past experience, the company thinks new revenues should be $50,000 annually. Sittin'-in-the-Sun will not expand unless the project covers its 14 percent cost of capital. The company's effective tax rate is 40 percent.

Inflation is a concern. The controller thinks that revenues and cash expenses will inflate by 5 percent per year. Round the discount rate to the next highest rate available in Table 2 in Chapter 12, page 536.

Required:

Using NPV, suggest whether the expansion project should be adopted.

13-13. Community Service.   Jon Jensen, president of Jensen Groceries, is evaluating several marketing and community charitable activities. The activities include:

Jensen's 10K Run for Food: This popular event gets 400 participants, raises about $10,000 for the local food bank, and costs Jensen about $5,000 in support costs. Jensen does worry about legal liability for race accidents.

United Way contribution: Jensen matches all contributions made by his employees to the local United Way. Jensen's contribution was $15,000 last year. The company receives a plaque and newspaper coverage.

Gourmet cooking classes: Jensen hires a local cooking expert to teach a series of ethnic foods classes. The classes cost about $6,000 per year and have helped give the store a reputation as a connoisseur's food center.

Jensen's helpers: The company encourages employees to give volunteer time to community organizations. If an employee gives forty hours to predetermined charities, Jensen gives the person two days of paid vacation time. Last year this cost Jensen $8,000 in vacation time and overtime for replacements.

Required:
Suggest how Jensen can evaluate these "investments" in the community.

13-14. Lease Versus Purchase Alternatives.   Al Williams in Freeport, Bahamas, is evaluating two similar machines. Both machines do the same tasks and generate the same revenues. Cash operating costs, however, differ and are as follows:

	Alternative A	Alternative B
Year 1	B$125,000	B$ 80,000
Year 2	100,000	80,000
Year 3	80,000	120,000
Year 4	80,000	100,000
Year 5	60,000	100,000
Year 6	40,000	100,000

Both alternatives can be leased under a 6-year contract for B$50,000 per year or purchased for B$200,000. Al's long-term funds have a cost of 14 percent. Borrowing against his bank line of credit costs him 10 percent.

Required:
1. Which alternative is the better operating decision?
2. Which financing alternative is better?
3. What should be done? Explain this decision.

13-15. Lease Financing.   Vehicle A can be leased under a 4-year contract for $16,000 per year or purchased with cash for $54,400. Vehicle B can be leased on a 6-year contract for $15,000 per year or purchased with cash for $74,900. Assume cash funds at a cost of 10 percent. The first payment is due today on both vehicles. Ignore taxes.

Required:
1. What is the embedded interest rate in each vehicle's contract?
2. If we want both vehicles, which should be purchased or leased?

13-16. Unequal Lives.   Having given the matter some thought, you decide that you would be equally happy buying and driving any of the following cars:

(a) A Supreme Deluxe and trading every sixth year.

(b) A Premium Fairmont and trading every third year.

(c) An Economy Delight and trading every second year.

You have decided to base your decision on the present value of the expected future costs. You have predicted your costs as follows:

	Supreme Deluxe	Premium Fairmont	Economy Delight
Original cost	$30,000	$20,000	$15,000
Market value at trade-in time	8,000	8,000	8,000
Annual cash operating costs	2,400	2,000	1,500
Overhaul, fourth year	2,000	0	0
Overhaul, second year	0	1,000	0

You believe that you will stick with this approach for at least six years. Your minimum desired rate of return is 10 percent. Ignore taxes.

Required:

Select the alternative that promises the greatest financial advantage.

13-17. Net Present Value and Expected Values.   Two competing investment alternatives are being considered by the Mills Company. One alternative costs $130,000. The other alternative costs $160,000. An investment of this type is expected to earn a discounted ROR of at least 14 percent. The two projects are each expected to last five years. Ignore taxes. Probabilities of annual revenues from each project differ as follows:

Annual Revenue Probabilities

$130,000 Investment		$160,000 Investment	
10%	$ 10,000	10%	$ 20,000
10%	20,000	20%	40,000
15%	30,000	40%	60,000
20%	40,000	20%	80,000
25%	50,000	10%	100,000
10%	60,000		
10%	90,000		

Required:

Determine the more desirable alternative by the NPV method.

13-18. Sensitivity Analysis of Future Estimates.   Yen Industries estimated the following figures on a bid for a 10-year government contract:

Investment in machinery	$800,000
Additional inventory (funds to be released when contract ends)	100,000
Cost of equipment overhaul at the end of sixth year	120,000
Machinery salvage value at the end of contract (in 10 years)	80,000
Annual revenue from the contract	200,000
Cost of capital	14%

Required:

Ignoring taxes, what impacts (amount and percentage change) will the following mistakes in estimation have on the NPV of this contract?

(a) An understatement of $20,000 in the investment in machinery.

(b) An understatement of $20,000 in the inventory needed.

(c) An understatement of $30,000 in the cost of the overhaul.

(d) An overstatement of $50,000 in the salvage value at the end of the contract.

(e) An overstatement of $4,000 in the annual revenue from the contract.

13-19. Value of MACRS.   Fletch Company plans to buy a piece of equipment that will cost $120,000 and have a useful life of ten years with no salvage value. The expected incremental annual cash inflows from using the new machine are $32,000, and the expected incremental annual cash outflows are $6,000. The tax rate is 40 percent. The company uses a 12 percent cutoff rate.

Required:

1. Using straight-line depreciation and ignoring the half-year rule, what is the net annual aftertax cash benefit? Find the NPV.

2. Assuming that the 5-year MACRS asset class is used, what is the net annual aftertax benefit? Find the NPV, and compare it to your answer to Part (1).

*P*ROBLEMS

13-20. Equipment Replacement.   Dodd Company owns a truck with the following attributes:

Book value	$55,000
Current market value	40,000
Expected salvage value (after 5-year remaining useful life)	0
Annual depreciation expense, straight-line method	11,000
Annual cash operating costs	18,000

The firm's cost of capital is 14 percent, and a 40 percent tax rate is applicable to all taxation items.

The firm plans to replace the truck with one costing $80,000 and having an expected salvage value net of taxes of $5,000, annual cash operating costs of $3,000, and a useful life of five years. Straight-line depreciation of $16,000 per year would be taken on the new truck. Additionally, because the new truck is more efficient, the firm could reduce its repair parts inventory by $15,000.

Required:
Determine whether the new truck should be bought. Use whatever capital investment methods you believe will best present the facts to Dodd's management.

13-21. Mutually Exclusive Alternatives. The Jason Company has $50,000 to invest in either of two alternatives. Investment I yields $12,000 a year in aftertax annual cash flows for ten years. Investment II yields a one-time, aftertax return of $180,000 at the end of ten years.

Required:
1. Using Tables 1 and 2 in Chapter 12, pages 535 and 536, find the PV for all interest columns from 4 percent through 25 percent, using the 10-year row.
2. Which investment is preferred over what ranges of minimum RORs?
3. At approximately what ROR would you reject Investment I and Investment II?

1-2-3

13-22. Incremental Investment. Welton Company is introducing a product that will sell for $10 per unit. Annual volume for the next four years should be about 200,000 units. The company can use either of two machines to make the product. Data are as follows:

	Machine X	Machine Y
Per unit variable cost	$ 4	$ 2
Annual cash fixed costs	725,000	850,000
Cost of machine	800,000	1,400,000

Both machines have 4-year lives and no anticipated salvage value. The firm uses straight-line depreciation, has a 40 percent income tax rate, and has a 14 percent cost of capital.

Required:
1. Determine which machine has the higher approximate IRR.
2. What is the approximate IRR on the incremental investment needed for Machine Y beyond Machine X's investment?

13-23. Comparing Unequals. Data relating to three possible investments are as follows:

	X	Y	Z
Cost	$34,000	$25,000	$75,000
Annual cash savings	8,111	7,458	14,011
Useful life—years	10	5	20

Required:
1. Ignoring taxes, rank the investments according to their desirability using the payback period, IRR, NPV with a discount rate of 12 percent, and the profitability index.
2. Comment on the impact that the unequal lives have on the rankings.
3. Comment on the impact that the unequal investments have on the rankings.

13-24. Sell or Use Equipment.   An offer of $130,000 has been received for equipment that Herrera Products has been using to make certain parts. The equipment is fully depreciated but can be used for five more years. After five years, it is expected to have little, if any, value.

The variable cost of producing the parts is $10 per unit. A total of 10,000 units are needed each year. If the parts are not manufactured, the company must buy them from an outside supplier at a cost of $15 per unit. Also, if the parts are not produced, the space occupied by the equipment can be rented for $12,000 per year. Income tax is estimated at 40 percent of the income before tax. The company uses a 12 percent hurdle rate on this type of investment.

Required:

Prepare a recommendation for Herrera's president on the proposed equipment sale.

13-25. Sensitivity of Key Variables.   The Richmond Company owns a machine that cost $50,000 five years ago, has a book value of $20,000, and has a current market value of $14,000. The machine costs $25,000 per year after taxes to operate and will have no market value at the end of five more years.

The firm has an opportunity to buy a new machine that costs $60,000, will last five years, have no salvage value, and costs $10,000 per year after taxes to operate. It will perform the same functions as the machine currently owned. The firm has a cost of capital of 12 percent.

Required:

1. Determine the approximate ROR that the firm would earn on the investment.
2. Suppose that the production manager is not sure of the cost savings. By what percentage could the cost savings change and still allow the company to earn a 12 percent return?
3. Suppose that the estimate of annual cash flows is considered reliable but that the useful life of the new machine is in question. How many years must the new machine last for the firm to earn a 12 percent return?

13-26. Required Investment in Current Assets.   An interesting project is being considered by Deer Creek, Inc. The project will require an investment of $300,000 in equipment that is expected to have a useful life of eight years with no salvage value. Initially, additional cash, accounts receivable, and inventory will be required in the amount of $100,000. This working capital will be released at the end of eight years. Annual cash inflows from this project before income tax have been estimated at $100,000.

Depreciation is to be deducted by the MACRS method assuming a 7-year MACRS class. Income tax is estimated at 40 percent of income before income tax. The minimum desired ROR is 14 percent.

Required:

Does the investment meet the ROR objective? Explain.

13-27. Equipment Replacement.   Guarantee Insurance Company has been operating a cafeteria for its employees at its headquarters, but it is considering a conversion to a completely automated set of coin vending machines. The old equipment would be sold, and the vending machines would be purchased immediately for cash. A reputable catering firm would take complete responsibility for servicing the vending machines and would simply pay Guarantee a contracted percentage of the gross vending receipts. The following data are available:

Current cafeteria:	
Cash revenues per year	$240,000
Cash expenses per year	265,000

Equipment (6-year remaining life):

Net book value	$ 60,000
Annual depreciation expense.	10,000
Disposal value now	10,000
Disposal value in six years	0

New vending machines:

Purchase price.	$120,000
Forecast disposal value	20,000
Expected annual gross receipts	180,000
Estimated useful life	6 years
Guarantee's percentage receipts	10%

Guarantee uses straight-line depreciation without the half-year rule and has a tax rate of 40 percent.

Required:

1. Evaluate the financial aspects of the change in Guarantee's approach to the cafeteria problem by measuring:

   (a) Expected change in net annual operating cash flow.

   (b) Payback period.

   (c) Approximate IRR.

2. Prepare a report highlighting your findings in Part (1) and any nonquantitative variables that you see impacting this decision. Comment on whether and how the nonquantitative variables can be quantified.

13-28. Life-Cycle Budgeting.   Will O'Connell, product development director of WM Labs, is meeting with the research, marketing, and finance directors tomorrow. His staff has brought together pieces of a financial puzzle on a potential new product. The research lab has spent $100,000 last year (1996) and $300,000 this year (1997) on a project that looks promising. The product, apparently environmentally safe, would cause ground moles to pack their bags and move on. Will's projections show a huge market and strong profits if final testing and production problems can be solved. The research lab forecasts continuing development costs of $500,000 next year (1998) and $300,000 in 1999. Production engineering costs will start in 1998 at $200,000 and continue in 1999 at $400,000. Equipment costs for production would be $2,000,000, incurred at the end of 1998 and depreciated over the next five years using straight-line depreciation.

The product will be introduced in 1999 with annual sales projected at $800,000, $3,000,000, $5,000,000, $4,000,000, and $3,000,000 through 2003, respectively. Cash production costs as a percentage of sales are expected to be 60, 55, 50, 40, and 40 percent through 2003, respectively. After an initial advertising campaign of $300,000 per year in 1999 and 2000, advertising expenses should be $200,000 per year. Will's reports show possible international licensing arrangements. Licensing fees would be 5 percent of international sales. Will thinks international sales will parallel U. S. domestic sales but will lag by one year and cease in 2003. Assume all cash flows occur at yearend. The tax rate is 40 percent.

Required:

1. Comment on the role of 1996 and 1997 expenditures in the project's analysis.

2. Prepare a product life-cycle project analysis showing cumulative expected cash flows through 2003.

3. Evaluate the project for capital investment purposes if WM Labs uses a 15 percent hurdle rate.

4. Comment on the impact of the discount rate on this project.

13-29. Acquisition of Equipment Using Expected Values.   A new product line is being considered by the Engram Company. Special equipment will be required for the manufacturing process. To handle the expected volume, Engram may need to purchase multiple machines if the project is to be accepted. Data with respect to the production of this product are:

Number of Equipment Units	*Product Unit Capacity*
1	60,000
2	120,000
3	160,000
4	200,000
5	240,000

The new product line will increase out-of-pocket annual fixed costs (excluding depreciation) by $140,000. It is estimated that this increase can be expected regardless of the number of machines purchased. The variable cost of producing a unit has been estimated at $6, and the selling price has been estimated at $10. The company has the physical space to install up to five units of equipment. Each machine sells for $300,000 per unit, and the useful life is estimated at six years with no salvage value.

A survey has been made to estimate the potential demand for this product. Probabilities of the estimated demand are as follows:

Sales Probability	*Units of Sales*
10%	40,000
20%	80,000
30%	120,000
20%	160,000
10%	200,000
10%	240,000

Required:

Using straight-line depreciation, a 40 percent tax rate, and a 16 percent discount rate, determine how many machines, if any, should be purchased.

13-30. Purchase vs. Lease Decision.   Cittin Farms is considering replacing a technologically obsolete and fully depreciated tractor currently used in farming operations. The tractor is in good working order and will last, physically, for at least six years. However, the proposed tractor is so much more efficient that Cittin Farms predicts cost savings of $25,000 a year. The tractor's delivered cost is $80,000. Its technological useful life is six years, although the physical useful life is 15 years. The salvage value of the tractor is $10,000 in six years and zero in 15 years. The 5-year class MACRS depreciation will be used on the new tractor. If the new tractor is acquired, Cittin Farms can sell the old tractor at a capital gain of $5,000.

Cittin Farms requires a minimum of a 14 percent aftertax return on all investments. The income tax rate is 40 percent. If Cittin Farms decides to acquire the new tractor, it has the option of purchasing or leasing the tractor. The distributor will sell the tractor outright for $80,000 delivered cost or will lease the tractor at $24,000 per year for six years. Under the lease, the first payment of $24,000 is due now; and, at the end of six years, the tractor reverts to the distributor.

Required:

1. Should Cittin Farms acquire the new tractor? Explain.

2. If Cittin Farms should acquire the new tractor, would the company prefer an outright purchase or a lease? Why?

13-31. Financing Alternatives.   Martin Hospital Corporation is a for-profit health care provider. The hospital's Capital Needs Committee has approved the acquisition of new magnetic resonance imaging (MRI) equipment. Before the final recommendation is sent to Martin's board of directors, financing choices must be evaluated. The equipment will cost $1,000,000, have a life of five years (assume straight-line depreciation), and have no salvage value. Three financing choices have been suggested.

Finance internally: Martin Corporation will pay the vendor from its cash balance on the date the machine is certified as ready for operations.

Finance with a bank loan: Martin would obtain a bank loan to finance 90 percent of the equipment cost at 10 percent annual interest. Five annual payments of $237,418 each would be due at the end of each year, beginning one year from the certification date. Martin will pay the remaining $100,000 from its cash balance at certification date.

Lease from a lessor: MedLease could lease the equipment to Martin for an initial $50,000 payment and five annual payments of $220,000 each starting one year from the certification date. At the lessee's option, the equipment can be purchased at the fair market value at the lease's termination. (The lessor is currently estimating a 30 percent residual value.) At this time, however, Martin does not plan to buy the machine.

Martin has a bank borrowing rate of 10 percent, a corporate hurdle rate of 12 percent, and a 40 percent income tax rate.

Required:

1. Prepare a PV analysis as of the certification date of the expected aftertax cash flows for the three financing choices.

   (a) Identify the discount rate(s) you used and explain why.

   (b) Recommend the preferred financing choice.

2. Discuss the qualitative factors Martin should consider before a final financing decision is made.

(ICMA adapted)

13-32. Inflation Impacts. Goslin Company designs and makes lighting fixtures. The sales manager is deciding whether to introduce a new line of lights. The lights will sell for $100 and have variable costs of $40. Volume is expected to be 2,000 units per year for five years. Additional fixed cash operating costs will be $50,000 per year. Additional machinery costing $200,000 is needed. The new machinery will have a 5-year life and have no salvage value. Goslin uses straight-line depreciation. Goslin's tax rate is 40 percent, and the company uses a hurdle rate of 15 percent.

The sales manager sees a serious threat to the project's profitability—inflation. He knows competition will allow only small increases in prices, perhaps 4 percent per year. But he knows labor and materials cost pressures could cause variable costs to increase by double that rate, probably 8 percent per year. Fixed costs are likely to increase by $2,000 per year. The general inflation rate is estimated to be 6 percent.

Required:

1. Evaluate the NPV of the project, assuming that inflation is included in the hurdle rate.

2. By adjusting each cost and revenue element by its estimated inflation factor, evaluate the project using NPV. Round the discount rate to the nearest whole percent.

3. Comment on the impact of inflation on the NPV of the project.

13-33. Sensitivity Analysis. Hillkirk-Lurie Corporation wants to expand a production facility because of increasing demand for its specialty line of cycling shorts. The following information is available for management's consideration in this decision:

Investment:	
Increase in fixed assets	$125,000
Increase in working capital	45,000
Recovery at the end of five years:	
Fixed assets	$ 25,000
Working capital	45,000
Project life	5 years

Annual operations:

Volume in units	10,000
Selling price per unit	$ 28
Variable cost per unit	15
Fixed cost, exclusive of depreciation.	24,000

Straight-line depreciation is used for tax purposes. Ignore salvage value and the half-year convention. The company's tax rate is 40 percent. On investments of this nature, the company uses a 15 percent aftertax ROR cutoff.

Required:
1. Determine the NPV of this investment proposal.
2. If variable costs are underestimated, by how much can the estimates be off and the investment still return 15 percent?
3. Holding costs and prices constant, by how much can unit volume fall and still have the firm earn 15 percent?
4. Given the original data, by how much can fixed costs increase (exclusive of depreciation on the new investment) and still have the project earn a 15 percent return?

C ASE 13A—DIVISIONAL PERFORMANCE IN THE CHAMBER CORPORATION

Chamber Corporation has four divisions, each in a different industry. Gettes Division manufactures appliances. Its management is preparing its capital investment requests for next year. Six projects have about the same degree of risk and are being reviewed for inclusion in Gettes' capital budget request sent to Chamber headquarters. The division manager must select which to forward. The six projects and their data are as follows:

	Project A	*Project B*	*Project C*	*Project D*	*Project E*	*Project F*
Economic life	6 years	8 years	5 years	8 years	6 years	8 years
Initial investment	$106,000	$200,000	$140,000	$160,000	$144,000	$130,000
PV of cash inflows (12%) .	175,683	223,773	(10,228)	234,374	150,027	199,513
IRR	35%	15%	9%	22%	14%	26%
Payback period	2.2 years	4.5 years	3.9 years	4.3 years	2.9 years	3.3 years

Projects A and D use the same excess capacity; therefore, both could not be accepted. Chamber has set its hurdle rate at 12 percent. The same hurdle rate is used for all four divisions.

Required:
1. If Gettes Division has no budget restrictions for capital investments and has been told to maximize its value to the Corporation, what projects should be recommended to Chamber? Explain your recommendation.
2. If Gettes Division will be restricted to $450,000 for capital investments and has been told to maximize its value to the Corporation, what projects should be recommended? Assume that any unused funds will be invested at the hurdle rate. Explain your recommendation.
3. Discuss the propriety of using the same hurdle rate for all four divisions.

(ICMA adapted)

C ASE 13B—PLASTIC PRODUCTIONS, INC.

On Monday morning, Joe Sequeira, owner and president of Plastic Productions, Inc. (PPI), sits in his office pondering the acquisition of a new machine for the company. PPI is in need of an additional plastic injection molding press, specifically a 175 ton Cincinnati Machining injection molding press. A former coworker, who now works at a large plastics firm on the East Coast, mentioned at a recent trade show that his firm was leasing new injection molding presses. In fact, Sequeira maintains a favorable relationship with BancTwo so that PPI can borrow needed cash for capital investments. Realizing he lacks knowledge about leasing, Sequeira somewhat reluctantly calls in Claudia Ringwald, his controller.

"Claudia," says Sequeira, "I wonder if it's possible for us to lease that press. Trouble is, I don't know the first thing about leasing. And to tell you the truth, I've always liked owning my equipment. But, I want you to show me whether my negative gut feeling on leasing is right or wrong."

"No problem," replies Ringwald. "Consider it done."

PPI is a small, closely-held firm that employs 50 people. As a job-shop plastics molder, PPI offers a full-service approach to its customers. The process starts when PPI receives an order from a buyer, typically a large original equipment manufacturer. An order is the design specifications for a mold. Once PPI's tooling engineers finish the mold, a product prototype is made and shipped to the buyer for inspection. When the prototype is approved, it is returned to PPI; and production begins.

Driving the decision to acquire the additional injection molding press is a major strategic decision based on two significant factors. First, the technical experience at PPI has grown greatly over the past several years to the point where the engineering staff and the production personnel feel that PPI is ready to tackle specialty low-volume, high-margin jobs that require considerably more technical and production expertise.

The second factor is the increasing control high-volume customers exercise over PPI. These customers are typically large original equipment manufacturers that face increasingly stiff foreign competition. To stay competitive, these customers employ just-in-time techniques. Basically, PPI has been forced to incur higher costs since it produces the entire contract amount in one run but only ships when the customer calls. Realizing that these JIT techniques will only become more prevalent with the high-volume buyers, PPI wishes to increase its flexibility.

The sales rep at Cincinnati Machining quotes Ringwald a price of $25,000 for the press. The company is willing to lease the press to PPI at $6,000 annually for six years, with the first payment due upon the arrival of the equipment at PPI. If the press is leased, Cincinnati will provide free maintenance. If purchased, PPI could enter into a series of one-year maintenance contracts with Cincinnati at the cost of $900 annually. The first annual maintenance payment would be due when the machine is delivered to PPI.

The bank officer at BancTwo tells Ringwald that the bank would make a loan to PPI for $25,000. The terms would be four years at a 10 percent annual rate. Equal annual payments are due at the end of each year.

Ringwald determines that the press will have a useful life of six years, with no salvage value, and will have to be replaced due to heavy use in spite of strong maintenance. She notes that the equipment is eligible for the MACRS using a 5-year class life. PPI's current marginal tax rate is 40 percent.

Required:

Prepare a memo to Mr. Sequeira from Ms. Ringwald evaluating the purchase or lease of the press and the financing alternatives. Provide spreadsheets that will support your analyses.

CHAPTER *14*

Analysis of Decentralized Operations

*L*EARNING OBJECTIVES

After studying Chapter 14, you will be able to:

1. Define the components of division net income, division direct profit, division controllable profit, and division contribution margin.

2. Describe the problems of selecting an investment base for evaluating performance.

3. Evaluate a division manager's performance using return on investment and residual income.

4. Identify the criteria for developing and evaluating transfer pricing policies.

5. Discuss the advantages and disadvantages of alternative transfer pricing methods.

6. Explain how the importance of intracompany dealings, the existence of external markets, the relative power positions of the divisions, the intent of managers, and other factors affect transfer pricing and divisional evaluations.

Dividing the Profit Pie: Whose Is Whose?

. . . a large Nigerian oil company . . . . . . .ne company has five operating . . . . . .uon & Production, Trading & Supply, Gas . . . . .ng, Refining, and Marketing & Distribution. Each division is responsible for generating a profit and for managing its investment in assets. Debates have raged among division managers about who earned what profits since, in many cases, "Your revenues are my costs."

The Exploration & Production Division has the task of finding, developing, and producing oil and gas reserves. Oil produced is sold to the Trading & Supply Division or to outside customers, depending on who offers the best prices. Gas produced is sold to the Gas Processing Division, petrochemical companies, or pipeline companies.

The Trading & Supply Division is responsible for meeting the crude oil needs of the Refining Division. It purchases crude oil from the Exploration & Production Division and the open market. Crude oil not sold to Refining is marketed overseas. Consequently, the division engages in speculative buying and selling as a major means of generating profits.

Although the Gas Processing Division may purchase gas from other companies, 90 percent of its gas needs are met by the Exploration & Production Division. Processing

results in liquid petroleum gas products such as ethane, propane, and butane. These products are sold to the Marketing & Distribution Division and to petrochemical companies.

The Refining Division has refineries in Kano, on the Niger River, and in Ibadan. The refineries have the capability to produce a full range of petroleum products. Finished products are sold either to the Marketing & Distribution Division or to an overseas wholesale market.

Marketing & Distribution sells to utilities and international resellers, plus industrial, governmental, commercial, and residential customers. It buys its products from the Refining and Gas Processing Divisions. If shortages occur, it may purchase from overseas wholesale markets. The division sells a wide range of products. It owns a barge fleet, tanker trucks, and some pipeline facilities for transporting the products. Other product shipments are contracted with shipping companies.

Since the divisions each generate profits and have tremendous investments in assets, Shagari Petroleum wants to develop an appropriate measure for evaluating the financial performance of the divisions and their managers. Also, a transfer price policy should value intracompany deals fairly.

One of the most striking characteristics of organizations over the past thirty years has been top management's desire to grow and yet retain the advantages of smallness. Companies have decentralized operations to retain this element of smallness, to build "entrepreneurial spirit," and to motivate division managers to act as the heads of their "own" companies.

In general, a **decentralized company** is one in which operating subunits (usually called divisions) are created with definite organizational boundaries and in which managers have decision-making authority. Thus, responsibility for portions of the company's profits can be traced to specific division managers. Even though the amount of authority granted to these managers varies among companies, the spirit of decentralization is clear—to divide a company into relatively self-contained divisions and allow them to operate in an autonomous fashion.

This chapter discusses two problem areas common to evaluating divisional performance. Evaluation measures and how these measures can be used are covered first. Then we discuss criteria, approaches, and problems associated with transfer prices for goods and services moving among divisions.

*R*EVIEW OF RESPONSIBILITY CENTERS

Before discussing decentralization and performance measures, it is essential to review the types of responsibility centers first introduced in Chapter 7. A **responsibility center** is any organizational unit where control exists over costs or revenues. Managers of **cost centers** have control over the incurrence of costs but not over revenues. Cost centers are usually found at lower levels of an organization but may include entire plants or even entire parts of an organization, such as manufacturing or the controller's office. In contrast, managers of **profit centers** have control over both costs and revenues. These managers are responsible for generating revenues and for the costs incurred in generating those revenues.

In **investment centers**, managers control costs, revenues, and assets used in operations. The investment represents plant and equipment, receivables, inventories, and, in some cases, payables traceable to the investment center's operations. Companies or subsidiaries could be investment centers or profit centers, depending on whether the corporate headquarters gives investment responsibility to these levels. Investment responsibility is defined as authority to buy, sell, and use assets.

Top management's intent often determines the type of responsibility center. In a large company, a data processing center could be a cost center, either absorbing its own costs or allocating its costs to users of the firm's computer operations. As a profit center, it would be allowed to charge a rate for data processing services it provides to internal users and be expected to earn a profit on its operations. To create an investment center, the manager would be given responsibility to acquire equipment and update services from funds generated by its charges for services provided. Often, organizational structures create natural cost, profit, or investment centers. But managerial intent is perhaps the most important factor in determining how a decentralized unit will be viewed and managed.

*A*DVANTAGES OF DECENTRALIZATION

Decentralization is the delegation of decision-making authority to lower management levels in an organization. The degree of decentralization depends on the amount of decision-making authority top management delegates to successively lower managerial levels. Advantages of decentralizing include:

1. **Motivated managers.**   Managers who actively participate in decision making are more committed to working for the success of their divisions and are more willing to accept the consequences of their actions, whether positive or negative.
2. **Faster decisions.**   In a decentralized organization, managers who are close to the decision point and familiar with the problems and situations are allowed to make the decisions. Consequently, decisions can be made faster without moving data up the organization and having a decision made by a manager far removed from the action.
3. **Enhanced specialization.**   Delegating authority permits the various levels of management to do those things each does best. For example,

top management can concentrate on strategic planning and policy development; middle management on tactical decisions and management control; and lower management on operating decisions.

4. **Defined span of control.**   As an organization increases in size, top management has more difficulty controlling the organization. Decentralizing the authority defines more narrowly the span of control for each manager and thus makes the control system more manageable.

5. **Training.**   Experience in decision making at low management levels results in trained managers who can assume higher levels of responsibility when needed.

To realize the full benefits of these advantages, top management must resolve the following issues:

1. **Competent people.**   Without competent people, the best policies break down; and a lack of control reduces the efficiency and effectiveness of operations.

2. **Measurement system.**   The same measurement system should be used for all divisions. Top management must develop policies that provide consistency in reporting periods, methods of reporting, and methods of data collection.

3. **Suboptimization.**   Left to themselves, division managers may work for their own interests without consideration of benefits to the entire organization. Top management needs to focus all managers' efforts on corporate goals through planning and incentive systems.

Formulating the best method for controlling and evaluating divisions is usually more complex than any other single control activity within a company. Motivation, control, and managerial behavior are broad topics and are far beyond the scope of this book.

*M*EASUREMENT OF FINANCIAL PERFORMANCE

In previous chapters, planning and control methods were discussed. We apply these to cost, profit, and investment center evaluations. Cost controls used in cost centers are also relevant for profit and investment centers. Revenue and profit measurements used in profit centers are also applied to investment centers. Thus, we can build the following planning and control structure:

	Cost Center	Profit Center	Investment Center
Expense budgeting	X	X	X
Flexible budgets	X	X	X
Plan versus actual expense comparisons	X	X	X
Standard cost variances	X	X	X
Revenue and profit budgeting		X	X
Plan versus actual controllable contribution margin		X	X
Plan versus actual direct contribution margin		X	X
Asset utilization and rate of return target setting			X
Plan versus actual asset utilization comparisons			X
Plan versus actual rates of return comparisons			X

It is rare that financial measures alone can evaluate the performance of a responsibility center. Product or service quality, delivery reliability, market share, and responsiveness to customers are all nonfinancial measures critical to the overall success of a firm. Both financial and nonfinancial goals are often parts of a manager's business plan. We discuss in detail nonfinancial performance measures in Chapter 15.

For profit and investment centers, selecting proper financial performance measures is not an easy task. The financial measures chosen:

1. Send messages to all managers about what is important to the firm's executive managers.
2. Are often the basis for calculating incentive compensation, personnel evaluations, and promotion decisions.
3. Influence the allocation of new capital and personnel resources.

Rate of return on investment is widely accepted as the primary measure of performance for investment centers.

Return on Investment

Return on investment (ROI) is defined as a ratio:

$$\text{Return on investment} = \text{Profit} \div \text{Investment}$$

We can decompose this ratio into two elements for better control and evaluation:

$$\text{Return on investment} = (\text{Profit} \div \text{Sales}) \times (\text{Sales} \div \text{Investment})$$

The first term is **return on sales (ROS)** (sometimes called the profit margin). It measures the percentage of each sales dollar that is turned into profit. The second term is **asset turnover** which measures the ability to generate sales from the assets a division employs.

Implementing the ROI concept raises a number of issues. Problems exist in defining the profit numerator, investment denominator, and the ratio itself. Even then, divisions within a company may be dissimilar, creating "apples and oranges" comparisons.

The Numerator—Division Profit. The choice of the profit figure is not simple. The first problem is how the profit number will be used. Will it be used to evaluate the division as an economic unit or to evaluate the division manager's performance? A different profit is appropriate for each. Once the purpose is decided, the next problem is how to construct the best measure from several profit concepts commonly available. Assume that a division reports the following profit and loss data (all numbers in thousands):

Revenue from division sales	$1,000
Direct division costs:	
Variable cost of goods sold and other operating costs	700
Fixed division overhead—controllable at the division level	100
Fixed division overhead—noncontrollable at the division level	50
Indirect division costs:	
Allocated (fixed) home office overhead	60

Four alternative income statements organize the data for different purposes. (The profit titles are also consistent with those used in Chapter 2.)

	Division Variable Contribution Margin	Division Controllable Contribution Margin	Division Direct Contribution Margin	Division Net Profit
Revenue	$ 1,000	$ 1,000	$ 1,000	$ 1,000
Direct costs:				
Variable costs	700	700	700	700
	$ 300			
Fixed controllable costs		100	100	100
		$ 200		
Fixed noncontrollable costs			50	50
			$ 150	
Indirect costs:				
Allocated home office overhead				60
				$ 90

Division Net Profit. The best profit measure for division performance may appear to be **division net profit**. However, the net profit calculation includes allocated home office overhead. An example of these costs would be the costs of operating the president's office. Although each division benefits from these costs, they are not controllable at the division level or traceable to specific divisions. Generally, net profit is a poor indicator of a division's performance. The main arguments for using net profit are that the division manager is made aware of the entire firm's operating costs and that these costs must be covered by the divisions' earnings. Another argument is that the allocated home office costs stimulate division managers to pressure corporate managers to control their costs.

Home office expenses that are traceable to specific divisions should be assigned directly to those divisions. Allocated home office expenses are likely to be arbitrary and open to question by the division managers. Often, division managers spend much time attempting to reduce their costs by getting top management to change the allocation procedure.

Division Direct Contribution Margin. **Division direct contribution margin** is defined as total division revenue less direct costs of the division. This concept avoids the main difficulty of division net profit since common costs of the firm are excluded. The direct contribution margin is the most useful profit measure for comparing divisions' performances, for resource allocation decisions, and for corporate planning purposes. All revenues and costs traceable to the divisions are included.

Often, corporate-level decision makers use the direct contribution margin to indicate where additional investments should be made to generate the greatest incremental returns. Certainly, specific projects must justify themselves as Chapters 12 and 13 demonstrate. But more attention will be paid to high-performing divisions.

Division Controllable Contribution Margin.   **Division controllable contribution margin** is defined as total division revenues less all costs that are directly traceable to the division and that are controllable by the division manager. This calculation is best for managerial performance measurement, because it reflects the division manager's ability to execute assigned responsibilities.   Any variances between actual and plan can be explained in terms of factors over which the division manager has control.

Sometimes direct costs are traceable to a division but cannot be controlled at that level. For instance, a division head's salary is controllable only at a higher management level. Also, some division costs, such as long-term leases and depreciation, are from past investment decisions that may have been made by higher level managers or previous division managers. These direct but noncontrollable costs should be excluded from the profit calculation for managerial evaluations. If this is not done, the division profit used for performance evaluation may be affected by actions outside the division or of prior managers.

Some factors in the division controllable contribution margin may be difficult for the division manager to influence; for example, the materials prices may increase. Even though the price cannot be changed, perhaps alternate materials can be used; or alternate sources of supply can be found. Problems of this nature may be difficult to solve, but they are part of the division management's responsibility. Failure to solve such problems is different from being unable to take action due to lack of authority.

Division Variable Contribution Margin.   The **division variable contribution margin** is defined as total revenues less variable costs. Although variable contribution margin is useful in decision making, for performance evaluation its defect is obvious; namely, direct and controllable fixed costs are excluded from the calculation. Variable costs do have an important role in intracompany pricing policies and decisions, which are discussed later in this chapter.

The Denominator—Investment.

   If divisions are to be evaluated by ROI, it is necessary to measure the investment base. The **investment base** may be total direct assets, net direct assets, or net direct assets managed. Net direct assets would be traceable assets minus any traceable liabilities.   Again, the distinction between direct and controllability is important. Certain assets may be traced to a division but not be in service or usable by the division manager.

Since ROI is a measure for a period of time, which date during that period should be chosen to measure the amount of assets? Usually, a simple average of the beginning and ending amounts is used.

Asset Identification.   The first task is to decide which assets to assign to each division. Many assets can be traced directly to a division. For example, much of a firm's physical property can be traced to a particular division. A division may handle its own receivables and inventory and may even have jurisdiction over its own cash. But sometimes, these traceable assets are centrally administered and controlled. By proper account coding, it is possible to trace receivables and inventories to specific divisions. Cash, as a corporate asset, is rarely traceable to specific divisions.

For assets that are common to several divisions, no amount of coding, sorting, or classifying will enable tracing them to the divisions. An example of a common asset would be the administrative offices used by two product divisions. Any basis of allocation would be arbitrary. As with home office expenses, avoiding these arbitrary allocations generally improves the analysis.

Asset Valuation. Once the assets have been identified with the divisions, the value of the assets must be determined. It may seem that the assets should be stated at some current value (e.g., replacement cost or original cost adjusted for price-level changes) rather than on a historical-cost basis. The obvious difficulty is measurement. How can replacement costs be determined? If a common-dollar base is desirable, which price-level index should be used? It is easier to raise questions than to give answers.

Preferred Relationships. Matching an income measure and an investment base is the next step. If the purpose is to evaluate the division itself, direct contribution margin would be the natural match with net division direct assets, which are assets traceable to the specific division less traceable liabilities. To evaluate the division managers, controllable contribution margin should be matched with net direct managed assets. Managed assets include the assets controlled by the division manager having the authority to acquire, use, and dispose of these assets.

Additional Problems With ROI. Using the ROI concept as a means of evaluating performance raises some concerns about how effective ROI can be and about potential undesirable impacts that may arise from its use.

Comparability Among Divisions. One of the major concerns is that ROI comparisons should use the same definitions for the same purposes. Divisions being compared should have the same or similar accounting methods.

The same depreciation method should apply to similar classes or categories of assets. Likewise, incorrect comparisons result when one division uses FIFO for inventories and another division uses LIFO. Also, each division being compared should have the same or similar policies for capitalizing or expensing costs. For instance, one division might expense tools whenever they are purchased. Another division might capitalize the original tools plus any increments and expense replacement tools. It would be inappropriate to compare these two divisions on the basis of ROI without making appropriate adjustments.

Motivational Impact on Managers. From top management's point of view, division managers should be working to achieve the overall objectives of the organization. This requires strategies, policies, techniques, and incentives to act as motivators for division managers. **Goal congruence** is the term often used to link each division manager's goals with top management's goals. Individual managers may have personal and organizational goals that differ from top management's goals. When designing managerial performance criteria, senior management must carefully select measures to promote goal congruence. Thus, managers should be motivated to work for their own benefit while, at the same time, benefiting the whole organization.

ROI may sometimes promote decisions that are not goal congruent. For example, suppose that one division of a company is currently earning 25 percent ROI. The division manager may be reluctant to make additional investments at, perhaps, 20 percent because the average return of the division would drop. However, if new investments in other divisions of the company yield only 15 percent, company management may prefer that the investment with a yield of 20 percent be accepted. The high-earning manager may still be reluctant to lower the average ROI from 25 percent even though company management has set 15 percent as the base rate for comparison. Thus, the use of ROI might restrict additional investment to the detriment of company-wide profitability.

Improving ROI.   Since division managers are expected to improve ROI, they look to components they can control. ROI can be improved in three direct ways: by increasing sales, by decreasing expenses, and by reducing the level of investment. To see how individual changes affect the ROI calculation, consider the following data for the Sports Division of Eddington Entertainment Corporation:

Sales	$2,500,000
Variable costs	1,500,000
Contribution margin	$1,000,000
Fixed costs	600,000
Net income	$ 400,000
Investment base	$2,000,000
Return on sales	16.00%
Asset turnover	1.25 times
ROI	20.00%

Increase Sales.   Looking at ROI as a product of return on sales and asset turnover might give the impression that the sales figure is neutral, since it is the denominator in return on sales and the numerator in asset turnover. However, suppose the Sports Division can increase ticket sales without increasing unit variable costs or fixed costs. The return on sales improves. This happens anytime the percentage increase in total expenses is less than the percentage increase in dollar sales. The increase in sales also improves the asset turnover as long as there is not a proportionate increase in assets. The objectives are to attain the highest level of net income from a given amount of sales and the highest level of sales from a given investment base.

Continuing the numerical example for the Sports Division, assume that ticket sales and total variable costs increase by 5 percent and that fixed costs and the investment base remain constant. ROI, return on sales, and asset turnover all increase, as follows:

Sales (105%)	$2,625,000
Variable costs (105%)	1,575,000
Contribution margin	$1,050,000
Fixed costs	600,000
Net income	$ 450,000
Investment base	$2,000,000
Return on sales	17.14%
Asset turnover	1.31 times
ROI	22.50%

Reduce Expenses.   Often, the easiest path to improved ROI is to implement a cost reduction program (focusing on certain expense areas or across-the-board cuts). Reducing costs is usually the first approach managers take when facing a declining return on sales. A rather typical pattern has emerged. First, review the discretionary fixed costs, either individual cost items or programs representing a package of discretionary fixed costs, and find those that can be curtailed or eliminated quickly. Second, look for ways to make employees more efficient by eliminating duplication, nonvalue-adding time, or downtime and by increasing individual workloads. Third, review costs of resource inputs for operations and seek less costly choices.

Reduce Investment Base.   Managers have traditionally sought to control sales and expenses. Their sensitivity to asset management, however, has not always been at the same high level. Managers, whose performances are evaluated using ROI, will find that trimming any excess investment can have a significant impact on the asset turnover and, therefore, on ROI. Reducing unnecessary investment often involves selling or writing off unused or unproductive assets. Recently, many companies have reduced investment in inventories, and also lowered nonvalue-added expenses, by changing to just-in-time inventory systems. Referring to the original Sports Division data, assume that its managers are able to reduce the investment by 4 percent but still maintain the same level of sales and expenses. As a result, both the asset turnover and ROI increase:

Sales	$2,500,000
Variable costs	1,500,000
Contribution margin	$1,000,000
Fixed costs	600,000
Net income	$ 400,000
Investment base (96% of original)	$1,920,000
Return on sales	16.00%
Asset turnover	1.30 times
ROI	20.83%

If the eliminated investment is a depreciable asset, depreciation expense will also be reduced. This causes a compound reaction: profitability increases, return on sales increases, and ROI increases by improvement in both the return on sales and the asset turnover.

Residual Income

The use of residual income has been proposed as an alternative to ROI. Residual income focuses attention on a dollar amount instead of a ratio. The maximization of a dollar amount will tend to be in the best interest of both the division manager and the company as a whole.

In general, **residual income** is defined as the operating profit of a division less an imputed charge for the operating capital used by the division. The same measurement and valuation problems encountered with ROI still apply to residual income. But motivational problems should be eased. Assume that a division's current controllable contribution margin (before any imputed capital charge) is $250,000 and the relevant investment is $1,000,000. The ROI, then, is 25 percent. Suppose top management wants division management to accept incremental investments so long as the return is greater than 15 percent. We refer to this rate as a **minimum desired rate of return**.

This minimum desired rate of return is then used to calculate an imputed charge for division investment funds. The residual income would be calculated as follows:

Division controllable profit (before imputed capital charge)	$ 250,000
Less imputed capital charge (15% x $1,000,000)	150,000
Division residual income.	$100,000

The advantage of this evaluation measure is that the division manager is concerned with increasing a dollar amount (in this case, the $100,000) and is likely to accept incremental investments which have a yield of over 15 percent. The division manager's behavior, then, is congruent with company-wide objectives. This would less likely be true with the ROI measure, since any incremental investment earning less than 25 percent pulls down the division's current ROI.

A disadvantage with residual income arises when comparing the performance of divisions of different sizes. For example, a division with $50 million in assets should be expected to have a higher residual income than one with $2 million in assets.

The stage of growth and other risk factors influence the potential profits that a division can generate. Consequently, top management might select different minimum desired rates of return for each division to recognize the unique role each plays in the organization. For example, a start-up division may be more expensive to operate than a division in the mature stage—justifying a lower initial rate of return.

Ethical Concerns Relating to Performance Measures

Division managers can increase short-run profits of divisions to the detriment of the company as a whole. For example, it may be possible to delay maintenance costs. Such an action will increase short-run profits but adversely affect long-run profitability of the division and the company. Expenditures that engender employee loyalty such as employee physical fitness programs may be eliminated. By reducing training costs, the division manager may not develop long-run top management personnel.

C O N T E M P O R A R Y   P R A C T I C E   1 4 . 1

International Comparison of Residual Income Usage

A recent article reported on the use of residual income by manufacturing companies in the U. S., Korea, and Japan. In the U. S., 13 percent of the surveyed companies indicated they used residual income; while in Korea and Japan, the figures were 20 percent and 6 percent, respectively.

Source: Kim, I., and J. Song, "U. S., Korea, and Japan: Accounting Practices in Three Countries," *Management Accounting*, August 1990.

CONTEMPORARY   PRACTICE   14.2

Bonuses Based on Residual Income

Businesses sometimes base executive bonuses on some form of residual income. The following excerpt relates to The Walt Disney Company:

"The agreement provides for an annual bonus equal to 2% of the amount (the "Bonus Base") by which the Company's net income for the fiscal year exceeds the amount representing a return on stockholders' equity of 11%."

Source: Proxy statement of The Walt Disney Company, December 28, 1992.

Our earlier discussion that the use of ROI may not promote goal congruent behavior has ethical implications also. A manager should consider whether it is ethical to reject an investment that would benefit the company even though it would reduce the manager's average ROI.

PERFORMANCE EVALUATION SYSTEMS IN SERVICE ORGANIZATIONS

Service organizations, like manufacturers and merchandisers, also need evaluation systems. Evaluation criteria and measures can depend on whether the service organization is commercial or not-for-profit.

Profit-oriented operations have an incentive to be profitable. They may use ROI or residual income, if an appropriate profit measure and an investment base are available. Obviously, organizations such as CPA firms, law firms, insurance agencies, and consulting firms do not have large investment bases. Personnel is their prime resource. Furthermore, they often lease equipment, space, cars, and other operating assets. Using ROI or residual income in these situations will not give a realistic measure of performance for the divisions within the organization. Return on revenue is a better measure and a greater management motivator than is ROI or residual income.

Not-for-profit organizations are different because profits are not the prime interest of managers. Moreover, revenues are often unrelated to services performed; rather, they come from funding agencies. For example, a police department obtains its operating funds from the local government. The department's mandate is to provide law enforcement services within the limits imposed by the operating funds. But how does one measure the level of services performed—by the number of cases investigated? by time spent on cases? by the number of arrests? Finding criteria for evaluating performance is not an easy task in not-for-profit settings.

INTRACOMPANY TRANSACTIONS AND TRANSFER PRICING PROBLEMS

In calculating division profit, problems arise when the divisions are not completely independent. If one division furnishes goods or services to another division, a **transfer price** must be set to determine the buying division's cost and the selling division's revenue.

The following list illustrates a variety of intracompany transactions:

1. A centralized accounting department serves all divisions of a company, and its costs are allocated to divisions based on the number of employees in each division.
2. One department provides repairs and maintenance for production departments' equipment in a factory and bills for those services at an average actual cost per hour of service.
3. A Data Processing Services Division provides computer-based information systems services to all other divisions in the company and allocates costs on the basis of predetermined prices for volumes of transactions and data handled.
4. Plant A produces components which are shipped to Plant B for assembly into an end product which is then transferred to the Sales Division for sale to outside customers. Components and products are billed at a "full cost plus a profit" basis between Plants A and B and between Plant B and the Sales Division.
5. Plant J sells strategic raw materials to a variety of customers, including Plant K in the same company. Managers negotiate a special price each year for the raw materials, depending on the supply and demand factors for each plant.
6. Division R sells an industrial product to a broad array of customers. Division S happens to need the product and buys from the sister division at the prevailing market price because of the product's high quality or the division's delivery reliability.

This continuum of accounting approaches for intracompany dealings is shown in Figure 14.1. While not representing any numerical measuring scale, this line does illustrate the range of accounting techniques for intracompany transactions. At one end is pure (arbitrary) cost allocation. At the other end is pure market-driven pricing.

On the left side of the continuum, overhead or administrative costs are being roughly redistributed to other units using cost drivers, benefits received, or even arbitrary rules. Commonly, service departments are

FIGURE 14.1   Continuum of Accounting Approaches for Intracompany Transactions

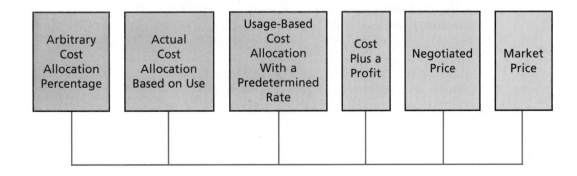

transferring costs to producing departments. The middle portion involves internal sales of goods and services where external markets do not exist or where company policies force the divisions to deal with each other internally. The right end of the continuum represents situations where external markets do exist and where market prices are used, in part or in total, as the exchange price. Buyers seek suppliers. Sellers seek customers. If an intracompany sale takes place, it is the best source for the buyer and a profitable sale for the seller.

Desired Qualities of Transfer Prices and Policies

No one transfer pricing method will be best for all situations. A manager who has spent years supervising internal sales and purchases for a major company has said: "Perhaps the optimal policy is one that will produce the least amount of dysfunctional behavior or, at best, an amount that we can tolerate." Hopefully, policies encourage positive behavior. But dysfunctional behavior, actions which hurt the firm's results, can be frequent by-products.

Let us first outline the criteria for creating a transfer pricing system; second, discuss alternative transfer prices; and third, identify the ability of each price to meet the criteria. Criteria for a transfer price can be reduced to four main elements:

1. **Goal congruence.**   Will the transfer price encourage each manager to make decisions that will maximize profits for the firm as a whole? In decentralized organizations, perhaps one of the most difficult tasks is to get everyone to pull toward the common goal—the financial success of the whole firm. Success of each division will not guarantee the optimal success for the whole firm.

2. **Performance evaluation.**   Will the transfer price allow corporate-level managers to measure the financial performance of division managers in a fair manner? How will power positions that certain divisions have over other divisions be neutralized? For instance, if one division sells its entire output to another division, the buyer can demand concessions from the seller that can cause the seller to appear unprofitable. If the two divisions are to remain independent, the pricing policy must allow the seller to get a reasonable price for its output.

3. **Autonomy.**   Will the transfer price policy allow division managers to operate their divisions as if they were independent businesses? If a division manager must ask for approval from some higher level, the firm's policies have diluted the autonomy of its managers. If autonomy is restricted greatly, the objectives of decentralization are defeated.

4. **Administrative cost.**   Is the transfer pricing system easy and inexpensive to operate? As with all accounting costs, incremental costs should generate a positive contribution margin. Where internal transaction volume is large and complex, a more extensive internal pricing system is justified. Administrative costs also include waiting for decisions, hours spent haggling, and internal divisiveness.

These four criteria should be prioritized when forming transfer pricing policies. Different situations will demand different transfer pricing policies.

Transfer Prices

The most common transfer prices are:

1. Market price.
2. Cost-based prices including:
   (a) Actual full cost.
   (b) Target or predetermined full cost.
   (c) Cost plus a profit.
   (d) Variable cost.
3. Negotiated price.
4. Dual prices.

Contemporary Practice 14.3 reveals the transfer prices used by a group of multinational companies. We now examine each method with comparison to the transfer pricing criteria.

Market Price.   **Market price** is a price set between independent buyers and sellers. Two contrasting conditions are typical:

1. A market price exists, and both buyer and seller have access to other sellers and buyers for the same products.

C O N T E M P O R A R Y   P R A C T I C E   1 4 . 3

Transfer Pricing Methods of Multinational Companies

A recent survey of U. S. multinational companies revealed the following transfer pricing methods used for domestic and international transfers:

	Domestic Transfers (%)	International Transfers (%)
Cost-based methods:		
Actual or standard variable production cost	3.6%	1.2%
Actual full production cost.	9.0	3.8
Standard full production cost.	15.2	7.0
Actual variable production cost plus a lump-sum subsidy.	0.9	1.3
Full production cost (actual or standard) plus a markup	16.6	26.8
Other.	0.9	1.3
Subtotal for cost-based methods.	46.2%	41.4%
Market-based methods:		
Market price	25.1%	26.1%
Market price less selling expenses	7.6	12.1
Other.	4.0	7.7
Subtotal for market-based methods	36.7%	45.9%
Negotiated price	16.6%	12.7%
Other methods	0.5%	0.0%
Total—all methods.	100.0%	100.0%

Source: Tang, R. Y. W., "Transfer Pricing in the 1990's," *Management Accounting*, February 1992, p. 24.

2. A market price is not readily available, but a pseudo-price is created either by using similar products or by getting outside bids for the same item.

Market price meets more of the transfer pricing criteria than any other method. But finding a market price may be difficult since one may not exist. Examples include intermediate components, industrial supplies, and "make or buy" jobs. The buyer's purchasing department may request bids from outside suppliers. If, because of company policy, the outside bidders are rarely considered seriously, the outside bidders will not play this game for long. Bidding is an expensive process. Some companies have a policy of considering outside vendors seriously and committing a certain percentage of business to these bidders to help keep the system viable.

Even if a market price exists, it may not be appropriate. For instance, catalog prices may only vaguely relate to actual sales prices. Market prices may change often. Also, internal selling costs may be less than would be incurred if the products were sold to outsiders.

Despite the problems of finding a valid market price, managers generally agree that market prices are best for most transfer pricing situations. A market transfer price parallels the actual market conditions under which these divisions would operate if they were independent companies.

Goal Congruence. When excess capacity exists, market prices may not lead to goal congruence. For instance, Division A, which has excess capacity and a mixture of fixed and variable product costs ($50 per unit and $100 per unit, respectively), could benefit greatly from additional production volume. Division A sells its output on the market for $200 per unit. Division B is looking for a supplier for a part that Division A can easily provide. Division B asks for bids from a variety of suppliers. Company C, an unrelated firm, may be selected because it has bid $160 per unit. This price is well above Division A's variable cost but below A's market-price bid. Managers in A and B are making the best decisions for their respective divisions as they see it, but total company profits are hurt. The firm as a whole would be better off by $60 per unit ($160 - $100) if Division B purchased from Division A. But Division B would need to pay Division A a $40 higher price ($200 - $160), or Division A would have to accept a lower contribution margin ($160 - $100 = $60) than its regular business generates ($200 - $100 = $100).

Many believe that this is a small cost to incur if the individual division managers act in an aggressive, competitive style. What is lost from suboptimization is gained in greater profits from highly motivated quasi-entrepreneurs. Depending on results in specific firms, this trade-off may or may not be justified.

Performance Evaluation and Autonomy. Market prices form an excellent performance indicator because they cannot be manipulated by the individuals who have an interest in profit calculations. A market price eliminates negotiations and squabbling over costs and definitions of fairness. If market power positions exist, they also exist in the general marketplace.

Where market prices are less clear and are either created or massaged, the pure advantage of market prices declines. In fact, as we move away from a true market price, the price becomes a negotiated price, which is discussed later.

Administrative Cost. As part of normal buying and selling, the transfer price is determined almost costlessly. As we move away from a clear market price, costs increase. Negotiations are expensive in terms of consuming executive time, getting outside bids, and creating support data for negotiating positions.

Cost-Based Prices. Unless market price is readily available, most transfer prices are based on production costs. Three issues stand out in **cost-based transfer pricing**:

1. Actual cost versus a target cost, such as standard or budgeted cost.
2. Cost versus cost plus a profit.
3. Full cost versus variable cost.

Actual Cost Versus a Target Cost. A primary problem with an actual **full-cost transfer price** is that it gives the selling division no incentive to control costs. All product costs are transferred to the buying division, "reimbursed" as revenue to the selling division. This can create a serious competitive problem for the vertically integrated firm that passes parts through numerous divisions before selling a product in a competitive market. Historically, this has been a problem for General Motors Corporation.

Moving to a target cost helps promote cost control but is not a perfect solution. If a budget or standard cost is used for cost control and also for transfer pricing, profit pressures may well subvert the cost system and damage its usefulness as a cost control device. Furthermore, who sets the standard? Is it a tight or lax standard?

Cost Versus Cost Plus a Profit. If cost only is used as a transfer price, the selling unit cannot earn a profit. Full cost plus a profit percentage is a popular solution. Adding a percentage to cost for a profit creates a question: "What percentage?" Somehow 10 percent seems attractive and common. This is, however, an arbitrary choice. Perhaps a markup percentage can be calculated that will cover operating expenses and provide a target return on sales or assets. Even here, these prices fail to produce the kind of competitive environment that decentralization promotes.

Full Cost Versus Variable Cost. Another version of cost-based transfer pricing is variable cost. With **variable-cost transfer prices**, only variable production costs are transferred. These costs are generally materials, direct labor, and variable overhead. Variable-cost transfer prices have the major advantage of encouraging maximum profits for the entire firm when excess capacity exists. This will be illustrated later. The obvious problem is that the selling division must absorb all of its fixed costs. That division is now a loss division, nowhere near a profit center.

With these issues in mind, how well do cost-based transfer prices match with the evaluation criteria?

Goal Congruence. Full-cost transfer prices generally produce suboptimal profits for the firm as a whole. Variable-cost transfer prices generate an optimal firm-wide profit when the selling division has excess capacity. Otherwise, market prices yield optimal firm-wide profits. In general, the definition of the most goal-congruent transfer price is out-of-pocket costs plus any opportunity cost of transferring to the next division. Usually, out-of-pocket costs are the variable costs. The opportunity cost is the contribution margin earned from best alternative use of the seller's capacity. When there is no excess capacity, the out-of-pocket cost plus opportunity cost equals the market price. These relationships are summarized in Figure 14.2.

The following example highlights these concepts. Assume that Division A sells to Division B. The output of Division A is Product A, which can be sold to an outside market or to Division B to be processed further and sold as Product B. One unit of Product B uses one unit of Product A. In Division A, variable costs are $100 per unit; and Product A sells for $175. In Division B, additional variable costs are $200 per unit; and Product B sells for $350. This scenario is diagramed in Figure 14.3. Arrows indicate costs flowing out of the divisions and revenues flowing into them.

Suppose Division A has excess capacity. Thus, there is no opportunity cost of transferring to Division B; and the company would receive a contribution of $50 per unit ($350 - $200 - $100), assuming that these units do not increase total fixed costs. A full-cost transfer price, however, might not promote a transfer. If the fixed costs per unit for Products A and B totaled more than $50, Division B would not accept a transfer since its costs would be more than $350 per unit. Consequently, the full-cost transfer price is not goal congruent. Using a variable-cost transfer price, Division B would accept the units since now its total cost of $300 per unit is less than $350. The variable-cost transfer price is, therefore, goal congruent.

Now suppose that Division A has no excess capacity—all units produced can be sold to the outside market for $175. By selling outside instead of transferring to Division B, the company would receive a contribution of $75 per unit ($175 - $100) rather than just $50 ($350 - $200 - $100). A variable-cost transfer price, however, would not achieve this higher profit because Division B would readily accept transfers to earn $50 per unit. In contrast, a market price would be goal congruent. With a transfer price of $175, Division

FIGURE 14.2   **Goal-Congruent Transfer Prices**

Goal-Congruent Transfer Price	=	Out-of-Pocket Cost	+	Opportunity Cost of Transferring

		Goal-Congruent Transfer Price
If Seller Has Excess Capacity →	Opportunity Cost Equals Zero	Out-of-Pocket Cost
If Seller Has No Excess Capacity →	Opportunity Cost Exists	Market Price

FIGURE 14.3   Diagram of Example Transaction Possibilities

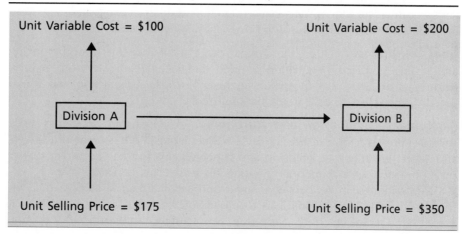

B's costs would total $25 more than its revenue ($350 - $200 - $175), so it would not take any units from Division A.

We summarize these analyses using the preceding decision rule:

Excess capacity:

Goal-congruent transfer price = Out-of-pocket cost + Opportunity cost = $100 + $0 = $100

No excess capacity:

Goal-congruent transfer price = Out-of-pocket cost + Opportunity cost = $100 + ($175 - $100) = $175

Performance Evaluation and Autonomy.   Clearly, a variable-cost transfer price provides little help in performance evaluation if the division is considered to be a profit center. Autonomy is also violated since close working relationships and much exchange of data are expected. When using full-cost transfer prices, an added profit percentage is necessary to get the seller to a profit position. It is difficult to support any cost-based approach as a strong performance evaluation method for profit centers. Cost-based transfer prices are best suited to cost centers.

Administrative Cost.   Cost-based transfer prices are easy to obtain since they are outputs of the cost accounting system. Perhaps this is why, in spite of its weaknesses, cost-based transfer pricing is the most widely used transfer pricing approach.

Negotiated Price.   The use of **negotiated transfer prices** is often suggested as a compromise between market-based and cost-based transfer prices. Real advantages may exist in allowing two division managers to arrive at the transfer price through arm's-length bargaining. The self-interests of the division managers may serve the company objectives. Negotiated prices are helpful when:

1. Cost savings occur from selling and buying internally.
2. Additional internal sales fill previously unused capacity allowing the buyer and seller to share any incremental profit.

As long as the negotiators have relatively equal power positions, negotiations can create a quasi-free market. Friction and bad feelings that may arise from centrally controlled transfer prices may be eliminated.

Goal Congruence.   Often, the company as a whole benefits from the buying and selling divisions negotiating a price that is agreeable to both parties. Fairness is an issue that must be weighed. The firm as a whole will win if the divisions elect to enter negotiations freely.

Performance Evaluation and Autonomy.   A negotiated price may be a suitable surrogate for a market price. A market atmosphere is created if buyers and sellers are free to go outside and if neither division has an unfair power position—such as a monopoly position for purchases or sales.

Negotiations can be between buyer and seller alone or involve the corporate office. If negotiations lead to arbitration by the corporate office or if corporate policies interfere with free negotiations, autonomy suffers. The corporate office has the delicate problem of keeping hands off and yet monitoring divisional dealings to prevent significant noncongruent behavior.

Administrative Cost.   Negotiations are often expensive, consume time of key executives, and may cause an internal unit to be created to handle these relationships. If intracompany sales are important to a division, its managers must put a high priority on these negotiations. Its sales and profit levels are at stake. In highly integrated companies, negotiation costs can be a major operating expense.

Dual Transfer Prices.   A **dual transfer pricing system** allows the selling division to "sell" at a real or synthetic market price (such as full cost plus a profit percentage). The transfer price to the buying division is usually the variable cost (plus perhaps identifiable opportunity costs). Use of dual transfer prices has been suggested as a way of creating a profit, and thus a positive motivation, in both the selling and buying divisions. Such a system, however, does expand the corporate office accounting task. Intracompany sales and duplicate profits have to be eliminated before total company profits can be determined.

Goal Congruence and Performance Evaluation.   The advantages of a dual transfer price system rest on being able to evaluate performance of both units as profit centers and to encourage behavior that will benefit the firm as a whole. Thus, the dual system provides the buying division with incremental cost information and at the same time allows the selling division to show a profit. Such a system encourages the congruence of divisional goals with company-wide goals.

If the selling division has substantial fixed costs to cover, a danger does exist that the buying division will sell at cut-rate prices and fail to cover all fixed costs. Here active corporate-level monitoring may be needed.

Autonomy and Administrative Cost.   Costs and corporate interference are the practical considerations and the major obstacles to the use of dual transfer pricing systems. From an accounting point of view, each division records its own transactions; and the central office must monitor, record, and track intracompany dealings, a clear violation of autonomy. In financial statements for the combined company, accounts representing intracompany transactions are eliminated. For example, a selling division will record a sale and establish a receivable; a buying division will record a purchase and set up a payable. In eliminating the intracompany accounts, any intracompany profits in the buying division's inventory will be adjusted out. The home office must have a special accounting system to track all transactions of a dual pricing system. These extra costs must be outweighed by the benefits of better performance evaluation and goal congruence.

Commonly, the dual transfer pricing system is an academic approach to solving transfer pricing conflicts. But occasionally, a real-world firm will put a dual pricing system in place. Given the right circumstances and intent of management, a dual system can generate the desired combination of benefits.

Grading Transfer Pricing Methods According to the Criteria

Having discussed the transfer pricing criteria and the methods commonly used, an assessment of the relative strengths and weaknesses is as follows:

	Goal Congruence	Performance Evaluation	Autonomy	Administrative Cost
Market prices..............	Strong	Very Strong	Very Strong	Low, if available
Cost-based prices:				
Actual cost..............	Poor	Poor	Poor	Very Low
Full cost plus profit	Poor	Average	Average	Low
Variable cost	Strong	Very Poor	Poor	Often Low
Negotiated prices...........	Strong	Strong	Strong to Poor	High
Dual prices...............	Strong (Variable Cost)	Strong (Market Price)	Poor	High

Remember that specific cases can produce very different answers in each area. Clearly, no one transfer price serves all purposes. Managers must rank their priorities and select transfer pricing policies that fit the situation. Perhaps the goal really is to select a transfer pricing policy that creates the least disruption or adverse managerial behavior.

SUMMARY

Many companies have sought to increase their financial performance by organizing themselves into an array of profit or investment centers. Decentralizing a company involves defining boundaries for organizational units, called responsibility centers, and delegating decision-making authority to the managers of these centers. Such a structure motivates managers to work for the benefit of the company, provides for frontline decision making by those nearest the action, enhances specialization by letting managers do what they do best, and reduces the span of control for management.

A control system is necessary if management wants to motivate its division managers and to evaluate performance. Measurements of expected performance level and of actual performance are the two essential ingredients for a control system. Since decentralized companies frequently place investment authority at the divisional level, performance measures should relate profitability to the amount of investment. Return on investment and residual income are approaches to divisional financial performance evaluation. Problems exist in defining both profit and investment. Possible profit definitions include direct and controllable contribution margins. Possible investment definitions include net direct assets and managed assets.

Divisions within a company do not operate in isolation from one another; rather, they frequently do business as buyer and seller. Any time intracompany transactions occur, a transfer price must be attached to the transaction. Criteria of goal congruence, performance evaluation, autonomy, and administrative cost are developed to measure the strengths and weaknesses of each type of transfer price. Transfer prices can be market based, cost based, negotiated, or dual. No one method meets all criteria. Each has strengths and weaknesses depending on the importance of intracompany dealings and the priorities of management.

P ROBLEMS FOR REVIEW

Review Problem A

A truck division of an auto company follows a pricing policy whereby normal activity is used as a basis for pricing. That is, prices are set on the basis of long-run annual volume predictions. They are then rarely changed, except for notable changes in wage rates or materials prices. You are given the following data:

Materials, wages, and other variable costs	$ 5,000 per unit
Fixed overhead	$ 30,000,000 per year
Desired rate of return on invested capital	20 %
Normal volume	40,000 units
Invested capital.	$ 90,000,000

Required:

1. What net income percentage based on dollar sales is needed to attain the desired rate of return?

2. What rate of return on invested capital will be earned at a sales volume of 35,000 units?

3. If sales were to drop to 35,000 units, by what percentage must each of the following variables change from the normal level of 40,000 units to achieve the 20 percent rate of return?

    (a) Sales price.

    (b) Fixed overhead.

    (c) Return on sales percentage.

    (d) Invested capital.

Solution:

1. Net income = Investment base x Return on investment

          = $90,000,000 x 20%

          = $18,000,000

To solve for the net income percentage, first find sales necessary to earn the $18,000,000 net income:

Net income	$ 18,000,000
Plus:	
Variable cost (40,000 x $5,000)	200,000,000
Fixed cost...	30,000,000
Sales	$248,000,000

Note: The selling price is $6,200 per unit ($248,000,000 ÷ 40,000 units). This value is needed later in the solution.

$$\text{Net income percentage} = \text{Net income} \div \text{Sales}$$
$$= \$18{,}000{,}000 \div \$248{,}000{,}000$$
$$= \underline{7.26\%}$$

2. Sales volume drops to 35,000 units:

Sales (35,000 x $6,200)	$217,000,000
Variable cost (35,000 x $5,000)	175,000,000
Contribution margin.......................................	$ 42,000,000
Fixed cost...	30,000,000
Net income	$ 12,000,000

$$\text{Return on investment} = \text{Net income} \div \text{Investment base}$$
$$= \$12{,}000{,}000 \div \$90{,}000{,}000$$
$$= \underline{13.33\%}$$

3. First, format the income statement for the normal level of sales, 40,000 units, with dollars and percentages:

Sales (40,000 x $6,200)	$248,000,000	100.00%
Variable cost (40,000 x $5,000)	200,000,000	80.65
Contribution margin.............................	$ 48,000,000	19.35%
Fixed cost....................................	30,000,000	12.10
Net income	$ 18,000,000	7.25%

Remember that this net income provides a 20 percent rate of return.

Assume a drop in volume to 35,000 units:

(a) Change in sales price:

Net income	$ 18,000,000
Plus:	
Variable cost (35,000 x $5,000)	175,000,000
Fixed cost...	30,000,000
Sales	$223,000,000
Divided by volume in units	÷ 35,000
New selling price per unit.............................	$ 6,372

This represents an increase of 2.77 percent over the original selling price of $6,200 per unit.

(b) Change in fixed overhead:

Sales (35,000 x $6,200)	$217,000,000
Variable cost (35,000 x $5,000)	175,000,000
Contribution margin....................................	$ 42,000,000
Less net income	18,000,000
New fixed overhead....................................	$ 24,000,000

This represents a decrease in fixed overhead of 20 percent over the original fixed overhead of $30,000,000.

(c) Change in return on sales percentage:

Dividing the sales figure of $223,000,000, from Part (a) above, into the net income figure of $18,000,000 gives a return on sales percentage of 8.07. This represents an increase of 11.16 percent over the original return on sales percentage of 7.26 ($18,000,000 ÷ $248,000,000).

(d) Change in invested capital:

$$\text{New investment base} = \text{Net income (from Part 2 above)} \div \text{ROI}$$
$$= \$12,000,000 \div .20$$
$$= \underline{\underline{\$60,000,000}}$$

This represents a decrease in investment base of 33.33 percent over the original investment base of $90,000,000.

Review Problem B

Patrick Corporation, manufacturer of specialized trailers for over-the-road and container shipping, is decentralized, with each product line operating as a divisional profit center. Each division head is delegated full authority on all decisions involving sales of divisional output both to outsiders and to other divisions of Patrick. The International Shipping Division (ISD) has always purchased its requirements for a particular trailer platform subassembly from the Highway Division (HD). However, when informed that the HD was increasing its price to $300, ISD management decided to purchase the subassembly from an outside supplier.

ISD can purchase a similar subassembly from a reliable supplier for $260 per unit plus an annual die maintenance charge of $20,000. HD insists that owing to the recent installation of some highly specialized equipment, which has resulted in high depreciation charges, it would not be able to make an adequate profit on its investment unless it charged $300. In fact, the ISD business was part of the justification for buying the new equipment. HD's management appealed to top management of Patrick for support in its dispute with ISD and supplied the following operating data:

ISD's annual purchases of subassembly	2,000 units
HD's variable costs per unit of subassembly	$220
HD's fixed costs per unit of subassembly	$ 65

Required:

1. Assume that no alternative use for HD's internal facilities exists. Determine whether the company as a whole will benefit if ISD purchases the subassembly from the outside supplier.

2. Assume that HD's internal facilities would not otherwise be idle. By using the capacity needed to produce the 2,000 units for ISD for other production, HD can earn $40,000 in contribution margin. Should ISD purchase from the outsider? Explain.

3. If the outside supplier drops the price by another $20 per unit, would your answer to either Part (1) or (2) change? If so, why?

Solution:

1. Since no alternative use for HD's internal facilities exists, its fixed costs are irrelevant to the decision to purchase the units internally or in the outside market. Only HD's variable costs are relevant to this "make or buy" decision:

Make Costs			**Buy Costs**		
HD's variable costs			Purchase cost		
(2,000 x $220)		$440,000	(2,000 units x $260)		$520,000
			Die charge		20,000
Total make costs		$440,000	Total buy costs		$540,000
Net make advantage		$100,000			

Therefore, the company as a whole would be worse off by $100,000 if ISD purchases the subassembly from the outside supplier.

2. If HD's internal facilities would not otherwise be idle, then its transfer price would be the variable cost per unit plus $20 per unit. The $20 per unit represents the opportunity cost to HD of producing the 2,000 units for ISD ($40,000 ÷ 2,000 units).

Make Costs			**Buy Costs**		
HD's variable costs			Purchase cost		
(2,000 x $220)		$440,000	(2,000 units x $260)		$520,000
Opportunity cost		40,000	Die charge		20,000
Total make costs		$480,000	Total buy costs		$540,000
Net make advantage		$ 60,000			

It is still in the best interests of the firm for ISD to purchase the 2,000 units from HD.

3. The answer to Part (1) would not change if the outside supplier drops its price by $20 per unit since the total buy costs would only fall by $40,000 (2,000 units x $20). The net make advantage is $60,000, instead of $100,000.

The answer to Part (2) would also not change since the total buy costs would only fall to $500,000, down from $540,000. The net make advantage is $20,000, instead of $60,000.

T ERMINOLOGY REVIEW

Asset turnover, *591*
Cost centers, *589*
Cost-based transfer pricing, *603*
Decentralization, *589*
Decentralized company, *588*
Division controllable contribution
   margin, *593*
Division direct contribution
   margin, *592*
Division net profit, *592*
Division variable contribution
   margin, *593*
Dual transfer pricing system, *606*
Full-cost transfer price, *603*

Goal congruence, *594*
Investment base, *593*
Investment centers, *589*
Market price, *601*
Minimum desired rate of return, *597*
Negotiated transfer prices, *605*
Profit centers, *589*
Residual income, *596*
Responsibility center, *589*
Return on investment (ROI), *591*
Return on sales (ROS), *591*
Transfer price, *599*
Variable-cost transfer prices, *603*

S UGGESTED READINGS

Cats-Baril, W., J. F. Gatti, and D. J. Grinnel, "Transfer Pricing Policy in a Dynamic Market," *Management Accounting*, Vol. 69, No. 8, pp. 30-33.

Dejong, D. V., R. Forsythe, J. O. Kim, and W. C. Uecker, "A Laboratory Investigation of Alternative Transfer Pricing Mechanisms," *Accounting, Organizations, and Society*, Vol. 14, No. 1/2, pp. 41-64.

Greenberg, P. S., R. H. Greenberg, and S. Mahenthiran, "The Impact of Control Policies on the Process and Outcomes of Negotiated Transfer Pricing," *Journal of Management Accounting Research*, Fall 1994, pp. 93-127.

Jacobs, F. A., and E. R. Larkins, "Management Control of a Foreign Sales Corporation: Some Special Considerations," *Journal of Management Accounting Research*, Fall 1992, pp. 99-115.

Leitch, R. A., and K. S. Barrett, "Multinational Transfer Pricing: Objectives and Constraints," *Journal of Accounting Literature*, 1992, pp. 47-92.

Strupeck, C. D., K. Milani, and J. E. Murphy, "Financial Management at Georgia Tech," *Management Accounting*, Vol. 74, No. 8, pp. 58-63.

Viator, R. E., C. D. Poe, and J. R. Strawser, "An Empirical Investigation of the Effect of Negotiation Strategy and Risk-Taking Behavior on Transfer Pricing Outcomes," *Advances in Management Accounting*, 1992, pp. 151-178.

Q UESTIONS FOR REVIEW AND DISCUSSION

1. What are the advantages of decentralization? What are the primary problems of decentralization?

2. Distinguish among a cost center, a profit center, and an investment center.

3. How is performance generally measured in a cost center? In a profit center? In an investment center?

4. Why is a cost budget not a good control measure in evaluating a division manager who has decision power on prices and marketing products?

5. What are some problems in using division profit as an evaluation measure?

6. Explain the difference between division controllable profit and division direct profit.

7. Identify and explain allocation problems involved in determining a profit measure and the investment base for calculating ROI.

8. When comparing various divisions, why is it important that the divisions have the same or similar accounting methods? Cite three examples of accounting methods that could cause divisions' profits to differ.

9. List the components of the ROI equation, tell how they are related, and identify an action a manager can take regarding each component to improve ROI.

10. How is residual income defined? What is the major advantage of using residual income versus ROI in performance evaluation?

11. Identify the major factors necessary in conceptually defining profit centers for promoting decentralization in an organization.

12. What is a transfer price? Under what conditions are transfer prices necessary?

13. Identify four criteria that are useful in evaluating transfer prices for intracompany transactions.

14. Using the criteria for evaluating transfer prices, evaluate each of the following transfer prices:

(a) Market price.

(b) Actual cost.

(c) Standard full cost.

(d) Cost plus a profit percentage.

(e) Variable cost.

(f) Negotiated price.

15. Explain and comment on the following paragraph from a recent publication:

A pseudo-profit center is one that is artificially carved out of an organization by management, such as making the maintenance department in a factory a profit center. The primary advantage of a pseudo-profit center is that it captures the motivational advantages of real profit centers. But an analysis of pseudo-profit centers shows that the transfer pricing techniques used to create them can cause motivational disadvantages that completely overshadow any perceived advantages. Frequently, pseudo-profit centers will motivate managers to act in a dysfunctional manner.

16. If a market-based transfer price can be determined, why is such a price usually considered the best one to use?

17. Briefly describe a dual transfer price. What are the advantages and disadvantages of implementing such a pricing system?

18. If the intermediate market is perfectly competitive, will a market-based transfer price ever lead to suboptimal profits in the producing division? Explain.

19. What is the disadvantage of negotiated transfer prices when no intermediate market exists for the producing division?

20. If a full-cost transfer price does not produce an optimal profit for the firm, why is it so popular?

E XERCISES

14-1. Profit Measures.   The following data are from the Courier Division of Ghosal Delivery Company:

Revenue from deliveries.	$50,000
Division variable cost	32,500
Allocated home office overhead	4,600
Fixed overhead traceable to division ($4,500 is controllable, and $8,000 is noncontrollable).	12,500

Required:

Calculate division variable contribution margin, division controllable contribution margin, division direct contribution margin, and division net profit.

14-2. Comparison of ROI and Residual Income.   The Electricity Division of Northern Alaska Utilities reported operating income of $2,400,000 per year based on an investment of $12,000,000. The company is considering the use of ROI or residual income as an evaluation measure. At the present time, the division manager is faced with a decision on an incremental investment of $4,000,000 which will increase annual operating income by $700,000 per year.

Required:

Provide calculations showing the difference between the two performance measures, and explain the possible advantage of using residual income assuming that a 16 percent ROI is considered minimally acceptable.

14-3. Valuing Assets. Joe Fisher, the president of Hoosier Company, has returned from an executive management seminar. He sees you in the office coffee lounge and says, "As I read and hear more and more on valuing assets, I am increasingly bewildered by the 'language of accounting.' Yes, I understand historical cost and its problems. But you accountants also mix and match terms like market value, replacement value, economic value, present value, opportunity value, disposal value, entry value, and more values! You seem to have extra time since I see you here in the lounge a lot. Maybe you could help clear up this confusion for me by describing how these terms can help us to make decisions about divisional performance and about keeping or selling these assets and to inform our shareholders about our performance."

Required:
Respond to the president's request.

14-4. ROI and Residual Income. Provide the missing data for the following divisions of La Societe du Quebec (monetary amounts are in Canadian dollars):

	Divisions			
	Un	Deux	Trois	Quatre
Net income	?	C$500,000	?	C$ 300,000
Investment base	C$1,500,000	?	C$2,000,000	C$3,000,000
ROI	?	20%	12.5%	?
Imputed rate	6%	18%	?	?
Residual income	C$ 15,000	C$?	C$ (50,000)	C$ 0

14-5. Transfer Price Based on Full Cost. The Stromberg Company has a division which produces a single product that sells for $26 per unit in the external market. The full cost of the product is $18, calculated as follows:

Variable materials and labor cost per unit $14
Fixed cost per unit 4*
    Total cost per unit $18

* Total fixed cost of $400,000 divided by current production and sales of 100,000 units.

Another division has offered to buy 20,000 units at the full cost of $18 per unit. The producing division has excess capacity, and the 20,000 units can be produced without interfering with the current external sales volume of 100,000 units. The total fixed costs of the producing division will not change as a result of the order. The producing division manager is inclined to reject the order, feeling that the division's profit position will not improve.

Required:
Explain to the producing division manager, supported by calculations, the impact of transferring 20,000 units at the full cost of $18 per unit.

14-6. Selecting a Transfer Price. Division 1 produces 100,000 units of a product with a variable cost of $5 per unit and a fixed cost of $3 per unit (based on $300,000 allocated to 100,000 units). These units can be sold in an intermediate market for $1,000,000 ($10 per unit) or transferred to Division 2 for additional processing to be sold in a finished market. The selling price of the fully processed units is $14 per unit, and the additional processing cost in Division 2 is $1.50 per unit. The fixed costs in Division 2 total $100,000. At this time, excess capacity exists in Division 2 if the units are not transferred.

Required:
Should the 100,000 units be sold by Division 1 or processed further and sold by Division 2? Would a transfer price based on either market price or variable cost be likely to lead to the right decision? Explain.

14-7. ROI and Transfer Pricing.   You are given the following data regarding budgeted operations for Nigrini Mining Division of Cape Town Industries (monetary amounts are in South African rand):

Average direct assets:	
Receivables	R 100,000
Inventories	300,000
Plant and equipment, net	200,000
Total	R600,000

Fixed overhead	R200,000
Variable costs	R1.00 per gram of ore
Desired ROI on average direct assets	20%
Expected volume	100,000 grams of ore

Required:

1. What average sales price per gram is needed to obtain the desired rate of return on average direct assets?

2. Assume that 30 percent of the 100,000 grams is sold to another division of the same company. The other division manager has balked at a tentative selling price of R4.00. He has offered R2.25, claiming that he can obtain the ore elsewhere for that price. The manager of Nigrini Mining Division has examined her data. She has decided that she could eliminate R40,000 of inventories, R60,000 of plant and equipment, and R20,000 of fixed overhead if she did not sell to the other division. Should she sell for R2.25? Show computations to support your answer and briefly explain your reasoning.

14-8. Transfer Pricing Problem.   The Tooele Company has a production division which is currently manufacturing 120,000 units but has a capacity of 180,000 units. The variable cost of the product is $22 per unit, and the total fixed cost is $720,000 or $6 per unit based on current production.

The Sales Division of the Tooele Company offers to buy 40,000 units from the Production Division at $21 per unit. The Production Division manager refuses the order because the price is below variable cost. The Sales Division manager argues that the order should be accepted since by taking the order the Production Division manager can lower the fixed cost per unit from $6 to $4.50. (Output will increase to 160,000 units.) This decrease of $1.50 in fixed cost per unit will more than offset the $1 difference between the variable cost and the transfer price.

Required:

1. If you were the Production Division manager, would you accept the Sales Division manager's argument? Why or why not? (Assume that the 120,000 units currently being produced sell for $30 per unit in the external market.)

2. From the viewpoint of Tooele Company, should the order be accepted if the manager of the Sales Division intends to sell each unit to the outside market for $27 after incurring an additional processing cost of $2.25 per unit? Explain.

14-9. Profit Centers and Transfer Prices.   A large automobile dealership is installing a responsibility accounting system with three profit centers: Parts and Service, New Vehicles, and Used Vehicles. The department managers were told to run their shops as if they were in business for themselves. However, interdepartmental dealings frequently occur. For example:

(a) The Parts and Service Department prepares new cars for final delivery and repairs used cars prior to resale.

(b) The Used Vehicle Department's major source of inventory is cars traded in as partial payment for new cars.

Required:

The owner of the dealership has asked you to outline criteria for a company policy statement on transfer pricing, together with specific rules to be applied to the common examples cited. He has told you that clarity is of paramount importance because your criteria will be relied on for settling transfer-pricing disputes.

14-10. Policy Implications.   Assume you are concerned about managing corporate profitability as well as divisional decentralization and autonomy. Comment on each of these:

(a) From the viewpoint of the corporation, does any general transfer-pricing rule lead to the maximization of corporate profits?

(b) Why might a division manager reject a cost reduction proposal with a positive net present value, preferring instead to retain an inefficient old asset?

(c) Many firms use cost-plus or negotiated transfer prices even though they do not lead to optimal results for individual products. Why?

(d) Competitive market prices are often thought to be ideal transfer prices. Is this true? Explain your answer.

(e) Why might it be said that the goal of a divisional manager performance evaluation system should be to "create the least amount of dysfunctional behavior" by the individual manager?

14-11. Evaluating Transfer Prices.   Newmill Enterprises runs a chain of drive-in hamburger stands in northern Michigan during the summer season. Each stand's manager is told to act as if the stand will be judged on its own profit performance. Newmill has set up a separate business to rent a soft ice cream machine for the summer and to supply its burger stands with ice cream for their frappes. Rent for the machine is $1,000. Newmill is not allowed to sell ice cream to other dealers because it cannot obtain appropriate licenses. The manager of the ice cream business charges the stands $3 per gallon. Operating figures for the machine for the summer are as follows:

Sales to the stands (10,000 gallons x $3)		$ 30,000
Variable costs, $1.60 per gallon	$16,000	
Fixed costs:		
Rental of machine	1,000	
Other fixed costs	4,000	21,000
Operating margin		$ 9,000

The manager of Clam Bar, one of the Newmill drive-ins, is seeking permission to sign a contract to buy ice cream from an outside supplier at $2.40 a gallon. The Clam Bar uses 2,000 gallons of soft ice cream during the summer. Frank Redmond, controller of Newmill Enterprises, refers this request to you. You determine that other fixed costs of operating the machine will decrease by $500 if Clam Bar purchases from an outside supplier. Redmond wants an analysis of the request in terms of overall company objectives and an explanation of your conclusion.

Required:
Evaluate these transfer prices: $3.00, $2.40, $2.10, and $1.60. Recommend a price. Explain.

14-12. ROI and Divisional Charges.   The following three charges are found on the monthly report of a division that provides financial services primarily to outside companies. Division performance is evaluated using ROI.

(a) A charge for general corporation administration at 10 percent of division revenues.

(b) A charge for the use of the corporate computer facility. The charge is determined by taking actual annual computer department costs and allocating an amount to each user based on the ratio of divisional hours used to total corporate hours used.

(c) A charge for services provided by another division. The charge is based on a competitive market price for similar services.

Required:

Are any of these charges consistent with responsibility accounting and managerial performance evaluation? Explain.

14-13. Dual Transfer Price System.   Aymara Chemical Company, based in La Paz, Bolivia, has two divisions, Positivo and Negativo. The Negativo Division produces a product at a variable cost (in pesos) of $B10 per unit and sells 50,000 units to the external market at $B15 per unit and 40,000 units to the Positivo Division at variable cost plus 50 percent. However, under the dual transfer price system in use, the Positivo Division pays only the variable cost per unit. The fixed cost of the Negativo Division is $B160,000 per year.

The Positivo Division sells 40,000 units of its finished product to the external market at $B30 per unit and has a variable cost of $B8 per unit in addition to the cost of the subassembly purchased from the Negativo Division at variable cost. The annual fixed cost of the Positivo Division is $B180,000.

Required:

Show the income statements for the two divisions and the income statement for the company as a whole. Assume the company consists of only the two divisions. Explain why, under the dual transfer price system, the net income for the company is less than the sum of the net income figures shown for the two divisions.

14-14. Market-Value Transfer Price.   Epsilon Company has two divisions, M and S. Division M manufactures a product, and Division S sells it. The intermediate market is competitive. But the product can be processed further and sold or stored for later processing and sale. Once the product is manufactured, some of it is sold by Division M; and some is transferred to Division S which decides whether to hold or to process and sell the product. The following information pertains to the current year:

Division M manufacturing cost for 1,200,000 units	$7,200,000
Of the 1,200,000 units produced:	
Sold by M in intermediate market—600,000 units	6,000,000
Held by S for later sale—200,000 units (no additional	
processing work done on these units in Division S).	2,000,000
Processed by S and sold—400,000 units	7,200,000
Intermediate market value of 600,000 units when transferred to S . .	6,000,000
Total additional processing costs of S	1,200,000

Assume no beginning inventories.

Required:

1. Prepare an income statement for the whole firm.

2. Prepare a separate income statement for each division using a cost-based transfer price.

3. Prepare a separate income statement for each division using a market-value transfer price.

14-15. ROI and Residual Income.   Puffino & Associates is a large insurance company headquartered in Milan, Italy. The company has a 25 percent minimum desired rate of return. Its Residential Insurance Division has an investment base of 800 million lira. In 1998, this division earned a residual income of 120 million lira and had a return on sales of 10 percent.

Required:

1. Compute the division's ROI for 1998.

2. Compute the division's asset turnover for 1998.

14-16. Performance Measurement and Ethics.   Minsk Brothers is a securities broker-age firm with four autonomous divisions. ROI is used to evaluate each division. Cash bonuses are given to division managers who have the highest ROI figures at year end. The firm's minimum desired rate of return is 15 percent. The Southeast Division's projected operating results for 1996 are as follows:

Revenues	$5,000,000
Variable expenses	3,000,000
Variable contribution margin	$2,000,000
Direct fixed expenses	1,600,000
Direct contribution margin	$ 400,000

The Southeast Division has $1,200,000 of total direct assets. Early in 1996, Donald Birnbrey, the manager of the Southeast Division, has been presented with the following investment proposal:

Additional direct assets required	$ 500,000
Additional revenues anticipated	$1,000,000
Additional variable expenses	60% of revenues
Additional fixed expenses	$ 300,000

Required:

1. Would Donald Birnbrey be likely to accept the proposed investment? Explain with supporting computations.

2. Discuss the ethical issues that Donald Birnbrey would face.

14-17. Choosing an Appropriate Transfer Price.   The Walker Oil Company has just decentralized its Refining and Marketing divisions. Refining is allowed to sell to outside wholesalers, while Marketing is permitted to buy from other refiners. Walker Oil produces only unleaded gasoline at a variable refinery cost of $0.30 per gallon and a fixed refining cost of $160,000 per month for a capacity of 400,000 gallons. The market price in the intermediate market is $1.00 per gallon. Marketing sells the fuel to independent service stations at $1.20 per gallon and incurs transportation costs of $0.10 per gallon.

Required:

Assuming all refined gallons are sold to Marketing, show the impacts on profits for Refining, Marketing, and Walker Oil Company as a whole when using each of the following transfer prices: (a) variable cost, (b) market price, and (c) full cost. What conclusion can you draw?

14-18. Decision Making in a Decentralized Operation.   Richardson Company is planning to build its own office building. The company has a division which constructs all buildings for the entire company. This division has requested bids on the elevators for the building from two companies. O Company gives a bid of $4,500,000, and U Company bids $4,000,000. However, O Company would buy materials for the elevators from the Fabricating Division of the Richardson Company. This order would result in the Fabricating Division earning $600,000 after covering all costs. Since Richardson Company is decentralized, the Construction Division is not aware of this possibility.

Required:

Which bid would you expect the Construction Division to take? Which bid would Richardson Company prefer to have the Construction Division accept? Show calculations.

14-19. Transfer Pricing Problem.   The tailor shop in a men's clothing store is set up as an autonomous unit. The transfer price for tailoring services is based on variable cost which is estimated at $12 per hour. The store manager feels that the Suit and Sport Coat Department is currently using too much tailor time and that this department could cut down on hours used by taking more care in fitting the garments.

The manager has decided to double the hourly tailor rate even though this new rate will be no reflection of the real variable cost. The idea is simply to provide an incentive to the Suit and Sport Coat Department to conserve on tailor time.

Required:

1. What possible disadvantages do you see in the store manager's action? Do you agree or disagree with this means of stressing the need to conserve tailor time? Why?

2. Would it make any difference if the various selling departments were not required to use the tailor shop and were allowed to take their work to some outside tailor shop? Explain.

14-20. Opportunity Costs.   The Cook Division of Colaianne Corporation expects the following results for the coming year on sales to outsiders:

Sales (100,000 units)		$600,000
Variable cost of sales	$300,000	
Fixed cost of sales	200,000	500,000
Profit		$100,000

Yesterday, the manager of the Cole Division requested a bid from Cook for 30,000 units. Cole would perform additional work on each unit at a cost of $4 per unit and sell the end product for $9 per unit. Cook can make only 120,000 units per year and would have to forego some regular sales if the Cole business is accepted. Cole has an outside bid of $4.50 per unit.

Required:

1. What is the minimum bid Cook should make to Cole, and what transfer pricing goal is being optimized?

2. What is the maximum bid Cook should make to Cole, and what transfer pricing goal is being optimized?

3. If Cole buys from the outside supplier, does Colaianne gain or lose and by how much?

14-21. Allocation of Central Corporate Office Costs.   Horton Company has several operating divisions which are largely autonomous as far as decision making is concerned. The central corporate office consists mainly of the president and immediate staff. The annual fixed costs are $1,000,000. In calculating division profit, these costs are allocated to divisions on the basis of sales. The current allocation rate is $0.04 per sales dollar based on the company-wide normal sales volume of $25,000,000 per year. Harold Wolf, the company controller, does not consider this to be a transfer price because he feels that the divisions are not really buying anything. In Wolf's view, the charge is a method of allocating costs which should be absorbed by the divisions when they calculate their annual net income.

Required:

Do you agree with Mr. Wolf? In what sense is the charge a transfer price? Could the charge affect the decision of a division manager considering a new product with a variable cost of $5.50 and a selling price of $8? Explain.

14-22. Intracompany Sales.   Nally Enterprises has three divisions: Fisk, Nied, and Zale. One of the products sold by Zale requires parts made by Fisk and Nied. Data on the product from Zale are as follows:

Selling price		$70
Variable costs:		
Fisk costs	$18	
Nied costs	12	
Zale costs	8	38
Contribution margin		$32
Factory fixed costs (based on volume of 10,000 units)		18
Profit		$14

Fisk charges Zale $26 per unit. Nied charges Zale $20 per unit. These prices are full manufactured cost plus $2 per unit markup. Fixed costs applied to the finished product are incurred equally by the three divisions.

Zale routinely gets outside bids on all parts used. Recent valid quotes were $21 per unit on the part made by Fisk and also $21 per unit on the Nied part.

Required:

1. Based on the preceding data, what profits are reported by each division?
2. What should be considered the maximum and minimum transfer prices for the Fisk and Nied parts?
   (a) What objective(s) would be met by the maximum price? Why?
   (b) What objective(s) would be met by the minimum price? Why?

*P*ROBLEMS

14-23. Transfer Price Based on Full Cost.   The Casper Division of Freddie Company produces a large metal frame which is sold to the Cody Division. Cody Division uses these frames in constructing metal lathes which are sold to machine tool manufacturers. In Casper Division, the frames are produced in a stamping process and are then run through a finishing process in which they are trimmed and polished before being shipped to the Cody Division.

The current estimate of the variable costs of materials and labor to produce a frame in the stamping process is $120 per frame. Fixed overhead associated with this process in the Casper Division is $700,000 per year. Current production is 50,000 frames, which is full capacity for both the stamping and the trimming and polishing processes.

The variable cost of labor in the trimming and polishing process is $12 per frame since labor in this process is paid on a piece-rate basis. (No additional materials are required.) The fixed overhead in this process is $300,000 per year and is largely due to equipment depreciation and related costs. The machines have almost no salvage value because of their special-purpose design.

The transfer price to the Cody Division is a full-cost transfer price and is calculated by prorating the current fixed cost in each process over the 50,000 frames being produced. The price is quoted for each process and is presented to the manager as follows:

Stamping process:		
Materials and labor cost per unit	$120	
Fixed overhead cost per unit ($700,000 ÷ 50,000 units)	14	$134
Trimming and polishing process:		
Labor cost per unit	$ 12	
Fixed overhead cost per unit ($300,000 ÷ 50,000 units)	6	18
Total cost per unit		$152

An outside company has offered to rent to Cody Division machinery which would perform the trimming and polishing process. The rental cost of the machinery is $200,000 per year. With the new machinery, the labor cost per frame would remain at $12. The Cody Division manager sees the possibility of obtaining the frames from the Casper Division for $134 by eliminating the $18 cost of trimming and polishing and of performing these processes in the Cody Division. An analysis is as follows:

New process:

Machine rental cost per year	$200,000
Labor cost ($12 x 50,000 units)	600,000
Total Cody Division trimming and polishing costs	$800,000

Current process:

50,000 units at $18 per unit (portion of the Casper Division transfer price attributable to trimming and polishing process)	$900 000

The manager of the Cody Division has approached the vice-president of operations for approval to acquire the new machinery.

Required:

1. As the vice-president, how would you advise the manager of the Cody Division?

2. Could the transfer pricing system be improved and, if so, how?

14-24. Allocation of Central Office Overhead. Wilbur Company has several departments which operate quite autonomously as far as decision making is concerned. The company allocates central office overhead to these operating departments based on the total labor dollars incurred by each. The central office overhead budget and the allocation rate are as follows:

Executive offices	$ 200,000
Legal	70,000
Advertising	60,000
Personnel	100,000
Accounting	70,000
Total	$ 500,000
Total estimated payroll in operating departments	$1,000,000

Allocation rate: $500,000 ÷ $1,000,000 = $0.50 per labor dollar

The central office overhead of $500,000 is considered to be a fixed cost. Also, once the rate is established, it is not changed for one year.

The Engineering Research Department conducts research on certain engineering problems related to the company's products and issues reports to clients who request this service. The manager of this department is faced with a need to hire two more technical assistants because of an increased workload. If the manager hires through the company's Personnel Department, these positions can be filled at a cost of $1,500 per month for each employee. However, the usual $0.50 per dollar of payroll will also be charged against the Engineering Research Department's budget for central office overhead. The manager discovers that it is possible to contract for technical services from an outside engineering firm which will furnish two technical assistants for as long as they are required. The cost would be considered a consulting cost and not part of the division's payroll. The cost will be $2,000 per month for each assistant.

Required:

1. Is the central office overhead charge a transfer price? Explain.

2. What is the manager of the Engineering Research Department likely to do? Show calculations to support your answer.

3. If Wilbur Company wants to continue to allocate central office overhead, advise the president how this might be done so as not to affect the hiring decisions of the various department managers.

14-25. Decision Making in a Decentralized Operation.   Broadway Company has several divisions. Division S produces (among other products) a metal container which is sold to customers who use it for shipping liquid chemicals. The main material used in manufacturing these containers is a metal which can be purchased from Division M, one of the other divisions of the company, or from several outside sources. Division S has received a customer order for 100 containers at $500 each. It will require two tons of materials to produce the 100 containers. The manager of Division S requests bids for the materials required from Division M and from two outside companies. Division M, using a transfer price based on full cost, bids a price of $8,000 per ton on the materials order. Division M's variable cost is only $4,500 per ton, and it has excess capacity. However, Division M regularly bases price bids on full cost, whether the order is from another division or from an outside customer.

The two outside companies bid $6,000 and $6,500 per ton. However, Gairer Company, which bid $6,500, would buy the manufacturing supplies necessary to produce the materials from Division P, another division of Broadway Company. The supplies would amount to $1,500 per ton of materials required. Division P's variable cost is about $800 per ton with a $200 freight charge for the total shipment.

Required:

1. What would you expect Division S to do? Explain.
2. Will Division S accept the right outside bid? Explain.
3. Should Division M's transfer pricing policy be changed? If so, how?

14-26. Changing a Cost Center to a Profit Center.   The president of Morris Company has just attended a seminar on the use of responsibility centers. He is very anxious to put "competitive zeal" into every part of the organization. He is especially interested in making some of the service centers within the company into profit centers. It is decided that the Maintenance Department will be the first to be made into a profit center, and it is hoped that the experience gained will be helpful if other service centers are converted to profit centers.

A meeting has been called to discuss setting prices to be charged by the maintenance department to units that it serves. The manager of the Maintenance Department suggests a cost-plus basis for pricing, with labor and materials costs plus a 10 percent markup being charged to the unit requesting maintenance services. He argues that a markup over cost is needed to allow the department to become a profit center; otherwise there is no point in changing from the current status—that of a cost center.

Some managers of operating departments argue that a fee schedule for each kind of maintenance job should be established. Some think a reasonable approach would be to survey local industrial maintenance firms and use their prices less a percentage for cost savings. Others think that the whole idea only creates an "artificial profit center" and that the maintenance budget should just be divided among the operating departments. Most do not seem to like the cost-plus idea.

Required:

1. Evaluate each position. Are there other choices? If so, what?
2. What recommendation can you make?

14-27. Transfer Pricing Problem.   Baltic National Bank of Vilnius, Lithuania, has a central computer facility which is used by several operating departments for data processing and problem-solving purposes. The facility's budget (in Lithuanian litas) for the current year is as follows:

Rentals	1,200,000 litas
Payroll, operators	260,000
Payroll, programmers	180,000
Payroll, supervision and secretarial	90,000
Miscellaneous supplies	120,000
Utilities	250,000
Total	2,100,000 litas

It is estimated that 20,000 computer time units will be available. All of the costs shown in the budget are considered to be fixed, except for utilities and miscellaneous supplies which are variable.

During the past five years, the computer facility has not been operated at full capacity. The percentage of capacity has increased from 40 percent in the first year of operation to an estimated 70 percent for the current year.

A transfer price policy has been established which calls for the use of a full cost per unit of time. Thus, an operating department that needs one half of a time unit would be charged at the rate of 52.50 litas [1/2 x (2,100,000 litas ÷ 20,000 time units)]. All operating departments do most of their own programming. The computer staff has four programmers who are used to solve special problems as they arise in the facility.

The associate director of the facility, Iluv Telshe, has approached Dora Litvak, the director, to revise the transfer price policy to include only the variable costs. His argument is that the operating departments would thereby be encouraged to make greater use of the facility. Litvak's response is that she sees no reason why this should be so. "After all," she points out, "the operating departments need only so much time anyway; and besides, the various managers cannot buy computer time outside of the bank. So how could the transfer price affect their behavior?"

The associate director's response is that he knows of several instances where the operating departments have secured outside programming services so that the program submitted would require less running time. "In fact," he says, "I know of one case where a commercial lending manager spent 300 litas on additional programming to save an estimated two time units of running time."

Litvak's response is, "He should have—after all, it cost us 105 litas every time we run the program!"

Required:

1. Do you agree with the associate director or the director? Explain.

2. Was the behavior of the commercial lending manager (as described by the associate director) optimal as far as the bank is concerned? Why or why not?

3. Assuming that the additional programming effort could not have been done inside the bank, what is the maximum price that the commercial lending manager should have paid?

14-28. Preparation of Divisional Income Statements.   Butler Packing Company has two divisions. Division 1 is responsible for slaughtering and cutting the unprocessed meat. Division 2 processes meat such as hams, bacon, etc. Division 2 can buy meat from Division 1 or from outside suppliers. Division 1 can sell at the market price all the unprocessed meat that it can produce. The current year's income statement for the company is as follows:

Sales		$2,600,000
Cost of goods sold:		
Beginning inventory	$ 0	
Processing costs:		
Livestock costs, Division 1	600,000	
Labor, Division 1	400,000	
Overhead, Division 1	500,000	
Processing supplies, Division 2	200,000	
Labor, Division 2	300,000	
Overhead, Division 2	100,000	
Cost of goods available for sale	$2,100,000	
Less ending inventory cost:		

Division 1	$ 0		
Division 2	200,000	200,000	1,900,000
Gross margin			$ 700,000
Operating expenses:			
Sales and administrative, Division 1	$ 120,000		
Sales and administrative, Division 2	100,000		
Central office overhead	100,000		320,000
Income before income tax			$ 380,000

The ending inventory of $200,000 is valued at the product cost incurred in Division 1. This inventory is as yet unprocessed. The market value unprocessed is $300,000. The sales for the year can be broken down as follows:

Division 1 (to outsiders)	$ 600,000
Division 2	2,000,000
	$2,600,000

The market value of the unprocessed meat actually transferred from Division 1 to Division 2 (exclusive of the ending inventory) was $1,800,000.

Required:

1. Prepare divisional income statements that might be used to evaluate the performance of the two division managers.
2. Explain the transfer pricing policy you have used in preparing the statements.
3. Can you see any conflict in the policy you have used if this same transfer price is to be used for decision making? Explain.

14-29. Preparation of Divisional Income Statements.   Kumar Farms, near Bombay, India, has two divisions; one produces grain, and the other sells the grain. As soon as the grain is produced, it is transferred to the Selling Division where it is stored in anticipation of future sales at a higher price.

During the year, three grain crops of 1,900,000 bushels each were produced. All three have now been sold, although some were held in inventory for various periods of time. The market prices (in rupees) at production time were Rs120 per bushel for the first crop, Rs150 per bushel for the second, and Rs90 per bushel for the third. Assume no beginning inventories.

The annual income statement for the entire company is as follows:

Revenue:		
Sales (5,700,000 bushels)		Rs 1,200,000,000
Cost:		
Producing Division labor and materials	Rs 130,250,000	
Selling Division labor	10,500,000	
Producing Division overhead	80,250,000	
Selling Division overhead	9,000,000	
Total cost		Rs 230,000,000
Net income		Rs 970,000,000

Required:

The company president is very pleased with the total profit but wants to determine whether the price speculation activities of the Selling Division are earning a profit. You are requested to prepare divisional income statements for the Producing Division and the Selling Division. Decide what type of transfer price, market or cost, to use. Explain which transfer price is better. Are the divisional income statements useful? Explain.

14-30. Capital Budgeting and ROI. Berman, Inc. has a division which performs telemarketing services for clients throughout the U. S. The income statement of this division is as follows:

Revenues		$ 17,000,000
Division costs:		
Variable cost	$12,000,000	
Fixed cost	4,000,000	16,000,000
Division contribution margin		$ 1,000,000
Allocated central office overhead		500,000
Net income		$ 500,000
Investment allocated to division		$ 5,000,000
ROI		10%

The management is disturbed about the low ROI. The corporate treasurer indicates that the company can earn at least 20 percent on investment funds from any number of other projects. Furthermore, the treasurer points out that the investment is actually understated because an office building carried at a cost of $5,000,000 could be disposed of for about $8,000,000.

An investigation reveals that 50 percent of the division's fixed cost of $4,000,000 cannot be eliminated even if the division is sold. The allocated central office overhead is a pro-rata share of operating the corporate offices, and sale of the division would not affect this cost either.

Required:

1. Assuming that an expenditure of $1,000,000 annually would maintain the facility in good operating condition for at least 10 years, should the division be sold? Explain.

2. If not, does a better way of reporting the ROI exist that would alert management to consider selling if volume begins to decline? Describe.

14-31. Internal or External Sales. Wittkamp Company has the capacity to manufacture 700 units of parts used in machine tool production. These parts are manufactured in batch lots of 100 units each. Division A makes these parts at a uniform variable cost of $5 per unit. The manufactured batches can be sold either to outside customers or to Division B where the parts are used in machine tool assembly.

Data with respect to prices per batch from outside sales are given below along with prices charged to outsiders after further processing in Division B:

Batch No.	Division A Price to Outside Customers	Division B Price to Outside Customers After Additional Processing	Division B Additional Processing Costs Per Batch
1	$16	$35	$13
2	15	32	13
3	14	30	13
4	13	26	12
5	12	22	12
6	11	20	12
7	10	20	11

Required:

Decide which batches should be sold after production in Division A and which batches should be transferred to Division B for further processing. Show computations.

14-32. Transfer Pricing Problem. Leisure Company has a producing division (Division 1) which supplies several parts to another producing division (Division 2) which produces the main product. These component parts are listed as follows with relevant cost information, including outside supplier prices:

Component No.	Variable Cost Per Unit	Quantity Produced	Outside Price
1	$11	25,000	$14.50
2	15	35,000	19.20
3	7	15,000	9.40
4	5	15,000	9.60

The out-of-pocket fixed costs of Division 1 amount to $270,000. These costs consist of salaries and other overhead. In addition, other fixed costs (consisting mainly of depreciation on machinery) amount to $90,000 per period. In calculating unit cost, total fixed costs of $360,000 are allocated based on units produced to arrive at a full cost.

A full-cost transfer price is used. In Division 2, which uses the four components, the manager has authority to buy inside the company or from an outside supplier. The outside prices vary somewhat throughout the year.

After calculating the full cost, the manager of Division 2 notices that outside purchase prices of Components 1 and 3 are lower than the transfer prices and places orders with outside suppliers. Division 1 stops producing these two components, reallocates fixed costs to the remaining units, and adjusts the full-cost transfer prices.

Required:

1. Reallocate fixed costs and determine the adjusted transfer prices based on full costs of the remaining products. If no communication between the two divisions occurs, what action will the manager of Division 2 likely take?
2. Comment on the deficiencies of the full-cost transfer price system.
3. What if the items transferred to Division 2 from Division 1 are 100 percent of Division 1's business? Devise a method of assigning the fixed cost of Division 1 to Division 2 that will not cause Division 2 to buy outside when the components could be produced by Division 1.
4. What if the items transferred to Division 2 from Division 1 are 4 percent of Division 1's total business? How would your answer to Part (3) change?

14-33. Evaluation of Alternative Transfer Prices. Stratton Company has a division that manufactures shafts, which are sold to other divisions and to outside customers. This division is organized into two sections as follows:

Section 1—Machining and Grinding: This highly mechanized section has much heavy equipment that is used to give shape to shafts and to perform grinding operations on shafts with special requirements.

Section 2—Cleaning and Packing: This section consists primarily of workers who clean and pack all shafts.

The costing system used by the company charges materials, direct labor, and overhead to each order. Labor, materials, and one-third of overhead in both sections are considered to be variable. The overhead is allocated on the basis of labor cost for normal activity levels. Furthermore, the rate is a division-wide rate, not by section. This rate is developed as follows:

	Direct Labor Payroll	Overhead
Section 1 (70% of capacity)	$200,000	$ 900,000
Section 2 (60% of capacity)	600,000	300,000
Total division	$800,000	$1,200,000

Overhead rate: $1,200,000 ÷ $800,000 = 150% of labor cost

The average wage for Section 1 is $15 per hour; for Section 2, $10 per hour. A full-cost transfer price is used for selling shafts to other producing divisions. If an order is placed by another producing division that calls for $100 of materials and 2 hours of labor time in each section, the price that is quoted would be arrived at as follows:

	Hours	Total
Labor:		
Section 1.	2	$ 30
Section 2.	2	20
		$ 50
Overhead (150% x $50).		75
Materials.		100
Transfer price		$225

The assistant to the controller has been considering a change in the costing system whereby an overhead rate would be developed for each section. It is believed that such a system would give a more equitable price for the work done for other divisions and would be a better basis for pricing outside sales. Since the shaft sold to outside customers is competitive, the price is determined by bid and negotiations; and the primary factor in deciding whether to accept or reject business is the order's profit. At times, the division is operating near enough to capacity that outside work must be stopped if inside work is to be done.

At the moment, two orders are being considered and are from another division that can buy either inside or outside the company. The details on the two orders are:

	Order 1	Order 2
Materials.	$500	$200
Labor:		
Section 1.	3 hours	6 hours
Section 2.	3 hours	1 hour

Required:

1. Calculate the transfer prices for the two orders under the present system. Then, calculate the transfer prices under the proposed system.

2. If the market prices were $700 for Order 1 and $600 for Order 2, how might management decisions in both buying and selling divisions be affected by the overhead system?

3. Recalculate the transfer prices for the two orders based on variable cost only. Assume a sectional variable overhead rate is used in the manufacturing division.

4. Which system do you prefer? Why?

14-34. Transfer Price Decision.   The Elkton Subsidiary of Nordic Instruments, Inc. manufactures small printed circuit boards and has the capacity to make 100,000 units of a given model each year. At the present time, only 75,000 units are being made each year and are sold to an outside customer for $7.50 a unit.

Fixed manufacturing costs are applied on the basis of an annual production of 100,000 units each year. Total fixed costs for the year are $175,000. The total unit cost of each circuit board is $6.50. The Reeves Subsidiary has been purchasing this type of circuit board from an outside supplier at a price of $7.50 per unit. The president of Nordic requests that the Elkton Subsidiary deliver 25,000 circuit boards to the Reeves Subsidiary at a price equal to the variable cost.

The superintendent of Elkton states that the division gains no advantage by selling at variable cost. No contribution is made to the recovery of the fixed costs. Furthermore, the superintendent states that the company gains nothing. The fixed costs of Elkton must be recovered, and Reeves should pay the full price of $7.50 as it would by buying outside.

Required:

1. Is the argument of the superintendent valid? Explain.
2. What is the variable cost of manufacturing each circuit board?
3. Describe a pricing system that should benefit the company and be acceptable to each division.

14-35. Internal Pricing Decision.   Alan William is the manager of the Sterling Division of Triple-A Machine Company. This division manufactures spring assemblies that are sold to various outside customers at a price of $32 per unit. Recently, the division has been operating at 550,000 machine hours. Normal capacity has been defined as 700,000 machine hours and is approximately equal to the practical capacity.

Each assembly requires 15 minutes of machine time. The direct materials and direct labor cost per assembly is $16.20, and overhead varies at the rate of $8.40 per machine hour. The total fixed overhead for the year is $3,521,000.

William's division has just been awarded a contract for the sale of 400,000 units in another country at a unit price of $26. This contract will not interfere with the regular sales at a price of $32, and it is anticipated that this contract can be renewed in future years.

The Jessop Division of the company has started production of a product line that will require 400,000 units of the spring assembly made by the Sterling Division. The president of Triple-A states that the assemblies should be transferred between the divisions at the variable cost to the Sterling Division. If Sterling Division does not furnish the units, the Jessop Division will be forced to purchase the assemblies on the outside market at $32 apiece. With higher costs, Jessop will have lower profits on the sale of the end products.

Required:

1. Determine the variable cost to produce each spring assembly.
2. Under the circumstances, should the Sterling Division supply the Jessop Division? Explain.
3. What price should be used for the internal transfer, assuming a transfer should be made?

 14-36. ROI and Residual Income.   Kimber-Zack Corporation is a highly diversified company organized into autonomous divisions along product lines. The autonomy permits division managers a significant amount of authority in operating their divisions. Each manager is responsible for sales, cost of operations, acquisition of division assets, management of accounts receivable and inventories, and use of existing facilities. Cash management is centralized at the corporate home office. Divisions are permitted cash for their normal operating needs, but all excess cash is transferred to the corporate home office.

Division managers are responsible for presenting requests for capital expenditures (to acquire assets, expand existing facilities, or make any other long-term investment) to corporate management for approval. Once the proposals are analyzed and evaluated, corporate management decides whether to commit funds to the requests.

Kimber-Zack adopted an ROI measure several years ago. The measure uses division direct profit and an investment base composed of fixed assets employed plus accounts receivable and inventories. ROI is used to evaluate the performance of each division, and it is the primary factor in assessing salary increases each year. Also, changes in the ROI from year to year affect the amount of the annual bonus.

ROI has grown over the years for each division. However, the company's overall ROI has declined in recent years. Cash balances are increasing at the corporate level, and investments in marketable securities are growing. Idle cash and marketable securities do not earn as good a rate of return as division capital investments.

The following data (with 000s omitted) show the operating results for the Apparel Division and the Sports Gear Division for the last three years:

	Apparel Division			**Sports Gear Division**		
	1996	*1997*	*1998*	*1996*	*1997*	*1998*
Estimated industry sales	$ 10,000	$ 11,000	$ 12,100	$ 5,000	$ 6,250	$7,500
Division sales	$ 1,200	$ 1,380	$ 1,587	$ 500	$ 650	$ 780
Division direct costs:						
Variable costs	$ 360	$ 396	$ 467	$ 160	$ 182	$ 203
Discretionary fixed costs	480	490	500	180	210	240
Committed fixed costs	250	300	375	150	215	260
Total division direct costs	$ 1,090	$ 1,186	$ 1,342	$ 490	$ 607	$ 703
Division net profit	$ 110	$ 194	$ 245	$ 10	$ 43	$ 77
Investment base	$ 1,100	$ 1,200	$ 1,300	$ 125	$ 195	$ 280
ROI	10.00%	16.17%	18.85%	8.00%	22.05%	27.50%

The managers of both divisions were promoted to their positions in 1996. John Harris had been assistant division manager of the Apparel Division for six years prior to his appointment as manager of that division. The Sports Gear Division was created in 1994. Rose Knolting had served as assistant manager of the Toy Division for four years prior to becoming manager of the Sports Gear Division, when the latter position suddenly became available in late 1995.

Required:

1. In general, is ROI an appropriate measure of performance? Explain.
2. Explain how an overemphasis on ROI can result in a declining corporate ROI.
3. Describe specific actions that might have caused this increase in 1998 divisional ROI while the corporate ROI declined.
4. Assuming the minimum desired rate of return is 12 percent for Apparel and 15 percent for Sports Gear, compute the residual income and the residual income as a percentage of the investment base for each division for each year.
5. Which division manager (Harris or Knolting) do you judge as the better manager? What are your reasons?

14-37. ROI and Residual Income. Raddington Industries produces tool and die machinery for manufacturers. The company expanded vertically in 1994 by acquiring one of its suppliers of alloy steel plates, Reigis Steel Company. To manage the two separate businesses effectively, the operations of Reigis are reported separately as an investment center.

Raddington monitors its divisions on the basis of both unit contribution and return on average investment (ROI), with investment defined as average operating assets employed. Management bonuses are based on ROI. All investments in operating assets are expected to earn a minimum return of 11 percent before income taxes.

Reigis' cost of goods sold is considered to be entirely variable while the division's administrative expenses are not dependent on volume. Selling expenses are a mixed cost with 40 percent attributed to sales volume. Reigis' ROI has ranged from 11.8 to 14.7 percent since 1994. During the fiscal year ended November 30, 1999, Reigis contemplated a capital acquisition with an estimated ROI of 11.5 percent; however, division management decided against the investment because it believed that the investment would decrease Reigis' overall ROI.

The 1999 operating statement for Reigis is presented below. The division's operating assets employed were $15,750,000 at November 30, 1999, a five percent increase over the 1998 yearend balance.

REIGIS STEEL DIVISION Operating Statement For the Year Ended November 30, 1999 ($000s omitted)		
Sales revenue		$ 25,000
Less expenses:		
Cost of goods sold	$16,500	
Administrative expenses	3,955	
Selling expenses	2,700	23,155
Income from operations before income taxes		$ 1,845

Required:

1. Calculate the unit contribution for Reigis Steel Division if 1,484,000 units were produced and sold during the year ended November 30, 1999.
2. Calculate the following performance measures for 1999 for the Reigis Steel Division:
   (a) Pretax return on average investment in operating assets employed (ROI).
   (b) Residual income calculated on the basis of average operating assets employed.
3. Explain why the management of the Reigis Steel Division would have been more likely to accept the contemplated capital acquisition if residual income rather than ROI were used as a performance measure.
4. Identify several items that Reigis should control if it is to be evaluated fairly by either the ROI or residual income performance measures.

(ICMA adapted)

14-38. Performance Evaluation and Ethics.   Pittsburgh-Walsh Company (PWC) is a manufacturing company whose product line consists of lighting fixtures and electronic timing devices. The Lighting Fixtures Division assembles units for the upscale and mid-range markets. The Electronic Timing Devices Division manufactures instrument panels that allow electronic systems to be activated and deactivated at scheduled times for both efficiency and safety purposes. Both divisions use the same manufacturing facilities and share production equipment.

PWC's budget for the year ending December 31, 2000, is shown on the next page. This budget was prepared under the following guidelines:

■ Variable expenses are directly assigned to the incurring division.
■ Fixed overhead expenses are directly assigned to the incurring division.
■ Common fixed expenses are allocated to the divisions on the basis of units produced which bear a close relationship to direct labor. Included in common fixed expenses are costs of the corporate staff, legal expenses, taxes, staff marketing, and advertising.

	Lighting Fixtures		Electronic Timing Devises	Totals
	Upscale	Mid-range		
Sales	$1,440	$770	$800	$3,010
Variable expenses:				
Cost of goods sold	720	439	320	1,479
Selling and administrative . . .	170	60	60	290
Contribution margin	$ 550	$271	$420	$1,241
Fixed overhead expenses	140	80	80	300
Segment margin	$ 410	$191	$340	$ 941
Common fixed expenses:				
Overhead	48	132	120	300
Selling and administrative . . .	11	31	28	70
Net income (loss)	$ 351	$ 28	$192	$ 571

Budget for the Year Ending December 31, 2000 (Amounts in Thousands)

- The production plan is for 8,000 upscale fixtures, 22,000 mid-range fixtures, and 20,000 electronic timing devices.

PWC established a bonus plan for division management that requires meeting the budget's planned net income by product line, with a bonus increment if the division exceeds the planned product line net income by ten percent or more.

Shortly before the year began, the CEO, Jack Parkow suffered a heart attack and retired. After reviewing the 2000 budget, the new CEO, Joe Kelly, decided to close the lighting fixtures mid-range product line by the end of the first quarter and use the available production capacity to increase production of the remaining two product lines. The marketing staff advised that electronic timing devices could grow by 40 percent with increased direct sales support. Increases above that level and increases in sales of upscale lighting fixtures would require additional advertising expenditures to expand consumer awareness of PWC as an electronics and upscale lighting fixture company. Kelly approved the increased sales support and advertising expenditures to achieve the revised plan. Kelly advised the divisions that for bonus purposes the original product line net income objectives must be met, but he did allow the Lighting Fixtures Division to combine the net income objectives for both product lines for bonus purposes.

Prior to the close of the fiscal year, the division controllers were furnished with preliminary actual data for review and adjustment, as appropriate. These preliminary yearend data, which follow, reflect the revised units of production amounting to 12,000 upscale fixtures, 4,000 mid-range fixtures, and 30,000 electronic timing devices.

The controller of the Lighting Fixtures Division, anticipating a similar bonus plan for 2001, is contemplating deferring some revenues into the next year, on the pretext that the sales are not yet final, and accruing in the current year expenditures that will be applicable to the first quarter of 2001. The corporation would meet its annual plan, and the division would exceed the ten percent incremental bonus plateau in the year 2000 despite the deferred revenues and accrued expenses contemplated.

Preliminary Actuals for the Year Ending December 31, 2000 **(Amounts in Thousands)**				
	Lighting Fixtures		**Electronic Timing Devises**	**Totals**
	Upscale	*Mid-range*		
Sales	$2,160	$140	$1,200	$3,500
Variable expenses:				
Cost of goods sold	1,080	80	480	1,640
Selling and administrative . . .	260	11	96	367
Contribution margin	$ 820	$ 49	$ 624	$1,493
Fixed overhead expenses	140	14	80	234
Segment margin	$ 680	$ 35	$ 544	$1,259
Common fixed expenses:				
Overhead	78	27	195	300
Selling and administrative . . .	60	20	150	230
Net income (loss)	$ 542	$ (12)	$ 199	$ 729

Required:

1. Segment (divisional) reporting can be developed based on different criteria. What criteria must be present for division management to accept being evaluated on a segment basis?

2. Why would the management of the Electronics Timing Devices Division be unhappy with the current reporting, and how should the reporting be revised to gain its acceptance?

3. Explain why the adjustments contemplated by the controller of the Lighting Fixtures Division are unethical by citing specific standards from the "Standards of Ethical Conduct for Management Accountants" from Chapter 1, page 21.

(ICMA adapted)

C ASE 14A—LORAX ELECTRIC COMPANY

Lorax Electric Company manufactures a large variety of systems and individual components for the electronics industry. The firm is organized into several divisions with division managers given the authority to make virtually all operating decisions. Management control over divisional operations is maintained by a system of divisional profit and return on investment measures which are reviewed regularly by top management. Top management of Lorax has been quite pleased with the effectiveness of the system it has been using and believes that the system is responsible for the company's improved profitability over the last few years.

The Devices Division manufactures solid-state devices and is operating at capacity. The Systems Division has asked the Devices Division to supply a large quantity of integrated circuit IC378. The Devices Division currently is selling this component to its regular customers at $40 per hundred.

The Systems Division, which is operating at about 60 percent capacity, wants this particular component for a digital clock system. It has an opportunity to supply large quantities of these digital clock systems to Centonic Electric, a major producer of clock radios and other popular electronic home entertainment equipment. This is the first opportunity any of the Lorax divisions has had to do business with Centonic Electric. Centonic Electric has offered to pay $7.50 per clock system.

The Systems Division prepared an analysis of the probable costs to produce the clock systems. The amount that could be paid to the Devices Division for the integrated circuits was determined by working backward from the selling price. The cost estimates employed by the division reflected the highest per unit cost the Systems Division could incur for each cost component and still leave a sufficient margin so that the division's income statement could show reasonable improvement. The cost estimates are summarized as follows:

Proposed selling price		$7.50
Costs excluding required integrated circuit (IC378):		
Components purchased from outsider suppliers	$2.75	
Circuit board etching—labor and variable overhead	0.40	
Assembly, testing, and packaging—labor and variable overhead	1.35	
Fixed overhead allocations	1.50	
Profit margin	0.50	6.50
Amount which can be paid for integrated circuits IC378 (5 x $20 per hundred) . . .		$1.00

As a result of this analysis, the Systems Division offered the Devices Division a price of $20 per hundred for the integrated circuit. This bid was refused by the manager of the Devices Division because he felt the Systems Division should at least meet the price of $40 per hundred which regular customers pay. When the Systems Division found that it could not obtain a comparable integrated circuit from outside vendors, the situation was presented to an arbitration committee which reviews such problems.

The arbitration committee prepared an analysis which showed that $0.15 would cover variable costs of producing the integrated circuit, $0.28 would cover the full cost including fixed overhead, and $0.35 would provide a gross margin equal to the average gross margin on all of the products sold by the Devices Division. The manager of the Systems Division reacted by stating, "It could sell us that integrated circuit for $0.20 and still earn a positive contribution toward profit. In fact, it should be required to sell at its variable cost—$0.15—and not be allowed to take advantage of us."

Lou Belcher, manager of Devices, countered by arguing, "It doesn't make sense to sell to the Systems Division at $20 per hundred when we can get $40 per hundred outside on all we can produce. In fact, Systems could pay us up to almost $60 per hundred; and it would still have a positive contribution to profit."

The recommendation of the committee, to set the price at $0.35 per unit ($35 per hundred) so that Devices could earn a "fair" gross margin, was rejected by both division managers. Consequently, the problem was brought to the attention of the vice-president of operations.

Required:

1. What is the immediate economic effect on Lorax Electric Company as a whole if the Devices Division were required to supply IC378 to the Systems Division at $0.35 per unit—the price recommended by the arbitration committee? Explain your answer.

2. Discuss the advisability of intervention by top management as a solution to transfer pricing disputes between division managers such as the one experienced by Lorax Electric Company.

3. Suppose that Lorax adopted a policy of requiring that the price to be paid in all internal transfers by the buying division would be equal to the variable cost per unit of the selling division for that product and that the supplying division would be required to sell if the buying division decided to buy the item. Discuss the consequences of adopting such a policy as a way of avoiding the need for the arbitration committee or for intervention by the vice-president.

(ICMA adapted)

CASE 14B—ERCULEAN ELECTRONICS

Erculean Electronics is a division of a major communications equipment supplier. It designs, manufactures, assembles, and tests a wide variety of electronic linking assemblies. The largest percentage of its business is internal, meaning that about 45 percent of its assemblies becomes part of the division's own end products. But in the past few years, sales have gone to a growing array of customers including:

1. Other sister divisions producing complementary products.
2. Other communications companies, often direct competitors, that use similar assemblies with minor engineering changes.
3. Automotive firms and automotive suppliers who are incorporating more electronic communications components into their products.
4. Appliance manufacturers who use specialized linkages in their electronic products.
5. Numerous international manufacturers in each of the above industries.

In short, Erculean is enjoying success in a very specialized market. The keys to its success are high-quality products, an ability to adapt to a customer's needs quickly (sometimes in days), and highly dependable delivery to most customers on narrow just-in-time schedules. Another factor has been Erculean's manufacturing prowess. It has always been cost conscious and on the edge of manufacturing technology and processes.

Manufacturing has expanded rapidly to meet the growth in demand. Also, since its original plants were in the high labor cost Midwest, it has sought relief in numerous ways. A brief description of its current manufacturing locations and capabilities introduces the problems facing Erculean managers:

1. The Jackson, Michigan, plant is older but highly automated; and its production employees work under an Automotive Workers Union contract that guarantees its members 2,000 hours per year of employment. It is within 200 miles of 40 percent of Erculean customers. The number of workers at this plant has dropped from over 800 in 1974 to about 225 today. Most of these workers are very experienced and have adapted very well to the increased automation and robotics introduced in the early 1990s. Worker classifications have been reduced in the latest contract by 75 percent. But the average cash wage is over $15 per hour, and the fully-loaded rate is nearly $30 per hour.
2. A Tulsa, Oklahoma, plant was built in the mid-1980s and is also highly automated; and, since 1990, employees are represented by the International Electric Workers Union. The average cash wage is about two-thirds of the Jackson plant, and the fully-loaded rate is about half of the Jackson plant. Few worker classifications exist, and the definition of "direct labor" differs considerably from the Jackson definition.
3. Outside subcontractors are used for certain products and when company plants are operating at capacity. Generally, Erculean controls materials quality by buying the materials, selling them to the subcontractors, and buying back the finished products. The subcontractors are suppliers of electronic subassemblies in other industries. These suppliers have different cost functions and may do different amounts of work depending on the contract requirements.
4. Six small Mexican plants near the U. S. border also produce the same linkages. These plants have extremely low labor rates, are labor intensive with little automation, produce lower volumes, but have very high quality. The wage cost is around $2.00 per hour, depending on the location and the peso exchange rate.
5. Other international production has not yet been needed, but Erculean is already negotiating for a Malaysian facility. Potential European customers are pushing for close proximity plants for sourcing.

In the U. S. plants, under recent labor contracts, new employees enter at lower wage rates or under a temporary status with no benefits. This adds to the already confusing labor costing situation.

Very fundamental questions need answers:

1. Should the cost accounting system define costs the same way for all plants?
2. How should labor cost be defined?
3. What are variable production costs?
4. How should "where to produce" decisions be made?
5. On which costs should bids for new business be based?
6. What transfer pricing policies are appropriate for intracompany business?

Required:
1. Suggest an approach in the form of a policy on how costs might be incorporated in the bidding and pricing procedures for external business.
2. Suggest an approach in the form of a policy to price intracompany transfers between Erculean and other divisions of the communications equipment firm.
3. Suggest an approach to match cost functions, types of production, volumes, sources of business, and sales revenues that might help Erculean optimize its profits.

Extensions in Managerial Analysis

Costs of Quality and Other Cost Management Issues

LEARNING OBJECTIVES

After studying Chapter 15, you will be able to:

1. Identify four categories of costs of quality.
2. Explain relationships among the costs of quality categories.
3. Understand the concepts of target costing and kaizen costing.
4. Distinguish between value-added and nonvalue-added activities.
5. Describe various types of nonfinancial performance measures.
6. Explain strategies to enhance productivity such as downsizing and business process reengineering.

TQM and the Need to Measure Quality Costs

Chuck Gaa, considered the ace trouble shooter for GreenCo Products, was sent to its Cleveland plant by "Big Jim" Thomas, president of GreenCo, about 15 months ago. What he found was "big trouble." The plant was losing about $400,000 per month—mostly from production waste, low productivity, and customer warranty claims. Sales were declining, and too many customers were unhappy. This was Spring 1993, long after Total Quality Management was a cliché and a norm in most firms. Yes, GreenCo had a TQM program that "Big Jim" had announced in late 1990. Signs had been posted about quality being "No. 1." A consulting firm had conducted seminars for workers; statistical control charts were maintained; and managers had increased inspection of incoming parts and outgoing products. Faster response to warranty claims had been implemented through a costly system to guarantee a 24-hour response to any customer problem.

Yet, productivity declined; scrap was up (reaching nearly 50 percent of output in certain weeks); and warranty costs soared. Workers saw the TQM program as a management project. And managers blamed much of the problem on the lack of union cooperation and of employee concern. No specific quality goals were set. Everyone lacked a sense of urgency. Chuck's arrival brought a sudden change: Meetings with line workers quickly pointed to key production problems; warranty claims were grouped to identify failure causes; product design and production engineers were brought together to analyze failures; and certain changes were made "overnight." A goal of cutting scrap by 50 percent in three months was set.

At every step, the same question came up—"What's this costing us?" Chuck, knowing that this question was key at other plants, sought out DeAnn Ricketts, the plant cost accountant. DeAnn was in the middle of an ABC study and had begun to define new activity centers and cost drivers. While not an easy task, DeAnn was able to modify her system rather quickly to identify quality costs—which, where, and how much. Chuck and DeAnn became allies, promoting each other's views to managers and employees alike. Within two months, DeAnn gave Chuck a 1994 costs of quality analysis. These costs totaled a surprising 15 percent of sales. Of this, little was spent on prevention; about 30 percent was spent on appraisal; nearly 45 percent went to fixing internal failures; and the rest were external failure costs. Lost sales because of bad product were not captured or estimated. In addition to many nonfinancial quality measures, the quality cost reports helped Chuck measure the impact of his recovery program.

Chuck is now gone, off to another problem plant. The Cleveland plant is now at breakeven. But the quality job is just now paying dividends. DeAnn's latest costs of quality report shows total costs still high at 12 percent of sales. But, the cost composition had changed already: 30 percent prevention, 30 percent appraisal, 25 percent internal failure, and 15 percent external failure. The target for 1996 was 10 percent of sales with percentages of 40, 40, 15, and 5, respectively. Long-term goals are 6 percent of sales and a percentage mix of 70, 20, 10, and 0, respectively. Incidentally, sales are rebounding.

In the 1990s, the competitive environment has forced a changed and improved focus on every business. Heightened customer service expectations, development of integrated systems, demands for cost reductions, advances in information technology, access to international markets, and speed of competitor reactions have all increased the demands on managerial accountants for relevant and timely data for decisions. This chapter examines a set of the more important areas of change in managerial accounting. These topics are heavily influenced by international competitors, particularly the Japanese. Product quality and process improvement have allowed Japanese automakers, electronics firms, and other consumer goods producers to capture major shares of international markets. Disciplined and team-oriented approaches brought market and financial success. Soon others, particularly U. S. firms, began to adopt and adapt similar concepts and strategies. JIT, quality circles, and continuous improvement programs are examples.

In this chapter, we focus on several of these topics that have strong managerial accounting ramifications. Specifically, measuring and monitoring quality costs are major parts of any total quality management program. Team approaches to design, costing, production planning, and process improvement have yielded huge dividends. These approaches have focused on linking customer needs to the design process, on identifying and eliminating any activity that does not add value to the product, and on organizing planning and control activities that truly measure performance. Many more topics could be included and more pages added on a weekly basis. Old accounting tools are redesigned, some are abandoned, and new concepts are tried and tested. The pace of change is exciting.

C OSTS OF QUALITY

"Quality is free" is a favorite saying of many who argue for efforts to improve quality. It may be difficult to accept the concept that spending more on quality improvement efforts will lower costs. But the facts tell an exciting story:

- Increased training of workers will reduce scrap and rework costs.
- Higher quality products improve customer satisfaction and generate higher sales.
- Narrower control limits force improved processes and greater utilization of capacity.
- With reduced waste, more product can be generated with the same equipment and workers.
- "Designing in" quality prevents production problems and the need for engineering changes to create "fixes." An error of $1 in design can easily cause $10 in production problems.
- Empowering employees through quality circles and other participation techniques to give them control over quality-related production decisions increases total commitment.
- Employee satisfaction from eliminating rework, downtime, and scrap increases productivity and further commitment to improvement, particularly if the benefits are shared with the employees.

These results reduce quality costs and, therefore, product costs. Quality efforts come in many forms and names, including:

- **Total quality management (TQM)**—an integrated effort of training, process controls, incentives, employee empowerment, product engineering and design, supplier involvement, and customer satisfaction measurement to achieve quality goals.
- **Statistical quality control**—the use of statistical techniques on processes to measure, monitor, and evaluate performance based on goals, control ranges, and performance percentages.
- **Continuous improvement programs**—efforts to establish quality targets that represent improvement over current performance through worker involvement in evaluation processes.

■ **Quality control through the guidance of quality experts—** specific approaches to quality management promoted by internationally recognized leaders such as Deming, Juran, Crosby, and Taguchi.

All of these focus on management commitment to bringing about a change in attitude and changes in processes.

Methods vary but include heavy management commitment to change. One Michigan firm's management, tired of customer complaints and nagging productivity problems, introduced an array of techniques to impress employees and managers with the need to work toward zero defects in its output. Every work station was made responsible for approving the quality of its work before sending it to the next station. When defects were detected, the entire line was halted; horns sounded; the problem diagnosed; and responsibility for the solution identified. The initial result was that very little was shipped from that plant for nearly two weeks because of the nearly constant stoppage of the line. But within two months, productivity was above any prior period and continued to rise. The costs of the early stoppages were nearly fatal to the firm, but the payoffs are substantial both internally and to customers, many of whom are automotive related and are using vendor certification programs to promote quality, delivery, and cost goals and to eliminate nonperforming suppliers.

Cost Categories

Four categories of costs are commonly identified. These are related and can be considered tradeoffs for each other. They, along with examples, are:

■ **Prevention costs** are incurred to prevent the production of products or services that do not meet specifications. As these costs increase, failure costs should decrease. These costs, often spent prior to production, include:

Job training	Design and process engineering
Supplier evaluation and approvals	Quality training
Development of specifications and standards	Preventive maintenance
	Promotion of quality
Employee quality circle teams	New equipment to reduce waste

■ **Appraisal costs** are incurred to monitor and inspect production. These costs are intended to detect products or services that do not meet specifications during the production process. As these costs increase, failure costs should decrease. Included are:

Inspections of materials	Internal auditing activities
Inspections during production	Quality control activities
Inspections of finished products	Production testing
Line personnel's self-checking activities	Statistical quality control
	Calibration of test equipment

■ **Internal failure costs** are incurred after a defective or substandard product or service is detected but before it leaves the plant. These costs increase as the number of defective units detected increases. Included are:

Rework, retesting, and rescheduling	Scrap
Lost production	Downtime
Lost contribution margin on defective units[*]	Increased inventory

- ■ **External failure costs** are incurred when the defective product or service gets to the customer. These costs increase as customers find defective units and reject them. These costs include two important groups: costs of handling customer complaints and costs of future lost sales because of poor quality and customer dissatisfaction. Included are:

Repairs	Logistics of returned units
Warranties (estimated and actual)	Processing recall programs
Contribution margin on replacement units	Lost contribution margin from damaged product reputation[*]
Liability claims	Lost contribution margin from price reductions[*]
Complaint departments	
Product service departments	

[*] These items are measurable only by making estimates of external impacts and are rarely part of a costs of quality accounting report. They are the most subjective of all quality costs yet, perhaps, the most important in a strategic sense.

While these lists seem straightforward, much judgment goes into the typical quality cost analysis. If a person's duties are part production and part inspection, what percentage should be considered to be quality costs? Each firm must decide on its own definitions. Also, as time passes, processes change; greater understanding of quality issues evolves; and accounting systems change. One danger behind this discussion is that an impression is created that cost measurement is precise and easily done. Activity-based costing, special studies, and improved charts of accounts have certainly detailed the trail of costs.

Traditionally, these costs have been buried in other cost categories. Prevention costs are "lost" in administrative overhead. Appraisal costs are spread among the many locations. Internal failure costs show up in efficiency and quantity variances and allowances for "normal scrap." External failure costs are selling and administrative costs or not captured at all. In many firms, it takes a major effort to identify, measure, and track these costs with reasonable accuracy.

Prevention and appraisal costs are considered tradeoffs to internal and external failure costs. Thus, stronger training programs are viewed as important costs that help reduce internal and external failure costs. Also, a stronger appraisal program should reduce both internal and external failure costs. Yet, in the long run, spending on prevention costs may allow a company to reduce both failure costs and appraisal costs. Better trained employees will produce much higher quality products which require less testing and inspecting, a result of producing few if any defective units. Implicitly, failure costs fall to near zero levels.

Diagraming Costs of Quality

Figure 15.1 illustrates the interaction of the four costs of quality categories. The horizontal or *X*-axis reflects either a decreasing defect rate or an increasing quality-assurance level. As can be seen, an optimal cost level can be drawn. The presumption is that increased prevention and appraisal spending will lower failure costs (internal plus external). We must be careful not to over-simplify the relationships here. For example:

- The optimal spending level can be drawn but can rarely be measured accurately. Also, this optimal level of spending implies that we should be satisfied with this level of quality (defects).
- This static drawing of the four cost categories reflects general trends but implies that they are substitutes for each other, are equally important, and are of approximately equal size. Rarely is this the case.
- The cost curves imply that cost functions can be defined quantita-tively to allow these costs to be plotted at various levels of quality assurance. While cost relationships do exist, they are difficult to quantify accurately.

FIGURE 15.1   Costs of Quality

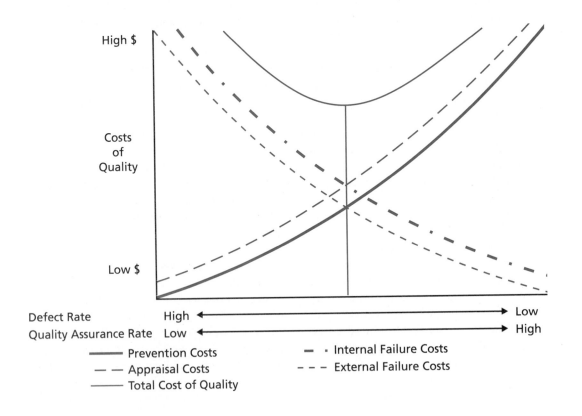

■ Too often, managers assume that by merely spending money on quality prevention and appraisal activities their quality goals can be achieved. Some TQM programs have been successful and sustainable; many others have achieved neither their quality nor cost reduction goals.

Any manager or managerial accountant who advocates finding the optimal spending and failure cost level and operating at that level fails to understand the interrelationships that exist. For example, prevention costs (i.e., training, education, and quality-enhancing investments) are in effect current investments in future defect reductions. More spending on training and vendor certification programs, for example, should reduce internal and external failure rates in the future. A highly trained workforce should reduce the need for inspections in the future.

As an offbeat example of this idea, compare the teenage driver accident rate in the U. S. with Japan. In the U. S., most teenagers take a short driver's training course with very limited coverage of driving laws, driver etiquette, and hands-on skill development. In Japan, compulsory driver education courses cost approximately $5,000 per person because of the amount of training required. Car accidents do occur but at a much lower level as compared to U. S. experiences. (To test the idea, survey your current class. Odds are that well over half of your fellow students have had an auto accident before they reached 20 years of age.) Japan has traded accident costs for training costs. Other social impacts must be considered; for example, many persons might not drive because they cannot afford the $5,000.

As a numerical example of Figure 15.1, assume that 100,000 units are produced with six possible levels of spending on prevention and appraisal efforts. The contribution margin is $10 per unit. Of the defects, 60 percent is detected internally; and 40 percent is discovered externally. All defects must be reworked at a cost of $8 per unit. External failures cause a loss of future sales at a ratio of three units of lost sales for each external defect found, or $30 of lost contribution margin for each external defective unit. All dollar and unit amounts are in thousands.[1]

Defect Rates	Prevention Costs	Appraisal Costs	Rework Costs		Lost Contribution Margin		Total Quality Costs
			Units	Costs	Units	Costs	
5.00%	$100	$100	$8 x 5.0	$40	$30 x 2.0	$60	$300
3.50	120	80	8 x 3.5	28	30 x 1.4	42	270
2.25	140	65	8 x 2.25	18	30 x 0.9	27	250
1.25	160	55	8 x 1.25	10	30 x 0.5	15	240
0.50	190	50	8 x 0.5	4	30 x 0.2	6	250
0.10	240	48	8 x 0.1	0.80	30 x 0.04	1.20	290

To explain these numbers, the first row assumes that 5 percent of the 100,000 units produced is defective. Also, we are now spending $100,000 each on prevention and appraisal costs. It will cost $8 per unit to rework the 5,000 defective units or $40,000. Lost contribution margin is found by taking the

---

[1] This example was adapted from an article by J. T. Godfrey and W. R. Pasewark, "Controlling Quality Costs," *Management Accounting,* March 1988, p. 72.

external failures (40 percent x 5,000 units) times the contribution margin of three lost units (3 x $10)—a lost sales cost of $60,000 in contribution margin. The total costs of quality are $300,000.

Based on these numbers, the managerial accountant would recommend that the current optimal cost level is $240,000. This assumes that we can quantify the relationship between higher prevention costs and lower defective percentages. It also assumes that appraisal costs can be reduced accordingly. Internal and external discovery rates for defective units and lost sales figures are clearly estimates. Contribution margins and rework costs are reasonably solid data. This, however, is a static picture of quality costs. As time passes, these relationships will change, resulting in a new optimal spending pattern.

Continuous Improvement

Can any firm be satisfied with a static quality level? No! Markets are demanding higher and higher quality assurance levels. Japanese auto quality levels of the 1980s well exceeded U. S. capabilities. U. S. firms now exceed those levels, but Japanese car makers have moved to still higher levels. Competition demands continuous improvement.

Prior to the implementation of a TQM program, appraisal costs and combined failure costs will likely be very high. For example, the mix of quality costs at the start of a major quality effort in a machine manufacturer was:

Prevention costs	4.5%	
Appraisal costs	41.7	
Internal failure costs	53.4	
External failure costs	.4	(excluding lost sales estimates)
Total costs of quality	100.0%	

Total costs were approximately 8 percent of total sales. As part of management efforts to get employee "buy in," figures were presented to show the impact on employee profit sharing if the percentage decreased to 6 percent.

As time passes, Figure 15.1 will be revised to reflect improvements in quality and changed cost relationships. Movement will be toward higher quality assurance and lower defect levels. Cost patterns will shift from failure to prevention. Even appraisal costs may decrease as more confidence is gained in the production processes. Figure 15.2 incorporates a sequence of Figure 15.1 diagrams and reflects this change in patterns over a series of years.

A line linking minimum cost points should always be shifting downward and to the right. Whether the company is ever at the exact optimal point each year or month is questionable. But aggressive TQM programs have produced results following this pattern. As an illustration of the shifting cost patterns, a set of summarized biannual data from a heavy equipment producer appears in Figure 15.3. The data are in millions and include an approximate 10 percent increase in sales each year. Definitions of what costs belong in each category rest with the company personnel.

Notice that, at the start of the total quality management program, internal failure is the highest percentage category; two years later, appraisal costs are the highest percentage; and finally, prevention costs become the highest

FIGURE 15.2   Annual Shifts in the Total Costs of Quality Line

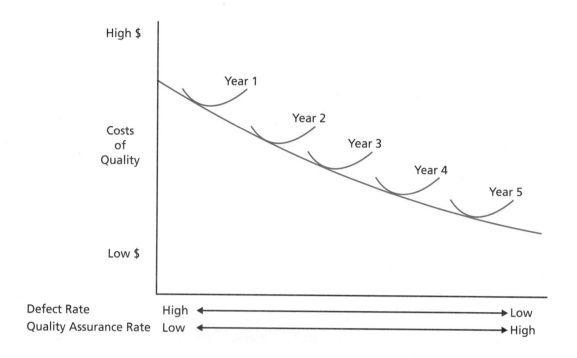

percentage. Of particular note is the steadily declining percentage of quality costs to sales. While significant reductions in these percentages are rather consistent, company management feels that the TQM program training effort is approaching a steady state. The forecast for 1996 shows a further dramatic decline in the costs to sales percentage and in total quality costs. These challenges have been met in the past, but the 1996 goal is particularly rigorous. Managerial and employee efforts will determine the result.

FIGURE 15.3   Shifting Patterns of Costs of Quality Over Time

	1988		1990		1992		1994		Forecast 1996	
Cost Categories	Costs	% of Total	Costs	% of Total	Costs	% of Total	Costs	% of Total	Costs	% of Total
Prevention	$ 2.5	14.7	$ 3.5	19.3	$ 5.9	36.2	$ 5.7	40.7	$ 4.5	45.5
Appraisal	6.0	35.3	6.8	37.6	4.8	29.4	3.9	27.9	2.9	29.3
Internal failure	6.2	36.5	5.6	30.9	4.4	27.0	3.6	25.7	2.1	21.2
External failure . . .	2.3	13.5	2.2	12.2	1.2	7.4	0.8	5.7	0.4	4.0
Total costs	$17.0	100.0	$18.1	100.0	$16.3	100.0	$14.0	100.0	$ 9.9	100.0
Costs as a % of sales		18.0%		15.8%		11.7%		8.3%		4.9%

Sources of Costs of Quality Data—ABC and Customer Inputs

Most traditional costing systems will find it difficult if not impossible to collect the type of data needed for the preceding analyses. ABC has been a timely innovation. Activity centers that focus on quality issues (i.e., training, rework and scrap, inspections, and quality assurance program costs) can separate these activities and the resources they consume. Cost drivers can help identify relationships between failure costs and their causes. Thus, ABC increases the ability to identify quality costs, focuses attention on costly activities, and even helps recognize cause and effect linkages.

Many companies must extend even ABC data to capture more quality costs. This might include account analysis, discussed in Chapter 3. With certain costs, allocations may be needed, which introduce difficulties when measuring improvement. As improvements occur, allocations must be redone, often introducing arbitrariness.

The tough measurement is still lost sales, part of external failure. Numerous firms have made customer satisfaction surveys important and routine parts of their marketing, service, and product planning and design functions. Quality councils have included both suppliers and customers to add critical external views of internal quality levels and efforts. In the past, lost sales estimates were only vague guesses, but greater articulation of customer and potential customer inputs can push this figure toward a more valid estimate.

Service and Other Nonmanufacturing Applications

While TQM programs are often linked to manufacturing and its quality, service organizations also find quality just as critical to customer satisfaction and to their long-term survival. The same categories of costs of quality apply to all organizations. Xerox, for example, has developed significant quality programs for its manufacturing, sales, and service activities. Training to increase service employee competence, to improve interactions with customers, and to raise the quality of services provided is similar to manufacturing tradeoffs. The focus is more heavily on customer satisfaction since providing the service, in many cases, is at the customer contact point. Lost sales, service reputation, and attributes such as "friendliness" are difficult to measure in a financial context. Yet, measuring costs of improving and sustaining quality and of eliminating service failures is critical. Hospitals, for example, have an obvious need for high levels of quality control activities. Monitoring quality costs, while important, becomes secondary to the need for assuring extremely high levels of operating quality regardless of cost. Yet, because of huge increases in health care costs, national health care policies will require measuring and analyzing operating costs including costs of quality.

International Impacts

Quality is an international issue. For the past twenty years, techniques implemented by Japanese companies have given the Japanese a competitive advantage in many markets. These techniques include statistical quality control, continuous improvement (kaizen), target costing, quality circles, and TQM programs. While not overt in each technique, managing quality costs is a vital element in international success.

C O N T E M P O R A R Y   P R A C T I C E   1 5 . 1

American Express and Total Quality Management

All American Express business units must include strategies for quality improvements as part of their annual budgets and business plans. Integrated Payment Systems (IPS) is a business unit that handles American Express Money Orders and other cash transfer services. A TQM program was instituted in 1990. This soon lead to an activity-based cost study and to implementation of a system to capture costs by customer, mission, person, expense type, cost of quality category, and cost driver. This study is known as the Functional Administrative Control Technique (FACT) and is driven by value engineering, not cost accounting. With this database, an accurate estimate of costs of quality within a particular TQM study area can be produced in a matter of hours. From these studies came restructuring plans that improved operations and yielded substantial savings. The CFO of IPS commented, "In addition to hard numbers, it helped us develop an understanding for mission-related activities—what's hot and what's not." Within two months of completing the FACT, $1 million in savings was identified while several equally dramatic customer service improvements were made—a win, win situation.

Source: Carlson, D. A., and S. M. Young, "Activity-Based Total Quality Management at American Express," *Journal of Cost Management*, Spring 1993, pp. 48-58.

In Chapter 16, we discuss the International Standards Organization which created the ISO 9000 standards for doing business in the European Community. These standards are spreading beyond Europe and require documentation of quality programs and of quality costs. Thus, to become qualified, a firm must measure its quality costs as a normal international business activity.

COST MANAGEMENT IN DESIGN AND PRODUCTION STAGES

Companies have traditionally emphasized cost management in the product production phase, while neglecting the design and development stages. Managers now recognize that most of the costs incurred in the production stage are in fact determined in the design and development stages. Accordingly, many companies are adopting target costing, a system initiated in Japan, to manage costs in the design and development stages for new (or redesigned) products. Another Japanese system known as kaizen costing is used to manage costs in the product manufacturing stage.

Target Costing

Historically, U. S. manufacturers have set their pricing strategies by adding required profit margins to the costs of already designed products. **Target costing** reverses this process. After a target selling price and a target profit are established, an allowable cost consistent with these targets is obtained for the product. The company then designs the product based on the allowable (target) cost. Figure 15.4, page 650, compares the target costing approach to the traditional approach.

FIGURE 15.4   Target Costing Compared to the Traditional Approach

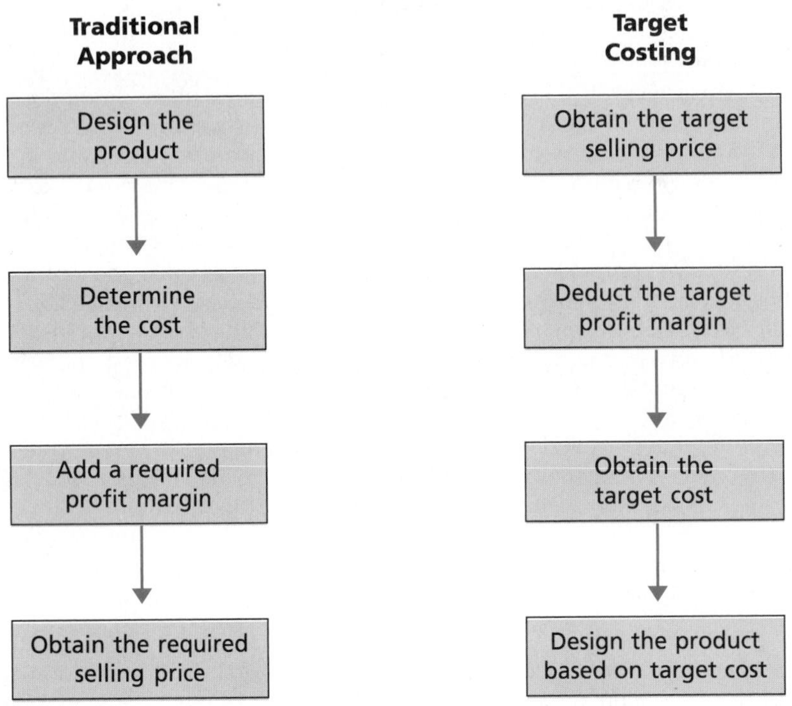

Traditional Approach

Design the product

↓

Determine the cost

↓

Add a required profit margin

↓

Obtain the required selling price

Target Costing

Obtain the target selling price

↓

Deduct the target profit margin

↓

Obtain the target cost

↓

Design the product based on target cost

In target costing, the process begins with a general plan to produce a product based on marketing research. This marketing research also suggests a target selling price by estimating what consumers will pay for the product. The company then determines the amount of profit that would be required for this product. From this target price and target profit, a target cost is obtained:

$$\text{Target cost} = \text{Target selling price} - \text{Target profit}$$

This overall target cost is then decomposed into specific cost elements for materials, subassemblies, direct labor, various manufacturing overhead categories, and various nonmanufacturing categories such as distribution and customer service. Finally, the design department establishes a blueprint according to the target cost for each element.

As an example of the target costing approach, suppose that Lylatove Sleepwear is considering the production of a new line of pajamas. Based on preliminary market research, management has decided that each pair of pajamas should be priced at $20. Furthermore, management believes that the profit margin should be 12 percent of sales revenue. Hence, the target profit would be $2.40 (0.12 x $20). The target cost, therefore, would be $17.60 ($20 - $2.40).

Kaizen Costing

Kaizen costing is a system to support cost reduction beyond the design and development stages. "Kaizen" is a Japanese word that refers to "continuous accumulations of small betterment activities rather than innovative improvement."[2] Innovative improvements are usually introduced in the design and development stages. In kaizen costing, the actual cost for the latest period becomes the kaizen cost target for the current period. To promote continuous improvement, these kaizen cost targets must be reduced in each successive period.

These techniques have allowed many Japanese firms to overcome the effects of the increased value of the yen in international markets. Lower costs and improved products have offset less competitive yen exchange rates.

To achieve cost reduction, many companies are adopting an **activity-based management (ABM)** approach. ABM is an outgrowth of activity-based costing (ABC) that emphasizes management of activities through ABC, activity analysis, and performance measurement. We discussed ABC in Chapter 6; the latter topics are discussed in the following sections.

ACTIVITY ANALYSIS

Companies are monitoring their activities to assess which add value to the customer, which, in turn, should add profit to the company. This technique is referred to as **activity analysis**. An emphasis on activities can help identify nonvalue-added costs and eliminate the activities that cause them. Any resource-using activity that does not add value is often called waste. Having value implies that a consumer would be willing to pay for the results of the activity. A key goal of production managers is to eliminate waste and, thereby, to have an efficient and productive operation.

Time is perhaps the most valuable manufacturing resource. Study of nonvalue-added time in manufacturing operations takes five forms: process time, inspection time, move time, wait time, and storage time.

Process time is the time during which a product is undergoing conversion activities which transform raw materials into finished products. Although most people view process time as the sum of many value-added activities, the presence of inefficiency or other nonproductive activities represents nonvalue-added time. Managers must continually review processes to catch inefficiencies that can creep in over time.

Just-in-time (JIT) production concepts are fundamental building blocks for reducing process time. Many companies have physically reorganized their factories to encourage faster process time. Figure 15.5, page 652, compares a JIT layout to a traditional factory layout. The traditional plant has large inventories, much materials movement within the plant, and a mixing of fabricating and assembly tasks. The JIT plant produces only when parts and products are needed, carries narrow safety stock inventories, has a north-to-south flow of production, and organizes production around product families (similar production requirements). The implication is that greater output can be achieved with the same equipment, people, and space—waste is reduced.

---

[2] Monden, Y., and K. Hamada, "Target Costing and Kaizen Costing in Japanese Automobile Companies," *Journal of Management Accounting Research*, Fall 1991, p. 17.

FIGURE 15.5   Traditional Factory Versus Just-In-Time Factory Layouts

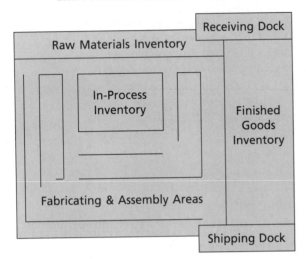

Traditional Factory Layout With Large Materials, In-Process, and Finished Goods Inventories

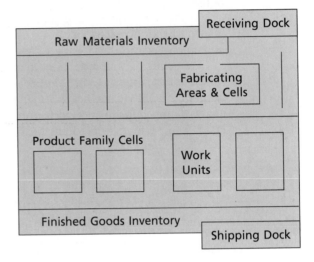

Just-In-Time Factory Layout With a Pull-Through Flow, Few Inventories, and Integrated Manufacturing

Inspection time is the amount of time spent ensuring that the product is of high quality. Typically, materials and components are inspected upon arrival. Then inspection occurs at various points during and at the conclusion of the production process. It is difficult to determine whether inspection procedures result in nonvalue-added costs without detailed knowledge of the production technology and inspection procedures. However, many companies are striving to reduce the costs of maintaining product quality and are working virtually to eliminate the costs of reworking defective products. Consequently, zero defects and total quality control programs sensitize employees to the need for eliminating spoiled and defective units. The argument is that quality is built into and not inspected into the product. Unless otherwise stated, we presume that inspection is a nonvalue-added activity.

Move time is the time spent moving raw materials, work in process, or finished products between operations within the plant. This includes the activities associated with receiving materials, moving them into storage, moving materials and components to the first production operation, moving partially completed products from one work center to the next, and moving the completed product to the finished goods storage area to await shipping. Many companies refer to these activities as materials-handling operations. Move time is a nonvalue-added activity. A certain amount of move time is necessary in any production process, but proper sequencing of operations and tasks and implementing automation technologies can significantly reduce move time. Figure 15.5 illustrates the importance of an efficient flow through the factory to minimize materials movement.

Wait time is the amount of time that materials or work in process spend waiting for the next operation. This includes the time that materials, components, and partially completed products remain in queues immediately preceding an operation and in holding areas located near each department waiting for the next production operation. Wait time potentially represents a significant nonvalue-added cost. A company's working capital is tied up in work in process, and space is unnecessarily wasted on numerous production queues and holding areas. Even in the simple diagrams in Figure 15.5, we see that space released from having inventory wait for the next production step can be used to expand production. The ultimate goal of the JIT philosophy is to eliminate wait time completely. Companies using JIT systems have proven that remarkable reductions in in-process inventories can be made. For example, a car assembly plant producing seventy cars per hour may have less than one hour's supply of car seats in the plant at any time. When a car begins its two-hour trip along an assembly line, an electronic message is received in a supplier's seating plant to trigger assembly of that car's seats. The seats are built and delivered to the car assembly line minutes before the car arrives at the seat installation point.

Storage time is the time during which finished products are held in stock before shipment to customers. It includes the time products spend in storage and the time spent packaging the products for shipment. Traditionally, companies have stored large inventories of finished products to avoid stockouts. Similar to waiting time, storage time ties up a company's working capital in inventories and requires large amounts of space devoted to storage activities. While not applicable to all manufacturing operations, produce-to-order is a goal—manufacture products only after a sales order is received. Improvements in order entry systems and shortened lead times in production scheduling can give the appearance of a produce-to-order operation.

The time required for an average unit to go from the beginning of the production process to completion and shipment is often referred to as **throughput time**. This time is equal to productive processing time plus nonvalue-added time. More specifically, it is the sum of all five activities previously discussed —process time, inspection time, move time, wait time, and storage time.

N ONFINANCIAL PERFORMANCE MEASURES

As changes occur in the operating environment, traditional measures of performance are being reexamined. New measures are being adopted to better fit the concepts of activity-based management. In addition, accountants are measuring performance in new areas of operations, areas that have normally been outside of the accountants' domain or are new because of needs that innovative and automated environments create. This section gives a glimpse of some of the critical changes taking place.

Accountants have traditionally focused on financial measures of performance, such as variations from budgeted or standard costs. Such measures are still important, but a broader evaluation including nonfinancial measures is necessary. For example, physical measures such as throughput time, value-added labor ratio, and defective product rates are playing greater roles in helping managers achieve high quality and competitive operations. Let's look at some nonfinancial performance measures that are commonly being used.

Measures of Manufacturing Productivity

Increasing pressure from global competition has caused many companies to focus on better measures of productivity. Traditionally, accountants have associated productivity with variances calculated for quantity, efficiency, mix, yield, and capacity. The goal was cost minimization. Other productivity measures commonly used were nothing more than quantities of output divided by quantities of input. Today, we are looking for more detailed, meaningful measures. Activity-based costing can pinpoint high-cost activities. Engineers can design for greater production efficiency and defect elimination. For example, a machine manufacturer might determine the number of machines produced per day per employee. A car assembly operation might ascertain the square footage required per day per car. An electrical generating plant might keep track of the tons of coal required to generate a thousand kilowatt hours of electricity. The measures are oriented toward specific activities and evaluate management control over these activities.

Manufacturing cycle efficiency (MCE) is a measure of the amount of throughput time that consists of process time. It is the following ratio:

$$\text{Manufacturing cycle efficiency} \ = \ \frac{\text{Process time}}{\text{Throughput time}}$$

Remember that throughput time is the sum of process time, inspection time, wait time, move time, and storage time. Assuming that inspection time is nonvalue-added time, then MCE measures the portion of throughput time which is value-added time. The goal is to have MCE as high as possible. Although 100 percent is the theoretical ideal, the operations of many manufacturing companies range from the 60 to 90 percent levels; and the percentage cannot improve without major restructuring.

Another widely used productivity measure is the **first-pass yield**. This measures the percentage of nondefective items that have gone through the production process one time only (i.e., without needing any rework).

Computer-integrated manufacturing (CIM) is an attempt to optimize the entire plant's production by planning which departments will produce which parts and products, in what order, and when. Formerly, each department's efficiency was measured, and keeping all departments running at full speed was the goal. Now in CIM, certain departments may be idled until their resources are needed. This is "pull-through" production and part of the JIT

C O N T E M P O R A R Y   P R A C T I C E   1 5 . 2

Effect of Work Cells on Productivity

Compaq Computer Corporation began using a work cell approach rather than assembly lines for its factory located in Erskine, Scotland. Unlike assembly line workers, each member of these three-person cells performs several tasks. Also, the work cells take up less total space. As a result, output per square foot of factory floor space rose 16 percent compared to assembly lines.

Source: Levin, D. P., "Compaq Storms the PC Heights," *New York Times*, November 13, 1994.

philosophy. Produce only what is needed immediately. Performance measures must therefore evaluate a unit based on its production assignment, not necessarily its capacity. Responsibility for productivity is now moved to higher management levels and away from the individual activity center or cost center manager.

Productivity of Labor

The total labor expended for the benefit of a product or service is segregated into direct and indirect labor. Direct labor is all labor that can be specifically identified with a product or service in an economically feasible manner. **Value-added direct labor** is that portion of direct labor that changes raw materials into a finished product or service that is delivered to a customer. For example, value-added direct labor fabricates, assembles, and finishes products. Nonvalue-added direct labor moves, inspects, stores, examines, or otherwise handles the products without adding customer value. Indirect labor is labor that is not readily traced to a product or service. Indirect workers supervise, repair, manage, purchase, inspect, record, advise, or otherwise support the direct workers. Traditionally, indirect workers are considered nonvalue-added labor. In labor-intensive activities, one measure of performance for labor is the **value-added labor ratio** or ratio of value-added time to total time:

$$\text{Value-added labor ratio} = \frac{\text{Value-added direct labor time}}{\text{Total direct and indirect labor time}}$$

The ratio also may be computed in terms of number of employees or payroll. One goal is to reduce the number of supervisors, managers, clerical staff, accountants, engineers, inspectors, and all others that are nonvalue-added workers. This is part of empowering workers to work as teams and to assume responsibility for production.

In many operations, direct labor is being replaced by automated equipment; and indirect labor now includes technicians needed to program, set up, and maintain the equipment. Often, the distinction between direct and indirect is blurred or eliminated. Team approaches to production (work units or product family cells as shown in Figure 15.5), guaranteed wage labor contracts, and broader job classifications have further eroded the importance of direct labor as a cost group. A labor-related performance measure that does not distinguish between direct and indirect is the percentage of total labor cost in the total product cost, called the **labor content percentage**:

$$\text{Labor content percentage} = \frac{\text{Total labor cost}}{\text{Total product cost}}$$

The goal is to reduce this percentage and increase the productivity of all labor dollars.

Product Quality

Earlier in this chapter, we discussed financial measures of product quality. Costs of quality enable us to aggregate various aspects of quality by using a common unit of measure—dollars. Furthermore, it allows us to assess the impact of quality on the company's profits. However, knowing the costs of quality does not enable us to pinpoint specific sources of quality problems. To diagnose and correct specific problems relating to quality, we need a variety of nonfinancial measures of quality.

Four categories of nonfinancial measures are helpful in assessing and maintaining quality. The first, customer acceptance measures, focuses on the extent to which a company's customers perceive its product to be of high quality. It includes such measures as counts of customer complaints, warranty claims, incidence of failures at customer locations, products returned, and repeat sales.

Design quality assesses how well a product has been designed. Frequency of engineering change orders is an important measure of design quality. Other measures include the number of parts in the product and the percentage of common versus unique parts. Since simplicity is desirable, the fewer the number of parts and the higher the percentage of common parts, the better is the design quality.

In-process quality measures look at product quality during production. Rework, defects, and scrap measures are used to keep these items to a minimum. Products are also selected for testing at random or statistically sampled during the various stages of production. Defect rates are measured, and corrective actions specified.

A fourth area of quality measurement relates to purchased materials and parts. Pressure is on purchasing agents to acquire high-quality inputs to meet materials requirements at low costs and on a timely basis. Common vendor performance measures include percentage of defects in the delivery (in terms of dollars as well as number of items), percentage of orders filled, and percentage of orders delivered on time. Many companies are now computing an overall rating of suppliers based on the quality of their materials, delivery performance, and customer service. Also, waste, scrap, and defects occurring during production that are traceable to materials are identified with specific suppliers. A growing number of companies now have vendor certification programs, where managers may purchase from only those vendors who have met the company's quality standards.

Inventory Reduction

Inventory investments, ordering costs, and carrying costs often include significant amounts of nonvalue-added costs. To remain price competitive, effort is necessary to reduce or eliminate inventories. The JIT philosophy focuses on keeping inventories at low or zero levels for materials and parts at every stage of production. Therefore, inventory control measures are used to minimize nonvalue-added costs. Such measures may include average inventory values, average time various categories of materials are held or inventories are standing in a production operation, and inventory turnovers (cost of goods sold divided by average inventory). Measures like manufacturing cycle efficiency also relate to inventory reduction because nonprocessing time—inspection, move, wait, and storage times—is much of the reason why inventories exist.

Machine Maintenance

If our efforts to reduce inventories are successful, we shift our focus to the company's capability of producing goods quickly. We must keep production equipment and machinery operating. Therefore, performance measures will look at unscheduled machine downtime, equipment repair time, tooling turnaround time, engineering change time, machine availability, and adherence to maintenance schedules. Some companies even make a distinction between bottleneck and nonbottleneck machinery. A bottleneck operation is one that limits the production capacity of the entire facility. It is vital that the machinery in bottleneck operations be available 100 percent of the time, excluding time for routine required maintenance. Managing bottleneck operations has received considerable attention in recent years and has become a central component of a management philosophy known as the **Theory of Constraints**. This philosophy emphasizes planning around constraining factors and working to relax the constraints.

Delivery Performance

As a final point, assume that we have done a super job of reducing many nonvalue-added activities and eliminating others. Still, we are not successful until quality products are delivered on time and at the right place to the customer. This is especially important for customers that have JIT systems.

Some companies have a goal of filling 100 percent of their orders on time. Common measures of delivery performance include the percentage of orders filled, the percentage of on-time deliveries, and the average time between the receipt of a customer order and the delivery of the goods. Monitoring customer back orders also tells how many orders were not filled from stock or on time and how long a customer had to wait for an order. A desirable piece of information often impossible to measure is business lost because of delivery failure. Many managers believe that the "competitive ballgame" is won or lost with product quality and delivery performance.

In Figure 15.6, page 658, we summarize the nonfinancial performance measures previously discussed.

*B*ENCHMARKING

To improve both quality and productivity, many companies are turning to **benchmarking**. This technique identifies activities as standards ("benchmarks") by which similar activities should be judged. Simply put, it is a process of finding better practices. Benchmarking can be done with internal sources—other parts of the company—or with other companies including competitors. The external candidates are often obtained by examining lists of companies cited in trade and business journals for excellence in their business practices.

Aside from trade and business publications, performance benchmarks can be gathered from electronic databases, professional conferences and trade conventions, commissioned studies, and site visits to companies. Benchmarking utilizes both financial and nonfinancial performance measures. But this information says nothing about the changes needed to improve quality and efficiency. Therefore, those doing the benchmarking must also obtain an understanding of these "best practices" so that they can implement them in their own organizations.

FIGURE 15.6 Summary of Nonfinancial Performance Measures

Manufacturing Productivity
Output per day per employee
Output per square foot of space
Energy required per unit of output
First-pass yield
Manufacturing cycle efficiency

Productivity of Labor
Value-added labor ratio
Labor content percentage

Inventory Reduction
Average inventory values
Average time inventories are held
Inventory turnovers

Machine Maintenance
Unscheduled machine downtime
Equipment repair time
Tooling turnaround time
Engineering change time
Machine availability
Adherence to maintenance schedules

Delivery Performance
Percentage of orders filled
Percentage of on-time deliveries
Time from customer order to delivery

Product Quality
Customer acceptance:
Number of customer complaints
Number of warranty claims
Incidence of failures at customer locations
Number of returned products
Repeat sales

Design:
Frequency of engineering change orders
Number of parts in the product
Percentage of common vs. unique parts

In-process:
Amount of rework
Defect rates
Amount of scrap

Materials and parts:
Percentage of defects in the delivery
Percentage of orders filled
Percentage of orders received on time

Ethics in Benchmarking

To promote ethical benchmarking, the International Benchmarking Clearinghouse and the Strategic Planning Institute Council on Benchmarking have adopted a common Code of Conduct. These rules of conduct cover such areas as:

- Legal matters (e.g., collusion to restrain trade).
- Integrity.
- Confidentiality.
- Proper use of information and names.
- Contacting policies.
- Preparation for benchmarking.

STRATEGIES TO ENHANCE PRODUCTIVITY

To achieve gains in productivity, many companies have turned to various strategies in recent years. Two of these strategies are downsizing and business process reengineering.

CONTEMPORARY PRACTICE 15.3

Benchmarking in a Finance Department

In 1992, Xerox Corporation's finance department in its U. S. customer operations division conducted benchmarking studies at 24 companies including Kodak, AT&T, Digital Equipment Corporation, Abbot Laboratories, IBM, and Hewlett Packard. In addition, internal benchmarking was done with its Canadian affiliate—Xerox of Canada. Benchmarking efforts focused on activities such as taxes, financing businesses, financial accounting, and financial systems. Usually, three to eight people comprised the benchmarking team, including the chief financial officer, senior analysts, first-line managers, and sometimes second-line managers.

Source: Camp, R. C., "A Bible for Benchmarking, by Xerox," *Financial Executive*, July/August 1993, pp. 24-25.

Downsizing

For many companies, particularly in service industries, a major portion of costs are labor-related costs. These include not only the wages and salaries of employees but also fringe benefits and overhead costs to support labor such as telephone expenses and office space. Thus, when companies look to reduce costs and improve efficiency, a prime candidate becomes the reduction of their workforce. This phenomenon, sometimes referred to as **downsizing**, can involve outsourcing one or more functions, consolidating certain functions, initiating across-the-board cuts in personnel, or eliminating business segments such as product lines or geographical territories.

While downsizing may reduce costs and improve efficiency in the short run, it can harm the company's long-run competitiveness and well-being. Remaining employees sometimes become overburdened, making more mistakes and declining in productivity. Morale suffers. They fear for their jobs, and company commitment takes a back seat to personal interests. Therefore, if downsizing is deemed necessary, it must be done with extreme care.

Often, downsizing is accompanied by fundamentally changing the way a company operates. This strategy is called business process reengineering.

Business Process Reengineering

A business process is a series of activities that are linked to achieve a specific objective. Business processes include both manufacturing as well as nonmanufacturing processes such as purchasing materials or handling customer inquiries and complaints. **Business process reengineering (BPR)** refers to changes made in management, organizational structure, and work practices to achieve significant improvements in quality, cost, speed, and service. BPR is not merely a marginal changing of processes; rather, it involves major restructuring of organizational forms, management procedures, job descriptions, work flows, control systems, and organizational cultures.

One of the main principles of BPR is to organize work around processes and outcomes rather than around tasks and departments. Instead of having a specialist for each separate task, one person or group is responsible for an entire process. This has led to the replacement of functional departments like sales and production with interdisciplinary teams that focus on performing an

CONTEMPORARY   PRACTICE   15.4

Benefits of Business Process Reengineering

"After Citibank reengineered a credit-analysis system, its employees were able to spend 43%, instead of 9% of their time recruiting new business. Profits increased by 750% over a two-year period. When Datacard Corporation reengineered its customer-service operations, its sales increased sevenfold. Bell Atlantic reduced both the time (15 days to a few hours) and the costs ($88 million a year to $6 million) required to connect customers to long-distance carriers."

Source: Romney, M., "Business Process Reengineering," *CPA Journal*, October 1994, p. 30.

entire process. For instance, at IBM Credit Corporation, the credit approval process formerly involved five different individuals. Credit requests were forwarded to someone to check the applicant's credit, then to another person to set the interest rate, and so on. IBM Credit reengineered this process so that one individual, called a deal structurer, completely processes an application; productivity has dramatically increased.[3]

Ethical Considerations

Enhancing productivity via downsizing or business process reengineering can be traumatic for individuals in the organization. Therefore, management must be careful to conduct these changes in an ethical manner. A key consideration should be to communicate the changes in an honest way. Decisions as to who gets terminated and how it is done can be subject to serious abuses. Those whose job duties are changed should be properly informed about new expectations and should be trained adequately for their new roles.

Major downsizing or business process reengineering can sometimes affect entire communities. Such is often the case with plant closings. Should management consider the impact of a plant closing on the welfare of the surrounding community? Many people believe that there is an ethical responsibility to do so.

SUMMARY

The focus on quality has caused the analysis of the costs of quality to become an important managerial task. These costs are broken into four components: prevention, appraisal, internal failure, and external failure. Often it is difficult to define these costs clearly. The goal is to reduce total quality costs. Often this is done by increasing prevention and appraisal costs to reduce or nearly eliminate failure costs. ABC systems have aided the measurement and reporting of these costs significantly.

---

[3] Romney, M., "Business Process Reengineering," *CPA Journal*, October 1994, p. 30.

Recognizing that most costs of production are determined when products are developed and designed, many companies are turning to a technique known as target costing. After a target selling price and a target profit are established, a target cost is obtained for the product. The company then designs the product based on the target cost. To promote continuous improvement in the manufacturing stage, kaizen cost targets are reduced in each successive period.

Activity analysis involves reviewing activities and eliminating those that do not add value to the product. Throughput time is composed of process time, inspection time, move time, wait time, and storage time. The most common place to look for nonvalue-added activities is in inspection, move, wait, and storage time.

Traditional measures of performance are being reexamined. New measures are being adopted to better fit the concepts of activity-based management. These are largely nonfinancial measures relating to manufacturing productivity, labor productivity, product quality, inventory reduction, machine maintenance, and delivery performance. Companies are also benchmarking their performance against best practices from other organizations. To achieve gains in productivity, many companies have turned to strategies such as downsizing and business process reengineering.

P ROBLEMS FOR REVIEW

Review Problem A

The following accounts were listed in the chart of accounts for Michienzi Machine Tooling:

Warranty Repairs	Depreciation on Machinery
Supplier Training and Certification Programs	Final Product Testing
	Rework Time
Cost Accounting Salaries	Planned Machine Maintenance
Engineering Design Reviews	Emergency Machine Repairs
Customer Returns and Allowances	Purchased Materials Inspection
Scrap	Direct Labor

Required:

Classify these accounts according to the appropriate costs of quality category—prevention, appraisal, internal failure, and external failure. Not all accounts will be included.

Solution:

Prevention costs:
   Supplier Training and Certification Programs
   Engineering Design Reviews
   Planned Machine Maintenance

Appraisal costs:
   Final Product Testing
   Purchased Materials Inspection

Internal failure costs:
   Scrap
   Rework Time
   Emergency Machine Repairs

External failure costs:
  Warranty Repairs
  Customer Returns and Allowances

Cost Accounting Salaries, Depreciation on Machinery, and Direct Labor may include elements of quality costs, but they are not normally considered costs of quality accounts. If quality costs are included in these accounts, they should be segregated by creating new expense accounts to track these costs directly.

Review Problem B

Lee Industries manufactured cash registers with an average throughput time of three hours during a recent quarter. Inspection time averaged 20 minutes; wait time was typically one-half hour; and move time usually totaled 15 minutes. The manufacturing cycle efficiency during this quarter averaged 50 percent. Other data were as follows:

	April	*May*	*June*
Average tooling turnaround time	1/4 hr.	1/3 hr.	1/2 hr.
Cash registers produced per day per employee	3.3	2.8	2.6
First-pass yield	78%	85%	88%
Unscheduled machine downtime	10 hrs.	9.5 hrs.	8.5 hrs.

Required:

1. Determine the amount of average storage time.

2. Based on the preceding data, why did the daily output of cash registers decline during the quarter?

3. What aspects of performance improved during the quarter?

Solution:

1. Amount of average storage time:

$$\text{Manufacturing cycle efficiency} = .50 = \text{Process time} \div 180 \text{ minutes}$$

$$\text{Process time} = .50 \times 180 \text{ minutes} = 90 \text{ minutes}$$

$$90 + 20 + 30 + 15 + \text{Storage time} = 180$$

$$\text{Storage time} = 25 \text{ minutes}$$

2. Daily output of cash registers declined because the average tooling turnaround time increased.

3. First-pass yields and unscheduled machine downtime improved during the quarter.

T ERMINOLOGY REVIEW

Prevention costs, *642*
Process time, *651*
Storage time, *653*
Target costing, *649*
Theory of Constraints, *657*

Throughput time, *653*
Total quality management, *641*
Value-added direct labor, *655*
Value-added labor ratio, *655*
Wait time, *652*

SELECTED READINGS

Banker, R. D., G. Potter, and R. G. Schroeder, "Reporting Manufacturing Performance Measures to Workers: An Empirical Study," *Journal of Management Accounting Research*, Fall 1993, pp. 33-55.

Carr, L. P., and L. A. Ponemon, "Managers' Perceptions About Quality Costs," *Journal of Cost Management*, Volume 6, No. 1, pp. 65-71.

Carr, Lawrence P., and Thomas Tyson, "Planning Quality Cost Expenditures, How Much Should a Company Spend on Improving Quality?" *Management Accounting*, October 1992, pp. 52-56.

Edmonds, Thomas P., Bor-Ui Tsay, and Wen-Wei Lin, "Analyzing Quality Costs," *Management Accounting*, November 1989, pp. 25-29.

Fisher, J., "Use of Nonfinancial Performance Measures," *Journal of Cost Management*, Volume 6, No. 1, pp. 31-38.

Godfrey, James T., and William R. Pasewark, "Controlling Quality Costs," *Management Accounting*, March 1988, pp. 69-72.

Heagy, C. D., "Determining Optimal Quality Costs By Considering Cost of Lost Sales," *Journal of Cost Management*, Volume 5, No. 3, pp. 64-72.

McNair, C. J., and W. Mosconi, "Measuring Performance in an Advanced Manufacturing Environment," *Management Accounting*, July 1987, pp. 28-31.

Nanni, A. J., J. R. Dixon, and T. E. Vollmann, "Integrated Performance Measurement: Management Accounting to Support the New Manufacturing Realities," *Journal of Management Accounting Research*, Fall 1992, pp. 1-19.

QUESTIONS FOR REVIEW AND DISCUSSION

1. Identify four categories of costs of quality. Give an example of each.

2. Production Manager Tim Battle asks Quality Manager John Bertin, "Isn't a failure cost a failure cost? Why break them into two components?" Respond to Tim.

3. Greg Chun, controller of Christoff Electronics, sees the four categories of costs of quality as substitutions for each other. Explain why he might believe this.

4. This chapter suggests that a total quality management program may cause the portions of total quality costs to shift over time as quality efforts take hold within an organization. Explain this possible shift.

5. What important cost of quality is missing from most cost accounting systems when these costs are being monitored? Why?

6. Why might the task of measuring, reporting, and analyzing costs of quality be difficult? Can these costs be easily benchmarked across firms? Explain.

7. Discuss the possible linkage between monitoring quality by measuring quality costs and by using nonfinancial measures of quality performance. Comment on which is most important.

8. Explain why minimizing the costs of quality in one time period may not be the optimal spending level for long-run quality improvement.

9. For most firms, is it possible to eliminate failures and, therefore, failure costs? Is it possible to push total quality costs to zero? Explain.

10. Comment on the importance of costs of quality in service organizations. Among the four categories, where might the major emphasis be placed?

11. How is target costing different from the traditional approach of setting costs and prices?

12. During which stages in a product's life cycle do target costing and kaizen costing apply?

13. What is meant by the term "nonvalue-added costs?" Provide three examples.

14. List and describe the five ways that time is spent in a manufacturing process. Which of these activities are likely candidates for nonvalue-added activities? Explain.

15. Define the term "manufacturing cycle efficiency." What does it represent?

16. Explain the value-added labor ratio.

17. Why are nonfinancial measures of quality needed in addition to costs of quality?

18. Describe the four types of nonfinancial measures related to product quality.

19. Provide two examples of nonfinancial measures that assess a firm's capability to keep equipment operating and to produce goods quickly.

20. Which measure of poor delivery performance is often impossible to determine?

21. What are the common external sources for obtaining performance benchmarks?

22. What forms can downsizing take?

23. Explain business process reengineering.

E XERCISES

15-1. Classifying Quality Costs. The following accounts and their costs are from Sengupta Textiles.

Customer design verification	$ 5,000
Machine testing after machine setup	10,000
Employee training	40,000
Raw materials testing	12,000
Scrap loss net of scrap sales	30,000
Materials reprocessing	28,000
Customer complaints and returns	40,000
Final product testing	20,000
In-process inspection	45,000
Routine machine maintenance	25,000
Nonroutine machine repairs	50,000
Discounts for missed delivery dates	33,000
Price reductions for product quality downgrades	68,000
Idle labor—downtime due to machine repairs	37,000

Required:

1. Classify these costs by the four costs of quality categories.

2. If sales were $5,000,000, show the costs of quality as a percentage of sales for each category and in total.

15-2. Comments on Costs of Quality. At a recent continuing education program, Chris Wozniak heard several speakers talk about measuring costs of quality. He asked questions and had good discussions with other managers. But several ideas still bothered him. He scratched some notes for further thought on his pad including:

A. Cost of quality is free. If we spend more to reduce failure costs than the failures cost us, how can it be free?

B. The second speaker said that the optimal cost of quality level can't be found in most cases. She also said that the optimal level is a moving target. If it is optimal today, isn't it optimal next year too?

C. Another (boring) speaker focused on how to design the chart of accounts and cost centers to better capture quality costs. That seems like a waste of time for us since we just implemented a new general ledger system last year.

D. The terms internal and external "benchmarking" were mentioned. What did this have to do with costs of quality?

Required:

Chris is back in his office. He asks your reaction to these thoughts.

15-3. Costs of Quality Trends. Schadler Enterprises, a consulting firm, recently studied its costs over the past three years. The partners of the firm have been promoting total quality management programs to its clients for years. They finally decided to apply the same concepts to their own business. After much discussion, they adopted certain definitions of quality costs and began to monitor them. They did acknowledge that internal failure costs also included costs of nonvalue-added activities that were not technically failure costs. Now, three years later, they show the following data as highly summarized results of their efforts.

	1994		1995		1996	
	1st Half	2nd Half	1st Half	2nd Half	1st Half	2nd Half
Prevention costs	$ 5,000	$ 20,000	$ 50,000	$ 60,000	$ 50,000	$ 55,000
Appraisal costs	40,000	60,000	65,000	70,000	72,000	70,000
Internal failure costs	120,000	130,000	120,000	123,000	110,000	105,000
External failure costs	43,000	30,000	25,000	26,000	18,000	15,000

Client billings have gone up modestly over the three years, perhaps 20 percent in total.

Required:

Comment on the results of the three-year effort.

15-4. Changes in Quality Costs. Volkmann Enterprises has reported the following data for 1997:

Prevention costs	$374,000
Appraisal costs	615,600
Internal failure costs	651,400
External failure costs	27,100

Required:

Comment on the following thoughts:

A. Prevention and appraisal spending has eliminated nearly all customer quality problems.

B. More should be spent on prevention to even the spending among the three internal cost categories.

C. A goal of reducing costs in each category by 10 percent (or by some specific dollar amount) should be set in next year's profit plan.

D. A good job has been done if the sum of the four costs as a percentage of sales declines somewhat.

15-5. Appraisal Costs Versus Failure Costs. In the Jessamy Company, a Lancaster, Great Britain firm, a production problem is being analyzed. Currently, 11,000 units of its Mark4 product are produced. All of these units could be sold. Good units sell for £100 per unit. Four production stages are required. Final inspection in Stage 4 typically finds a 10 percent failure rate. Of these, half are scrapped; and half can be reworked and sold as off-brand units to a discount house at a price equal to the normal per unit production costs. Scrap and rework costs are taken directly to cost of goods sold. Costs for the four stages are:

	Stage 1	Stage 2	Stage 3	Stage 4	Rework
Materials	£88,000	£22,000			£1,000
Labor	66,000	44,000	£33,000	£44,000	2,000
Variable overhead .	66,000	88,000	99,000	44,000	2,000
Cost per unit	£20	£14	£12	£8	

Anurag Kumar, production manager, is considering adding an inspection step to each production stage. He feels that this will reduce the scrapped units to nearly zero. It will add £1 per unit to Stages 1, 2, and 3 to cover inspections, testing, and rework needed. Costs in Stage 4 would shift but remain the same in total since inspection is already being done there.

Required:

1. Estimate the costs of internal failure in the current process.
2. Evaluate Mr. Kumar's proposal. What advantages does this approach offer aside from financial concerns?

15-6. Costs of Quality. The Hackman Company processes financial contracts for several major banks. Accuracy is essential. Errors cause inconvenience to the parties involved, legal entanglements, and embarrassment. The financial arrangements are complex and difficult to check manually. Thus, self-checking software is being considered to eliminate much of the calculation evaluation, word processing reviews, and checks for missing items. The software purchase, modification, and installation will cost $300,000. Annual updating and routine monitoring will cost $30,000 per year. It is estimated that three clerical positions can be eliminated at a "loaded" cost of $40,000 each. It is estimated that the rate of errors in finished documents can be cut by 80 percent. Correcting one error costs an estimated $100. A review of one sample month's work last year showed that 50 errors slipped through the review processes and had to be corrected. These errors resulted in a loss of $50,000 in costs and legal fees. This was thought to be a typical month in terms of activity and results.

Required:

Assuming a three-year cycle for this computer system, evaluate the costs and benefits of the new software.

15-7. Target Costing. Professor Fruitcake has surveyed a group of companies on their needs for accounting software and the prices they are willing to pay. Based on this survey, he has developed an idea for a specialized software product which can be reasonably priced at $500. Professor Fruitcake believes that the particular product he designs and manufactures should allow him a profit of 25 percent of the product's cost.

Required:

What is Professor Fruitcake's target cost for this new software product?

15-8. Kaizen Costing. In 1996, Heights High School incurred the following costs in its athletic department:

Event	Cost Per Event
Track meet	$600
Swim meet	950
Soccer game	820
Water polo match	980

The school has recently begun a system of kaizen costing. Accordingly, the principal has asked Jim Nasium, the head of the athletic department, to reduce costs by 2 percent each year for the foreseeable future.

Required:

Assume that Jim Nasium reduces costs according to the plans set by the school principal. Compute the projected kaizen cost targets in the year 2000 for each of the preceding events.

15-9. Nonvalue-Added Costs.   El Paso Denim Jeans, Inc. manufactures denim jeans in a process that passes through three departments. The output of each department is immediately transferred to the next department to await further work. Output from the last department in the process represents the completed product, which goes to finished goods inventory to await shipping. Specifically, dyed denim cloth bales are released from the storeroom (materials inventory) and moved to the Cutting Department where the fabric is cut to patterns. The cut pieces are sorted into sets of jeans. Any miscut pieces are scrapped. The sets move to the Stitch and Form Department where the pieces are sewn together. Thread, zippers, and snaps are added during this process to make the completed jeans. The jeans are sent to the Inspection and Finishing Department. Inspection makes certain jeans meet quality standards; spoiled and defective jeans are removed from the process. Spoiled jeans go to the scrap pile. Inspectors must determine the extent of defect in those jeans considered defective. If the defect can easily be corrected, the jeans go back into the process where the work will be done. If the defect cannot be corrected, the jeans are treated as seconds and are sold unlabeled in factory outlets and discount stores. Those jeans successfully passing inspection move to the labeling tables where brand labels are stitched on each pair of jeans. The completed jeans move to the warehouse where they become part of the finished goods inventory.

Required:

1. Identify the activities in the denim jeans production process that fall into process time, inspection time, move time, wait time, and storage time.
2. List the activities in the denim jeans production process that are candidates for nonvalue-added activities.

15-10. Nonvalue-Added Costs in a Doctor's Office.   Dr. Wally Johnson has his own medical practice. He specializes in the treatment of diabetics. His staff consists of a receptionist, two nurses, a lab technician, and a dietitian. As patients enter the outer office, they check in with the receptionist. The patient then waits until called by a nurse. When called, the patient moves from the waiting room to the inner offices. The patient must weigh in and is then assigned a room for the rest of the work and conferences. The nurse assigning the patient to a room gathers all the personal data for updating the medical records, such as insulin dosage, medication, illnesses since last visit, and so forth. The nurse also takes an initial blood sample for blood sugar testing and performs a blood pressure test. The patient then waits until the doctor comes in. After the doctor's conference, the nurse returns to take more blood samples, depending on what is ordered by the doctor. The patient then waits until the dietitian comes to review eating habits and talk about how to improve eating and weight control. The patient returns to the receptionist to pay for the office visit and to schedule the next visit.

Required:

1. Identify the activities in the doctor's office that fall into process time, inspection time, move time, wait time, and storage time.
2. List the activities in the doctor's office that are candidates for nonvalue-added activities. Explain why you classify them as nonvalue-added activities.

15-11. Value-Added Labor.   Borodovsky Company produces air pumps in a small factory about 30 kilometers south of Moscow, Russia. The company employs eleven people with nine direct and two indirect laborers. The plant manager, Vladimir Oliker, describes the tasks of the nine direct workers as follows:

(a) Three fabricators who cut and grind metal parts from raw steel, aluminum, and brass.

(b) One parts inspector who examines and approves parts produced.

(c) One warehouse stocker who keeps parts in inventory and fills bins used by assembly workers.

(d) One molder who makes vinyl seals and plastic fittings by using an injection molder.

(e) Two assemblers who assemble parts into product.

(f) One product inspector who approves the final product.

Required:

1. Categorize each of the nine workers as value-added or nonvalue-added workers.

2. Compute the value-added labor ratio.

15-12. Value-Added Labor. KATT Country is an FM radio station with the current country hits. The station has the following employees and wages for September 1998:

	Number of Employees	Wages & Salaries	Totals
Lead disc jockeys	8	$2,000	$16,000
Support disc jockeys	9	1,500	13,500
News and weather staff	3	1,700	5,100
Engineering staff	5	2,100	10,500
Supervisors/managers	5	2,300	11,500
Account executives	6	1,200	7,200
Clerical/office staff	4	1,100	4,400
Totals	40		$68,200

Required:

1. Compute the ratio of value-added employees to total employees in terms of number of employees.

2. Compute the ratio of value-added employees to total employees in terms of total compensation paid.

15-13. Production Efficiency—Nonfinancial Data. Adrian Sargent's Advanced Plastics (ASAP) manufactures a wide range of plastic-based products for automobiles, airplanes, and boats. The company has the reputation for delivering high-quality products on time. Each month the CFO issues a production efficiency report. The data compiled on these reports for the third quarter of 1999 are as follows:

	July	August	September
Manufacturing cycle efficiency	94%	96%	92%
Total setup time (in hours)	62	60	58
Overtime hours	70	73	76
Power consumption in kilowatt-hours (000s omitted)	802	832	838
Machine downtime (hours)	15	10	20
Number of unscheduled machine maintenance calls	0	0	1
Inventory value/Sales revenue	4%	4%	5%
Number of defective units received in raw materials orders . . .	2	1	0
Number of defective units—in-process	35	40	55
Number of defective units—finished goods	18	12	24
Percentage of customer orders filled	100%	100%	100%
Percentage of on-time orders delivered	99%	98%	94%
Number of products returned by customers	0	0	1

Required:

Categorize each of the preceding nonfinancial performance measures as one of the following:

1. Manufacturing productivity
2. Product quality
3. Delivery performance
4. Inventory control
5. Machine maintenance

15-14. Measures of Delivery Performance. International Communications Products (ICP) is a Maryland-based company that manufactures fax machines in two of its four wholly-owned subsidiaries located Kuala Lumpur, Malaysia, and Jakarta, Indonesia. ICP wishes to compare the delivery performance between these subsidiaries. Operations managers for both subsidiaries have provided the ICP vice-president for operations with the following data for a recent month:

	Malaysian Subsidiary	*Indonesian Subsidiary*
Number of customer orders	3,000	5,500
Number of orders delivered	2,895	5,250
Number of orders delivered on time	2,540	5,100
Average time from order to delivery	3 weeks	4 weeks

Required:

Which of the two subsidiaries is performing better delivery service? Provide support for your answer.

15-15. Business Process Reengineering. Fishwrap, Inc. owns a chain of 20 similar-sized newspapers. A decentralized purchasing system is used whereby each newspaper obtains its own newsprint. On average for all newspapers, 70 percent of the newsprint is delivered on time.

The following average cost data per newspaper have been obtained for the past year:

Cost of newsprint	$980,000
Purchasing Department salary costs	240,000
Other Purchasing Department costs	125,000

Of the purchased newsprint, an average of $7,200 turned out to be defective.

Because of the decentralized purchasing system, Fishwrap has been unable to take advantage of quantity discounts. Therefore, the company reengineered the purchasing process by introducing a corporate Purchasing Department. Each newspaper continued to purchase its own newsprint from approved vendors. However, the corporate offices began to track the purchases of all 20 newspapers and used that data to negotiate quantity discounts and resolve problems with vendors. The on-time delivery rate improved to 85 percent. The defect rate (in terms of dollars) decreased by 60 percent. The average quantity discount amounted to 2.8 percent of newsprint cost. After reengineering, the average salary and other purchasing costs for the local departments decreased from $365,000 to $190,000. The annual cost of the centralized Purchasing Department is $1,800,000.

Required:

Evaluate whether reengineering the purchasing process was worthwhile.

15-16. Downsizing, Kaizen Costing, and Ethics. Biltmore Insurance Corporation instituted kaizen costing in 1997 for all of its divisions. During 1996, the Claims Division incurred costs of $5.6 million. Seeking to dramatically reduce costs, the manager of the Claims Division, Gail Norman, thought about cutting $200,000 in payroll costs for 1997 by eliminating all part-time claims adjuster positions. However, she soon realized that her kaizen cost target for 1998 would then be

$5.4 million. Therefore, she decided to institute her reforms much more slowly and, consequently, reduced payroll costs by only $40,000 during 1997.

Required:
Discuss the ethical dimension of Gail Norman's dilemma.

PROBLEMS

15-17. Trends in Quality Costs.   White and White, Inc. has just finished a study of its quality costs. Based on recent accounting reports, quality costs for the 1997 fiscal year are as follows:

Prevention costs	$100,000
Appraisal costs	300,000
Internal failure costs	400,000
External failure costs (including lost sales)	300,000

These costs are 11 percent of sales. The firm plans to implement a program called "TQM Victory" to reduce quality costs in total and as a percentage of sales. Sales are expected to expand by 10 percent per year. By 1999, it expects to spend $300,000 on prevention costs by substantially expanding employee training. Improved inspection efforts will add $100,000 to appraisal costs. By 1999, each failure cost category will be reduced by 10 percent.

By 2001, continued efforts will hold prevention and appraisal costs constant; but external failure costs are expected to drop to 1 percent of sales. Internal failure costs will drop 30 percent from 1999 levels.

By 2003 (the target year of the TQM effort), prevention costs should fall to $200,000; appraisal costs could be cut in half from 1999 levels. Internal failure costs should drop another 40 percent from their 2001 levels. And, external failure costs are targeted to be no higher than 0.3 percent of sales.

Required:
1. What are total quality costs targeted to be in year 2003?
2. Can the firm get to a 4 percent of sales target by 2003? Explain.
3. Comment on at least three key assumptions you see from the data provided.

15-18. Ethics, Hiding a Problem.   Avesian, Inc. produces complex printed circuits for stereo amplifiers. The circuits are sold primarily to major component manufacturers.

A common product defect that occurs in production is a "drift" that is caused by failure to maintain precise heat levels. Rejects from the 100 percent testing program can be reworked to acceptable levels if the defect is drift. However, a recent analysis of customer complaints shows that normal rework does not bring the circuits up to standard. Sampling shows that about one-half of the reworked circuits will fail after extended, high-volume amplifier operation—about 10 percent per year over the following five years. Unfortunately, which circuits will fail cannot be determined by testing. The rework process could be changed to correct the problem, but cost-benefit analysis of the change indicates that it is too expensive.

Avesian's marketing analyst has indicated that this problem will have a significant impact on the firm's reputation and on customer satisfaction if the problem is not corrected. Consequently, Avesian's board of directors would view this problem as having serious negative implications on the firm's profitability.

George Wilson, cost manager, has included the circuit failure and rework problem in a report prepared for the upcoming board meeting. Following a long-standing practice, he has highlighted the problem as having serious adverse economic impacts. After reviewing the reports, the plant manager was disturbed and met with the controller. He said, "We can't upset the board with this kind of information. Tell Wilson to tone it down. Maybe we can get through this meeting and work on a solution. People who buy these cheap systems and play them that loud shouldn't expect them to last forever."

The controller called Wilson into his office and said, "George, bury this. You can refer to it in your oral comments, but it shouldn't be mentioned or highlighted in the written report." Wilson is perturbed and feels strongly that the board will be mislead, particularly if a serious loss of business and, therefore, net income results. He talks with the quality control manager who helped evaluate the rework data. His response is, "That's your problem, George."

Required:

1. Comment on the ethical responsibilities of the controller, the plant manager, and the quality control manager.
2. What should George do in this situation? Explain your answer.

(ICMA adapted)

15-19. Vignettes on Costs of Quality.   Steve Fan, a quality assurance manager for Lynx Motors, has seen a lot of proposals for spending money on quality projects. He wants to "get his money's worth" from the investments he approves. He has the following on his desk now:

A. Manager A recommends a $50,000 expenditure to modify equipment which will reduce the tolerances in a metal grinding operation. The equipment is expected to last another five years. Eventually, reject rates will be lowered by 50 percent. Annually, this will save 500 units from being scrapped. The manufactured per unit cost is:

Prime costs	$ 8
Variable overhead	2
Fixed overhead	8
Unit cost	$18

Fixed overhead is common costs. Scrap revenue is $4 per unit.

B. Manager B wants to expand output of saleable units by 1,000 monthly. For these units, incremental costs will be $120,000. Current production capacity is 50,000 units. Typically, only 45,000 good units are produced and sold. Ten percent of the output has to be reprocessed and is sold at a price that recovers the incremental and reprocessing costs only. Steve thinks that improved training of employees would reduce the need for reprocessing by 40 percent. The training over the next year will cost $80,000.

C. Manager C wants to increase the number of inspectors to reduce defects leaving the plant. The plan calls for $200,000 for a testing lab and $100,000 for personnel to test every fifth item on the assembly line. Most defects are caused by adapting complex engineering designs to the production equipment. Last year, ongoing engineering changes cost $60,000 to create and another $135,000 to implement. Scrap from testing processes after each engineering change costs $36,000.

Required:

Suggest an analysis format to evaluate each case.

15-20. Analyzing Quality Costs.   Management of Merritt Software Services (MSS) has recently implemented a TQM program to eliminate a serious level of "program bugs" that have plagued its recent product releases. The following activities and their costs were taken from MSS's records. The data are for 1996 (the year prior to the TQM program) and 1998 (the year after the start of the TQM program).

	1996	1998
Design documentation standards development	$ 0	$100,000
Documentation of customer training process	0	20,000
Documentation of changes to software	5,000	20,000
Customer training	100,000	130,000
Software testing—customer site	130,000	80,000
Software testing—prerelease	50,000	140,000
Telephone "on-line" customer problem support	90,000	60,000
Software corrections and redesign	50,000	20,000
Field "trouble shooting" for customer support	140,000	80,000
Costs of contract cancellations	180,000	30,000
Revenues lost due to delivery date delays	0	120,000
Training for systems designers/programmers	100,000	250,000
Training for sales staff	10,000	80,000

Required:

1. Categorize the costs of quality for both years.
2. Evaluate the two years. Develop a scenario to explain the major differences in costs between the two years. In other words, what happened?
3. If 1996 showed an operating loss and 1998 showed a small operating profit, would this change your scenario in Part (2) or confirm it? Explain.

15-21. Classifying Costs of Quality. Jackie Hill, controller of Detroit Medical, has reviewed the costs of quality records for the past year. Detroit Medical provides calibration and maintenance services for sophisticated medical equipment in the midwest. Training, testing, and service calls are major costs that seem to grow each year. Jackie is trying to measure possible ways of reducing the total costs of quality as part of a review of all processes and activities within the firm. She assembled the following costs.

Parts warranty, including replacement labor	$ 92,000
Emergency trips to service client machines	86,000
Rental of substitute equipment to cover client downtime	43,000
Training of repair technicians (time and travel)	196,000
Inspection of finished repairs	45,000
Testing and certifications of calibration equipment	15,000
Development of client testing processes and diagnostics	31,500

She is aware of two contracts that were cancelled this past year because of client complaints about poor service response. These contracts totalled $60,000.

Required:

1. Classify these costs according to prevention, appraisal, internal failure, and external failure.
2. Comment on the difficulty that Ms. Hill likely has in analyzing these and other costs that might be costs of quality.

15-22. Ethics and Quality Costs. Watts Dairy Products operates a network of 30 dairy processing plants across the eastern United States. A portion of the bonus system considers improvements in reducing waste and costs of quality. The payment is 5 percent of the annual improvement over the prior year. The company defines the categories of improvement as follows:

Lost product due to operational problems (waste, production yield, or scrap)
Product returns
Prevention costs
Inspection costs
Operational efficiency savings

The results are reported as part of the overall responsibility accounting process with most of the initial transaction classification and recordkeeping done at the plant level. The data are then transferred to the corporate office for report preparation purposes. The controller is concerned about several issues:

- In several plants, the patterns of earned bonuses are erratic for certain managers—high in some years and none in others. In fact, the pattern often includes high gains in prevention and inspection cost reductions and strong efficiency savings one year, with the reverse occurring the next year.

- In another case, a frequently promoted manager (and as a result frequently moved manager) has had a record of generating high quality bonuses each year. Yet, in each case the next manager who takes over that location after a transfer seems to have quality problems.

- In a recent executive staff meeting, several vice-presidents mentioned problems with product yields, customer satisfaction surveys, and several small product recalls.

Required:

1. Comment on the bonus system and how the issues of concern to the controller might be interrelated.

2. Suggest ways the system might be improved (using both accounting and operational methods) to help resolve the issues.

15-23. Target Costing and Downsizing.   Blossom Enterprises manufactures mah-jongg sets that sell for $100 per set. In 1997, the following manufacturing costs were incurred to produce 12,000 sets:

Direct materials	$120,000
Direct labor	210,000
Energy costs—variable	144,000
Energy costs—fixed	130,000
Other fixed overhead	175,000
Other variable overhead	96,000
	$875,000

In addition, Blossom incurred $145,000 in marketing and administrative expenses (all fixed) during 1997.

These sales and cost figures are expected to be the same during 1998. However, to achieve a 1999 sales level of just 11,000 sets, the increasing competition from Marcy's Gaming Corporation will necessitate a price reduction from $100 to $90. To maintain the same net profit margin percentage, Blossom plans to produce 11,000 sets by downsizing the direct labor workforce in 1999.

Required:

1. What is Blossom's target cost for 1999?

2. Compute the planned percentage reduction of the direct labor workforce for 1999.

15-24. Nonvalue-Added Activities.   Donut Depot manufactures donuts that are available fresh every day at several stores throughout Dallas. Donuts left over at the end of the day are packaged and sold at a reduced price as day-old donuts. Donuts not sold by the end of the second day are contributed to the local food bank (a food supply to help welfare families in the metroplex). The production process consists of the following steps:

(a) Ingredients such as flour, sugar, and cooking oil are received, inspected, and placed in the storeroom until requisitioned by production.

(b) Upon requisition, the ingredients are transported from the storeroom to the production area and staged at the Mixing Department.

(c) Ingredients are blended into a dough mixture in 40-pound batches in six heavy-duty mixers.

(d) The dough is rolled out on large boards and left to rise in a holding area.

(e) When the dough is ready, the boards are moved to the cutting machines; and the donuts are cut. Leftovers from each cutting are accumulated, rerolled on another board, and processed through the cutting machine. At the end of the production day, leftovers and unprocessed dough on boards are thrown in the trash.

(f) The cut donuts and donut holes are placed on wire trays and taken to the cooking area, where the trays are stacked until ready for cooking.

(g) The cooks empty the trays into large vats of hot cooking oil where the donuts and donut holes are, in effect, fried in a sea of oil.

(h) The cooked products are removed from the vats and placed on drying pads which absorb the excess oil from the donuts. While the product is drying, it is inspected. Misshaped donuts are removed from the good batch and set aside for disposal. What the crew doesn't eat is thrown out at the end of the production shift.

(i) After drying, the products are placed on large square boards and moved to the finishing area where they will be coated with glaze, icing, powdered sugar, coconut, candy chips, etc.

(j) After allowing the coating to settle or dry, whichever is the case, the donuts are placed in boxes of four dozen each. Donut holes are packed in boxes with 100 donut holes per box. The boxes are moved to the shipping area to await the trucks that will deliver them to the various retail outlets.

(k) Each morning the delivery trucks return the unsold donuts delivered the previous day. (For some reason donut holes are always sold out.) The day-old donuts are repackaged in plastic bags. Each bag contains one dozen donuts and is marked "day old." The packages are then returned to the retail outlets. On the second day, any unsold packages are returned to the shipping area. At the end of the day, these packages are delivered to the food bank.

Required:

1. Identify the activities in the donut production process that fall into process time, inspection time, move time, wait time, and storage time.

2. List the activities in the donut production process that are candidates for nonvalue-added activities. Explain your rationale.

15-25. Nonvalue-Added Costs. HomeTech Manufacturing, Inc. specializes in making products that represent the latest materials and technologies available. The company has a reputation for excellent quality and for entering the market with the best products at reasonable prices.

The Cookware Division has two product lines: Chef's Delight, a 9-piece set, and Gourmet Ease, a 20-piece set. Chef's Delight is top quality, featuring anodized solid-spun aluminum for fast, even heat conductivity and a satin finish for easy cleaning. It has bright stainless steel lids and nickel-plated cast iron handles. Stamping operations are needed for the pots, frying pans, and lids. Handles attached to all pots and pans require a molding operation. The handles for each lid are made from stainless steel rods that are bent to shape and flattened where attached to lids. In finishing and assembly, holes are drilled into each pot, pan, and lid so handles can be attached with screws. The pieces are polished and assembled and placed in the finished goods warehouse.

The production costs for the set of Chef's Delight are as follows:

	Total 9 Pieces	Average Per Piece
Materials	$ 92.70	$10.30
Stamping and molding:		
Direct labor	10.80	1.20
Overhead	32.40	3.60
Finishing and assembly:		
Direct labor	18.00	2.00
Overhead	27.00	3.00
Total	$180.90	$20.10

Inspection takes place at the end of each major operation. The outlines and trimmings resulting from the stamping, molding, and drilling are scrap, which is sold for the value of the materials. Work from the drilling operation through final assembly that does not meet quality standards is either spoilage or defective work, depending on the inspector's decision. Spoilage goes with the scrap. Defective units are reworked.

Required:

1. List the activities in the Chef's Delight production process that are probable candidates for nonvalue-added activities.

2. It is often said, "There is no free lunch." Where in the costs of the product will the costs of scrap, spoilage, and rework appear?

3. List some of the things the company might do to eliminate nonvalue-added activities.

15-26. Costs of Breakage and Defective Customer Service. Bangkok Trucking Co. hauls goods throughout Thailand. The company guarantees arrival at the designated place within an agreed two-hour period. Penalty for late arrival is 10 percent off the shipping rate. The penalty for being a day late is 20 percent off shipping rates. Each additional day costs an additional 20 percent. The following portion of shipments will arrive late:

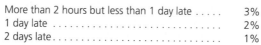

More than 2 hours but less than 1 day late	3%
1 day late	2%
2 days late	1%

Breakage of shipped goods results in additional costs related to replacing the goods, reshipping them to their destination, and the disruption of the customer's business. The company follows the policy of paying replacement costs on all broken goods, refunding shipping charges on damaged shipments, and paying a 30 percent surcharge on the replacement cost for business interruption. Approximately one percent of goods shipped (in sales value) will be damaged in shipment.

During July 1997, Bangkok Trucking expects to make 642 shipments with total revenues (before breakage and defective service) amounting to 6,420,000 baht. The average shipment is expected to have an 8,000 baht replacement cost. The variable costs of shipping are 70 percent of the billed shipping rate. Fixed costs are 900,000 baht per month.

Required:

1. Prepare an estimate of the penalties, or revenue lost, from late shipments during July 1997.

2. Prepare an estimate of the cost of shipments with breakage.

3. Assume the company can make systems changes and implement training programs that will reduce the late shipments to:

More than 2 hours late but less than 1 day	2%
1 day late	1%
More than one day	0%

The percentage of goods shipped that would be damaged would be cut in half. How much could the company afford to pay for such changes and programs?

15-27. Value-Added Labor Concept.   Following is a listing of different business enterprises.

(a) Airline

(b) CPA firm

(c) Radio station

(d) Clinic specializing in sports injuries

(e) Rehabilitation and therapy center for accident and surgery patients

(f) Member of a nationwide budget motel chain

(g) Travel agency

(h) Retail department store

(i) Automobile garage for repairs and servicing

(j) Funeral home

Required:
For each of the organizations, identify the value-added direct workers.

15-28. Manufacturing Productivity Measures.   Alvarez Biological Enterprises is a company located in San Jose, Costa Rica, that produces various blood products for use by hospitals throughout Central America. According to the operations manager, Ricardo Odio, the process for producing a blood coagulant used for treating hemophiliacs is as follows:

Procedure	Average Time Required
Blood is drawn from a donor at a clinic	20 minutes
Blood is tested	30 minutes
Placing into proper blood group	10 minutes
Blood is separated into red cell concentrate and plasma	45 minutes
Waiting for delivery of plasma to fractionation plant	2.5 hours
Transportation to fractionation plant	15 minutes
Incoming plasma is shelved	20 minutes
Plasma sits on shelf	35 minutes
Plasma is taken to centrifugation center	5 minutes
Plasma is pooled into batches, prepared, and centrifuged	1.5 hours
Solids (cryoprecipitate) are processed further	2 hours
Cryoprecipitate is frozen	25 minutes
Cryoprecipitate waits for inspection	15 minutes
Cryoprecipitate is inspected	10 minutes
Heat treatment	10 minutes
Movement to packaging center	5 minutes
Packaging	15 minutes
Completed coagulant is taken to storage area	5 minutes
Waiting for delivery to hospital	3 hours

A typical batch of plasma transported to the fractionation plant weighs 80 kilograms. Of this, about half results in cryoprecipitate; the other half—a liquid residue—is transformed into other blood products. When the cryoprecipitate is inspected, about two kilograms are typically sent back to the beginning of the centrifugation procedure.

Required:
1. Classify the preceding activities into the five categories of throughput time.
2. Compute the manufacturing (processing) cycle efficiency for the entire process.
3. Compute the first-pass yield for the cryoprecipitate.

15-29. Nonfinancial Measures of Product Quality. Howard Pen Company manufactures expensive calligraphy pens in two of its Ohio plants. One plant is located in Cleveland, and the other is in Columbus. The pens produced are similar but not identical. Moe Howard, the president, wishes to evaluate the quality of production in each plant. He has asked the two plant managers, Larry Fine of Cleveland and Jerome (Curly) Howard of Columbus, to provide certain performance measures for the most recent year. After he threatened to tear their tonsils out, he received the following data from his two plant managers:

	Cleveland Plant	Columbus Plant
Number of pens produced and sold	20,000	20,000
Number of parts in each pen	7	5
Number of unique parts in each pen	3	1
Percentage of pens returned by customers . . .	2%	5%
Dollar amount of scrap	$250	$370
Percentage of defects in parts received	3%	4%
Dollar percentage of defects in parts received .	3.5%	3.2%
Number of warranty claims	22	39
Amount of pens that needed rework	950	1,400

Required:

Provide an analysis of product quality performance for the two plants.

15-30. Nonfinancial Performance Measures. Robert Newman Associates manufactures transducers in one of its plants. The number produced and sold between 1996 and 1998 has remained steady. Specific performance data for these three years are as follows:

	1996	1997	1998
Time from customer order to delivery	3 weeks	2.5 weeks	2.2 weeks
Number of failures at customer locations	76	88	91
Transducers produced per day per employee . . .	25.6	29.1	30.6
Number of returned transducers	111	114	142
Manufacturing cycle efficiency	80%	89%	90%
Costs of scrap	$1,897	$1,995	$2,066
Percentage of customer orders filled	85%	89%	91%
Average time inventories are held	20 days	26 days	28 days
First-pass yield	77%	72%	68%
Unscheduled machine downtime	10 hrs.	9.5 hrs.	8.5 hrs.
Number of engineering change orders	5	3	2
Costs of rework	$8,144	$8,993	$9,857
Percentage of defects in delivered components .	1.5%	1.9%	2.2%

Required:

1. Did product quality improve from 1996 to 1998? Explain.
2. Did manufacturing productivity improve from 1996 to 1998? Explain.
3. Did inventory control improve from 1996 to 1998? Explain.
4. Did delivery performance improve from 1996 to 1998? Explain.

*C*ASE 15—RADISON DEVICE, INC.

Radison Device, Inc. produces cathode ray tubes (CRT) for use in televisions and computer monitors. The company has been profitable until the last few years when foreign competition has eroded Radison's market share. Radison's management responded two years ago by implementing controls and systems to achieve lower production costs, improve quality, and shorten delivery times.

The company's organizational and reporting structure has been instrumental in accomplishing these overall objectives. Bob Pleshman, manager of manufacturing, and Viola

Walters, manager of quality control, report to Paul Bruckman, vice-president of production. The production supervisors for each product line report to Pleshman.

These production supervisors have, in the past, received only a listing of the orders to be filled during the month and measured their performance by how many orders they were able to fill. High quality was always stressed, and they all worked together even if it meant some unfilled or reworked orders at the end of the month. Production data received from the floor were primarily used for accounting, financial reports, product pricing, and materials purchasing. Management reports went only to top management and the manager of quality control for scrap performance.

To improve its competitive edge, Radison developed a new monthly productivity report for each product line that compares the company-established goals for the quantity of materials used in production to the amount of actual scrap and the actual number of good units completed. This performance report is presented at a monthly meeting that includes Pleshman, Walters, the production supervisors, and a cost accounting representative.

Initially, the production supervisors, who are proud of their work, were pleased with this system as it gave them an opportunity to participate and make suggestions. However, four months after the productivity measurement system and monthly meetings began, the following conversation occurred among three of the production supervisors.

Richards:	"I really dislike these monthly meetings. The accounting people present data on last month's production that we have never seen before, and Pleshman expects us to have immediate answers."
Green:	"It's like an ambush by the enemy. When the accounting people have finished with us, Walters hits us with her data."
Richards:	"Where do the standards for materials cost usage come from anyway?"
Green:	"I'm not sure. I think the Bill of Materials has something to do with it."
Richards:	"But the data they present are in dollars and the Bill of Materials is in units. And how does the scrap rate data Walters hits us with affect the accounting data? Let's talk to Pleshman about how all this information is assembled."
Green:	"Do you really want to talk to the boss right now after he just criticized us in the meeting?"
Richards:	"But he criticizes us every month. All the departments are always at least 20 percent below the financial standards. In fact, I consider it a good month when my department performs at 75 percent of standard."
Green:	"Let's just forget it. At next month's meeting, we can look amazed at the results again, apologize, and say that we will do better next month. That's what we have been doing for the last four months."
Richards:	"I'm tired of looking bad at every monthly meeting. I'm going to find a way to look good at next month's meeting. Here comes Tilman. I wonder what he thinks."
Tilman:	"After the meeting, Pleshman gave me the production schedule requirements for my department for the rest of the month. I told him the schedule far exceeded the capability of my department. He told me that he was sure that I could find a way to meet the schedule. I told him that the product specifications had not yet been received from the Quality Control Department for many of the orders that the Sales Department had committed to ship before the end of the month. He just smiled and walked away."

Required:

1. Based upon the conversation among the three production supervisors of Radison Device, Inc., discuss the likely motivation and behavior during the coming months of
    a. the production supervisors.
    b. the employees who work for each of the production supervisors.

2. Based upon the conversation among the three production supervisors of Radison Device, Inc., identify and explain several weaknesses in Radison's productivity measurement system and monthly meetings; and present a recommendation for correcting each identified weakness. Use the following format to present your answer:

Identification and Explanation of Weakness	Recommendation for Correcting Weakness

(ICMA adapted)

International Implications in a Changing Environment

*L*EARNING OBJECTIVES

After studying Chapter 16, you will be able to:

1. Describe the essential environmental factors influencing companies doing business internationally.

2. Identify and describe the major methods used to conduct business internationally.

3. Outline the basic methods to minimize taxes and maximize profits and cash flows in global operations and understand how transfer prices can be used to meet these goals.

4. Describe major differences among countries in financial reporting, taxation, and tariffs and duties that affect managerial decisions.

5. Calculate and record foreign exchange gains and losses on international purchase and sales transactions.

6. Describe the use of hedging operations to mitigate the risk of foreign exchange losses.

7. Identify and describe the major issues relating to performance evaluation in and control of global operations.

All Roads Lead to South Korea

Douglas Carr is chief financial officer of International Machining Equipment (IME), which has 16 foreign subsidiaries and affiliates operating in various locations around the world. Sales to customers in South Korea are developing rapidly. But, the company has no manufacturing or distribution operations tied directly to South Korea. After IME's last executive committee meeting, the CEO asked Carr to evaluate creating a presence in South Korea. Carr completed his annual financial review of IME's Pacific rim operations. He has five likely alternatives to discuss with the CEO:

1. A large family-owned and operated business could be available for purchase at a rather high price. It has a customer base, skilled workforce, little computer-based technology, and no modern manufacturing facilities.

2. A major South Korean manufacturer will consider forming a joint venture for producing machining equipment aimed at niche markets. Joint management, control of proprietary technology, and long-term expansion are concerns.

3. IME could license a Korean firm that wants to expand into machine tool equipment. The main concerns are the Korean firm's lack of experience and the control of IME's leading-edge technology.

4. While an excellent site is available where IME can build its own "greenfield" manufacturing facilities, many governmental approvals are needed to do business in South Korea without a domestic partner.

5. IME can continue to serve Korean customers from its Taiwan facilities but put service personnel and a parts distribution center in Seoul.

Even after an alternative is selected, Carr knows he has to deal with a number of other issues. For example: How will the Korean unit fit into IME's overall planning and control program? How will managers be evaluated? Who will be sent to Korea? Is it cost effective to import components from Taiwan or to buy from Korean suppliers? Will products manufactured in South Korea be sold outside the country? Will Korean international sales be denominated in Korean won or one of IME's other currencies? Can cash move in and out of the country? These are only a few of the questions that Carr must resolve.

Given the influence of a global economy, a chief financial officer of a multinational company should be aware of international business issues and be able to interpret international accounting issues for top management. A few of the major concerns with which the executive must deal include:

1. Establishing control systems for strategic planning, budgeting, and investment analysis at the multinational level.
2. Interpreting differences in accounting and reporting practices which affect financing and investing decisions.
3. Coping with economic events within countries where the company operates and dealing with the impacts on investors, creditors, international bankers, and government regulators.
4. Managing pricing and costing to optimize cash, tax, and profit positions.
5. Evaluating trends that are taking place in the areas of international corporate finance, financial markets, and financial services.

The subjects related to global managerial accounting are diverse and would require more than one chapter to explain in detail. Therefore, this chapter presents an overview of the international environment, how companies expand operations into other countries, the differences in accounting issues, and selected managerial accounting concerns of a multinational company. Many international issues already have been woven into other topics in nearly every chapter.

GLOBAL ENVIRONMENT

Technological developments during the 1980s and 1990s accelerated what many have called a "shrinking world." Political boundaries are changing or disappearing; economic alliances among countries are expanding; and multinational businesses view the world as a global marketplace. Company executives know that a market confined to a home country limits their ability to grab market share, to meet world-class competitors, and to be profitable. Internationalizing the value chain begins with economic sourcing of materials and extends to serving customers, wherever and whomever they may be. For example, labor is cheaper in Mexico than in the United States. Many companies moved processing facilities to Mexico to lower costs. But now, the North American Free Trade Agreement has opened Mexican markets to U. S.-made goods, creating new sales opportunities.

Since customers expect high-quality products, JIT delivery, low cost, and extensive service, internationalization adds even more complexity. Changing a company to thrive in a world-wide environment involves overcoming communications, cultural, and environmental differences (economic, political, and business).

Communications Differences

One does not have to travel far to realize that different languages create communication challenges. Local companies manage with a great deal of face-to-face interaction and written communication in a common language. In international operations, communications become complicated and time consuming. Recruiting personnel with language skills is vital to multinational firms. Distance makes face-to-face meetings more time-consuming, less frequent, and more expensive when they do occur. Normal links become phone conferences and faxes operating with up to 12-hour time differences. In addition, information processing technology varies among countries. Many documents must be translated into all languages in which the company does business. In the U. K., personal computers may be commonplace. While in Japan, word processing is just now becoming widespread; yet most Japanese trading companies operate satellite-linked telecommunications systems.

Cultural Differences

Managers in most global companies agree that qualified local managers are preferred to expatriates. Managers from specific cultural backgrounds may have culture-related attributes which impede their effectiveness in other cultures. For example, in some countries, companies are like families. Historically, large Japanese firms hire young college graduates for life. Teamwork and consensus building are the decision norm. Employees develop a strong loyalty to the company and know that they will have considerable input on decisions. In other countries, decisions flow from a hierarchical organizational structure.

Other differences exist that make managing a far-flung operation difficult. German discipline, Italian sociability, and British structure can be viewed as stereotyping; but it does cause the European Community to be many markets in one. Time, and thus a deadline, may be of no consequence to a manager in one country, while being minutes late for a meeting can kill a contract in another.

Environmental Differences

Managers must treat individual country environments as variables in decision making, planning, control, and cost management. For example, large U. S. refrigerators will not fit into small Chinese homes. Failure to redesign the product for specific customer needs has allowed other international competitors to grab a large share of this market.

Inflation. One of the most difficult aspects that a multinational manager must face is inflation. Germany, Brazil, and the United States are examples of countries with diverse inflationary patterns. A high rate of local inflation means that local managers are preoccupied with continually finding new sources of working capital, protecting the values of local monetary assets, and reevaluating product-line pricing daily or weekly.

Political and Business Differences.   The diversity of political and business differences within a country's environment creates challenges for the multinational managers. Differences exist in legal and tax systems, business customs and practices, types of government, types of government regulations, and national traditions. Kickbacks and bribes are normal practice in one country and illegal in another country. For example, for a company to build a plant in certain South American countries, the company must make monetary gifts to

C O N T E M P O R A R Y   P R A C T I C E   1 6 . 1

YKK Comes to Georgia

Japan's largest zipper manufacturer, YKK, came to Macon, Georgia, in 1974, building a $15-million plant. Today YKK runs 11 plants in Macon with 825 employees, of which 50 are Japanese on long-term assignments. The remainder are locals.

   Both Japanese and Georgian employees had to unlearn several misconceptions about each other. For example, the company at first encouraged Japanese management practices, such as mandatory uniforms and long, convivial evenings to build team spirit among managers. The Japanese drive to make the world's best zippers, coupled with their poor English, bewildered U. S. workers. Problems led, in 1979, to a union winning representation rights. In response, YKK started a personnel department, largely staffed by locals. Changes started to occur. The blue uniforms became optional. YKK also gave control of the daily management of the plants to locals, believing that the workers would accept locals as bosses more readily. Japanese technicians remained in charge of maintaining the YKK-designed machinery. In 1984, workers dropped the union.

   After work, Japanese employees now enjoy life with their families, American style. Some men even attend PTA meetings. Macon, meanwhile, is just a little bit more Japanese. For nine years, YKK has supported an annual cherry blossom festival. Tad Yoshida, executive VP of the parent company and son of the founder, says, "My father tells people assigned to Macon, 'Forget you are a Japanese and think like an American.'"

Source: Louis Kraar, "Japanese Pick Up U. S. Ideas," *Fortune,* Vol. 123, No. 12, Spring/Summer 1991, p. 67.

local and provincial government employees to get construction permits, inspections, and other approvals expeditiously. Such practices are forbidden in the U. S. by federal law and are not permitted to be committed by representatives of U. S.-based multinational firms.

SETTING UP BUSINESS IN OTHER COUNTRIES

Companies expand into other countries in a variety of ways. Approaches companies have used include branching, direct investment, equity investment in other companies, joint ventures, franchising and licensing, and barter exchanges and countertrade. The specific entry method will depend on the intent of management, country laws and regulations, tax rules, and cash-flow restrictions.

Branching

One common approach is to establish a **foreign branch** or sales office which is responsible for marketing the company's products in that country. Its organization may consist of a sales manager and salespersons or merely a sales manager who coordinates activities with various wholesalers and jobbers. A branch is simpler in structure than other forms. It will pay taxes in the foreign country but may not need to publish financial statements there. This is merely an extension of exporting from the firm's home country.

Direct Investment

A **direct investment** means the company enters a foreign country and invests in its own operations. A direct investment may be an expensive alternative, and it may be one of the most difficult alternatives. Many countries discourage alien firms from coming into their country to establish a wholly foreign-owned business. Motorola, however, is presently one of a handful of companies to own 100 percent of its People's Republic of China operation. Governments want foreign investment dollars; but encourage local ownership and management.

Another approach is to buy an existing company. Such companies usually have a well-established customer base and a reputation in that country. A multinational company may also choose to build manufacturing and marketing operations from scratch. These are known as **greenfield facilities**.

Equity Investment in Other Companies

An equity investment usually means buying an interest in an established foreign firm. The investment can be managed as a subsidiary similar to that of a domestic subsidiary. The multinational company may not actually perform world-wide manufacturing and marketing functions itself. Rather, it can leave such functions to subsidiaries and their managers. Certain management functions may be centralized, but most operating activities are decentralized. The parent coordinates intracompany activities and manages cash, tax positions, and foreign currency risk.

Joint Ventures

A **joint venture** is an entity that is owned and operated by a small group of investors who are termed venturers or partners. Joint ventures often bring together partners with complementary resources and common goals. Capital, facilities, personnel, market access, and technology are among the contributions made by specific partners. Partners usually play an active role in the management of the joint venture. Control is usually joint in the sense of joint property, joint liability for losses and expenses, joint participation in profits, and joint voting power in decisions relating to major issues.

Joint ventures may be incorporated and function as a corporation, or they may be a literal partnership. Joint ventures have been used with increasing frequency in recent years as a means of entering foreign markets, often because of government limits on direct entry.

Franchising and Licensing

Franchising and licensing are two vehicles for expanding into new markets. **Franchising** is an approach where a company goes into an area and sells the right to use its name, its products, and its system of conducting business operations. Perhaps the most famous franchise in the world is McDonald's and its golden arches. McDonald's is now in Moscow and is moving into other eastern European countries. The Hard Rock Cafe in Beijing is owned by a wealthy and well-connected Chinese and is probably selling as many T-shirts as hamburgers.

Licensing requires less direct management involvement. A license allows another company to use a proprietary process, patent, brand name, and other intellectual property. Technology is transferred between companies for a fee. The advantage to the licensor is the international use of the technology without the costs and risks of entering the foreign markets. The disadvantage is the possible loss of competitive advantage by developing a potential future competitor. Intellectual property rights in many countries are not as well developed or policed as in the United States.

Barter Exchanges and Countertrade

Bartering is simply an exchange of products or services involving something other than cash. Internationally, bartering provides a way for companies to swap their abundant resources for needed resources, while conserving cash or avoiding foreign exchange and transfer problems.

Countertrade is a reciprocal trade arrangement required as a condition of a sale and is sometimes used by firms as a marketing device. Basically, it is a swap of goods. The generic term, countertrade, describes any reciprocal trading arrangement. A more specialized meaning is a financing technique used by companies dealing with countries which lack an easily converted currency. For example, the Russian ruble in the 1990s has moved from an official exchange rate of over one dollar per ruble to a free market exchange rate of over 2,700 rubles to the dollar. Russia has little "hard currency" reserves (international funds denominated in easily traded currencies). Thus, commodities themselves become a currency. The People's Republic of China, wanting to conserve its foreign exchange reserves, encourages foreign firms who want to import machinery and technology for use in their Chinese operations to offset those purchases with exports of Chinese-made products. Typical countertrade includes in-country sourcing, encouragement of exports to build "hard currency" reserves, and technology transfers.

Countertrade is the environment of the true global merchant. The great Japanese **sogo shoshas**, or trading companies, have grown into world-wide economic giants. Mitsubishi Corporation, Mitsui & Company, Summitomo Corporation, and C. Itoh are huge trading companies that serve a multitude of companies connected to a keiretsu. A Japanese **keiretsu** is an informal group of firms with interlocking ownership that tends to work for the common good of the group. The keiretsu members produce a wide variety of goods that are sold and traded internationally by the trading company. Years ago, the merchant bankers of Great Britain and Italy served roles in international commerce similar to today's sogo shoshas.

*I*NTERNATIONAL FINANCIAL REPORTING AND THE NEED TO KNOW

Since our focus is on managerial actions, we need to understand how global managers view financial data used to plan, control, and make decisions. While many structures could be used, a three-way view may be useful.

1. **Global economic perspective.** This broad viewpoint attempts to look past country-specific issues such as taxes, cash-flow restrictions, tariffs, currency exchange problems, and inflation. It looks at the net economic impact on the well-being of the entire multinational enterprise.
2. **Responsibility perspective.** This viewpoint is segment or segment manager specific. It evaluates performance of a segment, given corporate policies and practices, country legal and environmental constraints, and the sphere of operations in that segment or the control delegated to that segment manager. Controllability and responsibility accounting concepts apply.
3. **Legal perspective.** This is the viewpoint of meeting local country requirements in the form of tax filings, duty and tariff rules, pricing controls, financial disclosures, and the business legal environment. Financial and taxation reporting requirements apply.

In fact, different sets of records are probably needed for each perspective and, perhaps, for levels sandwiched between these three. Therefore, the question "Why do you want to know?" takes on a new and more complex meaning.

Accounting rules and business philosophies underlying financial structures vary by country. Rules that seem reasonable in the United States might be inappropriate elsewhere because of differences in the legal and business systems. Several organizations have emerged with the goal of harmonizing international accounting standards. Perhaps the most notable is the work of the **International Accounting Standards Committee (IASC)**. The IASC is composed of representatives from a variety of accounting rule-making groups and international business organizations. To date, IASC standards have received varying degrees of acceptance. They are influential in countries which have little formal accounting standard setting activity and in reducing conflicts among existing standards in various countries.

Accounting Rules

Studies of accounting practices around the world show differences in how costs and revenues are treated by multinational companies. The following are a few examples:

1. The use of discretionary reserves on balance sheets and income statements.
2. The valuation of investments in subsidiaries.
3. Accounting for varying inflation rates in many countries.
4. Accounting for deferred income taxes.
5. Accounting for leases.
6. The treatment of gains and losses from foreign currency transactions and from translations of financial statements.

Let's look at the first two items to understand a few differences.

Discretionary Reserves.   In the United States, discretionary reserves were largely abandoned years ago. However, reserves are used extensively internationally. These reserves are either contra-asset or quasi-equity accounts. They result in a more conservative balance sheet encouraging relatively higher liquidity, understated asset values, or stronger capital positions. Adjusting reserve levels allows managers to smooth net income from year to year or to report whatever earnings level they choose.

Valuation of Subsidiary Investments.   Generally, subsidiary financial reports are consolidated with the parent's financial results if the parent has control through more than 50 percent ownership. And, ownership that gives significant influence (between 20 and 50 percent) is accounted for using the "equity method." The equity method recognizes the parent's share of the subsidiary's net income or loss and dividends on the parent's books. Other investments are carried at cost, with only dividends recognized on the parent's books. Specific rules are complex and different for each country.

Japanese firms have extensive intercompany ownership linkages but rarely prepare consolidated statements or equity-method statements. Each company in a keiretsu may own three to five percent of other keiretsu members, often adding to control of the member firm by the group. Many Japanese firms carry these investments at cost. This significantly understates the asset values and the equity base. For example, assume that six companies in one keiretsu each owns five percent of each other's stock. Thus, 25 percent of each firm is owned by the "group." If these five percent investments each cost $1 million in 1960 and each investment is now worth $500 million, each firm's assets and equity are undervalued by $2.495 billion. But each firm continues to report the investments at cost, $5 million, recognizing income only when dividends are received from another keiretsu firm. Also, another 25 percent of ownership is probably distributed among other keiretsu members in smaller portions.

Financial Structure—Relative Importance of Debt and Equity

Different accounting rules are related to different financial structures common to specific countries. Let's look at a few of examples of how the financial structure is influenced.

A commonly used ratio is the debt to equity ratio—total liabilities divided by total assets. Since liabilities must be paid using company assets, the lower the ratio, the greater is the company's ability to pay its debts, and the lower the risk for investors in the company. From the U. S. lending perspective, creditors are more willing to lend money to and investors are more willing to invest in companies with lower debt to equity ratios. However, Japan is a different situation. Japanese companies tend to have high debt relative to reported assets. In Japan, the debt to assets percentage is an indication of how much confidence banks have in a company. Troubled companies have lower debt to assets percentages because banks are reluctant to extend credit.

In most European countries, the common equity plays a much narrower role in financing a firm. Instead, heavy reliance is placed on internal cash flow and debt financing. Creditors are protected by high liquidity, and banks tend to have easy access to financial information through positions on boards of directors and long-term working relationships. Therefore, accounting rules are less influenced by information needs of external investors than in the United States.

In Germany, law requires that at least 50 percent of the net income of a company must be available to shareholders at the annual meeting. To limit dividend payouts and to strengthen liquidity and capital positions, managers have incentives to keep reported earnings low. Also, German tax laws require that the same methods be used to value assets for both book and tax purposes. Therefore, companies tend to follow accounting practices that minimize tax payments. Assets may be undervalued, reserves may be overstated, and the equity available for dividends will be minimized—a very conservative view of the firm.

*M*AXIMIZING INTERNATIONAL PROFITS: THE ROLE OF TRANSFER PRICES

"Buy low, and sell high" is the proverbial route to profits. However, other factors determine how much profit is kept and how much is taxed or restricted in global business. Income taxes, import duties, and limits on repatriation of profits are major components in creating complex international financial management problems. In a truly global world, goods and cash should flow across borders without restriction and without tariffs being imposed. Also, tax rates would be the same in all countries with little inflation and minimal changes in currency exchange rates. Absent these ideals, the controller must develop strategies to minimize financial risks and to maximize profits and cash flow. Historically, transfer pricing has been used to manipulate profit levels internationally.

As discussed in Chapter 14, a transfer price is used to value goods or services that are bought and sold between subunits of a firm. Because the transfer does not occur at arm's length, manipulation of the price can occur. Cost-based transfer prices can include, at management's discretion, more or fewer costs. Transfer prices for a multinational company are more complex because conditions differ in each country in which the company does business. Governments are concerned because transfer prices affect tax revenues. Companies are concerned because transfer prices affect direct cash flows for payments of goods, taxes, prices, and management performance evaluations.

Naturally, we want managers to make decisions that enhance company goal congruence. However, international transfer pricing goes beyond domestic needs to include:

1. Minimization of world-wide income taxes and import duties.
2. Avoidance of financial restrictions, including the movement of cash.
3. Approvals from the host country.

Assume that Firm A in Country A and Firm B in Country B are subsidiaries of the same holding company. The following cases could exist:

1. If income tax rates are high in Country A and low in Country B, use a low transfer price for sales from Firm A to Firm B. More profits will be shifted to Firm B, lowering total tax payments.
2. If import duties are high for imports into Country B, use a low transfer price for sales from Firm A to Firm B. Lower duties are paid; profits are higher.
3. If Country B restricts cash withdrawals from the country or imposes a tax on dividends paid to the holding company, use a high transfer price on sales from Firm A to Firm B. This allows a greater cash outflow from Country B through payments for purchases.

When these simple cases are fused and more issues are added, situations quickly become complex, particularly when revenue-hungry governments are involved.

Minimization of World-Wide Taxes

Manipulation opportunities in the transfer price setting process mean taxable profits can be shifted from a country with high income tax rates to a country with lower taxes. For example, assume that the tax rate in Brazil is 50 percent, while the tax rate in the U. S. is 35 percent. A U. S. subsidiary of a multinational company sells a product to its sister subsidiary in Brazil. If we assume that a normal transfer price is $16 per unit but that the transfer price for units going into Brazil is set at $20 per unit, the U. S. subsidiary's profit will be higher by $4 per unit ($20 - $16) which is taxed at 35 percent. When the Brazilian subsidiary sells the units, its cost of goods is higher and profits are lower by $4 per unit. Therefore, $4 per unit is taxed at 35 percent, not 50 percent.

International taxation occurs when a domestic government imposes taxes on income or wealth generated within its boundaries by a company based in a foreign country. Also, taxes are levied on income earned by a domestic company from activities in foreign countries. A multinational company is thus taxed in the foreign country and in its home-base country. For example,

C O N T E M P O R A R Y   P R A C T I C E   1 6 . 2

Japanese Land Values

Mitsubishi Estate Company has substantial holdings in the Marunouchi District in Tokyo. The land is carried on the balance sheet at the 1890 acquisition cost of $1 million. An estimate of market value in 1986 was $50 billion. Since 1986, the yen to dollar exchange rate has fallen from ¥240 to $1 to under ¥100 to $1, raising the land's value in dollars by over 200 percent. While the land value of these properties has not been reported in the mid-1990s, it still meets a real estate agent's criteria for value: location, location, and location—downtown Tokyo. All this appreciation is unreported on Mitsubishi's financial reports.

Source: "Tokyo's Nicest Landlord," *Forbes*, June 16, 1986, pp. 32-33.

Upjohn Company is a U. S.-based pharmaceutical firm with extensive global operations. It must comply with U. S. tax laws and tax laws of each country in which it does business.

International taxation has dramatic impacts on management decisions, such as where a company should invest; what form of business organization is used; what products are produced where; how prices and transfer prices are set; which currency should be used to denominate transactions; and what financing should be used. A firm must have professional expertise on its staff or available to review its tax status and the impacts that changes in tax treaties, agreements, laws, and regulations will have.

Governments and taxpayers are equally aware of tax minimization strategies. Tax laws in each country reduce the management accountant's flexibility. Even if we assume that they have a desire to be inherently fair, governments want to generate revenue, plug tax and cash-flow loopholes, get at least their share of tax revenues, promote specific types of economic growth, and perhaps build in subtle biases in favor of domestic firms.

The European Community (EC), General Agreement on Tariffs and Trade (GATT), North American Free Trade Agreement (NAFTA), and other bilateral and multilateral agreements have as their main themes encouraging free trade. While "free" means loosening many barriers, reducing or eliminating import duties and other cross-border taxes and fees is of major importance.

Avoidance of Financial Restrictions

Foreign governments often place financial restrictions on international subsidiaries operating within their boundaries. Government restrictions are placed on the amount of cash that may leave the country and for management fees charged by the parent company. Thus, moving profits and, therefore, "stuck" cash by high transfer prices can reduce those restricted profits and increase firm-wide liquidity and financial mobility.

Gaining Host Country Approval

Governments are not naive. They are becoming sophisticated and aware of the results of using high or low transfer prices. Prices are compared to arm's-length sales prices elsewhere. Products are analyzed for content. Price controls may be based on the transferred-in cost. For example, price increases may be limited by government regulators to cost increases. In the long run, companies find that transfer pricing policies which satisfy foreign authorities may be in the best interest of the company when compared to the greater profits that might be sacrificed. A foreign government's requirements about domestic ownership, percentage of locally produced content, and approval for government sales can be significant factors in determining how an international market is entered and how a company will operate there.

ACCOUNTING FOR TRANSACTIONS IN FOREIGN CURRENCY

The management accountant must facilitate business activity wherever it occurs. Therefore, a basic understanding of currency trading and exchange is expected. Global business basically means buying and selling goods and services across national borders. For example, a manufacturer of computer-aided design equipment may expand its market by selling to foreign customers. Or, it might try to lower its costs by buying memory chips from a less expensive source in another country. These transactions are commonly denominated in the currency of the country in which the transaction takes place. Thus, an international transaction typically involves two currencies. The values of currencies rise and fall daily in relation to each other. An international transaction itself may earn a profit. But, because the foreign currency exchange rates change, a risk of loss exists.

Foreign currency exchange rates are quoted in both currencies, such as 100 Japanese yen per one U. S. dollar (¥100 = $1) or one hundredth U. S. dollar to one yen ($0.01 = ¥1). On U. S. exchanges, the latter expression is more common. A sample of currency rates as of a specific date for several years is shown in Figure 16.1. Notice the significant changes for Britain, China, and particularly Mexico between 1994 and 1995. Of note is the fact that the March 1993 date comes three days after the bombing of the World Trade Center in New York City, a disruptive event for foreign exchange markets.

A **foreign currency transaction** is one in which settlement is in the currency of another country. A transaction with a foreign company that is settled in a domestic currency is an international transaction but not a foreign currency transaction. The more common foreign currency transactions are:

1. Importing (buying) or exporting (selling) goods or services on credit with the amount to be paid or received denominated in a foreign currency.
2. Borrowing from or lending to a foreign company with the amount to be paid or received denominated in a foreign currency.

A third transaction type commonly undertaken to reduce foreign exchange risk is:

3. Hedging operations.

These types of transactions create a payable or receivable with time elapsing before cash changes hands to complete the deal. This time interval creates the opportunity for **exchange gain or loss** from foreign currency transactions.

FIGURE 16.1   Sample of Foreign Exchange Rates as of the First Monday of March

Country	Currency	U. S. Dollar Equivalent			
		March 1992	March 1993	March 1994	March 1995
Australia	Dollar	$ 0.7533	$ 0.7045	$ 0.7130	$ 0.7367
Britain	Pound	1.7530	1.4380	1.4896	1.6275
Canada	Dollar	0.8430	0.8009	0.7403	0.7113
Chile	Peso	0.0030	0.0026	0.0024	0.0024
China (PRC)	Yuan	0.1830	0.1712	0.1149	0.1186
Germany	Mark	0.6086	0.6040	0.5855	0.7005
Hungary	Forint	0.0130	0.0117	0.0097	0.0090
India	Rupee	0.0390	0.0305	0.0322	0.0316
Israel	Shekel	0.4225	0.3662	0.3339	0.3376
Japan	Yen	0.0077	0.0084	0.0096	0.0106
Mexico	Peso	0.3270	0.3237	0.3145	0.1586
Saudi Arabia	Riyal	0.2674	0.2670	0.2670	0.2666
Singapore	Dollar	0.6088	0.6078	0.6317	0.6920
Sweden	Krona	0.1679	0.1281	0.1248	0.1376
Thailand	Baht	0.0392	0.0393	0.0395	0.0403

Source: *Wall Street Journal*, March 2, 1992; March 3, 1993; March 2, 1994; March 2, 1995.

Importing or Exporting Goods or Services

The most common form of foreign currency transaction is importing or exporting goods or services. Let's look at the financial impacts of these transactions.

Foreign Exchange Purchases. When a domestic company purchases goods or services abroad, it pays either in its own currency or in the foreign currency. If both billings and payments are in the domestic currency, no foreign exchange accounting problem exists. A normal payable and a cash payment are recorded.

Assume that our U. S. company buys memory chips from a Japanese company in yen at a cost of ¥20,000,000 when the exchange rate is $0.0100 per yen, or $200,000. Our accounting records would reflect the purchase as follows:

If the Japanese company bills our U. S. company in yen and requests payment in yen, the U. S. company incurs an exchange gain or loss if the exchange rate changes between the dates of purchase and payment. Assume that the yen exchange rate moves from $0.0100 to $0.0105 at the settlement, or payment, date. At the payment date, we spend $210,000 to buy ¥20,000,000 (¥20,000,000 x $0.0105). The payment is recorded as follows:

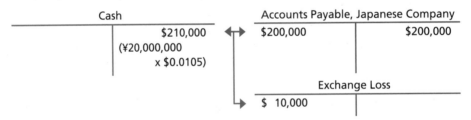

Here, the U. S. company incurred an exchange loss of $10,000 because it agreed to pay ¥20,000,000; and, between the dates of purchase and payment, the exchange value of the yen relative to the dollar increased. More dollars were required to buy the same number of yen.

Foreign Exchange Sales. Sales are the opposite of purchases. Although the same rationale applies to sales, exchange gains or losses are reversed. If the billing and subsequent payment are made in U. S. dollars, no exchange accounting problems arise.

Assume that our U. S. company sells computer products to a German company in marks for DM1,000,000. If the exchange rate is $0.60 per mark, we record a sale of $600,000 as follows:

Sales		Accounts Receivable, German Company	
	$600,000 ↔	$600,000	

Using German marks (DM) for the transaction, the U. S. company will incur an exchange gain or loss if the exchange rates change between the dates of billing and settlement. Assume that the exchange rate on the settlement date is $0.61, changed from the $0.60 per mark rate. The sale is still recorded as

$600,000 and represents DM1,000,000 of revenue. On the settlement, or collection, date, we receive DM1,000,000. But, the marks are now worth $610,000 (DM1,000,000 x $0.61). The transaction is recorded as follows:

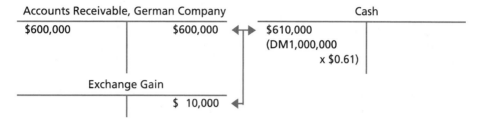

The U. S. company incurred an exchange gain of $10,000 because it agreed to receive DM1,000,000 and the exchange rates changed between the billing and collection dates. In this case, the German marks convert into more dollars at the collection date.

Dates of Concern to Accountants. Because exchange gains and losses occur and must be reported properly, three dates concern accountants. The dates and the proper exchange rates used in translating foreign currencies are as follows:

1. **Transaction date:** Each asset, liability, revenue, expense, gain, or loss arising from the transaction is measured and recorded in the domestic currency at the current foreign exchange rate.
2. **Balance sheet date:** Balances that are denominated in a foreign currency are adjusted to reflect the exchange rate at any interim balance sheet date. This date is important to apportion the gains and losses to the proper reporting period. This is a requirement of current financial accounting reporting under SFAS 52.
3. **Settlement date:** In the case of a foreign currency payable, a domestic company must convert the domestic currency into foreign currency units to settle the accounts payable. For an accounts receivable in which foreign currency is received, the foreign currency must be converted to domestic currency.

To illustrate the impacts of these dates, assume that in 1998 our U. S. company sold computer products to a French company for Fr500,000 when the franc exchange rate was $0.18. The billing to the French company was for Fr500,000. The **spot rate**, the rate of exchange between two currencies that are being bought and sold for immediate delivery, for francs at the three dates is as follows:

Transaction date (December 1)	$ 0.180
Balance sheet date (December 31)	0.165
Settlement date (March 1)	0.170

1. On December 1, the U. S. company records a sale and accounts receivable at the domestic equivalent of $90,000 (Fr500,000 x $0.180).
2. On the balance sheet, December 31, the receivable denominated in foreign currency is adjusted using the exchange rate in effect at the balance sheet date. The receivable is $82,500 (Fr500,000 x $0.165). The foreign exchange loss is as follows:

Initial receivable recorded (December 1)	$ 90,000
Value of receivable at yearend (December 31).	82,500
Foreign exchange loss	$ 7,500

We record the receivable decrease and an exchange loss of $7,500 in 1998.

3. On the settlement date, March 1, 1999, the U. S. company receives Fr500,000 and must convert them into U. S. currency. With a conversion rate of $0.170, the U. S. company receives $85,000 (Fr500,000 x $0.170). The foreign exchange gain is as follows:

Value of francs received at settlement date (March 1)	$ 85,000
Value of receivable at yearend (December 31).	82,500
Foreign exchange gain	$ 2,500

The receivable is collected, and a 1999 exchange gain of $2,500 is recognized. For the total transaction, the company realizes a net exchange loss of $5,000 ($90,000 - $85,000).

When a balance sheet date comes between the transaction and settlement dates, U. S. accounting rules require companies to identify exchange gains and losses with the proper time interval.

Borrowing or Lending

Accounting for borrowing or lending in foreign currencies follows the same approach as for trade payables and receivables. Any cash flow, asset acquired, or revenue earned is accounted for independent of the loan receivable or note payable. For example, if machining equipment is purchased from a foreign company using long-term credit, the cost of the asset is recorded at the acquisition date using the spot rate at the transaction date. The machine's cost is not adjusted for subsequent changes in the exchange rate, but the liability is adjusted at each balance sheet date using the spot exchange rate on that date. Any currency adjustment creates a foreign exchange gain or loss on the income statement. The interest expense recorded is the translation of the foreign currency needed to pay interest expense for the time interval. If a loan receivable is involved instead of a liability, a periodic adjustment is made to the receivable account.

This accounting treatment suggests that companies need to develop policies covering borrowings and lendings (investments) internationally. Judgments about how currencies will move relative to each other are speculative at best. Over time, a strong currency may weaken; or a weak currency may strengthen. International economics, global politics, and the economic health of any particular country relative to the others influence the value of currencies.

Hedging

As we have seen, a domestic firm doing business with companies in other countries and engaging in foreign currency transactions faces an exchange risk.

To minimize this exchange risk, companies use hedging. **Hedging**, in its broadest sense, is any transaction with the specific purpose of offsetting losses or locking gains from transactions already under contract. In this case, the gains and losses are due to foreign currency exchange rate changes. The hedging transaction dates usually match the dates of the transaction to be hedged.

Hedges can occur in a number of ways. Perhaps the most common hedge is a **forward exchange contract (forward contract)**. It is an agreement to exchange currencies of two different countries at a specified rate (the forward rate) on a stipulated future date. A **forward rate** is the rate of exchange between two currencies being bought or sold for delivery at a future date.

A forward contract can be written for a specific amount. Other hedges commonly used internationally are buy or sell options or currency swap contracts in futures markets. Brokers deal in contracts with standard terms and notional amounts to facilitate buying and selling. In most developed countries, futures markets exist for commodities, interest rates, and currencies. The variety of financial instruments and contracts is growing dramatically. Two simple examples using forward contracts follow.

Hedge for a Foreign Currency Exposed Liability. In a foreign purchase transaction where settlement occurs on a future date, a liability is created on the transaction date. If the transaction is denominated in a foreign currency, we create an exposed liability. To illustrate the accounting necessary for a forward exchange contract to hedge an exposed liability position, the same data from the foreign purchases section presented earlier are used. The assumptions are:

1. Memory chips were purchased for ¥20,000,000 payable in yen.
2. Exchange rates: Transaction date:

Spot rate	$ 0.0100
Forward rate (60 days) . . .	$ 0.0101
Settlement date spot rate . . .	$ 0.0105

3. The transaction is denominated in yen.

The U. S. company made a purchase on credit. The exchange rate for this transaction is the spot rate on the purchase date. The liability will be settled in 60 days in yen. The company could do nothing and assumes the risk of a foreign exchange loss. The company could immediately purchase yen at a cost of $200,000, but this ties up cash for 60 days. The treasurer could also go into the foreign currency market and purchase a 60-day forward contract to buy ¥20,000,000 at $0.0101. The forward rate differs from the spot rate because of differences in the relative market interest rates between the two countries, not because the foreign currency is expected to strengthen or weaken over the next 60 days. A completed hedging transaction consists of two parts: (1) a premium or discount paid which is the difference between the spot rate and the forward rate on the transaction date; and (2) an exchange gain or loss which is the difference between the spot rates on the transaction and settlement dates.

For our illustration, assume the U. S. company entered into a forward contract to buy ¥20,000,000 on the settlement date for $0.0101. The hedging transaction is treated separately from the actual memory chip purchase. (See the purchase entry made earlier.) Recording all elements of a hedging transaction is straightforward but includes several accounts with which managers are not usually familiar. Therefore, we will deal only with the calculations of the appropriate amounts related to the forward exchange contract. The relevant amounts on the hedging transaction date are as follows:

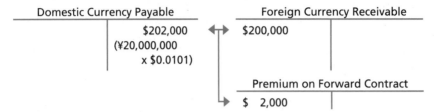

The ¥20,000,000 is translated into its present value, $200,000, using the spot rate of $0.0100 in effect at the transaction date. Note that the liability is for a fixed amount of dollars ($202,000) and is based on the forward contract rate. In future periods, the liability is not adjusted; however, the receivable is based on the foreign currency's value and is subject to exchange rate fluctuations. Any premium or discount amount is amortized to the income statement over the life of the forward exchange contract on a straight-line basis. Exchange gains and losses are identified with accounting periods between the transaction date and the settlement date using end of period spot rates. At the settlement date, the accounts appear as follows:

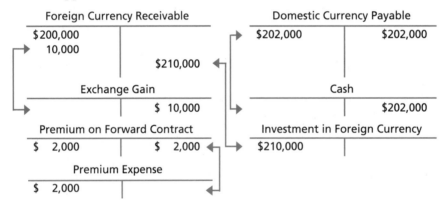

Notice that the exchange gain here offsets the loss on the transaction recorded earlier. Also, the investment in foreign currency is now used to pay the Japanese vendor in yen.

For managerial purposes, we are more concerned about the results of the whole transaction including both the exchange and hedging events. A summary follows:

Exchange loss on purchase transaction (computed earlier in chapter) .		$ 10,000
Premium amortized to expense		2,000
Received from dealer at settlement date (¥20,000,000 x $0.0105). . .	$210,000	
Receivable from dealer at transaction date (¥20,000,000 x $0.01) . . .	200,000	
Exchange gain on forward contract		(10,000)
Net foreign exchange transaction cost		$ 2,000

Notice that the net cost is the premium paid on the forward contract. The exchange gain on the hedge offsets the exchange loss on the original transaction.

Hedge for a Foreign Currency Exposed Asset. In a foreign sales transaction with a future settlement date, foreign currency will be received at a future date. This is an exposed asset. The hedging transaction sells the foreign currency today for dollars to be received at that same future date. Hedging an exposed asset is similar to hedging an exposed liability.

To cover the exposure, a forward exchange contract can be arranged that gives the U. S. company dollars for the foreign currency with delivery at the settlement date. The forward contract rate sets the amount of the dollars to be received from the dealer. The company's obligation to the dealer, on the other hand, is denominated in a foreign currency which translates into dollars using the current spot rate. The difference between the receivable and liability at the transaction date is a premium or discount on the forward exchange contract.

To illustrate the accounting for a forward exchange contract that hedges an exposed asset position, we use the data from the sale of computer products to a German company in our earlier example. The assumptions are as follows:

1. Computer products were sold for DM1,000,000 denominated in German marks.
2. Exchange rates: Transaction date (December 1, 1998):

Spot rate	$ 0.600
Forward rate (90 day)	$ 0.594
Settlement date spot rate (March 1, 1999) . .	$ 0.610

3. The transaction is denominated in marks.

The U. S. company has sold its products on credit and in marks. Therefore, it will go into the foreign currency market on that future date and exchange the marks to be received for U. S. dollars. The exchange rate for this transaction is the spot rate on the date the U. S. company makes the exchange for dollars. The hedge for this transaction is to contract today to sell the marks to be received on March 1, 1999, at a specific exchange rate (the forward rate).

For our illustration, assume the U. S. company entered into a forward exchange contract to sell DM1,000,000 on the settlement date for $0.594. The hedging transaction is treated separately from the transaction to sell the computer products. (See the entry to record the sale.) The relevant amounts on the hedging transaction date are as follows:

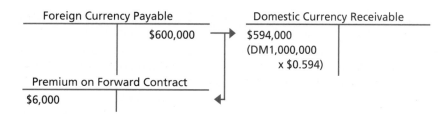

On March 1, the forward contract is closed. The entries needed are:

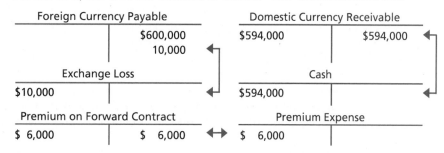

Notice that the marks (valued at $610,000) received from the customer are used to fulfill the Foreign Currency Payable and that the gain from the transaction offsets the loss on the forward contract. Also, because hedge transactions record offsetting payables and receivables, many firms record only the exchange gain or loss and the premium or discount amortization to avoid having large offsetting amounts distort financial ratios.

A summary of the results in total of all transactions is as follows:

Exchange gain on sale transaction (computed earlier)		$ (10,000)
Premium amortized to expense		6,000
Due to exchange dealer at end (DM1,000,000 x $0.610)	$610,000	
Due to exchange dealer at beginning (DM1,000,000 x $0.600) .	600,000	
Exchange loss on forward contract		10,000
Net loss on exchange		$ 6,000

Again, the gains and losses from the transaction and the forward contract offset each other. The net cost of the contract is the premium paid as part of the forward contract.

The accounting for foreign exchange tools to limit risk can be extremely complex. We have shown only the simplest of tools here—the forward contract. Futures, options, and swap contracts are becoming increasingly popular, are exchange traded, and are valued daily with gains and losses recorded. Complex securities introduce derivatives with many attendant advantages and significant risks, particularly for the naive. These instruments combine foreign exchange, interest rate markets, and borrowing and lending across borders. The prudent financial manager must be knowledgeable about methods to lessen and hedge currency risks. Yet, the temptation to use these same tools to speculate introduces huge risks that often violate company policies, common sense, and basic management controls.

*P*ERFORMANCE EVALUATION IN THE MULTINATIONAL COMPANY

How can managers compare cross-border performance statistics? How does a U. S. financial executive communicate performance measures with an investor in Germany, a potential joint venture partner in Eastern Europe, or a government trade official in Japan? All of these persons are thinking in terms of their "local" definitions. Suitable performance measurement of individuals, divisions, subsidiaries, or the entire multinational company is never simple. A manager must remember the basic planning and control perspectives defined earlier: global economics for the entire firm, responsibility for segment or country managers, and legal for local taxation and legal purposes. But from a managerial accounting perspective, designing incentive programs, budget systems, and reports to encourage congruence of global economic and responsibility perspectives is of paramount importance. The same issues relevant to increasing domestic congruence apply to international organizations. Yet, several issues are unique to the international environment that confound the use of measures commonly employed domestically.

Financial Measures

Chapter 14 discussed various measures to evaluate the results of operations at home and abroad. Various levels of profit and contribution margin, return on investment (ROI), and budget comparisons are key financial measures. Local currencies versus foreign currencies complicate the issues. For example, ROI uses an investment value in the denominator. Should ROI be computed using the local currency or the currency where the multinational company is based? Translating local currencies raises issues of which exchange rates to use for which assets. The most basic approach is to separate what is controllable by local managers from what they cannot or do not control, such as currency exchange rate fluctuations. Therefore, managers in the various countries are responsible for profits, investments, etc., in local currency, leaving responsibility for exchange gains and losses to someone at the multinational's corporate office.

Managers around the world are becoming cash-flow conscious. As a result, managers at all levels of the multinational organization place a heavy emphasis on cash flows and evaluate cash flows in periodic reports, most often against a cash-flow forecast.

Profits are important as an overall measurement. However, the various types of contribution margins discussed in Chapters 2 and 14 are becoming more useful in evaluating foreign managerial talent and in assessing the corporate investment in a foreign subsidiary or affiliate. Contribution margins are more reliable measures for planning and decision making, performance evaluation and control, and cost management. This is the responsibility perspective.

Nonfinancial Measures

As in other areas of performance measurement, multinational companies are increasingly using nonfinancial performance measures in evaluations. Common measures for international operating units are:

1. Increasing market share and market size.
2. Relationship with host country government.
3. Quality assurance.
4. Productivity improvement.
5. Cooperation with other company units and the parent.
6. Environment compliance.
7. Employee training and development.
8. Employee safety.
9. Labor turnover.
10. Community service.

Notice that for some of these measures a company will have difficulty attaching numerical values. These measures are very important in comparing performances, particularly over time and against planned target levels.

The implication is that the corporate office is in close touch with the international operation, can assess budget and planning targets astutely, and can link successful performance in the local environment with global economic goals of the corporation.

Budgets

As we have discussed in earlier chapters, budgets are a prime tool for planning and controlling operations. The budget provides a baseline for comparing the actual results of operations. This comparison produces variances that can be analyzed to evaluate performance and improve the efficiency of future operations. The same basic budgeting rules apply internationally—participation, goal oriented, etc. We can extend these concepts to international settings as long as several basic points about currency and tracking results are recognized.

Use of Local Currency. Should the multinational use the local currency or translate results into the domestic currency for budgeting and budgetary control purposes? In most cases, the local currency gives a more meaningful picture of the activities. The local currencies recognize differences within countries and also differences in the relationship of the subsidiary or affiliate to the parent. One potential difficulty with using local currencies is that senior managers of the multinational may not interpret results properly because of local country differences. They may not link the effects of currency exchange gains and losses.

Another problem can occur when comparisons of all world-wide operations are made and all local currencies are translated into the multinational's home country currency. If the subsidiary and the parent operate in countries with stable currencies, translation into the domestic currency should not affect comparisons. However, possible distortions can occur when currencies are unstable. In that case, management can either exclude those results or build another basis for comparison. These alternative evaluation bases often develop over time after biases and misinterpretation problems are identified.

Tracking Results. When budgets and performance results are translated into a home-country-based currency, questions arise as to which exchange rate to use in tracking actual results. Three rates might be used for budgeted data, and three rates might be used for tracking actual results. Various combinations of these rates could be used in performance evaluations. The exchange rates are:

Developing the Budget

B_1	Rate at budget preparation date.
B_2	Projected rate for the coming year at budget preparation date.
B_3	Actual rate at end of budget period (through updating).

Tracking Actual Results

A_1	Rate at budget preparation date.
A_2	Projected rate for the coming year at budget preparation date.
A_3	Actual rate at end of budget period.

The combinations that make the most sense to consider are those that use the same rate to develop the budget and to track results. They are: B_1-A_1, B_2-A_2, and B_3-A_3. All three of these combinations hold the manager accountable for local activities and environmental changes while eliminating the effects of exchange gains and losses. B_2-A_2 does require a forecast of future exchange rates at the time the budget is prepared. However, that forecast may not have much credibility, given the volatility of exchange rate movements. B_3-A_3 requires the budget to be revised for the actual exchange rate once it is known.

From a conceptual point of view, the use of projected rates is the most preferred combination because it gives the best information as the period is progressing and is completely independent of actual price changes.   Managers using B_3-A_3 may place less emphasis on the budget and certainly attach less importance to actions that may place the firm at risk if the exchange rate were to change.

Combinations B_1-A_3 and B_2-A_3 introduce exchange rate changes into the evaluation, since the rate used to develop the budget is different than the rate used to track actual results.   In B_1-A_3, the manager is held responsible for the entire rate change between date of budget and end of period.   Few companies give a country manager complete control of (and responsibility for) currency exchange.   The B_2-A_3 combination holds the manager responsible only for the difference between the projected and the actual end-of-period rates, again a noncontrollable component.

If senior managers want information on the exchange gains and losses, one possibility is to use B_1-A_1 to determine the operating variance and B_1-A_1 minus B_1-A_3 to determine the exchange gain or loss.   Another variation would be B_1-A_3 and B_3-A_3.   A report can then explain the reason for the exchange rate change and discuss the impact of the change on the business for the year.   Now, someone has to explain what changed and why.

As an example, consider a multinational company based in the United States that has a German subsidiary with the following situation:

Expected sales volume	1,200 units
Expected price in local currency	DM3
Beginning exchange rate	$0.65
Projected end of period exchange rate	$0.62
Actual sales volume	1,000 units
Actual price in local currency	DM3
Actual end of period exchange rate	$0.60

The variances will be computed using various combinations of budget and actual exchange rates as follows:

					Foreign Exchange Rate Combinations Applied to Budgets	
	B_1-A_1	B_2-A_2	B_3-A_3	B_1-A_3	B_1-A_1 & B_1-A_3	B_3-A_3 & B_1-A_3
Budgeted sales (1,200 x DM3 x Rate)	$2,340	$2,232	$2,160	$2,340	$2,340	$2,160
Actual sales (1,000 x DM3 x Rate)	1,950	1,860	1,800	1,800	1,950	1,800
Operating variance (unfavorable)	$ 390	$ 372	$ 360	$ 540	$ 390	$ 360
Less B_1-A_3 variance					540	540
Exchange rate variance (unfavorable)					$ (150)	$ (180)

Clearly, different combinations of budget, expected, and actual exchange rates create different variances.   The matched combinations (B_1-A_1, B_2-A_2, and B_3-A_3) focus on the operating variance.   Arguments can be made for and against each:

B_1-A_1: Based on the original approved budget, but now somewhat out of date.

B_2-A_2: Based on expected conditions and rates, but not tied to actual outcomes.

B_3-A_3: Based on actual performance in the marketplace, but includes adjustments to the original approved budget.

The combination columns report both the operating variance and the exchange rate variance. Managers may not control exchange rate gains or losses, but perhaps they should know how exchange rates impact their results. Another combination of B_2-A_2 and B_2-A_3 would allow use of expected exchange rates for operating performance evaluation and would also identify how exchange rates varied from the expected levels. Different situations, firm traditions, and specific performance evaluation systems may determine a preferred model.

Quality: International Standards and Cost Measurement

In Chapter 15, costs of quality were discussed. An important international force is driving many firms to establish systems to measure quality costs and to document quality levels achieved. The European Community (EC) has directed that companies doing business in their member countries have an established quality system. The International Standards Organization has created the **ISO 9000 standards** to measure firm compliance. While quality standards are beyond this text's scope, the management accountant's role is worthy of discussion. A complying firm will have access to the European Community markets, be identified as a quality producer, and obtain the benefits of better quality systems. Other vendors are also indicating their intent to use ISO standards.

A complying firm must document its quality costs and their measurement processes. The ISO 9000 objectives reflect these data needs in that the organization should:

- Achieve and sustain the quality of product or service produced so as to meet the purchaser's stated or implied needs continuously.
- Give its own management confidence that the intended quality is being achieved and sustained.
- Give the purchaser confidence that the intended quality is achieved in the delivered product.

C O N T E M P O R A R Y   P R A C T I C E   1 6 . 3

Budget Goals for Division Managers

A recent survey of Japanese and American firms showed that their international managers were evaluated on different criteria. The top three budget goals for Japanese division managers were sales volume, net profit after corporate overhead, and production costs. The highest ranking budget goals for American division managers were return on investment, controllable profit, and net profit after corporate overhead.

Source: Bailes, J. C., and T. Assada, "Empirical Differences Between Japanese and American Budget and Performance Evaluation Systems," *The International Journal of Accounting*, Vol. 26, No. 2, 1991, p.137.

Five standards have been published and include three levels of possible registration:

ISO 9000   Quality management and quality assurance standards—guidelines for selection and use.

ISO 9001   Quality systems—model for quality assurance in design/development, production, installation, and servicing. This level of registration is for use when conformance to specified requirements is to be assured by the supplier during multiple product stages. For engineering, construction, and complete life-cycle manufacturers.

ISO 9002   Quality systems—model for quality assurance in production and installation. This level of registration is for use when conformance to specified requirements is to be assured by the supplier during production and installation. For process manufacturers.

ISO 9003   Quality systems—model for quality assurance in final inspection and test. This level of registration is for use when conformance to specified requirements is to be assured by the supplier solely at the final inspection and test (for smaller manufacturers who deliver a finished and tested product).

ISO 9004   Quality management and quality system elements—guidelines.

To meet the data requirements of these standards, management accounting systems must include the measurement and reporting of life-cycle costs, quality costs, and continuous improvement assessments. These include preproduction costs such as market research, engineering, procurement, and process planning and post-delivery costs such as technical assistance, maintenance, and disposal. Documentation and verification are keys to sustaining registration. ISO 9000 is a powerful force in quality management and is placing significant demands on accounting systems to generate evidence of quality assurance systems and costs.

E THICS IN INTERNATIONAL BUSINESS

The concept of a global view toward ethical business practices is a far-away goal. The very nature of diverse cultures, legal systems, and society norms complicates the creation of ethical standards for multinational firms. What is an accepted way of doing business in one country is viewed as bribery in another. Nearly every major industrial country has had embarrassing cases of payoffs to government officials or to other companies to obtain favorable treatment or approved contracts.

The U. S. has attempted to take a leadership role in legislating moral conduct of U. S.-based firms. The Foreign Corrupt Practices Act (FCPA) was passed in 1977. The intent was to stop representatives of U. S. firms from making questionable payments to foreign officials. Many of the payments were never recorded, came from "slush funds," or were hidden inside other transactions.

A major emphasis was placed on internal controls and adequate recordkeeping. Many corporations took actions to create policies, establish internal controls, and educate their personnel on appropriate and legal behavior in international business activities. Violations of the FCPA bring fines and jail sentences.

The array of problem areas ranges from clearly illegal acts to quasi-legal, to questionable, to customary, and to expected. Bribery was the major target of the FCPA. The complaint about the FCPA is the unfair position in which U. S. firms find themselves when competing for international business. Evidence to support these fears is unclear. Many businesspersons report that the FCPA is a convenient shield to protect them against demands for bribes and illegal payments. Yet many other countries do appear to condone and even encourage behavior that would be considered illicit in the U. S. on the part of firms based in their countries to obtain international business.

Management accountants play an important role internally to affirm compliance with FCPA requirements. These include creating internal controls that offer "reasonable assurance" of compliance by use of the "prudent man" test to show that:

- Transactions have the general or specific authorization of management.
- Transactions are recorded to prepare proper financial statements and to maintain accountability of assets.
- Asset access has the general or specific authorization of management.
- Asset records are compared to the assets themselves periodically.

The gist is that internal controls should prevent bribery. And, if illegal payments are detected, they must be recorded and disclosed.

Yet, getting important items through customs quickly often requires facilitating payments to officials who should be expected to perform their normal duties. Tips, gratuities, free dinners, trips, and use of facilities are annoying costs of getting work done in many countries. The degree and the level of official may make the acts illegal or permissible under the FCPA, but the issues hang over many international managers who must get work done.

*S*UMMARY

More and more companies are moving into the international business arena. Before actually doing business in another country, managers must assess the complexities resulting from communication, cultural, inflation, political, and business differences.

Accounting rules differ among countries. Items like accounting for goodwill, asset valuation, and reserves vary around the globe. These differences relate to political, cultural, and business philosophies within each country. As a result, the financial structure of any subsidiary or affiliate is dependent on the country in which it operates. Transfer pricing of goods and services moving among units of the same company and across international borders takes on a meaning different from that of domestic transfer pricing.

As companies engage in purchase and sell transactions between countries, currency exchange rates become important. Companies face the possibility of exchange gains and losses. To minimize the uncertainty in exchange rate fluctuations, some companies engage in hedging operations, including forward exchange contracts and futures, options, and swap trading.

At some point, the individual, operation, subsidiary, or company must be evaluated. Performance measurement in international firms is more complex than in the domestic setting. Also, international pressures for improved quality can be typified by the EC's ISO 9000 quality standards. Quality costs and documentation are the management accountant's responsibility.

Because of wide cultural and socioeconomic diversity, international business raises many ethical issues. The Foreign Corrupt Practices Act is an attempt by the U. S. to influence the behavior of U. S.-based multinational firms.

P ROBLEM FOR REVIEW

Internet Machine had these international transactions during January:

Jan. 11   Sold two machines to a company located in Columbia for 7,000,000 pesos. The spot rate on this date was $0.0027 per peso. Payment was made in Columbian pesos on February 10 (a 30-day arrangement).

11   Entered into a 30-day forward exchange contract from a broker at a forward rate of $0.003 as a hedge on the Columbian transaction.

Required:

1. Using T-accounts, record in U. S. dollars the January 11 transaction. Ignore the hedging transaction.
2. Using T-accounts, record the events on the settlement date for the sale and purchase ignoring the hedge transaction. On the settlement date, the exchange rate for Columbian pesos was $0.0029.
3. Calculate the exchange gain or loss from the hedging transaction.
4. Summarize the total exchange gains and losses for all transactions covering the period of January 11 through February 10.

Solution:

1. Transaction date, January 11:

   Columbian transaction: 7,000,000 pesos x $0.0027 = $18,900

Sales		Accounts Receivable	
	$18,900	$18,900	

2. Settlement date, February 10:

Accounts Receivable balance	$ 18,900
Value of transaction at February 10 (7,000,000 x $0.0029)	20,300
Exchange gain	$ 1,400

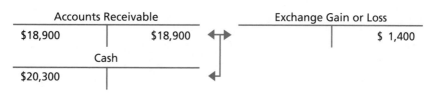

3. Exchange gain or loss on the hedging transaction:

Internet sold Columbian pesos on a 30-day forward contract:

Internet will receive U. S. dollars on February 10 at a forward rate of $0.003. This is an asset account called Domestic Currency Receivable. (7,000,000 x $0.003)	$21,000
Internet will pay the broker Columbian pesos with a current spot rate value of $0.0027. This is a liability account called Foreign Currency Payable. (7,000,000 x $0.0027)	18,900
Discount received on the contract. This is an contra-asset account called Discount on Forward Contract	$ 2,100

At settlement date:

Value of foreign currency owed to broker on settlement date (7,000,000 x $0.0029)	$20,300
Value of pesos on transaction date (7,000,000 x $0.0027)	18,900
Exchange loss on hedging	$ 1,400
Net gain from hedging contract ($2,100 - $1,400)	$ 700

4. Summary of exchange gains or losses on foreign currency transactions:

Exchange loss ÷ (gain) on transaction	$ (1,400)
Exchange loss ÷ (gain) on hedging	1,400
Less discount on hedging	(2,100)
Net gain on transactions	$ (2,100)

*T*ERMINOLOGY REVIEW

Balance sheet date, *693*
Bartering, *685*
Countertrade, *685*
Direct investment, *684*
Exchange gain or loss, *691*
Foreign branch, *684*
Foreign currency transaction, *691*
Forward exchange contract (forward contract), *695*
Forward rate, *695*
Franchising, *685*
Global economic perspective, *686*
Greenfield facilities, *684*
Hedging, *695*

International Accounting Standards Committee (IASC), *686*
International taxation, *689*
ISO 9000 standards, *702*
Joint venture, *685*
Keiretsu, *686*
Legal perspective, *686*
Licensing, *685*
Responsibility perspective, *686*
Settlement date, *693*
Sogo shoshas, *686*
Spot rate, *693*
Transaction date, *693*

*S*UGGESTED READINGS

Borthick, A. F., and Harold P. Roth, "Will Europeans Buy Your Company's Products?" *Management Accounting*, July 1992, pp. 28-32.

Chow, C. W., Y. Kato, and M. D. Shields, "National Culture and the Preference for Management Controls: An Exploratory Study of the Firm-Labor Market Interface," *Accounting, Organizations, and Society*, Vol. 19, No. 4/5, pp. 381-400.

Euske, K. J., M. J. Lebas, and C. J. McNair, "Performance Management in an International Setting," *Management Accounting Research*, December 1993, pp. 275-299.

Evans, T. G., M. E. Taylor, and O. J. Holzmann, *International Accounting & Reporting*, South-Western Publishing Co., Cincinnati, OH, 1994.

Hamer, J., and L. Kistler, "The Impact of Foreign Currency Translations on the New FASB Statement of Cash Flows," *International Journal of Accounting Education and Research*, Vol. 23, No. 1, pp. 129-144.

Mannino, P. V., and K. Milani, "Budgeting for an International Business," *Management Accounting*, February 1992, pp 36-41.

Meyer, P. E., and M. L. Gosman, "MNC Judgment, Foreign Currency Disclosures, and Financial Results," *Accounting Enquiries*, August 1992, pp. 35-39.

QUESTIONS FOR REVIEW AND DISCUSSION

1.   Describe two global environmental differences that can affect the manner of managing a company in a foreign country.

2.   Why are inflation rates in the various countries where multinational companies operate important to corporate management?

3.   How might a multinational company make a direct investment in a foreign country?

4.   What is meant by an "equity investment?"

5.   Why is the joint venture form of business attractive as a vehicle to enter a foreign market?

6.   What advantages does franchising have as a method of entering an international marketplace?

7.   What is a barter exchange? How might a multinational company use such an exchange?

8.   Why would a country with many natural resources and a desire to develop economically be interested in countertrade?

9.   Explain the difference among global economic perspective, responsibility perspective, and legal perspective. Suggest how these views of international business may be needed in a company such as Upjohn, a multinational pharmaceutical firm based in the U. S.

10.   The United States accounting profession largely abandoned discretionary reserves years ago. Why would a company want to use discretionary reserves?

11.   What is a discretionary reserve? How might it be used to modify reported net income?

12.   Describe how the business environment of an individual country will influence a company's financial structure.

13.   Why are international accounting standards especially relevant for multinational corporations?

14.   Why is an international transfer price often not the result of an arm's-length transaction?

15.   How might product costs be changed to produce higher or lower costs per unit?

16.   Give an example of how transfer prices could be used to minimize world-wide taxation.

17.   Explain why a company is exposed to an added risk when it enters into a transaction that is to be settled in a foreign currency.

18. If an American company does business with a German company and all of its transactions take place in German marks, which firm may incur an exchange gain or loss?

19. What does it mean if the exchange rate of a French franc in terms of the U. S. dollar is $0.16? If a bottle of French perfume costs 200 francs, how much will it cost in U. S. dollars?

20. Distinguish between spot and forward rates of exchange. Why do they differ?

21. Name the three dates that are important to an accountant in handling foreign currency transactions. Explain the accounting at each date.

22. When do exchange gains and losses occur on foreign purchases and foreign sales transactions?

23. Briefly explain how hedging is achieved through forward exchange contracts.

24. What is the difference between realized and unrealized exchange gains and losses?

25. Under what conditions should the local currency be used in developing budgets within a multinational company?

26. Why would a manager of an Italian subsidiary not want the budget developed using actual exchange rates at the time of budget preparation and actual operating results stated at actual exchange rates at the end of the period?

27. Why might nonfinancial measures of performance be attractive in evaluating international subsidiaries and managers?

28. What is ISO 9000? What has promoted its importance?

29. Why are ethical issues difficult to assess and ethical standards difficult to implement in international environments?

30. Comment on whether it is fair or unfair for U. S.-based firms to be required to abide by the Foreign Corrupt Practices Act, when non-U. S.-based firms can act as they please.

31. Given the extreme diversity of cultural, political, and social customs world-wide, how can a multinational firm develop and implement a corporate policy on ethical standards? Is it realistic to expect managers in these diverse locations to abide by the same policies?

E XERCISES

All exercises are international.

16-1. Foreign Exchange. The Hartstock Company sold $1,000,000 of equipment to Agency Ltd. of London, England. The sale was billed in pounds at an exchange rate of $1.50 per pound. The terms were net 90 days. The exchange rate at settlement date was $1.45.

Subcomponents for the equipment sold were purchased from a Canadian producer for C$200,000. The exchange rate at the purchase date was $0.75 per Canadian dollar. When Hartstock paid the Canadian producer, the exchange rate was $0.72.

Required:
Record the transactions in T-accounts to show the gain(s) or loss(es).

16-2. Entering an International Market. Bettridge Enterprises is developing sales contacts in several Pacific rim countries. As Bettridge products use sophisticated technology and require in-country customer service capabilities, knowledge of local businesses is essential. David Bettridge, the CEO, is reviewing several alternatives for establishing a presence in at least five different countries. David has asked you to analyze several approaches for entering these countries.

Required:

Outline several entry approaches and highlight advantages and disadvantages, given the characteristics of the products.

16-3. Impact of Inflation. Stinmark Company operates a sales subsidiary in Venezuela. Its Venezuelan assets and liabilities for the beginning and the end of year were exactly the same and appear as follows in thousands of bolivars:

Cash	B 50,000		Accounts payable	B120,000
Accounts receivable	200,000		Borrowings	200,000
Inventories	150,000			
Supplies	30,000			
Equipment	130,000			

Inflation was about 100 percent during the year in Venezuela. The exchange rate for the Venezuelan bolivar was $0.01 per bolivar at the beginning of the year and $0.005 at yearend.

Required:

1. Ignoring profits or losses for the year and using the exchange rates given, show the impact of the change in exchange rates on Stinmark's equity position in its Venezuela subsidiary.
2. Comment on possible strategies Stinmark might follow to protect itself.

16-4. Foreign Exchange. Anthony Microsystems has experienced the following transactions with Japanese suppliers and customers in the past year. Assume that the Japanese yen exchange rate was $0.01 at the transaction dates and $0.009 at the settlement dates. All transactions were on account.

(a) Sold controller boards for $500,000, denominated in U. S. dollars.

(b) Sold completed medical monitoring units for $300,000, denominated in yen.

(c) Purchased semiconductors for $400,000, denominated in yen.

(d) Purchased electronic subsystems for $200,000, denominated in U. S. dollars.

Required:

Determine the net cash flows from these transactions.

16-5. Transfer Pricing Problem. Volkswerke is a Swiss subsidiary of a German company. In a normal month, Volkswerke produces 100,000 units of product with a variable cost of SFr12 per unit and fixed costs of SFr8 per unit (based on SFr800,000 of fixed costs allocated to production). These units can be sold in Switzerland for SFr26 per unit or transferred to the German subsidiary for additional processing and sold in a processed form. The selling price processed is DM34. The cost to complete the additional processing is DM6 per unit. The fixed cost of processing is DM300,000. The current exchange rate between francs and marks is one Swiss franc to 0.90 German marks. If the product is not transferred, the German subsidiary would have excess capacity.

Required:

1. Should the Swiss production be transferred to the German subsidiary or sold locally? Explain your answer.
2. Explain how a transfer price could be used to move cash from Switzerland to Germany, assuming Switzerland does not like to see money leave the country.

16-6. Evaluating Fixed Overhead Relationships. Juarez Medical Center, a Mexican subsidiary of a U. S. corporate hospital chain, has a radiology department which scheduled 2,800 standard hours last year. The standard is 5 patients per hour, and the department actually handled 9,000 patients. Fixed overhead data are given as follows:

Fixed overhead charged to patients	M$ 630,000
Unfavorable capacity variance	350,000

This information was transmitted to the U. S. home office and was translated into U. S. dollars. Budgeted amounts were translated at the exchange rate at the time of preparing the budget (1 peso = $0.35), and the amounts charged to products were translated at the exchange rate at the end of the year (1 peso = $0.32).

Required:

1. What were the fixed overhead budget and the fixed overhead rate per patient last year in pesos?
2. Translate the appropriate information into U. S. dollars.
3. How does the translation affect the unfavorable capacity variance?
4. Where in the translated numbers can be found any exchange gain or loss?

16-7. Budget Variance for Individual Costs. Suzanne Stephens, manager of the Machining Department at the German subsidiary of U. S.-based Mayfield Industries, has estimated overhead costs for August at an expected operating level of 6,000 machine hours as follows:

1-2-3

Variable Costs:		Fixed Costs:	
Lubrication	DM1.50	Supervision	DM 4,500
Supplies	.60	Indirect labor	11,500
Power	.50	Heat and light	3,200
Repairs	1.00	Taxes and insurance	1,600
Maintenance	1.60	Depreciation	1,800

During August, the department produced output in 5,500 hours that should have taken 5,000 hours and incurred the following overhead costs:

Lubrication	DM 3,900
Supplies	1,700
Power	1,500
Repairs	2,800
Maintenance	4,300
Supervision	4,000
Indirect labor	12,000
Heat and light	3,200
Taxes and insurance	1,400
Depreciation	1,600
Total	DM 36,400

Required:

1. Compare the actual overhead costs with a revised budget for 5,000 machine hours. Show budget variances for each item.
2. The budget comparison in Part (1) is translated into U. S. dollars for review by a corporate-level manager. Use the exchange rate of $0.50 at the time the budget was approved for both the budget and the actual results to prepare a budget comparison.
3. Translate the budget at the $0.50 rate and the actual at the end of period exchange rate of $0.55. Prepare a budget comparison.
4. Comment on the comparison of results in Parts (2) and (3). What is the amount of foreign exchange gain or loss in the variances?

16-8. Variances for Individual Operating Expenses. Amia Manufacturing Company, a U. S. subsidiary of a British corporation, uses a budget formula for estimating its marketing and administrative expenses. The fixed and variable components of this formula for individual costs are:

Cost Category	Fixed Cost Per Month	Variable Cost Per Unit Sold
Salary and wages	$1,750	$ 0.90
Rent of space	1,000	0.60
Freight out	0	0.15
Miscellaneous	250	0.05
Total	$3,000	$ 1.70

The subsidiary budgeted 10,000 units of sales for the month. Actually, 9,200 units were sold, and the following expenses were incurred:

Salary and wages	$10,230
Rent of space	6,710
Freight out	1,280
Miscellaneous	680
Total	$18,900

At month end, numbers are sent to the home office in London for comparison and variance analysis. There, Siphiwe Mashinini, the corporate controller, oversees their translation into British pounds. The budgeted information is translated at the projected exchange rate ($1 = £0.70). The actual amounts are translated at the actual end-of-month exchange rate ($1 = £0.66).

Required:

1. Ms. Mashinini has asked you to:
   (a) Compute, for each of the individual cost categories, the spending and volume variances, and indicate whether they are favorable or unfavorable.
   (b) Translate the subsidiary data according to home office policy.
2. What impact does the translation have on how you evaluate the spending and volume variances?
3. What is your suggestion for translating the numbers so the results of the translation will be evaluated the same as the U. S. dollar results?

16-9. Recording a Foreign Purchase and Sale.   Macon Manufacturing, a U. S. corporation, had the following two transactions with foreign companies during this year:

(a) Purchased a special-purpose machine from a German company on credit in German marks for DM30,000. At the transaction date, the exchange rate was $0.59 per mark. On the settlement date, the exchange rate was $0.61.

(b) Sold a product on account to a British company for £200,000. Payment was made in British pounds. The pound was $1.50 on the transaction date and $1.58 on the settlement date.

Required:

Using T-accounts, record the events related to Macon Manufacturing's purchase and sale. Recognize any foreign exchange gain or loss.

16-10. T-Accounts and Foreign Purchases and Sales.   MARKAR Tools, Inc., a U. S. corporation, is a well-known importer/exporter of industrial tools, equipment, and supplies. The following transactions occurred during June:

June 3   Purchased power tools on account from a Japanese wholesaler at an invoice price of ¥1,400,000. The exchange rate for yen was $0.0092.

5   Sold supplies on credit to Machwerke, a German company, invoiced in dollars for $2,800. The exchange rate for German marks was $0.6634.

9   Sold hand tools on credit to Dodds Retailers in New Zealand, invoiced in New Zealand dollars for NZ$14,200. The exchange rate for New Zealand dollars was $0.676.

11   Purchased electric drills on account from a manufacturer in Belgium. The billing was for BF746,270. The exchange rate for Belgium francs was $0.0268.

16   Paid ¥900,000 yen on account to the Japanese wholesaler for the purchase on June 3. The exchange rate for yen was $0.0097.

18   Settled the accounts payable with the Belgium manufacturer. The exchange rate for Belgium francs was $0.0284.

22   Received full payment from the Dodds Retailer invoice of June 9. The exchange rate for New Zealand dollars was $0.625.

30   Completed payment of the June 3 purchase. The exchange rate for yen was $0.0098.

Required:
Show any exchange gains and losses relating to these transactions.

16-11. Ethics and Foreign Exchange. Rob Rheinhart, the controller for the German subsidiary of a U. S.-based firm, has noticed a consistent move in the exchange rate between the German mark and the Austrian shilling during certain holiday periods. He's not sure why this happens but thinks it is related to the large number of Germans who go to Austria to ski. He is aware that his company normally has about DM1,000,000 in its cash account. He decided to take advantage of this exchange rate movement during the Easter holiday week. His maneuver worked, and he made DM8,000.

Required:
1. If Rheinhart did this to benefit his company, should he be rewarded or fired? Explain your answer.
2. If Rheinhart did this on his own behalf, comment on the possible risks.
3. How might the U. S. firm control this type of speculation?

16-12. Yearend Adjustments for Foreign Currency Transactions. Clancy Wool Products, a U. S.-based import/export company, had the following transactions during March:

March 6   Purchased products from a Swiss company for SFr500,000. The exchange rate for Swiss francs was $0.786.

15   Sold products to a German company located in Dresden for DM100,000. The exchange rate for the German mark was $0.607.

18   Sold products to a British company for £100,000. The exchange rate for British pounds was $1.505.

20   Purchased products from Wool-Made, a British company, for $120,000. The exchange rate for British pounds was $1.498.

The firm's fiscal year ends on March 31. All of the foregoing transactions were open on March 31. The exchange rates on this date were: SFr1 = $0.760, DM1 = $0.598, and £1 = $1.472.

Required:
1. Determine the amount Clancy Wool Products would report for each unsettled receivable and payable on March 31.
2. Determine the exchange gain or loss on each unsettled receivable and payable as of March 31.

16-13. Calculation of Exchange Gains and Losses. Georgia Timberline, Inc. is a North Carolina company that has substantial import/export operations. The following transactions occurred in November:

Nov. 1   Purchased products on account from a manufacturer in Edinburgh, Scotland, at an invoice price of £1,000. The exchange rate for pounds was $1.50.

5   Purchased products on account from British Hi-Tech. The invoice was stated at $2,000. The exchange rate for pounds was $1.51.

7   Sold products to a Canadian wholesaler in Quebec City. The invoice was stated at C$4,000. The exchange rate for Canadian dollars was $0.80.

Nov. 15 Paid £500 on account to the Edinburgh manufacturer. The exchange rate for pounds was $1.52.

20 Paid the amount due to British Hi-Tech. The exchange rate for pounds was $1.49.

25 Returned merchandise to the Edinburgh manufacturer and received credit of £100. The exchange rate for pounds was $1.45.

28 Received full payment on account from the Canadian wholesaler. The exchange rate for Canadian dollars was $0.76.

30 Remitted final payment to the Edinburgh manufacturer. The exchange rate for pounds was $1.46.

Required:
Calculate the foreign exchange gains or losses on the transactions for each supplier and customer.

16-14. Hedging Foreign Exchange Fluctuations. Overseas Products Company billed a customer in a foreign country at 600,000 units of that country's currency. The exchange rate at that time was 50 units of local currency to one dollar. Overseas Products Company hoped to collect the equivalent of $12,000 from the customer in three months. Economic conditions changed in three months, and the currency was quoted at 120 units to the dollar when the company received payment.

Required:
1. Compute the loss in foreign exchange to Overseas Products Company.
2. Explain what measures could have been taken to guard against the loss in foreign exchange.

16-15. Foreign Exchange Gains and Losses With Hedging. Pagley Quality Exports is a wholesaler engaged in foreign trade. As a wholesaler, the company both buys and sells in international markets. The following transactions with companies in Hong Kong are typical of the company's business:

March 1 Purchased merchandise from Chang, Ltd., a Hong Kong manufacturer. The invoice was for HK$190,000, payable on June 1. The exchange rate on this date for the Hong Kong dollar was $0.1285.

1 Acquired a forward exchange contract, as a hedge, to buy 190,000 Hong Kong dollars on June 1 for $0.1294.

31 Sold merchandise to TSAI Retailers for HK$150,000. No hedging was involved. The exchange rate for Hong Kong dollars was $0.1256.

April 30 Received HK$150,000 from TSAI Retailers. The exchange rate for Hong Kong dollars was $0.1372.

June 1 Submitted full payment of HK$190,000 to Chang, Ltd., after obtaining HK$190,000 on its forward exchange contract. The exchange rate for Hong Kong dollars was $0.1430.

Required:
Calculate the exchange gains or losses associated with each of the transactions.

16-16. Foreign Exchange Gains and Losses With Hedging. Huseman Enterprises buys and sells products in the international marketplace. As a U. S. corporation, Huseman uses the U. S. dollar as its functional currency. However, all billings are denominated in a foreign currency. The following transactions are typical of the company's business activities:

(a) Sold merchandise to an Italian company for L2,000,000 when the exchange rate for lira was $0.00052. Huseman also sold L1,000,000 for future delivery at $0.00052.

(b) Received payment from the Italian company in (a) when the exchange rate for the lira was $0.0006. The lira sold in (a) are delivered to the exchange broker.

(c) Purchased merchandise from a British company for £5,000 when the exchange rate for pounds was $1.50. Concurrently, the company purchased £5,000 for future delivery at $1.48.

(d) Received the pounds in (c) from the exchange broker. The company then paid the British company for the merchandise purchased in (c) using these pounds. The exchange rate for pounds was $1.55.

(e) Sold merchandise to a Mexican company for M$100,000 when the exchange rate for pesos was $0.35.

(f) Purchased merchandise from another Mexican company for M$200,000 when the exchange rate for the peso was $0.33.

Required:
Calculate the exchange gains or losses associated with each of the transactions. The last two transactions are still open. Assume that on the date you are making your calculations, the exchange rate for the peso was $0.32.

16-17. Performance Evaluation After Translation. Herb Gonzalez is the manager of a South American subsidiary of MDE International. In a recent meeting of subsidiary managers in the western hemisphere, Herb learned he was one of only a few managers in world operations to meet or exceed budget projections. The actual sales exceeded the budgeted sales, and cost of goods sold and operating expenses were lower than projected. Herb acknowledged how easy it was to meet budgeted numbers when his budget was denominated in local currency. He knew what he had to do.

The next day, the president of MDE International made a presentation of operating results of all subsidiaries world-wide. To bring comparability to the presentation, the results of all subsidiaries were translated into U. S. dollars. The subsidiaries were ranked according to operating net income after translation. Herb found, to his astonishment, that his subsidiary was listed in the bottom ten performing subsidiaries. How could he be one of the top managers one day and the next day be one of the ten worst managers?

Required:
1. Give an explanation for why Herb's performance looks good in local currency but looks poor after translating the results into U. S. currency.
2. What are the problems associated with making comparisons of subsidiaries operating in different countries?

All problems are
international.

 ROBLEMS

16-18. Transfer Pricing Problem. A large farming company has two units: the Mexican Division produces grain, and the U. S. Division sells the grain. As soon as the grain is produced, it is placed in storage areas until sold by the U. S. Division. A transfer price is used to charge the U. S. Division and to recognize the Mexican Division as a profit center.

During the year, three grain crops of 1,900,000 bushels each were produced. All three have now been sold, although some were held in inventory for various periods of time. The market prices at production time were M$10 per bushel for the first crop (M$1 = $0.34), M$12 per bushel for the second (M$1 = $0.35), and

M$8 per bushel for the third (M$1 = $0.33).   No beginning inventories were on hand.   The Mexican producer uses a transfer price equal to the market price in pesos.

The results for the period are:

Total company revenues (5,700,000 bushels)	$ 22,300,000

Costs:
Producing division (M$1 = $0.33):	
Labor and materials	$ 13,200,000
Division overhead	5,610,000
Selling division:	
Labor	900,000
Division overhead	900,000

The company president is pleased with the total profit (stated in U. S. dollars) generated by the two divisions.   He wants to determine whether the price speculation activities of the selling division are earning a profit.

Required:

1. Prepare income statements for each division, using the currency of the country where each operates.   Which division is more profitable?
2. Would you use the market price or the cost for the transfer price?   Explain.

16-19. Overhead Variances for a Department.   Flexible budget information and actual expenses for May for the Fabrication Department of Abbott Industries, a Canadian subsidiary of a U. S. corporation, are as follows:

	Flexible Budget	Actual Results
Machine hours	5,000	4,650
Units of production	50,000	48,530
Variable overhead:		
Indirect labor......................	C$ 3,500	C$ 3,400
Supplies	2,500	2,200
Repairs and maintenance	1,000	960
Electricity, other than lighting	5,000	4,740
Total variable overhead	C$ 12,000	C$ 11,300
Fixed overhead:		
Supervision	C$ 3,000	C$ 3,100
Supplies	1,700	1,650
Repairs and maintenance	3,000	3,200
Depreciation on machinery	6,500	6,500
Insurance and property taxes	2,800	3,000
Heating and power	1,000	1,250
Total fixed overhead	C$ 18,000	C$ 18,700
Total factory overhead.................	C$ 30,000	C$ 30,000

Factory overhead is applied on the basis of machine hours.   The standard calls for ten units of product per machine hour.   Budget variances are based on actual output.

The budget was translated into U. S. dollars when the budget was approved (C$1 = $0.90).   When actual results are sent to headquarters, amounts are translated into U. S. dollars (C$1 = $0.80 for May 31).

Required:

1. Prepare a report that compares actual to an adjusted budget and that shows budget variances and efficiency or capacity variances.   Comment on the variances.
2. Translate the amounts into U. S. dollars according to the preceding rules and redo the variance report in Part (1).

3. Explain what differences occur in variances between Parts (1) and (2).

4. Would you recommend a different approach to translation? Why? Explain your approach.

16-20. Discussion of Alternative Budget Comparisons.   The text discussed three exchange rates that could be used for actual and budget amounts to evaluate performance of an international subsidiary. These were B_1, B_2, and B_3 for budgets and A_1, A_2, and A_3 for actual results.

Required:

Assume that you have been asked by your boss, Nikki Stathopoulos who is the corporate controller of a U. S.-based firm with subsidiaries in 22 countries, to prepare a report on the usefulness and problems with each combination of a budgeted exchange rate and an actual exchange rate.

Nikki has asked you to evaluate each possible combination (i.e., B_1 and A_3). Give at least one positive and one negative for each combination.

16-21. Transfer Prices.   Company Z operates in three countries, Countries A, B, and C. All company divisions sell to other company divisions in the other two countries. The following is known about tax rates, import duties, and sales.

	Country A	*Country B*	*Country C*
Tax rates on profits earned	60%	20%	40%
Import duties	10	70	40
In-country sales (in millions).........	$ 50,000	$100,000	$ 200,000
In-country cost of sales	40,000	80,000	160,000
Sales:			
To Country A..................		10,000	9,000
To Country B..................	10,000		3,000
To Country C..................	5,000	28,000	

A number of assumptions must be made:

1. All intercompany sales figures include a 25 percent markup over costs. Also, variable costs are 40 percent of costs of sales for all sales.

2. Costs of sales does not include import duties.

3. Import duties are applied to the transfer price for imported goods.

4. Costs of imported goods are included in the costs of sales for each country. No inventories exist.

Required:

The corporate controller of Company Z is considering a change in intercompany sales pricing practices to minimize global taxes and duties. Assuming that the controller decides that all intercompany sales must show at least a 10 percent profit on variable costs, suggest a transfer price that will minimize global taxes and duties.

 16-22. Sales and Marketing Expense Variances.   Trujillo Distributors, a wholly-owned Mexican subsidiary of a U. S. corporation, is evaluating its selling and marketing expenses. Management has estimated that its relevant range of operations is 40,000 to 60,000 sales units. At each of these levels, management has established the following budgets:

	Sales Units	
	40,000	*60,000*
Sales and marketing expenses:		
Transportation..........................	M$110,000	M$150,000
Credit and collections	57,000	65,000
Direct selling	19,800	26,200
Advertising and promotion	11,000	14,000

The company planned to operate at 48,000 units during 1998. Actual output for the year was 50,000 units. Although the president is not confident that his managers are good cost estimators and are controlling costs, the accounting systems are able to differentiate between variable and fixed costs. Actual costs incurred for sales and marketing activities are:

	Variable	*Fixed*
Transportation	M$109,000	M$ 31,000
Credit and collections	23,505	42,185
Direct selling	18,730	7,485
Advertising and promotion	7,248	4,690

The budgeted and actual financial results are submitted to the U. S. headquarters at the end of each year. All amounts are translated into U. S. dollars using the projected exchange rate for the end of the year (M$1 = $0.30).

Required:

1. Identify the budget formula for each individual sales and marketing expense.

2. Prepare an analysis for each expense that shows spending and volume variances.

3. Restate the analysis in terms of U. S. dollars according to company policy. Does this translation change the evaluation you would make of the subsidiary's performance? Explain.

16-23. Budget Translation.   Goforth Drugs has a subsidiary in Belgium. The budget is set in late November each year with final approval at the Goforth headquarters in the U. S. in early December. The 1998 budget and the actual results for 1998 are as follows in Belgium francs:

	Budget	*Actual*
Sales (in millions of francs)	BF 2,000	BF 1,980
Cost of sales	(1,200)	(1,250)
Selling expenses	(250)	(220)
Administrative expenses	(230)	(240)
Taxes	(100)	(120)

The relevant exchange rates for the Belgium franc at various dates were:

November 1997	$ 0.0300
Forecast for 1998 when the budget was prepared	0.0290
Actual at the end of 1998	0.0285

Required:

1. Compare the results of translating budget and actual amounts using:

   (a) $B_1 - A_3$

   (b) $B_2 - A_3$

   (c) $B_2 - A_2$

   (d) $B_3 - A_3$

2. Comment on the differences in the results.

1-2-3

16-24. Comprehensive Operating Expense Variance Analysis.   Pannex Manufacturing Company is a U. S. subsidiary of a Japanese company. It budgeted 180,000 sales units for November. The product has a budgeted selling price of $21 and a manufacturing cost of $11.50 per unit. The company's flexible expense budget for operating expenses and actual operating expenses for November are:

	Flexible Budget		*November Actual Expenses*
Administrative salaries and wages .	$ 50,000 +	$0.04 per unit sold	$ 56,800
Sales salaries and wages	20,000 +	0.06 per unit sold	33,600
Utilities	11,500 +	0.15 per unit sold	38,500
Supplies		0.10 per unit sold	19,560
Travel and entertainment		0.95 per unit sold	183,250
Depreciation	61,000		61,000
Property taxes	2,000		1,850
Total			$394,560

At the end of November, the accounting records showed that the company had sold 195,000 units for a total of $4,000,000 and that the cost of goods sold was $2,240,000.

At the end of each month, the accountant translates the budgeted and actual information into yen and sends the reports to the headquarter's office in Tokyo. The company uses the budgeted exchange rate for the year ($1 = ¥100) for budgeted information and the exchange rate at the end of the month ($1 = ¥105) for actual information.

Required:

1. Prepare an income statement showing columns for both actual and budgeted results with spending and volume variances for each of the individual income statement items.
2. Using the translation rules given, recompute the budgeted and actual results and the spending and volume variances.
3. Is your evaluation of the variances different in the translated amounts? If yes, explain why.

16-25. T-Account Recording of International Transactions. Harley Import/Export, Inc. has considerable foreign business dealings. Over the three months of August, September, and October the company engaged in the following transactions:

Aug. 15 Purchased goods from a Japanese company for $110,000; terms denominated in U. S. dollars (¥1 = $0.0095).

17 Sold goods to a German company for DM140,000; terms denominated in marks (DM1 = $0.65).

21 Purchased goods from a Mexican company for $120,000; terms denominated in pesos (M$1 = $0.30).

25 Paid for the goods purchased on August 15 (¥1 = $0.010).

31 Sold goods to an Italian company for $200,000; terms denominated in lira (lira = $0.0006).

Sep. 5 Sold goods to a British firm for $56,000; terms denominated in U. S. dollars (£1 = $1.50).

7 Purchased goods from a Japanese company for $162,000; terms denominated in yen (¥1 = $0.0095).

15 Received payment for the sale made on September 5 (£1 = $1.45).

16 Received payment for the sale made on August 17 (DM1 = $0.64).

17 Purchased goods from a French company for $66,000; terms denominated in U. S. dollars (Fr1 = $0.18).

20 Paid for the goods purchased on August 21 (M$1 = $0.31).

22 Sold goods to a British company for $84,000; terms denominated in British pounds (£1 = $1.40).

Oct. 7 Paid for the goods purchased on September 7 (¥1 = $0.0094).

19 Paid for the goods purchased on September 17 (Fr1 = $0.19).

22 Received payment for the goods sold on September 22 (£1 = $1.45).

30 Received payment for the goods sold on August 31 (1 lira = $0.00058).

Required:

Analyze the preceding transactions for Harley Import/Export, Inc. for gain and loss purposes.

16-26. Foreign Exchange Gains and Losses. Marlow Implements of Kansas City conducts a considerable amount of its business through foreign suppliers and customers. It is a calendar year company. The following are several typical transactions for 1997 and 1998:

Oct. 14   Sold products to a Mexican company for $20,000; terms denominated in U. S. dollars (M$1 = $0.30).

26   Purchased goods from a Japanese firm for $40,000; terms denominated in yen (¥1 = $0.009).

Nov. 4   Sold products to a British company for $39,000; terms denominated in pounds (£1 = $1.50).

14   Received payment in full for October 14 sale (M$1 = $0.32).

15   Paid for the goods purchased on October 26 (¥1 = $0.0094).

23   Purchased goods from an Italian company for $28,000; terms denominated in U. S. dollars (1 lira = $0.0005).

30   Purchased products from a Japanese company for $35,200; terms denominated in yen (¥1 = $0.0099).

Dec. 2   Paid for the goods purchased on November 23 (1 lira = $0.00055).

3   Received payment in full for goods sold on November 4 (£1 = $1.46).

8   Sold products to a French company for $66,000; terms denominated in francs (Fr1 = $0.20).

17   Purchased products from a Mexican company for $37,000; terms denominated in U. S. dollars (M$1 = $0.33).

18   Sold products to a German company for $90,000; terms denominated in marks (DM1 = $0.66).

Jan. 7   Received payment for goods sold on December 8 (Fr1 = $0.18).

16   Paid for goods purchased on December 17 (M$1 = $0.32).

17   Received payment for goods sold on December 18 (DM1 = $0.64).

28   Paid for goods purchased on November 30 (¥1 = $0.0101).

Required:

1. For each completed transaction, show the total exchange gain or loss incurred between transaction date and settlement date.

2. What is the total net exchange gain or loss for all completed transactions?

16-27. Foreign Exchange Gains and Losses and Hedge. On June 1, 1998, University Research Labs, a domestic research and development operation, placed an order for special laboratory equipment with a company in Holland. The purchase price was stated in florins at F400,000 and was payable in 60 days (July 30, 1998). The exchange rate for florins on June 1 was $0.50.

On this same date, University Research Labs decided to hedge its foreign currency commitment by purchasing F300,000 for delivery in 60 days at a price of $0.49 in the futures market.

These transactions were both settled on July 30, 1998. The exchange rate for florins on that date was $0.51.

Required:

1. Calculate the exchange gains and losses associated with these transactions. Include in your computations, the effects of any premium or discount on the hedging transaction.

2. Comment on the wisdom of the hedging activities.

16-28. Hedging Transactions. Intermountain Grain Importers/Exporters, located in Salt Lake City, buys and sells grains in the international market. The following transactions were handled:

Sep. 1   Sold 1,000,000 bushels of wheat to a French cooperative for 18,000,000 francs (Fr1 = $0.1864). Payment is due October 30.

1   Negotiated a forward contract with an exchange broker to sell 18,000,000 francs on October 30 for $0.1842, as management felt the franc might decline in value.

5   Sold 2,000,000 bushels of wheat to a company in Spain for $5,300,000 (P1 = $0.0074). The account is to be settled in U. S. dollars on November 5.

15   Purchased rice from an exporting company that operates in Japan. The contract provided for payment of ¥16,000,000 on October 15. Exchange rate for yen on September 15 was $0.00943.

15   Entered into a forward contract to buy 16,000,000 yen on October 15 for $0.00965 per yen.

18   Sold 500 tons of soybean meal to Quebec Meal and Flour, Ltd. for C$52,000 (C$1 = $0.8245). The account is to be settled December 17.

Oct.   15   Received ¥16,000,000 under terms of the forward contract and then submitted payment for the rice purchased on September 15 (¥1 = $0.00945).

30   Received Fr18,000,000 from the French company and settled the forward contract (Fr1 = $0.1857).

Nov.   5   Received payment in full for the wheat sold on September 5 to the Spanish company (P1 = $0.0073).

Dec.   17   Received payment from Quebec Meal and Flour, Ltd. for the September 18 sale (C$1 = $0.8246).

Required:
Compute the exchange gain or loss at time of settlement for each purchase or sale transaction and the related hedging transaction.

16-29. Transaction Gains and Losses on Hedging a Purchase.   Darby Refineries of Houston, Texas, purchased 2,000,000 barrels of oil from a company in Venezuela on November 15, 1998. Darby agreed to pay (in bolivars) B160,000,000 on January 14, 1999 (60 days later). To ensure that the dollar outlay for the purchase would not fluctuate, Darby negotiated a forward contract to buy B160,000,000 on January 14 at the forward rate of $0.0565.

Important dates and exchange rates for bolivars are: November 15: $0.0533; December 31: $0.0530; January 14: $0.0589.

Required:

1.   Compute the dollars to be paid on November 15, 1998, to acquire B160,000,000 from the exchange dealer.
2.   Compute the premium or discount on the forward contract.
3.   Compute the total exchange gain or loss on the exposed liability and the hedge related to the oil purchase.
4.   Did the hedging transaction minimize the effects of currency fluctuations? Explain.

Both cases are international.

C ASE 16A—JOE SCANLAN, THE ETHICS TEACHER

Joe Scanlan, corporate controller of Harper Enterprises, is responsible for reporting under the Foreign Corrupt Practices Act. He develops policy materials, conducts seminars for senior management, includes FCPA materials in all training programs for international personnel, and responds to ethical inquiries from anyone in the company. At a recent meeting of international general managers (GMs), he reemphasized several corporate goals that he thinks apply to international ethical problems. These were:

- Do the right thing.
- Have respect for others.
- Resolve conflicts constructively.
- Accept ownership for your actions.

Over cocktails and later at informal "bull sessions," he was dismayed to hear many "war stories" from several key GMs about how they really got things done in their respective countries. Several implied that favors, if not payoffs, were given to get approvals for important expansion plans. Others almost bragged about their contacts and ability to get to the right people. Stories about clearing goods through customs, getting approvals to raise prices, finding scarce resources, and beating out competitors with "unique" deals were great entertainment. Any number of these connivances, if exposed, could embarrass the company greatly and threaten Joe's job, since he is the FCPA enforcer, and the job of the GM is involved.

Joe is a savvy manager, since he spent two years as country controller in South America. He knows the pressures and the risks. Yet, he is clearly worried.

Required:

What should he do? What more can he do? What can he recommend to heighten the visibility of the ethical policies and practices of his company? Is his own neck on the line? Explain.

C ASE 16B—BOSCO COMPANY

In August 1997, Bosco Company, the British subsidiary of U. S.-based Nitrate Components, Inc., completed a proposal to expand its manufacturing facilities. The estimated cost is £15,000,000. The subsidiary has had a very spotty financial performance over its ten years of operation. New products and increased sales potential justified the proposed expansion. But, it has very little funds to pay for the expansion.

After the proposal was presented to Nitrate officials, the subject of financing arose. Because of its limited financial capabilities available, Bosco must depend on Nitrate to lead the financing effort. Should Nitrate provide the funds from internal sources? Should Nitrate borrow from British sources? From American sources? After extensive analysis, negotiations with a British bank were conducted. Terms included a 5-year loan and an 8 percent interest rate. The loan would be made effective January 1, 1998, with interest paid annually starting on December 31, 1998.

Nitrate officials believe a similar loan could be executed in the U. S. with a major bank. The money would then be transferred to Bosco as an intercompany loan at 9 percent, to cover the cost of funds and for arranging the deal.

At January 1, 1998, the British pound exchange rate was $1.50.

Required:

1. Compare the loan alternatives for Bosco if the exchange rate moves to $1.60 by yearend.
2. Compare the loan alternatives for Bosco if the exchange rate moves to $1.40 by yearend.
3. Comment on the results of Parts (1) and (2). What alternatives might you suggest to Nitrate to avoid the possible volatility of exchange rate moves?

Financial Performance Analysis

After studying Chapter 17, you will be able to:

1. Understand how financial statement analysis can give insight into the financial strengths and weaknesses of an organization.

2. Identify the key questions in each risk area of liquidity, capital adequacy, and asset quality and in each return area of earnings, growth, and market performance.

3. Identify and calculate specific ratios in each risk and return area.

4. Understand how financial leverage can improve returns to owners.

5. Show how earning-power ratios can be used to improve operating profitability.

6. Know why ratio analysis has certain limitations and caveats that must be recognized.

Why Do They All Want to Know My Business?

Maynard Hogberg operates CAD Creations, a computer-aided engineering firm doing contract work for automotive companies and other engineering firms. His firm is now six years old. He used his own money plus venture capital firm funds to start the company. He has just received his quarterly financial statements.

"It's like they have radar! As soon as these statements show up, everybody wants to see them. We're doing okay; I can pay the bills; and we're making a buck." Who are "they," and what do they want to know? Here's a sampling:

■ **Venture capital firm and its backers.** These people own 40 percent of the stock in CAD Creations. Their primary motive is to reap large gains from an initially risky investment. They want to see the revenues and the earnings growth rates from last quarter and last year.

■ **Major Motors' procurement office.** Major Motors is negotiating a long-term contract with CAD Creations and wants a financially stable supplier.

■ **Supplier of computer equipment.** The equipment seller wants to collect the cash from the sale. Normally, a seller will do a credit check on a prospective customer. In this case, the computer supplier is concerned about the large amount of equipment CAD Creations has purchased on credit.

■ **Friendly banker.** Maynard has a close working relationship with a commercial lending officer at Detroit National Bank. DNB's Credit Department maintains detailed files on the financial status of each borrower. The bank wants to assist Maynard in meeting his cash needs and yet wants to be sure that CAD Creations debt service can be paid from operating cash inflows.

■ **Mike, Maynard's 21-year-old son.** Mike received a few shares of CAD Creations stock as a gift from his dad. Mike is planning to attend an expensive graduate school after his days at Major University. Without sounding too presumptuous, he asks if he can expect any cash dividends soon.

Financial statements, blessed by the firm's CPA auditor, are management's representations. Management must approve the statements, understand their contents, and communicate them to the many financial interests facing the firm.

Financial performance analysis is like painting a picture. Blending colors, using different strokes, drawing certain abstractions, integrating foreground and background, and linking focal points, settings, and shapes are a few of the artist's skills which combine to bring art to life. The task of financial analysts is to utilize all the elements of their craft properly to pull the greatest understanding possible from the available data.

The primary vehicles of financial performance analysis are financial ratios. Finding the magnitude and direction of change of ratios gives the analyst insight into (a) what causes specific ratios to change; (b) how these changes are related; and (c) what impacts these changes have on the firm's financial condition. The firm's performance is evaluated relative to its financial plan, to other firms in its industry, and to the financial marketplace in general.

USES AND USERS OF FINANCIAL PERFORMANCE ANALYSIS

Financial performance analysis interprets financial statement data and presents information in summary form to simplify users' analyses. Primary users are existing or potential investors, creditors who may extend trade credit or lend cash, and customers who are trying to determine financial stability.

Financial performance analysis can be useful for many purposes, including:

1. To set goals and targets.
2. To compare the firm's performance to others.

3. To measure financial strength for credit granting purposes.
4. To measure profitability for return-on-investment purposes.
5. To spot trends, weaknesses, and potential problem areas.
6. To evaluate alternative courses of action.
7. To understand interactions that financial changes have on a firm's financial position.

The novice analyst sees one dimension, then two, and so on. Expert financial analysts have an amazing "feel" for financial statement relationships and underlying issues and seem able to read "between the lines."

*A*N EXAMPLE COMPANY—AMBERG LIGHTING

As an illustration, a comprehensive example is used throughout the chapter. Amberg Lighting is a major distributor of electrical fixtures for commercial and retail use. It is December 31, 1998. Management has approved a profit plan for 1999. Figure 17.1 presents balance sheets for three years and a forecast for December 31, 1999. Figure 17.2 presents income statements for 1997 and 1998 and the 1999 forecast.

F I G U R E   1 7 . 1   Forecast and Actual Balance Sheets and Other Financial Data

Balance Sheets as of December 31 (in Millions)				
	Forecast 1999	*Actual 1998*	*Actual 1997*	*Actual 1996*
Cash and marketable securities...	$ 230	$ 236	$ 180	$ 121
Accounts receivable (net)........	363	345	300	284
Inventories...................	524	356	320	287
Total current assets...........	$1,117	$ 937	$ 800	$ 692
Plant and equipment (net)	$ 439	$ 396	$ 369	$ 370
Land........................	139	127	119	98
Total noncurrent assets	$ 578	$ 523	$ 488	$ 468
Total assets.................	$1,695	$1,460	$1,288	$1,160
Accounts payable	$ 418	$ 275	$ 197	$ 151
Bonds payable—10 percent......	400	400	400	400
Total liabilities..............	$ 818	$ 675	$ 597	$ 551
Paid-in-capital ($5 per share)	$ 400	$ 400	$ 400	$ 400
Retained earnings.............	477	385	291	209
Total equity	$ 877	$ 785	$ 691	$ 609
Total liabilities and equity ...	$1,695	$1,460	$1,288	$1,160
Shares outstanding (in millions) ..	80	80	80	80
Dividends paid (in millions)......	$56	$48	$40	
Average price per share.........	$17.25	$16.75	$15.00	

FIGURE 17.2 Forecast and Actual Income Statements

Income Statements for Years Ending December 31 (in Millions)			
	Forecast 1999	Actual 1998	Actual 1997
Sales	$2,848	$2,454	$2,084
Cost of goods sold	1,721	1,461	1,210
Gross margin	$1,127	$ 993	$ 874
Operating expenses:			
Selling and administration expenses	$ 773	$ 672	$ 587
Depreciation expense	65	45	38
Total operating expenses	$ 838	$ 717	$ 625
Operating net income	$ 289	$ 276	$ 249
Interest expense	42	40	46
Net income before taxes	$ 247	$ 236	$ 203
Income taxes expense (40 percent)..........	99	94	81
Net income after taxes.....................	$ 148	$ 142	$ 122

In addition to Figures 17.1 and 17.2, much more information is included in the annual report, such as footnotes, a ten-year summary of financial data, and the auditors' report. These are not included here for simplification.

T YPES OF FINANCIAL STATEMENT ANALYSIS

Financial analysts examine financial statement data in every manner possible to gain insight. Traditional formats include:

1. **Comparative statements.** Data from two time periods are compared. Comparisons between actual and budget, two versions of a budget, and last period and this period are done routinely. As an example, the Amberg data show:

	Forecast 1999	Actual 1998	Difference	Percentage Change
Sales	$2,848	$2,454	$394	16.1%
Cost of goods sold	1,721	1,461	260	17.8
Gross margin	$1,127	$ 993	134	13.5

The Percentage Change column is found by dividing the difference between the values for 1999 and 1998 by the 1998 base-year value.

2. **Percentage composition statements.** All statement values are expressed as a percentage of a base number, which is set equal to 100 percent. The base is total assets on the balance sheet and sales on

the income statement. These are often called **common-sized statements** and are used for comparing multiple years of data, companies of various sizes, and one company to industry averages. A summarized presentation is:

	Forecast 1999	Actual 1998	Actual 1997	Actual 1996
Cash and marketable securities	13.6%	16.2%	14.0%	10.4%
Accounts receivable (net)	21.4	23.6	23.3	24.5
Inventories	30.9	24.4	24.8	24.7
Total current assets	65.9%	64.2%	62.1%	59.7%
Total noncurrent assets.	34.1	35.8	37.9	40.3
Total assets	100.0%	100.0%	100.0%	100.0%

If ideal mixes of assets, liabilities, and equity can be defined for an industry, percentage composition statements can quickly highlight deviations.

3. **Base-year comparisons.** Base-year comparisons fix a base period at 100 percent and express amounts in other periods as percentages of the base. As an example, 1997 is the base; and 1998 and 1999 figures are percentages of the base year, as follows:

	Forecast 1999	Actual 1998	Actual 1997
Sales	136.7%	117.8%	100.0%
Cost of goods sold	142.2	120.7	100.0
Gross margin	129.0	113.6	100.0

4. **Ratio analysis.** Ratio analysis is defined as selecting one variable as the numerator and another variable as the denominator—a ratio of two values. Ratios are expressed as a percentage (%), a ratio (X:Y), or merely a number.

In reality, all four formats are ratio based. A ratio is a numerator divided by a denominator. A few simple rules help in calculating ratios from balance sheet numbers (for a point in time) and income statement numbers (for a time period):

1. When calculating a ratio using balance sheet numbers only, the numerator and denominator should be from the same balance sheet, not from balance sheets for different dates.
2. When a balance sheet number and an income statement number are used in a ratio, the balance sheet number should be an average for the time period, at least an average of the beginning and ending balance sheet numbers.
3. Generally, the number of days in a month or year is simplified to ease calculations and analyses. For example, a year is 360 days, 52 weeks, or 12 months. A month is 30 days.
4. Analysts should use consistent definitions for terms and accounting rules.

*F*INANCIAL PERFORMANCE ANALYSIS: RISKS AND RETURNS

Instead of merely calculating ratios, measuring financial performance requires a framework. "Why do you want to know?" and "What do you want to know?" frame an attack. Answering the "why" defines the viewpoint of the questioner: creditor, shareholder, regulator, employee, etc. The "what" question leads to specific concerns and ratios. These concerns are grouped by *risks* and *returns* as follows:

Risks	*Returns*
Liquidity	Earnings
Capital adequacy	Growth
Asset quality	Market performance

Risks areas measure the financial safety of the firm. Returns areas measure the financial success of the firm. Risks and returns are interrelated. Reducing a risk can improve a return measure, and poor financial returns can cause a more risky financial position.

Every ratio can get too high or too low. This is the "Goldilocks paradox." Remember that papa bear's porridge was too hot, momma bear's porridge was too cold, but baby bear's porridge was just right. Generally, the "just right" level is difficult to find precisely. But if a ratio is too high or too low, financial risk grows. Benchmarking, comparative financial analysis, and monitoring common stock prices can help define the optimal area.

Liquidity

Liquidity is the availability of cash, other near-cash assets, and assets that can be converted into cash easily. The key liquidity question is:

What liquid assets are available or accessible to meet demands for
cash from expected and unexpected sources?

C O N T E M P O R A R Y   P R A C T I C E   1 7 . 1

When Financial Ratios Look Really Bad

"Cease and desist orders" carry the force of law and are issued by government regulators of banks when regulatory guidelines for safe and sound management are violated. Ratios for **C**apital adequacy, **A**sset quality, **M**anagement, **E**arnings, and **L**iquidity (**CAMEL**) are evaluated by bank regulatory auditors during bank examinations. In troublesome cases, regulators will sign an agreement with the bank's board of directors to make immediate changes. The changes often attempt to rebuild the bank's capital, create a strategic plan and master budget to improve financial ratios, develop a plan to improve management quality, respond to specific problems, and require frequent progress reports. Failure to do so can result in fines, loss of ownership, and a possible "cease and desist order."

Source: Takser, J., "What to Do When Regulators With a Cease and Desist Order Come Knocking," *Bottomline*, November-December, 1991, pp. 40-42.

Can the bills be paid on time? The answer comes from ratios that measure assets which can be converted quickly into cash for short-term needs. Traditional measures are the current and quick ratios.

Current Ratio. The **current ratio** indicates how many dollars of current assets are available for each dollar of current liabilities and is defined as:

$$\frac{\text{Current asset}}{\text{Current liabilities}} = \text{Current ratio}$$

Current assets can be converted into cash within the operating cycle, often a one-year timeframe. From the Amberg case, yearend numbers are:

	Forecast 1999	Actual 1998	Actual 1997	Actual 1996
Current assets	$1,117	$937	$800	$692
Current liabilities	418	275	197	151
Current ratio	2.7:1	3.4:1	4.1:1	4.6:1

Generally, firms want a safety cushion of more liquidity than is really needed to cover unexpected or sudden cash needs. At the end of 1998, $3.40 of current assets was available for each dollar of current liabilities. The difference between current assets and current liabilities is called **working capital**. These funds are needed to keep day-to-day operations working smoothly.

A 2:1 current ratio is often suggested as ideal but rarely is. Different industries have different needs for liquidity. Steel warehousers may need a 4:1 ratio to cover large inventories that "turn" slowly. Other firms with very predictable cash flows, few receivables, and low inventories can operate with a 1:1 ratio. Industry averages give an indication of what this ratio should be.[1]

Quick Ratio. The **quick ratio**, or **acid test ratio**, tests a firm's ability to pay its bills quickly from available cash and near-cash assets and is defined as:

$$\frac{\text{Cash, marketable securities, and receivables}}{\text{Current liabilities}} = \text{Quick ratio}$$

Inventories are excluded because they are less liquid. Receivables must still be collected, but at least cash is owed to the firm. For Amberg Lighting, the quick ratio has declined each year, from 2.7:1 to 1.4:1, a potentially serious concern.

	Forecast 1999	Actual 1998	Actual 1997	Actual 1996
Cash and marketable securities	$230	$236	$180	$121
Accounts receivable (net)	363	345	300	284
Total quick assets	$593	$581	$480	$405
Current liabilities	$418	$275	$197	$151
Quick ratio	1.4:1	2.1:1	2.4:1	2.7:1

[1] Sources of ratios for comparison purposes include publications of Dun & Bradstreet, Standard & Poors, and Robert Morris Associates. Many industry trade associations also publish financial data and statistics about member firms.

Other Liquidity Considerations. Liquidity commonly deals with cash flows. In particular, cash from operations is the amount of cash generated from normal operations and is discussed in Chapter 18.   Often, cash from operations is measured against cash needed to pay interest and principal on debt.

A missing element is the firm's ability to borrow cash when needed, called **off-balance-sheet financing**. These liquidity sources are lines of credit, other borrowing agreements, and borrowing against inventories or other assets. Often, off-balance-sheet sources are more important than on-balance-sheet liquidity.

A firm can have too much or too little liquidity. Generally, the more liquid, the lower is the earning power—low risk, low return. One job of a corporate treasurer is to minimize idle cash and maximize investment returns.

Capital Adequacy

Liquidity is closely tied to capital adequacy.   Even if a firm has a liquidity problem, a strong capital position allows it to borrow easily. And vice versa, if a firm's capital position is weak, it should maintain more liquidity to avoid any possible cash-flow troubles.   Capital is equity ownership, which is paid-in capital plus retained earnings. Two questions define capital adequacy:

1. How much capital is necessary to protect creditors and shareholders against losses?
2. How little capital is necessary to allow shareholders to enjoy maximum favorable returns on equity and dividends?

These are conflicting positions—more capital for protection and less capital for higher rates of return. Creditors want more; owners want less. But if capital as a portion of total assets or debt drops too low, creditors stop lending money or demand higher interest rates. If capital portions go too high, owners are disappointed by low rates of return on the large equity base.   The capital adequacy ratios examined are debt to equity, equity multiplier, times interest earned, and dividend payout percentage.

Debt to Equity. The definition of the **debt to equity ratio** is:

$$\frac{\text{Total liabilities}}{\text{Total equity}} = \text{Debt to equity ratio}$$

	Forecast 1999	Actual 1998	Actual 1997	Actual 1996
Total liabilities	$818	$675	$597	$551
Total equity	877	785	691	609
Debt to equity ratio	93.3%	86.0%	86.4%	90.5%

The debt to equity ratio is a percentage. Other ratios such as equity to total assets, debt to total assets, and equity to debt reveal similar information. Debt is often defined as long-term debt, excluding current liabilities.

Capital Multiplier. The **capital multiplier** indicates how much total investment can be financed from owner-provided equity and is defined as:

$$\frac{\text{Total assets}}{\text{Total equity}} = \text{Capital multiplier}$$

	Forecast 1999	Actual 1998	Actual 1997	Actual 1996
Total assets........................	$1,695	$1,460	$1,288	$1,160
Total equity	877	785	691	609
Capital multiplier	1.93:1	1.86:1	1.86:1	1.90:1

As the capital multiplier decreases, more equity money is used to finance assets; and more safety is assumed. A higher capital multiplier indicates an ability to lever "our" equity into more assets, using "other people's money" to finance the firm.

Times Interest Earned.   A measure of capital adequacy is the ability of a firm to earn enough from operations to pay for the cost of debt—more debt, more interest. **Times interest earned** is defined as:

$$\frac{\text{Net income before interest expense and taxes}}{\text{Interest expense}} = \text{Times interest earned}$$

	Forecast 1999	Actual 1998	Actual 1997
Net income before interest expense and taxes	$289	$276	$249
Interest expense...............................	42	40	46
Times interest earned........................	6.9	6.9	5.4

The risk is not having cash to pay the interest. A higher times interest earned number means more safety, and a lower number (particularly under 1.0) means more risk.

Dividend Payout Percentage.   The **dividend payout percentage** shows what portion of earnings was paid in dividends to shareholders. The definition is:

$$\frac{\text{Dividends paid}}{\text{Net income}} = \text{Dividend payout percentage}$$

	Forecast 1999	Actual 1998	Actual 1997
Dividends paid	$ 56	$ 48	$ 40
Net income after taxes	148	142	122
Dividend payout percentage	37.8%	33.8%	32.8%

A ratio of 30 or 40 percent is normal for a mature firm with a stable earnings record. Rapidly growing firms have lower percentages to save cash for reinvestment. If this ratio nears or exceeds 100 percent, dividend payments are using funds that the firm may need to expand or to pay bills.

Other Capital Adequacy Considerations.   As was mentioned, capital adequacy and liquidity often offset each other. Firms with large capital bases will find borrowing much easier than heavily levered firms. Yet, liquidity has a very short-term horizon; while capital adequacy has a longer-term timeframe.

Liquidity problems can arise and must be solved quickly. Capital is built from earnings which may take years to accumulate.

Asset Quality

Asset quality examines two questions dealing with balance sheet assets:

1. Are assets used efficiently?
2. What risk exists that the book values will not be recovered?

Measures of efficiency are plentiful and examine accounts receivable, inventories, and total assets. Often the second question must be answered using external data to ensure finding market values for assets. Increasingly, market values are being added to financial statements either through footnote disclosure or inclusion on the balance sheet itself.

Accounts Receivable Turnover and Days Sales in Receivables. **Accounts receivable turnover** and **days sales in receivables** computations are:

$$\frac{\text{Sales}}{\text{Average accounts receivable}} = \text{Accounts receivable turnover}$$

$$\frac{\text{Average accounts receivable}}{(\text{Sales} \div 360 \text{ days})} = \text{Days sales in receivables}$$

Both ratios are commonly used and express the same idea. Accounts receivable turnover times days sales in receivables yields 360 days.

	Forecast 1999	*Actual 1998*	*Actual 1997*
Sales	$2,848	$2,454	$2,084
Average accounts receivable	354	323	292
Accounts receivable turnover. . . .	8.0	7.6	7.1
Days sales in receivables	44.7	47.4	50.4

Over the past three years, the days sales in receivables has decreased. Amberg is speeding up collections. These numbers must be compared to credit terms extended to customers. Also, the portion of receivables that is past due and the bad debts expense percentage must be monitored carefully. Ratio trends and comparisons to industry leaders will help evaluate performance.

Inventory Turnover and Days Sales in Inventory. **Inventory turnover** and **days sales in inventory** are:

$$\frac{\text{Cost of goods sold}}{\text{Average inventory}} = \text{Inventory turnover}$$

$$\frac{\text{Average inventory}}{(\text{Cost of goods sold} \div 360 \text{ days})} = \text{Days sales in inventory}$$

Inventory turnover ratios use cost of goods sold, not sales. Sales and accounts receivable are valued using sales prices. Cost of goods sold and inventory use purchase prices at cost (or the cost of goods manufactured).

	Forecast 1999	Actual 1998	Actual 1997
Cost of goods sold	$1,721	$1,461	$1,210
Average inventories	440	338	304
Inventory turnover	3.9	4.3	4.0
Days sales in inventory	92.0	83.3	90.4

The 1999 forecast shows a large inventory increase with inventory turnover dropping below 4.0. A higher turnover indicates more sales are generated from the same amount of inventory. At high levels, frequent stock-outs occur; and sales may be lost. A low number implies that inventory is poorly used. Perhaps too much inventory is sitting around or is out-of-date.

Asset Turnover.   One way to increase profits on a given set of assets is to increase the ratio of sales to total assets—assuming a constant return-on-sales percentage. The **asset turnover** is:

$$\frac{\text{Sales}}{\text{Average total assets}} = \text{Asset turnover}$$

	Forecast 1999	Actual 1998	Actual 1997
Sales	$2,848	$2,454	$2,084
Average total assets	1,578	1,374	1,224
Asset turnover	1.8	1.8	1.7

As assets are used more efficiently, this ratio will increase. More sales, and presumably profits, can be earned from the same dollar amount of assets.

Other Asset Quality Considerations.   Asset quality ratios use balance sheet amounts that are assumed to be valid financial accounting amounts—not overstated. For example, it is essential that bad debts accounting is handled properly and that inventories are at cost and can be converted into sales within the normal business cycle. Often, financial analysts will automatically deduct intangible asset amounts from asset and equity totals, ignoring them in analyses.

Earnings

The key earnings question is:

Is net income adequate to satisfy investors' dividend and rate-of-return expectations and to support growth?

Profitability is often the focus of analysts. Announcements of financial performance emphasize quarter-to-quarter or year-to-year changes in net income. Earnings per share receive disproportionate attention. Clearly, long-term trends in earnings reflect success or difficulties in a firm's competitive markets. Rates of return are major indicators of earnings performance: return on sales, assets, and equity. Growing in importance is the cash flow per share, which indicates how much cash was generated per share from operations. Gross margin and operating expense percentages are examined for trends in operating profitability.

Return on Sales. The **return on sales (ROS)** is defined as:

$$\frac{\text{Net income}}{\text{Sales}} = \text{Return on sales}$$

As shown in the following table, Amberg Lighting's ROS shows a continued decline into the forecast year. Internal and certain external analyses use operating net income instead of net income.

Return on Assets. The **return on assets (ROA)** is defined as:

$$\frac{\text{Net income}}{\text{Average total assets}} = \text{Return on assets}$$

As seen in the following table, Amberg Lighting's ROA hovers around 10 percent but is forecast to drop to its lowest point in 1999. In 1999, assets appear to grow faster than net income.

Internal analyses would use **managed assets**, as discussed in Chapter 14, for the denominator to evaluate investment center managers. The numerator should be controllable or direct contribution margin—excluding allocated common costs.

Return on Equity. The **return on equity (ROE)** is defined as:

$$\frac{\text{Net income}}{\text{Average equity}} = \text{Return on equity}$$

Because shareholders' equity finances only a portion of total assets, the ROE percentage is larger than the ROA percentage. The returns numbers for Amberg Lighting are as follows:

	Forecast 1999	Actual 1998	Actual 1997
Net income	$ 148	$ 142	$ 122
Sales	2,848	2,454	2,084
Return on sales	5.2%	5.8%	5.9%
Average total assets	$ 1,578	$ 1,374	$ 1,224
Return on assets	9.4%	10.3%	10.0%
Average equity	$ 831	$ 738	$ 650
Return on equity	17.8%	19.2%	18.8%

Earnings per Share. **Earnings per share** is defined as:

$$\frac{\text{Net income}}{\text{Average number of shares outstanding}} = \text{Earnings per share}$$

	Forecast 1999	Actual 1998	Actual 1997
Net income after taxes	$148	$142	$122
Average shares outstanding	80 mill.	80 mill.	80 mill.
Earnings per share	$1.85	$1.78	$1.53

Earnings per share is increasing, but slowly. Investors prefer this number to grow at a steady rate and will probably be disappointed in the 1999 forecast.

Cash Flow per Share. With increased visibility, **cash flow per share** is becoming a leading indicator of the cash generating capabilities of operations. The definition is:

$$\frac{\text{Cash flow from operations}}{\text{Average number of shares outstanding}} = \text{Cash flow per share}$$

The calculations to determine cash flow from operations are discussed in Chapter 18. Although not explained here, the data for Amberg Lighting are:

	Forecast 1999	Actual 1998	Actual 1997
Net income	$148	$142	$122
+ Depreciation and other amortizations	65	45	38
± Changes in operating current assets	(186)	(81)	(49)
± Changes in operating current liabilities	143	78	46
Cash flow from operations	$170	$184	$157
Average number of shares outstanding	80 mill.	80 mill.	80 mill.
Cash flow per share	$2.13	$2.30	$1.96

The 1999 forecast growth in inventory will use cash and cause the forecast cash flow per share to decline.

Gross Margin and Operating Expense Percentages. The **gross margin percentage** provides information about prices (sales) relative to costs of products made or purchased (cost of goods sold) and is examined for trends. Have cost increases been passed along in price increases? Is the gross margin percentage improving or deteriorating? The **operating expense percentage** monitors the portion of revenue that the firm spends on selling, marketing, and administrative expenses. Definitions are:

$$\frac{\text{Sales - Cost of goods sold}}{\text{Sales}} = \text{Gross margin percentage}$$

$$\frac{\text{Operating expenses}}{\text{Sales}} = \text{Operating expense percentage}$$

	Forecast 1999	Actual 1998	Actual 1997
Sales	$2,848	$2,454	$2,084
Cost of goods sold	1,721	1,461	1,210
Gross margin	$1,127	$ 993	$ 874
Gross margin percentage	39.6%	40.5%	41.9%
Operating expenses	$838	$717	$625
Operating expense percentage	29.4%	29.2%	30.0%

Gross margin percentages are declining—a cause for serious concern. Often, very slight changes in the percentage are significant. This decline is probably the major reason that net income is not growing as fast as assets or sales and the cause of drops in the ROS and ROA ratios. Operating expenses, however, seem to be in control.

Other Earnings Considerations. Strong earnings overcome many other financial problems. But changes in earnings patterns create uncertainty. Volatile earnings bother analysts, who like to see stable earnings percentages and growing earnings dollar amounts. Declining earnings trends are particularly upsetting. Often earnings impacts are the result of changes in other financial performance areas. Studying the impacts on earnings of other financial and operating changes is an important part of analysis, particularly in financial forecasting and modeling, as discussed in Chapter 8.

Growth

The key growth questions are:

1. Is growth adequate given conditions in the firm's markets?
2. Are the firm's growth patterns balanced or at least within planned growth patterns?

The first question needs external economic and market growth data and cannot be answered from financial statement data. The second question compares growth rates across a variety of balance sheet and income statement accounts. Balance implies the same relative growth rates for accounts like assets, equity, sales, and profits. The argument can be made that nearly all financial problems arise from nonbalanced growth.

The basic definition for all growth ratios is:

$$\frac{\text{Year 2 balance - Year 1 balance}}{\text{Year 1 balance}} = \text{Growth rate percentage}$$

	Forecast 1999	Actual 1998	Actual 1997
Growth in assets	16.1%	13.4%	11.0%
Growth in equity	11.7	13.6	13.5
Growth in sales	16.1	17.8	
Growth in operating expenses . . .	16.9	14.7	
Growth in net income	4.2	16.4	

If net income growth lags behind asset growth, equity cannot be built quickly enough to support more rapid sales and asset growth.

Market Performance

The key market performance question is:

How do financial markets evaluate the financial condition of the firm?

Stock prices and debt instrument prices give an assessment by investors and analysts of the firm's financial risks and returns. Ratios commonly used are the price-earnings ratio and dividend yield.

Price-Earnings Ratio. The definition of the **price-earnings ratio** is:

$$\frac{\text{Average market price per share}}{\text{Earnings per share}} = \text{Price-earnings ratio}$$

	Forecast 1999	Actual 1998	Actual 1997
Stock price (average market price per share)	$17.25	$16.75	$15.00
Earnings per share	1.85	1.78	1.53
Price-earnings ratio	9.3:1	9.4:1	9.8:1

The price-earnings ratio (or multiple) is monitored intensely by investors, shareholders, and the firm's management itself. Generally, the higher the ratio, the greater the investors' expectation of future growth in earnings and dividends. The lower the ratio, the less trust investors have in future earnings and dividend growth.

Dividend Yield. Cash dividends paid relative to share market price is the **dividend yield** and is defined as:

$$\frac{\text{Cash dividends per share}}{\text{Average market price per share}} = \text{Dividend yield}$$

	Forecast 1999	Actual 1998	Actual 1997
Stock price (average market price per share)	$17.25	$16.75	$15.00
Dividends paid	$56	$48	$40
Average number of shares outstanding	80 mill.	80 mill.	80 mill.
Dividend yield	4.1%	3.6%	3.3%

Basically, the dividend yield is the cash payout on the share price. Firms with high dividend yields are attractive to investors who need immediate cash income.

*I*NTERRELATIONSHIPS OF RISKS AND RETURNS

As a firm becomes more risky in one area, it compensates with safety in another area. Aggressive risk taking must be offset by strong fall back positions and backup alternatives. Financial problems arise when this balance tilts too far.

Ethics in Financial Analysis

Ethics come into play in many financial reporting issues and are addressed by auditors and the chief financial officer. These are of concern to management accountants because the same issues occur when evaluating business segments and their managers. Concerns in ratio analysis include:

- Doing yearend "window dressing" to make our balance sheet look better than it normally appears to be. For example, using reserve cash balances to pay bills at yearend to increase the current ratio.
- Failing to record all payables at yearend or shipping merchandise and recording revenue when a sale may not have occurred.
- Defining ratios consistently from period to period and across firms.

- Using off-balance-sheet financing to distort the picture of the underlying financial strength of the firm.
- Valuing assets that will directly affect the equity position of the firm.

The same issues arise in divisional performance measurement, as discussed in Chapter 14. Internally, the misstatements are ethical issues, but externally the specter of legal violations, audit fraud, and legal liability becomes involved quickly.

Financial Leverage

Financial leverage uses borrowed funds to enhance the rate of return to equity owners. If only equity capital is used for long-term financing, equity owners get all profits. If owners can substitute borrowed funds, profits earned above the cost of the debt accrue to equity owners. The rate of return on equity should increase—perhaps dramatically. To illustrate, Common Company and Debt Company have identical operations. Condensed average balance sheets and operating results are:

	Common	*Debt*
Total assets	$1,000,000	$1,000,000
Liabilities and equities:		
Current liabilities	$ 200,000	$ 200,000
Bonds payable (8%).	0	400,000
Equity.	800,000	400,000
Total liabilities and equity.	$1,000,000	$1,000,000
Income before interest and taxes.	$ 125,000	$ 125,000
Interest on bonds payable	0	32,000
Income before taxes	$ 125,000	$ 93,000
Income taxes (40%).	50,000	37,200
Net income after taxes	$ 75,000	$ 55,800
Return on total assets	7.5%	5.6%
Return on equity.	9.4%	14.0%

Return on equity increases from using debt. Several observations can be made:

1. If the cost of debt is less than the return on the additional net investment, financial leverage will benefit the common equity owners.
2. If the cost of debt and the preferred dividend rate are similar, debt is less expensive because interest is deductible for tax purposes and dividends are not.
3. As the proportion of debt increases, lenders will tend to increase the debt interest rate because the risk of default is greater.

Again, too much of a good thing can turn bad. Financial leverage benefits end when interest on borrowed funds exceeds the returns on investments.

Earning-Power Model

Another extension of the ratio interrelationships and the leverage concept is the **earning-power model**, which combines return on sales, asset turnover, and capital multiplier ratios to yield return on equity. To earn a given return on equity, interrelationships among net income, sales, and asset and equity commitments can be analyzed. The basic format is:

$$\frac{\text{Net income}}{\text{Sales}} = \textbf{Return on sales}$$

$$\frac{\text{Net income}}{\text{Sales}} \times \frac{\text{Sales}}{\text{Average total assets}} = \textbf{Return on assets}$$

$$\frac{\text{Net income}}{\text{Sales}} \times \frac{\text{Sales}}{\text{Average total assets}} \times \frac{\text{Average total assets}}{\text{Average equity}} = \textbf{Return on equity}$$

$$\textbf{Return on sales} \times \textbf{Asset turnover} \times \textbf{Capital multiplier} = \textbf{Return on equity}$$

Using the 1999 forecast data for Amberg Lighting:

$$\frac{\$148,000}{\$2,848,000} \times \frac{\$2,848,000}{\$1,577,500} \times \frac{\$1,577,500}{\$831,000} = 5.2\% \times 180.5\% \times 189.8\% = 17.8\%$$

To improve ROE, the following changes could be made:

1. Increase ROS by reducing expenses while holding sales constant.
2. Increase sales relative to total assets while holding ROS constant.
3. Reduce total assets while holding sales, ROS, and capital multiplier constant.
4. Replace equity with debt to increase leverage while holding asset turnover and ROS constant.

Thus, improving any of the three ratios while holding the others constant will improve ROE. These ratios are compared to those of other successful firms and to industry averages to identify problems and relative strengths and

C O N T E M P O R A R Y   P R A C T I C E   1 7 . 2

Financial Ratios Can Foretell Hospital Closures

A study of open and closed hospitals shows that certain leverage, liquidity, capital adequacy, and cash-flow ratios can predict hospital closure up to two years in advance of a hospital's closure with an accuracy of nearly 75 percent. Timely detection of critical problems could prompt earlier or more aggressive development of financial, tactical, and strategic courses of action to improve a hospital's financial health.

Source: Lynn, M. L., and P. Wertheim, "Key Financial Ratios Can Foretell Hospital Closures," *Healthcare Financial Management*, November 1993, pp. 66-70.

weaknesses.   Leveraging net income, sales, total assets, and equity financing into high returns to owners is a major financial management task.

Strategic Profit Model

Another approach to evaluating and testing financial ratio relationships is a very traditional model, often called the Du Pont formula. A modified version, called the strategic profit model, is illustrated in Figures 17.3 and 17.4, pages 740 and 741. All components of ROA and ROE can be modeled. The model can:

1. Show earning-power ratios sensitivity from changes in account balances.
2. Identify financial structure and financial performance differences among firms and industries.
3. Test the impacts of proposed changes in operations, debt structure, and working capital policies and guidelines.
4. Help set long-range and near-term financial goals and targets.

Improved understanding has made this simple analytical framework popular in financial performance analysis for over 50 years.

Impact of the New Manufacturing Environment

While manufacturing and costing changes have had a dramatic impact on cost analysis and decision making, their impacts on financial performance analysis are less obvious but still present. The primary changes seen in firms at the edge of manufacturing excellence are:

- Much higher inventory turnovers as a result of just-in-time processing and the elimination of wasted time in all stages of production and distribution.
- Lower inventory investment that frees funds for other needed investments or debt reduction and strengthens both working capital and long-term financing positions.
- Higher investments in fixed assets due to the substitution of capital investments for labor.
- Shifts in expense and revenue patterns due to global sourcing, sales, and distribution. These are difficult to detect without more detailed analyses.
- Product pricing and costing changes as firms use value chain advantages of low-cost production, product quality, flexible manufacturing capabilities, and customer service to capitalize financially.

Differences in strategic approaches to sourcing, producing, and marketing can often be seen in comparative analysis of financial ratios. Major and subtle changes in financial results can be measured by astute observers. Trends can confirm these shifts and advantages.

International Implications

While financial performance analysis is international in scope, some differences do exist among countries and cultures. Among these are:

FIGURE 17.3 Strategic Profit Model—Return on Assets

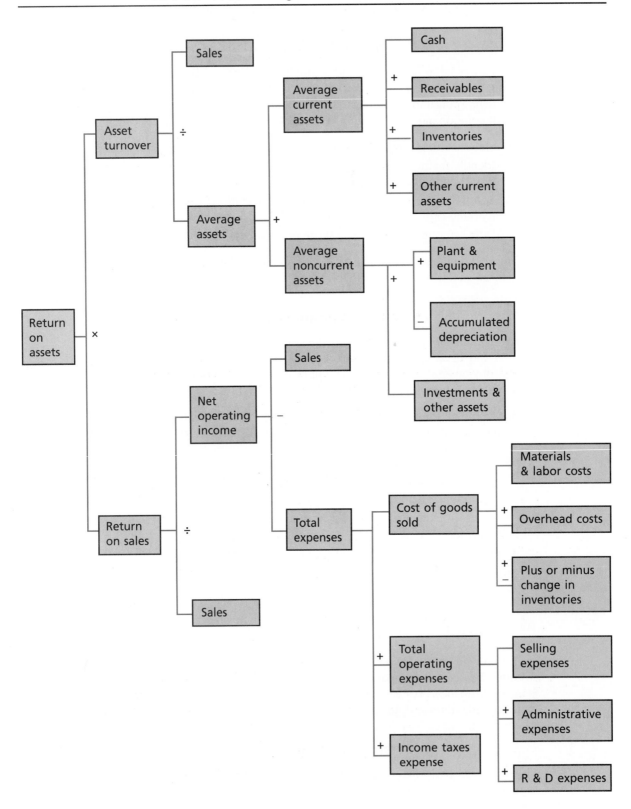

FIGURE 17.4 Strategic Profit Model—Return on Equity

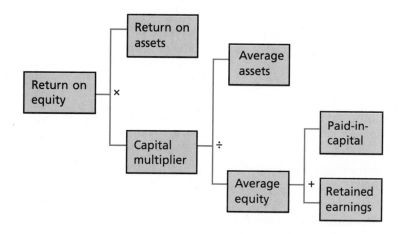

- Japanese managers tend to focus on sales growth, market share, and return on sales as opposed to return on equity.

- Managers in the United States tend to worry more about short-term profits and earnings per share than do most other managers.

- European companies tend to focus on safety of the creditor rather than on the returns of the common shareholder.

- In Germany, workers' councils are represented on boards of directors of companies. This gives a different thrust to financial reporting.

- Different accounting principles will influence the meaning of financial ratios. In Japan for example, undervalued land and intercompany investments will cause assets and, therefore, equity to be undervalued. Debt to equity ratios will be dramatically different than in the U. S.

For comparison purposes, these international differences must be recognized and incorporated into any analyses.

CAVEATS IN USING FINANCIAL PERFORMANCE ANALYSIS

As with any tool, the strengths and usefulness of performance analyses are tempered by limits and dangers of inappropriate application. Assumptions must always be tested; underlying data must have credibility; and care must be taken in generalizing from basic ratio findings. Among the caveats are:

- **No consistently valid rules of thumb exist.** Specific industries have different acceptable ranges for certain ratios. An individual firm's strengths and weaknesses cause ratios to be case specific.

■ **No one ratio can tell a story.**   Sets of ratios over a series of time periods are needed to paint a firm's financial picture. Knowing one number tells little about existing interrelationships.

■ **Industry averages are just that—averages.**   Strong firms and weak firms are averaged. Big and little firms often have different characteristics. A group of strong peer firms (similar size, industry, competitive environment, geography, etc.) provides a more powerful comparative base.

■ **Ratios must be defined uniformly and consistently.**   Using multifirm ratio data is dangerous unless common definitions and accounting are used.

■ **More ratios do not necessarily make a better analysis.**   A carefully selected set of ratios should be reported routinely with internal financial reports.

■ **Off-balance-sheet events and factors impact the interpretation of financial ratios.**   Nonfinancial links, contracts, or business events can influence a firm's financial condition with no obvious impacts on statement numbers.

■ **The goal of financial performance analysis is to diagnose the firm's financial health.**   Ratio analysis is not an exercise unto itself but should measure performance.

These caveats bring ratio analysis back to reality. Care must be taken to avoid pitfalls and yet to pull maximum understanding from the firm's financial data.

S UMMARY

Financial performance analysis should be a proactive tool—part of management's financial planning and control processes. Managers can also use ratios to capitalize on strengths and detect areas of needed improvement.

Financial performance analysis focuses on the financial risks and returns areas of liquidity, capital adequacy, asset quality, earnings, growth, and market performance. Key ratios in each area are defined and illustrated.

Interrelationships among various ratios and areas of risks and returns exist. Strengths in one area can offset a weakness in another area. Financial leverage as a concept that uses debt instead of equity to finance assets is illustrated. Earning-power ratios are composed of return on sales, asset turnover, and capital multiplier ratios. A strategic profit model is presented as a means of testing the sensitivity of relationships and the impacts of changes on rates of return.

Advantages of ratio analysis began the chapter. Caveats on the use of ratios ended the discussion.

P ROBLEM FOR REVIEW

Firestone Company has provided the following set of financial statements.

Average Balance Sheets as of December 31 (in Thousands)		
	1998	*1997*
Assets:		
Cash	$1,233	$ 686
Accounts receivable, net of allowance	635	584
Inventories	1,392	1,705
Total current assets	$3,260	$2,975
Plant and equipment, net of depreciation	2,085	1,895
Total assets	$5,345	$4,870
Liabilities and shareholders' equity:		
Accounts payable	$ 487	$ 612
Notes payable	650	650
Total current liabilities	$1,137	$1,262
Long-term notes payable	450	315
Total liabilities	$1,587	$1,577
Capital stock	$1,500	$1,500
Retained earnings	2,258	1,793
Total shareholders' equity	$3,758	$3,293
Total liabilities and shareholders' equity	$5,345	$4,870
Dividends declared and paid	$ 300	$ 200
Shares outstanding (in Thousands)	200	200

Income Statements for the Years Ended December 31 (in Thousands)		
	1998	*1997*
Net sales	$7,100	$6,850
Cost of goods sold	4,682	4,794
Gross margin	$2,418	$2,056
Operating expenses	1,047	1,020
Operating income	$1,371	$1,036
Interest expense	96	84
Income before income taxes	$1,275	$ 952
Income taxes expense (40%)	510	381
Net income	$ 765	$ 571

Required:

Compute the following ratios for 1997 and 1998. Comment.

(a) Return on assets

(b) Return on equity

(c) Gross margin percentage

(d) Debt to equity ratio

(e) Times interest earned

(f) Dividend payout percentage

(g) Days sales in receivables

(h) Inventory turnover

(i) Current ratio

(j) Quick ratio

Solution:

Ratios:

		1998	1997
(a)	Return on assets	14.3% ($765 ÷ $5,345)	11.7% ($571 ÷ $4,870)
(b)	Return on equity	20.4% ($765 ÷ $3,758)	17.3% ($571 ÷ $3,293)
(c)	Gross margin percentage	34.1% ($2,418 ÷ $7,100)	30.0% ($2,056 ÷ $6,850)
(d)	Debt to equity ratio	42.2% ($1,587 ÷ $3,758)	47.9% ($1,577 ÷ $3,293)
(e)	Times interest earned . . .	14.3 times ($1,371 ÷ $96)	12.3 times ($1,036 ÷ $84)
(f)	Dividend payout percentage	39.2% ($300 ÷ $765)	35.0% ($200 ÷ $571)
(g)	Days sales in receivables .	32 days [$635 ÷ ($7,100 ÷ 360)]	31 days [$584 ÷ ($6,850 ÷ 360)]
(h)	Inventory turnover	3.4 times ($4,682 ÷ $1,392)	2.8 times ($4,794 ÷ $1,705)
(i)	Current ratio	2.9:1 ($3,260 ÷ $1,137)	2.4:1 ($2,975 ÷ $1,262)
(j)	Quick ratio	1.6:1 ($1,868 ÷ $1,137)	1.0:1 ($1,270 ÷ $1,262)

The earnings and rates of returns have all improved in 1998. Equity has grown from earnings in spite of the higher dividend payments. Debt is a small portion of the long-term financing, and interest payments have greater protection. Inventory turnover has improved greatly.   The firm has more liquidity protection since both the current and quick ratios have improved. (This assumes that they are not getting too high.) Overall, 1998 appears to have strengthened the firm's financial position.

*T*ERMINOLOGY REVIEW

SUGGESTED READINGS

Brief, R. P., and R. A. Lawson, "The Role of Accounting Rate of Return in Financial Statement Analysis," *Accounting Review*, April 1992, pp. 411-426.

Chen K. H., "A Comparison of Financial Ratios: Historical Cost Versus Price-Level Adjusted Disclosures," *Advances in Accounting*, Vol. 3, 1986, pp. 233-254.

Hopwood, W. S., and T. F. Schaefer, "Incremental Information Content of Earnings and Nonearnings Based Financial Ratios," *Contemporary Accounting Research*, Vol. 5, No. 1, pp. 318-342.

Mielke, D. E., and D. E. Giacomino, "Ratio Analysis Using the New Statement of Cash Flows," *Corporate Accounting*, Vol. 6, No. 1, pp. 10-17.

Thomas, J. K., "Unusual Patterns in Reported Earnings," *Accounting Review*, October 1989, pp. 773-787.

Zavgren, C., "The Prediction of Corporate Failure: The State of the Art," *Journal of Accounting Literature*, Vol. 2, 1983, pp. 1-38.

QUESTIONS FOR REVIEW AND DISCUSSION

1. Is the usefulness of financial ratios restricted to analysis of historical financial statements? Explain.

2. What is asset turnover? What does a very low ratio imply? What is the danger of a very high ratio?

3. What are the risks and returns areas in financial performance analysis? How does a strong area offset a weak area? Give two examples of these tradeoffs.

4. What is the disadvantage of having more liquid assets than are needed? What is the disadvantage of having too few liquid assets?

5. What are the two conflicting questions used to assess capital adequacy? How is this conflict resolved?

6. What is the key question in assessing liquidity? What ratios are used to help answer the question? What additional off-balance-sheet data might be useful?

7. What are the primary concerns in assessing asset quality? What ratios are used to answer the concerns? What do too high and too low asset quality ratios mean?

8. What is the key question regarding earnings and profitability? Explain how short-term and long-term investor viewpoints may be in conflict.

9. What are the concerns about growth? Are these easily answered from financial statement data? Explain.

10. Why should management be concerned about how external financial markets assess the firm's financial position?

11. What is financial leverage? Explain how it works.

12. Explain the earning-power ratios. What actions can management take to increase return on equity?

13. List five caveats about financial statement analysis that limit its usefulness.

14. In general, what is being measured by the current ratio and by the quick ratio? What is the difference between the two ratios?

15. Describe the strategic profit model's structure. How can it be used to help set and achieve financial goals?

16. If return on assets is used to evaluate a manager of an operating segment, what adjustments should be made to net income and to assets? Comment.

17. What may be indicated by:

(a) A sharp increase in the current ratio?

(b) A return on shareholders' equity that is nearly equal to return on assets?

(c) A large increase in the dividend payout percentage?

(d) A drop in inventory turnover and an increase in days sales in inventory?

(e) A decline over several years of the gross margin percentage?

(f) An increase in the earnings per share?

(g) A decline in the price-earnings ratio?

E XERCISES

17-1. Rate of Return.   Three Rivers Stores earned $1,500,000 on net sales of $50,000,000 in 1996. Beginning total assets were $10,000,000; and ending total assets were $12,000,000.

Required:
1. Compute the return on sales. How could this ratio be improved?
2. Compute the return on assets. How could this ratio be improved?
3. Compute the asset turnover. How could this ratio be improved?

17-2. Ratio Patterns.   Assets are growing at an annual rate of 10 percent, sales by 15 percent, net profits by 8 percent, and equity by 6 percent.

Required:
What financial problems will eventually appear for this company if these trends continue?

17-3. Current Asset Use.   Analyze the following situations:

(a) If net credit sales for the year is $15,000,000 and average accounts receivable is $3,000,000, how many days of sales are in accounts receivable on the average? What is the receivables turnover?

(b) If the cost of goods sold is $7,200,000 and average inventory of merchandise is $600,000, how many days of sales are in inventory on the average? What is the inventory turnover?

(c) If accounts receivable should be collected in 40 days and inventory turns over six times per year, how long is the operating cycle?

17-4. Turnovers.   The following data are taken from Woolly Company's accounts:

Sales in 1998	$357,000
Cost of goods sold in 1998	216,000
Accounts receivable, 1/1/98	220,000
Accounts receivable, 12/31/98	242,000
Inventory, 1/1/98	130,000
Inventory, 12/31/98	70,000

Required:

1. Find the inventory turnover and the days sales in inventory.

2. Find the accounts receivable turnover and the days sales in receivables.

3. If industry averages for the turnover ratios are 3.0 for both inventory and accounts receivable, how is Woolly doing? Suggest possible causes.

17-5. Capital Ratios. The following data are available from the McCarthy Shipping Company. No shares were issued in 1998.

Net sales for 1998	$ 6,360,000
Net income for 1998	398,000
Cash dividends—preferred	36,000
Cash dividends—common	120,000
Average market price per common share	150
Average balance amounts:	
Common stock—par value, $100	1,500,000
Paid-in-capital in excess of par—common	100,000
Preferred stock—par value, $100, 6%	600,000
Retained earnings	500,000

Required:

Five ratios with their 1997 values in parentheses appear in the following list. Calculate the 1998 values and comment on the changes:

(a) Earnings per share of common stock ($17.60).

(b) Dividend yield per share of common stock (5.0 percent).

(c) Price-earnings ratio for common stock (13.2).

(d) Return on total equity (12.0 percent).

(e) Return on common equity (13.9 percent).

17-6. Statements From Incomplete Data. George Bernthal of Bernthal Company found these pieces of his average balance sheet and key ratio report in his gerbil cage:

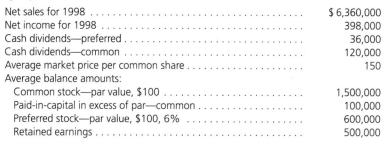

Cash	$?	Gross margin percentage . . .	25%
Accounts receivable . .	?	Debt to equity ratio	.25:1
Inventory	80	Current ratio	3:1
Fixed assets (net)	?	Inventory turnover	15 times
Current liabilities	100	Days sales in receivables	15 days
Common stock	100	(based on 360 days)	
Retained earnings	?		

Required:

Add as much to his balance sheet as possible from the data provided.

17-7. The Good News and Bad News. A change in any financial ratio can contain good news and bad news. Financial results of 1997 and 1998 have caused the following three ratio values to change:

Ratio	*1998*	*1997*
Current ratio	3:1	4:1
Inventory turnover	6	5
Dividend payout	30%	40%

Required:

1. For each ratio, what might be the good news; and what might be the bad news?

2. Create a scenario for the combined changes in the three ratios.

17-8. Common-Size Statements. Dan Schulte, president of Health Products Company, says that large dollar amounts on financial statements are confusing. However, he finds that percentage relationships are helpful. For example, he expects cost of goods sold to be 60 percent of net sales, operating expenses to be 20 percent, income taxes to be 7 percent, and net income to be about 10 percent. Operating results in summary form for 1997 and 1998 are as follows:

	1997	1998
Net sales	$15,140,000	$18,534,000
Cost of goods sold	9,175,000	11,523,000
Gross profit	$ 5,965,000	$ 7,011,000
Operating expenses	3,421,000	3,906,000
Operating income	$ 2,544,000	$ 3,105,000
Income taxes	1,036,000	1,233,000
Net income	$ 1,508,000	$ 1,872,000

Required:

1. Prepare percentage composition statements for both years.

2. Prepare a base-year comparison using 1997 as the base year.

3. What trends exist? Were the president's expectations realized? Should he worry about certain specific trends?

17-9. Liquidity and Capital Adequacy Ratios. X Business and Y Business have the following ratios:

	X Business	Y Business
Current ratio	4.5:1	1.5:1
Debt to equity ratio	0.2:1	1.0:1
Quick ratio	2.5:1	0.8:1
Times interest earned	10 times	3 times

Required:

What are the financial strengths of X Business and of Y Business?

17-10. Liquidity Impacts. A company's current and quick ratios have moved as follows:

	1996	1997	1998	1999
Current ratio	2.0:1	2.5:1	3.0:1	4.0:1
Quick ratio	1.5:1	1.0:1	0.8:1	0.6:1

Required:

Comment on the validity of the following statements:

(a) The stronger current ratio in 1999 reflects improved profitability.

(b) A large obsolete inventory may be a serious problem.

(c) The quick ratio change reflects a desire to pay bills on time.

(d) The current ratio in 1999 is clearly too high.

(e) The company is more liquid in 1999 than in 1996.

17-11. Equity and Market Ratios. At December 31, 1998, Richmond Company had 100,000 shares of £10 par value stock issued and outstanding. Shares outstanding during 1998 did not change. Total shareholders' equity at December 31, 1998, was £2,800,000. Net income for the year ended December 31, 1998, was £400,000. During 1998, Richmond paid £3 per share in dividends. The quoted market price of Richmond's stock on a London stock exchange averaged £32 during 1998.

Required:

1. What is the price-earnings ratio at the end of 1998?

2. What is the dividend yield at the end of 1998?

1-2-3

17-12. Creating Financial Statements From Ratios. Assume that net income was $6,000. No other information is known, except the following:

Return on equity	10%	Return on sales	4%
Gross margin percentage	60%	Income tax rate	40%
Current ratio	3:1	Return on assets	5%
Inventory turnover	4	Days sales in receivables	90
Long-term debt to equity	2:3		

Required:

Using the preceding ratios, construct an income statement and a balance sheet with as much detail as possible.

17-13. Impacts on Risks and Returns Areas. Business events impact each of these financial performance areas:

1. Liquidity   **4.** Growth

2. Capital adequacy   **5.** Earnings

3. Asset quality

Required:

Indicate the major impacts that the following business events have on the firm's financial performance categories. Will these impacts strengthen (S), weaken (W), or not change (NC) each area? List each event as a row and each performance category as a column. Make a brief note in each cell to explain your answer.

(a) Credit terms to customers lengthened from 30 to 60 days.

(b) Dividend declared and paid.

(c) Long-term debt issued for cash.

(d) Shares issued in trade for production equipment.

 17-14. Logical Relationships. In each of the following situations, compute the information requested:

1. What is the return on sales if the asset turnover is 2.6 and 13 percent is earned on assets?

2. Sales for the year were $28,000,000, and the average asset investment was $8,000,000. Determine the asset turnover.

3. Assets are turned over 0.8 times in earning 15 percent on the sales dollar. What is the return on assets?

4. With an asset turnover of 2.5, what must be the return on sales if the return on assets is 15 percent?

5. If shareholders' equity is equal to 60 percent of total liabilities and shareholders' equity, what is the rate of return on shareholders' equity if 9 percent is earned on total assets invested?

6. The return on assets was 16 percent, and 8 percent was earned on net sales. What was the asset turnover?

7. The return on assets has been computed at 14 percent. The net income was $840,000, and the asset turnover was 2. Determine the amount of sales and the return on sales.

8. If the total cost of operations, excluding income tax, amounts to $2,600,000, compute sales if net income is 5 percent of sales. The income tax has been computed at $250,000.

9. The return on sales has remained at 6 percent for the past two years. The asset turnover in the first year was 2.4 and declined to 1.8 in the second year. Compute the return on assets for each of the two years.

10. Net sales for the year were $9,600,000. Assets turned over 1.2 times during the year. Cost of goods sold and operating expenses, including income tax, amounted to $8,880,000. Compute the return on net sales and on total assets.

 17-15. Financial Leverage Effects. Deep River Brands, a Swiss company, earned net income before interest and taxes of SFr1,500,000 on sales of SFr30,000,000 and an average asset investment of SFr20,000,000. Total debt averaged SFr5,000,000 at 8 percent interest.

Valley Brands, a French competitor, also reported net income before interest and taxes of Fr1,500,000 on sales of Fr30,000,000 and an average asset investment of Fr20,000,000. However, total debt averaged Fr15,000,000 at 8 percent interest. Taxes are 40 percent for both firms.

Required:

1. Compute the return on equity for Deep River Brands.
2. Compute the return on equity for Valley Brands.
3. Comment on the differences in return on equity between the two firms.

17-16. Market Performance Ratios. Last year, Rapid Data Company reported a net income of $4,500,000 and paid a dividend of $0.90 per share on 2,000,000 shares of common stock outstanding. The market value of each share of stock averaged $45.

Required:

1. Compute the earnings per share, price-earnings ratio, dividend payout percentage, and dividend yield.
2. Comment on possible reasons that the market price changed (a) from $38 the previous year to $45 last year or (b) from $50 the previous year to $45 last year.

17-17. Growth in Working Capital. Wilhelm Company has been in operation for 20 years. Growth has been rapid in the past but is leveling off. The sales manager, who has been with the firm for 17 years, persuaded the president that the firm should carry larger inventory and grant more liberal credit terms to increase sales. The new controller believes that larger inventories and receivables are too expensive.

Required:

Prepare a brief statement indicating how you interpret the sales manager's arguments versus the controller's views. Include any added information you need.

17-18. Effects of Improved Inventory Turnover. In 1997, Achram Company earned a net income of $270,000 on an average asset investment of $3,300,000. The controller noted, however, that the inventory turnover of six represented 60 days of sales. Average inventory was $900,000 and thought to be too high. By eliminating obsolete inventory and planning target inventory levels, inventory was reduced to $600,000. Before the inventory reduction, current assets averaged $1,500,000; and current liabilities averaged $600,000. Assume that accounts payable will decrease by half of the inventory reduction and borrowings will decline by an amount equal to the other half. After the inventory reduction, 1998 operations will yield a $276,000 net income, the same as in 1997 except for interest expenses which are expected to decline by $6,000 after taxes.

Required:

1. Find the inventory turnover before and after the inventory reduction.
2. Find the current ratio before and after the inventory reduction.
3. What is the expected return on assets before and after the inventory investment cutback?

17-19. Inventory Turnovers. New management at Bosanac Supplies noted that materials inventory turned over every 18 days. Materials used during the year cost $18,000,000. The work in process inventory turnover was 24. Production costs for the year were $48,000,000.

Steps were taken to obtain more frequent deliveries from suppliers so that operations could be conducted efficiently with only a 12-day supply of inventory. In addition, bottlenecks in production were eliminated, with the result being that the production costs will be 30 times the work in process inventory.

Required:

1. What was the average materials inventory investment with a turnover every 18 days? Every 12 days?
2. What was the average work in process inventory investment with a turnover of 24? Of 30?
3. Explain why reducing inventory levels can improve the return on assets.

17-20. Current Asset Turnovers. Tech Products Company is a wholesaler and has very few noncurrent assets. It has been growing rapidly. Operating net income increased from $130,000 in 1997 to $288,000 in 1998. Cost of goods sold and operating expenses amounted to $1,300,000 in 1997 and $4,800,000 in 1998. The average investment in current assets was $650,000 in 1997 and $1,600,000 in 1998. The company had some difficulties in meeting delivery schedules in 1998 and in making payments to creditors. Ignore taxes.

Required:

1. Compute the return on current assets each year.
2. Compute the current asset turnover each year, using sales as the numerator.
3. Explain why the company may be having trouble in meeting delivery schedules and in making payments to creditors.

17-21. Accounts Receivable Turnovers. Dundee Health Services has been having difficulty paying current obligations on time and has obtained additional short-term credit from its bank. Collections on accounts receivable from health insurers have been slower than usual. Ordinarily, accounts receivable are turned over in 60 days. With the longer collection periods, the company is chronically short of cash to pay creditors promptly. Data with respect to a sales and receivables are:

	1998	1997	1996
Cash patient revenues	$12,000,000	$15,600,000	$21,000,000
Third-party insured patient revenues	97,600,000	83,200,000	67,600,000
Average accounts receivable	28,100,000	15,400,000	8,000,000

Required:

1. Compute the accounts receivable turnover for each of the three years.
2. Compute the number of days sales in receivables.
3. From the information given, what are possible impacts on the financial condition of the center?

17-22. International Segments. Amity International has three international divisions: electrical wiring in Germany, flexible conduits in Korea, and fiberglass control boxes in Sweden. Each of these lines is manufactured in a separate division. Data pertaining to operations for last year are as follows:

Divisions	Exchange Rates	Division Net Income	Average Assets
Electrical wiring	DM1.6 per $	DM192,000	DM3,840,000
Flexible conduits	W800 per $	W696,000,000	W4,640,000,000
Fiberglass control boxes	SKr8 per $	SKr816,000	SKr6,800,000

The average assets given are the assets directly identifiable with the divisions. In addition, corporate assets averaged $1,080,000 and are not directly identifiable with any division. For analysis purposes, corporate assets have been allocated evenly to all divisions. Expenses (after income taxes) that are common to the total operation are $250,000 and are not deducted in computing the division net income shown above. Historically, these expenses are allocated on a 40, 40, and 20 percent basis, respectively.

Required:

1. Compute the direct return on assets for each division and rank the divisions.
2. Allocate the common assets and expenses. Compute return on assets and rank the divisions.

3. Comment on:

(a) The role of common assets and expenses in the ROA analysis.

(b) Whether the analysis should be done in dollars.

17-23. Ethics and Ratio Manipulation.   Assume that Woodhouse Enterprises has 20 divisions reporting to a corporate office. A number of services such as data processing, cash management, personnel, and legal are performed at the corporate office. Most accounting is done at the division level. Corporate evaluates the earning-power ratios to rank divisions. The corporate capital multipler is used by each division. Only traceable assets are assigned to the division. Corporate expenses are not allocated to the divisions.

Required:

Assume that Division 15 is an average performing division. Using the earning-power ratios, how might the division manager and division controller work to make the division "look good" on paper? On a short-term basis? On a long-term basis?

P ROBLEMS

17-24. Rate of Return Relationships.   Red Ball Delivery Service reported a net income of $140,000 on net sales of $2,800,000 in 1997. Average investment in assets was $1,400,000. The president of the company plans to reduce the asset investment next year, observing that the company is holding some unproductive assets. Budget plans for 1998 show a net income of $150,000 earned on net sales of $3,000,000. The average investment in assets is to be $1,200,000.

Required:

1. Compute the return on sales, the asset turnover, and the return on assets for 1997.

2. Compute the return on sales, the asset turnover, and the return on assets from the 1998 budget. Comment on the impact of the asset reduction.

17-25. Relationships.   Steinhour Company's 1998 condensed income statement and 1997 and 1998 partial balance sheets are as follows:

Sales		$ 98,000
Expenses:		
Cost of goods sold	$ 56,000	
Interest	2,900	
Other operating expenses	26,000	84,900
Net income		$ 13,100

	12/31/1998	12/31/1997
Current assets:		
Cash	$ 1,200	$ 800
Accounts receivable	15,000	13,000
Inventory.	23,500	18,000
Other current assets	1,400	1,600
Total current assets	$ 41,100	$ 33,400
Current liabilities:		
Accounts payable	$ 8,000	$ 7,500
Current portion of long-term debt	2,000	2,100
Total current liabilities	$ 10,000	$ 9,600

Required:

1. Examine Steinhour's liquidity position for 1998. Assume that high-performing firms in this industry have a current ratio of 2.5:1 and a quick ratio of 1:1. Comment.

2. If the industry average for return on sales is 15 percent, for gross margin is 60 percent, and for times interest earned is 10, comment on Steinhour's performance.

17-26. Financial Ratios.   The following financial statements are from Rainey Company:

	12/31/1998	12/31/1997
Cash	$ 14,000	$ 16,000
Accounts receivable (net)	22,000	28,000
Inventories	65,000	55,000
Fixed assets (net)	85,000	79,000
Total assets	$186,000	$178,000
Accounts payable	$ 30,000	$ 15,000
Bonds payable	60,000	75,000
Common stock (par value $10)	60,000	60,000
Retained earnings	36,000	28,000
Total liabilities and equity	$186,000	$178,000

	1998
Sales	$ 360,000
Less:	
Cost of goods sold	240,000
Operating expenses	100,000 (Includes $20,000 of depreciation expense)
Income taxes	8,000
Income after taxes	$ 12,000

Required:
Find the following ratios:

(a)   Inventory turnover for 1998.

(b)   The average market price of Rainey stock, if the price-earnings ratio is 8.

(c)   The earning power ratios for 1998.

(d)   The current ratio by the end of 1998.

(e)   Cash flow per share from operations in 1998.

(f)   Gross margin percentage for 1998.

17-27. Rate of Return on Shareholders' Investment.   Secure Products Company reported net income of $4,200,000 on net sales of $70,000,000 in 1998. Selected balance sheet data for 1998 follow:

Average assets	$ 50,000,000
Average liabilities	8,000,000
Average shareholders' equity	42,000,000

Chance Enterprises reported net income of $6,000,000 on net sales of $100,000,000 in 1998. Selected balance sheet data follow for 1998:

Average assets	$ 50,000,000
Average liabilities	26,000,000
Average shareholders' equity	24,000,000

Required:

1. Compare the two companies by computing the following percentages and ratios:

(a) Return on sales.
(b) Return on assets.
(c) Asset turnover.
(d) Return on shareholders' equity.

2. Identify the company that earns a better return for shareholders. Explain the factors that enhance shareholders' rate of return.
3. Which company has more risk? Why?

17-28. Percentage Composition Statements. Park Medical Services had a good year in 1998, but its earnings fell slightly from 1997. Darrell Washington, a member of Park's board of directors, thinks that a revised presentation of income statement data would show basic relationships. Income statements for 1997 and 1998 are:

	1998	1997
Revenue	$91,000,000	$85,000,000
Operating costs:		
Materials and supplies	$ 5,920,000	$ 5,500,000
Wages and salaries	40,200,000	36,500,000
Rent	725,000	725,000
Taxes and insurance	4,200,000	3,400,000
Heat and light	980,000	850,000
Advertising	1,480,000	1,275,000
Other operating costs	13,880,000	12,700,000
Interest expense	7,250,000	7,350,000
Income taxes	6,250,000	6,300,000
Total expenses	$80,885,000	$74,600,000
Net income	$10,115,000	$10,400,000

Required:

1. Prepare percentage composition (common-sized) income statements for 1997 and 1998.
2. Comment on expense trends. What items might the board want to investigate further? What was the change in the return on revenue?
3. Would a base-year comparison show similar relationships? Why or why not?

17-29. Industry Averages. Jimmie Gilbert has recently compared his company's financial ratios to a set of average ratios for his industry that he obtained from the National Association of Financial Ratio Analysts (NAFRA). He has lined up his data, two local competitors' data, and NAFRA data as follows:

	Gilbert	Competitor 1	Competitor 2	NAFRA
Receivables turnover	6.3	4.9	5.6	5.8
Inventory turnover	4.2	2.6	3.1	3.1
Asset turnover	2.2	1.3	1.5	1.6
Gross margin percentage	37.0	40.6	40.3	39.6
Return on sales	0.3	7.2	4.9	9.2
Return on equity	12.2	11.0	10.6	17.1
Current ratio	1.6	2.9	2.1	1.9

Required:

1. Comment on the relative strengths and weaknesses of Gilbert as compared to the two competitors and to the NAFRA data.
2. Using only this data, what might explain Gilbert's low return on sales?
3. Why might the three businesses in this local area have such a low return on sales when compared to the NAFRA data?

17-30. Benefits of Financial Leverage. A majority shareholder of Okemos Products has forced the company to hold debt to a minimum. Net income each year has been approximately $7,200,000. A summary balance sheet for a typical year is:

Current assets	$ 80,000,000
Plant and equipment (net)	40,000,000
Total assets	$120,000,000
Current liabilities	$ 30,000,000
Shareholders' equity	90,000,000
Total liabilities and shareholders' equity	$120,000,000

A younger member of the board, Carla Freed, is irritated with such a cautious policy. "We would be better off to liquidate and invest in government securities," she protests. She states that with new product lines and an aggressive sales stance, net income could easily grow to $15,000,000 a year. She admits that $30,000,000 in additional assets would be needed and states, "The additional assets should be financed by long-term notes." Other balance sheet relationships would remain unchanged.

Required:
1. Compute the typical rate of return on assets and shareholders' equity.
2. Compute the revised rate of return on assets and shareholders' equity by following the younger member's proposal.
3. Comment on the two strategies. What will be the primary arguments on both sides at the board meeting? Which do you favor?

17-31. Rates of Return by Segments, Manager Behavior, and Ethics.   The president of Metro Products Company is reviewing 1998 financial data and is concerned that one operating division is not doing as well as the others. The company has three separate divisions. Managers are rewarded according to divisional ROA. Financial data from 1998 are as follows:

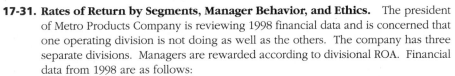

	Product Divisions		
	1	*2*	*3*
Net sales	$ 1,700,000	$ 2,000,000	$1,800,000
Cost of goods sold	$ 780,000	$ 940,000	$ 720,000
Operating expenses	590,000	860,000	810,000
Total expenses	$ 1,370,000	$ 1,800,000	$1,530,000
Net income	$ 330,000	$ 200,000	$ 270,000
Direct asset investment	$ 1,600,000	$ 2,000,000	$1,080,000
Return on assets	21%	10%	25%

Closer examination reveals that certain operating expenses are common to the total operation and have been allocated to the divisions. Also, included in direct assets are amounts pertaining to the total operation but not identifiable with any particular division. The amounts allocated to divisions are as follows:

Divisions	Allocated Expenses	Allocated Assets
1	$160,000	$200,000
2	350,000	500,000
3	140,000	100,000

Required:
1. From the information given, recompute the ROA for each division.
2. What type of behavior is the company trying to encourage by using divisional ROA to evaluate managers?
3. What negative or unethical behavior might result from this system? Why?

17-32. Rates of Return and Liquidity. Pam Ferrerio, vice-president of finance of Pacific Trade Company, is concerned that the company is growing too rapidly and is unable to support further growth by debt financing.

"We are enjoying an embarrassment of riches," she states. "Each month we must incur more costs to serve our ever-increasing sales. At the same time, we are increasing debt and must face the fact that we should sell more capital stock." Financial data (stated in thousands) for several years are:

	1999	1998	1997	1996
Current assets	$1,030	$ 870	$ 720	$ 580
Plant assets (net of depreciation)	3,150	1,770	860	770
Total assets	$4,180	$2,640	$1,580	$1,350
Current liabilities	$ 889	$ 550	$ 230	$ 210
Long-term notes payable	1,000	450	50	0
Shareholders' equity	2,291	1,640	1,300	1,140
Total liabilities and equities	$4,180	$2,640	$1,580	$1,350
Net sales	$9,870	$4,750	$3,240	
Cost of goods sold	$7,930	$3,640	$2,380	
Operating expenses	930	490	335	
Interest expense	100	45	5	
Total expenses	$8,960	$4,175	$2,720	
Income before income taxes	$ 910	$ 575	$ 520	
Income taxes	364	230	208	
Net income	$ 546	$ 345	$ 312	

Additional data:

Average outstanding shares	500	500	500	500
Depreciation expense	$ 220	$ 140	$ 60	
Current portion of long-term debt .	400	300	50	$ 0

Required:

1. Calculate the earning-power ratios for each year. What is happening?

2. For each year, examine the liquidity and capital adequacy positions. Comment on your findings.

3. Do you agree with the vice-president of finance? Why or why not?

17-33. Inventory and Accounts Receivable Turnovers. The president of Oberlin Stores, Charles Gaa, notes that collection of accounts receivable should be improved. He proposes that inducements be given to customers to pay promptly. This, he argues, will increase costs somewhat; but, in the final analysis, the rate of return should increase. Also, he believes that the company is holding a larger inventory than necessary and can improve the rate of return by inventory reduction.

Financial data for last year are summarized as follows along with a budget for next year as prepared by the controller:

	Last Year	Budget Year
Net sales	$4,200,000	$6,000,000
Cost of goods sold	$3,000,000	$4,500,000
Operating expenses	500,000	650,000
Total	$3,500,000	$5,150,000
Income before income taxes	$ 700,000	$ 850,000
Income taxes	300,000	380,000
Net income	$ 400,000	$ 470,000

	Average Balances	
Current assets:		
Cash	$ 500,000	$ 650,000
Accounts receivable	700,000	600,000
Inventory	600,000	450,000
Total current assets	$ 1,800,000	$ 1,700,000
Plant assets (net)	1,400,000	1,300,000
Total assets	$ 3,200,000	$ 3,000,000

Required:

1. Find the following relationships for last year and the budget year:

    (a) Return on sales and return on assets.

    (b) Accounts receivable turnover and inventory turnover.

2. What impacts could you imply resulted from the changes?

17-34. Measures of Liquidity. Denny Fink, a member of the board of directors of Egerdal Products, states that the company is becoming overextended in attempting to support a larger operation with insufficient working capital. Vera Amick, president of the company, states that results speak for themselves. Sales volume has increased, profits have increased, and return on shareholders' equity has increased. Financial data for the past three years are summarized as follows:

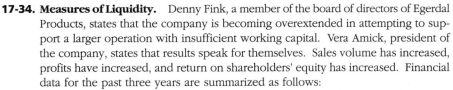

	1998	1997	1996
Net sales	$ 4,000,000	$ 2,000,000	$ 1,200,000
Less:			
Cost of goods sold	3,400,000	1,600,000	900,000
Operating expenses	180,000	150,000	140,000
Depreciation expense	50,000	40,000	30,000
Interest expense	80,000	30,000	0
Income taxes	120,000	70,000	60,000
Net income	$ 170,000	$ 110,000	$ 70,000

	Average Balances		
	1998	1997	1996
Current assets	$ 1,930,000	$ 1,780,000	$ 1,680,000
Current liabilities	1,250,000	970,000	760,000
Long-term debt	800,000	300,000	0
Common stock ($10 par)	600,000	500,000	500,000
Retained earnings	430,000	290,000	210,000

Required:

1. Determine these ratios for each year:

    (a) Return on sales, return on assets, and return on shareholders' equity.

    (b) Current ratio, cash flow from operations per share, and earnings per share.

    (c) Percentage of debt to equity and the common equity multiplier.

2. Do you share Denny Fink's concern? Or is Vera Amick's statement of assurance on target? Comment on the trends revealed by your analysis.

CASE 17A—GALLAGHER, GRUNEWALD, AND GUSLITS

Ben Guslits, vice-president of sales, has recommended adding a new product line. A market study and cost analyses show that the new line should yield the following annual results:

Net sales	$ 2,800,000
Cost of sales	$ 1,600,000
Operating expenses	200,000
Total expenses	$ 1,800,000
Income before income taxes	$ 1,000,000
Income taxes (40%)	400,000
Net income	$ 600,000

Depreciation of $150,000 is included in total expenses. Cost of sales and operating expenses include only direct costs of the new line.

Financial data for last year, considered to be a typical year, are:

Net sales	$12,000,000
Cost of sales	$ 7,500,000
Operating expenses	1,800,000
Total expenses	$ 9,300,000*
Operating income	$ 2,700,000
Interest expense	100,000
Income before income taxes	$ 2,600,000
Income taxes (40%)	1,040,000
Net income	$ 1,560,000
Total assets	$12,000,000
Current liabilities	$ 3,000,000
Long-term debt	1,000,000
Shareholders' equity	8,000,000
Total liabilities and equities	$12,000,000

* Depreciation expense included totals $400,000 for the firm.

The investment in additional equipment for the production and sale of the new product line has been estimated at $3,000,000. "The new product line will yield a 20 percent return on assets," Guslits states.

Steve Grunewald, the vice-president of production, interrupts. "Are you talking about a cash-flow return, Ben?" he asks. "No," Guslits answers. "When depreciation is added back, the cash-flow return will be even greater."

The vice-president of finance, Jude Gallagher, asks, "How do you think we should finance the investment?"

"We should be able to issue long-term notes," Guslits responds. "Our debt at the present time is modest. And, with debt financing, we gain the advantage of leverage."

"In your estimate, Ben, you forgot to include any interest cost. It will cost us $150,000 after income taxes to finance $3,000,000," Gallagher replies.

Required:
1. What impacts will the new product line have on profit measures and cash flows?
2. Examine and comment on Guslits' strategy to finance the investment. Is it likely that shareholders will be impressed with the investment? Why?
3. In your opinion, is the investment attractive? Explain your answer.

CASE 17B—LIZ WEBER'S ANALYSIS

Liz Weber has been doing research on the electronic components manufacturing industry. She has developed the following financial data:

	Percentage of Total Assets				
	1995	1996	1997	1998	1999
Cash and equivalents	6.6	6.9	7.7	7.9	8.9
Trade receivables	30.0	29.6	28.2	29.0	27.4
Inventory..................	31.7	32.9	32.6	27.8	26.4
All other current assets	2.5	1.9	1.2	2.3	2.2
Total current assets	70.8	71.3	69.7	67.0	64.9
All noncurrent assets	29.2	28.7	30.3	33.0	35.1
Total assets	100.0	100.0	100.0	100.0	100.0
Notes payable	11.9	12.7	11.6	12.3	12.4
Trade payables	15.3	14.2	13.3	14.0	13.6
All other current liabilities	13.0	13.4	12.4	12.3	11.9
Total current liabilities	40.2	40.3	37.3	38.6	37.9
Long-term debt.............	17.8	17.3	17.5	17.0	18.0
Equity	42.0	42.4	45.2	44.4	44.1
Total liabilities and equity ...	100.0	100.0	100.0	100.0	100.0

	Percentage of Net Sales				
	1995	1996	1997	1998	1999
Net sales	100.0	100.0	100.0	100.0	100.0
Less:					
Cost of goods sold	66.9	65.1	65.5	65.9	66.6
Operating expenses	25.8	26.7	26.0	26.7	27.4
Interest expense	1.3	1.7	1.7	1.6	1.8
All other net expenses (income)	.0	(1.3)	(.3)	(.2)	(.1)
Income taxes.............	1.8	2.5	2.3	1.9	1.4
Profit after taxes	4.2	5.3	4.8	4.1	2.9

	Ratio or Percentage Values				
	1995	1996	1997	1998	1999
Current ratio	1.8	1.8	1.9	1.9	1.8
Receivables turnover	6.3	6.1	6.6	6.4	6.8
Inventory turnover...........	4.0	3.9	3.6	4.0	4.6
Times interest earned	5.6	5.2	5.2	3.7	3.1
Debt to equity ratio	1.4	1.3	1.2	1.2	1.3
Return on equity	20.1	22.1	20.9	16.5	14.3
Return on assets	8.5	8.9	8.4	6.9	6.1
Asset turnover..............	1.8	1.8	1.8	1.8	1.8
Growth in net sales	5.3	6.2	7.3	5.1	6.9
Growth in assets	3.2	4.2	5.7	7.7	7.3
Growth in profits............	5.7	8.3	6.2	5.1	3.2

Because nearly 300 firms' data are summarized in the preceding numbers, the ratios do not correspond exactly to financial statement numbers of any individual firm.

Required:
1. What characteristics appear to cause 1996 to be a high returns year and 1999 to be a low returns year?
2. What do the growth ratios tell Ms. Weber about the industry?
3. As a potential investor in this industry, identify five key factors you would monitor during the year 2000.

The Statement of Cash Flows

After studying Chapter 18, you will be able to:

1. Prepare a statement of cash flows for a firm from its balance sheet, income statement, and additional key data.

2. Identify cash flows by operating, investing, and financing activities.

3. Explain why cash flow from operations is different than net income.

4. Understand the relationship between historical cash-flow reporting and forecasting.

5. Assess a firm's ability to generate cash flows and how its cash is used.

6. Measure cash flows for use in many managerial decisions.

The Case for Cash Flows

Lori Crandall, a partner in a CPA firm specializing in financial planning for small business clients, is preparing a speech for a local chamber of commerce meeting. She is recalling a number of recent cash-related incidents:

Case A: In a recent article about bankruptcies, insufficient cash flow was listed as the cause of over half of all small business failures. Lack of profits, low sales, and poor business decisions and planning accounted for much smaller percentages.

Case B: At a planning retreat with key managers of a small metals firm, Lori found good and bad news. The good news was a new long-term contract with a major customer. The bad news was a sudden need for cash. The customer uses a JIT system, but her client has not implemented JIT completely and has built safety stocks to meet delivery dates. The customer wants to be billed once a month for parts shipped and promises payment within 60 days of billing. So far, payments are at least 30 days late. Profits are up nearly 50 percent in the past six months, but the firm's bank line of credit is exhausted. It's having trouble just meeting the payroll each week.

Case C: A client news release announced the sale of $5,000,000 of new common stock to a major customer for a 15 percent ownership interest. The move was made to repay borrowings and reduce interest payments by $600,000 per year.

Case D: A recent news report said that a major local employer had purchased $10,000,000 of new equipment. The company's CFO is quoted as saying, "We are paying for this from current operations and short-term borrowings."

Case E: A friend who owns a fast-growing swimming pool and spa equipment company called and started the conversation with "Why am I always out of cash? I'm making money; sales are great; but I'm always overdrawn. Where's the cash?"

Lori has heard "cash" stories from many clients. She remembers that one of her professors always announced three rules of finance: "One, get the cash! Two, get the cash! Three, get the cash!" Yes, she thinks, every manager she knows has cash worries: Where's the cash? Where did it come from? Where did it go?

Cash flows contain important information. Knowledge of historical cash inflows and outflows helps us understand past events. Forecasting cash flows is often even more important since decision makers use cash-flow information to select financing sources, investments, and day-to-day operating strategies. In managerial accounting, cash flows are relevant to nearly every business decision. The size, direction, and source of cash flows largely determine a business deal's success.

Chapter 18 explains cash-flow reporting. The basic report format is primarily a historical and external reporting tool. But when linked to the financial planning discussions in Chapters 7 and 8, a time continuum is created for measuring cash flows for an organization's major activities and events—whether in the past or for the future.

CASH AND CASH REPORTING—A PERSPECTIVE

Managing cash is a major activity of a firm's financial officers. Cash is an important asset with some unusual characteristics. Cash has little or no earning power and, therefore, is an undesirable investment. However, cash balances are necessary to conduct business on a daily basis and to cover the mismatch of receipts and payments. Also, a firm can increase its return on assets by minimizing its nonearning assets like cash.

Cash is defined for cash-flow reporting as currency, bank demand deposit and savings balances, and any highly liquid securities (often U. S. Government securities or high-grade certificates of deposit with maturities under 90 days). Cash and near-cash assets, called **cash equivalents**, should be available for use and free of restrictions.

Financial Accounting Standards Board **Statement of Financial Accounting Standards No. 95, "Statement of Cash Flows"** requires publicly reporting companies to disclose cash flows and suggests using three groups of cash flows—operating, financing, and investing.

The balance sheet is a snapshot of the firm at a specific point in time. The income statement reports revenues and expenses from operating activities plus other gains and losses between snapshots. Changes in balance sheet accounts are partly explained by revenue and expense flows—operating activities. But many balance sheet changes arise from investing and financing activities. Also, other important transactions and cash flows are not reported directly or completely on either primary statement. Thus, the statement of cash flows should report all significant financial transactions and cash flows for a specific time period. A timeframe for the three financial statements appears as:

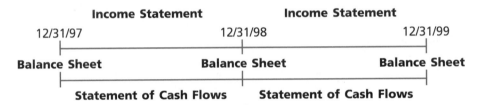

The **statement of cash flows** reports on three groups of cash flows—operations, investing, and financing—as defined in Figure 18.1. Figure 18.2

FIGURE 18.1   The Three Groups of Cash Flows

OPERATIONS

Activities:	Cash generated from normal activities of the firm. Cash received from customers and paid for purchases and operating expenses.
Accounts affected:	Operating current assets (accounts receivable, inventories, and prepaid expenses) and operating current liabilities (accounts payable and accrued expenses).

INVESTING

Activities:	Cash paid for purchases of noncurrent assets and received from sales of noncurrent assets plus purchases and sales of short-term investments.
Accounts affected:	All noncurrent assets and investment-type current assets.

FINANCING

Activities:	Cash received from issuing long-term debt and capital stock, paid to retire debt securities, and paid to shareholders for cash dividends, plus short-term debt borrowings and repayments.
Accounts affected:	All long-term debt and equity accounts and short-term borrowing and dividends payable accounts.

links the three cash-flow groups directly to the balance sheet. First, other than cash itself, every balance sheet account is included in one of the three groupings. Second, a change between balance sheet dates is explained by using additional information from within the firm or, if none is available, by making the obvious assumption about the change. For example, if the Land account increased by $100,000 and no other information is available, we assume that land costing $100,000 was purchased for cash.

*F*ORMAT OF THE STATEMENT

The statement's format frames the three cash-flow groups. The "bottom line" or the **"answer"** is the change in the cash balance between balance sheet dates. The cash from operating, investing, and financing activities must sum to the change in the cash balance.

Figure 18.3, page 764, shows the statement's outline and implies that operations will have a positive net cash flow, that investing is negative, and that financing is positive. For a profitable and growing firm, these assumptions are commonly true. Operations should generate cash for reinvestment in earning (noncurrent) assets. Negative investing cash flows are purchases of earning assets. These assets are generally consumed in normal business operations. Generally, new assets are purchased; and old assets are sold. Therefore, investing cash outflows commonly exceed investing cash inflows.

F I G U R E   1 8 . 2   Balance Sheet Account Groups for Cash-Flow Reporting

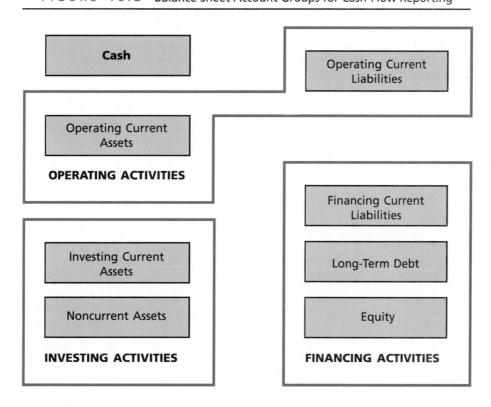

FIGURE 18.3 Framework of the Statement of Cash Flows

Cash flow from operating activities:		
(assumes the indirect method discussed on pp. 765-766)		
Net income (loss)	$	
Plus (minus) adjustments to convert accrual net income to cash	$	
Net cash flow from operating activities		$
Cash flow from investing activities:		
Purchases of noncurrent assets	($)	
Purchases of marketable securities	($)	
Sales of noncurrent assets	$	
Sales and maturities of marketable securities	$	
Net cash flow from investing activities		($)
Cash flow from financing activities:		
Issue long-term debt	$	
Issue common stock	$	
Increases in short-term borrowings	$	
Retirements of long-term debt and short-term borrowings	($)	
Payments of cash dividends	($)	
Net cash flow from financing activities		$
Net change in cash and cash equivalents		$
Schedule of noncash investing and financing activities:		
Trades of equity, debt, or assets for equity, debt, or assets	$	

The direction of financing cash flows is less certain. If the firm is growing and needs more cash than can be generated from operations, more debt must be incurred or more stock must be sold, producing cash inflows. The net cash flows will be positive. Yet, successful firms generating large cash inflows from operations might be able to finance all investment needs internally and still pay dividends to shareholders. Financing cash flows commonly shift from positive to negative and back.

A few major events do not impact cash—most involve trades of equity, debt, and assets. Statement readers need to know about these events, but they do not fit into the three cash-flow groupings. These major **noncash investing and financing transactions** are reported in memo form at the bottom of the statement of cash flows.

O PERATING CASH FLOWS

Normally, a business will buy merchandise on account, sell on account, pay for purchases, and then collect the receivables. This is the operating cycle. Operating current assets and liabilities facilitate this cycle. Accrual accounting measures the amount of revenue earned and expenses incurred to calculate net income. If all sales are for cash and all expenses are paid in cash when incurred, operating net income will be the same as cash flow from operations. But accounts receivable, inventories, accounts payable, accruals, and other operating accounts increase and decrease over the time period. Also, certain expenses, such as depreciation expense, are noncash expenses and have no impact on the cash account.

To find cash from operations, the accrual income statement must be converted to a cash basis. Two methods can be used:

1. **Indirect method:**   The starting point is net income, and adjustments are made to convert accrual-based net income to cash flow from operations.
2. **Direct method:**   Each income statement amount is adjusted to a cash basis, and all cash-basis items are summed for cash flow from operations.

Both approaches produce the same cash flow from operations amount. The goal of the operations section is to show the cash generated by or spent on the normal operating activities. Both methods do this. We will discuss the indirect method logic first, then apply the same logic to the direct method.

Indirect Method

Figure 18.4 presents a format for cash flow from operations using the indirect method. We will use the indirect method as the primary approach.

The starting point is net income from the income statement. The task is to convert this accrual-basis number to a cash basis. This means reversing adjustments made to convert the original cash-based transactions to accrual data. Accounts receivable represents sales not collected. For example, assume that accounts receivable increased from $60,000 to $75,000 and that sales were $800,000. The increase in receivables means that cash collections were less than sales. Some of the $800,000 of sales was not collected. If all other amounts on the income statement came from cash transactions, cash flow from operations would be $15,000 lower than net income. Thus, the $15,000 is subtracted from net income because cash received was less than revenue recognized by $15,000.

Any noncash expense on the income statement is "added back" to net income to eliminate this expense. Depreciation, depletion, amortization, and bad debt expenses are examples of noncash expenses appearing on many income statements. Any noncash revenue, such as revenue earned during this period and collected in another period, is subtracted to remove it from net income.

Gains or losses on the income statement that arise from investing or financing transactions are also eliminated from net income. Gains are subtracted, since the gain increases net income when it is included on the income

FIGURE   18.4   **Indirect Method for Finding Cash Flow From Operations**

Net income (loss).	$
+ Decreases in current operating assets	$
+ Increases in current operating liabilities	$
- Increases in current operating assets	($)
- Decreases in current operating liabilities	($)
+ Noncash-using expenses	$
- Noncash-providing revenues	($)
+ Losses on financing and investing transactions	$
- Gains on financing and investing transactions	($)
Net cash flow from operating activities	$

statement. Likewise, losses are added, since a loss decreased net income. The cash impacts of the gains and losses appear in the investing and financing sections of the cash-flow statement. Allowing the gains and losses to remain on the income statement will double count their impact.

Direct Method

The direct method goal is the same as the indirect method goal—find cash flow from operations. But instead of adjusting net income, each income statement account is converted from an accrual to a cash basis. Certain balance sheet accounts are tied to certain income statement accounts. The add or subtract logic is difficult and depends on algebra. An increase in accounts receivable is subtracted from sales. But because cost of sales is a negative in calculating net income, an increase in inventories is added to cost of sales (the same impact as a subtraction to net income). Handling positives, negatives, increases, and decreases algebraically solves these apparent inconsistencies. Figure 18.5 illustrates the links between account balance changes and the pluses and minuses.

P REPARING A STATEMENT OF CASH FLOWS—THE SEVEN STEPS

A key to preparing a statement of cash flows is organization. Two balance sheets, an income statement, additional data, and many cash flows going in opposite directions can cause confusion and errors. A structured approach, as

FIGURE 18.5   Calculating Cash Flow From Operations—Direct Method

Income Statement	Statement Amount		Adjustment Amount	Adjustments		Operations Cash Flow
Sales	$	+	$	Decrease in Accounts Receivable		
				or		
			($)	Increase in Accounts Receivable	=	$
Cost of sales	($)	+	$	Decrease in Inventory		
			$	Increase in Accounts Payable		
				or		
			($)	Increase in Inventory		
			($)	Decrease in Accounts Payable	=	($)
Operating expenses	($)	+	$	Decrease in Prepaid Expenses		
			$	Increase in Accrued Expenses		
				or		
			($)	Increase in Prepaid Expenses		
			($)	Decrease in Accrued Expenses	=	($)
Depreciation expense	($)	+	$	Depreciation expense	=	0
Gains on sales	$	+	($)	Gains on asset sales	=	0
Losses on sales	($)	+	$	Losses on asset sales	=	0
Net income	$					
Cash flow from operations						$

with any analysis, is essential. A set of steps should be followed to organize the data, statement, and procedures to complete the task. These steps are:

1. Format the statement.
2. Find the changes in balance sheet accounts between statement dates.
3. Enter the "answer" to the statement of cash flows.
4. Analyze any additional data available.
5. Use T-accounts to explain balance changes in more complicated accounts.
6. When a change in an account is explained, check it and move to the next data item or account until all balance sheet accounts are checked.
7. Total the operating, investing, and financing sections; and balance to the change in cash—the "answer."

Following these steps will not guarantee a complete and accurate statement, but a structured effort eliminates most errors. These steps approach the task very pragmatically. A methodology is established.

A COMPREHENSIVE EXAMPLE

The financial statements in Figure 18.6, page 768, are from the Hettiger Company. The content of the statement of cash flows in Figure 18.7, page 769, is developed using the previously presented steps. Additional data from various financial statement footnotes and management comments in the annual report relevant to cash flows include:

1. Declared cash dividends of $21,600.
2. Converted bonds payable of $20,000 into common stock.
3. Sold additional common stock with proceeds of $15,000.
4. Purchased an investment in Mace, Inc. for $26,000.
5. Sold equipment costing $12,000 with a book value of $7,000 for $10,200.

All other account balance changes arose from normal transactions and flows of cash during 1998. A reference to the seven steps is given for each balance sheet account and each statement of cash flow item.

CONTEMPORARY   PRACTICE   18 . 1

Investors Interest in Cash Flows Is Growing

In a recent survey, investors indicated that their understanding of cash-flow statements is growing. Reportedly, this is due to improved comparability across companies and easier-to-understand definitions and formats required by SFAS, No. 95. Investors said that they are more aware of the importance of cash flows and they have decreased confidence in accrual earnings figures. Investors want more background for the cash-flow numbers. Yet, only 28.5 percent of the respondents indicated that they had difficulty understanding the statement's data.

Source: Epstein, M. J., and M. L. Pava, "How Useful Is the Statement of Cash Flows," *Management Accounting*, July 1992, pp. 52-55.

FIGURE 18.6   Financial Statements for Comprehensive Example

HETTIGER COMPANY
Comparative Balance Sheets as of December 31, 1998 and 1997

	1998	1997	Increase or (Decrease)	Step	Text Page Reference
Cash and cash equivalents..........	$ 22,100	$ 18,300	$ 3,800	3	770
Marketable securities	14,000	15,000	(1,000)	6	772
Accounts receivable	38,200	39,900	(1,700)	6	772
Inventories.......................	71,600	64,000	7,600	6	773
Prepaid expenses	4,600	3,100	1,500	6	773
Investment in Mace, Inc.	26,000	0	26,000	4(4)	771
Plant and equipment	96,000	76,000	20,000	4(5)	771
Accumulated depreciation........	(14,000)	(12,000)	(2,000)	4(5)	771
Land	5,000	5,000	0	6	773
Total assets	$263,500	$209,300	$54,200		
Accounts payable	$ 50,200	$ 51,400	$ (1,200)	6	773
Wages payable	8,500	8,100	400	6	773
Taxes payable	11,200	7,500	3,700	6	773
Dividends payable................	6,000	5,000	1,000	4(1)	770
Bank notes payable	30,000	20,000	10,000	6	773
Bonds payable...................	0	35,000	(35,000)	4(2)	771
Common stock	50,000	15,000	35,000	4(2,3)	771
Retained earnings................	107,600	67,300	40,300	4(1)	770
Total liabilities and equity........	$263,500	$209,300	$54,200		

HETTIGER COMPANY
Income Statement for the Year Ended December 31, 1998

Sales		$ 326,400
Cost of sales	$149,800	
Operating expenses	88,400	
Depreciation expense................................	7,000	
Interest expense	4,000	
Total costs and expenses		249,200
Net income before gain and taxes		$ 77,200
Gain on sale of equipment		3,200
Net income before taxes		$ 80,400
Taxes expense		18,500
Net income		$ 61,900

Step 1: Format the Statement

The first step is to lay out the statement so that cash-flow items can be entered. Using a blank workpaper, enter the main headings as follows:

Cash flow from operating activities:
Net income . . . . $ 61,900
  •
Cash flow from investing activities:
  •
Cash flow from financing activities:
  •
Net change in cash and cash equivalents:
  •
Schedule of noncash investing and financing activities:

Step 2: Find the Changes in Balance Sheet Accounts

In Figure 18.6, Step 2 is shown in the Increase or (Decrease) column. These are the balance changes we need to explain.

FIGURE 18.7   Statement of Cash Flows

HETTIGER COMPANY Statement of Cash Flows for the Year Ended December 31, 1998		Step
Cash flow from operating activities:		
Net income	$ 61,900	1
Adjustments for noncash transactions:		
+ Depreciation expense	7,000	4(5)
- Gain on sale of equipment	(3,200)	4(5)
+ Decrease in accounts receivable	1,700	6
- Increase in inventories	(7,600)	6
- Increase in prepaid expenses	(1,500)	6
- Decrease in accounts payable	(1,200)	6
+ Increase in wages payable	400	6
+ Increase in taxes payable	3,700	6
Net cash flow from operating activities	$ 61,200	7
Cash flow from investing activities:		
Purchased stock in Mace, Inc.	$(26,000)	4(4)
Sold equipment	10,200	4(5)
Purchased plant and equipment	(32,000)	4(5)
Sold marketable securities	1,000	6
Net cash flow from investing activities	(46,800)	7
Cash flow from financing activities:		
Paid cash dividends to shareholders	$(20,600)	4(1)
Retired bonds payable	(15,000)	4(2)
Sold common stock	15,000	4(3)
Borrowed using additional bank notes	10,000	6
Net cash flow from financing activities	(10,600)	7
Net change in cash and cash equivalents	$ 3,800	3/7
Schedule of noncash investing and financing activities:		
Bonds payable converted into common stock	$ 20,000	4(2)

Step 3: Enter the "Answer" to the Statement of Cash Flows

From Figure 18.6, the change in cash is obvious, $3,800. This same amount is the sum of the cash flows from operations, investing, and financing—the "answer" to the cash-flow statement.

Step 4: Analyze Additional Data

Step 5: Use T-Accounts to Explain Balance Changes

Step 6: When a Change in an Account Is Explained, Check It and Move to the Next Data Item or Account Until All Balance Sheet Accounts Are Checked

Steps 4, 5, and 6 function together. They are repeated until all changes in balance sheet accounts are explained.

Often in textbook problems, additional data are merely listed. Also, supporting schedules and footnotes may yield relevant data. In real-world situations, the statement preparer may know certain facts not apparent from account balances. Within the firm, the treasurer and controller may provide additional data. In the Hettiger Company, five additional data items were found (Step 4).

For an account with any complexity, the easiest approach to analyze the balance change is to set up a **T-account** and enter the beginning and ending balances plus all transaction information known (Step 5). Now proceed to Step 6 activities of explaining and checking. Then repeat the cycle.

1st Item. Declared cash dividends of $21,600. Wording is important. Terms like "paid" and "received" mean cash flowed. Here, declared means cash flowed, unless a Dividends Payable account appears on the balance sheet. One does exist in this case. To find the cash flow, we look at the accounts affected. In Retained Earnings, two types of transactions are found: Dividends reduce the balance, and net income increases (or net loss decreases) the balance.

Retained Earnings				Dividends Payable		
		12/31/97	67,300		12/31/97	5,000
Declared cash				Paid dividend **20,600**	Declared cash	
dividend	21,600	Net income	61,900		dividend	21,600
		12/31/98	107,600		12/31/98	6,000

Bonds Payable				Common Stock		
		12/31/97	35,000		12/31/97	15,000
Converted to					Issued for	
stock	**20,000**				bonds	
					payable	**20,000**
Retired bonds	**15,000**				Sold stock	**15,000**
		12/31/98	0		12/31/98	50,000

By entering the beginning and ending balances for Retained Earnings and Dividends Payable in T-accounts, dividends declared *and* paid can be tracked. The $21,600 is deducted from Retained Earnings and added to the payable.

Dividends Payable had a $5,000 balance at December 31, 1997. This was probably paid in early 1998. Other cash dividends were declared and paid during 1998. Late in 1998, more were declared and are to be paid in early 1999. In the Dividends Payable T-account, we know the beginning balance, the dividends declared, and the ending balance. With no other information about cash dividends, the cash paid to shareholders is assumed to be: $5,000 + $21,600 - $6,000 = $20,600 cash paid (in **bold** in the T-account).

Since this is a financing account (see Figure 18.3), the paid cash dividends appear as an outflow in the financing section. The Dividends Payable account can now be checked. We have explained this account's change.

2nd Item. Converted bonds payable of $20,000 into common stock. Here is a significant noncash financial transaction. As no cash changed hands, it is presented as a memo item. Common shares were issued to debtholders, and $20,000 of long-term debt was eliminated. But, we can see from Figure 18.6 that the entire $35,000 of bonds was eliminated. Having no other information about Bonds Payable, we assume that in 1998 the remaining $15,000 of bonds has matured or was repurchased from the holders, apparently at book value. This is a financing cash outflow and completes the explanation of the Bonds Payable change. Check it.

3rd Item. Sold additional common stock with proceeds of $15,000. A financing cash inflow of $15,000 from sale of common stock is entered on our statement. Since no other information is available about Common Stock, we could assume that the sale netted $15,000. The T-account shows that, beyond the debt swap, the Common Stock account increased by $15,000. This transaction now completes the explanation of the Common Stock change. Check it.

4th Item. Purchased an investment in Mace, Inc. for $26,000. Since the account changed from zero to $26,000, we assume that this is an outflow for an investment. Investment in Mace, Inc. can be checked.

5th Item. Sold equipment costing $12,000 with a book value of $7,000 for $10,200. Typically, noncurrent assets and accumulated depreciation accounts have numerous transactions that must be sorted—purchases and sales. T-accounts are often essential even for the experienced accountant.

Accumulated Depreciation must have been $5,000. Since $10,200 was received in cash, the gain was $3,200 and appears on the income statement:

Original cost	$12,000
Less accumulated depreciation	5,000
Book value	$ 7,000
Gain on sale	3,200
Sale price (cash proceeds)	$10,200

The investing inflow of $10,200 is entered, and the gain on sale of equipment is subtracted from net income to eliminate this gain from the operating section.

In the Plant and Equipment and Accumulated Depreciation T-accounts, the sold asset and its accumulated depreciation must be removed. These T-accounts show that our work here is not complete. Since no other Plant and Equipment information is available, we assume additional plant and equipment was purchased for cash. The beginning balance minus the sale is subtracted from the ending balance. The difference is the amount purchased, $32,000, and is an investing cash outflow. The change of $20,000 is explained. Check it. The following T-accounts explain the changes and highlight the cash flows reported.

Plant and Equipment				Accumulated Depreciation—Plant and Equipment			
12/31/97	76,000					12/31/97	12,000
Purchased		Sold equipment	12,000	Sold equipment	5,000	Depreciation	
equipment	32,000					expense	7,000
12/31/98	96,000					12/31/98	14,000

Gain on Sale of Equipment		
	Sold equipment	3,200

In the Accumulated Depreciation account, we need to remember that the 1998 depreciation expense is added to the beginning balance. The income statement shows depreciation expense as $7,000. The beginning balance, plus the expense, and minus depreciation on the sold equipment equals the ending balance. Depreciation expense is added to net income in the operations section as a noncash expense. The change in Accumulated Depreciation is explained. Check it.

Please note that adding depreciation expense to net income does *not* generate cash. In financial analysis, depreciation expense is often added to net income to provide a crude estimate of cash from operations. *Assume that all other income statement items are cash flows.* If depreciation expense was $17,000 and not $7,000 for 1998, net income would decrease by $10,000. When depreciation expense is added back, both alternatives give the same operations cash flow. Therefore, depreciation is merely a noncash expense.[1] The numbers show:

	1998	**With Depreciation Expense at $17,000**
Cash revenue minus cash expenses (assumed).......	$ 68,900	$ 68,900
Less depreciation expense	(7,000)	(17,000)
Net income	$ 61,900	$ 51,900
Add back depreciation expense	7,000	17,000
Cash flow from operations	$ 68,900	$ 68,900

Remaining Accounts. Now that all additional data items have had their cash impacts recorded, the remaining balance sheet accounts can be analyzed. This continues the Step 6 cycle. Start at the top of the balance sheet.

Marketable Securities is a current asset and an investing account. (See Figure 18.3.) In the absence of any gain or loss, the decrease in this account assumes the sale of $1,000 of marketable securities. The securities may have matured or were sold at face value. We assume a cash inflow of $1,000.

An Accounts Receivable decrease means that the amount of cash collected from our customers this year was greater than the amount of sales. The rule from Figure 18.4 states that a decrease in a current operating asset is added to net income.

---

[1] We must distinguish between depreciation expense and the tax benefits of the depreciation deduction. Depreciation expense is an allowable tax deduction. In a given year, a higher tax deduction results in a lower tax payment. But depreciation expense itself generates no cash. See Chapters 12 and 13.

In Inventories, purchases were $7,600 more than cost of sales. In Prepaid Expenses, the increase of $1,500 implies that more supplies and prepaid items were purchased than were expensed in 1998. Both increases used additional cash and are subtracted from net income.

Since the Land account balance did not change, no land transactions apparently occurred.

Accounts Payable is an operating current liability which decreased by $1,200. An amount equal to all of this year's plus $1,200 of last year's purchases was paid. The decrease used cash and is subtracted from net income.

Wages and many other expenses are part of operating expenses. The $400 increase in Wages Payable indicates that actual wages paid are $400 less than the wages expensed. Thus, the increase is added to net income. Taxes Payable is tied to taxes expense. The increase in Taxes Payable means that the cash paid for taxes was less than the tax expense. This increase in a current operating liability is added to net income.

The last account not checked is Bank Notes Payable and may include short-term or long-term bank borrowings. The balance increased by $10,000 in 1998. Given no other information, we assume that new notes were signed for $10,000 and that no old notes matured. These are important assumptions. If, for example, $5,000 of the notes owed at December 31, 1997, had matured and $15,000 of new notes added, both the repayment and the new borrowings would appear in the financing section.

All balance sheet accounts are now checked. Steps 4, 5, and 6 are complete.

Step 7: Total the Operations, Investing, and Financing Sections; and Balance to the Change in Cash—the "Answer"

As shown earlier, Figure 18.7 presents the completed statement of cash flows. The three sections are added, and their totals sum to the change in cash: $61,200 + $(46,800) + $(10,600) = $3,800. With this equation in agreement, the statement is complete; and the financial analysis of the cash flows can begin.

The Operations Section Using the Direct Method

The operations section in Figure 18.7 uses the indirect method. The explanations developed earlier for operating activities change very little when the direct method is used. However, it is worthwhile to report the adjustments needed to prepare a direct method cash flow from operations. Figure 18.8, page 774, uses the format given in Figure 18.5. The direct method calculations result in cash from operations of $61,200, the same as in the indirect method. Figure 18.9, page 774, shows the operations section as it would appear using the direct method.

W HAT IF THE STATEMENT DOES NOT BALANCE?

Step 7 came to a happy end in the analysis just completed. What if the operating, investing, and financing cash flows do not balance to the change in cash? With no promises or guarantees, a few suggestions can be offered:

1. Check for items entered as negatives instead of as positives or vice versa. Divide the difference by two, and check any item equalling that amount.

FIGURE 18.8   Calculation of Cash Flow From Operations Using the Direct Method

Income Statement	Accrual Amount		Adjustment Amount	Adjustment		Operations Cash Flow
Sales	$ 326,400	+	$ 1,700	Decrease in Accounts Receivable	=	$ 328,100
Cost of sales	(149,800)	+	(7,600)	Increase in Inventories		
			(1,200)	Decrease in Accounts Payable	=	(158,600)
Operating expenses	(88,400)	+	(1,500)	Increase in Prepaid Expenses		
			400	Increase in Wages Payable	=	(89,500)
Depreciation expense	(7,000)	+	7,000	Depreciation Expense	=	0
Interest expense	(4,000)	+	0		=	(4,000)
Gain on equipment sale	3,200	+	(3,200)	Gain on equipment sale	=	0
Taxes expense	(18,500)	+	3,700	Increase in Taxes Payable	=	(14,800)
Net income	$ 61,900					
Cash flow from operations						$ 61,200

2. Check to see if an account was omitted from the analysis.
3. In complex accounts, ensure that all aspects of a transaction are recorded.
4. Recheck addition. Numerous pluses and minuses can be confusing.
5. Recheck the operations section rules of increase and decrease.

Often the error is simple but difficult to find. It is here that the discipline of following the seven steps becomes invaluable. By repeating the steps and checking for completeness and accuracy, you *will* find the discrepancy.

*T*HE STORY THE STATEMENT TELLS

The story the statement of cash flows tells is sometimes obvious and other times subtle. In this case, operations clearly generated cash that allowed Hettiger to purchase more equipment and to invest in Mace, Inc. Changes in current asset and liability accounts did not have much impact on the cash from operations.

FIGURE 18.9   Cash Flow From Operations Section—Direct Method

HETTIGER COMPANY
Operations Section Using the Direct Method
For the Year Ended December 31, 1998

Cash flow from operating activities:	
Cash collected from customers	$ 328,100
Cash paid to suppliers for merchandise	(158,600)
Cash paid for operating expenses.	(89,500)
Cash paid for interest on debt	(4,000)
Cash paid to government for income taxes.	(14,800)
Net cash flow from operating activities	$ 61,200

Cash "savings" from the noncash depreciation expense was offset by inventory growth. Debt and equity transactions allowed the firm to increase its equity position and reduce its long-term debt position. The net cash from common stock sales and bank borrowings was used primarily to retire debt. Shareholders received cash dividends, requiring about a third of the cash from operations. To get a fuller picture of Hettiger Company's cash trends, several years of cash flows should be compared.

Typically, the statement highlights major cash flows and points to strengths and weaknesses. Among many relevant questions are:

1. Is cash, needed for expansion, being used to pay dividends to shareholders?
2. What happened to profits that the firm generated?
3. Is cash generated from issuing stock or long-term debt being spent to support cash-consuming operating activities?
4. Are operations causing accounts receivable and inventories to grow too fast?
5. Is cash from operations growing as fast as sales?
6. Is investment in noncurrent assets causing debt to grow too rapidly?
7. Can operations generate enough cash to repay maturing debt obligations?
8. Can needed growth in noncurrent and current assets be supplied by internal cash flow (operations) or must external cash inflows (financing) be found?
9. Are assets being sold to cover cash needs in operations or for debt repayment and dividends?
10. Is the cash balance itself too low, or has it declined too far to handle normal business activities of the firm?

Answers to these questions may require nonfinancial information and several years of data. But financial analyses are incomplete without the cash-flow statement.

Cash-Flow Forecasting—The Timeframes

Managers are often more concerned with forecasting the firm's cash-flow position than with history. Several versions of cash planning exist:

1. **Long-term planning:** The timeframe is three to five years or more. Major cash events are identified. Plant expansion, new products, and debt maturities cause large cash needs that require advance planning.

C O N T E M P O R A R Y   P R A C T I C E   1 8 . 2

What Lenders Require

A survey of commercial loan officers asked about their credit evaluation practices. All require historical balance sheets and income statements. Ninety percent requires a statement of cash flows. Eighty percent requires a separate cash-flow schedule using the lender's format. Stability of cash flows over time and net income are the most important risk elements. Other important factors are size, reputation, and key ratios. The business ethics reputation of top management was rated as the most important qualitative characteristic by a third of the respondents.

Source: Fulmer, J. G., T. A. Gavin, and W. J. Bertin, "What Factors Influence the Lending Decision: A Survey of Commercial Loan Officers," *Commercial Lending Review*, Winter 1991-1992, pp. 64-70.

2. **Annual planning:** The annual financial plan includes a cash budget. Cash forecasts are much like historical statements of cash flows. Operations is often the primary provider and user of cash—sales, production, inventories, credit, and collections.

3. **Daily and weekly planning:** Is Friday's payroll covered? Knowing exactly when bills must be paid, getting receipts to the bank quickly, borrowing for short-term needs, and keeping cash balances as low as possible are key near-term cash actions.

Chapters 7 and 8 developed the budgeting and cash planning concepts and methods. The same basic cash-flow reporting reaches across past and future time lines.

The Ethics of Cash Flows

Management manipulations of accrual accounting reports are age-old practices. Recognizing revenue before it is earned and deferring expenses or losses to later periods are common improper actions. Cash flows, on the other hand, are much more objective and verifiable, unless blatant theft or fraud is involved. Either you got the cash or you did not. Cash reporting often deters accounting gamesmanship. Yet, nothing is foolproof; even here managers can delay paying and recording incurred expenses. Moving cash, paying bills to reduce liabilities, and borrowing to eliminate perpetually overdrawn checking accounts are done to improve the appearance of yearend statements. This is "window dressing."

Cash is a very liquid asset. Many controls are required over physical cash, cash bank accounts, who handles or signs for cash, and spending limits. The increased interest in cash-flow reporting is due in part to the investment community's feeling that, by combining accrual income and expense and cash-flow data, a truer picture of a firm's operations can be seen and evaluated.

Often, divisionalized companies use a centralized cash treasury function. Basically, this is intended to make more efficient use of cash balances that might otherwise be scattered in many banks in many locations. But central control of cash gives the corporate office subtle and powerful control. The corporate office knows about every cash transaction. Often, cash-flow budgets are integral parts of subsidiary performance evaluation systems.

In most acquisitions, the buying company almost immediately puts one of its own managers in the treasurer or controller position and takes control of the new subsidiary's cash flows. This is particularly true of international operations.

Other Managerial Implications

Cash is the basic ingredient in nearly all business transactions. Often knowing the "where and when" of cash flows is critical to understanding the business problem. In other chapters, incremental revenues and costs imply cash flows. In capital investment decisions, timing of cash flows is absolutely critical in selecting a project from among many choices available.

The financial health of the firm as a whole is partly measured by its ability to generate and sustain cash flows. The term "cash cow" refers to a business segment that can generate large cash flows, even if its relative profitability is not high. Ability to generate cash is perhaps the primary factor that banks evaluate prior to extending credit. Debt coverage, which is the ability to pay interest and principal when due, is as vital for companies in international money markets as it is for a student with a car loan.

S UMMARY

This chapter presented the statement of cash flows. The format, the procedures for preparing the statement, the logic of understanding cash flows, and the interpretations of the statement were discussed. Cash-flow reporting can have a future or a historical orientation. Underlying the formal statement is a multitude of uses and users. History has shown that the usefulness and, therefore, the importance of cash flows have grown tremendously in the past few decades. This trend will likely continue.

P ROBLEM FOR REVIEW

Financial statements for Wade Construction Company are given for 1998 and 1999 in summary form. Max Wade, the president of the company, is considering expansion and would like your views on the firm's ability to generate cash.

WADE CONSTRUCTION COMPANY Income Statement for the Year 1999 (in Thousands of Dollars)	
Net revenue...	$8,400
Costs of construction billed...........................	$5,552
Operating expenses, excluding depreciation..............	1,085
Depreciation expense..................................	232
Interest income.......................................	(170)
Interest expense	290
Gain on sale of equipment	(146)
Expenses (net of gains and losses)	$6,843
Net income	$1,557

WADE CONSTRUCTION COMPANY Balance Sheets as of December 31, 1998 and 1999 (in Thousands of Dollars)			
	1998	*1999*	*Increase (Decrease)*
Cash and cash equivalents.........	$ 386	$ 607	$ 221
Temporary investments	920	1,320	400
Accounts receivable	1,472	1,890	418
Inventory	746	1,046	300
Plant and equipment (net)	3,762	3,816	54
Total assets	$7,286	$8,679	$ 1,393
Accounts payable	$ 856	$ 831	$ (25)
Bank loans payable	482	643	161
Long-term notes payable	1,800	1,200	(600)
Common stock..................	2,500	3,700	1,200
Retained earnings	1,648	2,305	657
Total liabilities and equities......	$7,286	$8,679	$ 1,393

Additional data:

1. Temporary investments of $400,000 were sold.

2. Plant assets costing $746,000 were acquired during the year.

3. Long-term notes payable of $600,000 were traded for 20,000 shares of stock.

4. Wade issued 20,000 shares of common stock at a price of $30 per share.

Required:

Use the seven steps to prepare a statement of cash flows, including the indirect method for operations. Comment on Wade's ability to generate cash for expansion.

Solution:

Step 1: Format the statement. See the **bold** items on the following statement.

Step 2: Find the changes in balance sheet accounts. See the balance sheets.

Step 3: Enter the "answer" to the statement of cash flows, a $221,000 increase.

Step 4: Analyze the additional data items. See the four items listed previously.

Step 5: Use T-accounts to explain balance changes. Use where and when needed.

Step 6: Check accounts as they are explained. Been there; did that!

Step 7: Total the operations, investing, and financing sections; and balance to the change in cash. Yes! It balances.

The complete statement of cash flows follows:

WADE CONSTRUCTION COMPANY Statement of Cash Flows for the Year 1999 (in Thousands of Dollars)		
Cash flow from operating activities:		
Net income...................................	**$1,557**	
+ Depreciation expense	232	
- Gain on sale of equipment	(146)	
- Increase in accounts receivable	(418)	
- Increase in inventories	(300)	
- Decrease in accounts payable	(25)	
Net cash flow from operating activities................		$ 900
Cash flow from investing activities:		
Sold temporary investments	$ 400	
Purchased temporary investments	(800)	
Sold equipment.......................................	606	
Purchased equipment.................................	(746)	
Net cash flow from investing activities		(540)
Cash flow from financing activities:		
Issued common stock	$ 600	
Paid dividends..	(900)	
Borrowed additional funds from bank	161	
Net cash flow from financing activities		(139)
Net change in cash and cash equivalents		$ 221
Schedule of noncash investing and financing activities:		
Long-term notes payable exchanged for capital stock		$ 600

Commentary:

Several comments about 1999 cash flows are relevant to Wade's expansion plans:

- Operations generated $900,000, but the entire amount was paid as dividends. Reducing dividends would retain this cash.
- Profits appear unusually strong, given revenues and total assets. Hopefully, this earning level can be maintained to generate operating cash flows.
- A concern is the growth in receivables and inventories. Reducing these to 1998 levels would generate over $700,000 for expansion.
- Temporary investments did increase by $400,000. These are expansion dollars.
- Wade has already purchased nearly $750,000 of new equipment in 1999.
- Selling $600,000 of common stock and converting existing long-term notes into stock reduce debt, increase equity, and further increase the firm's ability to negotiate larger long-term borrowings for expansion.
- The Cash account itself increased by $221,000. No information is given about Wade's minimum cash balance needs.

Sizeable amounts of cash could be available to expand Wade Construction in 2000.

T ERMINOLOGY REVIEW

Cash equivalents, *762*
Cash flow from financing activities, *763*
Cash flow from investing activities, *763*
Cash flow from operating activities, *763*
Direct method, *765*
Financing activities, *762*
Indirect method, *765*
Investing activities, *762*

Noncash financing and investing activities, *764*
Operating activities, *762*
SFAS No. 95, "Statement of Cash Flows," *762*
Statement of cash flows, *762*
T-account, *770*
The "answer," *763*

S UGGESTED READINGS

Edwards, J. D., and C. D. Heagy, "Relevance Regained: FASB Modifies Cash Flow Statement Requirements for Banks," *Journal of Accountancy*, Vol. 171, No. 6, pp. 79-90.

Largay, J., and C. Stickney, "Cash Flows, Ratio Analysis, and the W. T. Grant Company Bankruptcy," *Financial Analyst Journal*, July/August 1980, pp. 51-60.

Nurnberg, H., "Inconsistencies and Ambiguities in Cash Flow Statements Under FASB Statement No. 95," *Accounting Horizons*, Vol. 7, No. 2, pp. 60-75.

Seed, A. H., *The Funds Statement Structure and Uses*, Financial Executives Research Foundation, Morristown, NJ, 1984.

Stephens, R. G., and V. Govindarajan, "On Assessing a Firm's Cash Generating Ability," *Accounting Review*, January 1990, pp. 242-257.

QUESTIONS FOR REVIEW AND DISCUSSION

1. How should the balance sheet accounts be grouped for reporting cash flows?

2. Is the change in the cash balance important to financial reporting and managerial analysis? Explain.

3. Explain why historical cash-flow reports are similar to cash-flow forecasts.

4. Statements of cash flows report changes in balance sheet accounts. Does the statement of cash flows explain all the changes? Comment.

5. Define "cash and cash equivalents."

6. Explain how the cash balance is increased or decreased by income statement transactions.

7. Name the common inflows of cash in each activity area: operations, investing, and financing.

8. Name the common outflows of cash in each activity area: operations, investing, and financing.

9. In using the indirect method, explain why losses are added to net income and gains are subtracted from net income.

10. If the cash balance increases by $10,000, does this mean that liabilities plus equity minus noncash assets decrease by $10,000? Explain.

11. Peter Leong operates a very successful and expanding party store. He received his yearly financial statements and tax return. He sees that profits are up, but he doesn't have enough cash to pay his taxes. What might be the problem?

12. Ralph heard someone say, "Depreciation is a source of cash." He needs more cash! He thinks he'll buy more equipment and get more depreciation expense. Comment.

13. This chapter suggests a seven-step approach to preparing a statement of cash flows. What are the steps?

14. In a normal growing firm, should we expect to see net cash inflows or outflows from operating activities? Investing activities? Financing activities?

15. "Accumulated depreciation creates a cash reserve for replacement of assets." Do you agree or disagree with the statement? Why?

16. Explain why a decrease in an accrued liability account indicates that the cash disbursement was greater than the related expense on the income statement.

17. The Hopp Company paid high dividends, had zero profits, and had an unchanging cash balance for the past few years. The company probably did which of the following:

(a) Sold assets to get cash to pay off long-term debt early.

(b) Financed the dividends by allowing accounts receivable to rise.

(c) Had very low operating expenses.

(d) Had lots of depreciation expense.

18. The manager of Best Fixtures Company states that cash dividends in the amount of $85,000 were declared but not paid this year. The manager sees that retained earnings decreased and insists that this decrease must appear in the financing activities section. Comment on the manager's thinking.

E XERCISES

18-1. Balance Changes and Cash. The following data are from the Sagesser Company:

	December 31, 1998	December 31, 1997
Accounts receivable	$ 20,000	$ 25,000
Accounts payable	15,000	18,000
Retained earnings	80,000	60,000

Net income for 1998	$ 60,000	
Purchase of equipment for cash during 1998	26,000	
Depreciation expense for 1998	15,000	

Required:

What is the change in cash based on the preceding information?

18-2. Cash Flow From Operations. Zwenger Company reported a net income of $132,000 for the year. Included as deductions on the income statement were depreciation of $46,000 and loss on the sale of equipment of $7,000. Accounts receivable increased by $6,000, and inventories decreased by $5,000.

Required:

Compute the cash flow from operations for the year.

18-3. Summing the Statement. The cash balance increased by $20,000, cash flow from financing activities was negative by $15,000, and cash flow from operations was positive by $50,000.

Required:

Which of the following is (are) correct?

(a)   Cash paid for purchases of investing assets must have exceeded cash from sales of investing assets by $15,000.

(b)   The company must have been profitable.

(c)   Depreciation expense must have been greater than net income.

(d)   Cash flow from investing activities must have been negative by $55,000.

(e)   The sum of operating, financing, and investing activities was $20,000.

18-4. Equipment Purchases. Lental Company's equipment account balance net of accumulated depreciation was $320,000 at December 31, 1998, and was $455,000 on December 31, 1999. Depreciation expense on equipment for 1999 was $60,000. Equipment sold during 1999 originally cost $80,000, had a net book value of $25,000, and realized $30,000 in cash. Lental also purchased equipment in 1999.

Required:

What did Lental spend for equipment purchases in 1999?

18-5. Direct Method Cash Flows. The following data are from the Freiburger Company:

(a)   Operating expenses for the year totaled DM60,000. Beginning accrued expenses were DM50,000, and ending accrued expenses were DM40,000. Operating expenses also included depreciation expense of DM30,000. How much cash was spent on operating expenses?

(b)   If cash inflow from operations was DM40,000, net income was DM32,000, depreciation expense was DM12,000, cash outflow from investing was DM120,000, dividends paid were DM20,000, and cash inflow from financing was DM66,000, what is "the answer" to the cash-flow statement?

(c)   Retained earnings increased by DM30,000. Net income was DM64,000. Dividends payable increased by DM7,000. How much cash was paid for dividends?

Required:

In each case, answer the question asked.

18-6. Finding Net Income.   For Kennedy Clothing Stores, cash outflow from investing was $50,000. Cash inflow from financing was $13,000. These account balances are known:

	Beginning	Ending
Cash	$10,000	$13,000
Accounts Receivable	32,000	40,000
Inventory	50,000	45,000
Accounts Payable	27,000	40,000

Required:

Apparently, what was net income? Explain.

18-7. Cash Flow With Loss From Operations.   Valley Mining Company reported a net loss of $247,000 for the year after deducting depreciation and depletion of $437,000. Credit sales exceeded cash collections by $55,000. Accrued operating expenses increased by $40,000 during the year.

Required:

Compute the cash flow from operations for the year.

18-8. Reporting Cash Flows.   Gosse Company's income statement for the year shows a net loss of $4,200. Depreciation expense was $8,500. In addition, a balance sheet comparison revealed these balance changes:

Increase in Inventory	$ 4,000
Decrease in Accounts Receivable	14,000
Increase in Accounts Payable	18,000

Required:

Why was Gosse still able to pay its bills despite the net loss?

18-9. Cash-Flow Reporting.   Key transactions, along with other relevant information for Newman Company, include:

(a) Net income was $100,000.

(b) Depreciation expense was $25,000.

(c) Dividends of $18,000 were paid.

(d) 10,000 shares of preferred stock were issued for $350,000 cash.

(e) Land was acquired for $20,000.

(f) Used equipment, which originally cost $20,000, was sold for $8,500 and had $11,500 of accumulated depreciation.

(g) The following changes in operating accounts occurred:

Accounts Receivable	$ 27,000 increase
Inventory	16,000 decrease
Accounts Payable	11,000 decrease

Required:

From a statement of cash flows, comment on the major cash inflows and outflows.

18-10. Summing Cash Flows.   The following information is provided by the Simcoe Company:

Proceeds from sale of building (book value $300,000)	$ 500,000
Proceeds from long-term borrowing	2,000,000
Purchases of fixed assets	1,600,000
Payment of dividends	400,000
Proceeds from sale of Simcoe common stock	1,000,000

Required:

What is the net change in cash based on the preceding events only?

18-11. Statement of Cash Flows From Basic Data.   Warren Lamont gives you his mixed-up trial balances as of June 30 for the past two years.

	June 30, 1999	June 30, 1998
Income Tax Payable	$ 8,130	$ 8,240
Plant and Equipment	54,600	51,400
Accumulated Depreciation	18,000	13,500
Accounts Payable	12,140	13,610
Inventory	14,280	12,430
Cash	16,400	17,250
Capital Stock	12,000	8,000
Accounts Receivable	18,920	16,480
Wages Payable	7,320	7,890
Notes Payable, due June 30, 2001	24,000	30,000
Unexpired Insurance	2,630	2,280
Retained Earnings	19,240	13,600
Short-Term Bank Loans	6,000	5,000

Required:

Prepare a statement of cash flows for the fiscal year ended June 30, 1999, using only the balances and the information Warren has given you. What are the major cash inflows and outflows?

18-12. Cash Flow From Operations.   Precision Instruments, Inc., a Glasglow, Scotland firm, reported net income of £216,000 for the fiscal year ended September 30, 1999. Included on the income statement were deductions for depreciation expense of £41,500 and amortization of patents of £5,600. Accounts receivable and accounts payable both decreased by £12,000. Inventories increased by £18,500, while prepaids dropped by £2,500. Dividends payable increased by £2,000.

Required:

How much cash was generated from operating activities?

18-13. Cash-Flow Transactions.   Siva Flavorings recorded these events:

(a)   Collected an account receivable.

(b)   Purchased merchandise inventory on account.

(c)   Sold a delivery truck for book value.

(d)   Exchanged common stock for elimination of a mortgage on the firm's factory.

(e)   Paid rent on computer equipment.

(f)   Purchased a new delivery truck and financed it by a bank loan.

(g)   Sold common stock.

(h)   Borrowed money from a bank for 6 months to finance inventories.

(i)   Sold merchandise on account.

(j)   Purchased common stock in a company that is a long-time vendor.

Required:

1.   For each of the above events, indicate whether the event is a cash inflow (I), a cash outflow (O), or has no cash effect (NE).

2.   Given each event's nature, indicate whether its activity is operations (Op), investing (In), financing (Fi), or none of these (N). (Do not indicate how each event is reported, merely what kind of activity it is.)

18-14. Transactions and Cash Flows.   Selected events of Goswin Parts Company from the past year are as follows:

(a)   Acquired equipment at a cost of $850,000.

(b)   Received $62,000 from the sale of land, which had a book value of $50,000.

(c) Issued common stock of $1,300,000 in exchange for an investment in common stock of Wait Machine Company.

(d) Decreased accounts payable by $54,000.

(e) Paid dividends in the amount of $240,000.

(f) Repurchased shares of its own stock for $50,500.

(g) Deducted depreciation expense of $138,000 on the income statement.

(h) Increased patents by $85,000.

(i) Sold Goswin common stock for $400,000 and used proceeds to retire $350,000 of long-term notes payable.

(j) Paid $200,000 to an advertising agency and recorded advertising expense of $160,000 and an increase in prepaid expenses.

Required:

For each transaction, indicate the correct letter(s) from the following list which describes how that transaction will be reported on a statement of cash flows.

A. Added to net income.

B. Subtracted from net income.

C. As an investing inflow of cash.

D. As an investing outflow of cash.

E. As a financing inflow of cash.

F. As a financing outflow of cash.

G. As a supplemental memo item.

H. Not reported on this statement.

18-15. Determining the Missing Amounts.   The following cases come from the Tecante Export/Import Services Company located in Tecante, Mexico:

Case 1:	Sales for the year	M$?
	Accounts Receivable, beginning	135,000
	Accounts Receivable, ending	92,000
	Cash collections during the year.	534,000
Case 2:	Cost of goods sold for the year	M$ 267,000
	Inventory, beginning.	62,000
	Inventory, ending	?
	Accounts Payable, beginning	38,000
	Accounts Payable, ending	29,000
	Cash payments to vendors during the year.	295,000
Case 3:	Operating expenses for the year.	M$ 145,000
	Prepaid operating expenses, beginning	8,000
	Prepaid operating expenses, ending	12,000
	Depreciation expense on operating equipment	?
	Accrued operating expenses, beginning	21,000
	Accrued operating expenses, ending	18,000
	Cash paid for operating expenses during the year	135,000

Required:

Fill in the missing figures, using Mexican pesos.

18-16. Financing Cash Flows.   Except for the additional data, assume that all other cash flows for the Chiddick Company are normal events.

	Beginning	*Ending*
Long-Term Debt	$ 40,000	$ 33,000
Common Stock.	40,000	80,000
Retained Earnings	40,000	35,000

Events for this year include:

1. Net income was $40,000.

2. $23,000 of Chiddick common stock was swapped to retire long-term debt.

Required:

What financing cash flows will be reported? What other financing transactions might have occurred in these accounts?

18-17. Measuring Cash Flows. These financial statements are from Abramson Stores.

	12/31/1999	*12/31/1998*	*Increase (Decrease)*
Cash	$ 12,000	$ 12,000	$ 0
Accounts receivable (net)	40,000	45,000	(5,000)
Inventories	65,000	45,000	20,000
Fixed assets	180,000	160,000	20,000
Less accumulated depreciation .	(45,000)	(50,000)	5,000
Total assets	$252,000	$212,000	$40,000
Accounts payable	$ 15,000	$ 20,000	$ (5,000)
Bonds payable	80,000	60,000	20,000
Common stock	120,000	100,000	20,000
Retained earnings	37,000	32,000	5,000
Total liabilities and equity . . .	$252,000	$212,000	$40,000

For the Year 1999	
Sales	$ 800,000
Cost of goods sold	(440,000)
Operating expenses	(300,000) (including $30,000 of depreciation expense)
Gain on assets sold	5,000
Net income	$ 65,000

In addition, Abramson sold fixed assets originally costing $50,000 and having a book value of $15,000.

Required:

1. As defined in the chapter, what is the "answer" to the cash-flow statement?
2. Based on the preceding data, what was the cash flow from financing activities?
3. How much cash was paid for purchases of fixed assets?

18-18. Incomplete Data and Cash Flows. Only these incomplete data from the McFall Company are available for 1999:

	12/31/1999	*12/31/1998*
Plant and equipment (net)	$286,000	$290,000
Long-term debt	160,000	0
Capital stock	300,000	200,000
Retained earnings	705,000	517,000

Dividends of $148,000 were declared and paid during the year. Depreciation of $32,000 was deducted on the income statement. Equipment having a net book value of $88,000 was sold at a loss of $30,000.

Required:

Prepare a statement of cash flows. Comment on the major cash flows.

18-19. Changes in Noncurrent Asset Accounts. Crumbleu Company has these entries in its Trucks account and the related Accumulated Depreciation account:

Trucks				Accumulated Depreciation—Trucks			
1/1/98	100,000					1/1/98	40,000
3/4/98	25,000	6/6/98	?	6/6/98	?	12/31/98	30,000
12/31/98	?					12/31/98	60,000

Required:

If a truck was sold on June 6, 1998, for $13,000, creating an $8,000 gain on the sale, what is the ending balance in the Trucks account?

18-20. Changes in Notes Payable. The following data were taken from Pilerno Company:

Notes Payable

	12/31/1999	280,000
	12/31/2000	350,000

Notes payable of $50,000 were traded for shares of common stock. $100,000 of old notes payable matured. A new dump truck was purchased for $80,000 by issuing a note payable to the truck dealer. The only other transaction affecting the account shown involved new borrowings from its bank.

Required:

How will the Notes Payable events be shown on the cash-flow statement?

P ROBLEMS

18-21. Cash Flow From Operations. Household Helpers, a home cleaning service in Oslo, Norway, presents the following summarized financial data in Norwegian krones:

Revenue	NKr 494,000
Salaries and wages	NKr 215,000
Supplies and other cash expenses	178,000
Depreciation expense	14,000
Income taxes	40,000
Total expenses	NKr 447,000
Net income	NKr 47,000

	December 31, 1999	December 31, 1998
Current assets:		
Cash	NKr 117,000	NKr 91,000
Accounts receivable	77,000	56,000
Inventory of supplies	54,000	42,000
Total current assets	NKr 248,000	NKr 189,000
Current liabilities:		
Accounts payable (purchase of supplies) . .	NKr 11,000	NKr 8,000
Salaries and wages payable	44,000	46,000
Income taxes payable	18,000	21,000
Total current liabilities	NKr 73,000	NKr 75,000

Required:

1. Develop the cash flow from operations using the direct method.

2. Comment on the differences between net income and cash flow from operations.

18-22. Cash Flows Using Incomplete Data. The marketing manager of Rose Industries hands you an envelope with a few dollar amounts listed on the back. He is temporarily handling the financial duties since the chief accountant took another job. He wants to know a few things about "cash." You look at the envelope and see:

Depreciation expense	$ 3,200
Decrease in accounts payable	4,000
Increase in tax liability	500
Cash from bank borrowings	19,000
Loss on sale of land	1,000
Net income	28,000
Cash from sale of land	10,000
Cash paid for acquisition of land	22,400
Cash dividends paid	15,000
Cash paid to retire preferred stock	18,500

Required:

1. What was the cash flow from operating activities?

2. Which of the following responses correctly describes the land transactions?

(a) A net loss of $2,200 would be recorded.

(b) Land transactions caused a net cash inflow of $9,000.

(c) Land transactions caused a net cash outflow of $12,400.

(d) The change in the Land account balance was $12,400.

18-23. Charitable Giving: Cash-Flow Ethics.   Summarized financial statements are as follows for Franklin County Caring Society (FCCS):

Membership dues	$263,100
Fundraising dinners	95,600
Donations received	212,800
Total revenue	$571,500
Wages and supplies expense	$ 99,600
Dinner expenses	77,200
Rent	15,000
Depreciation of fixtures	11,200
Benefits provided	294,200
Total expenses	$497,200
Net income	$ 74,300

	1999	1998		1999	1998
Cash	$100,900	$132,000	Accounts payable	$ 12,900	$ 9,100
Temporary investments	311,000	215,000	Wages payable	5,800	6,400
Dues receivable	54,100	58,100	Total current liabilities	$ 18,700	$ 15,500
Supplies inventory	9,200	7,900	FCCS capital	611,400	537,100
Prepaid rent	3,500	2,000	Total liabilities and equities	$630,100	$552,600
Total current assets	$478,700	$415,000			
Fixtures (net)	151,400	137,600			
Total assets	$630,100	$552,600			

Additional data: Computers and software costing $25,000 were acquired in 1999.

Required:

1. Prepare a statement of cash flows for the year.

2. If a donor asks what happens to all the cash receipts, what would you say?

3. Assume that community needs are great.   Comment on FCCS's financial position.

18-24. Estimated Cash Flow.   Yoder Mills, Inc. is expected to make a payment of $500,000 on equipment notes payable by December 31, 1999.   Sales volume is down, and it is difficult to collect accounts receivable.   The cash balance on January 1, 1999, was $130,000 and is at an absolute minimum to meet operating obligations.

The controller estimated net income for 1999 to be only $18,000. Depreciation of $270,000 was deducted in estimating net income. Other estimates are:

1. Accounts receivable are to be reduced by $20,000.

2. Inventories are to be reduced by $30,000.

3. Accounts payable will increase by $10,000.

4. Equipment with a net book value of $12,000 will be sold for that amount.

Required:

From the information given, does it appear that the debt payment can be made while holding a cash balance of no less than $130,000? Prepare an estimated statement of cash flows to support your position.

18-25. Reconciling Net Income and Cash From Operations. The following items are from the accounts of a local firm.

Gain on sale of long-term investment	$ 133,500
Increase in accounts receivable	14,300
Increase in land	48,000
Increase in accrued expenses payable	6,800
Decrease in inventory	21,700
Decrease in accounts payable	12,000
Decrease in prepaid insurance	1,500
Increase in common stock	85,000
Net income	124,800
Depreciation of building for year	48,000
Decrease in cash	14,000
Cash received from sale of long-term investment	228,800
Cash from operations	43,000

Required:

Select from the preceding list those items that would be relevant to a reconciliation of net income and cash from operations, and prepare such a reconciliation.

18-26. Operating Cash Flows. Data from the beginning and ending balance sheets for Donaldson Machine Company are as follows:

	Ending	Beginning		Ending	Beginning
Cash	$ 27,000	$ 23,000	Accounts payable	$ 23,000	$ 29,000
Accounts receivable	54,000	48,000	Accrued expenses	18,000	7,000
Inventory	46,000	71,000	Current liabilities	$ 41,000	$ 36,000
Current assets	$127,000	$142,000			

The income statement for the year shows net sales of $620,000, cost of goods sold of $385,000, and operating expenses of $112,000. Included in operating expenses is depreciation of $14,000. Also, a gain of $8,000 is reported from the sale of equipment. Equipment costing $248,000 was acquired, and equipment sold had a net book value of $23,000 at the date of sale. The company sold its common stock for $60,000.

Required:

1. Prepare a statement of cash flows using the direct method.
2. Does this explain the change in cash? Comment.

18-27. Cash Flows From Operating Activities. The Brown Company provided the following data from its 1998 activities:

Comparative Balance Sheets			
	12/31/98	*12/31/97*	*Increase (Decrease)*
Cash	$ 34,000	$ 50,000	$(16,000)
Accounts receivable	68,000	60,000	8,000
Inventory	90,000	99,000	(9,000)
Plant and equipment	240,000	180,000	60,000
Accumulated depreciation	(80,000)	(65,000)	(15,000)
Total	$352,000	$324,000	$ 28,000
Accounts payable	$ 55,000	$ 66,000	$(11,000)
Bonds payable..............	90,000	50,000	40,000
Common stock	70,000	60,000	10,000
Retained earnings...........	137,000	148,000	(11,000)
Total	$352,000	$324,000	$ 28,000

Income Statement for the Year Ended December 31, 1998	
Sales..	$ 300,000
Cost of goods sold	(200,000)
Operating expenses	(72,000)
Loss on sale of equipment.................................	(8,000)
Net income	$ 20,000

Additional data:

Equipment costing $30,000 with a book value of $18,000 was sold for $10,000. Investors swapped $10,000 of bonds payable for $10,000 of common stock.

Required:

1. What was cash flow from operations in 1998?

2. What items would Brown report in its investing and financing activities sections of its statement of cash flows in 1998?

3. If Brown has a significant noncash transaction, explain why it should appear on the statement of cash flows.

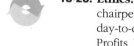

18-28. Ethics: Suspicions, Guesses, and Conjectures. Joan Arch, board of directors chairperson, never worried about cash flows until recently. Joan is not active in the day-to-day activities of the firm. She has heard some rumors that concern her. Profits had been strong for the prior five years. She did see a yearend bank statement that showed a near zero balance. The following data are from this year's financial statements. No other current data are available to her.

Sales.	$450,000
Cost of goods sold	(350,000)
Gross margin.......................	$100,000
Operating expenses..................	(124,000)
Net loss	$ (24,000)

	12/31/1998	*12/31/1997*
Accounts receivable	$ 50,000	$ 80,000
Inventory	60,000	85,000
Equipment	100,000	130,000
Accumulated depreciation—equipment	(48,000)	(20,000)
Accounts payable	68,000	32,000
Dividends payable	10,000	10,000
Bank borrowings	120,000	80,000
Retained earnings	48,000	89,000

Required:

1. Suggest two scenarios of what could be happening. What facts support your theories?

2. Of the data that Joan probably already has in her files and given what you know, what additional data would you like to see immediately?

18-29. Revising a Cash-Flow Statement.   Mr. Dunny thinks cash flow is critical. He has tried to express his own company's cash flow in the following statement:

Cash generated:		Cash paid out:		
Net income	$26,000	Dividends paid		$15,000
Depreciation expense	2,000	Inventory increase		400
Amortization expense	1,000	Long-term notes payable		1,000
Accounts receivable decrease	200	Gain on sale of land	$500	
Accounts payable increase	500	- Loss on sale of investments	(200)	300
Sale of land	3,000	Purchase of buildings		16,000
Sale of investments	1,300	Purchase of equipment		4,300
Sale of stock	4,000	Change in cash		1,000
Total	$38,000	Total		$38,000

Required:

Help Mr. Dunny get squared away with a better cash-flow statement.

18-30. Statement Preparation—Cash Basis.   Following is a list of items that occurred during 1999 in the Harrol Company.

Net income for the year	$ 356,000
Dividends paid during the year	75,000
Proceeds from sale of a 10-year bond issue	200,000
Amortization of patents	15,000
Depreciation expense	125,000
Cash received on sale of land	130,000
Decrease in inventory	44,000
Increase in accounts receivable	96,000
Loss on the sale of land	20,000
Increase in accrued expenses	18,000
Cash purchase of new equipment	500,000
Cash purchase of a long-term investment	158,000
Decrease in income taxes payable	24,000
Increase in accounts payable	47,000
Purchase of buildings by issuing 20-year notes	300,000

Required:

1. Prepare a statement of cash flows for 1999 using the items given. The treasurer of the Harrol Company indicates that cash increased by $102,000.

2. Comment on the major causes of the cash balance increase.

18-31. Cash Flows From Financial Statement Data.   The following statement of income and selected balance sheet data are given for the Lichtman Company:

Income Statement for the Year Ended December 31, 1999		
Sales		$450,000
Cost of goods sold		300,000
Gross profit		$150,000
Operating expenses:		
Depreciation expense	$10,000	
Cash expenses	90,000	100,000
Net income before taxes		$ 50,000
Tax expense		20,000
Net income		$ 30,000

	December 31				**December 31**	
	1999	*1998*		*1999*	*1998*
Cash	$10,000	$ 6,000	Accounts payable . . .	$30,000	$22,000
Accounts receivable . .	90,000	80,000	Taxes payable	4,000	6,000
Inventory	60,000	55,000	Retained earnings . .	60,000	55,000

Required:

1. How much cash did Lichtman pay to suppliers for purchases in 1999?

2. Prepare an operating section of the cash-flow statement.

3. How much did Lichtman pay in cash dividends?

18-32. Decrease in Cash Balance.   Jon Walgren, the president of Dunbar Instruments, Inc., cannot understand why the firm's cash balance decreased by $37,000 during the last fiscal quarter, when the cash flow from operations for the quarter was $71,000. He had expected the cash balance would increase by that amount. Depreciation expense of $25,000 was deducted on the income statement and was the only difference between net income and cash from operations.

Noncurrent balance sheet items from the statements at the beginning and at the end of the quarter follow:

	Beginning of Quarter	**End of Quarter**
Plant and equipment (net)	$386,000	$404,000
Long-term debt	200,000	160,000
Retained earnings	317,000	338,000

Required:

Write a memo that will show Mr. Walgren why Dunbar's cash decreased.

18-33. Cash Flow and Acquisitions.   The president of Van Horn Appliances cannot understand how a competing company, Murphy Appliances, can invest $12,000,000 in new plant and equipment in 1999 and yet not increase debt or capital stock. Furthermore, dividend payments to shareholders were not reduced. The president asks you to determine how the competitor was able to finance these additions without borrowing or issuing capital stock.

You also find that, during 1999, equipment having a net book value of $3,150,000 was sold at a gain of $420,000, net of income tax. No other plant assets were sold. Financial data from the statements for Murphy Appliances for the past three years are as follows (in thousands of dollars):

	Year Ended December 31		
	1999	*1998*	*1997*
Operating net income (excluding gain)	$3,153	$2,732	$2,068
Depreciation deducted for the year	1,835	887	936
Dividends declared and paid	500	500	500

Required:

1. Explain to the president how cash might have been acquired for the plant and equipment additions made by Murphy Appliances.
2. For your answer to Part (1) to be true, what assumptions are you making about the current operations of Murphy Appliances?

18-34. Cash Flow From Operations. "Net income is fine—over 10 percent of sales!" exclaims the president of Armitage Parts Company. "But I want to know why we have to reduce our cash balance just to pay our bills on time." An income statement for 1999 for Armitage Parts Company follows:

Income Statement for the Year Ended December 31, 1999	
Net sales	$ 5,230,000
Cost of goods sold	$ 2,890,000
Operating expenses	940,000
Income taxes	630,000
Total expenses.	$ 4,460,000
Net income	$ 770,000

Depreciation of $147,000 is part of operating expenses. Current assets and current liabilities as of December 31, 1998 and 1999, are:

	12/31/1999	12/31/1998		12/31/1999	12/31/1998
Cash	$ 203,000	$ 474,000	Accounts payable	$ 801,000	$ 719,000
Accounts receivable	941,000	846,000	Accrued payables.	267,000	293,000
Inventory	982,000	928,000	Taxes payable.	137,000	188,000
Prepaid expenses	16,000	12,000	Dividends payable	180,000	260,000
Total.	$ 2,142,000	$ 2,260,000	Total	$ 1,385,000	$ 1,460,000

Dividends of $400,000 were declared in 1999. A new building was constructed at a cost of $850,000. A mortgage of $290,000 was obtained to make the final payment to the building contractor. No other transactions affected these accounts.

Required:

1. Prepare a statement of cash flows. Show the cash-flow effect of each item on the income statement.
2. Is the president's concern about the cash position justified? Explain.

18-35. Operating Cash Flows. White Company has completed preparation of the income statement and the balance sheet at yearend, December 31, 1998. A statement of cash flows must be developed. The following data are available:

		12/31/1998	12/31/1997
(a)	From the balance sheet:		
	Cash	$17,000	$ 8,000
	Accounts receivable	17,000	12,000
	Inventory	15,000	18,000
	Accounts payable	10,000	12,000
	Notes payable, short term	18,000	13,000
(b)	From the income statement for 1998:		
	Net income		$ 20,000
	Depreciation expense		6,000
(c)	From other records:		
	Purchase of long-term investment		$ 15,000
	Payment of long-term note		5,000
	Sale of capital stock		10,000
	Payment of cash dividend.		8,000
	Purchase of land, issued capital stock		25,000

Required:

Prepare a statement of cash flows. Comment on the major cash flows.

18-36. Cash Flows—Incomplete Data. Gibbons Transport Company plans to acquire new trucks in 1999 at an estimated cost of $4,000,000. The company president hopes that the past year's operations can produce cash to finance at least half of the acquisition. Temporary investments should pay for the other half.

The company controller is out of town, but you have been able to obtain the following information from the assistant controller. The assistant's numbers are solid for current assets, but the noncurrent accounts' events and balances are only estimates. All figures are in thousands of dollars.

	June 30, 1999	June 30, 1998
Assets:		
Cash and cash equivalents	$ 2,667	$ 1,168
Temporary investments	3,000	1,000
Accounts receivable	2,460	2,274
Prepaid taxes and insurance	78	64
Supplies on hand	290	316
Total current assets	$ 8,495	$ 4,822
Terminal buildings (net)	1,700	1,400
Trucks and equipment (net)	6,000	7,500
Total assets	$16,195	$13,722
Liabilities and equities:		
Accounts payable	$ 2,633	$ 2,027
Wages and salaries payable..............	734	812
Interest payable.......................	52	68
Income taxes payable	218	357
Total current liabilities	$ 3,637	$ 3,264
Mortgage payable.....................	1,800	1,900
Long-term notes payable	1,500	500
Capital stock.........................	4,000	4,000
Retained earnings	5,258	4,058
Total liabilities and equities	$16,195	$13,722

The assistant controller also told you the following:

1. An addition to the terminal buildings cost $500,000 in March 1999.

2. Trucks with a book value of $1,100,000 were sold in April 1999, incurring an aftertax loss of $230,000. No trucks were purchased.

3. Net income for the year ended June 30, 1999, including the loss on truck sales, was $1,600,000.

Required:

1. From the information given, prepare a statement of cash flows for the fiscal year ended June 30, 1999.
2. What is the source of the additional temporary investments?
3. If a minimum cash balance of $1,500,000 is considered necessary, does it appear that the president's goal can be achieved? Explain.

18-37. Cash Flow From Divisions. Wear-Well Fabrics Company, Inc. operates with three divisions: an apparel division, a sports division, and a novelty division. Each division is autonomous with a minimum of control exercised by the corporate headquarters. At the end of each fiscal year, divisions are expected to remit to corporate offices half of the cash flow generated by operations in that division. This requirement may be suspended if it can be shown that the funds are needed by the division for future operations.

Account balances (in thousands) traceable to each division as of February 1, 1998, for the fiscal year, and as of January 31, 1999, are:

	Apparel	Sports	Novelty
February 1, 1998:			
Accounts receivable	$ 326	$ 68	$ 89
Inventories	636	240	277
Equipment, net	784	472	217
Accounts payable	502	145	103
Accrued expenses	32	15	15
For the fiscal year:			
Net sales	$ 3,670	$1,720	$ 840
Cost of goods sold	$ 2,936	$1,204	$ 504
Cash operating expenses	342	286	138
Depreciation expense	65	73	34
Interest expense	30	15	6
Loss on sale of fixtures	37	0	0
Income taxes	130	71	79
Total expenses	$ 3,540	$1,649	$ 761
Net income	$ 130	$ 71	$ 79
Equipment purchases	$ 96	$ 29	$ 19
January 31, 1999:			
Accounts receivable	$ 390	$ 105	$ 115
Inventories	630	368	301
Equipment, net	759	423	202
Accounts payable	432	155	70
Accrued expenses	55	20	4

Required:

1. Prepare a statement that will show the cash flows from operations and investing for each division and for the company in total for the year.
2. Determine the amount to be remitted to corporate offices.
3. Comment on the possible impacts of this system of corporate cash control.

C ASE 18A—DENNING COMPANY

The Denning Company has seen its balance sheet (in millions) grow over the past five years as follows:

	12/31/2000	12/31/1995
Cash and equivalents	$ 2	$ 37
Receivables, net	60	3
Inventories	100	50
Plant assets, net	300	100
Total assets	$462	$190
Current operating liabilities	$105	$ 30
Long-term debt	150	0
Shareholders' equity	207	160
Total equities	$462	$190

The total net income for the five years was $104 million. Cash dividends paid were $57 million. Depreciation was $80 million. Fixed assets were purchased for $280 million, of which $150 million was financed with long-term debt.

Jeff Denning, the president and majority shareholder, is an effective operating executive but has little patience with financial matters. After examining the most recent balance sheet and income statement, he muttered, "We've enjoyed five years of steady growth and strong profits. We're in the worst cash position in our history and deep in debt. This is ridiculous! The harder we work, the deeper in debt we get. Who stole our cash?"

Required:

1. Prepare a statement of cash flows for the 5-year period.

2. Using the cash-flow statement and any other information available, outline the major causes for such a squeeze on cash.

3. As a planning strategy, suggest a cash planning process to Mr. Denning that would hopefully prevent a similar meeting in another five years.

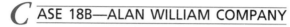

*C*ASE 18B—ALAN WILLIAM COMPANY

1-2-3

Alan William Company, a Wellington, New Zealand firm, plans to construct a building and to make some major changes in its operations in 1999. In anticipation, the company has conserved cash and has not paid dividends during the past year.

Estimates show that the building will probably cost NZ$23,000,000 and that furnishings and equipment may cost another NZ$5,000,000. A member of the board of directors states that, by the time the building is constructed, the cost may be NZ$30,000,000 with the furnishings and equipment costing NZ$6,000,000.

Other actions planned for 1999 are as follows:

1. Issue capital stock for an estimated NZ$4,000,000 cash.

2. Sell old plant assets having a net book value of NZ$1,680,000 for an estimated NZ$3,460,000. Disposal costs of NZ$100,000 will be incurred.

3. Sell an investment in Vero, Inc. for an estimated NZ$4,800,000.

4. Have at least NZ$3,000,000 in cash by yearend.

5. Partially finance the building by a long-term loan of NZ$15,000,000 at 12 percent interest. First-year interest will be deducted, leaving the net proceeds at NZ$13,200,000. In later years, annual interest of NZ$1,800,000 will be paid until the loan matures in 2006.

6. Achieve the following 1999 operating levels:

   (a) Net turnover (sales) are to be NZ$52,000,000.

   (b) Cost of sales and operating expenses combined, excluding depreciation, are estimated to be 70 percent of net sales.

   (c) Depreciation expense has been estimated at NZ$2,300,000. Depreciation will be NZ$3,000,000 if the building's cost is the higher estimate.

   (d) Income taxes have been estimated at 40 percent for all taxation items.

Balance sheet data as of December 31, 1998, are:

Cash and cash equivalents . .	NZ$ 1,972,000	Accounts payable	NZ$ 5,420,000
Temporary investments.	6,000,000	Short-term bank loans . . .	500,000
Accounts receivable	4,763,000	Accrued expenses	860,000
Inventories	6,211,000	Interest payable	230,000
Investment in Vero, Inc.	3,000,000	Common stock	12,600,000
Plant and equipment (net) . .	10,300,000	Retained earnings	12,636,000
Total	NZ$32,246,000	Total	NZ$32,246,000

The president of Alan William states that sales revenue for 1999 may be only NZ$45,000,000 but cost of goods sold and operating expenses would still be budgeted at 70 percent of net sales.

Required:

1. Prepare forecast statements of cash flows under four assumptions:

    (a) Lower building and equipment costs with the optimistic sales estimate.

    (b) Lower building and equipment costs with the lower sales estimate.

    (c) Higher building and equipment costs with the optimistic sales estimate.

    (d) Higher building and equipment costs with the lower sales estimate.

2. Will the company need all or part of the long-term loan under each of the assumptions stated? Comment.

CHECK FIGURES

C HECK FIGURES

CHAPTER 2

2-2	1. Cost of goods manufactured = $201,000	
2-4	Cost of goods manufactured = $99,000	
2-6	Direct materials for Department 2 = $150,000	
2-11	Cost function is £2,000 + £5 per unit	
2-14	b. Ending work in process = $38,000	
2-15	Cost of goods sold for Kawasaki = ¥66,000	
2-17	Operating income = $73,000	
2-22	Gross profit for 1998 = $47,500	
2-25	1. Total cost per pie = $2.60	
2-27	3. Total controllable costs = $584,000	
2-28	3. $142,000	
2-29	2. Total actual cost per rivet for February = M1.0619	
2-31	Variable contribution margin = $56,000	
2-34	Gross profit for Firm 2 = $11,800	
2-35	2. Cost of goods sold = $128,000	
2-38	Operating income = $90 million	
Case 2A	1. Total costs for Alternative C = $1,394	
Case 2B	1. Segment contribution margin for Freight = $600	

CHAPTER 3

3-2	Fixed cost = $200	
3-4	1. Total cost estimate = $3,400	
3-5	2. Variable cost per hour = $9.78	
3-7	2. 3,681,818 gallons	
3-9	2. 3,133 visits	
3-10	1. 8,182 units	
3-12	2. $3,750,000	
3-14	3. 360 tables	
3-16	1. 35,625 units	
3-17	2. Increase in sales revenue = 500,000 pesos	
3-19	2. Profit = $125,000	
3-24	1. Fixed cost = $20,000	
3-25	2. Expected cost for November = $2,775	
3-26	2. Variable cost = $2.08 per hour	
3-27	2. 4,175 subscriptions	
3-28	2. 31,500 units	
3-29	2. Operating leverage at 3,000 units = 3.0	
3-31	1. $54,000	
3-32	2. Selling price = $4.50	
3-35	3. $1,230 additional profit each	
3-37	1. Weighted contribution margin ratio = 36.95%	
3-38	1. Summer profit = $181,400	
3-39	4. Total net income = $3,347.34	
3-43	2. Range is from $1.7539 million to $2.0283 million.	
Case 3A	1. Total fixed cost = $3,380,000	
Case 3B	2. Contribution margin per unit for Napkins = $1.90	

CHAPTER 4

4-1	Total cost of order #723 = $69.20
4-4	1. $3.00 per hour
4-6	Overapplied overhead = $5,000
4-7	Direct labor cost = 498,000 shekels
4-10	Direct materials charged to Job #232 = $4,250
4-13	1. Plant-wide rate = $20.00
4-15	2. Total overhead applied = $300
4-16	1. Overhead rate for Producing Dept. A = $6.05
4-17	2. Overhead rate for Finishing = $4.4221
4-18	Cost allocated to Producing Dept. 1 = $32,000
4-19	Cost allocated to Freight = $2,309,699
4-20	2. Total unit cost = 37.00 pesos
4-23	3. Total cost of goods sold in August = $432,800
4-24	1. Cost of contracts completed = $8,905,000
4-26	3. $41,000
4-27	4. Unit cost = $40.08
4-30	2. $20.705 per machine hour
4-31	3. (b) Total overhead costs for Alaska = $954
4-32	1. Plant-wide overhead rate = $20.55 per direct labor hour
4-35	Total overhead costs for P&C = $177,936
Case 4A	1. Total applied overhead = $193,520
Case 4B	1. Total Civil Dept. costs = $569,000

CHAPTER 5

5-3	Cost of jobs completed = $85,000
5-7	2. 29,600 equivalent units
5-9	2. Cost of units in ending inventory = $48,000
5-10	March 30 work in process (total) = $2,588
5-12	Unit cost for materials = $5.448
5-14	1. Total cost of completed units = $51,800
5-15	1. Cost of units completed = $51,748
5-19	2. Total costs transferred = NZ$25,440
5-23	3. $145,000
5-24	1. May 31 work in process (total) = $34,000
5-25	1. July 31 work in process (total) = $326,080
5-27	2. Total cost of completed units = $859,017
5-28	1. Cost per unit for materials = $20.95948
5-29	1. Cost per unit for materials = $1.60
5-30	2. Unfavorable variance in conversion costs = $47,097
5-31	1. Conversion costs per unit = S$3.20
5-32	2. April 30 work in process (total) = $34,570
5-35	2. Unit cost for overhead = $0.39515
5-36	2. (a) Conversion cost per unit = $2.23
5-37	1. Unit cost for labor = 2.20 balboas
Case 5B	4. Variable cost per unit = $2.80

CHAPTER 6

6-9	26,000 shekels
6-10	2. Total costs for Low-Unit = $79,750
6-11	2. Unit cost for Overnighter = $78.30
6-13	1. Cost per unit for SuperPro = Rs202.91
6-14	$11,800
6-16	Unit cost for LE = $213.65
6-17	Overhead cost per unit for Propane = $1,483.23
6-18	2. $397,000 debit balance

6-24	2. Total for #TK451 = $21,189
6-26	Overhead cost with ABC = $11,000
6-27	1. Total for Standard = $253,050
6-28	2. Cost per unit for Y = $19.52
6-29	2. A$42,335
6-30	3. Total overhead for Gears (ABC) = $3,914,805
6-31	1. Unit cost for Large = $0.30
6-32	2. Total cost per pound for Malaysian Coffee = $7.54
6-33	1. Predetermined rate for Report Generation = $0.036 per page
6-35	2. Underapplied conversion costs = $10,000
Case 6A	2. (a) Unit contribution = $39.34
Case 6B	1. Total manufacturing overhead = $6,107,000

CHAPTER 7

7-3	March purchases = $16,500
7-4	Purchases required during second quarter = 2,300 pounds
7-6	Total June payments = $115,200
7-7	1. Cash receipts during May = £160,480
7-8	1. January purchases = $3,120
7-10	Cash payments in November = $91,400
7-13	Budgeted net profit for March = $26,000
7-19	March 31 cash balance = A$33,880
7-25	3. Total cost of goods sold (materials) = W8,208,000
7-26	3. Maximum sales forecast = 260,000 units
7-30	May 31 cash balance = $62,000
7-31	1. January purchases = $45,200
7-32	2. Break-even occupancy = 29.8%
7-33	1. Total direct labor cost for fourth quarter = $16,000
7-34	2. Adjusted budget net income = ¥25.0 million
7-36	3. Total costs for November = $136,900
7-37	3. Total labor savings (20% reduction) = M$49,775
7-38	1. Fourth-quarter sales = 623 units
7-40	Expected net income = $2,402
7-42	2. Expected cash flow for Alternative 2 = $465,000

CHAPTER 8

8-1	1. Third-quarter purchases = 138,000 units
8-2	2. Second-quarter cash collections = $760,000
8-4	Cash payments for February = $33,600
8-5	1. March purchases of Material 08 = 21,600 units
8-7	2. June cash receipts = $57,000
8-9	1. December cash collections = $84,000
8-10	1. Total March disbursements = $68,000
8-12	Total cash payments = $398,000
8-13	Cost of materials used during first quarter = $290,000
8-15	Accounts receivable = $196,000
8-18	1. July purchases = $910,000
8-20	1. Total cost per unit = $26.50
8-22	1. Ending cash balance for April = $271,480
8-23	Ending cash balance for May = F258,285
8-26	1. Unit cost for Red product line = $10.2333
8-27	2. Ending first quarter cash balance = $225,000
8-30	1. First quarter net income = $74,940
8-34	2. Estimated cash balance after payments = $148,000
Case 8A	1. Balance of loans at end of December = $95,073
Case 8B	1. Forecast 1998 net income = $22,440

CHAPTER 9

9-2	Standard cost per unit = $6,000 drachmas
9-5	2. 8,600 units of product manufactured
9-7	1. Standard quantity allowed = 1,200 kilograms
9-8	3. Actual cost per assembly = $0.912
9-11	2. Unfavorable labor efficiency variance = $6,250
9-13	3. Favorable budget variance = $8,000
9-15	1. Total overhead costs = $35,600
9-18	Loss on proposal = $61.30
9-19	3. Unfavorable variable overhead spending variance = $20,000
9-22	Total standard cost per workstation = $194.61
9-24	2. Standard cost per unit = $8.80
9-25	1. Actual price = 8.475 pesos
9-26	1. Favorable materials price variance = $7,500
9-27	1. Total variance for June = $140,000 Unfavorable
9-29	1. Total overhead cost per unit = $0.14
9-30	1. (d) Labor efficiency variance = $400,000 Unfavorable
9-31	3. (b) Overhead capacity variance = $1,100 Unfavorable
9-34	1. Total standard cost = $30.20 per batch
9-35	2. Direct labor cost per order with 90% learning curve = $75,980.80
9-38	1. Unfavorable capacity variance = 1,600,000 pesos
9-39	3. Variable spending variance = $1,460 Favorable
Case 9A	4. Standard cost per unit = $116.41

CHAPTER 10

10-3	Total price variances = $136,000 Unfavorable
10-4	Cost of lace variance = £888.5 Favorable
10-6	2. Total revenue mix variances = $80,000 Favorable
10-11	1. Profit before taxes = $15,000
10-12	Profit after taxes = $165,000
10-13	1. Total unit cost = $30
10-14	2. Profit = $840,000
10-16	1. Total revenue quantity variances = $60,121 Favorable
10-17	Total interest income rate variances = $1.30 Unfavorable
10-18	1. Total staff mix variances = $69,000 Favorable
10-20	2. Total quantity variances for gross margin = $142,500 Favorable
10-23	2. Total manufacturing cost for Rakes = $2.25
10-24	2. Net loss = $90,000
10-25	1. Manufacturing profit for Utility = $920,000
10-27	1. 1999 profit = $22,000
Case 10A	2. Contribution margin gain (relative to market) for Plastic chairs = $7,000
Case 10B	1. Contribution margin for Handles (all three formats) = $276,000

CHAPTER 11

11-1	Selling price = $23
11-4	Incremental net income = $6,000
11-8	Additional profit from special sale = $800
11-10	Variable cost per packet = $3
11-14	1. Contribution margin per hour for Baker = $30
11-16	2. Maximum amount = $85,000
11-17	Direct segment contribution margin = $125,000
11-19	1. Contribution margin per hour for C = $20
11-20	Incremental contribution from additional processing = $13,000
11-23	Incremental income for Department A = $15,000

11-25   2. Net disadvantage of accepting special order = HK$10,000
11-26   1. Net make advantage = $9,000
11-29   2. Markup on total costs = 9.4%
11-31   Profit is $16,000 higher if Department 2 is kept
11-32   Net make advantage = $125,000
11-33   1. Net additional profit from special sale = ¥35,500,000
11-34   1. Incremental disadvantage of closing Store 54 = $30,000
11-35   1. Total variable cost per unit = NT$180
11-37   1. (c) Lease revenue = $660,000
11-41   1. (b) Total contribution margin = $2,950,000
11-44   1. Incremental net income for Garden Supplies = $24,000
11-45   Variable contribution margin per hour for Iron Frames #10 = $3.50
Case 11A   1. (d) Incremental profit = $615
Case 11B   1. Net make advantage = ƒ73,894

CHAPTER 12
12-3   Accounting rate of return = 12.5%
12-4   2. Payback period = 3.125 years
12-5   3. Net present value = -$10,680
12-9   Year 5 net cash flows = £140,000
12-10   Cash balance after one year for Investment (a) = $65,520
12-11   3. Net present value = $22,436
12-15   1. Payback period for Project 98-G3 = 5.2 years
12-16   1. Net cash inflow after taxes = $18,400
12-17 $70,000
12-20   Project 3 annual cash inflow = $12,197
12-23   2. Net present value for choice 2 = $4,143
12-25   1. Net present value = $29,258
12-27   Case 4: Annual cash inflow = $100,000
12-28   2. Necessary sales volume = 26,541 units
12-29   1. Net present value for Proposal 1 = -$15,900
12-32   2. Profitability index = 1.06
12-33   Net present value = HK$862,756
12-34   1. Net present value = $247,664
12-36   2. Net present value = $4,823
12-39   Net present value = $81,898
Case 12A   2. Annual cash flow = $14,000
Case 12B   2. Profitability index = 0.92

CHAPTER 13
13-3   Net present value = £125,200
13-4   1. Net present value for Alternative 2 = ¥700
13-5   Net present value = $30,472
13-8   2. Net present value = $21,536
13-10   Net present value = -$3,916
13-14   1. Present value of operating costs for Alternative A = B$337,265
13-15   2. Net lease advantage for Vehicle B = $3,035
13-16   Net present value of (b) = -$34,655
13-17   Net present value of $130,000 Investment = $17,619
13-19   2. Net present value = $23,584
13-20   Net investment = $19,000
13-22   1. Annual net cash flow for Machine X = $365,000
13-23   1. Profitability index of X = 1.35
13-24   Net present value = -$4,194
13-25   1. Present Value factor = 2.906

13-28	3. Net present value = $637,474
13-30	1. Net present value = $6,626
13-32	2. Net present value = -$7,619
13-33	1. Net present value = $111,497

CHAPTER 14

14-4	C. Imputed rate = 15%
14-7	1. Average sales price = R4.20 per gram
14-8	1. Profit at 120,000 units = $240,000
14-13	Net income for Negativo Division = B$290,000
14-14	1. Net income for Epsilon Company = $6,000,000
14-15	2. Asset turnover = 4
14-16	1. ROI for proposed investment = 20%
14-20	1. Minimum bid = $4.00 per unit
14-22	1. Zale net income = $100,000
14-27	1. Variable cost per time unit = 18.50 litas
14-28	1. Division 1 net income = $1,080,000
14-29	Producing Division net income = Rs473,500,000
14-30	1. Net present value = $384,000
14-32	2. Cost of buying parts internally = $1,340,000
14-33	1. Transfer price for Order 2 = $450
14-34	2. Variable unit cost = $4.75
14-35	1. Variable unit cost = $18.30
14-36	3. Asset turnover in 1996 for Apparel Division = 1.09
14-37	2.(b) Residual income = $153,750
Case 14A	1. Net advantage if clock system is produced by Systems Division = $1.00 per unit

CHAPTER 15

15-1	Internal failure costs = $140,000
15-5	2. Total costs under revised system = £627,000
15-6	Total costs after installation = $786,000
15-11	2. 66.7%
15-12	2. 41.5%
15-15	Cost savings provided by centralized purchasing department = $4,135,200
15-17	Total quality costs in 2003 = $591,100
15-20	1. Total prevention costs in 1998 = $740,000
15-23	1. Target cost = $841,500
15-26	1. Total loss from late shipments = B70,620
15-28	3 First pass yield = 95%

CHAPTER 16

16-4	(c) Currency gain = $40,000
16-6	4. Unfavorable capacity variance = $122,500
16-7	1. Total variance = DM12,200
16-10	June 11 currency loss = $1,194
16-12	March 6 accrued currency gain = $13,000
16-14	1. Currency loss = $7,000
16-15	March 31 currency gain = $1,740
16-16	(e) Unrealized loss on open contract = $3,000
16-18	Selling Division net income = $1,044,000
16-19	2. Total applied overhead = $25,110
16-22	3. Total volume variance = $1,722U
16-23	1. (d) Actual net income = $4.275
16-24	2. Total volume variance = ¥12,300,000F

16-25   September 22 currency gain = $3,000
16-27   1. Total net gain = $2,000
Case 16B   2. Loan cost if made in U.S. dollars = $2,025,000

CHAPTER 17

17-1   3. Asset turnover = 4.6
17-3   (c) Operating cycle = 70 days
17-5   (b) Dividend yield = 5.33%
17-6   Average accounts receivable = $67
17-11   2. Dividend yield = 9.375%
17-12   Net income = $6,000
17-14   6. Asset turnover = 2.0
17-15   2. Return on equity = 30.0%
17-18   3. Return on assets after reduction = 9.2%
17-20   1. 1998 return on current assets = 18.0%
17-22   2. Return on assets for Flexible Conduits = 12.5%
17-24   2. Return on sales = 5.0%
17-25   2. Times interest earned = 5.5
17-26   (f) Gross margin percentage = 33.3%
17-31   1. Return on assets for Division 3 = 41.8%
17-32   1. 1999 return on equity = 27.77%
17-34   1. (a) 1998 return on assets = 5.5%
Case 17A   1. Cash-flow rate of return from present operation = 16.3%

CHAPTER 18

18-2   Net inflow = $184,000
18-4   Purchased equipment = $220,000
18-5   (c) Cash paid for dividends = DM27,000
18-7   Cash inflow = $175,000
18-9   Net change in cash = $423,500
18-11   Net change in cash = -$850
18-12   Cash inflow = £247,100
18-17   2. Cash flow from financing = -$20,000
18-18   Net change in cash = $452,000
18-21   1. Cash flow from operations = NKr26,000
18-22   1. Cash flow from operations = $28,700
18-23   1. Net change in cash = -$31,100
18-26   1. Cash paid for operating expenses = $87,000
18-27   1. Cash flow from operating activities = $45,000
18-29   Net change in cash = $1,000
18-30   1. Net change in cash = $102,000
18-31   3. Dividends paid = $25,000
18-34   1. Net change in cash = -$271,000
18-36   1. Net change in cash = $1,499,000
Case 18A   1. Net change in cash = -$35 million
Case 18B   1. Net income for (c) = NZ$8,568,000

I ndex